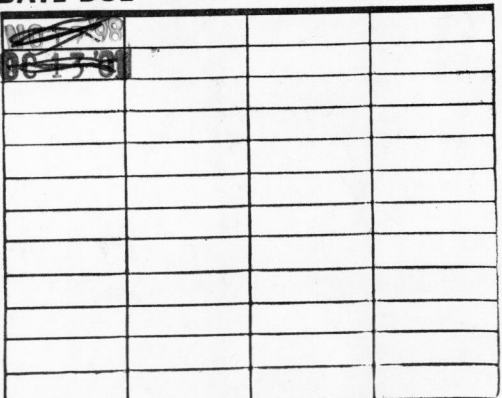

Slave Populations
   of the
   British
   Caribbean
   1807–1834

JOHNS HOPKINS STUDIES IN ATLANTIC HISTORY AND CULTURE

Richard Price, General Editor

The Guiana Maroons: A Historical and Bibliographical Introduction
Richard Price

The Formation of a Colonial Society: Belize, from Conquest to Crown Colony
O. Nigel Bolland

Languages of the West Indies
Douglas Taylor

Peasant Politics: Struggle in a Dominican Village
Kenneth Evan Sharpe

The African Religions of Brazil: Toward a Sociology of the Interpretation of Civilizations
Roger Bastide, translated by Helen Sebba

African and the Caribbean: The Legacies of a Link
Margaret E. Crahan and Franklin W. Knight

*Behold the Promised Land: A History of Afro-American Settler Society
in Nineteenth-Century Liberia*
Tom W. Shick

*"Alas, Alas, Kongo": A Social History of Indentured African Immigration into
Jamaica, 1841–1865*
Monica Schuler

"We Come to Object": The Peasants of Morelos and the National State
Arturo Warman, translated by Stephen K. Ault

A History of the Guyanese Working People, 1881–1905
Walter Rodney

The Dominican People, 1850–1900: Notes for a Historical Sociology
H. Hoetink, translated by Stephen K. Ault

Self and Society in the Poetry of Nicholás Guillén
Lorna V. Williams

Alantic Empires: The Network of Trade and Revolution, 1713–1826
Peggy K. Liss

Settlements, Trade, and Politics in the Seventeenth-Century Gold Coast
Ray A. Kea

*Main Currents in Caribbean Thought: The Historical Evolution of Caribbean Society in its
Ideological Aspects, 1492–1900*
Gordon K. Lewis

The Man-of-Words in the West Indies: Performance and the Emergency of Creole Culture
Roger D. Abrahams

First-Time: The Historical Vision of an Afro-American People
Richard Price

Slave Populations of the British Caribbean, 1807–1834
B. W. Higman

Slave Populations of the British Caribbean 1807–1834

B.W. HIGMAN

THE JOHNS HOPKINS UNIVERSITY PRESS
Baltimore and London

For Bloss

© 1984 by The Johns Hopkins University Press
All rights reserved
Printed in the United States of America

The Johns Hopkins University Press, Baltimore, Maryland 21218
The Johns Hopkins Press Ltd., London

Library of Congress Cataloging in Publication Data

Higman, B. W., 1943–
Slave populations of the British Caribbean, 1807–1834.

(Johns Hopkins studies in Atlantic history and culture)
Bibliography: p.
Includes index
1. Slavery—British West Indies—History—19th
century.   2. Slavery—Caribbean Area—History—19th
century.   I. Title.   II. Series.
HT1091.H5 1984   306'.362'09729   83–22203
ISBN 0–8018–3036–2

Contents

List of Figures   xi
List of Tables   xv
Preface   xix
Abbreviations   xxi
Metric Conversion Table   xxiii

1. Slavery and Comparative History   *1*

2. Materials and Methods   *6*

Slave Registration: Origins and Administration   *6*
Slave Registration: The Nature of the Data   *11*
Slave Registration: An Assessment   *36*
Methods of Analysis   *37*

3. Physical and Economic Environments   *40*

Physical Environments   *40*
Settlement Histories   *43*
Types of Economic Activity   *46*
A Classification of the Colonial Economies   *66*

4. Growth and Distribution of the Slave Populations   *72*

Population Growth and Decline   *72*
Intercolonial Slave Movements   *79*
Spatial Distribution   *85*

5. Structure of the Slave Populations   *100*

Masters and Mistresses   *100*
Males and Females   *115*
Africans and Creoles   *121*
Age Structure   *135*
Color   *147*

6. Rural Regimes *158*

    Occupations *158*
    Hours of Work and Seasonal Demands *179*
    Occupational Allocation *188*
    Incentives to Labor *199*
    Food *204*
    Housing *218*
    Clothing *223*

7. Urban Regimes *226*

    Occupations *227*
    Work Organization *242*
    Occupational Allocation *247*
    Food *251*
    Housing *255*
    Clothing *257*
    The Character of Urban Slavery *257*

8. Health *260*

    Medical Care *261*
    Etiological Theories *272*
    Smallpox *278*
    Indicators of Health Status *280*
    Sickness and the Rhythm of the Seasons *298*

9. Fertility, Mortality, and Natural Increase *303*

    Natural Increase *307*
    Mortality *314*
    Fertility *347*
    Conclusions *374*

10. Refuge and Resistance *379*

    Manumission *379*
    Marronage *386*
    Rebellion *393*

11. Slavery and Population History *395*

STATISTICAL SUPPLEMENT   *399*

1.   Geographical Distribution   *409*
2.   Ownership   *431*
3.   Birthplace   *442*
4.   Age   *459*
5.   Color   *526*
6.   Stature   *532*
7.   Occupation   *547*
8.   Births and Deaths   *603*
9.   Vital Rates   *636*
10. Manumissions   *687*
11. Land Use and Labor Use   *696*

Notes   *705*
Bibliography   *739*
Index   *767*

List of Figures

1.1. The Caribbean c.1807–34   *xxvi*
1.2. British Honduras and Jamaica c.1820: Parishes   *xxvii*
1.3. The Bahamas and the British Virgin Islands c.1820   *xxviii*
1.4. St. Kitts, Nevis, Antigua, and Montserrat c.1820: Parishes and Divisions   *xxix*
1.5. Dominica, St. Lucia, St. Vincent, and Barbados c.1820: Parishes, Quarters, and Districts   *xxx*
1.6. Grenada, the Grenadines, and Tobago c.1820: Parishes   *xxxi*
1.7. Trinidad c.1834: Quarters   *xxxii*
1.8. British Guiana c.1831: Parishes   *xxxiii*

2.1. Age by Single Years, Africans and Creoles: Trinidad, 1813   *19*
2.2. Age by Single Years, Africans and Creoles: St. Lucia, 1815   *20*
2.3. Age by Single Years: St. Michael, Barbados, 1817   *21*
2.4. Infant Mortality of Slaves per 1,000 Live Births: St. Kitts, St. Vincent, Tobago, and Berbice, 1817–21   *28*

3.1. Sugar Production, 1800–1834   *51*
3.2. Mustique, 1804   *57*
3.3. Production of Cocoa, Coffee, and Cotton: Trinidad, 1800–1833   *60*
3.4. Land Use: Trinidad, 1832   *61*

4.1. Slave Populations: Total British Caribbean, Barbados, and Demerara-Essequibo, 1807–34   *73*
4.2. Percentage Change in Slave Population per Annum: Classes of Colonies, 1817–34   *75*
4.3. Slave Population Density in the Old Sugar Colonies   *86*
4.4. Slave Population Density in the Windward Islands and Tobago   *89*
4.5. Distribution of Rural Slaves in Trinidad, 1808 and 1832   *91*
4.6. Distribution of Rural Slaves in Demerara-Essequibo and Berbice c.1820   *91*
4.7. Distribution of Slaves, Whites, and Freedmen: Bridgetown c.1830   *96*
4.8. Georgetown, Demerara c.1830   *98*

5.1.   Slave Sex Ratios, 1816–34   *117*
5.2.   Slave Sex Ratios by Age: Classes of Colonies c.1817   *121*
5.3.   Rural and Urban Slave Sex Ratios by Age: Barbados, 1817, and Trinidad, 1813   *122*
5.4.   Distribution of African-born Slaves: Trinidad, 1813   *125*
5.5.   Origins of African-born Slaves: St. Kitts, 1817   *129*
5.6.   Origins of African-born Slaves: St. Lucia, 1815   *131*
5.7.   Origins of African-born Slaves: Trinidad, 1813   *132*
5.8.   Origins of African-born Slaves: Berbice, 1819   *133*
5.9.   Percentage of Slaves African-born by Age: Classes of Colonies c.1817   *134*
5.10. Slave Age Profiles: Classes of Colonies c.1817   *137*
5.11. Slave Age Pyramids: Classes of Colonies c.1817 and 1834   *138*
5.12. Slave Age Pyramids by Colony   *139*
5.13. Male Slave Age Profiles by Crop-type: Trinidad, 1813   *144*
5.14. Slave Age Pyramids: Bridgetown, 1817 and Castries, 1815   *145*
5.15. Age Pyramids of African-born Slaves by Holding-size: St. Kitts, 1817   *146*

6.1.   Peruvian Vale and Henry's Vale Estate, St. Vincent, 1809   *185*
6.2.   Occupations of Slaves by Sex and Age: Rural Trinidad, 1813   *190*
6.3.   Occupations of Slaves by Sex and Age: St. John, Barbados, 1817   *191*
6.4.   Occupations of Slaves by Sex and Age: Rural St. Lucia, 1815   *193*
6.5.   Occupations of Slaves by Sex and Age: Anguilla, 1827   *194*
6.6.   Occupations of Slaves by Sex and Age: Berbice, 1819   *195*
6.7.   Field Slaves by Sex, Age, and Color: St. John, Barbados, 1817   *196*
6.8.   Domestic Slaves by Sex, Age, and Color: St. John, Barbados, 1817   *197*
6.9.   Occupations of Male Slaves by Age and Birthplace: St. Lucia, 1815   *198*

7.1.   Occupations of Slaves by Sex and Age: Urban St. Lucia, 1815   *248*
7.2.   Occupations of Female Slaves by Age: Urban Trinidad, 1813   *249*
7.3.   Occupations of Male Slaves by Age: Urban Trinidad, 1813   *250*
7.4.   Occupations of Slaves by Sex and Age: Bridgetown, 1817   *251*
7.5.   Bridgetown Market Prices, 1812–14   *253*

8.1.   Heights of Creole Male Slaves by Age: Trinidad, 1813, St. Lucia, 1815, Berbice, 1819, and the Bahamas (Trinidad Imports), 1819–25   *284*
8.2.   Heights of Creole Female Slaves by Age: Trinidad, 1813, St. Lucia, 1815, Berbice, 1819, and the Bahamas (Trinidad Imports), 1819–25   *285*
8.3.   Heights of Creole Male Slaves by Age and Color: St. Lucia, 1815   *286*

8.4. Heights of Creole Female Slaves by Age and Color: St. Lucia,
      1815 *287*
8.5. Heights of Rural and Urban Creole Male Slaves by Age: St. Lucia,
      1815 *288*
8.6. Heights of Rural and Urban Creole Female Slaves by Age: St. Lucia,
      1815 *289*
8.7. Heights of Creole Male Slaves by Occupation: St. Lucia, 1815 *290*
8.8. Heights of Creole Female Slaves by Occupation: St. Lucia, 1815 *291*
8.9. Seasonal Morbidity of Slaves: St. Vincent (Peruvian Vale), 1807–8,
      Jamaica (Rose Hall), 1830–31, Barbados (Newton), 1797–98, Baha-
      mas (Farquharson's), 1831–32 *301*

9.1. Natural Increase of Slaves by Colony, 1815–34 *312*
9.2. Age-specific Mortality of Males: Model Life Table Populations (Coale
      and Demeny) *318*
9.3. Age-specific Mortality of Male Slaves Compared with Model Life Table
      Rates: Tobago, St. Kitts, and Anguilla *320*
9.4. Age-specific Slave Mortality by Sex and Colony *321*
9.5. Age-specific Slave Mortality by Sex and Birthplace: Berbice, St. Lucia,
      St. Kitts, and the Virgin Islands *323*
9.6. Age-specific Slave Mortality by Parish: Grenada, 1817–19 and
      1830–32 *327*
9.7. Age-specific Slave Mortality by Sex: Rural and Urban St. Lucia,
      1815–19 *330*
9.8. Seasonality of Slave Deaths: Dominica (Select Plantations), 1817–32,
      Berbice, 1819–22, and Tobago, 1819–21 *336*
9.9. Slave Deaths by Month: Tobago and Berbice, 1819–21 *337*
9.10. Age-specific Slave Mortality by Cause of Death: Tobago,
      1819–21 *345*
9.11. Age-specific Slave Fertility: Berbice, 1819–22, Tobago, 1819–21,
      and St. Lucia, 1815–19 *359*
9.12. Age-specific Slave Fertility by Occupation: Berbice, 1819–22 *363*
9.13. Seasonality of Slave Births: Tobago, 1819–21 and Berbice,
      1819–22 *364*

List of Tables

2.1. Slave Registration Dates *8*

2.2. Data Available in the Initial Slave Registration Returns *12*

2.3. Data on Births and Deaths Available in the Subsequent Registration Returns *13*

2.4. Preference for Digits of Age in the Slave Registration Returns, Shown by the Blended Method: Trinidad, 1813 and St. Lucia, 1815 *18*

2.5. Intraregistration Birth-Deaths as a Percentage of Total Registered Births *27*

2.6. Parameters Used for the Selection of Model Life Tables *31*

2.7. Underregistration of Births: Estimated Directly and by Model Life Tables *32*

2.8. Underregistration of Deaths: Estimated Directly and by Model Life Tables *35*

3.1. The British Colonies in the Caribbean c.1834 *41*

3.2. British Caribbean Slave Population as Classified for Compensation, 1834 *47*

3.3. Distribution of Slaves between Compensation Categories by Colony, 1834 *48*

3.4. Tons of Sugar Produced per Slave by Colony, 1815–34 *51*

3.5. Employment of Slaves in the Virgin Islands, 1815 and 1823 *54*

3.6. Distribution of Slaves by Crop-type: St. Lucia, 1815 *59*

3.7. Distribution of Slaves by Crop-type: Trinidad, 1810 and 1813 *62*

3.8. Estimated Distribution of Slaves by Crop-type and Colony, 1810, 1820, and 1830 *68*

3.9. Estimated Distribution of Slaves by Crop-type: Classes of Colonies, 1810, 1820, and 1830 *71*

4.1. Distribution of the Slave Population by Classes of Colonies, 1807–34 *74*

4.2. Estimated Slave, Freedman, and White Populations by Colony, 1810 and 1830 *77*

4.3. Ranking of Colonies by Average Compensation Payments per Slave, 1834 *79*

4.4. Major Town Slave Populations, 1813–34 *94*

5.1. Distribution of Slaves and Owners by Slaveholding Size and Colony,
        c.1832 *102*
5.2. Distribution of Slaves by Slaveholding Size-group: Sixteen Colonies
        c.1817 and c.1834 *105*
5.3. Slaves per Holding by Crop, in Five Colonies *106*
5.4. Percentage of Slaveowners Unable to Sign Their Registration Returns by
        Sex and Slave-holding Size: Virgin Islands, St. Lucia, Tobago, and
        Berbice, 1815–19 *110*
5.5. Percentage of Slaves Transferred to New Owners by Sex: Select Col-
        onies, 1815–34 *114*
5.6. Slaves Transferred by Sex, Slave-holding Size-group, and Crop:
        St. Lucia, 1815–19 *115*
5.7. Slave Sex Ratios and Percentages African and Colored by Colony, c.1817
        and c.1832 *116*
5.8. Slave Sex Ratios and Percentages African and Colored: Major
        Towns *118*
5.9. Demographic Characteristics by Crop-type: Trinidad and St. Lucia, 1813
        and 1815 *120*
5.10. Birthplaces of African Slaves: St. Kitts, St. Lucia, Trinidad, Berbice, and
        Anguilla, 1813–27 *127*
5.11. Sex Ratios of African Slaves by Birthplace: St. Lucia, Trinidad, and Ber-
        bice, 1813–19 *130*
5.12. Mean Age of Slaves by Sex, Birthplace, and Type of Enterprise:
        St. Lucia, 1815 *143*
5.13. Demographic Characteristics by Slaveholding Size-group: Barbados,
        1832–34 *151*
5.14. Percentage of Slaves Colored by Slaveholding Size-group: Select Col-
        onies, 1815–32 *152*
5.15. Color of Slaves: Eight Colonies, 1813–27 *155*

6.1. Occupations of Slaves: Trinidad, St. Lucia, Berbice, Cayman Islands,
        Anguilla, and British Honduras, 1813–34 *159*
6.2. Occupations of Rural Slaves: Barbados, St. Lucia, and Trinidad,
        1813–17 *160*
6.3. Distribution of Labor on Sugar Estates during Crop: Demerara-Essequibo,
        1832 *165*
6.4. Seasonal Allocation of Slaves to Tasks: Peruvian Vale Estate,
        St. Vincent, 1807–8 *186*
6.5. Percentage of Female and Colored Slaves by Occupation: Rural Bar-
        bados, St. Lucia, and Anguilla, 1815–27 *192*

7.1. Occupations of Urban Slaves: Barbados, St. Lucia, St. Vincent, and Trinidad, 1813–17 *228*

8.1. Heights of Slaves Aged 25–40 Years by Sex and Birthplace: Trinidad, St. Lucia, Berbice, Cuba, and the United States *281*
8.2. Heights of Creole Slaves Aged 25–40 Years Imported into Trinidad, 1819–25, by Sex and Birthplace *283*
8.3. Heights of Male Police Aged 25–40 Years: Jamaica, 1835 *293*
8.4. Physical Deformities and Disabilities by Sex and Birthplace: Berbice, 1819 *293*

9.1. Slave Birth Rates, Death Rates, Rates of Natural Increase, and Sex Ratios by Colony, 1815–34 *308*
9.2. Slave Birth Rates, Death Rates, and Rates of Natural Increase in Towns and Urban Parishes, 1815–34 *313*
9.3. Correlation Coefficients: Twenty Colonies, 1820 *315*
9.4. Correlation Coefficients: Twenty Colonies, 1830 *316*
9.5. Slave Infant Mortality: Model Life Table Estimates *319*
9.6. Slave Birth Rates, Death Rates, Rates of Natural Increase, and Sex Ratios, by Crop-type: St. Lucia, 1815–19 *326*
9.7. Slave Birth Rates, Death Rates, and Rates of Natural Increase by Crop-type: Demerara-Essequibo, 1829–32 *326*
9.8. Causes of Slave Deaths: Grenada, Dominica, Tobago, Demerara-Essequibo, and Berbice, 1817–32 *340*
9.9. Slave Child-Woman Ratios by Colony *356*
9.10. Age-specific Slave Birth Rates by Birthplace: St. Lucia, 1815–19, Tobago, 1819–21, and Berbice, 1819–22 *358*
9.11. Age-specific Slave Birth Rates by Type of Enterprise: St. Lucia, 1815–19 *361*
9.12. Slave Family Types by Enterprise: St. Lucia, 1815 *367*
9.13. Spatial Separation of Slave Mates *370*
9.14. Age-specific Slave Birth Rates by Family Type: St. Lucia, 1815–19 *372*

10.1. Manumission Rates by Colony, 1808–34 *381*

Preface

IT IS MY AIM IN THIS BOOK TO PROVIDE A COMPREHENSIVE ANALY-
sis of the major demographic features of slavery in the British Caribbean between
the abolition of the Atlantic slave trade in 1807 and the abolition of slavery in
1834. The work is complementary to my *Slave Population and Economy in
Jamaica, 1807–1834* (Cambridge University Press, 1976), but there are differences in coverage resulting both from changes in my interests and from differences
in the availability of source materials. Most important, the rich Jamaican data
on economic activity have no real counterpart in the other colonies, so that the
study of economic-demographic relationships is necessarily limited. The emphasis here is more definitely demographic. The slave registration returns, on which
the analysis so largely depends, were in some colonies a great deal more detailed
than those for Jamaica and in others much less informative. My attempt to produce
a truly comparative analysis has been inhibited by such differences in source
materials as much as by the essential difficulty of dealing with the many and varied
territories with their contrasting geographies and settlement histories. Many loose
ends remain. But variation in the nature of slave life is at the core of the present
work, just as it was central to my study of Jamaica. Here, Jamaica is included in the
broad comparative analysis of the British colonies, but variation within the island
is not discussed in any detail.

This book contains many numbers. For convenience, most of the detailed tables
have been gathered together at the end of the volume in a Statistical Supplement. I
cannot claim to have extracted all that can be learned from those tables, and they
are intended to serve as a sourcebook as well as to provide support for arguments
advanced in the text. To an even greater extent, the vast mass of material available
in the original slave registration returns remains underexploited, and I have
certainly left much for others to do. Although I have studied the data for all the
colonies in a general way, it has been possible to treat only a selection of places and
periods in detail. The returns for Demerara-Essequibo have hardly been touched,
for example, and much is to be learned from following through particular colonies,
parishes, or plantations over the entire registration period. It is also to be hoped
that further work along similar lines can be carried out for other regions of the
Americas, so that a broader comparative synthesis of the character of New World
slavery can ultimately be achieved.

A great deal of the labor required to derive the quantitative data for this book can only be described as tedious, boring hack work. Other aspects of the enterprise have been a pleasure, not least the assistance and encouragement I have received from colleagues and friends. For their comments on the final manuscript as well as long-term support I am especially grateful to Stanley Engerman, Merle Higman, Franklin Knight, and Barry Smith. I also benefited from the reading of earlier versions of parts of the work by Carl Campbell, Colin Clarke, Michael Craton, Elsa Goveia, Neville Hall, Jerry Handler, Howard Johnson, David Lowenthal, Herman McKenzie, and Arnie Sio. Useful pieces of data and specialized advice were generously provided by Warren Alleyne, Roberta Delson, Barry Gaspar, Jean Lindsay, Elizabeth Pigou, Gail Saunders, and Richard Sheridan. Financial support over the long period during which I have been involved with this project came from the University of the West Indies, the University of Liverpool, Princeton University, the Australian National University, the American Philosophical Society, the Economic History Association, the Leverhulme Trust, the Research Institute for the Study of Man, and the Social Science Research Council. Help with computing problems was always willingly given by the staffs of the computer centers at the University of the West Indies, Princeton University, and the Australian National University. Most of the writing was done at the Australian National University, and I wish particularly to thank Helen Macnab for her work in producing the script, Leona Jorgensen for preparing camera-ready copy of the supplementary tables, and Lio Pancino for drafting the figures. For permission to quote documents in their possession I thank Columbia University Library and Her Majesty's Customs and Excise Department. Work in archives great and small in the Caribbean and elsewhere was, almost always, made a pleasure by the custodians. I remember particularly the kindness of the many West Indian churchmen who allowed me to use their records and occupy their vestries or living rooms, fortifying me with tea and rum. I recall too the generosity of those who helped me see so much of the Caribbean's beauty, scene of such an extreme example of man's inhumanity to man.

Abbreviations

B.M.H.S.	Barbados Museum and Historical Society
C.O.	Colonial Office
D.A.B.	Department of Archives, Barbados
M.B.C.	Minutes of the Board of Cabildo, Port of Spain (City of Port of Spain Archives)
M.C.P.B.G.	Minutes of the Court of Policy, British Guiana (N.A.G.)
M.C.P.D.E.	Minutes of the Court of Policy, Demerara and Essequibo (N.A.G.)
n.a.	not available
N.A.B.	National Archives, Belize
N.A.G.	National Archives of Guyana
n.c.	not calculated
p	probability
P.P.	*Parliamentary Papers* (Great Britain)
P.R.O.	Public Record Office, London
r	correlation coefficient
S.C.R.B.	Supreme Court Registry, Belize
S.D.	Standard Deviation
S.K.G.A.	St. Kitts Government Archives, Basseterre
T.A.	Tobago Archives, Scarborough
T.71	Slave Registration and Compensation Records (P.R.O.)
U.W.I.	University of the West Indies

Metric Conversion Table

Inch (English)	2.54 cm
Inch (Rijnland)	2.62 cm
Pouce (French)	2.71 cm
Foot	30.5 cm
Yard	0.914 m
Ell	1.15 m
Chain	20.11 m
Mile	1.61 km
Acre	0.405 ha
Quarrée	1.3 ha
Square mile	2.59 km^2
Cubic foot	28.3 dm^3
Pint	568 mL
Gill	0.7 litre
Gallon	4.55 litre
Pound	454 g
Ton	1.02 tonne

Note: £1 sterling = £1.4 currency

Maps

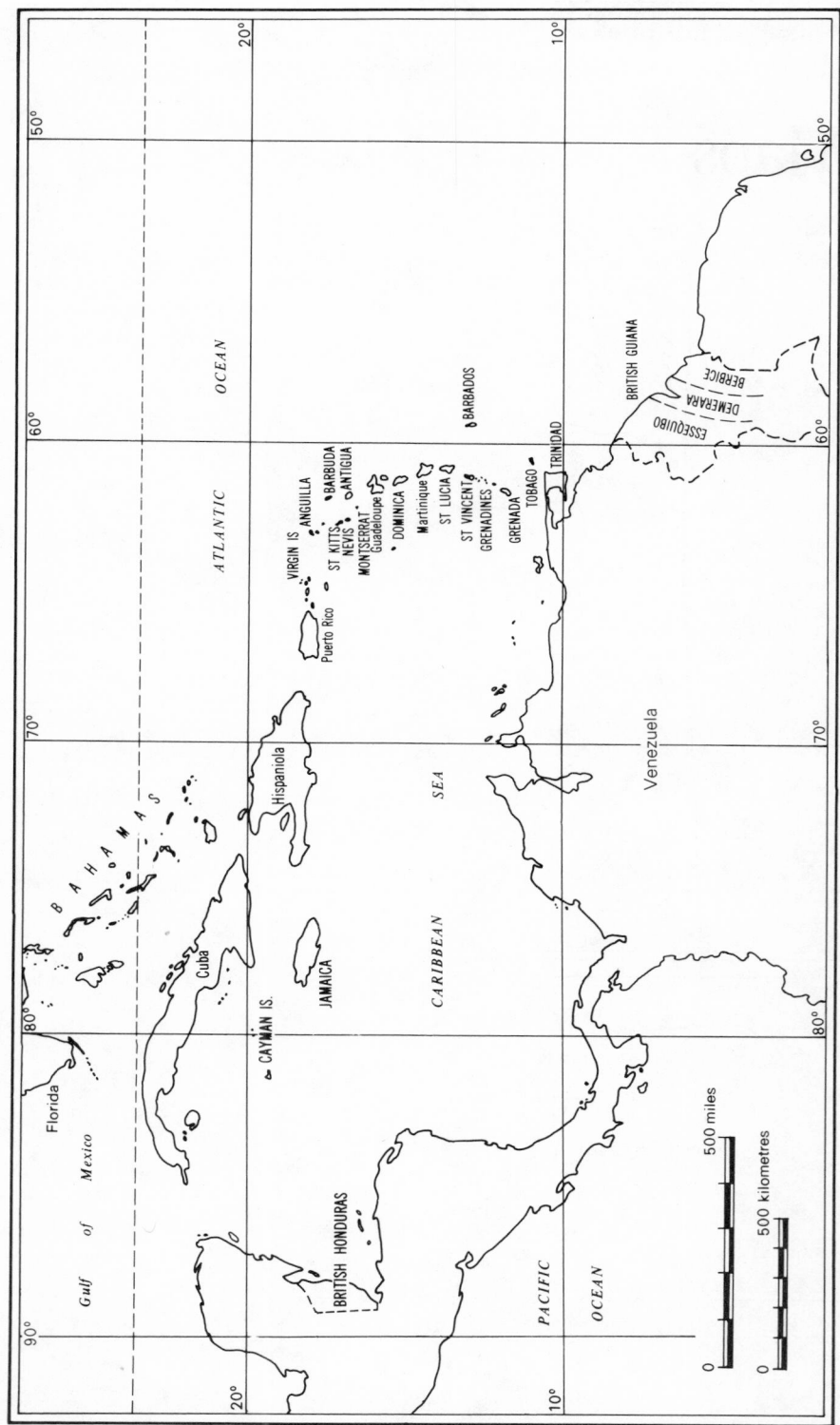

Fig. 1.1. *The Caribbean c.1807–34. The names of the British colonies are shown in capital letters.*

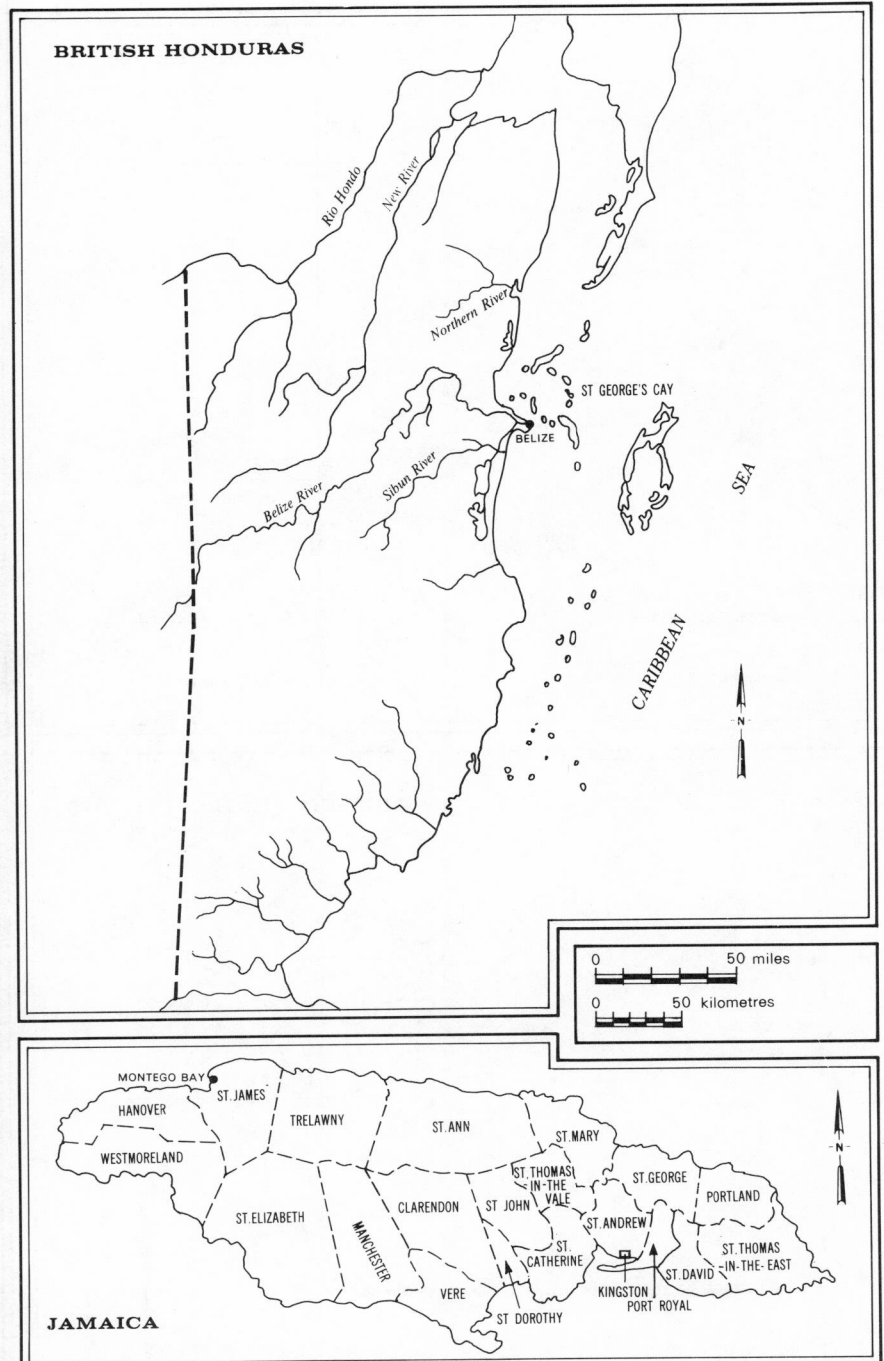

Fig. 1.2.   *British Honduras and Jamaica c.1820: Parishes*

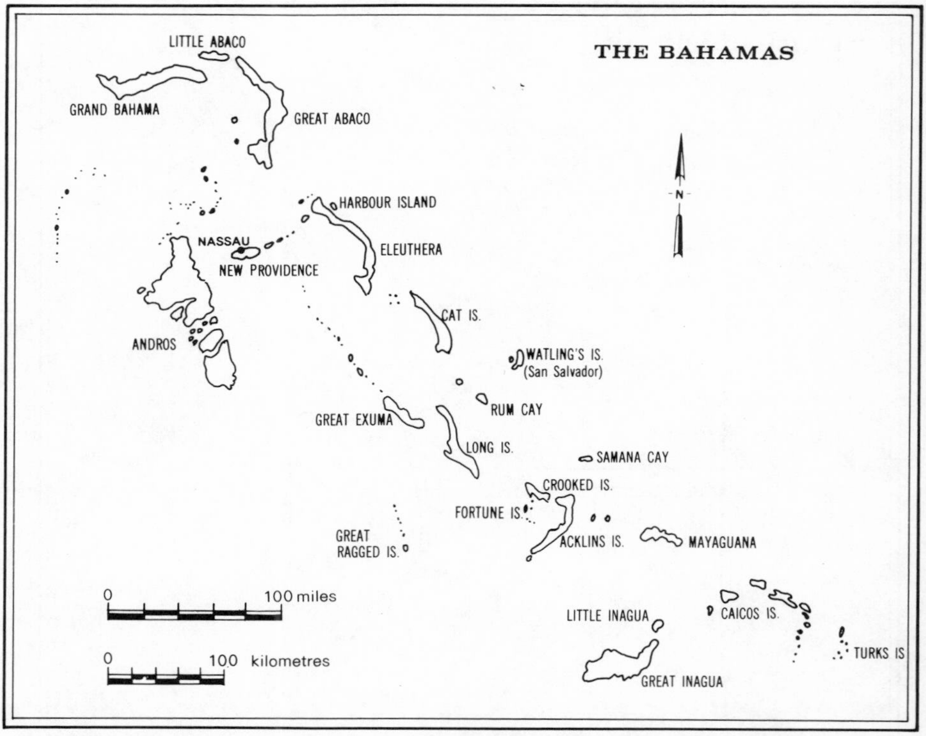

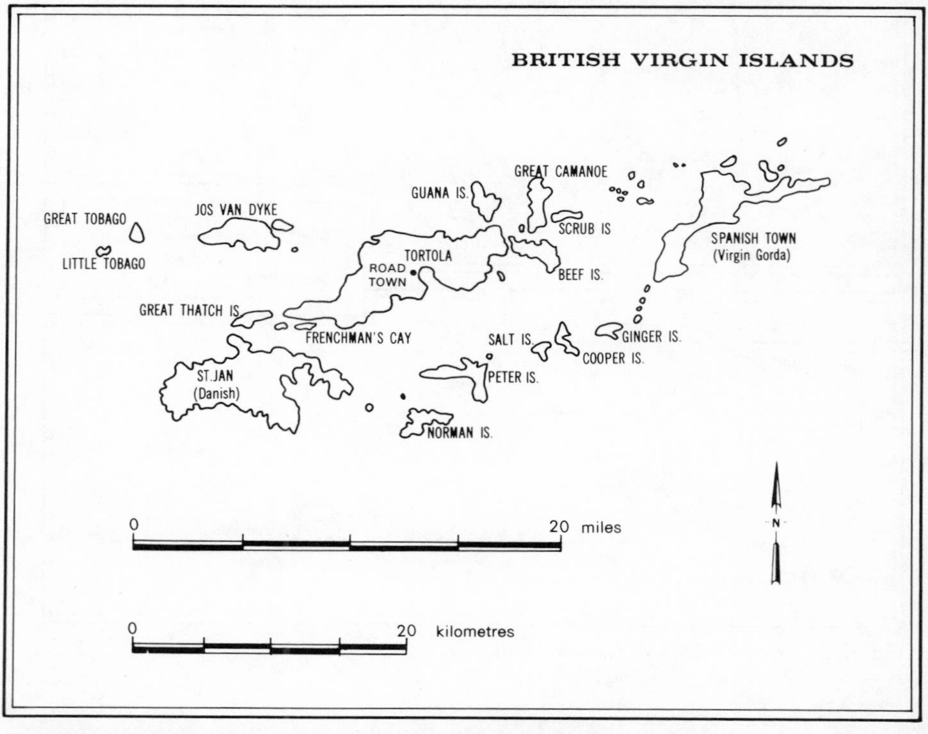

THE BAHAMAS

LITTLE ABACO
GRAND BAHAMA
GREAT ABACO
HARBOUR ISLAND
NASSAU
NEW PROVIDENCE
ELEUTHERA
CAT IS.
WATLING'S IS.
(San Salvador)
ANDROS
RUM CAY
GREAT EXUMA
LONG IS.
SAMANA CAY
CROOKED IS.
FORTUNE IS.
GREAT
RAGGED IS.
ACKLINS IS.
MAYAGUANA
LITTLE INAGUA
CAICOS IS.
TURKS IS
GREAT INAGUA

0   100 miles

0   100 kilometres

BRITISH VIRGIN ISLANDS

GREAT CAMANOE
GUANA IS.
GREAT TOBAGO
JOS VAN DYKE
SCRUB IS
LITTLE TOBAGO
TORTOLA
ROAD
TOWN
BEEF IS.
SPANISH TOWN
(Virgin Gorda)
GREAT THATCH IS.
FRENCHMAN'S CAY
SALT IS.
GINGER IS.
COOPER IS.
ST.JAN
(Danish)
PETER IS.
NORMAN IS.

0   20 miles

0   20 kilometres

N

Fig. 1.3.   *The Bahamas and the British Virgin Islands c.1820*

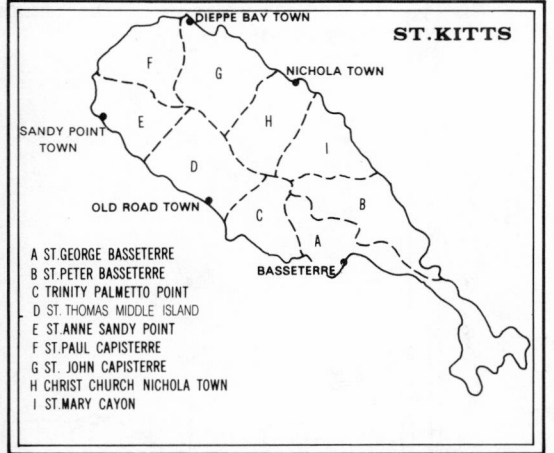

ST. KITTS

DIEPPE BAY TOWN
NICHOLA TOWN
SANDY POINT TOWN
OLD ROAD TOWN
BASSETERRE

A ST. GEORGE BASSETERRE
B ST. PETER BASSETERRE
C TRINITY PALMETTO POINT
D ST. THOMAS MIDDLE ISLAND
E ST. ANNE SANDY POINT
F ST. PAUL CAPISTERRE
G ST. JOHN CAPISTERRE
H CHRIST CHURCH NICHOLA TOWN
I ST. MARY CAYON

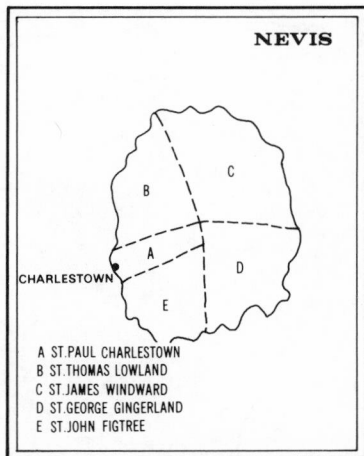

NEVIS

CHARLESTOWN

A ST. PAUL CHARLESTOWN
B ST. THOMAS LOWLAND
C ST. JAMES WINDWARD
D ST. GEORGE GINGERLAND
E ST. JOHN FIGTREE

ANTIGUA

DIVISIONS

ST. JOHN'S PARISH

1 Dickinsons Bay

2 St. Johns

3 Five Islands

ST. MARY'S PARISH

4 New

5 Bermudian Valley

6 Old Road

ST. GEORGE'S PARISH

7 New North Sound

ST. PETER'S PARISH

8 Old North Sound

9 Mercers Creek

ST. PHILIP'S PARISH

10 Belfast

11 Nonsuch

ST. PAUL'S PARISH

12 Willoughby Bay

13 Falmouth

14 Rendezvous Bay

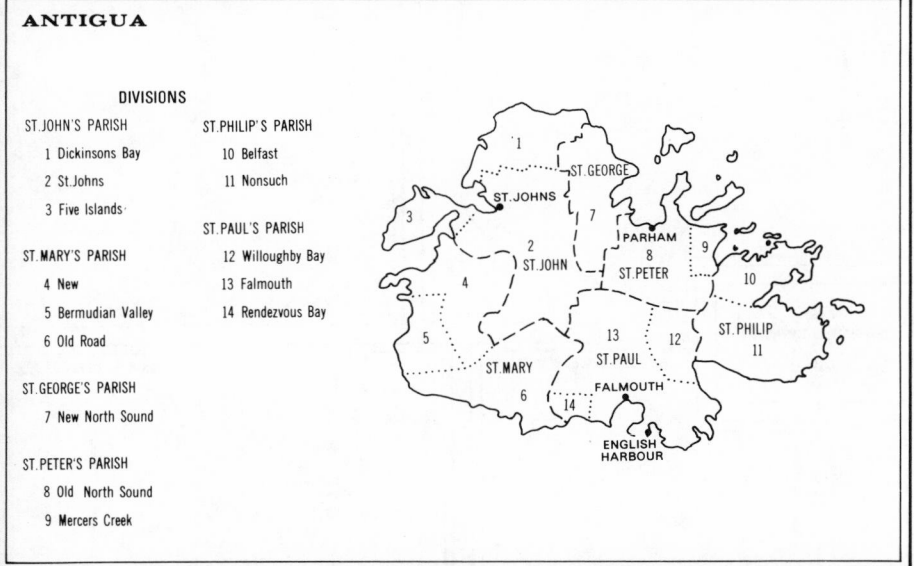

MONTSERRAT

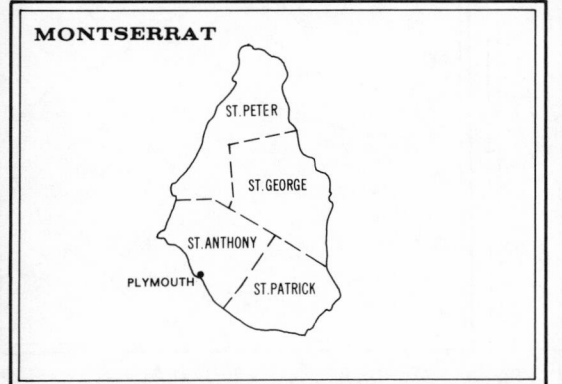

ST. PETER
ST. GEORGE
ST. ANTHONY
PLYMOUTH
ST. PATRICK

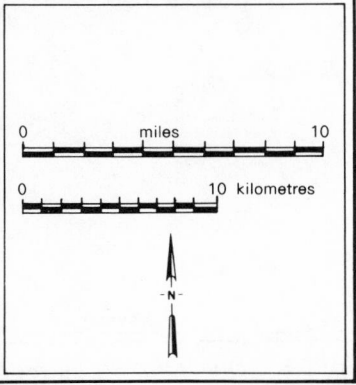

0 miles 10

0 10 kilometres

-N-

[xxix]

Fig. 1.4.   *St. Kitts, Nevis, Antigua, and Montserrat c.1820: Parishes and Divisions*

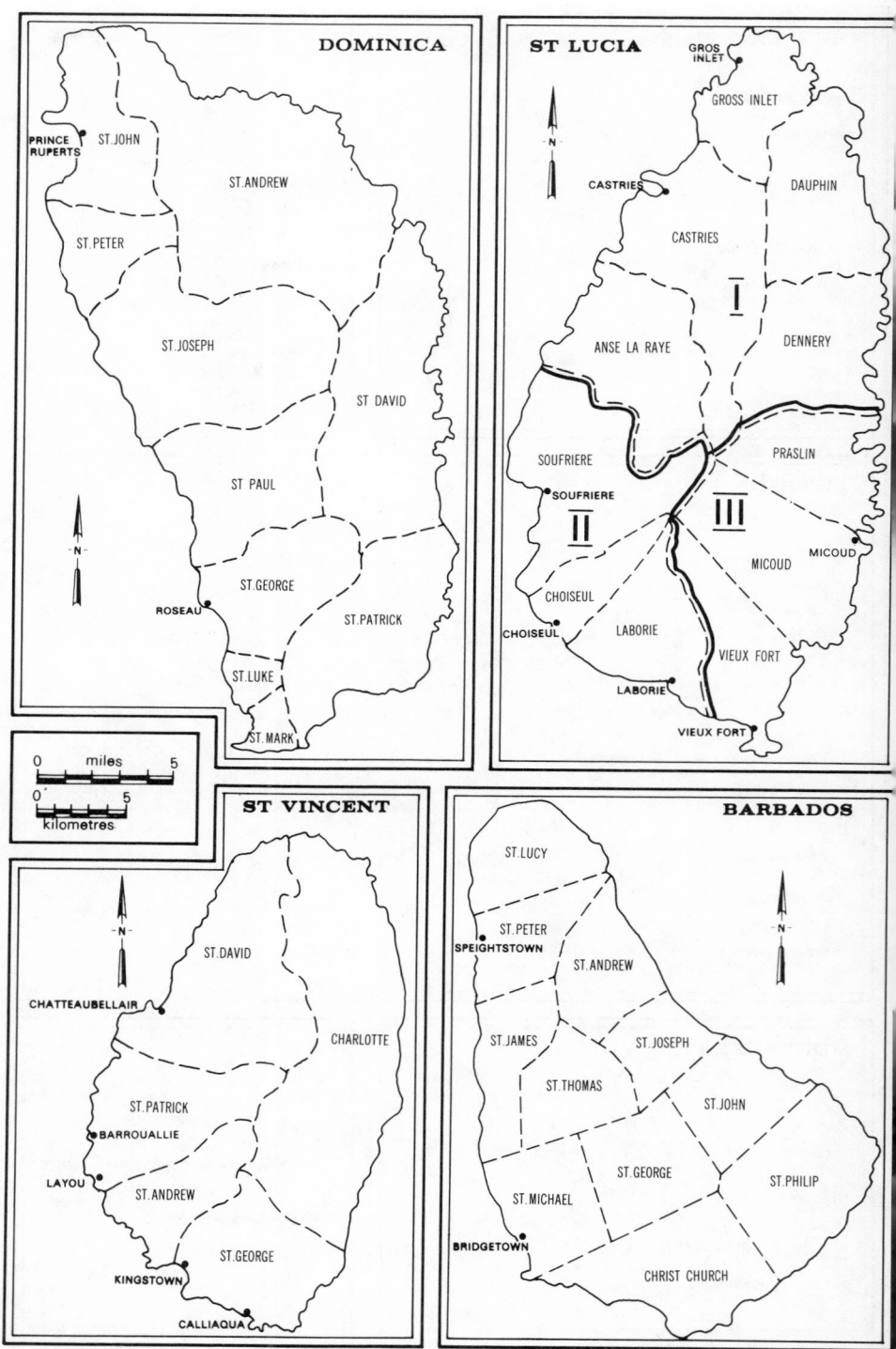

Fig. 1.5. *Dominica, St. Lucia, St. Vincent, and Barbados c.1820: Parishes, Quarters, and Districts*

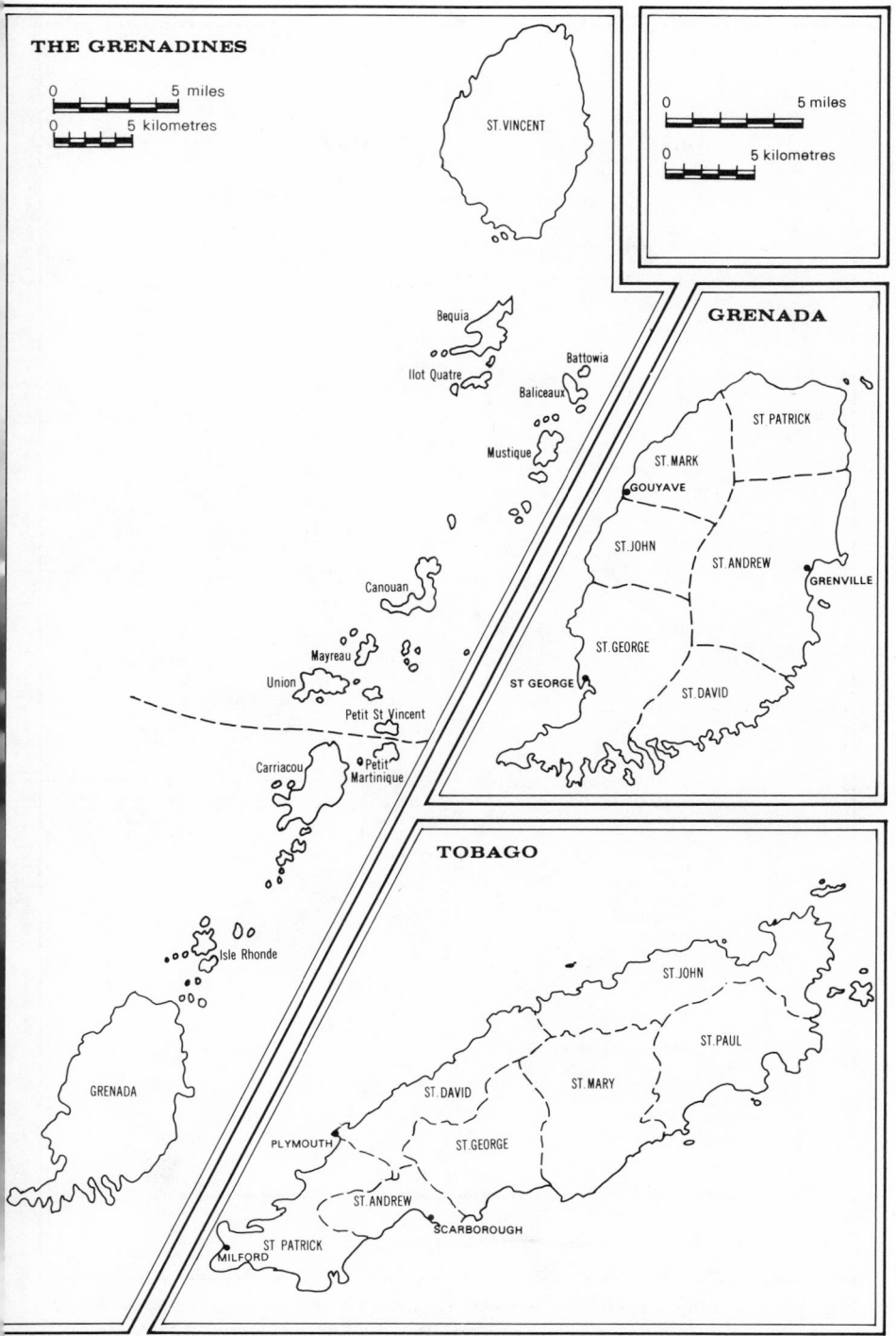

THE GRENADINES

0 ——— 5 miles

0 ——— 5 kilometres

ST.VINCENT

0 ——— 5 miles

0 ——— 5 kilometres

GRENADA

Bequia

Battowia

Ilot Quatre

Baliceaux

Mustique

ST PATRICK

ST.MARK

GOUYAVE

ST.JOHN

ST.ANDREW

GRENVILLE

Canouan

Mayreau

ST.GEORGE

Union

ST GEORGE

Petit St Vincent

ST.DAVID

Carriacou

Petit
Martinique

TOBAGO

Isle Rhonde

ST.JOHN

ST.PAUL

GRENADA

ST.MARY

ST.DAVID

PLYMOUTH

ST.GEORGE

ST.ANDREW

SCARBOROUGH

ST.PATRICK

MILFORD

Fig. 1.6.   *Grenada, the Grenadines, and Tobago c.1820: Parishes*

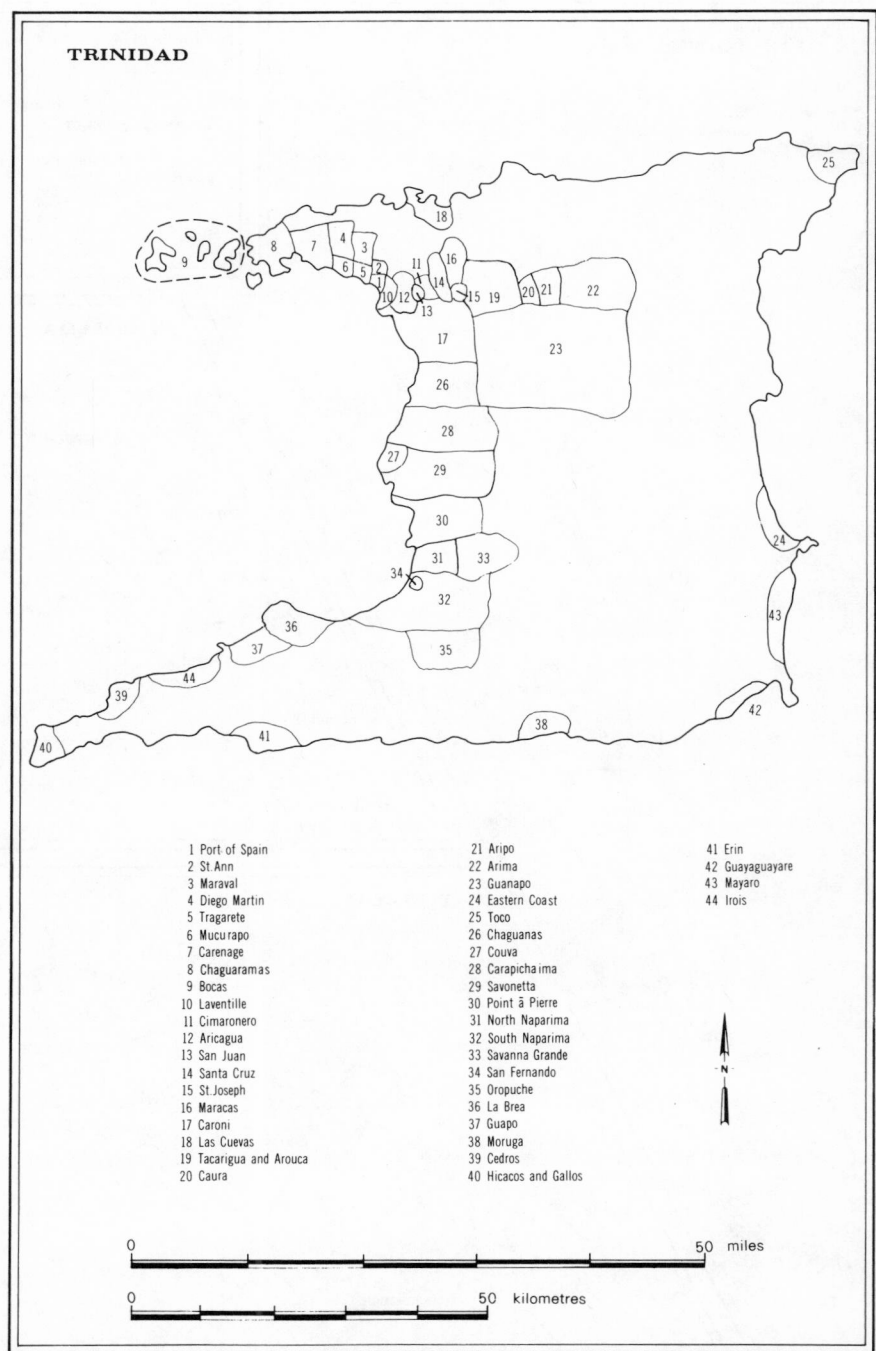

TRINIDAD

1 Port of Spain	21 Aripo	41 Erin
2 St.Ann	22 Arima	42 Guayaguayare
3 Maraval	23 Guanapo	43 Mayaro
4 Diego Martin	24 Eastern Coast	44 Irois
5 Tragarete	25 Toco	
6 Mucurapo	26 Chaguanas	
7 Carenage	27 Couva	
8 Chaguaramas	28 Carapichaima	
9 Bocas	29 Savonetta	
10 Laventille	30 Point à Pierre	
11 Cimaronero	31 North Naparima	
12 Aricagua	32 South Naparima	
13 San Juan	33 Savanna Grande	
14 Santa Cruz	34 San Fernando	
15 St.Joseph	35 Oropuche	
16 Maracas	36 La Brea	
17 Caroni	37 Guapo	
18 Las Cuevas	38 Moruga	
19 Tacarigua and Arouca	39 Cedros	
20 Caura	40 Hicacos and Gallos	

0 _____ 50 miles

0 _____ 50 kilometres

Fig. 1.7. *Trinidad c.1834: Quarters.* (Sources: *The quarters are those listed by the Compensation Commissioners* [Port of Spain Gazette, *24 March 1835*]. *The area of each quarter was given in the Bluebook* [C.O.300/46, *p. 118*]; *the boundaries are derived by locating the property names in the detailed lists of* ''*estates and proprietors*'' *for each quarter* [Trinidad Almanack, 1830, *pp. 72–86*] *and plotting on the cadastral map of 1936.*)

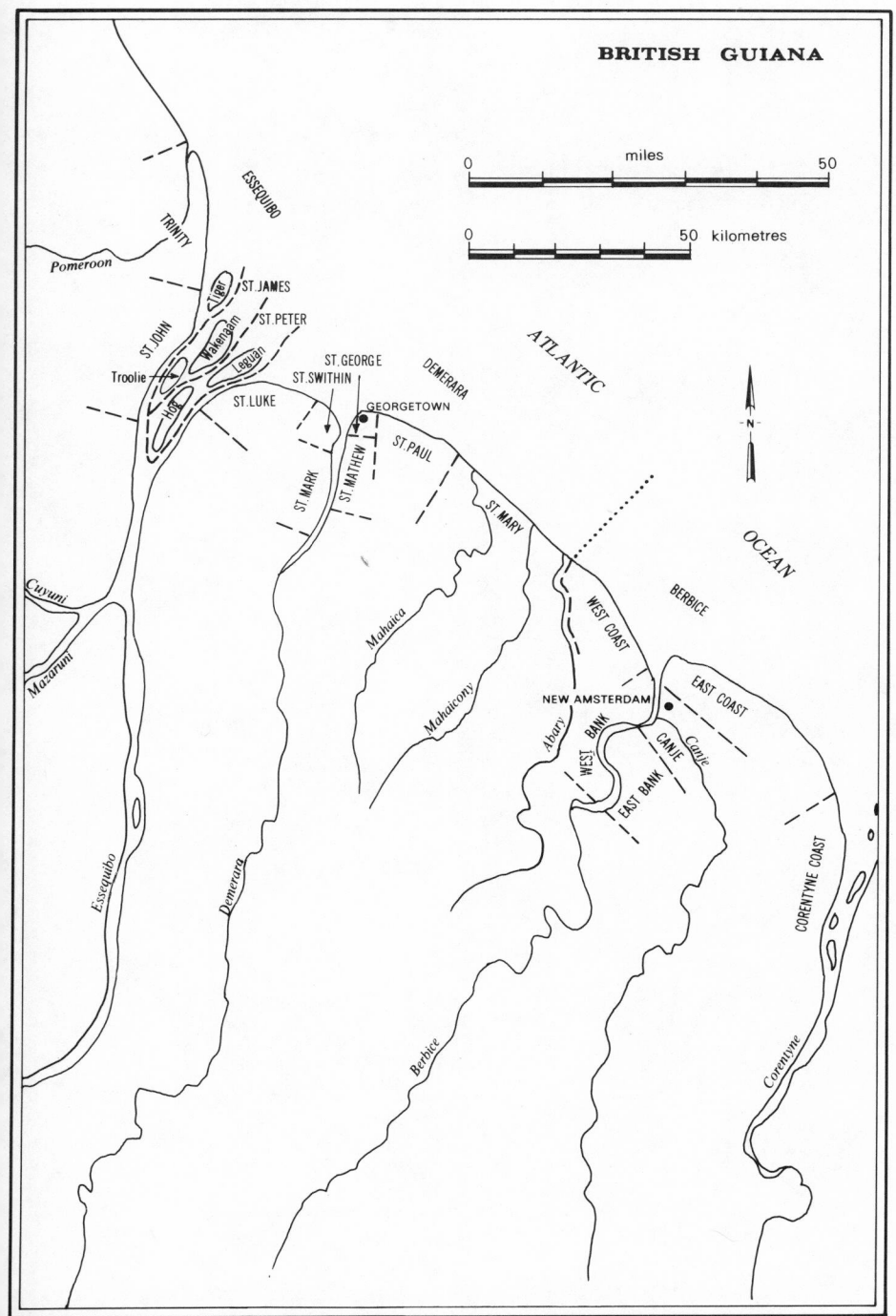

Fig. 1.8. *British Guiana c.1831: Parishes.* (Sources: *M.C.P.D.E.*, 1825,
vol. 2, p. 660; ibid., 1826, vol. 2, p. 165; Demerara Vade-mecum, 1821,
pp. 73–76.)

1.
Slavery and Comparative History

VARIATIONS IN THE DEMOGRAPHIC EXPERIENCE OF WEST INDIAN slaves were determined principally by their material conditions of life. Those material conditions, it will be argued, were the product of essentially economic forces rather than any particular characteristics of the slaveowners such as personal temperament and religion or laws and state systems. The exploitation of slave labor in the New World and the Old took certain characteristic forms, which cut across these superstructural variables and were rooted in distinct combinations of productive forces. In the Caribbean the typical form of exploitation was the sugar plantation. This dominance was of fundamental importance, since the large-scale plantation was commonly associated with extreme demands on labor throughout the history of slave societies.[1] But even in the British Caribbean a significant proportion of the slave population lived and worked in situations beyond the plantation boundaries, and their demographic experience differed in consequence.

To attempt any comparative analysis of slavery, it is essential to recognize the importance of the contexts in which particular slave populations existed, and to appreciate the fact that these contexts were products of the actions of slaves and non-slaveowning free people as much as slaveowners. West Indian slaves could, and did, make decisions that affected the structure of their material world, not merely within the context of rules imposed by their masters but as a contribution to the very creation of that context. Further, slave societies were constructed on the assumption that the presence of slaves could always affect the outcome of the behavior of free as well as slave people. In view of this complex web of interactions, a recognition that slavery cannot be abstracted from its context may seem to erect impossible obstacles to comparative analysis. As Moses Finley argues, in the case of the classical slave societies of the ancient world, ultimately "a genuine 'synthesis' of the history of ancient slavery can only be a history of Graeco-Roman society."[2] The same might be said of the history of almost any institution or class, however. At one level, comparative history may be seen merely as the comparison of contexts, but the advantage of the approach is that it permits an understanding of the range of forms an institution may take and provides a means of explaining such variations.[3]

In the study of slavery in the Americas, the comparative method has been directed primarily at variations in the treatment of slaves.[4] As well as suggesting a one-way relationship, it has become clear that the method is likely to be invalid in the absence of precise definition of what is meant by "treatment" and "stages" of social and economic development.[5] Causal factors determining regional and temporal variations are too readily confused in the grander interpretations. Eugene Genovese has usefully distinguished three meanings of "treatment".[6] The first covers "day-to-day living conditions," including "such essentially measurable items as quantity and quality of food, clothing, housing, length of the working day, and the general condition of labor." The second meaning, which Genovese terms "conditions of life," covers the ability of slaves to develop an independent cultural life, particularly in terms of family organization, religion, and personality development. The third category concerns "access to freedom and citizenship," the ease with which slaves could obtain manumission and find a place in free society. To a certain extent, these three separate aspects of the treatment of slaves varied independently. Thus, grand interpretations based on any one category, at the scale of the imperial system or nation, do not necessarily match findings based on another. It is difficult, if not impossible, to make general judgments as to which slave system was the most harsh, since the answer may vary with the category selected for analysis. Certainly there was no clear relationship between the demographic experience of New World slave populations and their relative access to freedom or their ability to practice religions, for example.

Scholars have, in cavalier fashion, compared Iberian and Anglo-Saxon slave-owners, Catholics and Protestants, the United States and Brazil. The underlying assumption is that slave societies were sufficiently uniform at such a scale that one can make useful generalizations. This is dubious. In the first place, it is known that slave societies and slave populations changed over time in response to economic change. In his study of Cuba, for example, Franklin Knight argues that the sugar revolution, which occurred in that island only after 1763, produced a slave society organized in much the same way as all societies based on the sugar plantation, from Brazil to Barbados, St. Domingue, Jamaica, and Louisiana. Metropolitan influences and timing were relatively insignificant. Thus, Knight concludes that comparative studies of slave societies "should be concerned less with concurrent time spans and metropolitan institutional influences than with equivalent stages of economic and social growth."[7]

The second major criticism that may be directed at the hemispheric systems in the comparative study of slavery concerns the spatial scale of generalization. Essentially, historians have thought in terms of the vast expanses of empires and nations, blissfully ignoring the considerable diversity contained within such large-scale geographical units. In part, this explains the early emphasis on legal systems and laws rather than practice. But critiques of recent works that break away from this pattern and focus on the conditions of life of the slave have tended to stress the ahistorical character of these works rather than their failure to recognize spatial diversity.[8] David Lowenthal argues that within the West Indies, "geography made more difference than nationality" in the treatment of slaves. But, he continues, "Most variations in slave treatment were trivial or inconsistent. The West Indian slave suffered much the same fate everywhere; differences reflect the character or circumstances of slave-owners more than any territorial distinctions."[9] There is a great need to test the validity of this common assumption of spatial homogeneity in the nature of slave systems.

Alongside the hemispheric comparative analysis of slavery, of course, there have always been local studies, particularly studies of individual plantations. In recent times some of these too have been cast in the comparative mold. This trend may be exemplified by Michael Craton's comparison of individual slaveholdings in the Bahamas and Jamaica and Richard Dunn's comparison of plantations in Virginia and Jamaica.[10] Although these studies are suggestive, they contain their own pitfalls. They rest on the invalid assumption that the plantation was a microcosm of the larger society and economy, and so ignore the variety of slave experience found in town and country. Again, they necessarily assume a degree of typicality which is not supportable. They are data-bound, so the comparisons often fail to interlock and questions are left hanging in the air for want of specific information. To understand the conditions of life of slaves it is necessary to take into account their relationships with other, nonplantation units, and this can be achieved only on a broader regional scale.

The analysis attempted in this book sails somewhere between these two extremes, the grand systems and the local studies. It comprehends all of the British colonies in the Caribbean and depends chiefly on systematic data covering entire populations rather than sample plantations or regions. It covers the period between the abolition of the Atlantic slave trade (1807) and emancipation (1834), when the total slave population of the colonies fell from roughly 775,000 to 665,000. This decline was matched by growth in other New World slave populations, so that the proportion of the total slave population of the Americas living in the British Caribbean dropped significantly during the period. The British Caribbean remained a very substantial component of the whole, however. The slave populations of the United States and Brazil, by far the largest in the Americas, barely exceeded 1,000,000 in 1807. In that year, then, the British Caribbean accounted for almost one-quarter of all slaves living in the Americas. Within the Caribbean, the importance of the British colonies was even more significant. In 1807 there were approximately 1,150,000 slaves in the Caribbean, two-thirds of them in British colonies. The subsequent decline of the British colonies together with the rapid growth of Cuba meant that by 1834, when the total slave population of the Caribbean was 1,300,000, the proportion in the British colonies had fallen to barely more than one-half.[11] But the British Caribbean remained of outstanding importance throughout the period.

Slavery existed in British colonies outside the Caribbean, so the British Caribbean was not equivalent to an imperial system, and events in other parts of the empire had ramifications for the Caribbean colonies. The most important of these other colonies were Bermuda, with a slave population of 4,000 in 1834, the

Cape of Good Hope (38,000), Mauritius and the Seychelles (70,000), and Ceylon (10,000).[12] These colonies have been excluded from this study in order to preserve the unity of the Caribbean as a geographical region and reduce the complexity of contextual variables.

The internal diversity of the British Caribbean must also be considered in terms of differences in the colonies' histories of imperial influence, some of them having been French, Dutch, or Spanish possessions to the end of the eighteenth century. Hence, the imperial factor is held constant only for the period 1807–34, and differences in previous patterns of European colonization and control had an important impact on stages of economic and social development. Thus, the internal diversity of the British Caribbean may have to be traced to differing stages of growth as well as to discrete economic and social structures.

Few historians of British Caribbean slave societies have been concerned with internal diversity.[13] Strongly contrasting studies of particular colonial units have been produced, but the differences lie more in the interpretation of the nature and place of slavery in these societies than in the recognition of genuine diversity.[14] Edward Brathwaite has advanced an analytical classification of Caribbean plantation societies, covering both slavery and the post-emancipation periods, but he argues that "with variations" processes observable in Jamaica applied to "the anglophone Caribbean plantation system as a whole."[15] In her seminal work on the Leeward Islands at the end of the eighteenth century, Elsa Goveia is careful to say that she regards those islands as "mature examples of the West Indian slave colony."[16] But here the identification of regional diversity emerges from a recognition of stages of development rather than fundamental structural differences. Colonies not based on the sugar plantation receive scant mention in Goveia's work. In his study of British Honduras, Nigel Bolland concludes only that "the conditions of slavery . . . differed somewhat from those on the Caribbean plantations."[17] Studies of slavery in the Windward Islands and the Bahamas have also been completed but remain unpublished, and there are as yet no comprehensive works on Barbados, Trinidad, or Guyana.[18]

It is perhaps not very surprising that in all of this work the colony has been the dominant unit of study. The British West Indies comprised a scattered set of territories, varying greatly in size and physical geography, and with complex political histories. But while these factors provide a ready explanation for the direction of research, the very difficulties underline the need for a broad survey if the particular studies are not to exist within a vacuum or an untested supposed unity. It is the primary aim of this book to provide the necessary demographic framework for comparative analysis. All 20 British Caribbean colonies are discussed, though variations in the available data prevent systematic comparisons on all points. The goal is to establish what was *typical* of the slave populations after 1807 and also to establish the limits of the *possible*.

The central feature of the experience of the British Caribbean slave population was the general failure to achieve a natural increase, to show more births than deaths. This failure threatened the population with eventual extinction. Before the abolition of the Atlantic slave trade to the British colonies, the population was constantly augmented by fresh recruits from Africa. But the continued harshness of the regimes under which the slaves labored after 1807 made ultimate extinction a real possibility. While the British colonies shared this experience with most of tropical America, it was quite the reverse in North America where the slave population grew as rapidly as the free.[19] More importantly, there were within the British Caribbean significant variations in the level of natural increase achieved between 1807 and 1834. The magnitude of these variations was at least as great as the difference between the two regions as a whole. Such variations were apparent at a number of levels within the British Caribbean and affected entire colonies as well as particular types of slaveholdings. Thus, it is necessary to explain this diversity of experience as much as the general failure of population growth.

2.
Materials
and Methods

SOURCE MATERIALS AVAILABLE FOR THE STUDY OF SLAVERY IN the British Caribbean between 1807 and 1834 are much more extensive than those for any earlier period.[1] In large part, this abundance results from the unprecedented interest shown in the slave population by abolitionists and missionaries. Abolitionism produced a voluminous literature of propaganda, parliamentary investigations, and, most important for the present study, the slave registration and compensation records. European missionaries reported regularly to their parent churches and compiled data on their slave congregations. The period was also distinguished by the number of books and pamphlets, written by travelers, planters, and other observers, describing West Indian society from both proslavery and antislavery perspectives. The West Indian press was more active than in the seventeenth and eighteenth centuries, particularly in the publication of newspapers and periodicals. The quantity of plantation records surviving from this period is unusually large, and the data they contain are generally richer than for earlier periods.

Use is made of each of these types of source material in this book. It is not necessary to supply a critique of each of them here, but one source, the slave registration records, is sufficiently systematic to deserve separate discussion. These records are fundamental to the analysis that follows, so it is useful to deal at once with the major technical problems they present. Specific features of the data will be considered as they arise, but the present chapter aims to provide an overview of the origins and administration of the registration system and to make a general assessment of the quality of the data.

SLAVE REGISTRATION: ORIGINS AND ADMINISTRATION

Slave registration was meant to identify slaves brought to the West Indies in the illicit Atlantic slave trade that continued after the British abolition of 1807. The abolitionists believed that by taking a complete census of the slave population and recording all subsequent movements resulting from birth, death, sale, or manumission, the failure to account for any slave through the registration system could be taken as presumptive evidence of illegal importation. Thus, the origins of slave registration lie in abolitionist attempts to effectively close off the Atlantic slave trade by policing the movement of slaves within the West Indies. At the same time, the abolitionists worked to plug the African end of the trade by promoting the act that made slave trading a felony in 1811 and working for international abolition at the Congress of Vienna.[2] The abolitionists' preoccupation with the slave trade, rather than with the institution of slavery itself, lay in their belief that amelioration would occur only when the West Indian planter could see no hope of replacing losses in his labor force by recourse to the Atlantic slave trade and would be forced to depend on natural increase in the population.

The abolitionists began to argue for the introduction into Parliament of a bill to require the registration of slaves in Trinidad as early as 1810, but the government avoided this by allowing James Stephen to draft an order in council in 1812.[3] The first registration of slaves took place in Trinidad in 1813. A similar order in council was applied to St. Lucia in 1814, and the slaves were registered the following year. The campaign for a general registration was delayed until 1815, but the assemblies of the legislative colonies objected to parliamentary interference in what they regarded as their internal affairs and eventually accepted responsibility for passing slave registration acts of their own. Jamaica and Barbados passed acts in 1816, and the other colonies in 1817, except that the Bahamas delayed until 1821, Anguilla until 1827, and British Honduras and the Cayman Islands until 1834 (table 2.1).

The orders in council for Trinidad and St. Lucia, and the various colonial acts, contained provisions for the administration of the registration system, set fines for the omission of slaves, and specified the data to be included in the returns. In most of the colonies, the system was administered by a salaried Registrar of Slaves, appointed by the government, who received the returns and employed clerks to copy them into volumes, or "registers." Duplicate copies of the latter were also made and sent to the central Slave Registry Office in London. Although many of the original registers no longer survive in West Indian archives, the duplicates exist as an intact series.[4]

The order in council that applied to Trinidad required that the Registrar of Slaves not be a slaveowner. Henry Murray, nominated by the Governor in 1812, sold his slaves and estates in order to qualify. The Privy Council at first refused to grant him the post, so Murray traveled to England to explain that it was impossible to find any person in Trinidad of sufficient "respectability" for the office who did not own slaves. In March 1813 Murray returned to Trinidad confirmed in his appointment, with a salary of £500 sterling and the right to fees.[5] Two days after his return, a proclamation was issued requiring all persons owning slaves to deliver their registration returns personally, on oath, either at the Registrar's office, on Brunswick Square in Port of Spain, or to a deputy in the appropriate district. Returns were supposed to be made within one calendar month, but the difficulties of travel within Trinidad resulted in an extension of the period to 14 October 1813.[6]

Table 2.1. *Slave Registration Dates*

Colony	Date of Original Registration Act or Order in Council	Date of Original Return (Census)		Dates of Subsequent Registration Returns[a]
Barbados	17 Dec. 1816	1817	(1 May)	*1820 1823* 1826 1829 1832 *1834* (1 Mar.)
St. Kitts	17 May 1817	1817	(1 June)	*1822* (1 Jan.) *1825 1828 1831 1834*
Nevis	16 Apr. 1817	1817	(1 July)	1822 (1 Jan.) 1825 1828 1831 1834
Antigua	18 Mar. 1817	1817	(1 Oct.)	*1821 1824 1828* (1 Apr.) *1832* (1 Jan.)
Montserrat	10 July 1817	1817	(31 Dec.)	*1821 1824 1828 1831*
Virgin Islands	6 Sept. 1817	1818	(1 Feb.)	*1822 1825 1828 1831 1834*
Jamaica	11 Dec. 1816	1817	(28 June)	1820 1823 1826 1829 1832
Dominica	10 Mar. 1817	1817	(1 Mar.)	*1820* 1823 1826 *1829* 1832
St. Lucia	26 Sept. 1814	1815	(1 Nov.)	1819 (1 Jan.) 1822 1825 1828 1831 1834
St. Vincent	28 Mar. 1817	1817	(27 Mar.)	1822 (1 Jan.) 1825 1828 1831 1834
Grenada	31 Mar. 1817	1817	(30 Apr.)	1818 (1 Jan.) 1819 1820 *1821* 1822 1823 1824 *1825* 1826 1827 1828 *1829* 1830 1831 1832 *1833 1834*
Tobago	8 Feb. 1817	1819	(1 Jan.)	1820 1821 1822 1823 1824 1825 1826 1827 1828 1829 1830 1831 1832 1833 1834
Trinidad	26 Mar. 1812	1813	(1 Apr.)	1815 (1 Jan.) 1816 1819 1822 1825 1828 1831 1834 (1 Mar.)
Demerara-Essequibo	18 Mar. 1817	1817	(31 May)	*1820 1823 1826 1829 1832*
Berbice	3 Sept. 1817	1817	(1 Nov.)	
		1819	(1 Jan.)	1822 1825 1828 1831 1834
British Honduras	1834	1834	(1 May)	
Cayman Islands	1834	1834	(2 Apr.)	
Bahamas	6 Apr. 1821	1822	(1 Jan.)	1825 1828 1831 1834 (31 July)
Anguilla	1827	1827	(1 Jan.)	1832 1834

Sources: P.P., 1835, vol. 51 (235), ''Slavery Abolition Proceedings,'' p. 289; *P.P.,* 1817, vol. 17 (338), ''Additional Colonial Laws Respecting Slaves''; T.71/678–1; T.71 Index (P.R.O.).

[a]Dates shown in italics indicate census-type returns together with returns providing data on movements. Exact dates are given only when changes occurred in the day of registration.

Murray employed two clerks, alternately relieved by two others, working twelve hours a day, transcribing the returns into two ponderous volumes, one for ''plantation'' slaves and the other for ''personal'' slaves not attached to agricultural units. The masters were given a month to make good omissions resulting from accidental causes. Then duplicate copies were made for the Colonial Slave Registry Office in London. In February 1814 Murray's clerks were still busy making indexes, eight of them working from 6 A.M. to 9 P.M. daily.[7]

This delay in the completion of the Trinidad registration created suspicion that the late returns comprised slaves imported illicitly, though the vast majority of the returns were in fact made in the first month.[8] By January 1817 some 58 judicial cases had been heard concerning defaulters in the initial Trinidad registration, but 49 of these returns were admitted by the Registrar and another three on appeal to the Governor.[9] Corrections were made to the original returns of some "absentees and incapacitated persons" by special commissioners who traveled around the island. This process was valuable, said the Governor, "for the original returns were generally defective and imperfect."[10]

Subsequent registration returns were designed to record all changes in the Trinidad slave population, whether resulting from birth, death, manumission, sale, purchase, marronage (desertion), or transportation. Slaveowners were also required to record changes in the stature of growing children, "by actual measurement," and changes in bodily marks.[11] After a brief attempt to obtain annual returns, in 1815 and 1816, Trinidad adopted a triennial system of registration. The principal reason for this change was the difficulty involved in travel within Trinidad; no arrangements were made for the collection of returns in the countryside after 1813, and masters had to deliver their returns personally to the Registrar's office in Port of Spain. But the process of copying the masters' returns into volumes and then sending authenticated duplicates to London was continued. In 1821 Henry Murray resigned the post of Registrar and was succeeded by his son Edward.[12] The final registration of slaves in Trinidad was carried out in 1834.

The registration procedures employed in Trinidad were followed quite closely in the other colonies, except that in Jamaica and the Bahamas no special registrar was appointed and the work was performed by the Secretaries of those colonies. In Barbados, the Registrar, Conrade Adams Howell (succeeded by his son Benjamin in 1824), also held the offices of Island Treasurer and Storekeeper, and was a lieutenant colonel in the militia. Thus, in 1817, when he called for the usual poll tax returns on slaves, in his role of Treasurer, he warned that "as Registrar I shall have it in my power to detect all those persons who did not heretofore give in their slaves."[13] The dates of registration were published in the parish churches of Barbados, on the two Sundays following receipt of the notice by the rectors, "between the prayers and the sermon," and then fixed to the church doors until the registration period had elapsed. The masters were required to swear their returns, within three months, at the Registrar's office in Bridgetown, though the Registrar spent one day at each parish church and also announced that he would "feel pleasure in attending any number of ladies in Bridgetown, or within one mile of it, on being required to do so."[14] Those who failed to make returns had a period of two months in which to petition the Governor, but thereafter were subject to prosecution.

The Court of Policy in Demerara-Essequibo, taking the Barbados Registration Act as its model, believed that the Registrar should be "an individual of weight and consideration in the colony and one to whom, if unavoidable the United Colony would safely commit the vindication of its integrity and humanity not only here, but at home."[15] James Robertson, the colony's Registrar from 1817 to 1832, did in fact take his duties very seriously. In 1824 he submitted a report on the slave population, but only to be told "that the Court of Policy cannot recognise in the

Registrar any power to publish any report connected with remarks relating to the state of the slave population."[16] Robertson complained that since he had been provided with no office building for the Registry he had to use his own house and had to employ four copying clerks at his own expense. He persistently petitioned the Court for an improved salary and began including detailed statistical analyses of the registration returns in his reports, some of them being printed in British *Parliamentary Papers*.[17] At least Robertson's importunity resulted in many valuable tabulations, not available for any other colony, which have been used by G. W. Roberts to construct a life table.[18]

Similar administrative machinery was set up in the small colonies of the British Caribbean. In most cases the Registry was located in the capital town. But some registrars traveled from parish to parish to collect returns, as in Grenada, and in the St. Vincent Grenadines returns were collected by resident Justices of the Peace.[19] Many of the Registrars held additional official posts, but some employed deputies who shared their salaries and fees. Some of them were substantial slaveowners.[20]

Dates of registration varied from colony to colony. Most adopted a triennial interval, but in Grenada and Tobago returns were made annually (table 2.1). The month of registration also varied from colony to colony, occurring at different points in the seasonal cycle. In some cases, the month of registration for a particular colony varied from triennium to triennium. In Grenada and Tobago masters were required to make their returns during January, providing data on events occurring in the preceding calendar year. Where the triennial pattern was followed, the masters were generally allowed three months in which to make their returns, resulting in some variability in the events included. In Berbice, for example, the return of 1822 was intended to cover the calendar years 1819, 1820, and 1821, but some masters included events occurring early in 1822, in the months before they actually made their returns. In the case of Berbice these events were dated precisely in the returns and so can be allocated to the appropriate period. Few other colonies required such exact dating, resulting in some ambiguity regarding the true temporal attribution of events. But the vast majority of returns were made within a single month, thus reducing the potential for distortion. In St. Lucia, for example, 80 percent of the 1,024 initial returns were made in December 1815; another 13 percent were returned in January 1816, and 3 percent in November 1815, while the remaining 4 percent were late returns, some of which did not come in until the end of 1817. Most of the latter related to small urban slaveholdings, however. In fact, 85 percent of St. Lucia's slaves were included in the returns made in December 1815, and only 2 percent in returns made later than January 1816. The legal extensions granted for making late returns at the initial registration were rarely applied to the subsequent triennial returns, so the problem was reduced. A full listing of the registration intervals is provided in table S8.1.

As well as providing data on changes in the slave populations, some of the subsequent annual or triennial returns also included complete censuses, comprising information comparable to that found in the initial registration (table 2.1). Such returns were taken regularly in Demerara-Essequibo, Antigua, Montserrat,

St. Kitts, and the Virgin Islands, every fourth year in Grenada, and in 1834 in Barbados. The second registration of slaves in Berbice, taken in 1819, consisted only of a census giving no data on changes in the population; it was much fuller than the return of 1818 and is regarded here as the initial registration.

Most of the colonial governments produced printed registration schedules and distributed them to the slaveowners for completion. Some of the slaveowners were illiterate, however, and some of them spoke only French or Spanish. The language used in the returns was English, except that in St. Lucia 912 returns were in French and only 112 in English. Elsewhere those slaveowners who could not write in English had their returns made out by agents. In Trinidad a small industry grew up in response to this need. The Cabildo of Port of Spain complained to the Registrar in 1830 that such people were "reduced to the necessity of employing others to make them out, some by the clerks of the Registrar of Slaves' office and others by a host of people, who surround the office at the period of registration for that purpose, all of whom exact excessive fees."[21] Absentee owners, minors, and others incompetent to make out their returns for various reasons also had to depend on agents, but generally these were kin, guardians, administrators, attorneys, or other regular employees.

SLAVE REGISTRATION: THE NATURE OF THE DATA

Because the British West Indian slave registration returns were the creation of separate colonial acts or orders in council, the data they contained and their format varied quite widely from colony to colony. Variations over time resulted from amendments to the acts. Further variations in the available data stemmed from differences between masters in the amount of information volunteered by them within the limits imposed by the acts. Thus, the returns do not constitute a truly systematic or consistent body of data. It is necessary, then, to consider the significance of this variability for comparative analysis and to assess the quality of the available data.

The initial registration returns comprised a census of the slaves living in a colony at a specified date. Table 2.2 sets out the major items of information regarding each slave recorded in these initial returns. Only two items were recorded consistently in every one of the colonies: the slaves' names and ages. In the subsequent returns, which detailed changes in the slave population during the interval, some colonies provided no more than the names of slaves who were born or died, but others recorded a wide range of data (table 2.3). The treatment of manumission, sale, purchase, removal, transportation, and marronage was equally variable. Trinidad and St. Lucia, operating under orders in council, provided the most detailed initial returns, but only minimal information in the subsequent returns. In general, the amount of detail available in the registration returns is greatest for the late-settled sugar colonies and least for the nonsugar marginal colonies, with the old sugar colonies falling somewhere between. This

Table 2.2. *Data Available in the Initial Slave Registration Returns*

Colony	The Slave											The Holding			
	Name	Sex	Age	Color	African or Creole	Birth-place	Bodily Marks	Stature	Occu-pation	Family	Re-lations	Plantation/Unattached or Personal	Plan-tation/Town Name	Parish or District	Crop
Barbados	X	X	X	X	X	0	0	0	X	0	0	0	X	X	0
St. Kitts	X	X	X	X	X	X	0	0	X	0	0	X	0	0	0
Nevis	X	X	X	X	X	0	0	0	0	0	0	X	X	X	0
Antigua	X	X	X	X	0	0	0	0	0	0	0	0	+	0	0
Montserrat	X	X	X	X	0	0	0	0	0	0	0	0	+	0	0
Virgin Islands	X	X	X	X	X	0	0	0	0	0	0	0	X	X	0
Jamaica	X	X	X	X	X	0	0	0	0	0	0	0	+	X	0
Dominica	X	X	X	X	X	0	0	0	X	0	+	0	+	X	0
St. Lucia	X	0	X	X	0	X	X	X	X	X	X	X	X	X	X
St. Vincent	X	X	X	X	X	X	0	0	X	0	X	X	X	X	X
Grenada	X	X	X	X	X	0	0	0	0	0	0	X	X	X	0
Tobago	X	X	X	X	X	0	X	0	X	0	0	X	X	X	0
Trinidad	X	0	X	X	X	X	X	X	X	X	X	X	X	X	X
Demerara-Essequibo	X	X	X	X	X	0	X	0	X	0	0	0	X	X	X
Berbice (1819)	X	X	X	X	X	+	X	+	X	+	+	0	X	+	0
British Honduras	X	0	X	X	0	0	0	0	X	X	X	0	0	0	0
Cayman Islands	X	0	X	0	0	0	0	0	X	0	0	0	+	0	0
Bahamas	X	X	X	X	X	0	0	0	X	0	0	0	+	X	0
Anguilla	X	X	X	X	X	X	0	0	X	0	0	0	0	0	0

Source: T.71.

X   given consistently
+   given sometimes
0   never given

Table 2.3. *Data on Births and Deaths Available in the Subsequent Registration Returns*[a]

Colony	Births							Deaths								
	Name	Sex	Color	Month of Birth	Age at Registration	Mother's Name	Father's Name	Name	Sex	Color	African or Creole	Age	Occupation	Month of Death	Cause of Death	Certified by Physician
Barbados	X	X	X	0	X	0	0	X	X	X	X	+	+	0	0	0
St. Kitts	X	X	X	0	X	0	0	X	X	X	+	+	+	0	0	0
Nevis	X	X	X	0	X	0	0	X	0	0	0	0	0	0	0	0
Antigua	X	X	X	0	+	0	0	X	0	0	0	0	0	0	0	0
Montserrat	X	X	X	0	+	0	0	X	0	0	0	0	0	0	0	0
Virgin Islands	X	X	X	+	+	0	0	X	0	0	0	0	0	+	0	0
Jamaica	X	X	X	+	+	+	0	X	X	X	X	X	0	+	+	0
Dominica	X	X	X	0	+	+	0	X	X	X	X	X	X	+	X	0
St. Lucia	X	0	X	0	X	X	0	X	0	0	0	0	0	0	0	0
St. Vincent	X	X	X	+	X	+	0	X	0	X	0	X	X	+	0	X
Grenada	X	X	X	+	+	X	0	X	X	X	X	X	0	+	X	0
Tobago	X	X	X	X	0	X	0	X	X	X	0	0	0	X	X	0
Trinidad	X	0	X	0	X	X	+	X	0	0	0	0	0	0	0	0
Demerara-Essequibo	X	X	X	X	+	0	0	X	X	X	X	X	X	X	X	X
Berbice	X	X	X	X	0	X	0	X	X	X	0	X	X	X	X	X
British Honduras	–	–	–	–	–	–	–	–	–	–	–	–	–	–	–	–
Cayman Islands	–	–	–	–	–	–	–	–	–	–	–	–	–	–	–	–
Bahamas	X	X	X	0	+	0	0	X	X	X	X	X	X	0	0	0
Anguilla	X	X	X	0	X	0	0	X	X	X	X	X	X	0	0	0

Source: T.71.

X   given consistently
+   given sometimes
0   never given

[a]There was some variation in the amount of data given at each registration, which is not necessarily indicated in this table.

tendency limits somewhat the range of comparative questions which may be asked of the data.

The physical structure of the registration returns also differed from colony to colony. Each return provided a certain amount of information about the slave-owner, and this was followed by a series of columns, the data for each individual slave belonging to the holding generally occupying a single line. In Trinidad, St. Lucia, and British Honduras "families" were listed first, the slaves being grouped under a common surname, followed by general lists of males and females not attributed to family groups. For Trinidad, changes occurring in 1815 and 1816, and in some cases as late as 1825, were added by the Registrar to the initial 1813 returns. Subsequent returns provided references to the original folio number, and indexes were made to the names of slaves, plantations, and slaveowners. Thus, the various Trinidad returns are readily related to one another. In St. Lucia the format of the subsequent returns was a replica of the original, with the addition of a column for "corrections." The initial (1819) returns for Berbice were not consistent in format, some of them bracketing slaves into "family" groups and others merely providing lists with a minimum of data. The remaining colonies made no attempt to group the slaves by "family" or "household" units, though the ordering of individuals may suggest that this is implicit in some cases.[22] Generally, males were listed before females, and the ordering within the sexes was often alphabetical or based on descending age or an occupational hierarchy.

The registration returns also included a variable amount of information about the slaveowners and the geographical location of their slaveholdings. Owners' names were always recorded, but other data about them varied from colony to colony. As with the slaves, the range of information about the owners was greatest in the new sugar colonies and least in the marginal colonies (table 2.2). Geographical location, in the form of plantation name, town name, or parish, was often lacking in the returns from the marginal and old sugar colonies. The crop produced by the unit was stated only for the new sugar colonies. The sex of the owners can generally be established from the syntax/grammar of the oath or heading, or be inferred from the name. Color was stated erratically. Literacy was indicated by ability to sign the oath. Most returns stated the name of the person making the return as well as that of the owner, where an agent was involved, and noted the relationship of the agent to the owner.

Some of the information about the slaves recorded in the registration returns was obtained by questioning the slaves, but all data were filtered by the owners, most of whom were white and male. Most of the errors made by the masters stemmed from ignorance or carelessness rather than deliberate falsification. Tax evasion was not directly involved and the cost of registration was slight, while fines imposed on defaulters were substantial. In Barbados, for example, a fine of £100 sterling was levied for each slave not registered, and if the slave was African-born he would be freed, on the assumption he had been imported illicitly. These fines were in fact imposed.[23]

Some of the colonial acts, however, made no provision for freeing slaves if their owners were convicted of importing them illicitly. The Demerara-Essequibo

Act provided that owners so convicted be fined 6,000 guilders and imprisoned for up to two years, but no regulations were made to ensure the freedom of the slaves. In Antigua such slaves were merely surrendered "to the use of His Majesty."[24] But Antigua, as well as Dominica, St. Vincent, and Grenada, offered rewards to informers. Dominica, for example, imposed a fine of £100 currency for each slave not registered, half this amount to go to the informer. The island also imposed a fine of £500 and prison for up to two years for holding an African slave illegally imported; such slaves were to be freed and paid £6.12.0 maintenance annually by the Treasurer. Fines were also levied for wrongful registration, but some duplication did occur when the hirer as well as the owner of slaves each made returns.[25] The person making a return was required to swear an oath as to its accuracy, "to the best of my knowledge and belief," under heavy penalties.[26] If this apparatus did not necessarily strike terror into the hearts of the slaveowners, it was sufficient to ensure that few actually omitted registering their slaves. But the owner's ability to provide accurate information about their slaves on each of the items required by the registration returns varied widely. These items will now be discussed seriatim.

Name

Most registration returns allowed only a single column for each slave's name, and the frequency with which slaves were attributed surnames varied erratically. In Trinidad, St. Lucia, and British Honduras, however, two columns were provided, one labeled "name" and the other "surname." The Trinidad Order in Council gave detailed instructions on the treatment of surnames.[27] It ordered the masters to insert "the surname or second name of the slave, if he or she has ever been called or known by any surname or second name, and if not, then, in cases of Family Slaves . . . the name of the superior relation." Males and females in the general lists were to be attributed such names as "the owner or party making the return shall think fit to insert." The owner was also advised that no two families on the same plantation should have the same surname. But once a slave's surname had been established in the Trinidad Registry, it was to remain fixed and be passed on to any descendants, so that its value as an identifier could be ensured.

The surnames listed in the returns seem often to have been invented by the masters simply to meet the requirements of registration, and their prior status is dubious. For example, the slave families on Plantation Malheureuse, Trinidad, had the surnames Infamie, Tiranie, Demoralisation, Bétise, Malimaginer, Malvue, Horeur, Compation, Chagrin, and Misere. In St. Lucia, slaves on Choc Plantation were given the surnames Janvier, Fevrier, Mars, Avril, and so on through the months. Those on Volet Plantation were surnamed Syrup, Limes, Rum, Punch, Sangree, Grog, Brandy, Gin, Champaign, Porter, Madeira, and so on.[28]

There is no way of knowing whether these names had any currency among the slaves themselves, or even whether they were employed in any other context by the masters, before or after registration. But they must be regarded skeptically. On the other hand, surnames given in those returns which did not specifically require them may be regarded less doubtfully. The first names given in the returns must generally have been recognized by both slave and master before registration. The Barbados Registration Act, for example, required the name "by which he or she has been usually called or known."[29] But, while the first names recorded in the returns were those used in master-slave communication, they were not necessarily the only names used within the slave community.

No attempt is made in this book to study the cultural significance of slave names. This is a particularly difficult area in the understanding of slave life, which will remain tortuous until it can be determined how far slave names were chosen by the slaves themselves and how far they were imposed on them by the masters.[30] The evidence of the names listed in the British West Indian registration returns seems unlikely to provide such a resolution. If the problem can be overcome, however, the study of slave-naming practices can be expected to provide significant insight into the functioning of the slave community.

Here, slave names are used primarily as identifiers, especially in order to link demographic events through the initial and subsequent registration returns and in tracing kin relationships. For this purpose, the major problem is the duplication of names within a single slaveholding. Since the masters also used the names as identifiers they generally attempted to avoid such duplication, but it could arise through sale or removal or through the recognition of slave preferences. Sometimes number labels were attached to names (such as Mary 1st, Mary 2d), or age labels (Mary old, Mary young), or relationship labels (Jemima's Mingo, Christian's Robert), or ethnic labels (Ebo Mary, Creole Mary), or occupation labels (Mary field, Mary cook).

Sex

The sex of the slaves was generally stated explicitly in the registration returns. In the Cayman Islands, the returns included no column for sex, but males (recognizable by name and occupation) were always listed first and females second, separated by a space. In Trinidad, St. Lucia, and British Honduras, the sex of slaves attributed to family groups was not stated, whereas males and females lacking kin were placed in separate, labeled lists. For the slaves in families, sex can usually be inferred directly from the stated kin relationships, or from occupation and name. Parents with ambiguous names and occupations have been assumed to be female. The sex of siblings and laterals (cousins) cannot be inferred in this way, however, and in cases of ambiguity the most plausible interpretation of the name has been accepted. But such cases are very rare, and the registration data on sex may be regarded as highly reliable.

Age

Although age was reported consistently in every one of the colonies, the resulting data were necessarily subject to a much wider margin of error than those characteristics that could be determined by physical observation. The slaves, particularly the African-born, were generally unable to provide data in the form required by the masters. As the Governor of Trinidad complained in 1815, while arguing that a simple list of names would be an adequate method of registration, "half of the Negroes dont or wont know their nation—none their age.''[31] The ages of Caribbean-born creole slaves were known where the masters kept records of their birth dates prior to registration, but it seems many did not maintain such lists. Thus, the ages reported in the registration returns were most often based on the masters' assessment of the slave's physical appearance. But the resulting data suggest that the masters were fairly consistent in performing this assessment, and there is nothing to support the cynical view of a Jamaica planter, stated in 1836, that "in the original register of 1817, the mother is, in many cases, registered as younger than her daughter; it is all confusion.''[32]

In the Leeward Islands, the age column was labeled "reputed age," and many individual owners added notes to their returns admitting a similar lack of certitude. An owner in Berbice, for example, noted that the ages stated were "as near as can be conjectured from appearance.''[33] Again, some masters provided a range rather than an exact age, generally of five or ten years (15–20 or 40–50, for example). In such cases the median age has been used in any calculations made in this book. Some returns, however, recorded the ages of creole slaves exact to the month, and in these cases it is certain that the data derive from sources prior to registration.

One measure of age-misreporting is the extent of heaping in single years. Heaping generally occurs at the digits 0 and 5 and at even numbers. It is certainly evident in the slave registration data and, not surprisingly, was most pronounced among the African-born and those over 30 years of age. By comparison with modern censuses from developing countries, however, the amount of age-heaping in the slave registration data was not excessive.[34] A useful measure of the extent of concentration at particular digits of age is the "index of preference," which equals one-half of the sum of deviations from 10 percent, without regard to sign; if there was no preference, each digit would account for 10 percent of the population.[35] In the St. Lucia slave registration returns of 1815, the index of preference was as low as 11.3. This compares well with an index of 10.4 in the United States census of 1880, for example. Other colonies generally showed higher indexes: Trinidad had an index of 23.0 in 1813, and the parish of St. Michael, Barbados, 24.3 in 1817. The overall differences between the colonies cannot be easily explained in terms of the proportion of African-born slaves, then, since Barbados had a much smaller percentage than either Trinidad or St. Lucia. Nor do the masters on the long-settled islands seem to have developed more exact record keeping than those in the newer colonies. The index of preference was higher for African-born slaves than for creoles in all of the colonies sampled, but there was no consistent pattern in the differences between males and females, suggesting that the masters did not find the age of one sex more difficult to estimate than that of the other (table 2.4). Table 2.4 also shows the ratio of the numbers of slaves registered at each digit to the digit 9, taking the population 10 years of age and above, according to the "blended" method proposed by Myers.[36] This demonstrates clearly that the greatest amount of

Table 2.4. *Preference for Digits of Age in the Slave Registration Returns, Shown by the Blended Method: Trinidad, 1813, and St. Lucia, 1815*

	Ratio to Digit 9 (10 years and over)							
	Trinidad 1813				St. Lucia 1815			
	Africans		Creoles		Africans		Creoles	
Digit of Age	Males	Females	Males	Females	Males	Females	Males	Females
0	5.34	5.03	4.62	4.58	2.54	3.79	2.20	1.91
1	0.72	0.68	0.97	0.79	0.82	1.08	1.08	0.95
2	2.66	1.87	2.25	1.85	1.42	1.31	1.48	1.23
3	0.85	0.86	1.23	1.29	0.96	1.11	1.26	1.24
4	1.64	1.51	1.90	1.73	1.15	1.18	1.38	1.22
5	3.28	3.04	2.89	2.72	2.00	3.10	1.67	1.60
6	2.25	2.05	2.13	2.02	1.35	1.50	1.42	1.39
7	0.93	0.88	1.16	1.06	0.95	1.12	1.17	0.93
8	2.67	2.62	2.58	2.33	1.45	2.06	1.54	1.28
9	1.00	1.00	1.00	1.00	1.00	1.00	1.00	1.00
Index of Preference	25.90	25.30	19.80	20.10	14.40	21.00	8.50	10.20

Source: T.71.

concentration occurred at the decadal ages, followed by the digits 5, 8, and 2, while 9 was rather more popular than 1 at the other end of the scale (figs. 2.1–2.3).

The absence of extreme age-heaping in the slave registration data does not, of course, mean that the absolute ages reported were generally correct. But it does suggest that the masters were conscientious in their efforts and achieved a tolerable degree of consistency. Most of the calculations in this book involving age data are based on five-year age groups, and when the data are plotted at such intervals the curves obtained are generally quite smooth and devoid of gross distortions. Unfortunately, some of the external tests that might be applied to the data are not suited to the registration returns. Some colonies did produce series of censuses, but there is little point in examining these for comparable age-heaping, since the ages established in the initial returns were merely carried forward to later registrations in order not to reduce their value for identification.

If the masters had a tendency to falsify ages deliberately, it probably worked toward inflating the ages of the oldest slaves, thus demonstrating that the slave system was not inimical to health and longevity. In fact, very few slaves were registered at ages above 70 years. But the masters often thought of slaves above 40 years as ''old,'' and it may be that there is some minor inflation in these age groups. Here, slaves over 70 years are always placed in one age group. Besides conscious falsification, it is difficult to determine the direction in which the masters' errors might have gone. Physical indicators of age, such as stature, breasts, facial hair, balding, and greying, showed variations between Europeans

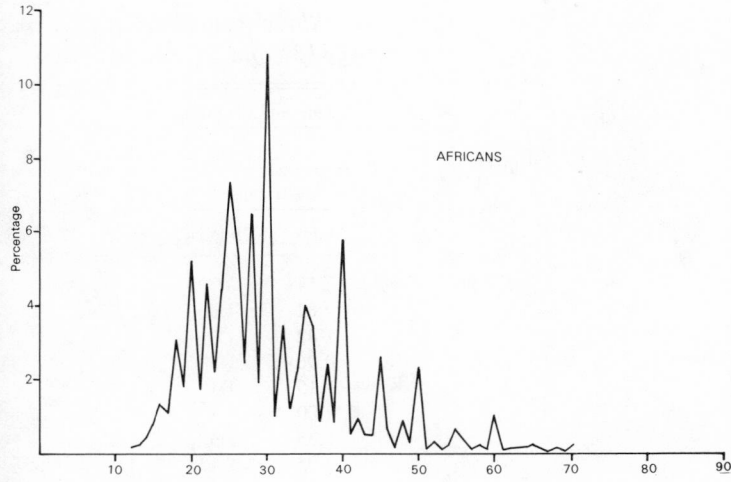

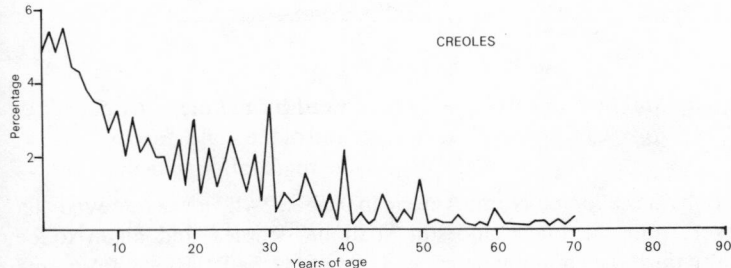

Fig. 2.1.   *Age by Single Years, Africans and Creoles: Trinidad, 1813.*
(Source: *T.71/501–3.*)

and blacks, between African ethnic groups, and between social classes. If the white masters applied standards from their own group, it is possible that they would have understated the ages of adolescents and overstated the ages of mature slaves. But it is unlikely that the planters saw themselves as an appropriate control group.

Color

Color was recorded in all of the slave registration returns, with the exception of the Cayman Islands. In some cases only a simple distinction between "black" and "coloured" was made. The Barbados Registration Act defined "coloured" as "all who are not black," and this practice was generally followed in the Leeward

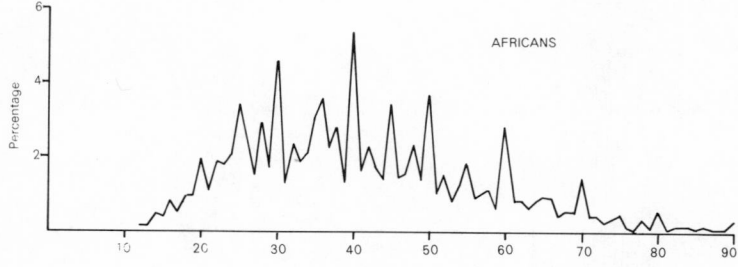

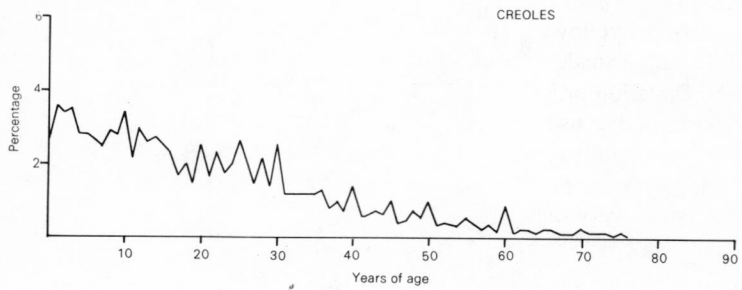

Fig. 2.2. *Age by Single Years, Africans and Creoles: St. Lucia, 1815.*
(Source: *T.71/378–79.*)

Islands.[37] The Bahamas adopted North American usage: "All slaves removed any degree whatever from the black ancestor shall be deemed and taken to be mulattoes."[38] But the most common practice, as set out in the St. Vincent Act, and following the Trinidad Order in Council, was to list the slaves as "Negro, Mulatto or Mustee, as the case may be, or such designation of intermediate shades of colour (if any) as are in use in these colonies."[39] This permitted the use of a wide range of terms, open to individual interpretation and not necessarily falling into a systematic gradation.

The major problem with the data on color is that they refer both to visible, perceived bodily characteristics and to known histories of miscegenation. Since color was basic to a person's social and legal status, these two referents sometimes came into conflict. In the Berbice returns, for example, one master noted that a male domestic belonging to him "appears to be a Negroe, but calls himself a sambo, altho' very dark indeed." The slave was listed as sambo.[40] In Antigua, a slave was "returned coloured but is in fact a white negro" (or albino).[41] Again, the terms "yellow," "yellowish," and "yellowskin" were applied to both creole and African-born slaves in the returns from Berbice and Tobago. The column for color occasionally identified a slave as "black" while the column for marks noted "yellowskin." One Berbice master felt constrained to explain that "the negroes

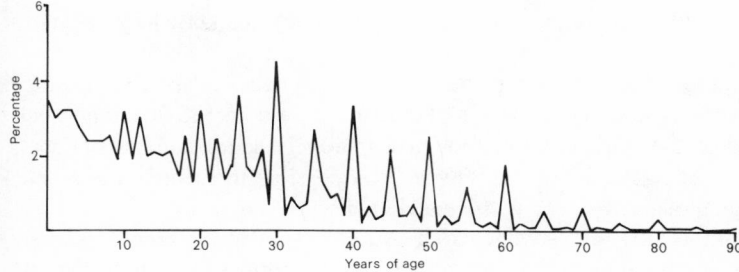

Fig. 2.3. *Age by Single Years: St. Michael, Barbados, 1817.* (Source: *T.71/ 520.)*

returned here above as yellowish are from black parents both father and mother being black but being a shade lighter than the others in order to fulfill as near as possible the Proclamation ordering to return black and yellow skin &c.''[42] But, with the exception of the use of the term yellow in Berbice and Tobago, the registration returns generally appear to provide a consistent identification of slaves of mixed race. If anything, they understate the number of the latter, since some masters simply listed every one of their slaves as black.

Birthplace

Only the registration returns of Antigua, Montserrat, British Honduras, and the Cayman Islands failed to distinguish clearly between slaves born in Africa and those born in the Americas (creoles). Very few of the colonies, however, provided more detailed information on the slaves' birthplaces. Some, such as Barbados, provided detailed data on creole slaves from other areas, in order to distinguish them from ''Barbadian'' or ''native'' slaves, but lumped all Africans together. There is little reason to regard the data on creole origins with suspicion, except that a slave shipped from colony to colony might sometimes be listed as belonging to the place from whence he came last; there are many cases in the registration returns to contradict the idea that such slaves were stripped of their true birthplaces, however, so this criticism cannot be an important one.

Much of the data on the birthplaces of the African-born probably came from the slaves themselves, since they cherished knowledge of links with particular ethnic groups. Those who passed into the Atlantic slave trade as children might have lacked this knowledge, but most slaves shipped from Africa were old enough to have acquired the information before enslavement. The statement, quoted above, that ''half the Negroes dont or wont know their nation'' was an exaggeration. Most of the ''country'' names listed in the registration returns referred to ethnic groups or tribes rather than broad regions or shipping points. This supports the view that the information came more often from the slaves than from the masters' slave-trading records. References in the registration returns to ''country marks'' make it clear that these were also used as identifiers, but whether the masters asked the origins of particular markings or relied on their own prior knowledge remains uncertain.

These variations in practice, together with idiosyncrasies of spelling, resulted in a proliferation of country terms. For Trinidad, more than 500 different labels were applied to the African-born, though a relatively small number of labels accounted for the vast majority of slaves. It is possible to identify the ethnic/regional origins of most slaves with considerable confidence.

Slaves born during the voyage from Africa, "salt-water creoles," were generally distinguished in the registration returns as "born at sea." In this study, such slaves are treated as creoles rather than Africans because their experience was confined entirely to the Middle Passage and the West Indian slave system. But whether these slaves regarded themselves as creoles or whether they recognized an attachment to the country of their parents is unknown.

Marks

Systematic data on the bodily marks of the slaves were recorded only in the new sugar colonies. No doubt this was a product of the high proportion of African-born slaves in those colonies. The Trinidad Order in Council specified that the masters should state "whether the slave has any, and what seams and marks on the face, or other parts of the body, such as African slaves commonly have, and which are usually called country marks, or any such brands or marks as are used in some of the colonies for distinguishing the owners property, or has any apparent bodily singularity, defect, or deformity, all which shall be specified, with convenient certainty, so as at least to mention the part of the face or body wherein the marks, brands, defects, or other singularity appears."[43] The most common marks recorded were the country marks of the Africans, which served also to identify the slaves' birthplaces. Most returns simply noted their presence or absence, but some specified that the marks were those characteristic of a particular ethnic group and, in Berbice, a few actually provided diagrams.[44]

As well as country marks and generalized references to tattooing, the "marks" column provided data of a wide variety: from "missing toes" to "nose bored" to "marks of smallpox" to "good looking." The data are not systematic, however. Since marks were intended only to identify the slaves, only the most conspicuous characteristic required mention. Thus, missing toes would not be specified for a slave listed as a "leper" and, in Berbice, stature might be omitted for slaves branded with their owner's initials, whereas the heights of unbranded slaves would be given. There was an order of precedence, the most conspicuous marks or deformities being the ones first noticed. This makes it difficult to use the data to study whole populations, even at the level of individual slaveholdings.

Stature

Height could be measured precisely. In Trinidad, the masters were required to record the heights of their slaves "by actual measurement," but critics of the registration system claimed that the heights of children were measured carelessly.[45] It appears that infants unable to stand were often not measured, and this resulted in a heaping at 2 feet for one-year-olds. The heights of decrepit slaves were sometimes omitted. In St. Lucia, for example, one slave was described as "trop courbé" and not measured.[46] A contemporary description of measurement for registration in Trinidad states that the slaves were made to stand against a wall; their heights were marked and then calculated using a foot rule.[47] They were probably measured barefoot (since few had shoes), but it is uncertain what account was taken of varying hair styles. Overall, there is little evidence of heaping in the data for those more than one year old, except that the heights 5 feet and 5 feet 6 inches were favored. This suggests that the vast majority of slaves for whom the data was recorded were in fact measured.

The most important problem with the height data is that they were not expressed in common units. English units (feet, inches, and fractions of an inch) were used systematically in Trinidad, but in St. Lucia and Berbice, the only other colonies to provide height data, French and Dutch measures were used alongside English. The difficulty is that it is not always clear which units were used in a particular return. Most of the St. Lucia returns, whether written in French or English, purportedly used French measures (pieds, pouces, and lignes).[48] In Berbice, all heights were recorded in units of feet and inches, though one owner noted that "the measured height of the adult slaves is taken in Dutch feet and inches," and another that they were "according to the Rhynlands measure."[49] The following conversion factors apply:

1 inch (English) = 2.54 cm
1 inch (Rijnland) = 2.62 cm
1 pouce (French) = 2.71 cm

Because individual returns rarely specified which of these units they employed, however, it is impossible to obtain precise results. It has been assumed here that the Trinidad and Berbice returns were all in English measure. In the case of St. Lucia, universal application of French measure produces obviously inflated results. This is most clearly seen in the African population, where the pattern of differences by sex and birthplace is almost exactly the same as in Trinidad but always about 7 cm greater in St. Lucia. Since it is unlikely that the heights of adult Africans of the same sex and ethnic group would differ so significantly and consistently by colony, a factor has been constructed by comparing the major African ethnic groups, and the pouce is taken to equal 2.59 cm throughout the St. Lucia returns. Thus, it appears that most St. Lucia returns in fact used English measure. There were no significant differences between returns written in French and those in English.

Height was recorded consistently in Trinidad and St. Lucia, but in Berbice there was considerable variation. Many returns omitted it for all slaves. Others recorded heights only for "adult" slaves and omitted it for those "still growing" or "probably still growing."[50] Only a few of the Berbice returns were complete, so the sample for children is small. There is no reason to suspect systematic bias in these variations.

Occupation

The Trinidad Order in Council instructed the masters to record "the particular trade, occupation, or ordinary employement of the slave, specifying, in the cases of mechanics, artisans, or handicraft-men, the particular art or business in which he or she is usually employed; in the cases of family slaves, the particular domestic service or department in which he or she is usually employed; and in cases of ordinary plantation slaves, describing them as labourers only."[51] There is no doubting the capacity of the masters to know the occupations of the slaves, but problems of definition remain. Some slaves, especially those belonging to small units, performed a wide range of tasks from day to day. In making their registration returns, the masters either spelled out this multiplicity or adopted portmanteau labels. Field workers were the most likely to be described in general terms. Thus the St. Vincent Act, following the Trinidad Order in Council, called for specific descriptions of the occupations of tradesmen and domestics, but "in cases of ordinary plantation slaves, describing them as labourers only."[52] This results in a relative lack of information on the distribution of slaves between particular field gangs and other agricultural tasks, compared to the richer detail on skilled and house slaves.

Of equal importance is the problem of seasonality in occupational patterns. Since the returns were made at a specific time of year, the occupations listed may have been weighted to that particular point in the seasonal cycle. For example, would a slave be described as a "sugar boiler" or a "fiddler" only if the return was made during crop or close to Christmas revelry? The Trinidad, Barbados, St. Kitts, and Anguilla regulations all called for "ordinary" or "usual" employment, but it seems probable that specific skills was more likely to be mentioned than manual work, even though the use of these skills was confined to one part of the year, because it was these skills that served best to identify the slave. The result, probably, is some overstatement of the amount of labor time spent in specialized occupations.

Family

In Trinidad and British Honduras slaves were grouped into "families," the names of which were the same as the surnames of the slaves in the group. No kinship relationships were noted between the family groups, or between the family groups and those slaves placed in the general lists of males and females. In St. Lucia, the registration returns did not separate kin (identified in the "relations" column) into distinct groups, though slaves with the same surname were generally listed together. In Berbice, only some returns noted kinship, and a wide variety of listing patterns occurred, not always placing identified kin in groups.

The Trinidad Order in Council required the masters to list all slaves who had husbands or wives, "either by actual marriage, or known and constant cohabitation, or who had parents or children, brothers or sisters, among the slaves of the said plantation."[53] The "families," then, approximated family household units. No doubt some of those in the general lists of males and females lived in the households of family slaves, and there was probably a general tendency to understate the number of extended families. But the Trinidad and British Honduras data provide a far more consistent picture of family and household structure than the returns from St. Lucia and Berbice.

More generally, the quality of the data may be criticized on the grounds that the masters lacked intimate knowledge of actual cohabitation patterns, or imposed their own preconceptions on the real patterns (either failing to recognize certain types of family structure because there were no precedents in their experience, or expecting the slaves to be promiscuous or constant). Where the data were obtained from the slaves themselves, these problems were minimized, but the returns give few hints as to the frequency with which the masters used slave-derived information. Another difficulty with the data is that families and kin relationships were almost always defined within the physical and legal boundaries of a particular slaveholding. Thus, the solitary slave owned by a poor master could by definition have no family or kin, even if he lived with slaves belonging to another master. This problem, of course, tends to distort comparisons between town and plantation.

Relations

Kin relationships were recorded more often than families, but generally the data were confined to the names of mothers. Only those colonies listing families identified fathers, husbands, wives, brothers, sisters, cousins, uncles, aunts, nephews, nieces, grandmothers, grandfathers, grandsons, and granddaughters. Such relationships were noted only when the kin were alive and resident on the same plantation, though rare references to widows and orphans do occur. In Trinidad, this information was placed in a column headed "relations," and in St. Lucia "parenté." But in British Honduras it came under "remarks," and in Berbice "remarks tending further to identify." The amount of detail given varied considerably, particularly in British Honduras and Berbice. Even in Trinidad the masters had a certain amount of latitude, being instructed to record "the relation that the slave bears to the superior relative, or slave, by whose name the Family Section of the List to which he belongs is entitled as aforesaid, with such further particulars of genealogy or family connection as the owner or party making the return shall think fit to add."[54] Once again, the capacity of the masters to report kin relationships may be questioned, especially on the terms in which they were understood by the slaves themselves.

Births

The detailed instructions provided for the completion of the initial registration returns were not always matched for the subsequent returns. With regard to fertility and mortality, the Trinidad Order in Council asked only for "a true and particular account of all births and deaths.'' This form of words was repeated in the registration acts of most colonies, including Barbados and Demerara-Essequibo, but the Jamaica Act called for a record of ''the total number of births and of deaths since the last return.''[55] The relative lack of guidance meant that the type and quality of data provided was more variable than in the initial returns, thus complicating the comparative analysis of movements in the population (table 2.3).

Whereas it is probable that most slaves living at the date of the initial returns were in fact registered, there is no doubt that a significant underregistration of births occurred. This did not result from any particular desire by the masters to conceal infants from the Registrars, since there was no incentive to do so. Nor did it relate to the masters' ignorance of the birth of slave children, most of whom were delivered by midwives appointed by the masters; slave women were encouraged to reveal their pregnancies in return for concessions in the amount of field labor required and, after 1807, most masters gave material rewards to slave mothers on the birth of their children. Rather, the underregistration of births resulted chiefly from the tendency of the masters to omit children born within a registration period but dying before its end. Where infant mortality rates were high, this meant the omission of a significant proportion of births. Births of this type were not universally omitted,[56] but variations in practice between individual masters and between colonies mean that the extent of underregistration is difficult to estimate exactly.

Although ''birth-deaths'' (children born within a registration interval but dying before its end) must in fact have comprised a larger proportion of total births the longer the interval, the registration data show only an erratic relationship. In a sample of 12 colonies (table 2.5), St. Lucia and the Virgin Islands, with quite long registration intervals, ignored birth-deaths almost totally. Elsewhere, birth-deaths accounted for roughly 10 percent of total registered births. Only in St. Vincent and St. Kitts, with long registration intervals of 55 and 57 months, did the proportion approach 20 percent. The ratio of registered birth-deaths to total births also varied by slaveholding size. In St. Kitts 1817–21, for example, the ratio increased fairly steadily from 14 percent in holdings of 1–10 slaves to 27 percent in the 301–400 group. This tendency could reflect actual differences in infant mortality, but it may also indicate a lower rate of birth registration in the smaller units due to inferior record-keeping practices and the confusion resulting from a relatively rapid turnover in ownership through sale and inheritance. Certainly, then, survival to the date of registration was not required for inclusion of births in the returns, but there was no clear relationship between the registration of birth-deaths and the length of the interval.

The major factor determining the registration of slave births was not survival to a particular date but survival to a certain age. Although there were significant differences in individual practice, and a few masters even registered stillbirths, most only bothered to record the fact of slave birth after the child had survived some minimum period. This in itself was a reflection of the high level of infant mortality among the slave population. Among the slaves high infant mortality

Table 2.5. *Intraregistration Birth-Deaths as a Percentage of Total Registered Births*

Colony	Registered Births	Registered Birth-Deaths	Percentage	Registration Interval (Months)
Anguilla, 1827–31	538	42	7.8	60
St. Vincent, 1817–21	2,702	506	18.7	57
St. Kitts, 1817–21	2,368	463	19.6	55
Nevis, 1817–21	1,064	140	13.2	54
Virgin Islands, 1818–22	549	2	0.4	48
St. Lucia, 1815–19	729	2	0.3	38
Berbice, 1819–21	1,664	193	11.6	36
St. Kitts, 1831–34	1,762	203	11.5	36
Jamaica, 1829–32*	438	49	11.2	36
Dominica, 1817–32†	220	21	9.5	36
Barbados, 1817–20	7,718	351	4.5	36
Anguilla, 1832–34	193	11	5.7	30
Barbados, 1832–34	6,084	698	11.5	22
Tobago, 1819–21	962	114	11.9	12
Grenada, 1817–34**	1,136	123	10.8	12

Source: T.71.

*St. James Parish only.
†Four plantations only.
**Nine plantations only.

resulted in a certain indifference and distancing in relation to the neonate, since emotional attachment was dangerous with the probability of early death so high. They treated the first nine days of life, regarded as the most risky period of all, with ritualized neglect; young children were denied funerals and their burial was generally casual, as in Africa.[57] This attitude on the part of the slaves reinforced the common neglect practiced in the record keeping of the masters.

Underregistration of births applied particularly to those children who died within the first month of life. In general, about 50 percent of infant deaths occurred in the first month, though the proportion tended to be less under conditions of heavy infant mortality.[58] John Hancock, who practiced medicine in Demerara-Essequibo, claimed that "at an average estimate" half of all slave infants died from tetanus, most within the first nine days.[59] He believed that a similar rate applied in the neighboring islands. Robert Renny, on the other hand, claimed that tetanus killed only one-quarter of those born in Jamaica, most of them between the fifth and fourteenth days of life.[60] It is difficult to test these contemporary impressions, to determine whether they reflect real regional differences, because most of the slave registration returns did not provide precise dates for births and deaths, and many omitted age at death (table 2.3). But where these data are available they permit more exact testing of the extent of underregistration.

Biometric analysis of infant mortality, using Bourgeois-Pichat's equation to subdivide total infant mortality into exogenous and endogenous causes of death, provides a valuable method for testing the registration data.[61] It is based on the fact that few endogenous deaths occur after the first month of life, and the empirical finding that the cumulative death rate between the first and twelfth months generally conforms closely to a straight line, when plotted on an axis showing the number of days since birth logarithmically transformed so that the distance of any point from the origin is proportional to $\log^3(d + 1)$, where d represents age in days. The data for Tobago, St. Vincent, and Berbice are plotted in figure 2.4. The first point to note is that arbitrary recording of age at death would result in a rather random scattering of points, but the slave registration data do in fact conform fairly closely to the expected straight line pattern. Secondly, the method demonstrates clearly that underregistration occurred at the colony level. Endogenous mortality

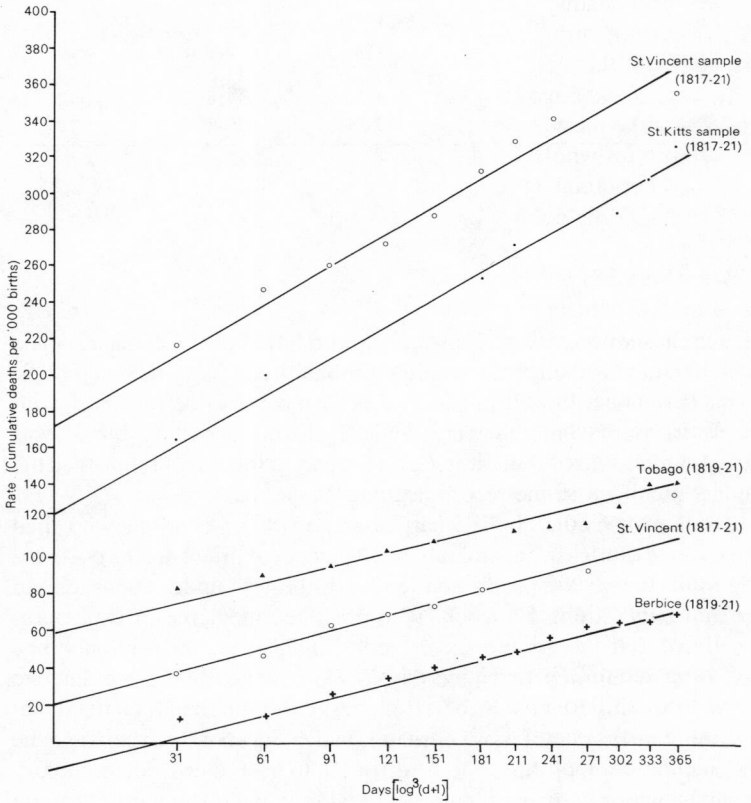

Fig. 2.4. *Infant Mortality of Slaves per 1,000 Live Births: St. Kitts, St. Vincent, Tobago, and Berbice, 1817–21. (Source: T.71/255, 440–41, 463–68, 495.)*

is determined by the point at which the line cuts the vertical axis, so the fact that the Berbice line actually cuts it below the point of origin is definite evidence of underregistration. The lines for St. Vincent and Tobago also cut the axis at improbably low levels. This may be taken as clear evidence of the under-registration of endogenous deaths occurring in the first month, but the method cannot establish the true extent of this mortality.

One way of estimating the actual extent of the underregistration of births is to compare recorded birth-deaths for entire colonies and for those slaveholdings where the data appear complete. For the latter, only returns stating precise dates of birth and death (or age at death exact to single days), and including deaths occurring before the seventh day of life, can be regarded as carefully prepared and usable. Very few returns qualify. Such data from three plantations in St. Vincent[62] and two in St. Kitts[63] are plotted in figure 2.4. These plantations were large, each having more than 250 slaves. In the St. Vincent sample, 40 percent of registered births comprised birth-deaths, and for St. Kitts 41 percent. But it is necessary to exclude births occurring during the final year of each registration period (1821), since the probability of these children surviving the first 12 months of life cannot be known. The expected straight-line pattern of cumulative infant deaths is again observed (fig. 2.4). The most obvious contrast between the lines for these sample plantations and those for whole colonies is the absolute difference in the level of mortality. Equally important is the difference in slope, indicating that under-registration of births at the colony level applied to exogenous as well as endo-genous deaths.

Of the children born 1817–20 in the St. Vincent sample, 36 percent died within the first year of life, 22 percent in the first month. Some 31 percent of infant deaths occurred in the first week, 15 percent in the second, 8 percent in third, and 7 percent in the fourth. Overall, 61 percent of infant mortality occurred in the first month. It seems probable, then, that these St. Vincent data are complete. If the sample plantations are excluded from the colony-level data, the proportion of birth-deaths to total registered births drops to 16 percent, compared to 40 percent in the sample. On the assumption that the slave population of St. Vincent experienced the same level of child mortality as the sample plantations, it follows that total registered births (less registered birth-deaths) must be multiplied by the ratio of birth-deaths to survivors in the sample (0.667) to give the actual number of birth-deaths, and hence estimated total births. The estimated number of birth-deaths in St. Vincent 1817–21 is 1,464 (compared to 506 registered), and total births 3,660 (compared to 2,702). This has the important effect of increasing the crude birth rate from 23.0 to 31.2 per thousand. According to this method, then, 26 percent of slave births occurring in St. Vincent 1817–21 were not registered.

A similar calculation applies to the two sample plantations in St. Kitts (fig. 2.4). On those plantations, 41 percent of births were birth-deaths; 33 percent of children born 1817–20 died in infancy, and 50 percent of infant mortality occurred within the first month. These ratios match very closely those observed in St. Vincent, and registered births must be inflated by an equivalent 27 percent.

It must be emphasized that this method of estimating the extent of under-registration of births depends for its validity on the universality of patterns found on a small sample of plantations. The sample data gain acceptability from their internal homogeneity and compatibility with contemporary calculations, but they are necessarily limited in their wider applicability. Three main factors inhibit their application to other colonies and other periods: (1) variations in the infant mortality rate, (2) variations in the proportion of birth-deaths to total registered births, and (3) variations in the length of the registration interval. Variations in the infant mortality rate are the most difficult to handle because of the paucity of reliable data and the possible permutations. Of tetanus, the major cause of infant deaths, one contemporary Jamaican physician reported that "in some parts of the island it is stated to be very uncommon, and there are districts where scarce a child can be raised; in towns less of it is seen than in the interior."[64] But estimates of the extent of underregistration of births can only be derived directly if a constant rate of child mortality is assumed. The rates established for the St. Vincent and St. Kitts samples can be used for this purpose, making allowance for variations in the length of registration intervals and in the ratio of birth-deaths to total births.[65] Direct estimates of the extent of underregistration, derived from these ratios, have been calculated for all colonies and all periods (see table 2.7, below). Overall, these estimates show an underregistration of about 30 percent, with a range from 40 percent in St. Lucia to 23 percent in Montserrat and Antigua.

Although these direct estimates of underregistration provide a much more realistic picture of fertility than the unadjusted registration data, they are founded on a relatively small sample of child mortality and incorporate some untested assumptions about the homogeneity of registration practices. An independent check on the plausibility of the direct estimates may be found in the use of model life tables. But this alternative approach to the problem has its own pitfalls, the most important being that model life tables are strictly applicable only to stable populations in which there is a constant age distribution and a constant rate of growth. It is obvious that in general the slave populations of the British Caribbean failed to satisfy these assumptions because of the distorting effects of migration through the slave trade and the heavy mortality experienced in some of the colonies. But, although the available model life tables may not be truly representative of all mortality patterns, they have been used successfully in much historical demography and provide results at least as good as those derived by alternative methods.[66] Model life tables have the advantage that they can be applied systematically to each of the West Indian colonies, rather than requiring us to accept as typical the experience of a small sample of plantations.

A number of parameters are available in the registration data for the selection of appropriate model life tables. Three age variables, subdivided by sex and the rate of natural increase, have been utilized, as set out in table 2.6. The age data in the registration returns are sufficiently robust for this purpose, and the rate of natural increase can be accepted even if the birth and death rates are erroneous, because movement in either one of these rates is counterbalanced by movement in the

Table 2.6. *Parameters Used for the Selection of Model Life Tables*

Colony	Natural Increase per 1,000	Percentage 15–44 Years		Population 0–4/15–44 Years		Population 5–14/5 + Years	
		Males	Females	Males	Females	Males	Females
Barbados, 1817–20	+4.8	47.1	46.7	0.344	0.304	0.306	0.261
St. Kitts, 1817–21	−5.7	49.6	47.9	0.234	0.242	0.255	0.232
Nevis, 1817–21	−3.7	49.6	46.4	0.214	0.250	0.266	0.225
Antigua, 1827–32	−2.0	48.0	45.8	0.259	0.241	0.251	0.219
Montserrat, 1828–31	+9.5	49.6	45.4	0.324	0.317	0.269	0.269
Virgin Islands, 1818–22	−6.3	49.5	48.7	0.240	0.231	0.271	0.240
Jamaica, 1817–20	−0.7	53.2	51.3	0.186	0.206	0.211	0.212
Dominica, 1829–32	+0.6	49.7	51.1	0.258	0.239	0.235	0.215
St. Lucia, 1815–19	−25.5	50.9	48.8	0.252	0.255	0.271	0.228
St. Vincent, 1817–21	−12.5	53.5	53.0	0.185	0.209	0.230	0.227
Grenada, 1817–20	−15.7	52.4	51.4	0.175	0.181	0.205	0.194
Tobago, 1819–21	−26.2	52.9	51.3	0.177	0.197	0.224	0.214
Trinidad, 1816–19	−18.5	68.1	62.8	0.147	0.206	0.138	0.179
Demerara-Essequibo, 1820–23	−9.7	58.3		0.191		0.209	
Berbice, 1819–22	−8.3	63.6	57.3	0.164	0.225	0.172	0.235
British Honduras, 1834	n.a.	47.2	53.5	0.181	0.241	0.147	0.236
Cayman Islands, 1834	n.a.	29.2	42.4	0.364	0.310	0.235	0.295
Bahamas, 1831–34	+13.9	42.8	43.9	0.401	0.369	0.285	0.309
Anguilla, 1827–31	+28.6	43.0	48.7	0.421	0.309	0.339	0.259
Barbuda, 1827–32	+22.2	38.3	38.5	0.500	0.346	0.335	0.365

Source: T.71.

n.a.: not available.

other. Stable populations and their associated model life tables have been selected for each of the British West Indian colonies by fitting all of these parameters. Where a good fit was difficult, primary reliance was placed on the rate of natural increase and the proportion 0–4/15–44 years, and on the pattern in the female population. The extreme negative rates of natural increase (below − 10.0) recorded in St. Lucia, St. Vincent, Grenada, Tobago, and Trinidad are not represented in the Coale and Demeny model life tables, and their birth rates had to be determined by graphical interpolation. Relatively poor fits were found for the parameters in the colonies of St. Lucia, Tobago, Demerara-Essequibo, Berbice, Jamaica, the Virgin Islands, and the Bahamas. The selection of model life tables involves fewer arbitrary assumptions than the direct method of estimation of underregistration, but the compromises necessary in the cases of poor fit increase the chances of error in determining true birth rates.

The model life tables selected for each colony are given in table 2.7, together with their associated crude birth rates. The latter are compared with the birth rates obtained by the direct method of estimation. These crude birth rates are then used to determine the numbers of births expected, according to the two methods of

Table 2.7. *Underregistration of Births: Estimated Directly and by Model Life Tables*

Colony	Model Life Table Mortality Level	Births per 1,000			Percentage Births Registered	
		Life Table Estimate		Direct Estimate		Life Table
		Males	Females	Total	Direct Estimate	Estimate
Barbados, 1817–20	West 3	49.4	45.4	47.3	69.8	69.9
St. Kitts, 1817–21	West 3	37.5	34.0	34.7	72.9	71.0
Nevis, 1817–21	West 3	39.7	36.1	36.3	69.1	66.2
Antigua, 1827–32	West 5	34.2	31.5	28.8	76.6	67.3
Montserrat, 1828–31	West 5	46.3	43.1	49.1	76.7	84.5
Virgin Islands, 1818–22	West 4	33.2	30.3	30.8	66.8	64.9
Jamaica, 1817–20	West 7	30.2	28.0	31.5	74.9	81.0
Dominica, 1829–32	West 6	33.8	31.3	37.0	74.0	84.3
St. Lucia, 1815–19	West 1	27.3	24.3	24.5	60.1	57.4
St. Vincent, 1817–21	West 3	30.6	27.7	31.2	73.8	78.9
Grenada, 1817–20	West 3	27.6	24.9	32.7	74.7	93.3
Tobago, 1819–21	West 1	26.8	23.8	28.1	75.0	83.5
Trinidad, 1816–19	West 1	33.4	29.7	27.8	68.8	60.2
Demerara-Essequibo, 1820–23	West 3	33.4	30.1	31.4	66.7	65.4
Berbice, 1819–22	West 4	31.3	28.4	35.4	67.9	80.2
British Honduras, 1834	West 8	30.0	30.0	–	–	–
Cayman Islands, 1834	West 8	35.0	35.0	–	–	–
Bahamas, 1831–34	West 5	51.4	48.0	37.1	74.0	55.3
Anguilla, 1827–31	West 9	55.0	52.5	63.6	65.1	77.2
Barbuda, 1827–32	West 9	48.0	45.6	43.3	76.9	71.4

Source: See text.

estimation, and these numbers are compared with the registration totals. In general, the estimated percentages of births registered are similar for the two methods, with the exceptions of Grenada and Berbice. Since the methods are quite independent, the overall similarity of the results encourages confidence in the estimates. The model life table estimate for Demerara-Essequibo (West 3) can be compared with a life table constructed by G. W. Roberts (which appeared in a pioneering article), who used the census-differencing method.[67] West 3 matches Roberts's life table quite closely, but implies an even heavier level of child mortality than assumed by him and hence a higher rate of underregistration of births. West 7, representative of Jamaica, compares with life tables prepared by Michael Craton for a number of Jamaican plantations.[68]

In arriving at a final estimate of the extent of underregistration of births, the model life table estimates have been preferred to the direct estimates. They are preferred because the model life table method of estimation involves fewer obvious arbitrary assumptions directly related to registration practice or child mortality and because it can be applied consistently throughout the colonies rather than extrapolating from a small sample of plantation experience. Patterns found by the model life table method are corroborated by these samples of actual West Indian slave experience, thus increasing confidence in their broader application. The use of model life tables also permits the estimation of a range of demographic measures not available directly. But all of these estimates are to be regarded critically, of course, within the framework of their assumptions and limitations.

The rates of underregistration of births accepted are those listed in the final column of table 2.7. These rates have been used to inflate the numbers of births registered in each period, and the adjusted totals are given in table S8.2, along with the mean populations.

It remains only to discuss briefly variations in the data relating to those births that were in fact recorded in the registration returns. Most of the children registered as births were named, except that those who died in the first few weeks of life often remained without names. In St. Vincent, for example, children who died within a week were sometimes listed as "infants without names," and a living child 36 days old at registration was said to be "not yet christened but to be called Nancy."[69] Children without names were often listed by reference to their mothers, for example as "Mary's child." Sex and color were recorded systematically, as in the initial returns. Month of birth and age at registration were recorded very erratically and were subject to considerable rounding (table 2.3). The names of mothers were listed consistently in most of the new sugar colonies but elsewhere were generally omitted. There is no reason to assume this information is not reliable, when given. The names of fathers were listed partially in the case of Trinidad but elsewhere were completely ignored, and it is not certain how these data were collected.

Deaths

The omission of deaths from the slave registration returns related almost entirely to children born and dying within a registration period. This problem has been dealt with in the section dealing with births. There was little incentive to omit adult deaths from registration. The masters may have wished to conceal the death of slaves in order to replace them with illegally imported Africans, but the range of characteristics used to identify slaves in the registration returns made such replacement difficult to hide. There is no external evidence to suggest that this in fact occurred and, during the period of registration, the illegal slave trade was rigidly controlled by the British so that the supply of such slaves was limited.[70] It is also possible that the slaves themselves could have reported a slave as dead who had in fact run away. But, because this possibility existed, the masters must have regularly inspected the bodies of the dead before burial. They also did this in order to determine the cause of death, especially in cases of accident or foul play. Any successful effort by the slaves to trick the master would have resulted in over-registration of deaths, of course. In general it seems improbable that either of these types of concealment could have been common. But some slave deaths were lost to the record because of the death of the owner, or through transfer within a registration period to a new owner after the death of the slave. The system was intended to cover these possibilities, and some slave deaths of this type were in fact registered. Omissions no doubt occurred, particularly in the smaller slaveholdings, as in the case of birth-deaths. But there is no reason to suspect any significant underregistration of adult deaths.

Adjustments to the death registration data can be confined to child mortality (birth-deaths). A direct estimate can be obtained by simply adding to registered deaths the numbers of birth-deaths found in the previous section and using these data to calculate crude death rates. Comparable death rates are found in the model life tables chosen as representative in the discussion of births (table 2.7). These death rates, together with an estimate of the extent of underregistration, are shown in table 2.8. A reasonably close agreement between the two estimates is found, with the exception of Grenada. The model life table estimates are accepted as the more plausible, for the same reasons as advanced in the case of births, and these are used to calculate estimated total deaths (table S8.2). It is important to notice that there were significant differences between the rates of underregistration for births and deaths in some colonies. These differences were most marked where mortality or fertility reached extreme levels. In St. Lucia, Trinidad, and Tobago, for example, a larger proportion of births than deaths went unregistered because these islands all suffered extremely high adult mortality. On the other hand, colonies with low adult mortality and high fertility, such as Anguilla and the Bahamas, showed a higher rate of underregistration for deaths than births, since birth-deaths comprised a large component of total deaths.[71]

The amount of data provided about those slaves whose deaths were registered varied widely from colony to colony (table 2.3). In Trinidad, St. Lucia, and most of the old sugar colonies, the returns rarely provided any more than the slave's name. Elsewhere, a range of characteristics was included, facilitating certain identification. Month and year of death were provided consistently only for Tobago, Demerara-Essequibo, and Berbice. There seems no reason to question the accuracy of these data. Age at death, however, when given, often did no more than repeat the slave's age at the date of the previous registration. The effects of such distortion are most obvious for children, but can be observed only where month and year of death are also given. Cause of death was noted consistently in the returns from some of the new sugar colonies, but only in Grenada, Demerara-Essequibo, and Berbice were these data certified by medical practitioners. The ability of the latter to properly identify causes of death was severely limited by the state of medical knowledge, of course. The data also suffer from individual variation in nomenclature, particularly where they were prepared by the masters themselves.

Sales, Purchases, and Transfers

The registration data relating to slaves transferred from one owner to another were similar to those provided in the initial returns. Considerable care was taken to specify the names of purchasers, sellers and those receiving slaves through

Table 2.8. *Underregistration of Deaths: Estimated Directly and by Model Life Tables*

| Colony | Deaths per 1,000 | | | | Percentage Deaths Registered | |
| | Direct Estimate | | Life Table Estimate | | Direct Estimate | Life Table Estimate |
	Males	Females	Males	Females		
Barbados, 1817–20	46.1	39.4	44.6	40.6	66.5	66.5
St. Kitts, 1817–21	42.2	38.8	43.2	39.7	76.7	74.9
Nevis, 1817–21	44.3	35.9	43.4	39.8	72.0	69.3
Antigua, 1827–32	32.0	29.6	36.2	33.5	78.2	69.2
Montserrat, 1828–31	41.6	38.1	36.8	33.6	71.1	79.7
Virgin Islands, 1818–22	40.9	33.8	39.5	36.6	72.4	70.8
Jamaica, 1817–20	33.9	30.5	30.9	28.7	75.5	81.6
Dominica, 1829–32	37.5	35.5	33.2	30.7	73.7	84.1
St. Lucia, 1815–19	59.2	42.4	52.8	49.8	80.5	78.7
St. Vincent, 1817–21	46.9	41.0	43.1	40.2	81.4	85.9
Grenada, 1817–20	51.0	45.8	43.3	40.6	82.9	95.6
Tobago, 1819–21	59.0	49.8	53.0	50.0	87.4	92.3
Trinidad, 1816–19	42.4	51.1	51.9	48.2	81.2	74.8
Demerara-Essequibo, 1820–23	41.1		43.1	39.8	74.6	73.6
Berbice, 1819–22	43.2	44.3	39.6	36.7	73.9	84.4
British Honduras, 1834	–	–	28.5	28.5	–	–
Cayman Islands, 1834	–	–	28.0	28.0	–	–
Bahamas, 1831–34	24.9	21.5	37.5	34.1	58.5	37.9
Anguilla, 1827–31	36.4	33.8	26.4	23.8	36.5	51.1
Barbuda, 1827–32	28.6	15.5	25.8	24.4	52.6	44.4

Source: See text.

inheritance, marriage, or gift. Some underregistration of slave sales occurred, especially when an owner completed a transfer and then died within that registration period. But the data for purchases are probably complete, since registration was required as proof of ownership. The information given about the slaves transferred was also fuller for purchases than for sales. As for deaths, some colonies merely listed slaves sold by name, whereas the purchasers generally included the same information as in the initial returns.

Manumission, Marronage, and Transportation

Data on slaves lost to the population by manumission, marronage (desertion), or transportation (beyond the West Indies, for criminal offenses) were similar to those provided for deaths. The only problems with them relate to definition and underregistration. Manumission was sometimes confused with sale and purchase. In Barbados, for example, some slaves were returned as "sold to himself/herself," "sold to be manumitted," or "sold to a free coloured (person) to be manumitted." The first two cases may be regarded as definite manumissions, though a less precise master might merely have written "sold" and so concealed a manumission. In the last two cases, however, it is not certain that the purchasers actually manumitted the slaves within the registration period; if they did, they may have regarded the transaction as strictly an act of manumission and not registered it as a purchase, so that the outcome is difficult to trace through the returns. Similar doubts surround slaves "left to be manumitted." In the Berbice returns some even vaguer notes occurred: "to be freed" and "free but not manumitted." But such comments relate to a very small number of cases.

Slaves were known to desert for periods of very variable length. A slave absent at the date of registration but who had been gone for only a few days was unlikely to be listed as a runaway. Thus, the returns underestimate marronage to some unknown extent and provide a sample only of those who were absent for long periods of time. The data must also suffer from significant individual variation between masters.[72]

SLAVE REGISTRATION: AN ASSESSMENT

A good deal of the preceding discussion of the slave registration returns has been critical, highlighting the various inadequacies of the data. It is perhaps necessary to reemphasize, then, that the returns comprise an extraordinarily rich and comprehensive collection of information, rarely surpassed in comparable slave societies and generally standing up to quite strict tests of reliability. Some items in the data stand up to criticism much better than others, however, and it is important to establish these distinctions rather than to accept or reject the data en bloc.

Variations in the reliability of the data stem largely from the role of slave registration as a system of identification. Thus, observable physical characteristics were likely to be the most accurately recorded: sex, color, bodily marks, and stature. Age and birthplace were less directly observable. Other items, such as name, occupation, and kin relationships, were open to a greater degree of distortion because they could change on the instant, according to the social context. The underregistration of births, probably the most important deficiency of the data, also stemmed from the purpose of identification: there seemed no need to list slaves who did not in fact exist at the date of registration. Further variations resulted from the ignorance of the masters or their slave informants. The items most affected by this simple lack of accurate knowledge were age, birthplace, and kin relationships. But there is little evidence of deliberate, systematic distortion of the data. Individual masters were concerned above all with the value of the information for identification and could hardly have spent much time pondering the ultimate propaganda uses of the data.

The origin of the slave registration records in separate legislation created considerable variation in the information provided for each colony, so that they do not constitute a truly systematic body of data. The constellation of identifiers differed from colony to colony. More importantly, the range of information was broader for the new sugar colonies than the older settlements of the British Caribbean, thus limiting the comparative value of the material. In some colonies there were also significant variations between the returns of individual masters. Thus, any analysis of the data must be based on a shifting sample of the population.

METHODS OF ANALYSIS

Analysis of the data in the slave registration returns has principally been aggregative, but a certain amount of nominal linkage and family reconstitution has also been carried out. Although total colony populations have generally been studied, some of the analysis derives from samples at varying levels of spatial generalization. In this section, the bases of this sampling will be stated, together with some technical notes on the treatment of the data.

The most detailed analysis has been performed on the returns for Trinidad 1813, St. Lucia 1815–19, Berbice 1819–22, Tobago 1819–21, and the parishes of St. Michael, St. Andrew, and St. John in Barbados 1817–20. This comprised a population of about 108,000 slaves, or nearly one-third of the total in the colonies other than Jamaica. Data for individual slaves in each of these five colonies were converted to machine-readable form and analyzed with the aid of computers. In the case of Trinidad, only the initial returns were studied. For St. Lucia, Berbice, and the Barbados parishes, the initial returns were linked with the data for individual slaves in the first subsequent return, so that movements in the population were also included. For Tobago, all movements recorded in the first three subsequent returns (dated 1 January 1820, 1821, and 1822) were linked with the data for individual slaves in the initial 1819 return, but the entire 1819 population was not coded for machine analysis. These colonies were chosen for detailed study because of the relatively wide range of data available in their returns. Unfortunately, all except Barbados were new sugar colonies, resulting in a relative neglect of the older settlements. Only three parishes were sampled from Barbados because the island's returns contained a fairly narrow range of data. St. Michael was chosen because it contained Bridgetown and the largest slave population of any parish on the island, and St. John and St. Andrew because they showed the greatest concentration of slaves in sugar cultivation.

Simpler varieties of hand-analysis have been applied to the other colonies. Attention has been concentrated on the early years of registration because very often the initial return was the only one to contain a census of the slave population. In a few cases, later census-type returns have been analyzed as well as the initial returns: Barbados 1834, St. Kitts 1834, and Anguilla 1834. For Antigua, Montserrat, and Dominica, only the later (1832) returns have been analyzed. Demerara-Essequibo is the only colony for which no work has been done on the original registration returns. This is because the detailed published reports of the Registrar, James Robertson, mentioned above, provide many basic tabulations of age structure, geographical distribution, mortality, and fertility, though the reports are somewhat erratic in terms of the categories and intervals employed.

Nominal linkage has been used chiefly as a means of relating births, deaths, manumissions, and transfers recorded in subsequent registration returns to individuals in the initial returns. Where the complete range of characteristics was included in the subsequent returns, such linkage is not required. But, as noted above, many returns provided only names in the case of deaths, and never gave any more than mothers' names for births. Linkages can be made directly as long as no duplication of names occurs within a return. Where duplication exists, some individuals can often be excluded as unlikely matches (five-year-old mothers, male mothers, and so on). If more than one candidate remains, the last resort is to choose the first listed. This will result in some age-weighting if the returns are consistently ordered by age, but a test of the data for Tobago suggests that the age structure would be little changed were the second or third case of the name selected. In Nevis the slaves were numbered as well as named in the returns, thus reducing the chances of improper linkage. The 1820 returns for Barbados provided complete lists of slaves, ordered as in 1817, but blanks were left in the columns for age and so on in the case of deaths; thus, the ordering of the names can be used to ensure certain linkages. A more general problem is that linkages can only be made if the correct owner's return is located. This becomes complicated when slaves had been sold or a master had died before a slave's death, for example. Most often the information on sales or deceased estates enables the initial returns to be traced, but a small number of owners and slaves remain unidentified.

The analysis has been carried out at a number of levels of spatial generalization. Within colonies, the data have generally been subdivided by administrative areas (most often called parishes) and by urban settlements. In St. Kitts, Antigua, and Montserrat, however, parishes were not identified in the registration returns. This lack of location data can be overcome for the final registrations by linking the returns to the claims for compensation made by the masters on the abolition of slavery in 1834. The compensation data are contained in three basic series: valuers' returns made by the Assistant Commissioners for Compensation, registers of claims, and indexes to claims.[73] The valuer's returns, in particular, provide parish and place-name notations for each claim, together with the name of the claimant and the status of his ownership. These have been used to identify the spatial location of slaveholdings in St. Kitts (1834), Antigua (1832), and Montserrat (1831). The gap between the date of registration and valuation creates problems because of changes in ownership, but most returns can be located satisfactorily.

Matching of the registration and valuers' returns also permits analysis at the level of the town or small region. It has been used to determine the population of Bridgetown, Barbados, by streets, in 1834. This method was used systematically in the writer's complementary study of Jamaica as the basis for analysis by a grid of small homogeneous spatial units (quadrats).[74] It has not been used for this purpose in the present book for a number of reasons. In the first place, the registration returns themselves permit the direct allocation of the slaves to almost 200 administrative areas for the British Caribbean as a whole, whereas Jamaica was divided into only 21 parishes (with a similar total population). Secondly, the insular character of the colonies means that any regular grid would contain a very large proportion of cut-off coastal areas, unless the quadrats were very small, in which case the problem of how to allocate plantations straddling their boundaries would become overwhelming. Thirdly, the separate colonial governments created significant variations in registration practice, so that it would be difficult to lump together for analysis a conglomerate of small units for the British Caribbean as a whole. Finally, matching of the registration and valuers' returns cannot be applied confidently to returns made before 1830. Thus, data recorded only in the initial census-type registrations, such as age and occupation, can rarely be analyzed on this small scale. These limitations restrict very considerably the value of using a grid of quadrats for the British Caribbean as a whole, and analysis is here confined to the "natural" units of plantation, island, parish, town, and colony.

It remains only to mention a few small technical points. As a general rule, calculations made by the writer from the original registration returns have been preferred to any contemporary tabulations. In some cases, these differences can be traced to obvious clerical errors in the contemporary calculations, such as incorrect addition or failure to notice duplicate returns. Clerical errors can also be detected in the registration returns themselves, and have been removed wherever possible. For example, the clerks sometimes listed "male, ditto, ditto, . . . male" when the names and occupations of some "ditto" slaves clearly show them to have been females. The same applies to cases such as "African, ditto, ditto, . . . African" where some "ditto" slaves were very young and the children or creoles. These errors can be removed with confidence. More difficult is the type "coloured, ditto, ditto, . . . coloured" where the "ditto" cases can be numerous; at some point the clerk should have changed a "ditto" or "black," but it is not certain exactly where. In such cases it is assumed that the first "ditto" was really "black," but this decision possibly understates the "coloured" numbers somewhat. A further problem is the rather vague use of brackets by some clerks to indicate a string of births or deaths. But overall the returns were carefully presented, and few subjective decisions of this sort need be made.

3.
Physical and
Economic Environments

VARIATIONS IN THE CHARACTER OF SLAVERY AND IN THE DEMO-graphic experience of slave populations may be traced, in part, to the contrasting physical and economic environments in which slaves were forced to live. In order to determine the nature of these parameters for the British Caribbean in the early nineteenth century, it is necessary to describe briefly the physical geographies and settlement histories of the colonies, the spatial distribution of the slave populations within these contrasting physical contexts, and distribution between the different types of economic activity. On the basis of these patterns, a typology of the colonies is advanced.

PHYSICAL ENVIRONMENTS

Differences in the physical geographies of the British Caribbean colonies related chiefly to the elements of size, slope, soil, and rainfall.[1]

Variations in size were great (table 3.1). The mainland colonies, British Honduras and British Guiana, exceeded the islands by far, but their slave populations were confined to narrow coastal and riverine belts. The Bahamas, the largest of the island colonies, was made up of some 700 islands and 2,000 cays and rocks spread through 90,000 square miles of sea; the largest of these islands were Andros (2,300 square miles), Inagua (599), Grand Bahama (530), and Abaco (395). Jamaica was easily the largest of the colonies occupying a single island, and its slave population was almost as numerous as that of the other colonies combined. The smallest of the island colonies, each with its own legislature, were Montserrat, Nevis, and Anguilla, in the Leewards. Thus, while some slaves lived on the fringes of massive hinterlands, most found themselves on small islands, only occasionally being able to see neighboring islands across the sea. But this had little significance for the mobility of the slaves, since the majority were tied to particular plantations or locations.

A systematic analysis of slope is not available, and maximum altitudes tend to be misleading at the colony level (table 3.1). The populated coastal strip of British Guiana was in fact largely below sea level and was protected by a sea wall; its

Table 3.1. *The British Colonies in the Caribbean c.1834*

Colony	Area (sq mi)	Maximum Altitude (ft)	Slave Population	Slaves per sq mi	Year of British Coloni- zation
Barbados	166	1,100	83,150	500.9	1627
St. Kitts	65	3,792	17,525	269.6	1625
Nevis	36	3,232	8,840	245.6	1628
Antigua	108	1,319	28,130	260.5	1632
Montserrat	39	3,002	6,400	164.1	1632
Virgin Islands	59	1,760	5,135	87.0	1672
Jamaica	4,411	7,402	311,070	70.5	1655
Dominica	305	4,672	14,165	46.4	1763
St. Lucia	233	3,145	13,275	57.0	1803
St. Vincent	150	4,048	22,250	148.3	1763
Grenada	133	2,756	23,645	177.8	1763
Tobago	114	1,860	11,545	101.3	1763
Trinidad	1,864	3,085	20,655	11.1	1797
British Guiana	83,000	9,000	83,545	1.0	1803
British Honduras	8,867	3,000	1,895	0.2	1670
Cayman Islands	100	165	985	9.9	1734
Bahamas	5,548	200	9,995	1.8	1648
Anguilla	35	200	2,260	64.6	1650
Barbuda	62	100	505	8.1	1685

Sources: B. W. Higman, *The Caribbean Today* (1975); table S1.2.

waterlogged agricultural lands were criss-crossed by canals. The mountains were far distant in the interior, known only to the Amerindians and a few explorers.[2] The slaves could not look unto the hills for strength. Along the coastline of British Guiana was a narrow clay lowland, rarely more than 30 miles wide, backed by a sandy lowland that took up about one-quarter of the territory. Further inland, to the west and south, were uplands under heavy forest cover.

The topography and settlement pattern of British Honduras were similar to those of British Guiana. The populated northern third of the territory was lowland, less than 500 feet above sea level. Along the entire length of the 200 miles of coast were many swamps, lagoons, and cays, covered by mangrove. Only in the southwestern third of the territory were there uplands rising above 3,000 feet.

Some of the island colonies were low-lying: the Cayman Islands, the Bahamas, Anguilla, and Barbuda. None of these rose above 200 feet. Made up of shallow limestone banks and coral reefs, many of them were covered by low scrub and surrounded by mangrove swamps. The islands and cays of the Bahamas stood on a shallow bank of limestone through which it was difficult for shipping to find a passage. The soil tended to be sandy and infertile, while the uplands weathered to create karstic landscapes. Anegada, one of the Virgin Islands, was simply a flat limestone block. Anguilla and Barbuda were coral islands with only occasional ridges interrupting their flatness. The soil was thin, and bare rock and sand common.

The remaining islands, in which local variations in relief were generally considerable, belonged to three partially submerged mountain systems. The most important of these stretched from the Virgin Islands in the east through Jamaica and southern Cuba to Central America: the Greater Antilles. The second extended southward from the Leeward Islands to Grenada: the Lesser Antilles. Here the volcanic peaks were separated by deep sea passages, creating a succession of small, mountainous islands. In the Leeward Islands the volcanoes were inactive and eroded to form relatively low-lying islands, as in the case of Antigua. In the Windward Islands volcanic activity continued, and the land was much more mountainous. The third mountain system was that extending from the South American mainland through Trinidad and Tobago. Tobago had a very limited fringe of level land, whereas the northern and southern ranges of Trinidad were separated by an extensive plain. Barbados rested on the same submarine ridge and was composed of coral terraces surrounded by barrier reefs. But, excepting the northeastern area where the terraces had been raised to create steep cliffs, the whole of Barbados was arable.

Temperatures in the Caribbean were uniformly high, in spite of the wide latitudinal spread of the colonies. Seasonal variations were also limited. Diurnal contrasts tended to be greater, occasionally exceeding those between summer and winter. Local variations were important, with altitudinal differences in the more mountainous islands having an effect on their patterns of settlement and land use.

Rainfall patterns were much less uniform. Great variations occurred both within and between colonies. Differences in altitude were basic, with the small low-lying islands receiving less than 60 inches per year. These islands also tended to suffer the longest droughts and to lose most by percolation. In Barbados rainfall exceeded 75 inches only in the most hilly area of the island. By contrast, the Windward Islands received less than 70 inches only in their coastal fringes, with rainfall being above 100 inches for the greater part of their area and exceeding 250 inches in Dominica. In Tobago the range was greater (40–150 inches), but in Trinidad less (50–100 inches). Coastal Guyana received an average 90 inches per year. But the greatest local variations occurred in Jamaica, with the southern plains receiving an average less than 70 inches while the eastern mountains received over 200 inches. It must be noted that all of these rainfall data derive from twentieth-century averages and take no account of secular change. There is evidence of change in rainfall levels since 1870, but no studies of the early nineteenth century are available, so it must be assumed that the pattern of variation found in modern times is similar to that in the last years of slavery.

The colonies of the British Caribbean, then, contained a variety of physical environments and contrasting landscapes. The colonies can be sorted roughly into types using these criteria, but the extremes of size mean that some colonies contained more than one of these types within their borders. Local, small-scale variation was common.

SETTLEMENT HISTORIES

Variations in the economic and demographic patterns of the British Caribbean colonies between 1807 and 1834 were also affected by their contrasting settlement histories. Some had been a part of the British Empire for the entire length of their colonial history; some had begun as Spanish, French, or Dutch colonies; and others were constantly passed back and forth between the European imperial powers. Some had been densely settled sugar colonies since the middle of the seventeenth century, some still possessed active frontiers in 1807, and others had never really moved beyond the presugar settlement pattern.

The British invasion of the Caribbean fell into three major phases: the second and third quarters of the seventeenth century, the 1760s, and the turn of the nineteenth century.[3]

In the first phase of British colonial expansion, settlements were established between 1625 and 1632 in St. Kitts, Barbados, Nevis, Antigua, and Montserrat; in Jamaica in 1655; and, rather more tenuously, in the Virgin Islands, Anguilla, Barbuda, the Bahamas, the Cayman Islands, and British Honduras (table 3.1). All of these settlements were largely the product of private enterprise rather than of government action. Jamaica was captured from the Spanish, the Virgin Islands from the Dutch, and St. Kitts was shared with the French until 1702. With the exception of British Honduras, all of these settlements were to remain in British possession, and they were firmly stamped with British influence. Barbados and the Leeward Islands, with high proportions of level land and moderate rainfall, were quickly transformed into full-blown sugar colonies. Jamaica, however, was never as strictly monocultural, and the expansion of settlement continued throughout the eighteenth century.

Jamaica's slave population continued to grow rapidly until the abolition of the Atlantic slave trade, whereas the populations of Barbados and the Leeward Islands leveled off after about 1710.[4] In the Virgin Islands the sugar revolution was retarded, gaining momentum only after 1750. The other colonies established in this first phase never endured the sugar revolution. The Bahamas experienced a short-lived plantation revolution based on cotton, following the influx of Loyalists after the American Revolution, but by 1800 the poor soil had been exhausted and salt raking and "wrecking" again became dominant activities. Anguilla depended on salt, British Honduras on logwood and mahogany, the Cayman Islands on turtles, and Barbuda on livestock. But none of these colonies produced major agricultural export staples, and they always remained marginal to the imperial plantation economy.

The sugar colonies established in the first phase all had their own planter-controlled legislatures by the end of the seventeenth century. The British attempted to establish a joint legislature in the Leeward Islands (including the Virgin Islands) in 1798, but it was dissolved in 1800, the island assemblies resuming their legislative autonomy.[5] The marginal, nonplantation colonies were much less successful in gaining control over their political affairs. Only the Bahamas established and maintained a legislative assembly, incorporating the Turks and

Caicos Islands from 1804. Anguilla's assembly was annexed to St. Kitts in 1825 and the island placed under a Deputy-Governor. Barbuda was effectively the private property of the Codrington family, and the Cayman Islands were administered from Jamaica. British Honduras, generally referred to in the early nineteenth century as "the British settlement in the Bay of Honduras," was aberrant since it existed within territory that remained legally Spanish until 1862. It was placed under a Superintendent rather than a Governor, and its legislation proceeded from a rough-and-ready "public meeting," not an elected assembly.[6] All of the nonplantation colonies lacking assemblies had small white populations and few slaves.

The second phase of British settlement in the Caribbean lacked the private enterprise characteristics of the first. All of the islands added to the empire in the 1760s were "conquered" colonies, acquired through European treaties rather than taken directly from Amerindians. The Peace of Paris, concluded in 1763, ceded to Britain the islands of Dominica, St. Vincent, Tobago, Grenada, and the Grenadines. Dominica and St. Vincent were "neutral" islands, still effectively occupied by the Caribs. Grenada, a French colony since 1645, had a partially developed plantation economy. Tobago was the scene of attempted settlement by the French and Dutch in the seventeenth century, but became "neutral" territory after 1690 and fell again into the hands of the French between 1780 and 1803. There was also a brief French occupation of Dominica in 1778–84. The total land area added to the British Empire through the cession of these islands was 702 square miles, much less than the area acquired in the seventeenth century.

This second phase of settlement took place during what Richard Pares called the "silver age" of sugar (the golden age being the 1640s).[7] Sugar prices were consistently high between 1750 and 1775, and British colonization transformed the ceded islands from diversified agricultural economies, producing cocoa, coffee, and cotton, into sugar colonies. But this transformation was nowhere as complete as it had been in Barbados and the Leeward Islands, the environments of the ceded islands being too mountainous and wet to permit the development of an encompassing sugar monoculture. The colonies of the second phase were, however, all granted elected legislatures, like the first-phase sugar colonies. The Grenadines were divided between the colonies of Grenada and St. Vincent.

In the third and final phase of British colonization, Trinidad was taken from the Spanish in 1797, St. Lucia from the French in 1803, and Demerara, Essequibo, and Berbice from the Dutch in the same year. Trinidad had remained a backwater until the *cédula* for population of 1783 opened the island to foreign Catholics, offering land in proportion to the number of slaves brought with them.[8] The result was a considerable influx of planters, slaves, and freedmen, most coming from the troubled French Antillean colonies. From a mere 1,500 (including only 200 slaves) in 1780, the population of Trinidad grew to 17,500 (10,000 of them slaves) by 1797. But the buoyancy of the 1760s sugar market had passed, and the British placed a restraining hand on the expansion of the sugar plantation and the slave trade. In order to effect this control, Trinidad was refused an elective legislature. It became the first crown colony, with its government originating in the imperial metropolis.[9] It was this direct control that made Trinidad the ideal colony for the first trial of the slave registration system.

St. Lucia had been the site of several abortive British settlements in the seventeenth century, but from 1748 was regarded as neutral. Britain occupied the island during the Seven Years' War, but it was ceded to the French in 1763. Between 1763 and 1803 St. Lucia was repeatedly lost and retaken by the French and British, until the final capture by the British in 1803. Sugar planting began only after 1763 and was interrupted by the uncertainty of control and supplies. As in the other Windward Islands, the firm establishment of the British led to the development of sugar at the expense of cotton, coffee, and cocoa, but the monocultural tendency was limited by the wet and mountainous character of the island. St. Lucia was not granted an assembly, and government was left largely in the hands of the Governor.[10]

Abortive British colonization of the Guianas in the seventeenth century had been followed by Dutch occupation between 1667 and 1803. At first settlement centered on the up-river regions, but by 1750 the locus shifted to the coastal clay soils protected by the sea wall. The British conquest of Demerara, Essequibo, and Berbice resulted in a large immigration of planters from colonies established in the first phase. The mainland colonies became the British Empire's leading producer of cotton and coffee for a brief period, but these crops were soon to fall off as sugar production was promoted and competition from United States cotton increased. Like Trinidad, the colonies possessed an open frontier in 1807. Similar forces operated to prevent the granting of an assembly, but pure crown colony government was not imposed. The Dutch legislative institutions, the Court of Policy and the Combined Court, were retained, together with their elective element. The colonies of Demerara and Essequibo were united in 1813 and combined with Berbice in 1831 to create British Guiana.[11]

By 1807, when the Atlantic slave trade was abolished, the territorial expansion of the British Empire in the Caribbean was complete. The phasing of this expansion over almost 200 years meant that the colonies were inevitably at different stages of economic and demographic development. They were also subject to differing political and cultural forces. But the plantocracy was generally strongest in the longest-settled, most monocultural, most British of the colonies, and weakest in the recently settled colonies of diversified agriculture and cosmopolitan population. Thus, the political power of the plantocracy was strongest where the ratio of slaves to free people was greatest. In general, the first-phase colonies tended to have the slighter slopes, the thinner soil, and the lighter rainfall, whereas the later-settled tended to be rugged and wet. The nature of the economic activities in which the slaves were employed was determined by the interaction of these contrasting physical environments with phases of settlement. Thus, any classification of the colonies based simply on stage of settlement is likely to prove inadequate as a basis for understanding variations in the character of slavery and economic-demographic relationships in the West Indian colonies.

TYPES OF ECONOMIC ACTIVITY

The primary object in this section is to determine the number of slaves employed in particular types of economic enterprise. The discussion begins with an overview of the structure of the slave labor force at about 1834, then treats the pattern of land and labor use in individual colonies for the period 1807–34. Finally, the colonies are classified into types according to their economic structure. The internal organization of the various types of economic enterprise is not discussed here but is taken up in chapters 5 and 6.

For an overall view of the occupational distribution of the British Caribbean slave population, the most comprehensive data available are those generated as a by-product of the compensation of the masters at emancipation. This compensation was calculated according to the money value of the slaves. The valuers' returns produced by this system have been discussed in chapter 2 as a source of data for the detailed geographical location of the population, but their main purpose was to classify the slaves belonging to the individual masters. This classification (table 3.2) was used to value the slaves on the basis of the average prices paid for slaves sold between 1823 and 1830 (a total of 74,000 transfers). The £20 million compensation money was then divided between the masters at a rate ranging from 42 to 55 percent of the valuation.[12] The slaves were classified after actual inspection by the Assistant Commissioners for Compensation, except that in the Bahamas the occupations listed in the registration returns of 31 July 1834 were used, to avoid the cost of visiting the scattered islands. The Cayman Islands were excluded entirely. The system required that slaves be classified according to their usual occupations before August 1834, but the masters had a monetary incentive to try to have slaves placed in a higher class.[13] There also seems to have been some inconsistency between colonies in the allocation of occupational groups. But in spite of these deficiencies, the compensation data do provide a very valuable picture of the total slave labor force (table S7.1).

In the British Caribbean as a whole, 81.7 percent of the slaves were classified as active in the labor force (table 3.3). Indeed, the only slaves excluded were children under 6 years of age (13.6 percent of the population) and those classed as "aged [70 years and over], diseased, or otherwise non-effective" (4.7 percent). There were some significant differences between the colonies, but only in Anguilla and Barbuda did the active labor force fall below 75 percent of the total population, and only in Trinidad, British Guiana, and the Virgin Islands did it exceed 84 percent. These variations were a product of differing age structures.

Predial slaves, who made up 85 percent of the total labor force, were those employed in agriculture or the extraction of other produce from the land (table 3.2). Many of the "non-predial" slaves lived on agricultural units, of course, but most of these served in the masters' households. The largest proportions of predials were found in the sugar colonies of Tobago and British Guiana (exceeding 90 percent of the active labor force), and the smallest in the marginal colonies of Anguilla and the Bahamas (less than 60 percent). Slaves working on lands owned

Table 3.2. *British Caribbean Slave Population as Classified for Compensation, 1834*

Compensation Classification	Number of Slaves	Percentage of Slaves	Percentage of Employed Slaves
Predial attached			
Head people	25,658	3.8	4.7
Tradesmen	18,735	2.8	3.4
Inferior tradesmen	5,999	0.9	1.1
Field laborers	241,177	36.2	44.3
Inferior field laborers	132,008	19.8	24.2
Predial unattached			
Head people	1,772	0.3	0.3
Tradesmen	1,639	0.3	0.3
Inferior tradesmen	643	0.1	0.1
Field laborers	22,218	3.3	4.1
Inferior field laborers	10,730	1.6	2.0
Non-predial			
Head tradesmen	4,151	0.6	0.8
Inferior tradesmen	2,439	0.4	0.5
Head people on wharves, shipping, etc.	3,335	0.5	0.6
Inferior people on wharves, shipping	3,928	0.6	0.7
Head domestic servants	29,387	4.4	5.4
Inferior domestic servants	40,718	6.1	7.5
Children under 6 years of age	91,037	13.6	—
Aged, diseased, or otherwise noneffective	30,088	4.5	—
Runaways	1,075	0.2	—
Total	666,737	100.0	100.0

Source: T.71/851 and 1522.

by their masters were classified as "predial attached" and those employed elsewhere as "predial unattached." The latter were hired out by their masters under a variety of arrangements. Some led relatively settled lives, working for years on a single plantation. Others belonged to jobbers who moved them about frequently, while some, especially tradesmen, were employed on a daily basis. In British Honduras, at one extreme, no slaves were defined as predial attached, since plantation agriculture was proscribed and the woodcutters divided their year between town and interior. High ratios of unattached predials also occurred in the Virgin Islands and Anguilla, together with high percentages of non-predials. But elsewhere this relationship did not hold, and in many of the more mature sugar colonies a settled agricultural labor force went together with a large non-predial class.

Table 3.3. *Distribution of Slaves between Compensation Categories by Colony, 1834*

Colony	Percentage of Employed Slaves					Percentage of Total Slaves		
	Field Laborers	Domestics	Tradesmen	Head People	On Wharves	Employed	Children under 6	Aged, Diseased
Barbados	70.8	18.8	5.7	3.0	1.7	80.2	17.7	2.1
St. Kitts	72.4	16.4	5.0	4.4	1.7	79.2	16.2	4.6
Nevis	64.1	16.8	6.8	3.9	8.4	82.0	14.3	3.7
Antigua	78.9	9.6	7.7	2.6	1.2	80.3	14.7	5.0
Montserrat	81.2	8.1	4.7	5.0	1.0	79.0	17.6	3.4
Virgin Islands	71.5	17.1	4.7	3.8	2.9	84.1	14.5	1.4
Jamaica	73.5	12.5	7.0	6.0	0.9	82.1	12.5	5.4
Dominica	81.3	9.2	3.6	5.4	0.5	82.3	14.9	2.8
St. Lucia	78.6	14.0	3.3	3.3	0.8	77.7	14.7	7.6
St. Vincent	75.5	12.2	5.0	5.2	2.1	81.4	13.3	5.3
Grenada	77.4	6.9	6.7	6.2	2.8	80.4	14.0	5.6
Tobago	82.1	6.9	7.3	2.4	1.3	78.3	12.8	8.9
Trinidad	67.4	18.6	6.1	6.8	1.1	84.9	10.9	4.2
British Guiana	82.8	7.0	4.9	4.9	0.4	84.2	11.8	4.0
British Honduras	48.1	46.4	2.8	1.5	1.2	83.7	11.5	4.7
Bahamas	54.5	31.8	2.7	0.9	10.1	77.2	19.9	2.9
Anguilla	67.9	28.4	1.4	0.7	1.5	74.9	20.3	4.8
Barbuda	80.4	5.3	8.4	2.0	3.9	72.5	23.0	4.5
Total	74.6	12.9	6.2	5.0	1.3	81.7	13.6	4.7

Source: T.71/851 and 1522.

Below these broad divisions, comparisons of the occupational composition of the colonies are affected more strongly by inconsistencies in classification. In particular, the principles used to separate "inferior" from other slaves in a class varied from colony to colony.[14] It is more useful to ignore this distinction and consider the five main occupational categories into which the slaves were grouped (table 3.3). Overall, "field labourers" accounted for almost 75 percent of the active labor force. Only in British Honduras and the Bahamas did this proportion fall below 60 percent. Low proportions were also found in Trinidad, Anguilla, and, surprisingly, Nevis.

After field laborers, the most numerous category comprised "domestics." In the marginal colonies of British Honduras, the Bahamas, and Anguilla, domestics made up more than 25 percent of the slave labor force. They were less numerous in the sugar colonies, where the proportion varied with the urban concentration of the slaves. More than half of the domestics lived in capital towns.[15]

Slave "tradesmen," employed in manufacturing processes or the production of intermediate goods on plantations, accounted for 6.2 percent of the labor force. The largest proportions occurred in the first-phase sugar colonies, whereas the marginal colonies with large numbers of domestics had the smallest. Although the compensation records rarely summarized the data by sex, it is clear that the trades were the occupations most strictly reserved for male slaves.

Slaves classified as "head people," the supervisors, overlapped the tradesman and field laborer categories. If they were distributed thus, there would be a significant inflation of the tradesman category (probably raising it to 10 percent of the labor force) and a slighter inflation of the field laborer class. Greater changes might result from this adjustment at the colony level, but there seem to have been inconsistencies in classification. It is obvious that head people would be most numerous in those colonies where the slaveholdings were large. In the Bahamas, for example, no headman was assigned to a master unless he owned at least 10 slaves.[16] In the sugar colonies the proportion of head people was inevitably larger, a reflection of the structure of slave ownership and of the internal hierarchy of the slave system.

The fifth major occupational category, accounting for only 1.3 percent of the labor force, comprised slaves "employed on wharves, shipping, etc." Such occupations were most important in colonies made up of small islands, the Bahamas having the largest proportion.

In broad terms, the occupational distribution of the slave labor force was determined by the extent to which a colony was dominated by sugar or other plantation crops. Of the nineteen British Caribbean colonies, only five were not significant producers of sugar in the period 1807–34: British Honduras, the Cayman Islands, the Bahamas, Anguilla, and Barbuda, with a total slave population of only 16,000 in 1834. The sugar colonies may be divided into three groups, according to their phase of settlement. The first-phase sugar colonies (Barbados, the Leeward Islands, and Jamaica) accounted for 463,000 slaves, the second-phase group 71,000, and the third-phase, frontier colonies 117,000.

Within these three groups of sugar colonies, however, there were significant differences in the dominance of the crop. A rough measure of its relative importance is the average production of sugar per slave. This ratio has been calculated for the years 1815 to 1834 (table 3.4). But the results are of limited value because the ratio contains three separate elements: the proportion of the slave labor force employed in sugar production, the proportion of the slave population comprising the active labor force, and the productivity of labor. The presence of the last two components weakens the ratio's ability to measure the first. In 1830–34 slaves in the first group of colonies produced only 0.14 to 0.30 tons of sugar per annum, those in the second 0.19 to 0.40, and those in the third 0.65 to 0.71. Obviously the long-settled monocultural colonies suffer in this comparison because of low labor productivity. Changes in the ratio over the period are more revealing but tend to mirror changes in total output. Barbados, the only colony in the first-phase group to show an increase in the ratio, also experienced a substantial increase in output (figure 3.1).

Although these gross data provide some insights into the employment and productivity of the slave labor force, they cannot elicit a precise picture of the distribution of the slave population between the different types of economic activity. In order to build up such a picture, it will be necessary to discuss the data for individual colonies seriatim, within the framework of the phases of settlement outlined above.

First-Phase Sugar Colonies

Barbados. Between 1807 and 1834 Barbados more than doubled its sugar production, but this gain in output was not won at the expense of other crops. A summary of the registration returns for 1834 defined 49.5 percent of the island's 82,807 slaves as "labourers in sugar cultivation," 5.8 percent as "labourers in cotton and other agriculture," 11.6 percent as "labourers not in agriculture," 13.0 percent as "domestics," and 20.1 percent as having no occupation.[17] Comparison with the 1834 compensation returns (table S11.1) shows, however, that these registration data understated the number of domestics (by about 2,000) and agricultural laborers (by 7,000). It appears that the group "labourers not in agriculture" included tradesmen living on rural holdings, and these should be redistributed to the agricultural and urban categories.[18] It is also necessary to distribute the domestics and those with no occupation according to the proportions found in the compensation records. The derivation of the estimated size of the urban population will be discussed fully in the next chapter. On the basis of these manipulations, it seems that no more than 78 percent of the Barbados slave population lived on sugar estates in 1834, while 11 percent lived on plantations or "places" producing cotton, provisions, ginger, and other crops, and 11 percent lived in towns.[19]

Sugar estates were spread almost uniformly throughout Barbados, thinning out only around Bridgetown, and in the rugged country of Mt. Hillaby, the Scotland District, and Hackleton's Cliff (see fig. 4.3). There were no significant changes in

Table 3.4. *Tons of Sugar Produced per Slave by Colony, 1815–34*

Colony	1815–19	1820–24	1825–29	1830–34
Barbados	0.16	0.17	0.19	0.21
St. Kitts	0.34	0.27	0.27	0.24
Nevis	0.34	0.24	0.27	0.27
Antigua	0.29	0.26	0.26	0.30
Montserrat	0.24	0.23	0.19	0.14
Virgin Islands	0.36	0.16	0.17	0.16
Jamaica	0.23	0.23	0.21	0.22
Dominica	0.12	0.13	0.15	0.19
St. Lucia	0.20	0.26	0.24	0.24
St. Vincent	0.50	0.49	0.56	0.47
Grenada	0.40	0.50	0.46	0.42
Tobago	0.41	0.41	0.39	0.40
Trinidad	0.29	0.35	0.53	0.71
British Guiana	0.20	0.32	0.63	0.65

Sources: Calculated from data in Noel Deerr, *The History of Sugar* (1949), and T.71.

distribution between 1807 and 1834, the number of mills remaining steady at around 340.[20] But, whereas the windward (eastern) parishes were rather less densely covered by sugar mills, there the concentration of slaves into the sugar sector was at a maximum. Cotton and other agriculture were relatively concentrated in the leeward parishes, especially around Bridgetown.

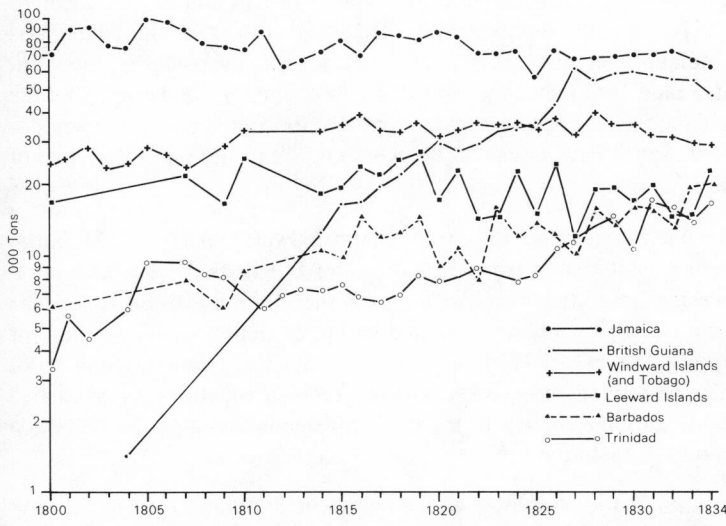

Fig. 3.1. *Sugar Production, 1800–1834. (Data from Noel Deerr,* The History of Sugar, *1949.)*

Barbados was effectively a vast sugar plantation, with sugar and its by-products, molasses and rum, accounting for almost 98 percent of the value of exports.[21] Molasses was more important than rum as an export item, the rum being largely consumed within the island, lubricating the internal market.[22] The only export other than sugar and molasses to exceed 1 percent of the total value was cotton. Ginger, arrowroot, and aloes were also exported on some scale, but were insignificant relative to sugar. The minor staples were produced by small settlers and slaves as well as planters.[23] In spite of the many acts passed to encourage the cultivation of these crops, the planters maintained a strictly monocultural orientation.[24] But the sugar planters of Barbados did use a significant proportion of their land space and the labor time of their slaves for the production of food crops to be consumed on the plantation, as will be discussed in detail in chapter 5. Even in such a monocultural economy, almost one-quarter of the slaves did not actually live on the sugar estates.

St. Kitts. Detailed data are not available for St. Kitts, but the distribution of slaves between economic activities must have been similar to that found in Barbados. Sugar, molasses, and rum accounted for 97 percent of the value of exports.[25] Between 1760 and 1810 St. Kitts had consistently produced more sugar than Barbados. It then entered a period of decline, but the ratio of sugar to slaves remained higher than in Barbados until 1834 (table 3.4). Few slaves in St. Kitts were employed in agriculture other than sugar, and only a small number were engaged in salt raking. Thus, the concentration of the slave population on the sugar estates was even greater than in Barbados.

The sugar estates of St. Kitts formed a fringe around the island's coast, interrupted only in the dry eastern peninsula where the salt ponds were located. According to William McMahon's map of 1828, 44 percent of the island was caneland, the remainder being taken up in ''works, negro huts, pasture, mountain, and uncultivated land.'' Some of the caneland was planted in food crops, but the planters became increasingly dependent on imported food and increasingly monocultural in orientation.[26] Few slaves on St. Kitts knew any life other than that of sugar cultivation.

Nevis. The land use pattern of Nevis was a simplified version of that of St. Kitts. Its conical form meant that there was almost no break in the succession of wedge-shaped estates, and the island lacked even the salt ponds of St. Kitts. The proportion of caneland (40 percent) matched that in St. Kitts, as did the ratio of sugar production to slaves. In 1765 some 75 percent of the slave population of Nevis was said to be located on sugar estates, and it is clear that this proportion had increased considerably by 1834.[27] In the early nineteenth century, Nevis was a sugar monoculture pure and simple.

Antigua. With its gentler slopes, Antigua approximated more closely the land use pattern of Barbados. Although it had been an important producer of cotton until the end of the eighteenth century, sugar gained complete mastery between

1800 and 1834, covering the greater part of the island.[28] Food crops were grown as a part of estate cultivation, as in Barbados, but Antigua imported most of its corn. An important contrast with Barbados, however, lay in the fact that some Antiguan properties were devoted to raising livestock for use on the estates. Sheep were also grazed, there being some demand for their wool.[29] Only in the more rugged southern parishes of Antigua were cattle and provisions properties numerous. Elsewhere sugar dominated. Antigua was the largest producer of sugar in the Leeward Islands for most of the period 1807–34, though the ratio of sugar to slaves did not exceed that in St. Kitts and Nevis until about 1830. Detailed data on the distribution of the Antiguan slave population are not available, but it can be estimated on the basis of these comparisons that almost 80 percent worked on sugar estates, while 10 percent were on holdings producing other crops and livestock, and 10 percent lived in towns.

Montserrat. Sugar, molasses, and rum were the only significant exports of Montserrat. Output remained fairly steady until 1820, then declined rapidly, so that by 1834 the sugar to slaves ratio was the lowest of all the British Caribbean sugar colonies (table 3.4). As in Antigua, cotton had declined rapidly in the late eighteenth century and reappeared only after 1838. The rugged topography of Montserrat confined sugar estates to the eastern and western coastal strips and the valley crossing the island. Food crops were rarely planted on the estates' limited potential caneland, and the slaves were expected to produce most of their own food on provision grounds allotted to them in the marginal hills.[30] The distribution of the slaves between enterprises was similar to that in Nevis.

Virgin Islands. In the Virgin Islands the sugar industry did not become dominant until 1800, and even then it was concentrated on one island, Tortola. Sugar exports increased rapidly between 1800 and 1819, but the extent to which this resulted from local production is uncertain. Tortola was declared a free port in 1801, permitted to import foreign sugar and coffee and reexport these goods to Britain. But since Tortola had to compete with free-trading St. Thomas, it is doubtful that it captured much non-British production.[31] In any case, by 1820 the Virgin Islands had become the smallest sugar producer in the Leeward Islands, rarely making more than 1,000 tons.

The most detailed source materials for the Virgin Islands are the tables prepared in 1823 by John Stobo for the Colonial Office.[32] Stobo provided data for 1815 and 1823, his intention being to show the great decline in the fortunes of the islands over the period. He named 47 islands, 15 being less than 10 acres in extent. In 1815 some 24 were under cultivation, but 2 (Ginger Island and Great Tobago) were abandoned by 1823. Four of the exploited islands had no people living on them, and others were occupied solely by slaves. Only a small proportion of the land was cultivated.

In 1823 only Tortola produced sugar, and even on that island scarcely more than 20 percent of the area was cultivated. The acreage under cane, according to Stobo, fell from 3,125 in 1815 to 2,400 in 1823 (table S11.2). By contrast, King's

Table 3.5. *Employment of Slaves in the Virgin Islands, 1815 and 1823*

	1815		1823	
Employment	Number	Percentage	Number	Percentage
In trade in town	178	2.4	159	2.5
Domestics in town	554	7.6	469	7.3
In fishing	136	1.9	124	1.9
Domestics in country	80	1.1	122	1.9
On sugar estates	4,569	62.6	4,131	64.1
On cotton plantations	1,725	23.7	1,343	20.8
Cultivating provisions	53	0.7	96	1.5
Total	7,295	100.0	6,444	100.0

Source: Stobo, "Statistical Table," C.O. 239/9.

map of 1798 showed 58 sugar estates on Tortola, covering the western two-thirds of the island.[33] Cotton, too, showed a minor decline in Tortola between 1815 and 1823, but in the Virgin Islands as a whole there was a slight increase, and cotton remained the major export staple of most of the smaller islands. Exports of cotton fluctuated but maintained a fair level until the end of the 1820s.[34] Land under cotton, according to Stobo, was valued at only half the amount for that under cane (£15 and £32 currency per acre, in 1815). Stobo also listed coffee produced in the larger islands, but most of this must have been imported from foreign colonies under the Free Port Act, the amount falling steeply after 1815. Salt was most important for Anegada, with 655 acres in salt ponds in 1815. Salt Island, Tortola, and Beef Island were also significant producers.

Stobo also provided estimates of the distribution of the slave population between these types of economic enterprise (table 3.5). The source of his information is not known, but the total populations conform closely to those found in the registration returns. In 1823 sugar estates accounted for almost 65 percent of the slaves, and cotton plantations for 21 percent. But, whereas the area under cane declined between 1815 and 1823, the estates increased their proportion of the slave labor force; hence the great fall in productivity. The dominance of sugar no doubt continued to increase, but even in 1834 the slaves of the Virgin Islands were employed in a much wider range of enterprises than those in the other sugar colonies of the Leeward Islands.

Jamaica. The use of land and labor in Jamaica has been discussed in detail elsewhere.[35] The available data are excellent, compared to those for the Leeward Islands and Barbados. Jamaica's economy was much more diverse than that of any of the other first-phase sugar colonies. This diversity resulted from the island's varied physical environments and the relatively slow movement of the frontier of settlement. Around 1832 slightly less than 50 percent of the slaves lived on sugar estates, 14 percent on coffee plantations, 13 percent on livestock pens, and 7 percent on minor staples plantations, while 6 percent belonged to mobile jobbing gangs, and 8 percent lived in towns.

2. Second-Phase Sugar Colonies

Dominica. Dominica was the least important sugar producer of all the colonies settled by Britain after 1763. But its level of output did remain fairly constant between 1807 and 1834, with a definite growth after 1825, and there was a steady increase in sugar production per slave. To a certain extent, the British did convert Dominica into a sugar colony from the coffee-cotton-cocoa-provisions economy it had been in 1763. Immediately following the cession of the island, sugar estates were established on a large scale by British planters, to the neglect of all other crops. By 1800 indigo, cotton, and ginger had all disappeared as significant crops.[36] Yet sugar failed to attain an absolute dominance, and coffee continued to employ a larger proportion of the slave population until 1834.

The most detailed data available for Dominica are found in the poll tax returns for 1827 (table S11.3). By that year, 80.6 percent of the slaves lived on sugar estates or coffee plantations. There were 42 sugar estates, 219 coffee plantations, and 11 properties that combined sugar and coffee in varying proportions. A few properties combined the production of coffee and molasses, but these may be placed with the coffee plantations since the quantity of molasses made was always small. If the slaves located on sugar-coffee units are divided equally between sugar and coffee plantations, it follows that 46.3 percent of the total slave population worked on coffee plantations and 34.3 percent on sugar plantations. If anything, this estimate overstates the proportion in sugar. It assumes 7,131 slaves in coffee and 5,271 in sugar, whereas a planters' petition of the late 1820s or early 1830s claimed 7,700 were in coffee and 4,500 in sugar.[37] The remaining predial slaves were employed on smaller holdings, producing minor staples such as cocoa and arrowroot,[38] and ground provisions. Thus, although there was a significant shift in land use patterns between 1763 and 1834, sugar never dominated the slave population of Dominica.

Coffee cultivation in Dominica was heavily concentrated in the windward parishes, the estates clinging to the limited level lands around river mouths. The sugar-coffee units were well scattered. They were relatively large, suggesting that they took advantage of diverse land types within their boundaries.

St. Vincent. For the greater part of the period 1807–34, St. Vincent was the leading sugar producer in the Windward Islands, with the highest ratio of sugar to slaves. Sugar had overtaken coffee and cocoa as the leading crop before 1800. Production increased until about 1828, after which there was a definite decline.

Detailed data on land and labor use in St. Vincent are available in the official annual returns made by the landowners to special commissioners.[39] These data show that sugar dominated in the windward parishes but was cultivated in coastal niches throughout the island (table S11.5). The windward parishes became increasingly monocultural, and by the 1830s coffee and cocoa production was largely confined to the leeward parishes of St. Patrick and St. David. Coffee output reached a peak about 1809 and then fell off steadily, while cocoa production increased until 1826. Arrowroot emerged as a significant crop during the 1820s, and by 1834 it accounted for as much as 50 percent of St. Vincent's minor exports (that is, excluding sugar, rum, and molasses). It was grown by slaves in their garden plots, as well as by small holders and planters, but the greater part of the crop came from St. Patrick parish.[40]

The data in the annual returns show that around 1830 some 70 percent of the slaves living on the island of St. Vincent worked on sugar plantations, and 20 percent worked on plantations and small holdings producing combinations of coffee, cocoa, arrowroot, and food crops. To this estimate must be added those slaves living on the islands of the Grenadines, divided between the colonies of St. Vincent and Grenada.

The Grenadines were miniature plantation economies dominated by sugar and cotton. Unlike St. Vincent and Grenada, they produced no coffee or cocoa. But the Grenadines experienced the same monocultural tendency as the larger islands in the early nineteenth century, sugar replacing cotton. The most dramatic decline in cotton production occurred in Carriacou, especially after 1820. In the St. Vincent Grenadines, cotton production fell from 225,000 lb in 1810 to 55,000 in 1831, though Union Island maintained a high level of output into the 1820s. Sugar production increased steadily after 1800, with particularly rapid growth in Carriacou (table S11.6). By 1830 sugar was produced only on Carriacou, Bequia, and Mustique. Using comparative labor output ratios, it can be estimated that by 1830 approximately 50 percent of the slaves in the Grenadines worked on sugar plantations and 35 percent on cotton plantations. The remaining 15 percent worked on small agricultural holdings or in fishing, shipping, or town occupations. The plantation system dominated only in Bequia, Mustique, Canouan, Union Island, and Carriacou. The other islands were all very small, supporting only rudimentary economies and tiny slave populations.[41] Even in the larger islands the pattern of landholding was simple: Mustique, for example, was divided up between only seven plantations (figure 3.2).

Grenada. The agricultural economy of Grenada was relatively diversified, though the nineteenth century saw the ascendancy of sugar. Sugar production rose rapidly after 1763, then more gradually after 1807, reaching a peak in 1828. Coffee went into decline from 1800, cotton from 1820, and by 1834 both crops dropped into insignificance. Cocoa production doubled during the 1820s, and Grenada also exported small quantities of arrowroot, ginger, and coconuts. The rugged topography meant that little estate land was planted in food crops, but the total area allocated to slave provision grounds was considerable, equaling the area under cane.[42]

Sugar occupied the coastal fringe of Grenada, penetrating more than two miles into the interior only in the northeastern corner of the island. The relative concentration of estates on the windward side of the island was matched by a relative decline in output in the leeward parishes of St. John and St. Mark during the 1820s (table S11.7). Most of the cotton plantations were located in the southwestern peninsula. Coffee and cocoa plantations were heavily concentrated in the leeward parishes on the steeper slopes behind the sugar estates, though there

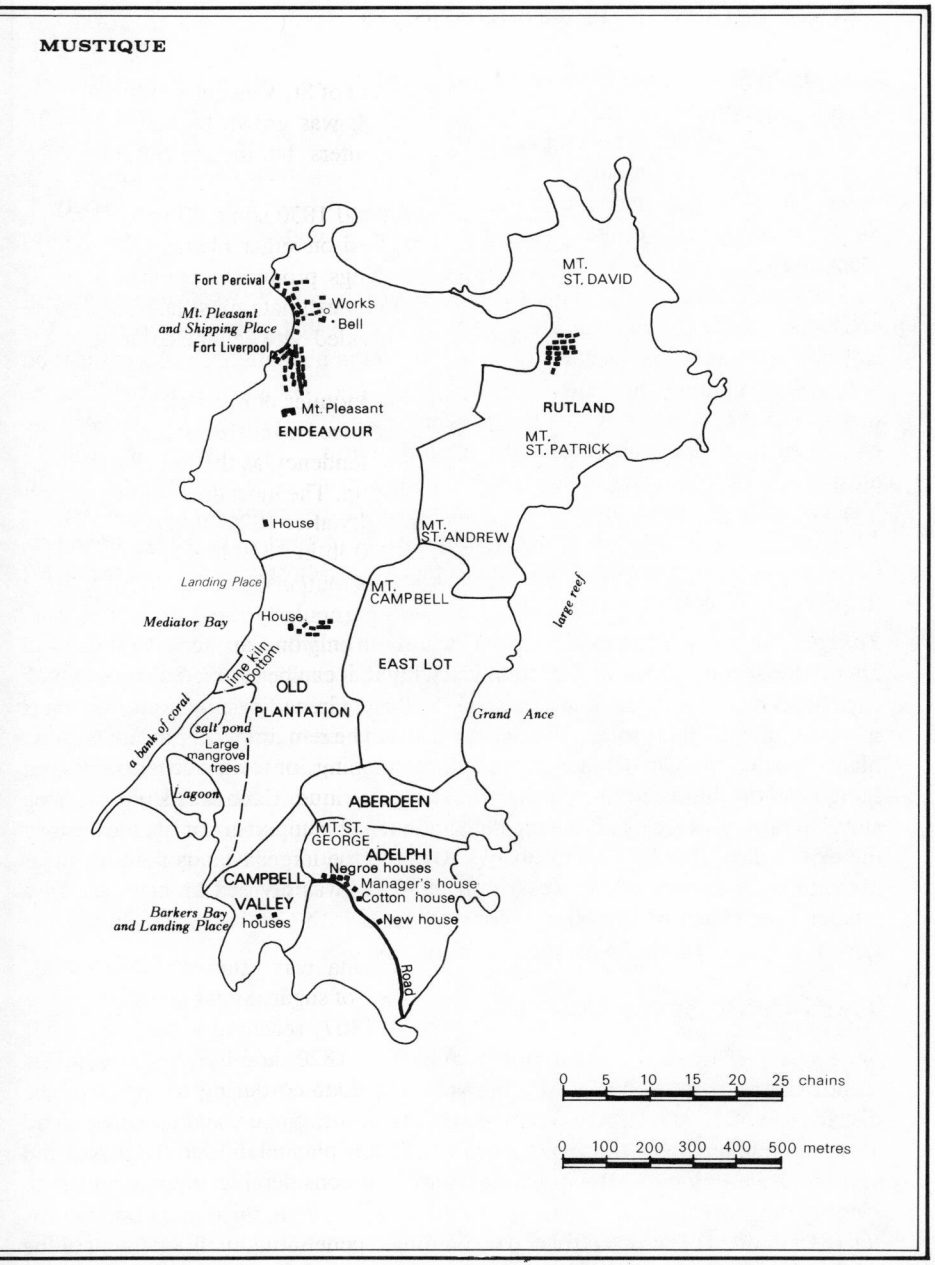

Fig. 3.2. *Mustique, 1804 (*Source*: MS plan [Survey Department, Kings-town, St. Vincent].)*

were also a few in the interior of the windward parishes. Coffee and cocoa were generally produced in combination, but it was very rare for sugar to be grown together with either of these crops or with cotton. An occasional holding combined coffee and cotton production.[43] Thus, the windward parishes were dominated by monocultural sugar estates, whereas the leeward parishes combined a variety of crops, monocultural estates being intermixed with diversified minor staples plantations.

The distribution of the slave population of Grenada between these types of enterprise can be calculated directly for 1819.[44] In that year, 83 percent of the slaves worked on sugar estates, 4 percent on cotton plantations, and 4 percent on holdings combining the cultivation of coffee, cocoa, and provisions. The remainder lived in the towns. As elsewhere, a small number of slaves were employed in fishing, charcoal burning, lime burning, and quarrying. The inclusion of the Grenada Grenadines, discussed in the section dealing with St. Vincent, changes these proportions somewhat. The proportion in cotton rises to 14.5 percent in 1819, while sugar drops to 72 percent. By 1834, however, Carriacou had come to resemble Grenada much more closely as sugar expanded at the expense of cotton.

Tobago. Sugar production increased steadily throughout the period 1800–34 in all of the second-phase sugar colonies with the exception of Tobago, which experienced a steady decline. In spite of this decline, Tobago was the most monocultural of the group. The island had developed very rapidly as a sugar plantation economy in the late eighteenth century, leading to the abandonment of indigo and the almost total collapse of cotton cultivation.[45] No detailed records on slave employment are available for Tobago, but it can be estimated, on the basis of the export data, that by 1834 probably 90 percent of the slaves worked on sugar plantations. This proportion was similar to that in Nevis and Montserrat. To a greater extent than in any other colony of the British Caribbean, the life of the typical slave in Tobago was one dominated by sugar.

Third-Phase Sugar Colonies

St. Lucia. The slave registration returns for the third-phase sugar colonies identified the crops cultivated by the slaves on each holding. Estimates of the distribution of the slaves between types of economic activity may thus be regarded as more reliable than those achieved by indirect methods for the first- and second-phase colonies. But problems remain because some masters failed to identify the crops produced on their holdings. In St. Lucia, the registration returns for 1815 omitted the crop cultivated on holdings accounting for 17.4 percent of the total slave population. All of these were defined as "plantation" slaves, so it is clear that they were all involved in agriculture. The owners of these slaves were not atypical in terms of their sex, color, or nationality, and the distribution of slaveholding size was very similar to that in the total population. Some 20.2 percent were defined as "personal" slaves, but only half of these lived in towns.

Table 3.6. *Distribution of Slaves by Crop-type: St. Lucia, 1815*

Crop	Number of Slaves	Percentage
Sugar	9,713	59.7
Coffee	3,256	20.0
Cocoa	586	3.6
Cotton	321	2.0
Other agriculture	640	3.9
Livestock	25	0.2
Lime	94	0.6
Personal: urban	1,647	10.0
Total	16,282	100.0

Source: T.71/378–79.

Thus, it is necessary to distribute these two unknown categories between the identified crop types pro rata, assuming that they were typical of the general pattern.

In St. Lucia in 1815, sugar accounted for barely 60 percent of the slave population, while 20 percent worked on coffee plantations (table 3.6). Cocoa and cotton were also significant, cultivated either as monocultures or in combination with coffee, sugar, cassava, and other provision crops. This land-use pattern was similar to that of Dominica, but sugar achieved a greater domination in St. Lucia. By 1831, cane covered 4,752 acres and coffee only 696 acres. Cotton was gradually abandoned, with only 18 acres planted by 1831. Cocoa production stagnated. A further 4,049 acres were under provisions in 1831, but it is uncertain how far this incorporated ground cultivated by slaves living on sugar estates.[46] Coffee cultivation was concentrated in the leeward parishes. Sugar also found its center here, especially in Castries and Soufriere parishes, but spread into the windward parishes.

Trinidad. Although it came to be dominated by sugar after 1800, Trinidad retained a relatively diversified agricultural economy. Sugar production grew very rapidly at first, but the peak of 1805 was not reached again until 1826, after which it once more expanded rapidly (figure 3.1). The cocoa industry expanded even more rapidly than sugar. But cocoa was a small holder's crop, largely cultivated by the considerable free colored and free black population of Trinidad and not dependent on slave labor in the same way as sugar. Unlike sugar and cocoa, the output of cotton fell drastically between 1800 and 1834, and coffee suffered a significant, though more gradual, decline (figure 3.3). By 1832 sugar and its by-products accounted for more than 90 percent of the total value of exports from Trinidad.[47] The island exported 90 percent of the sugar it produced, 99 percent of the molasses, and only 3 percent of the rum. Cocoa, in spite of its meteoric rise, contributed only 6.2 percent of total exports, and coffee a mere 2 percent.

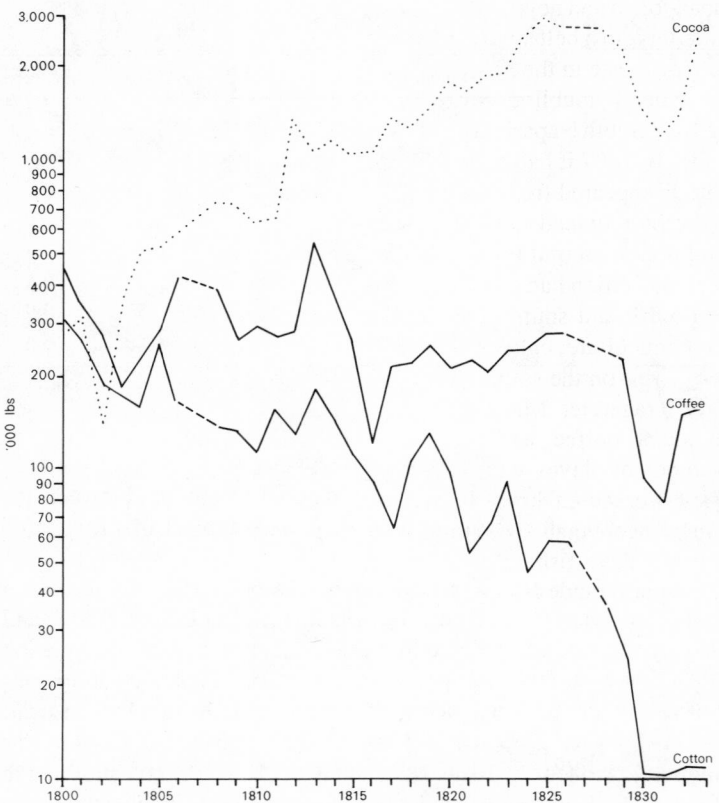

Fig. 3.3. *Production of Cocoa, Coffee, and Cotton: Trinidad, 1800–1833.*
(Source: *R. M. Martin,* Statistics of the Colonies of the British Empire,
1839, p. 34.)

The area planted in sugar cane doubled between 1808 and 1832, as did the area
in food crops (table S11.8). But for the greater part the cultivation of food crops
was contained within the plantation economy, since almost two-thirds of the
provisions seem to have been produced on "Negro grounds," and at least a
proportion of the remaining third must have been cultivated by planters rather than
free small holders. Land under food crops was valued as highly as land under
cane.[48] A considerable area of Trinidad was under pasture, but this too was
contained within the plantation sector and it did not give rise to independent
livestock pens.[49] Tobacco, annatto, nutmeg, cloves, and coconuts were all produced on a small scale, in combination with the more important minor staples.[50]
    Agricultural settlement in Trinidad was restricted to the western edge of the
island, fringing the Gulf of Paria, throughout the period 1807–34. But within this
zone there was a major southward shift in the location of the sugar industry.[51] Old

estates were abandoned and new ones established on fertile virgin soils. In many of the northern quarters, in a belt stretching from Bocas to the Maracas Valley, there was an absolute decrease in the area under cane. The regions of greatest growth, exceeding the general doubling, were Chaguanas, Point à Pierre, and South Naparima. By 1832 South Naparima alone was cultivating more than 20 percent of the island's cane. In 1807 it had been a leading coffee producer, but by 1832 the crop had all but disappeared from the quarter. The expansion of cocoa took place mainly in the northern upland interior quarters, while coffee survived best in the northern upland region around Port of Spain. Thus, by 1832 a distinct pattern of agricultural regionalization had emerged in Trinidad (figure 3.4), with a sharp line drawn between north and south at about Chaguanas. The southern region was strictly a sugar monoculture, cultivating only provision crops as a subsidiary. Only in the quarter of Erin, on the southern coastal uplands, was cocoa significant. In the north, only Tragarete, Mucurapo, and Carenage remained sugar mono-cultures, with cocoa, coffee, and provisions dominating elsewhere.

A small number of slaves were employed in manufacturing and extractive industries. They worked in lime, brick, and tile kilns, and in quarrying and charcoal burning.[52] More than 100 fishing boats operated out of Port of Spain, but there were only 63 slave fishermen in the town in 1813. A whale fishery was established at Gaspar Grande Island in 1826, but it was said to be difficult to find

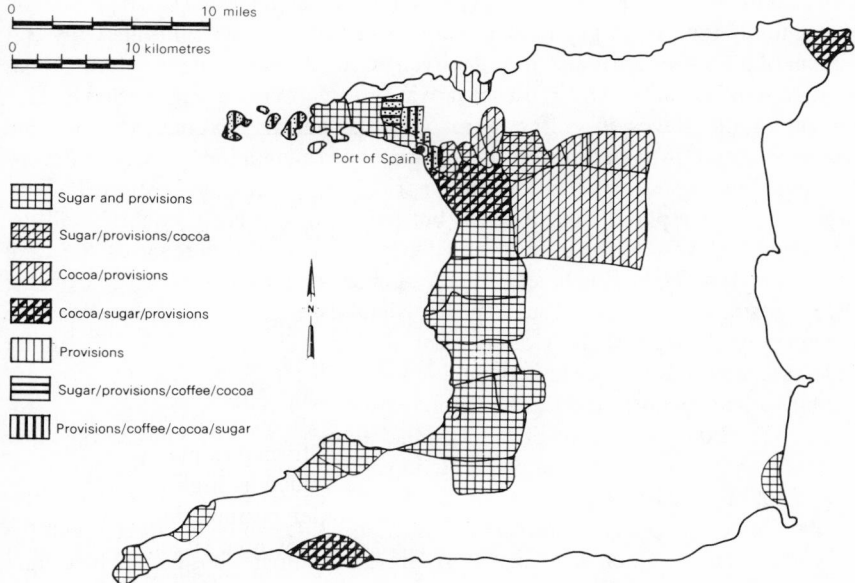

Fig. 3.4.　*Land Use: Trinidad, 1832. (Source: C.O.295/46, p. 158. Crops are included only if they covered more than 10 percent of the total culti-vated area of a quarter, and they are ordered in terms of area.)*

Table 3.7. *Distribution of Slaves by Crop-type: Trinidad, 1810 and 1813*

Crop	1810		1813	
	Number of Slaves	Percentage	Number of Slaves	Percentage
Sugar	13,219	60.1	14,498	56.4
Coffee	1,732	7.9	1,742	6.8
Cocoa	859	3.9	1,421	5.5
Cotton }	2,492	11.3	765	3.0
Other agriculture }			971	3.8
Fishing, shipping	—	—	128	0.5
Personal: urban	3,680	16.8	6,171	24.0
Total	21,982	100.0	25,696	100.0

Sources: 1810: C.O. 295/23, f.57: Hislop to Liverpool, 16 Apr. 1810. 1813: T.71/501–3.

men accustomed to whaling in Trinidad, and schemes were proposed to bring forty slaves from Bermuda; so it is doubtful that the station employed many slaves.[53]

The distribution of the slave population of Trinidad between types of economic activity can be established directly from the slave registration returns for 1813. In table 3.7, slaves belonging to units combining more than one crop have been allocated to the leading, first-named crop, but these account for a small proportion of the total since most plantations were described as monocultural. Only 3.4 percent of the slaves attributed to sugar lived on sugar-cocoa, sugar-coffee-cocoa, or sugar-coffee units. Diversification was greater outside sugar. Some 22.7 percent of the slaves in coffee were on units that also produced cocoa and provisions, and 14.6 percent on diversified cocoa plantations. Provision crops dominated the units attributed to "other agriculture." Trinidad possessed a very large urban slave population in 1813, but the towns did not account for all the "personal" slaves on the island, and the remainder (9.6 percent of the total population) have been distributed pro rata. A check on the pattern derived from the 1813 registration returns is found in an official estimate of 1810, based on the annual returns made to the Commissary of Population (table 3.7). The latter underestimated the urban slave population, but otherwise the pattern was very similar to that found in the more comprehensive registration returns.

In 1813 about 56 percent of the Trinidad slave population worked on sugar estates, and another 19 percent on plantations producing combinations of coffee, cocoa, cotton, and provisions. The pattern in 1830 cannot be determined directly, but the data on output and cultivated area (figure 3.4) can be compared with the geographical distribution of the slaves to derive an estimate. It is certain that sugar increased its share significantly, to about 70 percent, at the expense of the towns and cotton and coffee. But the growth of cocoa meant that the minor plantation staples still accounted for 14.5 percent of the slaves and created a clear regional distinction between sugar monoculture and small-scale diversified agriculture.

Demerara-Essequibo and Berbice.   At the end of the eighteenth century Demerara, Essequibo, and Berbice (combined to form British Guiana in 1831) were
the leading British colonial producers of coffee and cotton. These two crops
reached their peaks about 1810 and thereafter were increasingly eclipsed by sugar.
Between 1810 and 1834 sugar output increased more rapidly than in any other
colony, leveling off only after 1827 (figure 3.1), and production per slave more
than tripled. But coffee production dropped from 19.2 to 1.4 million lb in
Demerara between 1810 and 1831, and from 2.3 million to a mere 27,000 lb in
Essequibo. Cotton production showed a similar pattern: between 1810 and 1831 it
fell from 5.8 million to 400,000 lb in Demerara, and from 1.3 million to 41,000 lb
in Essequibo. A similar decline in cotton and coffee occurred in Berbice, though
sugar proved far less dominant than in Essequibo, where the shift was most
marked. Some of the old cotton and coffee plantations were converted to sugar
estates or cattle farms but, particularly in Berbice, great tracts of land were simply
abandoned and left in waste.[54]
   The distribution of the slave population between the major agricultural activities can be established for Demerara-Essequibo in considerable detail, using
data provided in the registration returns. But Berbice is less well served, the
returns giving no real clues as to the crops cultivated. Table S11.9 summarizes the
data for Demerara-Essequibo in 1832, the nonurban "unattached" or "personal"
slaves being distributed pro rata by parish. In Essequibo 97.2 percent of the slaves
lived on sugar estates, very few of which grew coffee as a subsidiary crop, and on
the islands in the mouth of the Essequibo River sugar monoculture was almost total
in its dominance. Coastal Demerara was much less completely dominated by
sugar, with cotton and coffee plantations remaining significant until the time of
emancipation, and some large estates produced coffee as well as sugar. But
overall, 78.5 percent of the slaves in Demerara-Essequibo lived on sugar estates by
1832, a proportion very similar to that found in Barbados. This pattern may be
compared with that in 1813, when only 32.6 percent of the slaves in Demerara-
Essequibo lived on sugar estates, 31.3 percent were on cotton plantations, and
22.3 percent on coffee plantations.[55] The contrast with 1832 is great.
   For Berbice, only total numbers of holdings are known, by simplified land
uses, and the slave populations attached to them must be estimated by applying the
mean holding sizes found in Demerara-Essequibo (table S11.10). These calculations show that less than 50 percent of the slaves lived on sugar estates in 1832,
while at least 35 percent were on plantations producing coffee, cotton, and
provisions. The contrast with Demerara-Essequibo is confirmed by production
data: in Berbice sugar production per slave was less than half that in Essequibo, but
in coffee and cotton the ratio was double that for Demerara. Berbice also had a
larger livestock industry, selling twice as many cattle as Demerara-Essequibo.[56]
   By 1832 sugar cultivation was spread throughout the settled coastland of British
Guiana, but it was everywhere mixed with other crops except on the islands in the
mouth of the Essequibo. Cotton, however, was chiefly concentrated in the coastal
belt between the Berbice and Demerara rivers. Up-river settlements tended to

combine sugar and coffee cultivation, the majority of coffee plantations favoring this location over the coast. Food crops, particularly plantains, were produced extensively, with Demerara the leading area.[57] Woodcutting, which employed only a small number of slaves, was most important in areas accessible to the Georgetown market.

4. First-Phase Marginal Colonies

British Honduras. Plantation agriculture and manufacturing enterprises were prohibited in the British settlement in the Bay of Honduras under the terms of the 1786 Convention of London. Thus, no slaves were classified as "predial attached" in the compensation returns of 1834. The occupational distribution of the slaves was quite simple, most males working as woodcutters and females as domestics.[58] But most of the boys, to about the age of 15 years, lived in town with their mothers, who were employed as domestics. Thus, almost exactly 50 percent of the slaves lived in town, working as domestics or tradesmen, the other 50 percent being employed as woodcutters. The latter did not live permanently in the interior and spent several months of each year in Belize Town.

The export of mahogany, the leading timber cut in British Honduras in the early nineteenth century, fluctuated from year to year but maintained a consistent level of about 5 million feet during the 1820s. The profitability of mahogany cutting led to the large scale cutting out of reserves by about 1830, especially on the Belize and Sibun rivers, and to the extraction of timber from outside the limits of settlement (north of the Rio Hondo) in spite of a heavy tax levied on it after 1818.[59] Logwood was relatively unimportant between 1807 and 1834, and the output of cedar was slight. Indigo production declined, but cochineal emerged as a minor export after 1828.[60] Some boats were built in Belize, using local timer, but the industry was hampered because such boats could not be registered as British shipping before 1820, and thereafter only under rigid restrictions, due to the ambiguous legal position of the settlement.[61]

Cayman Islands. The Cayman Islands were known in the early nineteenth century for their turtle meat and shell, otherwise producing only a little cotton, logwood, and livestock for export.[62] But the occupational data in the 1834 registration returns, the only material available on the distribution of the slaves between activities, suggest that few slaves were fully employed in fishing. Only 29 of the 490 male slaves were listed as fishermen or mariners. Another 25 were carpenters, sawyers, caulkers, mechanics, and coopers, who may have been employed in boat building. The great majority of the slaves were field laborers or domestics, and it seems that most were engaged in an agriculture primarily directed toward food crops for domestic consumption. Some cane was grown for home sugar processing, but the more important products were yams, plantains, and cassava, and pigs, poultry, and goats. All of the holdings were small, with fewer than 50 slaves.

It may be estimated, rather crudely, that in 1834 some 80 percent of the slaves in the Cayman Islands lived on diversified food-producing holdings, 15 percent in town (Georgetown),[63] and 5 percent in units directed toward the sea (fishing, turtling, sailing, and boat building).

Bahamas.   In the Bahamas, the collapse of the cotton plantation economy had occurred by about 1800, the crop surviving in the following decades only as part of a diversified agriculture similar to that of the Cayman Islands. In 1816 the assembly complained that "our almost worn out islands" were reduced to the export of a few tons of cotton, dyewoods, salt, and turtle, and the scavenging of stranded cargoes.[64] By 1829 salt was declared the only real staple, the exhausted soil yielding but meager crops of cotton and provisions.[65]

The occupational data in the 1834 compensation returns show that, in the working age groups, about 55 percent of the slaves were field laborers, 32 percent domestics, and 10 percent employed in fishing and shipping.[66] It can be estimated, then, that 15 percent lived in the towns, 10 percent belonged to sea-oriented units, and 75 percent worked on agricultural and salt-raking holdings. It is difficult to separate the slaves involved in salt raking, since the activity was seasonal, but they may have comprised 10 percent of the total. Thus, the pattern in the Bahamas was similar to that in the Cayman Islands, except that there was a greater emphasis on fishing and shipping. The scattered nature of the islands of the Bahamas and the concentration of trade in Nassau were the major causes of this contrast.

Salt ponds were found on six of the islands, the largest being on Rum Key, Long Island, and Exuma, but the leading producers were Turks and Caicos. By 1832, cotton production was concentrated on Exuma and Long Island, and the nearby Rum Key and Crooked Island (table S11.11). Elsewhere cotton was never more than a marginal part of the land use pattern. Most islands cultivated a diversity of crops, but some were able to specialize to some degree by supplying the town and port markets of Nassau. Eleuthera was the leading producer of provision crops, harvesting one-third of the corn, half of the yams and potatoes, half the cassava and arrowroot, one-third of the pumpkins and lemons, and one-quarter of the peas, beans, garlic, onions, and eschalots. Eleuthera also supplied almost all of the pineapples produced for the emerging export trade (40,000 dozen in 1832).[67] Fishing, turtling, and sponge gathering were carried out on the Bahama Bank, off the coast of Cuba. The banks also provided favorable conditions for that other prop to the Bahamas economy in the nineteenth century, "wrecking," gathering up stranded goods from unfortunate vessels.[68]

Anguilla.   Less than one-tenth of Anguilla's land area was cultivated, only a fringe around the central pond, which in the eighteenth century had been a leading supplier of salt to the American trade. In the early nineteenth century the annual yield of salt was 3 million bushels. Sugar was cultivated, but even in favorable seasons the crop amounted to little more than 100 tons of inferior quality, and most of it was consumed locally. A trifling amount of cotton was produced, but the major crops were corn, yams, potatoes, and other ground provisions. Cultivation was diffused over many small parcels of land.[69] Anguilla struck contemporary travelers in the West Indies by its lack of typicality, the landscape forming "the exact antipode of large plantations of sugar."[70]

The American Revolution destroyed the market for Anguilla's basic resource, salt, and even when restrictions on British West Indian–United States trade were relaxed in 1822 Anguilla was overlooked, so that American vessels went elsewhere. In the same year the island was affected by drought, and the ports were opened to foreign vessels to prevent famine. In 1823 no salt was made, heavy rains dissolving it in the pond just when it was ready for gathering, but in 1824 the ports were opened to dispose of an abundant salt crop.[71] In 1832 it was said that the salt crop, "the staple commodity of the island," had failed for the past six years, and that the provision crops had been destroyed by an intense year-long drought, resulting in actual starvation. Subscription lists were opened in the British colonies of the eastern Caribbean for the relief of the ill-fated Anguillans.[72]

The occupational distribution of the 2,260 slaves living on Anguilla in 1834 is uncertain. But the failure of salt, the apparent small scale of sugar production, and the absence of any urban settlement or even a store on the island, suggest that at least 90 percent of the slaves must have lived on small diversified agricultural holdings.

Barbuda.   Sir Bethel Codrington's lease on Barbuda meant that the island comprised a single economic unit, an adjunct to his Antiguan sugar estates. It supplied the estates with livestock, harness and leather goods, timber, meat, fish, and provisions. But it produced no export staples, and the island developed a life of its own. The economy was essentially self-sufficient.[73] The livestock—cattle, horses, sheep, and deer—roamed wild and were run down by mounted slave "huntsmen." The provision grounds were fenced to protect them from the animals. Some slaves were fishermen, drawing the seine in the lagoon; others were sailors; and a small group of domestics tended the few supervisory whites who occupied the "castle." Thus, it is difficult to categorize Barbuda.

A CLASSIFICATION OF THE COLONIAL ECONOMIES

An attempt can now be made to classify the colonies in terms of the types of economic environments in which the slaves were employed. Table 3.8 summarizes the estimates made for each colony at about 1810, 1820, and 1830. These estimates relate to the number of slaves living on particular types of units, not their actual occupations. Slaves attributed to "sugar," for instance, all lived on sugar plantations, but some worked as domestics or cattle keepers rather than in the cane field or mill. Slaves attached to diversified agricultural holdings have been distributed according to the leading crop, where this was sugar, coffee, or cotton; but those in which cocoa, provisions, or other minor staples predominated have been allocated to "other agriculture." The problem of definition is least in the case of sugar, which was usually cultivated as a monoculture, and greatest in those small holdings in which slaves were variously employed in fishing, agriculture, and salt raking. It must also be emphasized that for only 11 of the 20 colonies are the estimates calculated directly from employment or labor use data. But these 11 colonies accounted for as many as 552,000 slaves around 1830, and the estimates for the largest colonies (Jamaica, Barbados, and Demerara-Essequibo) all rest on strong data. For the remaining 9 colonies, with 133,000 slaves, the estimates are derived from output/export data, applied to the labor-output ratios found in comparable colonies. Again, the data are generally stronger for 1830 than for the earlier years, except in Trinidad, St. Lucia, Grenada, and the Virgin Islands. In most cases, the data permit an exact estimate for only one of the reference years, and the estimates for the others are based on extrapolations within the general trends established in the discussion of individual colonies. The slave populations for 1820 and 1830 are derived from the registration returns, but those for 1810 are extrapolations.

In spite of these reservations about the data, the general patterns that emerge are quite clear. The phase-of-settlement classification employed in this chapter thus far is shown to be inadequate, in terms of economic environments. Of the first-phase colonies, it is patent that the "marginal" colonies had a very different pattern from that in the sugar colonies, but it is also apparent that Jamaica must be separated from the other sugar colonies because of its diversification. The second- and third-phase sugar colonies can be combined to form a single class, the "new sugar colonies." The pattern in the latter class was, however, distinct from that in Jamaica and that in the old sugar colonies. Within the four classes of colonies, the Virgin Islands approached the pattern of the new sugar colonies, and Tobago that of the old sugar colonies, but it seems more useful to retain the settlement history element of the classification rather than moving these two colonies. Thus, the colonies can be classified efficiently as follows: old sugar colonies, new sugar colonies, Jamaica, and marginal colonies.

It is obvious that the principal factor underlying this typology is the relative dominance of sugar (table 3.9). In 1830 roughly 80 percent of the slaves in the old sugar colonies worked on sugar estates, compared to 71 percent in the new sugar colonies, 53 percent in Jamaica, and none in the marginal colonies. The proportion changed little between 1810 and 1830, except in the new sugar colonies where the crop significantly increased its share of the population. There was also a clear pattern of agricultural diversification outside of sugar, with cotton predominating in the old sugar colonies; coffee, pimento, and livestock in Jamaica; and coffee, cotton, and cocoa in the new sugar colonies. But it is probable that this pattern, especially in the years immediately before emancipation, was the most mono-cultural in the history of the British Caribbean, since the peasantry that emerged after 1838 was quick to restore minor staples to a more important place in colonial agriculture. Thus, the dominant role of the sugar estate in determining the character of slavery was at its most intense in this period. Even in 1830, however, more than one-third of the slaves were not employed in sugar, but lived and worked in a variety of economic, social, and physical environments, each with a differing potential for shaping their demographic experience.

Table 3.8. *Estimated Distribution of Slaves by Crop-type and Colony, 1810, 1820, and 1830*

Colony	Percentage of Slaves								Number of Slaves
	Sugar	Coffee	Cotton	Other Agriculture	Live-stock	Salt, Timber	Fishing, Shipping	Urban	
1810									
Old sugar colonies									
Barbados	76.5	—	4.0	7.0	—	—	0.5	12.0	75,000
St. Kitts	87.0	—	1.0	2.0	—	0.5	0.5	9.0	20,800
Nevis	90.0	—	—	1.5	—	—	0.5	8.0	10,400
Antigua	73.5	—	5.0	5.0	5.0	—	0.5	11.0	35,650
Montserrat	80.5	—	8.0	2.0	—	—	0.5	9.0	6,800
Virgin Islands	60.0	—	27.0	0.5	—	0.5	2.0	10.0	7,500
Jamaica	51.5	17.0	—	8.0	14.0	—	0.5	9.0	347,000
New sugar colonies									
Dominica	30.0	50.0	0.5	10.0	—	—	0.5	9.0	19,000
St. Lucia	55.0	22.0	3.0	9.3	0.2	—	0.5	10.0	18,500
St. Vincent	60.0	5.0	8.0	16.0	—	—	2.0	9.0	27,400
Grenada	70.0	1.0	15.0	3.5	—	—	1.5	9.0	30,000
Tobago	88.0	—	2.0	2.5	—	—	0.5	7.0	18,000
Trinidad	55.0	8.0	4.0	7.5	—	—	0.5	25.0	26,200
Demerara-Essequibo	58.0	10.0	20.0	3.0	0.5	0.2	0.3	8.0	80,000
Berbice	18.0	35.0	30.0	1.5	5.0	0.2	0.3	10.0	27,300
Marginal colonies									
British Honduras	—	—	—	—	—	50.0	—	50.0	2,900
Cayman Islands	—	—	—	80.0	—	—	5.0	15.0	850
Bahamas	—	—	5.0	60.0	—	10.0	10.0	15.0	10,000
Anguilla	—	—	—	90.0	—	8.0	2.0	—	1,700
Barbuda	—	—	—	90.0	5.0	—	5.0	—	350

1820

Old sugar colonies

Barbados	77.0	—	3.5	7.5	—	—	0.5	11.5	78,350
St. Kitts	87.0	—	0.5	3.0	—	0.5	0.5	8.5	20,000
Nevis	90.0	—	—	1.5	—	—	0.5	8.0	9,350
Antigua	77.0	—	2.0	5.0	5.0	—	0.5	10.5	30,850
Montserrat	85.0	—	4.0	2.0	—	—	0.5	8.5	6,550
Virgin Islands	64.0	—	22.0	1.5	—	0.5	2.0	10.0	6,600
Jamaica	52.0	16.0	—	9.0	14.0	—	0.5	8.5	342,380

New sugar colonies

Dominica	33.0	48.0	—	10.0	—	—	0.5	8.5	16,550
St. Lucia	64.0	17.0	1.0	7.4	0.1	—	0.5	10.0	14,750
St. Vincent	66.0	1.0	6.0	16.0	—	—	2.0	9.0	24,750
Grenada	72.0	—	14.0	4.0	—	—	1.5	8.5	26,900
Tobago	90.0	—	—	2.5	—	—	0.5	7.0	15,050
Trinidad	65.0	4.0	0.5	10.0	—	—	0.5	20.0	23,400
Demerara-Essequibo	72.0	6.0	10.0	2.0	0.5	0.2	0.3	9.0	77,400
Berbice	32.0	30.0	20.0	3.0	4.5	0.2	0.3	10.0	23,400

Marginal colonies

British Honduras	—	—	—	—	—	50.0	—	50.0	2,560
Cayman Islands	—	—	—	80.0	—	—	5.0	15.0	900
Bahamas	—	—	—	65.0	—	10.0	10.0	15.0	11,000
Anguilla	—	—	—	90.0	—	8.0	2.0	—	2,100
Barbuda	—	—	—	90.0	5.0	—	5.0	—	400

Table 3.8. *Estimated Distribution of Slaves by Crop-type and Colony, 1810, 1820, and 1830 (continued)*

Colony	Percentage of Slaves								Number of Slaves
	Sugar	Coffee	Cotton	Other Agriculture	Live-stock	Salt, Timber	Fishing, Shipping	Urban	
1830									
Old sugar colonies									
Barbados	77.5	—	3.0	8.0	—	—	0.5	11.0	82,000
St. Kitts	87.0	—	—	4.0	—	0.5	0.5	8.0	19,100
Nevis	90.0	—	—	1.5	—	—	0.5	8.0	9,200
Antigua	79.5	—	—	5.0	5.0	—	0.5	10.0	29,120
Montserrat	89.5	—	—	2.0	—	—	0.5	8.0	6,300
Virgin Islands	65.0	—	17.5	5.0	—	0.5	2.0	10.0	5,150
Jamaica	52.7	15.2	—	9.9	13.7	—	0.5	8.0	319,000
New sugar colonies									
Dominica	35.0	45.0	—	12.5	—	—	0.5	7.0	14,700
St. Lucia	72.0	10.0	—	7.5	—	—	0.5	10.0	13,400
St. Vincent	68.5	0.5	4.0	16.0	—	—	2.0	9.0	23,100
Grenada	80.0	—	4.5	6.0	—	—	1.5	8.0	23,880
Tobago	90.0	—	—	2.5	—	—	0.5	7.0	12,550
Trinidad	70.0	2.0	—	12.5	—	—	0.5	15.0	22,750
Demerara-Essequibo	78.5	4.4	5.9	0.0	0.7	0.2	0.3	10.0	68,160
Berbice	48.3	21.7	9.7	5.5	4.3	0.2	0.3	10.0	20,700
Marginal colonies									
British Honduras	—	—	—	—	—	50.0	—	50.0	1,900
Cayman Islands	—	—	—	80.0	—	—	5.0	15.0	1,000
Bahamas	—	—	—	65.0	—	10.0	10.0	15.0	9,500
Anguilla	—	—	—	90.0	—	8.0	2.0	—	2,600
Barbuda	—	—	—	90.0	5.0	—	5.0	—	480

Sources: See text.

Table 3.9. *Estimated Distribution of Slaves by Crop-type: Classes of Colonies, 1810, 1820, and 1830*

Colony	Percentage of Slaves								Number of Slaves
	Sugar	Coffee	Cotton	Other Agriculture	Live-stock	Salt, Timber	Fishing, Shipping	Urban	
1810									
Old sugar colonies	77.5	—	4.8	5.0	1.1	0.1	0.6	10.9	156,150
Jamaica	51.5	17.0	—	8.0	14.0	—	0.5	9.0	347,000
New sugar colonies	54.7	14.2	13.4	5.8	0.7	0.1	0.7	10.4	246,400
Marginal colonies	—	—	3.2	54.0	0.1	16.4	6.9	19.4	15,800
Total	56.8	12.3	5.4	7.6	6.8	0.4	0.7	10.0	765,350
1820									
Old sugar colonies	78.9	—	3.4	5.5	1.0	0.1	0.6	10.5	151,700
Jamaica	52.0	16.0	—	9.0	14.0	—	0.5	8.5	342,380
New sugar colonies	64.2	10.5	8.1	5.7	0.6	0.1	0.7	10.1	222,200
Marginal colonies	—	—	—	59.9	0.1	14.9	7.1	18.0	16,960
Total	60.1	10.6	3.2	8.5	6.9	0.4	0.7	9.6	733,240
1830									
Old sugar colonies	79.9	—	2.2	6.2	1.0	0.1	0.5	10.1	150,870
Jamaica	52.7	15.2	—	9.9	13.7	—	0.5	8.0	319,000
New sugar colonies	70.5	8.0	4.0	6.2	0.7	0.1	0.7	9.8	199,250
Marginal colonies	—	—	—	63.0	0.2	13.6	6.9	16.3	15,480
Total	62.7	9.4	1.7	9.2	6.8	0.3	0.7	9.2	684,600

Source: Calculated from data in table 3.8.

4.
Growth and Distribution of the Slave Populations

POPULATION GROWTH AND DECLINE

THE PERIOD 1807–34 WAS UNIQUE IN THE HISTORY OF THE BRITISH Caribbean slave population, being marked by continuous absolute decline. In the first phase of population development, during the second half of the seventeenth century, the slave population multiplied five times. It doubled in the first half of the eighteenth century and doubled again in the second half. The expansion of the plantation system into the third-phase sugar colonies at the end of the eighteenth century was followed by rapid growth in the years immediately preceding the abolition of the Atlantic slave trade in 1807. Between 1807 and 1834, however, the slave population declined from roughly 775,000 to 665,000, a decrease of 14 percent, or 0.5 percent per annum. This decline was the direct result of the abolition of the Atlantic slave trade. The maintenance of the slave trade at a high pitch, together with territorial expansion, had been the major cause of growth in the preceding centuries. The contribution of natural increase was always minor and generally operated in a negative manner.

Significant differences existed between the colonies in the rate of decline they experienced, however, and some even showed growth in the period after 1807. The general lack of reliable censuses of the slave populations before the implementation of the registration system hinders the precise charting of these movements between 1807 and 1817. But reasonable estimates can be generated from the trends shown in poll tax and census data for many of the larger colonies, together with extrapolation from the registration statistics. Annual population estimates can be found by linear interpolation within the registration period. These methods have been used to determine the estimates of annual slave population for each colony presented in table S1.2. For the British Caribbean as a whole, the resulting curve is very smooth for the period 1816–34, showing that the rate of decline was relatively constant in spite of the transfer of slaves from colony within the system (fig. 4.1).

The rate of decrease was greatest in the new sugar colonies (25.3 percent between 1807 and 1834), followed by Jamaica (10.8 percent), the old sugar colonies (4.4 percent), and the marginal colonies (0.1 percent). Thus, it is clear

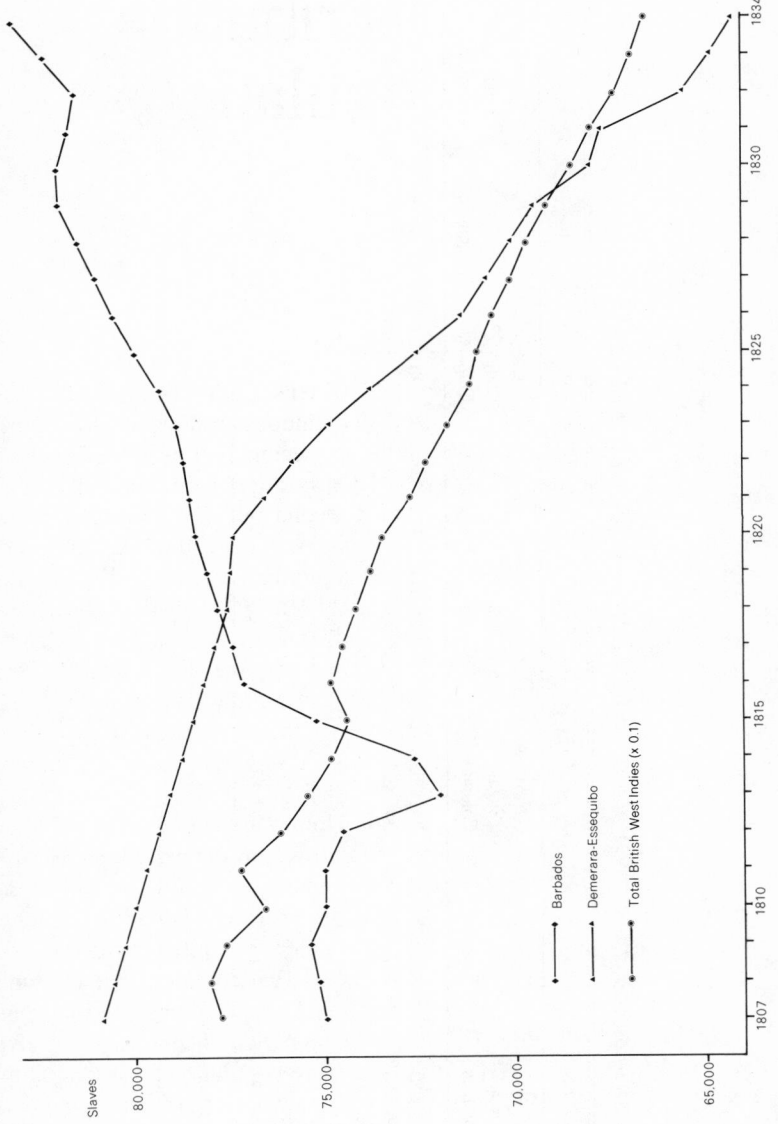

Fig. 4.1. *Slave Populations: Total British Caribbean, Barbados, and Demerara-Essequibo, 1807–34.*
(*Source: table S1.2.*)

Slaves

80,000
75,000
70,000
65,000

1807   1810   1815   1820   1825   1830   1834

Barbados
Demerara-Essequibo
Total British West Indies (x 0.1)

Table 4.1. *Distribution of the Slave Population by Classes of Colonies, 1807–34*

	Number of Slaves					Percentage of Slaves			
Year	Old Sugar Colonies	Jamaica	New Sugar Colonies	Marginal Colonies	Total	Old Sugar Colonies	Jamaica	New Sugar Colonies	Marginal Colonies
1807	158,615	348,825	252,995	15,670	776,105	20.5	44.9	32.6	2.0
1810	156,150	347,000	246,400	15,800	765,350	20.5	45.3	32.2	2.1
1815	152,245	339,840	234,635	16,385	743,105	20.5	45.7	31.6	2.2
1820	151,700	342,380	222,200	16,960	733,240	20.7	46.7	30.3	2.3
1825	150,210	332,830	210,070	15,490	708,600	21.2	47.0	29.6	2.2
1830	150,870	319,000	199,250	15,480	684,600	22.0	46.6	29.1	2.3
1834	149,180	311,070	189,080	15,640	664,970	22.4	46.8	28.4	2.4

Source: Calculated from table S1.2.

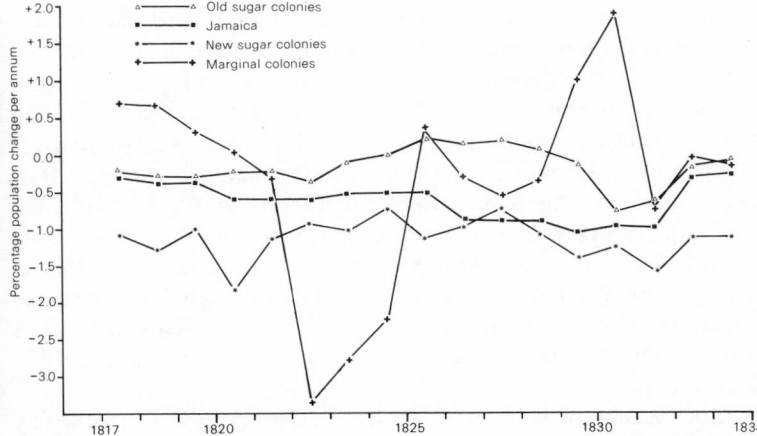

Fig. 4.2. *Percentage Change in Slave Population per Annum: Classes of Colonies, 1817–34.*

that there was no simple correlation between the rate of decrease and the economic structure of the classes of colonies, at least in terms of the relative dominance of sugar. But the variations in the rate of change meant that over the period 1807–34 the proportion of the slave population living in the new sugar colonies declined significantly, while there was a steady increase in the old sugar colonies and erratic growth in Jamaica and the marginal colonies (table 4.1). Even at the time of emancipation, however, fewer slaves lived in the old sugar colonies than in the new, while almost half of them were in Jamaica. The slave populations of the new sugar colonies and Jamaica never experienced absolute growth in the period, but positive growth did occur in the old sugar colonies between 1825 and 1829 (fig. 4.2). The pattern in the marginal colonies was rather more complicated. Positive growth probably occurred between 1807 and 1820, but this was followed by a rapid decrease in the early 1820s as a result of the transfer of slaves to the new sugar colonies. Once the latter trade was cut off, strong growth emerged again, only to be limited by the subsistence crisis in Anguilla.

Of the sugar colonies, only Barbados experienced an absolute increase in its slave population over the period 1807–34 (fig. 4.1). Even that colony suffered setbacks, caused chiefly by drought-induced food shortages in 1813 and the hurricane of August 1831. Montserrat and the Virgin Islands entered a period of increase only after about 1830, while St. Kitts, Antigua, and Nevis declined steadily throughout the period. The decline in Antigua was almost as great as that in the new sugar colonies as a group. Philip Curtin's interpolations from c.1805 and 1834 data lead him to show absolute increases for St. Lucia and St. Vincent,[1] but in fact all of the new sugar colonies experienced persistent decline between 1807 and 1834. Any increases were limited to the years before about 1810, when the new sugar colonies received large numbers of slaves through the Atlantic slave trade and through movement from the older plantation areas. Indeed, the smallest absolute decrease in the new sugar colonies occurred in Demerara-Essequibo (20.6 percent for 1807–34), since that colony paid high prices for slaves and so attracted movement from other colonies. The largest absolute decreases occurred in Tobago (38.7 percent), St. Lucia (33.1 percent), and Berbice (32.0 percent). A much wider range of variation was experienced in the marginal colonies. Barbuda's slave population increased rapidly (50.6 percent for 1807–34), as did that of Anguilla (41.3 percent) and, probably, the Cayman Islands (18.0 percent). On the other hand, British Honduras showed a decrease even greater than that in Tobago (40.7 percent). The Bahamas slave population appears to have increased steadily to about 1820. It then declined, due to the export of slaves, until 1828 when it returned to a position of growth, though failing to regain the peak of 1820 before emancipation.

The decline in the slave populations of the British Caribbean was exceeded by the decline in the white populations of the colonies. Between 1810 and 1830 the white population decreased by about 12 percent, while the slaves decreased by only 10 percent (table 4.2). It is perhaps ironic that the population statistics available for the masters are far inferior to those available for their slaves, but the general trends are not in doubt (see table S2.1). Whereas the slave populations had grown absolutely before 1807, however, the white populations often entered steady decline much earlier, as sugar monoculture drove out the small holder and slaves replaced white artisans in a wide variety of occupations. Only in the new sugar colonies and the marginal colonies was there growth in the white population after 1807. Yet whites comprised twice as large a proportion in the old sugar colonies as in the new. Around 1830 the ratio of slaves to whites was lowest in the marginal colonies (2.6:1) and highest in the new sugar colonies (17.6:1). This was a direct product of the contrasting economic structures of these groups.

While the slave and white populations declined, the free colored and free black (or "freedman") population increased dramatically. Between 1810 and 1830 the freedman population grew by approximately 70 percent. In 1810 there were fewer freedmen than whites; by 1830 the freedmen were almost twice as numerous. Freedmen comprised a larger proportion of the total population in the marginal colonies, but there they were less numerous than whites. Of the sugar colonies, Trinidad had the largest freedman proportion by far, with 16,000 freedmen in 1830 and only 22,750 slaves. Many freedmen were free by birth rather than the children of slaves, of course; thus, the growth of the freedman population cannot entirely account for the decline in the slave population. Even if all freedmen had been the children of slaves, manumission could explain only half of the decrease in the slave population between 1807 and 1834. Clearly, manumission was in fact a considerably less important factor.

In order to understand these differences in the growth and decline of the slave populations, it will be necessary to explain variations in the rate of natural increase and in the movement of slaves between colonies. In the period after the abolition of the Atlantic slave trade, no colony achieved absolute growth in its slave population

Table 4.2. *Estimated Slave, Freedman, and White Populations by Colony, 1810 and 1830*

Colony	Percentage Slave 1810	Percentage Slave 1830	Percentage Freedman 1810	Percentage Freedman 1830	Percentage White 1810	Percentage White 1830	Total Population 1810	Total Population 1830
Old sugar colonies								
Barbados	80.6	80.3	2.7	5.2	16.7	14.5	93,040	102,150
St. Kitts	85.4	81.6	7.8	12.0	6.8	6.4	24,350	23,400
Nevis	90.0	83.2	5.2	12.7	4.8	4.1	11,550	11,050
Antigua	89.6	80.0	5.2	14.9	5.2	5.1	40,200	37,000
Montserrat	88.9	84.0	5.2	11.3	5.9	4.7	7,650	7,500
Virgin Islands	85.4	69.1	9.1	22.8	5.5	8.1	8,780	7,450
Total	84.3	80.3	4.5	9.3	11.2	10.4	185,570	188,550
Jamaica	85.7	84.4	7.4	10.6	6.9	5.0	404,200	378,050
New sugar colonies								
Dominica	83.7	77.4	10.6	18.9	5.7	3.7	22,700	19,000
St. Lucia	84.8	72.8	9.2	21.7	6.0	5.5	21,800	18,400
St. Vincent	91.8	82.5	4.4	12.5	3.8	5.0	29,850	28,000
Grenada	92.5	84.1	4.9	13.4	2.6	2.5	32,450	28,400
Tobago	91.8	88.7	4.1	8.1	4.1	3.2	19,600	14,150
Trinidad	75.1	54.1	17.8	38.0	7.1	7.9	35,270	42,065
Demerara-Essequibo	93.8	87.7	3.5	8.3	2.7	4.0	85,300	77,500
Berbice	94.8	89.6	3.5	7.8	1.7	2.6	28,800	23,100
Total	89.4	79.4	6.7	16.1	3.9	4.5	275,770	250,615
Marginal colonies								
British Honduras	70.7	45.2	24.4	47.6	4.9	7.2	4,100	4,200
Cayman Islands	69.1	66.7	6.5	10.0	24.4	23.3	1,230	1,500
Bahamas	68.9	55.8	8.3	14.8	22.8	29.4	14,500	17,030
Anguilla	73.9	78.8	8.7	12.1	17.4	9.1	2,300	3,300
Barbuda	99.2	99.4	—	—	0.8	0.6	353	503
Total	70.3	58.4	11.0	19.2	18.7	22.4	22,483	26,533
TOTAL	86.2	81.2	6.6	12.2	7.2	6.6	888,823	843,698

Sources: Calculated from data in table S2.1; and Jerome S. Handler, *The Unappropriated People* (1974), p. 18; Douglas Hall, *Five of the Leewards* (1971), p. 8; Elsa V. Goveia, *Slave Society in the British Leeward Islands at the End of the Eighteenth Century* (1965); Stobo, "Statistical Table of the British Virgin Islands," C.O.239/9; Gad J. Heuman, *Between Black and White* (1981), p. 7; J. F. X. Pugnet, *Essai sur la topographie de l'ile de Sainte-Lucie* (1804), p. 35; Robert Montgomery Martin, *Statistics of the Colonies of the British Empire* (1839); O. Nigel Bolland, *The Formation of a Colonial Society* (1977), p. 51; *P.P.*, 1823, vol. 18 (89), "Slave Population."

Note: Amerindians and Chinese are excluded.

SLAVE POPULATIONS OF THE BRITISH CARIBBEAN 78

without showing a positive natural increase (an excess of births over deaths). The internal slave trade was never on a scale sufficient to sustain absolute growth by countering the negative natural increases experienced in most sugar colonies. The supply of slaves was too limited, and differentials in profitability too small, to draw slaves from the declining colonies. Only Trinidad managed a brief period of growth, around 1825, on the basis of slave imports. Not all colonies showing positive natural increase achieved absolute growth, however, being drained by the intercolonial slave trade and, to a lesser extent, manumission.

Variations in absolute growth depended also on the relative ratio of slave imports to population in the years before 1807. Colonies that depended heavily on the Atlantic slave trade in the decade immediately before its abolition tended to show relatively slight rates of decrease up to about 1815, but the aging of the African-born populations resulted in heightened mortality and reduced fertility after 1820. In the old sugar colonies, however, the slave populations leveled off between about 1750 and 1807, since they occupied small islands capable of only limited expansion. Thus, the proportion of African-born slaves was relatively small at the time of abolition, and the sex and age structure of the populations was better suited to the generation of positive natural increase.

The decade 1797–1807 was marked by heavy slave imports to the sugar colonies. But it is impossible to quantify the ratio of imports to population with any precision, because the available data are often contradictory and contain numerous gaps. No data have been found for the important years 1806 and 1807, with the exception of Jamaica.[2] Several colonies reexported a large proportion of the slaves they imported through the Atlantic slave trade; thus, it is necessary to consider only net imports. In 1802, the year for which the data appear most complete, the new sugar colonies had net imports of approximately 57 slaves per 1,000 population, compared to a ratio of 18 in Jamaica and 16 in the old sugar colonies (table S1.18). But over the entire decade before abolition Jamaica's ratio was considerably higher, reaching peaks in 1800 and 1807. Only in the marginal colonies and the old sugar colonies of Nevis and Montserrat does the slave trade appear to have been insignificant, while the Bahamas continued to play a leading role in the redistributive trade. But the Atlantic slave trade remained an important prop to the populations of Barbados, St. Kitts, and Antigua. Slave traders were quick to forewarn planters in these islands that cargoes brought from the Gold and Windward Coasts in 1807 would be the last.[3] Curtin has argued that the flow of slaves into the new colonies may have come "in large measure" from other West Indian islands.[4] He attaches this argument specifically to Trinidad, for which colony he estimates a total import of 12,400 slaves between 1797 and 1807. But at least 9,000 slaves were brought to Trinidad from Africa in the years 1802, 1803, and 1805, suggesting a much heavier dependence on the Atlantic slave trade (table S1.19). Thus, it seems probable that the greater part of the growth in the slave populations of the new sugar colonies before 1807 rested directly on the volume of imports from Africa. After 1807, however, with the African supply effectively cut off, the growth of these populations did come to depend on the scale of the intercolonial slave trade.

INTERCOLONIAL SLAVE MOVEMENTS

The movement of slaves between the colonies of the British Caribbean after 1807 resulted from regional inequalities in the market value of their labor. These inequalities reflected variations in the productivity of slave labor, particularly in terms of the average output of sugar (table 3.4). But the intercolonial slave trade was never of sufficient volume to significantly alter these ratios, so that the regional inequalities retained their relative pattern until 1834. Their extent can be determined directly from the value of the average compensation payments made to the masters, since these payments were calculated from the prices paid for slaves sold in each colony between 1823 and 1830 and were equivalent to approximately 50 percent of those prices.[5] Table 4.3 ranks the compensation values for employed slaves, for children under 6 years of age, and for the class "predial unattached field labourer." This ranking shows a great disparity, particularly between the old and new sugar colonies. In none of the old sugar colonies did the field laborer yield more than £30 sterling in compensation money, less than half the average for British Guiana. Only two of the new sugar colonies, Dominica and Tobago, had averages below £30. The Leeward Islands had the lowest averages by far, with the exception of the Bahamas. In general, the differences are explained quite ade-

Table 4.3. *Ranking of Colonies by Average Compensation Payments per Slave, 1834*

Average £ Sterling per Slave					
Employed Slaves		Children under 6 Years		Predial Unattached Field Laborers	
British Honduras	60.9	Trinidad	22.2	British Honduras	82.0
British Guiana	58.5	British Honduras	21.6	British Guiana	65.2
Trinidad	55.5	British Guiana	19.0	Trinidad	49.2
St. Vincent	30.6	St. Vincent	10.9	Jamaica	37.2
Grenada	30.0	Grenada	10.3	St. Vincent	35.7
St. Lucia	29.9	St. Lucia	8.4	Grenada	34.4
		Jamaica	7.7	St. Lucia	33.5
Barbados	24.9				
Jamaica	22.9	St. Kitts	5.6	Barbados	29.1
Dominica	22.7	Tobago	4.8	Dominica	26.8
Tobago	22.3	Dominica	4.6	Tobago	26.5
Nevis	21.4	Bahamas	4.4		
Montserrat	20.0	Nevis	4.0	Montserrat	22.8
St. Kitts	19.0	Barbados	3.9	Nevis	22.7
Antigua	17.8	Virgin Islands	3.3	Antigua	22.6
Virgin Islands	16.3	Montserrat	2.5	St. Kitts	22.3
Bahamas	15.4	Antigua	2.4		
				Virgin Islands	18.2
				Bahamas	15.2

Source: Calculated from Martin, *Statistics of the Colonies*, pp. 38–139.

quately in terms of the relative regional prosperity of the sugar plantation economy. British Honduras was aberrant: although it was a marginal colony, its slaves were valued more highly than any other colony's, because of the large proportion of adult males in the population and their productivity in timber getting. If prices paid for slave children are considered, however, Barbados moves down in the ranking, while the Bahamas moves up, and Antigua drops to the bottom of the scale, thus providing a more telling perspective on the masters' expectations.

These considerable regional inequalities in slave prices created the potential for a significant redistribution of the slave population within the British Caribbean. Where the staple crops were failing, as in the case of cotton, masters saw a relatively profitable exit from the system in selling their slaves to planters in the new sugar colonies. Others moved together with their slaves, establishing new plantations in the frontier regions. Such a pattern of movement was well established even before the abolition of the Atlantic slave trade.

The abolition act of 1807 provided that slaves could be carried from one British colony to another only under license from the governor or customs collector of the exporting colony.[6] Slave fishermen, sailors, and domestics were exempt from this licensing, to the extent of two for each free passenger on board a vessel. But slaves taken to the new sugar colonies also required a license from the importing colony, and they were to be permitted to enter at the rate of only 3 percent of the existing slave population per annum. This last provision was relaxed in 1818 by an act permitting the licensed movement of slaves into Demerara-Essequibo from the Bahamas and Dominica. The act of 1818 stated, in the face of already well-known facts to the contrary, that ''it might tend to ameliorate the condition'' of slaves by moving them from the exhausted lands of Dominica and the Bahamas where the masters could not find ''profitable employment and subsistence'' for them. But the masters had to enter into a bond to move the slaves in families and ensure their comfortable passage.[7] In 1819 the act establishing the central Slave Registry Office in London provided that only registered slaves might be moved between colonies. But this period of relatively free movement was brought to an end in 1825, in response to the general policy of amelioration. From 1825 until mid-1828, licenses could be granted only by the British Privy Council and only in cases in which removal was supposedly essential to the welfare of the slaves. After 31 July 1828 all movement was prohibited, excepting that of domestics and fishermen. The latter exceptions resulted in the development of a fraudulent movement of domestics, but on only a relatively small scale.[8]

Quantitative data on the intercolonial slave trade are rather scrappy, particularly for the years immediately following 1807. The best set of statistics available is that collected by David Eltis, but it contains numerous gaps and omits entirely the years after 1830.[9] The latter omission is rectified in table S1.20. It seems certain, however, that the greatest numbers of slaves were moved between 1815 and 1825, and that the only colonies to gain significantly from this movement of slaves were Demerara-Essequibo and Trinidad. Between 1808 and 1825 net imports of slaves into Demerara-Essequibo amounted to about 7,500, while Trinidad had net imports of around 6,000 between 1813 and 1825. The major exporters of slaves were the Bahamas, Dominica, and Berbice, each of these colonies showing net exports of 3,000 slaves in the period of relatively free movement between 1815 and 1825. Overall, more than 20,000 slaves were moved permanently to new colonies in this decade.

The pattern of movement fits only very roughly the one expected on the basis of the regional slave price differentials. Certainly the major importers were new sugar colonies, but Berbice and Dominica were net *exporters* on a large scale. Although the Bahamas, and probably the Virgin Islands, were net exporters as predicted, surprisingly few slaves came from Barbados and the Leeward Islands. There is nothing to suggest that the growth in the Barbados population was engendered by the masters to feed a supply of slaves to the new sugar colonies. The Barbadian masters retained their slave population, in spite of its great density. When in 1828 a planter asked permission to move his slaves to Trinidad, on the grounds that it would benefit their welfare, the Privy Council of Barbados responded that ''we cannot in candour pretend that the population has yet arrived at that degree of density which renders such removal 'essential to the well being of the slaves.' ''[10] On the other hand, an unexpectedly large number of slaves were exported from the Windward Islands. In part the cause was simple propinquity, most of the slaves exported from Grenada going to neighboring Trinidad, for example. Again, the Windwards contained a transilient planter class, more willing to move into new regions than the rooted planters of Barbados or the often absentee planters of the Leeward Islands. In any case, it is apparent that the intercolonial movement of slaves was never large relative to the total populations, except in the cases of the Bahamas and Dominica, and that it did no more than modify the rate of decline in Demerara-Essequibo and produce a brief interlude of absolute growth in Trinidad.

For Trinidad, annual returns of slaves imported under license, specifying place of origin, are available for the years 1813 to 1825 (table S1.18). These data are not directly comparable with those of Eltis, but help to fill out the details of the pattern. Over the whole period 1813–25, Grenada and Dominica were the leading suppliers of slaves to Trinidad, accounting for 39 percent of the total. The Virgin Islands, missing from Eltis's table, also emerge as significant suppliers, along with Barbados, St. Vincent, and the Bahamas. Montserrat, Nevis, and Anguilla, also missing from Eltis, sent modest numbers of slaves to Trinidad.

The planters in the new sugar colonies sought an intercolonial slave trade that was not only significant in its absolute volume but also demographically selective. Their preference was for young adult males, a preference satisfied by the Atlantic slave trade. Of course, the abolition of that trade created a long-term interest in establishing a self-supporting creole slave population, but this concern was outweighed by the short-term economic considerations of individual planters. Beginning in 1818, the statutes regulating the intercolonial slave trade specified that such movement should not separate husbands or wives, or parents and children under 14 years of age,[11] so inhibiting the ability of the planters to structure their labor force as desired. It is difficult to assess the success of the masters in manipulating the intercolonial movement to match their preferences, but an approach can be made through an analysis of the age- and sex-specific character of the movement.

In the peak period of movement, 1815–25, the available evidence suggests that the intercolonial slave trade was not sex- or age-selective, and that the slaves moved were in fact representative of the total populations from which they were drawn. According to the registration returns, the 538 slaves exported from the Bahamas in 1822 had a sex ratio of 107 males per 100 females, compared to 104 in the total Bahamas slave population.[12] Of the slaves exported, 22 percent were African-born, compared to 21 percent in the total population. In 1821 the Bahamas had exported 333 slaves, 15 percent of them African-born, with a sex ratio of 87.[13] The age structure of these slaves was not aberrant; if anything, it is surprising that such a small proportion fell into the prime working age groups (table S1.21). Only one-third were between 20 and 45 years of age. A similar pattern emerges from the data for the 2,500 slaves imported into Trinidad between 1822 and 1825 (table S1.19). In that period the slave sex ratio of Trinidad was 124 but for the slaves imported only 115. Thus, the masters failed to maintain the high sex ratios typical of the Atlantic slave trade. But they did manage to pull a relatively large number of males from the old sugar colonies, where the total slave populations were dominated by females. The major exception to this tendency was the Virgin Islands, the largest supplier in this period, where the sex ratio of the exported slaves was 80, compared to 85 for the total population.

At the height of the intercolonial slave trade, then, the planters in the new sugar colonies were unable to fulfill their desire for a demographically selective movement. Even where absolute growth in the slave population was effected, as in Trinidad around 1825, the trade failed to change its structure significantly. Thus, the planters saw it as a poor substitute for the Atlantic slave trade. The main reason for the failure of the masters to generate a selective flow of slaves was that most of the slaves moved belonged to large slaveholdings. Of the 320 slaves taken to Jamaica from the Bahamas in 1821–22, for example, 305 belonged to only four units.[14] The movement to Trinidad and Demerara-Essequibo was similar. In 1821, Burton Williams, son of a Loyalist cotton planter, left the Bahamas for Trinidad with 105 slaves. He petitioned the Trinidad government for a grant of land to establish a sugar plantation and livestock estate, promising to bring the remaining 365 of his slaves. By the end of 1823 he had brought in 324 slaves,[15] more than half of the total involved in the movement from the Bahamas to Trinidad. In 1826, after the closure of the intercolonial trade, Williams was asking leave to bring the remainder of his slaves to Trinidad, saying that in the Bahamas they could scarce raise provisions sufficient for their maintenance.[16] Similarly, in 1828 Lord Rolle was futilely seeking permission to transfer his 317 slaves from Exuma to Trinidad, and Dennistoun and Co. of Glasgow wished to move 650 from Tortola.[17] A large proportion of the slaves actually moved to new colonies were members of units of more than 100 slaves.[18]

The initiative for the movement of these large groups of slaves generally came from owners in the depressed colonies, with the intention of establishing new plantations. It was a matter of transfer rather than speculative slave trading, and it lacked the economic organization of the Atlantic trade. Thus, so long as the slaves were kept as a unit in the new colony, interference in the internal family structure of the slaves was limited, especially in cases in which the slaves had few kin relationships beyond the community of their owner's holding.[19] The movement of individual slaves, however, offered greater possibilities of achieving the age-sex structure desired by the masters and hence resulted in greater disruption of slave kinship. In the period 1815–25 small groups of slaves were most likely to come from the towns, where ownership was highly dispersed and fluid. Further, the registration system tended to camouflage the kinship networks of these town slaves, since it recognized only links between the members of a single slaveholding. Thus, the movement of such slaves met few challenges from the regulations. But, because of its urban focus, it provided relatively few of the agricultural laborers most demanded in the new sugar colonies.

In Barbados, for example, the vast majority of slaves exported between 1817 and 1820 came from the urban parish of St. Michael, and hardly any from the plantation parishes.[20] Within St. Michael, roughly 80 percent of the slaves exported came from Bridgetown. They had a high sex ratio of 125 males per 100 females, compared to only 78 for the total slave population of the parish, and they contained a relatively small proportion of children (table S1.21). Thus, the age-sex structure of these slaves came nearer to that of the Atlantic slave trade than did the large holdings transported from the Bahamas. But 37 percent of the males and 70 percent of the females were domestics, and only 9 percent field laborers. Occupations were not fixed, of course, and purchasers of these slaves in the new sugar colonies often moved domestics into field labor as the labor force dwindled. But slaves who had begun life as house slaves were never seen as ideal field laborers.

After 1825, the intercolonial slave trade was limited almost entirely to the movement of domestics. This trade depended on the continued freedom of masters to travel with domestics. There was no obligation to return the slaves to their home colony,[21] but the masters were required to produce official certificates showing that the slaves were registered as domestics. Limits to the number of domestic slaves accompanying their owners were unclear. In 1828 a Mr. Fox traveled from Trinidad to Dominica, where he purchased six slaves and attempted to take them to Trinidad as the "domestics" of persons to whom he offered a free passage as the nominal owners. This was exposed as fraudulent, but the Trinidad Collector of Customs observed that it was common practice in other British islands to permit nonresidents to purchase and remove one or two domestics, so long as they provided the certification required by the Consolidated Slave Act.[22] In 1829, a Mr. Hobson and a Dr. Birmingham purchased 29 slaves belonging to the field gang of a coffee plantation in Dominica and registered them as "domestics of all work." Eight of these slaves were sent to Trinidad, and the others to Birmingham's sugar estate in Dominica, where they were employed as field laborers. But the slaves sent to Trinidad were seized, and legal action under the Consolidated Slave Act led to their manumission in 1832.[23] The fraudulent movement of "domestics" from

Barbados seems to have been more successful. Of the 250 domestics sent to Trinidad in 1827, for instance, some 12 were registered as agricultural laborers in the returns of 1828, and others were employed as laborers in Port of Spain.[24] By 1830, however, the movement of domestics had been reduced to a trickle, and, although it was more selective of age and sex, it was never large enough to alter the demographic structure of the importing or exporting colonies.

In addition to the permanent transfer and trading of slaves between the colonies, there was a certain amount of short-term movement. Slaves as well as masters were aware of the regional variations in economic health within the British Caribbean. Thus, Barbadian "working out" slaves (such as hucksters, cooks, laundresses, carpenters, tailors, maids, and sailors, who were allowed to find their own employers and required only to pay their masters a fixed periodic sum) were said to be anxious to find work where the wages were highest, in Demerara-Essequibo. Around 1830, mechanics in Demerara received 7s. 6d. to 8s. 8d. per day, compared to only 3s. in Barbados.[25] The Demerara collector of customs also noted that huckster slaves were "often entrusted with goods to a large amount by their owners to sell in other colonies, in the benefit of which both partake," and occasionally "a confidential domestic is sent to bring back a child or relative, recover a debt etc. for their owners." Sick slaves were sent from Demerara for a change of air or medical treatment.[26] But such movement can hardly have accounted for any large number of slaves.

There were complaints from the masters, especially in the Bahamas, that the Consolidated Slave Act prevented the natural movement of slaves even within the islands. It was said that the regulations prevented slaves from the out islands traveling to Nassau to sell provisions in the market or to visit friends.[27] And "slaves often hire themselves from their owners, and join in fishing trips with other slaves or with free people 'on shares,' " though never venturing far in their small vessels.[28] Harbour Island was completely barren but was inhabited by men with small plantations or farms on nearby Eleuthera, who spent half of each week at the farms and the other half in fishing or turtling, always accompanied by their two or three slaves. Similarly, Hog Island, opposite Nassau, was the site of country houses belonging to town merchants. The salt pond on Fortune Island was provisioned from Crooked and Acklins Islands, the slaves moving from task to task.[29] By 1832, however, all such movements within the Bahamas were permitted without official clearances.

It may be concluded that the intercolonial movement of slaves, resulting from regional inequalities in economic health within the British Caribbean, was never of sufficient scale to alter those inequalities. It did no more than retard the rate of population decline in the new sugar colonies, and it caused absolute population decline in the face of natural increase only in the Bahamas. The structure of the slave populations of the exporting colonies was not altered significantly, since the movement was demographically selective only in the years after 1825, when the volume was small. But it did mean that more than 20,000 slaves were moved to new colonies, a number equivalent to the entire slave population of Trinidad at the time of emancipation. It meant movement from colonies producing cotton, coffee, and provisions to monocultural, sugar plantation economies. In spite of pious protestations from the planters it almost always meant movement into relatively hostile environments, inimical to the material welfare of the slaves and associated with extreme mortality levels.

SPATIAL DISTRIBUTION

The movement of slaves within colonies was not regulated in the same way as movement between colonies. Thus, the spatial distribution of slaves within particular colonies reached an equilibrium more rapidly. But the growing dominance of sugar monoculture in the British Caribbean after 1807, and the abolition of the Atlantic slave trade, created a flow of slaves into the sugar sector from other types of agricultural units and from the towns, which paralleled the pattern of movement observed in the intercolonial slave trade.

There was an imperfect relationship between the density of the slave populations and the economic classification of the colonies (table 3.1). Of the marginal colonies, only Anguilla had more than 10 slaves per square mile in 1834. In the old sugar colonies, on the other hand, there was everywhere a density of more than 200 slaves per square mile, excepting only Montserrat (164) and the Virgin Islands (87). Barbados, with more than 500 slaves per square mile, was the most densely populated colony by far. The new sugar colonies fell between the marginal colonies and the old sugar colonies in the density of their slave populations, but they showed a greater range of variation. Only Grenada (178), St. Vincent (148), and Tobago (101) had densities exceeding 100 per square mile in 1834; Dominica and St. Lucia averaged about 50, and Trinidad had as few as 11 to the square mile. The calculation of any density index for British Guiana is artificial, because the slave population was concentrated in a dense but narrow coastal strip while the vast hinterland remained terra incognita to the colonists. Jamaica had 70 slaves per square mile but showed considerable internal variation.

Despite these complications, it is apparent that by 1834 the density of the slave population was essentially a function of the ratio of potential sugar land to total area in each colony. Within the regions dominated by sugar the densities were similar, though Barbados had a higher ratio of slaves to acres of cane than the other colonies, in particular the newly settled. This was a result of long-term population growth in Barbados, the perceived need to apply closer attention to the old "exhausted" lands by manuring, and the use of plantation lands to produce food crops. Beyond these variations in the ratio of slaves to acres of cane, the differences in colony-level density were largely a direct response to the relative availability of level, well-watered land. But length of settlement was also important. Rather than attempting to adjust for such differences in physical-environmental factors at the colony level, it is more useful to consider patterns of spatial distribution *within* particular types of colonies.

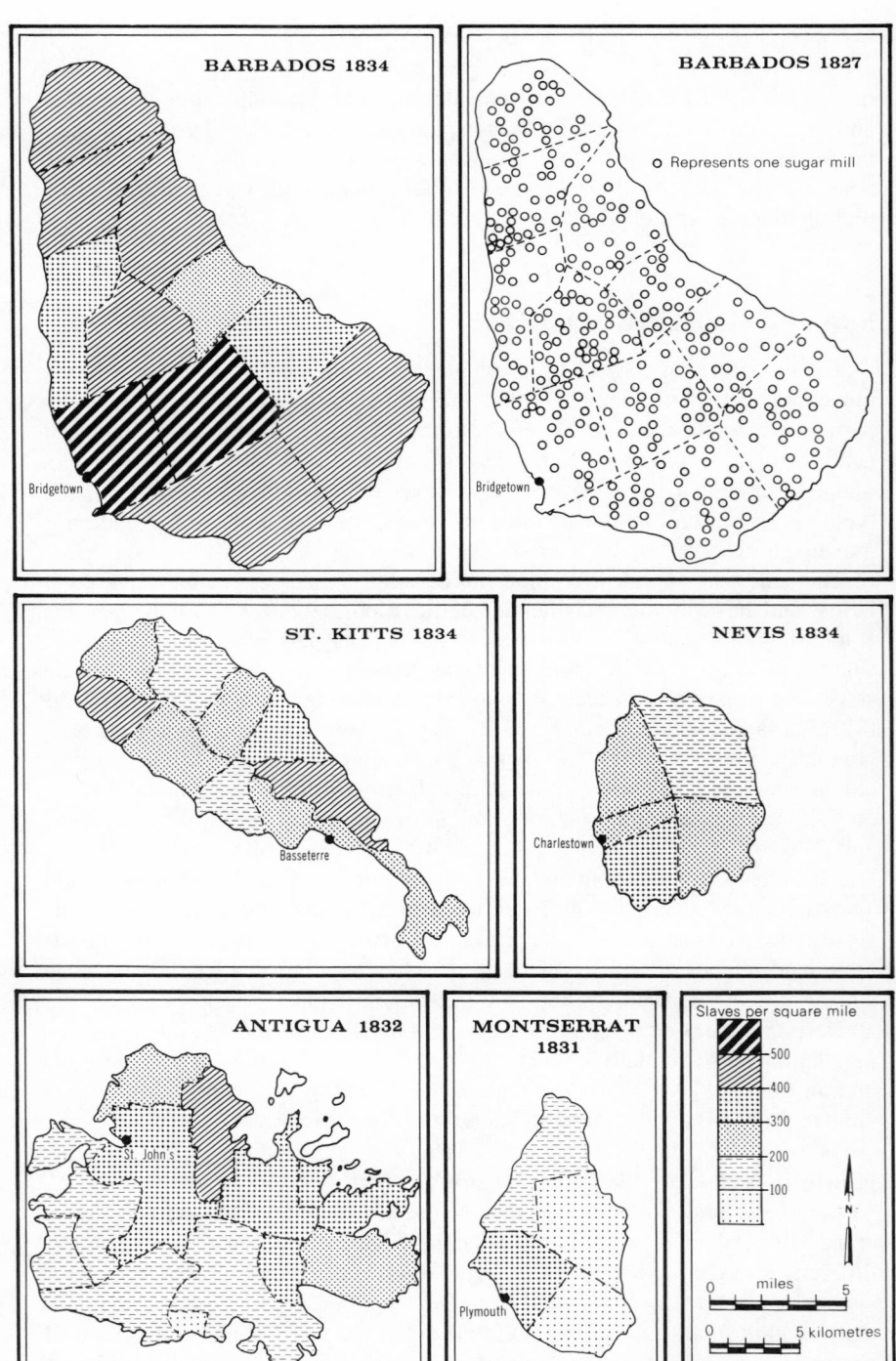

Fig. 4.3. *Slave Population Density in the Old Sugar Colonies.*

To begin with the simple case of Barbados, it is clear that the virtually uniform distribution of sugar mills was matched by only slight variations in the density of the slave population (fig. 4.3). In most parishes the density hovered around 400 slaves per square mile in 1834. It reached 974 in the urban parish of St. Michael and was as low as 298 in the relatively rugged parish of St. Joseph. But the central block of five parishes with more than 60 percent of their slaves employed in sugar (St. George, St. John, St. Joseph, St. Andrew, and St. Thomas) comprised a range of densities, including the most thinly populated areas. Thus, even at the local level, in the archetypal sugar island, the relationship between population density and concentration in sugar cultivation was ambiguous.

A certain amount of population redistribution occurred within Barbados between 1807 and 1834, a redistribution not readily explained by differential natural increase. Between 1817 and 1834 the island's slave population grew by 6.9 percent, but the parishes containing urban settlements lost population. St. Michael declined by 5.7 percent and St. Peter, containing Speightstown, by 4.7 percent (table S1.3). The greatest increases, exceeding 20 percent, occurred in St. Andrew and St. George. It is more difficult to reconstruct trends in the distribution of slaves before 1817, but the poll tax data suggest a similar flow of slaves out of the urban parishes into the central-windward parishes.[30] Over the whole period 1807–34, the slave population of Barbados grew by about 10 percent, but St. Michael lost 4 percent and St. Peter and St. James increased only slightly, while the central-windward parishes all increased by more than 20 percent. Thus, it is possible to identify an increasing concentration of the slave population in the sugar-producing regions of Barbados, together with a definite decline in the urban areas.

In the Leeward Islands the pattern of population distribution was complicated by variations in topography. The elongation of St. Kitts meant that the parishes at the extremes had somewhat higher densities than those in the middle of the island, which contained larger proportions of mountain land (fig. 4.3). Only the relatively level parishes of St. Anne and St. Peter approached densities typical of Barbados. The parish of St. George, containing the capital town of Basseterre, was less densely populated because it also included the island's dry, salt pond peninsula. It suffered a much more rapid loss of population than the St. Kitts average after 1807 (table S1.4), thus paralleling the pattern of urban loss observed in Barbados. A similar correlation between slave population density and the amount of relatively level potential sugar land occurred in Nevis, where the southwestern parish of St. John Figtree had the highest density. Again, the slave population of the urban parish of St. Paul Charlestown declined at almost twice the average for the island between 1817 and 1834.[31]

In Antigua there was a clear distinction between the northeastern limestone uplands and the southwestern volcanic mountains (fig. 4.3). The former region was dominated by sugar and had densities approaching those typical of Barbados, whereas the latter was devoted chiefly to the production of livestock and provisions and was quite sparsely settled. It is probable that the clay plain that separated these two zones was as heavily populated as the limestone uplands.

Thus, the slave population of Antigua was concentrated in the relatively level, and relatively dry, sugar-producing zone. Montserrat's slave population was similarly concentrated, with low densities in the rugged windward parishes and a high density only in the relatively level parish of St. Anthony, which contained the town of Plymouth. But a redistribution of population was taking place in Montserrat in the last years of slavery, with a decline in St. Anthony and growth in the other parishes.[32]

In the Virgin Islands, only Tortola was densely settled (table S1.6). Even Tortola's density of 158 slaves per square mile in 1831 was only equivalent to the lowest densities found elsewhere in the Leewards. It was the only sugar producer in the group, but contained a large proportion of steeply sloping land. With the exception of Thatch Island and Frenchman's Cay, all of the islands lost population after 1815, but there is no clear evidence of population redistribution within the Virgin Islands.

Around 1832, few of Jamaica's parishes had densities exceeding 100 slaves per square mile, but there was a strong correlation between sugar cultivation and high density.[33] Again, there was an absolute decline in the slave population of the urban parish of Kingston after 1807 and a relative redistribution to the agricultural regions.

Thus, the old sugar colonies had several features in common. The density of the slave population varied with the proportion of land under cane. Where there was little steep land, the density was commonly 300 to 400 slaves per square mile. With the exception of the Virgin Islands, and possibly Antigua, absolute decline in the urban parishes was matched by growth in the rural areas, but this was a product of movement rather than of differential rates of natural increase.

This equilibrium between the density of the slave population and the slope of the land, via the dominance of sugar, had not been achieved in the new sugar colonies by 1834. Large areas remained unsettled, regardless of their physical qualities or potential as cane land. The pattern of urban decline was much less uniform.

In Dominica, population density was in fact greatest in the parishes dominated by coffee, which were located in the southwestern corner of the island, around the town of Roseau (fig. 4.4). The windward parishes, where sugar dominated, contained much more rugged, very wet land; but it is probable, of course, that local densities in the limited areas devoted to sugar exceeded those in the coffee regions, variations in parish size creating artificial contrasts. Since Dominica was subject to heavy out-migration in the 1820s, it is difficult to identify any clear pattern of population redistribution (table S1.7). Between 1817 and 1834 the slave population of Roseau fell by 58 percent, more than twice the island average of 26 percent, but the town experienced relatively heavy mortality and some of the movement may have reflected the intercolonial trade in domestic slaves rather than a flow to the rural parishes.

In St. Vincent there was a definite correlation between the density of the slave population and the dominance of sugar (fig. 4.4). But in St. Lucia the densely

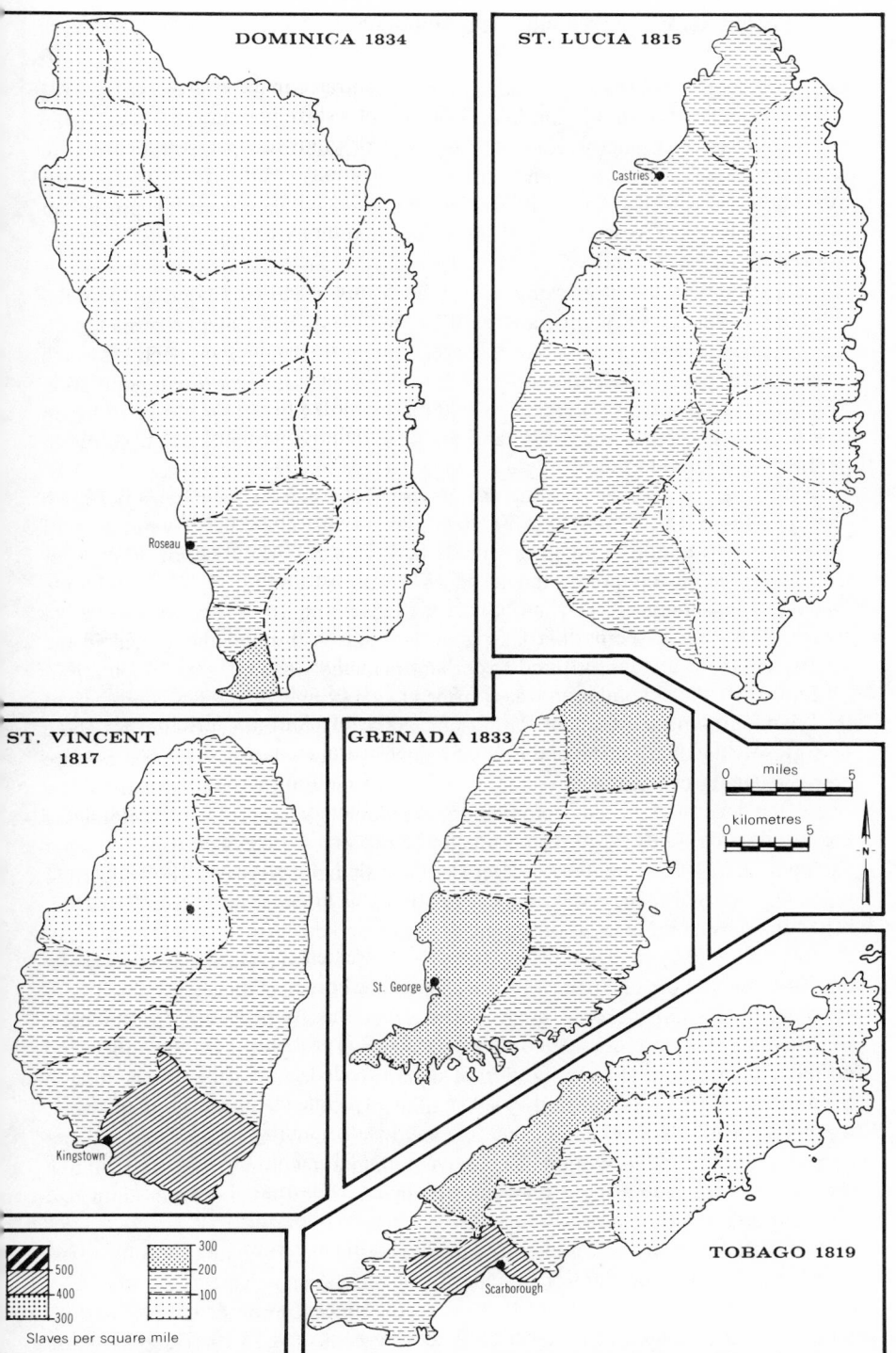

DOMINICA 1834

ST. LUCIA 1815

Castries •

Roseau •

ST. VINCENT 1817

GRENADA 1833

miles
0   5

kilometres
0   5

N

St. George •

Kingstown •

Scarborough •

TOBAGO 1819

500
400
300

300
200
100

Slaves per square mile

Fig. 4.4. *Slave Population Density in the Windward Islands and Tobago.*

[89]

populated leeward parishes produced both sugar and coffee. High densities were always associated with the dominance of sugar in Grenada, but contrasts at the parish level were gradually reduced between 1817 and 1834 with absolute growth occurring only in the cocoa and coffee parishes (table S1.10). In Tobago the overwhelming role of sugar resulted in high population densities being confined to the relatively level western end of the island. Only in the urban parishes of St. George (St. Vincent) and St. Andrew (Tobago) did the density exceed 400 slaves per square mile. It is impossible to establish any pattern of population redistribution in Tobago or St. Lucia after 1807, but the official island returns for St. Vincent show that the parish of St. George, containing Kingstown, declined much more rapidly than the island average.[34] A more exact picture of urban population loss can be obtained for Grenada, where the town of St. George declined by 38 percent between 1817 and 1833, and the periurban parish of St. George by 26 percent, compared to the colony's average decrease of 16 percent (table S1.10).

Within the Grenadines, Carriacou appears to have had the most densely settled slave population, with more than 300 to the square mile in 1820.[35] Several other of the sugar- and cotton-cultivating islands had densities in excess of 100. After Carriacou, the most populous islands in 1817 were Bequia (1,412 slaves), Union Island (598), Canouan (354), and Mustique (325) (table S1.9). The data are rather fragmentary, but it seems that Carriacou lost slaves through movement in the 1820s, and that Canouan suffered an earlier drastic decline in its slave population.

Trinidad's slave population was confined to a narrow belt in the western part of the island, ringing the Gulf of Paria (table S1.12). This concentration reflected very closely the distribution of the sugar industry, since relatively few slaves were employed in the cocoa and coffee industries. But even in the quarters dominated by sugar, the density of the slave population was much less than in the old colonies or the Windwards. Only North Naparima had a density in excess of 100 slaves per square mile in 1832, and most quarters had less than 50. Between 1807 and 1834 there was a significant redistribution of the slave population within Trinidad, reflecting the changing locus of sugar cultivation and the growing concentration of the slave labor force in that industry (fig. 4.5). There was a flow of slaves out of the capital town of Port of Spain, but the proportion of urban slaves remained very high until 1834. In the rural quarters there was a definite decline in the slave population in the northern settled region, a result of the decline of the cotton and coffee industries and of the migration of sugar estates to the south. The decline in the northern region was matched by substantial growth in the newer sugar quarters, the Naparimas, Carapichaima, and Savonetta. No movement into the east occurred. Thus, the redistribution of the slave population within Trinidad meant that the slaves were increasingly concentrated in low-lying areas in the south and elevated areas in the north.

For British Guiana it is impossible to measure slave population density at the parish level, since the interior boundaries of the parishes were generally indeterminate. But there is no doubting the coastal concentration of the population, with penetration inland confined entirely to river banks (fig. 4.6). The population

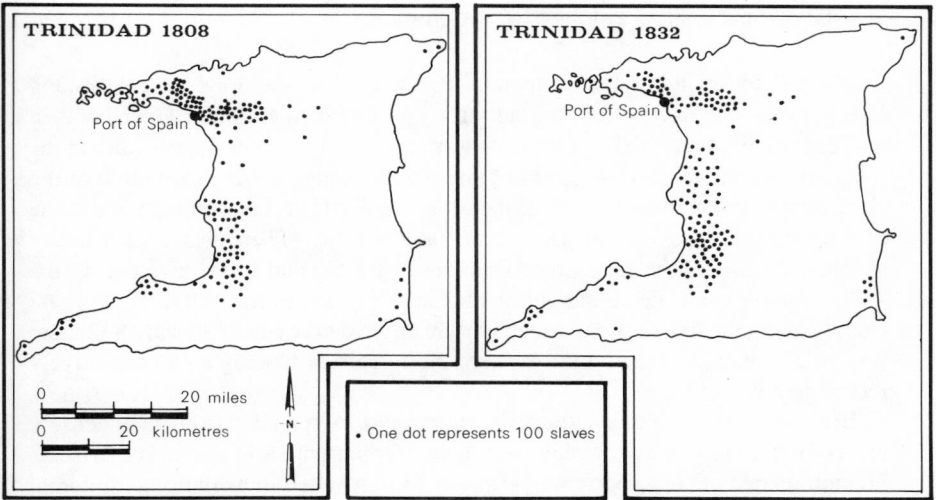

Fig. 4.5. *Distribution of Rural Slaves in Trinidad, 1808 and 1832.*
(Sources: *C.O.295/21, f. 107; C.O.300/46, f. 118.*)

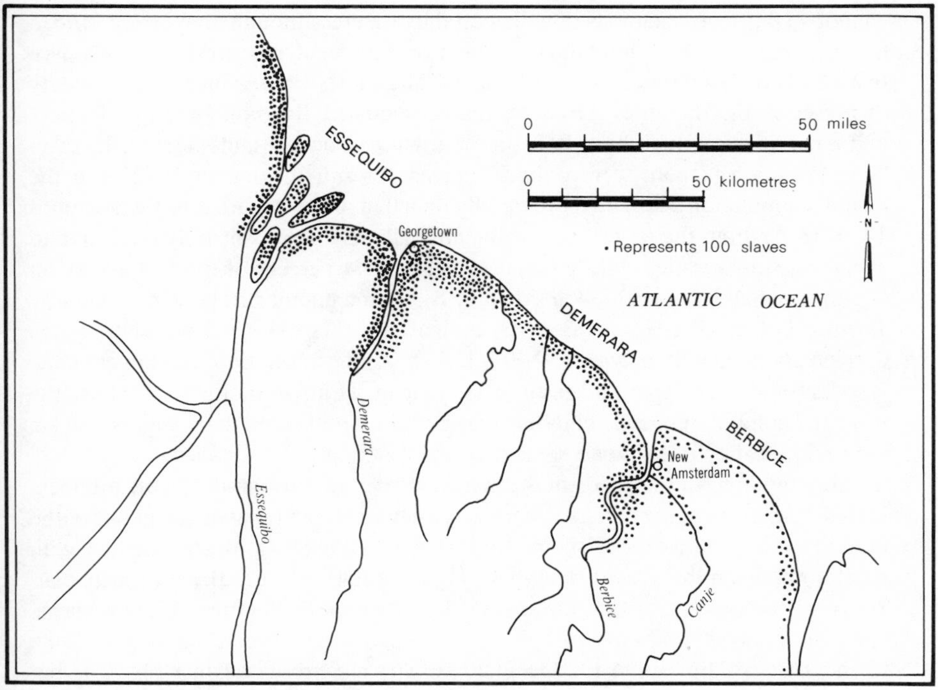

Fig. 4.6. *Distribution of Rural Slaves in Demerara-Essequibo and Berbice*
c.1820. (Sources: *tables S1.13–1.14.*)

was most dense along the Demerara River and on the East Coast, around Georgetown, and quite thinly spread throughout most of Berbice. The islands in the Essequibo estuary had densities of more than 100 slaves per square mile. In the period before emancipation, the most significant change in the distribution of the slave population was the growth of the urban parish of St. George and the decline of the other parishes on the Demerara (table S1.13). There was also a heavy absolute decline in the East Coast Demerara parishes and in Berbice during the 1820s, the region of declining cotton and coffee production.[36] But the Essequibo Islands maintained their populations fairly well, and between 1826 and 1832 there was an absolute increase on the Pomeroon, a sugar-producing area of relatively recent settlement.

In the new sugar colonies, then, the slave population tended to be most densely settled in the sugar-growing regions, but with important exceptions. The increasing dominance of sugar between 1807 and 1834 resulted in a significant internal redistribution of the population, characterized by the general decline of urban parishes and movement from coffee and cotton to sugar regions. These trends meant that the slave population was increasingly concentrated in rural environments of relatively low-lying land, along coastal fringes.

The spatial distribution of the slave population within the marginal colonies cannot always be established with certainty. But, although they were spread thinly, there was throughout the margnal colonies a tendency for the slaves to live in a small number of nucleated settlements. The slaves were probably most widely dispersed in the Bahamas, but more than one-quarter lived on New Providence, and most of these must have been in the town of Nassau (table S1.15). Even in New Providence there were only 50 slaves per square mile in 1822, and the island's population declined more rapidly than that of the Bahamas as a whole until 1834. In Andros, the largest of the Bahama Islands, there was only one slave to every ten square miles. In the Cayman Islands, 44 percent of the 974 slaves on Grand Cayman lived at Bodden Town in 1834, and another 16 percent at George Town.[37] For British Honduras, it is known only that the slave population was divided about equally between "North Belize" and "South Belize," but even the woodcutting slaves spent a season each year in the town of Belize.[38] Thus, the marginal colonies tended to combine concentration into towns and hamlets with an otherwise scattered and sparsely settled environment.

Although long-term trends in the marginal colonies are somewhat uncertain, it is clear that in the sugar colonies there was a general movement of slaves out of the urban parishes between 1807 and 1834. It is necessary now to establish with greater precision the size of the urban slave population in the British Caribbean. The registration returns did not always provide data distinguishing town slaves from rural slaves, and only in a few cases was the parish coterminous with the town. The available data for the major towns are presented in table 4.4, but Charlestown, Roadtown, Nassau, and Belize are omitted, and these towns might also have had populations exceeding 500 slaves. All of the towns in table 4.4 were capital towns except Kingston and Montego Bay. Another six Jamaican towns

(Lucea, Savanna la Mar, Falmouth, Port Royal, Port Antonio, and Morant Bay) had more than 500 slaves in 1832.[39] The slave populations shown for Bridgetown, St. Johns, Montego Bay, Spanish Town, Basseterre, and Plymouth around 1832 have been calculated by linking the compensation valuers' returns to the slave registration returns. Elsewhere the populations derive from direct identifications in the registration returns, except that the 1817 population for Bridgetown is an aggregation of the slaveholdings in St. Michael parish which did not contain any slaves engaged in agriculture.

Around 1830, some 9 percent of the British Caribbean slave population lived in settlements described as "towns" by contemporaries. Almost 6 percent lived in the eight largest towns, each of which had a slave population of more than 2,000. This urban concentration was less than in the Hispanic Caribbean, but significantly greater than in the United States.[40] Only 2.4 percent of the United States slave population lived in the South's eight largest towns in 1830, and a decade earlier the contrast with the Caribbean had been even greater. The total populations of the British Caribbean towns were smaller, however, with slaves making up about 50 percent of the whole, so that the nature of the urban experience was somewhat different.

Secular trends in the size of the urban slave populations are difficult to establish. In general, the towns seem to have increased their share of the population during the eighteenth century and probably reached a peak around 1810, when British West Indian ports were given a special role in trade with Spanish America under the Free Port Acts. Kingston, an important free port and surrounded by an active frontier, accounted for only 4 percent of Jamaica's slave population between 1730 and 1830, except for the period 1800–1820 when it reached 5.2 percent. But Kingston was complemented by other Jamaican towns, and many of these grew rapidly in the late eighteenth century, so that the total urban proportion probably increased until 1810.[41] Bridgetown increased its share of the Barbados slave population from 4 percent in 1680 to 12 percent in 1820.[42] The pattern of urban decline in the early nineteenth century has been discussed already, but there were some significant variations in its chronology. These variations resulted from differences in the nature of the free port trade and in the profitability of particular plantation crops. The greatest relative decline occurred in Roseau, where the town's share of Dominica's slave population fell from 12.7 to 5.4 percent between 1800 and 1834, but most of this loss occurred in the years after 1815.[43] Elsewhere, the decline commenced later and was less dramatic.

The most important aberration from the general pattern of urban decline was the case of Georgetown, which more than doubled its share of the Demerara-Essequibo slave population between 1812 and 1832 (table 4.4). It achieved this growth in the face of competition for slave labor from the colony's thriving sugar plantations, which were offering the highest prices for field slaves in the British Caribbean. One explanation for this pattern may be that the elasticity of demand for slave labor was greater in the towns than in the plantations.[44] Thus Georgetown, accumulating governmental and commercial roles for an expanding ter-

Table 4.4. *Major Town Slave Populations, 1813–34*

Town	Number of Slaves		Percentage of Colony's Slave Population	
	c.1815	c.1832	c.1815	c.1832
Kingston, Jamaica	17,954 (1817)	12,551 (1832)	5.2	4.0
Bridgetown, Barbados	9,284 (1817)	8,585 (1834)	12.0	10.3
Port of Spain, Trinidad	6,040 (1813)	2,927 (1832)	23.5	13.4
Georgetown, Demerara	3,589 (1812)	6,676 (1832)	4.5	10.2
St. Johns, Antigua	—	2,621 (1832)	—	9.0
Kingstown, St. Vincent	2,255 (1817)	—	9.0	—
Montego Bay, Jamaica	—	2,237 (1832)	—	0.7
Spanish Town, Jamaica	—	2,104 (1832)	—	0.7
St. Georges, Grenada	2,632 (1817)	1,632 (1833)	9.5	6.9
Castries, St. Lucia	1,408 (1815)	—	8.6	—
New Amsterdam, Berbice	—	1,400 (1827)	—	7.0
Basseterre, St. Kitts	—	1,283 (1834)	—	7.3
Roseau, Dominica	1,838 (1817)	827 (1832)	10.2	5.7
Scarborough, Tobago	888 (1819)	—	5.7	—
Plymouth, Montserrat	—	490 (1831)	—	7.7

Sources: Kingston, Montego Bay, Spanish Town: Higman, *Slave Population and Economy in Jamaica,* p. 58; Bridgetown: T.71/553–54, linked to T.71/790–803 and 895; Port of Spain: T.71/501–3, and C.O.300/46, p. 118; Georgetown: M.C.P.D.E., 1817, pp. 484–85, and *P.P.*, 1833, vol. 26 (700), p. 432; St. Johns: T.71/250, linked to T.71/735–38; Kingstown: T.71/493; St. Georges: see table S1.9; Castries: see table S1.8; New Amsterdam: Robert H. Schomburgk, *A Description of British Guiana* (1840), p. 46; Basseterre: T.71/740–42, linked to T.71/260; Roseau: see table S1.7; Scarborough: T.71/461; Plymouth: T.71/451, linked to T.71/766.

ritory, competed successfully in a market already stretched by plantation demand. Elsewhere, after 1807 the plantations were able to draw slaves from the towns, in spite of the depressed state of the market for export staples. Few towns were able to retain more than 10 percent of any British Caribbean colony's slave population. Nassau and Belize were probably successful in doing this, but in the sugar colonies only Port of Spain maintained a proportion significantly larger than 10 percent by 1834. In both Georgetown and Port of Spain the white and freedman populations grew significantly, so that the slave:free ratio declined. Slaves made up 61 percent of the total population of Georgetown in 1812 but only 53 percent in 1832, in spite of their absolute increase. In Port of Spain the proportion of slaves fell from 50 percent in 1808 to only 25 percent by 1832.[45]

In most colonies the capital town was overwhelming in its dominance, smaller settlements accounting for only a small proportion of the total urban population. Only in Jamaica did the secondary towns match the slave population of the primary town, Kingston, which was anomalous in not being the island's capital. Spanish Town, Jamaica's capital, was the only town of any importance not to serve a port function. The metropolitan orientation of the British Caribbean economy meant that only a discontinuous hierarchy of service centers developed, few of them linked by overland routes. Many plantations had their own wharves, reducing to a minimum their dependence on the towns for goods and services. Many slave villages on plantations exceeded in size and population the second-order towns and hamlets. In St. Vincent, for example, the seven minor towns accounted for only 18 percent of the island's urban slave population in 1817; none of them contained more than 200 slaves, whereas 30 plantations exceeded that population (table S1.9). Kingstown, however, supported a slave population several times that of the largest plantation on the island. In Antigua the minor towns accounted for 15 percent of the urban slave population and in Trinidad a mere 2 percent, but in St. Lucia the proportion rose as high as 31 percent (tables S1.5, S1.8, and S1.12). The secondary towns appear to have increased their share of the urban slave populations between 1807 and 1834, however, not suffering the same loss to the plantations as the capital towns.

The spatial distribution of slaves within the towns is not readily established. Most contemporary travelers reported a haphazard mixing of slave, white, and freedman housing. It is difficult to identify the existence of residential segregation at the district level.[46] Kingstown, for example, was described by Bayley as long and narrow, comprising only three streets.[47] The principal stores were on Bay Street; drygoods shops, small shops kept by freedmen, and rum shops occupied Middle Street; while Back Street contained few stores, and the houses belonged to persons not engaged in commerce, with ten to twelve huts intervening between the better-class residences. Thus, in 1820 a dwelling house was offered for rent "in a healthy, airy, situation in the Back-street with the offices detached, negro-houses, stable, bathing-house. . . ."[48] In the same year premises were offered on the bay, consisting of a large hall, a parlor and three chambers, an upstairs gallery and pantry, and in the yard a fireproof kitchen, stable, backstores, sickhouse, and negro rooms, together with a longboat and its crew of ten slaves.[49] Thus, it appears that most slaves lived on the premises of their owners, though in separate rooms or outbuildings, while others lived in huts scattered between the masters' residences. This pattern was common to all of the smaller towns.

In some of the larger towns, a greater degree of residential segregation occurred, especially where masters paid slaves a weekly allowance in cash, known as "board-wages," and required them to find and pay for their own accommodation and food. This practice resulted in the emergence of concentrations of slave housing, termed "negro yards." These yards were most numerous in Kingston, where they were located largely on the fringes of the town.[50] But even in Kingston, the great majority of the slaves lived in rooms on their owners' premises and were concentrated in the harborside commercial zone.

For Bridgetown, it is possible to establish the location of the slave population by streets, using the compensation valuers' returns of 1834, for all but 6 percent of the slaves.[51] The distribution of slaves within the town limits established by law in 1822 is mapped in figure 4.7, together with the distribution of whites and freedmen paying taxes in 1828.[52] Since exact locations are not known, all of these people

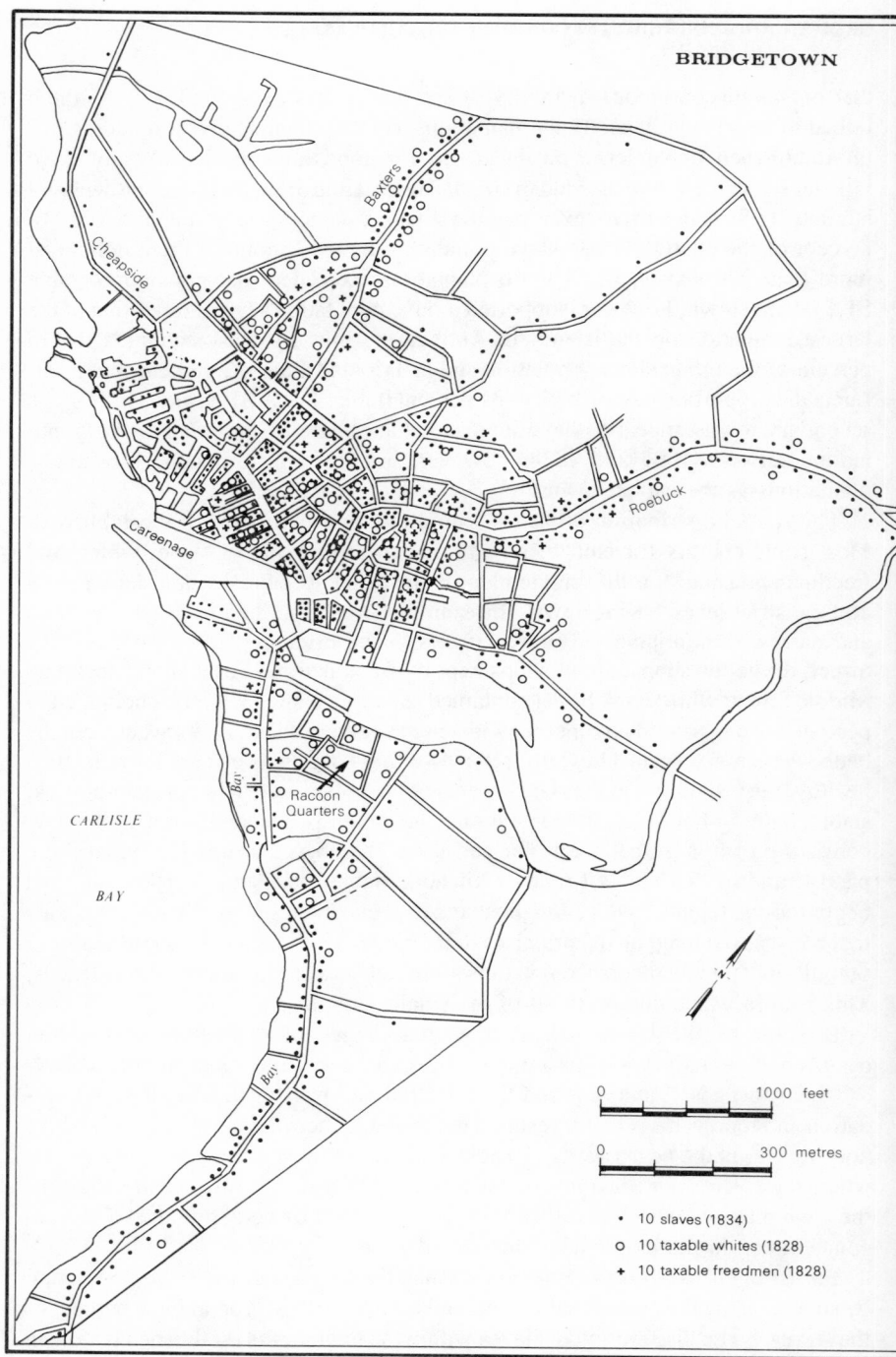

Fig. 4.7. *Distribution of Slaves, Whites, and Freedmen: Bridgetown c.1830.*
(Sources: *table S1.16; C.O.700/Barbados 14; St. Michael Levy Book,*
1823–29 [D.A.B.])

must be distributed evenly along the streets, which necessarily results in some distortion, especially where the streets were long. But it is certain that the slaves were widely dispersed, as were their owners. Concentration around the wharf area of the Careenage was less obvious than in Kingston, and there was a marked attenuation along the major routes leading out of the town, particularly Bay Street, Roebuck Street, Baxters Road, and Cheapside, where "negro yards" may have existed on a limited scale.[53] The white and freedman populations included in figure 4.7 comprise only those who paid taxes on trade, rents, offices, or professions; thus, they are chiefly confined to the propertied classes. The ratio of taxable whites to slaves seems to have been relatively high in the wharf area and at Racoon Quarters, while the ratio was relatively low toward Cheapside and "the Roe-bucks." Taxable freedmen, however, showed a much more definite concentration, particularly in the area around Marl Hill Street toward Roebuck. No data are available to indicate the spatial distribution of those many whites and freedmen who possessed neither taxable property nor slaves, and it is possible that they were more often fringe-dwellers. But the density of the slave population matched quite closely the density of the street pattern in Bridgetown, so there is no reason to suspect that the slave population was segregated into particular zones of the town.

It is uncertain whether the decline in the slave population of Bridgetown after 1807 resulted in any redistribution of the population within the town. In the case of Georgetown, Demerara, the data are relatively abundant, but this town was unusual in showing absolute growth rather than decline. Between 1812 and 1824 the total population of the town increased from about 6,000 to 10,500. The commercial and administrative core of Georgetown was in Stabroek, New Town, and Robb Town (fig. 4.8). In 1812, 40 percent of the slaves were located within this core, but by 1824 only 23 percent (table S1.17). New Town and Robb Town declined absolutely, and Stabroek showed only a small gain. The white and freedman populations behaved similarly. In 1812 this core area contained 47 percent of the whites and 38 percent of the freedmen, but by 1830 only 21 and 11 percent.[54] The greatest increase in the slave population of Georgetown took place in the outlying residential districts of Kingston, Cumingsburg, and Charles Town, while Werk en Rust and Lacy Town showed slower expansion. Once again, the growth rates were similar for all of the population groups, the most rapid growth occurring on the urban fringes.

The core of Georgetown was transformed into a commercial zone, with warehouses and shops replacing residences. During the 1820s it was also the center of public building. Drainage trenches, "in the highest degree offensive," intersected the area, and a building attached to the hospital housed the colony's deranged, "whose cries disturb the neighbourhood in the most disagreeable manner."[55] Small wonder that gentlemen established themselves in the new, spacious residential districts. There was little room for expansion within the core, other than the mud lots fronting the Demerara River. The front lands of Plantation Vlissengen were divided 196 town lots in 1804, forming Columbia District and,

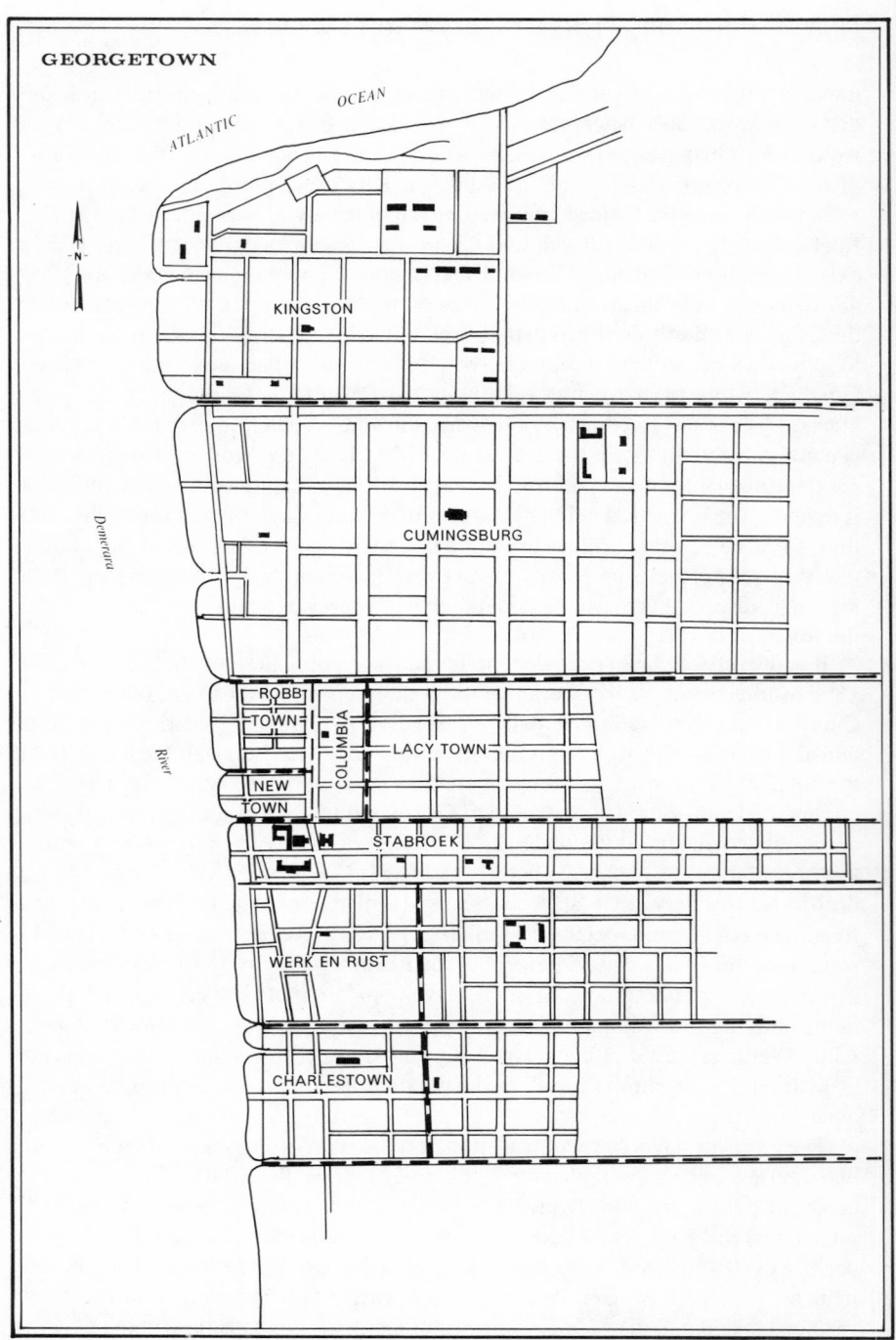

Fig. 4.8. *Georgetown, Demerara, c.1830.* (Source: Local Guide of British Guiana *[Demerara, 1843].)*

later, Lacy Town.[56] But even in this fluid situation the movement of population did not result in any significant residential segregation. All of the districts of George-town had similar proportions of slaves, whites, and freedmen throughout the period. In 1812 only Kingston had a low proportion of slaves and a large proportion of whites, probably because of the military barracks in the district. Freedmen were relatively less numerous in New Town and Robb Town, whereas slaves were fewer in the new district of Lacy Town and freedmen numerous. But all of these variations were minor.

The lack of residential segregation in the towns of the British Caribbean during the period of slavery resulted primarily from the domestic occupations of most slaves. Their functions could be fulfilled only if they were on hand. Slaves employed as laborers or tradesmen, most of them males, might live in separate huts or yards, but most were allowed to live no farther from their masters than the "negro rooms" within the house yard.

5.
Structure of
the Slave Populations

THE ATLANTIC SLAVE TRADE HAD BEEN DEMOGRAPHICALLY selective in response both to factors affecting the supply of slaves in Africa and to the preferences of the West Indian market, where the highest prices were paid for youthful males. Thus, abolition had important consequences for the sex and age structure of the slave population, as well as for its ethnic composition. Further, since almost all slaves supplied by the Atlantic slave trade were black, abolition meant an increase in the proportion of colored slaves and had more subtle implications for the pattern of miscegenation. These changes in the structure of the slave populations, together with changes in the distribution of ownership and location consequent on abolition, had broad implications for the organization and profitability of slave labor and for modes of behavior and attitudes within the slave community. The present chapter discusses the pattern of slaveownership and changes in the sex ratio, birthplaces, age structure, and color of the slave populations as a prelude to consideration of labor organization, mortality, and fertility.

MASTERS AND MISTRESSES

The growth of sugar monoculture at the expense of other plantation crops had the effect of concentrating the slave populations of the British Caribbean into relatively large slaveholdings. In the years after 1807, the flow of slaves from the towns to the countryside had a similar effect, reducing the number of small units. But the general decline in the white populations, which was in itself partly a response to the more limited possibilities of slaveownership after 1807, meant that slaveowning remained widespread among whites. The rapidly growing freedman population owned relatively few slaves, however, so that the ratio of slave to free declined significantly.

Around 1832 there were approximately 50,000 whites and 100,000 freedmen in the British Caribbean, but only 32,500 slaveowners (tables 5.1 and S2.1). No reliable data are available for an estimate of the extent of slaveowning among freedmen, as discussed below, but it is improbable that they were more than 20 percent of the owners in 1832, and it is certain that they owned a much smaller proportion of the slave population. If freedmen did constitute as many as 20 percent of the owners, it follows that only 6.5 percent of freedmen were slave-owners, compared to 52.0 percent of whites.

The widespread ownership of slaves by the white population meant that the average holding comprised only 20.9 slaves around 1832 (table 5.1). Eric Williams argued that "the large number of slaveowners and the small number of slaves held on an average by each one of them made the British West Indian slave system in 1833 more like a system of household management than a commercial plantation economy," and concluded that the colonies "still lived in the eighteenth century" because they were "producing for export with an economy geared to subsistence production."[1] But this interpretation is misleading, since it results from a false perspective on the pattern of slaveholding size. While it is certainly true that the great majority of slave owners possessed few slaves and that the mean holding was therefore small, most slaves lived and worked on large units. Whereas around 1832 the typical master owned fewer than 10 slaves, the typical slave belonged to a unit of more than 100 slaves.

Table 5.1 provides a comprehensive picture of the pattern of slaveownership derived from the registration returns for 1832 or thereabouts. It is based largely on contemporary tabulations, which unfortunately failed to distinguish among holdings larger than 30 slaves, so these data are more useful for understanding the distribution of owners than of slaves. A caution must be entered at this point. The "owners" included in table 5.1 are equivalent to separate registration returns. Some owners made several returns, since they possessed slaves located on different plantations or in different parishes or even colonies. Thus, the number of returns exceeds the true number of owners. On the other hand, slaves who worked on a single unit or plantation might be owned by several individuals, most often the planter's relatives, and registered separately. This practice artificially increased the number of slaves apparently working on small units. Similarly, small groups of slaves were sometimes leased and worked on large plantations, but returned only by their owners. It is generally difficult to identify these patterns in the registration returns, but those for plantation slaves in St. Vincent do permit such an analysis. In 1817, for example, the plantation slaves of Charlotte Parish were divided between 46 owners, almost half of whom owned fewer than 50 slaves each, accounting for 5.8 percent of the slaves.[2] But only 1.6 percent of the slaves in fact worked on units of less than 50 slaves. At the other end of the scale, some large planters lumped together separate plantation units, creating holdings significantly larger than those on which the slaves in fact worked. In Charlotte Parish this inflated the number of slaves attributed to units of more than 500 slaves. Thus, in reality, 89.3 percent of the slaves in Charlotte Parish worked on plantations of 101–500 slaves, compared to the 68.4 percent indicated by the registration returns. In general, then, the registration returns tend to weight the data toward the extremes of slave holding size. This distortion was greater for the distribution of slaves than for the

Table 5.1. *Distribution of Slaves and Owners by Slaveholding Size and Colony, c.1832*

Colony	Percentage of Slaves				Percentage of Owners				Mean Slaves per Holding
	0–10 Slaves	11–20 Slaves	21–30 Slaves	31+ Slaves	0–10 Slaves	11–20 Slaves	21–30 Slaves	31+ Slaves	
Old sugar colonies									
Barbados	17.4	10.4	5.4	66.8	69.8	10.1	3.0	17.1	14.0
St. Kitts	10.3	3.4	0.9	85.4	71.4	4.8	1.0	22.8	20.7
Nevis	8.7	4.5	1.1	85.7	59.2	8.7	1.2	30.9	27.5
Antigua	8.1	3.5	0.9	87.5	77.2	6.9	1.0	14.9	28.8
Montserrat	9.7	4.5	0.8	85.0	71.3	7.7	0.8	20.2	24.3
Virgin Islands	14.7	9.1	4.4	71.8	54.1	8.8	2.6	34.5	14.0
Total	13.7	7.5	3.5	75.3	69.8	9.0	2.4	18.8	17.2
Jamaica	8.7	6.3	3.8	81.2	69.1	11.2	3.9	15.8	25.1
New sugar colonies									
Dominica	14.8	6.9	5.7	72.6	59.2	6.0	3.0	31.8	13.2
St. Lucia	17.4	10.9	4.0	67.7	75.8	12.2	2.5	9.5	15.9
St. Vincent	7.6	3.9	1.7	86.8	58.0	7.2	1.9	32.9	26.4
Grenada	10.8	2.7	1.3	85.2	74.5	4.1	1.1	20.3	21.8
Tobago	5.7	2.3	1.1	90.9	69.4	5.1	1.6	23.9	32.2
Trinidad	22.5	9.5	6.0	62.0	77.6	6.9	2.4	13.1	10.2

Demerara-Essequibo	8.3	3.8	1.9	86.0	74.9	8.1	2.3	14.7	30.5
Berbice	6.9	2.7	2.0	88.4	53.5	5.3	2.3	38.9	28.1
Total	11.0	4.9	2.7	81.4	70.4	7.0	2.2	20.4	20.7
Marginal colonies									
British Honduras	41.5	12.9	8.3	37.3	89.2	5.2	2.0	3.6	6.3
Cayman Islands	37.5	23.3	15.5	23.7	75.9	13.8	5.2	5.1	8.5
Bahamas	31.0	19.9	10.7	38.4	73.5	10.1	3.6	12.8	8.4
Anguilla	25.8	20.8	10.2	43.2	73.8	15.2	4.8	6.2	12.0
Total	32.6	18.9	10.5	38.0	76.4	10.1	3.6	9.9	8.5
TOTAL	10.9	6.4	4.3	78.4	70.1	9.3	3.0	17.6	20.9
Numbers	74,176	43,038	29,064	531,442	22,747	3,027	972	5,725	

Sources: T.71/683, bundle 16, "Classified Statement . . ."; T.71/254 (British Honduras); T.71/261 (Anguilla).
Note: Barbuda is included with Antigua.

distribution of owners, and applied to the rural areas rather than the towns where the great majority of small units were located.

With these limitations in mind, it is possible to obtain a fairly clear picture of the distribution of slaveholding size. In the British Caribbean as a whole, at about 1832, 70.1 percent of the "owners" (returns) held 10 slaves or fewer, but only 10.9 percent of the slaves belonged to such units (table 5.1). Only 17.6 percent of the units comprised more than 30 slaves, but these accounted for 78.4 percent of the slaves. There were significant differences between the classes of colonies. In the marginal colonies, excepting Barbuda, only 38.0 percent of the slaves were in units of more than 30 slaves, and only 9.9 percent of the owners held such units. The new sugar colonies and Jamaica had a larger proportion of large holdings than the old sugar colonies, with the largest mean size occurring in Jamaica. The concentration of slaves into large holdings was greatest in Tobago, Demerara-Essequibo, Berbice, and Antigua, and least in Trinidad, Barbados, and the marginal colonies. Although the correlation between slaveholding size and the concentration of slaves in sugar was not perfect, it increased in strength after 1807 to reach a peak about 1830 (at the colony level, $r = .71; p = .00$).

A more detailed picture of the pattern of slaveownership has been calculated from the registration returns for a sample of colonies, comparing the years 1817 and 1834 (table 5.2). It has already been established that only in the marginal colonies did more than 50 percent of the slaves belong to holdings of 1–20 slaves around 1834, but it is now also apparent that very few lived in units of more than 100. Barbuda, with a population of 500, was of course exceptional. Of the sugar colonies it seems that only in Dominica, Trinidad, and St. Lucia did less than 50 percent of the slaves live in units of 100 or more by 1834. St. Kitts, Antigua, St. Vincent, Grenada, Tobago, and, probably, Berbice all had more than 70 percent of their slaves living on plantations of this size. In terms of really large holdings, those of more than 200 slaves, the new sugar colonies and Jamaica were most important. But about one-third of the slaves in Antigua, the Virgin Islands, Jamaica, St. Vincent, and Tobago belonged to such units. Once again, it is clear that the correlation with sugar was far from perfect (in 1830, for holdings of more than 200 slaves, $r = .78; p = .00$). Certainly Dominica, St. Lucia, and Trinidad had relatively diversified economies, but so did Jamaica and the Virgin Islands.

Although the pattern of slaveholding was complex, failing to match directly the distribution of the slaves between types of economic activity, there were distinct differences between the major crops in average slaveholding size. Data are available for only a few colonies, but it is clear that sugar was always produced on the largest holdings, followed by cotton, coffee, livestock, cocoa, and provisions (table 5.3). Differences between the colonies were considerable, with the average sugar plantation in Demerara-Essequibo and Jamaica being twice as large as that in St. Lucia or Dominica and four times as large as in Trinidad. The average Jamaican coffee plantation had twice as many slaves as a Trinidad sugar estate and almost twenty times as many as Trinidad coffee plantation. Only four sugar estates in Trinidad matched the Jamaican average by exceeding 200 slaves. These

Table 5.2. *Distribution of Slaves by Slaveholding Size-group: Sixteen Colonies, c.1817 and c.1834*

	Percentage of Slaves					
Colony	1–10 Slaves	11–50 Slaves	51–100 Slaves	101–200 Slaves	201–300 Slaves	301+ Slaves
1817						
Barbados (1817)	19.0	25.0	11.6	28.6	13.9	1.9
St. Kitts (1817)	12.7	7.6	9.6	41.8	14.2	14.1
Nevis (1817)	8.1	8.9	12.4	48.7	21.9	—
Virgin Islands (1818)	9.6	14.3	15.1	31.6	2.9	26.5
St. Lucia (1815)	17.5	32.6	23.2	17.6	7.0	2.1
St. Vincent (1817)	8.8	9.2	7.6	30.3	20.6	23.5
Tobago (1819)	5.7	5.7	6.9	42.0	19.4	20.3
Trinidad (1813)	26.1	34.4	24.5	11.4	3.6	—
Berbice (1819)	6.1	7.9	14.3	41.4	16.3	14.0
1834						
Barbados (1834)	19.0	22.5	10.3	28.8	15.9	3.5
St. Kitts (1834)	11.0	7.0	13.2	46.0	19.4	3.4
Nevis (1834)	8.0	12.6	12.4	47.7	19.3	—
Antigua (1832)	9.1	8.6	5.5	40.6	24.1	12.1
Montserrat (1831)	9.6	8.7	13.7	41.6	20.5	5.9
Virgin Islands (1831)	15.5	15.0	17.9	17.6	15.0	19.0
Jamaica (1832)	8.7	15.8	14.0	25.6	21.5	14.4
Dominica (1832)	14.9	23.3	24.2	27.5	10.1	—
St. Vincent (1834)	8.7	10.2	11.0	32.7	25.9	11.5
Grenada (1834)	10.4	8.9	8.5	45.5	20.9	5.8
Tobago (1834)	5.7	6.2	16.3	39.2	26.1	6.5
British Honduras (1834)	47.5	26.0	14.2	—	12.3	—
Cayman Islands (1834)	37.8	62.2	—	—	—	—
Anguilla (1827)	25.8	36.5	16.9	9.3	11.5	—

Source: T.71.

examples are sufficient to show that the distribution of slaveholding size could not be predicted directly from the pattern of land and labor use, since the scale of enterprise differed so considerably between colonies, even where the same crops were produced. But it is certain that the growing dominance of sugar was associated with an increasing concentration of the slaves in large units, in which the ratio of slaves to whites was always high and the size of the plantation population provided the basis for the development of an extensive social network within the slave community.

Change in the pattern of slaveowning between 1807 and 1834 had the overall effect of increasing the proportion of slaves attached to units of 101–300 slaves and reducing the proportion in the smallest and largest holdings. No data have been found for the period between 1807 and the beginnings of registration, and

Table 5.3. *Slaves per Holding by Crop, in Five Colonies*

	Mean Slaves per Holding				
Crop	Demerara-Essequibo, 1832	Jamaica, 1832	St. Lucia, 1815	Dominica, 1827	Trinidad, 1813
Sugar	233	223	121	112	56
Coffee	87	128	33	30	7
Cotton	149	—	23	—	12
Cocoa	—	—	24	—	12
Provisions	—	—	12	—	9
Livestock	28	99	—	—	—

Sources: PP., 1833, vol. 26 (700), pp.4–11 (Demerara-Essequibo); B. W. Higman, *Slave Population and Economy in Jamaica, 1807–1834* (1976), p. 13; T.71/378–79 (St. Lucia); *Dominica Almanac 1828*, "Returns of Produce"; T.71/501–2 (Trinidad).

comparative data have been extracted for only six colonies (table 5.2). But the general tendencies noted above were common to these colonies, with the exception of the Virgn Islands. In St. Kitts, for example, the proportion of the slave population held in units of 1–50 slaves fell by 2.3 percent between 1817 and 1834, and in units of more than 300 slaves by 10.7 percent, while the proportion in units of 51–300 slaves increased substantially. In Jamaica growth was most significant in groups of 51–200 slaves.[3] A similar trend occurred in St. Vincent and Tobago, except that an increase also took place in units of 11–50 slaves, and in Nevis this was the one group to show growth. Only the Virgin Islands showed relative growth in units of 1–10 slaves, but there was also growth in holdings of 11–100 and 201–300, balanced by decline in units of 101–200 and over 300 slaves. Barbados was unique in experiencing growth in units of more than 300 slaves, and decline was confined to units of 11–100, but the amount of change was relatively minor.

These changes in the distribution of the slave population by slaveholding size resulted chiefly from the movement of slaves out of the towns, the decline of cotton and coffee cultivation, the movement of slaves to the new sugar colonies, and the low levels of natural increase experienced on large sugar plantations. The movement out of the towns had a dramatic impact on the numbers of holdings of less than 10 slaves, while the growth of sugar at the expense of other staple crops drew slaves from units of less than 100. Movement of slaves to the new sugar colonies involved large holdings in its first phase and small units in the later "domestics" phase. In most of the sugar colonies, decline in the largest holdings was associated with high mortality and low fertility, so that these units merely shrank, the owners being unable or unwilling to purchase sufficient slaves to restore their numbers. In Barbados, however, the unusually high rate of natural increase meant that plantation populations expanded into the higher size groups (tables S2.9 and S2.10).

Variations in the size of slaveholdings were associated with differences in the sex, color, and nationality of the owners. White men of British origin were the major owners of slaves in the British Caribbean. But there were areas in which women, freedmen, and other nationalities were relatively important, and came to have a significant role in shaping the slave experience. Sex, color, and nationality were correlated with wealth, of course, and hence with types of economic enterprise and environments.

Women rarely possessed large slaveholdings, but they did own a substantial share of the smaller units and hence a significant proportion of the total slave population. Around 1815 females owned 25.1 percent of the slaves in St. Lucia, 22.2 percent in Trinidad, and 6.6 percent in Berbice (table S2.6). These were slaves possessed by females in their own right; but females also held slaves jointly with males. Few owned large plantations, however, and those who did were often widows, their estates being managed by male attornies and overseers. In St. Lucia females owned 13.1 percent of the slaves belonging to units of more than 50 slaves, in Trinidad 6.8 percent, and in Berbice a mere 1.8 percent. In the parishes of St. Michael, St. Andrew, and St. John, Barbados, in 1817 only two of the 74 holdings of more than 50 slaves were owned by females (table S2.9). The extent of female ownership of units of 10 slaves or less, however, rivaled that of males. Since in 1832 such holdings accounted for more than 70 percent of British West Indian slaveowners, females inevitably made up a substantial proportion of the slaveowning class, though possessing a much smaller proportion of the slave population. In St. Lucia 49.9 percent of the owners of 1–10 slaves were females, and in Trinidad 45.8 percent. In Barbados, 53.8 percent of the owners of such units were females in the urban parish of St. Michael, and even in the rural parishes of St. Andrew and St. John they accounted for 39.3 percent.

The small scale of female slaveownership was associated with a heavy concentration in the towns, where more than half of the slave population belonged to units of 1–10 slaves (table S2.9). In Bridgetown, for example, 57.0 percent of the slaveowners were female in 1817, and they owned 53.6 percent of the slaves in the town. Females owned few units of more than 20 slaves, but their dominance in the small units was sufficient to outweigh the males overall. In Scarborough, Tobago, 55.0 percent of the slaveowners were females in 1819, but women owned no units of more than 50 slaves.

Slaveowning freedmen were even more heavily concentrated in the towns. They rarely possessed holdings of more than 10 slaves but, unlike the white population, females owned more slaves than males. It is impossible to establish precisely the number of slaves owned by freedmen, because the registration returns obviously fail to identify all such owners. In the case of Trinidad, where freedmen were a highly visible and wealthy component of the population, the registration returns for 1813 identified only a handful of "free colored" and "free black" owners, possessing a total of but 39 slaves. Using additional sources, Carl Campbell has found at least 38 free colored planters in North and South Naparima, owning 862 slaves or 30.1 percent of the slave population of those quarters in

1813.[4] The Naparimas contained some of the largest sugar estates in Trinidad, and in 1813 freedmen owned two of the three holdings of more than 100 slaves, as well as a large proportion of the smaller coffee and provisions plantations. This pattern was repeated, with variations, throughout rural Trinidad, and the extremely large slave population of Port of Spain suggests that freedman slaveowning must have been extensive there.

The registration returns identify only 77 freedman slaveowners for St. Lucia in 1815, 25 for Berbice in 1819, and 13 for Tobago in the same year. All of these numbers appear much too small, but it is difficult to tell whether the omission of identifications followed any systematic pattern. In the case of St. Lucia an additional 22 owners can be identified from other sources,[5] increasing the total number of slaves held by freedmen to 483 in 1815. But John Jeremie, an antislavery writer who had served as President of the Royal Court of St. Lucia, claimed that around 1830 freedmen owned 2,350 slaves on the island.[6] It is probable that freedmen increased their share of the slave population between 1815 and 1830, but a leap from 3 to 17 percent seems unlikely. Jeremie believed that 1,202 of the slaves belonging to freedmen around 1830 were "plantation" slaves and 1,148 "personal" slaves, suggesting that freedmen held almost half of the personal slaves. Two or three freedmen were sugar planters, according to Jeremie, while a large number were coffee, cocoa, and provisions planters, each owning 10–40 slaves. There were two "first-rate" merchants, and many second-rate merchants and retail dealers, who monopolized the dry-goods trade and had one-third of St. Lucia's trade in their hands. Few freedmen of such status can be identified directly from the registration returns, however.

Although the data are not complete, the registration returns for Barbados do appear more consistent in their identification of freedman slaveowners. In part this may result from the fact that Barbados was the only sugar colony in which freedmen were much less numerous than whites (table S2.1). Even in Barbados identifications were somewhat erratic, not being repeated in every triennial return. In spite of the relatively small size of the freedman population in Barbados, and the limited extent of its landownership, some 650 slaveowners were identified as freedmen in 1817 (table S2.8). They owned 2,553 slaves, or only 3.3 percent of the total, but they were 12.1 percent of the owners. It is impossible to determine precisely what proportion of the freedmen owned slaves, since the official population returns provided conflicting estimates of the total freedman population.[7] But no more than 20 percent of freedmen were slaveowners. Contemporary white commentators tended to overstate the extent of freedmen slave-ownership to improbable proportions. Jerome Handler, in his major study of freedmen in Barbados, could conclude only that "there may have been a few hundred freedman slaveowners by the beginning of the nineteenth century . . . and by emancipation the number may have approached 2,000."[8] Thus, the registration returns provide a much firmer foundation than any other source. It can be assumed that the number of 650 freedman slaveowners in 1817 is a lower-limit estimate, since all owners not identified as freedmen have been regarded as whites, and it is improbable that whites were incorrectly identified as freedmen. As a comparative benchmark, it is reasonable to believe that freedman slaveowning was near to its minimum in Barbados and that in the sugar colonies of the British Caribbean the proportion was generally larger.

The pattern of freedman slaveowning in Barbados, as revealed by the registration data for 1817, is of considerable interest. As noted above, few freedmen owned land in Barbados, and 80.9 percent of those who owned slaves lived in Bridgetown. A further 5.5 percent were in rural St. Michael (table S2.8). Freedmen owned 21.2 percent of the slaves in Bridgetown and were 28.8 percent of the slaveowners in the town. What is perhaps more surprising is the fact that although the sex ratio of the freedman population was fairly evenly balanced, females held 74.2 percent of the slaves. Male slaveowners showed a somewhat greater rural concentration than females but did not approach the white pattern of overwhelming rural dominance. Within the freedman population, there was a strong contrast between the "free mulatto" and "free negro" groups. The mulatto group was only slightly more numerous, but it possessed greater wealth, much of it inherited from white ancestors, and owned almost four times as many slaves as the free blacks. Females dominated in each group, however, and there was relatively little difference in their spatial distribution. In Bridgetown there was little difference in the pattern of slaveownership for white and mulatto females, so that the free mulatto woman was a prominent figure among the town's slaveowners.

The pattern of freedman slaveowning in Barbados was probably typical of the old sugar colonies, but in the Windward Islands, Trinidad, and Jamaica it seems certain that they owned a larger proportion of the slave population and more often employed their slaves in agricultural work. In St. Lucia, for example, only half of the identified freedman slaveowners lived in the towns, but few owned more than 20 slaves and the "femme de couleur" dominated as in Barbados. Very similar patterns occurred in Berbice and Tobago. Only two free colored male slaveowners were identified in Berbice, and in Tobago none. In Berbice one female slaveowner was identified as "Indian." Information on the freedman slaveowners of Dominica is limited, but they are said to have held 22 percent of the slave population in 1820 and to make 30 percent of the sugar and 19 percent of the coffee produced in the island.[9] But outside of Trinidad and some of the Windward Islands, the free colored planter was very much the odd man out.

In the old sugar colonies, Jamaica, and the marginal colonies, most slaveowners were British. But in the new sugar colonies a large proportion of owners were French, Dutch, Spanish, or creoles surviving from earlier phases of imperial control. They can be identified in the registration returns by their names. In St. Lucia 92.0 percent of slaveowners had French surnames in 1815. There was little difference in this proportion between whites and freedmen or males and females, but English men did own the four plantations with more than 200 slaves, and 63.0 percent of the slaves belonging to the English were employed in sugar cultivation, compared to only 36.7 percent of those held by the French. In Berbice in 1819 34.9 percent of owners had Dutch surnames and 3.2 percent French, with the Dutch

Table 5.4. *Percentage of Slaveowners Unable to Sign Their Registration Returns by Sex and Slaveholding Size: Virgin Islands, St. Lucia, Tobago, and Berbice, 1815–19*

| | Male Slaveowners | | | | Female Slaveowners | | | | |
Colony	1–10 Slaves	11–50 Slaves	51 + Slaves	Total	1–10 Slaves	11–50 Slaves	51 + Slaves	Total	T
Virgin Islands, 1818	19.0	8.8	0.0	13.3	34.2	37.5	100.0	35.5	2
St. Lucia, 1815	24.1	1.5	0.0	14.9	46.1	10.3	0.0	39.1	2
Tobago, 1819	0.8	3.7	0.0	0.9	60.8	25.0	—	56.6	2
Berbice, 1819	1.5	0.0	0.0	0.8	48.4	27.3	—	45.4	1

Sources: T.71/370, 378–79, 461–62, 438–39.

retaining a more tenacious hold on the larger plantations in the declining colony than the French in St. Lucia. In Trinidad, an official report of 1810 showed that the English owned fewer sugar estates than the French but more slaves, while the French clearly dominated in coffee and the Spanish in cocoa.[10]

The registration returns provide little systematic information about the slaveowners beyond their sex, color, and nationality, and even these data can often be established only by inference. But the owners were required to swear to the truthfulness of their returns by signing their names or making their marks, and where this information was copied exactly in the registers it provides interesting data on literacy in the slaveowning population. Obviously the ability to sign is only a limited index of functional literacy, but it can be quantified and so has the advantage of comparability. In the British Caribbean, slaveowners were the most wealthy and hence the best-educated members of the free population. In the colonies of the Virgin Islands, St. Lucia, Tobago, and Berbice around 1817 the proportion of owners unable to sign their registration returns ranged from 14.7 percent in Berbice to 26.2 percent in St. Lucia (table 5.4). But there were significant differences in the ability to sign in terms of the sex, color, and wealth of the owners. The percentage of males unable to sign varied from a low 0.8 percent in Berbice to 14.9 percent in St. Lucia. For females the range was from 35.5 percent in the Virgin Islands to a high 56.6 percent in Tobago. This strong contrast reflected differences in the education of free males and females, but it also indicated differences in wealth. Virtually all owners holding more than 50 slaves were able to sign their returns. The rate of literacy fell rapidly as slaveholding size decreased. Females were always less literate than males, regardless of the number of slaves they possessed. In Tobago, at one extreme, 60.8 percent of the females owning 1–10 slaves were unable to sign their names, compared to a mere 0.8 percent among the men. Since female slaveownership was concentrated in the smaller units, the contrast with males was further accentuated. The low literacy rate of freedman slaveowners was the product of a similar lack of access to education and wealth. In St. Lucia 50.5 percent of the identified freedmen were unable to sign their returns, in the Virgin Islands 81.8 percent, and in Berbice 92.0 percent. Unlike white slaveowners, however, free females of color were able to sign almost as often as their male counterparts, since they were frequently more wealthy.

West Indian society in the period of slavery has generally been portrayed as lacking in education and intellectual life.[11] This is a fair assessment in terms of formal schooling, since the slaves, the vast majority of the population, were almost entirely illiterate and the freedmen, many of them recently released from slavery, showed very high rates of illiteracy even among the relatively wealthy. But by the early nineteenth century, when West Indian whites rarely performed manual labor and their numbers had been drastically reduced by emigration, the whites showed low levels of illiteracy when compared with European societies. In England and Wales 33 percent of males and 50 percent of females were unable to sign their names at marriage as late as 1839, but the level of illiteracy was only 12 percent for males in Scotland around 1800 and as high as 46 percent for males in France.[12] These statistics are not directly comparable with those obtained from slave registration, of course. But in St. Lucia, to take the colony with the highest proportion of owners unable to sign (and the largest proportion of Francophones), only 13.1 percent of white males and 37.3 percent of females could not sign their returns; and making the extreme assumptions that all literate whites were slaveowners and all whites were of marriageable age, the proportion unable to sign reaches only 50 percent for the entire white population of St. Lucia. Thus, by the early nineteenth century at least, the white populations of most colonies of the West Indies were relatively literate, even if lacking an intellectual focus. More important, the dominance of white males in slaveownership meant that most slaves belonged to literate masters. In St. Lucia, for example, although 26.2 percent of the slaveowners could not sign in 1815, only 6.4 percent of the slaves on the island belonged to such illiterates. This pattern contributed further to psychosocial differences in the character of slaveholding. The planter owning large numbers of slaves was distant in space, education, and authority, his power often mediated by other white men. At the other extreme, the poor urban female slaveowner was spatially close and little better educated than her slaves.

Although few exact data are available, it is certain that slaveowners of British origin increased their share of the slave population between 1807 and 1834, particularly in the large holdings of the expanding sugar sector. Rapid growth in the freedman population was similarly associated with increasing slaveownership, though many freedmen remained poor throughout the period.[13] Change in the proportion of female owners was probably slight, though the growth of freedman slaveownership augmented their number in some colonies.

The nationality, sex, and color of slaveowners have often been linked with differences in their treatment of slaves. In the British Caribbean the remnant effects of any relevant aspects of ''national character'' seem unlikely to have been of great significance, since there were few apparent differences between the owners in terms of slaveholding size, spatial distribution, or types of economic enterprise. It has sometimes been argued that freedmen were the most vicious masters and that slaves felt "humiliated" to be the slaves of ex-slaves and their descendants. Similarly, it has been argued that white women, as an oppressed group and facing competition for their husbands' attentions, were more brutal than white men in their treatment of slaves.[14] There is no doubt that freedmen tended to identify culturally with the whites and that they were committed to slaveowning as the only route to wealth in a slave society. But their slaves were rarely employed on sugar estates and most often worked in urban occupations generally regarded as relatively light work. Some of the slaves belonging to freedmen were kin, purchased with the intention of ultimate manumission. A distinction may also need to be made between free colored and free black slaveowners, the latter less conspicuously oriented to white culture. Thus, the significance of the slave-owner's sex and color remains uncertain.

The personal characteristics of slaveowners were important in determining the nature of the slave experience only if the owners were directly responsible for the management and control of their slaves. It had always been the ultimate aim of the British sugar planter to return home once he had amassed his fortune and to put his estates in the hands of attorneys and overseers. Many achieved this goal, though it often took several generations. By the beginning of the nineteenth century a very significant proportion of the slave population was owned by absentee proprietors, who rarely had any form of direct contact with their slaves. This process was furthest advanced in the old sugar colonies. Barbados was exceptional in retaining a rooted residential plantocracy, a result of the moderate scale of its sugar estates and the large white population of the island.[15] The owners of small slaveholdings had little expectation of becoming absentees, so relatively few absentees owned slaves in the new sugar colonies or the marginal colonies. But extremely large units were everywhere managed most commonly by overseers, creating a distancing in the master-slave relationship. This distancing proceeded steadily in the period after 1807, as the declining profitability of sugar forced many planters to surrender their estates to merchant creditors and corporate ownership.

By 1832 more than half the slaves of Jamaica belonged to absentees, most of them on large plantations.[16] In 1819, some 53 of Tobago's 81 plantations were in the hands of attorneys or managers and another five managed by trustees or executors, the owners almost all being absentees.[17] The extent of absenteeism in the other colonies is difficult to establish, since the registration returns are not very helpful on this point, but it was probably most common in Demerara-Essequibo and the Leeward Islands.[18] The significance of absenteeism for the efficiency of the plantation economy and the colonial political system has been the subject of some controversy.[19] In the period 1807–34 it is apparent that absentee merchant-planters were the most willing to invest in technological change, particularly in Demerara-Essequibo where sugar planting was most profitable. Thus, there was a tendency for resident proprietorship to be associated with relatively antiquated technology and smaller plantation units, which were functions of the slaveowner's relative lack of wealth rather than characteristics such as sex, color, or nationality.

The significance of absenteeism varied with differences in the broader economic context in which the slaves existed.

The ownership of slaves changed frequently. Any one slave was likely to belong to a number of owners over his life span, though the significance of these changes varied greatly. In the case of slaves living on large plantations belonging to absentees, transfer of ownership rarely meant removal to a new location or disruption of the slave community, and the group of supervisory whites on the plantation with whom the slaves had direct contact often remained unchanged. At the other extreme, slaves belonging to the owners of small slaveholdings might experience changes in the whole range of personal characteristics of their owners, in addition to changes in location and employment.

The Commissioners of Compensation appointed in 1834 based their valuations on an examination of the transfers of 74,000 slaves in the British Caribbean between 1823 and 1830.[20] On the average, then, 1.3 percent of the slaves were sold each year. But this must be regarded as a lower-limit estimate of the number of slaves transferred in the period, since the commissioners excluded all judicial sales and were not at all concerned with slaves transferred by means other than sale. Data available in the registration returns, however, cover all types of transfer and show a much higher rate of change in ownership. Table 5.5 presents data from eight colonies, indicating an average annual transfer of about 3 percent. The highest rate seems to have occurred in the Virgin Islands and the lowest in St. Lucia, suggesting that ownership change was related to the economic health of the colonies.

In general, transfers of ownership were twice as frequent in towns as in rural areas. Slaves living in capital towns could expect to be transferred to new owners once every 10 to 15 years. A similar rate applied in secondary towns. No doubt this high turnover in the towns reflected absolute decline in the urban slave populations and movement to the agricultural sector after 1807, but much of it was strictly internal to the towns. The relative poverty of many urban slaveowners meant that they often made speculative purchases of slaves and often were forced to sell in order to cover debts. Again, many were footloose, and this transience, as well as the very high rates of white mortality within the towns, resulted in frequent transfers. In the case of Bridgetown, the Commissioners of Compensation explained that causes of relatively low slave prices in the town "are to be found in the greater circulation of money in Bridge Town—the frequent changes, which amongst persons only temporarily resident necessarily take place, and from the mass of the slaves there sold being all of one description, namely non-praedial—a description of slave never looked upon as equally valuable with an agricultural slave, and of which there is a very redundant supply in this town."[21] The commissioners also noted that most of those sold in Bridgetown were in small lots of one, two, or three slaves, often including children. This observation is confirmed by the evidence of the registration returns.

The rate of transfer decreased steadily as slaveholding size increased. In St. Lucia, for example, 3.4 percent of those belonging to units of 1–10 slaves were

Table 5.5. *Percentage of Slaves Transferred to New Owners by Sex: Select Colonies, 1815–34*

Colony	Percentage of Slaves Transferred per Annum		
	Males	Females	Total
Barbados, 1817–20			
Bridgetown	4.1	3.2	3.6
Rural St. Michael	4.3	4.1	4.2
St. Andrew	1.2	1.2	1.2
St. John	2.6	2.5	2.5
Barbados, 1832–34	4.6	4.5	4.5
Bridgetown	7.9	7.7	7.8
St. Kitts, 1831–34	5.3	5.1	5.2
Basseterre	6.0	4.8	5.4
Antigua, 1828–32	2.3	2.1	2.2
Montserrat, 1828–31	2.5	2.5	2.5
Virgin Islands, 1828–31	8.8	8.1	8.4
Dominica, 1829–32	4.0	3.8	3.9
Roseau	8.2	7.7	8.0
St. Lucia, 1815–19	1.7	1.8	1.8
Castries	6.4	6.3	6.3
Grenada, 1823–33	2.1	2.2	2.2
Town of St. George	8.3	8.0	8.2

Source: T.71.

transferred each year, in comparison to only 0.4 percent of those in units of more than 200 slaves (table 5.6). This meant that a relatively high proportion of "personal" slaves were transferred, but very few of those attached to sugar plantations were. Slaveowners who were not also landowners were much more likely to sell their slaves. Masters holding a few slaves seem to have been involved in transfers more often than mistresses, but there were no significant differences between whites and freedmen.

It is possible to identify some general tendencies in the pattern of slaveowning. There was a very strong contrast between rural and urban patterns. Most rural slaves belonged to white men, generally British and generally absentee, and lived in relatively stable communities of 100 and over. Urban slaves, however, belonged to small, fluid units, most of the owners being women and many of them

Table 5.6. *Slaves Transferred by Sex, Slaveholding Size-group, and Crop: St. Lucia, 1815–19*

Slaves per Holding	Percentage of Slaves Transferred		Crop	Percentage of Slaves Transferred	
	Males	Females		Males	Females
1–10	12.8	9.3	Sugar	1.4	1.9
11–50	7.3	8.8	Cocoa	4.3	9.0
51–100	2.7	3.5	Coffee	6.3	7.8
101–200	1.2	1.6	Cotton	9.6	12.4
201–300	1.4	1.8	Provisions	4.1	2.0
301–400	0.5	0.7	Personal	14.8	12.5
Total	5.4	5.8	Total	5.4	5.8

Source: T.71/378–79.

freedmen. The decline of the urban populations, together with negative natural increase on the larger plantations, resulted in a general concentration into holdings of about 50–200 slaves. But in some colonies, chiefly those described as marginal, the slaves typically lived in units of less than 10, and very few belonged to holdings of more than 50 slaves. In some of the relatively diversified new sugar colonies there was a concentration in units of less than 100 slaves. Few of the sugar estates were really large, although they sometimes dominated isolated regions.[22] In Jamaica, very large holdings, medium-sized plantations, and small units were intermixed in most regions of the island. The unusual size of the white population of Barbados resulted in a similar range of variations, but holdings of 101–200 slaves dominated in the old sugar colonies of the Leeward Islands.

The number of slaves possessed by a free person was determined chiefly by the individual's wealth. It depended on the rate of natural growth or decline in the slave population, but a slaveowner could always alter the extent of his holding through selective sale and purchase, within the constraints imposed by prevailing prices in the market for slaves. Slaveowners also had definite preferences regarding the characteristics of their slaves, particularly in terms of sex, age, color, and birthplace. These preferences were determined partly by the type of work a slaveowner wanted performed and partly by ideas and prejudices based upon notions about biology. In consequence, there were significant differences between the types of slaveholdings in terms of their internal demographic structure as well as in their absolute numbers.

MALES AND FEMALES

British West Indian planters showed a clear preference for males as agricultural laborers, and this was reflected in the prices paid for slaves. In response to this demand, and also in response to supply conditions within Africa, the Atlantic slave trade brought considerably more males than females to the New World. In the last decades of the trade to the British Caribbean, slave cargoes had sex ratios varying between 150 and 180 males per 100 females.[23] Thus, the sex ratios of the slave populations differed according to the proportions of Africans they contained, and these differences in turn were determined chiefly by variations in stage of settlement. Abolition of the slave trade resulted in a gradual removal of the imbalance in the sex ratios, but the significance of this tendency varied according to the colonies' differential dependence on the slave trade in the period 1780–1807.

By 1817, when the first reliable data became available through the registration system, the slave sex ratio for the British Caribbean as a whole was in fact quite evenly balanced at about 101 males per 100 females (table 5.7). At the time of emancipation the sex ratio stood at 95, so it is clear that between 1807 and 1834

Table 5.7. *Slave Sex Ratios and Percentages African and Colored by Colony, c.1817 and c.1832*

Colony	Males per 100 Females		Percentage African		Percentage Colored	
	1817	1832	1817	1832	1817	1832
Barbados	83.9	86.3	7.1	2.9	14.9	14.0
St. Kitts	92.4	91.9[10]	16.1	n.c.	10.3	n.c.
Nevis	95.3	98.1[10]	14.5	n.a.	14.0	n.a.
Antigua	87.4	90.0[10]	n.a.	n.a.	n.c.	10.3
Montserrat	85.5	89.1[10]	n.a.	n.a.	n.c.	12.5[10]
Virgin Islands	88.1[4]	87.3[10]	14.9[4]	n.c.	6.6[4]	n.c.
Jamaica	100.3	94.5	37.0	23.5	n.c.	n.a.
Dominica	92.4	92.7	n.c.	15.3	n.c.	n.a.
St. Lucia	82.8[5]	84.6[10]	21.4[2]	n.a.	12.9[2]	n.a.
St. Vincent	102.1	95.2[10]	38.8	n.a.	4.4	n.a.
Grenada	96.1	93.7	32.5	15.8[9]	7.3	8.6[9]
Tobago	97.4[5]	86.4	38.9[5]	n.a.	3.3[5]	n.a.
Trinidad	123.9[3]	112.6[8]	54.4[1]	n.a.	6.0[1]	n.a.
Demerara-Essequibo	130.9	110.2	54.7	34.5	n.c.	2.9
Berbice	128.4	114.5[10]	53.9[5]	n.a.	2.2[5]	n.a.
British Honduras	n.a.	162.5[11]	n.a.	n.a.	n.a.	8.4[11]
Cayman Islands	n.a.	99.0[11]	n.a.	n.a.	n.a.	n.a.
Bahamas	104.7[6]	99.7[10]	21.1[6]	9.4[11]	n.c.	9.7[11]
Anguilla	n.a.	87.4[10]	n.a.	2.6[7]	n.a.	17.3[7]
Barbuda	n.c.	75.1	n.a.	n.a.	n.c.	37.0

Source: T.71.

Notes: [1]1813, [2]1815, [3]1816, [4]1818, [5]1819, [6]1822, [7]1827, [8]1828, [9]1829, [10]1831, [11]1834.

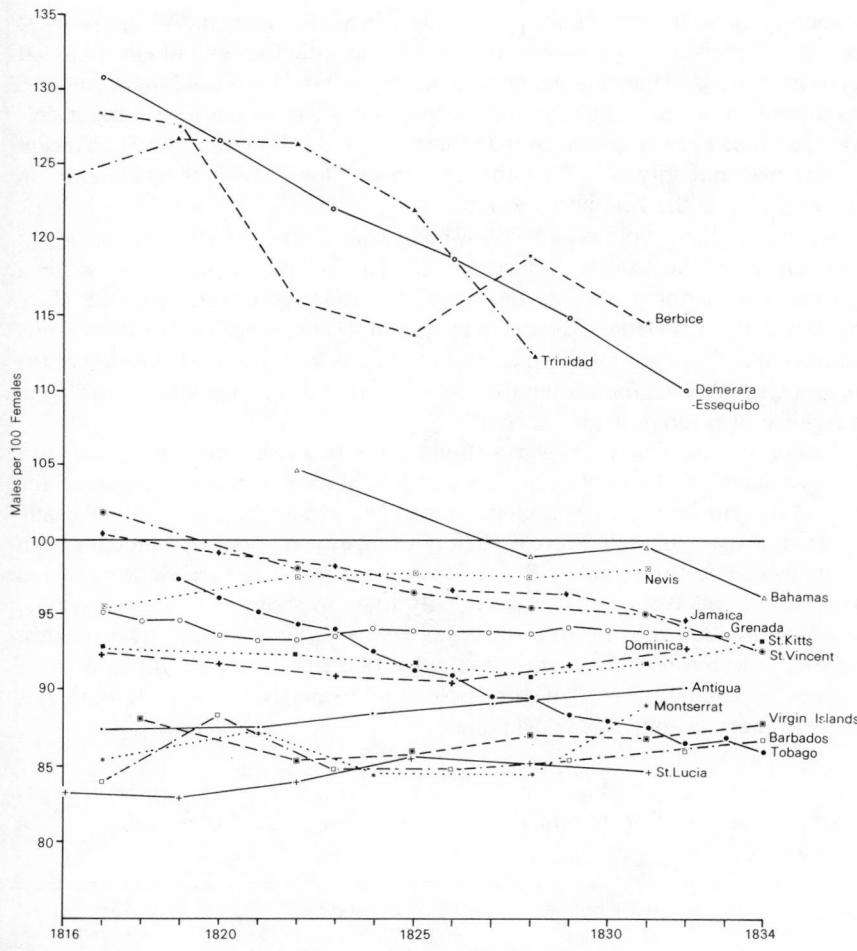

Fig. 5.1.   *Slave Sex Ratios, 1816–34. (Source: table S1.1.)*

there was a definite movement from male to female predominance. But there were
significant differences between the colonies (fig. 5.1). In the third-phase sugar
colonies of Trinidad, Demerara-Essequibo, and Berbice, where slaves were
imported at a high rate before and after abolition, males outnumbered females
throughout the period. More surprisingly, the same was true of the marginal
colonies. But the latter contained a large degree of individual variation, with
British Honduras showing by far the highest sex ratio of all the colonies and
Barbuda the lowest. In the first-phase sugar colonies, on the other hand, the sex
ratio actually increased between 1817 and 1834, though these settlements maintained a lower ratio than in any other group of colonies, with females out-

numbering males throughout the period. Only in St. Kitts and the Virgin Islands, which had relatively large proportions of Africans, did the sex ratio decrease. It can be hypothesized that this tendency to higher sex ratios in the old sugar colonies was a product of declining mortality differentials. The second-phase sugar colonies had much lower sex ratios than those of the third-phase, only St. Vincent having a male majority in 1817, with St. Lucia and Dominica showing increases in the same way as the first-phase group.

In general, then, abolition was followed by convergence toward a balanced sex ratio. Only in Jamaica, St. Vincent, and, particularly, Tobago was there a significant deviation from this tendency. By 1834, however, only the slave population of British Honduras approximated the sex ratio idealized by the masters and this, of course, was reflected in its peak slave prices. But the balancing of the sex ratio provided the foundation for a less distorted slave community and for the emergence of positive natural increase.

Within the colonies, there was a strong contrast between the rural and urban slave populations. The towns always had low slave sex ratios because of the demand for females in domestic employment. No town had a male majority at any registration date, though Port of Spain, Georgetown, New Amsterdam, and Kingstown came close (table 5.8). The lowest sex ratios occurred in Roseau and Bridgetown, and Bridgetown was the only town to show an increase over the period 1817–32, following the trend for Barbados as a whole. The greatest disparity between urban and rural sex ratios occurred in the third-phase sugar colonies. In Trinidad in 1813 the rural ratio was 130 and the urban 99. In Barbados the difference was only about 10 points.

Table 5.8. *Slave Sex Ratios and Percentages African and Colored: Major Towns*

Town	Males per 100 Females		Percentage African		Percentage Colored	
Kingston	81.4 (1817)	78.5 (1832)	42.1 (1817)			
Bridgetown	72.4 (1817)	73.0 (1832)	15.7 (1817)	6.2 (1832)	25.0 (1817)	24.3 (1832)
Port of Spain	99.5 (1813)	50.4 (1813)		10.3 (1813)		
Georgetown		95.7 (1832)				
St. Johns		84.7 (1832)				17.9 (1832)
Kingstown	98.7 (1817)		39.9 (1817)		4.4 (1817)	
St. George	86.1 (1817)	83.4 (1833)	42.3 (1817)	26.0 (1829)	13.0 (1817)	16.0 (1829)
Castries	92.9 (1815)		23.9 (1815)			
New Amsterdam	95.2 (1819)					
Basseterre		83.1 (1834)				
Roseau	79.5 (1817)	71.2 (1834)		13.0 (1832)		
Scarborough	89.7 (1819)		46.3 (1819)		4.3 (1819)	
Plymouth		78.2 (1831)				23.5 (1831)

Source: T.71.

Thus, the extensive female ownership of slaves in the towns was matched by the unusually high proportion of females in the slave population. Further, female slaveowners generally owned more female slaves than did male slaveowners. In Bridgetown in 1817, for example, the sex ratio of slaves belonging to males was more than double that for female slaveowners. Indeed, the male slaveowners actually held a majority of males. The sex ratio of slaves belonging to males was 111 and that for slaves belonging to females a mere 49. White male slaveowners showed the highest sex ratio among their slaves (113), but the ratios were also high for free mulattoes (90) and free Negroes (109). Among female slaveowners the ratios were 53 for whites, 40 for free mulattoes, and 41 for free Negroes.[24] In rural Barbados the contrasts were less strong than in Bridgetown, but the pattern was similar, the slaves of white men always showing the highest sex ratios. In Berbice in 1819 slaves owned by males had a sex ratio of 132, while those owned by females had a ratio of only 81. This association between female slaves and slaveowners can be attributed to the concentration of female owners in enterprises requiring large numbers of domestics.

It has already been established that males dominated in the ownership of large slaveholdings, while females generally held small units. This relationship explains, to some extent, the high sex ratios in urban slaveholdings belonging to males. In Bridgetown the sex ratio increased rapidly, along with slaveholding size, from less than 65 in units of 1–4 slaves to over 200 in units of more than 40 slaves. In Port of Spain the sex ratio increased similarly, from 75 in the smallest units to 245 in units of more than 20 slaves. Thus, in the towns, the free person of limited wealth was likely to purchase a female slave rather than a male. Females were cheaper, and their reproductive capacities provided possibilities of future profit, whereas the children of males became the property of others. Females could also play the immediate status-increasing role of domestic service. Males were concentrated in the largest urban slaveholdings because these units generally belonged to merchants, and they performed specialized tasks around the wharves and warehouses of the ports.

In rural areas the slave sex ratio exhibited a tendency to decrease after reaching a peak in units of about 50 slaves (table S2.11). The larger sugar plantations often had relatively low sex ratios, as a consequence of differential mortality.[25] But in some colonies, such as St. Kitts and Tobago, the largest holdings had higher sex ratios, probably a product of selective purchase. In the third-phase sugar colonies, where the expansion of sugar planting continued after 1807, sugar estates generally had the highest sex ratios. The ratio reached 140 on sugar estates in Trinidad in 1813, but was 144 on cocoa plantations. In St. Lucia the ratio was 98 on both sugar and coffee plantations in 1815 (table 5.9). Thus, the planter's demand for male slaves was not always matched in practice.

These urban and rural contrasts in the slave sex ratio were everywhere affected by the age structure of the populations. Where Africans were only a small proportion of the slave population, as in the old sugar colonies, the sex ratio declined quite steadily with increasing age (fig. 5.2). This decline must be

Table 5.9. *Demographic Characteristics by Crop-type: Trinidad and St. Lucia, 1813 and 1815*

Crop-type	Slaves per Holding		Males per 100 Females		Percentage Slaves African		Percentage Slaves Colored
	Trinidad	St. Lucia	Trinidad	St. Lucia	Trinidad	St. Lucia	St. Lucia
Sugar	56	121	140	88	58	24	12
Coffee	7	33	112	88	52	17	16
Cotton	12	23	120	61	47	13	19
Cocoa	12	24	144	83	57	13	17
Provisions	9	12	123	72	52	19	18

Sources: T.71/378–79, 501–3.

attributed to differential mortality, though the sex-selective movement to new colonies also played a part. The consequence was that in the old sugar colonies there were at least three women to every two men in all age groups above 50 years by about 1817. In Barbados this ratio was reached by age 40, and among slaves over 60 there were two women for every man (table S4.1). Within Barbados there was a strong contrast between the urban and rural populations. In Bridgetown the ratio of one male to two females was reached as early as age 40, suggesting a definite movement of adult males to the plantations (fig. 5.3).

Where Africans made up a substantial proportion of the slave population, as in the third-phase sugar colonies of Trinidad, Demerara-Essequibo, and Berbice, the sex ratio rose rapidly to reach a peak around 1817 of almost 200 males per 100 females at age 45. The ratio fell even more rapidly after this age, to be evenly balanced among the oldest slaves. But in these expanding colonies there was a much more spectacular contrast between the rural and urban populations than occurred in the old sugar colonies. In Trinidad, for example, the rural sex ratio remained high in all the adult age groups, but in Port of Spain the ratio fell away after age 15 to reach a minimum of 62 at age 55 (fig. 5.3). Thus, the urban slave populations of Trinidad and Barbados were much more similar, in terms of their sex composition, than the rural populations.

Around 1817 in Jamaica, the second-phase sugar colonies, and St. Lucia, the sex ratio was fairly evenly balanced until about age 40, but fell to 70 in the oldest age groups. The trend in the marginal colonies can be established only for the last years of slavery, and the variations within the group were extreme (table S4.1). Barbuda and Anguilla showed a steady decrease in the sex ratio with increasing age, but the Bahamas and the Cayman Islands had relatively high ratios in the age groups above 40 years. British Honduras had a male majority in every age group, and males outnumbered females by at least two to one in all age groups above 40 years. These high ratios suggest the existence of relatively large African contingents in British Honduras and the Cayman Islands.

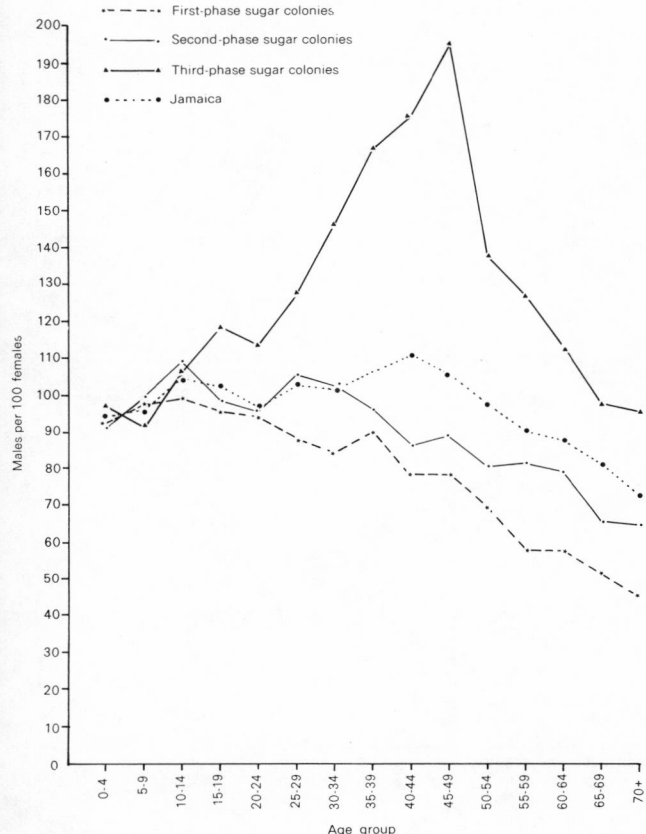

Fig. 5.2. *Slave Sex Ratios by Age: Classes of Colonies c.1817.* (Source: Table S4.1. Data for Antigua, Montserrat, Dominica, and Demerara-Essequibo are estimates.)

AFRICANS AND CREOLES

The declining proportion of African-born slaves in the slave populations of the British Caribbean after 1807 was the most obvious result of the abolition of the Atlantic slave trade. But the volume of imports from Africa varied significantly between the different types of colonies, chiefly in response to the amount of land available for plantation expansion. Thus, the first-phase sugar colonies had relatively small African-born slave populations in 1807 because expansion had reached its limit by about 1750 and slaves were imported only to supply losses due to negative natural increase. The largest proportion of Africans in the first-phase sugar colonies occurred in St. Kitts (16.1 percent in 1817) and the smallest in

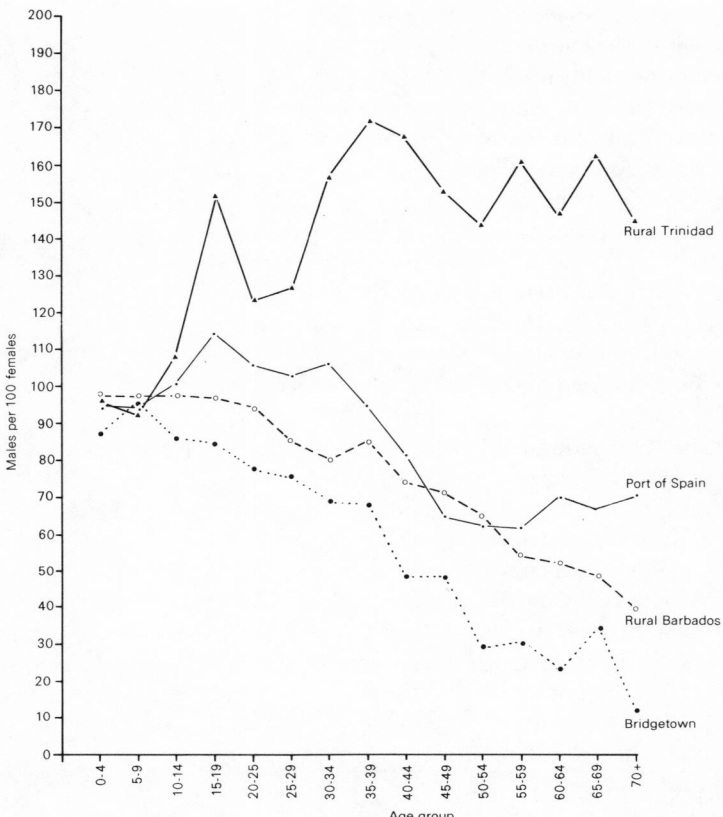

Fig. 5.3.   *Rural and Urban Slave Sex Ratios by Age: Barbados, 1817 and Trinidad, 1813.* (Sources: *tables S4.2 and S4.13.*)

Barbados (7.1 percent) (table 5.7). In the Windward Islands and Jamaica, however, the proportion exceeded 35 percent around 1817; and in Trinidad, Demerara-Essequibo, and Berbice, it exceeded 50.0 percent. The smallest proportion in these colonies occurred in St. Lucia, which was strictly a third-phase settlement but experienced only limited expansion. The position in the marginal colonies is less certain, but around 1817 the proportion of Africans in the Bahamas was similar to that in St. Lucia, and the evidence of the sex ratios shows that British Honduras must have had a very high proportion. Anguilla and the Cayman Islands also had significant African populations, while Barbuda probably had the smallest proportion in the entire British Caribbean.

These comparisons are necessarily centered on 1817, when the first systematic registration data became available. The proportion of Africans in the slave population must have been considerably higher in 1807, probably approaching a maximum of about 75 percent in Demerara-Essequibo and a minimum of 10 percent in Barbados. The rate of decline in the proportion of Africans depended on the colony-specific mortality rates of the Africans and creoles and on the fertility of the population. By 1817–34, when the extreme losses due to seasoning no longer applied, the rate of decline in the African population was generally 3 percent per annum. But where fertility rates were relatively high, as in Barbados and the Bahamas, the growth of the creole component was as important as African mortality, and the rate of decline in the proportion of Africans was therefore more rapid. As late as 1832, 25 years after abolition, Africans made up 34.5 percent of the slave population of Demerara-Essequibo, but in Barbados they had shrunk to a mere 2.9 percent (table 5.7). Thus, the Africans tended to disappear most rapidly in those colonies where they already formed only small contingents at the time of abolition, but they remained highly visible throughout the period in the colonies with expanding frontiers.

In view of this association between the size of the African populations and plantation expansion, it is surprising to find that there was a relatively large urban concentration of African slaves. This pattern is equally surprising in view of the low sex ratios of the towns and the high sex ratio within the African population. Of the eight capital towns for which the data are available, all but two contained larger proportions of Africans than the rural populations (table 5.8). The exceptions were Port of Spain and Roseau. In both of these towns the proportion was only marginally below the colony average, and in Port of Spain it stood as high as 50.4 percent in 1813. The largest urban concentration probably occurred in Bridgetown, where in 1817 15.7 percent of the slaves were Africans, compared to 7.1 percent for the island as a whole. At the same time, Bridgetown had the lowest sex ratio of all the capital towns. But the relatively large African slave populations in the towns did not mean a concentration of African females. In fact, the sex ratio of the Africans differed little between town and country. Only in St. George and Bridgetown were there more female than male Africans, and in the case of Bridgetown this merely reflected the pattern in the island as a whole. Thus, the male population of the towns contained a larger proportion of Africans than the female, and the African population differed sharply from the creole in having high sex ratios.

The urban concentration of African slaves was associated with relatively large African proportions in the smaller slaveholdings. In Barbados, St. Kitts, and Nevis there was a neat pattern, with the proportion African declining steadily as slaveholding size increased. In Barbados in 1817, for example, 11.4 percent of those in units of 1–10 slaves were Africans, compared to only 1.1 percent of those in units of more than 400 slaves (table S3.6). The pattern was very similar in 1832, though the percentages had fallen to 4.9 and 0.9, respectively. In the new sugar colonies and Jamaica the pattern was less consistent, but only in St. Lucia and Trinidad was there a clear tendency for the proportion of Africans to increase along with slaveholding size. The pattern in the marginal colonies is uncertain, but in Anguilla, at least, there was a concentration of Africans in units of more than 100 slaves. The general tendency for the smaller slaveholdings to contain relatively large proportions of Africans was repeated in the towns, so that the high sex ratios found in the larger urban units were not always associated with large proportions of Africans. In Bridgetown, for example, the units of more than 50 slaves, which had a majority of males, contained few Africans (table S2.10). But in Port of Spain a similar trend in the sex ratio was associated with very high proportions of Africans in the larger slaveholdings, no doubt a result of the scarcity of male creoles in Trinidad. Thus, it is evident that the high sex ratios of the larger urban slaveholdings were the product of a specific demand for males and not directly related to the overall size of the African population.

Female slaveowners, particularly whites, generally owned fewer Africans than did male slaveowners. In Bridgetown in 1817, for example, Africans were only 9.2 percent of the slaves belonging to white women, but they were 19.6 percent of those held by white men. Among the freedman slaveowners of Bridgetown differences by sex and color were slight, with about 16.0 percent of the slaves belonging to each group being African. In rural areas the contrast between white males and females was similar to that found in the towns, but freedmen tended to hold larger proportions of Africans. Variations in terms of crop types seem to have related directly to chronological differences in their establishment and decline. In St. Lucia in 1815, the proportion of Africans living on sugar estates was twice that on cotton and cocoa plantations. But in Trinidad the synchronous rise of sugar and cocoa meant that plantations cultivating these crops had very similar African populations, whereas the declining cotton and coffee plantations had much smaller proportions (table 5.9). In Jamaica Africans were most common on coffee plantations because of the recent introduction of that crop.[26] These variations resulted in some significant regional concentrations of Africans. In Trinidad, for example, Africans were relatively numerous in the expanding southern sugar belt as early as 1813, and it is probable that this concentration increased in the following decade (fig. 5.4). In the mature sugar colonies, however, there was little regionalization of the African and creole populations.

Reasons for variation in the distribution of Africans and creoles within the rural slave populations can readily be found in differences in settlement chronology, but the general concentration of Africans in the towns requires further investigation. It has often been assumed that the urban slave populations contained relatively large proportions of creoles and that the towns were consequently "creolized." Thus, Michael Craton holds that the slaves of Spanish Town, Jamaica "were largely creole" by the 1770s, and Peter Hogg argues that by the early nineteenth century, "many European cultural elements had been adopted, particularly by the urban and domestic slaves who where mostly born locally, while the majority of rural slaves retained more of the African cultural traditions."[27] The reality was quite different, however, with the towns retaining relatively large African populations in the early nineteenth century in spite of losing slaves to the plantations in this period of urban decline. One explanation for this seeming paradox lies in the poverty of many free town dwellers. Not all free people could afford to own slaves,

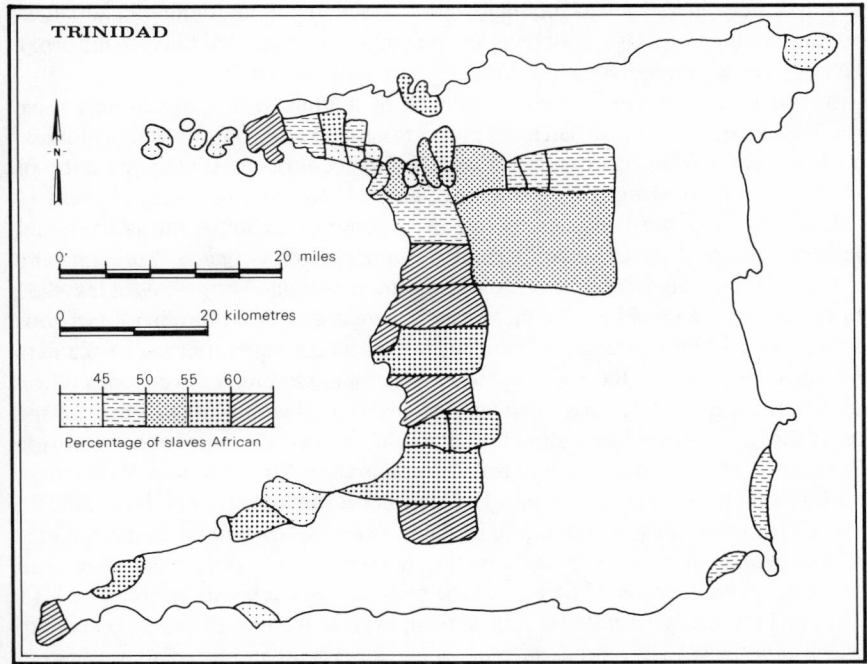

Fig. 5.4.   *Distribution of African-born Slaves: Trinidad, 1813.* (Source:
T.71/501–3.)

and those who could had a propensity to purchase one or two at a time and to sell
them when in need. As noted earlier in this chapter, slaves belonging to the owners
of small slaveholdings were transferred much more frequently than those held by
large planters, and the proportion of African slaves was greatest in such units. It
was this poorer class of slaveowners (boatwomen, tailors, hucksters, shopkeepers)
who bought sick, feeble, and "yellowish" slaves directly from the slave ships.
The slaves were called "refuse negroes" and were incapable of surviving the
journey to a rural plantation, but were taken "on a hand-cart or on the shoulders"
to be coaxed back to health "either for labor or advantage or by a subsequent
sale."[28] It was also relatively easy to purchase Africans singly, whereas creoles
were more likely to be offered for sale in family groups. Where plantations were
being established in new regions, the planters were more likely to purchase large
groups of slaves directly from the slave ships. Once this initial demand had been
satisfied, however, the town dwellers were able to compete for small lots, and
merchants requiring slaves to work as porters, tradesmen, or sailors had always
been able to compete successfully against the planters in securing male Africans;
hence the relative concentration of African slaves in the towns of the old sugar
colonies. It is also probable that slave traders coming from Africa increasingly

confined their operations to the major ports, once plantation demand had slackened, rather than visiting major bays and plantation wharves, thus giving the urban slaveowners a competitive advantage.

By the early nineteenth century, as well as having large African-born slave populations, the towns also had large proportions of creoles born in other colonies. In 1817 creoles from other colonies were 3.2 percent of the slave population of Bridgetown, numbering 297, while only another 48 lived in the rural areas of Barbados.[29] The most numerous of these creoles came from Martinique, Demerara, Antigua, Bermuda, Dominica, Guadeloupe, Grenada, Surinam, and St. Vincent, but a further eighteen colonies were represented by groups of less than ten slaves each. The majority of these slaves were domestics, brought to Barbados by footloose urban masters. In Trinidad, however, the general influx of planters and slaves meant that the majority of non-Trinidadian creoles were located on plantations. Yet Port of Spain managed to retain a disproportionate share of the slaves. In 1813 some 27 percent of Port of Spain's slaves were creoles born outside Trinidad, compared to 15 percent for the rural areas.[30] Since the non-Trinidadian creoles actually outnumbered the Trinidad-born, the latter were less than 25 percent of the town's population. Only slaves from the marginal colonies, chiefly brought in large units from the Bahamas, were as numerous on the plantations as in the town. Overall, about 37 percent of the creole slaves living in Trinidad in 1813 had been born elsewhere, 22 percent of them in British colonies and 14 percent in French colonies. Elsewhere, the proportion was considerably smaller, ranging from 8.5 percent in St. Lucia to less than 1 percent in Barbados around 1817 (tables S3.1–S3.5). But, like the African-born, "foreign" creoles were a diminishing proportion of the slave populations of most colonies as emancipation approached.

The regional/ethnic origins of the African-born slaves are known for only five colonies (table 5.10). Although the proportion whose birthplace cannot be identified from the data in the registration returns varied considerably from colony to colony, there is little reason to suspect bias in their distribution. The patterns derived from the registration data match fairly well the general trends projected by Roger Anstey, Philip Curtin, and Herbert Klein on the basis of shipping data for the period 1790–1807.[31] The calculations of these three authors are based entirely on the decade 1791–1800 and assume a similar pattern between 1801 and 1807. Revisions of Curtin's original estimates by Anstey and Klein have had the effect of increasing the proportions coming from the regions between Senegambia and the Gold Coast and considerably reducing the role of Central Africa. The registration data, however, show that the importance of Senegambia remains grossly underestimated and, to a lesser extent, so does that of the Bight of Benin. This divergence may result from changes in the pattern of the slave trade after 1800 or from differential reexportation.[32]

Slaves from the Bight of Biafra and Central Africa dominated the African populations of the British Caribbean after 1807. In most colonies these two regions accounted for approximately two-thirds of the African-born. The proportion was apparently somewhat less in Berbice and Anguilla, but the available data for these

Table 5.10. *Birthplaces of African Slaves: St. Kitts, St. Lucia, Trinidad, Berbice, and Anguilla, 1813–27*

| | Percentage of Africans | | | | | |
Birthplace	St. Kitts, 1817	St. Lucia, 1815	Trinidad, 1813	Berbice, 1819	Anguilla, 1827	Total British Slave Trade, 1790–1807
Senegambia	19.2	9.6	12.2	10.1	43.4	0.7
Sierra Leone	4.7	1.3	4.5	8.2	1.9	4.7
Windward Coast	4.8	9.2	6.6	5.7	—	7.5
Gold Coast	2.4	6.3	8.2	14.8	5.7	13.8
Bight of Benin	1.1	3.4	8.1	22.2	—	1.7
Bight of Biafra	21.1	47.4	41.2	16.5	7.5	40.5
Central Africa	46.7	22.8	19.1	22.5	41.5	30.8
Mozambique	—	—	0.1	—	—	—
Total	100.0	100.0	100.0	100.0	100.0	100.0
Region unknown	10.9	24.4	4.3	91.4	19.7	?

Sources: Tables S3.1–3.5; and Roger Anstey, "The Volume and Profitability of the British Slave Trade, 1761–1807," in *Race and Slavery in the Western Hemisphere,* ed. Stanley L. Engerman and Eugene D. Genovese (1975), p. 13.

colonies derive from small populations. In the southern Caribbean the Bight of Biafra was the most important source of slaves, but in the Leeward Islands Central Africa and Senegambia dominated. This pattern was distinct from that which applied in the period before 1750, when the Windward Coast, Gold Coast, and Bight of Benin accounted for two-thirds of the British slave trade.[33] Thus, the old sugar colonies, Jamaica, and the marginal colonies received a changing mix of ethnic groups throughout their histories, while the third-phase sugar colonies had a much briefer period of heavy slave importation in which particular source regions were more likely to dominate. But it is important to emphasize that each colony had a heterogeneous mixture of Africans in the early nineteenth century, and that this mix showed relatively slight spatial variation, with only minor differences between the rural and urban populations. Further, slaves arriving in the British Caribbean in the last two decades of the Atlantic slave trade generally found themselves in established creole societies, the main characteristics of which had been forged in much earlier encounters between Africans and Europeans.[34] Only on the sugar frontier of Trinidad and the coffee frontier of Jamaica did slaves entering the British Caribbean after about 1790 find themselves in a relatively open system, and even there they worked alongside creoles from a variety of colonial situations. Thus, any potential "retentions" or "Africanisms" of particular African ethnic groups could only emerge or submerge within this complex context.

A significant proportion of African slaves in the West Indies carried the evidence of some form of body mutilation, either "country marks" or "filed teeth," but few passed on these practices to their creole children. In Berbice in 1819, for example, at least 3,874 African slaves were registered as possessing country marks or tattoos (30.1 percent), while only 21 creoles showed evidence of cicatrization. Similarly, in St. Lucia in 1815 some 649 Africans bore country marks (18.6 percent), but only four creoles did.[35] Of the 57 slaves listed as having filed teeth in Berbice, only three were creoles, and in St. Lucia only one of the thirteen with "dents pointues" was a creole. Some of these cases of creole body mutilation may be attributed to possible scribal error, of course, but it is certain that the practice was essentially abandoned. In the late eighteenth century an observer wrote that "The Creoles sometimes disfigure themselves, but less than the Africans, as they only scarify the temples."[36] The filing of teeth was abandoned even more quickly. This abandonment was common throughout New World slave populations and may be interpreted as an adaptive response to the negative values placed on African identification in slave societies.[37] In both Berbice and St. Lucia, slaves from Central Africa and the Bight of Benin were the most likely to possess country marks or filed teeth, and those from the Windward Coast the least likely to do so.

Each region of Africa supplying slaves to the British Caribbean contained a variety of ethnic or tribal groups, widely scattered spatially but rarely located more than 200 miles from the coast. The distribution of ethnic groups and shipping points accounting for more than 0.1 percent of the Africans in each of St. Kitts, St. Lucia, Trinidad, and Berbice has been mapped (figs. 5.5–5.8). Full lists of birthplaces are given in tables S3.1–3.5. The maps demonstrate the extensive spread of source areas, but also show that a single ethnic group often accounted for a large proportion of the slaves from a particular region. Malinke (Mandingo) slaves dominated in Senegambia, Temne in Sierra Leone, Canga and Kwakwa in the Windward Coast, Chamba and Popo in the Bight of Benin, Igbo, Ibibio, and Northwestern Bantu (Moco) in the Bight of Biafra, and Kongo in Central Africa. Only the Kongo, Igbo, Moco, and Malinke constituted more than 10 percent of the African slaves in any colony. The Kongo and Igbo were by far the most important groups, reflecting the dominance of Central Africa and the Bight of Biafra. In St. Kitts almost half of the slaves were Kongo, and in St. Lucia one-third were Igbo. It was slaves from the larger ethnic contingents who had the best chances of retaining particular cultural habits, but even these slaves were spread widely and rarely concentrated on a single plantation.

The potential for cultural cohesiveness depended also on the sex and age structure of the African populations. In addition to the contrast in sex ratios between Africans and creoles as a whole, there were differences between the African regional groups. Most significant was the relatively low sex ratio of slaves from the Bight of Biafra, which was almost evenly balanced in Trinidad by 1813 and actually favored females in St. Lucia by 1815 (table 5.11). Slaves from

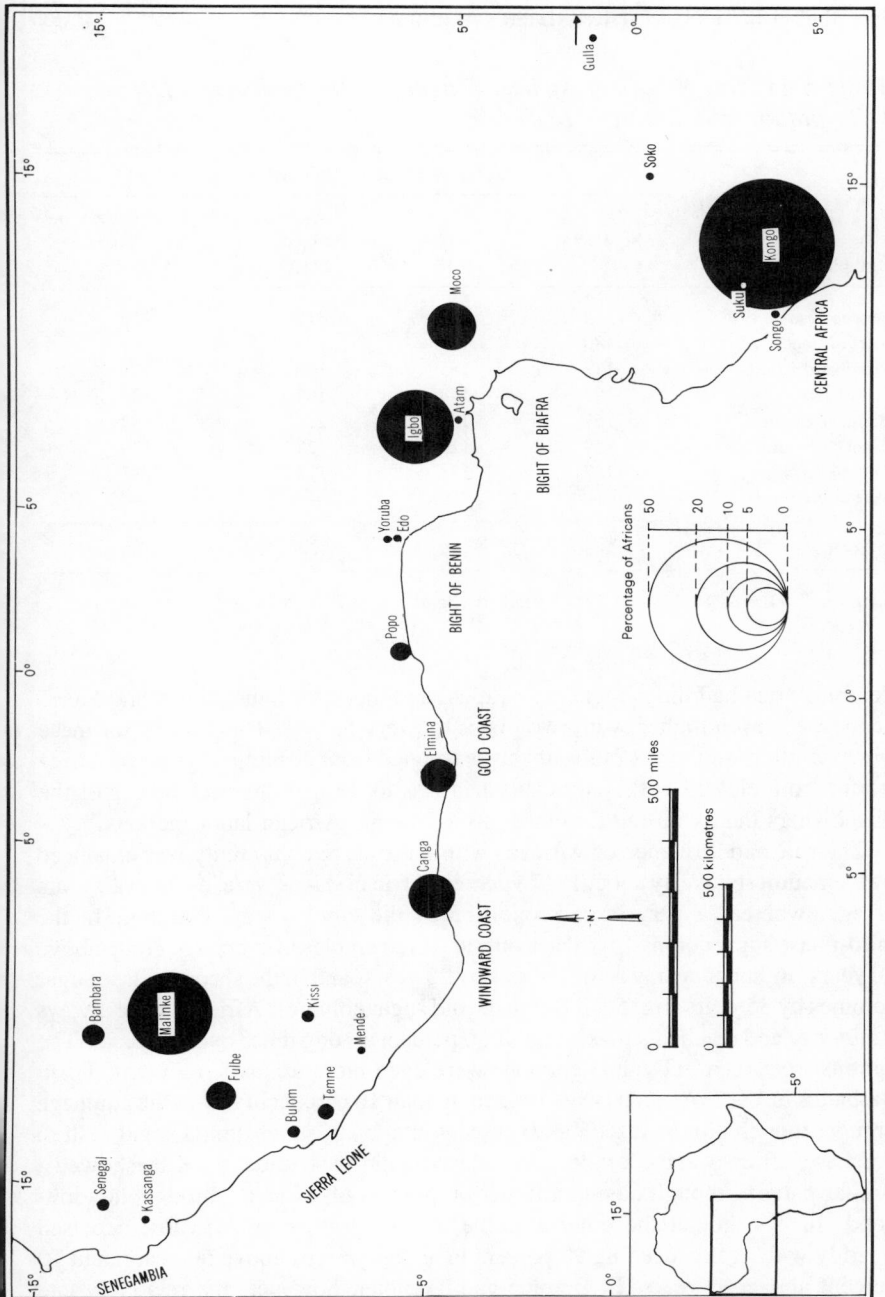

Fig. 5.5. *Origins of African-born Slaves: St. Kitts, 1817.* (Source: *table S3.1.*)

Table 5.11. *Sex Ratios of African Slaves by Birthplace: St. Lucia, Trinidad, and Berbice, 1813–19*

	Males per 100 Females			
Birthplace	St. Lucia, 1815	Trinidad, 1813	Berbice, 1819	Total British Slave Trade, 1791–98
Senegambia	134	187	311	210
Sierra Leone	180	173	203	211
Windward Coast	112	165	110	208
Gold Coast	97	148	165	184
Bight of Benin	57	131	227	187
Bight of Biafra	59	120	125	139
Central Africa	137	173	170	217
Mozambique	—	300	—	—
Total	93	146	164	183

Sources: T.71/378–79, 438–39, 501–3; Herbert Klein, *The Middle Passage* (1978), p. 150.

Central Africa had much higher sex ratios, and those for Senegambia and Sierra Leone were even higher, with two males to every female. The reasons for these wide variations in the sex ratios of slaves shipped from different regions of Africa are far from clear, but they probably had less to do with the preferences of the slaveowners than with the structure of the internal African labor markets.[38]

The role and influence of Africans within the slave community was enhanced by their adult status. By about 1817 very few African slaves were less than 20 years of age, whereas a very large proportion of the creoles were children. In the third-phase sugar colonies Africans outnumbered creoles in every age group above 20 years, in Jamaica they achieved this by 25 years, and in the second-phase sugar colonies by 35 years (fig. 5.9). But in the old sugar colonies, Africans were always a minority and reached a maximum of 30 percent among those over 70 years. The contrasts between individual colonies were even more dramatic (table S4.1). In Barbados in 1817, Africans were little more than 10 percent of any of the adult age groups, though almost reaching 20 percent at age 30, suggesting a small rush to purchase Africans in the last decade of the Atlantic slave trade. St. Kitts showed a similar pattern, though having a larger proportion of Africans throughout adulthood. In Tobago, at the other extreme, the proportion of Africans increased steadily with age, exceeding 90 percent in all age groups above 50 years, and 70 percent above 40 years. In Berbice and Trinidad, however, the relatively late development of the plantations meant that Africans made up more than 80 percent of the population as early as age 25, but declined after age 35 to fall as low as 60 percent among those over 70 years. It has already been established that the sex ratio tended to fall quite sharply with increasing age, except in the third-phase

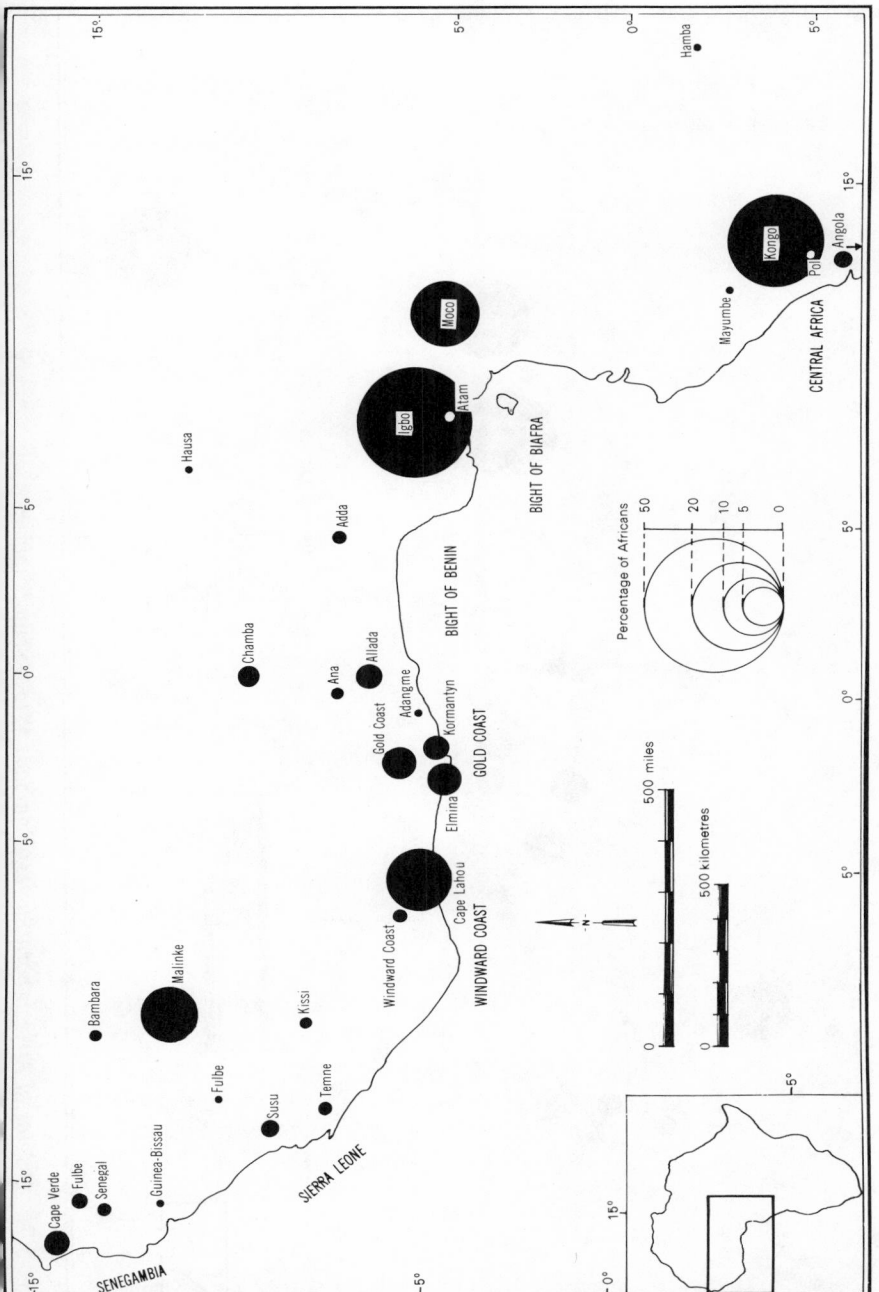

Fig. 5.6. *Origins of African-born Slaves: St. Lucia, 1815. (Source: table S3.2.)*

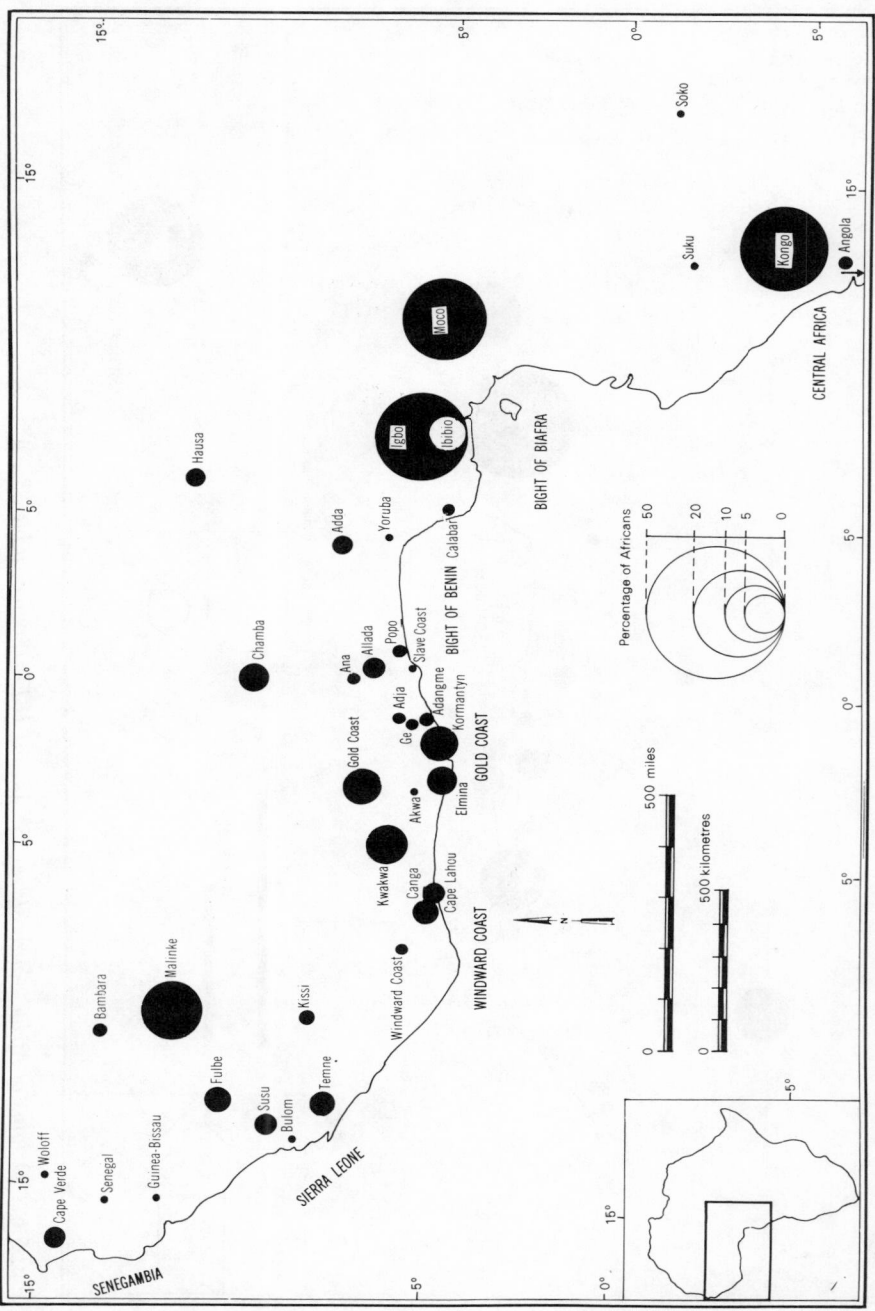

Fig. 5.7. *Origins of African-born Slaves: Trinidad, 1813. (Source: table S3.3.)*

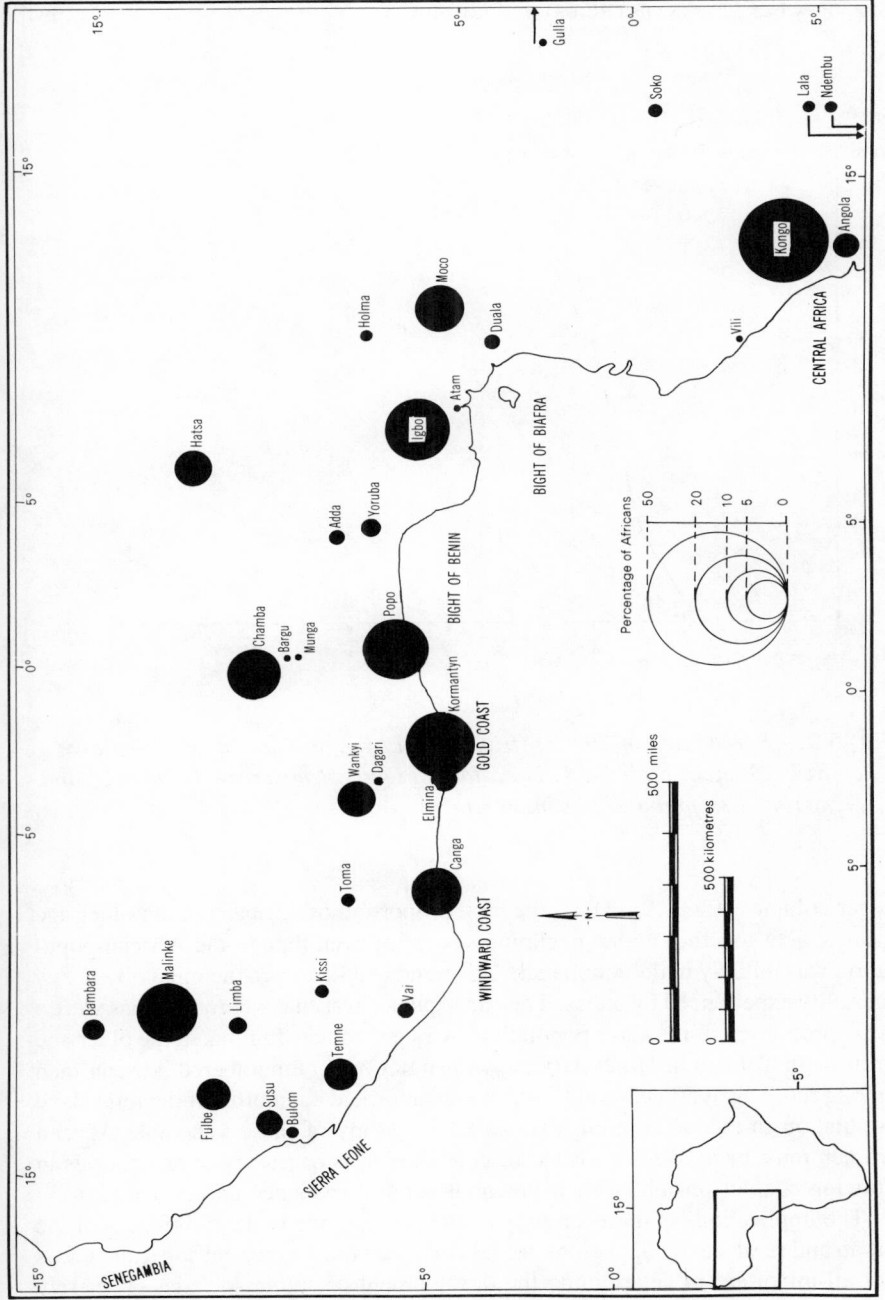

Fig. 5.8. *Origins of African-born Slaves: Berbice, 1819.* (Source: *table S3.4.*)

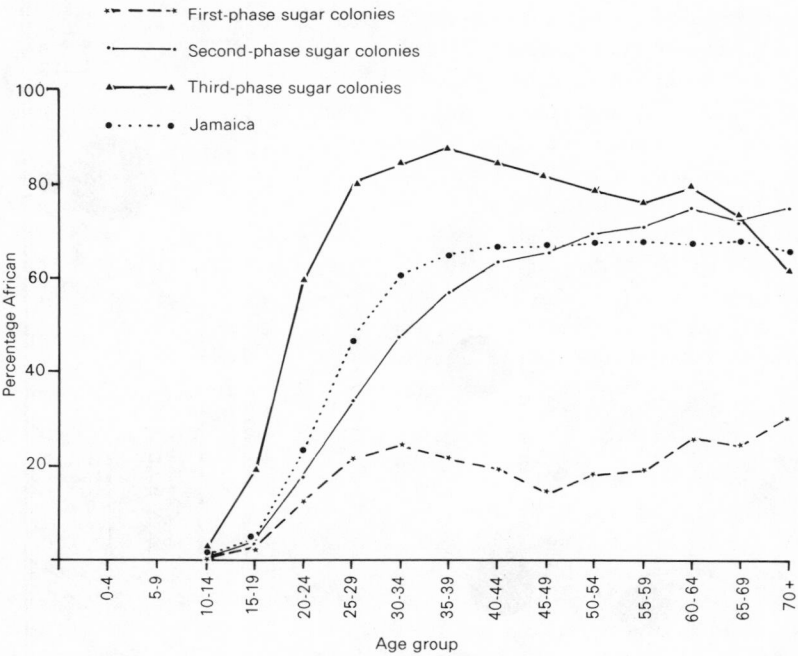

Fig. 5.9. *Percentage of Slaves African-born by Age: Classes of Colonies c.1817. (Source: table S4.1. Data for Antigua, Montserrat, Dominica, and Demerara-Essequibo are estimates.)*

sugar colonies (fig. 5.2). Thus, the high proportion of Africans in the older age groups went together with a declining sex ratio, even though the African population was initially male-dominated. This trend resulted from the relatively heavy mortality experienced by males. The consequence was that where Africans were a large proportion of the slave population, African women dominated the older age groups. In Tobago in 1819, African women not only outnumbered African men among those aged 50 years and over, but also formed a majority of the total slave population in these age groups (table S4.1). Many of these venerable African women must have lived in towns, of course, so it is necessary to be cautious in drawing conclusions about their potential cultural influence and authority.

The implications of these strongly contrasted patterns in the birthplaces of the urban and rural slave populations are less than certain. Numerical superiority was not all-important in determining the development of creole societies. It merely placed limits on the possible. For example, even if creoles outnumbered Africans on a plantation, the latter may still have constituted a larger, potentially more cohesive-conservative group than those Africans attached to small urban units. Alternatively, the absolute size of the African populations of the capital towns may have permitted slaves with common ethnic and linguistic backgrounds to regroup, taking advantage of the less rigid supervision and fluid residential arrangements existing within the towns. It has been argued, for example, that in Bahia the African religions and languages are purer and richer in the large cities than in the rural areas, as a consequence of this potential.[39] Comparative studies of African cultural "retentions" in rural and urban settings have not been carried very far in the British Caribbean, but there is some evidence to suggest that town slaves were not necessarily the first to adopt "European cultural elements," contrary to the argument of Hogg.[40] Again, differences in the age and sex composition of the African and creole populations were important only within the context of general rules, established by the slaveowners or the slave community itself, governing the roles and authority attributable to males and females, old and young.

AGE STRUCTURE

The age structure of the slave population of the British Caribbean was determined, in large measure, by the African-creole ratio. Variations in the level of fertility, age-specific mortality, and migration were also important but tended to be strongly correlated with the proportion of Africans in the population. The Atlantic slave trade was organized to supply young adults, since these slaves fetched the highest prices in West Indian markets, but every slave ship carried some children and older people. At the end of the eighteenth century the Jamaica Assembly legislated a tax on the importation of slaves over 25 years of age.[41] No attempt seems to have been made to regulate the proportions of children carried from Africa, but in the last decades of the Atlantic trade "boys" and "girls" (under about 18 years) made up less than 15 percent of total imports to the West Indies.[42] In Trinidad, five years after abolition, fewer than 9 percent of the Africans on the island were under 20 years, and less than 1 percent under 15 years (table S4.1). Thus, the continual addition of Africans to the slave population produced a bulge in the age groups over 20 years, the size and shape of this bulge depending on the relative proportion of creoles in the population and the chronological spread of the slave trade.

The reliability of the age data included in the slave registration returns has been discussed in detail in chapter 2. They suffered from heaping at the decadal ages, particularly among the Africans. Minor kinks in the graphs presented in this section must be interpreted with this problem in mind. A more significant problem for comparative analysis is that the registration returns do not provide age data for any one year and, at the extremes, the available samples are 20 years apart. Table S4.1 presents the data extracted for each colony, including estimates based on large samples for Jamaica and Antigua. Using these data, it has been possible to estimate total age structures for the marginal colonies only at about 1834, and for the other groups of colonies at 1817.[43] Since data on the African-creole ratio, fertility, and mortality are deficient for most of the marginal colonies, an estimate of the age structure in these colonies at 1817 has not been attempted.

The only comprehensive age data available for the British Caribbean are those derived from the compensation records of 1834, and these merely distinguished slaves under 6 and over 70 years (table 3.3). These data do show clearly that the largest proportions of young children were to be found in the marginal colonies of Barbuda, Anguilla, and the Bahamas, followed by the old sugar colonies of Barbados, Montserrat, and St. Kitts. The smallest proportions occurred in the new sugar colonies of Trinidad, British Guiana, and Tobago, together with Jamaica and British Honduras. But the distribution of "aged" slaves appears much more erratic, with the largest proportion occurring in Tobago and the smallest in the Virgin Islands. Thus, although these compensation data point to some broad contrasts related to stage of settlement, their value is limited.

The age data derived from the registration returns provide a much more detailed picture. Figure 5.10 compares the total age profiles for each of the four sugar-producing classes of colonies at about 1817. At this level, the patterns are quite smooth, with decadal kinks appearing only above 50 years of age. But the contrasts between the colonies are stark. Most obvious is the shape of the bulge in the 25–39 years groups, reflecting the African component of the population. In the third-phase sugar colonies of Trinidad, Demerara-Essequibo, and Berbice, 41.1 percent of the slaves were in these age groups around 1817, but in the first-phase sugar colonies, only 24.2 percent were. Only in the third-phase sugar colonies did the proportion of Africans decline after age 40 (fig. 5.9). The age pyramids presented in figure 5.11 clearly show the differences in the structure of the African populations, the first-phase colonies having only a minor bulge at 25–39 years and the third-phase colonies a prominent one.

In the age groups below 25 years, the positions of the classes of colonies were reversed. Slaves under 25 constituted 53.9 percent of the population in the first-phase sugar colonies around 1817, 47.4 percent in the second-phase colonies, 44.2 percent in Jamaica, and only 41.8 percent in the third-phase colonies. These differences were less pronounced than in the 25–39 groups and were most obvious among adolescents. Thus, these contrasts had clear implications for the future fertility of the populations, just as differences in the proportions over 25 years had implications for mortality. In the age groups above 50 years, differences between the classes of colonies were less marked, except that the third-phase sugar colonies had significantly fewer old people.

The age structure of the marginal colonies has been ignored thus far because of the lack of comparable data for 1817, but it is certain that it was even younger than that for the first-phase sugar colonies. By 1834 some 58.5 percent of the slaves in the marginal colonies were less than 25 years of age, and only 19.5 percent were 25–39 years (fig. 5.11). But individual differences between colonies were greater in the marginal group than in any other class (fig. 5.12). Barbuda had an extremely young age structure around 1834, as did the Bahamas and, to a lesser extent, Anguilla. But British Honduras had a top-heavy age structure, with a large proportion of males over 40 years. This, together with the high sex ratio of the population, confirms that British Honduras contained a considerable African

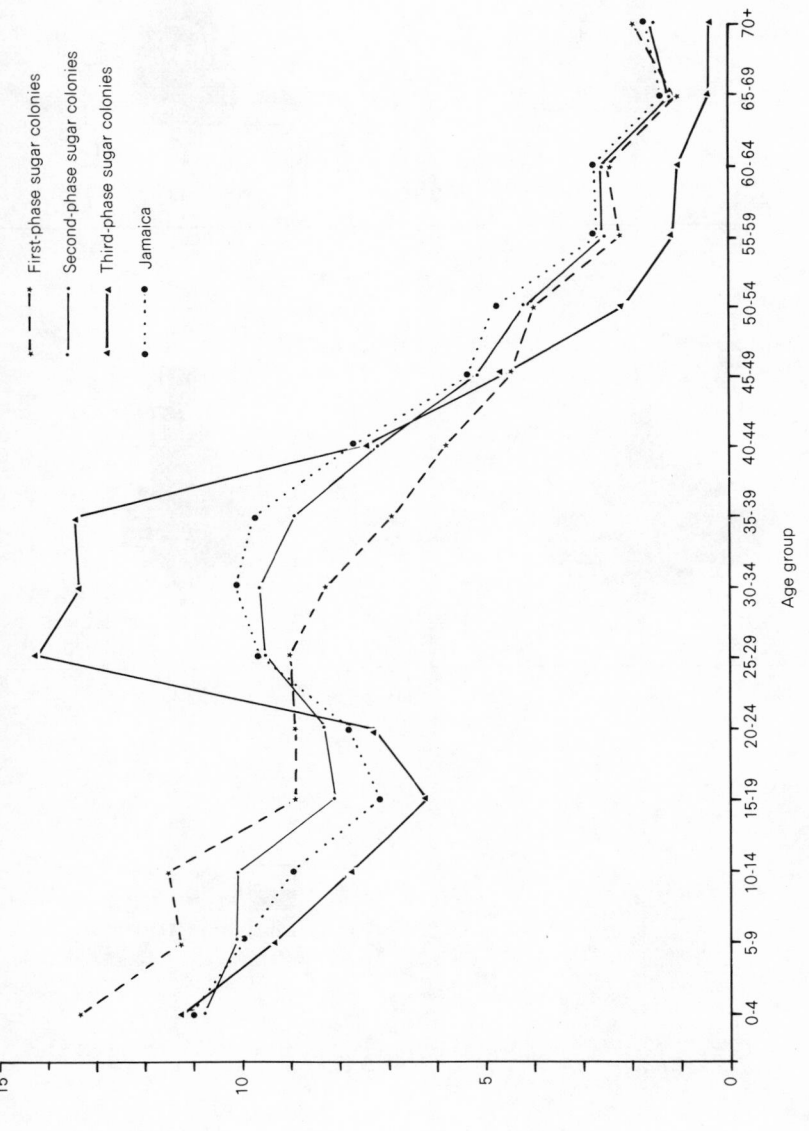

First-phase sugar colonies
Second-phase sugar colonies
Third-phase sugar colonies
Jamaica

Percentage

Age group

Fig. 5.10. *Slave Age Profiles: Classes of Colonies c.1817.* (Source: *table S4.1.*)

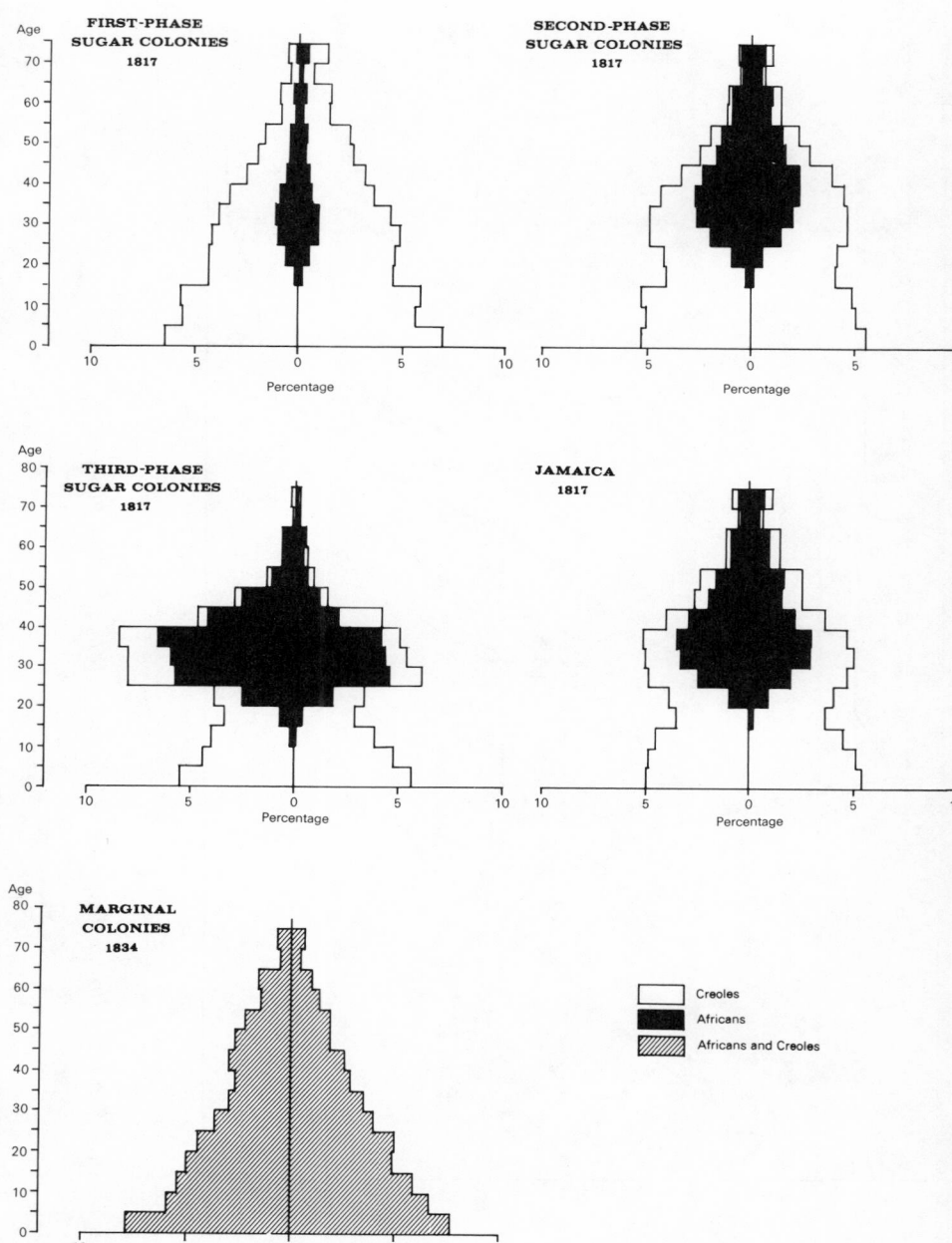

Fig. 5.11. *Slave Age Pyramids: Classes of Colonies c.1817 and 1834.*
(Source: *table S4.1.*)

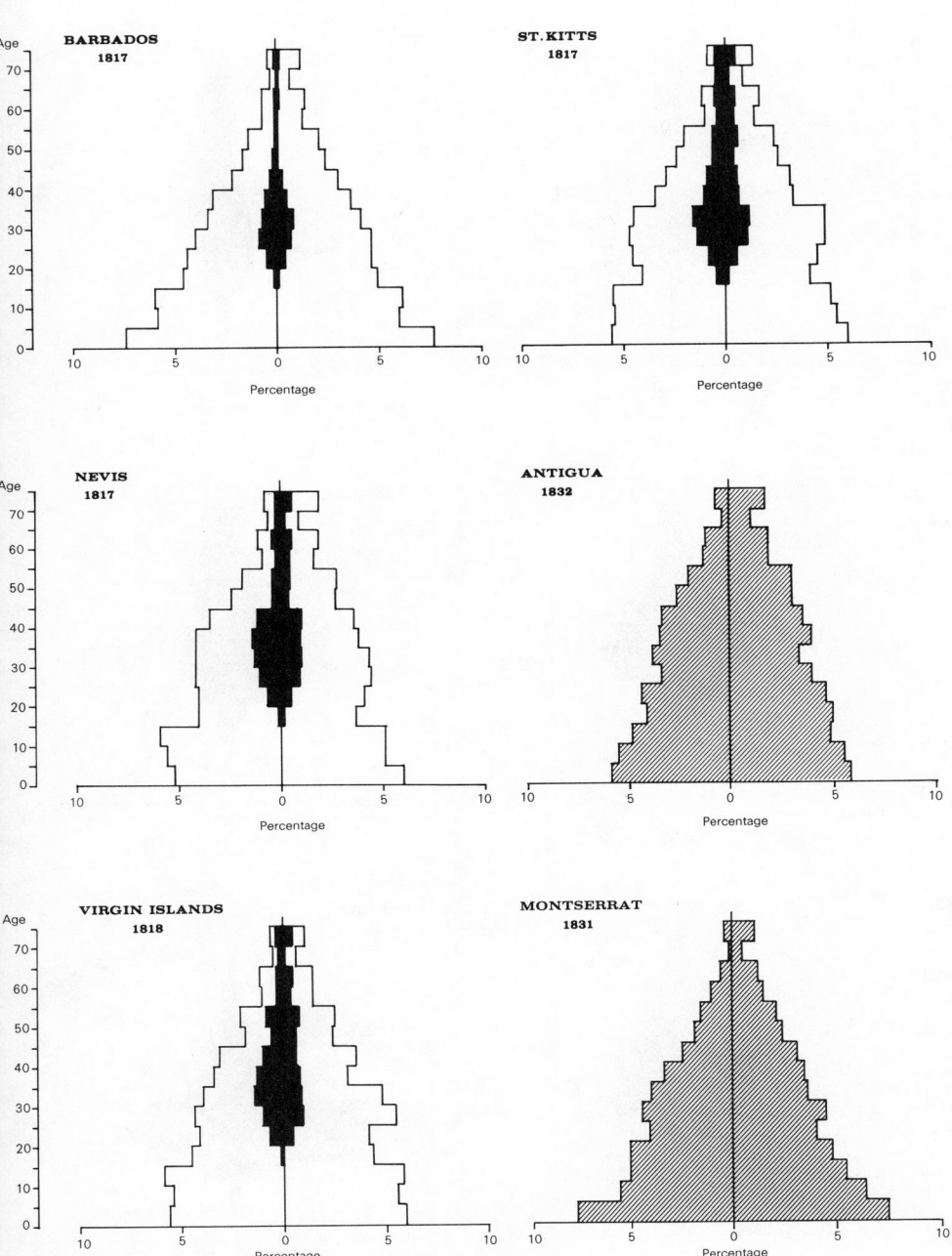

Fig. 5.12. *Slave Age Pyramids by Colony.* (Source: *table S4.1.*)

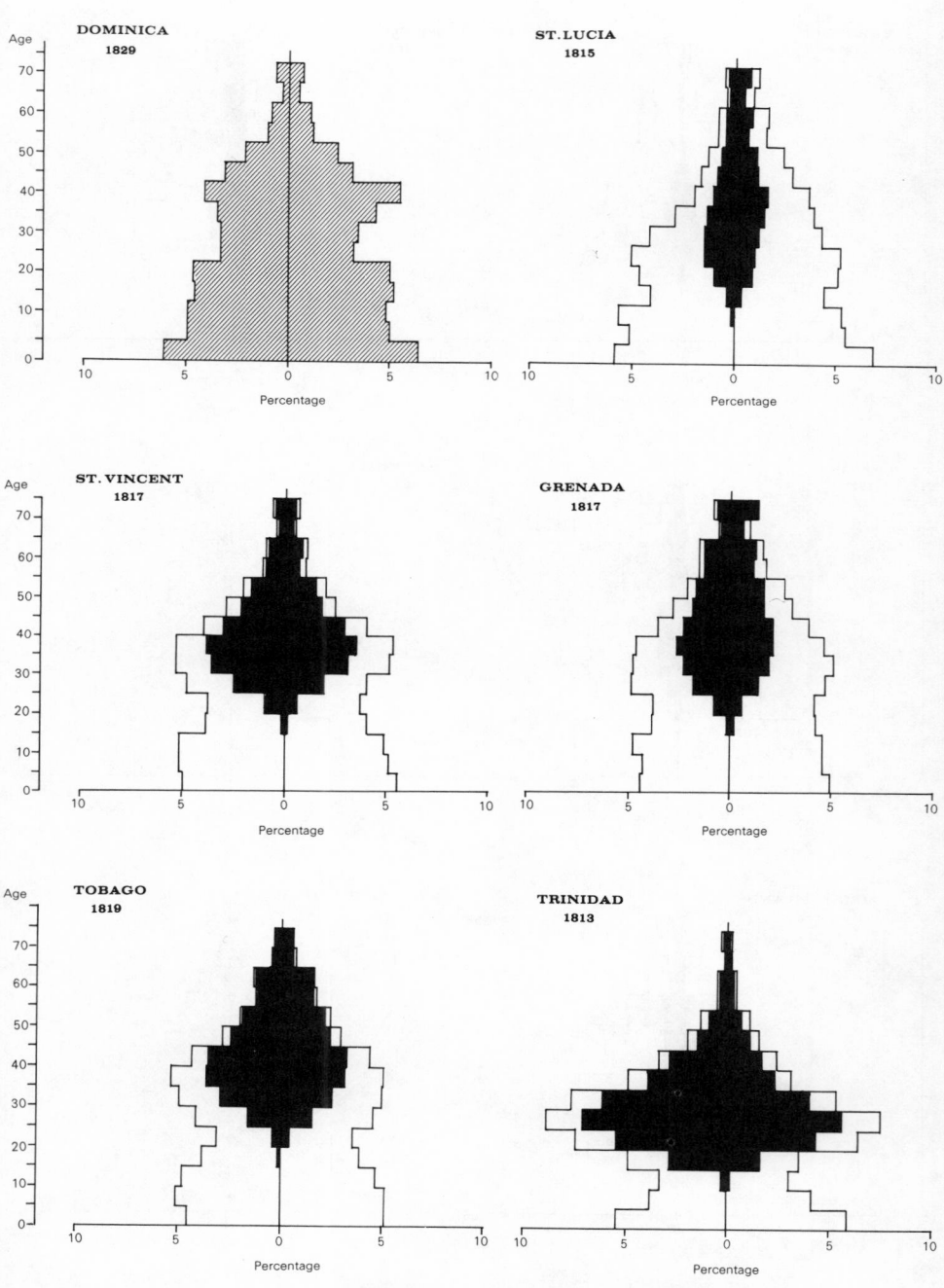

Fig. 5.12. *continued*

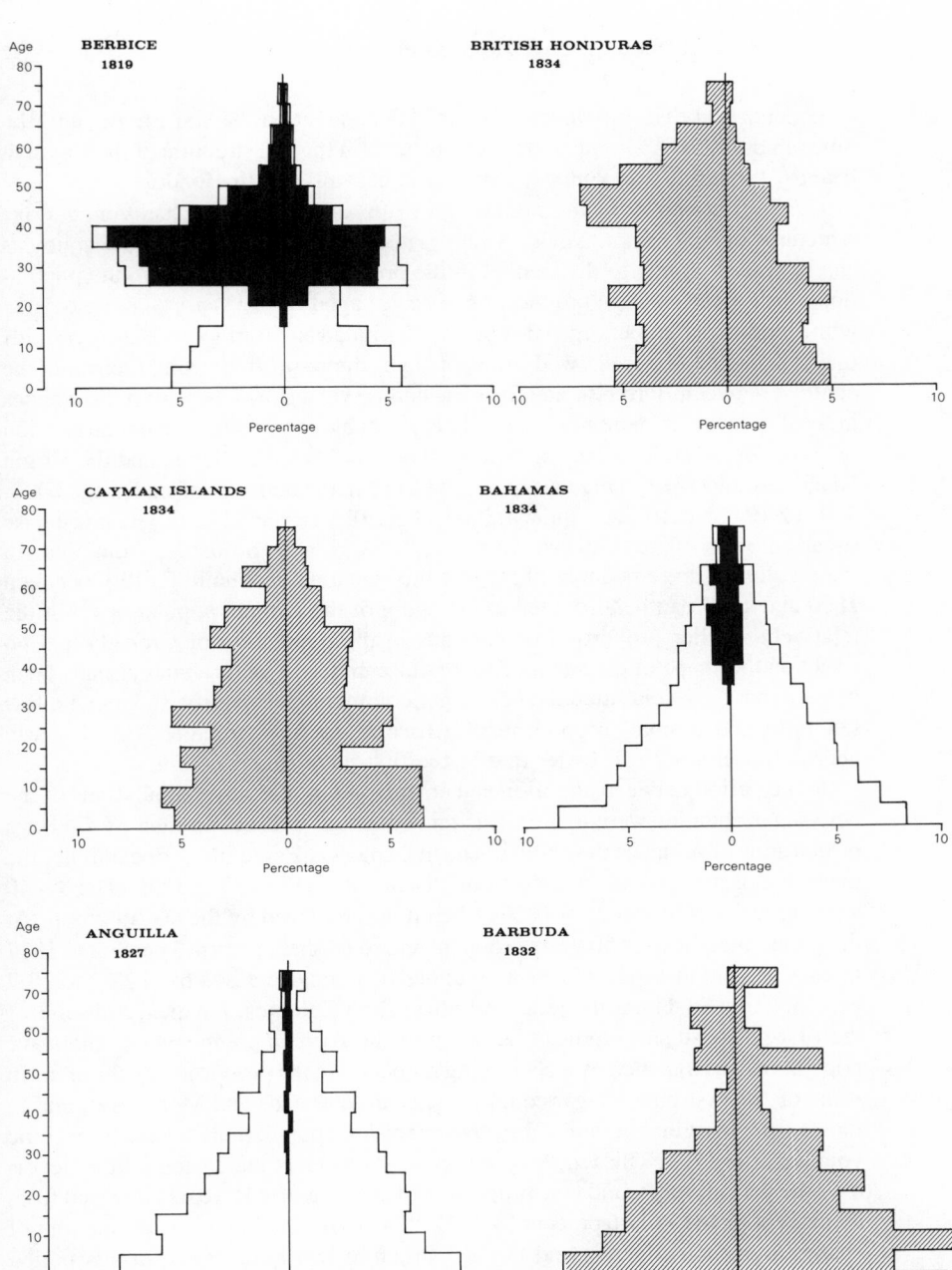

Fig. 5.12. *continued*

component and that growth had remained dependent on the slave trade until the time of abolition. A similar pattern can be seen in the age structure of the Cayman Islands, though it was younger than in the case of British Honduras.

Of the first-phase sugar colonies, Barbados and Montserrat had younger age structures than St. Kitts, Nevis, Antigua, and the Virgin Islands. These contrasts can be traced largely to differences in the proportions of Africans in the populations. But whereas large proportions of slaves aged 25–39 years were associated with significant numbers aged 0–4 years in Trinidad and Berbice, the age pyramids of St. Kitts and Nevis showed little spread at the base. It appears, then, that the contrast between Barbados and St. Kitts and Nevis resulted also from differences in fertility levels that are not obviously attributable to variations in the proportion of slaves in the childbearing age group. Thus, in St. Kitts, Nevis, and the Virgin Islands around 1817, there was little difference in the numbers of slaves aged 0–4, 5–9, or 10–14 years. A similar failure of fertility occurred in the second-phase sugar colonies of St. Vincent, Grenada, Tobago, and, probably, Dominica. In these colonies it seems more likely that this apparent decline in fertility between 1800 and 1817 can be attributed to the aging of the African populations, but the relatively smaller proportion of Africans in the population of Grenada had no effect on the shape of the age profile for those under 15 years. It has already been noticed that St. Lucia fitted the new sugar colony models poorly, in having a low sex ratio and a small proportion of Africans. Its age structure was similarly aberrant, seeming to fit better that of the first-phase sugar colonies.

In the period between abolition and emancipation, the slave populations of the new sugar colonies were aging. This tendency was a direct product of the large proportions of Africans they contained. In Demerara-Essequibo, for example, the mean age of the slaves increased from 25 years in 1817 to 30 in 1832. The 30–40 years group was modal until 1826, when it was replaced by the 40–50 group. At the same time, the over 50 years group increased its share from 4.3 percent in 1817 to 14.1 percent in 1832, while slaves under 10 years decreased from 22.3 to 18.7 percent (table S4.1). As in the second-phase sugar colonies, Jamaica, and some of the first-phase sugar colonies, the aging of the African component of the slave population was matched by a continuing reduction in the proportion of children. In some of the first-phase sugar colonies, such as Barbados and Montserrat, and in most of the marginal colonies, however, the slave populations tended to become younger after 1807. This tendency was chiefly a result of increasing fertility levels over the period. In Barbuda the proportion of slaves under 15 years increased from 39 percent in 1817 to 46 percent by 1832.[44] In Barbados, however, the amount of change was such slighter, and the age structure was quite stable in this period (tables S4.2 and S4.3). Essentially there was a continuum, stretching from the third-phase sugar colonies through the second and first-phase colonies to the marginal colonies, in which the slave populations became increasingly youthful after 1807. But the gradual disappearance of the African bulge in the age structure had the short-term effect of reducing the proportion of young children, so that the slave populations containing large proportions of Africans experienced a period of

Table 5.12. *Mean Age of Slaves by Sex, Birthplace, and Type of Enterprise: St. Lucia, 1815*

| | Africans | | Creoles | | |
Enterprise	Males	Females	Males	Females	Total
Sugar	39.7	45.3	20.7	23.3	27.0
Coffee	39.2	44.2	18.4	21.9	23.9
Cotton	41.1	47.2	20.1	23.0	24.9
Cocoa	39.4	47.6	15.4	21.8	22.2
Provisions	30.9	47.0	16.4	21.0	23.7
Personal	33.4	37.4	17.0	21.0	22.6
Total	38.7	43.5	19.0	22.3	25.2

Source: T.71/378–79.

aging. Thus, the differences in age structure between 1807 and 1834 must be explained largely in terms of stage of settlement.

Differences in age structure by type of economic enterprise, within colonies, were relatively slight. In St. Lucia, for example, the mean age of the slave population was 25.2 years in 1815, with a range from 22.2 on cocoa plantations to 27.0 on sugar estates (table 5.12). The range on coffee, cotton, and provisions plantations was even more limited. These relatively minor variations reflected quite accurately differences in the proportions of Africans in each enterprise (table 5.9). Similar patterns are evident in the case of Trinidad (figure 5.13). Elsewhere the relationship between age and type of enterprise can be studied only at the parish level, and here the pattern is inevitably ambiguous. Around 1817 in Barbados, the population of the archetypal cotton parish (St. Lucy) was only slightly younger than that of the archetypal sugar parish (St. John) (table S4.2). Of the leading coffee parishes in Dominica around 1829, St. Peter had a relatively youthful age profile, while St. Luke and St. George were quite mature. St. David and St. Patrick, the parishes most heavily dominated by sugar, also had mature profiles, though with more obvious African components (table S4.6). In Jamaica the recently-settled coffee parishes of Port Royal and Manchester, where more than 50 percent of the slaves were Africans in 1817, had significantly younger age profiles than the long-established sugar parishes, as did the livestock-producing parishes.[45] Thus, although sugar estates generally seem to have had the most mature slave populations, differences in age structure were more obviously related to stage of settlement factors than to the crops produced.

Whereas differences between the age structures of the slave populations attached to the various crop types were not marked, the contrast between urban and rural populations was quite strong. Because they contained relatively large proportions of Africans, the urban populations displayed a more prominent bulge around 1817 in the 20–34 years age group. But in some cases the bulge in these age

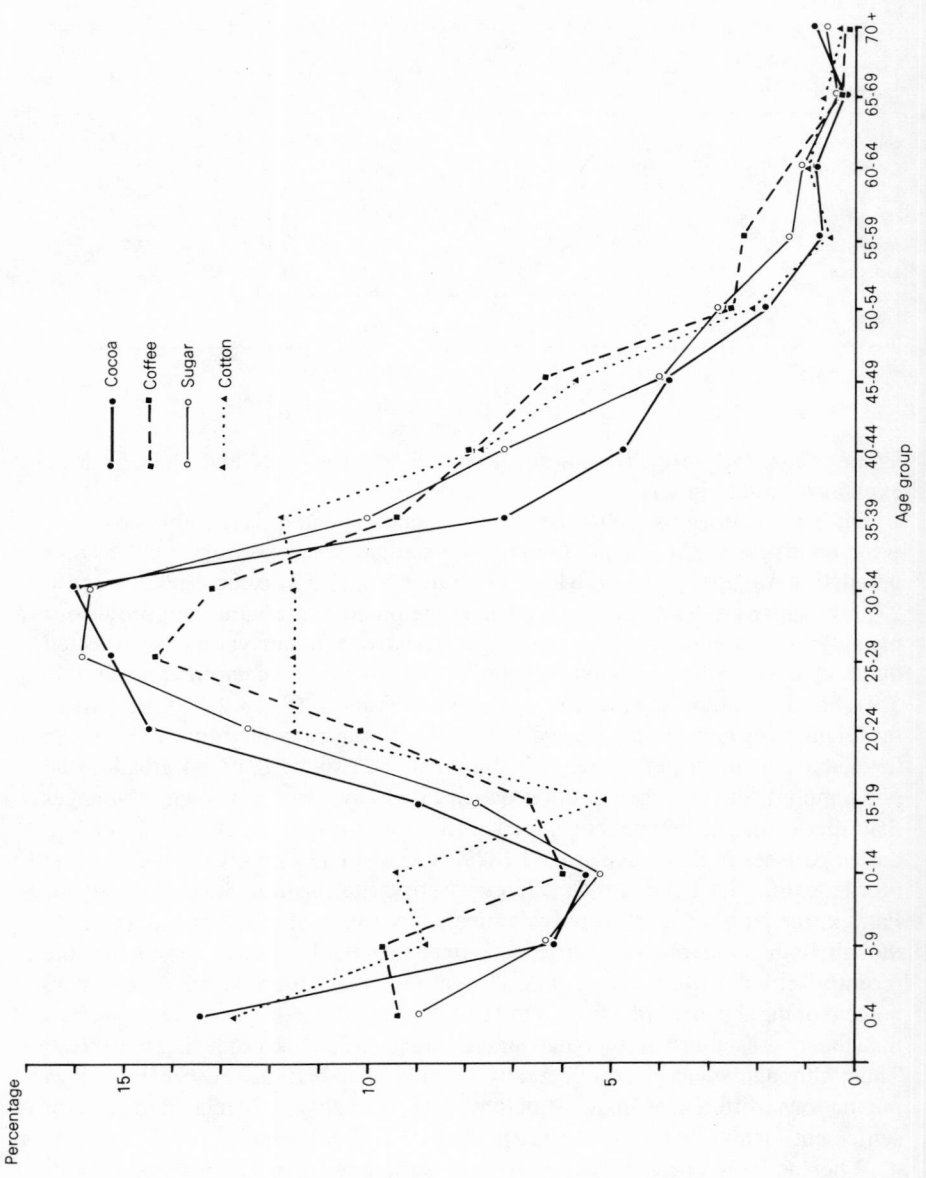

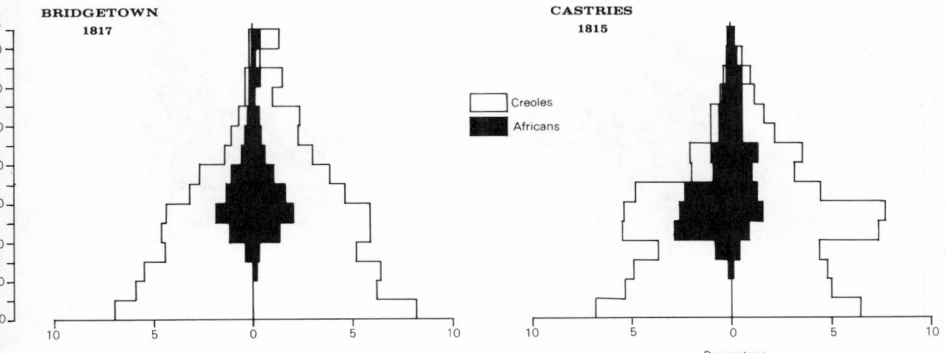

Fig. 5.14. *Slave Age Pyramids: Bridgetown, 1817 and Castries, 1815.*
(Sources: *tables S4.2 and S4.7.*)

groups was composed mainly of creoles, particularly among the females. This pattern was apparent in Castries and, to a lesser extent, Bridgetown (fig. 5.14). Thus, it is clear that the towns had a specific demand for females in their twenties, and that this demand was not determined by the birthplaces of the slaves. It is equally important to notice that in spite of the large proportions of Africans, which in the case of the sugar estates produced mature populations, the urban populations were relatively youthful. This resulted primarily from the youthfulness of the African component. In the case of St. Lucia, for example, in 1815 the creoles in Castries were only 1.5 years younger than creoles living on the plantations, but the Africans, both males and females, were 7.5 years younger. This pattern also occurred in Bridgetown and Kingstown (tables S4.2 and S4.8).[46] It supports the argument advanced in the previous section of this chapter that the large proportions of Africans found in the towns of the older colonies were created by direct, and relatively recent, purchase from the slave ships. As noted at the colony level, a large and relatively young African component generally meant a large proportion of children, and in the towns, this went together with a small proportion of old people. But in towns affected heavily by transfer to the plantations, the younger age groups were significantly eroded, both directly through sale and indirectly through the shrinking of fertility. This tendency was most obvious in Roseau (table S4.6), but it had an impact on all of the towns which experienced decline after 1807.

Variations in age structure by slaveholding size reflected the ambiguity of the relationship between age and economic activity. It has already been noticed that the highest mean age in St. Lucia occurred on the sugar estates (table 5.12), so it is not surprising to discover that mean age increased fairly steadily along with holding size (table S4.24). This pattern applied equally to Africans and creoles, except that creoles belonging to units of only one or two slaves were older than those in the largest holdings. The latter tendency is easily explained by the relative absence of young children in these very small units: as soon as a solitary female

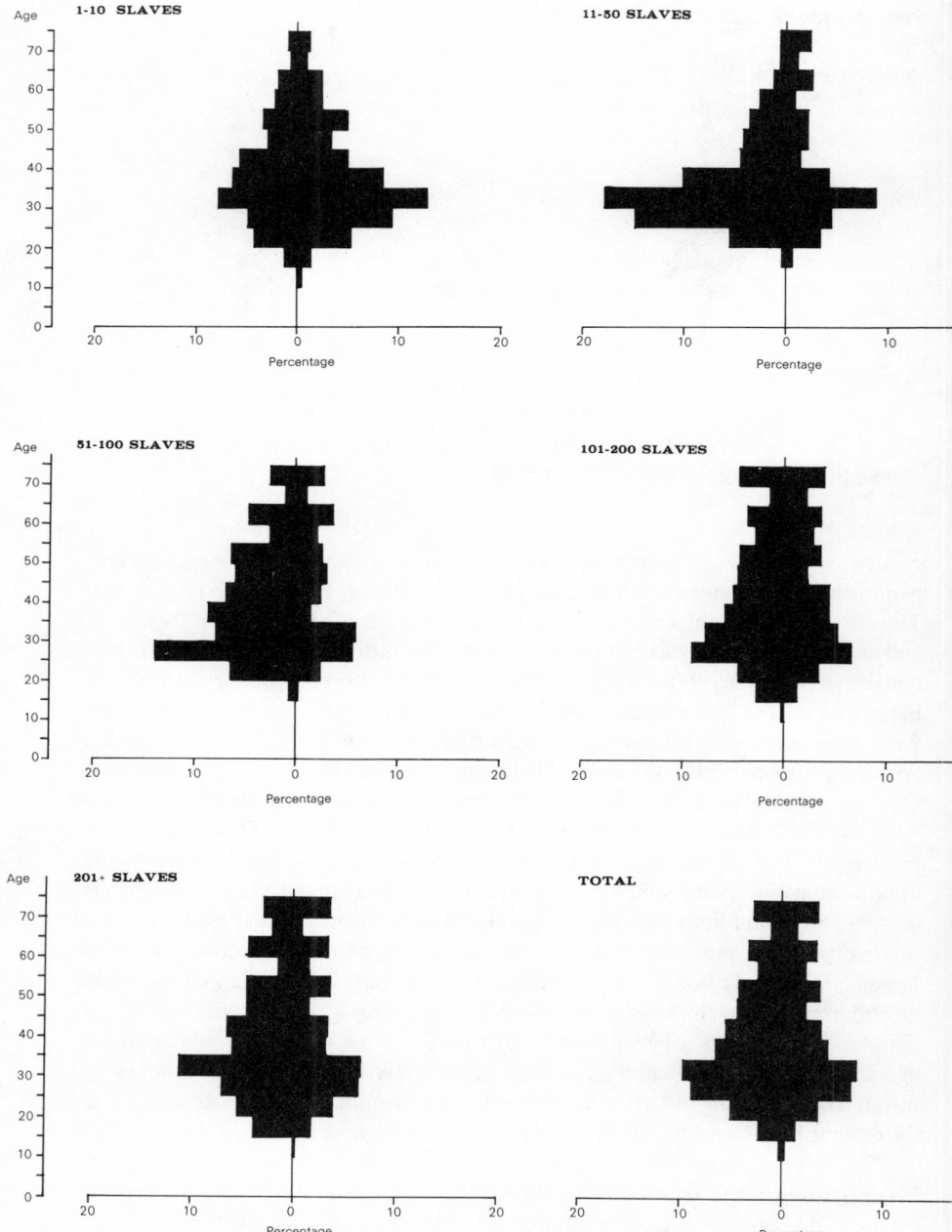

Fig. 5.15. *Age Pyramids of African-born Slaves by Holding-size: St. Kitts, 1817.* (Source: *table S4.15.*)

slave had a child, the holding shifted into a higher class. Again, the higher mean age of slaves belonging to the very small units may be explained by the large proportions of Africans in such holdings, as noted in the previous section. In general, youthfulness in the African section of the slave population was associated with youthfulness in the creole, so variations in age structure by slaveholding size are best considered in terms of the African population, which presented the most vivid contrasts. St. Kitts in 1817 provides a useful example, the proportion of African slaves decreasing along with increasing slaveholding size (fig. 5.15). The African age profiles were ordered similarly, shifting from youthfulness to maturity with increasing holding size. The same applied to the creoles (table S4.15). Among the Africans, females were dominant only in units of 1–10 slaves, reflecting their strong urban concentration, though the age profiles differed relatively little by sex. But the large proportion of African females aged between 20 and 40 years in the smaller slaveholdings had obvious implications for fertility, and this fact emphasizes the link between the age structures of the African and creole populations.

COLOR

Children of slave mothers and free fathers inherited the slave status of their mothers unless they were more than four generations removed from black (Negro) ancestors.[47] Only a proportion of these "slaves of color" were freed through manumission, so that miscegenation resulted in the gradual growth of a significant minority of slaves with white ancestors. Virtually no African slaves were defined as "colored," so the size of this subpopulation depended largely on the size of the creole population and hence on the stage of settlement of a particular colony. Decline in the African component of the slave populations meant an inevitable increase in the proportion of colored slaves.

The proportion of slaves of color in the slave populations has been calculated for at least one year for each of the colonies except Jamaica and Dominica (table 5.7). For the latter colonies, the proportions of colored births and deaths are known. These calculations exclude all slaves described as "yellow" or "red" in the registration returns for St. Lucia, Berbice, Tobago, and Nevis, since these designations were applied to Africans as well as creoles and did not serve to distinguish slaves of mixed race.[48] But it is clear that around 1817 slaves of color made up roughly 12 percent of the total slave population in the first-phase sugar colonies, 10 percent in the marginal colonies, 8 percent in the second-phase sugar colonies, and 4 percent in the third-phase sugar colonies. It has been estimated, from the registrations of births and deaths by color, that 10 percent of Jamaica's slaves were colored in 1832.[49] Edward Brathwaite and William Green hold that the latter figure is too high but derive their own estimates indirectly, from contemporary statements about the size of the free colored population at disparate dates.[50] These contemporary statements were often contradictory and provide a far less systematic statistical foundation than the direct testimony of the slave registration returns. As argued in chapter 2, the registration data seem more likely to provide an underestimate of the size of the slave colored population than an overestimate, and the validity of the Jamaica estimate is strongly supported by the pattern found for a larger sample of colonies.

Although the precise numbers may remain uncertain, there is no doubt that the proportion of colored slaves increased with length of settlement and that this proportion varied between 4 and 12 percent around 1817. The differences between the colonies are reduced somewhat if the focus is shifted to the proportion of the creole population composed of colored slaves, but the ordering of the colonies remains much the same. In St. Lucia and Nevis 16.4 percent of the creole slaves were colored around 1817, in Barbados 16.0, in Trinidad 13.2, in St. Vincent 7.2, in Tobago 5.4, and in Berbice 4.8 percent. Once again, St. Lucia proved aberrant among the new sugar colonies, having a large proportion of colored slaves as well as a relatively small proportion of Africans and a low sex ratio. Thus, the demographic structure of St. Lucia meant that it had more in common with the old sugar colonies than the new. And the relatively large proportion of colored slaves in Trinidad as well as St. Lucia distorted the relationship between stage of settlement and the number of slaves of color.

Variations in the proportion of colored slaves related also to the size and sex ratio of the white and freedman populations. In general, the proportion of colored slaves declined along with the ratio of slaves to whites, so that the proportion was highest in the towns and on small rural slaveholdings, and lowest on large plantations supervised by small groups of whites. The urban concentration of freedmen and the small scale of their slaveholdings operated in the same way. But the white sex ratio was always high on large plantations and low in the towns. Since white men but not white women could be the progenitors of slaves, this pattern complicated the simple relationship between miscegenation and the slave-white ratio. Thus, colony-level correlations between the percentage of colored slaves in 1817 and the ratio of slaves to whites or slaves to freedmen do not produce statistically significant results. This outcome matches that found for Jamaica at the quadrat level.[51] At the colony level there were significant negative correlations between the proportion of colored slaves in 1817 and the percentage of slaves attached to holdings of more than 300 slaves in 1832 ($r = -.68; p = .02$) and mean slaves per holding ($r = -.44; p = .03$), and positive correlations with the percentage in units of 11–20 slaves ($r = .55; p = .01$) and the percentage of holdings of this size ($r = .66, p = .00$). Thus, there was a clear relationship between slaveholding size and the proportion of colored slaves, which was not obviously related to the ratio of slave to free. And at the colony level, correlation with the percentage of slaves living in towns was not significant, though there is no doubt that the towns always contained more colored slaves than did the plantations. There was, however, a fairly strong positive correlation between the proportion of colored slaves and the percentage of slaves employed in non-plantation agriculture in 1820 ($r = .66; p = .00$), and negative correlations with the percentage employed on sugar estates ($r = -.39; p = .04$) and average sugar production per slave in 1820 ($r = -.57; p = .00$). But all of these colony-level correlations are distorted to some extent by the inclusion of Barbuda with its unusually large population of colored slaves, its very small white population, and its unique economy. Unfortunately, those who have studied Barbuda in detail have failed to provide any explanation for the high proportion of colored slaves or to consider its implications for the unusually high rate of natural increase on the island.[52]

In spite of the difficulties involved in colony-level correlation, little is to be gained by shifting analysis to the slaveholding because it is impossible to incorporate external variables such as the slave-white ratio at this level. But stepwise regression on a variety of economic, social, and demographic variables shows that it is difficult to develop an efficient explanation for variation in the proportion of colored slaves at the colony level. The largest coefficient of multiple correlation obtained ($r = .68$; $p = .04$) implies an explanation of only 46 percent of the variation, but the exercise is important because it reveals that the slave sex ratio can by itself account for this amount of the variation in the proportion of colored slaves. This correlation was negative: the greater the proportion of females in the slave population, the larger the proportion of colored slaves. The latter result matches that found in Jamaica at the parish level. Although there was a strong correlation at the colony level between the sex ratio and the African-creole ratio in 1817 ($R = .84$; $p = .00$), the relationship with color did not merely reflect the size of the creole population. This is made clear by the case of Jamaica, where the relationship can be established with colored births, not merely the total colored slave population. Reasons for the correlation between color and the slave sex ratio can be found in the relative lack of black male mates and the character of slave family life on small holdings, particularly in the towns. This suggests that the pattern of miscegenation depended on the internal structure of the slave population as much as the size and sex ratio of the white population.

Changes in the proportion of slaves of color between 1807 and 1834 are difficult to establish with certainty. The proportions of colored slaves in both 1817 and 1832 have been calculated only for Barbados and Grenada and are calculable for no more than another five colonies (table 5.7). Barbados showed a decrease, from 14.9 to 14.0 percent, and Grenada an increase, from 7.3 to 8.6 percent. But this apparent contrast may be attributed largely to the difference in the proportion of Africans in the two populations. In fact, the colored slaves decreased in both colonies, as a proportion of the creole populations, from 16.0 to 14.4 percent in Barbados and from 10.8 to 10.2 percent in Grenada. Thus, the overall growth of the colored slave populations resulted more from the decline of the (black) African populations after the abolition of the Atlantic slave trade than from any increase in miscegenation. The very rapid growth in the freedman populations between 1807 and 1834 depended on relatively high rates of manumission as well as on natural increase, and manumission removed many more colored than black people from the slave populations (see chapter 10). The growth of the freedman populations also meant the establishment of viable subpopulations, and this may have reduced mating between freedmen and slave women. Further, the general decline of the white populations must have meant a decrease in white paternity.

In the case of Barbados, which had by far the largest white population of any of the sugar colonies, many planters attempted to prohibit "improper intercourse" between their white employees (servants) and slaves.[53] In 1824 Sir Reynold A. Alleyne, the owner of 525 slaves on four plantations, stated that white servants forming connections with slaves were discharged, and that only one slave child had been fathered by a white on his estates since 1811. William Sharp, claiming that illicit connections were confined generally to the inferior young white servants on estates, observed that on two of his estates, with more than 400 slaves, only two slave children had been fathered by whites since the beginning of registration in 1817.[54] Analysis of the Barbados registration returns shows there was truth in these assertions, at least to the extent that the proportion of colored births was well below average in the larger slaveholdings, especially those of more than 100 slaves. In 1832–34, for example, 14.8 percent of the slaves born in Barbados were colored, the proportion falling steeply from 24.8 percent in units of 1–10 slaves to a mere 1.7 percent in units of more than 400 slaves (table 5.13). A similar tendency was evident in the total populations, the proportion of colored slaves falling from 20.3 percent in the smallest units to 8.0 percent in the largest. In terms of secular trends, it is important to observe that whereas the percentage of colored births was significantly less than the proportion of living colored slaves on the largest plantations, and in all units of more than 100 slaves, the reverse was true for the smaller slaveholdings. This shows that colored slaves were an increasing population in the smaller units, while they were a decreasing and already small proportion in the largest units. This growing concentration of the slave population on large plantations and the decline of the urban population thus contributed to the overall reduction in the proportion of colored slaves in Barbados in the early nineteenth century. These tendencies of urban decline and plantation concentration were common to all of the sugar colonies except Demerara-Essequibo, but the pattern of resident proprietorship and the evenly balanced white sex ratio of Barbados were not shared.

The attempt to prohibit miscegenation on large plantations was not repeated outside Barbados, and the groups of transient single white men employed to manage the increasingly absentee-owned estates continued to father large numbers of slave children. In Jamaica the proportion of colored births reached a peak in units of 301–400 slaves.[55] In Nevis, the Virgin Islands, St. Lucia, and Berbice, the relationship between slaveholding size and the proportion of colored slaves was much more ambiguous than in Barbados, especially when the rural population is isolated (table 5.14). Thus, the increasing concentration of the slave population on large plantations did not inevitably lead to a reduction in the size of the colored component. On the contrary, there is evidence to suggest the reverse. In St. Kitts, for example, only 10.3 percent of the slaves were colored in 1817, but by 1831–34, 10.5 percent of deaths and 15.7 percent of births were colored. Similarly, in the Virgin Islands only 6.6 percent were colored in 1818, but 7.2 percent of deaths and 16.9 percent of births were colored by 1828–31. But the proportion of colored births and deaths varied relatively little at the colony level. In Jamaica 18.4 percent of births and 7.3 percent of deaths were colored in 1829–32,

Table 5.13. *Demographic Characteristics by Slaveholding Size-group: Barbados, 1832–34*

Slaves per Holding	Males per 100 Females	Percentage African	Percentage Colored	Percentage Births Colored	Births per 1,000	Deaths per 1,000	Natural Increase per 1,000
1–10	74.9	4.9	20.3	24.8	39.8	23.9	15.9
11–50	88.7	3.5	17.2	18.9	42.0	22.8	19.2
51–100	94.2	3.4	10.9	12.4	37.3	24.4	12.9
101–200	87.8	2.2	10.8	9.3	40.6	29.2	11.4
201–300	86.3	1.3	11.9	10.6	39.6	27.6	12.0
301–400	93.2	0.2	8.8	5.3	41.5	29.4	12.1
401–500	81.1	0.9	8.0	1.7	47.1	23.6	23.5
Total	86.2	2.9	14.0	14.8	40.3	26.0	14.3

Source: T.71/553–64.

Table 5.14. *Percentage of Slaves Colored by Slaveholding Size-group: Select Colonies, 1815–32*

Slaves per Holding	Barbados, 1832	Nevis, 1817	Virgin Islands, 1818	St. Lucia, 1815	Berbice, 1819
1–10	20.3	25.7	12.6	17.6	10.1
11–50	17.2	25.4	13.0	15.6	5.2
51–100	10.9	12.6	2.7	10.0	3.8
101–200	10.8	12.5	5.0	9.4	2.2
201–300	11.9	17.5	6.4	4.3	1.7
301–400	8.8	—	6.6	4.7	2.4
401 +	8.0	—	4.8	—	1.3
Total	14.0	15.8	6.6	12.6	3.1

Source: T.71.

in Dominica 15.6 and 8.9 percent in 1829–32, in St. Lucia 15.8 and 11.2 percent in 1815–19, and in Barbados 14.8 and 10.0 percent in 1832–34. It may be concluded that the proportion of colored slaves increased in almost all of the colonies after 1807, but that since this growth was partly a function of the decline in the African populations, the proportion of creole colored often showed a minor reduction.

The most striking contrast in the distribution of the colored slave population was that between town and plantation. In general, colored slaves were almost twice as numerous in the towns as in the rural populations (table 5.8). Only in Kingstown and Scarborough did the proportion approximate that in the surrounding countryside. As at the colony level, the largest proportions of colored slaves were to be found in the towns of the old sugar colonies and the smallest in the new. In Bridgetown and Plymouth roughly 25 percent of the slaves were colored in 1817, but in Kingstown and Scarborough less than 5 percent were. These contrasts are reduced if the African-born are excluded, but the gap remains wide. It must be recalled here that the towns, especially in the old sugar colonies, had larger proportions of Africans than did the rural populations. This means that the urban slave populations comprised not only a large colored component but also a large African section.

The coexistence of large African and colored slave populations in the towns was not matched in the plantation system. In St. Lucia, for example, large proportions of Africans were associated with small proportions of colored slaves on sugar estates, while the largest proportion of colored slaves occurred on cotton plantations, which had the fewest Africans (table 5.9). A similar relationship occurred in Jamaica, where sugar estates had relatively many colored and few Africans, and coffee plantations had few colored and many Africans.[56] On the plantations, of course, low proportions of Africans generally meant low sex ratios. In the towns, however, very low sex ratios went together with relatively high proportions of Africans. Thus, the large colored slave populations of the towns are not unexpected, in view of the presence there of the major concentrations of whites and freedmen and the predominance of adult females in the slave population. It is the existence of the large African component in the same environment that is more remarkable.

Change in the size of urban colored slave populations mirrored that at the colony level. For example, the proportion fell slightly in Bridegetown, from 25.0 percent in 1817 to 24.3 percent in 1832, while in St. George it increased from 13.0 to 16.0 percent between 1817 and 1829 (table 5.8). Thus, it seems that the overall decline of the urban populations had little effect on their internal structure. The common allocation of colored female slaves to domestic occupations meant that they were relatively unlikely candidates for removal to the plantations, but they were more likely to be manumitted than blacks. Any losses of these types were quickly made up, because the urban slave populations showed particularly high proportions of colored births. In Barbados 1832–34, for example, only 13.3 percent of births were colored in the rural population, compared to 28.7 percent in Bridgetown. The relevant proportions for deaths were 8.4 and 23.4 percent. In Roseau 1829–32 some 32.9 percent of births and 18.5 percent of deaths were colored, while in Basseterre these percentages stood as high as 51.1 and 30.9. A consequence of these high birth rates was that the colored slave populations tended to be relatively youthful, particularly in the towns. This tendency was greater where there were also large African populations. In Bridgetown in 1817, for example, 62.4 percent of the colored slaves were under 20 years of age, compared to 44.1 percent of the blacks (table S5.4). In St. Lucia and Berbice around 1817, colored creoles had a mean age 2 years less than that for black creoles, so the difference was not simply a function of the proportion of Africans. To the extent too that the colored slave populations contained relatively large numbers of children, their potential cultural significance should not be exaggerated. But the youth of the populations bore visible testimony to their growth in the towns.

A relatively large proportion of colored slaves belonged to freedmen, but this merely reflected the urban concentration of the two groups. In Barbados, where the registration data were most complete, the few rural freedman slaveowners generally owned about twice the proportion of colored slaves as did whites in 1817. But in Bridgetown 25.1 percent of the slaves belonging to whites were colored, compared to 24.5 percent for freedmen. The breakdown of ownership reveals a more complex pattern, however. Only 13.8 percent of the slaves held by free blacks were colored, compared to 27.5 percent for free colored owners. Among the white owners, 28.8 percent of the slaves belonging to women were colored, compared to only 21.9 percent of those held by men. Thus, the association between colored slaves and free colored slaveowners may be explained principally by the domestic occupations in which the slaves were employed and their urban concentration. Where free colored slaveownership was more extensive, as in St. Lucia, Dominica, and Trinidad, the association was much less obvious. The proportion of colored slaves on sugar estates or coffee plantations owned by free colored planters differed little from that on similar properties belonging to whites. Slaves of color owned by white men had higher sex ratios than those owned by white women or freedmen, both in town and country, but the same applied to black slaves. It may be concluded that slaveowners rarely purchased slaves on the basis of their color, and that sex and occupation were much more significant characteristics.

Thus far, "slaves of color" have been treated as a homogeneous group. But the slave societies of the British Caribbean made much finer distinctions, placing each individual along a gradation between white and black. This system had legal implications, being used to determine slave status, and implications for the allocation of slaves to particular occupations. But no uniform system of gradations was accepted throughout the British Caribbean, and significant variations emerged from the systems employed by the earlier French, Spanish, and Dutch masters. Further, the registration returns for some colonies provided only a generalized "coloured" or "mulatto" category, even though finer distinctions were used in law and custom. This practice was followed in Barbados, Antigua, Montserrat, and the Bahamas, while the Cayman Islands returns omitted color altogether. It is tempting to interpret the whites' lack of recognition of gradations as a response to their unusual numerical strength, together with the relatively small proportion of freedmen. A similar theory has been used to account for the development of "two-tier" and "three-tier" systems of stratification within the Americas.[57] In this case, however, the theory fits Barbados, the Bahamas, and the Cayman Islands, but can hardly work for Antigua or Montserrat.

Table 5.15 presents a simplified list of the major color categories used in the registration returns for eight colonies. The categories are ordered roughly in terms of the gradation from black to white, but it seems that many of the terms were used without any genealogical precision and merely served as labels for generalized categories. (More detailed lists are provided in tables S5.1–S5.3.) There was considerable variation between colonies in the popularity of particular labels. In Jamaica, where genealogical rules were followed more rigidly, the word *mulatto* was used to describe the offspring of white-black unions, *quadroon* for the children of white-mulatto unions, *mustee* for the children of white-quadroon unions, and *sambo* for the children of mulatto-black unions.[58] This system was employed in St. Kitts, Nevis, and Anguilla, except that these colonies omitted the term quadroon. The omission is confusing since the ratio of mustee to mulatto slaves was very similar to that found in Jamaica, and it is improbable that quadroons were covered by the term *yellow* because this word was widely applied to "black" Africans as well as creoles. The label *cabre* (cobre, capre, copper) accounted for about 40 percent of the colored slaves in St. Lucia and Trinidad, and 8 percent in Tobago. Its genealogical position is uncertain, but it seems to have approximated most nearly to the sambo of Jamaica and the Leeward Islands. The Trinidad registration returns certainly provide clear examples of mulatto-black couples having cabre children,[59] but the term was probably used more loosely. In St. Vincent cabre was displaced by the portmanteau *mongrel*. As in the Leeward Islands, the new sugar colonies had no use for the term quadroon. In Tobago mulatto appears to have been generalized, the only other terms used being mestee

Table 5.15. *Color of Slaves: Eight Colonies, 1813–27*

Color	St. Kitts, 1817	Nevis, 1817	St. Lucia, 1815	St. Vincent, 1817	Tobago, 1819	Trinidad, 1813	Berbice, 1819	Anguilla, 1827
Black	18,100	8,057	13,836	24,116	13,748	24,152	21,097	2,071
Yellow	379	194	5	3	1,224	4	1,966	186
Red	—	2	346	1	—	—	212	—
Sambo	655	707	8	1	—	43	49	153
Cabre	—	—	937	13	38	574	22	—
Mulatto	911	571	1,017	758	408	864	370	83
Quadroon	1	1	1	—	—	1	—	—
Mustee	110	64	65	80	52	38	43	4
Mongrel	10	5	9	237	—	16	1	1
Brown	—	—	1	9	—	—	42	5
Castee	3	—	—	—	—	4	—	—
Indian	—	1	—	—	—	—	11	—
Unknown	—	—	57	—	—	—	69	—
Total	20,168	9,602	16,282	25,218	15,470	25,696	23,881	2,503

Source: T.71.

and cabre. It is possible, however, that the label yellow was applied to some slaves of mixed race as well as black creoles and Africans, in which case the proportion of colored slaves in Tobago and Berbice should be increased beyond the 3.3 and 2.2 percent calculated in table 5.7. The same may apply to some proportion of the *red* slaves of Berbice and St. Lucia.

These local variations in classification and the generalization of color categories make it difficult to estimate the extent of white paternity in the slave populations. If it is assumed that all mulatto and mustee slaves had white fathers, it follows that the proportion of the slave population fathered by whites varied from 1.7 percent in Berbice to 6.6 percent in Nevis and St. Lucia around 1817 (table 5.15). In terms of the colored slave populations, however, only 35.3 percent had white fathers in Anguilla in 1827, compared to 92.3 percent in Tobago in 1819. Without pressing the data too hard, it is at least clear that whites fathered a larger proportion of the colored slave population in the new sugar colonies than in the old sugar colonies. This pattern is not surprising, since the role of black and colored men in fathering slaves of mixed race was limited by the size of the population of colored female slaves. The mulatto sons of white fathers were unable to compete with whites in seeking the favors of mulatto, quadroon, or mustee women, so they most often turned to black women and fathered sambo or cabre children. As a slave population became increasingly creole, so its colored component became increasingly internal and its growth less dependent on white intervention. But this process also meant long-term change in the composition of the colored slave population, the sambo category often constituting a majority in the old sugar colonies after 1807. To the extent that the various categories of colored slaves were treated differently by the slaveowners, and so had different expectations and roles within the slave community, these changes had significant implications for their place within slave society.

The presence of "Indian" slaves in the registration returns of Berbice and Nevis deserves brief comment. Amerindian slaves existed in some numbers in the British Caribbean during the seventeenth and early eighteenth centuries, but their enslavement was declared illegal in various ordinances. A few masters were brought to court for offenses after 1807, particularly in Demerara-Essequibo, Berbice, and British Honduras.[60] In view of this, the most surprising thing about the inclusion of a handful of Amerindians in the slave registration returns is the fact that the masters chose to make their existence public. In terms of defining the limits of enslavement, an extraordinary advertisement appearing in a Barbados newspaper of 1805 is relevant here.[61] It offered for sale "a European white man named Cane," explaining that "this man was some months past purchased, and considered a mulatto of very fair complexion," but since identified as being from a poor part of Scotland. The advertiser continued, "It is repugnant to the feeling of his owner that a white man in this island shall be a slave; and do not chuse it shall be to him, and will part with the said man at half the price given for him, to a person who will put him to no meanly office and treat him with lenity." This suggests that the definition of color gradations had as much to do with perceived physical characteristics as with known histories of miscegenation, and that the limits of slavery were as flexible as the rules governing the treatment appropriate to slaves at different points within the hierarchy of color.

To summarize, the proportion of colored slaves in the West Indian colonies increased with length of settlement, ranging from about 4 percent in the third-phase sugar colonies to 12 percent in the first-phase colonies. Slaves of color were particularly common in the towns and on small holdings producing crops other than sugar. Variations in the slave sex ratio were very important in determining the pattern of miscegenation, however, and white paternity became relatively less significant as the slave population became increasingly creolized and slaves of color developed a network of kin in the rapidly growing freedman community.

6.
Rural Regimes

PREVIOUS CHAPTERS HAVE ESTABLISHED THE DISTRIBUTION OF slaves between particular types of economic activities and physical environments and have discussed variations in the demographic structure of the slave populations. The objective here is to draw these strands together by considering the material conditions of life of slaves living on rural holdings, as well as the interaction between the demographic characteristics of the slaves and the demands made of them by their owners. Chapter 7 provides a similar discussion for slaves living in towns. The principal topics to be considered are the allocation of slaves between occupations, the nature of the tasks they were required to perform, the systems used to organize and coerce their labor, material treatment in terms of food, shelter, and clothing, and the seasonal rhythms of the rural regimes. Although the slaveowners had ultimate control over all of these aspects of slave life, they had to operate within the framework of a fixed physical environment and, after 1807, a closed slave population and increasing legislative controls. Slaveowners could always sell or purchase slaves, change location, or plant a different crop, of course. But once a particular slave population was placed on a plantation organized to produce a particular crop, the slaveowner's options were greatly reduced, and this resulted in the emergence of characteristic patterns of material conditions. It is these patterns, essentially internal to the slaveholding, that are the focus of the following analysis.

OCCUPATIONS

Each type of rural enterprise had its own peculiar specialized requirements and tasks, but the majority of the West Indian slave population was almost everywhere employed in unskilled field labor with hoe or bill. This is made clear by the data collected in 1834 for compensation purposes, which were discussed in chapter 3 (tables 3.2 and 3.3). It is possible to advance beyond these gross categories for a number of colonies by analyzing the occupational data provided in the registration returns. Detailed classified lists for Barbados, St. Lucia, Trinidad, Berbice, and Anguilla are presented in tables S7.2–7.6 and summarized in tables 6.1 and 6.2. The occupational descriptions employed by the slaveowners were sometimes idiosyncratic and, more important, any classification of occupations is somewhat

Table 6.1. *Occupations of Slaves: Trinidad, St. Lucia, Berbice,*
Cayman Islands, Anguilla, and British Honduras, 1813–34

| | Percentage of Slaves | | | | | |
Occupation	Trinidad, 1813	St. Lucia, 1815	Berbice, 1819	Anguilla, 1827	Cayman Islands, 1834	British Honduras, 1834
Field laborers	47.5	44.0	49.2	40.9	45.7	2.5
Drivers	1.3	1.0	1.4	0.4	0.0	0.4
Skilled tradespeople	8.8	5.4	7.2	5.1	2.5	4.8
Domestics	18.8	16.5	8.0	14.7	39.9	33.6
Stockkeepers	1.3	2.1	1.5	2.3	0.0	0.6
Transport workers	1.3	1.4	0.6	0.6	1.4	0.8
Watchmen	0.4	1.8	0.9	0.6	0.0	0.0
Fishermen	0.3	0.4	0.1	1.0	1.5	0.0
Sellers	0.7	0.4	0.1	0.1	0.0	0.1
Laborers	0.6	1.0	4.4	0.0	0.0	43.0
Hired	0.0	0.3	0.0	0.0	0.0	0.0
Nurses	0.5	0.6	1.2	0.3	0.2	0.3
Sick or disabled	0.6	1.8	3.8	1.1	0.1	0.0
Absent	0.8	0.5	0.3	0.0	0.0	0.0
None	17.1	22.8	21.2	32.9	8.7	13.9
N	25,571	16,078	23,760	2,503	985	1,923

Sources: Calculated from tables S7.3–7.6 and S7.8, and O. Nigel Bolland, *The Formation of a Colonial Society* (1977), pp. 108–9 (British Honduras).

Note: Unspecified occupations are excluded.

subjective. No doubt criticisms can be made of the classification adopted here, but it derives fairly directly from contemporary ideas and focuses on the nature of the tasks performed rather than the materials or locus of production. The most problematic category occurring in the registration returns is laborer. In French usage *laboureur* signified an agricultural worker, distinquished from the generalized *ouvrier* or *travailleur*, whereas in English "labourer" was the generalized term and distinguished clearly from "field," or "field labourer." The returns for St. Lucia, most of them written in French, present few problems, but those for Trinidad, written in a form of English heavily influenced by French usage, are more difficult to interpret. All slaves listed as "labourer" in Trinidad have been allocated to the field laborer category, but it is obvious that some proportion of them were not in fact employed in agricultural work, especially those belonging to urban slaveowners. It must also be recalled that the "rural" population of St. Michael Parish, Barbados, has been distinguished from Bridgetown strictly on the basis of the presence of field laborers in any slaveholding, so that it probably contains some peri-urban units.

Table 6.2. *Occupations of Rural Slaves: Barbados, St. Lucia, and Trinidad, 1813–17*

| | Percentage of Slaves | | | | |
| | Barbados, 1817 | | | St. Lucia, | Trinidad, |
Occupation	Rural St. Michael	St. John	St. Andrew	1815	1813
Field laborers	40.2	53.8	57.4	48.9	56.8
Drivers	1.2	1.8	1.7	1.2	1.6
Skilled tradespeople	6.3	4.5	3.9	4.8	7.4
Domestics	19.2	10.1	8.5	11.9	10.6
Stockkeepers	4.4	5.0	4.1	2.3	1.6
Transport workers	0.7	0.3	0.4	0.9	1.0
Watchmen	0.7	0.9	1.1	2.0	0.6
Fishermen	0.2	0.0	0.0	0.3	0.1
Sellers	0.3	0.0	0.0	0.2	0.1
Laborers	0.3	0.6	0.1	0.7	0.4
Hired	0.1	0.0	0.0	0.3	0.0
Nurses	0.7	1.0	0.9	0.7	0.6
Sick or disabled	1.0	1.3	0.9	1.9	0.7
Absent	0.1	0.1	0.1	0.6	0.8
None	24.6	20.6	20.9	23.3	17.7
N	8,979	5,464	3,392	14,121	19,401

Sources: Calculated from tables S7.2–7.4.

Although Barbados, St. Lucia, and Trinidad had distinct patterns of crop production and demographic structure, the distribution of their rural slave populations between occupations showed little significant variation (table 6.2). The proportion of field laborers was least in St. Lucia, but this may be explained by variant practice in the attribution of occupations to children and the relatively large proportions of watchmen and sick or disabled. Trinidad had a larger proportion of skilled tradespeople, possibly as a result of the small scale of the plantations, but fewer stockkeepers. Overall, however, differences between the sugar colonies were surprisingly slight. Even the marginal colonies of Anguilla and the Cayman Islands do not appear to have been notably aberrant, since the apparently large proportion of domestics in the Cayman Islands was inflated by the inclusion of young children. British Honduras did differ significantly, however, because of its unique concentration on woodcutting, the urban focus of the colony's female slaves, and the proscription of plantation agriculture (table 6.1). But at the colony level the similarities in occupational structure were much more striking than the differences, so it is necessary to look beyond them to the nature of the work performed on different types of rural holdings.

Comprehensive data on occupational structure by crop type are available only for St. Lucia in 1815 and Trinidad in 1813, but these examples do have the advantage of covering a broad range of crops (tables S7.9–7.10). The most significant difference between these holdings was that sugar plantations had two to three times as many skilled tradespeople as did plantations producing coffee, cocoa, cotton, or provisions, but only half as many domestics. The contrast in the distribution of domestics applied equally to male and female slaves, but differences in the proportion of skilled tradespeople were confined to males. Variations in the proportion of field laborers were less clear-cut. Males were less often employed in the field on sugar than on the other types of plantations, but for females the position was reversed. Sugar plantations also employed relatively large proportions of their slaves as watchmen and nurses. The other occupational categories involved few slaves and varied rather inconsistently by crop. Similarly, differences between coffee, cocoa, cotton, and provisions plantations were fairly slight and inconsistent. Thus, the most striking contrast was that between sugar, with its large scale of operations and relatively complex processing technology, and the minor staples plantations, most of them small-scale affairs making simple demands on skilled labor.

Rather than examining the organization of slave labor crop by crop, the following discussion focuses on the tasks performed by slaves employed in particular occupations. The purpose of the analysis is to describe the nature of the work performed and attempt to establish the physical demands involved. Subsequent sections of this chapter discuss hours of work, seasonal demands on labor, demographic determinants of occupational allocation, and work organization, while later chapters consider the significance of differential labor demands for fertility and mortality in the slave populations. This approach has the disadvantage that it does not provide a coherent account of the internal workings of particular types of plantation units, but descriptive material of this sort is readily available for sugar estates and, to a lesser extent, for the minor staples.[1] It must also be admitted that with the available data the physical demands of particular tasks cannot be precisely quantified in terms of energy expenditure, but it is possible to order the occupations roughly in terms of effort.[2]

Field Laborers

Field laborers were the backbone of almost every type of rural enterprise and performed the most physically demanding work. In frontier regions they were required to clear the land and prepare it for cultivation. Few areas of expansion existed in the British Caribbean after 1807, but sugar plantations were established on virgin lands in southern Trinidad, and coffee plantations in western Jamaica. Most slaves lived on established units, however, and unlike slaves of earlier periods were not required to perform the rigorous tasks involved in establishing new plantations. Slaves living on sugar estates were generally divided into three or sometimes four field gangs, according to their age and strength, and the tasks allotted to each gang were graded accordingly. A similar system was employed on large coffee or cotton plantations or livestock pens with 100 or more slaves, but smaller agricultural holdings, especially those producing cocoa or provisions, had less clearly defined hierarchies within their field labor force. It also seems probable that many of Trinidad's sugar estates, with an average of only 56 slaves per holding in 1813, must have lacked this internal differentiation (table 5.3 and S7.4).

First gang: sugar estates. On sugar estates, the first gang was required to prepare the soil, plant and manure the canes, cut them when mature, and perform manual labor in the mill during crop (harvest) season. Cultivation was largely carried out with hand-held hoes and bills, the plough remaining rare in the early nineteenth century. The registration returns identify only two "ploughman" slaves in Trinidad in 1813, and two in rural St. Michael and two in St. John, Barbados, in 1817 (tables S7.2 and S7.4). No ploughmen were listed in St. Lucia, but 568 slaves *à la houe* were distinguished from the general mass of *au jardin* and *cultivateur* slaves (table S7.3). White ploughmen were brought to the West Indies in the late eighteenth century, but few remained after 1807, and many planters abandoned the use of the plough where soil conditions were unsuitable or an abundant supply of field laborers was available as in Barbados and the Leeward Islands.[3] Ploughing matches held by the Grenada Agricultural Society in the 1820s and 1830s were regularly won by slave ploughmen who received medals. In 1830, for example, there were ten ploughs in the competition, "each drawn by eight oxen, held by two negro men, and attended by three boys."[4] But the plough remained an exotic implement in all of the colonies except Antigua, where it was widely adopted.[5]

Cane land was prepared for planting either by trenching or the digging of cane holes. Contemporary planters generally talked of "holing," but sometimes they used this term to cover continuous trenching as well. Trenching was relatively uncommon in the early nineteenth century, except on those estates that made use of the plough. In Antigua some planters prepared and banked the soil entirely with the plough, but elsewhere trenches, generally six feet apart, were dug with hoes rather than spades or shovels. In Demerara-Essequibo and Berbice, the low-lying fields were covered with an intricate grid of trenches and ditches for drainage and irrigation, which had to be prepared afresh at each planting; but it is uncertain whether the canes were planted in trenches or merely pushed into the wet soil as in later periods.[6] The digging of cane holes proper involved the excavation of four- to five-foot squares to a depth of six to nine inches. The number of holes dug in a day varied between 60 and 100, or even 120, depending on the dimensions of the holes and the stiffness of the soil. Thus, the slave digging an average of 80 holes moved between 640 and 1,500 cubic feet of earth per day.[7] It was the task of the "liner," under supervision of the driver, to set out the field in geometric squares, using light surveyors' chains to standardize their dimensions and placing stakes at their corners.[8] In some cases every square in the grid was dug, as on the Pinney estates in Nevis, but in others a "checker hole" system was used, taking out alternate squares, as a method of conserving topsoil. In 1832 John Baillie of Jamaica described the digging of four-foot checker holes as follows: "There is four feet not turned up, and four feet which is turned up. There is only half of that, or somewhat more, which ought to be turned up; for that is turned upon what we call the bank. That which is taken out is taken to cover the cane, when we give the cane what we call the bank.''[9] In Antigua some planters used hoes to make cane holes in ploughed land, while others used the hoe to "cross-hole" after banking the soil.[10]

Cane holing was generally regarded as the heaviest work required of field slaves. In 1812 Dr. Jones, M.D. communicated a paper to the Barbados Agricultural Society in which he traced the prevalence of "diseases of debility" in the slave population to constant hard labor and the great strain on the constitution experienced in cane holing. "It has often occurred to me," said Jones, "that a gang of Negroes in the act of holing for canes, when hard driven appeared to be as formidable as a phalanx of infantry by the rapid movement of their hoes, . . . while I have been astonished how such habit could enable beings to persevere, so many hours in such a violent effort.''[11] Similarly, William Taylor of Jamaica stated in 1832 that "cane-hole digging is fearfully severe" but also observed that the effort required varied with the stiffness of the soil.[12] Stiff clay soils were the most demanding, both because of the effort involved in digging the cane holes and the frequency of the planting process.

Where the soil was light and well drained, several "ratoon," or second-growth, crops could be taken from a field of canes, so that only a small proportion of the cultivated area had to be entirely replanted each year. But in stiff and poorly drained soils, the canes tended to rot and needed to be replanted regularly. In Jamaica "ratooning" estates were spread along the south side of the island, while "planting" estates predominated on the north coast and in the interior valleys.[13] The light, ashy loams of most of the British colonies in the eastern Caribbean permitted extensive ratooning, but because the yield from ratoon crops was always less than that obtained from plants and declined steadily over time, planters preferred to maximize the area in plant canes wherever they had large first gangs. The second crop generally yielded only half as much sugar as the first. In Barbados, where cane was rotated with food crops, few estates permitted more than three cycles. At Colletons, for example, there were 352 acres in cultivation in December 1811, worked by 268 slaves: 45 acres were under first-crop canes, 48 acres under second-crop canes, and 14 acres under third-crop canes to be reaped and replanted, while 45 acres were in preparation for plant canes. Of the latter, 12.5 acres had yams or eddoes planted on the banks separating the cane rows, and an additional 110 acres were under Guinea corn, 17 acres under potatoes, and 15 acres under peas.[14] Thus, roughly one-third of the cane land at Colletons was holed each year. This proportion was common in Barbados after 1810, but exceeded somewhat the one-quarter (40 of 160 acres) recommended as a maximum in the 1780s for an estate with 120 slaves.[15] The growth of the slave population permitted a greater application of labor, and hence increased yields from plant canes. But Barbados was exceptional in this growth, and after 1807 most planters had to choose between accepting an increased proportion of ratoons or forcing their first gangs to work even harder.[16]

Pressure on the first gang was increased by the fact that cane holing overlapped with the reaping of the crop. Barbadian planters advocated the early preparation of the soil and recommended the use of hired jobbing gangs to hole one-half of the new cane land by the end of May in order not to interrupt the crop.[17] On some estates in Jamaica cane holing was performed entirely by jobbing gangs, and most planting estates employed such gangs to a significant extent.[18] As well as preventing interruptions to the reaping of the crop, this practice was seen as a means of reducing the amount of effort required of the estate's first gang. But this meant that field laborers belonging to jobbers, who did not themselves own land, were regularly employed in the heaviest physical work.[19] Planters paid as much as £7.5 currency per acre for cane holing in Jamaica, but only £4 in Barbados.[20] This difference reflects both the relative abundance of slave labor in Barbados and the demand for constant replanting in Jamaica. But in 1811 Barbadian planters complained that jobbing gangs employed by the task often dug shallow cane holes, and agreed that they should require day laborers to come to work earlier than usual.[21]

The work of planting and manuring was lighter than cane holing and was often shared by the second and first gangs. Whereas slaves were expected to dig only a maximum of 120 cane holes in a day, or 90 if the land had not been ploughed, the planting of 350–400 canes was regarded as a day's task.[22] Dung was carried in baskets from estate cattle pens, but often livestock were simply penned on the holed land to provide a random spread of manure.

During the crop season first-gang field laborers were required to cut the cane, assist the estate carters in transporting it to the mill, and perform a variety of manual and skilled tasks in the sugar factory. Thus, many slaves had dual, seasonal occupations. Field slaves worked also as mill feeders, stokers, firemen, sugar boilers, clarifiers, rum distillers, and mill boatswains. The registration returns identified only small numbers of slaves with such dual occupations, so it is probable that some are concealed among the skilled tradespeople (tables S7.2–7.5). But a slave listed as a "boiler," for example, did not necessarily work in the first gang out of crop, so it is impossible to make any accurate adjustment to the numbers employed in field labor. The tasks of slaves employed in skilled occupations during crop will be discussed in a later section, but it is important to emphasize that the vast majority of field laborers performed only unskilled manual labor in the sugar factories.

First-gang slaves were required to perform the heavy work of cutting the canes, using a bill or cutlass, and trimming off the tops for plants or cattle fodder and the leaves for trash. Although this work involved considerable exertion, it was regarded as less exhausting than cane hole digging. The cut canes were tied into bundles and carried to the mill on the slaves' heads or, more often, in carts drawn by oxen or on the backs of asses. In Demerara, Essequibo, and Berbice, the canes were transported in punts pulled by cattle, using the internal drainage and irrigation canals of the estates. While this system eased the labor of transportation, the digging and cleaning of these canals, six feet wide and six to seven feet deep, meant heavy labor in shoveling mud, the slave often working up to his hips in water.[23]

During crop roughly one-half of the active slave labor force was employed in the sugar factory, but two-thirds of the first gang remained in the field. An idealized version of the distribution of labor during crop in Demerara-Essequibo around 1832 is given in table 6.3. First-gang slaves provided all of the cane cutters and carriers in the field, and most of the firemen, cane carriers, and mill feeders. Very often a slave had to cut cane during the day and then perform manual labor in

Table 6.3. *Distribution of Labor on Sugar Estates during Crop: Demerara-Essequibo, 1832*

Task	Number of Slaves
Field	
Cane cutters and carriers	66
Punt men	10
Superintendent	1
Water carrier for cane cutters	1
Superintendent of cane-cutting gang	1
Cook for gang	1
Total	80
Mill	
Fire man for engine	1
Engineer	1
Clarifier men	5
Boilers, including headman	11
Fire men	3
Cane carriers	12
Mill feeders	2
Megass carriers	12
Fuel carriers	15
Packers of megass in logie	2
About liquor pump and wheel	1
Engineer's attendant (apprentice)	1
Superintendents of outdoor work	2
Cooks for people about buildings and creoles	3
Total	71
Distillery	
Fire men, 2 stills	2
At mixing cistern	1
At pumps	2
Superintendent at liquor vats	1
Can room	1
Head distiller	1
At pumps for water tank	2
Fuel carriers	1
Total	11

Source: M.C.P.D.E., 1832, vol. 1, pp. 422–28.

the mill at night. But on small estates, particularly in Demerara-Essequibo, Berbice, and Trinidad, it was often necessary to cut on one day and grind the next, and by the 1830s it was said that even "the very largest estates are often reduced to the necessity of stopping grinding from their inability to furnish a sufficient number of adults to relieve the fields of the cane trash and continue manufacturing operations at the same time."[24] One reason for this problem was that the introduction of steam engines to drive the mills created a voracious appetite for cane, compared to the less efficient wind, water, and cattle mills used on most sugar estates of the British Caribbean. Steam engines were generally applied to cane-crushing mills in Demerara-Essequibo after 1807, and in Trinidad the number increased from 5 to 18 between 1805 and 1829. The older sugar colonies were slower to accept the new technology, however, and in Barbados there were no steam mills as late as 1831.[25] But the steam mill merely replaced another machine, or animal power, and steam was not substituted for manual labor until it was used to operate mechanized cane carriers and megass elevators in Demerara in 1833, and was applied to the vacuum pan introduced by John Gladstone in the same year.[26] Throughout the slave period, then, steam power meant little more than an increased demand for cane and an improved efficiency in crushing, which created a greater output of juice to be boiled. It did nothing to reduce the heavy manual labor involved in sugar making. As the Demerara attorney Hugh Hyndman said in 1828, "I do not think that it supersedes manual labour; it economizes labour; but the work done by steam was formerly done by wind or water, or by cattle."[27]

On most sugar estates, first-gang slaves fed cut canes to the mill rollers by hand, a hazardous task that occasionally caused the loss of limbs or even death when an exhausted slave's clothing or hand was drawn into the unstoppable machine.[28] They fed dried cane trash or coal to the furnaces heating the boiling pans of sugar and fired the steam engines. The boiling houses became so hot that slaves were often employed to spray water on their shingled roofs to prevent them from catching fire.[29] First-gang slaves also performed much heavy work in the sugar factory, carrying pails of sugar from the coolers and moving hogsheads of sugar weighing up to a ton and puncheons of rum and molasses containing up to 120 gallons from the boiling house to the curing house, or the distillery to the rum store. Carrying was the most common task allocated to first-gang slaves, and it was without doubt the most physically demanding within the sugar factory.

Second-gang: sugar estates.   Second-gang slaves, most of them adolescents, performed a range of lighter field tasks. They worked with hoes and bills molding, weeding, "trashing," and "cleaning" the canes. This was described by William Taylor as "very light work," especially when compared with cane-hole digging, but again the effort involved varied with the stiffness of the soil.[30] In Barbados second-gang slaves sometimes planted food crops, especially Guinea corn, and carried manure to the fields.[31] During the crop season they worked in the field removing trash for use as fuel. At the sugar factory they carried crushed cane stalks to the trash house, or logie, where they dried them and eventually carried them to the furnaces. Only in Demerara-Essequibo did the shortage of labor result in the use of trucks running on iron rails to move the trash from the mill.[32]

Third gang: sugar estates.   The tasks assigned to the third gang, composed chiefly of children, overlapped with those of the second. But where a third (or fourth) gang was distinguished on the larger sugar plantations, it was given the specific task of gathering grass for the estate livestock and carrying it to the pens. Thus, it was often called the "grass gang" or "meat gang" (tables S7.2–7.5).

In addition to the field gangs proper, some slaves were employed in carrying drinking water for the laborers or cooking their food. Others minded the young children of mothers working in the field gangs, especially those up to three years old, who were breast feeding.

Coffee, cotton, cocoa, pimento, and provisions plantations.   On established coffee, cotton, cocoa, or pimento plantations the range of tasks required of field slaves was less than on sugar estates, and most contemporaries were agreed that the work was considerably less arduous. Only cotton needed annual replanting for high yields, and many planters avoided this by harvesting "ratoon cotton." In any case, replanting involved no more than the second gang dropping seeds into small holes made in land prepared by ploughing or hoeing.[33] The work of clearing new land for coffee, cocoa, or pimento plantations, as in Trinidad and Jamaica, was certainly heavy, but once the trees were established little replanting was required and the tasks of the field slaves were restricted to weeding, pruning, picking the crop, and processing it.[34] Coffee trees needed to be replanted only every 12–30 years, and in the meantime it was necessary merely to replace the weakest, while cocoa only required replanting after 100 years.[35] Thus, the work of cultivation on coffee, cocoa, and pimento plantations was similar to that performed by second-gang field laborers on sugar estates, though the slaves on large coffee plantations were often divided on the same three-gang system. The other advantage of work in these three tree crops was that it was largely performed in the shade. Whereas the cane or cotton field was barren of trees, although planters sometimes built huts or put up tents for occasional protection from sun and rain, coffee and cocoa groves were generally planted under taller shade trees.

Although contemporaries were agreed that the cultivation tasks involved in coffee, cocoa, cotton, and pimento were less demanding than those needed for sugar, there was some dispute over the heaviness of the work in harvesting. For example, William Shand, attorney for a large number of Jamaican estates between 1791 and 1826, claimed that the work on coffee plantations during crop was even harder than that on sugar estates.[36] A similar argument has been advanced by Warren Dean for nineteenth-century Brazil. Dean contends that "harvesting and processing the two crops required about the same amount of effort," and believes that the difference between the demands of coffee and sugar must be traced entirely to cultivation practices.[37] There seems little merit in this argument. The physical effort involved in cutting cane is certainly greater than that required to pick coffee berries, and often it was necessary only to pick the berries off the ground. The latter task was tedious rather than exhausting, and it seems that an all-out effort was required only when the coffee ripened all at the same time, in which case the crop season was brief. Very often the picking was left to the second or third gangs.[38] The volume and weight of produce to be carried to the drying platforms (known as "barbecues" in Jamaica and "drogeries" in Berbice), or to the logie or "coffee lodge" was small, relative to that involved in sugar processing. And the work of drying coffee berries by turning them on the platforms required much less heavy lifting and took place in a less torrid atmosphere, though fanning produced a good deal of dust. Pimento, cotton, and cocoa were dried on similar platforms, but, though the cocoa had to be "broken," these crops probably made even smaller demands than did coffee in terms of harvesting and processing labor.

Field laborers employed in the production of provisions performed heavy labor with the hoe in the preparation of the soil, but this work involved less arduous movement of soil than did cane-hole digging. Harvesting also involved some digging, where root crops were grown, but plantains, corn, and peas required less effort. None of the provision crops needed extensive processing. There is no evidence of the use of a gang system on holdings dominated by provisions production. Most of these units were small and concentrated in the marginal colonies. Planting was regarded as heavier work than weeding, as on sugar estates, and very often the entire labor force was employed in weeding or harvesting.[39]

Field laborers on all types of plantations were also employed in a variety of general laboring tasks other than the cultivation and processing of crops. Most of this work was performed in the out-of-crop season, and much of it involved considerable energy expenditure and heavy lifting. Field slaves collected stones for the estate masons, and were themselves frequently employed in building the stone walls that formed field boundaries in all colonies other than Demerara-Essequibo and Berbice. In the latter colonies they had the heavy work of digging and cleaning the canals that divided the fields on all types of plantations. Field slaves cut wood to fuel the factory furnaces and obtained timber for the construction and repair of estate buildings and slave houses.

Drivers

Field slaves were directly supervised by nonlaboring slaves known as "drivers," "superintendents," "overseers," or "rangers." Wherever the labor force was sufficiently large to be divided into gangs a driver was appointed to each gang, and where the first gang was extremely numerous it was sometimes supervised by two drivers, one called "head driver" and the other "under driver" (table S7.5). Drivers were rarely distinguished in holdings of 1–10 slaves, but as a proportion of the slave population they reached a peak in units of 51–100. Thus, it appears that the slave system reached a critical limit in units of this scale, encouraging the differentiation of the slave labor force into gangs and requiring the establishment of a hierarchy of authority. In smaller units it was not profitable to withdraw slaves from actual labor to act as drivers, and the owners performed most supervision directly. In units of more than 100 slaves, however, drivers were expected to supervise increasingly large gangs as the population of the unit rose, to a limit of about 400 slaves. In both St. Lucia and Berbice, for example, only 0.3 percent of male slaves were employed as drivers in units of 1–10 slaves, but the proportion rose steeply to 2.9 percent in units of 51–100, then fell to 2.0 percent in units of 301–400 in Berbice and 1.6 percent in St. Lucia (tables S7.12–7.13). In Berbice there was a slight rise to 2.3 percent in units of more than 400 slaves, suggesting that a new critical point was reached in such massive plantation populations. A very similar pattern occurred in Barbados (table S7.11). The complexity of the relationship between the supervisory class and slaveholding size meant that sugar estates, which had the largest populations, did not always have the largest proportions of drivers. In Trinidad, where the average sugar plantation had only 56 slaves in 1813, sugar did have the largest proportion of drivers (3.3 percent of males), but cocoa (2.9) and coffee (2.3) were not far distant (table S7.10). In St. Lucia, where the average sugar estate had 121 slaves in 1815, only 2.6 percent of male slaves were drivers, compared to 3.4 percent on the island's much smaller coffee plantations (table S7.9).

The drivers of field gangs were expected to ensure that the slaves kept up a certain rate of labor and performed their tasks in a manner acceptable to the slaveowner. As Robert Scott, attorney in Jamaica between 1802 and 1829, observed: "It is the duty of the driver to see that the people do their work. . . . It is his duty to see that they are diligent in the field."[40] It was the driver's job to see that the slaves turned out on time in the mornings and worked throughout the day, or completed the tasks set by the master or overseer. The driver had the power to modify or equalize the amount of work expected of individual slaves. When slaves were digging, said William Taylor, "the drivers duty is to walk about, and if he observes that one man is coming to a bad piece of ground, and that the man is working diligently, he orders another man to assist him; he shortens the line of work."[41] The role of the driver in coercing labor will be discussed more fully in a later section of this chapter, and it is enough to notice here that authority was exercised through a variety of negative and positive incentives. It was the driver's task to administer most of the corporal punishment carried out on the plantation. He carried a rod or switch as well as a whip. Whipping was generally performed on report to an overseer or master, but the driver was expected to use his rod or switch to lash slaves turning out late in the mornings or failing to keep pace in the field.[42]

Drivers were also appointed to supervise slaves employed in transportation or as skilled tradespeople. The position of the supervisor as a nonlaborer was less certain in such occupations than it was in the field. Relatively few supervisory tradespeople were described as "drivers" in the registration returns, and it was more common to find the principals termed "heads." In Berbice, for example, only one slave was called "carpenter driver," while thirteen were listed as "head carpenter," "first carpenter," or "chief carpenter." One slave's occupation was given as "head carpenter and driver" (table S7.5). It seems likely that head tradespeople frequently spent a certain amount of time prosecuting their trades as well as supervising the work of qualified tradespeople and instructing apprentices. The role of drivers supervising carters or puntmen was similarly ambiguous. Mill boatswains supervised grinding operations within sugar factories, controlling the feeding of canes to the rollers and regulating the motion of the mill whether it be powered by wind, water, or animals. Overall, it is certain that supervisory slaves generally performed few tasks involving significant physical exertion.

The slave "ranger" stood between the driver and the slaveowner or his free representatives. Handler and Lange believe that the position emerged in Barbados by the late eighteenth century, and it certainly existed in Jamaica and Berbice in the early nineteenth century.[43] One slave was listed as "ranger and driver" in the Barbados registration returns of 1817, and most rangers probably served as drivers before being moved to the top supervisory position. Augustus Beaumont, a nonslaveowner of Jamaica, stated in 1836 that the white manager generally learned the practical side of planting from slave tradespeople, and "he in general performs his duties through the negro headmen, who know the routine of the business a great deal better than he does." He continued, "I have known estates managed for weeks together entirely by the blacks, and very well managed."[44] In British Honduras, where the term "driver" was not used, woodcutting gangs were supervised by slave "captains" or "overseers" given discretionary powers to coerce their labor when the slaveowners left the works.[45]

Skilled Tradespeople

The most common skilled tradespeople on rural slaveholdings were carpenters, coopers, and masons. Sugar estates also employed specialist sugar boilers and rum distillers, but these slaves often worked as field laborers out-of-crop. The proportion of skilled tradespeople was considerably larger on sugar plantations than on other types of agricultural enterprises, partly because of the importance of these manufacturing functions and partly because of the scale of operations. But there was no clear relationship between the proportion of skilled tradespeople and slaveholding size at the colony level, since many small units contained one or two specialists (tables S7.11–7.13).

Around 1817, carpenters accounted for 27 percent of the skilled tradespeople in rural St. Lucia, 29 percent in Trinidad, 32 percent in Barbados, and 58 percent in Berbice (tables S7.2–7.5). This strong contrast between Berbice and the islands is explained by the lack of building stone on the low-lying coast and the propensity to build entirely in wood. Excellent timber was available in the colony's forests, and some plantations used it for staves, heading, and building, though most building timber was imported from North America.[46] British Honduras showed a similar concentration, with 83 percent of the male tradespeople working as carpenters in 1834.[47] There were no slave masons at all in British Honduras or the Cayman Islands, and in Berbice they were only 4 percent of the skilled. But they accounted for 11 percent in rural Trinidad, 16 percent in Barbados, and 19 percent in St. Lucia. These carpenters and masons were responsible for constructing and repairing the substantial factory buildings, hospitals, workshops, great houses, livestock pens, bridges, aqueducts, and walls found on most large plantations. Carpenters were also employed at times in building slave houses or barracks, as were masons where stone was used.[48] Carts and boats for estate use, as well as functional pieces of furniture, were built by the carpenters, but joinery was more often an urban occupation. Coopers were almost as numerous as carpenters in rural Trinidad and St. Lucia, though they accounted for only 10 percent of the skilled in Berbice and 14 percent in rural Barbados. Their work was highly specialized, being confined to the production of casks of various shapes and sizes for sugar, rum, molasses, coffee, and other produce. However, cotton was generally shipped in bales, and pimento in bags.

The heaviness of the work performed by carpenters, coopers, and masons depended to some extent on whether they were required to obtain their own materials. Cask staves were imported ready-made, and hoop making was often performed by estate blacksmiths, so the coopers' work was fairly straightforward and strictly an indoor activity. Much of the timber used by slave carpenters was imported sawn, and some plantations employed specialist sawyers. But some carpenters doubled as woodcutters and sawyers, especially in the new sugar colonies where local timber was available. Specialist stone quarriers were identified in the Trinidad registration returns, but elsewhere it is uncertain whether masons were obliged to perform the heavy manual labor of quarrying and dressing stone or whether this work was largely done by field slaves. Masons, working largely outdoors, certainly expended more effort than carpenters or coopers, but all tradespeople enjoyed a more independent regime than field laborers. The observation of the Reverend John Barry, Wesleyan missionary in Jamaica for seven years, that "if I were a negro, from what I have seen, I would infinitely rather dig cane holes than work as a country carpenter," can be dismissed as nonsense.[49]

After carpenters, coopers, and masons, the most important groups of skilled tradespeople were the sugar boilers and rum distillers. But these slaves were specialists only for the duration of the crop and generally spent the remainder of the year performing field labor. The juice expressed from the canes was carried in a gutter from the mill to the boiling house and tempered with lime to separate the dirt, in an "upper range" of coppers known as clarifiers and siphons. Very few slaves were described as specialist "clarifiers" in the registration returns (table S7.2), and it appears that some estates, especially small ones, did not use specialized clarifying vessels.[50] The clarified juice passed next to a set of coppers, three to five in number, in which it was boiled and the sugar granulated. On large estates there was a slave to each copper, equipped with a long-handled skimmer, "to clean and keep the liquor from flowing over." But, stated William Shand, "on a small estate, I should suppose there may be from two to three negroes skimming the copper; a negro skims the copper, and after a time puts down his skimmer and rests himself, but he very seldom sits, he is not allowed to sit down during the time he is there."[51] These slaves were supervised by a "head boiler" who determined the amount of lime to be added to the juice, controlled the rate of evaporation, and decided when to "strike" the sugar at the point of crystallization. He had "the charge of the whole boiling house" and was depended on by the planters to make correct decisions in what required "practical chemical knowledge" but remained more an art than a science.[52] When Sturge and Harvey visited a Jamaican sugar factory in 1837, they reported: "One of the hogsheads of sugar had been spoiled by the carelessness of the boiler-man. The book-keeper told us that they never interfered with the negros in the manufacture of the sugar, and that a book-keeper is stationed in the boiling house, merely to see that the negros commit no depredations on the syrup or sugar."[53] The rum distiller's task, on the other hand, was relatively simple, and he had far fewer chances to affect a plantation's profitability.

Plantations other than those producing sugar employed relatively few slaves in skilled tasks to process their crops. A small number of slaves on cotton plantations in Berbice were involved in ginning, spinning, and weaving, but most of them also worked in the field (table S7.5). Cocoa, coffee, and pimento, however, seem to have required no skilled specialists.

The only other group of skilled occupations employing significant numbers of slaves outside the towns was that related to the production of clothing. Most of this output was intended for the use of the masters, rather than for sale. Seamstresses, tailors, and shoemakers accounted for 5 percent of the rural skilled in Barbados, 6 percent in Trinidad, and 8 percent in St. Lucia (tables S7.2–7.4). Their tasks were sedentary, involving relatively small amounts of physical exertion. Very often, especially for the seamstresses, they worked within the domestic environment and were sometimes made to perform other duties in the great house.

Few other skilled occupations employed enough slaves to merit attention here. Some sugar estates in Barbados, Trinidad, and St. Lucia employed potters, who manufactured the conical earthenware vessels used in the process of refining "clayed" sugar.[54] Others had blacksmiths, coppersmiths, and millwrights to produce hoops for the hogsheads and repair factory equipment. There were cartwrights, wheelwrights, saddlers, and farriers to attend to the needs of transport. Slaves made baskets for the carrying of dung and canes. Almost all of these specialists were found only on the largest plantations.

Domestics

Slaves employed in providing personal service to their owners or other supervisory free people necessarily worked almost entirely within the great house complex and very rarely had dual occupations involving work in field or factory. The number of domestics on particular rural holdings increased with size, but as a proportion of the slave population the reverse was true. Thus, relatively few of the slaves living on large sugar estates worked as domestics, compared to those on small, minor staples plantations. Among female slaves, only about 10 percent were domestics on sugar estates, compared to 20 percent on coffee, cotton, cocoa, or provisions plantations (tables S7.9–7.10). In the rural parish of St. Andrew, Barbados, the proportion of female domestics fell steadily from 42 percent in units of 1–10 slaves to only 6 percent in units of more than 200 (table S7.11). For males, the proportion fell from 11 to 3 percent. Only in Berbice is there evidence of an increase in units of more than 300 slaves (table S7.13). Thus, it appears that while every slaveowner desired at least one domestic as evidence of status, there was a definite upper limit to the number required to signify opulence. This tendency was perhaps reinforced by the frequency of absentee ownership in the larger slaveholdings, though the comparison of Barbados and Berbice fails to support this line of argument.[55]

Domestic slaves have sometimes been portrayed by historians as "nonproductive" or "expendable," and contemporary observers often referred to them as "useless" or "idlers."[56] No doubt there is some truth in these assertions. Domestics were certainly more numerous in the West Indies than in Great Britain during this period, though the contrast with the land-owning bourgeoisie and aristocracy was far less marked.[57] But it is important to remember that the domestics did in fact perform a variety of productive functions, making bread and butter as well as beds, and relatively few of them were mere liveried flunkies serving decorative roles. The registration returns distinguished only a small proportion of specialists, most slaves being listed simply as "domestic," "house servant," or "servant." These slaves were expected to perform a wide range of tasks. Of the specialists, however, by far the most numerous on rural holdings were cooks and washerwomen (tables S7.2–7.4). In rural Trinidad in 1813, for example, 40 percent of the specialists were cooks and 50 percent washers. In the parishes of St. John and St. Andrew, Barbados, 49 percent were cooks and 28 percent washers. Only in rural St. Lucia were valets more numerous than cooks or washers. Butlers, housekeepers, and footmen were rarities on plantations. Nurses attended the free children of slave owners in the great house. But they also watched over the young children of slaves, and it is not always possible to distinguish the two functions in the registration returns. Domestics were also occasionally appointed to wait on slave drivers or housekeepers, as well as on free overseers and estate managers. Others held positions of trust, acting as messengers, gatekeepers, and keykeepers.

The tasks performed by domestics were less physically demanding than those of field laborers or most skilled tradespeople. Slaves are supposed to have preferred working in the house, and "demotion" to field work was considered sufficient punishment for the misdemeanors of domestics.[58] Domestic occupations were correlated with status within the slave hierarchy for reasons other than the heaviness of the work, but there is no doubt that slaves were well aware of the latter differential. The domestic was subject to a more constant, often brutal, supervision, however, working directly under the eye of master or mistress. This applied particularly in the small holdings of the marginal colonies. A minor distinction may be made between the work of washers and other domestics. The work of the washer was relatively heavy, but permitted a certain independence since it was often carried out beyond the house. George Pinckard described the process in Barbados as follows:

The linen is first put into a tub, and rubbed through some water, then it is taken out and sprinkled with sand, previous to being pressed and beaten with a piece of wood, upon a coarse large stone, by the side of the river; after which it is rubbed out in the open stream. Next it is sprinkled with the fine white sand of the shore, and spread out by the sea to whiten; then it receives another dipping in water, and, finally, is rinced out in the running stream of the river.[59]

Stockkeepers

Cattle and horses were vital to the plantations, since they provided the main source of power for drawing carts and punts, turned animal mills on sugar estates, and transported free people from place to place. But only in Jamaica were livestock raised on specialized, large-scale pens.[60] Elsewhere, most animals were either imported or raised on the plantations themselves. Slaves employed in tending livestock were generally most numerous on sugar estates, but the proportion varied somewhat erratically with slaveholding size (tables S7.11–7.13). On large properties the number of livestock was sufficient to permit the employment of specialist cowherds, mule keepers, ass minders, shepherds, goat keepers, pig drivers, rabbit keepers, fowl keepers, and turkey keepers. Cattle keepers were the most numerous of these specialists in Barbados and St. Lucia but were outnumbered by mule boys in Trinidad. Other slaves were employed as grooms, ostlers, stable boys, jockeys, dairy women, and milk maids. In Barbados cooks were employed to prepare food for plough cattle and hogs (tables S7.2–7.5). The tasks of these stockkeeper slaves require little explanation, but it is necessary to note that their work was generally less physically demanding than that of field slaves and involved a relatively large degree of independence and skill.

Transport Workers

On rural holdings, especially sugar estates and units of more than 50 slaves, a small proportion of the slaves were employed as specialist transport workers. These slaves were required to move goods within the boundaries of the plantation and to carry produce and imported supplies to and from the wharves. On rural holdings carters, mule drivers, sailors, and canoe men were most common within this class. Some of these slaves also worked in the field, or as stockkeepers or fishermen, but the vast majority were specialists (tables S7.2–7.5). The movement of goods within plantations generally involved only land transport, but in Demerara-Essequibo and Berbice the internal canal systems were used. In either case the task of the slave was chiefly to drive or lead the animals pulling carts, wagons, or punts.

Movement beyond the plantation boundaries required that transport workers have a wider range of skills, because the generally bad state of the colonies' road networks meant that a large proportion of the goods were carried by coastal shipping. In Trinidad, for example, travel to Port of Spain from the southern, northern, or eastern settlements was almost entirely by sea until the time of emancipation.[61] Movement along the coast of Demerara-Essequibo and Berbice also tended to be by sea, though slaves were employed on the ferries that crossed the wide estuaries of the colonies. Indeed, enterprising slave boatmen used plantation punts and boats to carry slaves to Georgetown on Sundays at half price, much to the distress of the lessee of the Demerara ferry.[62] In the eastern Caribbean and the Bahamas, slave sailors had even greater mobility, some of them becoming expert pilots. In 1815, for example, an Antiguan slaveowner offered for sale "a stout negro man, a good sailor and fisherman, capable of taking charge of a vessel, and a good pilot for this and all the neighbouring islands."[63] Such slaves had a far greater independence of action than the estate carter, but the tasks performed by all transport workers were fairly similar in their physical demands. Even the carter, who like the driver carried a cartwhip, had a certain authority within the slave hierarchy.

Watchmen

The demand for slave watchmen was greatest on rural holdings cultivating staple export crops. None at all were listed in the registration returns for the Cayman Islands and British Honduras, but in St. Lucia they accounted for as many as 1.8 percent of the slaves (table 6.1). The largest proportions were found on sugar estates, and the proportion generally increased steadily with holding size (tables S7.9–7.13). In St. Lucia in 1815, for example, 4.7 percent of male slaves on sugar estates were watchmen, compared to 2.0 percent on coffee plantations, 1.1 percent on cocoa plantations, and none on cotton or provisions plantations. In the parish of St. Andrew, Barbados, the proportion of watchmen increased from zero in units of 1–10 slaves to 4.7 percent of males in units of 201–300. Thus, it appears that the need for watchmen was greatest where the threat to export crops, whether from theft, arson, or the depredations of livestock, was greatest. The large number of livestock on sugar estates also required protection, to prevent the slaves from slaughtering them for meat. Of the specialist watchmen distinguished in the registration returns, very few were employed to guard mill buildings or work-shops. But watchmen were specifically employed to guard pastures, orchards, kitchen gardens, and slave provision grounds, as well as export crops (table S7.3). To some extent the work of watchmen was seasonal, and some held dual occupations. Their work was largely sedentary, and their authority was limited to report insofar as they had to deal with other slaves. In Berbice the watchman "may sometimes have a gun, for the purpose of driving away birds, or to kill the wild animals that injure the provisions," but "he is usually armed only with a cutlass, which he is strictly ordered never to use but in self defence."[64] As John Barry put it, watchmen, "in consequence of their situation on properties, are almost entirely excluded from human society."[65]

Fishermen

The fish caught by slaves belonging to rural holdings were either sold in the internal markets or served at the master's table. In Barbados some of their catch (salt flying fish) found its way into the slaves' diet.[66] But fishermen were always a minor group. They were relatively numerous in the marginal island colonies, where the sea was always close. In the sugar colonies they were most common on cotton plantations, but the reason for this concentration is not obvious (tables S7.9–7.10). Some of them also worked as sailors, tradespeople, or field laborers. No specialists were listed in the registration returns, except that in St. Lucia a distinction was made between *pecheur* and *seineur* slaves (table S7.3). Most fish seem to have been taken with nets, but baskets, hooks, and harpoons were also used. Sturge and Harvey described the use of seines in Dominica:

Three or four canoes, loaded with stones, take a large net about ten feet deep, and from sixty to one hundred yards in length, to some distance from the shore, which they let down; the lower edge being weighted with lead, and the upper supported by pieces of cork. The stones in the canoes are then thrown with great violence into the sea in such a direction as to frighten the fish towards the shore, when a canoe at each extremity drags the net rapidly to the beach, and the fish is secured.[67]

This was certainly not light work, though it lacked the inexorable pace of field labor and permitted a degree of independence. The most hazardous of the techniques used by slave fishermen was diving for conchs, which sometimes resulted in drowning.[68]

Sellers

Most of the slaves employed in retailing goods for their owners worked in the towns, and those belonging to plantations were generally attached to holdings on the urban fringes. The activities of these slaves will be discussed in chapter 7.

Laborers

The slaves included in this category performed a variety of unskilled tasks other than field labor. In some occupations, such as firemen, they were employed in sugar factories, and their tasks have been discussed in earlier sections as part of dual occupations. Huntsmen, rat catchers, lime burners, charcoal burners, and castor oil makers also generally belonged to plantations. Lime was required both for building mortar and for clarifying cane juice, but lime burners, and the other slaves in this group, led a relatively independent existence even on plantations with permanent kilns. The heaviest part of the work was the quarrying of limestone rock or coral and shell, using drills and hammers, for burning.[69] Brickmakers were most common in Trinidad, where there was small brick and tile factories on the Caroni River and at Barancon.[70] Work in these factories was as hot and heavy as in sugar mills. Chain gang slaves labored at public works, performing heavy earthmoving tasks or sawing planks, their legs weighed down by chains fastened by a string to the waist.[71] Pioneers attached to military units were required to perform similarly heavy tasks.

Woodcutters were most numerous in Demerara-Essequibo, Berbice, and British Honduras. In 1813 William Reed petitioned the Lieutenant Governor of Demerara-Essequibo for a license to cut wood, stating that "your petitioner has resided for twenty years in these colonies in the several capacities of overseer and manager and has from his savings acquired a few Negroes whom, with some others hired, he wishes to employ in cutting timber on the banks of Mahaicony Creek."[72] By 1821, however, the proprietors of a boat-building establishment at Mahaicony (Park Benjamin and James Albouy) were arguing that the timber had all been cut down; they had moved their works to Georgetown and applied for a license to cut mora and other timbers on creeks up the Demerara. Yet another timber cutter moved his slaves up this river beyond the rapids, "conceiving that a few loads of wood might possibly be brought over them about the night of the rainy season."[73] Over the period, then, timber getting was steadily pushed into the interior, the small groups of slaves becoming increasingly isolated. George Pinckard, traveling on the remote upper Demerara, came upon

a party of sixteen naked slaves, male and female, in the act of dragging the trunk of an immense tree out of the forest, with ropes. They were conducted by a driver with his whip; and pulled on the load by mere strength of arm, having no assistance from any machinery, and only availing themselves of the simple expedient of placing billets of wood under the tree, at short distances from each other, in order to prevent it from sinking into the dirt, and doubling their toil.[74]

Here was extreme physical exertion to rival anything on the coastal estates. Yet the planter, attorney, and timber getter Park Benjamin could inform a Boston client in 1813 that he had sent her slaves up river to cut timber, since this was more healthful than hiring them on a plantation, and the slaves had refused the latter alternative.[75] This was a self-interested assessment.

The mahogany cutters of British Honduras also worked in shifting, isolated camps, but followed a more clearly defined seasonal cycle than the woodcutters of Demerara. Around August, the gangs left Belize for the up-country works, or "banks," where they built huts and penned livestock. The cutting concessions stretched back from the rivers or, occasionally, covered entire islands.[76] Each gang contained slaves with specialized occupations. The trees to be cut were located by a skilled "huntsman" and felled 12 feet above the ground by axmen standing on platforms. When sufficient trees had been cut, the gang made roads to them, clearing the underwood with cutlasses, the larger trees with axes and fire, and the stumps and rocks with hoes and pickaxes. This task accounted for two-thirds of the total cost of the operation. The roads stretched up to 10 miles inland from the river bank. After spending Christmas in Belize, the gangs returned to the banks in February, when the timber was cross-cut and squared. The roads were firm enough for use only in the dry season, in April and May, so this period was one of great activity. A gang of 40 men was capable of working six trucks, each with seven pairs of oxen and two drivers, 16 men cutting cattle fodder, and 12 loading the trucks. Logs were loaded from temporary platforms that were inclined planes. The work was carried out at night, the trucks leaving camp about 6 P.M. and returning to the river by 11 A.M. The logs, marked with the owner's initials, were then floated down river for up to 200 miles, the gang following in flat-bottomed canoes, or "pitpans," to release the logs from snags. At Belize the logs were halted by a boom across the river, then tied into rafts, taken to the wharf, and smoothed for shipping.[77] Most of the tasks performed by mahogany cutters involved considerable physical exertion, but unlike woodcutting in Demerara, the driver and his whip were absent.

Salt rakers also performed heavy labor on a seasonal basis. In the Bahamas the salt ponds were opened annually to all free people, who were required only to give lists of all "negroes and servants" to be employed by them in raking the salt.[78] In Anguilla the council appointed Commissioners for each division of the island, who inspected the salt pond and appointed constables to keep out trespassers. When the reaping day came, less than an annual occurrence in the early nineteenth century, a gun was fired early in the morning and the slaves rushed forward to gather as much as they could for their owners. A gun was fired again at 2 P.M. when the laborers, it was said, could reap for themselves.[79] The slaves carried out this feverish activity standing in salt water, filling a half-barrel with a shovel. Sometimes the salt was simply heaped on to wooden rafts. The slaves then shoveled the salt into heaps on dry land, pushing heavy wheelbarrows through the sand, and covered them with palmetto thatch.[80] But salt raking generally occupied only a small part of each year, and in the registration returns for Anguilla not one salt raker was listed; the work was performed chiefly by "field" slaves (table S7.6).

Nurses

The tasks of nurses included the care of young and old as well as sick and disabled slaves. Their numbers were greatest on sugar estates and large slaveholdings, where the sick or disabled were concentrated (tables S7.9–7.13). Large plantations also had sufficient young children to warrant the employment of specialist nurses, so the proportions of nurses caring for the sick and the young tended to be equivalent. The tasks of sick nurses, hospital nurses, yaws house nurses, doctors, apothecaries, and midwives will be discussed in detail in chapter 8, in the context of slave medical attention. Nurses attending the young worked either in the field, feeding and playing with children while their mothers labored, or in the slave village. These were known as children's nurses, creole nurses, or field nurses (tables S7.2–7.5). Only large plantations established specialized nurseries. Bayley described the nursery at Colville Estate, Barbados, as "a large and airy room, full of young negroes. Some old and stout enough to crawl about, or even to stand upon their legs, and others lying kicking in their trays."[81] On the plantations of the largest slaveowner in Berbice young children were left with nurses, "whose sole duty is to keep them together in a nursery and playground prepared for that purpose." The nurses washed the children, cooked the food eaten during the day, and sometimes acted as wet nurses.[82]

HOURS OF WORK AND SEASONAL DEMANDS

The great variations in the amount of energy expended by West Indian slaves in performing the tasks described in the previous sections gain increased significance when related to differences in the amount of time spent at work. Hours of work varied according to the occupation and strength of the slave, as well as the pattern of work organization and seasonal demands of rural holdings.

Most slaves were forced to work set hours, but it became increasingly common after 1807 for rural labor to be organized on a task-work system, in which slaves were given specified tasks measured in terms of distance, area, or volume. Thus, it was applied only to tasks in which output could be quantified according to these parameters. The reasons for the spread of the system in the British Caribbean in the early nineteenth century are not entirely certain, but it appears the planters believed task work increased productivity and reduced costs of supervision. Some planters paid cash to slaves for additional work performed after the task was completed.[83] The system might be seen as a response to a labor shortage, but it was used in densely-populated marginal colonies as well as new sugar colonies with declining populations.

Task work seems to have emerged first in the marginal colonies. In 1823 Bahamian slaveowners claimed that task work had been universal in the islands, "within the memory of the oldest of us," for all slaves except those employed as domestics, sailors, or tradespeople.[84] The work of mahogany cutters in British Honduras was said to be almost entirely on a task basis by the 1830s, but it seems more likely that it was largely confined to the clearing of roads in the forests.[85] In Grenada task work was first introduced by the planters of Carriacou.[86] The use of the system in the sugar colonies, however, seems to have been confined largely to the crown colonies of Trinidad, Demerara-Essequibo, and Berbice, where it emerged in response to efforts by the British government, beginning in 1823, to place legal controls on hours worked and the use of the whip. Indeed, the development of the task-work system received active encouragement from government.[87] By 1826 the system had been adopted on sugar estates wherever it could be introduced in Trinidad and was widespread in Berbice, and by 1828 it was said that in Demerara it was "becoming pretty general."[88] But it seems that the system was poorly defined in Demerara, many planters inflating the tasks beyond a normal day's labor to ensure that they could barely be completed within the time.[89] In Jamaica, after 1820 the digging of cane holes and the planting of canes was occasionally performed on a task basis, but the system was used systematically only in the cultivation and harvesting of coffee and pimento.[90]

The amount of work set for any task varied with the strength of the slave and local conditions, such as the stiffness of the soil. A task was supposed to equal the work normally completed in a day. In Trinidad, slaves commencing work at the usual time of 6 A.M. were said to generally complete their tasks by 1:00–2:30 P.M., though "indolent persons" took longer. In Demerara-Essequibo they finished by 2:00–3:00 P.M., except on estates where the so-called tasks were inflated to ensure that the slave labored until 6 P.M.[91] It is not possible to give anything like a comprehensive listing of variations in the amount of labor required by the task. In Jamaica, for example, the number of cane holes to be dug in a day task ranged from 80 to 120, depending on the preparation of the soil. In Trinidad, 350–400 canes were to be planted. In Demerara, 90 rods (500 yards) of weeding and molding, 36 rods of banking, or 20 rods of trenching (if two feet wide), were expected. In Berbice 90–100 coffee trees were to be cleaned. In British Honduras, 100 yards of underwood or larger trees were to be cleared.[92] Although the slaveowners seem to have been satisfied with work done by slaves under the task system, and slaves generally were able to reduce the amount of time they spent in supervised labor, the system had definite limitations. It was difficult to operate during crop season, especially on sugar estates, and could not be applied to certain occupations at any time of the year. The concept of job work, as opposed to the daily task, might have been applied to some of the skilled trades but was not used until after emancipation. The work of watchmen, fishermen, or domestics, however, was not adaptable to either of these systems.

By the end of the eighteenth century it was customary, and occasionally codified in colonial slave laws, that West Indian slaves should not be required to perform labor for their masters on Sundays or the Christmas holidays. The number of days given at Christmas varied from two to four, and some colonies also gave Good Friday, Easter Monday, and Whitsuntide. Beyond Sundays and these traditional holidays, masters gave days largely at their own discretion, though fines were sometimes imposed for permitting too many or too few free days. But it was a general rule that the slaves were granted more "free" days where they were required under the provision ground system to produce their own food, and fewer where the masters distributed regular allowances.

One of the first acts of the British after the conquest of Trinidad was to abolish the "custom" of giving slaves Saturdays in lieu of food rations and to impose a fine of $50 on delinquent masters. From 1800 Trinidad slaves got only Sundays, Christmas, New Year's, Good Friday, and Corpus Christi, as well as Saturday afternoons, to work their provision grounds, from July to December on sugar plantations or January to June on coffee, cocoa, or manioc plantations. But the ordinance of 1800 proclaimed that "this regulation shall not extend to watchmen or pasture boys (who will continue as heretofore to do that duty in turn), nor to family domestics, the intention being simply to assure the field Negro the free enjoyment of his holiday to work his own grounds."[93] The customary practice of giving only occasional afternoons, rather than whole Saturdays, was common in Barbados and the Leeward Islands where slaves were given rations rather than being expected to produce their own food, and the Trinidad ordinance was based on the assumption that the planters should move toward the ration system.[94] But the slave laws of Barbados did not specify the granting even of Sundays until 1826, and it remained customary for the slaves to be given their allowances on Sunday mornings when they were expected to bring a bundle of grass.[95] In the Bahamas, the slaves belonging to Charles Farquharson of Watling's Island worked Monday to Saturday every week of the year in 1831 and 1832, excepting four days at Christmas, and were given only one Saturday in each of these years in return for working Sundays.[96]

Few plantation journals provide the data necessary for a calculation of the number of days actually worked, so that detailed comparative analysis is impossible. Handler and Lange calculated that the slaves of Newton Plantation, Barbados, had 54 days off in 1796/97, and those on Seawell Plantation at least 56. Farquharson's slaves, in the Bahamas, had 56 days in 1831/32. At Peruvian Vale Estate, St. Vincent, the slaves had 67 days in 1807/8. Rose Hall Estate, Jamaica, gave 78 days in 1830/31.[97] A small number of additional days were lost to the planters as a result of bad weather, and occasionally individual slaves were listed as "taking day." But the differences in the number of days given on these five plantations must be explained largely in terms of the absence of the provision ground system in Barbados and the Bahamas, and its presence in St. Vincent and Jamaica. The extra days given in the latter colonies were "free" only in the sense that the slaves were not required to work in gangs under the supervision of drivers. The time was given only because the planters had relinquished the responsibility for ensuring the slaves' subsistence and had shifted the onus for food production to the slaves themselves. Thus, the slaves spent much of this time performing agricultural work, albeit at their own pace and without the driver's lash.

The early nineteenth century saw some reduction in the hours worked by West Indian slaves. This reduction resulted primarily from the ameliorative legislation forced on the colonies by the British Parliament. In 1823 an order in council was introduced in Trinidad prohibiting the performance of any labor (other than that of watchmen or domestics) between sunset on Saturday and sunrise on Monday, and abolishing the Sunday markets.[98] Since the latter were crucial to the marketing of food for both free and slave, and were largely supplied by the slaves, these two prohibitions effectively abolished most forms of Sunday labor and forced the owners to permit slaves to attend markets on Saturdays. Similar legislation was introduced in all of the colonies by the end of the 1820s. It was not completely effective. Some masters continued to exact a certain amount of labor on Sundays, and unofficial Sunday markets persisted on a small scale. In Tobago, for example, the slaves were given Thursdays as well as Sundays out of crop, but even the use of military force merely pushed the markets held on Sundays from the road leading to Scarborough to the beach.[99] But in some cases colonial legislation was in advance of that promoted by Parliament. The Jamaican slave law of 1816, for example, prohibited Sunday labor during crop, stating that no mill should be worked between 7 P.M. Saturday and 5 A.M. Monday and imposing a fine of £20 on offenders. A law passed in 1809 had already established that Jamaican slaves should be granted one day in every fortnight out of crop, as well as Sundays, to cultivate their provision grounds, and the 1826 law specified that the number of such days should be at least 26 in each year.[100] In Nevis some estates provided no allowances of food but gave the whole of every Saturday in lieu. In St. Vincent during the 1820s it was customary to give the slave Saturday afternoons out of crop.[101] In Barbados the granting of Saturday afternoons, including alternate days during crop, was introduced on the Codrington plantations from 1819. The crop-over, or harvest-home, holiday became increasingly common in the early nineteenth century, and slaves were also given several hours to attend the funerals of their relatives. Occasional days were set aside for the celebration of deliverance from hurricanes or epidemics.[102]

As well as a reduction in the number of days worked by slaves there was also some shortening of the working day in the early nineteenth century. Generally, slaves worked from sunrise to sunset, but these limits were very flexible, particularly during the crop season. The most important change was the partial abandonment of night work in some of the colonies. At one extreme, the sugar factories operated around the clock for six days in the week. This system was followed very generally in Jamaica and some of the Windward Islands, but was rare in Barbados and the Leeward Islands, and disappeared in Trinidad, Demerara-Essequibo, and Berbice as a consequence of the introduction of steam power and regulatory legislation. Where mills worked around the clock, the slaves were organized according to a variety of systems of "spells." In the "long spell," practiced in Jamaica until the 1830s, slaves worked from midday until shell-blow (about 4:30 A.M.) the next morning, when they had a break of two hours, then worked until dark, and turned out again at daylight the following day. This meant periods of up to 30 hours of continuous labor. In St. Lucia slaves on some estates worked three spells, or watches, as follows: work 24 hours, rest 6, work 12, rest 12, work 12, rest 6, work 24, rest 6, and so on. This work was divided between spells in the field and the factory, but all of the night work and the 24-hour watches were confined to the mill.[103] It was performed by all first-gang slaves, both males and females. The long spell meant a total of 96 hours of actual work time in a six-day week. But the "double spell" was more common. In this system the slave spent the daylight hours working in the field, then went more or less directly to the mill and worked there until midnight. The second day was spent in the field; on the third, work commenced in the mill at midnight and continued in the field until sunset.[104] Although the double spell limited the periods of continuous labor to 18 hours, it still meant three days of night work and a total work time of 90 hours per week. Thus, the spread of the double spell system in Jamaica did little to reduce hours of work. It is also important to notice that the number of spells worked by a slave depended on the size of the holding, since a certain minimum work force was required to keep the factory operational. Slaves belonging to small units inevitably worked more spells and longer hours. The long spell or double spell continued throughout the crop season, for up to six months of the year.

In Barbados sugar factories rarely operated around the clock, and most slaves finished work by 9 P.M. The outer limits were 5 A.M. to 10 P.M.[105] The reason for the general absence of night work in Barbados probably lies in the relatively small cane acreage on most of the plantations and their large populations, as evidenced in the low level of output per slave. A similar tendency accounts for the later decline of night work in the Leeward Islands. The decline of night work in the Windward Islands is more difficult to explain, but as early as 1816 the Assembly of Tobago reported "the total relinquishment of all night-work upon the estates."[106] The order in council of November 1831, which restricted work time to 9 hours per day in the crown colonies, was an important factor in reducing night work in Trinidad, Demerara-Essequibo, and Berbice. But it appears that most sugar factories in those colonies had already ceased to operate around the clock. Henry Gloster, Protector of Slaves in Trinidad, reported in 1830 that the factories generally finished boiling by 7 or 8 P.M., though if the fuel was wet and the weather bad they might go on until 11 P.M. The slaves employed in the factories were changed every night or every other night.[107] A similar report came from the British Guiana Protector of Slaves, stating that the factories generally stopped work by 10 P.M. In British Guiana there was no regular crop season, and most estates manufactured sugar for a concentrated period of about 10 days in every month. The practice was to light the fire at 4 A.M. and extinguish it at 10 P.M., but variations in the extent of mechanization resulted in differing work schedules for the slaves.[108] The relative insignificance of around-the-clock sugar making in British Guiana can be explained by the absence of a concentrated crop season, the efficiency of the steam-powered mills, and mechanization of some processes, while in Trinidad it may be explained by the smallness of the plantation populations as well as the partial use of steam power. In any case, the order in council of 1831 effectively removed the possibility of even this limited system of night work in the crown colonies.

The length of the crop season depended on the amount of cane to be processed and the efficiency of the sugar factory's technology. It also depended on weather conditions, which affected the yield of cane and interrupted cutting and milling operations. With the exception of Demerara-Essequibo and Berbice, where crop extended throughout the year, the sugar harvest generally took place between January and June. Some estates began milling before Christmas, but it was a common practice to commence work as soon as the excitement of the holidays had passed. In drought years, and on small estates, the crop was often complete by May, but where the yield of cane was heavy, or cutting was interrupted by rain, it might continue into July. This pattern was universal in the eastern Caribbean and was followed on the south side of Jamaica, but on the north side the sugar crop generally extended from March to November.[109] On most estates, however, the crop occupied fully six months of each year. The use of steam-powered mills and improved boiling techniques helped to concentrate the duration of the crop, especially in Trinidad, Demerara-Essequibo, and Berbice.[110] On Jamaican coffee plantations the crop season generally lasted four to six months, October to March, but might be concentrated into as little as six weeks. In British Guiana the coffee crop began in June and lasted for nine weeks. In Trinidad the cotton crop was harvested in the first half of the year, and coffee and cocoa in the second. Pimento crops were taken off between July and September.[111]

An example of the annual work cycle on a sugar estate may be helpful. Peruvian Vale Estate was located on the Petit Yambou River, on the southern coast of Charlotte Parish in St. Vincent.[112] Around 1807 it occupied 521 acres and was worked by 200 slaves. It was linked with Henry's Vale Estate, with 112 acres and 130 slaves. Some 260 acres of Peruvian Vale were under cane, divided into 45 "pieces," and caneland stretched continuously along the coast and along the river into the interior (fig. 6.1). On the interior slopes, 193 acres were in wood and provision land, 16 acres were in pasture, and the remainder of the estate was taken up by the works, the slaves' houses, and broken ground. The works and houses were located on the river, where it was crossed by the coastal highway; the great house was 20 chains away, perched on a knoll.

The annual cycle at Peruvian Vale in 1807/8 was as follows. The first and second gangs spent the greater part of July, August, and September weeding the growing canes, the third or "small" gang carrying dung to the pieces. October and November were the months for digging cane holes and for commencing the planting of new canes. Cane holes were dug by both the first and second gangs. The maturing canes were also stripped of their leaves, but weeding was then generally abandoned. Crop began on 4 December 1807 and continued until the last sugar was potted on 27 May 1808. Most of the cutting was done by the second gang, the first gang being employed throughout the crop in "hoe-ploughing," holing, and planting. The third gang had a wider range of tasks during the crop season: stripping, dunging, weeding, tying trash, carrying trash to the mill furnaces, carrying ashes from the stills, digging yams, and "relieving" young cane sprouts. Once the crop was complete (308 hogsheads of sugar and 24,000 gallons of rum), the first and second gangs were employed in hoe-ploughing and the third in weeding.

This seasonal cycle at Peruvian Vale affected the distribution of slaves between gangs and tasks. Table 6.4 shows the numbers in each grouping on the first Monday of every month from July 1807 to June 1808. The increase in the total labor force in December 1807 resulted from the addition of 36 slaves from another holding, Rabaca. The first and second gangs fluctuated in size because members were drawn off to perform tasks in the works or to drive carts during crop and because they were partly composed of hired slaves. It is also apparent that the number of slaves employed as watchmen increased significantly in the months immediately before crop. The domestics and tradespeople, however, remained fixed groups through the year.

Only slaves living on sugar estates were subject to the regime of extended night work during crop. Although coffee planters in Brazil sometimes employed slaves as late as 11 P.M., sorting coffee beans and preparing food, those in the British Caribbean seem not to have exacted this form of night labor.[113] Planters in

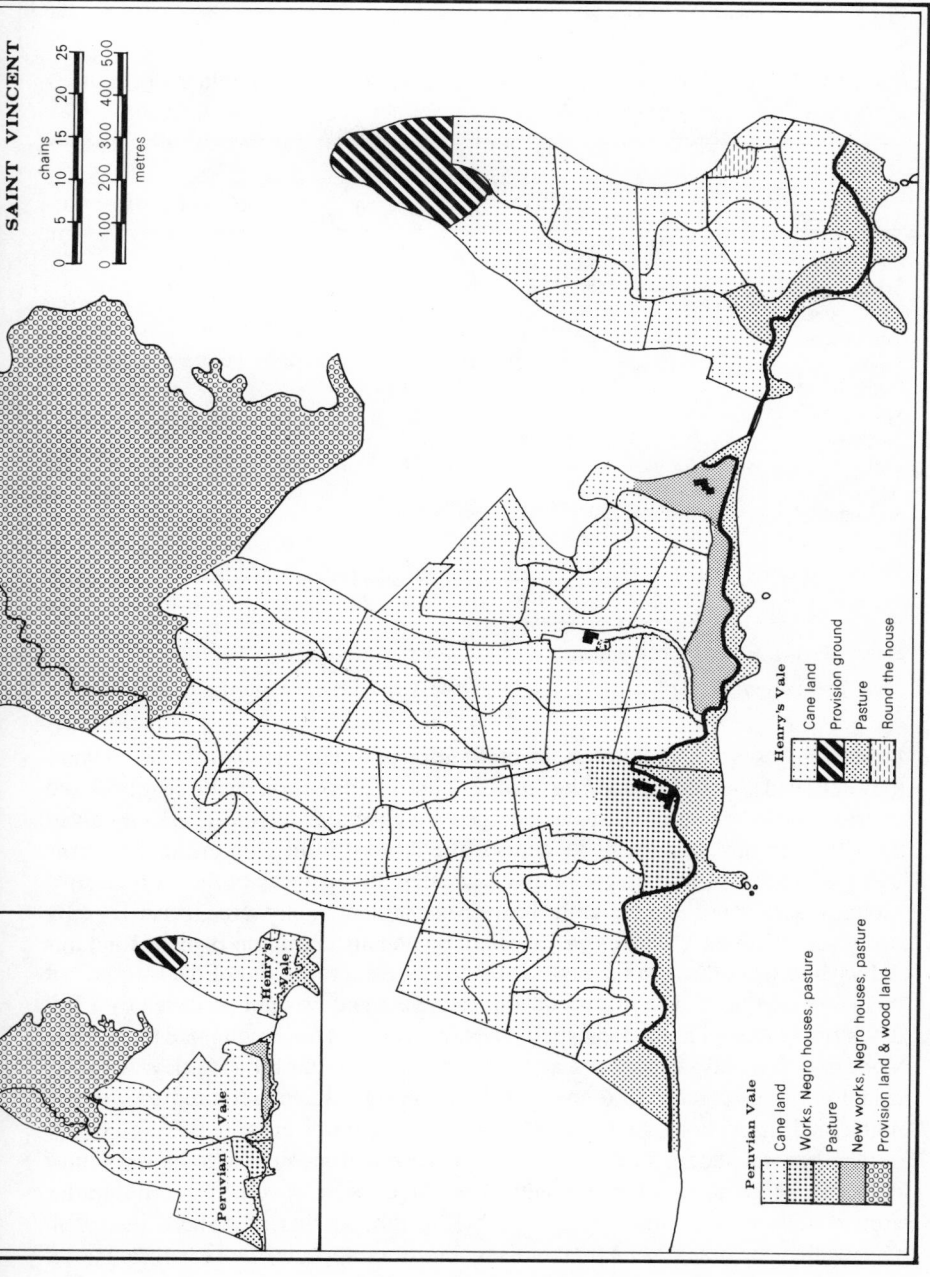

SAINT VINCENT

chains
0 5 10 15 20 25

metres
0 100 200 300 400 500

Peruvian Vale
Cane land
Works. Negro houses, pasture
Pasture
New works. Negro houses. pasture
Provision land & wood land

Henry's Vale
Cane land
Provision ground
Pasture
Round the house

Fig. 6.1. *Peruvian Vale and Henry's Vale Estate, St. Vincent, 1809. (Source: MS plan [Survey Department, Kingstown, St. Vincent].)*

Table 6.4. *Seasonal Allocation of Slaves to Tasks: Peruvian Vale Estate, St. Vincent, 1807/8*

	Months											
	J	A	S	O	N	D	J	F	M	A	M	J
First gang	40	38	35	30	27	40	39	38	28	32	38	48
Second gang	40	38	35	30	26	20	20	20	26	20	26	33
Third gang	36	35	30	31	30	33	30	27	30	30	30	30
Tradesmen	8	8	8	8	7	9	9	11	11	11	11	11
Jobbers }	18	13	21	20	16	7	15	14	13	23	15	15
Domestics }					7	8	8	8	8	9	9	9
Watchmen	5	9	12	12	12	11	9	8	8	8	8	8
Stockkeepers	4	5	4	4	4	4	3	3	3	3	3	4
Cart and mule boys	5	6	6	2	2	8	9	12	12	12	6	3
At works	—	4	3	—	—	17	18	20	28	20	14	4
Superannuated	6	6	6	6	5	4	4	5	4	4	4	4
Children	30	30	30	30	31	34	34	34	34	30	34	34
Sick	18	15	14	15	21	29	27	24	18	19	21	18
Total	210	207	204	188	188	224	223	224	223	224	222	222

Source: Peruvian Vale Estate Journal, 1807–8 (Supreme Court Registry, Kingstown).

Note: These data show the number of slaves thus employed on the first Monday of each month.

Demerara-Essequibo did protest the prohibition of Sunday labor in 1825, because they believed it would hamper the turning of coffee and cotton on the drogeries and interfere with the potting of sugar, but they did not claim that these tasks involved the slaves in any significant amount of night work.[114] In Dominica, the slaves living on coffee plantations were given one day in every week to work their own grounds, as well as Sunday, while those on sugar plantations were given a day only every second week.[115] Slaves employed in mahogany cutting in British Honduras did have to work through the night when logs were trucked out of the forests, but this work was limited to two months in each year and was not preceded by a full day's field labor as in the long spell on sugar estates. These men were required to work only five days each week and received half a dollar for Saturday work, by custom.[116] Watchmen and domestics were the only slaves required to work at nights and throughout the week regardless of season or crop.

The general statement that field slaves worked from sunrise to sunset out of crop can be refined to some extent. The slaves were wakened before sunrise around 4:30 A.M. by the ringing of a bell or the blowing of a shell. In British Guiana they ate breakfast in their houses before commencing work between 6 and 7 A.M., but in Jamaica they went directly to the field and began work by 5 A.M. The Jamaican field slave's breakfast was prepared by a field cook and eaten around 9 A.M., when the slaves stopped work for half an hour. At midday the slaves rested for 1½ hours in Jamaica (12:30–2:00 P.M.) and 2 hours in British Guiana (11 A.M.–1 P.M.). Work ended for the day at 6 P.M. in British Guiana and at 6:45

P.M. in Jamaica.[117] The St. Kitts slave law of 1798 stated that the slaves should not work before 5 A.M. or later than 7 P.M., and allowed them 1½ hours for breakfast in the field and 2 hours at noon. The same absolute limits to the day were established by the Jamaican law of 1809.[118] The Trinidad ordinance of 1800 limited the field slave's day to 5 A.M. to 6 P.M. out of crop, with half an hour for breakfast and 2 hours at noon, but also required them to "throw grass" at noon and night.[119] In Barbados the typical work day out of crop in the 1820s was said to be from 6 A.M. to 6 P.M., with 1 hour for breakfast at 9 A.M. and 2 hours for dinner at 1 P.M.[120] This matched exactly the pattern established in the crown colonies by the order in council of 1831, except that the breaks were to begin an hour earlier and it was intended to apply in crop as well as out. Once work ceased in the field, most planters required their slaves to carry bundles of grass to the livestock pens, but this practice became relatively uncommon after 1807 as the "grass gangs" grew in proportion to the creole populations.[121]

Although there was a degree of individual variation in the hours worked by field slaves on particular sugar estates out of crop in the years between 1807 and 1834, it appears that the typical day was 12 hours in Jamaica and 10 hours in most of the eastern Caribbean, except that in Barbados it was nearer to 9 hours. Whereas the length of the work day was reduced somewhat during the crop season after 1807, little change seems to have occurred in the out-of-crop period. The exception to this rule was the imposition of a 9-hour day on the crown colonies after 1831. This regulation of the hours of work was viewed by the planters of Trinidad and British Guiana as the most "subversive" of all the objectionable clauses in the order in council, but they were particularly upset because these hours were to apply throughout the year and not only out of crop.[122] It is improbable that the order was in fact followed during crop.

Hours of work also varied for individual slaves. Those described in the preceding paragraph applied principally to the first and second field gangs and other "able" manual laborers on sugar estates. Mothers with children at the breast were said to turn out two to three hours later than the main body of gang laborers. Children employed in grass gangs also worked shorter hours.[123] The hours worked by skilled tradespeople out of crop were probably less than those of field laborers, but here there is little hard evidence. Mechanics were said to work an average 8 to 9 hours per day in the Bahamas during the 1820s.[124] But it is uncertain whether this pattern was confined to the marginal colonies. The hours of work required of field laborers in the marginal colonies, as well as plantations producing crops other than sugar, are equally uncertain, but it is probable that they were very similar to those of laborers on sugar estates out of crop. Thus, the shortening of the working day after 1807 was confined almost entirely to the crop season and affected only slaves belonging to sugar estates.

Timekeeping remained in the hands of the planters throughout the period. The ringing of bells and blowing of shells that regulated the periods of work and rest was always controlled by the masters, and slaves had few means of checking the time other than the position of the sun. Unlike the factories of industrializing

Britain, West Indian sugar works never sported clocks, and sundials were rare and generally hidden in the great house garden. When, in Jamaica around 1835, apprentices used an hourglass, it was broken by the overseer.[125] This lack of time-keeping devices provided the planters with an ultimate weapon in exploiting the slaves' labor time and helps explain the popularity of the task-work system.

It is difficult to make general statements about the total hours worked by slaves in the course of a year. The demands of plantation labor varied with the colony, the crop, the use of the task system, the length of the crop season, the size of the slaveholding, the existence of the provision ground system, and the sex, age, and strength of the slaves themselves. The task system was most common where the normal hours of gang labor were longest, while days of work were longer and fewer where the slaves had to produce their own food on provision grounds. For slaves working on sugar estates, who were the majority of the rural population, the extremes were represented by Jamaica and Barbados. A rough calculation of total annual hours worked can be made for first-gang field slaves, using the parameters established above.[126] This results in an average annual 3,200 hours for the Barbadian slave, and 4,000 for the Jamaican. The Barbadian slave spent less time than the Jamaican in estate labor out of crop, and the contrast was even greater during crop. Thus, the provision ground system was simply an added imposition for the Jamaican slave, in no way compensated by extra "free" days. It is impossible to fix the other colonies between these extremes with precision, but first-gang field laborers must have spent about 3,500 hours in estate labor in most colonies of the eastern Caribbean, except that Trinidad and British Guiana gradually came nearer to the Barbados pattern after 1823. Apart from the crown colonies, the reduction in hours over the period 1807–34 did little to alter the ordering of the colonies. But slaves working on coffee, cocoa, cotton, or pimento plantations, or on livestock pens, probably worked only 3,100 hours for their owners, slightly less than the hours on Barbadian sugar estates. These annual work times may be compared with the 1,500 hours of the modern factory worker, the mandatory 2,300 hours worked by British West Indian apprentices 1834–38, the 2,900 hours of factory workers in Britain around 1830, and the 3,000 hours of rural slaves in the ante-bellum United States.[127] West Indian slaves located on plantations of any type worked more hours than all of these groups, and those on sugar estates spent vastly more time in supervised labor. Yet these hours were less than those worked at the peak of the British West Indian slave system in the seventeenth and eighteenth centuries or on contemporary Cuban estates.[128]

It is important to notice that the slaves with the longest annual work times also performed the heaviest tasks, worked the longest continuous spells, and most often had to produce their own food outside the time spent in estate labor.

OCCUPATIONAL ALLOCATION

The heaviness of rural labor depended not only on the nature and duration of the tasks performed by the slaves but also on the strength of those allocated to particular occupations. At the end of the eighteenth century, a group of Barbadian planters instructed their fellow planters that "a judicious division of negroes into gangs" was essential to good plantation management, since "the application of their labor to works suited to their strength and ability requires the strictest attention." The first task of a new manager, they said, was "to examine individually the state and condition of every negro; and then to assort them in such manner, that they may never be employed upon any work to which their powers are not equal."[129] The planter's evaluation of the slaves' "strength and ability" was based chiefly on the demographic characteristics discussed in chapter 5: age, sex, birthplace, and color.

The general principles of occupational allocation on rural slaveholdings can be stated fairly simply. Females were totally excluded from skilled trades other than sewing, and very rarely worked in transportation or fishing, or served as "watchmen." Males were excluded only from washing and sewing. Color was less exclusive than sex, but colored males were generally allocated to domestic work or skilled trades, and colored females to domestic occupations. Ethnic origin was of only minor significance and never accounted for actual exclusions. Within the framework of these fixed characteristics, occupational allocation depended above all on age. Children generally worked in the third gang between 5 and 12 years of age. The second gang comprised children of 12 to 18 years and weak adults, most of them over 40 years of age. The first gang comprised the strongest slaves on the holding, those aged between 18 and 45 years. Domestics and stockkeepers also commenced work from an early age. Skilled tradespeople, transport workers, and fishers were generally drafted from the field labor gangs and domestics during their teens. Drivers gradually emerged from the first gang, most them over 35 years of age. The duties of watchmen were confined to the old and weak. All of these general tendencies were affected by short- or long-term illness or physical disability, of course. The size and demographic structure of particular slaveholdings also imposed constraints on the flexibility of the rules, as did changes in demographic structure consequent on the abolition of the Atlantic slave trade. Obviously, the range of tasks varied with the type of enterprise.

Field labor accounted for the majority of rural slaves between the ages of 10 and 60 years in the new sugar colonies of Trinidad and St. Lucia. But slaves entered the field much earlier in Barbados, and left earlier as well. More than 40 percent of Barbadian slaves were in the field by age 9 and more than 70 percent by age 14, compared to only 5 and 25 percent in Trinidad (figs. 6.2–6.4). Although the concentration of slaves in field labor in the marginal colony of Anguilla was not as great as in the sugar colonies for any age group, the slaves tended to remain longer in field work because there were fewer alternative occupations for the aging (fig. 6.5). In Anguilla there was little difference in the concentration of males and females in field work, but in the sugar colonies it is striking that a larger proportion of females than males worked in the field after about 20 years of age and until they reached 50. Indeed, the proportion of males in the field declined from an early peak of about 65 percent at 20 years in all of the sugar colonies, while females reached a higher peak of more than 80 percent only by about 30 years. The peak was reached earlier in Barbados than in the new sugar colonies, probably because

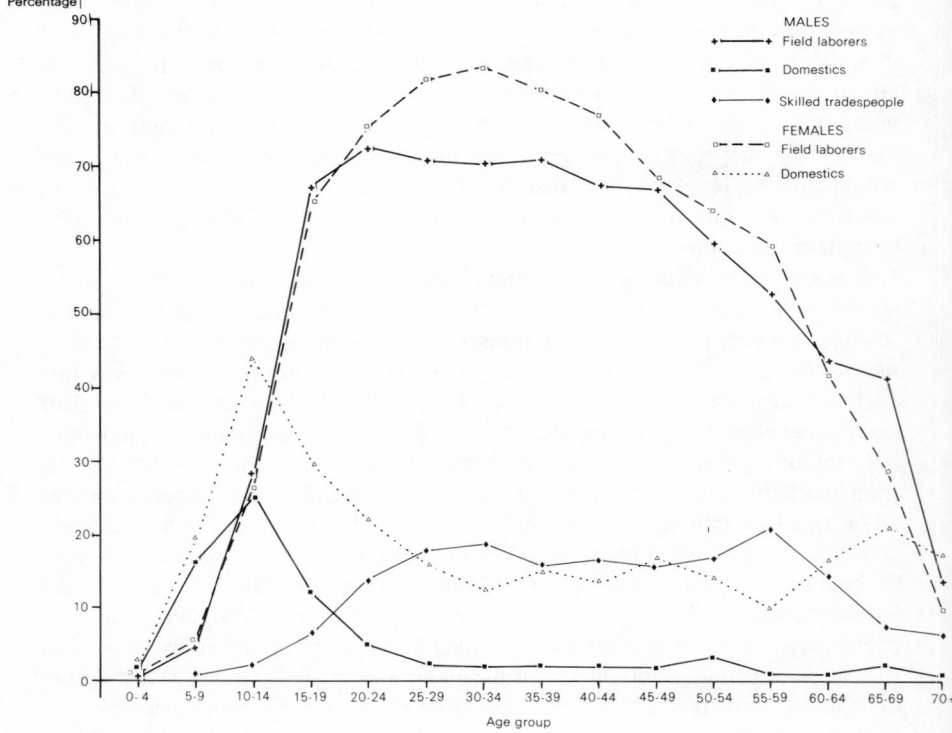

Fig. 6.2. *Occupations of Slaves by Sex and Age: Rural Trinidad, 1813.*
(Source: *table S7.18.*)

Barbados had a larger proportion of young creoles in the population by 1817. It is important to note that the graphs discussed here are based on the cross-sectional registration data and reflect the life experiences of individual slaves as well as long-term trends in the structure of the slave populations. The concentration of females in field labor, then, does not mean that they necessarily outnumbered males in the gangs. Where the sex ratio was relatively high, as in the third-phase sugar colonies, males continued to dominate the field labor force. In Trinidad females were only 43.6 percent of the field slaves in 1813, compared to 43.5 percent of the total rural population; and in Berbice in 1819 females accounted for 44.9 percent of field slaves, compared to 43.8 percent overall. Where the sex ratio was low, as in the old sugar colonies, Jamaica, and the marginal colonies excepting the Cayman Islands, females did indeed attain a numerical superiority in the field gangs soon after 1807 (table 6.5). The important point here is that females were always overrepresented in the field labor force, and that as the slave populations became increasingly creole and the sex ratio fell to low levels females came to dominate. The reason for this tendency is that males were put to a fairly

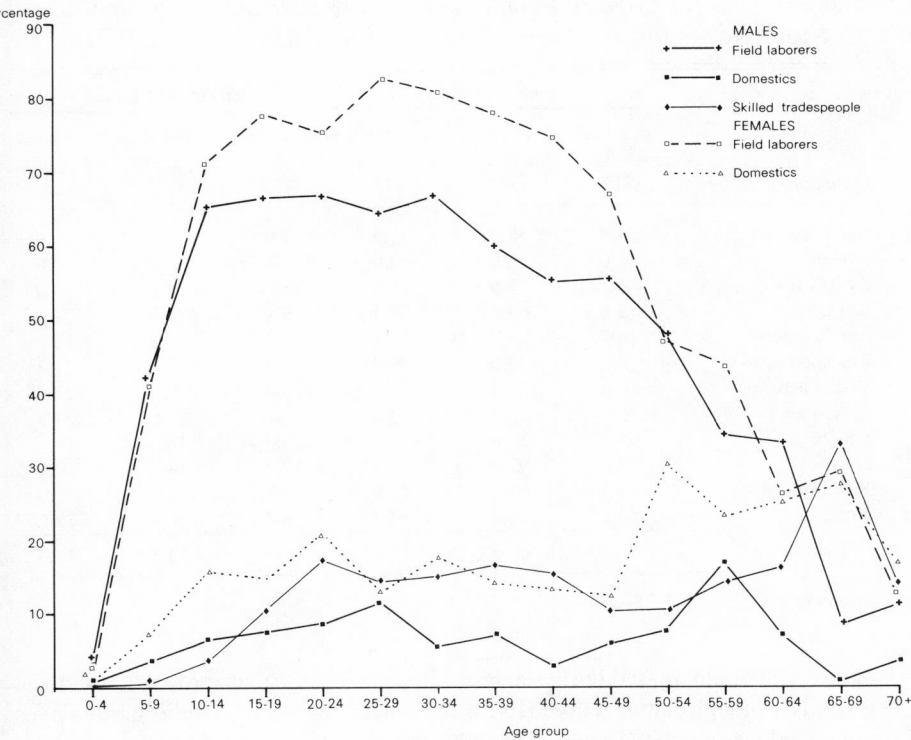

Fig. 6.3. *Occupations of Slaves by Sex and Age: St. John, Barbados, 1817.*
(Source: *table S7.17.*)

wide range of occupations, whereas females were confined almost entirely to field
or domestic tasks.

Females also dominated among the house slaves. In general, 70 percent of rural
domestics were females, though the proportion was as high as 86.4 percent in
Anguilla in 1827 (table 6.5). In the new sugar colonies, a large proportion of the
domestics were young. This pattern was most obvious in Trinidad, where 44
percent of rural females aged 10–14 years were employed as domestics in 1813, as
were 25 percent of males (fig. 6.2). The proportion dropped rapidly until it leveled
out at about 30 years of age, when only 15 percent of females and 2 percent of
males were domestics. A similar pattern occurred in St. Lucia and Berbice, though
the early peaks were lower than in Trinidad (figs. 6.4 and 6.6). In these new sugar
colonies, then, many young slaves spent a few years in domestic work before
being drafted into the field gangs or skilled trades. Anguilla showed a similar
pattern, except that males never accounted for so many domestics and the
concentration of females was clear at all ages (fig. 6.5). In the parish of St. John,
Barbados, however, the proportion of the female slave population employed in

Table 6.5. *Percentage of Female and Colored Slaves by Occupation: Rural Barbados, St. Lucia, and Anguilla, 1815–27*

	Percentage Female			Percentage Colored		
Occupation	St. John, Barbados, 1817	Rural St. Lucia, 1815	Anguilla, 1827	St. John, Barbados, 1817	Rural St. Lucia, 1815	Anguilla, 1827
Field laborers	56.8	58.8	55.3	11.0	5.6	10.6
Drivers	51.6	3.0	0.0	6.6	14.8	0.0
Skilled tradespeople	6.7	7.9	21.1	33.3	26.2	37.0
Domestics	72.8	69.3	86.4	36.4	32.0	24.0
Stockkeepers	26.7	28.7	21.1	9.1	12.2	10.2
Transport workers	0.0	0.0	0.0	0.0	10.2	24.3
Watchmen	0.0	31.8	26.7	8.3	7.6	25.0
Fishermen	—	2.2	0.0	—	20.0	24.3
Laborers	68.6	36.6	—	0.0	18.3	—
Nurses	100.0	97.1	100.0	17.5	14.7	0.0
Sick or disabled	64.3	65.2	51.9	5.7	7.1	7.4
None	50.6	54.9	50.3	18.2	18.9	19.2
Total	53.2	54.2	54.6	15.8	13.5	17.3

Sources: T.71/261, 377–78, 521.

domestic work increased fairly steadily with age, and the male proportion showed a similar, though flatter, curve (fig. 6.3). Since the overall proportion of slaves employed was much the same in St. John and rural Trinidad (table 6.2), it is clear that the Trinidad domestics contained significantly fewer adult slaves. This contrast between the old and new sugar colonies can be explained by the greater demand for "able" field laborers in the expanding plantation frontier and the desire to minimize the loss in productivity resulting from the use of scarce labor in domestic service. It matched the significantly earlier entry of slaves to field work in Barbados.

The skilled trades were confined almost entirely to male slaves, and the few females included in this category were usually seamstresses. In the sugar colonies females accounted for only about 7 percent of tradespeople. Seamstresses were often quite young, but skilled males were generally older than male field laborers or domestics and increased as a proportion of the population with age. Skilled males were drawn from the domestics or field gangs as they entered their later teens, while females employed as domestics or seamstresses in their youth were drafted to field labor. Apprentice carpenters, coopers, masons, and wheelwrights distinguished in the Barbados registration returns were aged between 8 and 18 years, but the "carpenter's boy" probably had the same role as the apprentice, learning by example and performing subsidiary manual tasks.

In most colonies all of the drivers were males. Not one female driver was identified in the registration returns of Trinidad or Anguilla, and only a handful

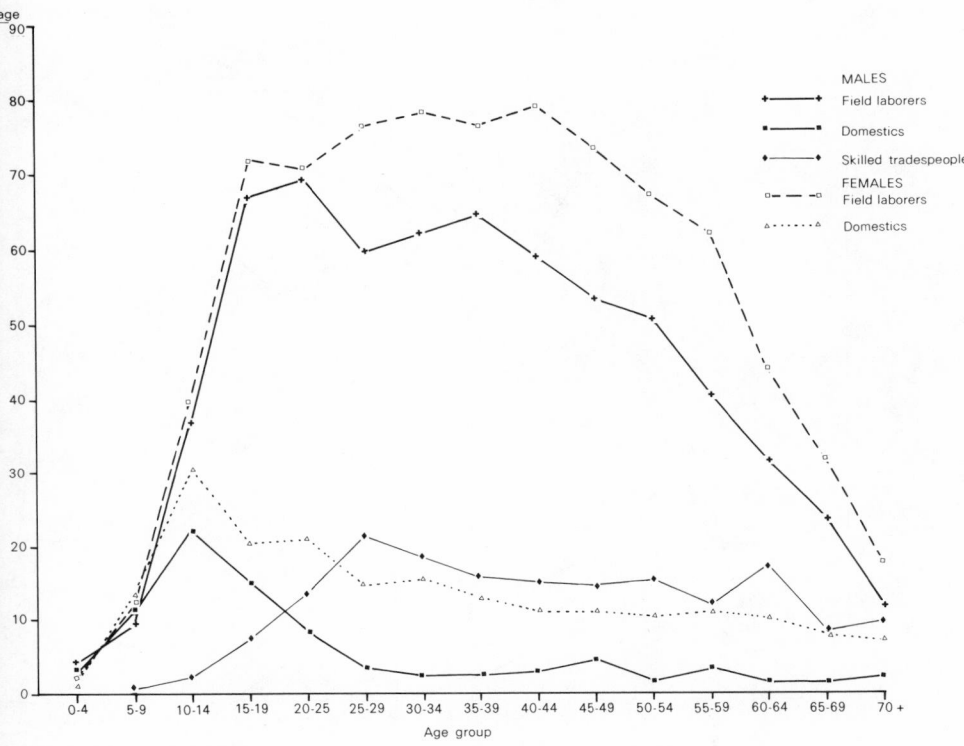

Fig. 6.4.   *Occupations of Slaves by Sex and Age: Rural St. Lucia, 1815.*
(Source: *table S7.14.*)

were listed for St. Lucia and Berbice. But they were common in Barbados.
Females accounted for 37.9 percent of the drivers in rural St. Michael, 44.8
percent in St. Andrew, and 51.6 percent in St. John. They were never employed as
drivers of the first gang, but in all of these rural parishes they easily outnumbered
males as supervisors of the second, third, or fourth gangs. Grouping the three
Barbadian parishes, females were 80.6 percent of second-gang drivers and 94.7
percent of third-gang drivers. Almost all of these females were over 40 years of
age, whereas males often began working as drivers in their thirties (table S7.17).
The unusual importance of female drivers in Barbados must be traced to the early
age at which Barbadian children were introduced to field labor and the resulting
large squads of children under 15 years of age to be supervised. These two
characteristics made the field labor system of Barbados unique, and they help to
explain how Barbadian planters were able to maintain productivity while extracting relatively low levels of work time from their first gangs.

Females accounted for about one-quarter of the slaves employed as stockkeepers, but they generally had responsibility for the smaller animals rather than

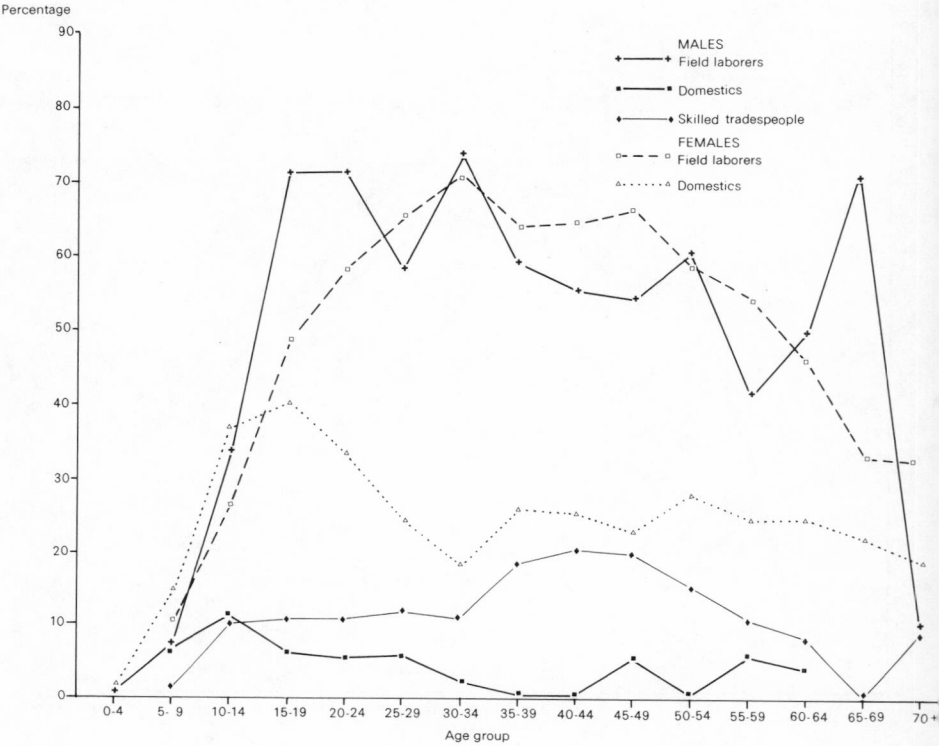

Fig. 6.5. *Occupations of Slaves by Sex and Age: Anguilla, 1827.* (Source: *T.71/261.)*

cattle and horses.[130] The age distribution of stockkeepers, both male and female, was bimodal, with peaks in the teens and over-50 age group (tables S7.14–7.18). The tasks of watchmen overlapped with those of stockkeepers to some extent, but females were generally not required to keep watch at night, and males employed in this occupation were older than any other active group. Fishermen tended to be mature adults. So did nurses, but the females, who predominated, were generally older than the males.

Color was a significant factor in occupational allocation, especially for domestics and skilled tradespeople, but slaves of color never outnumbered blacks in any occupation. In St. Lucia, for example, 57.5 percent of employed colored slaves worked as domestics or skilled tradespeople in 1815, yet they were only 32.0 percent of domestics and 26.2 percent of skilled tradespeople (table 6.5). Slaves of color were also overrepresented among the drivers, fishermen, and nurses of St. Lucia. In Anguilla slaves of color were overrepresented among domestics, skilled tradespeople, transport workers (most of them sailors), fishermen, and watchmen. A relatively large proportion of slaves of color remained unemployed, both

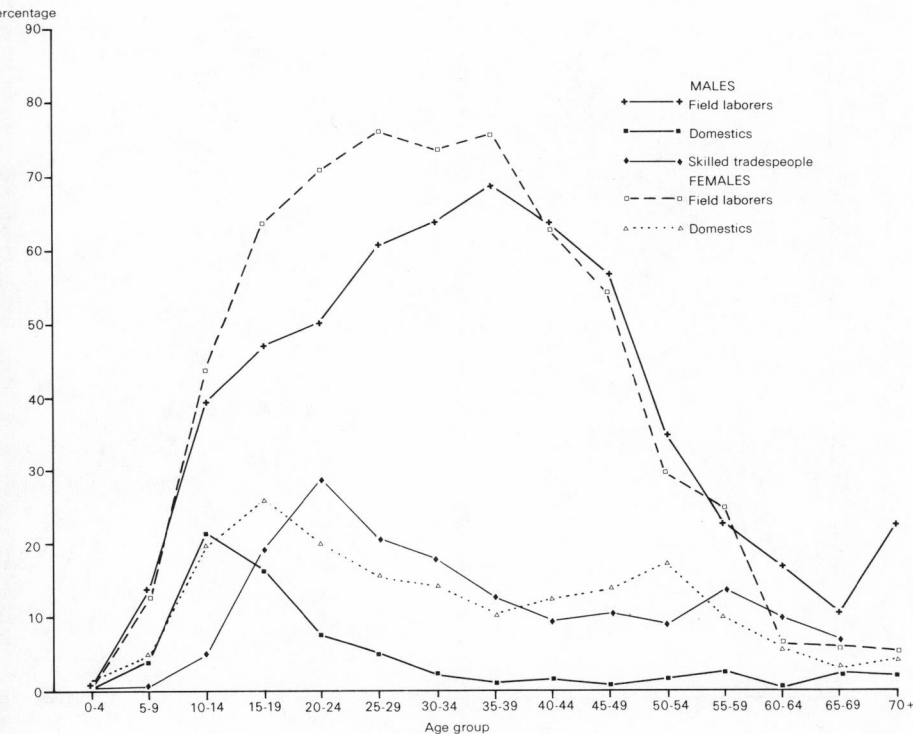

Fig. 6.6.   *Occupations of Slaves by Sex and Age: Berbice, 1819.* (Source:
    table S7.16.)

because they tended to be younger than blacks and because they were sheltered
from the rigors of plantation life. Slaves of color were everywhere underrepresented in the field gangs, though they followed the pattern for blacks in being
introduced to field labor earlier in Barbados than elsewhere (fig. 6.7). The contrast
between the sexes applied to colored as well as black slaves, so that colored males
least often found themselves employed in the field, followed by colored females,
black males, and black females (tables S7.14–7.17). The proportion of colored
males in the field began to decline at an earlier age than for any other group.
Although females predominated overwhelmingly among domestics, a larger
proportion of the male colored population than of the female black population was
employed in the house (fig. 6.8). Only a slightly larger proportion of colored
females than colored males worked as domestics. On the other hand, females of
color were somewhat more likely to find themselves in the field than were males of
color, reflecting the greater alternatives for male employment. Female drivers
were always black, but a small proportion of the males were colored. Seamstresses
were much more likely to be colored than were skilled tradesmen. In St. Lucia in

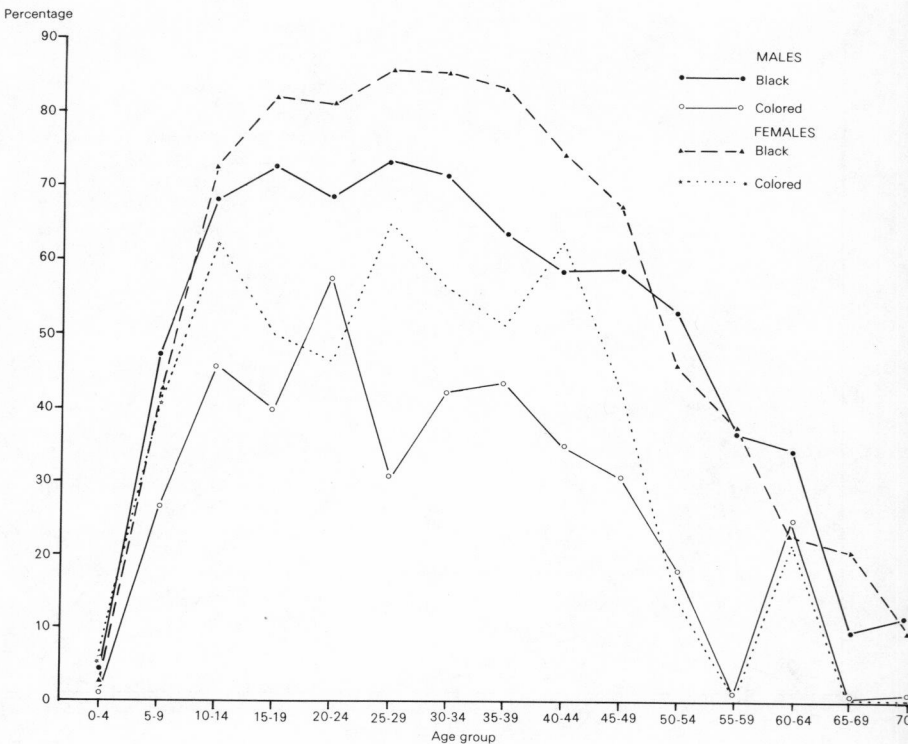

Fig. 6.7.   *Field Slaves by Sex, Age, and Color: St. John, Barbados, 1817.*
(Source: *table S7.17.*)

1815, 46.3 percent of seamstresses were colored, compared to 24.6 percent of tradesmen. In Berbice in 1819, 42.9 percent of seamstresses were colored, but only 4.7 percent of tradesmen. Among female slaves, however, a significant distinction was made between washerwomen and other domestics. In 1817 in St. John, Barbados, for example, only 13.8 percent of washerwomen were colored, compared to 36.8 percent of other domestics. In St. Lucia in 1815, 21.9 percent of washers were colored, as were 31.9 percent of other domestics. Thus, it appears that washerwomen were rarely selected on the basis of color, and this, together with their relative maturity, is clear evidence that the strenuous nature of their work was generally recognized.

The preference given to colored slaves as domestics, skilled tradespeople, and nurses reflected the slaveowners' perception of them as relatively weak and unfitted for the hard work of field labor. In some cases it also reflected a conscious recognition of the obligations of paternity or an essentially unconscious appreciation of the hierarchy of status in the broader slave society. According to Augustus Beaumont, ''The number of domestics is generally in proportion to the

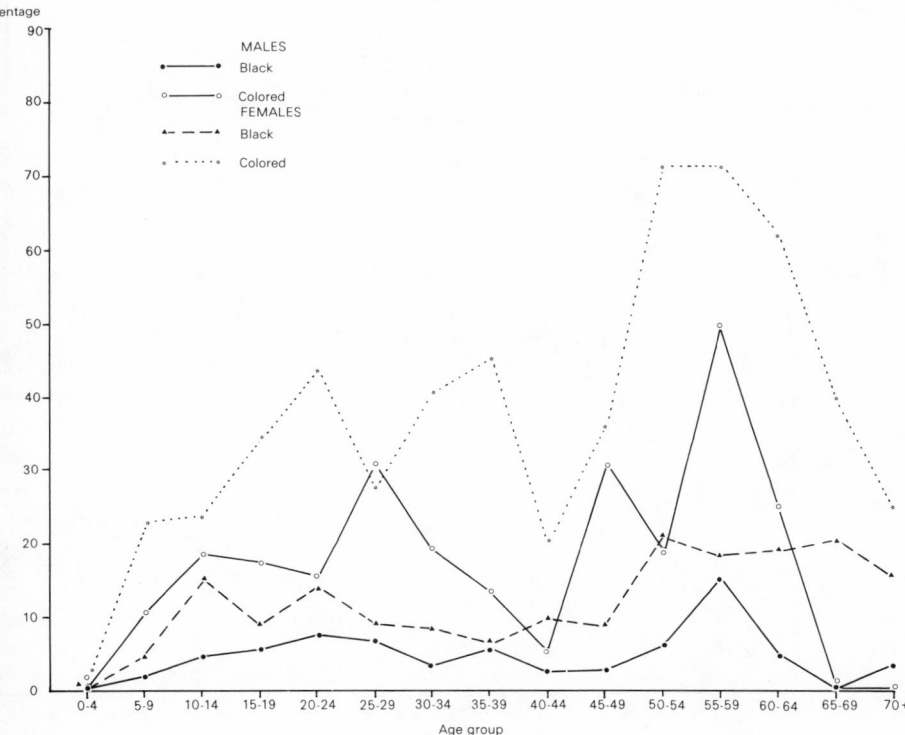

Fig. 6.8. *Domestic Slaves by Sex, Age, and Color: St. John, Barbados, 1817.* (Source: *table S7.17.*)

number of females of fair complexion on an estate, and who are rarely put to field labour in consequence of their approach to the aristocracy of complexion.'' In 1815 a Barbadian overseer told his employer that a mulatto girl on his plantation had never done any work because ''she is as white as either of us and in fact I could not find an occupation for her.''[131] The conviction that slaves of color made poor field laborers and should be employed as domestics or skilled tradespeople was placed under stress in the period after 1807 as the source of black field laborers was cut off and the proportion of colored slaves grew in most colonies.

Birthplace was the least important of the demographic factors controlling occupational allocation. Creole slaves were generally regarded by planters as more ''intelligent'' than Africans, but this was believed to give them an advantage only in the skilled trades. According to Alexander McDonnell of Demerara, speaking in 1831, creoles exhibited ''greater intelligence, greater skill and better moral feeling, because the proprietor had endeavoured to train up his people in the best manner possible adapted to the circumstances of the colony.'' But McDonnell also held that ''the Africans are physically a strong race of men, and it is frequently

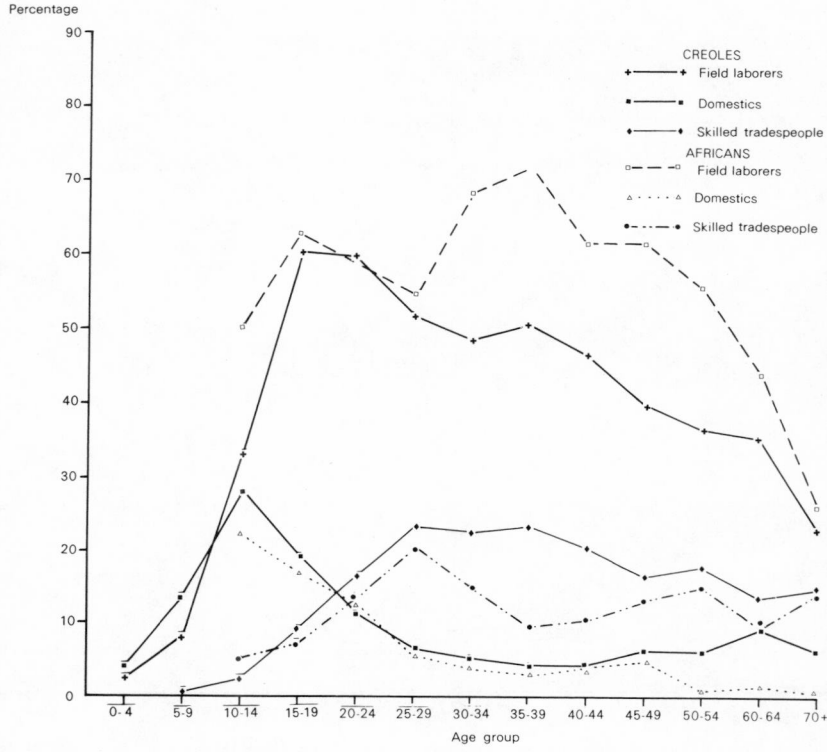

Fig. 6.9.   *Occupations of Male Slaves by Age and Birthplace: St. Lucia,*
1815. (Source: T.71/378–79.)

found that imported Africans, in certain descriptions of labour, will perform more
than Creoles,'' and commented that ''I think a great many planters would like to
have Africans for field labour.''[132] Another Demerara planter, Peter Rose, agreed
that the African was ''equally efficient as the Creole'' in work ''such as weeding,
trenching or cane-holing, where manual labour is required,'' but William Henery
of Berbice believed Africans less ''athletic'' than creoles. All of these planters
were agreed that creoles made the better tradesmen.[133] These assessments are
supported by the evidence of the registration returns from Berbice, where creole
males were much more likely to be skilled tradesmen than were Africans, even if
the slaves of color are excluded from the creole group. A similar pattern occurred
in St. Lucia (fig. 6.9). Africans and creoles of similar age were equally likely to be
domestics, but Africans over 25 years of age were more often employed as field
laborers, and creoles as skilled tradesmen. In the other occupations birthplace
mattered little. Among the Africans, particular regional or ethnic origins seem not
to have been considered in allocating slaves to occupations. Although planters
may have been aware of the technological skills of Africans, these were of no

account in their selection of slaves for purchase, and in general their objective was to remake the slaves, teaching them European methods of carpentry, potting, and so on. This is not to say that Africans with particular skills failed to inject them into the products of their labor. But they were not allocated to occupations on the basis of these abilities.

It can be concluded that rural slaveowners did allocate slaves to occupations on the basis of their "strength and ability," with some notable exceptions. The most important of these aberrations were the tendency to keep slaves of color from field work and other types of heavy manual labor and the failure to recognize the particular skills of Africans. In the field gangs females performed the same tasks as males, including the digging of cane holes and night work in the factories, though pregnant women were put to lighter work, and mothers performed lighter work or shorter hours for up to three months after delivery.[134] The early age at which children were put to work did not appear unusual to the slaveowners of this period, nor did the long hours children had to labor. There were few significant differences between colonies in the principles used to allocate slaves to occupations, except that the Barbadian system of large gangs of children supervised by female drivers was unique.

INCENTIVES TO LABOR

The labor of rural slaves was extracted by means of a complex combination of negative and positive incentives. Physical coercion was fundamental, but it was combined with the imposition of extra tasks, the withholding of material goods or customary "indulgences" or free time, and the granting of special allowances, occasional monetary payments, and short-term freedoms. The particular combination of negative and positive incentives employed by the masters varied with the occupations of the slaves, the nature of the work organization on particular types of holdings, and the character of the slaveowner.

Perhaps the most elaborate discussion of the combination of negative and positive incentives used in the extraction of slave labor was that contained in the report of a committee of the Barbados Agricultural Society "appointed to draw up a plan for the regulation of plantations with a particular reference to the treatment of slaves" in 1812.[135] The committee observed that, unlike free people, slaves were not stimulated by a concern for their future prospects:

From these facts it is clear that a system of discipline is necessary which will keep the slave in a state of pupilage; and yet awaken his mind to those objects of ambition which bounded as they are, yet are worth his attainment. With these views a system of rewards as well as punishments should be held forth; and those punishments should be calculated to make him feel that it is his interest to be a good member of the plantation to which he belongs, rather than to depress his spirits and produce despondence and despair.[136]

Slaves should never be struck in anger or by white masters or overseers, and all punishments should be seen as "the act of cool deliberation" rather than petulant malevolence, argued the committee. Corporal punishment was always to be inflicted with "formality," by the driver, using only rods. Any heavier punishment was to be sought through the public magistrate. The committee recommended solitary confinement as an effective mode of punishment within the plantation. Positive incentives should consist of material rewards, as a means of appealing to the "ambition and vanity" of the slaves. But the committee also noted that the differential treatment of slaves, in terms of rewards received by headpeople, tradesmen, and field laborers, created feelings of "inequality" and "depression" within the slave community. It believed that slaves "should be placed as nearly as possible on an equality and be taught to think as highly as possible of themselves as human beings in such a state can. They should be guarded from the oppression of their brother slaves who happen of necessity to be placed over them and by being encouraged to realize a comfortable peculium of their own, feel themselves to have an interest at stake and a regard for home."[137]

West Indian slaveowners of the early nineteenth century did not have the power of life and death over their slaves, but their effective control of the legislative and legal machinery meant that they could both protect themselves from prosecution for brutality and ensure the punishment of slaves who resisted.[138] On the plantation the master and his representatives could use a variety of methods of physical coercion without recourse to any external authority. Of these methods, whipping was the most important. Thus, the Jamaican overseer William Taylor could say in 1832 that "the stimulous to labour is decidedly the fear of the lash" and that "physical coercion I conceive to be necessary to the production of labour through the instrumentality of slaves." He believed that this applied to all types of occupations: "The carpenter or the cooper knows that if he will not go to the shop and do his work he will be flogged."[139] Fear of the lash was also basic to the task-work system, but that system did permit a degree of self-regulation within the day, and it lacked the constant threat of the driver's whip felt by field gang laborers who temporarily slackened effort.

The Trinidad ordinance of 1800 limited the use of flogging as follows:

Owners or attorneys shall not punish slaves by more than thirty-nine lashes; and managers and overseers shall not punish by more than twelve lashes for any one offence; the slave who has received thirty-nine lashes shall not be flogged again on the same day, nor until he be recovered from the effects of that punishment. . . . Should the crime of the slave however, be of a nature to deserve a severer chastisement, he shall be conducted before the Commandant of the District, who will order such corporal punishment as the case deserves; it being well understood that it cannot extend to death or mutilation.[140]

Although the limitation to 39 lashes was common in the British colonies, the Trinidad ordinance replaced the Spanish law of 1789 in which the limit was 25 lashes. Just as the British initially increased the hours to be worked by slaves in Trinidad, so they increased the level of punishment. The Spanish limit of 25 lashes was reinstated in 1815. In 1823 an order in council prohibited the carrying of the whip or cat in Trinidad for the purpose of coercing slaves to work or to "exhibit it as an emblem of authority," and prohibited the whipping of females, except those under 10 years of age, who might be flogged like any schoolgirl. Imprisonment in stocks was recommended as a substitute for whipping. Males were to be flogged only 24 hours after an offense and in the presence of one free or six slave witnesses. All punishments were to be recorded. These controls on the use of the whip in Trinidad were extended by the order in council of 1831, which reduced the number of lashes a male might receive to fifteen. All of these limitations on the use of the whip were regarded by the slaveowners as violations of the rights of private property.[141]

The control of whipping proceeded more rapidly in Trinidad than in the other crown colonies, and progress was even slower in the colonies with planter-controlled legislatures. Legal limitations on the use of the whip were not necessarily followed by the slaveowners, of course, and examples of abuse are easy to find. The cases of Huggins in Nevis and Hodge in Tortola were the most notorious in the period after 1807, but the execution of Hodge in 1811 for murdering several of his slaves brought to an end the belief that masters could do what they willed with their slave property.[142] Most examples of extreme planter brutality, and the "official" brutality of the cage, treadmill, chain gang, or hangman's noose, were responses to slave "crimes" such as rebellion, marronage, violence, or theft rather than short-term reluctance to labor. Slaves removed themselves from the labor force by running away, of course, but their actions generally symbolized a much deeper form of protest than the simple desire to escape the rigors of plantation labor. Marronage and rebellion will be discussed in detail in chapter 10, but it is important to note here that the ultimate public power of the planters to exercise social control through extreme physical pain lay behind the milder forms of punishment used to extract labor day by day. Since planters were interested in maximizing their profits by maximizing labor inputs, they were reluctant to make use of magistrates who might remove slaves from the labor force for public punishment. The planters preferred to use the whip relatively lightly but with great regularity because it meant minimal interruption to the work regime and retained authority in their own hands.[143]

It is impossible to estimate how often slaves were whipped for refusing to work or failing to keep pace. No West Indian planter seems to have kept detailed records, and the driver's authority to whip slaves in the field in the absence of the owner meant that any records would be incomplete. Contemporary observers provide conflicting evidence, some saying that the whip had virtually disappeared from the field by the 1820s and others reporting that it was in constant use.[144] The registration returns are of no value, only a handful of slaves being listed with whip marks. The Protectors of Slaves in the crown colonies made six-monthly reports on "offences" committed by slaves after 1826 but did not relate the offenses to particular types of punishment. In Trinidad in 1827–28, when the total slave population was 24,000, some 3,535 offenses were reported. Of these offenses, 35 percent clearly related to resistance to the labor regime: neglect of duty, not coming to work in proper time, refusing to work, bad work, neglect to throw grass, and neglect of stock. Disobedience and insolence, common offenses, may also relate to the labor regime.[145]

Slaveowners were particularly anxious to remove examples of excessively liberal or excessively harsh discipline, so that slaves might be encouraged to see the rigors of their regime as a normal state of affairs. Thus, they were hostile to planters who introduced ameliorative measures on an individual basis. But examples of extreme ill-treatment were equally threatening to the regime. For instance, the Court of Policy of Demerara-Essequibo decided in 1819 to banish a Mr. Benny, part-owner and manager of Turkeyen Estate, because of his harsh treatment of the slaves on that estate. Benny had set fire to the old range of slave houses on Turkeyen without providing new ones, had failed to supply medical attention, had forced the slaves to work on Sundays, and had given short time for meals. As a result of this harsh treatment the whole gang absconded for several weeks. Such an example of mass protest was seen as dangerous to the entire neighborhood. Thus, the court decided to banish Benny from the colony, since "the Negroes on that estate have got into that state of insensibility and desperation they quite disregard every punishment he had inflicted, which they appear to endure rather than submit to Mr. Benny's management or remain under his control."[146] He was banished for the "safety" of the colony at large.

While slaveowners wished to make the infliction of punishment appear dependent on the behavior of the slaves, the giving of rewards was to be seen as following from the generosity of the master. Rewards and indulgences were not to become entrenched rights, since this would remove their value as positive incentives to labor. Richard Pares has explained how John Pinney attempted to prevent the development of such customary rights on his Nevis plantations at the end of the eighteenth century. Pinney

told one manager to change, from time to time, the day of the week upon which the negroes got their half-holiday for tending their own provision-grounds, or even to suspend it altogether for a week or two, so that they should not come to think they had a customary claim to Saturday afternoon. In the same way he forbade another to increase their basic allowance of food, but encouraged him to supplement it where the circumstances of a particular negro made it necessary to do so.[147]

By the early nineteenth century, however, many of the "indulgences" of the previous century had indeed become entrenched in law or custom. The most important of these related to holidays, special allowances of material goods, and cash payments. The provision of food, housing, clothing, and certain other goods was basic to survival, but the amount distributed could be varied so as to serve as a positive or negative incentive to labor. These items will be discussed in detail in the following sections of this chapter. But it is important to note that the differential allocation of such rewards on the basis of the slaves' status in the occupational hierarchy was at the root of that "inequality" observed by the Barbadian planters within the slave community.

Some slaves came to receive cash payments from their owners as a matter of custom. The practice was most widespread in British Honduras. In 1809 Henderson reported only that Saturday labor was "invariably the privilege of the slave," who was "generally engaged by his owner" at an established rate of 3s. 4d. (or £8 13s. 4d. per annum), though the owners often substituted inferior goods for the amount. By 1833, however, it was said that the slaves received this sum whether sick or well.[148] Elsewhere, cash payments were confined to individual slaves of high status. In the 1780s, first-gang drivers on the Codrington plantations, Barbados, received cash rewards of 6s. 3d., but in the nineteenth century these annual gifts amounted to £20.[149] From 1798 the manager of Newton Estate "gave the drive man as an encouragement for his good behaviour and attention to the Negroes" a "salary" of £10.[150] The white overseer of Newton received £250 per annum. The journals of other plantations rarely record such payments, so it may be assumed that they were not standard and might be altered with circumstances. Occasional small payments were also made to masons, carpenters, coopers, and even field slaves in return for specific job work or for labor on customary free days. The only other slaves who regularly received cash payments from their owners were midwives, but these payments were designed to encourage fertility rather than to serve as direct incentives to labor. Planters sometimes purchased provisions and small livestock from slaves, for cash, and made special grants to cover the costs of funerals and house building.[151] But the latter grants were generally made in kind rather than as cash.

Some slaves were permitted to work independently, hired to themselves and required only to make fixed periodic payments to their owners. This practice was common in the towns but rare in the rural areas, where it was confined mostly to skilled slaves. It was generally frowned on by the planters, since it threatened the driving system. At Newton Estate, Barbados, for example, a mulatto carpenter named John Thomas was permitted to "work out" at a certain daily hire but fell in arrears. He asked for his freedom, but when this was refused he ran away and was not heard of for three years, when he turned up on his absentee master's doorstep in London in 1813. The overseer reported that the whole family of John Thomas was disaffected, and that three other slaves had run away in the same fashion when allowed to work out.[152] The slaveowners of British Honduras expressed their fears about the development of self-hire with much greater force. A resolution carried by a public meeting in 1805 clearly revealed the roots of concern:

That no owner of negro men slaves be permitted to suffer such slave or slaves to hire himself to himself with a view to pursue trade, or for the purpose of cutting mahogany, logwood, or fustic; as thereby such slave being under no controul of his master, becomes subject to no authority but what results from his own will, which naturally tends to create insubordination thereby diminishing respect to his proprietors, and destroying that spirit of industry which so strongly conduces to good order, regularity and due obedience.[153]

A penalty of £500 was imposed, but a committee reported in 1810 "a continuation of such evil practices" and recommended a further extension of the law, so that ''slaves of either sex shall not be permitted to hire themselves to themselves *for any purpose whatever*.''[154] It was fundamental to the West Indian planters' theory of slavery that labor could be extracted only under the discipline of direct supervision. The Malthusian incentive of hunger was seen by the masters as inadequate to the maintenance of any significant level of output in the West Indies. Although they changed to some extent the relative importance of the negative and positive incentives to labor, they believed that only direct supervision and strict discipline could maximize productivity. But significant exceptions to these rules came to be accepted long before 1807. One of the most important of these exceptions occurred in the area of food production.

FOOD

West Indian slaveowners followed three quite distinct methods in providing nutrition for their slaves. Some purchased food and distributed it in regular rations. These planters devoted all of their arable land to the production of export staples. The second method also involved the distribution of rations, but most of the food was produced on the plantations and cultivated under the same system of gang labor as used for export staples. The third group of slaveowners simply provided the slaves with land, generally known as provision grounds, on which to produce their own food, though they did distribute rations to a limited extent. All rural slaveowners possessing land permitted their slaves to cultivate garden plots around their houses and to raise small livestock.

The first of these three methods of provisioning was rarely practiced after 1807. Subsistence crises, resulting chiefly from the interruption to trade consequent on the American Revolution, caused the death of thousands of slaves in the British islands and led the planters to avoid dependence on external sources.[155] The Napoleonic Wars had a similar effect. Where almost all land was potential cane land, as in Barbados and some of the Leeward Islands, the planters kept control of the system of production but allocated part of their resources of land and labor to the cultivation of food crops. Where land types were more varied, planters were reluctant to devote potential export crop land to food crops and merely provided lands on which the slaves were expected to produce what they could when they could. This system was seen by the planters as far less costly than purchasing imported food or taking land out of profitable export crops. In some cases the provision grounds fell within the boundaries of the plantation; in others the planters purchased separate areas for that purpose, requiring the slaves to travel distances of up to 15 miles to tend their crops. In some cases the provision grounds comprised marginal, unproductive land; in others the soil was ideal for food crops. These physical and economic factors led to the emergence of the provision ground system in Jamaica long before 1776, but there is no doubt that the subsistence crises of the late eighteenth century gave it an added impetus. The system also became firmly established in the Windward Islands and Trinidad. The situation in the marginal colonies is less certain. The slaves of Barbuda had extensive grounds, but those in British Honduras, Anguilla, the Bahamas, and the Cayman Islands seem to have had only limited access and generally cultivated food crops while under the direct supervision of their masters. Indeed, they often produced little else after the failure of export crops in these islands.

Recent attempts to establish the caloric intake of slaves in the British Caribbean, carried out by Robert Dirks and the Kiples, have been based largely on the rationed allowances prescribed by colonial slave laws.[156] Neither of these studies produces systematic estimates for all of the colonies, but it is obvious that precision is impossible because of the variable importance of rations in the slave diet. The slave laws provide a poor guide to actual practice, and Dirks notes major anomalies. Further, there is little hard evidence available on the output of provision grounds and gardens, and much of this produce was in any case retailed by the slaves in public markets and not necessarily consumed or exchanged for food items. Thus, it is difficult to know what to make of Dirks's finding that the "average estate ration" in the late eighteenth century was between 1,500 and 2,000 calories per day, whereas "the average energy demand placed on a young man in a first gang must have been in excess of 3,500 calories per day, perhaps 150 calories per day less for a woman."[157] There are two problems here. The first is that it is uncertain how many calories were obtained from sources other than rations, though it is certain that these supplementary sources became increasingly important after 1807. The second problem is that Dirks's estimate of energy demands derives from an underestimate of slave stature and an admitted understatement of the hours worked by slaves (which he estimated as a daily average of eight hours).[158] There seems no way of resolving these problems with real precision. The approach of the Kiples, who appear simply to assume that adult slaves must have received an average 3,000 calories per day, is even less fruitful. The analysis that follows makes no claim to greater quantitative precision, and for the moment this aspect of the question remains insoluble. Rather, it attempts to establish a firmer comparative foundation, emphasizing differences in food supply between colonies, differences between slaves within the hierarchy of occupational statuses, and differences between seasons.

Rationed Allowances

In Barbados, where the dependence on rations was greatest, the "usual allowances" described by planters match quite closely those prescribed by the abolition act of 1834 and are corroborated by the evidence of actual practice on large plantations.[159] In 1824 the planter Forster Clarke claimed that "grown" Barbadian slaves received daily allowances of 1½ pt of Guinea corn (sorghum) or 2 pt of Indian corn (maize), making 4.5–5.0 lb when dressed, or the same weight in roots, and weekly allowances of 1 lb of salt fish, 1 pt of molasses, and ½ pt of salt. Each day, he said, the slaves were given 1 pt of tea in the morning before starting work, an allowance of "weak diversion" (rum and water sweetened with molasses) once or twice a day, and 1 pt of molasses and water beverage, "in addition to which a plentiful meal is provided for every one at dinner [midday].''[160] The abolition act of 1834 was rather more limited in its prescriptions, stating only that laborers over 10 years of age were to have weekly allowances of not less than 10 pt of Indian or Guinea corn or 30 lb of plantains, potatoes, yams, or eddoes, and 2 lb of codfish, herring, shad, or pickled fish. Children under 10 were to get half rations.[161] Thus, the allowances of corn or root crops were almost exactly the same in the act and Clarke's report, but the amount of salt fish was double in 1834, matching what appears to have been the upper limit of practice.

Although these systems of providing food contained a variety of options, Barbadian planters regarded Guinea corn as the staple. It was fed to cattle as well as slaves, but rarely eaten by whites. On sugar estates the area planted in corn frequently exceeded that under cane and generally accounted for more than one-third of the total cultivated area. Root crops ("ground provisions"), plantains, and pigeon peas rarely occupied more than one-tenth.[162] Overall, food crops commonly accounted for more than half of the cultivated area but occupied no more than one-third of the time spent in estate labor.[163] They formed part of a rotational cycle, and fields were rarely left in cane for more than three years at a stretch. Corn could be harvested within six months, so was often interplanted. Indian corn and bonavist peas were planted on the banks of land holed for canes, while Guinea corn and pigeon peas were sown through ratoon crops. Poorer land often remained in Guinea corn for four or more years.[164] In spite of the large area devoted to Guinea corn, most estates purchased additional supplies from other planters or from the slaves themselves, and occasionally had to fall back on imported corn in times of drought.[165] Planters, however, gave allowances of root crops, pigeon peas, maize, and plantains only occasionally, and most of this produce was sold in the local market. Thus, a Grenadian planter visiting Barbados in 1823 noted that "the yams being very profitable are seldom given as an allowance, but chiefly sold to assist in defraying the expenses of the estate which the rum alone seldom does," and yams and sweet potatoes were exported to neighboring islands.[166] The principal occasions for the distribution of these special foods were Christmas and harvest home, when the planters might also provide a barrel of imported salt pork or kill an ox on the estate. During crop slaves could chew cane and drink sugar syrup in the boiling houses, but it is not clear whether there was any regulation of the volume consumed. Meat was sometimes obtained from injured estate cattle and stranded whales.[167]

The rations of Guinea corn and salt fish, molasses, and salt were given out on a daily or, less often, a weekly basis.[168] One of the reasons for this frequency was a desire to prevent the sale of food items in the internal markets. But the monotony of Guinea corn and salt fish did lead Barbadian slaves to barter these items for other provisions or sell them for money to buy salt meat or vegetables. According to Pinckard, when slaves were asked why they sold their rations they replied, "Massa gib me Guinea corn too much—Guinea corn to-day—Guinea corn to-morrow—Guinea corn eb'ry day—We no like him Guinea corn—him Guinea corn no good for gnhyaam [eat].''[169] This attitude may be compared with the

Jamaican slaves' hymn in praise of Guinea corn, but in that island the grain was no staple.[170] Barbadian slaves also supplemented their rations with fruit, vegetables, and livestock produced in their house gardens. These gardens remained very small throughout the period. A new village established on the Codrington estates in the 1820s was to provide 100 square feet of garden space to each household, but this was generous.[171] Most slave gardens were said to include a hencoop and many a hogsty. At Spendlove Plantation, Pinckard observed pigs, goats, Guinea fowls, ducks, chickens, and pigeons, though often these were raised for sale rather than consumption. Provisions from the gardens were sold in internal public markets, and it was said that "the markets of the island depend almost wholly upon this mode of supply." The slaves also contrived to produce small quantities of arrowroot, cotton, and aloes in their garden grounds, for the export market.[172] But it is important not to overemphasize the significance of these house gardens, for Barbadian slaves depended very heavily on estate rations for their subsistence.

Food supplies were not equally distributed in Barbados. The giving of half-rations to children under 10 years of age has been noted already. Special allowances other than those given on holidays were distributed chiefly to head people on sugar estates, further buttressing the hierarchy of status and increasing the potential nutrition of those performing the smallest amounts of heavy manual labor. There is little quantitative evidence for Barbados on the extent of this difference, but it is clear that much of the corn purchased by planters from estate slaves came from slaves of status, drivers, and mulattoes, suggesting that they had more extensive grounds.[173] In 1812 the Barbados Agricultural Society recognized the giving of extra rations to hired tradespeople as a "grievance" and agreed not to exceed 2 pt of corn or 6 lb of ground provisions, 0.25 lb of salt fish, 0.5 pt of molasses, and 1 gill of rum per day, except that master workmen or foremen might have more.[174] Sick slaves also received special foods such as rice, cocoa, flour, biscuits, and poultry, but only so long as they remained sick. Aged slaves and women not working in the field may have received less than the usual allowances, but the position of high-status domestics, who had direct access to the master's larder and leftovers, is less certain.[175] It was said that slaves belonging to poor masters received smaller allowances than those on large sugar plantations, but again there is no quantitative evidence of the extent of this contrast for Barbados.[176]

St. Kitts, Nevis, and Antigua followed the basic outlines of the Barbados food supply system. The Leeward Islands slave law of 1798 prescribed weekly allowances of 9 pt of corn or equivalent quantities of beans, peas, wheat flour, rye flour, Indian corn meal, oatmeal, rice, cassava flour, biscuits, yams, potatoes, eddoes, tanias, plantains, or bananas, and 1.25 lb of herring, shad, mackerel, or other salted provisions, or 2.5 lb of fresh fish or provisions. These allowances were repeated exactly in the Nevis abolition act of 1834.[177] They were significantly less generous than the 10 pt of corn and 2 lb of salt fish allowed by the Barbados act, though very similar to those said to be usual in Barbados during the 1820s. But the availability of marginal mountain lands in St. Kitts and Nevis provided the base for more extensive separate provision grounds than in Barbados or Antigua. The slave law of 1798 required the planters to provide only 40 square feet of garden grounds per household, and in some cases the slave village was so cramped with houses that even these gardens were located elsewhere. Where provision grounds were provided to the extent of one acre per ten slaves, however, the law permitted planters to reduce rations by one-half, though maintaining allowances of salt or fresh provisions.

In St. Kitts and Nevis most sugar estates were wedge-shaped, with a sea frontage, cane fields extending almost to the 1,000-foot contour and provision grounds occupying the more rugged inland. But the local markets were relatively poorly supplied with small stock and vegetables, so the contrast with Barbados was less than might be expected.[178] Less than 15 percent of the cultivated area on estates in these islands was devoted to food crops, particularly yams and sweet potatoes. In Antigua, however, nearer to 30 percent of cultivated estate land was in provision crops. All of these islands depended heavily on corn imported from North America.[179] Thus, yams and sweet potatoes rather than corn tended to be the staple foods. St. Kitts planters followed the Barbadian practice of planting Angola (pigeon) peas on the banks, and it was said by the planters that since "the Negroes have in this island an unrestricted access to this part of the plantation, it forms not only an unlimited article of excellent food, but of profit also by its sale in the market."[180] Yet the continued dependence on imported corn led to the giving of short allowances. In 1820, for example, an estate manager in St. Kitts was fined £573 for giving only 3 pt of corn and no salt provisions for a period of six weeks. The slaves had received none of the yams and sweet potatoes grown on the estate and normally given as allowances.[181]

A similar system of rationed allowances was followed in Demerara-Essequibo and Berbice. The slaves on most estates had grounds as well as gardens, but the grounds were small and the planters put a much greater area of estate land under food crops. This is somewhat surprising, in view of the extensive uncultivated backlands available in these colonies. Probably it resulted from the high cost of impoldering land and maintaining drainage and irrigation canals on the estates, as well as the planters' desire to maximize productivity and retain close supervision of labor. Planters were required to plant one acre of provisions for every five slaves, these grounds being inspected annually by the burgher captains.[182] The system was nearer to that followed in St. Kitts than Barbados, but the staple was the plantain rather than corn or root crops. Plantains were cultivated in groves, or "walks," on the estates, the planters occasionally purchasing and impoldering backlands for this purpose. Abandoned cotton plantations in Mahaica were converted to plantain lots. Some small holdings specialized in the crop and, together with plantations producing a surplus, supplied a large internal market. In 1832, for example, plantains to the value of 705,845 guilders were sold in the three colonies.[183] The average cost of a bunch was half a guilder, so roughly 20 bunches were traded per slave. Plantains were affected by a mysterious disease throughout the 1820s, but it never became general.[184] Plantain walks occupied more than one-quarter of the total cultivated land on estates. At Wales, on the west bank of the Demerara, 355 acres were in cane and 60 in coffee in 1832, but plantains occupied 152 acres, and the 289 slaves were given only 30 acres in gardens. Vreedestein, with 209 slaves, had 20 acres in grounds, 75 in plantains, and 246 in cane.[185]

In 1830 the weekly allowance to adult working slaves in Demerara-Essequibo was set at 2 lb of salt fish, herring, shad, or mackerel, or 4 lb of fresh provisions plus 0.5 pt of salt, and 1.5 bunches of plantains (weighing not less than 45 lb) or 9 pt of corn or its equivalent.[186] The list of equivalents and their quantities matched exactly that in the Leeward Islands law of 1798, except that the latter specified 30 lb of plantains or bananas. But comparison is complicated because the Leeward Islands law prescribed average quantities, the planter being allowed to distribute the total as he wished, and the Demerara-Essequibo act provided that invalids and children of 10–15 years should receive only two-thirds of the rations prescribed for working adults, children 5–10 years one-half, and children under 5 years one-third. Thus, the total quantity of food supplied on particular plantations depended on the age structure of the slave population. Taking the age structure of the colonies as typical, it follows that if the legal allowances were given, a plantation of 200 slaves would receive 340 lb of salt fish weekly in Berbice and only 250 lb in St. Kitts, around 1820. The Berbice plantations had fewer children, of course, but there is no doubt that the legislated allowances were more liberal than in the Leeward Islands and came close to those specified by the Barbados abolition act. According to the calorie values used by the Kiples, the 20 lb of yams or sweet potatoes specified in the Leeward Islands would yield 7,880 calories weekly, the 10 pt of corn in Barbados 8,840 calories, and the (dressed) 30 lb of plantains in Demerara-Essequibo and Berbice 16,200 calories. But the corn and plantains yielded about the same amount of protein, and twice as much as yams or sweet potatoes.[187]

The manager of the Katz plantations in Berbice claimed in 1831 that every Saturday adult slaves on these holdings received 1.75 lb of salt fish and 2 bunches of plantains. Drivers and tradespeople got double the amount of fish, while children of about 10 years got 1.5 lb of fish and 1.5 bunches of plantains, and infants received "some" of these items. But during crop all of the slaves were given a double alllowance of fish, he said, though the quantity of plantains remained standard. Rum, up to three glasses a day, was given according to work and weather. On holidays the slaves were said to get 2 lb of salt pork each, and an ox was killed. On their grounds the slaves cultivated yams, cassava, corn, and rice, and in their gardens they planted vegetables and reared poultry[188] but were given only every fourth Saturday for such work. No doubt this was an optimistic description, but it does make clear the differential treatment of slaves in terms of age and occupation. The giving of increased rations during crop is of interest, especially because the Leeward Islands law permitted a one-fifth reduction in allowances on sugar estates during crop (though excepting the Virgin Islands). It may be that slaves in Demerara-Essequibo and Berbice were denied the ready access to cane juice permitted in Barbados and the Leewards. Some slaves received rations of cassava flour cakes, but the emphasis on plantains created a monotony as great as that of Guinea corn in Barbados, and the slaves sought to supplement their diet from garden and ground. As in Barbados, it could be said that "the supply of the market with vegetables, poultry and pigs, and articles of that kind, is almost entirely in the hands of the Negro population."[189]

Provision Grounds

The system of rationed allowances prevailed throughout Barbados, St. Kitts, Nevis, Antigua, Demerara-Essequibo, and Berbice, with only minor variations in the relative significance of supplements obtained from provision grounds. In the remaining sugar colonies of the British Caribbean the provision ground was everywhere more important than the master's store in the early nineteenth century. It is a revealing fact that the Jamaican abolition act of 1834 made no mention of food. The Montserrat act stated only that the planters were to provide food if the provision grounds failed, and the Tobago act merely stipulated that apprentices over 12 years were to have half an acre of provision grounds within a mile of their houses and children under 12 were to have a quarter acre. The St. Vincent abolition act was unique in specifying quantities: slaves over 10 years were to receive 4 qt of wheat flour or farina or the flour of Indian or Guinea corn or 20 lb of yams or potatoes, and children were to have half-rations.[190] Earlier laws were generally equally vague. The Jamaican slave law of 1816, for example, was careful to specify that the slaves should have sufficient time to cultivate their grounds, but beyond this merely called for a monthly inspection "in order to see that the same are cultivated and kept up in a proper manner," and required that where no suitable land was available or where grounds had been made unproductive by drought the planters should "make good and ample provision" equivalent to 3s. 4d. per week per slave.[191] In Grenada all slaves over 14 years, except domestics, were to be allotted provision grounds as well as one-fortieth of an acre for gardens, but if land suited to provision grounds was unavailable the planter could provide "a weekly allowance of provisions, completely adequate to their maintenance."[192] The Tobago slave law of 1794 stated that every plantation should have one acre for every five slaves "well planted with provisions," but this seems to have been neglected as provision grounds became increasingly important.[193] In Dominica the slave law of 1821 did stipulate that adults should receive 2 lb of salt provisions weekly, and chilren half that amount, but the earlier law of 1799 had stated only that masters should provide either "a sufficient quantity of good and wholesome food" or sufficient land and time to produce it. The masters claimed that slaves with provision grounds got "not less than half an acre" each.[194]

The Trinidad Ordinance of 1800 was more specific. It required planters to cultivate one quarrée (3.2 acres) per 10 working slaves in provisions, and to give a weekly allowance of 3 lb of salt meat or 4 lb of salt fish to each slaves aged 14 years or over. In addition, each of these slaves was to have "a portion of land allotted to him, adequate to produce, by cultivating it, a sufficiency of ground provisions for himself and his family," to be cultivated on Saturday afternoons out of crop. Slaves without grounds were to be given 60 plantains or 6 qt of cassava meal weekly, or 3 bits to purchase provisions, in addition to the allowances of salt meat or fish.[195] But Trinidad planters soon began to complain about the high cost of provisions, and sugar estates neglected the cultivation of provision crops. In 1817 it was said that most large estates complied with the ordinance in giving Saturday afternoons, but generally gave only 3 lb of fish. On smaller holdings, however, the slaveowners tended to give no fish but allowed the slaves every Saturday to cultivate their grounds.[196] Thus, there was a rapid shift to heavy dependence on the provision ground system. In 1830 the Protector of Slaves in Trinidad, Henry Gloster, claimed that adult plantation slaves received 3.5 lb of salt cod weekly, as well as three drams of rum per day during crop and a glass a day out of crop. But slaves were given only 4–6 qt of farinaceous food weekly if their provision grounds proved unproductive. Head people got double rations of fish. Children under 14 years had only half-rations but were fed a mess from the owner's kitchen. Special allowances were given at Christmas.[197] For most of the period 1807–34, then, slaves on large plantations in Trinidad received relatively generous allowances of salt fish but little else, and those on small holdings were totally dependent on their provision grounds.

Although the slave laws of the Windward Islands and Jamaica were generally silent on the distribution of rationed allowances, it was customary in most of these colonies for the planters regularly to provide limited quantities of pickled fish and to supply occasional allowances at holidays. In Jamaica, adult slaves got 6–8 pickled herring weekly. The distribution of fish was said by some proslavery observers to have increased after about 1800, but contemporary calculations for Dominica and Jamaica showed that the amount of fish imported was only about half that required to supply the supposed allowances.[198] In Jamaica salt and pickled fish were sometimes termed "indulgences," which might be withheld for bad conduct, in contrast to rightful "allowances."[199] On sugar estates slaves were allowed to consume cane juice during crop, as in the rationed colonies, and also received rum and molasses out of crop. With the significant exception of the parish of Vere in Jamaica, where the slaves had only limited grounds and depended on allowances of Guinea corn cultivated on the sugar estates as in Barbados,[200] the vast majority of slaves in the Windward Islands and Jamaica relied heavily on the produce of their provision grounds.

In the Virgin Islands slaves had both provision grounds and limited allowances. Around 1830 George Richardson Porter claimed that they received weekly 4–6 pt of corn meal and 6 herring, as well as salt, pork, and flour at Christmas. The slave law of 1798 prohibited the reduction of rations during crop but permitted a reduction of one-fifth out of crop where the grounds were adequate.[201]

The internal organization of the provision grounds was left very largely to the slaves themselves. The planters might subdivide the grounds and allocate them to particular individuals, but beyond this they took little interest, apart from making occasional inspections. In 1814 some planters in Dominica began "working the

gangs on their grounds on the days allotted for that purpose, under the super-
intendence of the overseers and drivers," but this was done to prevent the
development of a trade between the slaves and maroons, and was very much an
exception.[202] Normally the grounds were worked by family groups or individual
slaves, with men, women, and children all performing labor. Aged and disabled
slaves were allotted grounds, and these were often worked for them by relatives or
fellow laborers. Head people, such as drivers and tradesmen, were often allocated
larger grounds, and in some cases they actually hired other slaves to work their
grounds.[203] The crops cultivated on the grounds varied with locality, but root crops
generally predominated, with corn and plantains as subsidiaries. In Dominica it
was said that the slaves cultivated "yams, plantains, bananas, cassada or manioc,
eddoes, potatoes, ocoraes [okra], Indian corn, cale, pigeon pease, and several
species of beans, and pine apples; and the higher grounds produce many kinds of
European garden stuff, such as cabbages, carrots, turnips, beet root, lettuce,
asparagus, artichoke, radish, cucumber, cellery, and herbs of all sorts, besides
tropical fruits."[204] Most of these vegetable crops were produced for sale in the
public markets, however, and some of the corn and other provisions was fed to
pigs and poultry kept in the slaves' garden plots. The slaves of the Windward
Islands and Jamaica played an even greater role in supplying the internal markets
than those in the rationed colonies, so it is impossible to know how much of the
produce of ground and garden entered the slaves' diet directly or was exchanged
for other food items and how much was exchanged for nonfood items or accumu-
lated as cash. The provision ground system certainly provided the basis for a more
varied diet, but even in the rationed colonies slaves were able to achieve variety by
selling produce from their gardens or exchanging their allowances in the market. A
simple example of such behavior was the exchange of pickled fish (herring, shad,
mackerel) for the salt cod preferred by slaves in most colonies.[205] Without doubt
the provision ground system created the framework for relatively independent
economic activity, and it was said to be preferred by the slaves themselves,[206] but
its ultimate effect on nutrition is less than certain.

The Marginal Colonies

Slaveowners in the marginal colonies practiced a variety of methods of
providing food supplies for their slaves. In British Honduras the provision ground
system was rarely practiced, and even the urban market seems to have been
supplied very largely from the provisions "plantations" of smallholders rather
than from the grounds or gardens of slaves. This pattern may be explained by the
seasonal migrations of the mahogany cutters. Slaves belonging to wood-cutting
gangs did sometimes contract with their masters to supply the gang and cultivated
food crops in their own time. But it was more common for the masters to allocate
several slaves specifically to the production of food. In 1816 it was said that
woodcutters received weekly allowances comprising 5 lb of salt pork, as well as
plantains, yams, rice, flour, and salt.[207] Plantains seem to have been the staple. The

quantity of salt meat was generous compared to the allowances commonly given in the sugar colonies, and the range of other food items was relatively varied. But the dependence of rural slaves on rationed allowances was at least as great as in Barbados.

Barbuda lay at the other extreme. There the slaves performed relatively little supervised labor and, according to Lowenthal and Clarke, "enjoyed an abundance of provisions from their large garden plots, from hunting game in the forests, and from fishing."[208] In 1824 the Codrington estates' manager claimed that "many" of the slaves had 10–11 acres in cultivation on their own account, where they produced "an immense quantity of potatoes"; they also raised poultry, pigs, and goats and used their own nets to fish. Much of this produce was sent to Antigua for sale. Corn and root crops were cultivated under supervision, and it was said that the slaves received rations of 10 pt of corn weekly. In 1834, however, the slaves complained that the customary granting of an "allowance of food from the stores of their master" when their potato crops failed had been withheld, that "their allowance of fresh meat and fish was latterly much curtailed and very irregularly afforded," and that they "were not permitted to fish or sell crabs or firewood as formerly they were allowed to do."[209] Although this suggests a definite attempt to straiten the slaves at the end of the period of slavery and shows that an "abundance" of provision crops was not always obtained from the slaves' grounds, it does appear that the slaves of Barbuda generally consumed relatively large quantities of fresh fish and meat as well as sweet potatoes and that this food was very largely produced by their own efforts and on their own grounds.

The organization of food supplies in the Bahamas, the Cayman Islands, and Anguilla is less certain. It has already been established that rural slaves in these colonies were largely employed in the production of food crops, but much of this produce was sold by the slaveowners in local markets, and it is not obvious that the slaves necessarily received large quantities of provisions even though the supplies were present. The rations distributed by slaveowners in the Bahamas were very limited. In 1825 Burton Williams, who had moved his slaves to Trinidad, stated he gave his field slaves only 8 qt of corn weekly in the Bahamas, as required by law, and half-rations to those under 12 years of age. He gave them nothing else, except for 3–4 lb of fresh or salt meat at Christmas. The allowance of fish required by the Trinidad ordinance he thought quite excessive.[210] Farquharson's journal for 1831–32 similarly makes reference only to the distribution of corn rations, but at Christmas his "grown hands" received 4 lb of pork and 4 lb of beef, a bottle of rum, and "a large cup full of sugar," with half-rations of meat and sugar to the children, and at the end of the cotton crop they had a harvest supper of "half a sheep and 2 flasks of rum." In 1831 the slaves also had the meat of two cows that broke their legs, one in February just four days after the harvest supper, the other in August.[211] Apart from these occasional treats, rural slaves in the Bahamas received only corn from their masters' stores. Williams claimed that he used Indian corn, keeping the Guinea corn in reserve, but Farquharson depended on Guinea corn.

Bahamian slaves were forced to depend largely on their own provision grounds and fishing. Williams said that his slaves generally cultivated only small gardens "but had as much land as they pleased." Farquharson's journal made only one reference to "Negro Grounds," and there is no indication of their extent. More importantly, it has already been noted that Bahamian slaves generally worked six days a week throughout the year, so most of the cultivation and fishing had to be performed on Sundays. Williams gave his slaves "one day in each month, to encourage them," but Farquharson made no such concessions.[212] The accessibility of the sea probably did mean a relatively plentiful supply of fresh fish, and the slaves could raise livestock and cultivate a variety of vegetable crops as in the rationed colonies. Even if the quality of produce was no greater, the proportion consumed probably exceeded that in colonies totally dependent on the provision ground system, since most rural Bahamian slaves had only limited opportunities for marketing any surplus.

In Anguilla slaves were given allowances of root crops but were expected to provide their own fish, as in the Bahamas. The provision ground system was less firmly systematized, however. In 1824 special commissioners were dispatched from St. Kitts to investigate the state of the island and provided a revealing critique of the system of feeding slaves:

As long as the ground provisions hold out they are fed, and we believe abundantly, from that source—but they have no allowance of fish, or of other salt provisions. When the stock of yam and potatoe is exhausted, we are informed that a day, sometimes two days in the week are allowed to them, and in some cases that corn meal is substituted. We cannot imagine a more mischevious system or one more ruinous to the planter and to the slave; . . . to let these people loose in order that they may seek their weekly subsistence can only be an inducement to idle and profligate habits and affords at once opportunity and encouragement to very extensive depredations.[213]

The St. Kitts commissioners believed that food production should be under the direct supervision of the slaveowner, as on their own island. Certainly they must have been aware of the established provision ground system of Jamaica and the Windward Islands, but they found the arbitrary pattern of Anguilla reprehensible because it was not governed by standard rules.

Seasonal Stress

One of the arguments presented by the planters of Barbados and the Leeward Islands in favor of the system of rationed allowances and estate cultivation of food crops was that it reduced the possibility of famine resulting from drought, hurricanes, or interruptions to trade. Anguilla suffered from all three of these hazards in the 1820s, and by 1832 actual starvation was said to affect all classes.[214] Elsewhere famine was kept at bay throughout the period 1807–34, but planters often feared the failure of food crops planted on estate land or had to supplement the produce of provision grounds. In 1812, for example, Barbados experienced a prolonged drought from June to November. Corn and provision crops could not be planted in May because of the drought and the covering of ash resulting from the eruption of Soufriere on St. Vincent. The crops were planted in June, but the corn and potatoes were attacked by worms, flies, and ants, and much had to be replanted in later months. By July provisions were scarce, and in August it was said that "the scarcity of food is very general, and is a subject of the most serious alarm." This scarcity continued throughout the year, and much corn was imported for sale. It was not until February 1813, when a good Guinea corn crop was harvested, that the Barbadian planters could feel secure.[215] In May of that year the attorney of Newton Estate reported that Barbados was extremely parched and on the verge of famine, but he felt confident that there was sufficient corn in the plantation's store to last for eight months. In general, emergency importations of food became rare in most colonies after 1815, except after hurricanes.[216]

The well-being of a population, it has been argued, is limited not so much by the average amount of food available but by the amount available at the time of year when food supply is at its minimum. West Indian slaves certainly did suffer from seasonal nutritional stress, as well as the subsistence crises resulting from prolonged drought, hurricanes, and interruptions to trade. The seasonality of food supplies was most pronounced on sugar estates, but it affected both the rationed colonies and those dependent on the provision ground system. The minimum period of food supply occurred in the out-of-crop season, which Barbadian slaves called the "hungry-time" or "hard-time."[217] This was evident during the scarcity of 1812. Although it might seem providential that the minimum did not overlap with the extreme exertions of the slaves during crop, one of the reasons for the minimum was that the slaves were forced to neglect their grounds in this season. Sugar planters were universally agreed that slaves appeared most healthy during crop.[218] The reason for this was not that crop was all good fun, as the planters would have it, but that the slaves had access to unusually large quantities of energy-rich food in sugar cane and syrup. They were also able to reap crops of ground provisions planted and tended during the sugar harvest. It was this relative abundance of food supplies that enabled the Leeward Islands slave law to permit the reduction of all rations by one-fifth and Barbadian planters to reduce their molasses rations during crop. Since the comparatively high nutritional status of slaves in the crop season was observed in the rationed colonies as well as those dependent on the provision ground system, this condition must be attributed chiefly to the availability of high-energy sugar in the diet. The eating of unripe fruits and vegetables out-of-crop was noted in all of the colonies, but it may be that seasonal nutritional stress was greatest in those sugar colonies using the provision ground system.[219]

Food Preparation

The preparation of food was generally left to the slaves themselves, but planters in the rationed colonies tended to intervene to some extent in this process. A few planters provided iron cooking pots and spoons, but the only utensils commonly distributed in most colonies were knives.[220] In the provision ground colonies only the cooking of food for young children was closely supervised, a common pot being prepared from plantation stores. For example, a Trinidad planter stated in 1825 that he kept back half of the children's ration of salt fish and had "a pot boiled for the children consisting of fish, plantains and yams, and occasionally salt beef and rice, of which I gave the children that are weaned two meals a day," while "the sucking infants are brought to the house, and get pap made of flour in my kitchen three times a day."[221] Otherwise the slaves could choose what to eat, within the limits of their resources, and how to cook it. When breakfast was prepared by field cooks, as in Jamaica, it was said that "the negro gives out his breakfast to this cook before he leaves his home, and the breakfast is carried out to the field about nine o'clock." This meal might consist of plantains, root crops, or breadfruit, boiled in a soup or roasted, and seasoned with salt fish. Little was eaten at dinner, and the main meal might not be cooked until after 9 P.M. Slaves performing night work in sugar factories would return briefly to the village, give out their supper to be cooked, and eat it in the boiling house. Pepperpots and broths, which enabled the stretching of scant supplies of protein, were particularly common. In the eastern Caribbean slaves prepared *coocoo*, "a very thick hasty pudding made of the meal of Indian, or Guinea corn, and used instead of bread," while Jamaican slaves produced a similar food, called *foo-foo*, from yams, cassava, or plantains boiled and pounded.[222]

In November 1812, during the period of near famine, the Barbados Agricultural Society heard a paper by one Dr. Caddell in which he argued that the diseases of slaves were caused not by an insufficiency of food but by its improper preparation. Some slaves lacked the energy to cook their food adequately, he said, and so ate too little or consumed it half-raw. Others ate to repletion and developed "depraved" appetites, bartering their rations for small quantities of more palatable food. Caddell recommended the provision of cooked food, including the main meal at supper, and advocated its soporific qualities.[223] These arguments obviously carried weight with the Society, and planters were advised to feed children and indolent slaves from a public kitchen, supervised by a white servant, and to serve two-thirds or the whole of the adults' food ready-cooked wherever the slaves proved negligent in cookery.[224] Either these recommendations were influential or they reflected current tendencies. John Cobham, a Barbadian planter who moved to Trinidad in 1823, told a committee in his new colony that "since 1812 it has been a general custom" in Barbados not only to give the slaves rations "but to have a dinner cooked and distributed to them, that we might be sure of their getting at least one good meal; for it was discovered during that year, when provisions were very scarce, that many of the negroes sold their allowance and starved themselves; and the children we never trust to the mothers but provide for them entirely."[225] Whether the planters' intervention resulted in any significant change in methods of cookery is uncertain, however. It seems most probable that pepperpots, broths, *coocoo*, and *foo-foo* predominated as in the provision ground colonies, the meals varying little from day to day or season to season.[226]

Dietary Adequacy

Although West Indian slaves did consume a wide variety of food items from time to time, the basic diet was monotonous even when it was relatively substantial in terms of quantity. Using an "ideal" diet for the British Caribbean as a whole, and one more varied than that typical for most field slaves, the Kiples conclude that the basic caloric and protein needs of the slaves were in fact supplied.[227] This general conclusion is probably too optimistic, since it fails to recognize important differences between colonies. But the significant point here is that the Kiples go on to argue that even this "ideal" diet concealed numerous nutritional deficiencies with epidemiological implications. These implications, together with the medical indications of malnutrition, will be discussed in chapter 8. Here it is necessary only to note some of the nutritional deficiencies suggested by the Kiples for their ideal diet. In the first place, this diet was poor in calcium. Milk could have remedied this deficiency but was in short supply, and in any case many of the slaves were lactose intolerant. Some slaves did own cattle in the British Caribbean after 1807, but they were generally kept for their meat and for sale; only in the Virgin Islands was it said that slaves benefited from keeping cattle "in the use and sale of the milk and butter."[228] More important than this calcium deficiency was the absence of fats, and this further increased the deficiency of vitamin A in the slaves' diet. But the introduction of the ackee and the mango at the end of the eighteenth century did help to reduce this vitamin A deficiency. The Kiples also argue that the dependence on corn, root crops, and plantains as the major energy source increased requirements for thiamine, since this is necessary for the metabolism of carbohydrates. The availability of thiamine in the slave diet was reduced by the salting and pickling of fish and meat and by the long boiling common in slave cookery. Thus, it may be concluded that even when the slaves' diet was relatively varied it remained deficient in calcium, vitamin A, and thiamine. In periods of seasonal nutritional stress it was also inadequate in calories and, more often, protein. These deficiencies were not evenly spread within the rural slave populations. It must be said, however, that the metabolic pathways of many nutrients remain poorly understood, and that some apparently healthy modern West Indian populations subsist on only 1600–2000 calories per day, significantly less than the level assumed by the Kiples for the slave population.[229]

Slave diets varied between individuals and plantations, but some generalizations can be attempted at the colony level. Among the rural populations, a system of rationed allowances supplied the greater part of the slaves' food in Barbados, St. Kitts, Nevis, Antigua, Demerara-Essequibo, Berbice, and British Honduras. Elsewhere the provision ground system was basic, though supplemented to some extent by rations. Anguilla and the Bahamas fell somewhere between these extremes, and in Trinidad there was a shift from rations to provision grounds within the period. Protein was supplied chiefly by salt fish in the rationed colonies (except that British Honduras depended on salt pork) and by pickled or fresh fish in the other colonies. The staple energy sources were Guinea corn in Barbados and the Bahamas, yams and sweet potatoes in the Leeward Islands, and plantains in Trinidad, Demerara-Essequibo, Berbice, and British Honduras. Elsewhere the staples varied regionally or from plantation to plantation. These local variations make comparative conclusions difficult, but overall the slaves of the marginal colonies probably consumed the least deficient diets in normal times. Of the rationed colonies, the plantain-based diet of Demerara-Essequibo and Berbice probably delivered more calories than that of Barbados, while the smaller allowances of fish given in the Leeward Islands made these colonies further deficient. Of the colonies based on the provision ground system, Trinidad was most generous in its fish rations, but the individual character of the system obscures general tendencies. Although Sidney Mintz asserts that "it seems quite likely that the provision ground-marketing complex . . . reduced the hunger of the slaves," Dirks is justified in concluding that "the available evidence seems to indicate that the praedial slaves' efforts to feed themselves were not as successful as many accounts of vigorous gardening, hunting, gathering, and trading activities might lead one to believe."[230]

Within each of the types of colonies, further variations in diet may have been related to the different crops produced on the plantations, but such variations were minor. To the extent that slave laws affected practice, a certain uniformity at the colony level was imposed from above. It has been noted that poor slaveowners with small holdings were said to give less food than opulent planters, but most of this testimony comes from the latter and may be suspect. Many of the smaller holdings were devoted to provision crops rather than export staples, but the presence of potential food supplies did not necessarily have any effect on the slaves' nutrition. In the same way, the presence of vast stores of energy-rich sugar did not mean adequate food supplies for slaves living on sugar estates.

Differences in diet between individual slaves on particular plantations related chiefly to age and occupational status. The young and the old were often directly dependent on food prepared in their owners' kitchens, but the old were likely to be neglected. Distinctions were not generally made between males and females in the distribution of food, but males occupied most of the supervisory and skilled posts, which were rewarded much more generously in rations or provision grounds than were field laborer positions. Certain occupations provided direct access to food supplies. For example, Richard Price contends that slave fishermen "undoubtedly dined relatively well, trading surplus fish for vegetables from their neighbors' kitchen gardens."[231] Domestics had access to great house larders but generally lacked productive provision grounds. Only the sick shared in the variety of food, wholesome and unwholesome, that covered the planters' groaning tables.

HOUSING

Whereas nutrition had a direct effect on the ability of slaves to perform the tasks set by their owners and on their health and demographic experience, the housing and clothing of the slaves had a more limited impact. The nature of slave housing affected health and disease patterns, and hence the ability to perform work, while its spatial organization played a role in determining family structure and fertility. Clothing was significant chiefly in terms of its effect on health. Housing and clothing obviously had a much broader significance for the cultural history of the slave societies, but since the concern here is with population history, they can be treated more briefly. The slave laws of the British West Indian colonies were generally silent on the question of shelter, and throughout the period slaves were generally required to build their own houses with a minimum of intervention by the planters. Individual planters adopted different attitudes about the matter, and it is relatively difficult to make generalizations at the colony level. Further, the descriptions provided by contemporary observers were most probably based on small samples, often viewed from afar. Archaeological investigations help to fill many of the present gaps in our knowledge, but such research remains too limited to provide a useful comparative perspective, and its long-term prospects are limited by the varied patterns of occupation and the disturbance of slave village sites since emancipation.[232]

Where slaves were left to build their own houses, as on most plantations, the masters simply set aside a tract of land for the village site and permitted the slaves to locate and construct houses as they wished. In some cases the slaves set out their houses in compounds, or "yards," surrounded by fences in a conscious attempt to recreate African forms of spatial organization. The evidence of such tendencies is strongest for Jamaica.[233] A vivid impression of the cramped character of slave villages was provided by George Richardson Porter in 1830. This description occurs in conjunction with his observation that the manure of the slaves' livestock was rarely used or collected. He wrote:

It must be confessed that the crowded and irregular way in which the negro-houses are, from the wayward and capricious choice of those who inhabit them, frequently built, is an obstacle to removing this essential part of the fund of manure from them; but, in some estates, they are so disposed, that wheel-barrows, or light one-horse carts, which turn in small spaces, either have access, or a narrow lane may be made between each row of houses so as to give them access.[234]

But Porter's recommendation that slave houses should be laid out according to such geometric principles had already been taken by many planters, especially during the 1820s. Slave villages were being relocated at a distance from the great house or overseer's house and the houses made to conform to straight-line patterns.[235] By the end of the 1820s it was said that on estates in Dominica, for example, the works were placed some distance from the great house "and the negro-houses are in rows, on a line with them."[236]

Intervention in the architecture of the slave villages was more limited than this growing desire to organize space. In British Honduras, where the proportion of Africans in the slave population remained large, the shelters built by slaves at the mahogany banks were said to differ according to their tribes.[237] But such cultural differences were rarely remarked after 1807, and the housing of creole slaves became increasingly uniform. Toward the end of the eighteenth century some planters began providing slaves with materials for house building rather than merely permitting them access to woods, grasses, canes, and clay. At first these materials were given only to slaves of high occupational status, but after about 1820 such provision became more general. In addition, slave carpenters and masons were increasingly employed in the construction of houses, often following standardized plans chosen by the masters. This tendency toward master-controlled building often went together with the imposition of geometrical regularity on the settlement pattern. It was also associated with a change in the fabric of the houses. During the seventeenth and eighteenth centuries almost all slave houses were wattle-and-daub structures thatched with canes or grasses, but in the period commencing about 1790 an increasing number were built of wooden planks or stone and roofed with shingles.[238]

It must be emphasized, however, that wattle-and-daub remained predominant throughout the period. As late as 1832 a proslavery writer was content to say that in St. Lucia the slaves' "houses were well thatched, wattled, plaistered and whitewashed."[239] Stone houses were reported during the 1820s in Jamaica and St. Vincent but seem to have been most common in Barbados.[240] Even there they remained relatively rare. In 1805 Pinckard described the typical slave house in Barbados as "a roof of plantain leaves, with a few rough boards, nailed to the coarse pillars which support it."[241] At the end of the 1820s Bayley described something very similar at Colville Estate, Barbados. Most of the "negro huts," he said, "were built of wattling, lined on the inside with a plaster of clay, and roofed with a thatchwork of palm or cocoanut branches: some, however, were of wood, and others had shingled roofs."[242] This description appears to fit quite well the general pattern in most of the sugar colonies. Bayley's observation that the houses were universally divided into two apartments, one a sleeping room, the other a "hall" or "parlour," also finds support in most colonies.[243]

The masters' growing interest in creating a disciplined, gridlike spatial order within the slave village rarely extended to the building of barracks. Most slaves continued to live in free-standing structures, with maximum dimensions of 18 by 27 feet and generally much smaller. The establishment of barracks accommodations on West Indian plantations was chiefly a post-emancipation development, but it is interesting that the system seems to have been used most extensively in Demerara-Essequibo and Berbice, where it was soon to be generally applied to indentured Indian laborers. Around 1823 it was said that "on some estates" in Demerara

the Negroes build their own houses being allowed time and the assistance of trades-men to do so, and furnished with materials. Each man in that case builds his house according to his own fancy, they are constructed of wood and generally thatched. But as such buildings are very liable to fire, are seldom well built, and durable, the Negro houses are more generally erected by the proprietor of wood boarded or wattled and plastered and covered with shingles. They are generally constructed in ranges from 50 to 100 feet in length 20 to 24 feet wide and one story high: such a range contains about 5 families if from 5 to 6 persons each including children, they are partitioned into sitting rooms and seperate bed-rooms, which is generally left to the fancy of the individual, only taking care that each family has its due proportion of room.[244]

This description clearly shows that the erection of barracks, or "ranges," occurred independent of changes in fabric and provided much the same amount of space as in separate slave houses. But the slaves disliked such housing. In 1832 John Baillie told a select committee that he and others had attempted to build stone "barracks" in Jamaica, "and made them a far superior description of house to the ordinary negro house," but the slaves "refused to occupy them, stating, that they were so much exposed to their neighbours, they did not like to let them know what they were doing on all occasions." Challenged, Baillie defined a "barrack" as "a range of houses, or a row of houses, not detached."[245] As well as the loss of privacy, the barrack system meant that each slave household had a much more confined garden space. This is probably an important reason why the system could be introduced more rapidly in the rationed colony of Demerara than in Jamaica. But the planters of Demerara had an industrializing tendency, and the hydraulic system of the colony engendered a linear mental geometry.

A more extreme type of barracks accommodation was described by the slave Mary Prince, who spent ten years raking salt on Turk's Island in the Bahamas. There, she said, she slept "in a long shed, divided into narrow slips, like the stalls used for cattle."[246] No instances of barracks accommodation have been found in the old sugar colonies. But one Barbadian planter was said to have built separate houses for the families on his estate, and a house with cabins in it for the "idle" and "the desolate who are at a loss for lodging."[247] Pinckard reported an apparently unique settlement pattern on a Barbadian plantation around 1805, where

a circular piece of ground had been appropriated as the negro-yard, but instead of the slaves being left to construct their own habitations, sixteen very neat and uniform cabins have been erected of wood, and well roofed with shingles. Placed in eight divisions they form a hollow octagon, a free opening being left for the breeze at one end of each hut. In the centre of the octagon is built a common kitchen, which serves for all the sixteen families. The huts are neat, and the whole premises wear an air of order, and of cleanliness, not common to the abode of slaves.[248]

This model suggests a close link between the Barbadian planter's desire to establish discipline and "pupilage" in the slave population and his desire to control nutrition. But this was very much an extreme case. Most slave villages remained internally-ordered communities in which the planters rarely intervened.

Within each plantation village there were some significant individual differences in the size and fabric of the slaves' houses. The most often remarked was the relative opulence of the houses of drivers and skilled tradespeople. This advantage in housing was directly related to the differential provision of building materials by the masters, noted above, but more generally reflected the superior access of such slaves to cash, goods, and grounds. Some of them, of course, had the immediate advantage of skills in carpentry or masonry. Thus, William Taylor of Jamaica could obseve in 1832 that "the wealth of the negro was chiefly amongst the tradesmen; in going through a negro village I could always tell a tradesman's house from its external appearance." Such houses were divided into three or more apartments, rather than the usual two, and often had separate kitchens and hogsties.[249] The relative advantage of domestics is less certain, however, as many of them were accommodated in rooms attached to the great houses on estates.[250] Watchmen often had no house in the village and generally occupied isolated, small, or dilapidated huts. Occasionally these huts were built of stone, but others were portable.[251] Slaves without families sometimes lived in rooms of houses "belonging" to other slaves on large plantations. This practice was reported in Barbados, Berbice, and Jamaica. The planters of Barbados complained in 1812 that "from the custom of one Negro giving lodging to another great hardships must arise. The only means of paying for it is in labour and the time when that labour is given is after he has performed his master's daily labour and should be at rest." Thus, they believed that "no Negro at the time of puberty should be without a house."[252]

The furniture of slave houses varied considerably, though head people and tradesmen certainly had more than field slaves. The most common item was some form of bed. In Grenada the slave law of 1797 was unusual in specifying that every planter should provide "to at least every head of a family of slaves thereunto attached, one good and comfortable house, with one or more cabanes or beds to sleep upon, raised at least one foot from the ground."[253] Most of these beds were merely rough planks. Mary Prince reported that in Turk's Island she slept on a bare board set on stakes, and this was the most common experience of plantation slaves.[254] The only significant development was that in earlier periods these bed boards had been placed directly on the floor. Elite slaves sometimes had "bedsteads" made of timber nailed together. Paillasses stuffed with plantain leaves or corn husks were used by some slaves, while others used mats, and some had bedclothes and sheets. Elite slaves sometimes had "mosquito curtains," and in British Honduras every slave was said to be issued a "mosquito pavilion."[255] Other items such as tables, chairs, and benches were found in slave houses, but it is difficult to generalize about their distribution beyond the fact that they belonged principally to head people and tradesmen.

The character of slave housing varied with plantation size. On large plantations the elite lived in relatively substantial and roomy houses, while domestics and slaves belonging to very small rural holdings often occupied rooms in their masters' houses. But most slaves lived in wattle-and-daub houses which were, said Pinckard, "dark, close, and smoky," prone to catch fire, easily flattened by hurricanes, and poorly waterproofed.[256] Generally, three to six slaves occupied each house and had an average living space of between 30 and 60 square feet each. Pressure on space was greatest where the slave populations continued to grow after 1807, but the rapid deterioration of wattle-and-daub meant that slaves living in declining communities were not necessarily better off. The process of rebuilding went on in most colonies regardless of the growth or decline of the slave population, and this meant a general improvement in the fabric of slave housing, though it was constrained within a spatial framework increasingly regulated by the masters.

CLOTHING

In contrast to the growing intervention of the masters in slave housing and settlement patterns, the nineteenth century saw an increasing tendency to leave the slaves to fashion their own clothes. During the eighteenth century slave clothing had been supplied ready-made or sewn by the slave seamstresses on plantations. After 1807, however, many planters simply supplied cloth, needles, thread, thimbles, and scissors and left the slaves to make up the material.[257] But items such as jackets, hats, and caps were supplied ready-made throughout the period.

The slave laws of the British Caribbean mentioned clothing much more often than they did housing, but the provisions were generally too vague to give an indication of actual practice. The Barbados slave law of 1825, for example, required only that masters provide each year "decent clothing according to the custom of the island" or the equivalent in cash, and imposed a fine of 20s. on defaulters.[258] The Bahamas law of 1824 called for "two suits of proper and sufficient clothing" per annum; and the Trinidad ordinance of 1800, "two shifts of clothing complete." The Jamaican law of 1816 merely prescribed "proper and sufficient" clothing.[259] The Leeward Islands law of 1798 was more specific, requiring masters to distribute clothing on 1 January and 1 August each year; males were to receive a woolen jacket and a pair of Osnaburg trousers, and females a wrapper of woolen cloth and an Osnaburg petticoat, though the master could give a blanket, hat, or cap in lieu, with the consent of the slave.[260] Although the slave laws did little to regulate the quantity and quality of clothing worn by the slaves, owners were occasionally fined in cases of extreme neglect.[261]

Clothing allowances varied considerably from holding to holding. As in the case of food, it was said that small slaveowners were less liberal than large planters, but even the latter rarely provided more than the bare minimum, and many slaves used their own resources to obtain basic items.[262] The allowances given by the masters, then, are only a rough guide to what the slaves actually wore, and the examples that follow are intended to provide only a broad idea of practice.

In 1825 Joseph Peschier, a Trinidad sugar planter, claimed that he gave his slaves each year "two suits, consisting in the whole of one blue jacket of pennistone, two shirts of duck and osnaburgh, and one duck and one osnaburgh trowsers, with a hat; and every other year a blanket." Osnaburg, a coarse linen, was the most common cloth throughout the period, while pennistone was a coarse wool, and duck an untwilled linen or cotton fabric, lighter and finer than canvas. Robert Mitchell, another Trinidad sugar planter, stated that he gave his men "a woollen jacket and trowsers, one shirt of check and another of red baize, with a pair of sheeting trowsers and a hat; every second year they have a blanket"; the women got "a woollen petticoat and long wrapper, two shifts, a handkerchief and a hat; blankets the same as the men.''[263] At Plantation Berenstein, Berbice, in 1822 the men were issued a lined jacket, a hat, 1 yard of salempore (a blue cotton cloth), and 4 yards of Osnaburg; the women received a lined jacket, a hat, 4 ells of check, and 4 ells of Osnaburg; "working creoles" got a lined jacket, a hat, check, and Osnaburg; and "young creoles," check and Osnaburg cloth.[264] The accounts of Spring Garden Plantation, on the west bank of Essequibo, with a population of about 100 slaves, show that it purchased in 1825 some 292 yards of Osnaburg, 154 yards of check, 2 pieces of salempore, 58 lined jackets, 50 pairs of blue trousers, 38 wrappers, 6 flannel shirts, 54 handkerchiefs, 6 boys' jackets, 10 boys' hats, 1 gross of needles, 36 scissors, and 2 lb of Osnaburg thread. In the following year this plantation purchased 294 yards of Osnaburg, 2 pieces of check, 4 pieces of salempore, 8 tradesmen's best jackets, 7 boys' jackets, 8 pairs of tradesmen's trousers, 47 pairs of Negro blue trousers, 47 pairs of Negro Dutch trousers, 14 pairs of boys' trousers, 33 wrappers, 33 blue petticoats, 119 Negro hats, 8 tradesmen's hats, 12 boys' hats, 92 Kilmarnock caps, 8 check shirts, 8 watch coats, 48 blue romals (silk or cotton handkerchiefs), 4 lb of Osnaburg thread, 38 scissors, and 98 blankets. Similar purchases were made in 1827.[265] In 1832 James Simpson claimed that every ''able-bodied'' slave on his Jamaican estates received 2 suits of baize, Osnaburg, or check, a hat, a cap, handkerchiefs, and a blanket. The Wesleyan missionary John Barry believed the usual allowance in Jamaica comprised 2 Osnaburg suits (a loose frock and trousers), a common hat, a Kilmarnock cap, and a coarse rug coat known as a contoon for bad weather. In British Honduras mahogany cutters were said to receive 2 suits of Osnaburg, a shirt, and a blanket.[266]

These examples from a variety of situations and sources suggest a fairly common minimum of dress, men most often having a jacket, shirt, trousers, and hat or cap, and women a jacket, petticoat, and hat. Handkerchiefs were generally used by the women as head ties, while men wore Kilmarnock caps. Watchmen and stockkeepers sometimes had heavy cloaks, but most slaves used their blankets for warmth. Boiler men, mill feeders, and trash turners got extra cloth for aprons. Drivers and head tradesmen often received greater quantities of cloth than other slaves, and occasionally they got material of superior quality and additional items. Domestics, especially liveried footmen, also tended to have superior clothing. Children, however, tended to be issued very small amounts of clothing or nothing at all, and many went naked up to 14 and 15 years of age. Even children employed as domestics complained that they sometimes got no clothing and wore only ''a small piece of cloth for decency sake.'' Some planters, however, issued baby clothes and baby linen to privileged slaves. Occasionally special items of clothing were given as incentives to labor, but some planters withheld the basic allowance as punishment.[267]

The standard allowance of clothing was unlikely to survive the long hours worked by slaves in all weathers. It rotted rapidly. Thus, field slaves frequently wore only ''a mere rag round their loins'' while at work, keeping what clothing they had for other occasions. Woodcutters also worked naked.[268] Very often slaves wore their daily clothes to bed, even when wet. Those working under cover were better able to preserve their clothes throughout the year, and some of them had more to start with. More important for the health of the slaves is the fact that the planters made no allowance for footwear. A few privileged slaves were given an occasional pair of shoes, but slaves universally worked barefoot. In Jamaica it was said that some slaves, both men and women, purchased shoes, and occasionally stockings, with their own money. These were kept for special occasions, but Jamaican slaves also made sandals known as "champouters," or "shampattens," from bull's hide and wore these when walking long distances or cutting timber in the woods.[269] In general, however, rural slaves wore little to protect them from the environment and its disease vectors.

7.
Urban Regimes

THE MATERIAL CONDITIONS OF LIFE OF SLAVES LIVING IN TOWNS contrasted sharply with those of rural slaves in a number of important respects. Whereas planters recognized that "an estate may be called a small community," the towns represented much broader, fluid networks.[1] The functions served by the towns inevitably created an occupational structure quite different from that of rural holdings, and the labor of the slaves was extracted by different methods. These contrasts were closely related to patterns of slaveownership and had significant implications for the food supplies, housing, clothing, and other material things used by the slaves.

It has already been established in chapters 4 and 5 that towns accounted for roughly 10 percent of the total slave population of the British Caribbean in 1807, and 9 percent in 1834. With the exception of Georgetown, Demerara, all of the major towns shared this tendency toward decline, and many urban slaves found themselves moved to plantations and field labor during the period. Most urban slaves lived in large towns, two-thirds of them in settlements containing more than 2,000 slaves. Unlike plantation slaves, urban slaves were often outnumbered by whites and freedpeople and mingled daily in towns that lacked significant large-scale residential segregation. Urban slaveowners were very often women and freedpeople possessing fewer than five slaves, whereas almost all planters holding more than 200 slaves were white men and frequently absentee. Slaves belonging to large planters were only rarely sold or moved, but those living in towns were frequently transferred to new owners. Compared to plantation populations, the urban populations contained large proportions of female, African-born, and colored slaves.

These demographic contrasts between urban and rural slaves had significant implications for their material conditions of life. Unfortunately, the data available for the study of urban slavery are less complete than those for large-scale plantation slavery, so comparisons cannot always be made with precision. In part, this situation results from the small scale of urban slaveownership and the illiteracy of many of the owners. There are no urban equivalents of the plantation journals. Parliamentary inquiries, which provided much detailed information on plantation slavery, rarely showed any great interest in the urban populations. The colonial newspapers based in the towns, do contain a wealth of data on urban slavery, though much of it is indirect and thrown up by way of complaint. Thus, it is not always possible to provide matching accounts of every aspect of the material conditions of life in town and country. The account of urban conditions presented in this chapter looks at the same topics as covered in the previous chapter on rural regimes, but the purpose is to emphasize the most outstanding contrasts, and where conditions appear to have been the same in town and country, the discussion will be brief.

OCCUPATIONS

Most urban slaves worked as domestics. In 1834 they accounted for 71 percent of the total slave population of Roseau, 66 percent in Kingston, 60 percent in St. Johns, and 49 percent in St. George.[2] On most plantations, by contrast, only 10 percent of slaves worked in the great houses. In St. Lucia, for example, 49 percent of urban slaves were domestics in 1815, compared to only 12 percent of the rural slave population. In Bridgetown 50 percent of the slaves were domestics in 1817, compared to 10 percent of the rural population of Barbados (tables 6.2 and 7.1). Apart from domestics, the towns also contained many more sellers and transport workers than did the rural slave populations, and roughly twice as many skilled tradespeople, fishermen, and general laborers. The towns, however, contained relatively few field laborers, drivers, stockkeepers, watchmen, and nurses. Within Bridgetown, for example, the most numerous occupational groups were, in descending order, domestics, skilled tradespeople, transport workers, laborers, fishermen, and sellers (table 7.1). By contrast, the order in the rural parish of St. Andrew, Barbados, was field laborers, domestics, stockkeepers, skilled trades-people, drivers, watchmen, and nurses (table 6.2).

The presence of field laborers in the urban populations requires some comment. In the cases of St. Lucia and Trinidad, problems of interpreting French usage, discussed in chapter 6, no doubt result in the inclusion of general laborers in the field laborer category. Thus, most of the field laborers included in table 7.1 were probably manual laborers performing a variety of nonagricultural tasks. This argument is supported by the fact that there were only two sugar boilers registered in Port of Spain and none in Castries, and that males made up a much larger proportion of the "field laborers" in the towns than they did in the rural population (table S7.18). Some urban slaveowners, however, especially those living on the fringes of the towns, employed small numbers of slaves to cultivate small gardens. The absence of field laborers is the basis of the definition of the Bridgetown slave population in 1817, but rural St. Michael certainly contained a number of such peri-urban holdings, and this is reflected in its occupational structure (table S7.2). Semirural holdings were also common on the fringes of smaller towns. For example, Merton Cottage in the "environs" of Speight's Town comprised three acres when offered for sale in 1818. On its lands were planted coconut, fruit, fustic, and other trees; there was a plantain walk, an enclosed poultry yard, and a fish pond. It was promoted as a desirable residence for a large and genteel family,

Table 7.1. *Occupations of Urban Slaves: Barbados, St. Lucia, St. Vincent, Trinidad, 1813–17*

Occupation	Bridgetown, Barbados, 1817	St. Lucia, 1815	Kingstown, St. Vincent, 1817	Trinidad, 1813
Field laborers	0.1	8.4	0.0	18.4
Drivers	0.0	0.0	0.0	0.2
Skilled tradespeople	11.8	9.3	12.5	13.3
Domestics	50.3	49.2	41.4	44.4
Stockkeepers	0.3	0.4	0.0	0.3
Transport workers	4.6	5.3	8.3	2.4
Watchmen	0.0	0.3	0.0	0.0
Fishermen	0.7	1.2	0.6	1.0
Sellers	0.6	2.2	1.1	2.4
Laborers	2.1	3.0	11.4	1.1
Hired	0.4	0.5	0.0	0.0
Nurses	0.2	0.0	0.3	0.1
Sick or disabled	0.6	0.8	0.9	0.3
Absent	0.3	0.2	0.5	0.7
None	28.0	19.2	23.0	15.4
N	9,254	1,957	2,255	6,170

Sources: Calculated from tables S7.2–7.4 and S7.7.

having its own bathing-house and shower-bath, a double coach house with a five-stall stable and loft, and an extensive range of boarded and shingled slave houses and kitchen.[3] The slaves attached to Merton Cottage performed a variety of domestic and agricultural tasks.

The relative absence of drivers from the towns was a function of the absence of field laborers. Urban slaves were never organized into gangs, though some of the units involved in transportation came close, and they were not forced to labor under the driving system. The reasons for this contrast with the rural population will be discussed below.

The almost total absence of slave watchmen from the towns is more difficult to explain. Only five watchmen were listed in the registration returns for urban St. Lucia, and none at all for Bridgetown, Kingstown, or Port of Spain. Bayley commented on the absence of watchmen in West Indian towns at the end of the 1820s, but he believed that house breaking and robbery were rare, though slaves would steal to obtain food.[4] Theft and arson were certainly not unknown in the towns,[5] though depredations by livestock were limited. It should be recalled that most plantation watchmen were involved in guarding crops and livestock, and few cared for estate buildings. The presence of a large white and freedman population meant a more direct surveillance was possible than on plantations, but the larger towns offered a certain anonymity. Many runaway slaves came to the towns and pretended to be freedmen.[6]

In most British West Indian colonies the establishment of professional police forces was a post-emancipation development and followed the imperial model.[7] The police function of the militia was aimed at a high level of social control in order to prevent rebellion and disorder. It did not serve the functions that might be expected of a police force or of private watchmen. Slaveowners did sometimes call for the establishment of urban police forces, but their complaints were generally directed toward the threat of rebellion and the "riotous and disorderly conduct" of the slaves rather than theft.[8] In Georgetown a limited night watch was established in 1822 to prevent arson and "for the protection of the lives and property of the inhabitants of the town, as well as for the safety of the colony in general, at this momentous and alarming crisis," but it was carried out by free rather than slave watchmen.[9] In Port of Spain there was a police force made up of two corporals, twelve constables, and fifteen watchmen in 1833 but, when the fear of hydrophobia in that year led to the destruction of dogs at large in the streets, shopkeepers complained that small dogs were often their only protection against theft at night.[10] Even if theft was less common in town than in the country, and the valuables contained in stores and warehouses could be shuttered more effectively than crops or livestock, it is surprising that so few slaves were employed as watchmen. An explanation for their absence may be provided in part by the demographic characteristics of the towns, particularly the shortage of the aged males who made up most of the watchmen in the countryside. The small numbers of slaves held by most urban slaveowners may also have been important, since this meant that relatively few owners could afford to employ slaves as specialist watchmen. Some slaves may in fact have worked as watchmen at nights and at some other occupation during the day, but there is no definite proof of this. Thus, the absence of slave watchmen in the towns remains difficult to explain.

Stockkeepers were less common in the towns than in the countryside because the towns lacked the large numbers of livestock used to provide motive power on plantations. Most of the urban stockkeepers tended the riding horses and mules of their owners or looked after poultry (tables S7.2–7.7). The numerous cattle keepers of the plantations were almost entirely absent from the towns, though a few women worked as milkmaids. Grooms were by far the most common among the urban stockkeepers, working on the fringes of domestic service.

Nurses were relatively rare in the towns. An immediate explanation for this may be found in the smaller proportion of slaves registered as sick or disabled in the towns than in the countryside, but the ratio of nurses to sick and disabled was significantly lower in the towns, so the difference was a real one (tables 6.2 and 7.1). Urban females generally belonged to small slaveholdings, however, so few could be spared to serve as specialist nurses. And at the level of the individual small urban slaveholding the number of sick was unlikely to be more than one or two at any time, so that the ratio of nurses to sick would be very high. Thus, urban slaveowners were generally unwilling to release slaves from other, more obviously profitable, occupations to act as nurses. The effects of slaveholding size also explain why so few of the urban nurses were specialized. Midwives, for example, were much rarer than in the rural populations. There were no urban slave hospitals to match those on large plantations. But the small proportion of nurses was also related to the presence of large numbers of free women in the towns, some of whom worked as nurses and midwives and could be employed on a short-term basis when required.[11]

Field laborers, drivers, watchmen, stockkeepers, and nurses were remarkable for their rarity in the towns. Domestics, skilled tradespeople, transport workers, fishermen, laborers, and sellers were all more common in the urban than the rural slave population, however, and these occupations deserve separate treatment.

Domestics

The small scale of urban slaveholding meant that many slaves were employed on minimal domestic staffs and so had to perform a wide range of tasks, whereas the large staffs of plantation great houses were more often internally differentiated and specialized. But the towns contained slaveowners who employed domestics in commercial establishments such as taverns, hostelries, and stores as well as in their private households. These commercial establishments provided the basis for a certain degree of differentiation and specialization of domestic tasks within the towns. Thus, the proportion of domestics performing the most generalized tasks, those slaves described in the registration returns merely as "domestic" or "servant," was in fact very similar in both town and country. This proportion was generally quite consistent, amounting to 75 percent of the domestic slaves (tables S7.2–7.7).

Urban slaveowners employed a significantly larger proportion of their domestics as washerwomen, chambermaids, and housemaids than did the planters, and this contrast may be attributed to the demands of the commercial establishments. The chambermaids and housemaids were employed in taverns and hostelries, cleaning and tidying the bedrooms and public areas. Barbers and hairdressers were also relatively common in the towns, especially in Trinidad. But the greatest contrast between town and country related to washerwomen. In most colonies there were as many washerwomen in the towns as in the entire rural population. In Trinidad 19 percent of the urban domestics were washerwomen in 1813, compared to only 10 percent of the rural domestics. In St. Lucia in 1815 these proportions were 9 and 4 percent. The demand for their services was a function of the size of the free population, including the crews and passengers of passing ships, and it seems that some slaveowners employed their slaves in laundering on a commercial basis rather than merely requiring them to wash their masters' dirty linen.

The only specialized domestic occupation less common in town than in the country was that of "housekeeper." This title was applied to women, generally free colored or slaves of color, who supervised the households of slaveowners or overseers. It usually served as a euphemism for mistress, and occasionally housekeepers were in fact called "housewives" (table S7.2).[12] The housekeeper rarely performed manual labor and enjoyed considerable status within the household. She also tended to have a reputation for treating slaves harshly.[13] The reason for the relative absence of slave housekeepers in the towns may be explained by the availability of free colored and white women and by the relative lack of single white men who were in a position, as overseers, to choose slaves for this role. The urban white male was more likely to be the head of a family group and hence less likely to have a housekeeper, though he might have slave mistresses. Free women were generally preferred for the role, since they were removed from the slaves and hence more acceptable as public mistresses in a slave society. In 1805, for example, a Bridgetown newspaper carried an advertisement seeking "a middle-aged free woman, of good character, as a house-keeper, unincumbered with children . . . : a preference will be given to a white person." Another was even more definite: "Wanted, a white woman, as housekeeper to a single gentleman in St. Vincent: she will receive good wages, and have little to do."[14]

The ambiguity of the slave housekeeper's position is seen clearly in the petition of the mulatto Catherine Bardon to the Court of Policy of Demerara and Essequibo in 1815, requesting gratuitous manumission. Brought to the colony, she said, she

became the property of the late E. Butler Esqr., and was his housekeeper until he married, when she became also housekeeper of John Ryan Esqr. planter of Leguan, to whom she bore two children and continued with that gentleman untill he married Miss Eliza Daly the sister of J. Daly Esqr. That some time after, she became the house-keeper and property of a worthy gentleman a Mr. Bardon, boat builder on Leguan, with whom she resided in perfect concord upwards of 15 years, whom she also bore two children.

Her entire life had been "faithfully and invariably devoted to the domestick duties, the perils, the anxieties, and toils of bearing a numerous progeny to gentlemen of respectability and rank in this colony." On the death of Bardon she had been permitted to work out for herself, had purchased three slaves and a small house in the Cumingsburg district of Georgetown. There she had lived twelve years, supporting herself by "laborious and honest industry . . . and to the utmost of her power conducting herself with prudence, discretion and humility, on every occasion demonstrating the most reverential, sincere respect and regard for all the white ladies and gentlemen whom she had the honour to be acquainted with."[15] She was placed by the court in a class of certified conditional freedom. But since the free colored populations of the British Caribbean expanded very rapidly in the towns after 1807, while the slave and white populations declined, it seems probable that urban housekeepers were increasingly drawn from the free colored. Thus, slave housekeepers became rare in the towns but remained relatively numerous on plantations.

Prostitution was common in the towns but rare on plantations. It was illegal, so no slaves were listed in the registration returns as prostitutes. But the inns and taverns of the towns were very often brothels as well, and the slaves attached to them were used as prostitutes as well as domestics.[16] In 1804 a widow in St. John's, Antigua was fined for having let her house to "evil disposed slaves and free persons of colour as well men as women of evil fame and name and of dishonest conversation, and the said slaves and free persons of colour then and there to be and remain drinking tippling whoring and misbehaving themselves unlawfully."[17] Other slave prostitutes were forced to work independently, paying fixed sums to their owners.[18] But whether they worked in taverns, brothels, or on the streets, urban prostitutes had no rural counterpart. They catered chiefly to transient white males, particularly sailors and military.

Although domestics formed such an overwhelming proportion of the urban slave population, it is no more possible to provide a detailed account of their daily tasks in the towns than it is for the plantations. They emptied the chamber pots of their owners, sometimes going no farther than the street gutter to do so, disposed of their garbage in vacant lots or threw it into the streets or the sea, and cleaned and polished their houses and utensils.[19] They purchased food from the markets and stores, prepared it, and waited on their owners and guests at the table. They looked after the children of the household, cared for the owners' clothes and helped them dress, served as valets and lady's maids, ran errands, and carried messages. Postillions, messengers, and slaves working in the offices and counting houses of their masters generally belonged to merchants. Butlers, valets, and footmen worked in the houses of the most wealthy urban slaveowners. Some domestics had dual occupations, working both in the house and going about the streets as itinerant sellers. Most urban domestics performed tasks that occasionally required them to leave their owners' houses, and they were generally less confined than those employed in plantation great houses.

Skilled Tradespeople

In the towns, skilled tradespeople generally accounted for more than 10 percent of the total slave population, double the proportion found on rural holdings. Although sugar boilers and distillers were absent, the urban skilled practiced a wider range of trades than those on plantations. Detailed comparisons of the proportions employed in particular occupations in town and country are possible for Trinidad, St. Lucia, and Barbados (tables S7.2–7.4). Carpenters were the most numerous skilled tradespeople in both the urban and rural slave populations, and their proportions varied little. In Trinidad, for example, 28.7 percent of the rural and 28.2 percent of the urban skilled were carpenters. There was a greater relative disparity in Barbados and St. Lucia, but carpenters always constituted well over 20 percent of the urban skilled slaves. Masons were next in importance, accounting for 19.8 percent of the urban skilled in Trinidad and 15.4 percent in St. Lucia, but only 5.4 percent in Bridgetown. In Trinidad masons were more numerous in the towns than on rural holdings, but in Barbados and St. Lucia they were fewer in number. Coopers, however, were everywhere only about half as common in the towns as on plantations. They generally accounted for about 10 percent of the urban skilled. In Trinidad and St. Lucia, carpenters, masons, and coopers together were more than 50 percent of the urban skilled, but in Bridgetown they were only

40 percent. In Kingstown, St. Vincent, carpenters alone made up 39.7 percent of the skilled in 1817, coopers 22.7 percent, and masons 8.9 percent, or 71.3 percent together (table S7.7). It is difficult to explain these variations, since they seem not to relate to the relative size or length of settlement of the towns. Some of these occupations may have been filled by whites or freedpeople in Bridgetown, but it is not clear why freedpeople should have failed to play a similar role in Port of Spain.

Seamstresses and tailors also made up a significant proportion of the urban skilled. In Bridgetown seamstresses accounted for 14.0 percent and tailors 11.0 percent. In Trinidad, St. Lucia, and Kingstown seamstresses accounted for 9.7 to 12.6 percent of the urban skilled, and tailors for 2.2 to 3.4 percent. Although Bridgetown contained an unusually large proportion of seamstresses and tailors, there were always three to four times as many of these tradespeople in the towns as on rural holdings. Whereas the plantation seamstress or tailor produced clothing chiefly for the planter's immediate family, those working in the towns frequently produced goods for sale and served a large market of free people. Shoemakers catered to a similar market and were always at least twice as common in the towns as in the countryside. In Bridgetown they accounted for a high 12.6 percent of the skilled slaves, so that the town clearly supported a substantial concentration in the production of clothing and footwear, with 169 seamstresses, 124 tailors, and 140 shoemakers in 1817 (table S7.2). In urban Trinidad shoemakers accounted for only 3.7 percent of the skilled slaves, while in Kingstown there were none. The few slave tanners, dyers, weavers, and hatters were similarly concentrated in the towns, though the wig makers and embroiderers of St. Lucia all belonged to rural masters.

Bakers accounted for 7.1 percent of the skilled slaves in the towns of Trinidad and St. Lucia, but only 1.6 percent in Bridgetown and 0.7 percent in Kingstown. These proportions far exceeded the rural maximum of 0.6 percent found in St. Lucia. In Barbados specialist bakers, bread bakers, and pastry cooks were virtually unknown in the rural parishes. Once again, it is clear that the slave bakers of the towns were employed to produce for a commercial market and not merely for their owners' tables. Butchers played a similar role, preparing meat for a market that did not exist on any scale in the rural areas. In Georgetown, Demerara, there were occasional complaints that slaves should not be employed to compete with free butchers, but in 1823 the Clerk of the Market reported that slaves were never permitted to slaughter or hold stalls in the market without producing papers from their owners for that particular purpose, and added that "the slave stall holders sell the best meat, and are most punctual in the payment of the stall rents."[20] In Port of Spain butchers were made responsible for the conduct of their "apprentices or slaves" who were permitted to assist in cutting up and retailing meat.[21] No action was taken to prevent the employment of slaves as butchers.

Smiths also tended to be concentrated in the towns. Blacksmiths made up 4.4 percent of the skilled slaves in urban St. Lucia and 3.9 percent in Kingstown, two to three times the proportion found on plantations. But they accounted for only 1.3 percent of the skilled in Bridgetown, less than a third of the rural proportion. No slave farriers were registered in Bridgetown, so it may be that these occupations were filled by free people. Coppersmiths showed a much stronger urban concentration than blacksmiths, while gold- and silversmiths were found only in the towns. There were ten slave goldsmiths in Port of Spain in 1813 and three in Bridgetown and two in Kingstown in 1817. Two slaves worked as watchmakers in Barbados; one in Bridgetown, the other in rural St. Michael.

Goldsmiths, silversmiths, and watchmakers performed highly skilled tasks and handled valuable materials. Very often they belonged to free people who practiced the same crafts, so they worked under close surveillance. The existence of apprentices shows that the slaves did not work as mere menials, though it is probable that they were required to perform routine tasks more often than were their masters. A similar pattern applied to slaves employed by printers. The registration returns for Kingstown lists two "printer" slaves, and those for Bridgetown distinguished a "printer's pressman," a "pressman at the printer's office," and a "printing press and waiter" slave. The work performed by pressmen was skilled, but it did not require literacy and it involved a large component of manual, routine labor. Most of the slaves employed in Jamaican printing houses also seem to have worked largely as pressmen.[22] But there is evidence that some slave "printers" did more than pull the arm of the press. In 1819 William Collins of Antigua stated in his will that

It has long been my intention to establish a printing office of my own in this island and I have for that purpose long since caused three young negro men named Tom, Charles and Cato belonging to me to be properly taught to read, write and spell and have placed them in the Gazette office where they have for several years been working as compositors and are now good workmen, and have for that purpose also placed three negro boys named Robert, George and Elyas, also belonging to me, at school to be instructed in the same manner.

When Collins died in 1824 Tom, Charles, and Cato were each listed in the appraisement of his property as "printer, can read and write" and valued relatively highly. Thus they continued to work as compositors. But Robert, then 18 years of age, was sick, and neither he nor George nor Elyas had fully acquired these skills. Collins also owned a tailor and five females, but these slaves probably did little work in his printing house.[23] The important general point is that slaves registered as printers or watchmakers, for example, did in fact perform many of the most complex tasks required by their trades, though some spent much of their time engaged in the most physically demanding, routine, and dirty operations.

Slaves employed in the more precise branches of carpentry also tended to be located in the towns. Cabinet makers and joiners were quite numerous in the towns but rare in the countryside, and once again it appears that they must have worked on a commercial basis. Ship carpenters, shipwrights, sail makers, and caulkers were almost exclusively found in the towns. Most of these slaves were employed in repairing vessels that called at the major ports rather than in building boats. Thus, they were most numerous in Bridgetown, the first port of call for most shipping from Europe. The town contained fourteen slave shipwrights, three ship carpenters, seventeen sail makers, and fourteen caulkers in 1817, or 4.4 percent of the total skilled (table S7.2). Bricklayers, plumbers, painters, wheelwrights, cartwrights, saddlers, and harness makers were less numerous and less definitely concentrated in the towns. Cigar makers, who probably also produced snuff,[24] accounted for 5.3 percent of the skilled in urban Trinidad, and there was a lone umbrella maker in Port of Spain.

Skilled slaves practiced a wider range of trades in the towns than on the plantations, though the general preponderance of carpenters, masons, and coopers was common to both situations. The amount of physical effort required of tradespeople differed little between town and country, though some urban slaves certainly possessed more precise skills and received more instruction. But skilled slaves were more likely to work alongside or be owned by free craftsmen in the towns, and they generally worked in smaller units so that few were distinguished as "head" or "first" tradespeople.

Transport Workers

In most towns of the British Caribbean around 1820, roughly 5 percent of the slaves were employed in transportation. This proportion ranged from 2.4 percent in urban Trinidad to 8.3 percent in Kingstown. Although transport workers were a smaller proportion of the slave population than were domestics or skilled trades-people, the rural-urban contrast was much greater for this group. In most colonies transport workers were less than 1 percent of the rural slaves. The main contrast in the occupations of these slaves was that in the towns a much larger proportion worked as sailors, boatmen, or porters, while carters and wagoners were more common on rural holdings. In Bridgetown and Port of Spain, 60 percent of the transport workers were sailors or boatmen; and in Kingstown and urban St. Lucia, a high 97 percent. In rural areas, however, only 20 to 50 percent worked on shipping. Carters generally accounted for a majority of the transport workers on plantations, but in Kingstown, Bridgetown, and urban St. Lucia they were less than 2 percent. Only in Port of Spain did carters approach one-third of the transport workers, and this proportion was still less than half that in rural Trinidad. Porters were unknown on rural holdings, but they accounted for 1 percent of transport workers in urban St. Lucia, 2.1 percent in Kingstown, 7.5 percent in urban Trinidad, and a high 37.5 percent in Bridgetown (tables S7.2–7.7). Thus, it appears that slaves carried goods on their heads or backs much more often in Bridgetown than elsewhere.[25] But Barbados had a relatively small freedman population, and it may be that elsewhere freedmen rather than slaves made up a much larger proportion of the porters, since it was an occupation requiring little capital or skill. In Port of Spain, where the freedman population was most numerous, the Cabildo declared in 1822 that it was necessary to limit the number of free persons and slaves employed as porters and laborers and ordered that such workers were to be licensed and issued three-monthly brass tickets to be worn on a chain around the neck. Similar orders were applied to slave and free boatmen in Port of Spain in 1822 and proposed for Georgetown in 1826.[26]

Transport workers performed heavier physical labor than any other group of urban slaves. Although some of them could operate with a certain independence, like their rural counterparts, they generally constituted the largest urban slavehold-ings and thus came nearer to a system of gang work than any other urban slaves. For example, the largest holding in Kingstown in 1817 comprised 57 slaves, 35 of them employes as sailors, two as sailors and sail makers, one as sailor and fisherman, two as porters, and one as porter and sailor (table S7.7). These large holdings generally belonged to merchants. In 1820 a Kingstown merchant offered for sale premises on the bay comprising a house with store below, "well adapted for the dry good or American line," together with a longboat capable of carrying eighteen "heavy hogsheads" and its crew of ten slaves.[27] Similarly, a Kingston, Jamaica, merchant owned 51 slaves at his death in 1825, including seven "sailor negroes" employed on his schooner, seven "wharf negroes," thirteen coopers, twelve carpenters, two storemen, and ten house slaves.[28]

Slave sailors worked on vessels carrying passengers and goods between the capital towns of the eastern Caribbean and sometimes traveled as far as North America, but most of them probably sailed in the smaller droghers that linked the outlying plantations and smaller towns with the capital in each colony. When the movement of slaves was curtailed by the laws designed to prevent the intercolonial slave trade, a group of Grenada shipowners claimed that hired slave mariners formed "a chief part" of the crews of vessels trading between the islands and North America. Thus, they saw the Collector of Customs' refusal to clear vessels with slave sailors unaccompanied by their owners as a great disadvantage to trade.[29] From 1832 it was legal to navigate only with slaves who were the property of the vessel's master or of the owner of the vessel.[30] Boatmen and porters were also frequently employed under systems of hire, which will be discussed below, and this practice led to public regulation of their fares.[31]

Fishermen

The proportion of slaves employed as fishermen in the towns was generally more than five times that in the rural population, yet they rarely exceeded 1 percent of the total. The demand for fresh fish, consumed chiefly by free people in the sugar colonies, was always limited on the plantations, but the towns supported a large market. In Trinidad, where slaves were given rations of imported salt fish, only 26 rural slaves were registered as fishermen in 1813, compared to 64 in the towns. In St. Lucia there were more fishermen in the rural population than in the towns, but the urban proportion remained relatively large. Although the tasks performed by fishermen were essentially the same whether they operated out of towns or plantations, those owned by urban masters more often belonged to small slaveholdings but worked on a larger scale in more highly specialized units.[32] Most of the more than 100 fishing boats working out of Port of Spain in the 1820s traveled relatively long distances to exploit the grounds off the mainland.[33] Urban fishermen were more likely to work alongside their owners.

Laborers

Although laborers were a substantial minority in most towns, their tasks were largely undefined. Only in the case of Trinidad does the category include a number of specific occupations, most of them involving the processing of agricultural products, bordering on the skilled trades. Slaves were employed in Port of Spain as cotton ginners, mattress makers, syrup makers, and bark dryers. The largest groups, however, were the lime burners and quarriers who supplied raw materials to the building industry. In Kingstown, where the category was significant, two slaves were employed in gathering and charring wood, but another 252 slaves were undifferentiated "laborers."

Sellers

The role of slaves in distribution, whether through public or informal markets, was one of the most striking features of West Indian town life. Urban slaves themselves produced relatively little that could be retailed, and it was plantation slaves who supplied the markets of the towns with food and other wares. Very often plantation slaves did their own selling in the urban markets, but town slaves sometimes served as intermediate purchasers and controlled the final retailing of the produce of provision ground and garden. More importantly, slaves were specifically employed in the sale of goods for the benefit of their masters. Thus, they competed directly with white and freedman storekeepers and hucksters as well as with plantation slaves in the markets and streets of the towns.

Sellers accounted for less than 3 percent of the urban slave populations, the proportion ranging from 0.6 percent in Bridgetown to 2.4 percent in urban Trinidad, but these proportions were always several times those found in the rural population (tables 6.2 and 7.1). Other slaves marketed goods as one of a broader range of tasks. The majority of the sellers listed in the registration returns were not distinguished as specialists, most being described simply as hucksters, sellers, or retailers. The only specialists noted were itinerant retailers of dry goods, and these slaves often left the towns to sell on the plantations. Slave shopkeepers or shopmen were also distinguished occasionally, because they worked in the stores of their owners rather than on the streets or in the public markets.

Wherever they plied their wares and whatever they marketed, the urban sellers generally enjoyed a relatively independent existence and were always responsible for dealings in cash or kind. They worked under a variety of systems. Some sellers were given a range of goods to sell and were expected to deliver their daily takings to their owners. Others were employed under the system of self-hire and were expected only to make fixed periodic payments to their owners, so that they were responsible for choosing and purchasing the goods they were to sell, and they retailed them by whatever mode they preferred. In either case, the seller was involved in a series of commercial transactions which could not be directly controlled by the owner and which provided experience of a way of life separate from the slave condition. In the urban context, this was as important as the provision ground system, which had created a rural proto-peasantry.[34] It was one of the touchstones of the contradictions inherent in slave society.

In the simplest version of the urban marketing system, slaves were sent out with wooden trays of goods on their heads to call at the doors of householders. Describing the system in Bridgetown at the end of the 1820s, Bayley observed that

From these people, eatables, wearables, jewellery, and dry goods, of all sorts, may be purchased; but those things for which they find the most ready sale, are pickles and preserves, with fruit, sweetmeats, oil, noyau, annisette, eau-de-cologne, toys, ribbons, handkerchiefs, and other little nick-knacks, exported from Martinique.[35]

In Dominica the hucksters' trays and baskets were filled with crockery, glassware, fruit, pickles, and sweetmeats, while jellies, pickles, and preserves were popular in Grenada.[36]

In Port of Spain the Cabildo ordered in 1816 that all hucksters were to take out licenses at the rate of 10s. per month, and these licenses were to be pasted to the bottom of the tray, giving the seller's name or, if a slave, the owner's. In 1818 it moved to enforce these regulations, specifying that licenses were required for the sale of all "dry goods, tin and iron ware, porcelain and earthen ware, confectionary and toys," but not for "milk, syrup, mawbey, spruce, candles, ground provisions, and fresh fruit; and when sold in the country, salt meat and salt fish."[37] This distinction was clearly an attempt to confine hucksters to the sale of locally produced goods or rural markets, leaving the control of imported items in the hands of free merchants and shopkeepers. In St. George, Grenada, slaves selling bread about the town were required to be licensed.[38] Similar attempts to limit the hawking of goods in Bridgetown by slaves and, more particularly, freedpeople were made during the period, but were widely ignored and some of the legislation was in fact repealed.[39] Shortly before the law of 1819 was passed in Barbados, the assembly received a petition from 100 inhabitants of Bridgetown, most of them white shopkeepers, seeking relief from the "pernicious" system of hawking goods about town and country. Their chief competitors were slave and free colored hucksters, as well as white servants sent out by gentlemen to peddle linen and haberdashery. Swarms of colored people infested the streets and roads of the island, complained the shopkeepers, dealing in stolen goods as well as honest trade and defrauding the revenue.[40] But during the early nineteenth century the legislature of most colonies were content to live with the system and merely attempted to control it and collect the license fees.

In Demerara-Essequibo the Fiscal argued in 1822 for the prohibition of itinerant hucksters from Georgetown and the colony generally, in order to stop the trading of goods stolen from plantations and to prevent the sale of coffee, sugar, and molasses in small quantities other than by license.[41] But the Court of Policy rejected this proposal and maintained only its prohibition of the employment of slaves or freedpeople to go into the country as hucksters or huckstering on plantations. Hucksters could accept payments only in money, livestock, or provisions, and never in coffee, cotton, sugar, cane, or plantains.[42] The latter prohibition was of long standing, and as early as 1808 slaves were allowed to sell plantains in Georgetown only on account of their owners and were required to carry passes specifically for this purpose.[43] But Georgetown was unusual in the growth of its slave population in the period after 1807, and this growth went together with the expansion of its commerical functions and of the merchant-storekeeper class. By the 1820s the owners of hucksters were complaining of competition from both retail stores and unlicensed peddlers. In 1824, for example, a group of free colored women petitioned the Court of Policy requesting a decrease in the tax on hucksters, since they could no longer make a living by sending their slaves out to sell. Formerly, they said, they had lived in comfort by purchasing packages of goods from merchants and transient traders and retailing them in town and country by sending out their own or hired slaves, properly licensed. In those palmy days there were barely 20 stores in Georgetown, none selling goods in quantities of less than a package. Now, in 1824, there were a host of stores making sales of less than a guilder, as well as innumerable slave, free colored, and white hucksters, most of them not paying taxes. Thus, the free colored women asked for a reduction in the license fees, observing that "the women usually employed as huckster's, acquire a habit of life, which renders them after wholly unfit either for the field, or domestic purposes, so that even there value is considerably diminished." The court refused their request.[44]

The second major method of organizing the work of slave hucksters was to permit them to set up semipermanent stalls so that they did not have to operate as peripatetics. As among the itinerants, slave sellers mingled with freedpeople and occasional whites, the customer often being unable to distinguish between the stalls of slave and free. Some slave hucksters set up their stalls outside the doors of their owners' houses, but most established themselves in the busiest streets or on bridges or wharves. In Georgetown hucksters' huts crowded the stellings during the 1820s, creating a fire hazard. This strategic location enabled the hucksters to buy up provisions in bulk from boats arriving from the plantations.[45] In Bridgetown there were periodic attempts to remove the stalls of unlicensed hucksters. On one Monday in 1833, reported *The Barbadian*, the Commissioners of Roads put the law in force

against the negroes who have so long made the town, particularly the Roebuck and Milk Market streets, a public market, to the great annoyance of passengers. The insolence of these people in completely filling the streets with their articles, is inconceivable to any but those who live in a slave country. . . . The Commissioners seized an immense collection of articles: several cart loads of all kinds of provisions, and dry goods, sent out for sale by persons who had not complied with the law in taking out licenses, were taken to Gaol, and legally condemned and sold.[46]

This account suggests that most of the street stalls in Bridgetown were operated by slaves rather than freedpeople. It is also clear that attempts to control the spread of semipermanent street markets were never a complete success.

The third method of selling was through pubic markets. New market buildings were constructed in Bridgetown in 1810, Georgetown (Stabroek) in 1811, and Port of Spain in 1817. These public markets were designed to keep hucksters off the streets, bridges, and wharves of the towns and to regulate their prices and practices. They were meant to contain the rural slaves who came to town on Sundays or, later, Saturdays to sell provisions and livestock from their grounds and gardens, as well as the town hucksters who often operated elsewhere on other days. In Bridgetown plantation slaves were sometimes abused, even on Sundays when laws generally regarded as no longer having any utility were strictly enforced. In 1808, for example, the Clerk of the Market reported that "the country Negroes who brought produce to the market on Sunday last, were not only shamefully plundered, but barbarously misused, by persons who either were, or pretended to be constables." The following Sunday few plantation slaves ventured to the market, and the town hucksters went into the fringes of the country, bought up the slaves, poultry, corn, and vegetables, and sold these items at an advanced price.[47] Since the free population of the town depended so heavily on the plantation slaves' provisions, in Bridgetown as elsewhere, they had little to gain by this practice. Thus, the public markets were supported as a means of preventing such occurrences. The market opened in Cheapside in November 1810 was said to be the first regularly established market in Bridgetown, though the ground allotted was insufficient "when we consider the vast influx of Negroes who resort to the market from the country on Sundays and other holidays."[48] But the market building itself was thought adequate for the venders of butchers' meat, poultry, and fish, and its nearness to the sea was seen as facilitating its being kept clean. Slaves selling sugar cane in the market were required to produce certificates from their owners. Intoxicated slaves were placed in the stocks until the market gates were about to be shut.[49]

The new market built in Georgetown in 1811 was intended to encourage the supply of provisions in the rapidly growing town and to prevent the current crowding by hucksters of the public streets and bridges. It was built on the site of the existing market, but included a shed specifically designed for the use of "all slaves habitually employed by their proprietors to expose goods for sale in the market" who were required to pay a monthly stall fee. On Sundays a free market was held "for the Negroes of estates coming to town with articles for sale." Weights and measures were regulated by commissioners, and the clerk of the market inspected all meat, fish, poultry, and provisions to prevent the sale of bad goods. Stocks were set up to confine slaves involved in disturbances, though whites and freedpeople were merely to be fined on conviction.[50] But the complaints of the 1820s make it clear that the public market of Georgetown failed to contain the town's hucksters, and they continued to spill out into the streets.

Port of Spain's new market house, built in 1817, had arches and pillars of freestone and a slate roof. As in Bridgetown and Georgetown it was intended particularly to control the sale of meat and fish. All butchers were licensed, and meat condemned as unfit for sale was given to the (free) poor of the town.[51] The fish house was let to a contractor who collected fees from fishmongers selling in the market as well as the tax on all fresh fish sold by hucksters either in the streets or the market. When Mrs. Carmichael saw the Port of Spain market around 1825, she described the butchers' market as "neat and commodious" and said "the market for fish excels in convenience, beauty, and regularity, anything of the sort I ever saw." Dr. McTear visited the market in the same year and reported that it was attended by several thousand people, most of them slaves or freedpeople as well as a few Chinese and Amerindians.[52] The slaves supplied most of the poultry, pigs, goats, sheep, and provisions offered for sale, but the cattle, which accounted for three-quarters of the weight of meat slaughtered for market, came from the planters. Prices were regulated quite rigidly.[53] In the marketing of fish, however, there was a prolonged struggle between the fish-house contractor and the town's fishermen and hucksters. The fishmongers found the contractor's fees excessive and argued that they should be allowed to huckster in the streets for the benefit of the poor "who subsisted principally upon fish" and could not send out slaves to purchase in the public market. Itinerant huckstering of fish was permitted at times, but in 1832, when it was temporarily prohibited, Awa, the Chinese fish-house contractor, complained to the Cabildo "of being defrauded of his dues by huckster women who continue to hawk fish about the town in spite of the orders of the Board to the contrary." When a member of the Cabildo visited the fish-house, he "found it in a most filthy state, and the conduct of the fish women most riotous."[54] As in Bridgetown and Georgetown, the public stocks used for the judicial punishment of slaves were set up in the market.[55] In spite of this exemplary symbol, the attempt to contain slave sellers within the public markets was nowhere a success.

The partial abolition of Sunday markets after 1825 gave urban slave hucksters an advantage in their competition with plantation slaves in the town markets. They were most successful in this competition where plantation slaves depended heavily on rationed allowances for their food supplies and had little free time other than Sundays in any season. In Barbados, for example, "a slave-owner" complained in 1828 that even when slaves were allowed to sell "their trifling commodities" on Saturdays, they were occasionally attacked by the constables. By 1831 the Sunday market was reviving in Bridgetown, though it was claimed that most large plantations gave Saturdays, and "we see many negroes in town during the week, and on Saturday a vast number, making the whole town a market." The rural slaves, it was said, were encouraged to come to town on Sundays by the town hucksters.[56] In Grenada, where the provision ground system dominated, the hucksters of St. George made a practice of buying up goods brought to the town and selling at inflated prices, particularly after about 1828. As in Barbados, there were frequent violations of the act abolishing the Sunday market during the 1830s. Slaves and freedpeople continued to hawk goods in the streets of St. George on Sundays, and shopkeepers, in response, often opened.[57]

Slaves were employed in four types of marketing in the towns: as hawkers, street-stall sellers, hucksters in the public markets, and in the stores of their owners. Most of the slaves employed in stores were probably menials and laborers, but the other three styles of marketing all involved the slaves in commercial transactions and made them directly responsible for the handling of money and bargaining with customers. It is impossible to say precisely how many of the sellers were engaged in each of these types of marketing, and very often the method adopted changed through the week. In particular, slaves who sold in the public markets on Saturdays or Sundays frequently worked as itinerant hucksters on other days of the week or had semipermanent stalls in the streets. The growing importance of regulated public markets after 1807 probably created some change in the pattern, but it is certain that they failed to contain or control all of the towns' sellers, who continued to spill into the highways and byways.

WORK ORGANIZATION

The system of negative and positive incentives employed to extract labor from urban slaves differed in many fundamental respects from that used on plantations. The most obvious of these differences was the almost universal absence of slave drivers and gang labor in the towns. Whereas the slaveowners' authority was generally enforced through slave intermediaries on large plantations, the small size of urban holdings meant that physical coercion was applied directly by masters and mistresses. This system was reinforced by the fact that urban masters were rarely absentees. The small scale of urban slaveownership in the towns also explains the rarity of the gang system. Thus, urban slaves were much more likely to work on an individual basis under the immediate supervision of their owners than were rural slaves. At the same time, urban slaves were more often employed under the system of self-hire than were rural slaves. This removed them from immediate supervision to a large extent and provided opportunities for a wide range of independent economic behavior. But, although self-hire was common after 1807, it was generally confined to certain occupations and rarely practiced by domestics, so it is fair to conclude that the great majority of urban slaves did work under the direct supervision of their owners.

By the early nineteenth century, there was a very clear distinction between the work performed by free people and by slaves on plantations. In the towns, however, slaves continued to perform many of the same tasks as whites and freedpeople, and this overlap was as important in determining the nature of work organization as the demographic facts of resident proprietorship and small slave-holding size. Few whites worked as domestics or porters in the town, but many freedpeople were employed in these occupations, and the skilled trades, huckstering, and fishing were practiced by all classes. In many cases the slaves employed as skilled tradespeople, fishermen, or sailors worked alongside their owners. While the owners reserved the most skilled tasks for themselves, and slaves were expected to perform the most menial, the strictly supervisory role of most owners and white employees on large plantations was not repeated in the towns.

Although urban slaves did not work under constant threat of the lash in the same way as plantation field laborers, physical coercion remained basic to the system of work organization. Town slaves were flogged and otherwise abused by their owners and, equally important, the towns contained visible symbols of public terror in the shape of workhouses, jails, cages, stocks, and treadmills which, apart from the stocks, had no exact equivalents on plantations.[58] In some cases it seems that urban slaves were more likely to suffer physical abuse than rural slaves. In 1816, for example, George Arthur, superintendent of British Honduras, reported that

So great is the kindness, the liberality, the indulgent care of the wood-cutters towards their negroes, that slavery would scarcely be known to exist in this country, was it not for a few unprincipled adventurers in the town of Belize who exercise authority over their one or two slaves, in a manner very different from the great body of the community.[59]

Arthur repeated this argument in 1820 and observed that "the extreme inhumanity of many of the lower class of settlers residing in the town of Belize towards their slaves" was a growing evil, while the recent rebellion had resulted in an "increasing severity and cruelty." In support of this claim he reported a number of cases of ill treatment. One Belize slaveowner, a free colored woman, handcuffed her slave Kitty, chained her by the legs to the foot of a bed with a double padlock in the loft of her house, and whipped her about the body and face. Another case involved a Belize magistrate, Dr. Manfield Bowen, whose slaves were chained to the foot of the stairs and to a post in the store under the apothecary's shop on his premises, and flogged in the yard.[60] It may be that the supposed good treatment of slaves at the mahogany banks of British Honduras exaggerated the contrast between town and country, but these cases do clearly show that urban slaves were subject to physical punishment at the hands, and in the houses, of their owners.

Public jails and stocks existed in most towns of the British Caribbean before 1807, but treadmills were introduced only during the 1820s. These were used to inflict physical punishment on slaves from the plantations as well as the towns, but their presence in the towns was a constant warning to those of the urban population. The common jails and stocks were used for free people as well as slaves, but the treadmills and chain gangs were confined almost entirely to slaves. The Demerara-Essequibo Court of Policy went so far as to state that "if it should unfortunately happen that any white person be condemned to be confined in the workhouse, a separate building on the premises thereof, shall be appropriated for that purpose."[61] Workhouse slaves were employed in heavy labor on the roads and other public works, so the chain gang was a highly visible portent in the streets. The chain gang was the only true form of gang labor in the towns, and the slaves worked under a driver who was a slave but not himself a convict. They wore light collars and chains, and, in St. Kitts, they were issued jackets and trousers on which a large letter C was painted. They were confined in stocks between sunset and sunrise.[62] Whereas the chain gangs were composed largely of slaves who had been sentenced to death but pardoned, the treadmill was applied much more generally. The first treadmill in the West Indies was erected in Port of Spain in 1823, soon after this innovation of the Industrial Revolution was introduced in Britain, and it was widely adopted during the 1820s.[63] Bridgetown did not erect one until 1830. It operated from 7 A.M. to 4 P.M. daily, excepting Sundays, Christmas Day, and Good Friday, the maximum spell being 10 minutes separated by 30 minutes. All slaveowners were able to substitute punishment on the treadmill for corporal punishment, so long as they first complained to a Justice of the Peace.[64] Since the treadmills were designed for short-term punishment, it is likely that they were more frequently used by urban slaveowners than planters, who preferred to impose their will directly through their own drivers. In any case, the presence of the public workhouse, jail, stocks, and treadmill in the town constituted a powerful symbolic incentive to labor, over and above the intimate corporal punishment administered by the slaveowners themselves. They played an important role in a system that contained significant elements of independent action for many slaves.

Self-hire was the most extreme form of independent economic behavior available to urban slaves. Under this system slaves were "permitted to engage themselves, and to pay their owners a weekly or monthly sum, appropriating their extra gains themselves."[65] It was a means by which the slaveowners' capitalization of slave labor could be molded to fit the fluctuating and dispersed demand for that labor in the urban economy. Along with the role of slave hucksters in commercial transactions, self-hire constituted a fundamental contradiction in the slave system. It admitted that economic efficiency required freedom in the market for labor and made the slave a free agent rather than a piece of property. It removed the slave from the direct authority and supervision of the master.

It was recognition of the contradictions involved in self-hire that led the colonial legislatures to attempt to prohibit the practice. In Tobago, for example, the slave law of 1794 stated that "no person whatsoever shall permit or give leave to any slave or slaves of their own or under their care, to hire out themselves."[66] A fine of £10 was imposed on errant masters. The attempts of the magistrates of British Honduras to prohibit self-hire, because it made the slave "subject to no authority but what results from his own will, which naturally tends to create insubordination," have been fully discussed in the previous chapter. The Consolidated Slave Law of Barbados, passed in 1825, imposed a fine of £5 on masters permitting their slaves "to go at large for the purpose of . . . paying hire for himself, herself, or themselves, or to follow any trade, business, or occupation for the benefit and advantage" of themselves or their owners. But such absolute prohibitions never worked, as the continuing need to legislate against the practice makes clear, and most slaveowners were content to attempt to control it. Thus, the Barbados law of 1825 went on to state that the prohibition of self-hire was not intended to apply to slaves "regularly settled in any house, shop, or place, in carrying on any kind of trade or business for the benefit of" their owners, so long as they were given half-yearly licenses for the purpose. Further, slaves were not to be employed by others without their owners' consent.[67] The purpose of these limitations was to prevent slaves from mingling too easily with freedpeople, and so passing themselves off as free, and to control the slave's ability to move as a free agent within the labor market. The 1795 slave law of Jamaica argued that the system under which slaves were "suffered and permitted by their owners and employees to work and employ themselves in what manner and wheresoever they shall think fit, provided they pay their owners a certain sum of money daily, weekly, monthly or yearly" led slaves to engage in theft and other evils, and so the law imposed a fine of £20 on owners allowing their slaves to work out without licenses.[68] An act passed in the Bahamas in 1808 went further, stating that it was no longer lawful for the owner of slaves on New Providence

to suffer or permit such slave or slaves to hire themselves out to work, either on board of vessels or on the shore, as porters or labourers, without first registering the names of such slaves in the police office, and obtaining therefrom a copper badge, with the number of such slave marked thereon; which badge is to be worn on the jacket or frock of the slave, in a conspicuous manner.[69]

A similar system of badges, tickets, and licenses was used in Georgetown.[70] Thus, most slaveowners seem to have been willing to acknowledge the advantages of flexibility in the labor market resulting from self-hire, and wished merely to make such slaves visible and hence subject to public control.

Attempts to limit self-hire were applied to rural as well as urban slaves but, with the exception of British Honduras, the occupations mentioned specifically in the slave laws were chiefly urban. The system was certainly much more widespread in the towns than in rural areas. Large plantations had self-contained labor forces and were able to find profitable employment for slaves with specific skills at most times by forcing them to perform dual occupations. Slaves were hired from plantation to plantation for short or long terms, but such hiring was generally contracted by the owners themselves, and the slave was not involved in seeking jobs, bargaining for payment, or handling money. Few rural slaves were permitted to rove the countryside on a self-hire basis. In the towns, however, the cost of finding jobs for slaves was often high. It was probably highest for porters, where an individual might perform several small tasks each day for different employers and where it was necessary to be on hand at the harborside or the merchant's door in order to contract work. Skilled tradespeople also tended to perform relatively large numbers of small jobs in the towns. In the case of hucksters, self-hire offered the advantage of simplifying accounting procedures and meant that the owner could be less concerned about the possibility that the slave was withholding the true returns on sales. In marketing, where competition was often fierce, the slaveowner ensured a regular and certain income. For the slave, however, self-hire meant pressure to compete for jobs or sales in what became an increasingly tight market after 1807. Although the numbers of urban slaves generally declined in the period, they faced a rapidly growing freedman population, and the frequent claims that working-out slaves engaged in theft to meet their periodic payments suggest that the system was profitable to the masters but of little benefit to the slaves.

The extent of self-hire in the towns is difficult to determine. The registration returns listed few cases, but it is certain that many slaves who were attributed specific occupations in the returns in fact worked under the system (tables S7.2–7.7). As many as one-third of the male slaves in Havana, Cuba, worked on their own account and lived separately from their masters, and in the United States perhaps more than 20 percent of the adult slave labor force of the towns worked under self-hire systems in the early nineteenth century.[71] But there seems to be no reliable comparative data for the British Caribbean. It is also difficult to establish precisely the occupations involved. Sellers, sailors, porters, tradespeople, and washerwomen were the most affected, while domestics, the vast majority of urban slaves, were rarely involved because of the constant labor they were required to perform.

There is little evidence available to permit an analysis of the internal workings of the self-hire system. The amounts slaves were required to pay to their owners are uncertain, except that Bayley reported they varied between £4 and £8 per month in the eastern Caribbean at the end of the 1820s.[72] This amounted to 25–50s. in Barbados. Barbadian slaveowners paid about 3s. per day and provided rations and accommodations when hiring skilled tradespeople from other owners, but they may have reduced these rates under self-hire.[73] Thus, the skilled working-out slave needed at least eight to seventeen days' work to cover the master's demands, while porters and laborers probably needed longer. It is not certain whether employers gave working-out slaves rations or accommodations, however, so self-hire may have left few days available for the slave to earn a surplus. Town merchants sometimes complained that self-hire permitted porters, laborers, and fishermen to earn an "easy subsistence" in the towns, making enough in a few hours to support themselves for several days, and so encouraged habits of idleness, drunkenness, and loitering. The competition for jobs meant that such behavior was probably rare, but it is equally difficult to show how hard-pressed the slaves might have been under self-hire. Just as rural slaves preferred the provision ground system to rationed allowances, so the urban slave preferred self-hire, because it meant an opportunity to work beyond the master's direct supervision and lash and to make independent decisions about how to use time and resources. But its effect on actual hours worked and the creation of a surplus remains unclear.

Hours of work varied widely in the towns. Domestics, the great majority of urban slaves, worked long and indeterminate hours and were at the beck and call of their masters and mistresses every day of the week. Most other urban slaves normally did not work for their masters on Sundays, though hucksters had to attend the public markets and sailors tended to work erratic regimes. There is no doubt that apart from the domestics, urban slaves worked shorter hours than plantation slaves. In Bridgetown the stores closed between 4 and 5 P.M. In Jamaican towns work generally ceased at 6 P.M. or earlier if the slaves took no noon break, "which is a very common thing."[74] There was no equivalent of the night work required on sugar estates. In St. Kitts, the law stated that slaves were not allowed to walk the streets of the towns between 10 P.M. and 5 A.M. without a ticket or a lighted candle in a lantern from their owners.[75] No doubt the law was not followed, and slaveowners and travelers frequently complained that their repose was disturbed by slaves "who sit up during the greater part of the moonlight nights," but this nocturnal activity was not a matter of work under the owners' supervision.[76] In addition to the absence of night work, urban slaves followed no seasonal regime like that experienced by plantation slaves. The sugar harvest did create a seasonal peak in activity at the wharves, but much of this activity was dispersed, and it had only a minor impact on the majority of urban slaves.

Patterns of work organization in the towns, then, contained extremes that inhibit general comparisons with rural regimes. The tasks of most urban slaves involved less physical exertion than that required of plantation slaves. The hours worked by urban slaves may have been longer overall, because of the large proportion employed as domestics, but those performing the heaviest manual labor in the towns generally worked the shortest hours, whereas heavy labor and long hours often went together on plantations. The large proportion of domestics in the towns and the small scale of slaveholding meant that most slaves worked under the immediate supervision of their mistresses or masters, but others worked on a relatively independent basis. The small scale of urban slaveholdings also meant a limited internal hierarchy of statuses, and this reduced the possibilities for receiving differential positive incentives. In any case, the opportunities for independent economic activity were limited for the majority of urban slaves, most of whom worked long hours as domestics under constant surveillance and lacked even the potential of creating a surplus from provision grounds.

OCCUPATIONAL ALLOCATION

Female slaves worked in a narrower range of occupations than males in both town and country. But whereas this meant large-scale allocation to field labor on plantations, in the towns it meant concentration in domestic work. The occupations of urban females were somewhat more diverse than those of rural females, however, so that only slightly more than 60 percent of adult females were employed as domestics in most towns. Fewer than 20 percent of adult males were domestics in the towns. In Trinidad, for example, only 16. 5 percent of urban males aged 30–39 years worked as domestics in 1813, compared to 2.0 percent of rural males, while 72.2 percent of urban females in this age group were domestics, compared to 13.4 percent of rural females (table S7.18). Thus, a relatively larger proportion of males than females worked as domestics in the towns as against the plantations, even though they were always a minority. Females accounted for all of the seamstresses and washers and most of the hucksters, while males had a monopoly of the skilled trades, fishing, and transport work. Thus, males and females were equally likely to work out and live separately from their owners.

In urban Trinidad and St. Lucia, large numbers of young children were employed as domestics, the proportion reaching a peak in the 10–14 age group for both females and males (figs. 7.1–7.3). There was also a minor peak in the sixties.

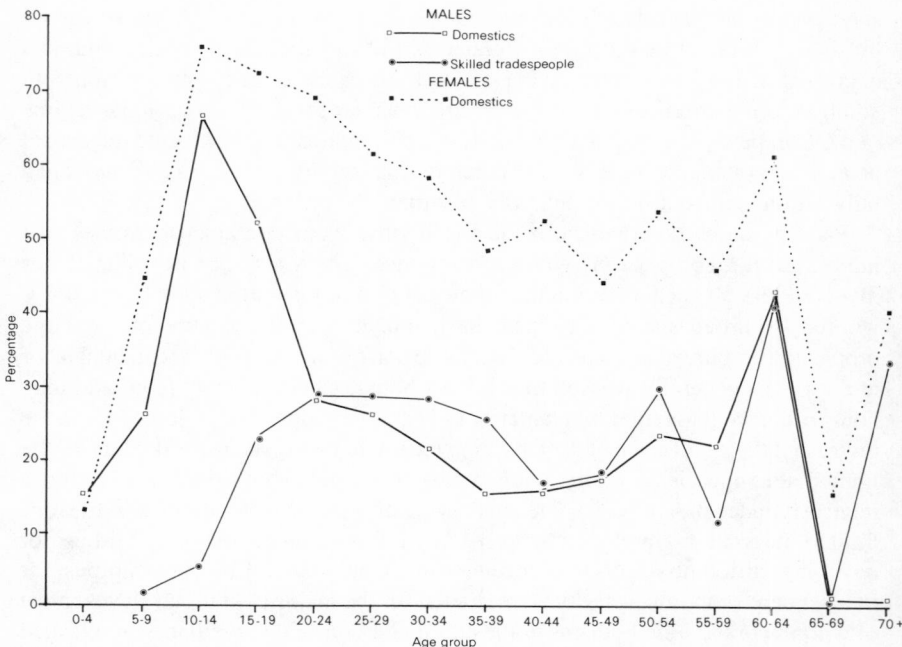

Fig. 7.1. *Occupations of Slaves by Sex and Age: Urban St. Lucia, 1815.*
(Source: *table S7.14.)*

In Bridgetown, however, the proportion of females employed as domestics increased steadily with age to a maximum at about 35 years, and only males shared the early peak observed in the newer colonies (fig. 7.4). Thus, while the planters of Barbados were particularly quick to introduce children to field labor, the slave-owners of Bridgetown were relatively slow to put them to domestic work. It is difficult to explain this contrast, though the perceived abundance of labor was greater in town than in the country. Among the domestics, washerwomen followed a distinct pattern, being concentrated in the 25–50 age groups, a recognition of the relative exertion required (fig. 7.2). Seamstresses, on the other hand, reached an early peak in the teens and then fell to a small proportion of the female population. This clearly suggests that sewing was viewed strictly as a part of domestic work. Male skilled tradespeople emerged at later ages, as on the plantations, and always accounted for a larger proportion of the population than domestics after age 20. Transport workers emerged at even higher ages, and in Bridgetown outnumbered domestics and skilled males only after age 35. In part, this reflected the concentration of African-born slaves in transportation, but it was determined also by the heavy nature of the work. Sellers also tended to be relatively old, approaching 10 percent of the female population only among those aged over 40 years (tables S7.14–7.18).

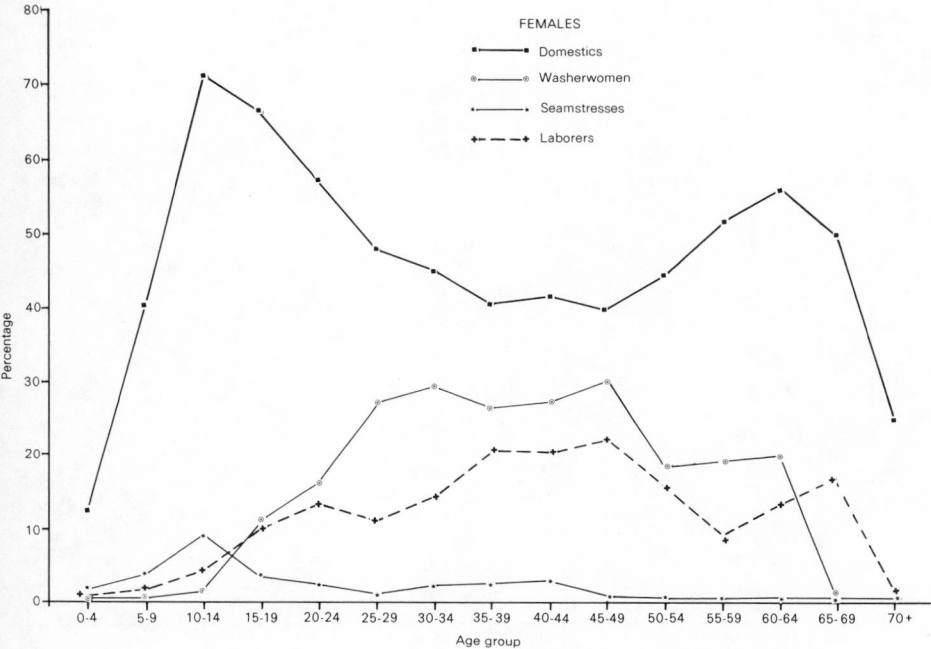

Fig. 7.2.   *Occupations of Female Slaves by Age: Urban Trinidad, 1813.*
(Source: *table S7.18.)*

Sex and age affected urban occupational allocation in much the same way as in the rural slave population. Color and birthplace, however, were less significant in the towns than on the plantations. Most importantly, the general rule that colored females should be employed as domestics was not followed in the towns. In Bridgetown, for example, 69.6 percent of black females were employed as domestics, compared to only 56.5 percent of the colored; and among the males, 28.6 percent of black slaves, but only 26.2 percent of the colored, were domestics (table S7.15). This pattern was little affected by differences in age structure, larger proportions of black than colored slaves working as domestics in almost every age group. In urban St. Lucia colored males and females did have a slight edge over black slaves, but it was nothing like that seen on plantations (table S7.14). This contrast between the rural and urban situations in the importance of color in occupational allocation existed in spite of the much larger proportions of colored slaves found in the towns. The reason for its relative insignificance can be traced to the small scale of urban slaveholding. The owners of very small numbers of slaves had few choices available to them and could not always afford to put colored slaves to domestic tasks or exclude blacks. The demand for male domestics was greatest in small holdings, while the proportion of females employed as domestics varied little with slaveholding size (tables S7.7 and 7.12). It has already been established

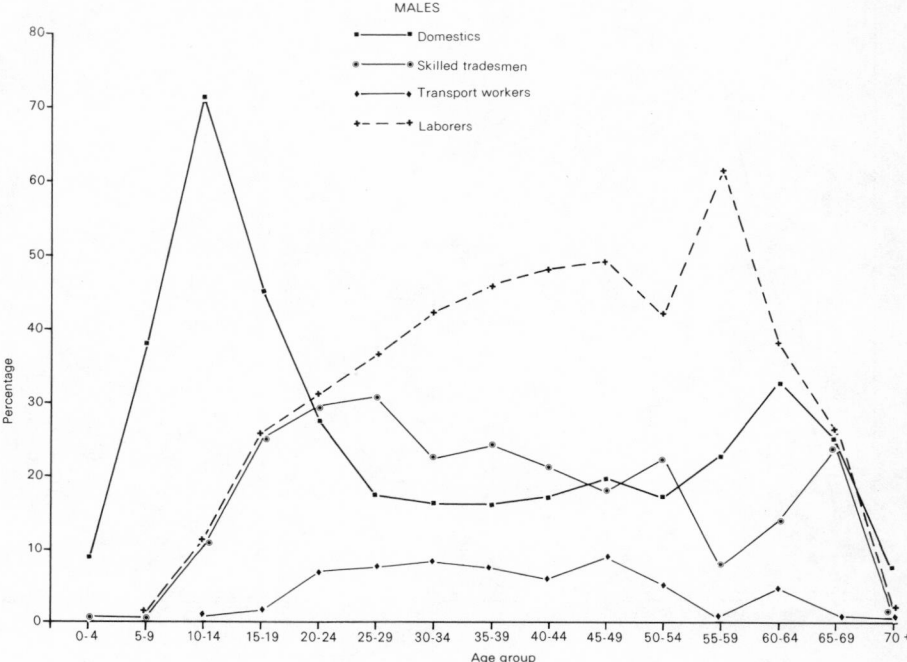

Fig. 7.3. *Occupations of Male Slaves by Age: Urban Trinidad, 1813.*
(Source: *table S7.18.*)

that small slaveowners tended to possess relatively large proportions of African-
born slaves, and this reinforced the role of black slaves in domestic labor in the
towns.

Skilled tradespeople and transport workers belonged to the larger urban
slaveholdings and were purchased more selectively than were domestics. Colored
male slaves were more often employed in the skilled trades than were blacks, and
less often as porters, sailors, fishermen, or laborers. But the contrasts were less
than seen on plantations. Colored females were more likely to work as seamstresses but were less likely to be sellers, most of whom belonged to small units
(tables S7.14–7.15). The sex and color of the owners had only a minor influence.
Skilled tradesmen and transport workers belonged most often to males, but
domestics were evenly distributed. Although it was sometimes said that hucksters
were generally the property of free colored women, the registration evidence from
Bridgetown shows that white and free colored women owned roughly equal
proportions of sellers.[77] Certainly, few belonged to males. In general, then, it may
be concluded that the structure of urban slaveownership, particularly its disper-
sion, meant that occupational allocation in the towns was determined very largely
by the slaves' age and sex but had relatively little to do with their color or
birthplace.

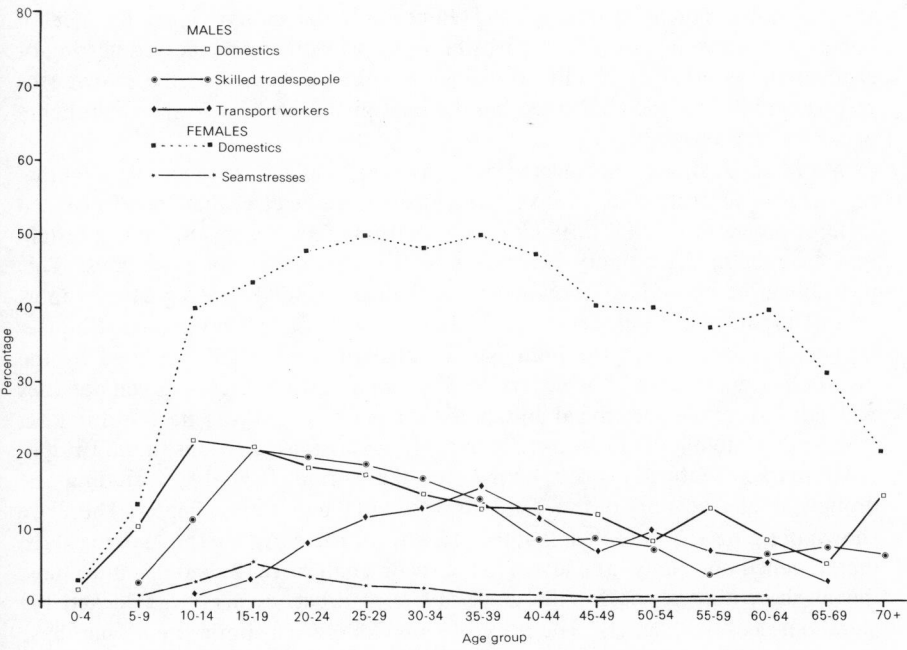

Fig. 7.4. *Occupations of Slaves by Sex and Age: Bridgetown, 1817.*
(Source: *table S7.15.)*

FOOD

Urban slaves generally depended on rationed allowances for their food supplies. The towns obviously lacked the necessary arable land to establish provision
grounds, but the slaveowners never followed the example of some planters in
purchasing nearby plots for the purpose, chiefly because the majority of urban
slaves worked as domestics and so lacked the time to cultivate grounds. Just as
urban slaves were sometimes involved in independent economic decisions through
the system of self-hire and their role in marketing, and thus participated in
commercial transactions, so they were sometimes given money by their owners
and required to find their own board and lodging.

Where slaves depended on their owners for rationed allowances of food, the
colonial regulations, discussed in chapter 6, were applicable to those living in
towns as well as those on plantations. There is little evidence to suggest deviations
from the rural pattern. But the position of urban slaves living in colonies where the
provision ground dominated and the slave laws contained no clauses relating to
food remains uncertain. In Jamaica, for example, the only clause in the slave law
of 1816 which concerned food was that setting the rations of slaves confined in
workhouses or jails. This specified that such slaves were to receive daily allow-

ances of not less than 1 qt of unground Guinea or Indian corn or 3 pt of the meal of either, or 8 plantains, or 8 lb of cocos or yams, as well as one pickled herring or shad or the equivalent in salt provisions.[78] This was less than the allowances provided in the rationed colonies, but the food given most urban slaves probably exceeded that of convicts.[79]

Many urban slaveowners were poor, however, and it was sometimes said that this meant that their slaves received less adequate allowances than those provided on large plantations.[80] It is difficult to test the truth of this assertion, but it is certain that drought in the countryside meant high prices in the town markets. This probably affected small slaveowners more than large, and hence a greater proportion of urban than rural slaves. In 1832, for example, a Georgetown "house-keeper" complained of the high cost of plantains, artificially inflated by the forestalling enterprises of hucksters, and reported that a houseboy given potatoes and salt fish refused the meal and called for plantains, saying he could not eat "backra [white man's] breakfast."[81] Weekly prices for provisions in the Bridge-town market (Saturdays) are known for the period 1812–14, including the drought-related scarcity of late 1812 discussed in the previous chapter. These are shown in figure 7.5. It is clear that the price of Guinea corn, the staple of the slave diet, reached unusually high levels in the second half of 1812, and this must have meant short allowances for the slaves of poor urban owners who lacked the storehouses of the planters. The price of yams followed a similar trend, but these were rarely included in slave rations. Plantains were less obviously affected by the drought, though they showed more erratic price movements. The prices of beef and poultry remained relatively stable throughout the period but played a small role in the diet of urban slaves.[82] Items included in the slave diet all showed a fairly definite seasonal trend in every year, reflecting the general scarcity of provisions in the "hungry time" of June to November.

Variations in market prices may have had relatively little effect on urban slaves whose owners provided fixed allowances throughout the year, but those given cash in lieu of food were certainly affected by these movements. Such payments, generally called "board-wages," were made by slaveowners who wished to avoid the responsibility of providing food for their own slaves and by persons hiring slaves. According to Bayley, the hired slave in Bridgetown at the end of the 1820s was "either fed, or receives half a dollar (about two shillings and twopence) per week to feed himself."[83] The five bits in half a dollar could purchase as much as 30 pt of Guinea corn in the Bridgetown market at the end of 1813 but only a mere 5 pt at the height of the 1812 drought. The usual rations on plantations, by contrast, amounted to 10 pt of Guinea corn, as well as 1 lb of salt fish, molasses, and other allowances. Thus, the Bridgetown slave receiving board-wages was relatively well-off in times of abundance but probably felt the hard times even more than the rural slave.

In Jamaica, it was said, "Negroes in the towns either receive a certain weekly stipend in money, or are allowed in lieu thereof, to work on Saturday for themselves."[84] But only tradesmen could regularly find profitable employment on

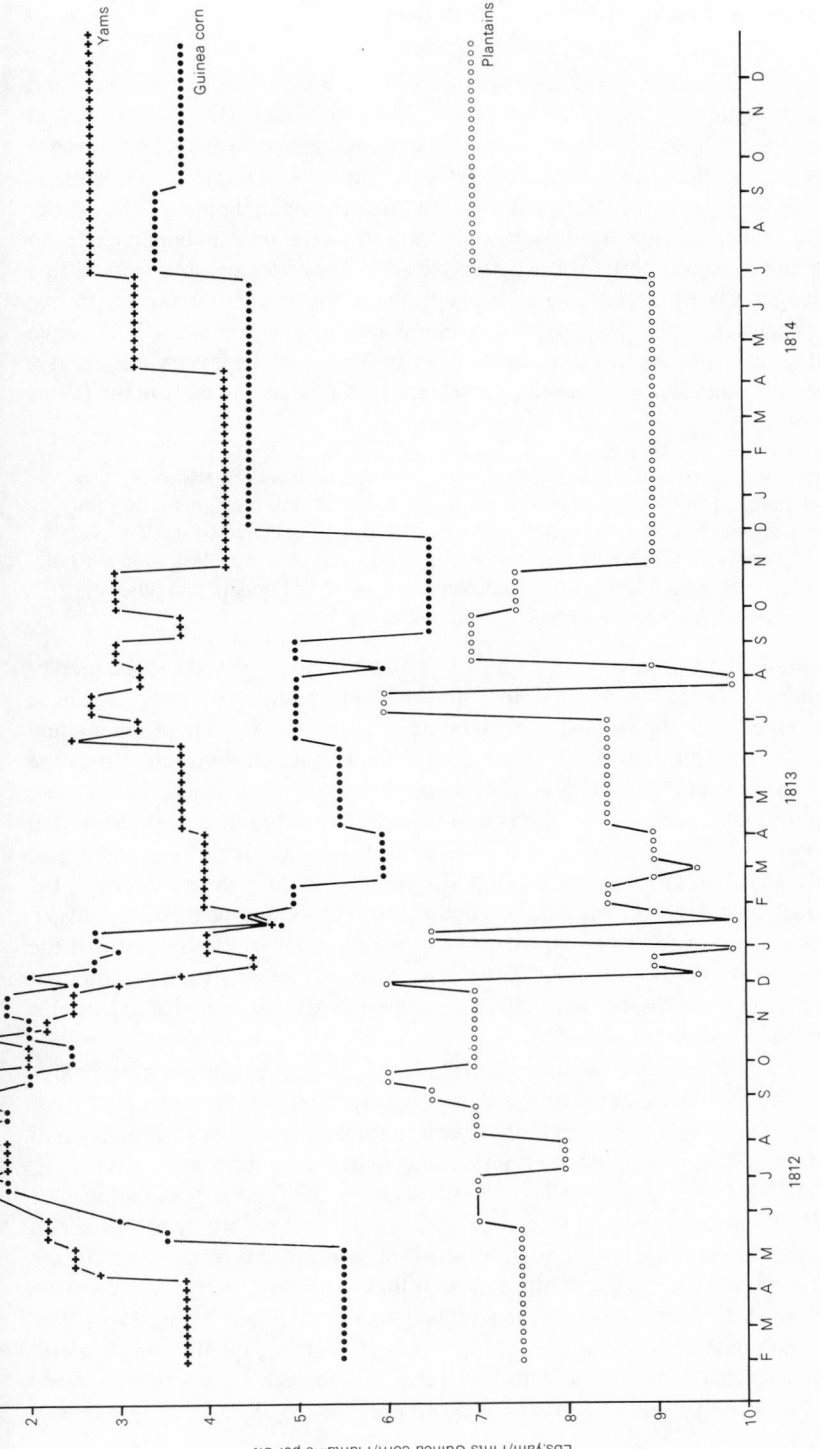

Fig. 7.5. *Bridgetown Market Prices, 1812–14.* (Source: Barbados Mercury, 8 February 1812 to 31 December 1814.)

Saturdays. In Kingston in 1825, domestics were "allowed from two shillings and threepence to three shillings sterling, per week," according to Bickell.[85] Earlier, at the end of the 1790s, one writer claimed that the Kingston slaves' "board wages are seldom more than sufficient for the purpose," and another, styled "Philanthropos," that they were "generally, and greatly, inadequate in their support; which, therefore, either subjects the unhappy creatures to starve amidst abundance, or to become the common pests of the community."[86] The latter writer observed that board-wages varied "according to capacity or disposition, from 1s. 8d. to one dollar per week" but accepted "a medium of 2s. 6d. per week." A slave subsisting on plantains had to spend 6s. 3d. to obtain the necessary 42 weekly, however. "Philanthropos" developed this argument by stating that, in the towns of Jamaica,

there are many ancient, and other reduced families, the members of which are too infirm or indolent to direct the labour—too weak to punish the transgressions—too proud or perverse to part with—and too poor to furnish subsistence for their slaves; the consequences of which are, that a stigma cruel as undeserved is cast upon a whole people—the community is daily pestered with new levies of higglers and other marauders, who watch with eager eye for plunder and for bread.

The solution to the problem, according to "Philanthropos," was the legislation of a minimum rate of allowance and fines for slaveowners failing to supply it. Those unable to feed their slaves adequately would ultimately be forced to sell them, and this would have the beneficial effect of shifting redundant domestics from the towns to the plantations. Those who could afford adequate board-wages, said "Philanthropos," would "be induced to recognise appetite; and to perform that part in compliance with *law*, which *inclination* would ever have been repugnant to." Although the urban populations of domestics certainly were reduced in the early nineteenth century, and Jamaica did legislate minimum board-wages of 3s. 4d. currency per week in 1809, the market prices of the 1820s suggest that the pressure on resources continued.[87] The Leeward Islands established a minimum of 4s. in 1798, but there as in Jamaica the owners frequently substituted inferior items of supposed equivalent value.[88]

As well as food obtained from hucksters, urban slaves subsisting on board-wages could purchase cooked food at rum shops. In Kingston, for example, it was said that "many houses are kept for their entertainment, where they have a meal of coarse bread, salted fish and butter, and a bowl of new rum and water for one ryal, which is about five pence sterling."[89] But slaves receiving the usual allowance could afford no more than six such meals per week. It seems highly probable that overall the board-wages system, like self-hire, placed severe pressure on the slaves' resources and in fact induced much theft and scavenging in the towns. Richard Wade has argued that in the ante-bellum United States urban slaves "ate better" than those in the countryside, in terms of quantity, quality, and variety, and contends that "even those who 'lived out' and 'boarded out' probably fared better than country house servants and certainly far better than field hands."

Similarly, Mary Karasch holds that domestic slaves in Rio de Janeiro "tended to receive better food" than other slaves in that city.[90] Domestics receiving rations or board-wages certainly had access to the larders and leftovers of their mistresses, but only under close surveillance, and those belonging to small slaveholdings were likely to have the least to pick over and worked under the most constant supervision. In the Caribbean, relatively large numbers of slaves belonged to poor whites and freedmen in the towns and did not share the wealth of the conspicuous rich. Thus, the statement of the free Mandingoes of Port of Spain that their slaves "have the same clothes and same table as ourselves" was intended more as proof of their own poverty than of the well-being of their slaves.[91] For the Caribbean generally it is necessary to remain agnostic on the question of whether urban slaves dependent on rations were better fed than those receiving board-wages, and it is equally difficult to establish that slaves in the towns had a real advantage over those living on plantations.[92]

HOUSING

The spatial distribution of slave housing within the towns of the British Caribbean has already been discussed in chapter 4. In general, town slaves were "resident in their masters' negro yards, every house having detached dwellings for their accommodation."[93] But the spread of the self-hire and board-wages system meant that many slaves were forced to seek lodgings separate from their owners' premises, in "negro yards" belonging to free people or in huts built by themselves on the fringes of the towns.

Most domestics, and hence most urban slaves, lived on their owners' premises. Their role was to perform more or less constant personal service, so they had to be on hand to do the bidding of master or mistress. At one extreme, domestics slept in the bedchambers of their owners or immediately outside the door. Others slept in special rooms contained within the owner's house or in the kitchen or store. In all of these cases the slaves were as well protected from rain, wind, and fire as their owners, though the space allotted may have been less than that in plantation houses. Larger slaveowners, however, generally built separate "negro rooms" in the yards behind their houses, shops, or stores. These rooms sometimes approximated barracks or ranges.[94] Their fabric was not always the same as that of the owner's house, but it was still likely to be more substantial than the typical slave housing found on plantations. For instance, premises on Henry Street, Port of Spain, were offered for sale in 1823, comprising a house of two floors, "with galleries above and below," the first floor containing a hall, pantry, and chamber, and the second two chambers and a closet. In the yard were a kitchen, store, three "Negro rooms," and a double chaise house with stabling for three horses. All of the buildings were of masonry and roofed with tiles, and the entire lot was enclosed by a wall.[95] Similar arrangements applied in the premises of relatively prosperous slaveowners in most towns, though there were significant differences in building materials.

In Belize the houses were all built of wood and were raised 8–10 feet above the ground on piles of mahogany. Stores and offices were located in the lower story, and dining and sleeping rooms in the upper. Until the great fire of 1806, most of the houses were thatched with palmetto, but it was then universally replaced by shingles.[96] This meant improved protection from the elements for slaves as well as owners. In Georgetown and New Amsterdam, most buildings were constructed of timber throughout the period. In Bridgetown, however, the great fires of 1766 resulted in legislation intended to ensure that all houses would in the future be built of brick or stone and not exceed three stories.[97] This growing tendency to build in brick or stone was also common in the towns of Jamaica and in the Leeward and Windward Islands, and it resulted in a general improvement in the fabric of slave housing wherever it was located on the slaveowner's premises. The threat of fire was also reduced by the introduction of fire engines in the towns and the establishment of fire companies. Slaves were required to play an active role in the latter, accompanying their owners to all fires. For example, each member of the Broad Street Fire Company, Bridgetown, was to be attended by two male slaves wearing blue jackets and red capes with the initials of the owner worked or painted on the back.[98]

Although the quality of urban slave housing varied with the wealth of the slaveowner, it is possible to accept the judgment of Bickell, who was highly critical of plantation housing, that in the towns "the domestic slaves are, generally speaking, comfortably lodged."[99] Slaves hired to other masters were similarly housed.[100] The quality of the shelter afforded urban slaves working under the self-hire and board-wages systems, however, was relatively inferior and much more comparable to that found on plantations. In spite of attempts to ensure that brick and stone were used in all construction in Bridgetown after 1766, for example, Bayley described a fire that destroyed twenty houses during the 1820s, "chiefly negro-houses, very small, and of no great value," all built of wood.[101] This suggests that these houses were grouped together and were possibly constructed by the slaves themselves. The link with self-hire was made clearly in the Jamaican law of 1795, which imposed fines on free people who permitted slaves "belonging to unknown persons"

not only to build cottages and huts in the savannas and waste grounds, but also do let or hire houses, cottages, huts, or lodgings unto the aforesaid slaves, by the day, week, month, quarter, year, or other greater or lesser term, who are suffered and permitted by their owners and employers to work and employ themselves in what manner and wheresoever they shall think fit.[102]

All houses built for this purpose were to be pulled down. Under the circumstances, it is not surprising that such slaves lived in relatively insubstantial housing. The frequency of changes in slaveownership in the towns, compared to the relative stability of life in plantation villages, meant that slaves could see little point in spending the scanty sums available from board-wages or self-hire to secure better shelter. Even working-out carpenters and masons might be reluctant to construct superior houses if their present location or owner was viewed as temporary. Thus, although the precise dimensions and materials of the shelters occupied by such slaves remain uncertain, it may be concluded that generally they were no better than the worst housing found on plantations and certainly inferior to that of slaves living at their owners' premises. Once again, however, it may well be that slaves preferred such arrangements. Even if the roof leaked more often and food was harder to come by, slaves on board-wages were beyond earshot of their owners and able, to a relatively great degree, to set their own rules of behavior.

CLOTHING

The clothing of urban slaves varied with their occupations. Because relatively few engaged in heavy manual labor, adults were less likely to work naked in the towns than on the plantations. Yet it was said that in Kingston "many negroes, while in their owners employ, totally neglect their dress; wearing the most ragged clothes in their possession, sometimes until they fall off, which however they protract as long as they can, by knotting their drapery to keep it hanging together."[103] There is little evidence to show precisely what clothing was given to urban slaves as allowance, but the high ratio of owners to slaves, and female owners to female domestics, meant that they were more likely than plantation slaves to receive cast-off items. Female domestics may have been largely supplied in this way. Thus, they wore clothes made of finer materials than the Osnaburg of most field laborers, but the quantity, style, and age of what they received depended heavily on the wealth of their owners. This conclusion fits Mary Karasch's finding that female domestics in Rio de Janeiro generally "possessed better clothing than other slaves because a master's prestige was enhanced by the sartorial elegance of his slaves."[104] Men were supplied most often with breeches and waistcoats, rather than the frocks of the plantations. For example, in Kingstown a male cook was given a blue cloth jacket, a pair of duck trousers, and a check shirt, when sold by his merchant owner.[105] Urban slaves were no more likely than rural slaves to wear shoes.[106] But some did manage to purchase a wide range of clothing items with their own money and "frequently have their cloaths made in the newest English fashion and sometimes exceed it fantastically."[107] The nature of urban life probably meant that clothing was more highly valued than on the plantations, especially for its symbolic value as evidence of status.[108] Although the specific data available are slight, it seems fair to conclude that urban slaves were generally better clothed than those on plantations.

THE CHARACTER OF URBAN SLAVERY

Slavery in the towns of the British Caribbean was characterized by contradiction and ambiguity. Most urban slaves lived in more intimate contact with their owners than did rural slaves, frequently sharing their houses, eating their leftovers, and wearing their castoffs. This intimacy went beyond that experienced by plantation domestics, chiefly because the small scale of urban slaveholdings and the high proportion of female owners resulted in an extreme degree of immediate supervision. At the same time, a significant minority of urban slaves worked and lived with a degree of freedom extremely rare in rural slave society. While they were not their own masters, slaves working under the system of self-hire did exercise a substantial ability to organize their own time and resources and worked beyond the immediate fear of the owner's tongue and lash. Similarly, slaves receiving board wages could exercise some degree of personal choice in where and how they lived and what they ate. Self-hire and board wages necessarily involved slaves in a range of commercial transactions with free people as well as other slaves, which went far beyond the retailing of goods in the public markets. They became part of an essentially free labor market, which theoretical defenses of slavery claimed to be an inefficient method of economic organization. Thus, they demonstrated the inherent contradictions of the system.

The towns of the British Caribbean contained visible symbols of the slaveowners' power to punish their slaves publicly. The freedom of economic behavior in the public market was matched by the presence of the stocks and cage for the confinement of slaves who exceeded the bounds of permitted self-indulgence. Drunkenness, gaming, and vice were associated with self-hire and separate residence. Treadmills were introduced to the towns after 1820, and jails and workhouses refurbished. Yet slaveowners remained unsure of their ability to retain full control in such a situation. In Bridgetown, for example, there were calls for a police force in the early 1820s to prevent the growth of disorder and rebellious meetings. According to one commentator,

As regularly as the Sabbath comes, so regularly at the approach of evening, are we annoyed with the sound of pumps, drums, tabors, etc.; and the continuance thereof, if not previously put an end to by brawls and combats among them, generally lasts to the approach of the subsequent morning; and this takes place now, not only on Sundays, but on other days of the week, to the no small interruption of business, the detention of servants sent out on domestic affairs, and the disturbance of the neighborhood. . . . The very confines of the consecrated church yard are not exempt from frequently becoming the scene of these revels, at which the most obscene and disgusting gesticulations are practised, without the slightest regard to decency, nay, even to the modest white females who may repair to their balconies, or be tempted to walk out for the purpose of enjoying the evening breeze.[109]

Another Bridgetown writer, in 1823, believed that "the riotous and disorderly conduct of the slaves who swarm about this town, loudly calls for some powerful combination on the part of their owners to repress their overbearing insolence." Slaves paraded the streets "at all hours of the night," singing, yelling, and making music, as well as playing cards and dice, fighting cocks, and holding weekly dances in the suburbs. These amusements, which in fact were the same as those of the free people, were dangerous in a slave society and, it was said,

nothing but a system of severity has any effect, and that system few indeed of the present day will pursue: although facts will bear us out in the assertion, that a strict discipline is the most conducive to the moral conduct, and to the happiness of the slave; a mild and indulgent government, in almost every instance, has been rewarded with insolence and ingratitude.[110]

This concern that urban slaveowners were losing control of their slaves is particularly interesting, since it had no real rural counterpart. A revealing advertisement by a Bridgetown owner in 1832 supports the point, admitting an incapacity to handle refractory slaves and offering them for sale:

The mother and sons are clever, intelligent people. To an owner in town they are, it must be confessed, great plagues; but in the country there is little doubt that they would be very serviceable labourers. Taking them out of this vile town would indeed be conferring a blessing on them.[111]

No doubt the movement of slaves from the towns to the country was chiefly motivated by economic factors, but the slaveowner's feeling that slaves were not easily controlled or disciplined in the urban context may be traced directly to the contradictions within the system, the distancing of slave and master, and the independence symbolized by self-hire and board-wages. Such complaints and attitudes were not confined to Bridgetown but were common to the larger towns of the British Caribbean.[112]

The impact of this relative social fluidity on the material conditions of life of urban slaves is less certain. Although the tasks they performed generally required less physical exertion than was required of plantation slaves, and they were not subject to a seasonal regime, the majority of urban slaves, the domestics, did work very long hours. Those who lived on the premises of their owners certainly occupied superior shelter and were probably better clothed than those who found their own, and it is doubtful whether those dependent on board-wages ate as well as those given rations. Thus, the numerous psychological and cultural advantages of the relative independence associated with self-hire and board-wages were not generally matched by material gains. But slaves working under these systems did at least have opportunities to enhance their welfare, which were largely denied the majority of the urban slaves employed as domestics who had no provision grounds, gardens, or marketable skills with which to generate an income.

The ambiguous and contradictory character of slavery in the towns of the British Caribbean was by no means peculiar to that region or the period after 1807. Indeed, virtually every feature of urban slavery in the West Indies was repeated with only minor variations in the towns of, for example, the United States, Cuba, the Danish Virgin Islands, and Brazil.[113] This common pattern very strongly supports the interpretation that the material bases of slavery were more important in determining the nature of the institution than were the religion, laws, or national character of any group of slaveowners, or even the phase of development of the population.

8.
Health

THE COMPARATIVE HEALTH OF THE SLAVE POPULATIONS OF THE
British Caribbean may be measured in terms of morbidity, mortality, fertility, and
life expectancy. Before the abolition of the Atlantic slave trade, rates of population
growth depended very much on the level of slave importation, but after 1807 these
variables, internal to the slave population, took on added significance.

It has often been argued that the rate of growth of a slave population was in the
masters' power to control. Thus, masters could make a "rational" economic
decision to work imported African slaves to death within, say, seven years and
then purchase replacements from the slave ships, rather than to support a population with a natural increase which would supply its own labor force. Alternatively,
they could adopt a pronatalist policy, offering rewards to women for bearing
children or even establishing "stud farms" for the breeding of slaves. Both of
these attitudes toward the manipulation of mortality and fertility are said to have
existed, in different times and places, in the Caribbean as elsewhere. But Stanley
Engerman, for example, has recently questioned the capacity of the masters to
effectively control the size and structure of the slave labor force.[1] Certainly
individual masters could determine the basic structure of their own slaveholdings
through selective purchase, sale, and manumission; and, by choosing particular
locations for their holdings, could determine the healthfulness of the physical
environment in which the slaves lived. They also had extensive control over the
physical exertions required of slaves, and their nutrition, shelter, and clothing, as
discussed in the last two chapters. But there seems no hard evidence for the
conscious breeding of slaves, which some have argued for Barbuda and
Barbados,[2] and after 1807 there was no longer any rational basis to the idea that it
was profitable to work or starve a slave to death in a short period of time.

In general, slaveowners believed they had a greater capacity to manipulate
mortality than fertility. Thus, they took a much more direct approach to the control
of morbidity and mortality levels. They built hospitals, hired physicians, employed slaves as nurses, procured medicines and special foods for invalids, and
recognized the inability of slaves to work when sick. Very often their intervention
did more harm than good, merely compounding the poor health of the slave
populations resulting from the extreme physical demands and inadequate nutrition
they experienced. But it is obvious that the masters' attitudes and approaches to the

control of health must be considered in attempting to explain patterns of slave morbidity and mortality. In this chapter the medical care provided by slaveowners will be discussed in the context of their attitudes toward public health and their understanding of etiology, alongside the slaves' ideas and independent actions. Indicators of the health of the slave populations, such as physical growth, abnormalities, and morbidity, are also discussed, but mortality and cause-of-death patterns will be considered in the following chapter.

MEDICAL CARE

A broad sketch of the medical treatment of slaves in the British Caribbean has recently been provided by Richard Sheridan. He argues that from the later eighteenth century the masters adopted a policy of amelioration, part of which involved improved medical attention, and that this, together with "medical progress," "did much to improve the health and longevity of slaves in the West Indies."[3] This conclusion may be doubted. Some of the doubts are implicit in Sheridan's essay. He notes, for example, that in Jamaica there was a very rapid decline in the ratio of European-trained doctors to population after emancipation, a period of substantial natural increase. One of Sheridan's prime examples of colonies with a large number of doctors is Antigua, but it will be shown that this island experienced the lowest rate of natural increase of all the first-phase settlements in the early nineteenth century. The rapid growth of the slave population on nearby Barbuda, however, seems to have occurred completely in the absence of any resident doctor. But Sheridan's conclusion must not be completely rejected, for there is evidence of limited medical progress from the end of the eighteenth century which had an impact on the health of the slaves. The use of inoculation and vaccination against smallpox is perhaps the most obvious example of this improvement. Generally, however, the ratio of slaves to doctors, or slaves to hospital beds, was of questionable significance for the survival of the slave population. It was not that the masters failed to take the provision of medical care seriously—they took it very seriously—it was simply that European medical knowledge of the period rested on weak foundations.

The numbers of physicians, surgeons, and apothecaries practicing in the British Caribbean between 1807 and 1834 are known only for a few colonies, so it is impossible to establish variations in the slave-doctor ratio. In Jamaica, where there were 209 legally authorized medical practitioners in 1833, the ratio averaged 1,500 slaves per doctor but ranged from only 350 in Kingston to more than 5,000 in some rural parishes.[4] In Trinidad in 1830 there were 29 licensed medical practitioners, a ratio of 780 slaves per doctor, and seven licensed apothecaries and four druggists.[5] There were about 60 "apothecaries" or "apothecarized doctors" in Barbados in 1820, a ratio of one to every 1,300 slaves, but their efforts were supplemented by an unknown number of physicians and surgeons.[6] In Georgetown, Demerara, thirteen "Gentlemen of the Faculty," a ratio of one to every 500 slaves, practiced medicine in the town in 1821, together with three apothecaries.

By 1823 there were ten "surgeons," four "M.D.'s," a "practitioner," and three "apothecaries" in the town.[7] In Berbice the deaths of slaves between 1819 and 1822 were certified by a total of 27 medical practitioners, a ratio of 900 slaves per practitioner. Of these practitioners, 21 signed as "doctor," while 14 further described themselves as "surgeons," four as "M.D.'s," three as "medical practitioners," two as "practitioners of physic," and one as "apothecary."[8] Although these ratios may appear quite acceptable, it must be remembered that the doctors served the white and freedman populations as well as the slaves. In terms of total population, the ratios were 1,800 persons per doctor in Jamaica, 1,450 in Trinidad, 1,600 in Barbados, and 1,000 in Berbice. In the case of Kingston the ratio was 700 and in Georgetown 750 persons per doctor. Thus, doctors were twice as common in the towns as on the plantations, but it is certain that their efforts were directed very much toward the white populations, which suffered high morbidity rates and paid higher fees.

Most large plantations employed doctors on an annual basis, paying a set fee for each slave regardless of his or her state of health. Doctors generally had contracts with a number of plantations and visited them regularly, either weekly or more frequently. Many worked on a partnership basis. Some attempted to accumulate rapid fortunes by contracting for large numbers of plantations, and served more than 4,000 slaves.[9] Physicians, surgeons, and midwives were called at need and were paid specific fees. Dentists were rare in the colonies, often serving several islands, and they probably had little to do with the rural slave populations.[10] On smaller slaveholdings, both in town and in the country, doctors were not generally retained at an annual salary but were called only when required. Slaves living on isolated islands or employed in woodcutting were even further removed from European medical practitioners.

In the seventeenth century Barbadian planters employed "apothecaries" as doctors. By the end of the eighteenth century, according to Handler and Lange, "plantations usually employed both apothecaries and 'physicians or surgeons,' and this system prevailed until the end of slavery."[11] Although there is clear evidence that this division of functions was followed on some plantations in Barbados, it appears that the apothecaries may have been supplanted by the physicians after 1807. In 1821, for example, "A Planter" complained in the Barbados press that the island's physicians were also surgeons and apothecaries and midwives, employed on estates at a fixed annual salary.[12] The system of "district doctors" removed the possibility of competiton, he said, contrary to Adam Smith's principles of the division of labor. Many Barbados-born whites had graduated from the medical schools of Britain, but the island's apothecaries no longer always brought up their sons as apothecaries because they were losing trade and were often maligned for their ignorance. Midwives had been completely given up, he wrote, while many doctors employed unsatisfactory partners. He feared that the island's apothecaries would be supplanted by young and inexperienced surgeons, since the returns of the work were insufficient to cover the £4–5,000 expense of a medical education.

In practice, a variety of systems were followed on Barbadian plantations between 1807 and 1834. At Colletons Estate in 1818, P. Greaves was paid 6s. 3d. per annum for the "care" of each of the 286 slaves on the plantation, while R. Caddell received £25 for four visits and prescribing for sick slaves. In 1826 Colletons paid Greaves and Greenidge £86 for the care of 275 slaves, at the same rate as in 1818, and R. C. Thomas received £22 10s. for medical and surgical attendance.[13] But in 1828 Drax Hall Estate merely paid the common rate of 6s. 3d. per slave to an "apothecary" and employed no physician or surgeon.[14] Mount Gay Plantation employed Thomas and H. Goodridge between 1811 and 1827 to perform a wide range of medical functions. In addition to "medical care" at 6s. 3d. per slave, they also presented annual accounts for surgical work, medicines, and appliances, as well as for medicines for horses and cattle on the estate. But in 1827 Mount Gay brought in R. C. Thomas to perform an instrumental delivery at a fee of £15.[15]

These examples may be supplemented by a continuous set of accounts for Newton Plantation, Barbados, covering the whole period 1807–34.[16] In 1807 and 1808 Newton employed John F. D. Jones as "physician and apothecary" at an annual rate of 7s. 6d. per slave, George Walwyn Shepherd as "surgeon" at £30, and Ann Crichlow as "sick nurse" at £15 per annum. Between 1809 and 1811 Shepherd was not called, but Jones's fee was raised to 10s. and by 1812 it specifically covered "medical and surgical" care.[17] In 1810 Crichlow was paid an additional 15s. for each of the six women she delivered. She was replaced as sick nurse and midwife by Frances Gibson in 1812, and in October of that year Jones was replaced by R. C. Thomas who was titled simply "apothecary" and was paid a reduced fee of 6s. 3d. Gibson worked as sick nurse until 1818 but was then replaced by a slave midwife belonging to Newton who received the lesser rate of 6s. 3d. per delivery. Thomas continued as apothecary until 1820, when he entered into a partnership with Edward H. Whitehall for 15 months, and in 1821 Whitehall took over the "care" of the slaves. But Thomas continued to present "surgical" accounts until 1825. In July 1825 Newton paid John H. Cutting £10 "for a general inspection of the Negroes; Opinion and advice," and separate sums for treating a woman's ulcer and, in 1830, for a case of midwifery. In 1832 Whitehall's annual fee was reduced to 5s. per slave. Between 1826 and 1830 Mrs. Elizabeth Birkett worked as the estate's sick nurse, at £15 per annum, while Margaret Birkett acted as midwife at 15s. per delivery. Within the period 1807–34, then, Newton Plantation employed three separate apothecaries or "doctors," the first two of whom, Jones and Thomas, graduated with experience into the more lucrative surgical field. But the estate employed a specialist "surgeon" on an annual basis only until 1808. This trend toward a new generalization of functions fits well the observations of "A Planter," noted above. White sick nurses and midwives were generally drawn from the estate tenantry but were generally used only when skilled slave women could not be found to perform these functions. The reduction in the annual doctor's fee over the period and the abandonment of a fixed surgical contract meant that Newton was able to cut its medical expenditure from £145 in

1807 to £71 in 1833, while the estate population declined only from 267 to 259 slaves.

The qualifications of the whites employed as medical practitioners were varied. Most of those trained in European medical schools were European-born, though a significant number of Barbadian creoles traveled to Britain, some 26 of them presenting dissertations at Edinburgh between 1807 and 1828.[18] Such doctors received as good a medical training as Europe could offer at the time. Many possessed large libraries of current medical literature and subscribed and contributed to the leading medical journals.[19] A few examples will suffice, since it is impossible to quantify the relative qualifications of practitioners in the different colonies. Alexander Cockburn (1739–1815), a Scot, "studied medicine" and set up in practice in Grenada in 1763 after a brief sojourn in the East Indies. In 1792 he returned to Britain to attend the classes of Drs. Cullen and Monro at Edinburgh University and the anatomical lectures of Dr. Hunter in London. Cockburn returned to Grenada in 1795 and eventually rose to the position of Physician General to the Militia.[20] Another Scot, William Wright (1735–1819), was apprenticed to a surgeon and in 1756 entered the Edinburgh Medical School. He worked as a naval and military surgeon's mate in the West Indies and after 1763 gained the degree of doctor of medicine at London. Wright then established a partnership in Jamaica and made sufficient money, chiefly from the treatment of slaves, to retire to Edinburgh after 1776.[21] The importance of Edinburgh as a center of medical education was considerable in the period, though some West Indian practitioners trained in Glasgow, London, Dublin, Leyden, and North America. Many of those practicing in the former French colonies had trained in France. Jean Bertrand Loubet, M.D., a Frenchman who died in Trinidad in 1827, was the brother of a surgeon practicing in France, and at his death left a library of almost 200 volumes treating medical and chirurgical matters. In 1823 he had established a "commodious house" for patients in Port of Spain.[22]

While many of the doctors employed to treat West Indian slaves were well qualified by contemporary European standards, some did not reach even this level. George Pinckard, M.D., a military physician, provided one of the most scathing condemnations. Many of the medical men of Barbados were highly skilled, he admitted, but others were grossly ignorant:

They are more illiterate than you can believe, and the very *negro doctors* of the estates too justly vie with them in medical knowledge. . . . Totally unprepared with a classical education, and, indeed, wholly devoid of the very rudiments of literature, they indolently waste a few years, in the house, or idly looking out at the shop-window of some uneduated apothecary of the island, and then in all the bold confidence of ignorance, they commence *Doctors*, feeling themselves fully qualified, without professional reading, without visiting the schools of Europe, without experience, and I might say, without thought, or judgment, to undertake the cure of all the direful maladies which afflict the human frame;—in short, without one necessary qualification do these creole *pretenders* feel themselves competent to exercise all the various branches of the healing art.[23]

In order to control the entry of such people to the practice of medicine, the colonial governments established licensing requirements. In Trinidad a Medical Board was reestablished in 1814, with the power to license all wishing to practice medicine or surgery or to sell medicine or drugs.[24] Practitioners were to produce "a certificate of medical degree, duly conferred upon them by some one or other of the universities of Europe and America, or some other body corporate, competent and entitled to confer the same," or "be fully examined by the Medical Board touching their fitness and ability" to practice. Heavy fines were to be imposed on any unlicensed practitioners. The Board was composed of four members appointed by the Governor, with Dr. Alexander Williams as President. Williams had practiced medicine for twenty years, he said, attending free families and slaves in town and country, but increasingly confining his efforts to Port of Spain.[25] Thus, the Board had the capacity to act as a closed shop and to control the kinds of medical attention offered. In 1816, for example, it licensed Vincent Monier to retail "such drugs as shall be authorized by the president and members of the Medical Board."[26] The following year Joseph Driggs, a native of Connecticut holding a diploma from the Royal College of Surgeons, London, was licensed to practice physic and surgery.[27] In 1820 Seth Driggs, wholesale and retail druggist, opened a "medical warehouse" in Port of Spain and announced his intention to import sufficient genuine fresh medicines to supply the whole island.[28] In 1826 Seth and Sherman Driggs took over the Trinidad Dispensary in Port of Spain and established a branch in San Fernando in 1830 called the Naparima Dispensary.[29] By 1831 the Driggses were involved in a court case during which collusion between apothecaries and medical practitioners, including members of the Board, was alleged. The owners of the Trinidad Dispensary charged that the prices of drugs had risen high because apothecaries now had to pay a percentage to physicians in order to influence their patients to patronize particular establishments.[30]

As well as seeking personal advantage from the system of licensing, the Trinidad Medical Board also used its power to exclude qualified practitioners. The most obvious examples of this power were its attempts to exclude freedmen from practice. Two sons of Louis Philip, the largest free colored planter of the Naparimas, were in fact admitted to practice, one of them the only doctor in southern Trinidad to hold a university degree. In 1822 Dr. Alexander Williams, President of the Board, sought to have a mulatto "protégé," Francisco Williams, admitted to practice. Francisco held a diploma from the College of Surgeons, London, but had been registered in 1813 as the property of Dr. Williams; and his mother, Sarah Williams, remained in slavery in 1822. The Board objected to his being licensed, chiefly because he was so close to slavery. But this refusal was reversed by the Colonial Office.[31]

A Collegium Medicum with powers similar to those of the Trinidad Medical Board had been established in Demerara in 1810.[32] Practitioners of physic and surgery were licensed in Grenada as early as 1821.[33] In Jamaica, however, a College of Physicians and Surgeons was not set up until 1832, and no proof of qualification was required before that date.[34] Elsewhere the situation is less certain. But it is clear that the qualifications of the European-trained doctors were generally respectable by contemporary standards, while many creole white practitioners merely learned by experience and only gradually boosted themselves to the upper levels of physic and surgery.

Medical care was also provided by slaves. Pinckard's comment that the "negro doctors" possessed as much medical knowledge as many of the white journeyman practitioners has already been noted. He was not alone in this view. In the early eighteenth century, James Knight had argued that the "negro doctors" were often more successful than the whites in obtaining cures through their use of hot baths of herbs, or fermentations. Knight observed that slaves lacked confidence in the white physicians and so were reluctant to take their medicine, and claimed that the slave doctors never prescribed anything to be taken internally.[35] This difference in practice may well have prevented slave doctors from doing as much damage as the whites.

Few slaves were listed as "doctors" in the registration returns, and it is difficult to determine exactly how their functions differed from those described as sick nurses or hospital nurses (tables S7.2–7.8). The most elaborate hierarchy occurred in the Berbice registration returns of 1819. Even there only 7 male slaves were listed as doctors and one as apothecary. But another 16 males were hospital attendants, assistants, or mates; and of the sick nurses, 38 were male and only 12 female slaves. It seems most likely that the plantation slave doctors worked under the irregular supervision of white practitioners, administering the medicines as prescribed but also being allowed to practice herbal remedies of their own in the first instance. Thus, there was only a fine line between doctor and sick nurse. Whereas in Berbice most sick nurses were males, slaves listed simply as nurses were almost all females, as were midwives and yaws house nurses.

The daily administration of hospitals on plantations was generally left in the hands of the slave sick nurses. On Sanderson's Estate in Antigua, reported John Johnson in 1824, the sick nurse was usually an old slave, "the extent of whose knowledge is perhaps an acquaintance with the peculiar virtues of some indigenous plants." The normal practice, he said, was as follows:

The Doctor attends the Estate (and) sees the several patients—prescribes for them in the Sick-Book, which is afterwards forwarded to his residence (unless it happens that medicines are provided by the property) and the messenger returns with the several compounds, most frequently made up by his attendant—these are transferred by the manager to the Sick Nurse who (not possessing a knowledge of letters) as she receives her directions places each packet between her several fingers each of which it is to be presumed represents in her mind the patients to whom they are to be administered.[36]

The sick nurse was also responsible for the general care of slaves in the hospital, though large plantations often employed slaves as hospital cooks who prepared special meals for the patients. The size of the hospital staff varied with the size of the slaveholding, and most urban or small rural units contained no specialist nurses.

Hospitals specifically designed for the care of slaves differed widely in their size and architecture. The hospital often was built in the same style as the works and great house on a large estate. Many of these were of two stories, constructed of cut stone, with boarded floors and shutters or glass windows on pulleys. In Demerara, hospitals built after 1807 were of wood but differed from the slave barracks in that they were raised on brick pillars and generally were of two stories.[37] Most often these substantial hospitals were divided into separate wards for males and females, lying-in rooms, rooms for those suffering from tetanus, and chambers for the sick nurse, medicines, and stores. The beds of the invalids were raised wooden platforms, supplied with mattresses and blankets and, frequently, stocks. The latter were used to prevent slaves' escaping from the hospitals. While some doctors claimed the stocks served a curative purpose, preventing movement, they were also designed to inhibit slaves' using the hospital as an escape from field labor and spreading disease within the slave village.[38]

At Sanderson's Estate, Antigua, John Johnson reported in 1824 that the hospital and lying-in room were housed in the old works buildings and were in a "satisfactory" state, except that the window shutters were decayed and admitted the wind, the beds needed repairs, and the rooms were not swept every morning. He proposed building a wall or fence to enclose the hospital yard, to prevent the sick running to the slave village. This was preferable to locking the hospital door, "which amounts to an undue check upon their liberty," he wrote.[39] At Fairhall and Brebner Estate in St. Vincent, however, Johnson found the hospital was wooden, comprising only two wards each 12 feet square, one for males and one for females. This was meant to serve for 240 slaves. There was no lying-in room, the women being delivered in their huts, and Johnson noted as a particular evil that the horse stable was immediately to windward of the hospital.[40] Elsewhere, even on large estates, the hospitals were often described as dark, unwholesome, stinking holes, with the sexes indecently mixed.[41]

As well as hospitals and lying-in rooms, many estates had separate yaws houses. Since yaws was a common and readily communicable disease, these houses were generally isolated, though a nurse was sometimes assigned specifically to care for the sufferers. The yaws house was generally a much less elaborate structure than the hospital, though few specific descriptions are available. On Plantation Maryshope, Berbice, however, the yaws house was 30 by 28 feet, occupying the old hospital in 1830; the new hospital was only 24 by 20 feet but had a gallery and two side buildings. Isolation was the principal motive, and the slaves themselves were well aware of its importance. In 1819, for example, the manager of Plantation Providence in Berbice sent three slaves suffering from yaws to stay in the isolated house of Brutus, the plantain walk watchman. But Brutus was reluctant to take the risk and, he said, "slept some nights in the open air, and built himself a small hut in the plantain walk, and covered it with dry leaves."[42]

The contention of the planters that every estate had its hospital is no doubt correct,[43] but there are no data available to permit a systematic analysis of variation from colony to colony of the adequacy of these structures, even in terms of the amount of space and protection from the elements they offered. The slave laws rarely specified that the masters should provide hospitals or medical care, and when they did it was only in the most general terms.[44] The only generalization that can be made with confidence is that the most substantial hospitals were found on the largest estates. There was probably an overall improvement in the size and structural qualities of the hospitals between 1807 and 1834. But even on large estates the hospitals must have been greatly overcrowded in times of epidemic. The general decline in the estate populations after 1807, however, meant that more space was available to the survivors. Small rural units did not have hospitals, and sick slaves were treated in their houses or rooms. Hospitals, therefore, were rare in the marginal colonies.

In the countryside hospitalization was strictly a private concern of the planters. In the towns, however, slaves were more likely to find themselves in public hospitals or the infirmaries of private doctors. This contrast resulted in part from the fact that the presence of a large white population with a high morbidity rate, living in close proximity to slaves, led to a greater concern for public health. Public hospitals became increasingly common in the capital towns from the end of the eighteenth century, but generally drew most of their patients from the poorer sections of the free population.[45] The wealthy, and most slaves, were treated at home. Even the free poor were reluctant to use the public hospitals. For example, M. Doyle of Georgetown petitioned the Demerara-Essequibo Court of Policy for free medicine and the aid of physicians, stating that he had "often seen and often relieved, several good, useful, and industrious inhabitants, of this United Colony, suffering under fever, and other maladies; but who thought it unbecoming them, to go to the Public Hospital: and whose funds were inadequate, either to purchase medicines, or to employ a medical practitioner."[46] Private hospitals did accept slaves, but their charges were high. For example, the Trinidad Infirmary and Marine Hospital, in Port of Spain, operated by Drs. Neilson and Finlay, increased its daily charges in 1829 to 15s. for sailors, 12s. for free persons, and 10s. for slaves.[47] Once again, it seems probable that the exposure of urban slaves to European medicine varied with the comparative wealth of their owners. But the treatment of working-out slaves dependent on board-wages is uncertain.

As on plantations, efforts were made in the towns to isolate sufferers from contagious diseases. In 1808, for example, Dr. Dunkin, Surgeon Major of the Colonial and Poor's Hospital in Georgetown, Demerara, argued the need for a small house in the back part of the town to be used as a lazaretto for those suffering from yaws and other infectious diseases, the existing hut being in a miserable state. In 1812 he described the yaws house as "a miserable hovel" and represented that separate apartments should be fitted up in the Colonial Hospital for white patients suffering from yaws or leprosy.[48] The Colonial Hospital also came to house the mentally ill.[49] Small islands off the coasts of Trinidad, Grenada, and St. Vincent were used as asylums for lepers for a time, but the practice was abandoned by about 1820.[50] In Port of Spain a special house was built in 1824 on the heights of La Ventille, overlooking the town, for slave and free lepers. But by 1827 the Governor of the colony admitted that the scheme was a failure, chiefly because "there were families in the island of a certain standing in society, who had members afflicted with this malady, who would never consent to allow of their separation." In 1828 the lepers at La Ventille comprised four slaves, three free persons, and a white woman, all living in an open shed. They received no attention, no allowance of clothing, and only a ration of bread and fish from the Cabildo.[51] Lepers continued to beg in the streets.

The medicines used by European-trained doctors in the treatment of slaves matched the pharmacopoeia of contemporary Europe and North America. Although physicians believed that blacks and whites reacted differently to certain drugs, they generally employed much the same range. Most of the drugs were imported. For example, a Bridgetown apothecary advertised in 1809 that he had imported from London, inter alia, yellow, red, and pale bark (cinchona), tincture of bark, musk, camomile flowers, Turkey and East India rhubarb, sarsaparilla, gum arabic, opium, camphor, ammoniaoum, myrrh, sassafras and elm bark, isinglass, senna, manna, lavender and rose water, opodeldoc, analeptic, calcined magnesia, spices, sago, tapioca, barley, oatmeal, barley sugar, honey water, balsam of honey, botanical syrup and nervous cordial, cardiac nervous tincture, and detergent pills.[52] In 1811 W. Reed, Doctor of Medicine and Surgeon, and G. Murray, Apothecary and Druggist, offered at their Bridgetown shop a range of specifics "prepared for occasional use": draughts to strengthen the stomach when a vomit was required, purging pills, febrifuge drops for a cold or fever whether attended with cough or diarrhea, worm powders and bitters to prevent the return of the disease, antiscorbutic drops to cure the first stage of consumption and to give relief in its later stages, drops for fever and ague, ringworm ointment, and specific antivenereal drops to be taken in the worst stages and pills for the more local stages.[53] Seth Driggs informed the public of Port of Spain in 1821 that he had received a new shipment of medicines, prepared by the chemists Savory, Moore, and Davidson of Bond Street, London, including genuine Peruvian bark, Turkey rhubarb, powdered jalap, sarsaparilla, sago, Epsom and Glauber salts, and much more.[54] In 1829 the Driggses advertised a variety of new French medicines such as sulphate of quinine, piperine, gentianine, acetate of morphine, sulphate of morphine, emitine, and strichnine, as well as a large supply of fine Lisbon leeches.[55] When Thomas Maitland left Carriacou for Europe in 1815, he offered for sale his entire stock of medicines: *powder* of jalap, rhubarb, yellow bark, pale bark, cremor tartar, ipecacuhan, seneka, aromatic, and savin; *tincture* of jalap, lavender, myrrh, sacrid, rhubarb, galbanum, opium, black hellebore, castor, assafetida, kino, valerian; *spirit* of hartshorn, turpentine, ammoniac, sweet nitre, aromatic volatile; *flowers* of sulphur, chamomile, zinc, benzoine; *oils* of olive, almonds, cloves, peppermint, anise, cinnamon, origanum, juniper, nutmegs, rosemary; Rochelle salts; Dragons' blood; and so on.[56]

Precisely how the European-trained doctors applied this pharmacopoeia in prescribing for slave patients is less certain, and each doctor tended to have his favorite cures. As noted earlier, medicines were sometimes supplied by the doctors, while other planters maintained their own stocks. Urban slaveowners probably purchased directly from apothecaries and may have attempted their own cures. In addition to medicines, the owners generally ensured that sick slaves received a more nourishing diet than usual. Mount Gay Plantation, Barbados, for example, made occasional special purchases of cocoa, rice, ginger, biscuits, flour, poultry, and port wine, while the attorney of Newton claimed in 1801 that sickly children on the plantation were "fed with our food, from our very table, and partake as our children."[57]

In Jamaica sick slaves were sometimes sent to take the mineral waters of the island's spas.[58] It is not clear whether slaves ever enjoyed the hot mineral baths of Nevis,[59] but the sick were sometimes sent from colony to colony in the eastern Caribbean for a "change of air" or surgery. In Demerara the Collector of Customs claimed in 1831 that he "almost daily" received requests for the movement of slaves for the sake of their health, "a sea voyage and change of climate being the only remedy for the low fevers of the colony."[60] In 1830 a Bermuda-born slave living in Grenada died at sea on the way to Quebec, "being sent away for the benefit of his health."[61] But such special treatment seems generally to have been reserved for domestics and the most valuable tradespeople.

The medical care provided by slaveowners was designed to preserve the health and fitness to labor of their slaves. Thus, the most expensive surgery was generally confined to young and healthy skilled slaves, and the aged could expect little concern. The attorney who could report to an absentee proprietor that "most of those dead were really people that did nothing and died of mere old age" felt well satisfied.[62] At the beginning of the nineteenth century some owners continued to evict aged, diseased slaves from their plantations, simply in order to avoid the expense of caring for them once they ceased to be productive.[63] On the other hand, slaves who promised years of potentially productive labor were worth preserving. Differential treatment also underlined the hierarchy of statuses within the slave community. For example, in 1816 Mount Gay Plantation paid the Goodridges £7 10s. for reducing a compound fracture of both bones in Fanny Princess's leg, £3 15s. for a double elastic steel truss for Sandy, and 30s. for a vial of Ruspino's Styptic for Mingo.[64] But whereas doctors found it profitable to provide basic treatment for slaves at cut rates, they made no distinctions in their charges for more complicated surgery, and this suggests that the market for major operations was limited. This pattern was shown clearly in the table of rates set by the Medical Board of Trinidad in 1821. Daytime visits in town cost 6s. for slaves, but 12s. for free colored people and 18s. for whites. The set rates for whites were double those for slaves in bleeding, opening abscesses, extracting teeth, vaccination, and midwifery in cases of natural labor. But the charge for midwifery in difficult labor was £36 for slaves and £45 for whites, and no distinction was made between slaves and whites when doctors were called to amputate, trepan, tap the abdomen, or heal fractures, dislocations, or venereal disease.[65] Most doctors regarded the treatment of slaves, at a fixed annual fee, as their bread and butter, but looked to the white population for anything more immediately lucrative.

Alongside these efforts of the masters to provide medical care for their slaves, the slaves themselves performed a variety of prophylactic and curative practices. The most spectacular of these were generally associated with magico-religious activities, but the slaves also made use of a wide range of less remarkable medical materials. It is difficult to establish whether there were any significant differences between the colonies in this respect, though it seems likely that the particular ethnic origins of the Africans and the proportion of creoles in the population had an effect. Whether there were differences between the practices of town and country slaves is even less certain.

The treatments employed by slaves were said to consist chiefly of hot baths of herbs.[66] But, although the slaves did not employ the "heroic" methods of contemporary European medicine, they did use the indigenous flora to produce emetics, for example. Dr. Titford recorded a wide range of uses of plants by the slaves of Jamaica, including cures for ulcers, venereal disease, and dropsy. In collecting this information, he said, "I was assisted by a negro doctress, whose fame was great in the Red Hills, and whose knowledge, in the opinion of the negroes, was far superior to that of physicians."[67] Slaves also employed inoculation as a preventive measure, particularly against yaws. Dr. David Mason reported in 1831 that "mothers inoculate their infants about the period of weaning, that they may be indulged in nursing them until their recovery; and many, from an African opinion and custom in that country, that children should undergo the disease at an early period of life." He also observed an African practice, "in use among the ignorant negro empirics," of immersing the feet of slaves suffering from crab yaws in a watery decoction of herbs kept near boiling point. This effectively removed the tubercles, but Mason thought the practice "dangerous."[68]

The slave *obeah*, or *confu*, man (sorcery man) sometimes exercised considerable power over a slave community in opposition to that of white medical practice. This conflict may be exemplified by the case of Willem, a creole field laborer on Plantation Buses Lust, Berbice, who was charged in 1821 with the murder of Madalon, a field slave "with African marks on the breast" who belonged to Plantation Op Hoop van Beter.[69] According to the slave Isaac, who described him as "a real Obiah man (Confou man)," Willem "was brought first to the estate by a negro of Op Hoop van Beter, named Fortuyn; he had one of his wives sick." Kees, the logie driver, stated that "I heard Willem tell Madalon she was the bad woman who caused so many strong healthy people on the estate to become sick." Madalon denied this, but was beaten by a group of slaves, on the orders of Willem. Another African field laborer, Adolff, made a revealing statement:

Denies having been present at the punishment of Madalon, he being confined in the hospital; but the man Willem, who said he was sent by God Almighty, came to the hospital. His child was sick, and his wife and another child were also in the hospital with him. Willem directed the children to be brought out, which they were by himself and his wife, and were washed by Willem, who took off two bits that were tied round the neck of one of them.[70]

All of this suggests that the obeahman was sought after by slaves for curative purposes, that he could overrule the authority of the planter's slave hospital, and that he could exact payment for his services.

In summary, the slaveowners of the British Caribbean provided a standard of medical care which was relatively good in terms of the contemporary European tradition. Many of the doctors they employed had only limited professional qualifications, but there were increasing efforts after 1807 to restrict entry through systems of licensing. These controls applied to apothecaries and druggists as well as physicians and surgeons. The physical architecture of slave hospitals also improved somewhat after 1807. There were significant, though not readily quantifiable, differences in the nature of the medical care provided, however. Slaves living on large holdings or belonging to wealthy townspeople probably were attended by practitioners with higher European qualifications than were those living on small holdings or in the marginal colonies. It also appears that the most valuable slaves received the greatest amount of attention. But in spite of the efforts of the masters to provide medical care, the slaves remained reluctant to accept the treatments they offered and continued to seek out the services of black doctors. The weakness of the system of medical care offered by the masters lay not so much in a lack of practitioners, hospital beds, or medicines, but in the very inadequate understanding of etiology in the contemporary European tradition of medicine.

ETIOLOGICAL THEORIES

In the early nineteenth century, European-derived understanding of the causes of disease was dominated by the concept of miasma, the influence of noxious exhalations from putrescent organic matter. This theory, which emerged in the seventeenth century, did not completely displace humoral theory or practice. It was associated with a renewed empiricism in European medicine which resulted in certain successes, notably the use of chichona bark to treat malaria, and inoculation and vaccination to prevent smallpox. But the empiricism associated with the development of miasmatic theory went together with the doctors' increased efforts to alter the body's internal, humoral balance in this so-called "heroic" age of medicine by bleeding, blistering, and purging. It was this practice, rather than the miasmatic theory, that ensured the doctors killed more often than they cured.

The miasmatic theory of etiololgy also led to some valuable empirical findings in the area of public health. Thus, the empirical linking of disease, especially "fevers," with areas of stagnant water and other sources of "poisonous effluvium" or atmospheric pollution led to improved levels of hygiene and health. But, since they remained ignorant of the germ theory of disease, doctors practicing in the period before 1850 universally failed to understand the reasons for their successes.

The miasmatic theory is a well-worn theme, and it does not seem necessary to describe in detail its explication in the writings of Europeans practicing medicine in the West Indies.[71] Rather, the theory will be illustrated here by looking at general attitudes toward public health and at the particular efforts made to meet the threat of cholera at the end of the period.

Public Health

Attempts to improve the public health of West Indian populations began in the towns. As in the case of the establishment of public hospitals, this urban focus may readily be explained by the presence there of a great concentration of whites and the need to impose a higher authority on the behavior of townspeople than was acceptable in the private world of the plantation. Most of the evidence comes from complaints about abuses, but this does provide a vivid picture of the poor state of urban sanitation and brings out the underlying concepts employed to counteract it. The complaints varied little in the major towns, and again it is possible to make a clear distinction between patterns of life in town and country.

In Port of Spain the Governor ordered in 1813 that all inhabitants of the town should clean the pavements in front of their lots and remove all dirt and rubbish each Wednesday morning and Saturday evening.[72] By 1814 it was clear to the Cabildo that stiffer penalties were needed to ensure the cleanliness of the town, since many people continued to throw their filth into the middle of the streets at night. Thus, it ordered that all persons so doing be fined £4, while slaves were to be given 25 lashes at the jail and remain imprisoned until the fine was paid by their master.[73] In the same year, the Cabildo began to make efforts to isolate the lepers who roamed the town, and the Medical Board was established.[74] The vacant lots of Port of Spain became the prime locations for people wishing to get rid of their filth and, said the governor in 1816, were covered in brushwood, which impeded the circulation of air. He ordered that all these lots be cleared, surrounded with brick walls, and cultivated as gardens or put under Guinea grass.[75] But in 1817 the Cabildo had to remark that ''a custom prevails and has of late increased among the inhabitants of this town in using the public streets and places, vacant unfenced lots etc., as receptacles for dirt and filth of every description,'' and reviewed the fines for such offenses. It also ordered that all houses in the town lacking privies should have them built.[76] In 1818 it specified that a pit was to be dug under each privy to a minimum depth of four feet, except where the land was so low that water was found at this level.[77] Filth remained a concern, however, and in 1819 an entrepreneur offered to set up an establishment of carts and slaves to remove dirt and dung from the houses of Port of Spain, in return for a ''liberal remuneration.'' But the Cabildo argued that the manure would be so valuable to the planters that it would be a paying concern and would not require official support.[78] Nothing came of the scheme, and by 1822 the Cabildo was complaining of a noxious and disagreeable nuisance ''in consequence of the filth and nastiness [ordure] of the town, being emptied into the sea, off the different wharves.'' Two locations in the town were set aside as dung heaps.[79] Finally, in 1824 the Cabildo decided to purchase two horses to pull carts through the main streets of Port of Spain, preceded by eight slaves sweeping the streets, and the townspeople were ordered to throw their dirt into the passing carts.[80] This acceptance of public responsibility was short-lived, for the Cabildo sold its slaves in 1828, employed a contractor until 1830, and then asked the inhabitants to resume the duty with a little help from the chain gang.[81] Only when cholera threatened in 1832 did the Cabildo send its cart back into the streets.[82]

As well as these erratic attempts to cleanse Port of Spain, the Medical Board through the Cabildo made efforts to ensure that bodies were buried promptly during epidemics. In 1831 it reduced the cost of interment to 30s. for an adult slave and £5 for a white.[83] The Cabildo sought to ensure that animals were slaughtered only in the public market and that the meat was carried in barrows and covered with clean cloths, rather than on the heads of slaves. It also recognized a need to enclose the market house with trellis work to prevent corbeaux entering, since "as soon as the market was over numbers of these birds flew into the market house and dirtied the tables, scales, chopping blocks, benches etc. etc. which it was very difficult to clean."[84] More importantly, the Cabildo took preventive measures against small-pox and cholera, which will be discussed separately.

The public health responsibilities of the Port of Spain Cabildo were matched with only minor variations in the other major towns of the West Indies, except that the Cabildo, inherited from the Spanish, constituted a more powerful town council than the parish vestries of the older British colonies. The Town Regulations of Georgetown, proclaimed in 1803, declared that

every person who occupies a house in the town of Stabroek or on the front lands of the plantations Werk en Rust and Vlissengen . . . shall within fourteen days of the publishing of these be obliged, to have such part of the road, street, dam or path, as is adjoining to his lot, cleared of dung or dirt that may be thereon, and have the same, as all filth from the lots on every subsequent day, carried to a punt, which is to lay every morning, from six till ten o'clock in the river near the landing place with the crane, from where the same will be carried and thrown into deep water.[85]

But many of the inhabitants, said the Governor in 1806, "neglected entirely to weed and cleanse their lots of land and the trenches that surround them, which may finally prove extremely hurtful to their own health."[86] The cleansing of the trenches was not made a matter of public responsibility, however, and some contemporaries actually argued that the tidal movement on the coast of Demerara created a relatively healthy environment.[87] Others related the lack of fresh water sources in Georgetown to "the mortality of the slave population, from diseases occasioned by the use of creek and trench water during the dry seasons."[88] While disease and miasma were associated with stagnant waters, breezes from the sea or large rivers were seen as especially healthful. Thus, the merchants of Georgetown argued in 1828 that the Colonial Hospital should be moved to "a more salubrious and remote spot," because the building up of the town meant that "the hitherto free current of air from the river will be shut out from the hospital the situation of which will be thus rendered more inappropriate for such an estabishment than what it now is.''[89]

It 1815 the Commissioners for the town of St. George, Grenada, called tenders for the cleaning and repairing of the streets by sections, threatened to prosecute all those throwing rubbish other than at two specified locations, and offered a reward for every pig killed at large in the town.[90] These arrangements continued until emancipation, though with some lapses in public concern.[91] The owners of slaves who emptied chamber pots in the streets were prosecuted.[92]

With the exception of St. George, Port of Spain, and Georgetown, however, urban sanitation remained essentially a private matter, public authority confining itself to occasional exhortation. Dirt and dunghills remained common landmarks in the townscape. Pigs wallowed in the garbage, and gentlemen traversed the streets with eyes and nose averted, hoping for a downpour to wash it all into the sea. Sewerage was unknown.[93] In all of this, of course, the colonies did little more than reflect metropolitan practice.[94] West Indian towns of the early nineteenth century were, however, somewhat less noisome than those of the previous century, and in the last years of slavery the threat of cholera resulted in a more self-conscious effort to cleanse town and country.

Cholera

The cholera pandemic of 1826–37 flowed into the Caribbean from North America in 1832. Only Cuba was seriously affected during that epidemic, but when cholera returned in 1850 it took 30,000 lives in Jamaica alone. In the United States cholera took an appalling toll of the slave population, whereas other epidemic diseases such as yellow fever and malaria tended to affect whites more than blacks.[95] So the fact that the slave population of the British Caribbean escaped the cholera epidemic of the 1830s was of great significance for its demographic experience. Here the cholera epidemic of 1832 is of special interest not because of its actual impact on mortality levels but because of the reactions of the colonial governments to the threat, and the light these throw on attitudes toward public health.

Cholera is characterized by an acute diarrhea causing great loss of salt in the body. Death often results from dehydration and toxemia within hours of the onset of the disease. The agent, the *Vibrio cholerae,* thrives in conditions of high temperature and humidity. It must be eaten or drunk by the host, and cholera is most often contracted through infected drinking water or foods contaminated by infected water. It is commonly associated with poor sanitation and water supplies.[96]

In the early nineteenth century, the etiology of cholera was not understood. The West Indies watched the progress of the disease through Europe, the United States, and the Caribbean with dread and foreboding. When cholera appeared in Britain in October 1831, the Privy Council advised the colonies of the preventive measures adopted there and urged that preparations be made. These instructions, which reached the West Indies in December, included the establishment of town Boards of Health, quarantine, the isolation of infected persons in separate houses, burning of all decaying matter, and the removal of filth, cleansing of drains and privies with chloride and lime, lime-washing of all woodwork in houses, ensuring the free flow of air, and the prevention of contagion.[97] Grenada seems to have been the first colony to react to these warnings and quickly ordered that all vessels entering the colony's port should anchor in the bay and be inspected by a medical practitioner.[98] Barbados did not introduce such simple quarantine measures until March 1832, when a Board of Health was established and the parish Commissioners of Public Roads were ordered to remove all filth and nuisances from the gutters. The streets of Bridgetown were filthy and full of puddles and cluttered with enormous piles of foul stuff, "the exhalations from which are enough to generate a pestilence without the Asiatic Cholera reaching us."[99] As the threat from the "grievous disease" increased, the Governor of Barbados proclaimed 16 May a public day of fasting and humiliation to be observed by all classes. Showing similar doubts about the efficacy of the preventive measures, the governor or Grenada proclaimed that 20 June,

be kept and observed as a day of general fasting, and of public humiliation throughout this Government, that every inhabitant thereof may humble himself before God, in order to obtain pardon of his sins, and in the most solemn and devout manner offer up his prayers at the Throne of Grace, that the Almighty, of his great mercy, may be pleased to avert and turn aside the heavy calamity which he has permitted to visit so many parts of this globe.[100]

But since the epidemic seemed not to have been turned aside, news of its spread into North America led to renewed practical efforts in the Caribbean. The Street Commissioners of Grenada, calling tenders for the cleaning of St. George in August 1832, asked the townspeople to assist, since the cholera was "always understood to be attended with the greatest fatality in places of a filthy and unwholesome description—the approach of which there is but too much reason to apprehend in these colonies."[101] At the same time the parish Boards of Health in Grenada continued to press the need to clean and ventilate houses, yards, and lanes and to remove all hog-sties and rubbish heaps likely to produce "foul air." Beyond the towns, it was directed that all hogs be removed from slave houses, and all sties and filth taken away. The slaves' houses, and hospitals and nurseries, were to be cleansed and whitewashed inside. Any brushwood preventing ventilation was to be removed.[102] In British Guiana Boards of Health were finally created in August 1832, and a Cholera Hospital established in Georgetown. These Boards made the usual recommendations regarding lime-washing, ventilation, and the cleaning of trenches, but also called for a completion of the drainage of Georgetown and the fumigation of vessels in the river.[103] Trinidad did not establish Boards of Health, but the Medical Board cooperated with the Cabildo in inspecting the barrios of Port of Spain. The Cabildo renewed its efforts to clean the streets and freely supplied lime for whitewashing and throwing in privies.[104] In September 1832 the the Trinidad Medical Society was established. Its aims were the advancement of medical science, including the investigation of epidemics, and most particularly the "spasmodic cholera."[105] After reading all the literature available, a committee of the society reported the following predisposing causes:

Dissipation and excesses of every kind, particularly in eating and drinking. Excessive fatigue of body; distress or over exertion of mind. Exposure to cold and damp. The use of acescent [sour] vegetable food and fruit. The habit of taking medicines unnecessarily, particularly nostrums and neutral salts. Want of sufficient clothing and wholesome food. The absence of personal and domestic cleanliness. Foul air. Panic, or apprehension of being taken ill.[106]

This list is a splendid illustration of the mixture of fact and fantasy which existed in the West Indies during the period of threatened cholera. While it shows an appreciation of some of the sources of the agent, though not the agent itself, this knowledge is confused with psychosomatic and miasmatic factors. A similar emphasis on the role of "atmosphere" was found elsewhere in the West Indies and may be symbolized by the New Amsterdam Board of Health's decree that "no person dying of cholera be admitted to burial in the yard of the English Church, it being to windward of the town."[107]

The Trinidad Medical Society did demonstrate a recognition of the social selectivity of cholera, and this was reflected in the precautionary measures it recommended. For the "upper classes" it advised the avoidance of panic, a moderate diet, free ventilation, keeping the body and feet warm and dry, wearing flannel or calico next to the skin, moderate exercise, and attention to symptoms of diarrhea. Faith in the flannel binder and "cholera belt" was related to the humoral theory of "obstructed perspiration."[108] For the "poorer classes" the Society recommended the same precautions that were directed to their superiors, together with a strict moderation in the use of liquors, but also noted that the indigent needed help to make their dwellings clean and comfortable.[109] Similarly, the St. George Board of Health believed that cholera's favorite localities were "low, overcrowded, narrow and filthy lanes and streets,"while "poverty, dissipated habits, drunkenness, or an abuse of rum, predispose in an especial manner to this disease."[110] The Board advised the use of castor oil, laudanum, and flannel binders. Bags of hot sand, water bottles, or hot bricks were to be applied to the feet, back, and belly to induce vomiting. Some believed that immediate bleeding was an effective cure for whites but not blacks.[111] Fortunately for the survival of the slave population, it did not have to suffer the full force of a cholera epidemic or the heroic attentions of the white doctors.

It is improbable that the preventive measures adopted by the masters had any role in diverting cholera in 1832, but they do show how basic public health measures emerged from a maze of environmental mystery. The system of quarantine was too loose to have been effective,[112] and although the cleansing of streets and trenches might have helped to avoid catastrophic levels of mortality, it did not strike at the root of the problem. Few of the towns had piped water, and most depended on public or private wells, while slaves often washed themselves in the same streams that were used for the washing of clothes.[113] There is every reason to believe that had cholera been introduced to the British Caribbean in 1832 it would have been at least as devastating as the epidemic of 1850, spreading rapidly through the towns and plantations and causing particularly heavy mortality among the slaves.

SMALLPOX

The etiology of smallpox was little better understood than that of cholera in the early nineteenth century, but the empirical knowledge that quarantine, inoculation, and vaccination could be used to control the diseases provided relatively effective preventive measures. These measures applied to slaves as well as free people because the masters wished to preserve their slave property and, equally important, because they feared contagion.

Inoculation was introduced to the West Indies in the 1770s, and Jenner's plan of vaccination spread rapidly after 1800.[114] The owners of large plantations usually employed the regular estate doctors to inoculate or vaccinate their slaves, at an additional fee of 6s. 3d. per slave.[115] But the smaller slaveowners, especially those in the towns, were more resistant to the innovation. As early as 1805 a Barbadian newspaper, noticing the death of a child from the "contagious disease," felt justified in pointing out "the criminality of those who, by refusing or neglecting to adopt *vaccine inoculation,* continue to subject themselves, their families, and the community, to all the horrors of the most pestiferous disease that ever scourged mankind."[116] There were also fears that the disease was being spread by inoculation with natural smallpox. This practice, which was the traditional method of building up immunities in African and Asian societies and was the origin of inoculation in European medicine, carried greater risks than inoculation with cowpox since it meant an actual culture of the disease. In 1808, when smallpox was detected on most slave ships coming to Demerara via Barbados and quarantine seemed unable to control the disease, the Court of Policy prohibited any planter or medical practitioner from inoculating with smallpox, and all cases of natural smallpox were to be confined and reported to the Colonial Officer of Health. At the same time, planters were advised to inoculate their slaves with cowpox.[117]

Jamaica created a Vaccine Establishment, modeled on the British National Vaccine Establishment, in 1813. It operated from the Kingston Public Hospital and provided vaccinations free of charge, but its chief aim was to ensure a continuous supply of lymph rather than depending on imports from Britain. The lymph was distributed to the country doctors and was applied to slave and free alike. Although there was some resistance to vaccination, smallpox had virtually disappeared from Jamaica by the early 1820s.[118]

Elsewhere, public concern with smallpox remained dormant until the disease reappeared on a large scale in most of the colonies at the beginning of 1819. In Demerara-Essequibo there was a rush to vaccinate the population when a slave imported from St. Vincent died and when smallpox raged in neighboring Surinam. The Court of Policy considered the success of the National Vaccine Establishment in Britain but concluded that legislation to enforce vaccination was unnecessary, since almost all planters had performed it at the first call. The evidence of medical practitioners, however, shows that this was not the case. F. Roose, whose practice included the infected estates, reported that he had vaccinated 2,103 slaves on seven estates, but that no provision had been made for vaccination on the other five estates in his practice.[119] The Court confined its activities to exhortation, vaccination in town by the Surgeon Major, and the erection of a building on the outskirts of Georgetown to house any patients. By 1825 it was said that the Smallpox Hospital was no longer needed, and a slave was put in charge of the building.[120] When smallpox again raged in the islands in 1827 and was described as "a disease so fatal to a black population," Demerara-Essequibo's precautions were confined to the searching of island vessels by the officer of health.[121]

More positive action was taken in the island colonies. In March 1819 an order of government required a general vaccination in Trinidad. Medical practitioners were ordered, "under pain of suspension of their licences," to extend vaccination "to the utmost of their power," and "all inhabitants are required to attend, and to cause their families, children, and servants to attend, and all proprietors of slaves are required to cause their slaves to attend to be vaccinated." A certificate of vaccination was to be given and fixed in the plantation journal. In Port of Spain all houses were to be visited by a doctor and alcalde (magistrate), and vaccination performed when necessary. A placard was placed on each house containing patients, and householders were fined if they appeared on the street. But it was believed that some people continued to inoculate their children with smallpox, believing vaccination to be ineffective, and a heavy fine was imposed on such offenders.[122] The number of smallpox cases in Port of Spain, slave and free, declined rapidly to less than 100, but a prejudice against vaccination remained. Thus, a Vaccine Establishment was created in June 1819, with a Public Vaccinator at a salary of £300. All persons arriving in the colony, including slaves, were to be vaccinated within one week of arrival. The Registrar of Slaves was to demand a certificate of examination by the Vaccinator for all imported slaves on registration. Children were to be vaccinated within a month of birth. Doctors attended the Vaccine Establishment on a weekly roster, receiving 12s. for each person vaccinated.[123] In the six months to August 1819 some 1,445 people were vaccinated in Port of Spain, but 202 of these were "doubtful or unsuccessful" cases. There were 1,226 cases of smallpox, 201 of them contracted after doubtful vaccination, 12 after supposedly successful vaccination, and 194 after vaccination in earlier years. Of the 128 deaths from smallpox, 56 percent of them slaves, 26 followed recent or previous vaccination.[124] Although vaccination in Trinidad and elsewhere drastically reduced smallpox mortality, it remained sufficiently risky to support the prejudices against it. Smallpox completely disappeared from the list of causes of death for all classes in Trinidad between 1823 and 1825, and when the disease reemerged in 1827 it was said that the island had little to fear since "a very large proportion of the population have been vaccinated." [125] The Vaccine Establishment continued to function until emancipation and beyond, but as late as 1831 the Public Vaccinator complained that the "lower orders" remained reluctant to have their children vaccinated. [126] This reluctance was probably confined to freedpeople, since slaves had no choice, though some small slaveowners may have been resistant.

Smallpox came to Barbados on a schooner from St. Lucia in May 1819. The island's assembly authorized the Commander in Chief to send away vessels carrying smallpox or any other contagious disease, while the Governor proclaimed that all inhabitants should seek vaccination as the only effective remedy. [127] But no Vaccine Establishment was created, and when the smallpox returned to Barbados in later years it was feared that many children were not protected. [128] In the smaller colonies vaccine lymph was not regularly available, however, and when cases were imported it was often necessary to obtain supplies from Trinidad or even Martinique. Grenada, St. Vincent, Dominica, Antigua, St. Kitts, and the Bahamas all suffered from this lack in the later 1820s and early 1830s. Large proportions of the populations remained unvaccinated, partly because of the shortage of lymph and partly because of the slaveowners' reluctance to pay the additional doctors' fees where vaccination was not compulsory. Antigua and Dominica, for example, also lacked any kind of quarantine legislation. In some cases, as in the Bahamas in 1829, smallpox was particularly destructive in the freedman and slave populations. [129] This relatively high mortality may be attributed to the much more limited scope of vaccination in the smaller colonies and the uncontrolled movement of people, which derived from a less developed sense of responsibility for public health.

INDICATORS OF HEALTH STATUS

Previous sections of this chapter have been concerned principally with the kinds of medical attention imposed on the slaves and the healthfulness of the environments in which they lived. What follows will consist of an attempt to analyze the interactions between medical care, infection, nutrition, and work regimes in terms of a number of indicators of the health status of the slave populations. Mortality and cause-of-death patterns will be discussed in chapter 9, and here only the following indicators will be considered: physical growth and deformities, morbidity, and evidence of malnutrition.

Physical Growth

The growth curves of children and the heights finally achieved by adults are valuable indicators of the health of a community, particularly in terms of nutri-

Table 8.1. *Heights (cm) of Slaves Aged 25–40 Years by Sex and Birthplace: Trinidad, St. Lucia, Berbice, Cuba, and the United States*

Birthplace	Males			Females		
	No.	Mean	S.D.	No.	Mean	S.D.
Trinidad, 1813						
Africans	4,911	163.3	8.1	3,331	153.9	8.1
Creoles	128	165.6	7.6	149	154.9	8.4
St. Lucia, 1815						
Africans	787	162.7	8.7	684	153.5	9.0
Creoles	1,284	164.8	9.1	1,688	155.4	9.1
Berbice, 1819						
Africans	2,127	163.6	7.4	1,318	154.1	7.6
Creoles	230	163.2	8.3	208	154.2	8.0
Cuba, 1855–59						
Africans	640	158.4	10.5	434	150.4	8.8
Creoles	280	161.5	8.1	281	154.2	7.6
United States, 1828–60						
Total (Engerman)	518	171.6	n.a.	299	158.6	n.a.
Total (Steckel)	780	170.8	8.0	508	159.5	8.1

Sources: T.71/501–3 (Trinidad); T.71/378–79 (St. Lucia); T.71/437–39 (Berbice); Manuel Moreno Fraginals, "Africa in Cuba," *Annals of the New York Academy of Sciences* 292 (1977): 198 (Cuba); Stanley L. Engerman, "The Height of Slaves in the United States," *Local Population Studies,* 16 (1976): 45–50; Richard H. Steckel, "Slave Height Profiles from Coastwise Manifests," *Explorations in Economic History* 16 (1979): 368.

tional status, infection, and psychological stress, though the precise nature of the interactions involved remain poorly understood.[130] Unfortunately, the slave registration returns do not provide complete data on the stature of slaves in the British Caribbean, so that the potential for comparative analysis is narrowed, but they do contain probably the largest sample available for any population in the early nineteenth century. Height data are available for more than 50,000 slaves in Trinidad, St. Lucia, and Berbice. Detailed results for Trinidad, together with a sample for Berbice and broad comparisons with modern Afro-American populations, have been reported elsewhere.[131] Here a complete comparative analysis is presented only for the slave populations.

In Trinidad and St. Lucia, adult creole slaves were taller than African-born slaves (table 8.1). An even larger differential has been reported for a sample of "men" and "women" slaves in Cuba later in the nineteenth century. But in Berbice in 1819 adult male creoles were somewhat shorter than male Africans, and there was no significant difference between the heights of female creoles and Africans. Another example of inferior creole stature has been reported by Orlando Patterson for Jamaican slaves between 1794 and 1814, but this sample was not controlled for age, and the fact that the creoles, both males (162.1 cm) and females

(152.4 cm), were shorter than most of the African groups identified may merely reflect their youth. In general, it seems that in most New World slave populations creoles, even of the first generation, exceeded the heights of slaves brought from Africa, but that in extreme conditions, as in Berbice, stature reduction occurred.

Within the African-born slave population, there were significant differences between the particular ethnic/regional groups (tables S6.2–6.4). The tallest adult males, exceeding 165 cm, came from Senegambia, Sierra Leone, and the Bight of Benin, while the shortest, under 162 cm, were those from Central Africa (Congo-Angola). Adult females followed a similar pattern, those from the first three regions exceeding 155 cm and those from Central Africa being less than 153 cm. These patterns closely match those found by David Eltis in his study of recaptives disembarked at Sierra Leone between 1819 and 1839 and also fit regional variations in twentieth-century Africa.[132] The importance of these differences for the present analysis lies in the fact that after 1807 the slave populations of the British Caribbean were largely dominated by slaves from Central Africa and the Bight of Biafra, though with significant minorities of Senegambians (table 5.8). As noted in chapter 5, all of the colonies had a heterogeneous mix of Africans in the early nineteenth century, but the first-phase sugar colonies and the marginal colonies earlier received large proportions of slaves from the Windward Coast, the Gold Coast, and the Bight of Benin. The third-phase sugar colonies, by contrast, experienced a much briefer period of heavy slave importation in which particular regions dominated to a greater degree. To the extent that genetic factors or heterosis ("hybrid vigor") were important to determining the growth of slaves, it might be expected that creoles would be taller in the long-settled colonies. This may seem to be supported by the fact that in late-settled Cuba African slaves were significantly shorter than Africans in the British Caribbean and that although the Cuban-born creoles showed a greater height gain they remained shorter than creoles in the British colonies (table 8.1). Within the British Caribbean, however, the Africans of Berbice were taller than those in Trinidad and St. Lucia, while the creole offspring were shorter in Berbice. Thus, it appears that genetic factors and heterosis were less important than nutrition, environmental conditions, and work regime.

Of the three colonies for which large samples are available, adult creole males were tallest in Trinidad and shortest in Berbice. But among the females, St. Lucia had the tallest creoles. Thus, differences in the ethnic mix of these colonies seem to have little to do with variations in final height. All of these colonies were third-phase sugar colonies, of course, so they provide only a limited comparative perspective. More valuable for this purpose are the data available for slaves imported into Trinidad between 1819 and 1825, most of whom came as large population groups and were not selected on the basis of stature (table 8.2). These data show that adult creole slaves from the marginal colonies were consistently taller than those from the old sugar colonies, while both of these groups were probably taller than the Trinidad-born. This may be taken as indirect evidence that nutrition, disease environments, and work regimes were much more favorable to

Table 8.2. *Heights (cm) of Creole Slaves Aged 25–40 Years Imported into Trinidad, 1819–25, by Sex and Birthplace*

	Males			Females		
Birthplace	No.	Mean	S.D.	No.	Mean	S.D.
British sugar colonies						
Barbados	55	167.5	6.4	27	159.1	6.2
Grenada	25	168.2	5.6	23	158.3	6.9
St. Vincent	11	170.4	8.4	10	160.5	4.7
Dominica	37	168.0	7.4	36	158.3	4.6
Antigua	31	166.6	7.3	13	158.7	5.3
St. Kitts	13	168.0	8.3	8	156.5	10.1
Nevis	9	167.9	6.0	2	153.7	3.7
Montserrat	4	166.4	9.8	4	156.8	7.8
Virgin Islands	100	166.5	6.8	106	158.1	6.9
Total	285	167.3	6.9	229	158.3	6.4
British marginal colonies						
Bahamas	21	172.8	6.6	32	159.1	8.2
Anguilla	8	170.2	5.1	6	157.9	5.2
Grenadines	28	169.9	8.7	36	159.7	8.0
Bermuda	21	169.5	6.9	17	161.1	8.0
Total	78	170.6	7.3	91	159.6	8.0

Source: T.71/510–13.

growth in the marginal colonies than in the sugar plantation economies. It also appears that the nutritional and health status of slaves from the Windward Islands may have been superior to that of those from the first-phase sugar colonies, but here the samples are small. A similar contrast between the sugar colonies and the marginal colonies was apparent in the initial registration data for Trinidad, St. Lucia, and Berbice (tables S6.2–6.4).

Creole growth patterns in Trinidad, St. Lucia, Berbice, and the Bahamas are shown in figures 8.1 and 8.2. The Berbice curve moves erratically because of the small size of the sample at some ages, though the standard deviations differ little from those for Trinidad or St. Lucia (table S6.1). It seems clear, however, that slaves in each of these four colonies grew at much the same rate until about age 7, after which those in the Bahamas outpaced those in the sugar colonies. The curves for Trinidad, St. Lucia, and, probably, Berbice showed no significant differences. Thus, the relative slowing of growth after age 7 in the sugar colonies suggests a correlation with the introduction of children to heavy field labor rather than a nutritional difference. Infant female creoles were taller in the Bahamas than in the sugar colonies, but this was not true for males, so the evidence for the superior nutrition of mothers in the Bahamas is equivocal.[133]

Black slave children with African parents and colored slave children with mixed Afro-European parents differed little in their growth patterns. In Trinidad in

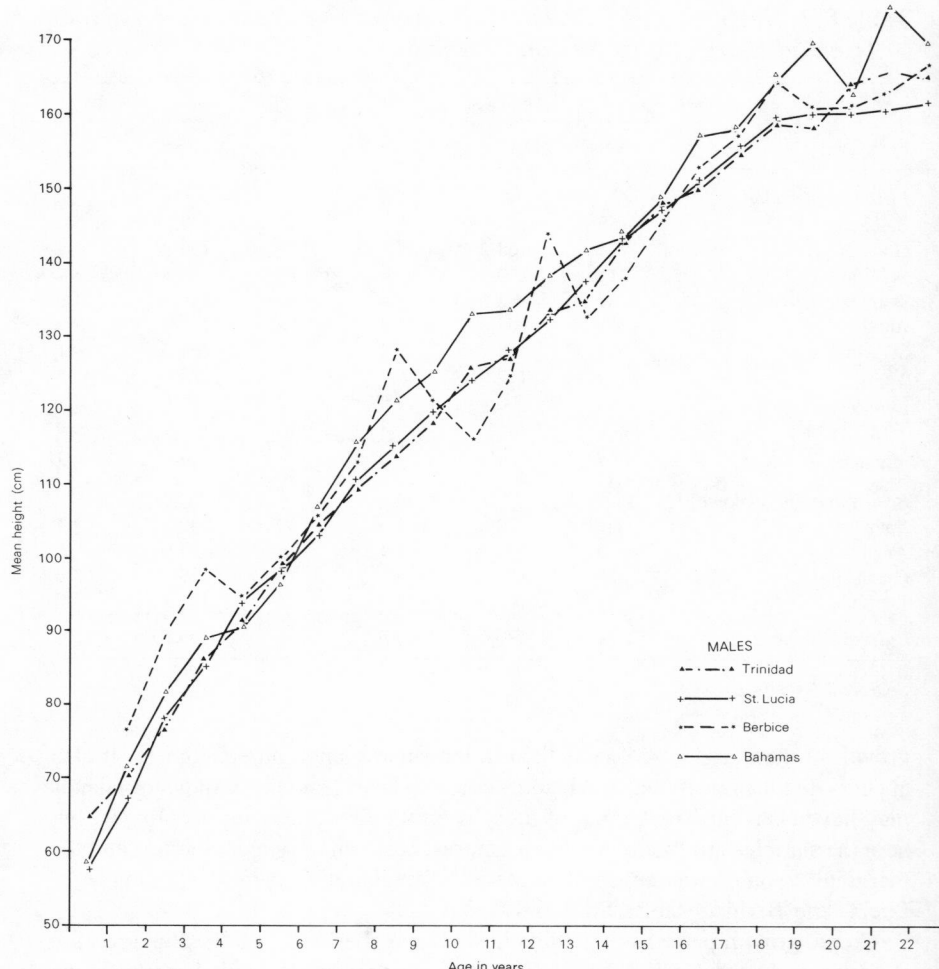

Fig. 8.1. *Heights of Creole Male Slaves by Age: Trinidad, 1813, St. Lucia, 1815, Berbice, 1819, and the Bahamas (Trinidad Imports), 1819–25.* (Sources: *table S6.1; T.71/510–13.*)

1813 male adult creoles aged 25–40 years achieved mean heights of 165.9 cm if black and 166.1 cm if colored; black females were 157.0 cm, and colored 156.1 cm. In Berbice colored males were slightly shorter than creole blacks, while colored females were taller than blacks (table S6.6). Only in St. Lucia did the colored show a clear superiority; in 1815 colored males were 2.2 cm taller than blacks, and colored females were 0.7 cm taller (table S6.5). But even in St. Lucia there were no significant differences between black and colored slaves in the

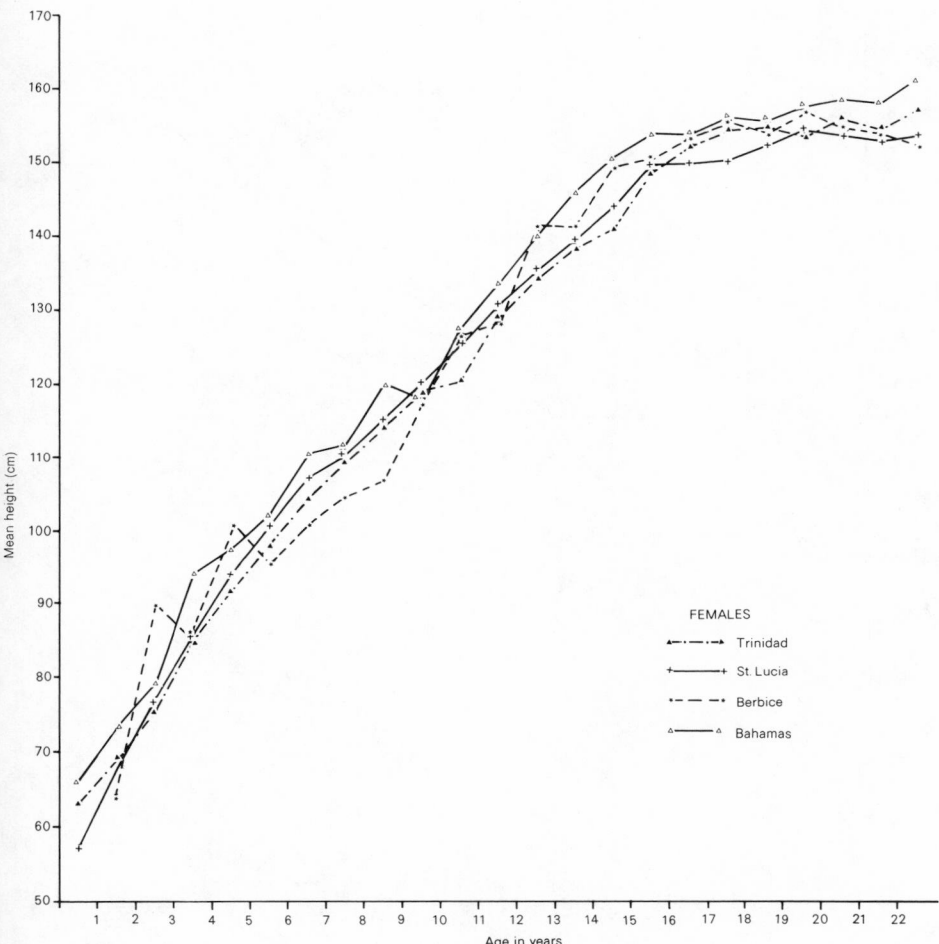

Fig. 8.2. *Heights of Creole Female Slaves by Age: Trinidad, 1813, St. Lucia, 1815, Berbice, 1819, and the Bahamas (Trinidad Imports), 1819–25. (Sources: table S6.1; T.71/510–13.)*

pattern of growth to maturity (figs. 8.3 and 8.4). Similar curves have been found in Trinidad.[134] Richard Steckel has found that color had no role in determining the heights of slaves in the United States.[135] These results fit the modern finding that Africans and Europeans have comparable growth potentials.[136] This suggests that heterosis was not important in determining the heights of slave children fathered by whites. Equally significant, it appears that the preference given colored slaves in terms of occupation and access to wealth did not result in any apparent growth differentials. It may be that the diets of colored slaves were much the same as for

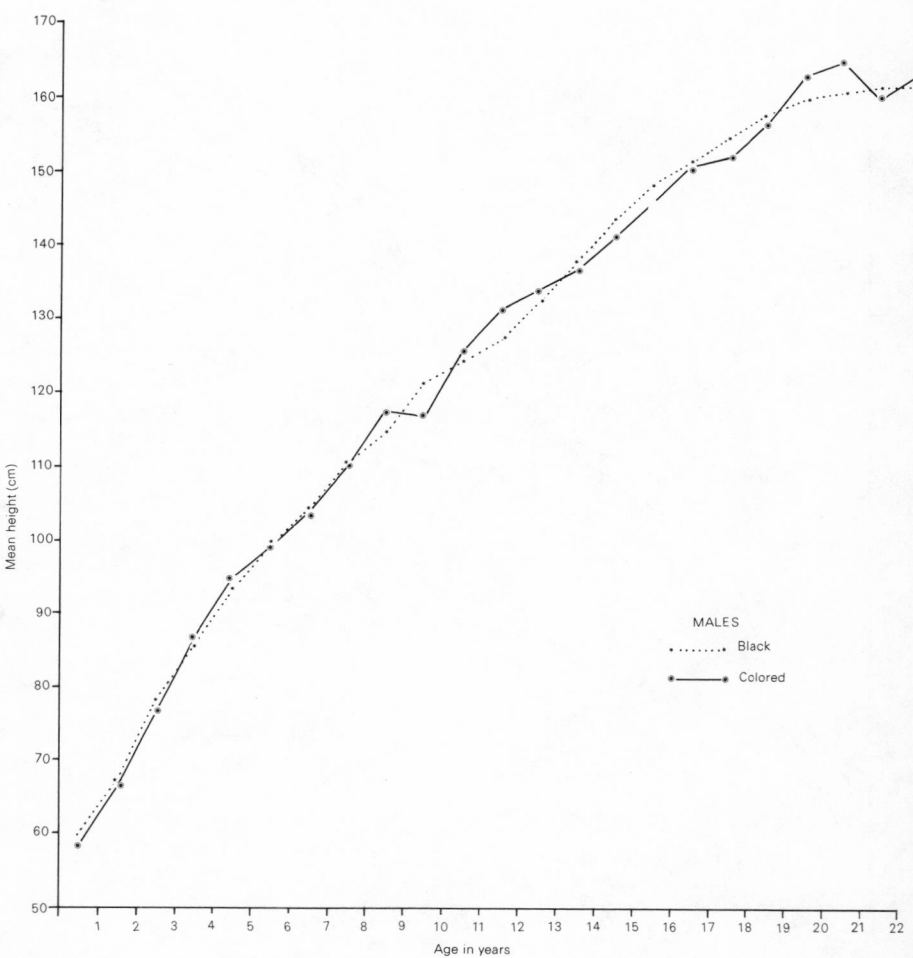

Fig. 8.3. *Heights of Creole Male Slaves by Age and Color: St. Lucia, 1815.*
(Source: *table S6.9.*)

blacks, or that colored slaves were increasingly refused preference in significant
numbers after 1807. Alternatively, nutritional advantages may have been confined
to the small group of "head people" among the colored.

Differences in the growth of slaves living in town and in the country were
similarly limited. In St. Lucia in 1815, adult male creoles aged 25–40 years were
taller in the towns (165.3 cm) than in the rural areas (164.6 cm), but urban females
(154.2 cm) were shorter than those in the countryside (155.6 cm). A similar
ambiguity was found in Trinidad. It must be noticed, however, that the heights of
slaves might have been taken into account in their allocation to particular occupations, stronger slaves possibly being chosen for plantation labor, so that any

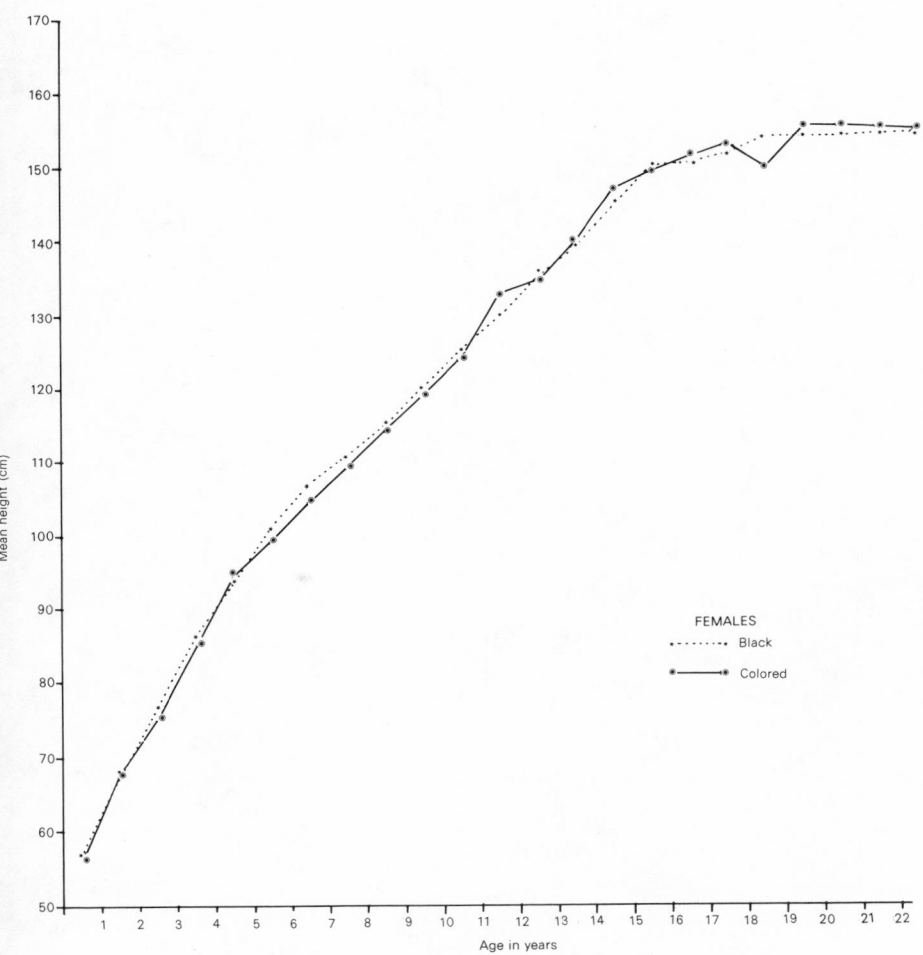

Fig. 8.4. *Heights of Creole Female Slaves by Age and Color: St. Lucia,*
    1815. (Source: *table S6.9.*)

differences in growth would be attributable to selective purchase rather than to the
long-term effect on growth of particular environments. This factor may be isolated
by comparing the heights of Africans, who did not grow up in the colonies but were
selected. In the case of St. Lucia it appears that although adult male Africans
working on plantations were 0.7 cm taller than those in the towns, female Africans
were 0.4 cm shorter. Thus, it seems that no systematic selection by height
occurred. Similarly, the growth curves of creoles in St. Lucia showed no significant differences between town and country (figs. 8.5 and 8.6). In general,
then, any differences in the nutritional health status of slaves livng in town and
country had no apparent impact on their patterns of physical growth.

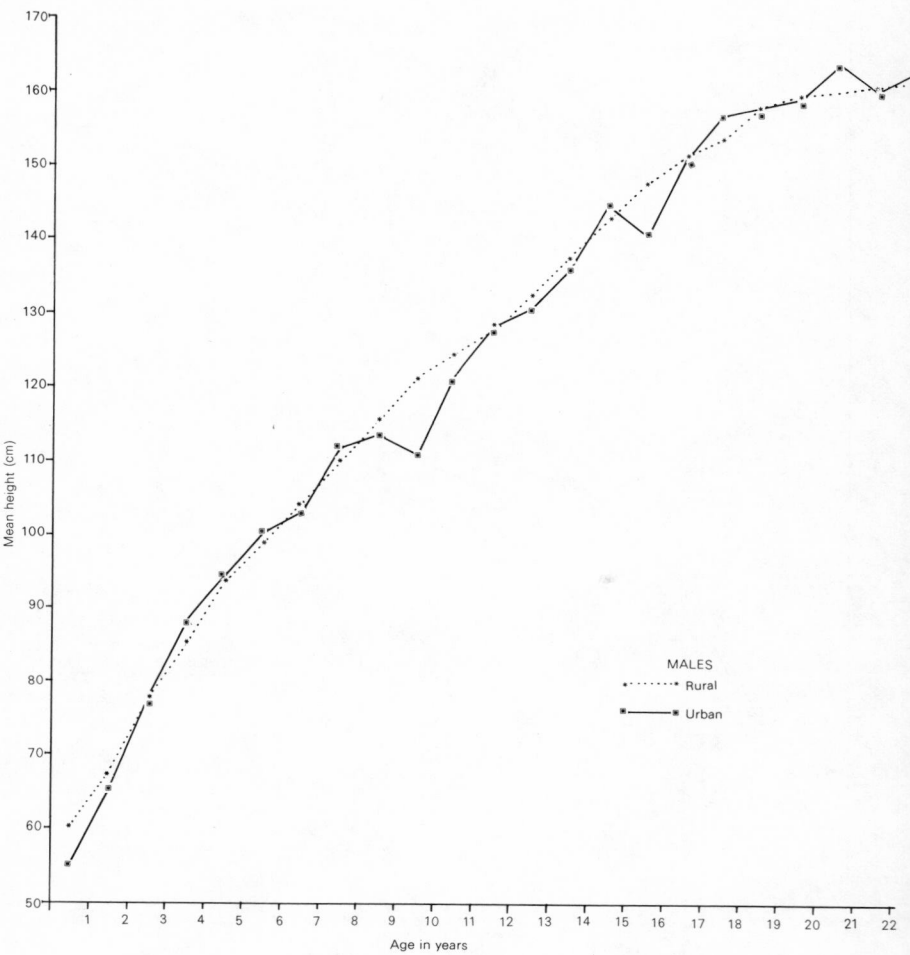

Fig. 8.5. *Heights of Rural and Urban Creole Male Slaves by Age: St. Lucia, 1815. (Source: table S6.10.)*

Occupational differences in height reflected the limited contrasts noted be-tween black and colored, and urban and rural, slaves. Some reasonably consistent differences in the heights of adult field laborers, domestics, and tradespeople did appear in St. Lucia and Berbice, but these were not observable in growth to maturity. In both of these colonies adult creoles employed as domestics were consistently taller than field laborers, while skilled tradespeople were even taller (tables S6.7–6.8). In Berbice, creole male drivers were taller than all of these groups, but in St. Lucia they were only as tall as the domestics. This pattern suggests that skilled tradespeople, both black and colored, enjoyed nutrition and

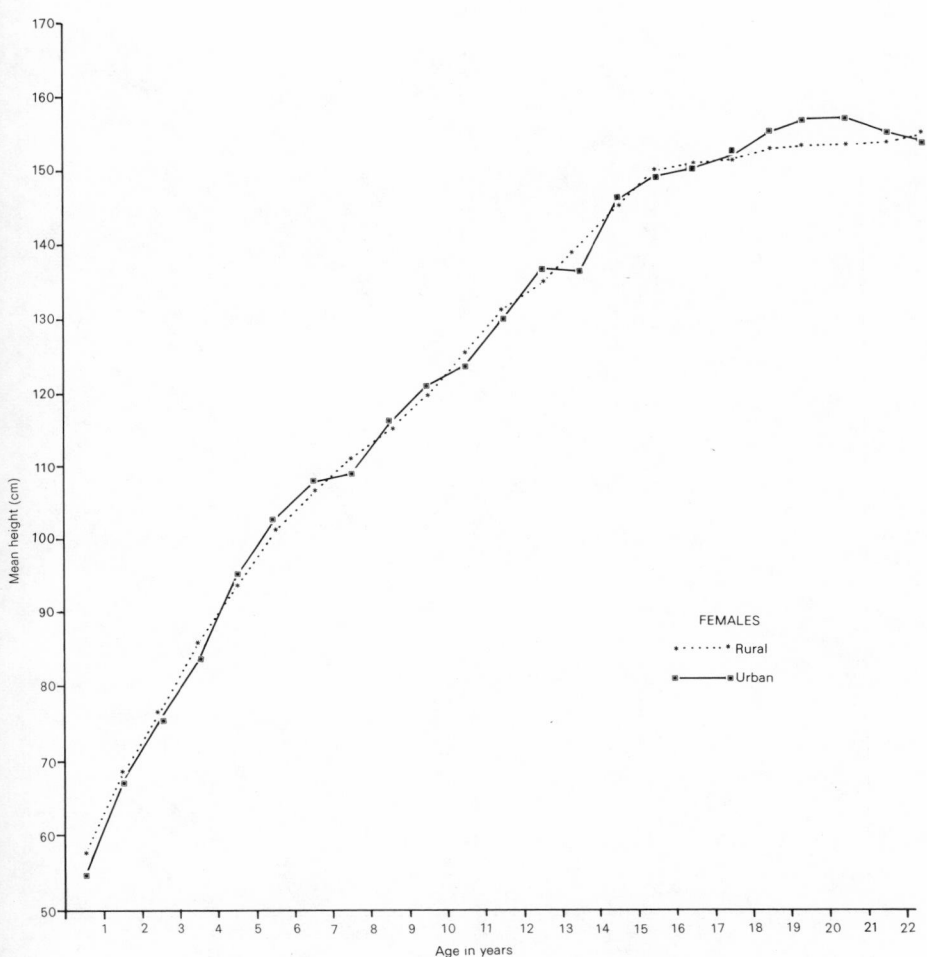

Fig. 8.6.   *Heights of Rural and Urban Creole Female Slaves by Age: St. Lucia, 1815. (Source: table S6.10.)*

health status superior to that of domestics and, to an even greater extent, field laborers. In general, drivers possessed a similar advantage, but they may have been selected more often on the basis of imposing stature. Thus, African-born domestics were shorter than field laborers.[137] The supposed nutritional advantage of fishermen is not revealed in any superiority in height. It is also apparent that differences in height between field laborers, domestics, and tradespeople did not emerge until slaves had reached about 16 years of age (figs. 8.7 and 8.8). This is not surprising, however, since there was a considerable fluidity in the occupational allocation of children.

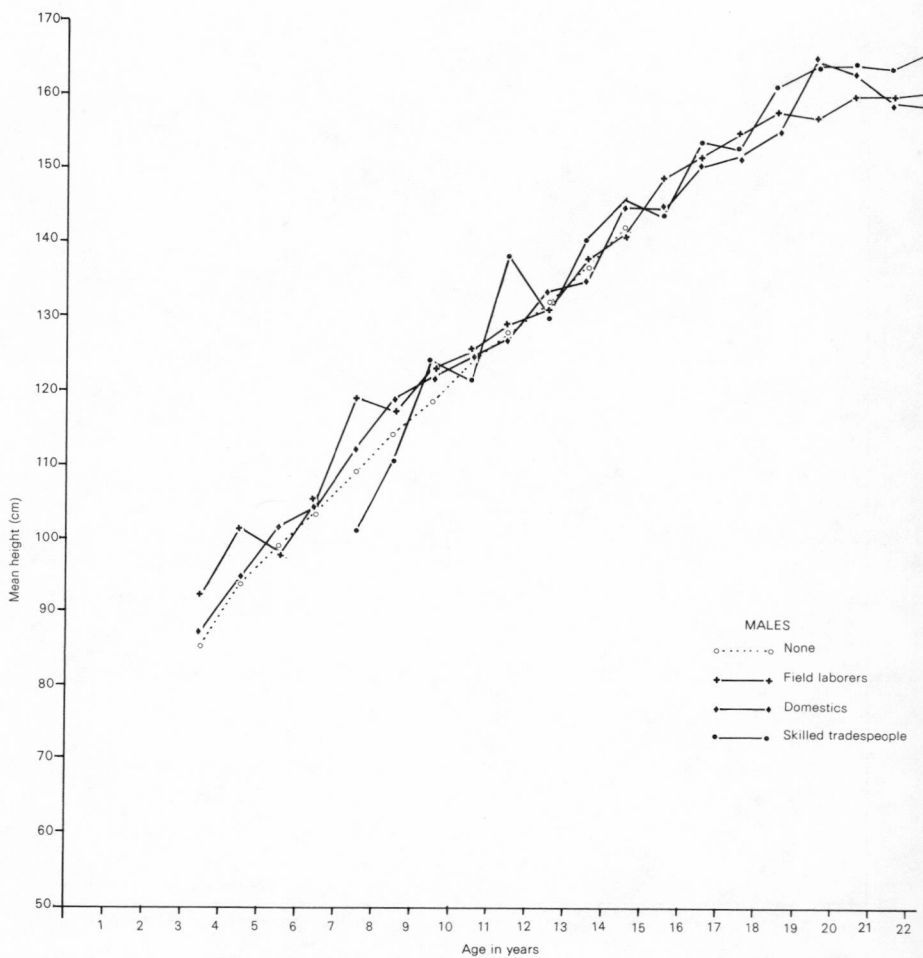

Fig. 8.7.   *Heights of Creole Male Slaves by Occupation: St. Lucia, 1815.*
(Source: *table S6.12.*)

    Within the rural slave populations, a significant difference in growth did appear
between slaves on sugar estates and those on other types of plantations. Surprisingly, adult creoles tended to be taller on sugar estates than on plantations
producing the minor staples. In St. Lucia in 1815, male creoles aged 25–40 years
averaged 165.5 cm on sugar estates and 162.7 cm on other plantations, and for
females the mean heights were 156.6 cm and 153.7 cm, respectively. A similar
differential applied to Africans, so a process of selection might have been
involved, but children on sugar estates also showed superior height in growth to
maturity (table S6.11). It needs to be noted that these data for St. Lucia show the

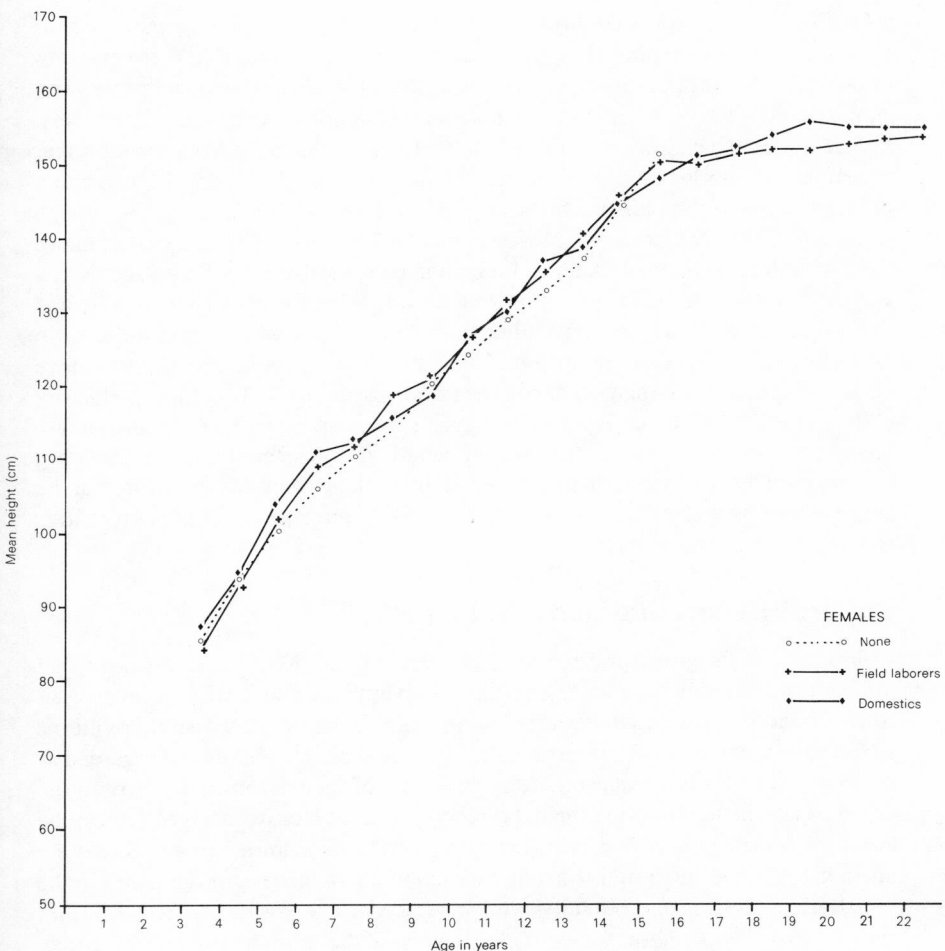

Fig. 8.8.   *Heights of Creole Female Slaves by Occupation: St. Lucia, 1815.*
   (Source: *table S6.12.*)

same pattern in holdings owned by French and British-named planters, so the difference is not simply an artifact of variations in measurement units. But the superior heights of slaves on sugar estates may have a genetic origin, derived from selective purchase, rather than indicating any significant difference in nutrition or health status. It might also reflect the larger proportion of skilled slaves on sugar estates, females as well as males.

   The most striking differences in slave heights within the British Caribbean, then, were those relating to birthplace, colony, occupation, and crop-type. Color and urban-rural differences, however, were largely nonexistent. This suggests that variations in nutrition and health status cut across the slave populations of plantations and towns, but also occurred as large-scale differences between types of colonies, particularly the sugar and marginal colonies. A broader comparison shows that British West Indian creoles were consistently taller than Cuban creoles. United States slaves were significantly taller than creoles in the West Indian sugar colonies, but shorter than those in the Bahamas (tables 8.1 and 8.2). It is more difficult to make comparisons between slave and free within the colonies, though some suggestive data are available for Jamaican police in 1835. These adult males were no taller than United States or Bahamian slaves (table 8.3). It also seems that free Afro-Jamaican males were shorter than free Afro-European Jamaicans, and that Jamaican-born whites were taller than British-born whites. But there is no doubt that slaves were shorter than free people in Jamaica. And it is clear that slave children in the West Indian sugar colonies were shorter by 2–3 cm than the factory children of industrializing Britain (even when possible differences in footwear are taken into account). If the children of the satanic mills suffered regimes that were harsher than those of slaves in the United States or the Bahamas, the children of the sugar colonies suffered even more, in spite of contemporary and modern British statements to the contrary.[138]

Physical Deformities and Disabilities

Physical deformities provide an indication of the debilitating diseases that affected the slave populations, and the disadvantages under which slaves continued to labor. Unfortunately, as noted in chapter 2, the slave registration returns supplied this information only erratically, and the available data can be regarded as no more than a lower-limit estimate of the extent of such deformities. Most of the colonies completely omitted the data, so no true comparative perspective can be obtained. Further, it is apparent that many of the deformities reported may be attributable to a number of distinct diseases. Several of the lesions described in the registration returns may equally well be traced to leprosy, venereal disease, rickets, yaws, or pellagra, for example. In view of these limitations, only the data for Berbice, which appear more systematic than for most colonies, will be discussed in any detail (table 8.4).

Some of the identifying "marks" listed in the Berbice registration returns for 1819 were the artifacts of former diseases and had no disabling effect on the slaves' capacity to labor. Smallpox was the most common cause of these, affecting at least 1.9 percent of the African slave population but only 0.7 percent of the creoles. This contrast may be explained in part by the relative youth of the creole population, but it probably also reflects the increasing success of inoculation and vaccination. Whereas the proportion of Africans bearing the marks of smallpox varied little with age, the proportion of creoles rose steadily from less than 1.0 percent for those under 20 years to more than 3.0 percent for those aged over 40. A similar pattern was observed in St. Lucia in 1815, when 1.9 percent of the total slave population bore the marks of smallpox.[139] But pockmarked slaves were allocated to

Table 8.3. *Heights (cm) of Male Police Aged 25–40 Years: Jamaica, 1835*

Ethnic group	No.	Mean	S.D.
African-born blacks	5	169.2	4.4
Jamaican-born blacks	63	169.7	6.5
Jamaican-born browns	141	172.1	6.4
Jamaican-born whites	27	171.2	5.9
British-born whites	125	170.2	6.6
German-born whites	12	171.2	4.6

Source: Jamaica, House of Assembly, Votes, 1835–36, pp. 356–82 (appendix 2).

occupations in just the same way as those bearing no visible markings, and they did not form a significant proportion among the sick. Even slaves suffering from more serious disabilities were kept at work, however. In Berbice 48 of those with leprosy continued to work in the field, as did ten of those who had lost a leg, and 14 of the blind. Others worked as skilled tradespeople.

The loss of extremities was particularly common in Berbice, affecting at least 2.6 percent of the slave population. But it is impossible to establish how these losses should be allocated among leprosy, yaws, and venereal disease. In some

Table 8.4. *Physical Deformities and Disabilities by Sex and Birthplace: Berbice, 1819*

Deformity or Disability	Africans			Creoles			Total
	Males	Females	Total	Males	Females	Total	Total
Smallpox	174	72	246	41	35	76	322
Yaws	69	43	112	72	69	141	253
Leprosy	88	52	140	21	14	35	175
Lost toes	143	76	219	114	91	205	424
Lost foot	2	2	4	3	3	6	10
Lost leg	25	12	37	4	1	5	42
Knock-kneed	230	81	311	94	56	150	461
Lost arm or hand	6	2	8	2	—	2	10
Lost fingers	43	6	49	13	10	23	72
Lost nose, palate, lips	25	21	46	8	9	17	63
Cripple	8	9	17	4	3	7	24
Humpbacked	8	7	15	6	—	6	21
Ruptured	80	1	81	13	1	14	95
Enlarged scrotum	7	—	7	—	—	—	7
Elephantiasis, swelled legs	70	44	114	18	12	30	144
Club feet	—	—	—	2	—	2	2
Blind	20	14	34	12	8	20	54
Deaf	3	—	4	—	—	—	4

Source: T.71/437–39.

cases, the returns explicitly related the loss of fingers or toes to leprosy, but others attributed the loss of toes to yaws. Knock-kneed, in-kneed, parrot-toed, duck-toed, bow-legged, bow-shinned, bandy-legged, or crooked-shinned slaves were noted very frequently (1.9 percent of the total population), but only in a few cases was the condition said to be caused by yaws. Toes, feet, legs, hands, and arms were sometimes described as being amputated or cut off because of sores, but such amputations were also evidence of punishments, particularly of maroons. When the returns contained explicit statements, the loss of nose, bridge of nose, palate, or lips was always attributed to venereal disease, but yaws and leprosy were equally likely causes. These complications prevent any real estimate of the proportions suffering from leprosy and yaws, but those said to show the marks of leprosy accounted for 1.1 percent of the Africans and 0.3 percent of the creoles, while those exhibiting the effects of yaws made up only 0.9 percent of the Africans and 1.3 percent of the creoles. Yaws was very much a disease of young creoles, while leprosy with its long incubation period affected mature Africans. The method of transmission of leprosy remains uncertain, but yaws is clearly associated with bodily contact in unsanitary living conditions.[140]

Elephantiasis affected at least 0.6 percent of the Berbice slave population, being most common among mature Africans. The disease was transmitted by mosquitoes carrying nematodes of the filaria group and was quite widespread within the sugar colonies. Another filarial parasite, the carrier of onochoceriasis, or "river blindness," was an unintended by-product of the Atlantic slave trade and may account for the few Africans in Berbice said to have enlarged scrotums and a proportion of the larger number of blind slaves in the population.[141]

Other disabilities affecting the slave populations were the result of accidents or severe labor. Rupturing was the most common of these in Berbice, but was confined to males. At least 1.0 percent of male Africans in Berbice were ruptured in 1819. In St. Lucia 27 slaves were described in the registration returns of 1815 as suffering from hernias, 8 had broken arms, and 43 showed the marks of burns. Most of these slaves were males.

In general, the prevalence of physical disabilities within the slave populations may be traced to the unsanitary conditions in which they lived and their inadequate clothing and footwear. Thus, they were exposed to parasites and infected persons. It may be that the waterlogged coast of Berbice provided a relatively bad environment in this respect, but there is much impressionistic evidence to suggest that the slave populations of the sugar islands were equally affected by disabling diseases. Those working in the drier climates of most of the marginal colonies, however, probably showed a lower incidence, and the absence of the sugar mill also meant a smaller propensity to disabling industrial accidents.

Mal d'estomac, Malnutrition, and Geophagy

The physical deformities and disabilities listed by slaveowners in the registration returns all related to visible features, so serving the general purpose of identification. But the masters were well aware of behavior in the slave population which may be used as an indicator of infection and nutritional deficiencies, though the masters often failed to recognize the relationships. The medical literature of the period was full of discussions of "mal d'estomac," or "cachexia Africana," and the association of this mortal disease with geophagy, or "dirt-eating." For example, Dr. Caddell of Barbados argued in 1812 that the cachexy associated with geophagy caused 75 percent of adult slave deaths in that island and was also the cause of low fertility. It led, he said, to dropsy and made its victims easy prey to dysentery, pleurisy, and cough or catarrh. He recommended improved nutrition as the best cure.[142] The masters, however, saw geophagy as evidence of a "depraved appetite" and resorted to brutal methods to prevent it. Thus, the contemporary literature provides an illuminating perspective on the slaveowners' ideas and attitudes as well as evidence of the extent of malnutrition in the slave population and its connection with infection.

The symptoms of mal d'estomac were frequently discussed by medical practitioners. David Mason, M.R.C.S.L., who practiced in Jamaica and preferred to term the disease "Atrophia a ventriculo," described the initial signs as indigestion and emaciation, a bloated countenance, a dirty yellow tinge in the eyelids, paleness of the lips and fingertips, whiteness of tongue, indolence, palpitation, difficult respiration, and giddiness. As the disease progressed, he said, a dropsical effusion occurred in the thorax or abdomen, the venous blood became pale and watery, and polyps were deposited in the heart.[143] Sufferers were generally geophagists. Most contemporary practitioners could readily agree with Mason's description of the symptoms of mal d'estomac, but the causes of the disease and its treatment remained matters of contention. Modern medical science has similarly failed to remove the confusion surrounding the origins of geophagy, and three competing hypotheses retain some vogue. The first sees geophagy as essentially a cultural trait or habit, the second as a response to hookworm infestation, and the third as a reaction to nutritional deficiencies.[144] The first and last of these hypotheses had currency in the early nineteenth century, but the second was rarely advanced.

Medical practitioners and planters often argued that African slaves ate earth "with a determination to kill themselves, firmly believing that after death they would return to their native homes."[145] This argument lost its weight after the abolition of the Atlantic slave trade, when it became clear that geophagy was practiced by creoles as well as Africans. Thus, James Maxwell, surgeon to the Annotto Bay Marine Hospital in Jamaica, observed in 1835 that

the moderate use of this [clayey] earth is considered by the negroes neither dangerous nor disgraceful; and those who eat it, take it as much to gratify an acquired taste, similar to that of chewing tobacco or opium, as to satisfy any morbid desire. Prepared in the manner described [baked in cakes], it is used by many as a social habit, under the name of aboo.[146]

The characteristics of the absorbent clay eaten by the slaves were described by Maxwell: "It occurs disseminated; colour chocolate brown; has an unctuous soapy feel; is soft; fractures roughly, and does not adhere to the tongue." A similar description was given by Colin Chisholm, a surgeon in Grenada. The clayey strata of the soil of Grenada, he wrote,

are called by the Creole whites and negroes, Aboo and Caioo; probably corruptions of the two French words *boue,* signifying dirt or clay; and *craie,* chalk: and by the African negroes, before they have acquired the language of their brethren in the West Indies, Trieng: an Ebo word, signifying a purer kind of pipe-clay, much used with food by most of the inhabitants of the coast of Guinea. All these varieties are eat with astonishing avidity by negroes of almost every description, but particularly the females: a pernicious custom, originally superstitious perhaps and certainly introduced from Africa.[147]

It was said that the prevalence of geophagy varied with the availability of the favored earths, but slaves traveled to gather them from the beds of rivers; and John Ferguson, M.D., recalled in 1836 having seen in Jamaica "a considerable excavation on the side of a hill along which passed the public road, where the negroes of the neighbouring properties were in the habit of supplying themselves with an absorbent earth to allay the cravings engendered by the Cachexia, or perhaps by other gastric disorders."[148] Further, slaves had individual preferences for particular earths, and were "overheard urging their companions to partake of their favourite material."[149] In general, the characteristics of the geophagical clays consumed by West Indian slaves were similar to those of potter's clay.

The preparation of earth for consumption was performed with as much care as its selection. Maxwell reported that in Jamaica

many of the agricultural negroes, especially the women, who are well fed, habitually consume moderate quantities of steatite made up into balls like chocolate, which are baked and sold in the market amongst themselves at the rate of two for five pence. Some eat it in its native state, and half an ounce in this way will suffice for a day; others mix it with a proportion of salt, and, after baking, preserve it in the smoke for occasional use.[150]

Similarly, in the late eighteenth century Edward Long had noticed that "*aboo,* or earth cakes are vended among the Negroes at Spanish Town in Jamaica."[151] Again, in 1837 Sturge and Harvey observed that "the alkaline earth which is so greedily sought for by dirt eaters, is sometimes made into cakes and sold in Kingston market."[152] Thus, it is possible that a trade developed, in Jamaica at least, in which slaves from areas lacking the favored earths were supplied through the markets by traders, either slave or free, who specialized in the excavation and preparation of earth for sale. Recent studies of geophagy among the Tiv of Nigeria and the Ewe of Ghana suggest significant parallels with West Indian practice.[153] Both the Tiv and the Ewe mine earth, particularly clay, from special pits. Among the Ewe, men mine the clay and sell it to women who pound and mold it into egg-shaped cakes, which are traded widely within West Africa. Salt is generally added to the earth when used by pregnant Tiv women, and it is mixed with water and drunk when taken by men as an antidiarrhetic.

There is considerable evidence, then, that geophagy among the slaves of the British Caribbean had a strong cultural focus. It was practiced in the face of a good deal of opposition from the planters. Geophagists were often locked up or forced to wear metal face masks. In Grenada an overseer made circular boards 26 inches in diameter, with a hole in the center, and placed them on the slaves' necks to prevent dirt eating. In Dominica a manager had the gang's faces smeared with ashes and excrement and had the driver force some of this mixture down their throats. This was resorted to when all other modes of punishment failed, said the manager, to prevent children from learning the habit from their mothers.[154] The tenacity of the slaves in clinging to the practice in the face of all this hostility suggests that its origin may be sought in some deeper physiological need.

Most often, geophagy has been traced to intestinal helminthiasis (hookworm).[155] But this explanation was unknown to contemporary medical writers, with the exception of John Hancock, and mal d'estomac was not thought to be a parasitic malady until 1853, when Bilharz related hookworm infection and certain anemias. The hookworm *Ancylostoma duodenale* was identified only in 1838, and *Necator americanus*, brought to the New World from Africa, in 1902. The theory was that the parasites sucked the host's blood, causing anemia and an irritation of the digestive organs, which was relieved by the ingestion of specific earths. Alternatively, geophagy has sometimes been seen as a source of hookworm infection.[156]

Not all geophagy can be related to hookworm infection, however, and a growing body of literature suggests a far stronger association with malnutrition, particularly deficiencies in calcium and iron. The Kiples argue that mal d'estomac was in fact beriberi, a disease of malnutrition specifically caused by thiamine deficiency.[157] There is no doubt that these deficiencies affected the West Indian slave population, while modern analyses of earths consumed by geophagists show them to contain high concentrations of calcium and iron.[158] Contemporaries also demonstrated an awakening understanding of the relationship between geophagy and nutrition. Mason, for example, held that "the habit of dirt-eating is most commonly brought on by long abstinence, bad food, and an irregular and inadequate supply." Slaves who produced sufficient provisions to carry to market a surplus never ate dirt, he said, whereas runaways were most subject to the disease. Similarly, John Imray of Dominica saw the slaves' neglect of their provision grounds as one of the first symptoms of mal d'estomac. Mason believed that the eating of absorbent earths did more than simply allay the sensation of hunger, since the craving was not generally removed by a regular and abundant supply of food. Thus, he concluded "that dirt-eating, instead of being a disease, or the cause of a disease, is actually a remedy; and probably the various earths, marl, and ashes made use of, really contain some useful ingredients mixed up with much hurtful matter."[159] Mason supported this perceptive remark with his observation that iron and alkalis proved of great curative power, together with adequate nourishment. Similarly, Imray believed that of the tonic medicines, carbonate and sulphate of iron, as well as tincture and muriate of iron, worked most effectively to neutralize the acids in the stomach. Hancock recommended mild purgatives and argued that "to amend the impoverished state of the blood and give tone and energy to the system, there is little doubt that preparations of iron should hold the first rank."[160]

Geophagy has always been particularly associated with children and pregnant women. This pattern was noted among the slave population by Mason in Jamaica and Imray in Dominica, for example. The physiological cost of pregnancy and lactation is great, in terms of calories, iron, and calcium. Iron deficiency is directly related to protein malnutrition (as is kwashiorkor), and during pregnancy the deficiency is exacerbated. Again, this deficiency could be made worse by hookworm infestation. The iron cost of pregnancy is about 540 milligrams, and of parturition about 50; blood loss from *N. americanus* is about 0.03 milligrams per worm per day (with infections of hundreds of worms being common).[161] Thus, especially for the pregnant slave, suffering from helminthiasis and dietary inadequacy, geophagy may well have been a response to iron deficiency.

Throughout the period of slavery most doctors and masters continued to see geophagy as a symbol of African barbarism, the product of a depraved mentality. Thus, although there is scant evidence that geophagy causes anemia, most West Indian whites believed this in the early nineteenth century.[162] As a result, their efforts to stop slaves from eating earth may have done more harm than good, preventing the slaves from continuing a practice that had its roots in physiological need, a need that was not abated by the slave's removal from Africa to the Caribbean. But the widespread character of geophagy in the slave population provides clear evidence of the extent of nutritional deficiencies.[163]

SICKNESS AND THE RHYTHM OF THE SEASONS

A systematic analysis of morbidity in the slave populations can be undertaken only in terms of cause-of-death data, and these will be discussed in the next chapter. Here it is possible only to describe briefly some broad variations in morbidity levels, and their relationship to seasonal trends.

The physical disabilities discussed in an earlier section concerned only visible bodily characteristics, which did not necessarily prohibit the slaves from full employment. An indication of the health status of the population may, however, be obtained from the registration returns by considering only those too ill to be employed, who were listed as "infirm" or otherwise disabled in the "occupation" columns of the returns (tables S7.2–7.7). Such slaves were not merely temporarily indisposed but chronic cases. It is uncertain how far variations in registration practice may affect the comparability of colonies, but of the available sample Berbice had by far the highest morbidity level, with 3.8 percent of the slaves described as invalids in 1819. The rate stood at 1.8 percent in St. Lucia in 1815, 1.1 percent in Anguilla in 1827, and 0.6 percent in Trinidad in 1813. The latter proportion is surprisingly low, but it does seem clear that the coastlands of Berbice were much less healthful than the islands. The proportion sick in Anguilla, on the other hand, appears high and may reflect the effects of food shortages rather than conditions typical of the marginal colonies.

Morbidity levels were significantly lower in the towns than on rural slavehold-ings. In general, the urban level was about half that experienced on rural holdings. In St. Lucia only 0.8 percent of urban slaves were listed as invalids in the registration returns for 1815, compared to 1.9 percent of rural slaves. In Trinidad in 1813 these percentages were 0.3 and 0.7, respectively. In Barbados in 1817 only 0.6 percent of the slaves living in Bridgetown were registered as invalids, compared to 1.1 percent in the plantation parishes of St. John and St. Andrew. Since it has been shown that there was no significant difference in the growth patterns of urban and rural slaves, it seems most probable that this contrast in morbidity levels resulted from differences in work regimes, shelter, and clothing rather than from poor nutrition. Sugar estates generally had higher morbidity levels did than other types of rural holdings, in Trinidad and St. Lucia at least, while small units producing cocoa or provisions tended to have larger proportions of invalids than did coffee or cotton plantations (tables S7.9–7.10). The latter contrasts are less readily explained in terms of work regimes, and they varied somewhat erratically, but the contrast between sugar and the minor staples cannot be accounted for simply by nutritional differences.

These differences between town and country and between crop-types were reflected in the tendency of morbidity levels to increase steadily with slaveholding size (tables S7.11–7.13). In St. Lucia, for example, the proportion of male invalids rose from 0.5 percent in units of 1–10 slaves to 2.7 percent in units of 301–400 slaves, while for females these percentages were 1.4 and 4.7, respectively.

The relatively high rate of morbidity among females indicated in this compari-son was common to all colonies, in both town and country (tables S7.9–7.18). In part, the higher morbidity levels of females may be explained by their reproductive role, since some slaveowners may have listed pregnant and nursing mothers as invalids. This appears to account for only a small proportion of the difference, however, because the greatest contrast between the sexes occurred in the age group above 40 years. In rural Trinidad in 1813, for example, morbidity rates were exactly the same for males and females until age 30, but among those aged 50–59 only 1.4 percent of males were sick, compared to 7.6 percent of females, and in the older age groups the percentages were 7.5 and 13.5, respectively (table S7.18). In the towns of Trinidad the differential emerged at even later ages. A similar pattern occurred in Berbice, where in 1819 the mean age of sick or disabled male creoles was 37.4 years, and of female creoles 40.6 years (table S7.20). In St. Lucia these mean ages were 39.5 and 44.5, respectively. Africans also showed this contrast between the sexes. The only exception found to the pattern of higher female than male morbidity occurred in the case of Anguilla, where 1.1 percent of the males and 1.0 percent of females were invalids in 1827. In general, however, the high level of morbidity experienced in the female slave populations may be traced to their concentration in field labor and their tendency to live longer than males. Thus, the relatively few males who survived beyond 50 years of age tended to remain in employment, while the large numbers of females were much more often invalids.

The relationship between occupation and morbidity cannot be established directly from the slave registration returns, since infirmity was listed under occupation, though detailed linkage of the few series that stated occupation at different times may prove revealing. But the clear contrast between urban and rural slave populations does suggest a definite connection between morbidity and field labor. This is supported by the sex differential, though this occurred in both town and country. The evidence of the relationship between morbidity and color is not clear-cut, but colored slaves appear to have had slightly higher rates than blacks (tables S7.14–7.17). This may mean merely that they were more readily indulged in sickness, rather than suggesting any link with occupation. But, as indicated by the lack of growth differentials between black and colored slaves, it seems that the general health status and nutrition of colored slaves as a group was not obviously superior to that of blacks.

Morbidity levels varied with the seasonal cycles of the plantations. The registration returns provide no direct evidence of this seasonality, of course, though it is possible that some of the differences in morbidity rates between the colonies may be traced to the seasons in which the returns were collected. The relatively low rates found in Trinidad in 1813, for example, may have been reduced somewhat by the taking of the returns largely in April, May, and June. But this effect must have been limited, since most slaveowners registered slaves as invalids only when their invalidism was of a more than temporary nature. To obtain a picture of these temporary fluctuations, it is necessary to make use of plantation journals. Very few of these journals provide daily data on the numbers of sick slaves, but four examples are given in figure 8.9. These show the weekly average number of "sick" slaves, those not actually working for a day or more. The curves apply strictly to particular plantations, which are not necessarily representative of their islands, but the pattern on the three sugar estates does suggest a certain uniformity of experience. No comparable data have been found for other types of plantations or for urban slaveholdings. Equally important, there seems to be no data for Demerara-Essequibo or Berbice, where there was no definite crop season on the sugar estates. Whereas long-term invalids made up only a maximum of 3.8 percent of the slave population of Berbice in 1819, the proportion of slaves affected by temporary (though sometimes mortal) illnesses reached almost 10 percent in the peak period on the sample estates for St. Vincent and Jamaica, 6 percent in the Bahamas, and 4 percent in Barbados.

In general, the number of sick slaves on sugar estates was at a peak at the commencement of the sugar harvest, fell fairly steadily during crop to reach a minimum about a month or two beyond crop-over, and then rose quite steeply during the out-of-crop season to reach a new peak shortly before the next crop

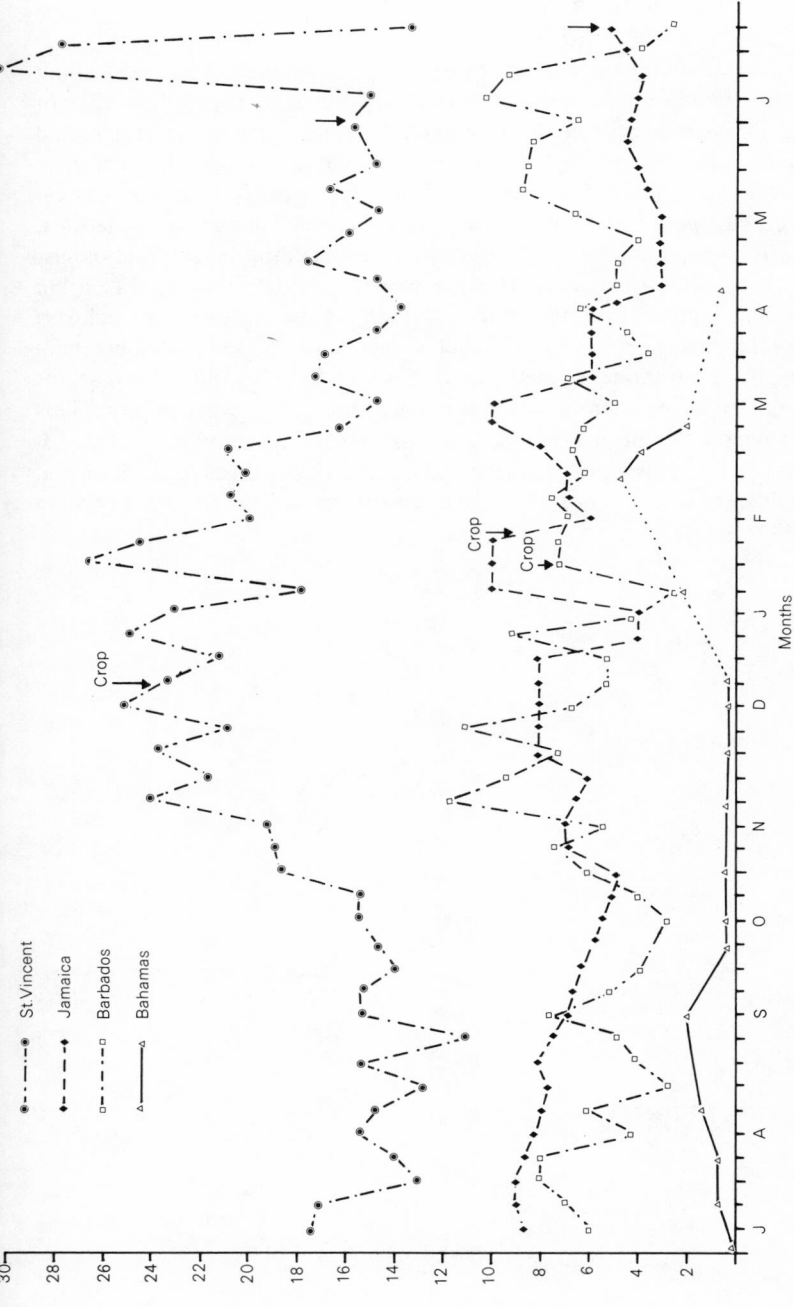

Fig. 8.9. *Seasonal Morbidity of Slaves: St. Vincent (Peruvian Vale), 1807/8, Jamaica (Rose Hall), 1830/31, Barbados (Newton), 1797/98, Bahamas (Farquharson's), 1831/32. (Sources: Peruvian Vale Estate Journal [Supreme Court Registry, Kingston]; Rose Hall Journal [Jamaica Archives, Spanish Town]; Newton Estate Papers, item 123, [University of London]; Farquharson's Journal [Nassau, 1957].)*

season. In the Barbados example, however, the number sick reached a peak about two months before the commencement of crop and rose again before the ending of the season. This pattern fits well that described in chapter 6: the out-of-crop period was commonly called the ''hungry-time,'' whereas the slaves were said to be most healthy during crop, when they had access to sugar cane juice and molasses. Alternatively, the peak period of sickness might be related to climatic variations. The period July–September was said to be the most healthful in the West Indies, generally, though the months around Christmas were called the ''sickly season'' in Jamaica.[164] This argument receives some support from the high levels of sickness noted in the Bahamas in February 1832, but no such seasonal peak was apparent in 1831. Overall, a nutritional-climatic explanation of the seasonal pattern seems much more convincing than one based on variations in the work regime. This conclusion contrasts with that reached in terms of chronic morbidity. Thus, it appears that minor illnesses were closely associated with changes in nutrition and weather, while the frequency of disabling disease depended chiefly on the relative rigor of labor regimes.

9.
Fertility, Mortality, and Natural Increase

THE ULTIMATE TEST OF THE WELL-BEING OF THE SLAVE POPULA-
tions of the British Caribbean lay in their capacity to survive. The significance of
this test was confirmed by both abolitionists and, sometimes reluctantly, slaveowners. It played a central role in the debate over slavery in the early nineteenth
century. Before the abolition of the Atlantic slave trade, slaveowners had been
able to attribute the general absence of a positive natural increase in the British
Caribbean to the distorting effects of that trade on the structure of the slave
populations, but after 1807 the argument became increasingly implausible. The
abolitionists in turn had believed that the institution of slavery was "created and
sustained" by the slave trade and hoped that it would simply fade away once the
trade was stopped. They also believed that the condition of the slave population
would be ameliorated as a result of the planters' need for a self-sustaining labor
force.[1] With some notable exceptions, the slave populations of the British Caribbean were slow to provide evidence of natural growth in the years following the
abolition of the slave trade, but the abolitionists clung to their proposition. Thus,
they first sought the registration of slaves, as a means of blocking the illegal slave
trade and forcing the planters to act in their own best interests, and in the 1820s
they promoted legislated amelioration. Only after these measures had failed to
create conditions favorable to the natural growth of the slave populations did the
humanitarians come to actively promote the abolition of the institution of slavery.

In 1832 the abolitionist Thomas Fowell Buxton argued that the decrease in the
slave population was "the best of all tests of the condition of the Negro" for a
number of reasons:

In the first place, because it cannot be liable to the imputation of any excitement of
feelings; it was a purely rational argument, it was addressed only to the understanding,
it was an arithmetical proposition. Again, I think it is the best of all tests, because the
facts we derive from the West Indians themselves . . . : also, perhaps my opinion has
been confirmed by seeing that the West Indians themselves, when they wish to establish a case of good conduct upon the part of an owner or overseer, . . . say the population upon that given estate has increased, and that is incompatible with any severe
treatment.[2]

Many slaveowners, particularly those in the long-settled colonies, did indeed accept the logic of Buxton's argument. For example, a group of Barbadian planters preparing a set of instructions for the management of plantations and slaves in 1786, before the abolition of the Atlantic slave trade, argued that "if negroes are fed plentifully, worked moderately, and treated kindly, they will increase in most places; they will decrease in no place, so much as to require any considerable expense to repair the loss, in number or in value. The increase is the only test of the care with which they are treated."[3] Similarly, the overseer of Newton Plantation, Barbados, was well satisfied to be able to tell its absentee proprietor that his estate was flourishing, "your Negroes under good discipline, but happy, and rapidly increasing, a certain sign of happiness and good treatment."[4] Later the overseer was presented with a piece of plate duly inscribed: "Presented to Mr. Robert Reece, for his particular attention, and humanity towards the Negroes on Newtons Plantation; (evinced by their increase since he was overseer) and, as a token of approval of his general-good-conduct by Thomas Lane Esq.: London October 1815."[5] When in 1812 the Barbados Agricultural Society debated the question "Is the slave population on well regulated estates likely to increase or not?" it answered in the affirmative.[6]

Slaveowners in the newly settled colonies were less ready to accept the logic of Buxton's argument that the rate of natural increase was a valid index of the well-being of the slave population. Thus, the Trinidad planter William Burnley observed that "probably, the most difficult of all subjects, satisfactorily to treat, is the theory of population; it presents anomalies at every step."[7] Similarly, a Jamaican planter argued that "a decrease may arise from a variety of adventitious circumstances having no relation even to the personal welfare of the individuals of a community."[8] The decrease in Jamaica's slave population, he said, resulted from the distorted age structure created by the Atlantic slave trade, the family structure of the slaves, African debauchery, and manumission. The unbalanced sex ratio, promiscuity, and induced abortion were frequently referred to by planters in this context.[9] These factors, of course, all related to fertility rather than mortality, and so enabled the planters to shift the blame for the failure to achieve natural increases from themselves to the slaves. Thus, they could contend that decreases should not be imputed to the masters' wanton and improper exercise of power. The argument led, as in the case of Burnley, to a doubt that any general theory was applicable to the case of the slave population.

The abolitionists, of course, were at odds with such skepticism and adopted at least the bare bones of Malthusian theory. Whereas the slaveowners preferred to attribute decrease in the slave population to preventive (fertility-reducing) checks, the abolitionists traced it to positive (mortality-increasing) checks. "I take it to be a maxim, as clear and certain as any maxim in political economy," said Buxton, "that in ordinary cases population will increase; that this is the law of nature, . . . and that increase can only be prevented by intense misery." He attributed the decrease in the West Indian slave population to "the excessive labour attendant upon sugar cultivation in a state of slavery," especially when coupled with "the natural disposition to languor and idleness" of the slaves. Carefully distinguishing between the positive and preventive checks on growth, Buxton continued, "My argument has never been that there was not a right proportion of births; my argument has been that there was an undue proportion of deaths." Indeed, he did not dispute data that seemed to show that on certain Jamaican plantations the fertility of the slaves was higher than in England, since he contended that in Jamaica and Demerara, "instead of having a population likely to decrease, you have a population which ought, under common circumstances, to increase rapidly, not only more rapidly than it does, but greatly more rapidly than it does in England, inasmuch as there is a greater proportion between the marriageable ages."[10] For Buxton, then, the preventive check was not crucial, while Malthusian misery, imposed on the slaves by the masters and clearly in their power to control, was at the root of the decrease.

James Stephen, too, saw the "excess of labour" associated with sugar cultivation under slavery as the cause of depopulation. "The best criterion of the good or bad condition of the labouring classes in any country," he wrote, "may be found in the increase or decline of their numbers." Emigration, famine, and war might produce exceptions to this rule, "but from these causes of depopulation, the slaves in our sugar colonies are pre-eminently exempt." In spite of this immunity, said Stephen, the decline in the predial slave population of the West Indies exceeded "any measure of the same calamity, that is elsewhere to be found, under ordinary circumstances, in the history of mankind."[11] Although it is perhaps surprising that the slaveowners rarely employed a catastrophic interpretation of slave population dynamics, they generally accepted the position of Stephen and Buxton that the slaves were not subject to calamities to any extent. Epidemic disease did not produce catastrophic mortality in the early nineteenth century, though cholera came close to doing so, and the numbers of slave deaths attributable to hurricanes, earthquakes, or volcanic eruptions remained a small proportion of total mortality. The important point here is that slave mortality was consistently high, and while the abolitionists could relate this experience to persistent malnutrition and severe labor, the slaveowners could not account for it by pointing to catastrophic fluctuations in mortality resulting from externally-generated subsistence crises. The population was in a state of permanent crisis.

Few contemporaries on either side of the debate over slavery placed their arguments in a comparative perspective. The evidence that some British West Indian slave populations did in fact achieve quite high levels of natural increase after 1807 was disquieting. For the abolitionists it created a theoretical difficulty. In spite of the apparatus provided by Malthus, it was harder to prove that rapid natural increase was not evidence of improved material welfare than to show that absolute population decline reflected extreme suffering and privation. Thus, when the abolitionists demonstrated the relative hardships of the British West Indian slave population by reference to rapid natural increase in the United States, they faced problems in attributing this contrast to the slave system rather than to exogenous factors. For example, after showing that the slave population of the

United States was growing as rapidly as the free (proof of "the great natural fecundity of the African race, when unsubdued by a pernicious excess of labour"), Stephen felt obliged to add; "For that the state of slavery is, even without this destructive species of oppression, unfriendly to the multiplication of our species, cannot admit of a doubt."[12] This argument fitted Malthus's statements on the slave populations of classical Greece and Rome but necessarily ignored the modern experience of the United States, Barbados, and the marginal colonies of the British empire.

For the slaveowner, rapid natural increase meant the threat of overpopulation and a future in which they would be heavily outnumbered while Malthusian misery stalked the land. Such a situation they saw as conducive to slave rebellion and a threat to their very lives. Not surprisingly, the fear of overpopulation was discussed most fully in Barbados. It was mentioned by some planters even before the abolition of the slave trade, and by 1833 a Barbados newspaper was prophesying that Malthus's "principle of population" would be verified in the island, it being "already overpopulated."[13] There were calls for permission to send surplus slaves to the fresh, fertile soils of the United States. Earlier, in 1828, when a Barbadian planter sought leave to move slaves to Trinidad on the grounds that it would benefit their welfare, the Privy Council of Barbados responded by saying that "we cannot it candour pretend that the population has yet arrived at that degree of density which renders such removal 'essential to the well being of the slaves.' "[14] The very fact that the Trinidad slave population decreased while that of Barbados increased, said the Privy Council, demonstrated that the Barbados plan of rationed allowances was superior to the provision ground system. The fear of overpopulation troubled the sleep of few slaveowners, even in Barbados.

In general, abolitionists and slaveowners shared the belief that the level of natural increase was a fundamental indicator of the well-being of a population. But they differed widely on the causes of the decreases observed in the slave populations of the West Indies. The abolitionists traced the decline to ill-treatment in terms of physical brutality and material welfare, and to the state of slavery itself. Although some slaveowners, particularly the planters of Barbados, were willing to accept the idea that ill-treatment might account for decreases on particular plantations, many attempted to explain the decline in terms of the behavior of the slaves themselves. As the planter Burnley noticed, some masters "attributed the decrease of the slave population to the national vices of the Negroes, in spite of the annual swarms proceeding from the African hive, testifying to the contrary."[15] The poverty of this argument was clear to most, especially to those planters who wished to contend that the slave's material welfare was superior to that of the African or the English laborer. The distortions created in the structure of the slave populations by the selectivity of the Atlantic slave trade offered firmer theoretical ground; but as 1807 receded, the planters were less able to advance this argument with conviction.

The contemporary debate over the decline of the slave populations of the British Caribbean was inhibited by the lack of a firm statistical base. Before the abolition of the Atlantic slave trade, both sides depended chiefly on the results of erratic censuses and figures from particular plantation journals. But there was no real dispute over the fact that deaths exceeded births. Indeed, the planters employed this fact as the foundation of their argument that the continuance of the slave trade was essential to the maintenance of the labor force, let alone population growth. The slave registration system provided a vastly improved set of data, though contemporaries exploited only the surface of it. Generally, the abolitionists were content to point to the excess of deaths over births, shown by the masters' own figures, as proof of their arguments. A few used the registration data to calculate crude mortality rates. Only James Robertson, the Registrar for Demerara-Essequibo, attempted to employ the data to determine the longevity, or "common probabilities of life," of the slaves.[16] In confining attention to the difference between births and deaths, contemporaries were on relatively firm ground. As shown in chapter 2, the registration data do permit a quite accurate estimate of natural increase but are less reliable for the comparative study of mortality and fertility. For both theoretical and practical reasons, the level of natural increase remains crucial.

NATURAL INCREASE

The pattern of growth and decline in the slave populations of the British Caribbean between 1807 and 1834 has already been discussed in chapter 4. It was noted there that of the sugar colonies only Barbados showed definite absolute growth over the period and that the pattern was affected to some degree by the differential effects of the intercolonial slave trade. Here the focus is confined to only one of the components of growth, natural increase.

Three distinct patterns of natural increase can be identified (table 9.1). The first was characterized by positive natural increase, the rate showing a general tendency to improve over the registration period. The second showed heavy but improving negative rates, and the third relatively light but deteriorating negative rates.

The first pattern was typical of the old sugar colonies and the marginal colonies. The position in the marginal colonies is not entirely certain, due to the lack of continuous registration records for British Honduras, the Cayman Islands, and Anguilla, but there is no doubt that Barbuda and the Bahamas experienced high rates of positive natural increase, generally exceeding 20 per 1,000. The Cayman Islands and Anguilla probably approximated these levels, except for the period of famine in Anguilla after 1830. The rate of natural increase in Anguilla stood at +28.6 per 1,000 in the period 1827–31 but collapsed to −1.6 in 1831–34. British Honduras seems likely to have experienced negative rates for most of the registration period, though probably emerging into a position of positive natural increase shortly before emancipation (tables 2.7 and 2.8). Thus, most of the marginal colonies showed high positive rates throughout the period after 1807. Of the sugar colonies, however, only Barbados managed to maintain a positive natural increase, a position it probably achieved by about 1810. Even Barbados

Table 9.1. *Slave Birth Rates, Death Rates, Rates of Natural Increase, and Sex Ratios by Colony, 1815–34*

Colony	Males per 100 Females	(Adjusted) Births per 1,000	(Adjusted) Deaths per 1,000			(Registered) Natural Increase per 1,000
			Males	Females	Total	
Barbados						
1817–20	86.1	47.2	46.1	39.3	42.5	+4.8
1820–23	86.5	50.0	48.0	38.4	42.8	+6.5
1823–26	84.9	57.5	46.7	38.4	42.2	+12.1
1826–29	85.1	54.3	46.9	37.9	42.5	+10.0
1829–32	85.8	58.2	58.2	48.0	52.7	+5.7
1832–34	86.5	57.8	42.8	36.0	39.1	+14.4
St. Kitts						
1817–22	92.3	35.6	43.2	39.6	41.4	−5.7
1822–25	91.9	39.8	42.2	34.7	38.3	−0.4
1825–28	91.2	41.3	40.6	33.2	36.7	+1.8
1828–31	91.5	39.8	38.1	32.3	35.1	+2.0
1831–34	92.5	44.6	36.7	35.7	36.2	+4.6
Nevis						
1817–22	96.6	37.9	44.8	41.0	42.9	−4.6
1822–25	97.9	36.1	37.6	34.4	35.9	−1.0
1825–28	97.7	34.7	34.4	30.8	32.6	+0.3
1828–31	97.8	35.2	36.3	34.8	35.5	−1.3
1831–34	97.8	38.6	28.7	28.1	28.4	+5.9
Antigua						
1817–21	87.4	27.5	36.7	29.7	33.0	−4.3
1821–24	87.9	40.3	44.3	35.9	39.8	−0.5
1824–28	88.8	32.5	33.4	29.3	31.3	+0.2
1828–32	89.6	32.8	36.0	33.6	34.7	−2.0
Montserrat						
1817–21	86.4	27.5	32.8	24.9	28.6	+0.5
1821–24	86.0	37.1	46.2	34.8	40.1	−0.6
1824–28	85.0	30.3	28.9	24.4	26.4	+4.5
1828–31	86.8	44.6	36.5	31.7	35.4	+9.5
Virgin Islands						
1818–22	86.7	31.7	49.1	35.4	41.8	−9.1
1822–25	85.4	40.4	28.8	20.2	24.2	+9.1
1825–28	86.2	43.5	29.5	20.3	24.5	+10.9
1828–31	87.1	40.5	34.6	37.0	35.9	+0.8
1831–34	87.5	38.1	37.0	30.0	33.3	+1.2
Jamaica						
1817–20	99.7	29.1	31.9	27.7	29.8	−0.7
1820–23	98.7	28.2	34.0	29.5	31.7	−3.1
1823–26	97.4	28.4	33.5	28.2	30.8	−2.1
1826–29	96.5	27.4	34.2	28.7	31.4	−3.4
1829–32	95.5	28.7	38.5	30.4	34.7	−4.8
Dominica						
1817–20	92.1	32.8	43.8	36.7	40.1	−6.1
1820–23	91.3	33.4	42.1	33.3	37.5	−3.4

Table 9.1. *Slave Birth Rates, Death Rates, Rates of Natural Increase, and Sex Ratios (continued)*

Colony	Males per 100 Females	(Adjusted) Births per 1,000	(Adjusted) Deaths per 1,000			(Registered) Natural Increase per 1,000
			Males	Females	Total	
1823–26	91.3	33.3	40.9	35.4	38.0	− 3.9
1826–29	91.6	35.3	36.9	31.3	34.0	+ 1.2
1829–32	92.1	35.3	32.6	31.4	32.0	+ 2.9
St. Lucia						
1815–19	83.0	25.6	61.4	42.5	51.1	− 25.5
1819–22	83.4	37.2	44.7	34.6	39.2	− 9.5
1822–25	84.8	51.0	37.3	27.5	32.0	+ 4.1
1825–28	85.3	50.6	39.4	23.9	31.0	+ 4.7
1828–31	84.9	48.6	39.1	27.6	32.9	+ 2.0
1831–34	n.c.	n.c.	n.c.	n.c.	n.c.	n.c.
St. Vincent						
1817–22	100.1	29.2	45.0	38.3	41.7	− 13.0
1822–25	97.3	32.6	37.9	30.3	34.0	− 3.5
1825–28	96.1	32.5	37.2	28.9	33.0	− 2.7
1828–31	95.4	32.2	41.9	33.6	37.7	− 6.9
1831–34	93.9	n.a.	n.a.	n.a.	n.a.	n.a.
Grenada						
1817	95.7	26.1	55.2	46.9	50.9	− 24.3
1818	94.9	25.6	42.1	39.4	40.7	− 15.0
1819	94.6	28.1	46.2	43.7	44.9	− 16.7
1820	94.1	25.5	38.8	30.9	34.7	− 9.4
1821	93.5	27.8	41.6	32.5	36.9	− 9.4
1822	93.4	30.2	30.8	25.0	27.8	+ 1.6
1823	93.6	30.3	33.8	33.9	33.9	− 4.1
1824	94.0	28.9	33.7	26.8	30.1	− 1.9
1825	94.0	29.1	34.5	29.3	31.8	− 3.3
1826	93.8	28.6	34.6	32.5	33.5	− 5.4
1827	93.8	30.8	31.8	25.5	28.5	+ 1.4
1828	93.7	30.2	33.3	28.0	30.6	− 1.1
1829	94.0	32.5	33.1	29.9	31.5	+ 0.2
1830	94.1	32.8	45.2	40.3	42.6	− 10.2
1831	94.0	30.9	45.5	36.6	40.9	− 10.3
1832	93.8	29.0	34.8	28.6	31.6	− 3.1
1833	93.6	36.9	32.1	26.5	29.2	+ 6.5
Tobago						
1819	96.8	23.8	60.1	53.6	56.8	− 32.5
1820	95.6	26.9	55.3	43.8	49.5	− 23.1
1821	94.8	26.3	56.6	44.2	50.2	− 24.4
1822	94.1	26.8	36.5	31.3	33.8	− 8.8
1823	93.1	27.9	60.1	43.7	51.6	− 24.4
1824	91.9	27.2	35.3	29.1	32.0	− 6.8
1825	91.1	29.0	60.7	50.0	55.1	− 26.7
1826	90.2	30.3	36.9	28.8	32.6	− 4.8
1827	89.4	34.1	51.2	39.5	45.0	− 13.1
1828	88.9	35.0	50.9	39.7	45.0	− 12.3

Table 9.1. *Slave Birth Rates, Death Rates, Rates of Natural Increase, and Sex Ratios (continued)*

Colony	Males per 100 Females	(Adjusted) Births per 1,000	(Adjusted) Deaths per 1,000			(Registered) Natural Increase per 1,000
			Males	Females	Total	
1829	88.1	30.3	52.7	35.4	43.5	− 14.9
1830	87.6	32.7	51.0	39.3	44.8	− 14.0
1831	86.9	29.9	56.8	41.9	48.8	− 20.0
1832	86.5	26.2	47.9	43.5	45.5	− 20.2
1833	86.4	31.7	47.6	33.6	40.1	− 10.5
Trinidad						
1813–16	123.1	44.1	47.2	40.9	44.4	− 6.6
1816–19	125.2	31.8	46.3	55.3	50.3	− 18.5
1819–22	126.5	35.1	44.3	47.4	45.7	− 13.0
1822–25	124.0	37.9	35.8	28.9	32.7	− 1.7
1825–28	117.2	33.7	37.0	30.8	34.1	− 5.2
1828–31	110.0	34.0	37.4	31.5	34.6	− 5.4
1831–34	104.4	31.0	39.4	35.2	37.4	− 9.4
Demerara-Essequibo						
1817–20	128.7	32.0	44.4	38.1	41.7	− 9.8
1820–23	124.4	30.2	46.4	38.2	42.7	− 11.7
1823–26	120.5	28.0	51.3	42.4	47.2	− 14.3
1826–29	116.9	33.9	42.0	30.9	36.9	− 5.0
1829–32	112.6	30.9	54.1	39.1	47.1	− 14.5
Berbice						
1817–19	128.0	n.a.	n.a.	n.a.	n.a.	n.a.
1819–22	121.9	30.0	38.9	37.5	38.3	− 7.9
1822–25	114.9	28.7	45.4	40.7	43.3	− 13.5
1825–28	116.3	35.1	35.7	28.5	32.4	+ 0.8
1828–31	116.8	31.8	38.5	32.8	35.9	− 4.8
1831–34	n.c.	n.c.	n.c.	n.c.	n.c.	n.c.
Bahamas						
1822–25	103.3	48.6	45.9	28.8	37.5	+ 12.7
1825–28	100.3	56.2	46.3	32.5	39.4	+ 16.1
1828–31	99.3	69.7	n.c.	n.c.	40.0	+ 23.3
1831–34	97.8	69.4	40.1	31.6	35.8	+ 24.8
Anguilla						
1827–31	85.3	53.6	24.2	25.7	25.0	+ 28.6
1831–34	84.6	39.5	86.1	52.0	62.7	− 1.6
Barbuda						
1817–21	89.6	37.3	n.c.	n.c.	23.6	+ 25.1
1821–24	80.5	61.6	n.c.	n.c.	21.6	+ 34.4
1824–28	77.3	47.5	n.c.	n.c.	26.3	+ 22.4
1828–32	77.8	46.7	n.c.	n.c.	25.0	+ 22.2

Source: Calculated from data in tables S1.1, S8.1, and S8.2.

Note: The rates of natural increase are derived directly from the unadjusted registration data, so that the adjusted birth and death rates do not always produce the same results.

showed a significant slowing in the rate of increase during the later 1820s, which is only partly explained by the hurricane of 1831 (fig. 9.1). Montserrat almost maintained a continuous positive natural increase throughout the registration period, while St. Kitts, Nevis, and Antigua moved from a modest decrease to a modest increase by 1825. The Virgin Islands rose rapidly from a heavy negative rate in 1818–22 to match the high rate of increase in Barbados by about 1827, but then declined steeply to a much lower positive rate. The low rate experienced in 1818–22 appears to have been aberrant, resulting chiefly from heavy mortality caused by a hurricane in 1819 and a measles epidemic in 1821.[17] In general, then, the old sugar colonies and marginal colonies improved their rates of natural increase fairly substantially between 1817 and about 1825, when they reached a peak; they declined again until 1830, then rose to a second maximum by emancipation.

The second group of colonies, showing heavy but improving negative rates, comprised most of the second- and third-phase sugar colonies. The colony with the heaviest negative rate of natural increase was Tobago, with a rate as low as −32.5 per 1,000 in 1819. As in the first group of colonies, this rate improved to a peak of −4.8 in 1826, declined to a new minimum of −20.2 in 1832, and rose again. Grenada, St. Vincent, and St. Lucia followed a similar trend but climbed much more rapidly, achieving positive rates by 1822 and never returning to the disastrously low rates typical of Tobago. Trinidad followed a similar course also but never achieved a positive rate. All of these colonies had rates significantly lower than Demerara-Essequibo and Berbice until about 1820, but the mainland colonies declined as the islands improved, and by 1825 Demerara-Essequibo's rate was as low as that of Tobago. Berbice's decline was less dramatic, and the colony actually achieved a bare excess of births over deaths around 1827. Dominica, however, was aberrant, approaching most nearly the tendency noted in St. Kitts and Nevis. In this as in its political history, Dominica demonstrated its wavering position between the Windward and Leeward Islands.

The third pattern of natural increase, characterized by relatively light but deteriorating negative rates, was typical only of Jamaica. Demerara-Essequibo and Berbice approached it more nearly than any of the other colonies, but they began from much lower levels and showed too great a tendency to improvement to be classed with Jamaica.

This threefold classification of the colonies in terms of natural increase fits well the classification of economic types established in chapter 3. The marginal colonies may readily be separated from the old sugar colonies, since they generally showed much higher rates of positive natural increase. The combining of the second- and third-phase sugar colonies, and the separation of Jamaica, on the basis of economic structure is clearly justified in terms of demographic experience. Dominica was the only real deviant.

Differences in the level of natural increase were also apparent on a variety of scales within particular colonies. Variations at the parish level in most colonies are detailed in tables S9.1–9.11. Here it is most important to notice that there was a

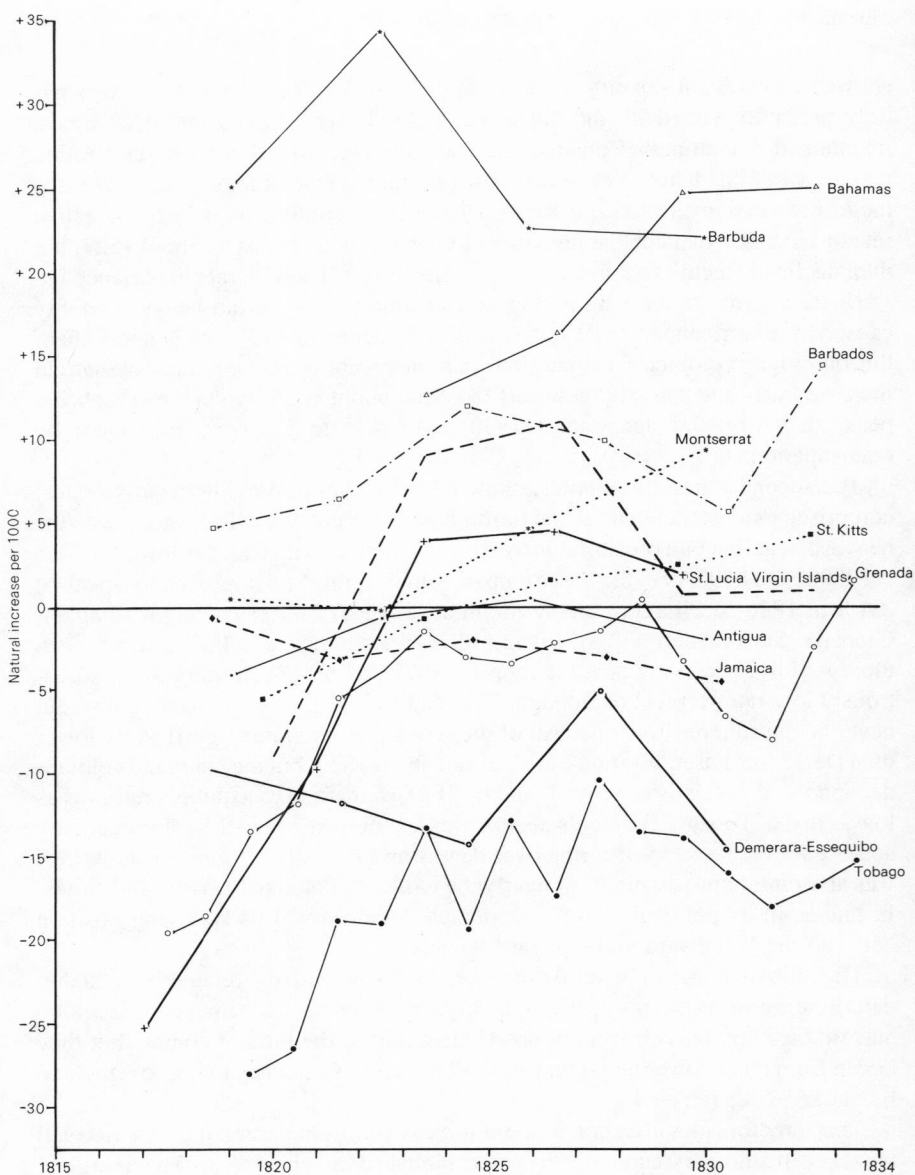

Fig. 9.1. *Natural Increase of Slaves by Colony, 1815–34.* (Source: *table 9.1.*
Grenada and Tobago are shown as three-year moving averages.)

consistent tendency for the rate of natural increase to be highest in the towns and the parishes producing crops other than sugar, while parishes dominated by sugar plantations had the lowest rates. These contrasts were clear within particular colonies but did not necessarily hold for the British Caribbean in general. Thus, the sugar parishes of the first-phase colonies generally experienced higher rates of natural increase than the coffee parishes of the later-settled colonies, for example. Not all urban slave populations showed positive rates, but with a few exceptions their rates were always higher than those common in the rural hinterlands of their particular colonies (table 9.2).

Before attempting to account for these variations in the pattern of natural increase, the relative importance of fertility and mortality must be weighed. In doing so it is important to recall that the slave registration data provide an accurate measure of natural increase but, because of the omission of many births and infant deaths, understate fertility and mortality by varying amounts. Thus, it is necessary to employ the adjusted rates, which are presented in table 9.1 and are derived from assumptions discussed fully in chapter 2. On the basis of these adjusted rates, for the year 1820 the coefficient of variation of the birth rate was 21.6 percent and of the death rate 20.2 percent. All eighteen colonies listed in table 9.1 are included in these calculations, but British Honduras and the Cayman Islands are excluded

Table 9.2. *Slave Birth Rates, Death Rates, and Rates of Natural Increase in Towns and Urban Parishes, 1815–34*

Town or Urban Parish	(Registered) Births per 1,000	(Registered) Deaths per 1,000	Natural Increase per 1,000	Colony Average: Natural Increase per 1,000
Towns				
Bridgetown, Barbados (1832–34)	40.4	27.8	+ 12.6	+ 14.3
Basseterre, St. Kitts (1831–34)	35.1	21.1	+ 14.0	+ 4.6
St. John's, Antigua (1828–32)	22.1	23.3	− 1.2	− 2.0
Plymouth, Montserrat (1828–31)	38.8	20.4	+ 18.4	+ 9.5
Kingston, Jamaica (1829–32)	19.4	21.1	− 1.7	− 4.8
Roseau, Dominica (1826–29)	23.2	27.6	− 4.4	+ 1.2
Roseau, Dominica (1829–32)	34.6	37.5	− 2.9	+ 2.9
Castries, St. Lucia (1815–19)	13.6	31.8	− 18.2	− 25.5
St. George, Grenada (1817–19)	28.8	28.2	+ 0.6	− 18.3
St. George, Grenada (1830–32)	30.3	28.0	+ 2.3	− 7.8
Scarborough, Tobago (1819–21)	20.3	29.7	− 9.4	− 26.0
Urban Parishes				
St. Michael, Barbados (1817–20)	34.6	26.7	+ 7.9	+ 4.8
St. George, St. Vincent (1817–22)	22.5	37.5	− 15.0	− 12.7
St. George and St. Andrew, Demerara (1829–32)	23.9	26.6	− 2.7	− 14.5

Sources: Tables S2.10 and S9.1–9.13, derived from T.71.

because of lack of data. Around 1820, then, fertility may have been slightly more important than mortality in determining the pattern of natural increase; but with a standard error of 4.7, compared to a difference between the means of 2.9, it is difficult to be confident of this result. By 1830 the coefficients of variations were 22.4 percent for the birth rate and 20.3 percent for the death rate, with a standard error of 4.8 and a difference between the means of 2.4. Similar results are obtained if the analysis is restricted to the 15 sugar colonies. To employ a further test, natural increase was more strongly correlated with mortality than with fertility in 1820, but by 1830 the position was reversed (tables 9.3 and 9.4). There was no clear correlation between fertility and mortality in either of these years. In general, it appears that mortality and fertility were of roughly equal significance in determining colony-level variations in the level of natural increase within the British Caribbean after 1807, though fertility differentials became increasingly important during the period of registration.

It has been argued by Stanley Engerman that in the contrast between the British Caribbean and the United States it was fertility rather than mortality that principally determined differential growth in the slave populations.[18] It is not necessary, of course, that there should be congruity between intra-Caribbean and extra-Caribbean comparisons, but the ambiguity of the evidence within the British Caribbean for the last years of slavery does suggest that more attention should be paid to fertility than has been common in most discussions.

MORTALITY

Analysis of mortality patterns is inhibited by the understatement of infant deaths in the slave registration returns. As discussed in chapter 2, this understatement chiefly pertained to children born and dying within a registration interval and so prevents direct comparisons of infant mortality levels. A solution to this problem has been sought in the use of model life tables as a means of estimating the extent of underregistration. Because of variations in registration practice it is necessary to regard the adjusted mortality rates presented in table 9.1 with caution, though they are undoubtedly a better guide to the reality than are direct calculations from the raw registration data. Age-specific mortality rates can, however, be calculated directly from the registration data for slaves 5 years of age and above.

Mortality differentials at the colony level did not conform closely to the threefold classification of colonies in terms of natural increase (table 9.1). In part, this lack of conformity resulted from the ambiguous correlations between mortality, fertility, and natural increase. It was also affected by the association, in many colonies, between high fertility and high infant mortality rates. Thus, some colonies achieved significant positive natural increase in the face of heavy mortality, through high fertility and a consequently high infant mortality rate. Barbados is the outstanding example of this pattern, experiencing mortality levels very similar to those characteristic of the third-phase sugar colonies. In the

Table 9.3. *Correlation Coefficients: Twenty Colonies, 1820*

	(1)	(2)	(3)	(4)	(5)	(6)	(7)	(8)	(9)	(10)	(11)
Natural increase per 1,000	(1)	1.00									
Births per 1,000	(2)	.70	1.00								
Deaths per 1,000	(3)	−.78	−.15	1.00							
Males per 100 females	(4)	−.42	−.28	.41	1.00						
Percentage African-born	(5)	−.66	−.50	.49	.84	1.00					
Tons sugar exported per slave	(6)	−.84	−.73	.53	−.04	.37	1.00				
Percentage slaves on sugar estates	(7)	−.72	−.52	.58	−.28	−.03	.77	1.00			
Percentage slaves on coffee plantations	(8)	−.17	−.16	.05	.04	.28	.03	−.13	1.00		
Percentage slaves on cotton plantations	(9)	−.28	−.37	.14	.08	.21	.36	.18	.11	1.00	
Percentage slaves in other agriculture	(10)	.85	.61	−.69	−.25	−.41	−.65	−.76	−.18	−.34	1.00
Percentage slaves in towns	(11)	−.48	−.05	.61	.84	.56	−.21	−.26	−.09	−.11	−.28	1.00

Note: Coefficients in italics are significant at the 99 percent level of probability.

Table 9.4. *Correlation Coefficients: Twenty Colonies, 1830*

		(1)	(2)	(3)	(4)	(5)	(6)	(7)	(8)	(9)	(10)	(11)	(12)	(13)	(14)	(15)	(16)
Natural increase per 1,000	(1)	1.00															
Births per 1,000	(2)	.70	1.00														
Deaths per 1,000	(3)	−.58	.07	1.00													
Males per 100 females	(4)	−.45	−.44	.29	1.00												
Percentage African-born	(5)	−.81	−.71	.26	.83	1.00											
Percentage colored	(6)	.72	.42	−.55	−.53	−.94	1.00										
Slaves per holding	(7)	−.64	−.62	.25	−.29	.87	−.51	1.00									
Tons sugar exported per slave	(8)	−.82	−.61	.46	.12	.80	−.62	.56	1.00								
Percentage slaves on sugar estates	(9)	−.70	−.32	.58	−.26	.48	−.43	.71	.61	1.00							
Percentage slaves on coffee plantations	(10)	−.12	−.25	−.16	.02	.21	−.41	.00	.14	−.09	1.00						
Percentage slaves in other agriculture	(11)	.76	.36	−.62	−.27	−.56	.73	−.48	−.56	−.79	−.15	1.00					
Percentage slaves in town	(12)	−.37	.09	.62	.90	.20	−.37	−.45	−.14	−.28	−.12	−.27	1.00				
Percentage field laborers, 1834	(13)	−.35	−.41	.04	−.58	.60	.08	.68	.44	.48	.34	−.14	−.68	1.00			
Percentage domestics, 1834	(14)	.42	.49	−.16	.62	−.70	−.12	−.76	−.49	−.56	−.26	.16	.73	−.94	1.00		
Percentage under 6 years, 1834	(15)	.89	.72	−.43	−.55	−.88	.82	−.33	−.70	−.45	−.21	.78	−.42	−.04	.05	1.00	
Percentage aged, 1834	(16)	−.37	−.33	−.05	−.07	.34	.06	−.39	.19	.18	−.12	−.06	−.04	.25	−.19	−.23	1.00

Note: Coefficients in italics are significant at the 99 percent level of probability.

marginal colonies, however, infant mortality accounted for a smaller component of total mortality, and so the latter was considerably less.

In the period after 1807 most colonies experienced a decrease in the crude death rate. But exceptions to this general decline came from all of the classes of colonies. The rise in mortality in Jamaica, Demerara-Essequibo, and Grenada after 1807 is not unexpected, but the same trend in Antigua and Montserrat is surprising. Anguilla also probably experienced an increase in the crude death rate toward the end of the 1820s, as a result of the island's subsistence crisis. In order to understand the apparent differences in the colonies' crude death rates, however, it is essential first to take into account the effects of variations in their age and sex structures. Mortality and the slave sex ratio were positively correlated at the colony level, though the correlations were not significant at the 99 percent level (tabes 9.3 and 9.4). Stronger correlations existed with the age structure. The crude death rate for male slaves was clearly associated with the proportion of males aged 15–44 years ($r = .62$), and to a weaker, though significant, degree for females ($r = .46$). Thus, differences in total mortality at the colony level may reflect contrasts in age structure.

Sex and Age

With few exceptions, crude death rates at the colony level were significantly higher for males than for females (table 9.1). This contrast occurs in most populations, of course, but it is important to recall that in the slave populations of the British Caribbean there was a substantial concentration of females in the field gangs of plantations and that females shared the heavy demands on labor. The significance of this relationship will be considered further in the discussion of occupation and mortality, below. Of the exceptions to the general trend, the most important occurred in Trinidad between 1816 and 1822. The reasons for this unusually high female mortality are not clear, but the period was unique in showing a rising sex ratio as the result of the movement of slaves to Trinidad from other Caribbean colonies. This may have created short-run distortions in age structure.

The extremes of mortality experience in the slave populations of the British Caribbean in the years after 1817 are represented by the model life tables West 1 and West 9 (figure 9.2). It was argued in chapter 2 that West 1 was typical of conditions in Tobago, Trinidad, and St. Lucia, while West 9 was typical of Anguilla and Barbuda. The other colonies fell between these extremes, West 3 being typical of Barbados, St. Kitts, Nevis, and Demerara-Essequibo, and West 6 of Dominica (see table 2.7). At most ages the death rate under West 1 conditions was double that experienced under West 9, though the differential narrowed with age. The use of model life tables is particularly helpful as a means of estimating the actual levels of infant mortality in the slave populations, in view of the inadequacy of the registration data. Here the extremes of mortality experience were widest. For male infants the death rate ranged from about 580 to 240 per 1,000, and for

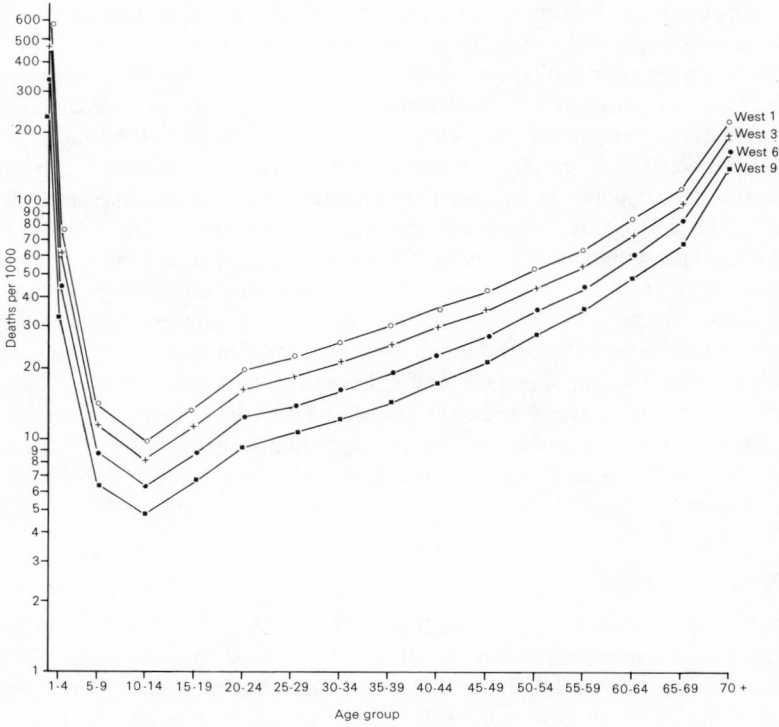

Fig. 9.2.   *Age-specific Mortality of Males: Model Life Table Populations*
   (Data from Coale and Demeny, Regional Model Life Tables, 1966*).*

females from 480 to 200 (table 9.5). These rates are only approximations and may
not fully take into account the prolonged breast-feeding periods typical of the West
Indian slave population, but they do show that there was a wide disparity between
the experience of the marginal colonies and the sugar colonies. The ordering of the
sugar colonies in terms of infant mortality is more difficult to explain, especially
the low rates for Jamaica. But the model life table estimates do suggest that rates in
excess of 400 per 1,000 were typical of most eastern Caribbean colonies and that
infant mortality levels in the old sugar colonies were not dramatically superior to
those in the new sugar colonies.

   A comparison of age-specific death rates for slaves 5 years of age and above,
calculated directly from the registration data, with rates indicated by the appropriate model life tables shows a very close correspondence in the middle range of
mortality levels, with wider disparities at the extremes (fig. 9.3). For slaves aged
5–69 years there is a close congruence between the two measures in the case of St.
Kitts at West 3, for example. But the high level of mortality experienced by adult
slaves in Tobago exceeded that predicted by West 1, while in Anguilla registered

Table 9.5. *Slave Infant Mortality: Model Life Table Estimates*

| Mortality Level | Infant Deaths per 1,000 | | Colonies |
	Males	Females	
West 1	583	479	St. Lucia, Tobago, Trinidad
West 3	459	381	Barbados, St. Kitts, Nevis, St. Vincent, Grenada, Demerara-Essequibo
West 4	411	341	Virgin Islands, Berbice
West 5	368	307	Antigua, Montserrat, Bahamas
West 6	331	276	Dominica
West 7	298	248	Jamaica
West 8	268	224	British Honduras, Cayman Islands
West 9	241	201	Anguilla, Barbuda

Source: Ansley J. Coale and Paul Demeny, *Regional Model Life Tables and Stable Populations* (1966), pp. 2–10. See also table 2.7, above.

mortality rates were lower than those expected for West 9. This suggests that there are limitations to the value of the model life tables as indicators of mortality patterns in the slave populations. This is hardly surprising. No doubt a similar range of error applies to the infant mortality estimates, but no independent check is available.[19] In the analysis of mortality at ages 5 years and above, however, rates calculated directly from the registration data provide a superior indication of reality and will be used in preference to the model life table estimates.

The broad contrast between the crude death rates of the sugar colonies and marginal colonies was equally obvious in terms of age-specific mortality levels (tables S9.14–9.16). It was apparent at all ages and affected males as well as females (fig. 9.4). But the relative ordering of the colonies is changed to some degree as a result of their differing age structures. Colonies with relatively large proportions of slaves aged over 40 or under 5 years generally showed high crude death rates because of the particularly high mortality affecting those age groups. These effects were complicated, but overall it appears that the adjusted crude death rates do provide a reliable indication of comparative mortality levels. Thus, the slave population of Tobago, with the highest crude death rate of all the colonies, suffered extreme mortality levels in almost all age groups among both males and females. Berbice showed relatively lower mortality among children, but its female slaves matched the Tobago rates after 35 years, and its males after 55 years. St. Lucia, however, came much closer to the Tobago rates among those under 20 years, while dropping below both Tobago and Berbice in the older age groups. The old sugar colony of St. Kitts was distinguished from those new sugar colonies by lower rates of mortality among children and old people. But in the principal working age groups, particularly among male slaves of 25–45, there was little difference between St. Kitts and Berbice or St. Lucia. Nevis and the Virgin Islands followed the same general trends as St. Kitts (table S9.14). The relatively low mortality levels that were reached in Dominica by the end of the 1820s were

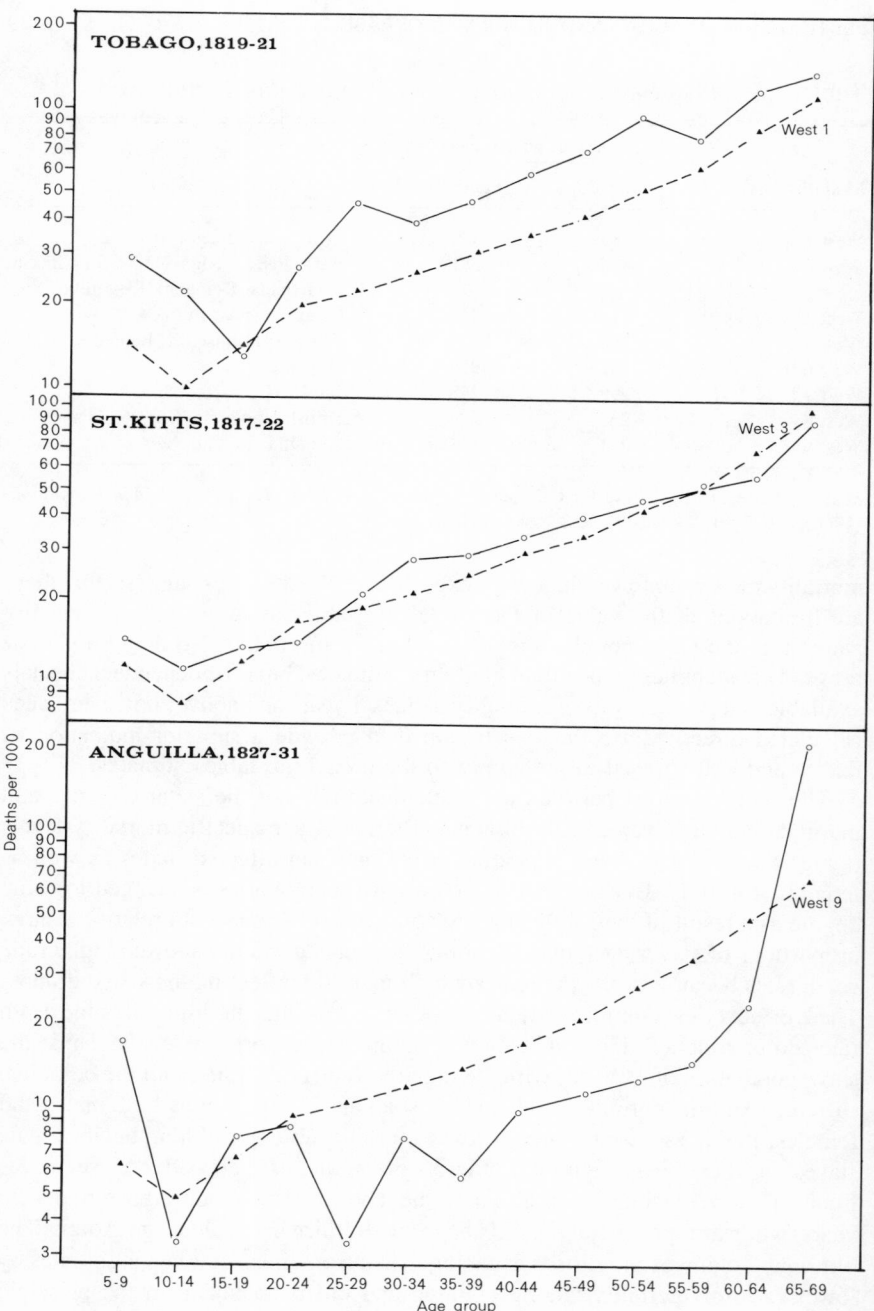

Fig. 9.3. *Age-specific Mortality of Male Slaves Compared with Model Life Table Rates: Tobago, St. Kitts, and Anguilla.* (Source: *table S9.14.*)

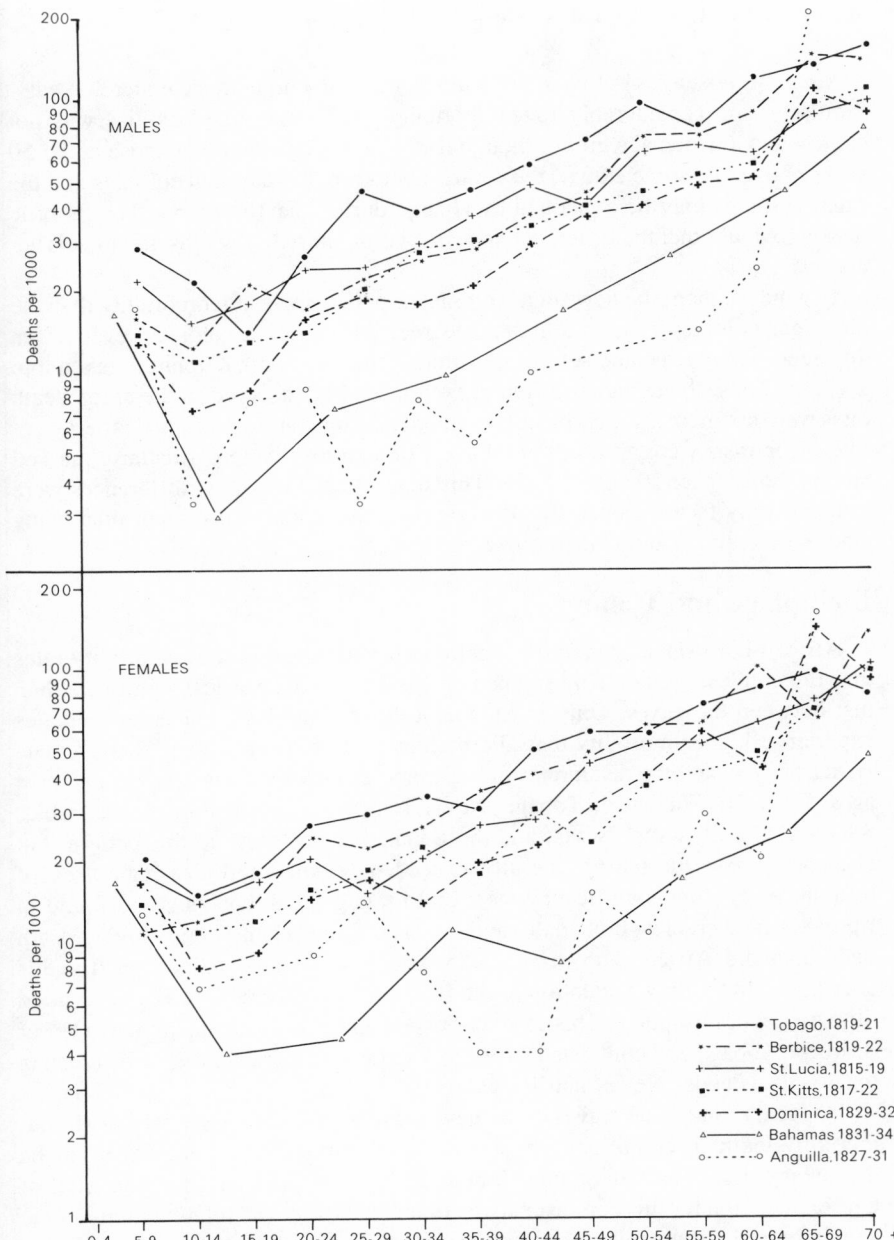

MALES

FEMALES

●———● Tobago.1819-21
■- - -■ Berbice.1819-22
+———+ St.Lucia.1815-19
■·····■ St.Kitts.1817-22
+- - -+ Dominica.1829-32
△———△ Bahamas 1831-34
○·····○ Anguilla.1827-31

Fig. 9.4.   *Age-specific Slave Mortality by Sex and Colony.* (Source: *table S9.14.*)

[321]

apparent at most ages but were particularly marked among those under 20 years. Similarly, the considerably lower mortality of the marginal colonies was not confined to any one age group, though it was most marked among those under 50 years of age. To some extent, the contrast between the marginal colonies and the sugar colonies may be explained by change during the 1820s, but there is little reason to doubt that the difference in age-specific mortality was as great in earlier periods.

In general, then, the new sugar colonies experienced heavier mortality than the old sugar colonies and, to a greater degree, the marginal colonies, even when differences in the age and sex composition of the slave populations are taken into account. Thus, the apparent differences in mortality observed in the crude death rates were not mere artifacts but represented real contrasts in mortality experience. These contrasts were apparent at all ages, though they were particularly marked among those under 20 years of age. This suggests that mortality differences were influenced by factors generally affecting the slave populations rather than being determined simply by labor regimes.

Birthplace and Color

African-born slaves generally experienced higher age-specific mortality rates than did creoles, though in most colonies this differential was less significant than that between the sexes. Only in St. Lucia did African-born males and females experience higher mortality than did creoles as a group, and even there female Africans exceeded the death rates of male creoles only by a slight margin at most ages (fig. 9.5). (For data on Tobago, Nevis, Barbados, and the Bahamas see tables S9.14–9.17). St. Kitts, Nevis, and the Bahamas came close to this pattern, but elsewhere male mortality generally exceeded female mortality regardless of birthplace. The one significant exception to this general tendency was found in Berbice where creoles, both males and females, showed consistently higher death rates than did Africans up to age 50 years. It is difficult to account for this aberration, but it draws attention to the fact that mortality rates in Berbice varied little by sex or birthplace. This close correspondence was also apparent to a lesser degree in Tobago and contrasted strongly with the much greater disparities seen in the Virgin Islands, Nevis, and Barbados.

It appears, then, that slaves in the new sugar colonies were exposed to similar mortality-inducing conditions regardless of sex or birthplace, while Africans in the old sugar colonies and marginal colonies suffered heavier mortality than creoles. One explanation for this contrast may be found in the creoles' relative immunity to certain mortal diseases. This advantage persisted, even though all Africans in the West Indies after 1810 were survivors of the "seasoning" process, which wreaked havoc among new arrivals in earlier periods. Further, the creole populations of the older colonies had had several generations to build up immunities, while creoles in the third-phase sugar colonies were commonly the children of African-born slaves. Alternatively, it might be argued that Africans, being concentrated in the

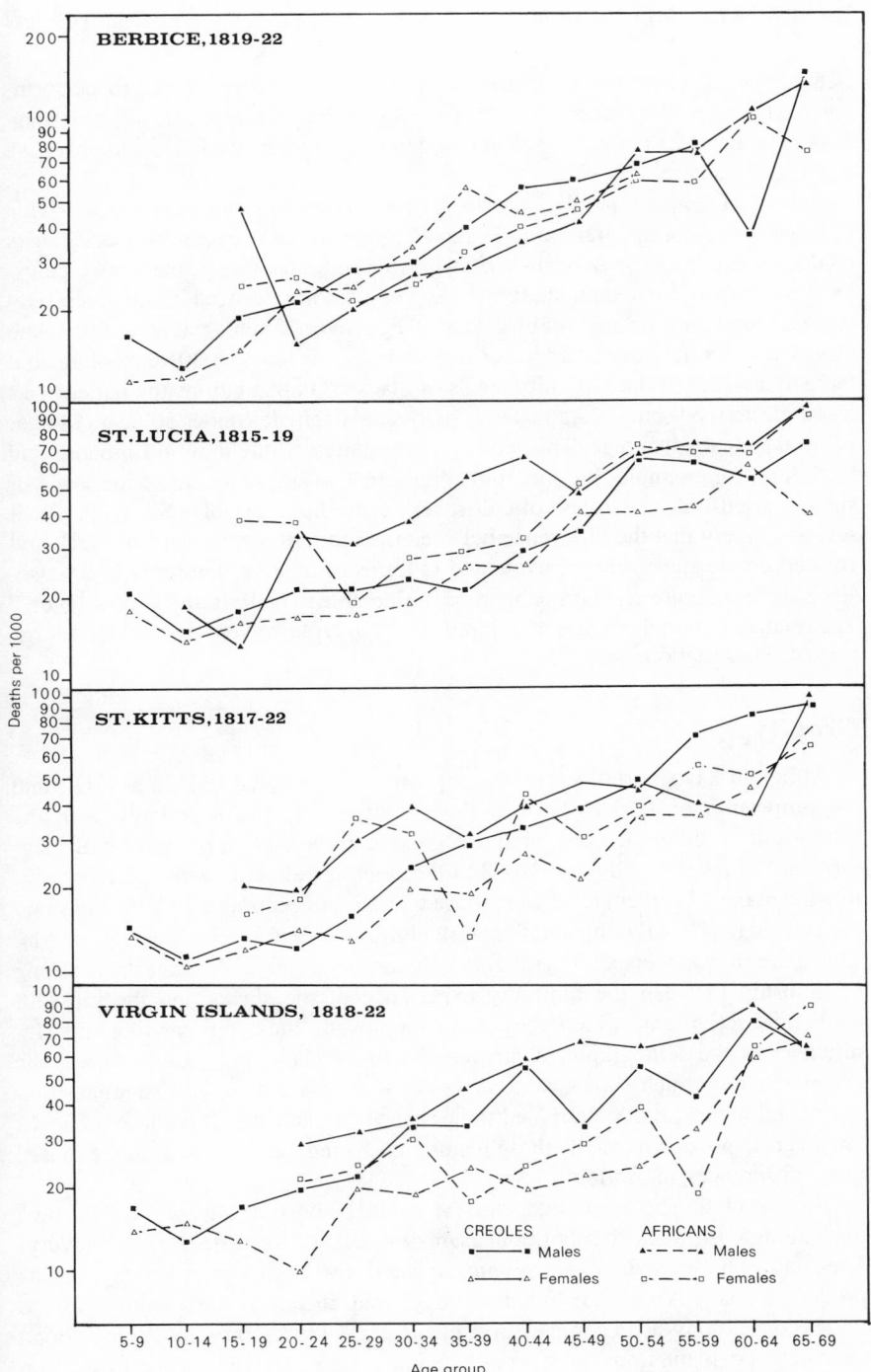

Fig. 9.5. *Age-specific Slave Mortality by Sex and Birthplace: Berbice, St. Lucia, St. Kitts, and the Virgin Islands.* (Source: *table S9.14.*)

field gangs of plantations, tended to be given the heaviest tasks to perform, whereas creoles were more often employed as skilled tradespeople or domestics. This hypothesis will be discussed below, but it does not by itself seem to provide a satisfactory answer.

Slaves of color generally had lower mortality rates than did blacks. This contrast was most apparent among slaves living in towns, because there blacks tended more often to be African-born, while the coloreds were virtually all creoles. In Bridgetown, for example, female slaves of color showed death rates only one-half to two-thirds those of blacks, at all ages over 20 years (table S9.20). Male slaves of color, however, had lower rates than blacks to about 30 years of age but thereafter matched the mortality levels of blacks. On plantations the pattern was less well defined, but colored slaves, particularly females under 50 years of age, showed a clear advantage. This tendency was quite definite in rural Barbados and St. Lucia, for example, but far from certain in Tobago, where the experience of slaves varied little regardless of color, sex, or birthplace (tables S9.21–9.22). It seems unlikely that the difference between the mortality experience of black and colored creole slaves can be explained in terms of relative immunity to disease, since slaves of color were probably more vulnerable to malaria and yellow fever.[20] The relative material welfare of colored slaves may, however, account for a large part of the variation.

Crop-type

Although slave mortality levels were positively correlated with the sex ratio and the proportion of African-born at the colony level, and negatively with the proportion of colored, none of these gross correlations were statistically significant (tables 9.3 and 9.4). In 1820 the only correlations with mortality significant at the 99 percent level were those with the concentration of slaves in sugar cultivation ($r = .58$), nonplantation agriculture ($r = -.69$), and towns ($r = .61$). This pattern was repeated with little change in 1830 and suggests a strong relationship between the mortality experience of the slaves and the types of economic activity in which they were employed, thus transcending the significance of the demographic characteristics of the slaves themselves. It was the regimes under which slaves worked, in activities associated with peculiar environmental niches, that determined their chances of survival. It is more difficult, however, to pin down exactly those features of the regimes which lay at the root of these differences in mortality levels.

The association between sugar cultivation and heavy mortality was well known to contemporaries, and the abolitionists made much of it in the debate over slavery. The contrast between the sugar colonies, old and new, and the marginal non-sugar-producing colonies was too obvious to be ignored. It is important to move beyond these broad colony-level comparisons, however, and to identify the patterns found on particular plantations or in small regions. Here it is necessary to rely on samples, since such detailed data are not available for most of the colonies. For

Jamaica, it has been shown that slaves living on coffee plantations and livestock pens had significantly lower mortality rates than those on sugar estates, even when adjusted for differences in sex and age composition.[21] The registration data for St. Lucia provide similar results. Between 1815 and 1819 the crude (registered) death rate on sugar estates in St. Lucia stood at 47 per 1,000, compared to only 37 on plantations producing coffee, cocoa, cotton, or provisions (table 9.6). An equally strong contrast existed in the age-specific death rates (table S9.25). There was little difference between the two types of agriculture before age 15 years, but thereafter the rates on sugar estates were consistently and substantially higher. Minor distinctions between the mortality levels of slaves attached to units producing coffee, cocoa, cotton, or provisions are less certain because of the relatively small populations. But cocoa and provisions were associated with lower crude death rates than were cotton or coffee. This ordering of crop-types in St. Lucia closely matches that found in the colony-level correlations for 1820 (table 9.3). It suggests a decline in mortality levels from sugar through cotton, coffee, cocoa, and provisions.

Each of these crops tended to occupy a particular ecological niche, sugar and cotton being most often produced on low-lying, level lands, and coffee and cocoa on elevated slopes. In order to minimize the effect on mortality of these factors, it is useful to turn to the case of Demerara-Essequibo, where there were no essential differences between the physical environments of the plantation-types. Plantations were intermixed along a homogeneous coastal and riverine strip. Of the major crops, sugar was associated with a crude (registered) death rate of about 40 per 1,000, compared to 32 on coffee plantations and 26 on cotton plantations (table 9.7). Cattle farms showed mortality similar to that on coffee plantations, while woodcutters had a surprisingly low death rate. Differences in age structure may account for the contrasting ordering of coffee and cotton in Demerara-Essequibo and St. Lucia, but the relatively heavy mortality of slaves employed in sugar remains outstanding and clearly cannot be explained in terms of environmental factors.

For most colonies, the crops produced by individual plantations are not readily identified, but parish-level analysis corroborates the general contrast between mortality levels on sugar and other types of plantations. In Grenada, for example, the sugar parish of St. Andrew had a crude (registered) death rate of 55 per 1,000 in 1817–19, compared to 43 in the sugar-coffee-cocoa parish of St. John and St. Mark, and 32 in the cotton-sugar island of Carriacou (table S9.9). Although Carriacou largely abandoned cotton for sugar cultivation during the 1820s, the gap between it and St. Andrew widened. St. John and St. Mark increased its production of cocoa but came to approach more nearly the mortality level of St. Andrew. Thus, the ordering of crop-types in Grenada, from sugar through coffee to cocoa and cotton, matched that found in Demerara-Essequibo. The pattern applied equally to both sexes, though St. Andrew was unusual in showing a higher death rate among females than males in 1817–19. It was not a function of differing age structures (fig. 9.6). The most pronounced differences in mortality levels

Table 9.6. *Slave Birth Rates, Death Rates, Rates of Natural Increase, and Sex Ratios by Crop-type: St. Lucia, 1815–19*

Crop	(1815) Males per 100 Females	(Registered) Births per 1,000	(Registered) Deaths per 1,000			(Registered) Natural Increase per 1,000
			Males	Females	Total	
Sugar	87.8	15.4	54.2	40.4	46.9	−31.5
Coffee	87.6	14.5	41.4	36.3	38.7	−24.2
Cocoa	82.5	15.5	37.8	21.2	28.7	−13.2
Cotton	60.6	11.5	57.1	34.6	43.1	−31.6
Provisions	71.6	14.4	17.3	40.2	30.7	−16.3
Combined	93.1	10.2	70.1	25.9	47.2	−37.0
Personal	74.9	13.1	38.1	17.6	26.4	−13.3
Total*	83.9	14.3	46.9	32.7	39.8	−25.5

Source: T.71/376–81.

*Includes 2,890 slaves for whom crop-type is unknown.

occurred among slaves under 40 years of age, though Carriacou showed unexpectedly high rates among those under 20 years in 1817–19. The improvement in mortality during the 1820s, common to all three parishes, particularly affected children and young adults.

In St. Vincent the pattern of mortality differentials was very similar to that in Grenada. Once again the sugar parishes showed much heavier mortality than the cotton- and sugar-producing islands of the Grenadines. In 1817–22 the crude (registered) death rate in the St. Vincent Grenadines was as low as 19 per 1,000, while in the sugar parishes the rate varied between 35 and 45, in spite of the very similar sex ratios found throughout the colony (table S9.8). The contrast was

Table 9.7. *Slave Birth Rates, Death Rates, and Rates of Natural Increase by Crop-Type: Demerara-Essequibo, 1829–32*

Crop	(Registered) Births per 1,000	(Registered) Deaths per 1,000	Natural Increase per 1,000
Sugar	20.2	40.4	−20.2
Coffee	17.3	32.0	−14.7
Cattle	23.4	31.2	−7.8
Timber	15.2	21.2	−6.0
Cotton	26.2	25.1	+1.1
Total*	20.2	34.7	−14.5

Source: PP., 1833, vol. 26 (700), "Slave Population," pp. 4–10.

*Includes unattached slaves and slaves attached to plantations producing combined crops.

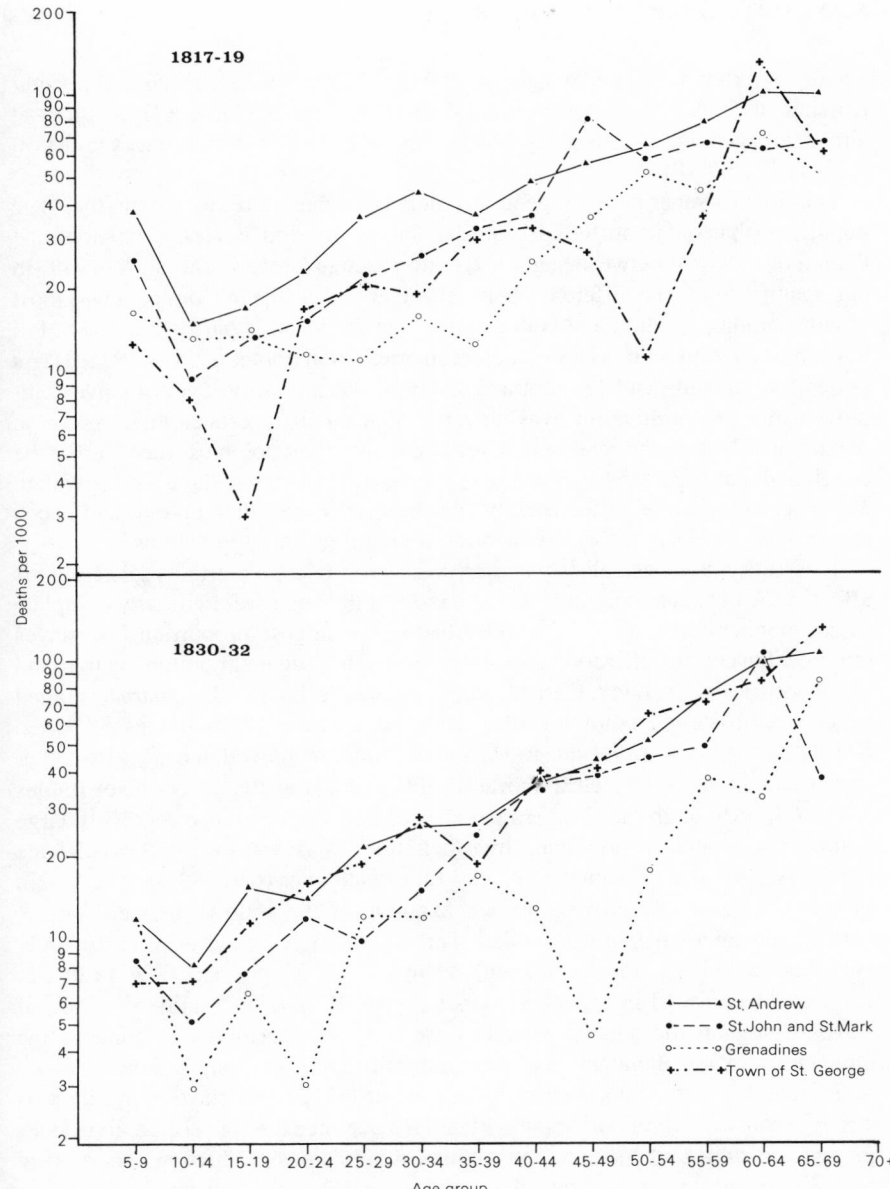

Fig. 9.6. *Age-specific Slave Mortality by Parish: Grenada, 1817–19 and 1830–32. (Source: table S9.19.)*

[327]

equally striking in terms of age-specific mortality. As in Grenada, the sugar parishes of St. Vincent showed much higher death rates than the Grenadines at almost all ages, but the disparity was particularly marked among slaves under 30 years (table S9.18).

Dominica's sugar parishes generally showed higher mortality among the slave population than did its coffee parishes, but the relationship was less clearly defined than in the contrast between sugar and cotton seen in Grenada and St. Vincent. In age-specific terms the difference between sugar and coffee in Dominica was most obvious among children and young adults, but the island's parishes failed to fall into a neat continuum in terms of their crop orientation (tables S9.6 and S11.3). As noticed in Grenada and Demerara-Essequibo, the mortality level of slaves employed in coffee cultivation was nearer to that on sugar estates than on cotton plantations. Within the relatively diversified new sugar colonies, then, it may be concluded that sugar was associated with substantially higher slave mortality than any other crop, while coffee usually showed higher rates than cotton, and cocoa and provisions showed the lowest rates among the rural populations.

It is difficult to establish whether these crop-related mortality differentials affected the old sugar colonies, because most of the latter were virtually complete sugar monocultures by 1807. In Barbados the largest proportions of slaves employed in cotton cultivation and other types of nonsugar agriculture were found in the parishes of St. Lucy, Christ Church, and St. Philip, but these parishes failed to show consistently below-average death rates in the 1820s (tables S9.1 and S11.1). In the Leeward Islands too few slaves were employed in enterprises other than sugar to show any clear mortality differentials at the parish level (tables S9.2–9.4). Although the southern parishes of Antigua contained relatively large numbers of properties producing livestock and provisions, even the small-scale divisions showed no advantage in their crude death rates (table S9.3). The Virgin Islands, however, do provide a clear example of the contrast between sugar, cotton, and minor plantation staples. Tortola, the only island devoted to sugar cultivation, had a crude (registered) death rate of 31 per 1,000 in 1828–31, compared to only 13 in the other islands (table S9.5). The conditions of life of slaves living on the smaller islands were very similar to those found in the Grenadines or the Bahamas, and their mortality rates were equivalent.

In general, then, the association between crop-type and slave mortality was strong. From a maximum in sugar cultivation it declined through coffee, livestock, pimento, cotton, and cocoa to a minimum in provisions production. There were few significant deviations from this ordering of crops, except that in St. Lucia cotton appears to have been associated with heavier mortality than coffee. The contrasting mortality levels were not merely a function of differences in the demographic characteristics of slaves attached to particular types of enterprise. They affected males and females, Africans and creoles, and were apparent at most ages. Nor can the mortality differentials be explained in terms of variations in the physical environments associated with particular crop types. This is made very clear by the case of Demerara-Essequibo, where the physical environment was uniform for all crops. Thus, it may be concluded that it is necessary to search for the reasons for these contrasts in slave mortality levels in the internal organization of the particular units. Before proceeding to this task, however, it is important to note briefly a further contrast in mortality patterns, that between the rural and urban slave populations.

Rural-Urban Differences

Urban slaves generally suffered lower mortality levels than rural slaves. Each of the capital towns listed in table 9.2 had a crude (registered) death rate lower than the average for its colony, with the one exception of Roseau in 1829–32. This contrast was also apparent where only the death rate of the larger parish containing the capital town is known, except that in St. Vincent the parish of St. George had a rate slightly higher than that in the entire colony (including the low-mortality Grenadines). The crude (registered) death rates varied from 20 per 1,000 in Plymouth to a maximum of 38 in Roseau, but rates of more than 30 seem to have been very rare in the towns, after about 1817 at least. Smaller towns sometimes showed even lower slave death rates than the capital towns. The minor towns of St. Lucia, for example, all had crude (registered) death rates of less than 25 per 1,000 in 1815–19, compared to 32 in Castries (table S9.7). But the pattern was not the same in all colonies, and in general there was relatively little difference between the towns in terms of size.[22]

Death rates were generally highest in the towns of the new sugar colonies, suggesting a relationship with age structure. It will be recalled that urban slave populations tended to contain relatively large proportions of young people, females, and slaves of color, all of whom had below-average mortality under rural conditions, but the urban populations also included large proportions of African-born slaves, whose death rates were above average. Adjustment for sex and age does remove some of the apparent differential between the urban and rural slave populations, though not by any means reversing their relative mortality positions. The case of St. Lucia was typical (fig. 9.7). Urban slaves under 20 years of age showed death rates less than half those of rural slaves. For females, the majority of the urban population, the differential remained wide until about age 60 years. Urban males, however, quickly caught up with rural males and suffered comparable death rates throughout their adult lives. A similar pattern occurred in Tobago (table S9.24). Thus, in new sugar colonies such as St. Lucia and Tobago, the mortality advantage of urban slaves was confined very largely to the young and to females. The relatively high rates for adult males resulted chiefly from the large proportion of Africans among them. Urban creole males did show a clear mortality advantage over rural creole males (tables S9.23–9.24). Birthplace had no obvious effect on the mortality of urban females, however, so it appears that factors such as occupation may have been crucial. Adult African-born males living in towns, it will be recalled, very often worked in the few large units performing the heaviest laboring tasks.

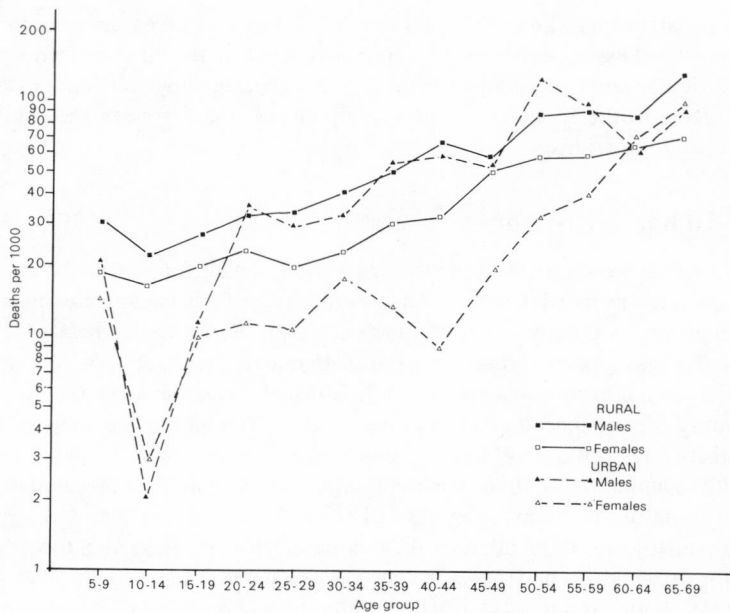

Fig. 9.7.   *Age-specific Slave Mortality by Sex: Rural and Urban St. Lucia,*
1815–19. (Source: table S9.23.)

Differences in slave mortality between town and country were less pronounced
in the old sugar colonies. In Barbados around 1817–20, for example, the age-
specific mortality curves for Bridgetown and the plantation parishes differed
relatively little up to age 40 years. Older slaves did have lower mortality in
Bridgetown than on the plantations, but the presence of the Africans was balanced
by the slaves of color, who had lower age-specific death rates in both town and
country (tables S9.17 and S9.20). In general, however, the mortality levels of
Barbadian slaves differed relatively little between town and country after 1807.
This narrowing of the gap probably resulted as much from the decline of mortality
on the plantations as from any change in the urban population. A similar narrowing
of the mortality differential occurred in Grenada between 1817 and 1832 (fig. 9.6),
placing the urban slave population much closer to the pattern typical on sugar
plantations and well above that of the Grenadines.

   The relatively low mortality of urban slaves in the British Caribbean after 1807
deserves emphasis, particularly since some recent writers have argued the opposite
position. Michael Craton contends that "seasoned slaves on established plantations were not more subject to fatality than most persons in the tropics—and
much less so than those living in towns in the lowlands." He believes that
"mortality rates in tropical towns were probably twice the average for whole
colonies, and higher than for any plantations."[23] The reason for Craton's error of

interpretation lies chiefly in the fact that his "urban" sample consisted of the Jamaican parish of St. Catherine, containing plantation populations as well as Spanish Town and including the mortality of whites and freedmen as well as slaves. There is no doubt that the total mortality of West Indian towns exceeded that on plantations, but the reason for this contrast related chiefly to the large proportions of whites found in the urban populations. As Craton recognizes, whites always showed higher death rates than blacks, chiefly because of their vulnerability to malaria and yellow fever. For example, white troops stationed in Jamaica had an average annual death rate of 121 per 1,000 between 1817 and 1836, compared to only 30 for black troops. In the Windward and Leeward Islands, the rates were 79 for whites and 40 for blacks.[24] Thus, Craton's sample population is heavily weighted by white mortality. His conclusions may therefore be rejected in view of the overwhelming specific evidence to the contrary presented here. This is not to say that the urban slave populations had mortality levels lower than those on all types of rural holdings. In fact, the towns appear to have fallen somewhere near the middle of the continuum, but significantly below the levels found on the dominant sugar plantations. It may be concluded that in the slave populations of the British Caribbean after 1807 the following ordering of mortality applied: sugar, coffee, livestock, pimento, towns, cotton, cocoa, and provisions.

Slaveholding Size

The grading of slave mortality levels by type of enterprise mirrored variations in terms of slaveholding size. It has been established above (table 5.3) that the typical ordering of slaveholding size, from largest to smallest, was as follows: sugar, cotton, coffee, livestock, pimento, cocoa, provisions, and towns. Thus, the major contrast between the gradation of slaveholding size and slave mortality related to cotton and the towns. There was a good deal of variation between colonies in terms of both slaveholding size and mortality patterns, so it is not surprising that a perfect equivalence is lacking. Where cotton was associated with relatively heavy slave mortality, as in St. Lucia, the slaveholdings were small, approximating the size of cocoa plantations (tables S2.3–2.4). The position of the urban populations is of more interest, since it seems that slaves living on small rural holdings had a mortality advantage over slaves attached to urban units of the same size. Thus, it may well be true that for slaves not subject to the conditions typical of large holdings, rural environments were indeed more healthful than the towns.

Beyond the direct correlation of slaveholding size and crop-type, there was a relationship between the size and mortality which operated independently of the effect of the conditions associated with particular crops. In most colonies, the death rate rose steadily along with slaveholding size to reach a peak and then fall again to relatively low levels in the largest holdings (table S9.12). In sugar-dominated colonies, the mortality maximum occurred as early as units of 51–100 slaves in Tobago and as late as 401–500 slaves in St. Vincent, but most often was found in holdings of about 200 slaves. Some colonies lacked a clear peak. In Berbice and St. Kitts the death rate climbed steadily with size to reach a maximum in the largest units, while in Anguilla the reverse was true, minimum mortality occurring in units of 201–300 slaves. To a limited extent, these variations may be explained in terms of differences in the age structure, sex ratio, and proportion of African-born slaves in the populations, but many ambiguities are apparent (see tables S2.11 and 3.6). In St. Lucia, for example, there was a fairly close correspondence between increasing mortality, sex ratio, and proportion of Africans with slaveholding size. In Anguilla, similar trends in the sex ratio and proportion of Africans were associated with a steady decline in mortality with increasing size. In most sugar colonies, particularly those of the first phase of settlement, sex ratio, proportion of Africans, and mean age peaked in smaller holdings than did mortality. In Tobago, where the mortality peak occurred in units of 51–100 slaves, the sex ratio and proportion of Africans peaked in holdings of only 11–50 slaves. Age-specific mortality curves for Tobago show that the heavy rates experienced by slaves in units of 51–100 were indeed higher at most ages, but the differential was greatest for males and was particularly pronounced among those under 40 years of age (table S9.13).

Although some of the variation in mortality with slaveholding size may be explained by strictly demographic characteristics, the mortality peak reached in units of about 200 slaves must also be seen as associated with a definite scale factor. The peak occurred in almost all of the parishes of Barbados, for example, so was independent of crop-type (table S2.10). It has been established that in the case of Jamaica the mortality peak in units of 201–300 slaves was associated with a peak in the value of production per slave.[25] This suggests strongly that such holdings approximated an optimum size for sugar estates, permitting the masters to maximize the output of the slaves through the most efficient organization of gang labor and the driving system, so making the heaviest demands on the slaves' physical exertions. The results of this maximization of labor productivity were seen in the maximization of mortality.

Occupation

While the association between mortality levels, enterprise-type, and scale can be established quite firmly, it is more difficult to determine precisely which features of these differing systems of organizing slave labor were responsible for the mortality differentials. When the mortality data are broken down, the differences often tend to be lost. In part, this is a technical problem. Once an attempt is made to measure the mortality levels of slaves in terms of sex-age-birthplace-occupation-scale-cause-specific death rates, the sample populations often become excessively small, even when selected from large colonies over periods of several years. Secondly, some important variables cannot be quantified at the level of the individual slave's actual experience: hours of work and nutrition, for example.

These variables can be taken into consideration only at a much higner level of generalization and are often only loosely quantifiable. Thirdly, factors determining the mortality of individual slaves often had their effect over a long period of time, and this prior experience is not always identifiable. Since slaves were frequently sold, moved from one location to another, and shifted between occupations, their physical environment and conditions of life at the time of initial registration were not necessarily typical of their previous experience. In the old sugar colonies such change was relatively limited, but in the new colonies and the towns it affected a large proportion of the slave population. Most of the measures of mortality employed here are cross-sectional, covering the experience of no more than about five years. Longitudinal analysis of the registration data for particular colonies may yield superior results, but linkage problems exist, and their maximum extent is limited to the experience of twenty years. All of these difficulties inhibit attempts to isolate the crucial factors involved in determining slave mortality differentials within enterprise-types. But in spite of these methodological problems, some clear associations can be established.

The most important occupational mortality differential was that between field laborers and "privileged" drivers, skilled tradespeople, and domestics. It is seen most clearly in age-sex-birthplace-specific death rates when account is taken of differences in enterprise-type. Such detailed analysis has been attempted only for St. Lucia in 1815–19 (table S9.28). In the case of creole males attached to sugar estates, the death rates of field laborers were more than double those of the privileged group at all ages over 30 years, and 50 percent higher among younger slaves. On plantations producing the minor staples—coffee, cocoa, cotton, and provisions—the differential was less consistent, creole male field laborers under 40 years of age having much higher death rates than the privileged, but in the older age groups (when the sample became small) there was little difference between the two groups. Privileged male creoles attached to "personal," generally urban, units showed death rates comparable to those experienced by the privileged on plantations. Thus, for creole males in St. Lucia the most striking contrast in mortality levels was that between field laborers on sugar estates and all other groups, whether in town or country. For female creoles, however, the differential between field laborers and privileged slaves on sugar estates in St. Lucia was much smaller, the death rates of field laborers actually falling slightly below those of the privileged between 20 and 40 years of age. In part, the contrast between creole females and males on sugar estates is explained by the concentration of privileged females in domestic work, while males were employed in a wider variety of occupations in adulthood with greater potential for improved individual material welfare. When the occupational groups are further disaggregated, the sample becomes too small to test this proposition crop by crop, but in the total male population there is no doubt that skilled tradesmen had lower death rates than domestics (table S9.30).

Female creole field laborers on minor staples plantations showed age-specific death rates at least as high as those experienced on sugar estates, and only somewhat higher than those for domestics. But female creole domestics attached to "personal" units did show lower rates than all of the rural groups at most ages. Similar patterns were observed for both males and females in the African-born population. In general, then, the high mortality observed on sugar estates in St. Lucia appears to have fallen particularly heavily on male field laborers. Gerald Friedman's analysis of the Trinidad registration data suggests that mortality differentials there were generally similar to those found in St. Lucia.[26]

In the case of Berbice, where it is impossible to distinguish occupational groups by enterprise-type, male and female field laborers had significantly higher death rates than domestics only among those under 40 years of age (table S9.31). Similarly, skilled tradesmen had lower death rates than male field laborers only to about 40 years. The greatest contrast between the mortality levels of particular occupational groups in Berbice occurred at about 20 years. At that age, field laborers suffered death rates more than double those of privileged slaves. Stock-keepers had even higher rates and maintained them at least until 30 years of age. Watchmen also had heavy mortality at all ages, particularly over 45 years, but this differential is expected, since it has been demonstrated that the slaves selected to work as watchmen were often chosen because they were too weak to perform field labor. Stockkeepers, especially those tending "small" and "feathered" live-stock, were sometimes selected on a similar basis. But neither watchmen nor stockkeepers suffered death rates as high as those for the sick and disabled.

As in Berbice, the differential mortality of field laborers and domestics in rural Barbados was most pronounced among slaves under 40 years of age, but continued somewhat longer for females than males (table S9.29). In the parishes of St. John and St. Andrew, male drivers and skilled tradespeople had lower mortality than field laborers, up to about age 50 years. In rural St. Michael, however, they showed relatively high mortality throughout, most particularly among young adults. Stockkeepers, especially those over 30 years, tended to have higher death rates than field laborers.

Although these examples drawn from Barbados, St. Lucia, and Berbice do not provide entirely consistent results, they do permit some generalizations about the differential mortality associated with the major occupational categories of rural slaves. There is no doubt that field laborers, especially those living on sugar estates, suffered significantly higher mortality than privileged drivers, tradespeople, and domestics. Stockkeepers and watchmen showed even higher mortality rates than field laborers, but such slaves were often selected because of their frailty. Generally, drivers and skilled tradespeople showed lower death rates than domestics. In rural slave populations, then, the ordering of mortality typically ranged from a maximum among the sick and disabled, through watchmen, stock-keepers, field laborers, domestics, and drivers, to a minimum among skilled tradespeople. The position of slaves employed in the minor occupations is less certain, but transport workers and fishermen may have been relatively long-lived (cf. tables S7.19, S7.20, S9.26, and S9.27). The differential mortality levels of the major occupational groups were apparent throughout the life cycle but were commonly most exaggerated among young adults and males. Of greater importance for the comparative analysis of mortality is the fact that the differentials were wider among sugar estate populations than other plantation types. Thus, the reasons for the high mortality associated with sugar cultivation must be sought principally among the field laborers and their conditions of life.

Occupational variations in mortality levels in urban slave populations differed from those found in rural situations, particularly in the relative position of skilled male tradespeople and domestics. This contrast was seen most clearly in Bridgetown, where skilled males showed death rates significantly higher than those of male domestics at most ages (table S9.29). Male transport workers had even higher death rates among those under 30 years in Bridgetown but generally suffered lower rates than skilled tradesmen in the older age groups. It will be recalled that an unusually large proportion of Bridgetown's transport workers were porters, carrying goods on their heads or backs, and it is not certain that the same differential applied where most were sailors or carters. Few comparisons can be made within the female urban populations, since they were highly concentrated in domestic service, but there is no doubt that female domestics had lower mortality levels than males.

The occupational differences in slave mortality established here have significance for broader comparisons at the colony level. Thus, although specific data are not presented for the marginal colonies, the relatively low mortality found in those colonies might be explained by the small proportion of slaves employed in plantation field labor and the large proportion working as domestics. Within the sugar colonies, however, occupational differences in mortality cannot directly account for variations found at the colony level. The mortality rates of creole field laborers working on sugar estates varied significantly between Barbados and St. Lucia, for example. No strictly demographic factor can explain this contrast. This suggests that variations in hours and conditions of work or in nutrition were more important than the actual tasks required of the slaves. Thus, the crucial difference between field labor on Barbadian and St. Lucian sugar estates lay in the extreme hours of work required on the latter, together with the additional demands of the provision ground system. The contrast between the minor staples and sugar within a single island system may be traced to broader differences in labor organization and demands: for the minor staples, significantly shorter hours of work, tasks that required less physical exertion, and the frequent absence of the direct brutality of the gang labor-driving system. In general, then, variations in the high mortality levels of field laborers depended on the physical demands of tasks they were forced to perform and the methods of coercion employed as much as on differences in work time. Domestics worked hours at least as long as field laborers, but their yoke was relatively easy and their burden light. Skilled tradesmen, however, had the advantage of generally short hours in combination with the performance of tasks which were much less physically demanding than those of field laborers. The gradation of mortality through field laborers, domestics, and skilled tradespeople also correlated with access to material goods, particularly food, but since the superior nutrition of domestics remains unproven, it may be concluded that the physical demands and associated brutality were of greater significance. This conclusion is not at odds with the interpretation of recent scholars, as well as abolitionists, that West Indian slaves in general were "overworked and under-fed."[27] But it greatly refines this blanket statement, providing an explanation for variations in mortality levels between colonies, enterprise-types, and occupational groups within the plantation status hierarchy.

Seasonality of Deaths

Further evidence of the association between mortality, overwork, and under-nutrition may be sought in seasonal patterns. Unfortunately, few colonies pro-vided data on the exact date of death of slaves in their registration returns, and those that did do not permit detailed analysis by type of enterprise. The three examples of seasonal mortality shown in figure 9.8, standardized as percentages of the daily average[28] for Dominica, Tobago, and Berbice, represent only the new sugar colonies. They do show remarkably similar general trends, but it is not

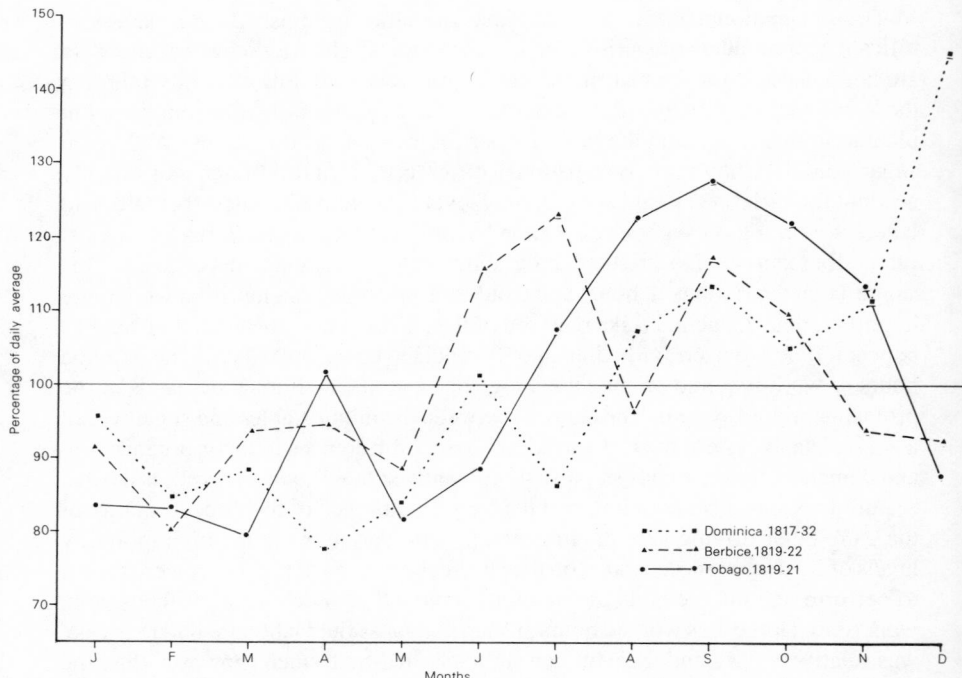

Fig. 9.8. *Seasonality of Slave Deaths: Dominica (Select Plantations), 1817–32, Berbice, 1819–22, and Tobago, 1819–21.* (Sources: *tables S9.32–9.33; T.71/337–63.*)

certain how far these might differ from patterns in the marginal colonies. The most important feature of the mortality curves is that they closely match the seasonal morbidity patterns established for particular sugar plantations in Barbados, St. Vincent, and Jamaica (fig. 8.9). Thus, slave mortality as well as morbidity tended to peak around September and fall to a minimum in March. Some minor erratic movements disturbed the smoothness of this trend, but these may be attributed to short-term fluctuations (fig. 9.9). In general, mortality was at near minimum levels at the commencement of the sugar crop around January and declined further in the early stages of the harvest. It rose fairly sharply at the end of the crop season in June, reached a maximum around the middle of the out-of-crop season, and then declined in the last months of the year. In terms of work demands, then, the extreme exertion required of slaves during the crop season cannot be seen as immediately causing high levels of mortality, but it had a cumulative and lagged effect, which was apparent only toward the end of crop and the months following its cessation. In terms of nutrition, the relatively abundant food supplies available during crop, together with access to cane juice, helped reduce mortality levels, while the "hungry time" associated with the first months of the out-of-crop season increased them.

The seasonal mortality curve for Berbice showed less pronounced peaks than did those for Tobago and Dominica. This may be explained by the lack of a concentrated crop season on Berbice's sugar estates and the inclusion of other

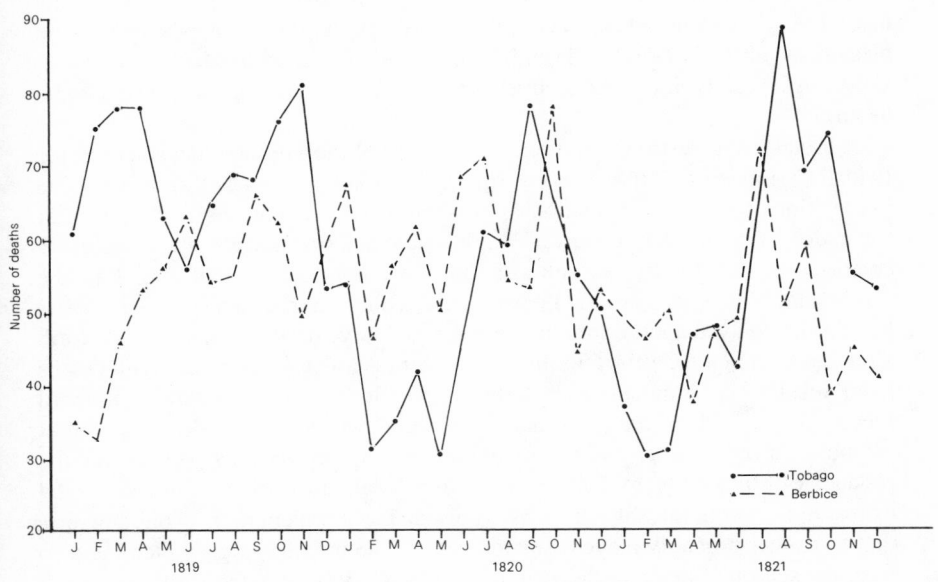

Fig. 9.9.   *Slave Deaths by Month: Tobago and Berbice, 1819–21.* *(Sources: T.71/440–41, 463–68.)*

plantation types. The dependence on rationed allowances may also be important, since it tended to reduce the seasonal pressure on food supplies observed in colonies relying on the provision ground system. In the case of Dominica, a comparison may be made between seasonal mortality patterns on sugar and coffee plantations in the sample.[29] On sugar estates, mortality increased quite steadily through the calendar year, reaching a maximum in December; but on coffee plantations it was at a maximum in the July–September quarter and at a minimum in April–June. It is uncertain how the latter pattern matched the crop cycle, however, since it is not known whether the coffee crop in Dominica occurred as in Jamaica (October–March) or as in British Guiana (June–August). But it is clear that the amount of seasonal variation in mortality was at least as great on coffee as on sugar plantations.

For Tobago, a comparison of seasonal mortality between town and country is possible (table S9.32). Although the urban peak occurred in August and the minimum in March, a pattern not unlike the rural extremes of September and May, the amount of short-term variation within this range was too great to show a consistent seasonal trend. In part, this may reflect the small size of the urban sample (89 deaths). But it is equally likely that the urban slave population was much less subject to a seasonal mortality pattern, and that this reflects the relative insignificance of seasonal rhythms in work demands and nutrition.

Occupational variations in the seasonality of mortality were not well defined. In the case of Berbice, the pattern for field laborers followed quite closely that for the total slave population (table S9.33). The sick and disabled also showed little deviation. Domestics experienced above-average mortality in November and December. Skilled tradespeople and drivers did so in February, March, and April, reflecting a peak period in the crop season and an associated high rate of accidental death.

A broader comparison of the seasonal pattern of mortality among slaves in the British Caribbean with that in North America is of interest, since it suggests some implications for the interpretation of seasonal rhythms. The seasonal pattern of slave deaths in the Chesapeake, Virginia, in the seventeenth and eighteenth centuries, for example, was almost the exact opposite of that found in the Caribbean, with a peak around February and a minimum in June.[30] This suggests that climate played a larger role in the timing of slave mortality in colonial North America than in the Caribbean, the mid-winter peak being associated with deaths from respiratory complaints. For the ante-bellum period, however, Richard Steckel identifies the "harvest months" of August–October as the peak period of mortality in the Southern slave population. He argues that this pattern was the product of "a variety of factors, including weather, work routine, diet, and exposure to communicable diseases from outside the plantation," but suggests that "weather probably played a major role"[31] The months August–October also were the season of peak mortality in the British Caribbean in the early nineteenth century, but there was no direct correlation with harvest activity. Climatic variation was less dramatic in the Caribbean, of course, so the lagged effect of work regimes and seasonal nutritional stress may have been more obvious. In order to proceed it is necessary to examine the causes of death particularly affecting the slave populations.

Causes of Death

Cause-of-death data are available in the slave registration returns for only a few places, all of them new sugar colonies. Thus, a systematic comparative analysis is impossible. Further, interpretation of the available data is hazardous because of the limited and variable nosological capacities of those describing the causes. Table 9.8 presents an attempt to classify the data for 12,701 deaths in five colonies, following the broad outlines of the system used by Todd Savitt in his study of ante-bellum Virginia.[32] Detailed listings of the contemporary descriptions found in the registration returns, in terms of this classification, are provided for Tobago and Berbice in tables S8.12 and S8.13. The data for Demerara-Essequibo derive from the contemporary classification published by the Registrar, James Robertson, but closely follow the original terminology of the returns. The data for Demerara-Essequibo, Berbice, Tobago, and Grenada cover the total slave populations, but those for Dominica 1829–32 relate only to 34 percent of the total, since most masters failed to provide the relevant information. The Dominica data are not biased in terms of sex or age, but accidental deaths do seem to have had a special propensity to be specified. In general, the proportions of deaths which were poorly defined or specified differed little between the colonies, though Dominica and Tobago, where deaths were not certified by medical practitioners, did show a slightly higher rate. It must be remembered that the registration returns omitted much infant mortality, thus weighting the data toward those causes of death which particularly affected adults.

Diarrheal diseases, chiefly dysentery, were the leading cause of death in every one of the five colonies included in table 9.8. The ordering of the other major causes of death varied from colony to colony, but there was a close correspondence between the patterns found in the neighboring islands of Grenada and Tobago and, not surprisingly, in the coastland colonies of Demerara-Essequibo and Berbice. In the table, the causes of death are ordered as they were in Grenada. The most significant deviations from this pattern were that measles and diseases of the digestive and respiratory systems were relatively uncommon in the other colonies, while tuberculosis, tetanus, leprosy, and accidents were more common. Measles was confined generally to epidemics, and outside Grenada its role was played by whooping cough in Tobago and smallpox in Dominica. The small proportion of slave deaths attributed to smallpox after 1817 is clear evidence of the success of the inoculation and vaccination campaigns discussed in the previous chapter. Deaths resulting from "old age" and general "debility" also accounted for large numbers, but it is not clear how these should be distributed, whether among the more precisely specified causes or separately. More than 5 percent of deaths were

Table 9.8. *Causes of Slave Deaths: Grenada, Dominica, Tobago, Demerara-Essequibo, and Berbice, 1817–32*

	Percentage of Deaths				
Cause	Grenada, 1817	Dominica, 1829–32	Tobago, 1819–21	Demerara-Essequibo, 1829–32	Berbice, 1819–22
Diarrhea	25.7	19.4	20.1	18.1	16.2
Dropsy	16.0	10.7	12.1	13.9	11.4
Fever	11.3	6.0	10.6	12.3	6.2
Digestive system diseases	9.3	5.6	6.5	3.5	4.7
Nervous system diseases	8.0	7.1	5.5	11.5	11.8
Measles	6.4	—	—	—	—
Tuberculosis	4.2	12.7	8.8	11.2	9.1
Worms	3.7	9.9	4.5	3.4	3.9
Respiratory diseases	3.7	2.8	1.5	3.3	10.0
Tetanus	2.4	6.0	2.4	3.9	2.7
Leprosy	1.9	—	4.5	5.8	5.9
Accidents	1.1	7.5	3.2	6.4	3.5
Maternity	1.1	1.6	1.5	0.9	1.4
Scarlet fever	1.1	—	1.4	—	0.9
Teething	1.1	—	0.6	—	0.1
Venereal disease	0.6	—	0.9	1.5	2.3
Rheumatism	0.5	—	0.4	—	0.3
Female diseases	0.5	—	—	—	0.3
Heart diseases	0.3	—	—	—	0.1
Yaws	0.3	4.0	2.7	3.9	6.7
Neoplasms	0.2	—	0.1	0.3	0.7
Violence	0.2	—	—	—	0.3
Suicide	0.2	—	0.4	—	1.2
Diphtheria	0.2	—	—	—	0.1
Cholera	0.2	—	—	—	0.1
Whooping cough	—	—	12.1	—	0.1
Smallpox	—	6.7	—	—	—
Total	100.0	100.0	100.0	100.0	100.0
Total number of deaths	902	401	2,146	7,016	2,236
Not included above:					
Unclassifiable, undefined	81	58	211	730	466
Mal d'estomac, cachexy	47	35	181	301	—
Old age	94	33	256 ⎫	1,342	92
Debility	54	23	107 ⎭		176
Percentage of Total	30.6	37.2	35.2	33.8	32.8

Sources: T.71/246–66 (Grenada), 363 (Dominica), 461–67 (Tobago), and 438–41 (Berbice); *P.P.*, 1833, vol. 26 (700), p. 438 (Demerara-Essequibo). See tables S8.12 and S8.13 for detailed lists (Tobago and Berbice).

caused by "mal d'estomac" or "cachexy," but again the precise nature of these diseases is uncertain.

In general, the most important causes of slave deaths in the new sugar colonies were ordered roughly as follows: diarrhea and dysentery, dropsy, fevers (malaria and yellow fever), tuberculosis, nervous system diseases, and digestive system diseases. These diseases accounted for 75 percent of all classifiable deaths in Grenada and 59 percent in Berbice, the other colonies falling within this range. Although the sample is relatively small, it is of interest to compare this pattern with that found in the plantation books of Newton and Colleton Plantations, Barbados, for the periods 1811–25 and 1819–34, respectively.[33] Of the classifiable deaths (189), the ordering was as follows: dropsy (14.3 percent), tuberculosis (12.2), diarrhea (9.0), marasmus (9.0), nervous system diseases (7.9), scarlet fever (6.9), and leprosy (5.8). The most obvious contrast with the pattern in the new sugar colonies is the relative unimportance of diarrhea and dysentery, digestive system diseases, and fevers in Barbados. The island was peculiar in remaining relatively free of malaria throughout its history. Causes accounting for relatively large proportions of deaths in Barbados were scarlet fever, teething, and diphtheria, reflecting the youthfulness of the creole population. The pattern of causes of death in Jamaica during the 1820s seems to have approximated more closely that found in Barbados than in the new sugar colonies.[34]

Comparison with the leading causes of slave deaths (6,284) in Virginia in 1850 suggests a much broader contrast.[35] In Virginia the ordering was as follows: respiratory diseases, tuberculosis, nervous system diseases, dropsy, typhoid, diarrhea, fever, cholera, accidents, digestive system diseases, diphtheria, suffocation, and scarlet fever. Thus, the major differences between the slave populations lay in the relatively great role of respiratory diseases, typhoid, and diphtheria in Virginia and the minor role of diarrhea and dysentery, dropsy, and, probably, fever. Differences in regional nosology mean that these comparisons should not be pressed too far. Typhoid fever's absence from the West Indian record, for example, may be balanced by intestinal diseases described as dysentery or flux. But as a group these intestinal diseases, having their roots in unsanitary living conditions, were clearly much more important in the Caribbean. Respiratory diseases (pleurisy, pneumonia, influenza, asthma) struck down 16.1 percent of all slaves dying in Virginia in 1850, but never more than 6 percent in the Caribbean. The concentration of such deaths in the winter months strongly suggests that the difference may be attributed to climatic contrasts.[36] It is more difficult to interpret the relatively large proportion of deaths attributed to dropsy in the Caribbean, since the swellings typical of the disease are really only indicators of deep-seated cardiovascular, respiratory, or liver disease and may conceal misdiagnosed tuberculosis, for example.[37]

Within the British Caribbean, cause-of-death patterns varied between town and country and between types of rural enterprises. In Tobago 1819–21 the major causes more common in town than in the country were dropsy, fever, tuberculosis, and accidents (table S9.36). Causes roughly twice as common in the rural slave population, however, included diarrhea and dysentery, whooping cough, leprosy, and respiratory diseases. A similar pattern occurred in Grenada. In the periods 1817–19 and 1830–32, more than double the proportion of slave deaths in the town of St. George resulted from tuberculosis, accidents, fever, venereal diseases, and heart disease, as in the sugar parish of St. Andrew (table S9.37). Diarrhea and dysentery, respiratory diseases, marasmus, and tetanus, however, were more common in St. Andrew than in the town. In Tobago and Grenada, then, it seems that the specifically urban causes of death were tuberculosis, fever, and accidents, whereas the most distinctly rural causes were diarrheal and respiratory diseases. The high rate of accidental death in the towns might appear surprising, but it can largely be explained by the drowning of town-based sailors. The relative urban concentration of tuberculosis and fever in the slave population probably resulted chiefly from the free circulation of people and contagious diseases in the towns. Plantation populations, however, were relatively closed, and the unsanitary living conditions of close-packed slave villages meant intestinal diseases rather than fever or tuberculosis.

For Grenada, a further comparison can be made between cause-of-death patterns in the high-mortality sugar parish of St. Andrew and the low-mortality cotton-sugar islands of Carriacou and the Grenadines (table S9.37). To a large extent, the pattern in the Grenadines had more in common with the town of St. George than with St. Andrew. Diarrhea, respiratory diseases, marasmus, scarlet fever, yaws, and rheumatism were all much less important in the Grenadines, whereas tetanus and leprosy accounted for a substantially larger proportion of deaths than on the island of Grenada. The relatively high rate of mortality from tetanus directly reflected the high fertility of the Grenadines' slave population. The large proportion of deaths from leprosy, however, may have been artificially inflated by the practice of establishing lazarettos on some of the smaller islands for slaves from Grenada. But the diseases closely related to unsanitary living conditions and malnutrition appear to have been much less common in the Grenadines. This pattern may well have been shared by the insular marginal colonies, and it accounts for the relatively low mortality rates found in those colonies.

Within Demerara-Essequibo, comparisons may be made between cause-of-death patterns in 1829–32 in the parishes of St. James (dominated by sugar cultivation), St. Mary (sugar and cotton), and St. George and St. Andrew (urban and sugar).[38] The urban parishes were most clearly distinguished from the rural by the small proportion of town slaves dying from diarrhea and dysentery, mal d'estomac, and, less importantly, respiratory diseases and leprosy. Town slaves were much more often the victims of fevers, tuberculosis, and accidents, however. This pattern of rural-urban contrasts matches very closely that found in the islands of Grenada and Tobago. Comparing St. James and St. Mary, it appears that cotton cultivation was associated with particularly high rates of death from diarrhea and dysentery and dropsy, while sugar was associated with mal d'estomac and, less importantly, ulcers and venereal diseases. The principal differences between these parishes in Demerara-Essequibo, then, lay in the role of mal d'estomac (associated with sugar cultivation), fevers (urban), and diarrhea and dysentery (cotton). As noted for Grenada and Tobago, the high proportion of slave deaths caused by fevers in the urban population resulted from the rapid circulation of people and vectors. Mortality in the white population resulted even more often from fevers; malaria was the great killer after the 1820s, yellow fever having largely disappeared. The importance of mal d'estomac on sugar estates, however, suggests that malnutrition and work demands played a significant role in determining relative mortality levels, though diarrhea and dysentery remained more important on sugar estates as well as cotton plantations.

Differences in cause-of-death patterns in terms of slaveholding size were complicated by variations in enterprise and demographic characteristics. In Tobago, diarrhea and dysentery were most prominent in units of 51–100 slaves, accounting for 20.4 percent of all deaths in 1819–21 (table S9.38). It will be remembered that mortality levels were maximized in units of this scale. Similarly, total mortality and the proportion of deaths caused by diarrhea and dysentery (31.1 percent) reached a maximum in units of more than 400 slaves in the case of Berbice (table S9.38; cf. table S9.12). In both Tobago and Berbice, dropsy, fever, and accidental deaths peaked as a proportion of total deaths in holdings of 11–50 slaves. Digestive system diseases reached a maximum in units of 11–100 slaves and tended to decline along with increasing holding size. Tuberculosis and respiratory and nervous system diseases tended to peak in the smallest holdings and then to decrease fairly steadily with size. Leprosy and yaws, on the other hand, increased their importance as causes of death as holdings increased in size. This last tendency may be explained by the role of cramped quarters in the spread of these communicable diseases, but if this argument is valid, it may be supposed that the high rates of diarrheal-disease mortality experienced in the "optimum" units were as much the result of extreme work demands as of unsanitary living conditions in the slave villages.

Within each of these types of enterprise units, cause-of-death patterns varied in terms of the slaves' sex, age, birthplace, color, and occupation. Sex was of only minor importance. In Tobago, for example, the only causes consistently affecting males at more than double the rate for females were accidents, suicide, and nervous system diseases (tables S9.36 and S9.39). The relatively high rate of accidental death for males resulted from their employment as sailors and in the mills. Apart from deaths resulting from maternity, females had significantly higher rates than males only in regard to debility and old age. The smaller sample for Dominica showed a similar pattern, except that males seem also to have been more heavily affected by smallpox and digestive system diseases, and females by tuberculosis.[39] In general, however, differences between the sexes were not remarkable, reflecting the similar conditions under which they lived and worked.

Africans and creoles did experience quite distinct cause-of-death patterns during the period of slave registration, but these differences were very largely a product of their contrasting age structures. Among adults the patterns were generally similar. In Berbice 1819–22, for example, African slaves aged 20–50 years had death rates more than 50 percent greater than those for creole adults only as a result of diarrheal diseases, nervous system diseases, and scarlet fever. Creoles, on the other hand, showed similarly high rates only for tuberculosis, fevers, old age, and suicide. The relatively high incidence of fevers among creole slaves may be attributed to the fact that the colored section of the population lacked to some degree the inherited immunity of the Africans, but this cannot be used to explain the differential impact of tuberculosis.[40] The prevalence of "old age" as a cause of death among creoles clearly reflects their greater longevity as well as the relatively large proportion of males in the African-born population. The incidence of suicide is of more interest, since it was confined almost entirely to males, yet proved less common among the male-dominated Africans. Probably this pattern did not occur as long as the Atlantic slave trade continued, but by the 1820s at least there is no doubt that anomie affected creole males to a greater degree than it did female or African slaves.

Slaves of color tended to suffer relatively more than blacks from fevers and respiratory diseases, for immunological reasons noted above (see also table S9.39). They were, however, less prone to diarrheal diseases, dropsy, tetanus, and suicide. This pattern is explained by the superior living conditions of slaves of color and the greater rewards they received within the slave hierarchy. In part, the superior well-being of slaves of color was a product of their urban concentration, but the pattern existed in both town and country.

As in all populations, cause-of-death patterns varied most dramatically in terms of the age structure of the slaves. Children were particularly affected by yaws, worms, teething, and whooping cough. Creoles dying from diarrheal diseases, dropsy, fevers, nervous system diseases, accidents, tetanus, respiratory diseases, and scarlet fever were generally in their teens, whereas tuberculosis, digestive system diseases, leprosy, venereal disease, suicide, and debility were most common among slaves over 20 years of age. Those dying of "old age" in the early 1820s, whether creole or African, had a mean age over 50 years. For causes of death other than old age, the African-born inevitably died at higher mean ages than the creoles, but the relative patterns were similar. These general tendencies in mean age at death have been established for Tobago and Berbice and for the Dominica sample, but colonies with older creole populations may have deviated somewhat (tables S9.41–9.42). The exclusion of much infant mortality from the registration data no doubt has the effect of inflating the mean age of slaves dying from tetanus, but it is clear that tetanus remained an important cause of death among mature slaves. It is equally important to notice that "debility" was not confined to aged slaves, but referred to nonspecific wasting diseases in slaves of all ages.[41]

A more exact picture of the relationship between age structure and cause-of-death patterns is obtained by considering age-specific death rates for particular causes. These have been calculated for Tobago and Berbice (table S9.43). The mortality resulting from diarrhea and dysentery exceeded that from all other causes at all ages, except that whooping cough, yaws, worms, and fevers affected a larger proportion among young children, and unspecified "debility" and "old age" accounted for more of those over 50 years of age (fig. 9.10). Whooping cough, worms, and yaws killed very few slaves over 10 years of age. The proportion dying from fevers remained fairly constant at all ages in Tobago, but in Berbice it dipped to a minimum among young adults before rising to a second peak in old age. This contrast between Tobago and Berbice may be explained by the relative insignificance of yellow fever on the coastlands after about 1810, while epidemics continued to plague the islands.[42] Tetanus also accounted for a fairly constant proportion of deaths throughout the life span. The mortality rates associated with diarrheal diseases, tuberculosis, dropsy, and leprosy increased steadily with age, but the rate of growth in diarrheal diseases was much more consistent, thus ensuring its dominant position in terms of overall mortality.

The association between cause-of-death patterns and sex, birthplace, color, and, particularly, age, was reflected in occupational differentials. In order to remove the effect of these demographic variables, it is most useful to consider only adults (aged 20–50 years) and to distinguish them by sex and occupation. Such an analysis is available for Berbice but is confined to differences between only the major occupational groups (table S9.40). The most obvious contrast suggested by this analysis is that while adult field slaves were struck down most often by diarrhea and dysentery, male skilled tradespeople and drivers suffered more

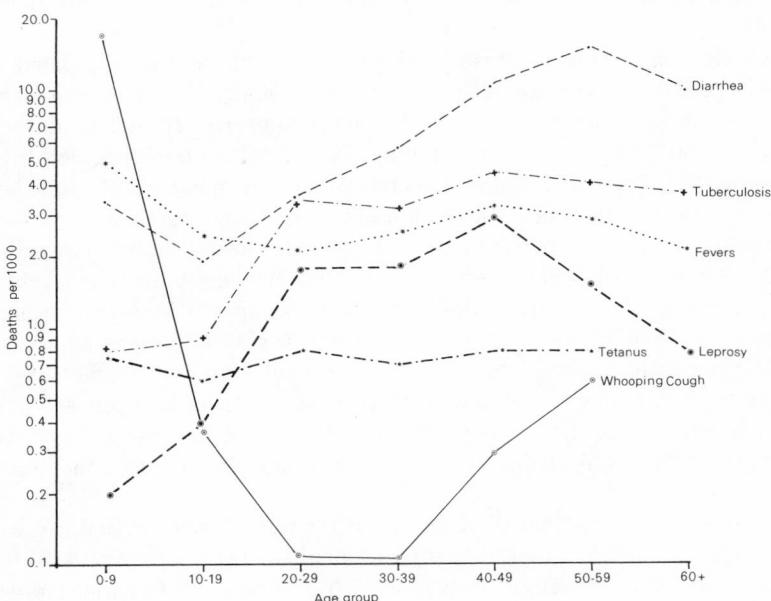

Fig. 9.10.   *Age-specific Slave Mortality by Cause of Death: Tobago, 1819–21.* (Source: *table S9.43.*)

heavily from dropsy, and female domestics from tuberculosis, respiratory diseases, and dropsy. The differential incidence of diarrheal diseases was most pronounced among the female population, affecting more than double the proportion of field laborers, while tuberculosis accounted for twice the proportion of domestics. Among the adult males, dropsy and accidents accounted for almost twice the proportion of skilled tradespeople and drivers, but the differential impact of diarrheal diseases on field laborers was less pronounced. The relatively high rate of accidental death among the skilled was a direct product of the hazardous character of some of their tasks. But the high rates of death from diarrheal diseases among field laborers, and dropsy/tuberculosis among privileged tradespeople, drivers, and domestics, must be traced to differences in their living and working conditions. Sanitation, housing, clothing, and physical exertion were probably most important. The connection with nutrition is more problematic, since tuberculosis is commonly associated with malnutrition, and the evidence suggests that the privileged occupational groups were at least as well nourished as field laborers. Tuberculosis may be contracted by drinking milk from infected cows, but again there is no clear evidence that privileged slaves consumed milk to any extent.[43] The privileged were somewhat more likely to be colored and to live in towns. Thus, the contrast between field laborers and privileged slaves in terms of the relative importance of diarrheal diseases and dropsy/tuberculosis may best be explained by the harsh labor regime and unsanitary living conditions of the mass of field laborers rather than by any obvious nutritional or occupational advantage of the privileged.

Beyond these major contrasts in the occupational patterns associated with causes of death, some minor differentials deserve notice. In the case of Berbice 1819–22, yaws, worms, venereal disease, and debility affected adult field laborers to a significantly greater extent than they affected skilled tradespeople, drivers, and domestics. These differentials may be explained largely in terms of the heavy labor regimes and inferior living conditions of field slaves. Tetanus, however, affected the privileged group more than it did field laborers. This may be explained by the propensity of skilled tradesmen to suffer cuts and bruises as a result of occupational accidents. Suicide was more common among field slaves than among the privileged groups. In general, then, suicide was most frequent among adult creole male field laborers, the group suffering the highest overall levels of mortality. Among the "sick and disabled," slaves not employed actively in productive labor, the most important cause of death for those aged 20–50 years was leprosy, followed by debility, dropsy, tuberculosis, diarrhea, and venereal diseases.

Seasonal variations in cause-of-death patterns were limited. In Berbice, where the seasonality of slave mortality was not marked, there were few significant deviations from the overall trend (table S9.35). Deaths resulting from respiratory diseases were relatively frequent in the months June–August and were rare between October and February. This pattern is difficult to interpret, since it does not appear to relate to the seasonality of rainfall or agricultural activity. Deaths attributed to "old age" were particularly common between January and March, possibly reflecting minor variations in temperature. Dropsy was relatively common April–August and rare September–January. Diarrhea was relatively rare February–April. But most of these variations were minor.

The seasonality of slave mortality was more marked in Tobago 1819–21, and some of the major causes of death did deviate significantly from the general trend (table S9.34). The most obvious example was whooping cough, which occurred as an epidemic, peaking in February and disappearing completely by September, so creating a major distortion in total mortality for 1819 (fig. 9.9). Diarrhea occurred at below-average levels throughout the crop season, January–June, but was particularly common in the months July to November. This pattern clearly demonstrates the association between relatively abundant food supplies during crop and shortages in the out-of-crop period where sugar cultivation and the provision ground system dominated. Digestive system diseases followed a similar pattern. Fevers, on the other hand, were relatively common January–May and rare September–December, but the extent of this deviation was less than that for diarrhea. Most of the remaining causes of death showed no consistent seasonality. In general, then, it was the causes of death particularly affecting field laborers that showed the greatest seasonality, and that seasonality was most pronounced where the sugar harvest was concentrated into a few months and the slaves were required to produce their own food supplies.

In concluding this discussion of cause-of-death patterns, it is important to emphasize that contemporary nosology was insecurely based and thus may distort the analysis, even in terms of the gross differentials stressed here. It is also necessary to draw attention to the relatively limited range of examples discussed in detail, most of them derived from the experience of the new sugar colonies. Although diarrheal diseases were clearly the major killers on the plantations of the new sugar colonies, the slave populations of the old sugar colonies, Jamaica, the marginal colonies, and, generally, towns seem to have suffered more heavily from dropsy and tuberculosis. This tendency may be explained only in limited degree by the decline in the African-born proportion of the slave population. But it was also evident among skilled tradespeople and domestics in the new sugar colonies. In general, analysis of the cause-of-death data suggests that the heavy relative mortality of field laborers living on sugar estates must be explained primarily by the harsh regimes under which they worked, the unsanitary living conditions of cramped slave villages, and the seasonal stress placed on their food supplies. The relationship between nutrition and infection was synergistic, however, and varied with labor demands.[44] A similarly complex set of interrelationships was associated with fertility differentials, and hence with the pattern of natural increase.

FERTILITY

Reproduction is more obviously a product of social behavior than is the pattern of mortality, though such behavior may often be explained by economic structure. Variations in the level of slave fertility were determined not only by work regimes and material well-being but also by the cultural forms of the slaves and the attempts of masters and missionaries to alter those forms. The slaves cherished systems of family organization learned in Africa, together with associated attitudes about the control of reproductive behavior, but these norms were partially transformed as a direct product of the slave system and the intervention of the masters, and indirectly as a result of the mixing of African ethnic groups with distinct cultural heritages and the growth of the creole population. The period following the abolition of the Atlantic slave trade saw a fairly rapid diminution in the size of the African-born population as well as increased efforts by the masters to control reproductive behavior. It has been demonstrated, however, that Africans maintained a dominant position among adult slaves in the new sugar colonies, and even in the heavily creolized old sugar colonies cultural practices with their origins in Africa continued to affect reproduction.

Pronatalism

The abolition of the Atlantic slave trade made slaveowners totally dependent on natural increase for the maintenance of their labor force. Thus, they adopted a variety of measures, complementary to those directed at the reduction of mortality, intended to increase fertility levels. But the social context of reproduction meant that the measures applied to fertility were generally less direct and often consisted of inducements rather than forcible intervention. The origins of this policy of pronatalism may be found in the late eighteenth century, particularly in the old sugar colonies, but there is no doubt that it became much more widespread in the period after 1807.

Slave breeding. Pronatalism took a variety of forms. At one extreme, it has been stated by a number of writers that Barbuda was used as a "stud farm" with the deliberate intention of "breeding slaves from selected stock," beginning in the middle of the eighteenth century. Lowenthal and Clarke, however, have argued that there is no hard evidence of such conscious manipulation, and they conclude that in Barbuda "slave numbers increased without any intervention by the proprietors, as a result of social and environmental circumstances conducive to low mortality."[45] Eric Williams holds the view that "slave breeding on a large scale" was practiced in Barbados between about 1807 and 1820, and R. Keith Aufhauser explains the lack of direct evidence of these activities in the documentary record by the fact that "it was better to keep breeding farms from the public's critical eye."[46] As in the case of Barbuda, the silence of contemporaries is hardly sufficient proof of the existence of slave-breeding systems, and the high levels of fertility found in these slave populations must be explained by a much broader range of factors.

Much of this controversy over slave breeding, in the British Caribbean as well as the United States, hinges on questions of definition. Fogel and Engerman contend that "*systematic* breeding of slaves for sale in the *market*" involved, firstly, "interference in the normal sexual habits of slaves to maximize female fertility through such devices as mating women with especially potent men, in much the same way as exists in breeding of livestock'' and, secondly, ''the raising of slaves with sale as the main objective.''[47] Gutman and Sutch, however, define breeding as ''any practice of the slave master intended to cause the fertility of the slave population to be higher than it would have been in the absence of such interference,'' including such things as ''the use of 'rewards' for childbearing, the encouragement of early marriage and short lactation periods, and the provision of both pre- and post-natal medical care, as well as practices more reprehensible to modern as well as to many nineteenth-century sensibilities.''[48] Both of these definitions are rather vague as to how far the analogy with livestock-breeding methods should be taken, but they do represent significantly different approaches. In the Caribbean context, arguments for and against the existence of slave breeding in Barbuda and Barbados must be viewed primarily in terms of the Fogel-Engerman definition. It is probable that such stud farm-style breeding was not practiced in the Caribbean or the United States to any significant extent.[49] If the broader Gutman-Sutch definition is adopted, however, there is no doubt that slave ''breeding'' was common in the British Caribbean after 1807. But most of the inducements to fertility included in the Gutman-Sutch definition have counterparts in the pronatalist policies of modern governments. Thus, the broader definition of breeding has little value as a means of distinguishing the manipulation of fertility in slave and free societies, and there seems little to be gained from pursuing this debate.

Positive incentives: rewards and awards.   The inducements to fertility offered by British Caribbean slaveowners related chiefly to giving cash and other rewards to women producing children, reducing working hours for pregnant and nursing mothers, providing medical care for mothers and children, and bestowing material advantages on slaves marrying or establishing nuclear families. Rewards were given to the overseers of absentee-owned estates showing natural increases. Incentives to fertility also included attempts to limit breast-feeding periods and to prevent the movement of slaves for purposes of extraplantation mating.

Barbadian planters were urged in 1786 to pay 5s. at the birth of each woman's first child, but the practice was not universal.[50] At Newton Estate the attorney, Sampson Wood, reported in 1798 that mothers of children surviving a month were given 6s. 3d., but the estate accounts suggest that payments to women ''upon coming out with their children, all well'' did not become universal until about 1805. In 1798 Wood told the absentee proprietor of Newton that ''I encourage their breeding as much as I can,'' but ''if we encrease as we *have* done, I am afraid, in a few years, we shall have too many.'' The estate continued to pay the standard rate of 6s. 3d. until emancipation.[51] Mount Gay, Colletons, and Drax Hall plantations paid the same amount to women ''bringing out'' their children, but it seems the practice may have been restricted before about 1813.[52] The condition that such payments be limited to mothers of children surviving at least a month reflected the high level of infant mortality and may have been viewed by the planters as a safeguard against infanticide.

The practice of making cash payments to slave mothers was not confined to Barbados. It certainly existed in Jamaica and the Leeward Islands from the end of the eighteenth century and, probably, in most other colonies. Some planters also made additional payments at Christmas, together with sugar and rum, and a favored few slaves received baby clothes and linen.[53] It may be that such practices were more common on large plantations than on small holdings, but it seems impossible to determine whether variations in their universality were sufficient to account for differences in the level of fertility between colonies, between rural and urban slaves, or between types of enterprise.

More important than these material rewards were the reductions in labor demands offered as an inducement to fertility. One Barbadian planter-attorney, Forster Clarke, contended in 1824 that women were commonly put to light work as soon as they were reported pregnant, were allowed to lie-in for a month after delivery, were required to perform little work for a further three months, and worked reduced hours until their children were weaned (generally at 18 months).[54] Similar advantages applied in other colonies, though sometimes more limited in duration.[55] The Leeward Islands slave law of 1798 stated that the owner of a female "five months gone with child, shall keep and detain such female slave upon the estate to which she belongs, at all times when the other slaves are at work, but not employ her otherwise than in taking care of the children on the estate, or other light work." This law was silent on the reduction of labor after the lying-in period. By contrast, the Trinidad Ordinance of 1800 was vague on prenatal treatment but prohibited women "being put to work before they are perfectly recovered from child-bed" and regulated hours of work for nursing mothers.[56] These regulations were not always respected, however. Certainly pregnant women were forced to continue at hard labor on some plantations and were subjected to the driver's lash. Nursing mothers on a Berbice coffee plantation complained in 1819 that they were given no reduction in tasks during crop and were flogged when they stopped to give suck.[57] There is, however, hard evidence that the month-long lying-in period was in fact followed rigidly on some estates, in Barbados at least.[58]

Beyond these short-term reductions in labor demands, some colonies legislated that the mothers of certain numbers of children should be completely released from heavy labor. The Jamaican slave law of 1792 stated that "every female slave who shall have six children living shall be exempted from hard labour in the field or otherwise," while her owner was to be exempted from the payment of poll tax. Similar legislation was passed in Grenada in 1797. This release from hard labor was extended by the Jamaican law of 1816 to include women who raised orphans from infancy as their "adopted children."[59] The Trinidad ordinance of 1800 provided that the mothers of three children were to have an additional free day out of crop, while those with seven were "exempted from all labour." They were to receive an annual reward of one dollar for each child.[60] In the Leeward Islands release from hard labor was confined to mothers of six living children, the youngest being seven years of age and all born during faithful "cohabitation."[61]

Barbados, however, passed no such legislation. On the Society for the Propagation of the Gospel's plantations it was proposed in 1825 only that exemption from labor be confined to mothers of six children "born in lawful wedlock," though no efforts had been made to perform marriages.[62] Thus, although Barbadian planters may have been liberal in the treatment of mothers in the pre- and postnatal periods as a means of encouraging fertility, their paternal stance meant that they could not countenance lapses from discipline exemplified by slaves released from hard labor.

All of the inducements to fertility discussed thus far were directed exclusively at the females in the slave populations. The most obvious reason for this concentration was that the ownership of slave children depended entirely on maternity. But the slaveowners did believe that "marriage" or faithful cohabitation raised fertility levels, and for this reason they provided incentives to males as well as females to live in such unions.[63] Most often this meant assistance in the construction of houses. Thus, a Barbadian planter instructed his attorney in 1786 that "upon the marriage of a young couple, who have not parents to establish them, I desire you will not only assign them a lot of land, but that you will have the house built for them altogether at my expence."[64] Similarly, the attorney of Newton Plantation wrote in 1798 that "when any marry in the estates [I] give them a couple of dollars to set up house-keeping, and buy a young goat and a pig—if they agree for a twelve-month a couple more (dollars)." He also noted that he encouraged the slaves into "intermarriages at home," so ensuring the augmentation of his particular plantation population.[65]

In the same year, 1798, the British government was advising the West Indian colonists that in order to promote natural increase among the slaves they should counteract dissolute manners, encouraging marriage by such means as

directing that the first establishment of married Negroes, to a certain extent to be specified, shall be made at the expence of the master, and bestowing some marks of distinction or favour, such as a difference of dress, or some pecuniary annual rewards on such parents as shall have reared a child; those rewards to increase with the number of children.[66]

This advice bore its most obvious fruit in the Leewards Islands slave law passed a few months later in 1798. That law regarded the marriage of slaves according to religious rites as "unnecessary and even improper" but directed the owners and managers of estates to assemble their slaves on New Year's Day and "enquire which of them have a husband or wife." This information was to be recorded in a book and read out each year, "at the same time extolling the good behaviour of those who have been faithful to their engagements, and reprobating the misconduct of those who have acted to the contrary." Slaves reaching maturity were to be encouraged to elect partners. The law also directed that the masters "give to every male and female slave, who shall live together faithfully and peaceably as aforesaid, as man and wife, one dollar each for every year that they shall live together.'' But the more generous rewards given on the birth of children were to be paid strictly to the mothers.[67] Thus, inducements offered to males were always minimal.

Some colonial governments attempted to encourage fertility by making awards to the owners or overseers of plantations. The Jamaican slave law of 1792 required that on estates showing a natural increase the owner was to pay the overseer three dollars for every slave birth, these amounts to be deducted from his parish tax bill. The money was to be divided equally between mother, midwife, and nurse. The legislation remained in force until emancipation.[68] In 1820 the Essequibo Agricultural Society awarded its ''first class Gold Medal'' to the manager of Plantation Union, ''having reared 11 out of 12 Negroe children during the year 1819.'' In presenting this award the Governor said that ''it is highly gratifying to me to be enabled to confer on you this distinguished mark of the sense the society entertains of the utility of your praiseworthy exertions.''[69] Silver and gold medals were proposed for owners and overseers in Trinidad in 1817.[70] The presentation of silver cups in 1816 to the overseers of Newton Estate, Barbados, in recognition of their efforts in producing a natural increase on that estate, has already been noted.

The giving of awards to slaveowners and overseers rather than to the slaves themselves suggests a recognition that low fertility was not only evidence of the ''promiscuity'' and ''vice'' so often referred to by planters but also of conditions of life inimical to reproduction created by the slave system. The reduction of working hours for pregnant and nursing women must be viewed in this light. The provision of midwives and nurses, and of white medicine, discussed in chapter 8, was similarly designed to maximize the chances of successful delivery and the survival of babies through the critical first weeks of life.

The building of special lying-in houses, separate from plantation hospitals, was further evidence of this growing sense of responsibility and concern. Many plantation hospitals lacked lying-in rooms, and in such cases women were usually delivered in their own houses.[71] Medical practitioners promoted the establishment of separate lying-in houses, but the slaves were often reluctant to use these facilities and seem generally to have preferred home delivery. Dr. William Sells, who practiced in Jamaica, recommended in 1815 ''the having proper lying-in houses with apartments according to the number of breeding women on the estate . . . ; the women to lie-in there, instead of going to their own houses, where they would be more likely to receive better attention than in their own houses from the manager and the medical practitioner.''[72] Planters, however, often claimed that the slaves, ''being family people,'' preferred being delivered in their own houses even when lying-in rooms were available, and ''a woman, generally one of their own relations or friends, is allowed to attend them when brought to bed, until they are able to get up, independent of the midwife.''[73] White medical practitioners had a vested interest in keeping childbirth within the ambit of the hospital complex and out of the separate world of the slave village, of course. But the slaveowner's reluctance to interfere indicates doubt that they could achieve superior results.

Lactation practices.   Slaveowners and white medical practitioners also believed that the prolonged breast-feeding practiced by slave mothers in the West Indies reduced their fertility. But, for a variety of reasons, they were unwilling or unable to take extreme measures to prevent this practice. This had important implications for patterns of childspacing and hence for total fertility. In a recent discussion, Klein and Engerman have hypothesized that the fertility differentials between the slave populations of North America and the West Indies "can be explained, at least in part, as a result of differences in the period of childspacing," and that the latter were partially determined by lactation practices.[74] They contend that in the nineteenth century, United States slave mothers were breast-feeding for about one year, while the period was a minimum two years in the West Indies.

Although the contrast between the United States and the West Indies seems clear enough, the evidence of planters and medical practitioners was by no means consistent, and the period of two years suggested for the West Indies may be somewhat too high as a typical minimum. Dr. Collins, whose experience was largely confined to St. Vincent, advised planters in 1811 that "Negroes are universally fond of suckling their children for a long time. If you permit them, they will extend it to the third year." Similarly the Jamaican planter Thomas Roughley stated in 1823 that "it is usually the wish of the female slaves, when they become mothers, to keep the infants suckling to an extraordinary or excessive time, sometimes for three years." Dr. McTear of Tobago put the breast-feeding period at two to three years, around 1825. In 1812 the Barbados Agricultural Society claimed that infants suffered from suckling over two years. Thus, planters and white medical practitioners seem to have agreed that breast-feeding in excess of two years was "too long" a period, at least as early as 1810.[75] But the typical period was probably shorter. In 1815 the Jamaican planter William Murray stated that "the children are generally weaned at the age of fifteen months, or if weakly it is allowed the comfort of the mother's milk to a later period." Another planter, William Shand, told a committee in 1832 that "the creole negro females in Jamaica, being very long in weaning their children, I think, is very much against their breeding: A woman will not wean her child till it is 16 or 18 months old, if she can prevent it." In 1823 one Barbadian planter claimed that slave children were "generally" weaned at 18 months, and another, when they cut their eyeteeth.[76]

These scattered, impressionistic data suggest a minimum breast-feeding period of 18 rather than 24 months. Some more direct evidence is available in the slave registration returns, but again it is limited. In 1817 the manager of Stone Castle Estate in St. Kitts listed as "sucking child" four slaves aged under one, six one-year-olds, and two two-year-olds; another two-year-old, together with those aged 3 and 4 years, was listed as "child."[77] This suggests that breast-feeding continued to at least 24 months for all slaves, and possibly months beyond, matching Klein and Engerman's period. In St. Lucia in 1815, however, eight slaves were registered as *à la mamelle*, one aged 3 years, one 14 months, and the others all under 10 months of age.[78] It seems most likely, then, that the breast-feeding period in the West Indies after 1807 was typically 18 months, though sometimes continuing to 36 months. There is no consistent tendency in the available data to suggest any reduction in the period between 1807 and 1834. Nor is there any hint of significant differences in lactation practices between the colonies, though unfortunately no data for the high-fertility marginal colonies have been discovered. Differences between town and country also remain obscure. Although the slaves' practice of "prolonged" breast-feeding had its roots in Africa, it is not clear that creoles adopted a shortened pattern.[79]

In Africa, breast-feeding was often associated with abstinence from sexual intercourse extending even beyond weaning. It is not certain that slaves practiced abstinence in the New World, but the limited contraceptive effect of continued lactation was sufficient to lengthen childspacing intervals and so to reduce fertility.[80] This was recognized by the slaveowners. Thus, Shand agreed that late weaning might "arise from a desire not to be with child again quickly." Collins argued that the slaves' motives were "habit, an idea of its necessity, the desire of being spared at their labour, or perhaps the avoiding of another pregnancy." He recommended weaning children at 14 to 16 months, and told planters that "if you neglect to do this, you not only lose some of the mother's labour, but you prevent their breeding so soon as they otherwise would do, in all probability."[81] Roughley believed that slaves prolonged breast-feeding "with the two-fold view of making the child strong, and having loitering, idle time to spend." It led, he said, to barrenness in the mother and dirt-eating in the child. To avoid these maladies, "I would never (except sickness intervenes) leave a child more than fourteen months sucking, but generally no more than twelve months."[82] The nurseries established on many plantations after 1800 were designed to facilitate such enforced weaning, but slave mothers continued to resist. In 1820 five women belonging to Orchard Plantation, Jamaica, complained to the magistrates that the manager "had directed their children to be taken from them and weaned from the breast and that they were too young for weaning; the said complaint was investigated when it appeared the whole of the children were at least twelve months old each, the women were reprimanded and directed to proceed back to the property to work."[83] John Baillie, a Jamaican planter, stated in 1832 that he offered mothers "two dollars if they would wean the child in twelve months; and I see by returns that since 1807 not one has applied for these two dollars."[84]

No doubt some mothers prolonged the breast-feeding period as a mode of pure resistance to the slave system. But they did no more than maintain African practices, and very probably with the same desire to avoid the high mortality suffered by children immediately after weaning by effectively extending the crisis date.[85] Slaveowners appear to have been aware that early weaning was commonly associated with high infant mortality, and it is for this reason that they were less draconian than they might have been in enforcing shortened lactation periods. Increasing conceptions and births did not necessarily mean an augmented population of surviving children, under extreme conditions of infant mortality.

Fertility Differentials

It is difficult to measure the role of the slaveowners' pronatalist policies in determining the general increase in fertility levels which occurred after 1807. These policies met resistance from the slaves themselves, most obviously in the refusal to alter lactation practices and also in the procuring of abortions and infanticide. More importantly, the slaveowners' pronatalism was only one element in the changing demographic and economic context of the period. Thus, the general reduction in working hours and improved housing, along with the growing proportion of creoles and females in the slave populations, may have been sufficient to account for all of the change which occurred in fertility levels. The pecuniary rewards offered mothers on the birth of their children were small, especially when compared with potential earnings from provision grounds, and few women could hope to produce and keep alive the numbers of children required to obtain any significant release from labor.

The general tendency toward higher fertility levels was more consistent than movements in mortality. While the West Indian colonies showed considerable divergence in their crude death rates during the registration period, all of them except Trinidad, Demerara-Essequibo, and Jamaica experienced improvement in their crude birth rates (table 9.1). Only in Trinidad was decline in fertility substantial, the adjusted crude birth rate falling from 44 per 1,000 in 1813–16 to 31 in 1831–34. In general, the improvement in fertility was most significant in the old sugar colonies, particularly Barbados and Montserrat, though Nevis barely managed to maintain its level. Of the new sugar colonies, only St. Lucia experienced an increase comparable to that of Barbados, and it will be remembered that St. Lucia had by far the smallest African-born population in that group of colonies (table 5.7). Movements in the birth rates of the marginal colonies are less certain because of the limited number of observations available. The Bahamas and Barbuda certainly experienced a substantial increase, but the two registration periods for Anguilla covering the years 1827–34 showed a significant decrease from an initially high rate, no doubt caused by the subsistence crisis on the island.

It is necessary to enter here a caution regarding the crude birth rates given in table 9.1. These rates have been adjusted for underregistration on the basis of principles discussed in detail in chapter 2. While the rates obtained by these adjustments are probably quite close to reality for the registration periods used to select the model life table estimates, the rates will diverge from reality in other registration periods if there was any significant change in the extent of underregistration. As noted earlier, the rates of natural increase obtained by differencing the adjusted birth and death rates do not always match the registered (unadjusted) rates of natural increase. Where substantial divergences occur, it may be assumed that the adjusted birth (and death) rates are incorrect. Thus, the adjusted birth rates obtained for the Bahamas after 1828 and Barbuda in 1821–24, for example, are no doubt excessive. Although the adjusted birth rates certainly provide a superior guide to reality, they must not be regarded too literally. For this reason, analysis of crude birth rates has been confined only to gross tendencies.

An alternative measure of fertility can be supplied by child-woman ratios, which derive directly from the age data and so avoid the difficulties associated with underregistration of births. These ratios can be calculated only for census dates, and lack complete comparability because of the changing age structure of the slave populations. The child-woman ratios shown in table 9.9 were strongly correlated with crude birth rates in 1820 ($r = .76, p = .00$) and 1830 ($r = .78, p = .00$), but the relationship was not perfect, particularly because the child-woman ratio was affected by differences in age structure and variations in infant mortality. Thus, although the birth rate in Barbados was at least as high as in the Bahamas, Anguilla, and Barbuda, the marginal colonies had higher child-woman ratios. The ordering of the colonies in terms of child-woman ratios was very similar to that found for crude birth rates, however, with the lowest ratios occurring in Grenada, Tobago, and Jamaica.

Few significant correlations with the crude birth rates can be established at the colony level (tables 9.3–9.4). Around 1820 there was a statistically significant, but not strong, correlation with the proportion of the slave population employed in

Table 9.9. *Slave Child-Woman Ratios by Colony (Children 0–4 Years of Age Divided by Females 15–44 Years)*

Colony	Ratio
Barbados, 1817	0.597
St. Kitts, 1817	0.469
Nevis, 1817	0.468
Antigua, 1832	0.484
Montserrat, 1831	0.633
Virgin Islands, 1818	0.446
Jamaica, 1817	0.399
Dominica, 1829	0.469
St. Lucia, 1815	0.475
St. Vincent, 1817	0.402
Grenada, 1817	0.352
Tobago, 1819	0.375
Trinidad, 1813	0.401
Demerara-Essequibo, 1820	0.431
Berbice, 1819	0.439
British Honduras, 1834	0.500
Cayman Islands, 1834	0.557
Bahamas, 1834	0.738
Anguilla, 1827	0.619
Barbuda, 1832	0.729

Source: Table S4.1.

nonplantation agriculture ($r = .61$). This relationship was not apparent in 1830, but there were then negative correlations with the size of slaveholdings ($r = -.62$) and per capita sugar production ($r = -.61$). Thus, it is apparent that in general, the level of fertility was highest in colonies where the slaves lived most often in small units, producing crops other than sugar or, to a lesser degree, coffee or cotton. But the proportion living in towns seems not to have mattered. Of the demographic variables, high fertility was more commonly associated with relatively large proportions of creoles than with low sex ratios. High fertility also tended to occur where there were large proportions of colored slaves. Thus, the low fertility of the new sugar colonies must be explained in part by the dominance of African-born males in their populations as well as their increasing concentration in sugar cultivation. Correlations with the child-woman ratio showed a very similar pattern.

In order to proceed beyond these rather gross colony-level correlations, it is necessary to consider age-specific fertility patterns. As noted in chapter 2, however, few of the colonies included the names of mothers in their registration returns, thus limiting the calculation of age-specific rates. More importantly, the only colonies to provide these data consistently were all new sugar colonies, so limiting the range of comparative questions that can be asked. Here the necessary nominal linkage has been carried out for the entire populations of St. Lucia 1815–19, Tobago 1819–21, and Berbice 1819–22, as well as select plantation samples from Dominica 1817–32 and Jamaica 1817–32. A similar analysis can be applied to the registration returns for Grenada, Trinidad, and St. Vincent, but not to any of the high-fertility old sugar colonies or the marginal colonies, other than through the erratic journals of particular plantations.

The age-specific fertility curves for St. Lucia, Tobago, and Berbice around 1820 were very similar in shape. The rates shown in table 9.10 and figure 9.11 have been adjusted for underregistration in order to permit comparison, but this adjustment does not affect their relative shapes. Berbice did achieve somewhat higher fertility than St. Lucia and Tobago, but this differential was evenly distributed. In general, fertility was at a peak among women aged 20–24 years but remained relatively constant between 15 and 39 years of age. Thus, the most obvious difference between these slave populations and modern West Indian populations is that fertility was less concentrated into early adulthood for the slaves, reaching relatively high levels before 20 and remaining relatively high beyond 40 years of age.[86] Although the slave curves may be distorted somewhat by the incorrect reporting of ages, it is improbable that this was sufficient to have a significant effect on their shape. There is no doubt that in spite of their relatively prolonged period of childbearing, the slave populations of the new sugar colonies failed to achieve high fertility.[87] This confirms that the patterns observed in the crude birth rates were not simply a product of variations in age structure. It seems most likely, then, that the contrasts between the colonies of high and low fertility are to be explained by differences in childspacing rather than by differences in age at first and last birth or in the relative youth of the slave populations.

Table 9.10. *Age-specific Slave Birth Rates by Birthplace: St. Lucia, 1815–19, Tobago, 1819–21, and Berbice, 1819–22 (Births per 1,000 Females, Adjuste͏ for Underregistration)*

Age group	St. Lucia, 1815–19			Tobago, 1819–21			Berbice, 1819–22		
	Africans	Creoles	Total	Africans	Creoles	Total	Africans	Creoles	Tota
10–14	—	17	17	—	8	8	—	16	1͏
15–19	50	86	84	—	103	102	122	156	15͏
20–24	72	115	108	99	154	147	133	177	15͏
25–29	85	115	109	90	109	106	125	171	13͏
30–34	41	104	87	90	96	93	103	115	10͏
35–39	67	72	70	53	99	71	79	103	82
40–44	14	44	31	32	49	36	34	38	3͏
45–49	18	35	28	13	13	13	19	18	1͏
50–54	8	10	9	10	21	11	3	—	2
General fertility rate	49	96	84	56	109	85	91	149	108

Source: Rates shown in table S9.44, multiplied by the ratios in table 2.7 to adjust for underregistration.

The fertility of creoles was significantly higher than that of African-born slaves.[88] This pattern was consistent throughout St. Lucia, Tobago, and Berbice around 1820 and in Dominica 1817–32, and seems to have been common to all of the colonies during the registration period at least.[89] The only real aberration occurred in Berbice and was confined to the low-fertility age groups, those over 45 years. Among females in the age groups of peak fertility, the creoles were everywhere almost half again as fertile as the African-born. A number of reasons may be advanced to explain this differential. In the first place, African-born females may have observed longer lactation periods than creoles. This practice would help explain the relatively high fertility of Africans in the older age groups, suggesting wider childspacing intervals over a long childbearing period. It might also be suggested that the differential had to do with mating patterns, younger Africans finding it more difficult than creoles to find mates. Thus, the differential between African and creole fertility tended to be greatest where Africans were the smallest proportion of the slave population, as in the contrast between St. Lucia and Berbice. It is more difficult to explain the differential in terms of labor demands, since birthplace was of relatively little significance in the allocation of slaves to particular tasks. But such distinctions were more common where slaves of color accounted for a significant proportion of the creole population, as in St. Lucia.

Colored creole females were no more fertile than black creoles in either St. Lucia or Berbice, but they did show significantly higher rates in Tobago (table S9.45). A small sample of Jamaican plantations suggests a differential at least as great as that in Tobago.[90] Although the available evidence is equivocal, it appears

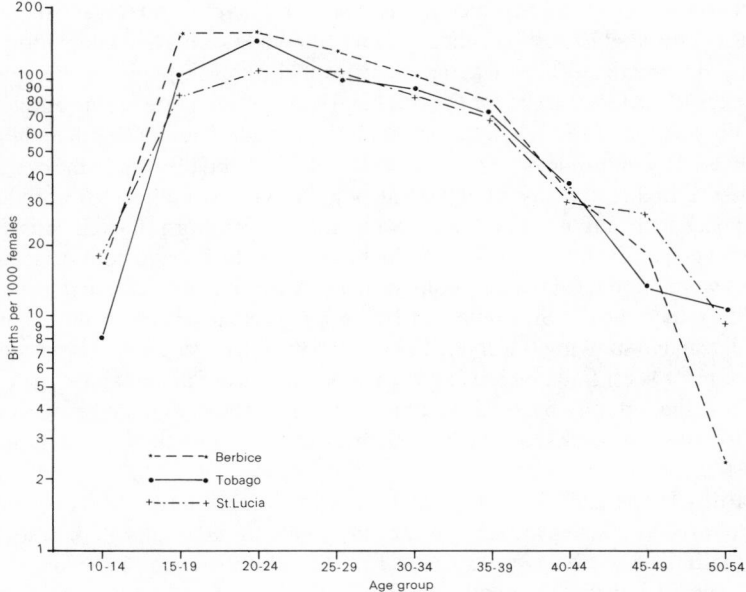

Fig. 9.11. *Age-specific Slave Fertility: Berbice, 1819–22, Tobago, 1819–21, and St. Lucia, 1815–19.* (Source: *table S9.44.*)

most likely that colored creoles generally were somewhat more fertile than black creoles, and that this pattern accounts for part of the African-creole differential. In the case of Tobago, the higher fertility of colored creoles was most apparent among females aged 15–24 years, whose fertility was more than double that of black creoles. At least half of the children born to colored creoles in Tobago 1819–21 were fathered by whites, another third by colored slaves or freedmen, and only 17 percent by blacks. On the other hand, 90 percent of the children born to black mothers were black. Thus, the fertility of the colored creoles had more to do with the physical and psychosocial compulsions of miscegenation than with forces strictly internal to the slave community. In Tobago, as in Jamaica, at least one-third of all children born to slave mothers under 20 years of age were colored. In St. Lucia and Berbice, however, this concentration of colored fertility into the early childbearing years was absent. The existence of a free colored population in St. Lucia permitted relatively stable unions, and this may explain the higher fertility of colored slaves in the older age groups. But the permutations seem too numerous to permit reaching any final conclusions on colored fertility. The important conclusion that does clearly emerge from the data is that creole blacks were consistently more fertile than Africans, so that it is not necessary to explain the African-creole differential in terms of the creole population's colored component.

African as well as colored creole slaves were relatively numerous in the towns, but the contrast between urban and rural environments seems to explain little of the fertility differential. There was no significant difference between the shape of age-specific fertility curves for the rural and urban slave populations of St. Lucia and Tobago around 1820, and the urban rates were consistently less than the rural, as indicated by the crude birth rates (tables S9.1–9.11 and S9.46). In the case of St. Lucia, the higher fertility of the rural population was entirely the product of differences in the creole populations, while the African-born showed consistently higher age-specific rates in town than in the country. In Tobago both Africans and creoles were more fertile in the country than in town. It is impossible to generalize from the experience of St. Lucia and Tobago, particularly because these colonies were unusual in showing lower fertility in town than in the country. The crude birth rates of most West Indian towns and urban parishes were in fact above the colony averages, though only by small amounts. In general, the contrast between urban and rural regimes seems to have had less impact on fertility than on mortality, but much remains to be learned.

Fertility levels tended to increase along with slaveholding size. This tendency was not always consistent, several colonies showing unusually high crude birth rates in units of 1–10 slaves (table S9.12). The clearest example occurred in St. Lucia, and even in that colony the units of 1–10 slaves were slightly aberrant. The reasons for the tendency of fertility to increase with holding size are not immediately obvious. The proportion of creoles in the slave population did generally increase along with slaveholding size, but surprisingly, St. Lucia showed the opposite pattern. The proportion of colored slaves decreased steadily as holding size increased, so the probable high fertility of the colored cannot account for the trend. Variations in sex ratios also failed to match the fertility trend. In some colonies, notably St. Lucia, the highest crude birth rates were associated with high sex ratios.

Thus, the tendency for fertility to increase with slaveholding size cannot readily be explained by the proportions of females, creoles, or colored slaves in the populations. Nor can it be explained by differences in age structure. In St. Lucia, Tobago, and Berbice, at least, age-specific fertility rates by holding size were ordered in the same way as the crude birth rates (table S9.47). The pattern was particularly clear in St. Lucia, the rates being quite similar to about age 25 years, then separating into distinct slaveholding size-groups; beyond age 25 the rates in units of greater than 300 slaves were more than double those in units of 1–10, the other size-groups falling between these extremes. The pattern was equally neat in Berbice. In Tobago, however, the age-specific fertility curve for units of 51–100 slaves fell below the curves for all other size-groups; it will be remembered that units of 51–100 slaves also showed the highest death rates in Tobago. This correlation suggests that the "optimum" conditions of labor exploitation existing in such units may have acted to reduce fertility in just the same way as they heightened mortality. But the correlation between maximum mortality and minimum fertility in particular slaveholding size-groups did not follow the same pattern in all colonies, nor can high mortality be explained simply as a function of high fertility and hence high infant mortality rates.

An alternative explanation for the general tendency of fertility levels to increase along with slaveholding size may be sought in the potentials for co-residential unions. It will be shown in a later section of this chapter that the proportion of slaves living in family units increased rapidly with increasing holding size, and that females living with mates on the same plantation tended to be more fertile than those separated from their partners. Within the rural populations generally, the tendency for fertility to increase with holding size may be viewed as a direct response to the local availability of potential co-residential mates in the context of the limited mobility permitted by the slave system.

A somewhat unexpected corollary of the association between fertility and slaveholding size is the finding that fertility was relatively high on large-scale sugar estates. In St. Lucia 1815–19, the crude birth rate for slaves living on sugar estates was almost the same as for those cultivating cocoa, and exceeded the rates associated with coffee, provisions, and cotton (table 9.6). This pattern occurred in spite of the relatively large proportions of Africans and males found on sugar estates. Sugar maintained its advantage in terms of age-specific fertility. The difference between sugar and the minor plantation staples was slight, but the fertility of "personal" slaves, unattached to rural holdings, was considerably lower after age 25 years (table 9.11). In the case of Demerara-Essequibo 1829–32 the crude birth rate was highest on cotton plantations, followed by sugar and coffee (table 9.7). On the basis of parish-level patterns, the ordering of fertility in Grenada was as follows: cotton, cocoa, coffee, and sugar (table S9.9). Although the ordering of crop-types was less consistent for fertility than for mortality, it is at least clear that sugar was not always associated with low fertility rates. This

Table 9.11. *Age-specific Slave Birth Rates by Type of Enterprise: St. Lucia, 1815–19 (Registered Births per 1,000 Females)*

Age group	Sugar	Coffee, Cotton, Cocoa, Provisions	Personal
10–14	15	14	4
15–19	53	56	48
20–24	67	53	56
25–29	73	71	44
30–34	61	49	36
35–39	42	50	20
40–44	21	17	20
45–49	15	24	—
50–54	3	7	7
General fertility rate	54	52	39

Source: T.71/376–81.

suggests that the harsh regimes found on sugar estates had their most direct impact on mortality patterns and that their effect on fertility was muted by the scale factors associated with plantation populations noted above. Hence, the emphasis placed on sugar cultivation's mortality-increasing tendencies is not misplaced.

In St. Lucia and Berbice, the fertility of field laborers exceeded that of domestic slaves (table S9.48). This difference applied to Africans as well as creoles, except that in St. Lucia African domestics were more fertile than field laborers. None of these differences were very strong, however, and the higher fertility of field laborers was confined almost entirely to females aged between 20 and 39 years (fig. 9.12). Some of the difference between domestics and field laborers may be explained by the contrast between rural and urban populations and by the associated contrasts in mating patterns. But where sugar estate populations can be isolated, in the case of St. Lucia, the difference between the two occupational groups appear largely a function of age structure. Domestics living on St. Lucian sugar estates 1815–19 showed a general fertility rate (births per 1,000 females living aged 15–49 years) of 124, compared to 82 for field laborers, but the age-specific fertility rates for the two groups were very similar between 20 and 39 years, as in the total population. Thus, it may be concluded that in St. Lucia and Berbice, at least, there was no really significant difference between the fertility of domestics and field laborers. The most likely explanation of this lack of variation is that the fertility-reducing labor regimes of the field laborers were balanced by the long hours spent by domestics in the great houses, isolated from the slave community. But it would be necessary to test the relationship between fertility and occupation in contexts of high fertility among colored slaves, such as occurred in Tobago, before reaching any final conclusion. For the moment it must be assumed that occupation-specific fertility differentials were limited and were certainly less marked than those relating to birthplace, enterprise-type, or slaveholding size.

Seasonality of Births

Births recorded in the slave registration returns showed a significant degree of seasonal variation. Figure 9.13 charts the pattern of births by month in Tobago and Berbice as percentages of the annual daily average. In these two colonies around 1820, births peaked in September and were at a minimum in February–April. Data are also available for a sample of plantations in Dominica 1817–32, but they show a more erratic pattern than that found for the seasonality of deaths (table S9.49). The peak did occur in September, as in Tobago and Berbice, but the minimum fell in October, and there was no clear distinction between the two halves of the year.

Analysis of the seasonality of births is more difficult than that of deaths, of course, because each event reflects a number of components.[91] Birth records may be lagged nine months to permit study of the seasonality of conception, but this overlooks possible variations in the seasonality of miscarriage and abortion. In the case of the slave registration data, it is also necessary to consider the potential impact on the recorded data of seasonal variation in the level of infant mortality.

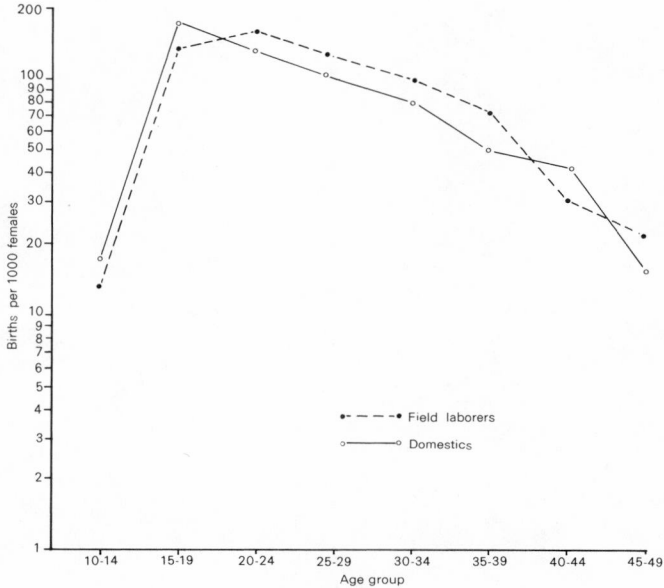

Fig. 9.12. *Age-specific Slave Fertility by Occupation: Berbice, 1819–22.* (Source: *table S9.48.*)

Thus, the patterns shown in figure 9.13 really display only the seasonality of conceptions which resulted in successful births and survival to about the fourth week of life. The nature of the registration data prevents accurate study of the seasonality of infant mortality. The seasonal spread of births of children born and dying within a registration interval did in fact match quite closely the pattern for total births. But the seasonality of deaths of young children differed strongly from the pattern for older slaves. In Tobago, for example, mortality was at a maximum in the months January–April for slaves under 3 years of age, while those over 10 years suffered the heaviest mortality between July and November. If the true seasonal pattern of infant mortality followed that for children under 3 years, this would significantly reduce the seasonality of births shown in figure 9.13. Manuel Moreno Fraginals has argued similarly that slave infant mortality in Cuba was "especially high in December, January, and February, the seasons of harvesting and cold."[92]

In view of these seemingly intractable difficulties, it is necessary to approach the available data on the seasonality of slave births with great caution. As in the case of mortality (fig. 9.8), Tobago exhibited stronger seasonality than did Berbice. This might be explained by the lack of a marked crop season in Berbice, but it may also mean that infant mortality was heavy during Tobago's crop season. If births are lagged nine months, it would seem that conceptions were at a peak in

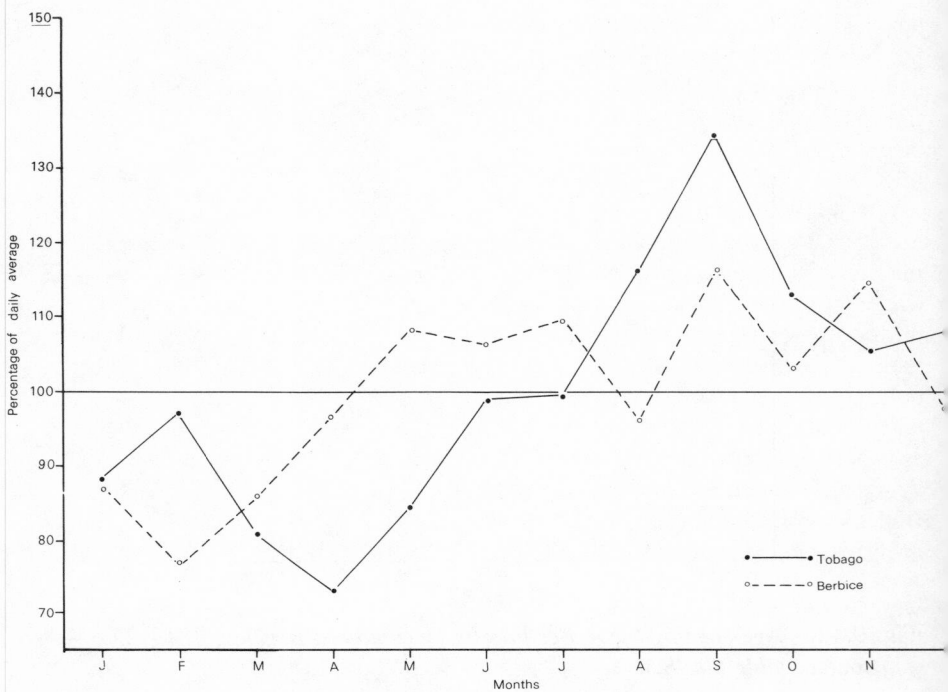

Fig. 9.13.   *Seasonality of Slave Births: Tobago, 1819–21 and Berbice,*
   1819–22. (Source*: table S9.49.)*

December, declined during crop to a minimum by July, the end of the crop, and
gradually increased again during the out-of-crop season. The extreme hours
worked during crop may have reduced coital frequency and conception, but the
impact of seasonal variation in nutrition is not obvious. Certainly births were more
common in the out-of-crop season. A comparison of the seasonality of births on
sugar and coffee plantations in Dominica suggests no significant differences by
crop-type (table S9.49). Similarly, the experience of field laborers and domestics
in Berbice was not obviously different. In Tobago, however, there was a strong
contrast between the rural and urban populations, the town slaves showing a
seasonal peak in the proportion of births occurring between November and March
(or of conceptions February–June). It is difficult to account for these variations.
They do not match findings from later periods.[93]

Family and Fertility

The nature of West Indian slave family structure is a complex issue and remains
the subject of controversy.[94] There is no doubt that the slave system disorganized
patterns of family and kinship organization, particularly through its narrow legal

emphasis on the mother-child link, the separation of kin by sale and transfer, the large-scale restriction of residential mobility, and the authoritarian role of master and overseer, most obviously symbolized by sexual intervention. At the same time, there is evidence of strong family bonds within the slave community, of parent-child affection, and of subtle variations of family patterns having their origins in Africa.

The existence of each of these tendencies in slave family organization can be documented in the literature produced by contemporary travelers, planters, and missionaries in the period after 1807. These sources provide impressionistic evidence of the frequency of particular types of family structure and also of differences between colonies and labor regimes. In order to quantify these variations, however loosely, it is necessary to use censuses of family and household groups. As noted in chapter 2, the slave registration returns provide systematic data of this sort only for Trinidad, British Honduras, and St. Lucia, as well as erratic materials for Berbice. The most valuable of these samples is that for Trinidad, and detailed analyses of these data have been presented elsewhere.[95] Bolland has made some use of the material for British Honduras, while Craton has analyzed family patterns implicit in a number of the Bahamas returns.[96] For Jamaica, three large holdings have been studied by linking a household census with the registration data.[97] It must be emphasized that each of these analyses is based on a different type of data, even though all depend on the registration returns, and that they involve peculiar methodological difficulties. Thus, they cannot be used for a truly systematic comparison of variations in slave family household structure between colonies. Only gross tendencies will be considered here. The results of these studies together with some new material for St. Lucia will be briefly reviewed, and, the implications of family patterns for slave fertility differentials in the early nineteenth century will be emphasized.

The proportion of the slave populations attributed to family units differed with the size of the holdings to which they belonged. In part, this relationship derived directly from the definition of "family" applied in the slave registration returns, kin being recognized only when they belonged to the same owner, but there was also a genuine tendency for the proportion in family groups to increase with holding size. In rural St. Lucia in 1815, for example, only 40 percent of those belonging to units of two slaves were attributed kin, but this proportion increased steadily to a maximum of 73 percent in units of 250 slaves. A very similar trend occurred in Trinidad in 1813, the proportion reaching a maximum of 74 percent in the largest holdings. In the towns of Trinidad and St. Lucia, however, the proportion of slaves living in family groups reached a maximum in units of about ten slaves and then declined with increasing holding size. The latter trend may be explained by the very high sex ratios of the largest urban units, which generally were composed of specialized transport workers. As a consequence of this trend and the typically small scale of urban holdings, slaves were much more likely to belong to family groups in the country than in town. In St. Lucia 69 percent of rural slaves were attributed to families in 1815, compared to 55 percent of town slaves, and much the same contrast occurred in Trinidad.

Beyond this contrast between town and country, there were also differences between types of rural holdings which did not simply reflect variations in slave population size. In St. Lucia, the percentage of slaves attributed to families was highest on cocoa and coffee plantations and least on cotton and provisions plantations, with sugar estates falling between these extremes (table 9.12). Since the sugar estates contained much larger populations than the other plantations, they might be expected to have held the largest proportions of slaves in families, so it may be concluded that sugar was in fact associated with a relatively high rate of familial disorganization.

As well as differences between town and country in the simple fact of belonging to a family unit, there were also variations in the types of family households in which slaves lived. In Trinidad and St. Lucia, mother-children units predominated in both town and country around 1815, but they were most common among the urban slave populations. In the case of St. Lucia, 32 percent of rural slaves lived in such units, compared to 39 percent in the towns. On the other hand, 4 percent of rural slaves were attributed to nuclear families (man, wife, and their children) in rural St. Lucia, compared to less than one percent in the towns. Although a larger proportion of slaves lived in nuclear families in Trinidad (14 percent, compared to 4 percent in St. Lucia), the contrast between town and country was the same.

Family types other than the matrifocal and nuclear accounted for much smaller numbers of slaves, but extended and polygynous units as well as families of more than two generations were always much more common among the rural than the urban slave population. Elaborated families were also most common on large-scale plantations, where the availability of potential mates was greatest. It should be remembered that slaves attached to large holdings suffered separation by sale or transfer less often than those belonging to small units, especially those in the towns. Thus, in St. Lucia extended family households were most common on sugar estates, and polygynous units were entirely confined to such large holdings (table 9.12). It is also important to note that women-children units accounted for a smaller proportion of the slaves living on sugar estates than on any other type of plantation. This pattern may be explained largely in terms of scale and the stability of plantation communities. Thus, the proportion of slaves living in woman-children units declined steadily with increasing holding size, while the proportion in nuclear families rose.

The analysis thus far has depended on the examples of Trinidad and St. Lucia, colonies for which the data are relatively consistent and interpretable. But it must be asked how far these examples, drawn from new sugar colonies with large urban, African-born, and freedman populations, were typical of the British Caribbean in the early nineteenth century. Craton's analysis of 25 holdings in the Bahamas suggests that as few as 15 percent of slaves may have lived outside family households in 1822. At Newton Estate, Barbados, roughly 20 percent of slaves had no family living on the plantation in 1796, while at Montpelier, Jamaica, the proportion was about 30 percent in 1825.[98] These proportions may be compared with the 31 percent found among rural slaves in St. Lucia in 1815 and the 44 percent in Trinidad in 1813.

Table 9.12. Slave Family Types by Enterprise: St. Lucia, 1815

				Percentage of Slaves				
Family Type	Sugar	Coffee	Cocoa	Cotton	Provisions	Combined	Personal	Total*
Man, wife, their children	4.1	5.8	2.9	—	2.9	6.3	1.1	3.6
Man, wife	0.9	0.2	0.5	—	—	3.1	0.1	0.6
Woman, her children	27.6	35.3	38.6	29.1	33.1	27.7	40.2	32.4
Man, his children	1.9	2.3	—	—	—	0.8	0.5	1.6
Woman, her children, her grandchildren	12.1	14.3	13.3	0.4	16.6	10.7	5.9	10.9
Man, wife, various children	2.2	—	—	1.4	2.9	4.6	0.5	1.6
Polygynists	0.2	—	—	—	—	2.2	—	0.1
Extended	7.5	2.0	1.2	—	1.7	9.7	1.1	5.0
Siblings and their children	11.8	12.3	20.4	3.2	5.7	6.5	8.0	11.0
No family	31.7	27.8	23.1	39.1	37.1	28.5	42.6	33.1
Total number of slaves	6,743	1,961	407	220	175	589	3,294	16,282

Source: T.71/378–79.

*Total includes slaves whose enterprise-type is unknown.

Although these proportions should not be regarded too literally, since they derive from different types of data and relate only to slaves belonging to the same master, they do suggest a rough correlation between the frequency of family membership and the size of the creole population. This might mean no more than a strictly biological relationship, lacking any co-residential basis, stability, or familial affection, of course. But there is literary and statistical evidence to suggest that nuclear and extended families were in fact relatively common in the high-fertility creole populations of the marginal colonies. In St. Lucia in 1815, slaves imported from the marginal colonies were found in nuclear families three times as often as the local creoles. Similarly, Craton's analysis of the slaves moved by Burton Williams from the Bahamas to Trinidad in the early 1820s shows that nuclear families were perhaps twice as common in the Bahamas as in rural Trinidad.[99] Interestingly, when Williams was questioned by a Trinidad committee in 1825 on the decrease of the island's slave population, he attributed it to the disproportion of the sexes and added that "I do not think sufficient care is given to their living together as man and wife, by giving a feast to the gang when they come together and a sharp punishment when they part."[100] At about the same time, it was said that although few slave marriages were solemnized, "it is pleasing to observe how seldom the matrimonial contract among them is violated, or dissolved except by death."[101] In the case of the high-fertility slave population of Barbuda, with 200 adults in 1830, the Incorporated Society for the Conversion and Religious Instruction of the Negro Population reported that 56 couples "were living as married persons faithfully with each other," most of them married many years before by the Wesleyans.[102]

No doubt, some of this evidence was self-serving, but it does seem that there was a significant difference between the slave family structures of the marginal colonies and the new sugar colonies. This contrast is not to be explained simply by the relative proportions of Africans and creoles in the slave populations. Indeed, in the Bahamas as well as St. Lucia and Trinidad, the African-born were found more often in nuclear families than were creoles. This pattern applied to both male and female adults, in town and country. The reason for this contrast is that the African-born were less likely than creoles to find themselves in any type of family, while creoles much more often belonged to units of several generations. Creoles also tended to dominate the mother-children units, giving a matrifocal tendency to the development of slave society. Thus, the relatively small proportion of slaves living in mother-children families in the marginal colonies was not simply a product of their creolization but must also have had to do with physical isolation and labor regimes.

In the sugar colonies, the relative importance of mother-children families among creole slaves resulted from the density of plantation populations and, possibly, the need to observe rules of exogamy. The high density of populations, particularly in the heavily creolized old sugar colonies, meant that many potential mates were available within short distances, resulting in "visiting" unions with no permanent co-residential base. Such unions were regarded by the slaveowners as mother-children family households. The estate manager who made up the New-ton, Barbados, list in 1796 stated that mothers appearing without the names of their husbands were partners of men belonging to other estates, but failed to distinguish these cases from those in which the male mates had died.[103] If the manager's assertion is taken at face value, only 20 mothers at Newton had husbands on the estate, while 35 had mates elsewhere; however, a similar percentage of fathers had no wives on the estate, and in most cases the mothers of their children were dead. These data, then, are ambiguous. But the manager certainly saw the matter as a problem. In 1798 he told Newton's absentee proprietor that "I endeavour to lead them likewise into intermarriages at home, for a Negro man will run after his wife to the other end of the island and be back next morning to his work."[104] Many whites noticed the night "rambling" of slaves, in Barbados and elsewhere, and some specifically distinguished between the "domestic" African and the "roving habit and unsettled disposition" of the creole slave.[105]

Better estimates of the extent of cross-plantation mating can be obtained from church records of slave marriages, partners, and baptisms. Priests of the Anglican and Roman Catholic churches baptized large numbers of slaves but rarely named the parents, and they performed relatively few marriages.[106] Although marriages performed by nonconformists were not recognized as legal until 1837, these churches were more active, and more particular.[107] Thus, the most useful records are those of the Moravians and Wesleyans. It is difficult to decide how the behavior of slaves joining such churches may be unusual, in terms of the separation of mates. The teachings of the missionaries emphasized the importance of matrimony and monogamy, rather than co-residence; and the slaves who joined the churches became part of a wider community of neighbors, expanding their range of potential mates.

Table 9.13 presents data from a sample of Moravian and Wesleyan church books, showing the proportions of slave mates who served different masters and, generally, did not live in co-residential unions. In the 1820s, with the exception of Barbados, no more than 30 percent of marriage partners belonged to different owners. Where plantations were relatively isolated, as in Dominica, the pro-portion was much smaller. In general, the proportion separated increased along with population density and creolization. For Jamaica, it has been shown that most of the marriage partners lived only a mile or two apart.[108] The Moravian data concerning "partners" of unmarried church members are more difficult to analyze, but it seems that roughly the same proportions were separated as in the case of marriages. At Sharon, Barbados, 55 percent of 114 men were separated from their mates, and 48 percent of 279 women.[109] The data relating to parents of baptized children may represent the extreme of separation (table 9.13). Although the proportions differ somewhat erratically, it must be concluded that in the old sugar colonies, at least, probably a majority of slave mates belonged to different masters. Most of these slaves were unable to establish co-resident households. It is not known how many of them were Africans and how many creoles, but the evidence from Trinidad and St. Lucia clearly shows that Africans were more likely

Table 9.13. *Spatial Separation of Slave Mates*

Colony	Number of Marriages/Baptisms	Percentage of Mates Belonging to Different Owners
Slave marriage partners		
Barbados (Moravian, 1827–34)	49	49.0
St. Kitts (Wesleyan, 1818–33)	345	29.6
Jamaica (Moravian, 1827–34)	189	28.0
Dominica (Wesleyan, 1820–34)	309	5.8
St. Vincent (Anglican, 1825–34)	121	22.3
Slave parents of baptized children		
Barbados (Moravian, 1824–34)	467	47.3
St. Kitts (Moravian, 1820–34)	1,081	71.7
Antigua (Wesleyan, 1816–34)	308	19.5
Antigua (Moravian, 1817–33)	296	67.2

Sources: Church Book of the Mission of the United Brethren among the Negroes in the Island of Barbadoes; Mount Tabor Moravian Church: List of Marriages in the Congregation (D.A.B.); Register of Marriages, 1818–44, Basseterre (Methodist Manse, Basseterre, St. Kitts); List of Marriages at Fairfield, Manchester, 1829–40; Carmel Church Book, 1813–37 (Moravian Church Archives, Malvern, Jamaica); Register of Marriages, 1820–37 (Methodist Manse, Roseau, Dominica); Register of Baptisms, Marriages and Burials, St. Vincent, 1820–34 (Parish Office, St. George's Cathedral, Kingstown); Moravian Baptisms, Marriages and Burials, 1769–1886 (D.A.B.); Children's Church Book, 1820–44 (Moravian Church, Basseterre, St. Kitts); Register of Baptisms, Parham and District, 1816–1921; Register of Baptisms, St. John's, 1823–1928 (Methodist Manse, St. John's, Antigua); Registers of Baptisms, 1807–26 and 1821–33 (Spring Gardens Moravian Church, Antigua).

to form co-residential unions, and the population of Barbados contained very few Africans after 1820, of course. Thus, the slaves' "propensity for rambling" increased as the population became densely settled and creolized, and the mother-children family household increased its dominance as a consequence.

Creolization also tended to be associated with relatively large proportions of female slaves of color, and the latter were particularly likely to be found in mother-children units. In part, this reflected the urban concentration of colored slaves. But the same pattern was found in rural St. Lucia, Trinidad, and Jamaica.[110] The reason for this was simply that the white or freedman mates of female slaves of color found no place in the owners' lists of slave family households, whatever the actual residential nature of the relationship. Even those colored female slaves who mated with black or colored slaves relatively rarely formed stable unions. The corollary of this relationship with color was that adult female field laborers were more likely than domestics to live in family households containing mates. Adult male drivers and tradesmen, however, lived in such households more often than did field laborers, suggesting that the male's status within the plantation hierarchy was reflected within the family structure of the slave community. Drivers in particular were found in nuclear, extended, and polygynous units much more often than was any other occupational group.

Before proceeding to consider the implications of slave family structure for fertility differentials, it may be useful to summarize the findings thus far. In the first place, it seems well established that the majority of African-born slaves were isolated from family life, and that the proportion of slaves living in family households increased along with the size of the creole population. Where the slave population lived in isolated communities composed largely of creoles, as in the marginal colonies, nuclear families predominated. In the densely populated sugar colonies, however, Africans tended to live in nuclear families more often than creoles, while the creoles were found more often in mother-children and extended units. Creolization in the sugar colonies was also associated with a considerable amount of cross-plantation mating. In all colonies, rural slaves were more likely than town slaves to live in any type of family and were less likely to belong to mother-children units. The potential for co-residential mating and the establishment of nuclear, extended, or polygynous families increased along with slaveholding size, particularly on sugar plantations. Female slaves of color and domestics more often lived in mother-children families than did blacks or field laborers, whereas privileged male slaves tended to be relatively common in nuclear, extended, and polygynous households.

The implications of these tendencies in slave family structure for fertility differentials can generally be established only by inference. Few data on the age-specific fertility of slaves belonging to different family types are available, and only those for St. Lucia (table 9.14) and sample plantations in Jamaica[111] will be considered here. But the broad conclusions that can be reached from these examples are quite uniform. The most important of these findings is that women living in co-residential unions were significantly more fertile than those living separately. This contrast is apparent in the general fertility rates (based on females 15–49 years of age) but emerges more clearly when smaller age groups are considered, since females living with mates were older than those without. The strongest contrast was that between females with no family at all and those with co-resident mates. The isolated women tended most often to be Africans, and their low fertility explains much of the difference between African and creole fertility discussed in earlier sections. Thus, this contrast was most obvious among women over 20 years of age. In terms of the contrast between the fertility of women living in nuclear and mother-children units, the difference in fertility was confined entirely to those over 20 years. But in St. Lucia, the fertility of women in the prime childbearing age group (25–29 years) was almost twice as great among those in nuclear families as in mother-children units. Women living in extended families with co-resident mates also tended to be relatively fertile, as did those in polygynous families, though here the sample becomes small.

The finding that slave women living in co-residential unions were more fertile than those who were separated from their mates is not particularly surprising, since it matches the relatively low frequency of sexual intercourse found in "visiting"

Table 9.14. *Age-specific Slave Birth Rates by Family Type: St. Lucia, 1815–19 (Births per 1,000 Females)*

Age Group	Man, Wife, Their Children	Man, Wife	Woman, Her Children	Woman, Her Children, Her Grand-Children	Man, Wife, Various Children	Polygynists	Extended	Siblings, Children	No Family	Total
10–14	—	—	12	8	29	—	9	7	17	10
15–19	—	205	60	68	51	—	56	60	24	48
20–24	89	82	70	91	—	—	141	57	33	62
25–29	124	164	70	61	103	410	89	95	22	63
30–34	84	—	69	98	59	—	59	44	7	50
35–39	72	—	50	52	51	137	88	53	12	40
40–44	19	—	16	42	—	—	26	53	7	18
45–49	63	—	23	26	—	—	—	14	3	16
50–54	—	—	9	8	—	—	—	—	3	5
General fertility rate	70	51	55	74	46	75	81	61	19	48
Total number of births	32	7	304	115	9	3	52	103	91	729

Source: T.71/378–79.

unions in modern West Indian societies.[112] The labor regime of slavery, together with the partially effective proscription of movement at night, must have meant an even wider differential. Some of the fathers of children living separately with their mothers belonged to the same slaveholding, of course, but in highly creolized populations such as Barbados a high proportion belonged to other owners. Differential mortality may also account for variations in the absence of fathers, but death rates were at a relatively low level among young adults, and the frequency of cross-plantation mating in Barbados occurred in spite of low mortality.

Variations in slave family structure help to explain some of the fertility differentials noticed earlier in this chapter. Thus, the relationship between fertility, slave-holding size, and sugar cultivation may be seen as a product of the potential for co-residential mating on large plantations. The importance of this factor should not be overstated, however, since the high-fertility marginal colonies were dominated by small holdings, yet appear to have had a high frequency of co-residential mating. Isolation as well as labor regimes may well have been more significant than holding size in determining the fertility levels of the marginal colonies. In the case of Barbados, where there were more small holdings than in most sugar colonies, the absence of an arduous night-work regime during crop season, together with the density of plantations, more than balanced the reduction of coital frequency resulting from cross-plantation mating.

The relatively low fertility of urban slave populations may also be explained in part by family structure. High proportions of urban slaves had no access to family life, since the majority of them were employed as domestics in small units, with little opportunity to escape their mistresses' surveillance. The low fertility of domestics on plantations may be traced to similar causes. Only slaves of color, whose children were very often fathered by whites or freedmen, showed relatively normal fertility levels among domestics in either town or country. Thus, the high fertility of field laborers, compared to domestics, must be explained largely in terms of their opportunities to establish co-residential unions within the slave community and had little to do with any differences in their material conditions of life.

The contrast between African and creole fertility levels also had to do with family structure, though the relationship was complex. It has been shown that slaves living with mates were more fertile than those not in co-residential unions and that Africans tended to live in nuclear families more often than did creoles, yet Africans were less fertile. The resolution to this seeming paradox lies in the fact that a majority of the African-born were completely isolated from the family system, even a decade after the abolition of the Atlantic slave trade, while most adult creoles were involved in mating of one sort or another. The relatively high fertility of the Africans who did live in nuclear families was insufficient to balance the infertility of these solitaries, while the fertility of creoles was more evenly spread. Thus, although the matrifocal tendency associated with creolization in the sugar colonies did operate to reduce fertility, slave populations dominated by creoles managed to achieve total fertility levels that were at least higher than the extremely low levels characteristic of populations dominated by Africans.

CONCLUSIONS

The complexity of the interactions involved in the strongly contrasting patterns of fertility, mortality, and natural increase found in the British Caribbean after 1807 suggests that any attempt at monocausal explanation is doomed to failure. The most that can be expected is a more precise ordering of the variables, only some of them quantifiable, and a clearer understanding of the differentials.

One route to an improved ordering of the variables is provided by regression analysis, but the results, at the colony level, do little more than separate the marginal colonies from the sugar colonies. Only three variables emerge as statistically significant as the result of stepwise regression on the rate of natural increase in 1820: the proportion of slaves employed in nonplantation agriculture, the African-creole ratio, and the sex ratio ($R = .92$). For natural increase in 1830, however, the only variables selected are the proportion employed as domestics and slaveholding size ($R = .98$). Although the level of explanation obtained is high, it is possible to conclude only that positive natural increase was strongly associated with small rural holdings producing crops other than the plantation staples, with employment in domestic occupations, and with large proportions of creoles and females in the slave population. The proportion of slaves employed in sugar cultivation or living in towns does not appear directly in the regression equations, but it is fair to conclude that the analysis points to the strong contrast between the chances of survival of slave populations in the marginal colonies and the sugar colonies. There is no doubting the significance of this contrast, but regression analysis at the colony level does little to help account for it.

In an early section of this chapter it was established that mortality and fertility were of roughly equal importance in determining variations in the rate of natural increase at the colony level, and that the role of fertility probably increased in the period after 1807. Dissection of the components, however, suggests that mortality differentials remained central. In the crucial contrast between sugar and other types of agriculture, fertility differentials were in fact relatively slight. Similarly, the contrast between urban and rural slave populations is to be explained by mortality rather than fertility. These relationships tended to be smothered at the colony level. In attempting to explain the essential differences in the demographic experience of slaves living in contrasting environments, however, it is clear that mortality must play a leading role.

The well-known association between sugar cultivation and high mortality can be traced to a number of factors, but most important were the extreme hours of heavy labor and the brutality of the gang-driving system. No other crop was produced under such arduous conditions of labor, and the demands of night work during crop season were unique to sugar. The tasks, hours of labor, and systems of work organization associated with coffee, livestock, pimento, cotton, cocoa, and provisions were much less demanding. These factors also explain much of the variation in natural increase found within the sugar colonies. Thus, the superior performance of the Barbadian slave population may be traced in part to relatively short hours of work, particularly the lighter load of night work.

A scale factor was also involved. Most sugar plantations were extensive units with large slave populations, and thus permitted a hierarchy of supervision and occupational differentiation that maximized the exploitation of labor. Large populations also meant cramped slave villages and unsanitary living conditions, which were breeding grounds for dysentery and communicable disease. The labor of slaves attached to small holdings producing the minor staples, however, could not be organized in such "efficient" forms, or the slaves exposed to such extreme demands.

The reason for this contrast between sugar and other forms of agriculture must ultimately be traced to the technical relations of production. There is every reason to believe that slaveowners producing crops other than sugar would have made similarly extreme demands on their slaves if the technological requirements had permitted such forms of organization. The crucial factor associated with sugar production was the importance of manufacturing processes. The limited technology available to sugar planters in the early nineteenth century meant that in the satanic mills of the Caribbean, manufacturing continued for at least six months of the year and was most profitably organized on a 24-hour basis. Investment in fixed capital was sufficiently massive to ensure large-scale enterprises, and hence investment in large slave labor forces. Planters took advantage of these factors. The demands of the manufacturing processes permitted the maximization of hours of work and physical exertion, while the standardization of cultivation permitted the development of gang labor and the driving system in the field. Gang labor was not unique to sugar, of course, but its combination with manufacturing created conditions that made demands on human endurance rarely matched on such a scale.

Differences in work organization also explain much of the contrast between rural and urban slave populations. Domestics living in towns certainly worked long hours, but their tasks were not as arduous as those performed by field laborers. Urban slaves hardly ever worked in gangs under the lash of the driver. Once again, these patterns must be traced to the technical relations of production and the material conditions of life that they generated. Differences in the slaveowners' sex, color, or nationality mattered little in the demographic experience of the slaves. Living in a town or on a small rural holding always meant greater chances of survival than living on a large sugar plantation.

The significance of variations in nutrition is more difficult to determine. At a gross level, there was no clear association between high mortality and either the rationed allowances or provision ground systems. The planters of Barbados were quick to argue that their paternal role in supplying rations and preparing food was basic to the natural increase in the slave population of that island,[113] but the system did not everywhere produce the same results. It may well be that slaves living in marginal colonies and in towns enjoyed superior nutrition. The evidence is ambiguous, however, being confused most obviously by the Anguilla subsistence crisis, so it must be concluded that differences in nutrition were probably less important than differences in labor demands. Within particular contexts, there were considerable differences in the food supplies of individual slaves derived from their status in the internal hierarchy, but these differences existed regardless of whether the provision ground or allowance system prevailed. Thus, although there is considerable evidence that malnutrition was widespread in the West Indian slave population and that this malnutrition was important in raising mortality levels, it is less obvious that differences in nutrition were crucial to variations in mortality other than individual differences within the slave hierarchy.

Differences in housing and clothing were most important in terms of the contrast between town and country and within the status hierarchy. The clearly superior housing and clothing of urban slaves may have helped protect them from diarrhea and dysentery, the great killers in the cramped plantation quarters. A similar pattern existed within the plantation populations. Slaves of high status, who occupied better houses and wore better clothes, died of diarrhea and dysentery much less often than the deprived field laborers and consequently showed lower overall mortality. It seems improbable, however, that differences in housing and clothing were of any great importance in the large-scale contrast between mortality levels on sugar plantations and other types of rural holdings. Nor is it clear that they can explain gross differences between colonies.

The most direct intervention of the slaveowner aimed at reducing mortality levels, the provision of European medical attention, probably had a negative effect. Slaves most definitely isolated from European medical practitioners, those living in the marginal colonies, survived longest. The attack on smallpox was successful and significant, but it cannot explain colony-level mortality differentials.

Factors affecting fertility were less clearly related to material conditions of life than those determining mortality differentials. Although the labor regime of sugar plantations must have had deleterious effects on reproduction, its impact was countered by other factors, and within the sugar colonies there was surprisingly little difference in the total fertility of slaves living on sugar estates, other types of rural holdings, or in towns. The lack of significant differences in the fertility of field laborers and domestics also suggests that variations in work regime, nutrition, housing, clothing, or access to European medical attention were of relatively little importance. The pronatalist policies of the slaveowners may have had some impact, but again it is impossible to link these incentives directly to fertility differentials. The symbiotic relationship of nutrition, infection, and fertility remains a controversial subject, even at a theoretical level.[114]

In the marginal colonies of Anguilla, Barbuda, and the Bahamas, high fertility was associated with small slaveholding size. In the sugar colonies, however, fertility tended to increase along with holding size. Since there was a similar relationship between holding size and the proportion of slaves living in the family types associated with high fertility, it may be argued that fertility was significantly affected by the availability of potential mates within plantation communities. This factor was particularly important because of the immobility, in terms of residence, imposed by the slave system. This immobility was mitigated to some extent where the slave population was very dense and where night work was relatively light. Thus, the Barbadian slave population showed high fertility in spite of high rates of cross-plantation mating. The relatively high fertility of slaves of color was a result of the psychosocial forces that controlled miscegenation and stemmed directly from the slave system. In general, fertility was less directly affected by material conditions of life than was mortality, but variations in fertility were very much a product of the slave system and the restraints it imposed on mobility and the development of relationships.

Differences in levels of fertility, mortality, and natural increase were not static, of course. They were influenced by changes in the material conditions of life of West Indian slaves after 1807, which in turn were responses to technological and demographic change and to the intervention of imperial government and humanitarianism. Further, Philip Curtin has argued that the demographic history of sugar colonies can be explained by a dynamic model of economic development.[115] In the early stages of plantation development, according to this model, the ratio of slave imports to population would be high; negative rates of natural increase resulted from the abnormal age-sex structure associated with this pattern. As the colony approached full production and further expansion of settlement became impossible, slave imports and population leveled off, the proportion of creoles increased, and the sex ratio became better balanced. Finally, the deficit between births and deaths diminished and disappeared. This, argues Curtin, was the position in Barbados by 1810 and in Jamaica by the 1840s.

Curtin's model has merits as a heuristic device, and it can accommodate the broad trends of economic-demographic development within the British Caribbean. But it fails to explain the significant differences in natural increase observed within colonies, most importantly the contrast between sugar and other crop-types, and between town and country. These differences existed without regard to stages of settlement. As Curtin recognizes, the contrast between the British Caribbean and mainland North America cannot be explained in these terms and must be traced to differing "physical and social environments." But similar qualifications must be made even within the British Caribbean. These result from the variable dominance of sugar in the "sugar colonies" and from independent variations in patterns of material conditions of life.

A further problem lies in defining what Curtin calls "full production." The first of the British sugar colonies, Barbados, reached a peak in production as early as the 1660s and from about 1730 entered a period of secular decline, from which it recovered only after 1810. Thus, the period of natural increase in the slave population of Barbados coincided with increasing productivity rather than with a situation of labor saturation. The appearance of natural increase in the Leeward Islands also seems decidedly tardy. It should not be taken for granted that the creole section of the slave population would grow naturally. In extreme conditions, even after 1807, it is clear that creoles suffered mortality levels at least as high as those suffered by Africans. This was the case in Berbice, for example. There is no doubt, however, that in all colonies creoles were more fertile than Africans, and this does support the general tendency of Curtin's model.

Although the secular trend was toward positive natural increase in the West Indian slave population, there was nothing inexorable about it. The rate of progress toward natural increase was regulated above all by the material conditions of life of the slaves and the types of enterprises in which they were employed. In the marginal colonies, where the sugar plantation never dominated, natural increase emerged early. Urban environments and nonplantation agriculture also permitted much earlier movement toward natural increase than did the sugar plantation with its extreme demands on labor and endurance. Thus, there was genuine diversity in the demographic experience of the British Caribbean slave population that was both independent of stages of development and rooted in differences in the material conditions of life associated with particular modes of the slave system.

10.
Refuge and Resistance

THE VAST MAJORITY OF WEST INDIAN SLAVES REMAINED SLAVES until death. A small proportion, however, escaped from slavery by manumission or marronage, and others were transported from the colonies as convicts. These losses to the slave populations were generally minor, relative to mortality, but they were of some significance in the marginal colonies, and everywhere they had a selective impact on demographic structure.

Only in Anguilla, in the registration period 1827–31, did the number of manumitted and maroon slaves exceed the number of registered slave deaths. During that period, 166 slaves were listed as having died, while 108 were manumitted and 83 ran away.[1] Some qualifications are necessary, however, since it is probable that a greater proportion of infant deaths went unregistered than of manumissions or maroons, and some of the latter may have been recaptured. Even in the case of Anguilla, the period 1827–31 may have been unique. During the subsistence crisis that followed, 203 slaves died between 1831 and 1834, but there were only 32 manumissions and 70 maroons. The only other colonies in which manumission and marronage approached the level of significance found in Anguilla 1827–31 were the Bahamas and, perhaps, the Cayman Islands, where mortality was low. In the sugar colonies, the mortality rates were overwhelming. Between 1829 and 1832 in Jamaica, for example, 26,700 slaves died, while only 1,362 were manumitted, and 446 ran away.[2]

MANUMISSION

Before discussing the pattern of manumission and its demographic selectivity, it is necessary to look briefly at the inadequacies of the available data. The numbers given in table S10.1 are those derived from slave registration records wherever such data are available, but these are in some cases significantly less than those found in published returns derived from other sources. Data provided for the period between 1807 and the commencement of registration are taken from the reports of colonial governments, which acknowledged these figures to be understated because of the frequent avoidance of manumission fees imposed in some colonies.[3] Fitting the two types of data together results in some obvious disjunction. Reasons for the underregistration of manumissions have been discussed in chapter 2, but no satisfactory method of adjustment seems to be available. Jerome Handler has usefully outlined the difficulties of the various sources of data for Barbados.[4] In general, it is important to emphasize that all the available data must be regarded as minimum estimates. Only gross comparisons between colonies and over time can be attempted, therefore, the most emphasis will be placed on internal, structural comparisons.

The frequency of manumission varied quite widely between the colonies, but there were no clear distinctions in terms of phase of settlement. The marginal colonies probably had the highest rates overall, followed by the old sugar colonies, the new sugar colonies, and Jamaica (table 10.1). This ordering may be confused by variability in the data, however, and it conceals a good deal of overlap. Although the Bahamas clearly had the highest manumission rate in the long term, some high rates also appeared in the new sugar colonies of Trinidad, St. Lucia, and Dominica. The Virgin Islands had the highest rates among the old sugar colonies. Demerara-Essequibo, Berbice, St. Vincent, and Jamaica had the lowest rates of all the colonies. This pattern suggests that variations in manumission rates can be explained only in part by differences in economic and political structure.

Manumission rates generally increased between 1807 and 1834, though the inconsistencies in the data prevent a precise charting of this tendency. Only Montserrat shows clear evidence of long-term decline in the rate, though several colonies probably experienced some decline in the period to about 1820 (tables 10.1 and S10.1). This initial decline may have represented a reaction to the abolition of the Atlantic slave trade and the expected shortage of labor, but it was of limited significance and duration. The principal reasons for the general increase in the manumission rates were the reduction or removal of fees, the growth of the creole and female components of the slave populations, the growth of the freedman populations, and the spread of the working-out system. In the crown colonies, the orders in council requiring compulsory manumission had some effect after 1825.[5] In order to understand the significance of these factors, it is necessary first to consider the demographic incidence of manumission and the means by which it could be obtained.

A number of routes to manumission were available in the British West Indies, but most slaves obtained their freedom by deed, purchase, or will.[6] Manumission by deed could be granted directly by a slaveowner as a favor or "gift," in recognition of special services or relationships. It also included the practice of self-purchase in which slaves paid their owners an agreed sum in order to have deeds executed. Other masters provided in their wills for manumission. Slaves could also be purchased by whites or freedmen with the specific intention of granting manumission. Special legislation provided freedom in some colonies, either to individual slaves for particular services, such as informing on slave rebels and conspirators, or to groups in recognition of a de facto status of freedom. With the exception of manumission by special legislation, however, the ultimate power

Table 10.1. *Manumission Rates by Colony, 1808–34* (*Manumissions per 1,000 Slaves per annum*)

Colony	1808	1820	1834
Barbados	1.7	1.2	4.9
St. Kitts	0.2	2.4	5.1
Nevis	0.1	1.0	2.1
Antigua	2.5	1.7	2.9
Montserrat	4.2	1.5	2.4
Virgin Islands	2.6	3.2	4.9
Jamaica	n.c.	1.0	1.4
Dominica	1.8	2.2	6.1
St. Lucia	n.c.	1.6	9.0
St. Vincent	n.c.	1.0	1.4
Grenada	n.c.	2.1	2.9
Tobago	2.0	1.1	2.7
Trinidad	1.6	6.6	5.1
Demerara-Essequibo	0.1	0.2	2.3
Berbice	0.2	0.3	1.9
Bahamas	3.1	4.5	11.4
Anguilla	n.c.	n.c.	5.1
Barbuda	n.c.	—	1.1

Source: Table S10.1

to grant or withhold freedom lay in the hands of the slaveowner. Only in the late 1820s was compulsory manumission introduced, and then only in the crown colonies.

The general increase in manumission rates after 1807 was related to a shift from those methods originating with the owners to methods in which the slaves themselves or other free people took an active role. This tendency was most obvious in Jamaica, where the number of manumissions purchased exceeded the number granted gratuitously from about 1826, and the owners seem to have manumitted a decreasing number of slaves after 1807, except in the last few years of slavery.[7] Manumission by purchase was more common than all other methods in Montserrat as early as 1808, but in Antigua gift remained more important than purchase at least as late as 1821. There is no doubt that bequest was of little significance, accounting for only 6 percent of manumissions in both Antigua 1808–21 and Barbados 1821–25.[8] The registration returns for Barbados, St. Lucia, Tobago, and Berbice suggest a similarly small role for manumission by will and the importance of purchase, but too large a proportion of the returns merely recorded that a slave had been "manumitted" to permit any precise assessment of frequency. In 1814 an investigation of claims to freedom presented to the Demerara-Essequibo Court of Policy showed that, *inter alia,* 164 were based on bills of sales, 89 on deeds of gift, 16 on wills, and 10 on "free passes." Some of these petitions were refused, but in 1815 the court promised manumission to all persons in the colony who had lived ten or more years in a "reputed state of freedom."[9]

Manumission was more common in the towns than on rural holdings. In Barbados, for example, 49 percent of the island's manumissions occurred in Bridgetown in the period 1817–20, when only 12 percent of the slave population lived in the town. Between 1832 and 1834, when Bridgetown's share of the slave population was reduced to 10 percent, some 32 percent of manumissions occurred there (table S10.2). In St. Kitts 1831–34 some 35 percent of manumissions affected slaves in Basseterre, although only 7 percent lived there (table S10.3). For Roseau, Dominica, in the period 1829–32, these percentages were 34 and 6, respectively (table S10.4). To give one more example, 22 percent of Jamaica's manumissions occurred in Kingston between 1829 and 1832, when only 4 percent of the slaves lived in that town.[10] In general, then, urban slaves were roughly five times more likely to be manumitted than were rural slaves.

The chances of manumission were also greatest for slaves belonging to small units, but this relationship was not simply a reflection of the urban concentration. In Barbados 1832–34, for example, when manumission ran at a relatively high rate, the proportion of slaves manumitted declined steadily as holding size increased in the plantation parishes, but in Bridgetown the proportion actually increased along with holding size (table S2.10). In the plantation parishes, slaves belonging to units of 1–10 slaves were twice as likely to be manumitted as other rural slaves. In Bridgetown the relatively few slaves in units of 51–100 were twice as likely to be manumitted as those in the smallest units. This contrast between the urban and rural patterns suggests that slaves belonging to relatively large units in towns were more likely to purchase their freedom, since it will be recalled that such units contained large proportions of male tradesmen and transport workers, whose chances of earning money were much better than those of the females commonly employed as domestics in the smallest urban holdings. Plantation slaves, however, had fewer opportunities to work out, and on a great proportion of the largest estates manumission was a rare occurrence.

In Barbados as a whole, 2.0 percent of slaves belonging to units of 1–10 slaves were manumitted between 1832 and 1834, but this proportion plunged to a mere 0.1 percent in plantations of 301–400 slaves. Although the provision ground system may have created superior opportunities for the accumulation of cash in other colonies, it seems unlikely that Barbados was unique in terms of this association between small slaveholdings and high manumission rates. The relationship was certainly apparent at the colony level. There was a strong negative correlation between mean slaveholding size and the manumission rate around 1820 ($r = -.73, p = .00$), and an even stronger correlation by 1832 ($r = -.80$, $p = .00$). By the last years of slavery, then, at the colony level belonging to a small slaveholding was even more important than urban location. But, although significant differences in scale were associated with particular rural enterprises, the type of crop produced was of little importance in determining manumission rates. In St. Lucia 1815–19, for example, the highest rates occurred on coffee plantations, followed by sugar and provisions, and the lowest on cocoa and cotton plantations.[11] The chances of manumission for rural slaves depended more on scale than on crop-type, while slaveholding size mattered much less for town slaves.

The concentration of manumission in small slaveholdings and towns was reflected in the demographic characteristics of the slaves manumitted. They tended to be female, creole, young, and colored, and to work as domestics. In the sugar colonies females were roughly twice as likely to be manumitted as males in the period before 1820, but this difference was narrowed significantly in many colonies as emancipation approached. In the last years of slavery in the Bahamas, males were actually manumitted at a higher rate than females. The sex ratio of manumitted slaves tended to be somewhat lower in the towns than on plantations, but it did not match the contrast between the total populations (tables S10.1–10.6). This means that an urban location was more important for the chances of males obtaining manumission that it was for females. Once again, this pattern points to the relative importance of self-purchase and working-out for urban males. Females, however, more often obtained manumission through sexual relationships with whites or freedmen, and such relationships were by no means confined to the towns.

Creoles obtained manumission more often than did African-born slaves, but this differential declined in importance after 1807 and can be explained partly in terms of sex, age, and color. African-born slaves were never the children of West Indian whites or freedpeople, were less likely than creoles to be the mistresses of whites or freedmen, and tended to be males. Even though they lived more often in towns, African females were less likely to be manumitted than were creoles. But, as for males generally, an urban location was more important for Africans than for creoles in increasing their chances of manumission (tables S10.2–10.6). Thus, an urban location was often vital to a male African's chances.

The role of color in determining manumission rates also showed a contrast between town and country which throws further light on the process. Although colored slaves were considerably more numerous in town than in the country, and although they tended to be manumitted more often than blacks, the proportion of colored slaves manumitted was greater in the rural slave populations. This pattern can be confirmed for Barbados, St. Kitts, Dominica, St. Lucia, and Jamaica, and no exceptions have yet been discovered (tables S10.2–10.7). In Bridgetown 1832–34 some 34 percent of slaves manumitted were colored, compared to 52 percent in rural Barbados.[12] In St. Lucia 1815–19 these proportions were 47 percent in the towns and 51 percent in the rural population. In Dominica 1829–32 they were 26 percent for Roseau and 38 percent in the rural population; and in St. Kitts 1831–34 the percentages were 45 in Basseterre and 46 in the rural population. But the contrast was most extreme in Jamaica 1829–32, when only 33 percent of the slaves manumitted in Kingston were colored, compared to 63 percent in the rural population.[13]

Most of these examples come from the last years of slavery, of course, and there is some evidence to suggest that in earlier years, when Africans made up a larger proportion of the total, color was of greater importance in the towns. In Bridge-town, for example, some 53 percent of the slaves manumitted between 1817 and 1820 were colored (table S10.7), 19 percent more than between 1832 and 1834. A similar shift from colored to black manumission in the towns can be identified in Jamaica. The existence of such a trend adds further support to the argument that purchase became more important than gift as a means of obtaining manumission during the 1820s and that this shift was related principally to the organization of slave labor in the towns.

In order to test this last argument it is necessary to consider the occupations and ages of the slaves who were manumitted, as well as the characteristics of their owners. Domestics and skilled tradespeople were much more likely to be manu-mitted than were field laborers. In part, this contrast reflected the urban con-centration of manumission, but it was apparent in plantation populations as well. In St. Lucia 1815–19, for example, only 11 percent of the slaves manumitted were field laborers, although they accounted for 44 percent of the slave population. On the other hand, 52 percent of those manumitted were domestics (17 percent of the population), and 15 percent were tradesmen (5 percent of the population). Sellers, hired slaves, and drivers also had above-average manumission rates, while no stockkeepers, watchmen, fishermen, or transport workers were manumitted during the period. Domestics, tradesmen, sellers, and hired slaves were three times more likely to be manumitted than any other occupational group.[14]

A similar pattern occurred in Barbados in the period 1817–20.[15] In rural St. Michael 23 slaves were manumitted, according to the registration returns, fourteen of them domestics, three tradesmen, two seamstresses, and four with no occu-pation. The eight blacks manumitted were all domestics. Not one field laborer was freed. In Bridgetown, however, domestics were relatively underrepresented. Only 37 percent of the 123 slaves registered as manumitted were domestics, although they made up 50 percent of the town's population in 1817. Skilled tradespeople accounted for 26 percent of the manumissions, but were only 12 percent of the population. Slaves with no occupation made up 34 percent of those manumitted, compared to 28 percent of the population. The only other slaves manumitted in Bridgetown were a stockkeeper, a transport worker, and a laborer. Thus, the opportunities available to tradesmen in the towns to accumulate wealth were at least as important as the presence of large domestic forces in creating the major contrast between town and country. This pattern also helps to explain the relatively high sex ratio of slaves manumitted in the towns and the relatively small proportion who were colored.

Age at manumission differed quite widely, reflecting the variety of modes of obtaining freedom. In general, the median age of slaves at manumission was similar to that in the population at large, though manumission tended to be particularly frequent at about 25 years of age (tables S10.5–10.6). These patterns were apparent in both town and country and affected males as well as females. Colored females were the only group to show a relatively youthful tendency, and this suggests strongly that they were most often the recipients of gratuitous manumission paid for by white fathers. The significant proportion of slaves with no occupation manumitted in Bridgetown 1817–20, noted above, was composed almost entirely of children under 10 years of age, and almost half of them were colored females. But young black children were also manumitted, most probably by freedman relatives. Slaves who purchased their own freedom, however, needed time to accumulate cash to pay for it, and domestics and mistresses had to build up many years of "faithful service" before benefactors went so far as to manumit them. Indeed, many of the colonial governments were forced to legislate against the practice of "freeing" aged slaves, the worn-out servants who were turned off plantations when they became a burden on the planters' stores.[16] Slaves who obtained manumission through wills had to wait for their owners to expire, and sometimes were required to remain the slaves of the owners' kin for set periods.[17] Thus, some of those manumitted spent very few years of their lives as slaves, while others were freed only in their last days.

The slave registration returns provided little systematic data on the owners of the slaves who were manumitted. If the number owned can be regarded as an accurate index of wealth, as it generally was in West Indian slave societies, it is at least clear that the frequency of manumission varied inversely with wealth. The manumitter was not always the slaveowner, of course, so factors beyond the capacity to be generous entered into the process of manumission. For present purposes the most useful registration returns are those for Barbados, since they identified a large number of freedman owners, as noted in chapter 5. These data demonstrate clearly that slaves belonging to freedmen were manumitted much more often than those owned by whites (table S10.7). In Bridgetown, where freedman slaveownership was concentrated, 2.6 percent of the slaves owned by freedmen were manumitted between 1817 and 1820, compared to only 1.0 percent of those belonging to whites. In rural St. Michael these percentages were 1.2 and 0.2, respectively. Thus, the slaves of freedmen were two to three times more likely to be manumitted than those of whites, both in town and in the country. The manumissions of some slaves belonging to freedmen may have been paid for by whites, but it is improbable that this was sufficiently common to account for such a wide difference, and in any event the owner's consent was required in most cases. Unless the period 1817–20 was unusual, it seems necessary to reject Handler's conclusion that in Barbados "freedmen manumitted at a rate that was roughly comparable to, or even somewhat below, that of whites, and . . . were not disproportionately inclined to manumit their slaves."[18] It is impossible to be certain how far the association between freedman ownership and manumission was peculiar to Barbados, but it is at least clear that the highest manumission rates occurred where freedmen were already relatively numerous, for example in Trinidad, St. Lucia, the Virgin Islands, and the Bahamas.

Beyond the gross contrast between freedmen and whites, the registration data also show that in Bridgetown slaves owned by free Negroes were manumitted more often than those owned by free mulattoes. In the period 1817–20 some 10.4 percent of the slaves owned by free Negro men were manumitted, followed by those belonging to free mulatto men (3.0 percent), free Negro women (2.7 percent), free mulatto women (1.6 percent), white women (1.5 percent), and white men (0.6 percent).[19] The fact that the slaves manumitted by free mulattoes and free Negroes most often belonged to the same color category suggests strongly that much of this manumission involved kin (table S10.7). The absence of any significant difference in manumission rates for slaves belonging to white and free mulatto women is of interest, since it has been shown that their patterns of slaveholding were very similar. To some extent, then, the variations in manumission rates may be explained by differences in wealth, but there seems little doubt that slaves belonging to freedmen least closely allied to whites had the best chances of being manumitted.

In general, then, the urban concentration of manumission is best explained as a product of the opportunities the towns provided for the accumulation of cash for the purchase of freedom, the relatively high proportion of slaves owned by freedmen, and, to a lesser extent, the large proportions of females and colored slaves found in the towns. But the towns always offered far greater chances of manumission than the plantations, regardless of the characteristics of individual slaves. Thus, although manumission was rarely common enough to affect the growth or decline of slave populations at the colony level, it did have an impact on the demographic structure of the towns, and to some extent the urban decline typical of the early nineteenth century reflected the differential incidence of manumission.

MARRONAGE

In the years before the abolition of the Atlantic slave trade, more slaves escaped from the slave system by becoming maroons ("runaways") than were released by manumission. This was due both to the low level of manumission and to the relative propensity of male Africans to become maroons. Many slaves left the plantations within days or weeks of their arrival from Africa, so the ending of the Atlantic trade and the growth of a creole population with links of kinship in the slave community were important factors in the relative decline of marronage as a source of loss to the slave populations.

Variations in the extent of marronage cannot be established with any real certainty. The reasons for this difficulty all relate, ultimately, to problems of definition. Some slaves left their owners for a few days at a time, most often going to visit relatives or friends, without any real intention of attempting to escape permanently. Others hoped to esatablish their freedom permanently, but unless they could escape completely from the colony they always faced the prospect of recapture. Marronage, unlike manumission, often had only a temporary effect on the slave labor force, and the owners necessarily applied arbitrary and variable rules in registering runaway slaves as losses to their populations. For example, many owners in St. Vincent added separate lists of runaways to their slave registration returns in 1817, generally including only those slaves who had been gone for five years or more, but excluding such slaves from their totals. Slaves who had been maroons for shorter periods were regarded by the owners as still their legitimate property, and very often they were simply listed with their original occupations rather than as "runaways." Generally, slaves were registered as lost to the population only when the masters despaired of recapturing them. Thus, there is no doubt that the registration returns understate the numbers of slaves who were maroons at any particular date, and the demographic characteristics of those registered must be taken to apply only to successful, long-term maroons.

Geographical factors were very important in determining the chances slaves had of becoming successful maroons. Conditions were best where slaves could conceal themselves in virgin forests or could escape by sea to islands colonized by other European nations. Thus, the possibilities were greatest in the new sugar colonies, Jamaica, and some of the marginal colonies, where population density was low and plantations were bordered by rugged or thickly forested land. Towns became increasingly important magnets for maroons, however, especially as the creole and freedman populations grew and slaves could more readily hope to pass themselves off as free people. The existence of these differences between colonies and between town and country is supported by a good deal of documentary evidence, but they cannot be systematically quantified from the registration returns or, apparently, any other source.

The largest proportion of maroon slaves identified in the initial registration was found in Trinidad (table 6.1). In 1813 some 0.78 percent of the colony's rural slaves were listed under the category "deserter," as were 0.73 percent of urban slaves (table S7.4). In St. Lucia in 1815 some 0.55 percent of rural slaves were placed in the category "marron," as were 0.20 percent in the towns (table S7.3). All of these slaves were still regarded as the owners' property, however, and no doubt they had been absent for very variable periods of time. The returns for Berbice in 1819 are somewhat more helpful. Only 0.29 percent of the slaves were listed in the classification "runaway," but about two-thirds of them were said to have run away before 1810, and only one-third between 1810 and 1819 (table S7.5).

The differences between Trinidad, St. Lucia, and Berbice may be partly explained by differences in chronology, since marronage seems generally to have declined after 1807. But there is no doubt that these new sugar colonies with large proportions of African-born slaves and extensive forested refuges had much higher rates of marronage than Barbados and, probably, the other old sugar colonies. In Barbados only 0.06 percent of rural slaves were "absent" in 1817, compared to 0.22 percent of those in Bridgetown (table S7.2). Some of those "absent" slaves were domestics traveling with their owners, so the proportion of maroons was even smaller. But the contrast between the new and old sugar colonies in the rural-urban ratio is of interest, suggesting that the towns constituted the major refuges or provided the best locations for escape by sea wherever the population was densely settled and heavily creolized. The large population of Port of Spain may have made it exceptional among the towns of the new sugar colonies, serving as a focus for internal marronage as well as for escape to the Spanish Main. There was no evidence of a decline in marronage in Trinidad after 1820.[20] A similar pattern of urban concentration emerged in Jamaica by 1834, when the proportion of maroons in Kingston was double that elsewhere in the island, some 0.35 percent of the total population being placed in the category "runaway."[21]

The rate of marronage in the marginal colonies is less certain. In Anguilla, only one slave was listed as "runaway" in 1827, but between 1827 and 1831 some 83 slaves (3.3 percent of the population) ran away.[22] On the other hand, only two slaves were described as having become maroons and registered as lost to the slave population in St. Lucia between 1815 and 1819, and in Berbice only four between 1819 and 1821. But 516 slaves (2.1 percent of the population) were punished for "absconding" in Trinidad during the year 1827/8.[23] The contrast between Anguilla and the new sugar colonies may be explained in part by the reluctance of sugar planters to surrender claims to their relatively valuable absent slaves. Alternatively, it may mean that slaves escaping from Anguilla had better chances of making their freedom permanent, since most left the island entirely and placed themselves beyond the powers of the colonial government. A few maroons were detained by the Dutch government of St. Martin and were returned to Anguilla, but most seem to have filtered into the fluid freedman populations of neighboring French, Dutch, and Danish colonies.[24] In general, it seems that creole slaves who could escape by boat and enter urban situations, where recognition was relatively unlikely and work readily obtainable, had greater chances of success in remaining free, within the restraints imposed by slave society, than those who attempted to live on the fringes of plantation society. This pattern contrasted with that prevailing in the seventeenth and eighteenth centuries, when few slaves could hope to pass unnoticed because the freedman populations were so small and because most of them were Africans, physically very visible and unlearned in the ways of creole society.

Africans continued to predominate among the maroons of the new sugar colonies until about 1820. In Berbice, for example, the registration returns of 1819 listed three African maroons for every creole, though Africans and creoles were by then equally numerous. In part, this contrast may be explained by differences in age structure, most maroons being adults, but it also reflects the fact that a large proportion of them had been absent for a decade, their escape occurring in days when Africans were even more numerous. In St. Lucia, however, Africans accounted for 21.6 percent of the maroons in 1815, when they made up 21.4 percent of the slave population. Thus, even in the new sugar colonies creoles became increasingly common among the maroons. By 1832, when Africans made up 23.5 percent of the slave population of Jamaica, they accounted for only 25.3 percent of the maroons.[25] In the old sugar colonies, the urban concentration of both Africans and maroons meant that Africans continued to be a relatively visible group. In 1817, for example, Africans made up only 15.7 percent of the slave population of Bridgetown but were 20.8 percent of the "absent"; in rural St. Michael, however, all of the long-term maroons registered were creoles. Similarly, in the marginal colony of Anguilla only 1.2 percent of the runaways registered in 1827–31 were Africans, when they made up 2.6 percent of the slave population. In all of the colonies, then, the general decline in marronage rates after 1807 may be seen as a direct product of the decrease in the proportion of African-born slaves, particularly "new Negroes" fresh from the Middle Passage, in the West Indian populations. The growing proportion of creoles among those who attempted to become permanent maroons after 1807, however, reflected the increasing urban orientation of marronage.

Males became maroons more often than did females. But this contrast became less obvious as the number of Africans declined, and largely disappeared in the marginal colonies. In Berbice 91 percent of the slaves registered as maroons in 1819 were males, contrasted with only 51 percent in Anguilla in 1827–31. Even in the new sugar colonies, females tended to be quite numerous among the urban maroons. In Kingstown all ten of the slaves "at large" in 1817 were females; but such an extreme contrast was not apparent in Port of Spain in 1813 (tables S7.7 and S7.18). In Bridgetown, female maroons were twice as common as males in 1817 (table S7.15), but on the plantations males continued to be predominant. Female slaves living in towns were more likely to work in occupations that had a potential for filtering into freedman society, and less likely to be restrained by family ties than plantation slaves. Hucksters employed under the working-out system had a head start.[26]

Slaves of all ages became permanent maroons, infants sometimes being carried by their parents. But young adults predominated, the mean age for creoles being about 30 years (tables S7.14–7.20). The registration returns tend to overstate the ages, however, since there was often a gap of several years between the slaves' desertion and the owners' registering the fact. Age also reflected earlier conditions. In Trinidad in 1813, for example, more than 20 percent of males aged 60 years were listed as deserters, in both town and country, a larger proportion than in any other age group. But the majority of slaves initiated their attempts to become permanent maroons during their twenties. Slaves of color were less well represented among maroons than were blacks, both in town and in country (tables S7.14–7.17). Variations in age structure accounted for some of this difference, but it is apparent that mulatto and mustee slaves were much less likely to desert than sambo or cabre slaves.[27] Maroons came from a very wide range of occupational groups, however, so it cannot be argued that privileged slaves in general were the least likely to desert. The increasing urban orientation of marronage worked against such a tendency.

Slaves attempting to become permanent maroons had a variety of choices. As noted above, chances of success were probably greatest where slaves could remove themselves beyond the jurisdiction of their owners, escaping by boat to other territories. Slaves who did not physically leave the colony could establish remote settlements, or attempt to blend into the freedman populations of the towns, or skip from place to place trying to keep ahead of owners and informers. The latter route was probably the least likely to succeed in the long run but was necessarily employed by rural slaves in the densely populated old sugar colonies. For instance, Appea, a slave of Mount William Plantation in Barbados, aged 50 years, had been gone twelve months when his master advertised for his return in 1815, stating that "he is perhaps one of the most notorious villains the country ever possessed; and a dangerous person to be at large amongst plantation negroes. He is famous for drawing the figure of negroes on paper, by which means he gets a subsistence, going from one estate to another; although he seldom stays long on any."[28] Another Barbadian slave, John, aged 28 years, "famous for playing the pump and singing at Negro dances and funerals," attempted to use his special skills in the same way when he deserted in 1808.[29]

More often, maroon slaves in the densely populated colonies attempted to establish their freedom by hiding out with relatives and friends. In 1809 a Congo woman able to speak both good English and French, formerly a slave in Dominica, was "supposed to be harboured by some of the Leeward Island people about Bridge-Town."[30] Creoles inevitably had much wider kinship networks than Africans, especially in the long-settled colonies, and after 1807 an increasing proportion of them had freedman relatives. Such links probably provided the greatest chances of success. Jacob, the son of a free mulatto, worked as a hairdresser in Bridgetown before being sold to Bromefield Plantation, where he was employed as a cooper; when he "absconded" in 1813 it was presumed he would head for Bridgetown and his many relations there.[31] When John Charles of Grand Bras Estate, Grenada, deserted in 1815 he was believed harbored by free blacks, since he used to "keep" a free black woman on the estate.[32] Other slaveowners showed a more precise awareness of the "numerous relations" of their slaves and their likely hiding places. For example, T. G. Armstrong of Speight's Town, Barbados, advertised in 1812 that his slave Kitty Pender, aged 13 years, had been gone for nine months. Her mother, Sally Walker, belonged to Edward Jemott, and her father, Sam Headley, was a slave on Rock Hall Plantation, but she had numerous other relations, stated Armstrong, including a brother in St. Thomas, two other brothers, an uncle, William Walker, who was a free mulatto living on a tenement at Cleland's Plantation, where he had a wife named Jenny Duck, and another uncle at Walker's Plantation in St. Andrew.[33] Cases of this sort were common in Barbados, where cross-plantation mating was frequent and the density of kin great.

In Jamaica and the new sugar colonies maroons were able to secrete themselves in independent settlements, with hopes of remaining undisturbed by the slaveowners. The maroons of Jamaica established their rights to an independent existence during the eighteenth century, but no new settlements were added after 1807.[34] The colonies in which attempts to form new settlements were most common in the early nineteenth century were Demerara-Essequibo, Berbice, and the Windward Islands.[35] Whereas maroons in Jamaica and the Windward Islands often had to raid the provision grounds of plantations to obtain food, those in the mainland colonies were able to achieve a greater self-sufficiency when they ventured into the vast forests that extended inland from the settled coastal fringe. The number of maroons living in these settlements is uncertain, but their subsistence base was considerable. In 1810 a bush expedition in the declining plantation region of Mahaicony in Demerara destroyed rice crops sufficient to feed 700 people for a year, as well as large amounts of yams, tanias, plantains, and tobacco.[36] Within a year the crops were established again, and planters complained of "the encreasing boldness" of maroons with encampments aback in enticing away slaves from the coast.[37] The continued growth of the camps and the arming of the maroons led to the call for all black and colored persons claiming freedom in Demerara-Essequibo to show proof of their status in 1814.[38] In 1818 "formidable" maroon settlements containing 22 cultivated fields at the heads of creeks west of the Demerara River were destroyed. These settlements were well known to slaves on the coast and served as a refuge for those deserting the plantations.[39] These settlements, as well as those in Mahaicony and on the islands in the Essequibo, continued to attract maroons until the rebellion of 1823.[40] After the rebellion the flow of slaves from the plantations seems to have become less substantial, and the maroon settlements ceased to pose a threat to the slave system.

Efforts by slaveowners to recapture maroons varied with the pattern of desertion. In Barbados, most seem to have depended on the maroons being captured and placed in the town cage, since owners provided detailed identifying information in newspaper advertisements only after slaves had been absent for several months. In some cases a pardon was offered if slaves returned of their own accord. Some owners threatened to punish slaves if they did not cause their runaway relatives to return to the plantations.[41] Occasionally, owners attempted to use the slaves' kinship networks to transmit messages to maroons. Late in 1815 the driver of Mount Wilton Plantation, Primus, was given a ticket of absence for ten days to search for a runaway slave, Prince. But Primus took advantage of this opportunity and three months later had not himself returned, "though invited to do so through his connections." His owner then employed the ranger of Pickering's Plantation, Frank, to seek out Primus where he had a wife, in St. Joseph; but Frank could not find Primus and, returning to Mount Wilton at midnight, was murdered by a group of men.[42] In general, slaveowners in Barbados and the other densely settled old sugar colonies depended on informal communication networks to ensure the identification and capture of maroons.

Where maroons could establish independent settlements, thus threatening the bases of slave society, slaveowners took a much more active role in their efforts to control slave desertion. In Demerara-Essequibo the government paid premiums for the apprehension or killing of "runaways" and "Bush Negroes," especially "in order to encourage the inhabitants to make Bush Expeditions with their own trusty Negroes."[43] But such efforts often failed, and it was complained that the use of trusty slaves, most of them highly valued tradesmen, was costly to the government when they were killed. After 1807 the Amerindians of Demerara-Essequibo were increasingly used by the slaveowners in such expeditions and were generally bribed to put pressure on maroon camps in the interior and prevent movement from the plantations.[44] These expeditions were designed to destroy the settlements of maroons, as well as to take prisoners. At first the recaptured slaves were usually transported from the colony or placed in chain gangs, but after 1823, when large numbers were jailed and the slave labor force dwindled rapidly, it was decided that those who had spent less than two years in the bush should be returned to their owners.[45]

In the Windward Islands slaveowners also took aggressive measures to prevent or contain the development of maroon settlements. In Grenada the colonial government employed a paramilitary group of Colony Rangers to apprehend maroons, and a similar system existed in Dominica.[46] By 1823, however, it was said that in Grenada there were no longer gangs of maroons in the woods and that there had been a great reduction in the tendency to desert since 1807. Some maroons were in fact taken by the Rangers in the island's woods, but most were apprehended on estates or estate provision grounds, or in the town of St. George.[47]

Slaveowners seem to have come to accept that individual slaves would always desert temporarily in order to visit kin or friends on other plantations or in the towns. What they really feared was marronage by entire gangs and the establishment of independent settlements. When the latter were permanent their locations became known to plantation slaves, who could use them as refuges. Very often a general trade between maroons and plantation slaves developed, the maroons exchanging ground provisions for salt provisions, clothes, arms, and ammunition.[48] In St. Vincent, where whites delighted in calling their rural picnics "marooning parties,"[49] the Chief Justice reminded slaveowners in 1827 that it was a transportable offense for a slave to be a runaway for more than six months and emphasized the seriousness of long-term marronage "in a country like this covered with woods and abounding in fastnesses." Maroons, he said, "remaining so long in a fugitive state must necessarily imbibe wild and ferocious habits, and consequently endanger the peace of society [and] constantly prey upon the provisions and stock of the plantation and of more domestic and orderly slaves."[50] The next day, the Chief Justice sentenced three maroons to transportation "beyond the seas" for the term of their natural lives.

Transportation was the most common punishment applied to long-term maroons, but the numbers lost to the slave populations in this way were always small. In Jamaica, less than 90 slaves were transported for marronage in the period 1829–32, whereas at least 450 slaves were regarded as lost to their masters as a result of successful marronage.[51] Elsewhere, in the new sugar colonies, the proportion transported was probably even smaller. Most of those transported went to Cuba or Bermuda, or to Pioneer Corps in other British Colonies. But an increasing number went to the hulks in England, and a few were sent to New South Wales.[52] An even smaller number of slaves were transported for theft, murder, or rebellion.

In general, slaveowners became increasingly reluctant to surrender any of their diminishing numbers of slave laborers, particularly after 1820 when marronage seemed less threatening. Many planters failed to report slave deserters, hoping no doubt that they would regain them without resort to public measures and the risk of losing their labor. Some enticed slaves back with promises of pardons. Others only sought court-ordered lashings for ''incorrigibles'' and had iron collars put around their necks to prevent future escape.[53] But the increasing severity of punishment applied to slaves firmly determined to escape did little to deter their efforts. The case of Sam, slave on the Jamaican pimento plantation of James Archer, M.D., is illustrative. In November 1828 Sam left the plantation for six days and was pardoned. In January 1829 he was gone for eight days and was pardoned on the intercession of Mrs. Archer. In February he was ''brought home by his mother'' after five days. In April he deserted for seven days and got 39 lashes from the driver. Sam then left the plantation from 20 May to 12 July, when he was again flogged and spent 22 days in the hospital. By August 1829 he had escaped his shackles and became a successful, permanent maroon.[54]

REBELLION

In the seventeenth and eighteenth centuries slave rebellions were frequently associated with marronage, as overlapping acts in defiance of the slave system. After 1807 marronage became increasingly individualistic, and rebellion took on creolized forms. No slave rebellion in the British Caribbean was successful, in the sense that the St. Domingue revolution was successful, but the 1831/2 rebellion in Jamaica played a crucial role in hastening emancipation, while less extensive rebellions in other colonies shook the structure of slave society.

The subject of slave rebellion in the British Caribbean is a large and important one and has been treated in detail in a recent study by Michael Craton.[55] Here it is possible only to review briefly some demographic implications.

Major slave rebellions occurred in Barbados in 1816, Demerara in 1823, and Jamaica in 1831/2. This wide geographical spread makes it clear that differences in stage of settlement or demographic structure were not of overwhelming importance in the origination of rebellion, though a large population was a necessary base and no major activity occurred in the marginal colonies. Confrontations on a smaller scale were widely scattered and remain to be catalogued and analyzed. Whether major or minor in scale, virtually all of the rebellions were confined to rural areas, generally at a distance from towns and in areas where the ratio of slaves to whites was high. Large, relatively isolated plantations provided the strongest bases for political organization within the slave community.

The Barbados rebellion of 1816 was confined to the parishes of St. Philip, St. John, Christ Church, and St. George. These parishes contained a slave population of 30,000, but the number actively involved is uncertain. About 100 slaves were killed in fighting with the militia and army, and 400 were put on board ships in the bay to await trial. Of these, 144 were executed and 170 transported. At least 123 of the latter were sent to British Honduras to work as mahogany cutters. Many of the rebel leaders were described as the most ''effective'' men on the plantations, those employed as drivers, rangers, and tradesmen. It is uncertain how many were slaves of color, but the free colored were said to be involved, and it is clear that creoles rather than Africans took a leading role.[56]

The Demerara rebellion of 1823 spread through the windward coast parishes of St. Paul and St. Mary, affecting about 20,000 slaves. Maroon camps existed near Mahaica, at the eastern end of this region, and some rebels made tactical retreats into the interior. Although slaves living in Georgetown were said to be well informed, they did not become involved. The number of slave deaths resulting from the rebellion are uncertain, but Craton states that "over a hundred" were killed and "dozens" executed. As in Barbados, the leaders were principally drivers and tradesmen. Africans were prominent, as might be expected from the slave population's age structure, but creoles also took leadership roles.[57]

The Jamaican slave rebellion of 1831/2 began in isolated plantation areas fringing maroon settlements and spread to cover a large part of the western end of the island. It had a broader geographical spread than the rebellions in Barbados or Demerara, affecting larger parish populations. At least 200 slaves were killed during the rebellion, 312 executed, and 35 transported. As in Barbados and Demerara, drivers and tradesmen played leading roles. African-born slaves were underrepresented among the rebels, but slaves of color played an important part.[58]

In general, the slaves who led these major rebellions tended to be adult male creoles with privileged positions within the plantation hierarchy. Thus, the demographic impact of the rebellions was confined primarily to the killing and execution of slaves in these groups. Such deaths were few relative to total mortality, and relatively insignificant when compared with losses to the slave population resulting from manumission or marronage, in the long term. But they did have important local and short-term effects on the sex and age structure of the slave populations.

The major slave rebellions of the period after 1807 were on a larger scale than those of earlier periods when the establishment of independent maroon settlements was a common goal. Thus, although the process of creolization may have operated to reduce marronage, this decline was not evidence of any easy accommodation to the slave system. Each of the rebellions had the overturning of slave society as its primary aim, not merely isolation for small bands of maroons. Whereas marronage and manumission were individualistic means of escape from slavery and required a degree of accommodation, the creolization of slave society after 1807 created rebellions that were by any reckoning more successful acts of resistance than those of earlier periods. They were responses to changing external conditions, created by the St. Domingue revolution and the transformation of metropolitan society, but they also depended for their impact on changes internal to the slave community and its demographic structure.

11.
Slavery and Population History

SLAVERY WAS DISTINGUISHED FROM OTHER FORMS OF COMPUL-
sory labor by the nakedness of the exploitation it entailed, by the slave's total lack
of rights and power. The material conditions of life of slaves, however, were not
always inferior to those of people toiling under other systems of labor, compulsory
or free.[1] Thus, it is difficult to distinguish the features of slave population
dynamics which were specific to the fact of slave status from those which reflected
independent variations in material conditions of life. It is equally difficult to locate
slave populations within the broad context of world population history.

The analysis of the West Indian slave populations presented in this book has
been essentially materialist in its approach. It is argued that the observed patterns
of similarity and differences in demographic experience are better explained in
terms of material conditions of life than by the ideas, beliefs, values, and
perceptions central to idealist paradigms. Ideology was not unimportant, of
course, but it did not operate independently and must be viewed within the context
of the causal primacy of material conditions of life.[2] In terms of the history of slave
societies, the study of ideology has largely been confined to the ideologies of
slaveowners (their religions, national characters, laws, and state systems), little
attention being given to the ideologies of slaves. This focus is consonant with the
view that the character of slave life was simply a function of the treatment meted
out by slaveowners rather than a product of the intimate interaction of master and
slave. No doubt much remains to be learned about the nature of slave ideologies
and their significance for demographic patterns, but it may be advanced that they
were no less rooted in material conditions than were the ideologies of the masters.

To argue that the wide variations in slave population patterns found within the
British Caribbean may be traced to material conditions of life recognizes the
humanity of the slave and sees slaves as people contending with a common
physical world. But the construction of that physical world was determined by the
fact that they lived in slave societies. The environments in which they existed were
a product of their slave status, for if they had not been made slaves they would have
lived in Africa rather than the Caribbean; and, with some notable exceptions, their
occupations and daily regimes were fashioned by the decisions of their owners.

Slaves had no significant role in deciding whether they were to be employed in towns or on sugar estates or on cocoa plantations, for example, but the characteristic material conditions of life associated with each of these types of situation had a profound impact on their demographic experience. Rarely were slaves able to choose their occupations, hours of work, clothing, type of housing, or means of obtaining food supplies. Once allocated to a particular occupation or issued a particular piece of cloth, however, slaves could and did inject their own ideas and attitudes into the way in which they worked and used their materials. The potential for independent action varied considerably, of course, with the working-out and board-wages systems providing the greatest range of possibilities in the towns, and the provision-ground and task-work systems in the countryside. Thus, the slaves' manipulation of their material conditions of life had a significance for their patterns of fertility and mortality which remains ambiguous and inadequately understood. But the parameters were always set by the masters.

Within the British Caribbean, and throughout the New World generally, slavery took a variety of characteristic forms, dependent on the types of economic activity in which the slaves were employed. It has been shown here that the material conditions of life of slaves living on sugar estates were similar, regardless of the planter's sex, color, nationality, or temperament. Differences in regimes did occur in terms of work organization and the supply of food, but the contrast between sugar and other types of plantations was stronger than that between the sugar estates of different colonies at different stages of development. The characteristic regimes of sugar estates were matched by a typically high mortality and a failure to show a natural increase. These patterns were repeated throughout the Americas, though the outlier behavior of Barbados remains a puzzle.[3] The material conditions of life associated with cotton, coffee, cocoa, pimento, and provisions plantations, as well as wood cutting and salt raking, each took on a characteristic form associated with typical patterns of demographic structure and natural increase. The contrast between rural and urban regimes was equally striking, and once again was echoed in other slave societies of the Americas. Urban slaves experienced lower death rates than rural slaves as a whole, and in this pattern the West Indies contrasted strongly with the contemporary experience of North American and European populations, not because Caribbean towns were particularly healthy, but because the typical sugar plantation slave suffered such extreme mortality. This rural-urban contrast was reversed in the West Indies after emancipation, but the characteristic patterns of mortality and fertility associated with the different types of rural enterprise largely persisted beyond 1838, affecting free and indentured laborers as well as slaves.[4] Ultimately, then, demographic variations within Caribbean slave societies must be traced to the technical relations of production.

West Indian slaves were not subject to genocide nor were they killed for sport. In this they were more fortunate than the indigenous inhabitants of the Caribbean and the slaves of ancient Rome, for example. But the everyday demands on human endurance associated with intensive sugar cultivation were extreme and created nonviable slave populations in most places.[5] The British West Indian colonies were distinguished, however, by the overwhelming dominance of sugar in their economies and by the concentration of the slave population on large-scale estates, so maximizing the physical demands of the system. Even at the peak of the slave system in St. Domingue and Cuba the dominance of sugar was never as great as in the British Caribbean, and the role of the large slaveholding was far greater in the British colonies than in the classical slave societies of Brazil and the United States.[6] Within the British Caribbean the dominance of the large sugar estate reached its climax during the period 1807–34, and its demographic impact was mitigated only by the external pressures of amelioration and the abolition of the Atlantic slave trade. Had the horrific conditions associated with the earlier "golden" and "silver" ages of sugar been continued after 1807, the prospect of extinction would have been even more real and imminent.

The dominance of sugar in the British West Indies means that the demographic experience of the slaves must be located toward the harsh extreme of the scale of modern world population history. Certainly some West Indian slave populations grew as rapidly as the free and slave populations of North America, as rapidly as the population of industrializing Britain and, probably, more rapidly than the free populations of Africa. For the overwhelming majority, however, labor in the fields and satanic mills of sugar estates, together with malnutrition and unsanitary living conditions and the disorganization of family life, meant a failure even to maintain their numbers. Few free populations in the New World or the Old were subject to such a persistent combination of conditions unfavorable to population growth in the early nineteenth century.

The population history of slave societies must not be conceived only in terms of their ability to survive and grow, of course. The fact that mere survival remained a central issue for so long highlights the extremity of the West Indian slaves' position, but for the survivors the demographic characteristics of slavery had a fundamental impact on every area of their lives. They had profound implications for social behavior and for the development of slave culture. In some respects these implications applied uniformly to all of the slave populations and were independent of differences in material conditions of life, but variations in mortality and fertility added a further dimension. Differential mortality, for example, affected sex and age structure and hence increased the potential role of venerable female Africans in the development of creole society. Variations in age at death affected the structure of slave family organization, the survival of spouses, the rate of orphanhood, the role of parents in selecting mates for their children, and the place of grandparents in the household. High infant mortality affected the emotional content of parent-child relations. It resulted in a certain indifference to the neonate, the first nine days of life being treated with ritualized neglect. Young children were denied funerals, and their burial was generally casual.[7] Children, however, were accustomed to the presence of death, with the majority of their siblings likely to die before reaching puberty. Differences in mortality related to occupation led to pressure to move slaves from the towns and the great houses and shops of plantations into field labor, and to move them from the marginal colonies to the new sugar regions, uprooting creoles and threatening the hierarchical superiority of the colored. In these and many other ways the contrasting material conditions of life of West Indian slaves meant not only differences in numbers, the mere ability to survive as a population, but shaped the entire fabric of slave society.

Statistical Supplement

LIST OF TABLES

SECTION 1.   Geographical Distribution

S1.1. Registered and Mean Slave Populations by Colony and Sex, 1813–34   *413*
S1.2. Estimated Annual Slave Populations by Colony, 1807–34   *417*
S1.3. Distribution of Slaves by Parish and Sex: Barbados, 1817, 1832 and 1834   *419*
S1.4. Distribution of Slaves by Parish and Sex: St. Kitts, 1812, 1816 and 1834   *419*
S1.5. Distribution of Slaves by Parish, Division and Sex: Antigua, 1832   *420*
S1.6. Distribution of Slaves by Island and Sex: Virgin Islands, 1815, 1823 and 1831   *420*
S1.7. Distribution of Slaves by Parish and Sex: Dominica, 1817, 1829, 1832 and 1834   *421*
S1.8. Distribution of Slaves by Quarter, Sex and Birthplace: St. Lucia, 1815   *421*
S1.9. Distribution of Plantation and Unattached Slaves by Parish and Sex: St. Vincent, 1817   *422*
S1.10. Distribution of Slaves by Parish: Grenada, 1817–1833   *423*
S1.11. Distribution of Plantation and Unattached Slaves by Parish and Sex: Tobago, 1819   *423*
S1.12. Distribution of Slaves by Quarter and Sex: Trinidad, 1808, 1813, 1824, and 1832   *424*
S1.13. Distribution of Slaves by Parish and Sex: Demerara-Essequibo, 1826 and 1832   *425*
S1.14. Distribution of Slaves by Parish and Sex: Berbice, 1819   *425*
S1.15. Distribution of Slaves by Island and Sex: Bahamas, 1822 and 1834   *426*
S1.16. Slave Population by Streets: Bridgetown, Barbados, 1832–34   *426*
S1.17. Distribution of Slaves, Whites and Freedmen by District: Georgetown, Demerara, 1812 and 1824   *428*
S1.18. Net Imports of Slaves by Colony, 1797–1807   *428*
S1.19. Slaves Imported into Trinidad, 1813–25   *429*
S1.20. Net Imports of Domestic Slaves, by Colony, 1830–34   *430*
S1.21. Slaves Exported from the Bahamas, 1821, and St. Michael, Barbados, 1817–20, by Age and Sex   *430*

SECTION 2.   Ownership

S2.1. White and Freedman Populations by Sex and Colony, c.1830   *433*
S2.2. Distribution of Slaveowners by Slave-holding Size-group and Parish: Barbados, 1817   *433*

S2.3. Distribution of Slaves by Slave-holding Size-group and Crop-type: Trinidad, 1813 *434*

S2.4. Distribution of Slaves by Slave-holding Size-group and Crop-type: St. Lucia, 1815 *434*

S2.5. Distribution of Urban and Rural Slaves by Slave-holding Size-group: Trinidad, St. Lucia and Barbados, 1813–17 *435*

S2.6. Distribution of Slaves by Sex of Owner and Slave-holding Size-group: Trinidad, St. Lucia and Berbice, 1813–19 *435*

S2.7. Distribution of Slaves and Owners by Slave-holding Size-group and Sex of Owner, Urban and Rural: St. Lucia, 1815 *436*

S2.8. Distribution of Owners and Slaves by Parish, Free Mulatto and Free Negro Slaveowners: Barbados, 1817 *436*

S2.9. Slaveowners by Sex, Color and Slave-holding Size-group: Barbados, 1817 *437*

S2.10. Demographic Characteristics by Slave-holding Size-group and Parish: Barbados, 1832–34 *439*

S2.11. Slave Sex Ratios by Slave-holding Size-group: Twelve Colonies, 1813–32 *441*

SECTION 3. Birthplace

S3.1. Birthplaces of Slaves: St. Kitts, 1817 *443*

S3.2. Birthplaces of Slaves: St. Lucia, 1815 *444*

S3.3. Birthplaces of Slaves: Trinidad, 1813 *448*

S3.4. Birthplaces of Slaves: Berbice, 1819 *454*

S3.5. Birthplaces of Slaves: Anguilla, 1827 *457*

S3.6. Percentage of Slaves African-born by Slave-holding Size-group: Ten Colonies, 1813 *458*

SECTION 4. Age

S4.1. Age Structure of Slaves by Sex, Birthplace and Colony, 1813–34 *462*

S4.2. Age Structure of Slaves by Sex, Birthplace and Parish: Barbados, 1817 *471*

S4.3. Age Structure of Slaves by Parish: Barbados 1834 *477*

S4.4. Age Structure of Slaves by Sex, Birthplace and Parish: Nevis, 1817 *477*

S4.5. Age Structure of Slaves by Sex and Parish: Montserrat, 1831 *480*

S4.6. Age Structure of Slaves by Sex and Parish: Dominica, 1829 *481*

S4.7. Age Structure of Slaves by Sex, Birthplace and Quarter: St. Lucia, 1815 *483*

S4.8. Age Structure of Slaves by Sex, Birthplace and Parish: St. Vincent, 1817 *490*

S4.9. Age Structure of Slaves by Sex, Birthplace and Parish: Grenada, 1817 *493*

S4.10. Age Structure of Slaves by Sex and Birthplace: Grenada 1829 and 1833 (St. Andrew and the Grenadines) *497*

S4.11. Age Structure of Slaves by Sex: Grenada 1829 (Town of St. George, St. John and St. Mark) *499*

S4.12. Age Structure of Slaves by Sex, Birthplace and Parish: Tobago, 1819 *500*

S4.13. Age Structure of Slaves by Sex and Birthplace, Rural and Urban: Trinidad, 1813 *504*

S4.14. Age by Sex, Birthplace, and Slave-holding Size-group: Barbados, 1817 *505*

S4.15. Age by Sex, Birthplace and Slave-holding Size-group: St. Kitts, 1817 *507*

S4.16. Age by Sex and Slave-holding Size-group: Montserrat, 1831 *509*

S4.17. Age by Sex, Birthplace and Slave-holding Size-group: Virgin Islands, 1818 *510*

S4.18. Age by Sex, Birthplace and Slave-holding Size-group: St. Lucia, 1815 *512*
S4.19. Age by Sex, Birthplace and Slave-holding Size-group: St. Vincent, 1817 *514*
S4.20. Age by Sex, Birthplace and Slave-holding Size-group: Tobago, 1819 *516*
S4.21. Age by Sex, Birthplace and Slave-holding Size-group: Berbice, 1819 *518*
S4.22. Age by Sex, Birthplace and Slave-holding Size-group: Anguilla, 1827 *520*
S4.23. Age by Sex, Birthplace and Slave-holding Size-group: Trinidad, 1813 *521*
S4.24. Mean Age of Slaves by Sex, Birthplace and Slave-holding Size-group: St. Lucia, 1815 and Berbice, 1819 *524*
S4.25. Age-specific Slave Sex Ratios by Colony, 1813–34 *524*

SECTION 5. Color

S5.1. Color of Slaves by Sex and Birthplace: St. Lucia, 1815 *527*
S5.2. Color of Slaves by Sex: St. Vincent, 1817 *528*
S5.3. Color of Slaves by Sex and Birthplace: Berbice, 1819 *529*
S5.4. Age Structure of Slaves of Color by Sex: Barbados, 1817 *530*
S5.5. Age Structure of Mulatto and Mestee Slaves by Sex: Tobago, 1819 *530*
S5.6. Age Structure of Creole Slaves of Color by Sex, Urban and Rural: Trinidad, 1813 *531*
S5.7. Age structure of Slaves by Color and Sex: Anguilla, 1827 *531*

SECTION 6. Stature

S6.1. Heights of Creole Slaves by Sex and Age: Trinidad, St. Lucia and Berbice, 1813–19 *534*
S6.2. Heights of Slaves Aged 25–40 Years by Sex and Birthplace: Trinidad, 1813 *536*
S6.3. Heights of Slaves Aged 25–40 Years by Sex and Birthplace: St. Lucia, 1815 *537*
S6.4. Heights of Slaves Aged 25–40 Years by Sex and Birthplace: Berbice, 1819 *538*
S6.5. Heights of Slaves Aged 25–40 Years by Sex, Birthplace and Color: St. Lucia, 1815 *539*
S6.6. Heights of Slaves Aged 25–40 Years by Sex, Birthplace and Color: Berbice, 1819 *539*
S6.7. Heights of Slaves Aged 25–40 Years by Sex, Birthplace and Occupation: St. Lucia, 1815 *540*
S6.8. Heights of Slaves Aged 25–40 Years by Sex, Birthplace and Occupation: Berbice, 1819 *541*
S6.9. Heights of Creole Slaves by Sex, Age and Color: St. Lucia, 1815 *542*
S6.10. Heights of Creole Slaves by Sex and Age, Urban and Rural: St. Lucia, 1815 *543*
S6.11. Heights of Creole Slaves by Sex, Age and Crop-type: St. Lucia, 1815 *544*
S6.12. Heights of Creole Slaves by Sex, Age and Occupation: St. Lucia, 1815 *545*

SECTION 7. Occupation

S7.1. Occupational Distribution of Slaves, as Classified for Compensation, 1834 *550*
S7.2. Occupations of Slaves: Barbados, 1817 *552*
S7.3. Occupations of Slaves, Urban and Rural: St. Lucia, 1815 *559*
S7.4. Occupations of Slaves, Urban and Rural: Trinidad, 1813 *565*

S7.5. Occupations of Slaves by Sex: Berbice, 1819 *571*

S7.6. Occupations of Slaves by Sex: Anguilla, 1827 *578*

S7.7. Occupations of Slaves by Sex and Slave-holding Size-group: Kingstown, St. Vincent, 1817 *580*

S7.8. Occupations of Slaves by Age and Sex: Cayman Islands, 1834 *584*

S7.9. Occupations of Slaves by Sex and Crop-type: St. Lucia, 1815 *585*

S7.10. Occupations of Slaves by Sex and Crop-type: Trinidad, 1813 *586*

S7.11. Occupations of Slaves by Sex and Slave-holding Size-group: St. Andrew, Barbados, 1817 *587*

S7.12. Occupations of Slaves by Sex and Slave-holding Size-group: St. Lucia, 1815 *588*

S7.13. Occupations of Slaves by Sex and Slave-holding Size-group: Berbice, 1819 *589*

S7.14. Occupations of Slaves by Sex, Age and Color, Rural and Urban: St. Lucia, 1815 *590*

S7.15. Occupations of Slaves by Sex, Age and Color: Bridgetown, Barbados, 1817 *594*

S7.16. Occupations of Slaves by Sex, Age and Color: Berbice, 1819 *596*

S7.17. Occupations of Slaves by Sex, Age and Color: St. John, Barbados, 1817 *598*

S7.18. Occupations of Slaves by Sex and Age, Urban and Rural: Trinidad, 1813 *600*

S7.19. Mean Age of Slaves by Occupation, Sex and Birthplace: St. Lucia, 1815 *602*

S7.20. Mean Age of Slaves by Occupation, Sex and Birthplace: Berbice, 1819 *602*

SECTION 8. Births and Deaths

S8.1. Registered Slave Births and Deaths, by Sex and Colony, 1815–34 *605*

S8.2. Estimated Slave Births and Deaths, Adjusted for Under-registration, by Sex and Colony, 1815–34 *609*

S8.3. Registered Slave Deaths by Age, Sex and Birthplace: St. Kitts, Nevis, Virgin Islands, St. Lucia, Tobago, Berbice and Anguilla, 1815–34 *613*

S8.4. Registered Slave Deaths by Age, Sex and Birthplace: Barbados, 1817–20 (Select Parishes) *615*

S8.5. Registered Slave Deaths by Age, Sex and Parish: Dominica, 1829–32 *616*

S8.6. Registered Slave Deaths by Age, Sex and Parish: St. Vincent, 1817–22 *618*

S8.7. Registered Slave Deaths by Age and Sex: Grenada, 1817–19 (Select Parishes) *619*

S8.8. Registered Slave Deaths by Age and Sex: Grenada, 1830–32 (Select Parishes) *619*

S8.9. Registered Slave Deaths by Age, Sex, Birthplace and Slave-holding Size-group: St. Kitts, 1817–22 *620*

S8.10. Registered Births and Deaths by Parish: Barbados, 1817–20 *621*

S8.11. Registered Slave Births and Deaths by Sex and Parish: Grenada, 1817–33 *622*

S8.12. Causes of Slave Deaths: Tobago, 1819–21 *624*

S8.13. Causes of Slave Deaths: Berbice, 1819–22 *630*

SECTION 9. Vital Rates

S9.1. Slave Birth Rates, Death Rates, Rates of Natural Increase and Sex Ratios, by Parish: Barbados, 1817–20 and 1832–34 *643*

S9.2. Slave Birth Rates, Death Rates, Rates of Natural Increase and Sex Ratios, by Parish: St. Kitts, 1831–34 *644*

S9.3. Slave Birth Rates, Death Rates, Rates of Natural Increase and Sex Ratios, by Parish and Division: Antigua, 1828–32 *645*

S9.4. Slave Birth Rates, Death Rates, Rates of Natural Increase and Sex Ratios, by Parish: Montserrat, 1828–31 *646*

S9.5. Slave Birth Rates, Death Rates, Rates of Natural Increase and Sex Ratios, by Island: Virgin Islands, 1828–31 *646*

S9.6. Slave Birth Rates, Death Rates, Rates of Natural Increase and Sex Ratios, by Parish: Dominica, 1826–29 and 1829–32 *647*

S9.7. Slave Birth Rates, Death Rates, Rates of Natural Increase and Sex Ratios, by Quarter: St. Lucia, 1815–19 *648*

S9.8. Slave Birth Rates, Death Rates, Rates of Natural Increase and Sex Ratios, by Parish: St. Vincent, 1817–22 *648*

S9.9. Slave Birth Rates, Death Rates, Rates of Natural Increase and Sex Ratios, by Parish: Grenada, 1817–19 and 1830–32 *649*

S9.10. Slave Birth Rates, Death Rates, Rates of Natural Increase and Sex Ratios, by Parish: Tobago, 1819–21 *649*

S9.11. Slave Birth Rates, Death Rates, Rates of Natural Increase and Sex Ratios, by Parish: Demerara-Essequibo, 1829–32 *650*

S9.12. Slave Birth Rates, Death Rates, Rates of Natural Increase and Sex Ratios, by Slave-holding Size-group: Barbados, St. Kitts, St. Lucia, St. Vincent, Tobago, Berbice and Anguilla, 1815–34 *651*

S9.13. Slave Age-specific Death Rates by Sex and Slave-holding Size-group: Tobago, 1819–21 *653*

S9.14. Slave Age-specific Death Rates by Sex and Birthplace: St. Kitts, Nevis, Virgin Islands, St. Lucia, Tobago and Berbice, 1815–34 *654*

S9.15. Slave Age-specific Death Rates by Sex: Dominica, 1829–32 *657*

S9.16. Slave Age-specific Death Rates by Sex and Birthplace: Bahamas, 1831–34 *657*

S9.17. Slave Age-specific Death Rates by Sex and Birthplace: Barbados, 1817–20 *658*

S9.18. Slave Age-specific Death Rates by Sex and Parish: St. Vincent, 1817–22 *659*

S9.19. Slave Age-specific Death Rates by Sex: Grenada, 1817–19 and 1830–32 (Select Parishes) *660*

S9.20. Slave Age-specific Death Rates by Sex and Color: St. Michael, Barbados, 1817–20 *661*

S9.21. Slave Age-specific Death Rates by Sex and Color: St. Lucia, 1815–19 *661*

S9.22. Slave Age-specific Death Rates by Sex and Color: Tobago, 1819–21 *662*

S9.23. Slave Age-specific Death Rates by Sex and Birthplace, Rural and Urban: St. Lucia, 1815–19 *663*

S9.24. Slave Age-specific Death Rates by Sex and Birthplace, Rural and Urban: Tobago, 1819–21 *664*

S9.25. Slave Age-specific Death Rates by Sex and Crop-type: St. Lucia, 1815–19 *665*

S9.26. Mean Age of Slaves at Death, by Sex, Birthplace and Occupation: St. Lucia, 1815–19 *666*

S9.27. Mean Age of Slaves at Death, by Sex, Birthplace and Occupation: Berbice, 1819–22 *666*

S9.28. Slave Age-specific Death Rates by Sex, Birthplace, Occupation and Crop-type: St. Lucia, 1815–19 *667*

S9.29. Slave Age-specific Death Rates by Sex and Occupation: Barbados, 1817–20 (Select Parishes) *668*

S9.30. Slave Age-specific Death Rates by Sex and Occupation: St. Lucia, 1815–19 *670*

S9.31. Slave Age-Specific Death Rates by Sex and Occupation: Berbice, 1819–22 *670*

S9.32. Seasonality of Slave Deaths by Sex, Rural and Urban: Tobago, 1819–21 *671*

S9.33. Seasonality of Slave Deaths by Occupation: Berbice, 1819–22 *671*

S9.34. Seasonality of Major Causes of Slave Deaths: Tobago, 1819–21 *672*

S9.35. Seasonality of Major Causes of Slave Deaths: Berbice, 1819–22 *673*

S9.36. Causes of Slave Deaths by Sex, Rural and Urban: Tobago, 1819–21 *674*

S9.37. Causes of Slave Deaths: Grenada, 1817–32 (Select Parishes) *675*

S9.38. Major Causes of Slave Deaths by Slave-holding Size-group: Tobago, 1819–21 and Berbice, 1819–22 *676*

S9.39. Causes of Slave Deaths by Sex, Birthplace and Color: Tobago, 1819–21 *677*

S9.40. Causes of Adult Slave Deaths by Sex and Occupation: Berbice, 1819–22 *678*

S9.41. Mean Age of Slaves at Death, by Sex, Birthplace and Cause of Death: Tobago, 1819–21 *679*

S9.42. Mean Age of Slaves at Death, by Sex, Birthplace and Cause of Death: Berbice, 1819–22 *680*

S9.43. Age-specific Slave Death Rates by Major Causes of Death: Tobago, 1819–21 and Berbice, 1819–22 *681*

S9.44. Age-specific Slave Birth Rates by Birthplace: St. Lucia, 1815–19, Tobago, 1819–21, and Berbice, 1819–22 *682*

S9.45. Age-specific Slave Birth Rates by Color and Birthplace: St. Lucia, 1815–19, Tobago, 1819–21, and Berbice, 1819–22 *682*

S9.46. Age-specific Slave Birth Rates by Birthplace, Rural and Urban: St. Lucia, 1815–19, and Tobago, 1819–21 *683*

S9.47. Age-specific Slave Birth Rates by Slave-holding Size-group: St. Lucia, 1815–19, Tobago, 1819–21, and Berbice, 1819–22 *684*

S9.48. Age-specific Slave Birth Rates by Occupation and Birthplace: St. Lucia, 1815–19, and Berbice, 1819–22 *685*

S9.49. Seasonality of Slave Births: Dominica, 1817–32, Tobago, 1819–21, and Berbice, 1819–22 *686*

SECTION 10. Manumissions

S10.1. Manumissions of Slaves by Sex and Colony, 1808–34 *689*

S10.2. Manumissions by Sex, Birthplace, Color and Parish: Barbados, 1832–34 *693*

S10.3. Manumissions by Sex, Birthplace, Color and Parish: St. Kitts, 1831–34 *693*

S10.4. Manumissions by Sex, Birthplace, Color and Parish: Dominica, 1829–32 *694*

S10.5. Manumissions by Sex and Age: St. Michael, Barbados, 1817–20 *694*

S10.6. Manumissions by Age, Sex and Color, Rural and Urban: St. Lucia, 1815–19 *695*

S10.7. Manumissions by Sex, Color, Birthplace and Owner: St. Michael, Barbados, 1817–20 *695*

SECTION 11. Land Use and Labor Use

S11.1. Employment of Slaves by Parish: Barbados, 1834 *698*

S11.2. Land Use: Virgin Islands, 1823 *698*

S11.3. Distribution of Slaves Living on Coffee and Sugar Plantations: Dominica, 1827 *699*

S11.4. Sugar and Coffee Production by Parish: Dominica, 1827 *699*

S11.5. Agricultural Production by Parish: St. Vincent, 1811–31 *700*

S11.6. Agricultural Production by Island: The Grenadines, 1819 and 1831 *700*

S11.7. Agricultural Production by Parish: Grenada, 1819 and 1831 *701*

S11.8. Land Use by Crop: Trinidad, 1808, 1824 and 1832 *701*

S11.9. Distribution of Slaves by Crop and Parish: Demerara-Essequibo, 1832 *702*

S11.10. Land Use by District: Berbice, 1832 *702*

S11.11. Agricultural Production by Island: Bahamas, 1832 *703*

SECTION 1

Geographical Distribution

Table S1.1. *Sources: P.P.,* 1833, Vol. XXVI (539), "Slave Registration," pp.473-77, and 1835, Vol. LI (235), p.289; supplemented by calculations from T.71, for particular colonies.

Notes: For exact dates of registration, see Table 2.1. The mean slave populations for Grenada and Tobago are at 30 June, the returns being made at 31 December or 1 January. Barbuda is extracted from Antigua. Errors in addition in the published data, for the Bahamas, have been corrected. Where calculations derived from the registration returns (T.71) differ from the published data, the former have been preferred.

Table S1.2. *Sources:* Calculated, by interpolation and extrapolation, from data in Table S1.1, and T.71/851; *P.P.,* 1823, Vol. XVIII (89), "Slave Population"; Jerome S. Handler, *The Unappropriated People* (Baltimore, 1974), p.18; B.W. Higman, *Slave Population and Economy in Jamaica, 1807-1834* (Cambridge, 1976), p.255; O. Nigel Bolland, *The Formation of a Colonial Society: Belize* (Baltimore, 1977), p.51; James Millette, *The Genesis of Crown Colony Government* (Port of Spain, 1970), pp.191-92; David Lowenthal and Colin G. Clarke, "Slave-Breeding in Barbuda," *Annals of the New York Academy of Sciences,* 292 (1977) 517.

Notes: Barbuda has been extracted from Antigua. All populations have been rounded to the nearest 5. The data for the years 1807-16 are relatively unreliable.

Table S1.3.   *Sources:* 1817: T.71/520-24; 1832: Index 10492 (P.R.O.); 1834: Index 10493 (P.R.O.).

Table S1.4.   *Sources:* 1812: St. Kitts Bluebook, 1832, p.118 (S.K.G.A.); 1816: C.O. 239/2, Probyn to Bathurst, 25 November 1816; 1834 (1 January): calculated from T.71/260, linked to locations in T.71/740-42; 1834 (Compensation, 1 August): T.71/740-42 (Valuers' Returns).

Table S1.5.   *Sources:* T.71/250, linked to locations given in T.71/735-38 (Valuers' Returns) and T.71/877 (Register of Compensation Claims).

Table S1.6.   *Sources:* 1815 and 1823: Stobo, "Statistical Table of the British Virgin Islands," C.O.239/9; 1831: calculated from T.71/374.

Table S1.7.   *Sources:* Dominica Registers of Slaves, 1817, f.612, 1834, f.584 (Archive Room, Old Ministerial Building, Roseau); T.71/361-63 (1829 and 1832).

Table S1.8.   *Source:* T.71/378-79.

Table S1.9.   *Source:* T.71/493-94.

Table S1.10.   *Source:* T.71/265-327.

Notes: For the dates 30 April 1817, and 31 December 1821 to 1833, the data are taken from the "abstracts" found in the slave registers at the end of the returns for each parish. The parish populations for 31 December 1817 to 1820 are calculated from the "increase" and "decrease" abstracts, but these appear somewhat low for St. John and St. Mark, St. Patrick and St. Andrew, and somewhat high for the Grenadines, St. George and Town of St. George. Notice that the total island population fell abruptly between 1820 and 1821, suggesting inadequacy in the former accounting.

Table S1.11.   *Source:* T.71/461-62.

Table S1.12.   *Sources:* Calculated from T.71/501-503 (1813); C.O.295/21, f.107, "A General Return of Population, Crop &c. of the Island of Trinidad, Extracted from the Returns of Commandants of Quarters, the 31st December 1808"; C.O.295/66, f.300, General Return, 1824; C.O.300/46, p.118 (1832 Bluebook).

Notes: The data for 1808, 1824 and 1832 are less complete than those for 1813, derived from the slave registration returns, particularly for the urban populations.

Table S1.13.   *Sources:* M.C.P.D.E., 1828, Vol. 2, p.157 (N.A.G.); *P.P.,* 1833, Vol. XXVI (700), "Slave Population," p.436.

Table S1.14.   *Source:* T.71/438-39.

Table S1.15.   *Source:* D. Gail Saunders, *The Slave Population of the Bahamas, 1783-1834* (M.Phil. thesis, University of the West Indies, 1978), p.97. (Calculated from the slave registration returns.)

Table S1.16.   *Sources:* Calculated from T.71/553-54, linked to T.71/790-803 (Valuers' Returns) and T.71/895 (Register of Claims).

Table S1.17.   *Sources:* M.C.P.D.E., 1817, p.484; 1824, Vol. 2, p.239 (N.A.G.).

Table S1.18.   *Sources: P.P.,* 1801-2, Vol. IV(88), "Accounts ... Respecting the Trade to the Coast of Africa, for Slaves," pp.47-51; *P.P.,* 1806, Vol. XIII (265), "Accounts . . . Relating to the African Slave Trade," pp.775-804. The "alternative data" for Barbados and Dominica come from *P.P.,* 1805, Vol. X (39), "Papers . . . Respecting the Slave Trade," pp.37-42, and for Jamaica, *Further Proceeding of the Honourable House of Assembly of Jamaica* (London, 1816), p.101.

Notes: It is not always possible to distinguish clearly between reported zero net imports and the lack of record. Surinam is included in the table because it probably accounted for imports to Berbice.

Table S1.19.   *Sources:* Calculated from C.O.295/55, f.356, and 295/70, f.189. See also *P.P.,* 1823, Vol. XVIII (89), "Slave Population," p.117.

Note: The "other" category included Bermuda (118 slaves 1813-21), Guadeloupe (226), Martinique (110), and numerous other small contingents from the islands and mainland.

Table S1.20.   *Sources:* Barbados: Customs 34/246, 247, 248, 250, 892, 893; St. Kitts: Customs 34/502, 515, 721, 733, 734, 737, 738, 740; Nevis: Customs 34/513, 515, 733, 734; Antigua: Customs 34/195, 198, 199, 513; Montserrat: Customs 34/502, 505; Virgin Islands: Customs 34/817, 820; Jamaica: Customs 34/440, 443, 445; Dominica: Customs 34/370, 372, 513; St. Lucia: Customs 34/247, 756, 758, 759, 762; St. Vincent: Customs 34/770, 893; Grenada: Customs 34/396, 399, 892; Tobago: Customs 34/247, 808, 809; Trinidad: Customs 34/835; Demerara-Essequibo: Customs 34/246, 358, 360, 361, 893; Berbice: Customs 34/246, 263, 893; Bahamas: Customs 34/221, 224 (H.M. Customs and Excise Archives, London).

Table S1.21.   *Sources:* Bahamas, Registers of Slaves, 1821 (Nassau Public Library); T.71/520 and 524 (Barbados).

Table S1.1. *Registered and Mean Slave Populations by Colony and Sex, 1813-34*

Colony	Registered Slaves			Mean Population		
	Males	Females	Total	Males	Females	Total
Barbados						
1817	35,354	42,139	77,493	36,044	41,876	77,920
1820	36,733	41,612	78,345	36,446	42,135	78,581
1823	36,159	42,657	78,816	36,577	43,107	79,684
1826	36,995	43,556	80,551	37,343	43,884	81,227
1829	37,691	44,211	81,902	37,727	43,974	81,701
1832	37,762	43,738	81,500	38,103	44,051	82,154
1834	38,443	44,364	82,807			
St. Kitts						
1817	9,685	10,483	20,168	9,595	10,398	19,993
1822	9,505	10,312	19,817	9,415	10,252	19,667
1825	9,324	10,192	19,516	9,261	10,152	19,413
1828	9,198	10,112	19,310	9,170	10,028	19,198
1831	9,141	9,944	19,085	8,903	9,627	18,530
1834	8,665	9,309	17,974			
Nevis						
1817	4,685	4,917	9,602	4,634	4,798	9,432
1822	4,583	4,678	9,261	4,587	4,687	9,274
1825	4,591	4,695	9,286	4,583	4,690	9,273
1828	4,574	4,685	9,259	4,550	4,651	9,201
1831	4,526	4,616	9,142	n.a.	n.a.	8,932
1834	n.a.	n.a.	8,722			
Antigua						
1817	14,864	17,013	31,877	14,563	16,661	31,224
1821	14,264	16,310	30,574	14,154	16,079	30,233
1824	14,043	15,848	29,891	13,952	15,680	29,632
1828	13,861	15,511	29,372	13,819	15,389	29,208
1832	13,778	15,267	29,045			
Montserrat						
1817	3,047	3,563	6,610	3,040	3,518	6,558
1821	3,032	3,473	6,505	2,955	3,437	6,392
1824	2,878	3,400	6,278	2,873	3,397	6,270
1828	2,867	3,395	6,262	2,931	3,378	6,309
1831	2,995	3,360	6,355			
Virgin Islands						
1818	3,231	3,668	6,899	3,103	3,577	6,680
1822	2,975	3,485	6,460	2,740	3,208	5,948
1825	2,505	2,931	5,436	2,508	2,910	5,418
1828	2,510	2,889	5,399	2,446	2,808	5,254
1831	2,381	2,727	5,108	2,404	2,746	5,150
1834	2,428	2,764	5,192			

Table S1.1. *Registered Populations, 1813-34 (continued)*

Colony	Registered Slaves			Mean Population		
	Males	Females	Total	Males	Females	Total
Jamaica						
1817	173,319	172,831	346,150	171,893	172,373	344,266
1820	170,466	171,916	342,382	168,531	170,787	339,318
1823	166,595	169,658	336,253	164,660	169,026	333,686
1826	162,726	168,393	331,119	160,490	166,280	326,770
1829	158,254	164,167	322,421	155,133	162,516	317,649
1832	152,011	160,865	312,876			
Dominica						
1817	8,624	9,335	17,959	8,272	8,985	17,257
1820	7,919	8,635	16,554	7,701	8,433	16,134
1823	7,482	8,232	15,714	7,422	8,131	15,553
1826	7,362	8,030	15,392	7,224	7,884	15,108
1829	7,086	7,738	14,824	7,002	7,602	14,604
1832	6,918	7,466	14,384			
St. Lucia						
1815	7,394	8,891	16,285	7,103	8,559	15,662
1819	6,811	8,228	15,039	6,554	7,863	14,417
1822	6,297	7,497	13,794	6,311	7,445	13,756
1825	6,325	7,392	13,717	6,303	7,386	13,689
1828	6,280	7,381	13,661	6,200	7,305	13,505
1831	6,119	7,229	13,348			
St. Vincent						
1817	12,743	12,475	25,218	12,375	12,360	24,735
1822	12,007	12,245	24,252	11,846	12,170	24,016
1825	11,685	12,095	23,780	11,634	12,106	23,740
1828	11,583	12,116	23,699	11,400	11,948	23,348
1831	11,216	11,781	22,997	10,935	11,649	22,584
1834	10,655	11,516	22,171			
Grenada						
1817	13,737	14,292	28,029			
1817	13,445	14,120	27,565	13,591	14,206	27,797
1818	13,328	14,087	27,415	13,387	14,104	27,491
1819	13,155	13,905	27,060	13,242	13,996	27,238
1820	13,007	13,892	26,899	13,081	13,899	26,980
1821	12,398	13,269	25,667	12,703	13,581	26,284
1822	12,355	13,231	25,586	12,377	13,250	25,627
1823	12,258	13,052	25,310	12,307	13,142	25,449
1824	12,101	12,871	24,972	12,180	12,962	25,142
1825	12,057	12,840	24,897	12,079	12,856	24,935
1826	11,896	12,685	24,581	11,977	12,763	24,740
1827	11,841	12,632	24,473	11,869	12,659	24,528
1828	11,777	12,565	24,342	11,809	12,599	24,408
1829	11,711	12,434	24,145	11,744	12,500	24,244
1830	11,572	12,306	23,878	11,642	12,370	24,012
1831	11,432	12,172	23,604	11,502	12,239	23,741
1832	11,322	12,089	23,411	11,377	12,131	23,508
1833	11,381	12,155	23,536	11,352	12,122	23,474

Table S1.1. *Registered Populations, 1813-34 (continued)*

Colony	Registered Slaves			Mean Population		
	Males	Females	Total	Males	Females	Total
Tobago						
1819	7,633	7,837	15,470	7,509	7,758	15,267
1820	7,384	7,679	15,063	7,246	7,577	14,823
1821	7,107	7,474	14,581	7,030	7,419	14,449
1822	6,952	7,363	14,315	6,882	7,313	14,195
1823	6,812	7,262	14,074	6,685	7,180	13,865
1824	6,558	7,098	13,656	6,545	7,125	13,670
1825	6,532	7,151	13,683	6,463	7,093	13,556
1826	6,394	7,034	13,428	6,266	6,948	13,214
1827	6,138	6,861	12,999	6,113	6,834	12,947
1828	6,088	6,807	12,895	6,027	6,782	12,809
1829	5,966	6,757	12,723	5,919	6,721	12,640
1830	5,872	6,684	12,556	5,821	6,643	12,464
1831	5,769	6,601	12,370	5,686	6,545	12,231
1832	5,603	6,488	12,091	5,534	6,395	11,929
1833	5,466	6,301	11,767	5,419	6,275	11,694
1834	5,373	6,248	11,621			
Trinidad						
1813	14,141	11,555	25,696	14,137	11,483	25,620
1816	14,133	11,411	25,544	13,644	10,897	24,541
1819	13,155	10,382	23,537	13,104	10,359	23,463
1822	13,052	10,336	23,388	13,243	10,677	23,920
1825	13,435	11,017	24,452	13,013	11,101	24,114
1828	12,591	11,185	23,776			23,068
1831			22,359			
1834						
Demerara-Essequibo						
1817	44,137	33,730	77,867	43,682	33,940	77,622
1820	43,227	34,149	77,376	42,226	33,951	76,177
1823	41,224	33,753	74,977	39,991	33,189	73,180
1826	38,758	32,624	71,382	37,950	32,475	70,425
1829	37,141	32,326	69,467	35,755	31,757	67,512
1832	34,368	31,188	65,556			
Berbice						
1817	13,802	10,747	24,549	13,565	10,594	24,159
1819	13,327	10,441	23,768	12,667	10,395	23,062
1822	12,007	10,349	22,356	11,715	10,195	21,910
1825	11,423	10,041	21,464	11,391	9,791	21,182
1828	11,358	9,541	20,899	11,189	9,583	20,772
1831	11,020	9,625	20,645			20,002
1834			19,359			
British Honduras						
1834	1,196	736	1,932	—	—	—

Table S1.1. *Registered Populations, 1813-34 (continued)*

Colony	Registered Slaves			Mean Population		
	Males	Females	Total	Males	Females	Total
Cayman Islands						
1834	490	495	985	–	–	–
Bahamas						
1822	5,529	5,279	10,808			
1825	4,670	4,594	9,264	5,099	4,937	10,036
1828	4,608	4,660	9,268	4,639	4,627	9,266
1831	4,876	4,892	9,768	4,742	4,776	9,518
1834	4,901	5,101	10,002	4,889	4,997	9,886
Anguilla						
1827	1,136	1,367	2,503			
1831	1,257	1,439	2,696	1,197	1,403	2,600
1834	1,064	1,305	2,369	1,161	1,372	2,533
Barbuda						
1817	189	203	392			
1821	190	221	411	190	212	402
1824	182	241	423	186	231	417
1828	205	262	467	194	251	445
1832	214	278	492	210	270	480

Table S1.2. *Estimated Annual Slave Populations by Colony, 1807-34*

Colony	1807	1808	1809	1810	1811	1812	1813
Barbados	75,000	75,200	75,400	75,000	75,000	74,570	72,000
St. Kitts	21,100	21,000	20,900	20,800	20,700	20,600	20,500
Nevis	10,700	10,600	10,500	10,400	10,300	10,200	10,100
Antigua	37,220	36,700	36,175	35,650	35,125	34,600	34,075
Montserrat	6,880	6,855	6,825	6,800	6,775	6,745	6,720
Virgin Islands	7,715	7,645	7,570	7,500	7,400	7,330	7,255
Jamaica	348,825	353,710	353,590	347,000	356,990	349,435	347,810
Dominica	19,445	19,300	19,150	19,000	18,850	18,705	18,555
St. Lucia	19,830	19,385	18,945	18,500	18,055	17,615	17,170
St. Vincent	28,335	28,025	27,700	27,400	27,090	26,775	26,465
Grenada	31,045	30,695	30,350	30,000	29,650	29,305	28,955
Tobago	18,845	18,560	18,280	18,000	17,720	17,440	17,155
Trinidad	26,100	26,150	26,200	26,200	26,200	26,000	25,695
Demerara-Essequibo	80,915	80,610	80,305	80,000	79,695	79,390	79,085
Berbice	28,480	28,085	27,695	27,300	26,905	26,515	26,120
British Honduras	3,200	3,100	3,000	2,900	2,865	2,830	2,800
Cayman Islands	835	840	845	850	855	860	865
Bahamas	9,700	9,800	9,900	10,000	10,100	10,200	10,300
Anguilla	1,600	1,620	1,660	1,700	1,740	1,780	1,820
Barbuda	335	340	345	350	355	360	370
Total	776,105	778,220	775,335	765,350	772,370	761,255	753,815

Colony	1814	1815	1816	1817	1818	1819	1820
Barbados	72,665	75,280	77,200	77,495	77,780	78,065	78,350
St. Kitts	20,400	20,300	22,250	20,170	20,110	20,055	20,000
Nevis	10,000	9,860	9,720	9,600	9,520	9,435	9,350
Antigua	33,550	33,025	32,500	31,975	31,600	31,225	30,850
Montserrat	6,690	6,665	6,635	6,610	6,590	6,570	6,550
Virgin Islands	7,185	7,115	7,040	6,970	6,900	6,750	6,600
Jamaica	344,050	339,840	343,020	346,150	344,890	343,635	342,380
Dominica	18,405	18,255	18,110	17,960	17,490	17,020	16,550
St. Lucia	16,725	16,280	16,285	15,870	15,455	15,040	14,750
St. Vincent	26,155	25,840	25,530	25,220	25,060	24,905	24,750
Grenada	28,610	28,260	27,915	27,565	27,415	27,060	26,900
Tobago	16,875	16,595	16,315	16,030	15,750	15,470	15,050
Trinidad	25,645	25,595	25,545	24,875	24,205	23,535	23,400
Demerara-Essequibo	78,780	78,475	78,170	77,865	77,710	77,555	77,400
Berbice	25,730	25,335	24,940	24,550	24,170	23,770	23,400
British Honduras	2,765	2,730	2,695	2,660	2,630	2,595	2,560
Cayman Islands	870	875	880	885	890	895	900
Bahamas	10,400	10,500	10,600	10,700	10,800	10,900	11,000
Anguilla	1,860	1,900	1,940	1,980	2,020	2,060	2,100
Barbuda	375	380	385	390	395	400	400
Total	747,735	743,105	747,675	745,520	741,380	736,940	733,240

Table S1.2. *Estimated Populations, 1807-34 (continued)*

Colony	1821	1822	1823	1824	1825	1826	1827
Barbados	78,505	78,660	78,815	79,395	79,975	80,550	81,000
St. Kitts	19,900	19,815	19,715	19,615	19,515	19,450	19,380
Nevis	9,305	9,260	9,270	9,280	9,285	9,275	9,270
Antigua	30,575	30,335	30,115	29,890	29,725	29,555	29,385
Montserrat	6,505	6,430	6,355	6,280	6,275	6,270	6,265
Virgin Islands	6,530	6,460	6,120	5,775	5,435	5,425	5,415
Jamaica	340,340	338,295	336,255	334,540	332,830	331,120	328,220
Dominica	16,270	15,995	15,715	15,605	15,500	15,390	15,205
St. Lucia	14,280	13,795	13,770	13,745	13,715	13,695	13,680
St. Vincent	24,500	24,250	24,095	23,935	23,780	23,750	23,725
Grenada	25,665	25,590	25,310	24,970	24,895	24,580	24,475
Tobago	14,580	14,315	14,075	13,655	13,685	13,430	13,000
Trinidad	23,395	23,390	23,745	24,095	24,450	24,225	24,000
Demerara-Essequibo	76,590	75,785	74,975	73,780	72,580	71,380	70,745
Berbice	22,870	22,355	22,060	21,760	21,465	21,275	21,085
British Honduras	2,530	2,500	2,470	2,450	2,430	2,410	2,280
Cayman Islands	910	920	930	940	950	960	970
Bahamas	10,900	10,810	10,200	9,700	9,285	9,280	9,275
Anguilla	2,160	2,215	2,275	2,330	2,390	2,445	2,505
Barbuda	410	415	420	425	435	445	455
Total	726,720	721,590	716,685	712,165	708,600	704,910	700,335

	1828	1829	1830	1831	1832	1833	1834
Barbados	81,450	81,900	82,000	81,750	81,500	82,300	83,150
St. Kitts	19,310	19,200	19,100	19,085	18,565	18,045	17,525
Nevis	9,260	9,230	9,200	9,140	9,040	8,940	8,840
Antigua	29,295	29,210	29,120	29,085	29,045	28,600	28,130
Montserrat	6,260	6,280	6,300	6,355	6,375	6,390	6,400
Virgin Islands	5,400	5,270	5,150	5,110	5,120	5,125	5,135
Jamaica	325,320	322,420	319,000	315,940	312,875	311,900	311,070
Dominica	15,015	14,825	14,700	14,545	14,385	14,320	14,165
St. Lucia	13,660	13,530	13,400	13,350	13,320	13,300	13,275
St. Vincent	23,700	23,400	23,100	22,995	22,750	22,500	22,250
Grenada	24,340	24,145	23,880	23,605	23,410	23,535	23,645
Tobago	12,895	12,725	12,555	12,370	12,090	11,765	11,545
Trinidad	23,775	23,265	22,750	22,360	21,790	21,225	20,655
Demerara-Essequibo	70,105	69,465	68,165	66,860	65,555	64,875	64,185
Berbice	20,900	20,800	20,700	20,645	20,215	19,790	19,360
British Honduras	2,155	2,025	1,900	1,840	1,785	1,830	1,895
Cayman Islands	980	990	1,000	1,000	995	990	985
Bahamas	9,270	9,290	9,500	9,770	9,845	9,920	9,995
Anguilla	2,535	2,570	2,600	2,695	2,560	2,430	2,260
Barbuda	465	470	480	485	490	500	505
Total	696,090	691,010	684,600	678,985	671,710	668,280	664,970

Table S1.3. *Distribution of Slaves by Parish and Sex: Barbados, 1817, 1832 and 1834*

Parish	1817			1832			1834		
	Males	Females	Total	Males	Females	Total	Males	Females	Total
St. Michael	7,985	10,294	18,279	7,657	9,591	17,248	7,702	9,539	17,241
St. James	1,836	2,072	3,908	2,074	2,245	4,319	2,148	2,259	4,407
St. Peter	2,872	3,260	6,132	2,916	3,344	6,260	2,725	3,120	5,845
St. Lucy	2,572	2,893	5,465	2,644	3,079	5,723	2,939	3,478	6,417
St. Andrew	1,631	1,762	3,393	1,821	2,157	3,978	2,000	2,339	4,339
St. Joseph	1,551	1,920	3,471	2,014	2,282	4,296	1,894	2,127	4,021
St. John	2,556	2,910	5,466	2,651	3,071	5,722	2,893	3,290	6,183
St. Philip	4,338	5,197	9,535	4,718	5,394	10,112	4,844	5,586	10,430
Christ Church	4,608	5,303	9,911	4,790	5,485	10,275	4,825	5,481	10,306
St. George	3,107	3,663	6,770	3,742	4,117	7,859	3,924	4,255	8,179
St. Thomas	2,390	2,773	5,163	2,735	2,973	5,708	2,562	2,877	5,439
Total	35,446	42,047	77,493	37,762	43,738	81,500	38,456	44,351	82,807

Table S1.4. *Distribution of Slaves by Parish and Sex: St. Kitts, 1812, 1816 and 1834*

Parish	Census Populations		Registered Slaves	Compensation, 1834		
	1812	1816	1834	Males	Females	Total
St. George: Basseterre	3,738	3,426	2,883	1,348	1,500	2,848
St. Peter: Basseterre	2,782	2,743	2,915	1,333	1,441	2,774
Trinity: Palmetto Point	1,543	1,395	1,179	541	569	1,110
St. Thomas: Middle Island	2,441	2,074	2,157	1,034	1,006	2,040
St. Anne: Sandy Point	1,997	2,176	2,255	1,105	1,125	2,230
St. Paul: Capisterre	1,588	1,433	1,419	658	737	1,395
St. John: Capisterre	1,151	1,511	1,282	589	620	1,209
Christ Church: Nichola Town	2,063	2,002	1,856	849	1,012	1,861
St. Mary: Cayon	2,222	2,068	2,028	969	1,042	2,011
Total	19,525	18,828	17,974	8,426	9,052	17,478

Table S1.5. *Distribution of Slaves by Parish, Division and Sex: Antigua, 1832*

Parish/Division	Males	Females	Total
St. John's			
St. John's Division	1,945	2,169	4,114
Town of St. John's	1,202	1,419	2,621
Dickinson's Bay Division	894	1,017	1,911
Five Islands Division	287	301	588
St. George's			
New North Sound Division	1,698	1,858	3,556
St. Peter's			
Old North Sound Division	2,006	2,067	4,073
Town of Parham	26	37	63
St. Philip's			
Belfast Division	776	819	1,595
Nonsuch Division	1,129	1,262	2,391
St. Paul's			
Falmouth Division	604	690	1,294
Town of English Harbour	128	137	265
Town of Falmouth	62	65	127
Willoughby Bay Division	598	755	1,353
Rendezvous Bay Division	31	44	75
St. Mary's			
New Division	699	762	1,461
Bermudian Valley Division	418	488	906
Old Road Division	625	673	1,298
Unknown	355	408	763
Total	13,483	14,971	28,454

Table S1.6. *Distribution of Slaves by Island and Sex: Virgin Islands, 1815, 1823 and 1831*

	Stobo's Estimate		1831 Registration			
Island	1815	1823	Males	Females	Total	Slave per Square Mile
Tortola	5,765	4,999	1,754	2,034	3,788	158
Spanish Town	507	436	179	188	367	41
Peters Island	132	116	44	47	91	30
Thatch Island	4	46	68	62	130	130
Anegada	115	109	30	51	81	6
Jos Van Dykes	376	403	36	43	79	20
Beef Island	130	148	40	48	88	37
Frenchman's Quay	36	7	20	23	43	36
Guana Island	105	164	18	20	38	19
Quaymanas	24	50	11	25	36	30
Salt Island	16	49	7	8	15	19
Other/Unknown	75	102	162	165	327	
Total	7,285	6,629	2,369	2,714	5,083	86

Table S1.7. *Distribution of Slaves by Parish and Sex: Dominica, 1817, 1829, 1832 and 1834*

Parish	1817			1829	1832	1834		
	Males	Females	Total	Total	Total	Males	Females	Total
Roseau	814	1,024	1,838	1,068	827	321	451	772
St. George	1,609	1,637	3,246	2,703	2,623	1,269	1,368	2,637
St. Paul	993	1,156	2,149	1,756	1,727	798	892	1,690
St. Joseph	989	1,057	2,046	1,458	1,426	633	677	1,310
St. Peter	590	612	1,202	1,049	871	418	461	879
St. John	703	843	1,546	999	1,130	589	581	1,170
St. Andrew	942	1,031	1,973	1,642	1,788	818	909	1,727
St. David	397	417	814	561	547	284	271	555
St. Patrick	1,059	1,090	2,149	1,684	1,675	809	836	1,645
St. Mark	600	594	1,195	860	927	455	470	925
St. Luke	422	472	894	838	843	423	454	877
Total	9,119	9,933	19,052	14,618	14,384	6,817	7,370	14,187

Table S1.8. *Distribution of Slaves by Quarter, Sex and Birthplace: St. Lucia, 1815*

Quarter	Africans		Creoles		Total*		
	Males	Females	Males	Females	Males	Females	Total
Castries	267	247	639	728	906	975	1,881
Gros Islet	136	160	492	629	629	796	1,425
Dauphin	136	93	243	313	380	407	787
Dennery	49	86	245	335	294	421	715
Praslin	89	96	191	224	283	321	604
Micoud	92	117	217	289	314	406	720
Vieux Fort	111	156	501	596	614	755	1,369
Laborie	155	199	673	846	829	1,045	1,874
Choiseul	68	110	377	437	445	547	992
Soufriere	284	256	1,205	1,406	1,492	1,663	3,155
Anse la Raye	73	67	258	311	337	382	719
Town of Castries	175	162	471	596	649	759	1,408
Town of Gros Islet	10	12	62	82	72	94	166
Town of Micoud	1	2	4	11	5	13	18
Town of Vieux Fort	2	2	5	11	7	13	20
Town of Laborie	6	6	20	42	26	48	74
Town of Choiseul	4	8	10	29	14	37	51
Town of Soufriere	18	31	101	138	119	169	288
Unknown	1	1	9	4	11	5	16
Total	1,677	1,811	5,723	7,027	7,426	8,856	16,282

* Includes 44 slaves whose birthplace is unknown.

Table S1.9. *Distribution of Plantation and Unattached Slaves by Parish and Sex: St. Vincent, 1817*

Parish	Plantation Slaves		Unattached Slaves		Total
	Males	Females	Males	Females	
Rural slaves					
St. George	2,878	2,800	263	259	6,200
St. Andrew	857	957	101	114	2,029
St. Patrick	1,157	1,128	35	61	2,381
St. David	837	848	29	24	1,738
Charlotte	3,694	3,353	146	141	7,334
Total	9,423	9,086	574	599	19,682
Grenadines: rural					
Bequia	630	558	118	106	1,412
Ilot à Quatre	38	43	–	–	81
Balliceaux	38	6	2	3	49
Mustique	171	147	4	3	325
Canouan	157	175	8	14	354
Mayreau	13	21	3	5	42
Union Island	277	311	4	6	598
Petit St. Vincent	3	8	–	–	11
Petit Bermuda	–	–	2	2	4
Total	1,327	1,269	141	139	2,876
Town slaves					
Kingstown, St. George	–	–	1,120	1,135	2,255
Calliaqua, St. George	–	–	90	100	190
Gomia, St. George	–	–	14	11	25
Mariaqua, St. George	–	–	11	9	20
Barrouallie, St. Patrick	–	–	47	49	96
Layou, St. Patrick	–	–	44	43	87
Princes Town, St. Patrick	–	–	9	7	16
Chatteaubellair, St. David	–	–	35	26	61
Total	–	–	1,370	1,380	2,750
TOTAL	10,750	10,355	2,085	2,118	25,308

Table S1.10. *Distribution of Slaves by Parish: Grenada, 1817-33*

Year	Town of St.George	St.George	St.John & St.Mark	St.Patrick	St.Andrew	St.David	Grenadines	Total
1817*	2,632	5,405	3,633	4,697	4,742	2,296	4,624	28,029
1817**	2,607	5,236	3,605	4,676	4,792	2,292	4,490	27,698
1818	2,602	5,017	3,386	4,719	4,854	2,266	4,505	27,349
1819	2,551	4,884	3,408	4,654	4,827	2,201	4,469	26,994
1820	2,487	4,908	3,356	4,622	4,847	2,225	4,388	26,833
1821	2,174	4,448	3,437	4,611	4,837	2,213	3,947	25,667
1822	2,112	4,426	3,467	4,662	4,844	2,230	3,845	25,586
1823	2,020	4,391	3,467	4,693	4,748	2,213	3,778	25,310
1824	2,072	4,411	3,449	4,610	4,903	2,153	3,374	24,972
1825	2,004	4,341	3,513	4,618	4,906	2,150	3,365	24,897
1826	1,875	4,373	3,486	4,552	4,840	2,106	3,349	24,581
1827	1,806	4,370	3,460	4,532	4,795	2,130	3,380	24,473
1828	1,800	4,264	3,468	4,496	4,747	2,120	3,447	24,342
1829	1,749	4,095	3,531	4,547	5,016	1,899	3,308	24,145
1830	1,715	4,155	3,457	4,415	4,922	1,890	3,324	23,878
1831	1,666	3,957	3,463	4,332	4,944	1,855	3,387	23,604
1832	1,606	3,922	3,452	4,313	4,759	1,851	3,508	23,411
1833	1,632	4,022	3,613	4,340	4,534	1,876	3,519	23,536

* At 30 April 1817.
** At 31 December (1817-33).

Table S1.11. *Distribution of Plantation and Unattached Slaves by Parish and Sex: Tobago, 1819*

Parish	Plantation Slaves		Unattached Slaves		Total
	Males	Females	Males	Females	
St. Andrew	1,086	1,182	58	62	2,388
St. George	950	891	36	35	1,912
St. Mary	430	466	16	14	926
St. Paul	730	732	28	29	1,519
St. John	667	678	25	17	1,387
St. David	1,644	1,629	107	98	3,478
St. Patrick	1,271	1,378	15	21	2,685
Town of Scarborough	–	–	420	468	888
Town of Plymouth	–	–	65	47	112
Town of Milford	–	–	15	17	32
Unknown	–	–	70	73	143
Total	6,778	6,956	855	881	15,470

Table S1.12. *Distribution of Slaves by Quarter and Sex: Trinidad, 1808, 1813, 1824 and 1832*

Quarter	Registered, 1813			Returns of Population		
	Males	Females	Total	1808	1824	1832
Rural slaves						
St. Anne's	450	415	865	756	449	221
Tragarete	138	86	224	340	293	255
Maraval	254	213	467	431	431	411
Mucurapo	78	79	157	232	179	108
Diego Martin	713	559	1,272	1,325	992	566
Carenage	711	593	1,304)		581	450
Chaguaramas	25	15	40}	1,346	276	116
Bocas	104	98	202)		442	236
Las Cuevas	134	105	239	88	65	27
Toco	103	79	182	215	100	52
Eastern Coast	—	—	—	—	—	9
Mayaro	212	176	388	338	566	563
Guayaguayare	90	56	146	229	—	—
Erin	15	7	22	—	353	124
Hicacos and Gallos	132	113	245	237	171	105
Irois	—	—	—	—	134	59
Cedros	224	166	390	457)	438	475
Guapo	230	121	351	—	710)	523)
La Brea	285	230	515	707)		
Oropuche	199	103	302	318	391	390
South Naparima	1,018	685	1,703	1,681	2,355	2,516
North Naparima	751	541	1,292	1,143	1,244	1,300
"Naparima"	102	80	182	—	—	—
Savanna Grande	—	—	—	—	876	977
Point à Pierre	508	365	873	670	884	936
Savonetta	284	199	483)			901
Couva	491	395	886)	2,334	2,349	—
Carapichaima	186	110	296	—	—	1,206
Chaguanas	584	400	984	183	491	621
Caroni	154	129	283	293	146	149
Guanapo	115	75	190	149	313	272
Arima	162	170	332	259	397	311
Caura	—	—	—	—	—	66
Tacarigua	447	383	830			
Arouca	320	226	546	1,408	1,097	1,281
St. Joseph	436	345	781	602	515	379
Maracas	153	103	256	235	333	268
Santa Cruz	333	279	612	653	649	448
Cimaronero	178	126	304	396	172	216
San Juan	38	52	90)	896	—	—
Aricagua	444	366	810}		701	476
Laventille	200	179	379)	396	189	169
Town slaves						
Port of Spain	3,012	3,028	6,040	3,680	3,683	2,927
San Fernando	51	48	99	—	—	—
Arima	—	—	—	—	24	31
St. Joseph	1	—	1	—	88	79
San Juan	10	24	34	—	40	46
Unknown	66	33	99	—	—	—
Total	14,141	11,555	25,696	21,997	23,117	20,265

[424]

Table S1.13. *Distribution of Slaves by Parish and Sex: Demerara-Essequibo, 1826 and 1832*

Parish	1826			1832		
	Males	Females	Total	Males	Females	Total
St. Mary	4,002	3,175	7,177	3,394	2,907	6,301
St. Paul	5,487	4,851	10,338	4,510	4,262	8,772
St. George	3,645	3,230	6,875	3,993	4,040	8,033
St. Matthew	3,762	3,277	7,039	2,934	2,670	5,604
St. Mark	3,137	2,553	5,690	2,570	2,063	4,633
St. Swithin	2,581	2,228	4,809	2,059	1,851	3,910
St. Luke	3,444	2,798	6,242	2,930	2,605	5,535
St. Peter	3,309	2,850	6,159	3,015	2,872	5,887
St. James	2,419	2,047	4,466	2,126	2,040	4,166
St. John	2,624	2,191	4,815	2,471	2,146	4,617
The Trinity	4,348	3,424	7,772	4,347	3,712	8,059
Total	38,758	32,624	71,382	34,349	31,168	65,517

Table S1.14. *Distribution of Slaves by Parish and Sex: Berbice, 1819*

Parish	Males	Females	Total
West Coast Berbice	2,205	1,707	3,912
West Bank Berbice River	1,775	1,543	3,318
East Bank Berbice River	1,796	1,534	3,330
Upper Berbice River	58	21	79
River Berbice	756	620	1,376
West Bank Canje Creek	227	171	398
East Bank Canje Creek	347	251	598
Lower Canje	29	25	54
Upper Canje	92	91	183
Canje Creek	555	489	1,044
East Coast Berbice	1,217	947	2,164
East Coastal Canal	165	128	293
West Coast Corentyne	475	331	806
West Bank Corentyne River	97	54	151
Corentyne Coast	957	613	1,570
New Amsterdam	40	42	82
Unknown	2,576	1,947	4,523
Total	13,367	10,514	23,881

Table S1.15. *Distribution of Slaves by Island and Sex: Bahamas,*
1822 and 1834

Island	1822			1834		
	Males	Females	Total	Males	Females	Total
New Providence	1,453	1,482	2,935	1,068	1,182	2,250
Grand Bahama	21	12	33	74	64	138
Abaco	124	93	217	194	201	395
Eleuthera	627	614	1,241	611	672	1,283
Harbour Island	234	224	458	230	281	511
Andros & Berry Islands	108	65	173	54	49	103
Cat Island	334	379	713	301	362	663
Watlings Island	197	158	355	185	172	357
Rum Cay	102	127	229	317	330	647
Exuma	353	348	701	439	429	868
Long Island	304	314	618	309	302	611
Crooked Island, Acklins and Long Cay	494	423	917	304	264	568
Inagua	25	26	51	30	20	50
Ragged Island	43	37	80	63	81	144
Turks and Caicos	1,074	872	1,946	698	678	1,376
St. George's Cay	12	17	29	24	14	38
Royal Island	6	3	9	–	–	–
Total	5,511	5,194	10,705	4,901	5,101	10,002

Table S1.16. *Slave Population by Streets: Bridgetown, Barbados, 1832-34*

Street	1834		Slaves, 1832						
						African-born		Colored	
	Slaves	Owners	Males	Females	Total	Males	Females	Males	Females
Alms House	1	1	1	–	1	–	–	–	–
Baxter's Road	347	71	155	225	380	4	12	41	51
Bay Street	1,109	241	431	579	1,010	29	50	102	148
Bolton Lane	1	1	1	–	1	–	–	1	–
Bridge Street	135	27	65	86	151	3	3	20	24
Broad Street	488	90	230	244	474	12	22	45	61
Bull Head Alley	17	1	10	7	17	3	–	–	2
Canary Street	130	31	50	78	128	3	8	8	12
Chapel Street	102	26	42	60	102	–	6	8	5
Cheapside	238	50	109	138	247	4	9	32	35
Church Street	101	23	45	58	103	–	1	13	14
Collymore Rock	298	41	102	141	243	9	4	28	31
Constitution	126	44	50	98	148	2	8	13	20
Crown Alley	6	2	1	5	6	–	–	–	–
Cumberland Street	157	22	69	98	167	1	8	21	25

Street	1834 Slaves	1834 Owners	Males	Females	Total	African-born Males	African-born Females	Colored Males	Colored Females
Dunn's Alley	23	5	6	15	21	—	—	—	2
Fontabelle	216	38	117	117	234	7	11	25	30
Gaol Street	48	5	20	23	43	—	3	4	3
George Street	16	3	5	6	11	—	—	1	3
Gulley	78	13	20	32	52	2	—	5	5
Henry's Lane	24	5	5	20	25	—	3	1	2
High Street	96	22	38	65	103	4	5	5	13
Holborn	27	2	10	15	25	—	—	1	—
James Street	168	28	76	73	149	1	4	7	14
Jassmine Alley	9	2	1	2	3	—	—	—	—
Jemmott's Lane	4	1	3	1	4	2	—	—	—
Lake's Folly	3	1	1	2	3	—	—	—	—
Lucas Alley	77	10	34	43	77	1	1	9	16
Magazine Street	16	8	7	9	16	—	1	3	4
Mahogany Lane	67	16	17	35	52	1	1	1	3
Maiden Lane	31	8	12	16	28	—	1	—	—
Marl Hill Street	149	24	70	72	142	2	9	10	15
Marshe's Alley	1	1	1	2	3	—	—	1	2
Mason Hall Street	25	7	9	15	24	2	2	3	7
Middle Street	69	16	22	43	65	—	8	4	9
Milk Market Street	154	36	51	88	139	2	10	9	22
Moll's Alley	11	3	4	15	19	—	2	—	5
My Lord's Hill	44	8	20	21	41	—	2	4	3
Nelson Street	127	41	41	79	120	1	8	11	17
Palmetto Street	106	19	34	40	74	—	2	5	13
Passage Lane	26	3	8	11	19	—	—	6	4
Pier Head	159	31	85	81	166	13	5	20	23
Pinfold Street	194	43	68	114	182	1	9	12	17
Reed Street	128	36	41	70	111	—	6	23	25
River Road	63	15	26	35	61	1	1	4	10
Roebuck Street	1,146	221	411	577	988	18	38	82	118
St. Mary's Street	55	17	17	34	51	—	2	6	6
St. Michael's Row	62	16	20	38	58	2	4	2	11
Slaughter Yard	9	2	4	10	14	—	1	1	6
Sober Lane	13	5	3	7	10	—	—	2	3
Spry Street	220	41	86	128	214	1	5	28	33
Stable Street	55	12	27	29	56	—	3	5	8
Suttle Street	185	48	79	97	176	3	4	21	22
Swan Street	288	76	111	176	287	3	10	31	75
Tudor Street	278	63	86	170	256	6	10	21	54
Upper Bay Street	5	2	2	4	6	—	2	—	2
Wharf	58	15	29	27	56	6	5	3	7
White Park Road	161	33	75	81	156	2	5	29	14
Windsor Road	20	2	10	10	20	—	—	8	6
Unknown	615	153	248	324	572	16	18	71	93
Total	8,585	1,827	3,421	4,689	8,110	167	332	816	1,153

Table S1.17. *Distribution of Slaves, Whites and Freedmen by District: Georgetown, Demerara, 1812 and 1824*

District	Slaves		Whites		Freedmen	
	1812	1824	1812	1824	1812	1824
Kingston	80	468	62	124	42	312
Cumingsburg	1,210	2,308	223	493	396	1,300
Robb Town	550	460	172	225	280	279
New Town	315	242	107	77	80	82
Stabroek	579	586	175	145	146	275
Werk en Rust	492	666	179	211	261	484
Charles Town	363	735	53	121	146	344
Lacy Town	–	234	–	116	–	240
Total	3,589	5,699	971	1,512	1,351	3,316

Table S1.18. *Net Imports of Slaves by Colony, 1797-1807*

Colony	1797	1798	1799	1800	1801[a]	1802
Barbados	702	1,969	369	295	–	208
St. Kitts	2	280	158	–	–	1,029
Nevis	- 30	–	–	–	–	–
Antigua	233	207	–	263	–	578
Montserrat	–	–	–	–	–	–
Virgin Islands	- 163	89	132	–	–	226
Jamaica	7,842	9,437	14,635	19,306	7,200	6,221
Dominica	289	545	746	932	362	603
St. Lucia	–	–	–	175	–	–
St. Vincent	863	2,366	1,546	460	234	981
Grenada	- 9	1,111	782	287	385	1,082
Tobago	323	721	1,463	38	255	172
Trinidad						4,630
Demerara-Essequibo	2,655	7,622	5,513	7,499	5,352	5,366
Surinam	–	–	–	2,674	2,280	1,529
Bahamas	n.a.	n.a.	n.a.	n.a.	n.a.	566
Alternative data						
Barbados[c]	567	458	477	40	–	208
Jamaica[d]	8,014	9,778	14,635	20,431	11,039	5,577
Dominica[c]	289	1,097	560	953	336	209

Table S1.18. *Net Imports of Slaves by Colony, 1797-1807 (continued)*

Colony	1803	1804[a]	1805[b]	1806	1807
Barbados	679	145	285	n.a.	n.a.
St. Kitts	566	286	–	n.a.	n.a.
Nevis	238	–	–	n.a.	n.a.
Antigua	89	251	101	n.a.	n.a.
Montserrat	–	–	–	n.a.	n.a.
Virgin Islands	207	–	334	n.a.	n.a.
Jamaica	4,299	369	5,169	n.a.	n.a.
Dominica	430	460	1,129	n.a.	n.a.
St. Lucia	–	–	372	n.a.	n.a.
St. Vincent	2,098	–	81	n.a.	n.a.
Grenada	1,108	–	–	n.a.	n.a.
Tobago	–	–	–	n.a.	n.a.
Trinidad	4,336	–	363	n.a.	n.a.
Demerara-Essequibo	–		6,630	n.a.	n.a.
Surinam	–	780	6,008	n.a.	n.a.
Bahamas	18	- 236	- 40	n.a.	n.a.
Alternative data					
Barbados[c]	679	145	n.a.	n.a.	n.a.
Jamaica[d]	5,810	4,168	4,608	8,321	15,927
Dominica[c]	976	1,378	n.a.	n.a.	n.a.

a   To 5 July only.
b   10 October 1804–10 October 1805.

c   All these data are for full calendar years.
d   Years ending 30 September.

Table S1.19. *Slaves Imported into Trinidad, 1813-25*

Origin	1813-14	1815-21	1822-25 Males	1822-25 Females	1822-25 Total	Total 1813-25
Barbados	15	222	258	119	377	614
St. Kitts	–	25	116	122	238	263
Nevis	4	1	26	9	35	40
Antigua	2	97	69	38	107	206
Montserrat	–	26	5	3	8	34
Virgin Islands	–	9	326	406	732	741
Dominica	67	1,013	23	10	33	1,113
St. Lucia	11	119	13	3	16	146
St. Vincent	10	186	230	193	423	619
Grenada	61	1,114	79	90	169	1,344
Tobago	3	23	2	2	4	30
Demerara-Essequibo	1	8	1	1	2	11
Berbice	–	–	–	–	–	–
Bahamas	1	300	123	112	235	536
Anguilla	–	8	25	26	51	59
Other	170	320	39	30	69	559
Total	345	3,471	1,335	1,164	2,499	6,315

Table S1.20. *Net Imports of Domestic Slaves, by Colony, 1830-34*

Colony	1830	1831	1832	1833	1834	Total 1830-34
Barbados	- 14	- 2	- 31	- 10	- 5	- 62
St. Kitts	n.a.	- 17	- 17	- 16	- 5	- 55
Nevis	n.a.	- 3	- 5	3	2	- 3
Antigua	- 5	2	4	- 2	4	3
Montserrat	1	—	1	—	4	6
Virgin Islands	n.a.	- 23	—	- 1	- 1	- 26
Jamaica	n.a.	- 16	—	- 1	- 3	- 20
Dominica	5	1	- 5	1	3	5
St. Lucia	- 8	- 8	- 9	- 2	3	- 24
St. Vincent	n.a.	5	- 2	- 11	- 10	- 18
Grenada	7	- 7	16	3	—	19
Tobago	n.a.	n.a.	—	- 5	- 1	- 6
Trinidad	2	13	4	- 7	- 7	5
Demerara-Essequibo	1	- 19	- 30	- 9	- 2	- 59
Berbice	5	- 3	1	- 1	- 6	- 4
Bahamas	- 13	- 9	—	—	3	- 19
Total	- 19	- 86	- 73	- 58	- 22	- 258

Table S1.21. *Slaves Exported from the Bahamas, 1821, and St. Michael, Barbados, 1817-20, by Age and Sex*

Age group	Bahamas, 1821		St. Michael, Barbados, 1817-20			
			Africans		Creoles	
	Males	Females	Males	Females	Males	Females
0-4	23	32	—	—	5	3
5-9	20	17	—	—	5	5
10-14	29	23	—	—	10	9
15-19	21	39	—	1	7	4
20-24	16	20	1	—	10	5
25-29	13	9	4	4	2	2
30-34	7	11	—	3	2	1
35-39	5	11	1	—	1	—
40-44	10	8	—	—	—	1
45-49	6	1	—	—	1	2
50-54	3	—	—	—	—	—
55-59	2	6	1	—	—	—
60-64	—	1	—	—	—	—
65-69	—	—	—	—	—	—
70+	—	—	—	—	—	—
Total	155	178	7	8	43	32

SECTION 2

Ownership

Table S2.1.   *Sources:* Barbados: Jerome S. Handler, *The Unappropriated People* (Baltimore, 1974), p.25. St. Kitts: St. Kitts Blue-book, 1832, p.118 (S.K.G.A.). Virgin Islands: Stobo, "Statistical Table of the British Virgin Islands," C.O.239/9. Jamaica: Gisela Eisner, *Jamaica, 1830-1930* (Manchester, 1961), p.127; B.W. Higman, *Slave Population and Economy in Jamaica, 1807-1834* (Cambridge, 1976), pp.142, 298; Gad J. Heuman, *Between Black and White* (Westport, 1981), p.7. Cayman Islands: Neville Williams, *A History of the Cayman Islands* (Grand Cayman, 1970), pp.34, 54. Anguilla: C.O.239/12, No.157, 10 Jan. 1825. Barbuda: David Lowenthal and Colin G. Clarke, "Slave-Breeding in Barbuda," *Annals of the New York Academy of Sciences,* 292 (1977) 515. All other colonies: Robert Montgomery Martin, *Statistics of the Colonies of the British Empire* (London, 1839).

                   Note: Amerindians and Chinese are excluded from the total populations.

Table S2.2.   *Source:* T.71/520-22.

                   Note: "Bridgetown" comprises all slave-holdings lacking field laborers.

Table S2.3.   *Source:* T.71/501-502.

Table S2.4.   *Source:* T.71/378-79.

Table S2.5.   *Sources:* T.71/378-79, 501-502, 520-22.

          Notes: "Urban" includes all towns, in Trinidad and St. Lucia; "Bridgetown" is defined above (Table S2.2.). There are 103 missing cases in Trinidad and 15 in St. Lucia.

Table S2.6.   *Sources:* T.71/501-502, 378-79, 438-39.

          Notes: Slaveowner's sex is unknown for 23 slaves in St. Lucia, and 1,077 in Berbice. Another 920 slaves were jointly owned by males and females in Berbice.

Table S2.7.   *Source:* T.71/378-79.

Table S2.8.   *Source:* T.71/520-28.

          Note: "Bridgetown" defined as for Table S2.2.

Table S2.9.   *Source:* T.71/520-28.

          Note: "Bridgetown" defined as for Table S2.2.

Table S2.10.   *Source:* T.71/553-64.

          Note: "Bridgetown" is defined as all holdings identified in the compensation claims (T.71/790-803). Number of slaves to percentage colored columns are as in 1834.

Table S2.11.   *Source:* T.71.

Table S2.1. *White and Freedman Populations by Sex and Colony, c. 1830*

Colony	Year	Whites			Freedmen		
		Males	Females	Total	Males	Females	Total
Barbados	1829	7,049	7,910	14,959	2,609	2,537	5,146
St. Kitts	1812	n.a.	n.a.	1,612	n.a.	n.a.	1,996
Nevis	1834	n.a.	n.a.	500	n.a.	n.a.	n.a.
Antigua	1821	1,139	841	1,980	1,706	2,360	4,066
Montserrat	1828	139	176	315	337	481	818
Virgin Islands	1823	275	258	533	716	732	1,448
Jamaica	1834	n.a.	n.a.	16,600	n.a.	n.a.	42,000
Dominica	1833	382	338	720	1,673	2,141	3,814
St. Lucia	1831	500	480	980	1,190	1,350	2,540
St. Vincent	1825	n.a.	n.a.	1,301	n.a.	n.a.	2,824
Grenada	1834	490	171	661	1,675	2,012	3,687
Tobago	1833	248	56	304	506	760	1,266
Trinidad	1831	1,870	1,449	3,319	7,733	8,552	16,285
Demerara-Essequibo	1829	2,100	906	3,006	2,530	3,830	6,360
Berbice	1827	431	139	570	681	980	1,661
British Honduras	1833	143	80	223	832	956	1,788
Cayman Islands	1834	n.a.	n.a.	350	n.a.	n.a.	150
Bahamas	1826	2,279	2,291	4,570	897	1,362	2,259
Anguilla	1819	162	203	365	150	177	327
Barbuda	1834	3	–	3	–	–	–
Total	1830			52,871			98,435

ble S2.2. *Distribution of Slaveowners by Slave-holding Size-group and Parish: Barbados, 1817*

ish	1-10 Slaves	11-50 Slaves	50-100 Slaves	101-200 Slaves	201-300 Slaves	301-400 Slaves	401-500 Slaves	Total
Michael: Bridgetown	1,954	186	–	–	–	–	–	2,140
Michael: rural	276	187	11	14	3	–	–	491
James	104	31	7	10	5	–	–	157
Peter	295	65	12	19	1	–	–	392
Lucy	160	74	8	16	2	–	–	260
Andrew	95	19	6	12	3	–	–	135
Joseph	139	46	5	6	3	–	–	199
John	122	39	7	14	5	–	1	188
Philip	292	101	13	14	13	1	–	434
rist Church	278	95	20	28	3	–	1	425
George	209	68	15	12	7	1	–	312
Thomas	172	62	14	11	2	–	–	261
Total	4,096	973	118	156	47	2	2	5,394

Table S2.3. *Distribution of Slaves by Slave-holding Size-group and Crop-type: Trinidad, 1813*

Slaves per holding	Number of Slaves					
	Sugar	Coffee	Cocoa	Cotton	Provisions	Combined
1-5	5	223	66	72	118	56
6-10	118	239	132	87	117	76
11-20	366	450	206	162	222	197
21-30	739	124	235	147	110	74
31-40	1,259	96	251	–	106	–
41-50	1,014	–	43	84	44	–
51-75	2,644	–	107	54	71	246
76-100	2,465	–	–	–	–	379
101-150	1,863	–	–	–	–	–
151-200	872	–	–	–	–	189
201-250	912	–	–	–	–	–
Total	12,257	1,132	1,040	606	788	1,217

Table S2.4. *Distribution of Slaves by Slave-holding Size-group and Crop-type: St. Lucia, 1815*

Slaves per holding	Number of Slaves					
	Sugar	Coffee	Cocoa	Cotton	Provisions	Combined
1-5	10	63	25	27	30	20
6-10	25	164	77	31	53	–
11-20	100	389	128	60	71	31
21-30	156	372	78	54	21	103
31-40	222	248	–	–	–	40
41-50	316	307	47	48	–	90
51-75	1,206	418	52	–	–	55
76-100	1,213	–	–	–	–	–
101-150	1,796	–	–	–	–	–
151-200	679	–	–	–	–	–
201-250	682	–	–	–	–	250
301-350	338	–	–	–	–	–
Total	6,743	1,961	407	220	175	589

Table S2.5. *Distribution of Urban and Rural Slaves by Slave-holding Size-group: Trinidad, St. Lucia and Barbados, 1813-17*

Slaves per holding	Number of Slaves							
	Trinidad, 1813		St. Lucia, 1815		Barbados, 1817			
	Urban	Rural	Urban	Rural	Bridge-town	Rural St. Michael	St. John	St. Andrew
1	378	243	66	85	656	39	32	40
2	468	289	109	145	700	52	46	32
3	479	323	102	177	752	102	45	27
4	396	316	120	168	837	111	44	44
5	464	322	135	189	670	135	55	25
6-10	1,587	1,413	691	864	2,684	962	243	103
11-20	1,663	2,031	508	1,490	2,208	1,602	357	151
21-30	469	1,620	217	1,281	562	1,068	188	119
31-40	103	1,712	35	693	179	758	168	–
41-50	44	1,229	44	1,029	49	408	137	88
51-75	120	3,247	–	2,213	–	373	72	248
76-100	–	2,842	–	1,563	–	434	550	283
101-150	–	1,862	–	2,038	–	646	989	1,379
151-200	–	1,061	–	832	–	1,529	909	188
201-250	–	912	–	1,135	–	469	659	666
251-300	–	–	–	–	–	295	553	–
301-350	–	–	–	338	–	–	–	–
351-400	–	–	–	–	–	–	–	–
401-450	–	–	–	–	–	–	419	–
Total	6,171	19,422	2,027	14,240	9,297	8,983	5,466	3,393

Table S2.6. *Distribution of Slaves by Sex of Owner and Slave-holding Size-group: Trinidad, St. Lucia and Berbice, 1813-19*

Slaves per holding	Number of Slaves					
	Trinidad, 1813		St. Lucia, 1815		Berbice, 1819	
	Male Owners	Female Owners	Male Owners	Female Owners	Male Owners	Female Owners
1	356	266	56	95	64	36
2	378	381	106	148	62	52
3	404	398	102	177	66	75
4	348	364	144	144	100	76
5	396	390	169	155	65	60
6-10	1,745	1,261	851	704	390	300
11-20	2,617	1,078	1,227	763	423	232
21-30	1,865	224	1,067	431	492	25
31-40	1,572	243	511	217	306	–
41-50	872	401	887	186	267	–
51-75	3,199	174	2,040	173	1,199	305
76-100	2,571	357	1,135	428	1,652	–
101-150	1,863	–	1,819	219	4,527	–
151-200	906	155	832	–	3,855	353
201-250	912	–	888	247	2,253	–
251-300	–	–	–	–	1,635	–
301-350	–	–	338	–	2,240	–
351-400	–	–	–	–	374	–
401+	–	–	–	–	401	–
Total	20,004	5,692	12,172	4,087	20,371	1,514

[435]

Table S2.7. *Distribution of Slaves and Owners by Slave-holding Size-group and Sex of Owner, Urban and Rural: St. Lucia, 1815*

Slaves per holding	Male Slaveowners				Female Slaveowners			
	Urban		Rural		Urban		Rural	
	Owners	Slaves	Owners	Slaves	Owners	Slaves	Owners	Slaves
1	24	24	30	30	41	41	42	54
2	26	52	25	50	28	56	46	92
3	12	36	21	63	21	63	38	114
4	13	52	23	92	17	68	19	76
5	11	55	22	110	16	80	15	75
6-10	50	382	58	438	39	296	53	408
11-20	18	251	64	937	18	257	33	506
21-30	3	70	34	869	6	147	12	284
31-40	1	35	13	476	–	–	6	217
41-50	1	44	17	754	–	–	4	186
51-75	–	–	29	1,805	–	–	3	173
76-100	–	–	13	1,135	–	–	5	428
101-150	–	–	13	1,527	–	–	2	219
151-200	–	–	4	669	–	–	–	–
201-250	–	–	4	888	–	–	1	247
251-300	–	–	–	–	–	–	–	–
301-350	–	–	1	338	–	–	–	–
Total	159	1,001	371	10,181	186	1,008	279	3,079

Table S2.8. *Distribution of Owners and Slaves by Parish, Free Mulatto and Free Negro Slaveowners: Barbados, 1817*

Parish	Mulatto Men		Negro Men		Mulatto Women		Negro Women	
	Owners	Slaves	Owners	Slaves	Owners	Slaves	Owners	Slaves
St. Michael: Bridgetown	91	264	42	144	297	1,271	96	296
St. Michael: rural	12	72	3	14	18	151	3	18
St. James	4	12	–	–	1	2	–	–
St. Peter	9	34	1	1	8	14	5	13
St. Lucy	–	–	–	–	–	–	–	–
St. Andrew	2	12	–	–	2	16	–	–
St. Joseph	–	–	–	–	–	–	–	–
St. John	3	7	2	4	3	13	1	1
St. Philip	6	33	6	14	5	18	4	20
Christ Church	3	8	2	9	3	19	1	4
St. George	2	15	2	10	5	24	2	6
St. Thomas	–	–	2	5	2	5	2	4
Total	132	457	60	201	344	1,533	114	362

Table S2.9. *Slaveowners by Sex, Color and Slave-holding Size-group: Barbados, 1817*

Slaves per holding	Number of Slaveowners					
	[White]		Free Mulatto		Free Negro	
	Males	Females	Males	Females	Males	Females
Bridgetown						
1	234	245	41	90	14	32
2	112	142	16	52	7	21
3	75	113	11	33	4	15
4	71	83	6	34	7	8
5	55	44	7	20	3	5
6-10	156	134	7	38	5	14
11-20	65	61	3	26	2	1
21-30	14	6	–	4	–	–
31-40	5	–	–	–	–	–
41-50	1	–	–	–	–	–
51-75	–	–	–	–	–	–
76-100	–	–	–	–	–	–
101-150	–	–	–	–	–	–
151-200	–	–	–	–	–	–
201-250	–	–	–	–	–	–
251-300	–	–	–	–	–	–
Total	788	828	91	297	42	96
Rural St. Michael						
1	20	17	–	1	1	–
2	8	16	–	1	–	1
3	15	13	3	3	–	–
4	13	12	1	2	–	–
5	9	14	1	3	–	–
6-10	61	46	7	4	2	2
11-20	70	40	–	3	–	–
21-30	32	12	–	–	–	–
31-40	19	2	–	1	–	–
41-50	5	4	–	–	–	–
51-75	6	–	–	–	–	–
76-100	5	–	–	–	–	–
101-150	4	1	–	–	–	–
151-200	9	–	–	–	–	–
201-250	2	–	–	–	–	–
251-300	1	–	–	–	–	–
Total	279	177	12	18	3	3

Table S2.9. *Slaveowners: Barbados, 1817 (continued)*

Slaves per holding	[White]		Free Mulatto		Free Negro	
	Males	Females	Males	Females	Males	Females
St. John						
1	14	16	1	–	–	1
2	11	9	1	–	2	–
3	8	6	–	1	–	–
4	5	5	1	–	–	–
5	3	6	–	2	–	–
6-10	16	14	–	–	–	–
11-20	15	8	–	–	–	–
21-30	4	4	–	–	–	–
31-40	4	1	–	–	–	–
41-50	1	2	–	–	–	–
51-75	1	–	–	–	–	–
76-100	6	–	–	–	–	–
101-150	8	–	–	–	–	–
151-200	5	–	–	–	–	–
201-250	3	–	–	–	–	–
251-300	2	–	–	–	–	–
401-450	1	–	–	–	–	–
Total	107	71	3	3	2	1
St. Andrew						
1	21	18	1	–	–	–
2	7	9	–	–	–	–
3	6	3	–	–	–	–
4	4	6	–	1	–	–
5	2	3	–	–	–	–
6-10	7	7	–	–	–	–
11-20	8	2	1	1	–	–
21-30	4	1	–	–	–	–
31-40	–	–	–	–	–	–
41-50	2	–	–	–	–	–
51-75	3	1	–	–	–	–
76-100	3	–	–	–	–	–
101-150	11	–	–	–	–	–
151-200	1	–	–	–	–	–
201-250	3	–	–	–	–	–
251-300	–	–	–	–	–	–
401-450	–	–	–	–	–	–
Total	82	50	2	2	–	–

Table S2.10. *Demographic Characteristics by Slave-holding Size-group and Parish: Barbados, 1832-34*

Slaves per holding	Slaves	Owners	Males per 100 Females	% African	% Colored	Births per 1,000	Deaths per 1,000	% Manu-mitted
Bridgetown								
1-10	5,668	1,654	67.4	6.9	24.8	40.6	27.7	2.6
11-50	2,808	171	81.6	5.1	23.6	41.3	28.4	2.8
51·100	109	2	104.8	3.5	19.2	15.9	19.0	5.2
Total	8,585	1,827	73.0	6.2	24.3	40.4	27.8	2.7
Rural St. Michael								
1-10	2,289	683	77.5	5.0	14.9	41.9	33.4	3.5
11-50	3,237	172	93.5	4.2	18.5	37.9	23.3	2.4
51-100	465	7	67.0	3.7	11.8	39.9	31.7	0.2
101-200	2,098	15	89.3	2.8	8.3	37.5	30.7	0.4
201-300	291	1	79.0	0.0	3.3	32.8	47.4	0.0
301-400	319	1	90.6	0.0	10.7	30.1	41.8	0.0
Total	8,699	879	87.0	3.8	13.9	38.5	29.7	1.9
St. James								
1-10	674	153	70.6	1.8	12.9	42.9	37.2	1.5
11-50	678	34	95.6	1.0	15.2	45.9	29.0	0.6
51-100	434	6	115.6	1.2	4.1	39.0	28.9	3.7
101-200	2,145	14	96.3	2.3	11.4	42.5	31.8	0.0
201-300	474	2	89.6	1.9	24.1	34.5	36.8	0.0
Total	4,405	209	93.4	1.8	12.4	41.9	32.4	0.7
St. Peter								
1-10	888	250	69.0	2.1	23.2	38.1	27.0	1.1
11-50	1,480	75	89.9	1.5	21.3	40.2	26.2	1.1
51-100	724	10	102.6	2.2	8.6	33.9	19.6	0.0
101-200	2,496	18	88.2	1.8	11.4	40.4	36.5	0.1
201-300	265	1	89.6	0.8	4.5	41.2	18.5	0.0
Total	5,853	354	87.4	1.8	15.0	39.2	29.5	0.5
St. Lucy								
1-10	845	190	73.6	1.8	14.8	61.7	23.0	0.5
11-50	1,685	79	84.9	0.8	14.0	46.1	15.3	0.2
51-100	532	6	92.0	2.1	9.3	29.0	20.7	0.2
101-200	2,429	17	86.4	3.0	11.9	43.5	26.9	0.5
201-300	527	2	85.4	4.2	8.5	42.1	33.6	0.0
301-400	399	1	87.0	0.0	6.2	48.1	19.0	0.3
Total	6,417	295	84.9	2.2	11.9	45.1	23.1	0.3

Table S2.10. *Demographic Characteristics: Barbados, 1832-34 (cont.)*

Slaves per holding	Slaves	Owners	Males per 100 Females	% African	% Colored	Births per 1,000	Deaths per 1,000	% Manu- mitted
St. Andrew								
1-10	308	84	92.4	1.6	24.6	45.5	8.7	0.6
11-50	374	19	82.9	1.7	13.7	52.5	27.0	2.1
51-100	563	7	95.9	4.0	9.5	37.8	21.8	0.4
101-200	1,827	13	82.5	1.8	9.2	46.5	35.6	0.0
201-300	957	3	85.6	0.2	9.3	34.1	19.0	0.5
301-400	304	1	85.3	0.0	11.9	34.3	30.7	0.0
Total	4,333	127	85.6	1.5	10.8	42.1	27.2	0.4
St. Joseph								
1-10	564	138	88.5	4.1	12.9	56.0	15.5	0.0
11-50	917	42	84.2	2.2	12.0	45.6	20.5	0.5
51-100	696	11	97.9	1.6	10.8	41.4	25.4	0.4
101-200	1,262	8	80.9	1.0	10.4	45.0	24.4	0.6
201-300	255	1	96.0	1.2	9.9	53.9	24.7	0.4
301-400	330	1	91.7	0.0	7.4	52.2	38.7	0.6
Total	4,024	201	87.4	1.7	10.8	46.9	23.9	0.4
St. John								
1-10	460	121	86.9	2.5	15.3	54.8	16.5	0.0
11-50	623	26	100.0	3.9	15.2	40.5	20.2	0.5
51-100	222	4	91.1	2.0	20.9	28.9	9.0	0.5
101-200	1,804	13	84.6	1.0	13.9	41.6	28.1	0.2
201-300	2,662	11	85.0	1.3	17.5	46.4	32.9	0.0
301-400	401	1	87.4	0.3	4.9	50.0	23.9	0.0
Total	6,172	176	86.9	1.5	15.4	44.1	27.4	0.1
St. Philip								
1-10	941	268	80.7	5.5	15.5	41.7	22.2	3.1
11-50	1,965	95	90.0	6.6	11.7	48.9	22.7	0.5
51-100	1,060	15	96.5	6.2	13.9	48.5	29.1	0.3
101-200	3,325	21	86.0	2.2	10.6	38.9	31.7	0.4
201-300	2,438	10	81.4	1.2	8.5	45.0	29.5	0.5
401-500	454	1	81.1	0.9	8.0	47.1	23.6	1.1
Total	10,183	410	86.1	3.6	11.2	47.7	30.4	0.7
Christ Church								
1-10	1,216	323	80.4	5.0	18.0	40.0	22.7	1.0
11-50	2,286	103	83.4	4.0	18.6	45.2	23.7	1.4
51-100	1,274	20	90.3	5.1	10.5	31.6	22.8	0.8
101-200	1,878	13	91.4	4.2	11.6	39.1	21.0	0.4
201-300	3,419	15	89.7	0.9	11.8	33.3	23.1	0.4
Total	10,073	474	87.7	3.2	13.7	37.5	22.8	0.8

Table S2.10. *Demographic Characteristics: Barbados, 1832–34 (cont.)*

Slaves per holding	Slaves	Owners	Males per 100 Females	% African	% Colored	Births per 1,000	Deaths per 1,000	% Manu- mitted
St. George								
1-10	1,047	235	95.3	2.4	16.6	42.7	20.8	1.1
11-50	1,462	73	96.0	2.6	16.1	48.8	22.5	0.3
51-100	1,050	13	89.6	2.5	10.0	42.2	25.6	0.1
101-200	2,760	19	87.7	2.0	8.9	44.5	29.2	0.4
201-300	1,166	5	89.0	3.0	7.7	40.8	33.2	0.0
301-400	663	2	107.4	0.6	10.8	43.0	29.5	0.0
Total	8,148	347	91.8	2.2	11.1	45.7	28.1	0.3
St. Thomas								
1-10	765	152	81.2	1.4	20.6	45.6	15.7	0.1
11-50	1,001	46	92.9	2.3	12.1	37.6	20.7	2.8
51-100	1,362	17	93.7	2.1	9.6	35.6	24.8	0.2
101-200	1,709	12	91.1	1.2	11.6	33.2	24.6	0.2
201-300	593	2	78.9	1.0	10.6	34.0	12.9	0.8
Total	5,430	229	89.4	1.6	12.1	36.5	21.4	0.7
Total								
1-10	15,665	4,251	74.9	4.9	20.3	39.8	23.9	2.0
11-50	18,516	935	88.7	3.5	17.2	42.0	22.8	1.5
51-100	8,491	118	94.2	3.4	10.9	37.3	24.4	0.6
101-200	23,733	163	87.8	2.2	10.8	40.6	29.2	0.3
201-300	13,047	53	86.3	1.3	11.9	39.6	27.6	0.3
301-400	2,416	7	93.2	0.2	8.8	41.5	29.4	0.1
401-500	454	1	81.1	0.9	8.0	47.1	23.6	1.1
Total	82,322	5,528	86.2	2.9	14.0	40.3	26.0	0.9

Table S2.11. *Slave Sex Ratios by Slave-holding Size-group:*
Twelve Colonies, 1813-32

Colony	Males per 100 females								
	1-10 Slaves	11-50 Slaves	51-100 Slaves	101- 200 Slaves	201- 300 Slaves	301- 400 Slaves	401- 500 Slaves	501 + Slaves	Total
Barbados, 1817	71.4	86.9	91.1	89.0	81.3	84.7	68.8	—	83.9
Barbados, 1832	74.9	88.7	94.2	87.8	86.3	93.2	81.1	—	86.3
St. Kitts, 1817	70.1	110.3	105.2	95.1	95.0	93.8	89.7	102.5	92.4
Nevis, 1817	82.1	95.7	113.5	93.1	94.4	—	—	—	95.3
Antigua, 1832	76.7	114.5	83.0	88.6	93.2	86.0	85.1	—	87.4
Montserrat, 1817	77.6	101.8	87.0	85.4	97.3	—	—	—	85.5
Virgin Islands, 1818	65.3	86.6	99.4	90.0	81.3	72.0	91.6	99.0	88.1
St. Lucia, 1815	67.7	87.3	86.3	87.8	83.1	125.5	—	—	83.2
St. Vincent, 1817	78.4	127.9	107.1	101.7	103.8	107.0	103.4	95.5	102.1
Tobago, 1819	84.0	104.1	101.7	97.4	99.0	93.8	111.8	—	97.4
Trinidad, 1813	89.6	135.4	139.9	134.0	130.9	—	—	—	122.4
Berbice, 1819	102.2	173.8	140.2	120.7	126.4	124.7	120.3	—	127.6
Anguilla, 1827	75.8	83.5	79.7	82.8	107.2	—	—	—	83.1

SECTION 3

Birthplace

Table S3.1.   *Source:* T.71/253. The ethnic identifications are based chiefly on material in George Peter Murdock, *Africa: Its People and their Culture History* (New York, 1959), Philip D. Curtin, *The Atlantic Slave Trade* (Madison, 1969), B. David, *Les Origines de la Population Martiniquaise* (Martinique, 1973), and Gabriel Debien, *Les Esclaves aux Antilles Francaises* (Basse-Terre, 1974).

    Notes: (1) Names in parentheses are the labels found in the registration returns and the numbers, where given, indicate their frequency. These are preceded by an ethnic/tribal identification, which may be the same as the label in the registration returns.
(2) * indicates a shipping point.
(3) ** indicates a geographic region.

Table S3.2.   *Source:* T.71/378-79.

    Note: See notes to Table S3.1.

Table S3.3.   *Source:* T.71/501-503.

    Note: See notes to Table S3.1.

Table S3.4.   *Source:* T.71/438-39.

    Note: See notes to Table S3.1.

Table S3.5.   *Source:* T.71/261.

    Note: See notes to Table S3.1.

Table S3.6.   *Source:* T.71.

Table S3.1. *Birthplaces of Slaves: St. Kitts, 1817*

AFRICANS	Number of Slaves
Senegambia	
Malinke (Mandingo, Madingo, Mundingo)	510
Bambara	31
Kassanga (Kassan)	2
Fulbe (Poulan)	1
Senegal**	8
Goree*	1
Total	553
Sierra Leone	
Fulbe (Foula, Foulah, Fuller)	57
Temne (Timmini, Temonay)	55
Bulom (Bolum, Bullama, Elbollom)	9
Kissi (Kissi, Issee)	8
Mende (Mendie, Minday)	3
Susu (Susa)	1
Limba (Limbu)	1
Guinea-Bissau** (Portuguese)	1
Total	135
Windward Coast	
Mesurado hinterland** (Canga, Conga, Congar, Congau, Cango)	140
Gold Coast	
Elmina* (Mine, Mina, Minna)	67
Kormantyn* (Cramantie)	1
Gold Coast**	1
Total	69
Bight of Benin	
Popo (Popo, Papa, Papaw)	24
Oyo Yoruba (Nargo)	3
Edo (Iddo, Edoo)	3
Chamba	1
Lusu (Loosoo)	1
Bariba (Barba)	1
Total	33
Bight of Biafra	
Igbo (Ibo, Ebo, Eboe, Ebbo, Ebooh)	440
Northwestern Bantu (Moco, Mucco)	164
Atam (Attam)	2
Duala (Joular)	1
Brinkum	1
Total	608

Table S3.1. *Birthplaces: St. Kitts, 1817 (continued)*

	Number of Slaves
Central Africa	
Kongo (Congo, Congra)	1,337
Suku (Sooka, Sukah, Sugua)	3
Songo (Soango, Sogno)	3
Gulla	3
Soko (Socho)	2
Total	1,348
Unidentified	
Manny	5
Shruga	3
Pusso	3
Wamey	2
Sugar	2
Surugar	2
Guinea	2
Carabaro, Idele, Nimmua, Bracham, Sundye, Shage, Corrobodre, Tibbency, Fulna, Comba (1 of each)	10
Total	29
Africans (so described)	325
TOTAL AFRICANS	3,240
TOTAL CREOLES	16,928
TOTAL	20,168

* indicates a shipping point.
** indicates a geographic region.

Table S3.2. *Birthplaces of Slaves: St. Lucia, 1815*

AFRICANS	Number of Slaves
Senegambia	
Malinke (Mandingue 129, Mandingo 39, Mandinga 13, Manding 3, Mondongue 3, Mandine 2, Mendigo 1)	190
Fulbe (Poulard 9, Poularde 4)	13
Bambara	6
Cape Verde** (Cap Verd 11, Calvére 11, Calvert 5, Calvaire 5, Calver 2, Calverd 1, Calverre 1, Calver Coast 1)	37
Senegal**	8
Total	254

Table S3.2. *Birthplaces: St. Lucia, 1815 (continued)*

	Number of Slaves
Sierra Leone	
Susu (Soso 11, Sosso 2, Sose 1, Sausau 1)	15
Temne (Temelin 2, Timme 2, Timini 1, Themanin1, Timminie 1, Timinee 1)	8
Kissi (Quissy 2, Quici 1, Kissy 1, Quissi 1, de terre qui'ci 1)	6
Fulbe (Fuller 1, Foula 1, Tamla or Fuller 1)	3
Guinea-Bissau** (Portugais 2)	2
Total	34
Windward Coast	
Akwa (Aquia 1)	1
Cape Lahou* (Caplaou 222, Caplahou 9)	231
Windward Coast**	10
Total	242
Gold Coast	
Elmina* (Mine 67, Minne 1)	68
Kormantyn* (Cormantyne 13, Cormantie 10, Cormantil 4, Cromonter 1, Cormantee 1, Coromatel 1, Coromantyne 1, Koromantiel 1, Coromantel 1)	33
Gold Coast** (Gold Coast 39, Cote D'or 27)	66
Total	167
Bight of Benin	
Allada (Arada 25, Rada 11)	36
Chamba (Quiamba 7, Yamba 7, Chamba 5, Quiemba 3, Camba 2, Kiambas 2, Kamba 1, Camauba 1, Guiamba 1, Quimba 1)	30
Adda (Ado 8, Adeau 1, Adou 1)	10
Ana (Annan 3, Ana 2)	5
Hausa (Howsa 3)	3
Adangme (Ada 1, Addow 1)	2
Agwa (Hagra 1)	1
Popo (Papau 1)	1
Boulala (Boula 1)	1
Total	89
Bight of Biafra	
Igbo (Ibo 814, Ebo 74, Ibboe 2, Terre Ibo 1, Ibo Rouge 1, Hibo 1, Hibeau 1)	894
Northwestern Bantu (Moco 290, Mocot 1)	291
Ibibio (Bibi 51, Biby 5, Terre Bibi 1, Byby 1, Bibie 1)	59
Atam (Otam 3, Otoom 1)	4
Duala (Joular 1)	1
Bornu** (Bornoux 1)	1
Total	1,250

Table S3.2. *Birthplaces: St. Lucia, 1815 (continued)*

	Number of Slaves
Central Africa	
Kongo (Congo 573, Congresse 1)	574
Pol (Pola 2)	2
Hamba (Ohamba)	2
Mayumbe (Mayombe 2)	2
Sena (Senna 1)	1
Bamba	1
Sorongo (Salanga 1)	1
Balolo (Balolas 1)	1
Angola** (Cote d'angole 12, Angole 1, Angola 1)	18
Total	602
Unidentified	
Guinea	89
Afrique du Nord	4
Africain de Septentrionale	4
De terre	4
Terre ferme	4
Mandille	3
Doncor	3
Ho de nation	2
Clamentine	2
Negre de terre	2
Bon Caca	2
Bouriqui, Bembard, Aloco, Cote d'Abane, Gobil, Cote ferme, Feemba, Pangel, Rany, Chimdin, Tinbou, Auron, Fiemba, Guinée meridionale, Annara, Mémi, Nibas (1 of each)	17
Total	136
Africans (so described)	714
TOTAL AFRICANS	3,488

CREOLES

	Number of Slaves
St. Lucia	9,821
British Sugar Colonies	
St. Vincent	163
Grenade	108
Barbade	43
Antigua	18
Trinite	14
St. Christophe	6
Demerary	3
Tortola	2
Montserrat	2
Tabago	1
Total	360

Table S3.2. *Birthplaces: St. Lucia, 1815 (continued)*

	Number of Slaves
British Marginal Colonies	
Canouan (Canouan 18, Cannawan 35)	53
l'Union	6
Anguilla	2
Bermuda	1
Cariacou	1
Total	63
French Colonies	
Martinique	322
Dominique	65
Guadeloupe	42
Marie Galante	10
St. Domingue	1
Total	440
Other	
St. Barthelemy	20
St. Thomas	7
St. Martin	6
Curacao	3
St. Croix	3
Surinam	2
Americain	1
Creole de la Cote D'Espagnol	1
Creole de la grifats	1
Amerique du nord	1
Total	45
Creoles (so described)	2,021
TOTAL CREOLES	12,750
Unknown	44
TOTAL	16,282

Table S3.3. *Birthplaces of Slaves: Trinidad, 1813*

AFRICANS	Number of Slaves
Senegambia	
Malinke (Mandingo 1,418, Mandinga 2, Malinga 1)	1,421
Bambara	42
Woloff (Waloff 6, Jaloff 1, Jollof 3)	10
Bram (Bola 2, Bramba 1)	3
Fulbe (Poulard 3)	3
Mayo	1
Wangara (Wanga 1)	1
Diola (Yola 1)	1
Goree*	2
Cape Verde** (Calver 134, Calbe 5, Cape de Verd 2)	141
Senegal**	15
Gambia**	2
Coromandel**	1
Total	1,643
Sierra Leone	
Fulbe (Foula, Foulah, Fulla, Fuller 171)	171
Susu (Soso, Sosoe, Suso 144, Souci 1)	145
Temne (Timini, Timmani, Timane, Timene, Timinin, Timiny 148, Temana 5, Theminin 3, Tibbeny 3, Timna 2, Teminin 1, Temmana 1, Timana 1, Timina 1, Timmena 1, Timmni 1, Tamine 1, Tamana 1)	169
Kissi (Kissi, Kissee, Kissy 51, Quissi, Quissy 3, Kiskee 2, Kissa, Kissiman 1, Kuisi 1, Quisi 1, Bekissey 1, Qusisy 1, Tisi 1)	63
Bulom (Bullam 4, Bullman 2, Bolom 1, Bolonn 1)	8
Limba (Limba, Limber 6)	6
Timbou	5
Koranko (Courango 2, Couwango 1, Curranco 1)	4
Mende (Mendé 2, Mendo 1)	3
Ngere (Doo 3)	3
Vai (Fye 1, Vea 1)	2
Mano (Mana 1)	1
Kru (Nana 1)	1
Toma (Tomba 1)	1
Kankan [town] (Cancan 1)	1
Guinea-Bissau** (Portugas, Portugee, Portugues 12, Portogai 1, Portuguese Guina 1)	14
Total	597
Windward Coast	
Kwakwa (Quaqua 473)	473
Akwa (Aquia 6, Aquia 2)	8
Cape Lahou* (Caplaou 121, Caplahoo, Caplahou 38, Caplahout 1)	160
Mesurado hinterland** (Canga 160, Conga 44, Cangar 2, Congar 1)	207
Windward Coast**	33
Ivory Coast**	3
Total	884

Table S3.3. *Birthplaces: Trinidad, 1813 (continued)*

	Number of Slaves
Gold Coast	
Bonda (Bonna 5)	5
Wankyi (Wangwee 3, Wangwing 1)	4
Kokofu (Cocoa 3)	3
Fanti (Fantee 2, Fonde 1)	3
Bargu (Bargo 2)	2
Akan (Quaco 2)	2
Abron (Bron 1)	1
Kamana (Camana 1)	1
Wassa (Woser 1)	1
Kormantyn* (Coromantee, Coromanti 354, Caramanti 32)	386
Elmina* (Mine, Minre 283, Mini 14)	297
Anomabu* (Anamabou 2)	2
Cape Coast castle* (Cape Coast 2)	2
Gold Coast**	385
Total	1,094
Bight of Benin	
Allada (Arada, Irada 200, Rada 78, Ardda 1, Ladda 1, Raddah 1)	281
Chamba (Chamba 233, Kiamba 8, Quiamba 8, Quimba 7, Camba 5, Jamba 3, Quamba 3, Tiamba 3, Jampa 2, Chiamba 1, Cuamba 1, Giamba 1)	275
Popo (Papa 104, Pappa 5, Papaw 2, Pawpau 1)	112
Hausa (Ahousa, Aousa, Housa 95, Hausa 5, Ousa 5, Arousa 1, Ausar 1, Canaou 1, Haoussa 1)	109
Adda (Adda 83, Addo 15, Adow 5, Addé 1)	104
Adangme (Ado 37, Ada 10)	47
Ge (Mina, Minna 33)	33
Adja (Aja, Ajah 13, Adja 6, Aga 5, Agar 1, Ajas 1, Ajo 1)	27
Ana (Ana 24, Anne 1)	25
Yoruba (Nago 8, Yolaba 1, Yruba 1)	10
Bariba (Barba 3)	3
Konkomba (Combah 2, Comba 1)	3
Wara (Guala 3)	3
Attam (Autan 2)	2
Dian (Dya 2)	2
Whydah (Whadah 1, Wydan 1)	2
Agwa (Agra 1)	1
Kumba (Cumba 1)	1
Edo (Eddo 1)	1
Manga	1
Munga	1
Apa* (Appa 9, Apa 5, Apay 1)	15
Slave Coast**	20
Dahomey** (Dahomet 1, Dahomin 1)	2
Total	1,080

Table S3.3. *Birthplaces: Trinidad, 1813 (continued)*

	Number of Slaves
Bight of Biafra	
Igbo (Ibo 2,729, Ebo 134)	2,863
Northwestern Bantu (Moco 2,239, Moko 1)	2,240
Ibibio (Bibi 367, Ibibia 3, Bibe 1)	371
Lumbo (Lumba 5)	5
Anang (Annan 4)	4
Ijaw (Aijo 1)	1
Bana (Bahna 1)	1
Banda	1
Banggolo (Bangolo 1)	1
Baji (Bolo 1)	1
Holma (Homa 1)	1
Wawa	1
Calabar* (Calabar 19, Calabay 1, Caravali 1)	21
Bonny* (Bonny 4, Bonni 1)	5
Gaboon**	4
Total	5,520
Central Africa	
Kongo (Congo 2,449, Gongo 1)	2,450
Soko (Socko 15, Soko 1, Soco 1)	17
Suku (Succo 13)	13
Samba	7
Vili (Loango 1, Vihi 4)	5
Ngala (Bangala, Bangara 3)	3
Mondonga (Mondongue 3)	3
Kasai (Bundu 2)	2
Hamba	2
Sorongo (Solongo 2)	2
Bachoko (Bacoco 1)	1
Ekonda (Baseca 1)	1
Kutshu (Bolono 1)	1
Cabinda (Cabonda 1)	1
Eton (Etton 1)	1
Kwese (Quesa 1)	1
Angola**	59
Total	2,569
Mozambique	
Yao (Ayo 1)	1
Nguni (Caffre 1)	1
Makoa (Macoua 1)	1
Mozambique**	8
Total	11

Table S3.3. *Birthplaces: Trinidad, 1813 (continued)*

	Number of Slaves
Unidentified	
Chique	9
Anooba	6
Morocco	6
Auca	5
Bouriqui	5
Bruckum	5
Gruma	5
Ossa	5
Alla	4
Aoia	4
Limbu	4
Capebon	3
Chababa	3
Jimba	3
Sicqui	3
Whougee	3
Abolou, Adaw, Afra, Agia, Attapa, Bassano, Bayon, Bayony, Bilicam, Bossa, Bourcam, Brekean, Bromé, Brucchi, Camisindo, Captaw, Caruba, Cataquoi, Chiqui, Dimba, Dinba, Doja, Gelingue, Guia, Guidon, Hido, Hiola, Immag, Inkerler, Keinsi, Kemba, Mamba, Mentic, Mimba, Nocobah, Quashy, Ramba, Remlis, Santin, Shava, Sisi, Sivomo, Tinsley, Wannawee, Whahou (2 of each)	90
Abai, Acola, Affa, Aguinia, Aio, Aloca, Ambaloer, Ambaloon, Angana, Angara, Anguia, Annaire, Aouix, Apas, Apouli, Arabe, Arian, Attanga, Auna, Avara, Aya, Ballyine, Bananda, Banbé, Bandy, Banqui, Bapa, Barbary, Bassett, Belumney, Bembi, Benga, Bobio, Bocou, Boino, Boisadore, Bononie, Boré, Borny, Bouba, Bouiebon, Boulican, Boulowon, Bournom, Bourrican. Bourriky, Boyas, Brickam, Brockham, Brogia, Brookham, Brooman, Brse, Brucum, Bruno, Bumbulo, Caive, Calvie, Cama, Candada, Caripe, Cavan, Cawao, Cezero, Cilbourn, Coeva, Cofin, Cola, Coli, Conaca, Conot, Copporo, Couci, Couna, Cribone, Cublin, Dabon, Daromain, Debo, Dibon, Dicky, Dogobia, Doibie, Douarou, Ecy, Eyo, Faveria, Ferrun, Folute, Frango, Froisi, Gain, Gesiba, Gonda, Gouamanoa, Goulmanken, Gourah, Grap, Grissy, Guiambas, Guilas, Guinea, Guramba, Gurmang, Hago, Haja, Iala, Igedda, Imaun, Jamy, Jola, Jolard, Kat, Kelebune, Keminee, Kiambo, Kimba, Kimina, Lancoma, Lanta, Leomi, Luger, Malabar, Malaquette, Mallamboo, Mamso, Mantee, Maraba, Martinboi, Massador, Matango, Mauloo, Mayaga, Mede, Min, Minda, Miso, Missibou, Mita, Mocombo, Modonte, Moiro, Molos, Molungo, Mombo, Mon, Mongueve, Monsolongo, Moquioco, Moseu, Nieve, Oco, Odu, Oreso, Oronso, Otame, Oubamai, Petty, Pouça, Quamende, Quida, Quinanco, Rhedoe, Riboo, Riddi, Rongo, Roui, Ruaco, Sadoin, Saso, Sauso, Sibbre, Siny, Solon, Sosola, Temimore, Timbla, Umbe, Uxo, Vivi, Wanee, Wangolo, Wangoo, Wanna, Wawee, Wayway, Willamalala, Wissal, Yamba, Youga (1 of each)	190
Total	353

Table S3.3. *Birthplaces: Trinidad, 1813 (continued)*

	Number of Slaves
Africans (so described)	233
TOTAL AFRICANS	13,984

CREOLES

Trinidad	7,088
British Sugar Colonies	
Grenada	746
St. Vincent	438
Antigua	257
St. Lucia	231
Barbados	160
St. Christopher	126
Montserrat	89
Tortola	61
Demerara (Demerara 56, Guiana 2)	58
Dominica	48
Nevis	37
Tobago	17
Jamaica	14
Total	2,282
British Marginal Colonies	
Grenadines (Mustique 58, Union Island 29, Bequia 21, Canouan 8, Becoya 8, Myro 4, Grenadines 4)	132
Bermuda	59
Carriacou	54
Bahamas	45
Anguilla	4
Total	294
French Colonies	
Martinique	962
Guadeloupe	428
Marigalant	35
The Saints	2
St. Dominique (St. Dominique 132, Dominique 30)	162
Cayenne (Cayenne 3, Cyanne 1)	4
Total	1,593
Spanish Colonies	
The Main (The Main 5, Spanish Main 45)	50
Cumana	22
Guiria	12
Margaritta	6
Rio Caribes	6

Table S3.3. *Birthplaces: Trinidad, 1813 (continued)*

	Number of Slaves
Baranca	4
Barcelona	4
Angostura	3
Caracas	3
Porto Rico	2
Puerto Cabello	1
Valencia	1
Cuba, St. Jago	
Hispaniola	1
Spanish St. Domingo	1
Deseada	1
Total	118
Other	
St. Martin	84
North America	41
St. Croix	25
St. Eustatius	22
Curacao	16
St. Thomas	15
St. Bartholomew	13
South America	2
Carupano	2
Carupa	2
Papaco	1
Madeira	1
Brazils	1
Jagurapo	1
Annah	1
Total	227
At Sea	31
TOTAL CREOLES	11,633
Unknown	79
TOTAL	25,696

Table S3.4. *Birthplaces of Slaves: Berbice, 1819*

AFRICANS	Number of Slaves
Senegambia	
Malinke (Mandingo 73, Mandinga 19, Mundingo 7, Madonga 2)	101
Bambara	10
Total	111
Sierra Leone	
Temne (Timini 7, Timinee 4, Timmany 3, Timmini 3, Timminy 2, Timme 2, Temine 1, Timine 1, Timina 1, Timne 1, Timmanee 1, Tamine 1)	27
Fulbe (Foulah 10, Foulla 8, Fulla 4, Foula 3, Fullah 1, Fuller 1)	27
Susu (Soso 17, Sasso 1)	18
Limba (Limba 6, Lemba 2)	8
Vai (Vie 1, Vay 1, Vye 1, Foi 1)	4
Kissi (Kissi 1, Kishee 1, Kissie 1)	3
Toma (Toma 2, Tomma 1)	3
Bulom (Bulon 1, Bullemy 1)	2
Total	92
Windward Coast	
Akwa (Aquilla 1)	1
Mesurado hinterland** (Canga 61, Conga 1)	62
Total	63
Gold Coast	
Wankyi (Waunwie 10, Wanwie 7, Wangwee 7, Waunawie 3, Wawe 2, Warwee 2, Wawee 1, Wamwee 1)	33
Dagari (Dagarie 11)	11
Kormantyn (Corromantin 45, Coromanti 39, Coromantee 29, Coromentie 10, Corremantie 4, Coromanty 3, Coromantie 2, Cromantie 2, Corimanti 2, Cromaty 1, Coramantee 1, Courmantin 1)	139
Elmina* (Amina 12, Momine 2)	14
Total	197
Bight of Benin	
Popo (Papa 61, Pappa 29, Papaw 20, Pappo 1, Pawpa 1, Papau 1)	113
Chamba (Chamba 48, Chiamba 16, Jamba 5, Chamber 5, Camba 3)	77
Hausa (Houssa 14, Aurissa 9, Ousa 5, Ausah 4, Hussa 3, Howsaw 2, Awisa 1)	38
Yoruba (Uraba 4, Euroba 4, Europa 1)	9
Adda (Addo 4, Adow 1, Adoe 1)	6
Munga (Mungo 1)	1
Bargu (Baraba 1)	1
Total	245

Table S3.4. *Birthplaces: Berbice, 1819 (continued)*

	Number of Slaves
Bight of Biafra	
Igbo (Ibo 76, Ebo 27, Hibo 5, Ebbo 2, Iboe 1)	111
Northwestern Bantu (Mocco 37, Moco 24, Moko 2, Mokko 1)	64
Holma (Hoa 3)	3
Duala (Joulla 1, Jolla 1, Joloa 1)	3
Atam (Attam 1)	1
Total	182
Central Africa	
Kongo (Congo 212)	212
Vili (Loango 11)	11
Soko (Sokko 2, Socko 1)	3
Lala (Balla 2)	2
Ndembu (Demba 2)	2
Gulla (Goolla 1)	1
Angola**	17
Total	248
Unidentified	
Nougoba	10
Conno	8
Berrai	4
Mumie	4
Mammena	3
Mammenie	2
Locco	2
Nungaba	2
Teckee, Dougoba, Doba, Iginy, Baracou, Zappa, Loco, Ookoo, Nemgoba, Morava, Boumy, Mammy, Nenno, Nimba, Surnah, Saracoorde, Meriba, Neguba, Goura, Curee, Toobe, Toopi, Benalley, Senuga, Coolah (1 of each)	25
Total	60
Africans (so described)	11,669
TOTAL AFRICANS	12,867

CREOLES

Berbice	10,071

Table S3.4. *Birthplaces: Berbice, 1819 (continued)*

	Number of Slaves
British Sugar Colonies	
Demerara	383
Barbados	180
St. Kitts	36
Grenada	30
Antigua	13
Tobago	5
Nevis	4
St. Vincent	4
Montserrat	3
Essequibo	2
Tortola	1
Dominica	1
Trinidad	1
Total	663
British Marginal Colonies	
Bermuda	6
Carriacou	4
Total	10
French Colonies	
Martinique	10
Guadeloupe	3
St. Domingo	1
Total	14
Other	
Surinam	30
St. Eustatius	6
Isle San Cruz	6
North America	2
St. Croix	1
America	1
Curacao	1
Virginia	1
St. Martins	1
Brasil	1
Total	50
Creoles (so described)	132
At sea	12
Islands	2
TOTAL CREOLES	10,954
Unknown	60
TOTAL	23,881

Table S3.5. *Birthplaces of Slaves: Anguilla, 1827*

AFRICANS	Number of Slaves
Senegambia	
Malinke (Mandingo)	22
Woloff (Jollow)	1
Total	23
Sierra Leone	
Fulbe (Fullo)	1
Gold Coast	
Elimina* (Minna)	2
Gold Coast**	1
Total	3
Bight of Biafra	
Igbo (Ebo)	4
Northwestern Bantu (Mucco)	2
Total	6
Central Africa	
Kongo (Congo)	20
Unidentified	
Buckoe	1
Africans (so described)	12
TOTAL AFRICANS	66

CREOLES	
Anguilla	2,344
British Colonies	
Barbados	7
St. Kitts	7
Antigua	4
Bermuda	3
Tortola	2
Dominica	1
St. Vincent	1
Trinidad	1
Spanish Town	1
Scrub Island	1
Total	28

Table S3.5. *Birthplaces: Anguilla, 1827 (continued)*

	Number of Slaves
Dutch Colonies	
St. Martin	33
Saba	1
Total	34
French Colonies	
St. Bartholomew	27
Danish Colonies	
St. Croix	4
TOTAL CREOLES	2,437
TOTAL	2,503

Table S3.6. *Percentage of Slaves African-born by Slave-holding Size-group: Ten Colonies, 1813*

Colony	Percentage African								
	1-10 Slaves	11-50 Slaves	51-100 Slaves	101-200 Slaves	201-300 Slaves	301-400 Slaves	401-500 Slaves	501 + Slaves	Total
Barbados, 1817	11.4	8.4	7.5	5.0	3.8	2.6	1.1	–	7.1
Barbados, 1832	4.9	3.5	3.4	2.2	1.3	0.2	0.9	–	2.9
St. Kitts, 1817	20.3	22.1	15.6	15.0	13.1	19.5	11.3	13.1	14.5
Nevis, 1817	22.7	19.1	17.0	12.3	13.2	–	–	–	14.5
Virgin Islands, 1818	16.6	16.2	20.7	12.8	5.9	4.7	16.5	14.2	14.9
St. Lucia, 1815	20.9	19.5	19.5	24.0	26.5	41.7	–	–	21.4
St. Vincent, 1817	35.8	43.4	41.4	37.0	38.3	42.3	40.9	32.3	38.8
Tobago, 1819	46.2	50.5	48.0	39.3	38.0	35.1	35.4	–	38.9
Trinidad, 1813	51.2	53.6	56.5	56.6	61.9	–	–	–	54.4
Berbice, 1819	53.4	62.6	57.9	50.9	55.2	50.6	71.8	–	53.9
Anguilla, 1827	1.4	1.6	3.1	6.4	4.9	–	–	–	2.6

SECTION 4

Age

Table S4.1.

Sources: Calculated from T.71, except that the data for Demerara-Essequibo are from *P.P.*, 1833, Vol. XXVI (700), "Slave Population (Slave Registries)," p.439, and those for the Bahamas are based on D. Gail Saunders, *The Slave Population of the Bahamas, 1783-1834* (M.Phil. thesis, University of the West Indies, 1978), Appendix 4.

Notes: (1) The *Antigua* data derive from a one-in-four sample of returns, stratified by slave-holding size.

(2) The *Jamaica* estimate is based on the registration data for nine parishes, containing 125,990 slaves or 36.5 per cent of the total population in 1817. See B.W. Higman, *Slave Population and Economy in Jamaica, 1807-1834* (Cambridge, 1976), pp.260-264. These parishes are used as models for the remaining twelve, matching them on the basis of similarity in mortality, fertility, sex ratio and African/creole ratio. St. John is used as the model for St. Thomas-in-the-Vale and St. Catherine, Vere for St. Dorothy, Clarendon for St. David and St. George, St. Elizabeth for St. Ann and St. Andrew, and St. James for Westmoreland, Hanover, Trelawny, St. Mary and St. Thomas-in-the-East. The age structure for each of these twelve parishes has been estimated by distributing the known population, by sex and birthplace, as in the model. The resulting island total has been corrected to match the known sex and African/creole ratios, by moving 4,059 slaves from the creoles to the Africans *pro rata*.

(3) The *Bahamas* data derive from calculations by Saunders for the nine largest islands, containing 8,209 slaves, or 82 per cent of the total. The remainder have been distributed *pro rata*, on the basis of the known sex and African/creole ratios.

Table S4.2.   *Source:* T.71/520-22.

                   Note: "Bridgetown" is distinguished from rural St. Michael by attributing all slave-holdings including agricultural slaves to the latter.

Table S4.3.   *Source:* Index 10493 (P.R.O.).

Table S4.4.   *Source:* T.71/364.

Table S4.5.   *Source:* T.71/451.

Table S4.6.   *Source:* T.71/361-62.

Table S4.7.   *Source:* T.71/378-79.

                   Note: The town populations are excluded from the following parish data.

Table S4.8.   *Source:* T.71/493-94.

                   Note: The populations of towns other than Kingstown are included in the parish data.

Table S4.9.   *Source:* T.71/265 and 267.

Table S4.10.   *Source:* T.71/304, 307, 319 and 322.

Table S4.11.   *Source:* T.71/305 and 310.

Table S4.12.   *Source:* T.71/461-62.

                   Note: The town populations are excluded from the parish data.

Table S4.13.   *Source:* T.71/501-502.

Table S4.14.   *Source:* T.71/520-22.

Table S4.15.   *Source:* T.71/253.

Table S4.16.   *Source:* T.71/451.

Table S4.17.   *Source:* T.71/370.

Table S4.18.   *Source:* T.71/378-79.

Table S4.19.   *Source:* T.71/493-94.

Table S4.20.   *Source:* T.71/461-62.

Table S4.21.   *Source:* T.71/438-39.

Table S4.22.   *Source:* T.71/261.

Table S4.23.   *Source:* T.71/501-503.

Note: Excluded from this table are 79 slaves for whom birthplace is unknown.

Table S4.24.   *Source:* T.71/378-79 (St. Lucia), 438-39 (Berbice).

Table S4.25.   *Source:* Calculated from Table S4.1.

Table S4.1. *Age Structure of Slaves by Sex, Birthplace and Colony, 1813-34*

Age group	Africans			Creoles			Total
	Males	Females	Total	Males	Females	Total	
Barbados, 1817							
0-4	–	–	–	5,742	5,959	11,701	11,701
5-9	–	–	–	4,460	4,616	9,076	9,076˙
10-14	8	7	15	4,622	4,794	9,416	9,431
15-19	115	62	177	3,515	3,750	7,265	7,442
20-24	362	320	682	2,987	3,317	6,304	6,986
25-29	604	555	1,159	2,444	3,081	5,525	6,684
30-34	561	588	1,149	2,009	2,668	4,677	5,826
35-39	448	388	836	1,946	2,500	4,446	5,282
40-44	233	238	471	1,461	2,148	3,609	4,080
45-49	127	101	228	1,165	1,781	2,946	3,174
50-54	94	113	207	959	1,620	2,579	2,786
55-59	40	73	113	489	947	1,436	1,549
60-64	62	131	193	441	912	1,353	1,546
65-69	22	52	74	207	432	639	713
70+	56	150	206	261	741	1,002	1,208
Unknown	1	–	1	4	1	5	6
Total	2,733	2,778	5,511	32,712	39,267	71,979	77,490
St. Kitts, 1817							
0-4	–	–	–	1,128	1,208	2,336	2,336
5-9	–	–	–	1,086	1,087	2,173	2,173
10-14	3	3	6	1,101	1,046	2,147	2,153
15-19	75	40	115	748	798	1,546	1,661
20-24	162	118	280	757	784	1,541	1,821
25-29	289	216	505	662	741	1,403	1,908
30-34	313	235	548	575	727	1,302	1,850
35-39	214	146	360	458	533	991	1,351
40-44	181	123	304	386	525	911	1,215
45-49	141	73	214	339	437	776	990
50-54	139	117	256	262	361	623	879
55-59	75	72	147	124	210	334	481
60-64	109	108	217	132	249	381	598
65-69	40	46	86	47	113	160	246
70+	94	106	200	72	181	253	453
Unknown	–	2	2	–	–	–	2
Total	1,835	1,405	3,240	7,877	9,000	16,877	20,117

Table S4.1. *Age by Colony (continued)*

Age group	Africans			Creoles			Total
	Males	Females	Total	Males	Females	Total	
Nevis, 1817							
0-4	–	–	–	500	575	1,075	1,075
5-9	–	–	–	545	497	1,042	1,042
10-14	1	–	1	572	490	1,062	1,063
15-19	14	7	21	373	347	720	741
20-24	63	48	111	319	352	671	782
25-29	104	85	189	301	335	636	825
30-34	128	95	223	281	315	596	819
35-39	138	85	223	272	282	554	777
40-44	115	92	207	225	254	479	686
45-49	41	26	67	189	234	423	490
50-54	43	40	83	144	219	363	446
55-59	26	35	61	55	114	169	230
60-64	49	47	96	67	123	190	286
65-69	27	23	50	29	59	88	138
70+	28	44	72	52	126	178	250
Unknown	–	–	–	6	6	12	12
Total	777	627	1,404	3,930	4,328	8,258	9,662

Age group	Males	Females	Total	Males	Females	Total	
	Antigua, 1832 (estimated)			*Montserrat, 1831*			
0-4	1,705	1,688	3,393	478	481	959	
5-9	1,638	1,597	3,235	353	412	765	
10-14	1,383	1,391	2,774	320	357	677	
15-19	1,217	1,429	2,646	321	304	625	
20-24	1,269	1,365	2,634	259	260	519	
25-29	999	1,127	2,126	278	291	569	
30-34	1,101	947	2,048	252	235	487	
35-39	1,005	1,130	2,135	209	222	431	
40-44	996	1,017	2,013	158	204	362	
45-49	773	886	1,659	117	150	267	
50-54	624	874	1,498	100	141	241	
55-59	369	537	906	67	98	165	
60-64	349	532	881	37	84	121	
65-69	113	299	412	8	31	39	
70+	192	494	686	19	71	90	
Unknown	–	–	–	4	1	5	
Total	13,733	15,313	29,046	2,980	3,342	6,322	

Table S4.1. *Age by Colony (continued)*

Age group	Africans			Creoles			Total
	Males	Females	Total	Males	Females	Total	
Virgin Islands, 1818							
0-4	–	–	–	384	415	799	799
5-9	–	–	–	373	384	757	757
10-14	–	–	–	400	400	800	800
15-19	5	–	5	301	306	607	612
20-24	51	35	86	233	259	492	578
25-29	71	66	137	225	313	538	675
30-34	100	65	165	174	272	446	611
35-39	90	55	145	138	169	307	452
40-44	69	42	111	143	211	354	465
45-49	40	43	83	81	127	208	291
50-54	54	56	110	90	127	217	327
55-59	21	27	48	47	76	123	171
60-64	24	35	59	53	70	123	182
65-69	12	8	20	12	40	52	72
70+	21	38	59	21	42	63	122
Unknown	1	–	1	–	1	1	2
Total	559	470	1,029	2,675	3,212	5,887	6,916
Jamaica, 1817 (estimated)							
0-4	–	–	–	17,199	18,237	35,436	35,436
5-9	–	–	–	16,993	17,594	34,587	34,587
10-14	23	44	67	15,985	15,203	31,188	31,255
15-19	735	314	1,049	11,932	12,026	23,958	25,007
20-24	3,592	2,732	6,324	9,774	10,945	20,719	27,043
25-29	8,745	6,694	15,439	8,234	9,667	17,901	33,340
30-34	11,429	9,789	21,218	6,361	7,510	13,871	35,089
35-39	12,063	10,051	22,114	5,431	6,389	11,820	33,934
40-44	10,207	7,687	17,894	3,768	4,899	8,667	26,561
45-49	6,910	5,342	12,252	2,589	3.632	6,221	18,473
50-54	5,861	5,387	11,248	2,372	3,056	5,428	16,676
55-59	3,161	2,978	6,139	1,145	1,802	2,947	9,086
60-64	3,055	3,034	6,089	1,149	1,751	2,900	8,989
65-69	1,367	1,388	2,755	451	858	1,309	4,064
70+	1,994	2,257	4,251	723	1,499	2,222	6,473
Unknown	33	31	64	38	35	73	137
Total	69,175	57,728	126,903	104,144	115,103	219,247	346,150

Table S4.1. *Age by Colony (continued)*

Age group	Males	Females	Total
Dominica, 1829			
0-4	896	930	1,826
5-9	715	734	1,449
10-14	717	708	1,425
15-19	691	763	1,454
20-24	684	736	1,420
25-29	485	473	958
30-34	489	490	979
35-39	509	630	1,139
40-44	615	805	1,420
45-49	452	464	916
50-54	310	358	668
55-59	144	170	314
60-64	122	154	276
65-69	46	67	113
70+	82	108	190
Unknown	29	42	71
Total	6,986	7,632	14,618

Age group	Africans			Creoles			Total
	Males	Females	Total	Males	Females	Total	
St. Lucia, 1815							
0-4	–	–	–	950	1,100	2,050	2,050
5-9	1	2	3	843	900	1,743	1,748
10-14	18	4	22	907	863	1,770	1,793
15-19	71	42	113	608	667	1,275	1,390
20-24	163	137	300	604	703	1,307	1,609
25-29	250	165	415	588	679	1,267	1,687
30-34	241	188	429	435	498	933	1,366
35-39	236	220	456	241	410	651	1,111
40-44	178	255	433	150	349	499	938
45-49	146	201	347	126	260	386	735
50-54	114	171	285	95	206	301	586
55-59	74	112	186	51	133	184	372
60-64	77	126	203	53	127	180	385
65-69	41	73	114	22	63	85	200
70+	62	114	176	33	61	94	271
Unknown	5	1	6	17	8	25	41
Total	1,677	1,811	3,488	5,723	7,027	12,750	16,282*

* Includes 44 slaves whose birthplace is unknown.

Table S4.1. *Age by Colony (continued)*

Age group	Africans			Creoles			Total
	Males	Females	Total	Males	Females	Total	
St. Vincent, 1817							
0-4	–	–	–	1,272	1,386	2,658	2,658
5-9	–	–	–	1,324	1,303	2,627	2,627
10-14	6	1	7	1,327	1,208	2,535	2,542
15-19	46	21	67	948	999	1,947	2,014
20-24	244	160	404	709	797	1,506	1,910
25-29	650	463	1,113	549	567	1,116	2,229
30-34	978	781	1,759	401	495	896	2,655
35-39	977	874	1,851	348	444	792	2,643
40-44	791	734	1,525	228	280	508	2,033
45-49	566	457	1,023	171	166	337	1,360
50-54	433	391	824	107	122	229	1,053
55-59	216	175	391	60	72	132	523
60-64	212	209	421	29	68	97	518
65-69	84	90	174	19	19	38	212
70+	114	134	248	20	43	63	311
Unknown	3	11	14	3	3	6	20
Total	5,320	4,501	9,821	7,515	7,972	15,487	25,308
Grenada, 1817							
0-4	–	–	–	1,257	1,332	2,589	2,589
5-9	–	–	–	1,218	1,264	2,482	2,482
10-14	1	2	3	1,336	1,253	2,589	2,592
15-19	45	35	80	1,037	1,116	2,153	2,233
20-24	230	153	383	846	997	1,843	2,226
25-29	491	361	852	873	956	1,829	2,681
30-34	654	506	1,160	704	900	1,604	2,764
35-39	744	586	1,330	554	689	1,243	2,573
40-44	642	581	1,223	369	473	842	2,065
45-49	521	480	1,001	249	356	605	1,606
50-54	482	464	946	155	282	437	1,383
55-59	359	322	681	98	157	255	936
60-64	354	336	690	84	102	186	876
65-69	131	164	295	29	80	109	404
70+	197	263	460	44	100	144	604
Unknown	4	1	5	6	7	13	18
Total	4,855	4,254	9,109	8,859	10,064	18,923	28,032

Table S4.1. *Age by Colony (continued)*

Age group	Africans			Creoles			Total
	Males	Females	Total	Males	Females	Total	
Tobago, 1819							
0-4	–	–	–	714	793	1,507	1,507
5-9	–	–	–	802	790	1,592	1,592
10-14	1	–	1	743	715	1,458	1,459
15-19	12	5	17	579	584	1,163	1,180
20-24	60	63	123	438	472	910	1,033
25-29	263	227	490	394	471	865	1,355
30-34	471	384	855	312	377	689	1,544
35-39	576	476	1,052	253	301	554	1,606
40-44	550	488	1,038	127	174	301	1,339
45-49	383	371	754	56	69	125	879
50-54	291	325	616	23	42	65	681
55-59	193	246	439	12	14	26	465
60-64	206	230	436	10	13	23	459
65-69	80	98	178	5	10	15	193
70+	65	88	153	2	6	8	161
Unknown	1	1	2	2	–	2	4
Total	3,152	3,002	6,154	4,472	4,831	9,303	15,457
Trinidad, 1813							
0-4	3	2	5	1,415	1,495	2,910	2,915
5-9	5	6	11	984	1,062	2,046	2,058
10-14	69	40	109	760	732	1,492	1,602
15-19	711	417	1,128	550	497	1,047	2,175
20-24	1,426	1,113	2,539	521	532	1,053	3,594
25-29	1,847	1,434	3,281	440	476	916	4,204
30-34	1,586	1,020	2,606	389	341	730	3,339
35-39	1,010	582	1,592	236	229	465	2,059
40-44	716	424	1,140	162	185	347	1,490
45-49	396	271	667	123	117	240	910
50-54	244	178	422	95	94	189	613
55-59	108	73	181	35	29	64	247
60-64	102	75	177	33	33	66	243
65-69	30	19	49	13	11	24	75
70+	50	27	77	22	22	44	172
Unknown	–	–	–	–	–	–	–
Total	8,303	5,681	13,984	5,778	5,855	11,633	25,696*

* Includes 79 slaves whose birthplace is unknown.

Table S4.1. *Age by Colony (continued)*

Age group	Africans			Creoles			Total
	Males	Females	Total	Males	Females	Total	
Berbice, 1819							
0-4	–	–	–	1,290	1,350	2,640	2,640
5-9	–	–	–	1,082	1,204	2,286	2,287
10-14	2	6	8	990	946	1,936	1,944
15-19	55	28	83	638	602	1,240	1,323
20-24	409	283	692	282	352	634	1,326
25-29	1,534	1,081	2,615	282	343	625	3,241
30-34	1,656	1,096	2,752	228	223	451	3,206
35-39	2,008	1,136	3,144	194	202	396	3,540
40-44	1,075	539	1,614	118	128	246	1,860
45-49	648	283	931	102	81	183	1,114
50-54	257	153	410	35	58	93	504
55-59	133	94	227	30	39	69	297
60-64	109	103	212	27	22	49	261
65-69	35	36	71	11	15	26	97
70+	32	32	64	16	25	41	105
Unknown	41	2	43	9	30	39	120
Total	7,994	4,872	12,866	5,334	5,620	10,954	23,865*

Age group	1817		1820			1823	1826	1829		1832
Demerara-Essequibo, 1817-1832										
< 2	3,044	< 3	4,868	< 3	Males	2,233	2,251	2,319		1,974
					Females	2,279	2,243	2,365		2,112
2-5	6,770	3-5	3,749			3,209	2,558	2,926		2,744
5-10	7,412		7,723			7,229	5,736	5,251		5,401
10-20	10,080		11,197			12,831	13,677	13,060	10-16	6,115
20-30	19,044		12,403			8,824	8,792	9,472	16-30 Males	8,008
									Females	8,005
30-40	19,998		21,169			17,872	15,524	10,835		8,345
40-50	7,414		11,185			14,074	14,623	14,856		13,585
50-60	2,470		3,553			4,640	4,505	6,239		7,179
60-70	714		1,191			1,409	1,193	1,621		1,613
70-80	111		234			299	218	417		363
80-90	17		44			44	31	56		40
90-100	11		12			5	6	8		7
>100	–		4			2	1	1		2
Unknown	78		44			27	24	41		24
Total	77,163		77,376			74,977	71,382	69,467		65,517

* Includes 45 slaves whose birthplace is unknown.

Table S4.1. *Age by Colony (continued)*

Age group	Males	Females	Total
Barbuda, 1832			
0-4	41	37	78
5-9	32	51	83
10-14	26	37	63
15-19	26	24	50
20-24	19	30	49
25-29	17	19	36
30-34	10	20 ˙	30
35-39	5	8	13
40-44	5	6	11
45-49	2	6	8
50-54	10	20	30
55-59	8	6	14
60-64	11	2	13
65-69	–	2	2
70+	2	10	12
Unknown	–	–	–
Total	214	278	492

Age group	Males	Females	Total	Males	Females	Total
	British Honduras, 1834			*Cayman Islands, 1834*		
0-4	102	95	197	52	65	117
5-9	84	81	165	59	63	122
10-14	77	70	147	44	64	108
15-19	84	73	157	50	27	77
20-24	111	95	206	35	46	81
25-29	78	76	154	54	50	104
30-34	79	47	126	33	28	61
35-39	83	47	130	30	29	59
40-44	130	56	186	26	30	56
45-49	135	40	175	36	32	68
50-54	98	23	121	29	18	47
55-59	59	15	74	10	17	27
60-64	44	9	53	21	11	32
65-69	13	3	16	8	10	18
70+	17	6	23	3	5	8
Unknown	2	–	2	–	–	–
Total	1,196	736	1,932	490	495	985

Table S4.1. *Age by Colony (continued)*

Age group	Africans			Creoles			Total
	Males	Females	Total	Males	Females	Total	
Bahamas, 1834							
0-4	–	–	–	841	827	1,668	1,668
5-9	–	–	–	608	712	1,320	1,320
10-14	–	–	–	550	607	1,157	1,157
15-19	1	–	1	516	514	1,030	1,031
20-24	3	–	3	426	491	917	920
25-29	1	–	1	350	362	712	713
30-34	8	1	9	281	346	627	636
35-39	34	14	48	224	269	493	541
40-44	79	63	142	175	181	356	498
45-49	81	58	139	138	118	256	395
50-54	112	61	173	73	106	179	352
55-59	65	43	108	71	84	155	263
60-64	87	66	153	50	47	97	250
65-69	36	36	72	17	18	35	107
70+	50	39	89	22	31	53	142
Unknown	–	–	–	2	7	9	9
Total	557	381	938	4,344	4,720	9,064	10,002
Anguilla, 1827							
0-4	–	–	–	206	206	412	412
5-9	–	–	–	155	163	318	318
10-14	–	–	–	160	138	298	298
15-19	–	–	–	122	144	266	266
20-24	–	–	–	102	141	243	243
25-29	2	–	2	82	118	200	202
30-34	6	1	7	67	107	174	181
35-39	1	4	5	48	69	117	122
40-44	4	1	5	55	81	136	141
45-49	2	2	4	33	37	70	74
50-54	5	5	10	28	52	80	90
55-59	3	5	8	14	35	49	57
60-64	6	6	12	18	22	40	52
65-69	2	2	4	5	7	12	16
70+	4	5	9	6	16	22	31
Unknown	–	–	–	–	–	–	–
Total	35	31	66	1,101	1,336	2,437	2,503

Table S4.2. *Age Structure of Slaves by Sex, Birthplace and Parish: Barbados, 1817*

Age group	Africans			Creoles			Total
	Males	Females	Total	Males	Females	Total	
St. Michael: Bridgetown							
0-4	–	–	–	655	751	1,406	1,406
5-9	–	–	–	552	576	1,128	1,128
10-14	3	5	8	508	589	1,097	1,105
15-19	31	20	51	379	463	842	893
20-24	111	121	232	319	431	750	982
25-29	169	184	353	244	364	608	961
30-34	124	149	273	175	286	461	734
35-39	101	97	198	146	265	411	609
40-44	59	57	116	77	225	302	418
45-49	34	33	67	63	166	229	296
50-54	18	29	47	44	188	232	279
55-59	7	11	18	22	83	105	123
60-64	10	37	47	22	101	123	170
65-69	4	13	17	11	31	42	59
70+	2	35	37	12	85	97	134
Unknown	–	–	–	–	–	–	–
Total	673	791	1,464	3,229	4,604	7,833	9,297
St. Michael: Rural							
0-4	–	–	–	668	743	1,411	1,411
5-9	–	–	–	471	518	989	989
10-14	2	–	2	549	549	1,098	1,100
15-19	10	17	27	393	414	807	834
20-24	51	29	80	361	400	761	841
25-29	92	76	168	240	368	608	776
30-34	72	88	160	238	280	518	678
35-39	56	42	98	192	260	452	550
40-44	28	30	58	171	227	398	456
45-49	16	12	28	148	205	353	381
50-54	8	23	31	127	209	336	367
55-59	4	11	15	61	113	174	189
60-64	3	18	21	63	116	179	200
65-69	3	4	7	22	42	64	71
70+	14	22	36	20	83	103	139
Unknown	–	–	–	–	–	–	–
Total	359	372	731	3,724	4,527	8,251	8,982

Table S4.2. *Age by Parish: Barbados, 1817 (continued)*

Age group	Africans			Creoles			Total
	Males	Females	Total	Males	Females	Total	
St. James							
0-4	–	–	–	267	274	541	541
5-9	–	–	–	195	216	411	411
10-14	–	–	–	238	243	481	481
15-19	–	2	2	198	177	375	377
20-24	4	8	12	151	155	306	318
25-29	14	4	18	125	119	244	262
30-34	20	13	33	114	127	241	274
35-39	22	7	29	109	144	253	282
40-44	7	6	13	108	161	269	282
45-49	3	2	5	67	109	176	181
50-54	7	3	10	58	81	139	149
55-59	1	2	3	37	64	101	104
60-64	8	6	14	38	61	99	113
65-69	–	2	2	21	26	47	49
70+	4	5	9	19	55	74	83
Unknown	–	–	–	1	–	1	1
Total	90	60	150	1,746	2,012	3,758	3,908
St. Peter							
0-4	–	–	–	467	483	950	950
5-9	–	–	–	323	338	661	661
10-14	–	–	–	366	369	735	735
15-19	12	4	16	288	282	570	586
20-24	17	14	31	249	285	534	565
25-29	26	33	59	207	241	448	507
30-34	49	29	78	144	178	322	400
35-39	37	23	60	172	211	383	443
40-44	22	14	36	142	167	309	345
45-49	8	3	11	111	149	260	271
50-54	8	5	13	78	120	198	211
55-59	4	3	7	44	98	142	149
60-64	5	9	14	46	84	130	144
65-69	6	1	7	16	41	57	64
70+	6	13	19	18	63	81	100
Unknown	–	–	–	1	–	1	1
Total	200	151	351	2,672	3,109	5,781	6,132

Table S4.2. *Age by Parish: Barbados, 1817 (continued)*

Age group	Africans			Creoles			Total
	Males	Females	Total	Males	Females	Total	
St. Lucy							
0-4	–	–	–	432	439	871	871
5-9	–	–	–	337	327	664	664
10-14	–	–	–	339	325	664	664
15-19	17	4	21	239	276	515	536
20-24	26	6	32	227	218	445	477
25-29	40	31	71	176	248	424	495
30-34	27	26	53	155	199	354	407
35-39	21	19	40	136	146	282	322
40-44	8	11	19	115	163	278	297
45-49	4	5	9	86	135	221	230
50-54	3	3	6	77	122	199	205
55-59	2	2	4	33	59	92	96
60-64	1	1	2	35	55	90	92
65-69	–	–	–	14	27	41	41
70+	1	4	5	21	42	63	68
Unknown	–	–	–	–	–	–	–
Total	150	112	262	2,422	2,781	5,203	5,465
St. Andrew							
0-4	–	–	–	222	216	438	438
5-9	–	–	–	208	217	425	425
10-14	–	–	–	180	182	362	362
15-19	1	3	4	160	158	318	322
20-24	10	4	14	142	137	279	293
25-29	5	10	15	153	162	315	330
30-34	26	8	34	105	119	224	258
35-39	15	16	31	109	97	206	237
40-44	6	5	11	77	99	176	187
45-49	3	1	4	61	90	151	155
50-54	3	3	6	46	73	119	125
55-59	1	3	4	30	42	72	76
60-64	1	2	3	28	38	66	69
65-69	–	4	4	13	23	36	40
70+	4	6	10	20	42	62	72
Unknown	2	2	4	–	–	–	4
Total	77	67	144	1,554	1,695	3,249	3,393

Table S4.2. *Age by Parish: Barbados, 1817 (continued)*

Age group	Africans			Creoles			Total
	Males	Females	Total	Males	Females	Total	
St. Joseph							
0-4	–	–	–	271	256	527	527
5-9	–	–	–	206	226	432	432
10-14	–	–	–	207	235	442	442
15-19	7	4	11	140	154	294	305
20-24	9	16	25	122	141	263	288
25-29	16	9	25	107	137	244	269
30-34	17	14	31	87	140	227	258
35-39	13	6	19	110	140	250	269
40-44	4	8	12	62	117	179	191
45-49	3	2	5	49	68	117	122
50-54	3	3	6	44	79	123	129
55-59	2	4	6	28	37	65	71
60-64	1	6	7	19	48	67	74
65-69	1	2	3	11	26	37	40
70+	2	7	9	10	35	45	54
Unknown	–	–	–	–	–	–	–
Total	78	81	159	1,473	1,839	3,312	3,471
St. John							
0-4	–	–	–	403	378	781	781
5-9	–	–	–	314	350	664	664
10-14	–	–	–	379	339	718	718
15-19	6	–	6	248	269	517	523
20-24	14	12	26	198	215	413	439
25-29	23	17	40	173	199	372	412
30-34	17	26	43	162	233	395	438
35-39	14	10	24	169	177	346	370
40-44	6	9	15	122	167	289	304
45-49	3	4	7	112	133	245	252
50-54	7	7	14	70	98	168	182
55-59	3	7	10	32	70	102	112
60-64	3	10	13	39	65	104	117
65-69	–	2	2	12	42	54	56
70+	4	8	12	23	63	86	98
Unknown	–	–	–	–	–	–	–
Total	100	112	212	2,456	2,798	5,254	5,466

Table S4.2. *Age by Parish: Barbados, 1817 (continued)*

Age group	Africans			Creoles			Total
	Males	Females	Total	Males	Females	Total	
St. Philip							
0-4	–	–	–	700	737	1,437	1,437
5-9	–	–	–	561	581	1,142	1,142
10-14	2	–	2	566	612	1,178	1,180
15-19	14	–	14	466	473	939	953
20-24	33	44	77	354	380	734	811
25-29	76	78	154	291	383	674	828
30-34	78	82	160	223	336	559	719
35-39	61	76	137	220	278	498	635
40-44	32	37	69	144	252	396	465
45-49	24	12	36	142	235	377	413
50-54	11	10	21	127	189	316	337
55-59	4	14	18	65	98	163	181
60-64	13	21	34	47	107	154	188
65-69	3	8	11	30	56	86	97
70+	9	16	25	41	82	123	148
Unknown	–	–	–	1	–	1	1
Total	360	398	758	3,978	4,799	8,777	9,535
Christ Church							
0-4	–	–	–	755	787	1,542	1,542
5-9	–	–	–	612	601	1,213	1,213
10-14	1	1	2	574	605	1,179	1,181
15-19	14	6	20	425	464	889	909
20-24	51	42	93	374	419	793	886
25-29	80	63	143	320	397	717	860
30-34	68	87	155	285	329	614	769
35-39	56	40	96	254	329	583	679
40-44	35	34	69	192	231	423	492
45-59	13	13	26	142	216	358	384
50-54	14	13	27	137	190	327	354
55-59	6	5	11	66	131	197	208
60-64	6	7	13	51	104	155	168
65-69	1	12	13	25	65	90	103
+70	6	15	21	44	97	141	162
Unknown	–	–	–	1	–	1	1
Total	351	338	689	4,257	4,965	9,222	9,911

Table S4.2. *Age by Parish: Barbados, 1817 (continued)*

Age group	Africans			Creoles			Total
	Males	Females	Total	Males	Females	Total	
St. George							
0-4	–	–	–	517	509	1,026	1,026
5-9	–	–	–	394	391	785	785
10-14	–	1	1	424	449	873	874
15-19	3	2	5	332	358	690	695
20-24	25	20	45	273	297	570	615
25-29	38	38	76	227	252	479	555
30-34	34	53	87	163	255	418	505
35-39	31	28	59	177	232	409	468
40-44	15	15	30	148	183	331	361
45-49	13	8	21	99	163	262	283
50-54	9	6	15	76	146	222	237
55-59	2	7	9	29	84	113	122
60-64	6	12	18	29	68	97	115
65-69	1	3	4	18	24	42	46
70+	4	10	14	20	49	69	83
Unknown	–	–	–	–	–	–	–
Total	181	203	384	2,926	3,460	6,386	6,770
St. Thomas							
0-4	–	–	–	385	386	771	771
5-9	–	–	–	287	275	562	562
10-14	–	–	–	292	297	589	589
15-19	–	–	–	247	262	509	509
20-24	11	4	15	217	239	456	471
25-29	25	12	37	181	211	392	429
30-34	29	13	42	158	186	344	386
35-39	21	24	45	152	221	373	418
40-44	11	12	23	103	156	259	282
45-49	3	6	9	85	112	197	206
50-54	3	8	11	75	125	200	211
55-59	4	4	8	42	68	110	118
60-64	5	2	7	24	65	89	96
65-69	3	1	4	14	29	43	47
70+	–	9	9	13	45	58	67
Unknown	–	–	–	–	1	1	1
	115	95	210	2,275	2,678	4,953	5,163

Table S4.3. *Age Structure of Slaves by Parish: Barbados, 1834*

Parish	Age in Years					
	Under 6	6-12	12-21	21-50	50+	Total
St. Michael	2,850	2,641	3,685	6,518	1,547	17,241
St. James	773	608	752	1,706	568	4,407
St. Peter	942	962	1,071	2,222	648	5,845
St. Lucy	1,158	1,024	1,150	2,455	630	6,417
St. Andrew	689	582	765	1,808	495	4,339
St. Joseph	700	529	711	1,659	422	4,021
St. John	1,045	810	1,080	2,569	679	6,183
St. Philip	1,853	1,427	1,903	4,153	1,094	10,430
Christ Church	1,743	1,499	1,992	3,979	1,093	10,306
St. George	1,388	1,133	1,450	3,382	826	8,179
St. Thomas	906	772	1,014	2,205	542	5,439
Total	14,047	11,987	15,573	32,656	8,544	82,807

Table S4.4. *Age Structure of Slaves by Sex, Birthplace and Parish: Nevis, 1817*

Age group	Africans			Creoles			Total
	Males	Females	Total	Males	Females	Total	
St. Paul							
0-4	–	–	–	13	46	59	59
5-9	–	–	–	34	17	51	51
10-14	–	–	–	25	27	52	52
15-19	–	–	–	20	18	38	38
20-24	–	–	–	14	9	23	23
25-29	–	1	1	8	24	32	33
30-34	2	9	11	13	12	25	36
35-39	6	7	13	24	23	47	60
40-44	7	2	9	17	19	36	45
45-49	2	1	3	10	15	25	28
50-54	1	2	3	6	23	29	32
55-59	2	1	3	1	12	13	16
60-64	–	2	2	5	8	13	15
65-69	3	–	3	1	4	5	8
70+	1	3	4	2	4	6	10
Unknown	–	–	–	–	–	–	–
Total	24	28	52	193	261	454	506

Table S4.4. *Age by Parish: Nevis, 1817 (continued)*

Age group	Africans			Creoles			Total
	Males	Females	Total	Males	Females	Total	
St. John							
0-4	–	–	–	86	103	189	189
5-9	–	–	–	119	109	228	228
10-14	–	–	–	120	114	234	234
15-19	–	–	–	92	86	178	178
20-24	1	1	2	86	84	170	172
25-29	16	12	28	88	61	149	177
30-34	19	9	28	69	66	135	163
35-39	27	20	47	60	53	113	160
40-44	23	20	43	46	57	103	146
45-49	9	4	13	52	49	101	114
50-54	15	12	27	37	44	81	108
55-59	6	16	22	13	23	36	58
60-64	16	11	27	25	28	53	80
65-69	4	7	11	5	18	23	34
70+	7	8	15	12	30	42	57
Unknown	–	–	–	6	5	11	11
Total	143	120	263	916	930	1,846	2,109
St. George							
0-4	–	–	–	105	128	233	233
5-9	–	–	–	129	105	234	234
10-14	1	–	1	138	106	244	245
15-19	8	4	12	75	78	153	165
20-24	9	5	14	63	66	129	143
25-29	21	8	29	53	56	109	138
30-34	26	12	38	64	68	132	170
35-39	40	17	57	55	74	129	186
40-44	42	32	74	68	63	131	205
45-49	9	5	14	39	50	89	103
50-54	5	1	6	30	50	80	86
55-59	3	6	9	15	29	44	53
60-64	6	6	12	10	32	42	54
65-69	4	3	7	8	8	16	23
70+	8	10	18	12	30	42	60
Unknown	–	–	–	–	1	1	1
Total	182	109	291	864	944	1,808	2,099

Table S4.4. *Age by Parish: Nevis, 1817 (continued)*

Age group	Africans			Creoles			Total
	Males	Females	Total	Males	Females	Total	
St. James							
0-4	–	–	–	98	117	215	215
5-9	–	–	–	65	77	142	142
10-14	–	–	–	118	98	216	216
15-19	1	1	2	54	66	120	122
20-24	24	19	43	57	69	126	169
25-29	19	14	33	78	80	158	191
30-34	18	18	36	53	59	112	148
35-39	15	9	24	59	63	122	146
40-44	6	10	16	40	42	82	98
45-49	5	7	12	44	50	94	106
50-54	8	8	16	39	48	87	103
55-59	5	4	9	16	17	33	42
60-64	6	6	12	17	25	42	54
65-69	10	7	17	10	18	28	45
70+	3	13	16	18	29	47	63
Unknown	–	–	–	–	–	–	–
Total	120	116	236	766	858	1,624	1,860
St. Thomas							
0-4	–	–	–	108	102	210	210
5-9	–	–	–	108	106	214	214
10-14	–	–	–	90	72	162	162
15-19	2	–	2	74	55	129	131
20-24	4	4	8	46	61	107	115
25-29	13	12	25	49	58	107	132
30-34	25	20	45	66	76	142	187
35-39	35	20	55	57	45	102	157
40-44	23	12	35	46	52	98	133
45-49	6	4	10	33	47	80	90
50-54	9	8	17	24	36	60	77
55-59	9	8	17	8	24	32	49
60-64	19	16	35	8	20	28	63
65-69	5	4	9	5	7	12	21
70+	9	9	18	8	27	35	53
Unknown	–	–	–	–	–	–	–
Total	159	117	276	730	788	1,518	1,794

Table S4.4. *Age by Parish: Nevis, 1817 (continued)*

Age group	Africans			Creoles			Total
	Males	Females	Total	Males	Females	Total	
Unattached (Parish Unknown)							
0-4	–	–	–	90	79	169	169
5-9	–	–	–	90	83	173	173
10-14	–	–	–	81	73	154	154
15-19	3	2	5	58	44	102	107
20-24	25	19	44	53	63	116	160
25-29	35	38	73	25	56	81	154
30-34	38	27	65	16	34	50	115
35-39	15	12	27	17	24	41	68
40-44	14	16	30	8	21	29	59
45-49	10	5	15	11	23	34	49
50-54	5	9	14	8	18	26	40
55-59	1	–	1	2	9	11	12
60-64	2	6	8	2	10	12	20
65-69	1	2	3	–	4	4	7
70+	–	1	1	–	6	6	7
Unknown	–	–	–	–	–	–	–
Total	149	137	286	461	547	1,008	1,294

Table S4.5. *Age Structure of Slaves by Sex and Parish: Montserrat, 1831*

Age group	Males	Females	Total	Males	Females	Total	Males	Females	Total
	Plymouth			*St. Anthony*			*St. Peter*		
0-4	44	35	79	197	182	379	94	99	193
5-9	26	44	70	150	177	327	77	78	155
10-14	27	32	59	135	141	276	54	82	136
15-19	36	34	70	123	124	247	75	60	135
20-24	23	25	48	90	93	183	48	52	100
25-29	23	24	47	103	107	210	49	50	99
30-34	13	27	40	115	106	221	50	35	85
35-39	6	6	12	81	91	172	60	52	112
40-44	5	14	19	61	95	156	28	42	70
45-49	6	14	20	52	63	115	23	36	59
50-54	5	10	15	54	61	115	24	27	51
55-59	–	5	5	37	45	82	10	25	35
60-64	1	3	4	19	48	67	6	14	20
65-69	–	1	1	5	12	17	–	7	7
70+	–	–	–	8	35	43	3	16	19
Unknown	–	1	1	3	–	3	–	–	–
Total	215	275	490	1,233	1,380	2,613	601	675	1,276

Table S4.5. *Age by Parish: Montserrat, 1831 (continued)*

Age group	Males	Females	Total	Males	Females	Total	Males	Females	Total
	St. George			*St. Patrick*			*Parish Unknown*		
0-4	72	87	159	69	72	141	2	6	8
5-9	53	59	112	42	48	90	5	6	11
10-14	59	62	121	38	38	76	7	2	9
15-19	54	36	90	32	48	80	1	2	3
20-24	45	46	91	51	40	91	2	4	6
25-29	50	67	117	45	41	86	8	2	10
30-34	41	37	78	33	29	62	–	1	1
35-39	33	34	67	26	37	63	3	2	5
40-44	35	35	70	24	17	41	5	1	6
45-49	16	25	41	19	11	30	1	1	2
50-54	7	26	33	10	16	26	–	1	1
55-59	14	12	26	6	11	17	–	–	–
60-64	8	11	19	3	8	11	–	–	–
65-69	2	3	5	1	7	8	–	1	1
70+	2	15	17	5	5	10	1	–	1
Unknown	–	–	–	1	–	1	–	–	–
Total	491	555	1,046	405	428	833	35	29	64

Table S4.6. *Age Structure of Slaves by Sex and Parish: Dominica, 1829*

Age group	Males	Females	Total	Males	Females	Total	Males	Females	Total
	Roseau			*St. George*			*St. Paul*		
0-4	42	78	120	174	165	339	86	117	203
5-9	46	53	99	143	122	265	88	84	172
10-14	54	64	118	131	134	265	87	89	176
15-19	63	79	142	133	129	262	82	89	171
20-24	49	73	122	120	140	260	66	70	136
25-29	41	39	80	82	98	180	47	53	100
30-34	39	39	78	83	90	173	60	63	123
35-39	35	41	76	111	111	222	59	92	151
40-44	34	65	99	114	115	229	77	116	193
45-49	22	26	48	87	92	179	57	61	118
50-54	15	18	33	53	79	132	53	43	96
55-59	6	9	15	37	31	68	27	26	53
60-64	3	12	15	24	31	55	11	15	26
65-69	–	1	1	10	10	20	3	7	10
70+	4	7	11	16	20	36	7	14	21
Unknown	3	8	11	9	9	18	4	3	7
Total	456	612	1,068	1,327	1,376	2,703	814	942	1,756

Table S4.6. *Age by Parish: Dominica, 1829 (continued)*

Age group	Males	Females	Total	Males	Females	Total	Males	Females	Total
		St. Joseph			*St. Peter*			*St. John*	
0-4	92	82	174	78	93	171	76	53	129
5-9	63	76	139	69	61	130	40	47	87
10-14	59	68	127	58	47	105	54	48	102
15-19	68	77	145	40	42	82	46	50	96
20-24	60	59	119	47	42	89	45	47	92
25-29	48	42	90	33	27	60	30	37	67
30-34	52	47	99	33	28	61	40	39	79
35-39	65	86	151	37	48	85	26	28	54
40-44	75	99	174	48	58	106	46	63	109
45-49	40	43	83	34	22	56	40	38	78
50-54	25	33	58	21	17	38	28	25	53
55-59	10	14	24	7	16	23	4	10	14
60-64	24	16	40	9	8	17	9	12	21
65-69	6	9	15	5	2	7	—	4	4
70+	2	5	7	9	6	15	3	9	12
Unknown	5	8	13	1	3	4	—	2	2
Total	694	764	1,458	529	520	1,049	487	512	999
		St. Andrew			*St. David*			*St. Patrick*	
0-4	87	103	190	28	41	69	104	101	205
5-9	71	81	152	17	26	43	78	87	165
10-14	83	64	147	34	20	54	83	95	178
15-19	82	90	172	24	35	59	83	81	164
20-24	86	96	182	29	24	53	98	106	204
25-29	69	64	133	19	10	29	58	53	111
30-34	46	55	101	28	25	53	48	40	88
35-39	55	76	131	18	31	49	49	70	119
40-44	67	91	158	27	28	55	72	78	150
45-49	51	47	98	21	15	36	53	66	119
50-54	36	49	85	8	10	18	33	35	68
55-59	11	11	22	4	4	8	19	18	37
60-64	14	19	33	3	2	5	8	16	24
65-69	2	5	7	5	10	15	8	14	22
70+	16	11	27	4	5	9	9	17	26
Unknown	2	2	4	3	3	6	2	2	4
Total	778	864	1,642	272	289	561	805	879	1,684

Table S4.6. *Age by Parish: Dominica, 1829 (continued)*

Age group	Males	Females	Total	Males	Females	Total
		St. Mark			*St. Luke*	
0-4	79	47	126	50	50	100
5-9	53	49	102	47	48	95
10-14	41	43	84	33	36	69
15-19	36	43	79	34	48	82
20-24	38	46	84	46	33	79
25-29	25	19	44	33	31	64
30-34	30	25	55	30	39	69
35-39	25	18	43	29	29	58
40-44	30	49	79	25	43	68
45-49	23	27	50	24	27	51
50-54	19	21	40	19	28	47
55-59	11	16	27	8	15	23
60-64	11	18	29	6	5	11
65-69	5	3	8	2	2	4
70+	5	5	10	7	9	16
Unknown	–	–	–	–	2	2
Total	431	429	860	393	445	838

Table S4.7. *Age Structure of Slaves by Sex, Birthplace and Quarter: St. Lucia, 1815*

Age group	Africans			Creoles			Total
	Males	Females	Total	Males	Females	Total	
Town of Castries							
0-4	–	–	–	96	90	186	186
5-9	–	–	–	75	70	145	146
10-14	2	1	3	68	66	134	137
15-19	11	6	17	41	56	97	114
20-24	39	27	66	52	78	130	196
25-29	36	36	72	53	72	125	198
30-34	32	18	50	35	45	80	130
35-39	13	15	28	16	30	46	74
40-44	14	19	33	16	32	48	83
45-49	8	8	16	5	24	29	45
50-54	8	8	16	6	15	21	37
55-59	6	9	15	2	8	10	25
60-64	3	8	11	3	6	9	20
65-69	2	4	6	1	4	5	11
70+	1	3	4	–	–	–	4
Unknown	–	–	–	2	–	2	2
Total	175	162	337	471	596	1,067	1,408*

* Includes 4 slaves whose birthplace is unknown.

Table S4.7. *Age by Quarter: St. Lucia, 1815 (continued)*

Age group	Africans			Creoles			Total
	Males	Females	Total	Males	Females	Total	
Other Towns (Gros Islet, Vieux Fort, Soufriere, Laborie, Choiseul, Micoud)							
0-4	–	–	–	38	47	85	85
5-9	–	–	–	32	39	71	71
10-14	1	–	1	39	41	80	81
15-19	–	–	–	21	36	57	57
20-24	6	8	14	27	32	59	74
25-29	10	8	18	17	34	51	70
30-34	7	7	14	15	23	38	52
35-39	5	11	16	5	18	23	39
40-44	6	5	11	–	15	15	26
45-49	1	8	9	3	12	15	24
50-54	1	4	5	2	3	5	10
55-59	–	4	4	1	3	4	8
60-64	–	2	2	1	7	8	10
65-69	1	2	3	–	3	3	6
70+	2	2	4	–	–	–	4
Unknown	1	–	1	1	–	1	2
Total	41	61	102	202	313	515	619*
Castries							
0-4	–	–	–	104	98	202	202
5-9	1	–	1	84	81	165	166
10-14	–	–	–	89	79	168	168
15-19	10	1	11	62	64	126	137
20-24	22	17	39	74	83	157	196
25-29	40	30	70	68	87	155	225
30-34	43	28	71	54	58	112	183
35-39	53	34	87	43	52	95	182
40-44	25	37	62	18	38	56	118
45-49	20	26	46	19	22	41	87
50-54	16	24	40	10	22	32	72
55-59	16	15	31	5	15	20	51
60-64	8	14	22	5	15	20	42
65-69	4	5	9	1	6	7	16
70+	7	16	23	2	8	10	33
Unknown	2	–	2	1	–	1	3
Total	267	247	514	639	728	1,367	1,881

* Includes 2 slaves whose birthplace is unknown.

Table S4.7. *Age by Quarter: St. Lucia, 1815 (continued)*

Age group	Africans			Creoles			Total
	Males	Females	Total	Males	Females	Total	
Gros Islet							
0-4	–	–	–	78	79	157	157
5-9	–	–	–	63	73	136	137
10-14	1	–	1	65	75	140	142
15-19	3	4	7	57	86	143	150
20-24	21	14	35	66	62	128	164
25-29	13	3	16	52	42	94	110
30-34	10	8	18	35	37	72	91
35-39	24	15	39	16	50	66	105
40-44	16	22	38	17	34	51	90
45-49	13	24	37	14	30	44	81
50-54	14	19	33	9	22	31	64
55-59	3	11	14	5	15	20	35
60-64	8	11	19	8	10	18	38
65-69	6	14	20	4	7	11	31
70+	4	15	19	2	6	8	27
Unknown	–	–	–	1	1	2	2
Total	136	160	296	492	629	1,121	1,424*
Dauphin							
0-4	–	–	–	43	56	99	99
5-9	–	1	1	40	44	84	85
10-14	7	2	9	38	39	77	86
15-19	14	6	20	28	25	53	73
20-24	6	1	7	24	36	60	67
25-29	18	2	20	20	35	55	75
30-34	24	3	27	20	17	37	64
35-39	14	7	21	10	9	19	41
40-44	12	9	21	4	13	17	39
45-49	8	18	26	5	8	13	39
50-54	12	12	24	6	11	17	41
55-59	11	12	23	1	5	6	29
60-64	4	11	15	–	4	4	19
65-69	2	6	8	–	7	7	15
70+	4	3	7	2	4	6	13
Unknown	–	–	–	2	–	2	2
Total	136	93	229	243	313	556	787**

* Includes 7 slaves whose birthplace is unknown.
** Includes 2 slaves whose birthplace is unknown.

Table S4.7. *Age by Quarter: St. Lucia, 1815 (continued)*

Age group	Africans			Creoles			Total
	Males	Females	Total	Males	Females	Total	
Dennery							
0-4	–	–	–	34	48	82	82
5-9	–	–	–	42	43	85	85
10-14	1	–	1	37	42	79	80
15-19	2	1	3	17	24	41	44
20-24	4	8	12	24	36	60	72
25-29	5	4	9	25	41	66	75
30-34	6	12	18	30	26	56	74
35-39	8	9	17	14	20	34	51
40-44	7	15	22	4	12	16	38
45-49	9	6	15	5	13	18	33
50-54	2	12	14	3	8	11	25
55-59	1	1	2	3	4	7	9
60-64	2	9	11	5	9	14	25
65-69	–	6	6	–	5	5	11
70+	2	3	5	1	4	5	10
Unknown	–	–	–	1	–	1	1
Total	49	86	135	245	335	580	715
Praslin							
0-4	–	–	–	34	42	76	76
5-9	–	–	–	23	24	47	47
10-14	1	–	1	41	20	61	62
15-19	6	–	6	20	36	56	62
20-24	6	9	15	23	33	56	71
25-29	11	4	15	17	14	31	46
30-34	13	5	18	11	13	24	43
35-39	9	7	16	6	11	17	34
40-44	11	14	25	5	8	13	38
45-49	11	14	25	3	5	8	33
50-54	4	8	12	1	7	8	20
55-59	2	6	8	2	6	8	16
60-64	6	15	21	3	1	4	25
65-69	5	4	9	–	–	–	9
70+	4	10	14	1	3	4	18
Unknown	–	–	–	1	1	2	4
Total	89	96	185	191	224	415	604*

* Includes 4 slaves whose birthplace is unknown.

Table S4.7. *Age by Quarter: St. Lucia, 1815 (continued)*

Age group	Africans			Creoles			Total
	Males	Females	Total	Males	Females	Total	
Micoud							
0-4	–	–	–	35	54	89	89
5-9	–	–	–	29	44	73	73
10-14	1	–	1	34	35	69	70
15-19	–	–	–	26	22	48	48
20-24	4	1	5	20	39	59	64
25-29	12	7	19	28	30	58	77
30-34	14	23	37	14	12	26	63
35-39	12	20	32	9	10	19	51
40-44	15	23	38	11	11	22	60
45-49	8	16	24	2	9	11	35
50-54	10	14	24	7	5	12	36
55-59	5	6	11	–	7	7	18
60-64	5	3	8	–	7	7	15
65-69	4	3	7	–	3	3	10
70+	2	1	3	1	–	1	4
Unknown	–	–	–	1	1	2	7
Total	92	117	209	217	289	506	720*
Vieux Fort							
0-4	–	–	–	88	95	183	183
5-9	–	–	–	70	81	151	151
10-14	1	1	2	89	70	159	161
15-19	1	4	5	61	42	103	108
20-24	2	8	10	39	51	90	100
25-29	11	6	17	53	63	116	133
30-34	15	16	31	41	58	99	131
35-39	26	26	52	21	41	62	115
40-44	8	30	38	10	27	37	75
45-49	15	18	33	9	27	36	70
50-54	11	15	26	6	11	17	43
55-59	10	9	19	5	8	13	33
60-64	4	9	13	4	11	15	29
65-69	3	11	14	2	5	7	21
70+	4	3	7	3	5	8	15
Unknown	–	–	–	–	1	1	1
Total	111	156	267	501	596	1,097	1,369**

* Includes 5 slaves whose birthplace is unknown.
** Includes 5 slaves whose birthplace is unknown.

Table S4.7. *Age by Quarter: St. Lucia, 1815 (continued)*

Age group	Africans			Creoles			Total
	Males	Females	Total	Males	Females	Total	
Laborie							
0-4	–	–	–	114	145	259	259
5-9	–	–	–	103	121	224	224
10-14	–	–	–	110	97	207	207
15-19	1	4	5	74	77	151	156
20-24	4	7	11	49	61	110	121
25-29	20	16	36	56	78	134	170
30-34	22	19	41	67	60	127	168
35-39	25	27	52	32	50	82	135
40-44	24	41	65	21	41	62	127
45-49	16	28	44	19	26	45	89
50-54	12	15	27	11	33	44	71
55-59	7	9	16	7	16	23	39
60-64	10	13	23	5	20	25	48
65-69	5	9	14	4	9	13	27
70+	8	11	19	1	12	13	32
Unknown	1	–	1	–	–	–	1
Total	155	199	354	673	846	1,519	1,874*
Choiseul							
0-4	–	–	–	59	77	136	136
5-9	–	–	–	72	57	129	129
10-14	–	–	–	52	60	112	112
15-19	2	4	6	31	38	69	75
20-24	7	15	22	33	28	61	83
25-29	10	16	26	43	46	89	115
30-34	12	6	18	21	31	51	70
35-39	9	7	16	14	23	37	53
40-44	3	12	15	12	22	34	49
45-49	9	8	17	16	20	36	53
50-54	2	14	16	6	10	16	32
55-59	2	7	9	3	7	10	19
60-64	5	12	17	4	11	15	32
65-69	4	1	5	2	2	4	9
70+	3	8	11	7	4	11	22
Unknown	–	–	–	2	1	3	3
Total	68	110	178	377	437	814	992

* Includes 1 slave whose birthplace is unknown.

Table S4.7. *Age by Quarter: St. Lucia, 1815 (continued)*

Age group	Africans			Creoles			Total
	Males	Females	Total	Males	Females	Total	
Soufriere							
0-4	–	–	–	185	232	417	417
5-9	–	1	1	179	187	366	367
10-14	3	–	3	203	195	398	401
15-19	17	8	25	136	128	264	289
20-24	32	18	50	136	125	261	311
25-29	50	26	76	122	114	236	314
30-34	30	34	64	75	103	178	242
35-39	29	31	60	46	71	117	177
40-44	28	21	49	28	77	105	154
45-49	26	23	49	21	52	73	122
50-54	18	17	35	23	50	73	108
55-59	7	20	27	17	32	49	76
60-64	20	16	36	13	19	32	68
65-69	4	6	10	6	10	16	27
70+	19	34	53	12	8	20	74
Unknown	1	1	2	3	3	6	8
Total	284	256	540	1,205	1,406	2,611	3,155*
Anse la Raye							
0-4	–	–	–	41	35	76	76
5-9	–	–	–	29	36	65	65
10-14	–	–	–	41	43	84	84
15-19	4	4	8	33	33	66	76
20-24	10	4	14	37	38	75	89
25-29	14	7	21	30	23	53	75
30-34	13	9	22	17	15	32	55
35-39	9	11	20	9	25	34	54
40-44	9	6	15	4	19	23	40
45-49	1	4	5	5	12	17	23
50-54	4	9	13	5	9	14	27
55-59	4	3	7	–	7	7	14
60-64	2	3	5	2	7	9	14
65-69	1	2	3	2	2	4	7
70+	2	5	7	1	7	8	15
Unknown	–	–	–	2	–	2	5
Total	73	67	140	258	311	569	719**

* Includes 4 slaves whose birthplace is unknown.
** Includes 10 slaves whose birthplace is unknown.

Table S4.8. *Age Structure of Slaves by Sex, Birthplace and Parish: St. Vincent, 1817*

Age group	Africans			Creoles			Total
	Males	Females	Total	Males	Females	Total	
Kingstown							
0-4	–	–	–	115	138	253	253
5-9	–	–	–	118	127	245	245
10-14	1	–	1	142	137	279	280
15-19	6	3	9	85	83	168	177
20-24	37	25	62	55	60	115	177
25-29	70	66	136	43	43	86	222
30-34	126	100	226	27	46	73	299
35-39	93	73	166	27	29	56	222
40-44	53	66	119	8	14	22	141
45-49	40	36	76	7	12	19	95
50-54	21	24	45	5	14	19	64
55-59	11	6	17	1	3	4	21
60-64	15	8	23	4	6	10	33
65-69	3	4	7	1	1	2	9
70+	4	3	7	1	2	3	10
Unknown	–	5	5	1	1	2	7
Total	480	419	899	640	716	1,356	2,255
St. George (rural)							
0-4	–	–	–	301	335	636	636
5-9	–	–	–	320	301	621	621
10-14	2	1	3	359	289	648	651
15-19	18	6	24	265	240	505	529
20-24	69	39	108	163	209	372	480
25-29	206	136	342	159	156	315	657
30-34	233	174	407	117	151	268	675
35-39	234	191	425	106	126	232	657
40-44	154	173	327	69	85	154	481
45-49	114	115	229	45	40	85	314
50-54	87	92	179	31	25	56	235
55-59	57	49	106	21	38	59	165
60-64	67	81	148	12	28	40	188
65-69	17	38	55	8	9	17	72
70+	19	33	52	3	18	21	73
Unknown	–	1	1	–	–	–	1
Total	1,277	1,129	2,406	1,979	2,050	4,029	6,435

Table S4.8. *Age by Parish: St. Vincent, 1817 (continued)*

Age group	Africans			Creoles			Total
	Males	Females	Total	Males	Females	Total	
St. Andrew							
0-4	–	–	–	100	111	211	211
5-9	–	–	–	105	98	203	203
10-14	–	–	–	85	105	190	190
15-19	10	3	13	72	96	168	181
20-24	18	25	43	67	56	123	166
25-29	54	48	102	48	41	89	191
30-34	68	49	117	33	54	87	204
35-39	54	56	110	38	66	104	214
40-44	40	58	98	18	24	42	140
45-49	27	29	56	16	17	33	89
50-54	23	32	55	10	14	24	79
55-59	11	14	25	6	5	11	36
60-64	16	16	32	3	7	10	42
65-69	8	14	22	1	2	3	25
70+	23	25	48	2	5	7	55
Unknown	1	–	1	1	1	2	3
Total	353	369	722	605	702	1,307	2,029
St. Patrick							
0-4	–	–	–	123	145	268	268
5-9	–	–	–	128	124	252	252
10-14	–	–	–	111	107	218	218
15-19	4	3	7	95	96	191	198
20-24	18	14	32	89	106	195	227
25-29	63	53	116	78	78	156	272
30-34	98	68	166	47	51	98	264
35-39	110	78	188	37	71	108	296
40-44	62	60	122	43	42	85	207
45-49	43	26	69	21	25	46	115
50-54	28	36	64	15	11	26	90
55-59	13	18	31	4	7	11	42
60-64	25	27	52	3	9	12	64
65-69	6	7	13	2	4	6	19
70+	19	12	31	7	6	13	44
Unknown	–	3	3	–	1	1	4
Total	489	405	894	803	883	1,686	2,580

Table S4.8. *Age by Parish: St. Vincent, 1817 (continued)*

Age group	Africans			Creoles			Total
	Males	Females	Total	Males	Females	Total	
St. David							
0-4	–	–	–	99	94	193	193
5-9	–	–	–	99	102	201	201
10-14	1	–	1	100	83	183	184
15-19	1	–	1	55	56	111	112
20-24	10	9	19	59	63	122	141
25-29	22	25	47	55	66	121	168
30-34	39	38	77	39	43	82	159
35-39	66	55	121	30	46	76	197
40-44	51	44	95	24	23	47	142
45-49	42	30	72	13	22	35	107
50-54	27	24	51	14	13	27	78
55-59	18	13	31	5	4	9	40
60-64	12	15	27	2	4	6	33
65-69	7	7	14	1	–	1	15
70+	6	14	20	2	3	5	25
Unknown	2	2	4	–	–	–	4
Total	304	276	580	597	622	1,219	1,799
Charlotte							
0-4	–	–	–	351	394	745	745
5-9	–	–	–	384	381	765	765
10-14	2	–	2	362	318	680	682
15-19	6	6	12	277	307	584	596
20-24	66	30	96	181	228	409	505
25-29	179	99	278	91	111	202	480
30-34	349	283	632	86	96	182	814
35-39	351	349	700	71	58	129	829
40-44	350	268	618	42	53	95	713
45-49	249	169	418	51	35	86	504
50-54	173	121	294	28	28	56	350
55-59	74	60	134	13	13	26	160
60-64	52	42	94	3	8	11	105
65-69	22	11	33	5	1	6	39
70+	19	23	42	2	2	4	46
Unknown	–	–	–	1	–	1	1
Total	1,892	1,461	3,353	1,948	2,033	3,981	7,334

Table S4.8. *Age by Parish: St. Vincent, 1817 (continued)*

Age group	Africans			Creoles			Total
	Males	Females	Total	Males	Females	Total	
St. Vincent Grenadines							
0-4	–	–	–	183	169	352	352
5-9	–	–	–	170	170	340	340
10-14	–	–	–	168	169	337	337
15-19	1	–	1	99	121	220	221
20-24	26	18	44	95	75	170	214
25-29	56	36	92	75	72	147	239
30-34	65	69	134	52	54	106	240
35-39	69	72	141	39	48	87	228
40-44	81	65	146	24	39	63	209
45-49	51	52	103	18	15	33	136
50-54	74	62	136	4	17	21	157
55-59	32	15	47	10	2	12	59
60-64	25	20	45	2	6	8	53
65-69	21	9	30	1	2	3	33
70+	24	24	48	3	7	10	58
Unknown	–	–	–	–	–	–	–
Total	525	442	967	943	966	1,909	2,876

Table S4.9. *Age Structure of Slaves by Sex, Birthplace and Parish: Grenada, 1817*

Age group	Africans			Creoles			Total
	Males	Females	Total	Males	Females	Total	
Town of St. George							
0-4	–	–	–	139	154	293	293
5-9	–	–	–	136	124	260	260
10-14	–	1	1	105	132	237	238
15-19	13	7	20	85	114	199	219
20-24	44	32	76	67	64	131	207
25-29	92	96	188	59	79	138	326
30-34	115	121	236	40	54	94	330
35-39	88	95	183	19	39	58	241
40-44	72	88	160	10	28	38	198
45-49	59	59	118	14	20	34	152
50-54	30	37	67	2	16	18	85
55-59	15	19	34	3	6	9	43
60-64	11	6	17	1	5	6	23
65-69	1	7	8	–	2	2	10
70+	3	3	6	–	1	1	7
Unknown	–	–	–	–	–	–	–
Total	543	571	1,114	680	838	1,518	2,632

Table S4.9. *Age by Parish: Grenada, 1817 (continued)*

Age group	Africans			Creoles			Total
	Males	Females	Total	Males	Females	Total	
St. George							
0-4	–	–	–	221	238	459	459
5-9	–	–	–	229	245	474	474
10-14	–	1	1	222	209	431	432
15-19	8	5	13	196	198	394	407
20-24	65	41	106	161	195	356	462
25-29	105	52	157	177	203	380	537
30-34	121	81	202	153	182	335	537
35-39	151	103	254	100	101	201	455
40-44	146	126	272	76	98	174	446
45-49	109	105	214	34	66	100	314
50-54	109	108	217	31	51	82	299
55-59	82	90	172	18	29	47	219
60-64	86	66	152	13	11	24	176
65-69	30	41	71	9	10	19	90
70+	28	44	72	5	14	19	91
Unknown	2	1	3	1	2	3	6
Total	1,042	864	1,906	1,646	1,852	3,498	5,404
St. John							
0-4	–	–	–	94	110	204	204
5-9	–	–	–	104	93	197	197
10-14	–	–	–	113	98	211	211
15-19	3	2	5	87	97	184	189
20-24	9	4	13	74	94	168	181
25-29	25	22	47	68	80	148	195
30-34	56	36	92	61	76	137	229
35-39	78	49	127	64	64	128	255
40-44	53	43	96	38	37	75	171
45-49	52	39	91	20	29	49	140
50-54	43	30	73	11	19	30	103
55-59	31	24	55	5	7	12	67
60-64	26	31	57	8	7	15	72
65-69	19	10	29	3	9	12	41
70+	22	34	56	4	10	14	70
Unknown	–	–	–	3	2	5	5
Total	417	324	741	757	832	1,589	2,330

Table S4.9. *Age by Parish: Grenada, 1817 (continued)*

Age group	Africans			Creoles			Total
	Males	Females	Total	Males	Females	Total	
St. Mark							
0-4	–	–	–	48	55	103	103
5-9	–	–	–	61	54	115	115
10-14	–	–	–	70	77	147	147
15-19	1	–	1	53	50	103	104
20-24	3	7	10	27	50	77	87
25-29	10	8	18	51	53	104	122
30-34	27	11	38	39	47	86	124
35-39	27	22	49	30	48	78	127
40-44	22	31	53	20	22	42	95
45-49	23	22	45	14	24	38	83
50-54	30	17	47	9	14	23	70
55-59	11	9	20	2	6	8	28
60-64	18	21	39	5	3	8	47
65-69	9	7	16	1	5	6	22
70+	10	9	19	3	6	9	28
Unknown	1	–	1	–	–	–	1
Total	192	164	356	433	514	947	1,303
St. Patrick							
0-4	–	–	–	199	206	405	405
5-9	–	–	–	193	193	386	386
10-14	1	–	1	230	203	433	434
15-19	6	11	17	162	166	328	345
20-24	43	19	62	139	153	292	354
25-29	109	58	167	156	158	314	481
30-34	116	80	196	103	177	280	476
35-39	137	84	221	107	138	245	466
40-44	94	93	187	76	81	157	344
45-49	63	61	124	52	62	114	238
50-54	76	74	150	29	58	87	237
55-59	51	45	96	21	44	65	161
60-64	67	54	121	20	36	56	177
65-69	16	21	37	8	18	26	63
70+	36	51	87	12	28	40	127
Unknown	1	–	1	–	1	1	2
Total	816	651	1,467	1,507	1,722	3,229	4,696

Table S4.9. *Age by Parish: Grenada, 1817 (continued)*

Age group	Africans			Creoles			Total
	Males	Females	Total	Males	Females	Total	
St. Andrew							
0-4	–	–	–	200	190	390	390
5-9	–	–	–	173	184	357	357
10-14	–	–	–	209	171	380	380
15-19	7	4	11	149	175	324	335
20-24	42	22	64	130	166	296	360
25-29	82	77	159	163	147	310	469
30-34	128	107	235	137	150	287	522
35-39	158	114	272	96	127	223	495
40-44	141	101	242	54	75	129	371
45-49	109	83	192	42	61	103	295
50-54	82	64	146	34	64	98	244
55-59	66	48	114	20	30	50	164
60-64	60	54	114	19	27	46	160
65-69	23	34	57	6	22	28	85
70+	34	45	79	12	23	35	114
Unknown	–	–	–	1	–	1	1
Total	932	753	1,685	1,445	1,612	3,057	4,742
St. David							
0-4	–	–	–	88	89	177	177
5-9	–	–	–	87	100	187	187
10-14	–	–	–	97	97	194	194
15-19	7	6	13	102	74	176	189
20-24	19	19	38	86	70	156	194
25-29	40	30	70	83	79	162	232
30-34	44	23	67	62	67	129	196
35-39	52	54	106	49	43	92	198
40-44	47	42	89	30	46	76	165
45-49	39	40	79	21	29	50	129
50-54	52	43	95	15	35	50	145
55-59	43	32	75	16	22	38	113
60-64	28	36	64	14	7	21	85
65-69	13	11	24	1	10	11	35
70+	14	23	37	6	17	23	60
Unknown	–	–	–	1	2	3	3
Total	398	359	757	758	787	1,545	2,302

Table S4.9. *Age by Parish: Grenada, 1817 (continued)*

Age group	Africans			Creoles			Total
	Males	Females	Total	Males	Females	Total	
Grenada Grenadines							
0-4	–	–	–	268	290	558	558
5-9	–	–	–	235	271	506	506
10-14	–	–	–	290	266	556	556
15-19	–	–	–	203	242	445	445
20-24	5	9	14	162	205	367	381
25-29	28	18	46	116	157	273	319
30-34	47	47	94	109	147	256	350
35-39	53	65	118	89	129	218	336
40-44	67	57	124	65	86	151	275
45-49	67	71	138	52	65	117	255
50-54	60	91	151	24	25	49	200
55-59	60	55	115	13	13	26	141
60-64	58	68	126	4	6	10	136
65-69	20	33	53	1	4	5	58
70+	50	54	104	2	1	3	107
Unknown	–	–	–	–	–	–	–
Total	515	568	1,083	1,633	1,907	3,540	4,623

Table S4.10. *Age Structure of Slaves by Sex and Birthplace: Grenada 1829 and 1833 (St. Andrew and the Grenadines)*

Age group	Africans			Creoles			Total
	Males	Females	Total	Males	Females	Total	
St. Andrew, 1829							
0-4	–	–	–	206	215	421	421
5-9	–	–	–	233	222	455	455
10-14	–	–	–	199	214	413	413
15-19	–	–	–	226	207	433	433
20-24	–	–	–	226	199	425	425
25-29	4	2	6	206	194	400	406
30-34	18	6	24	144	183	327	351
35-39	45	46	91	145	160	305	396
40-44	108	69	177	139	150	289	466
45-49	104	85	189	97	133	230	419
50-54	90	77	167	51	102	153	320
55-59	60	53	113	35	45	80	193
60-64	41	35	76	21	41	62	138
65-69	27	23	50	10	16	26	76
70+	37	29	66	8	26	34	100
Unknown	–	–	–	–	–	–	–
Total	534	425	959	1,946	2,107	4,053	5,012

Table S4.10. *Age Structure: Grenada, 1829 and 1833 (continued)*

Age Group	Africans			Creoles			Total
	Males	Females	Total	Males	Females	Total	
St. Andrew, 1833							
0-4	–	–	–	197	208	405	405
5-9	–	–	–	171	184	355	355
10-14	–	–	–	216	194	410	410
15-19	–	–	–	192	203	395	395
20-24	–	–	–	198	191	389	389
25-29	–	–	–	212	167	379	379
30-34	4	3	7	176	168	344	351
35-39	17	13	30	122	154	276	306
40-44	41	39	80	128	135	263	343
45-49	85	54	139	97	127	224	363
50-54	66	72	138	68	109	177	315
55-59	70	48	118	33	68	101	219
60-64	44	42	86	25	32	57	143
65-69	17	18	35	8	31	39	74
70+	34	27	61	16	15	31	92
Unknown	–	–	–	–	–	–	–
Total	378	316	694	1,859	1,986	3,845	4,539
Grenada Grenadines, 1829							
0-4	–	–	–	261	255	516	516
5-9	–	–	–	177	199	376	376
10-14	–	–	–	156	168	324	324
15-19	–	–	–	126	130	256	256
20-24	–	–	–	157	163	320	320
25-29	–	–	–	123	129	252	252
30-34	2	–	2	106	94	200	202
35-39	12	5	17	70	92	162	179
40-44	21	15	36	63	81	144	180
45-49	20	30	50	53	63	116	166
50-54	28	29	57	47	78	125	182
55-59	30	28	58	37	30	67	125
60-64	25	38	63	16	20	36	99
65-69	20	17	37	11	8	19	56
70+	27	45	72	3	5	8	80
Unknown	–	–	–	1	–	1	1
Total	185	207	392	1,407	1,515	2,922	3,314

Table S4.10. *Age Structure: Grenada, 1829 and 1833 (continued)*

Age Group	Africans			Creoles			Total
	Males	Females	Total	Males	Females	Total	
Grenada Grenadines, 1833							
0-4	–	–	–	307	273	580	580
5-9	–	–	–	219	237	456	456
10-14	–	–	–	165	174	339	339
15-19	–	–	–	140	165	305	305
20-24	–	–	–	122	128	250	250
25-29	–	–	–	142	150	292	292
30-34	1	–	1	107	113	220	221
35-39	3	2	5	86	88	174	179
40-44	15	6	21	67	78	145	166
45-49	16	16	32	51	76	127	159
50-54	19	33	52	59	71	130	182
55-59	27	17	44	33	51	84	128
60-64	34	26	60	30	27	57	117
65-69	16	23	39	13	10	23	62
70+	28	40	68	7	7	14	82
Unknown	–	–	–	1	–	1	1
Total	159	163	322	1,549	1,648	3,197	3,519

Table S4.11. *Age Structure of Slaves by Sex: Grenada 1829 (Town of St. George, St. John and St. Mark)*

Age Group	Males	Females	Males	Females	Males	Females
	Town of St. George		*St. John*		*St. Mark*	
0-4	91	104	139	118	71	83
5-9	98	97	103	114	77	55
10-14	99	94	87	81	39	66
15-19	81	88	85	77	58	58
20-24	71	85	110	71	75	90
25-29	47	70	97	81	64	58
30-34	52	67	65	81	47	54
35-39	67	85	61	78	43	52
40-44	62	96	78	88	71	56
45-49	46	75	85	70	45	47
50-54	41	49	75	55	27	53
55-59	15	23	45	42	23	23
60-64	13	13	21	24	13	19
65-69	3	8	20	17	7	7
70+	1	4	19	29	10	14
Unknown	–	–	–	–	–	–
Total	787	958	1,090	1,026	670	735

Table S4.12. *Age Structure of Slaves by Sex, Birthplace and Parish: Tobago, 1819*

Age Group	Africans			Creoles			Total
	Males	Females	Total	Males	Females	Total	
St. Andrew							
0-4	–	–	–	106	124	230	230
5-9	–	–	–	111	144	255	255
10-14	–	–	–	118	103	221	221
15-19	1	–	1	73	98	171	172
20-24	6	6	12	55	58	113	125
25-29	30	18	48	52	64	116	164
30-34	66	59	125	50	56	106	231
35-39	86	76	162	41	63	104	266
40-44	91	84	175	35	33	68	243
45-49	65	64	129	17	8	25	154
50-54	50	55	105	5	13	18	123
55-59	30	45	75	3	3	6	81
60-64	34	34	68	1	3	4	72
65-69	8	12	20	–	2	2	22
70+	10	19	29	–	–	–	29
Unknown	–	–	–	–	–	–	–
Total	477	472	949	667	772	1,439	2,388
St. George							
0-4	–	–	–	88	99	187	187
5-9	–	–	–	108	93	201	201
10-14	–	–	–	87	85	172	172
15-19	1	–	1	68	36	104	105
20-24	7	6	13	49	36	85	98
25-29	37	39	76	39	48	87	163
30-34	77	54	131	36	41	77	208
35-39	110	74	184	28	36	64	248
40-44	89	72	161	17	23	40	201
45-49	35	53	88	5	9	14	102
50-54	38	44	82	5	4	9	91
55-59	28	28	56	3	2	5	61
60-64	18	21	39	1	1	2	41
65-69	9	12	21	1	3	4	25
70+	2	5	7	–	2	2	9
Unknown	–	–	–	–	–	–	–
Total	451	408	859	535	518	1,053	1,912

Table S4.12. *Age by Parish: Tobago, 1819 (continued)*

Age Group	Africans			Creoles			Total
	Males	Females	Total	Males	Females	Total	
St. Mary							
0-4	–	–	–	34	45	79	79
5-9	–	–	–	46	48	94	94
10-14	–	–	–	48	38	86	86
15-19	–	–	–	43	44	87	87
20-24	8	9	17	33	34	67	84
25-29	19	20	39	20	30	50	89
30-34	24	25	49	23	15	38	87
35-39	32	34	66	16	20	36	102
40-44	38	31	69	10	15	25	94
45-49	15	12	27	4	4	8	35
50-54	7	15	22	2	5	7	29
55-59	8	13	21	2	–	2	23
60-64	6	11	17	1	1	2	19
65-69	2	5	7	1	1	2	9
70+	4	5	9	–	–	–	9
Unknown	–	–	–	–	–	–	–
Total	163	180	343	283	300	583	926
St. Paul							
0-4	–	–	–	51	76	127	127
5-9	–	–	–	61	61	122	122
10-14	–	–	–	68	50	118	118
15-19	–	1	1	62	51	113	114
20-24	7	7	14	46	38	84	98
25-29	28	29	57	51	62	113	170
30-34	72	46	118	32	45	77	195
35-39	60	67	127	24	29	53	180
40-44	64	53	117	15	18	33	150
45-49	46	28	74	2	8	10	84
50-54	28	26	54	–	2	2	56
55-59	10	17	27	–	–	–	27
60-64	18	25	43	–	1	1	44
65-69	5	9	14	1	–	1	15
70+	6	11	17	–	1	1	18
Unknown	–	–	–	1	–	1	1
Total	344	319	663	414	442	856	1,519

Table S4.12. *Age by Parish: Tobago, 1819 (continued)*

Age Group	Africans			Creoles			Total
	Males	Females	Total	Males	Females	Total	
St. John							
0-4	–	–	–	49	51	100	100
5-9	–	–	–	52	64	116	116
10-14	–	–	–	53	69	122	122
15-19	2	1	3	70	81	151	154
20-24	2	1	3	46	43	89	92
25-29	15	7	22	51	46	97	119
30-34	49	25	74	36	29	65	139
35-39	42	32	74	26	33	59	133
40-44	61	51	112	12	21	33	145
45-49	41	54	95	2	4	6	101
50-54	28	24	52	–	5	5	57
55-59	15	16	31	1	1	2	33
60-64	21	24	45	–	–	–	45
65-69	12	7	19	–	–	–	19
70+	6	6	12	–	–	–	12
Unknown	–	–	–	–	–	–	–
Total	294	248	542	398	447	845	1,387
St. David							
0-4	–	–	–	185	185	370	370
5-9	–	–	–	213	164	377	377
10-14	–	–	–	179	179	358	358
15-19	4	–	4	124	127	251	255
20-24	18	10	28	109	127	236	264
25-29	64	39	103	86	108	194	297
30-34	79	87	166	60	100	160	326
35-39	122	90	212	52	44	96	308
40-44	101	88	189	13	29	42	231
45-49	99	72	171	13	15	28	199
50-54	89	80	169	2	4	6	175
55-59	50	65	115	2	3	5	120
60-64	42	61	103	2	4	6	109
65-69	20	33	53	1	2	3	56
70+	21	17	38	1	2	3	41
Unknown	–	–	–	–	–	–	–
Total	709	642	1,351	1,042	1,093	2,135	3,486

Table S4.12. *Age by Parish: Tobago, 1819 (continued)*

Age Group	Africans			Creoles			Total
	Males	Females	Total	Males	Females	Total	
St. Patrick							
0-4	–	–	–	150	153	303	303
5-9	–	–	–	153	154	307	307
10-14	–	–	–	138	145	283	283
15-19	–	1	1	99	99	198	199
20-24	1	1	2	75	103	178	180
25-29	11	19	30	75	92	167	197
30-34	36	29	65	62	70	132	197
35-39	78	58	136	61	68	129	265
40-44	64	68	132	20	29	49	181
45-49	57	68	125	8	16	24	149
50-54	41	64	105	6	4	10	115
55-59	45	56	101	1	4	5	106
60-64	59	53	112	5	3	8	120
65-69	23	17	40	1	1	2	42
70+	15	23	38	1	1	2	40
Unknown	–	–	–	1	–	1	1
Total	430	457	887	856	942	1,798	2,685
Towns (Scarborough, Plymouth, Milford)							
0-4	–	–	–	45	54	99	99
5-9	–	–	–	57	57	114	114
10-14	–	–	–	50	44	94	94
15-19	4	2	6	37	42	79	85
20-24	10	20	30	20	29	49	79
25-29	50	52	102	18	21	39	141
30-34	64	52	116	10	18	28	144
35-39	42	41	83	4	7	11	94
40-44	32	33	65	4	6	10	75
45-49	23	19	42	3	5	8	50
50-54	9	15	24	3	4	7	31
55-59	5	6	11	–	1	1	12
60-64	8	1	9	–	–	–	9
65-69	–	1	1	–	1	1	2
70+	1	–	1	–	–	–	1
Unknown	1	1	2	–	–	–	2
Total	249	243	492	251	289	540	1,032

Table S4.12. *Age by Parish: Tobago, 1819 (continued)*

Age group	Africans			Creoles			Total
	Males	Females	Total	Males	Females	Total	
Parish Unknown							
0-4	–	–	–	6	6	12	12
5-9	–	–	–	1	5	6	6
10-14	1	–	1	2	2	4	5
15-19	–	–	–	3	6	9	9
20-24	1	3	4	5	4	9	13
25-29	9	4	13	2	–	2	15
30-34	4	7	11	3	3	6	17
35-39	4	4	8	1	1	2	10
40-44	10	8	18	1	–	1	19
45-49	2	1	3	2	–	2	5
50-54	1	2	3	–	1	1	4
55-59	2	–	2	–	–	–	2
60-64	–	–	–	–	–	–	–
65-69	1	2	3	–	–	–	3
70+	–	2	2	–	–	–	2
Unknown	–	–	–	–	–	–	–
Total	35	33	68	26	28	54	122

Table S4.13. *Age Structure of Slaves by Sex and Birthplace, Rural and Urban: Trinidad, 1813*

Age group	Africans			Creoles			Total
	Males	Females	Total	Males	Females	Total	
Rural Slaves							
0-4	1	1	2	1,072	1,131	2,203	2,205
5-9	3	2	5	759	825	1,584	1,589
10-14	45	20	65	565	538	1,103	1,168
15-19	485	212	697	389	365	754	1,451
20-24	1,030	782	1,812	380	362	742	2,554
25-29	1,413	1,057	2,470	314	310	624	3,094
30-34	1,310	801	2,111	284	210	494	2,605
35-39	868	471	1,339	191	147	338	1,677
40-44	617	336	953	118	104	222	1,175
45-49	361	215	576	102	88	190	766
50-54	222	145	367	77	63	140	507
55-59	101	62	163	29	19	48	211
60-64	88	58	146	26	20	46	192
65-69	28	16	44	11	8	19	63
70+	40	24	64	22	19	41	105
Unknown	–	–	–	–	–	–	–
Total	6,612	4,202	10,814	4,339	4,209	8,548	19,362*

* Excludes slaves whose location is unknown

Table S4.13. *Age, Rural and Urban: Trinidad, 1813 (continued)*

Age group	Africans			Creoles			Total
	Males	Females	Total	Males	Females	Total	
Urban Slaves							
0-4	2	1	3	338	358	696	699
5-9	2	4	6	330	232	452	458
10-14	24	20	44	191	193	384	428
15-19	225	205	430	160	132	292	722
20-24	390	330	720	139	170	309	1,029
25-29	422	365	787	125	166	291	1,078
30-34	262	215	477	105	131	236	713
35-39	137	111	248	45	82	127	375
40-44	93	88	181	44	81	125	306
45-49	34	56	90	21	29	50	140
50-54	22	33	55	18	31	49	104
55-59	7	11	18	6	10	16	34
60-64	14	17	31	7	13	20	51
65-69	2	3	5	2	3	5	10
70+	9	3	12	–	3	3	15
Unknown	–	–	–	–	–	–	–
Total	1,645	1,462	3,107	1,421	1,634	3,055	6,162

Table S4.14. *Age by Sex, Birthplace, and Slave-holding Size-group: Barbados, 1817*

Age group	Africans		Creoles		Total	Africans		Creoles		Total
	Males	Females	Males	Females		Males	Females	Males	Females	
	1-10 Slaves					*11-50 Slaves*				
0-4	–	–	1,154	1,192	2,346	–	–	1,656	1,677	3,333
5-9	–	–	861	969	1,830	–	–	1,258	1,308	2,566
10-14	5	5	890	1,028	1,928	2	2	1,159	1,148	2,311
15-19	28	30	659	814	1,531	37	14	868	896	1,815
20-24	116	161	531	703	1,511	129	94	762	836	1,821
25-29	159	213	383	604	1,359	211	166	566	713	1,656
30-34	115	213	261	428	1,017	163	182	474	618	1,437
35-39	80	136	264	406	886	152	96	415	554	1,217
40-44	57	85	142	350	634	65	67	325	484	941
45-49	34	39	111	244	428	35	27	212	368	642
50-54	14	41	97	320	472	24	25	176	330	555
55-59	10	19	47	138	214	10	22	91	205	328
60-64	7	43	37	173	260	15	32	100	219	366
65-69	6	19	24	49	98	4	10	27	77	118
70+	5	34	24	116	179	12	29	42	146	229
Unknown	–	–	1	1	2	–	–	1	–	1
Total	636	1,038	5,486	7,535	14,695	859	766	8,132	9,579	19,336

Table S4.14. *Age by Slave-holding Size-Group: Barbados, 1817 (continued)*

Age group	Africans		Creoles		Total	Africans		Creoles		Total
	Males	Females	Males	Females		Males	Females	Males	Females	
	51-100 Slaves					*101-200 Slaves*				
0-4	–	–	686	656	1,342	–	–	1,466	1,571	3,037
5-9	–	–	504	479	983	–	–	1,172	1,160	2,332
10-14	–	–	543	532	1,075	1	–	1,294	1,292	2,587
15-19	7	2	382	379	770	39	13	1,044	1,042	2,138
20-24	38	25	354	381	798	58	33	874	909	1,874
25-29	89	72	316	354	831	111	72	790	876	1,849
30-34	104	63	240	312	719	137	74	663	844	1,718
35-39	62	45	247	268	622	114	81	649	824	1,668
40-44	30	25	172	267	494	59	48	532	658	1,297
45-49	14	11	147	252	424	26	17	460	578	1,081
50-54	11	13	150	209	383	31	25	352	493	901
55-59	6	7	66	106	185	14	14	177	324	529
60-64	6	10	56	88	160	22	28	148	272	470
65-69	2	4	24	52	82	8	14	79	163	264
70+	10	20	28	81	139	16	47	103	255	421
Unknown	–	–	–	–	–	–	–	1	–	1
Total	379	297	3,915	4,416	9,007	636	466	9,804	11,261	22,167
	201-300 Slaves					*301-400 Slaves*				
0-4	–	–	691	772	1,463	–	–	46	46	92
5-9	–	–	573	612	1,185	–	–	39	30	69
10-14	–	–	642	678	1,320	–	–	51	45	96
15-19	4	3	499	527	1,033	–	–	38	53	91
20-24	18	4	412	427	861	3	2	28	25	58
25-29	32	28	337	468	865	1	1	29	29	60
30-34	40	53	334	395	822	2	3	19	35	59
35-39	38	30	336	392	796	1	–	10	26	37
40-44	22	13	257	347	639	–	–	17	18	35
45-49	18	7	207	294	526	–	–	9	15	24
50-54	13	9	168	232	422	1	–	4	13	18
55-59	–	10	98	151	259	–	1	1	10	12
60-64	11	17	92	140	260	–	1	2	10	13
65-69	2	5	43	66	116	–	–	7	7	14
70+	10	19	52	134	215	2	–	6	3	11
Unknown	–	–	1	–	1	–	–	–	–	–
Total	208	198	4,742	5,635	10,783	10	8	306	365	689

Table S4.14. *Age by Slave-holding Size-group: Barbados, 1817 (continued)*

Age group	Africans		Creoles		Total
	Males	Females	Males	Females	
		401-500 Slaves			
0-4	–	–	43	45	88
5-9	–	–	53	58	111
10-14	–	–	43	71	114
15-19	–	–	25	39	64
20-24	–	1	26	36	63
25-29	1	3	23	37	64
30-34	–	–	18	36	54
35-39	1	–	25	30	56
40-44	–	–	16	24	40
45-49	–	–	19	30	49
50-54	–	–	12	23	35
55-59	–	–	9	13	22
60-64	1	–	6	10	17
65-69	–	–	3	18	21
70+	1	1	6	6	14
Unknown	–	–	–	–	–
Total	4	5	327	476	812

Table S4.15. *Age by Sex, Birthplace and Slave-holding Size-group: St. Kitts, 1817*

Age group	Africans		Creoles		Total	Africans		Creoles		Total
	Males	Females	Males	Females		Males	Females	Males	Females	
			1-10 Slaves					*11-50 Slaves*		
0-4	–	–	158	196	354	–	–	85	94	179
5-9	–	–	157	145	302	–	–	87	86	173
10-14	–	2	141	169	312	–	–	91	80	171
15-19	6	7	88	137	238	1	2	66	49	118
20-24	22	27	88	126	263	19	11	68	57	155
25-29	25	49	68	96	238	50	15	38	57	160
30-34	40	67	45	89	241	60	30	41	59	190
35-39	33	45	31	58	167	34	14	29	26	103
40-44	30	26	24	57	137	15	5	35	31	86
45-49	15	17	20	50	102	14	7	14	25	60
50-54	17	26	12	28	83	12	7	13	17	49
55-59	11	13	6	15	45	9	3	4	7	23
60-64	10	13	3	17	43	4	9	6	12	31
65-69	2	5	–	5	12	2	4	–	6	12
70+	3	8	1	11	23	2	8	1	4	15
Unknown	–	2	–	–	2	–	–	–	–	–
Total	214	307	842	1,199	2,562	222	115	578	610	1,525

Table S4.15. *Age by Slave-holding Size-group: St. Kitts, 1817 (continued)*

Age group	Africans		Creoles		Total	Africans		Creoles		Total
	Males	Females	Males	Females		Males	Females	Males	Females	
	51-100 Slaves					*101-200 Slaves*				
0-4	–	–	102	94	196	–	–	455	501	956
5-9	–	–	100	81	181	–	–	460	452	912
10-14	–	–	101	112	213	3	–	452	396	851
15-19	2	1	61	79	143	35	15	321	328	699
20-24	19	7	69	66	161	57	40	331	325	753
25-29	42	17	67	62	188	115	83	289	288	775
30-34	24	18	50	67	159	98	65	238	319	720
35-39	26	4	70	62	162	73	56	190	228	547
40-44	21	7	50	45	123	63	56	158	224	501
45-49	18	9	44	59	130	57	27	167	189	440
50-54	19	8	30	43	100	54	46	130	147	377
55-59	8	6	11	26	51	35	37	72	90	234
60-64	14	11	18	21	64	46	46	70	118	280
65-69	3	3	8	10	24	17	27	18	64	126
70+	8	8	9	19	44	58	51	33	86	228
Unknown	–	–	–	–	–	–	–	–	–	–
Total	204	99	790	846	1,939	711	549	3,384	3,755	8,399
	201-300 Slaves					*301-400 Slaves*				
0-4	–	–	178	166	344	–	–	79	82	161
5-9	–	–	147	175	322	–	–	66	66	132
10-14	–	1	159	146	306	–	–	71	72	143
15-19	20	10	107	92	229	10	5	56	59	130
20-24	17	17	117	110	261	19	13	42	41	115
25-29	32	32	97	106	267	17	12	49	62	140
30-34	33	25	98	88	244	38	17	37	48	140
35-39	19	11	65	79	174	15	11	35	31	92
40-44	20	15	55	76	166	22	9	25	35	91
45-49	13	7	51	64	135	14	1	16	30	61
50-54	13	18	45	69	145	12	8	13	39	72
55-59	4	7	18	43	72	3	5	6	14	28
60-64	15	13	21	34	83	11	6	8	26	51
65-69	11	2	13	17	43	2	3	1	6	12
70+	8	9	11	28	56	6	16	10	11	43
Unknown	–	–	–	–	–	–	–	–	–	–
Total	205	167	1,182	1,293	2,847	169	106	514	622	1,411

Table S4.15. *Age by Slave-holding Size-group: St. Kitts, 1817 (continued)*

Age group	Africans		Creoles		Total	Africans		Creoles		Total
	Males	Females	Males	Females		Males	Females	Males	Females	
	401-500 Slaves					*501-600 Slaves*				
0-4	–	–	45	53	98	–	–	26	22	48
5-9	–	–	47	56	103	–	–	22	26	48
10-14	–	–	53	36	89	–	–	33	35	68
15-19	1	–	29	36	66	–	–	20	18	38
20-24	1	1	23	35	50	8	2	19	24	53
25-29	1	5	32	40	78	7	3	22	30	62
30-34	12	11	36	35	104	8	2	30	22	62
35-39	5	4	22	25	56	9	1	16	24	50
40-44	5	2	24	37	68	5	3	15	20	43
45-49	4	2	17	10	33	6	3	10	10	29
50-54	10	3	10	15	38	2	1	9	3	15
55-59	3	1	6	6	16	2	–	1	9	12
60-64	8	7	1	14	30	1	3	5	7	16
65-69	2	1	5	5	13	1	1	1	–	13
70+	4	5	5	13	27	5	1	3	9	18
Unknown	–	–	–	–	–	–	–	–	–	–
Total	56	42	355	416	869	54	20	232	259	565

Table S4.16. *Age by Sex and Slave-holding Size-group: Montserrat, 1831*

Age group	Males	Females	Total	Males	Females	Total	Males	Females	Total
	1-10 Slaves			*11-50 Slaves*			*51-100 Slaves*		
0-4	44	41	85	53	51	104	64	63	127
5-9	33	57	90	32	32	64	49	55	104
10-14	36	39	75	25	27	52	38	58	96
15-19	36	45	81	40	17	57	38	34	72
20-24	29	38	67	20	24	44	34	29	63
25-29	31	27	58	24	22	46	46	44	90
30-34	20	28	48	28	14	42	29	30	59
35-39	12	11	23	26	20	46	29	39	68
40-44	8	17	25	9	11	20	23	27	50
45-49	7	19	26	6	16	22	21	18	39
50-54	6	9	15	7	12	19	13	25	38
55-59	–	6	6	4	9	13	10	18	28
60-64	2	2	4	3	9	12	5	12	17
65-69	–	2	2	–	3	3	2	2	4
70+	2	1	3	–	5	5	2	9	11
Unknown	–	1	1	–	–	–	–	–	–
Total	266	343	609	277	272	549	403	463	866

Table S4.16. *Age by Slave-holding Size-group: Montserrat, 1831 (continued,*

Age group	Males	Females	Total	Males	Females	Total
	101-200 Slaves			*201+ Slaves*		
0-4	199	225	424	118	101	219
5-9	136	158	294	103	110	213
10-14	127	144	271	94	89	183
15-19	123	123	246	84	85	169
20-24	111	106	217	65	63	128
25-29	110	127	237	67	71	138
30-34	93	99	192	82	64	146
35-39	88	102	190	54	50	104
40-44	79	92	171	39	57	96
45-49	43	58	101	40	39	79
50-54	39	51	90	35	44	79
55-59	32	47	79	21	18	39
60-64	14	36	50	13	25	38
65-69	4	12	16	2	12	14
70+	9	38	47	6	18	24
Unknown	4	–	4	–	–	–
Total	1,211	1,418	2,629	823	846	1,669

Table S4.17. *Age by Sex, Birthplace and Slave-holding Size-group:*
Virgin Islands, 1818

Age group	Africans		Creoles		Total	Africans		Creoles		Total
	Males	Females	Males	Females		Males	Females	Males	Females	
	1-10 Slaves					*11-50 Slaves*				
0-4	–	–	48	43	91	–	–	73	78	151
5-9	–	–	41	39	80	–	–	58	66	124
10-14	–	–	36	42	78	–	–	67	54	121
15-19	–	–	29	39	68	1	–	43	42	86
20-24	2	10	17	36	65	10	9	26	35	80
25-29	4	11	12	34	61	13	13	39	40	105
30-34	12	21	12	15	60	19	15	13	42	89
35-39	6	11	8	17	42	15	10	21	19	65
40-44	2	8	15	14	39	3	11	13	22	49
45-49	2	6	5	12	25	2	6	10	8	26
50-54	–	6	–	12	18	5	9	7	12	33
55-59	3	2	–	9	14	4	4	4	12	24
60-64	2	2	3	5	12	1	6	9	7	23
65-69	–	–	1	4	5	3	1	–	2	6
70+	–	–	1	1	2	–	1	1	7	9
Unknown	–	–	–	1	1	–	–	–	–	–
Total	33	77	228	323	661	76	85	384	446	991

Table S4.17. *Age by Slave-holding Size-group: Virgin Islands, 1818 (cont.)*

Age group	Africans Males	Africans Females	Creoles Males	Creoles Females	Total	Africans Males	Africans Females	Creoles Males	Creoles Females	Total
			51-100 Slaves					*101-200 Slaves*		
0-4	–	–	57	50	107	–	–	107	121	228
5-9	–	–	54	68	122	–	–	105	106	211
10-14	–	–	51	51	102	–	–	138	139	277
15-19	1	–	42	54	97	1	–	117	90	208
20-24	7	3	47	38	95	15	1	59	71	146
25-29	15	15	37	42	109	14	3	68	95	180
30-34	30	11	23	38	102	16	4	75	108	203
35-39	28	11	18	23	80	17	13	57	68	155
40-44	23	8	19	34	84	26	9	43	59	137
45-49	9	13	13	15	50	14	9	30	37	90
50-54	8	5	10	11	34	25	23	31	51	130
55-59	4	3	3	6	16	2	13	17	21	53
60-64	3	3	7	7	20	8	20	11	26	65
65-69	2	–	2	1	5	6	6	7	22	41
70+	5	8	2	6	21	13	21	10	15	59
Unknown	1	–	–	–	1	–	–	–	–	–
Total	136	80	385	444	1,045	157	122	875	1,029	2,183
			201-300 Slaves					*301-400 Slaves*		
0-4	–	–	9	12	21	–	–	20	26	46
5-9	–	–	12	22	34	–	–	18	20	38
10-14	–	–	9	14	23	–	–	9	17	26
15-19	–	–	5	4	9	–	–	7	25	32
20-24	–	–	14	7	21	–	–	15	7	22
25-29	1	–	6	10	17	–	2	14	18	34
30-34	1	2	4	9	16	1	–	8	12	21
35-39	–	–	3	6	9	1	1	5	10	17
40-44	5	1	8	10	24	–	–	10	11	21
45-49	–	–	2	6	8	4	–	5	10	19
50-54	1	1	5	2	9	2	–	9	8	19
55-59	–	–	–	2	2	–	–	4	1	5
60-64	–	–	5	3	8	1	–	1	3	5
65-69	–	–	1	–	1	–	–	–	5	5
70+	–	–	–	1	1	–	3	–	7	10
Unknown	–	–	–	–	–	–	–	–	–	–
Total	8	4	83	108	203	9	6	125	180	320

Table S4.17. *Age by Slave-holding Size-group: Virgin Islands, 1818 (cont.)*

Age group	Africans Males	Africans Females	Creoles Males	Creoles Females	Total	Africans Males	Africans Females	Creoles Males	Creoles Females	Total
			401-500 Slaves					*601-700 Slaves*		
0-4	–	–	50	48	98	–	–	20	37	57
5-9	–	–	55	43	98	–	–	30	20	50
10-14	–	–	42	41	83	–	–	48	42	90
15-19	–	–	26	23	49	2	–	32	29	63
20-24	6	1	30	35	72	11	11	25	30	77
25-29	15	12	22	47	96	9	10	27	27	73
30-34	15	9	21	28	73	6	3	18	20	47
35-39	21	7	15	16	59	2	2	11	10	25
40-44	5	4	22	42	73	5	1	13	19	38
45-49	9	7	9	26	51	–	2	7	13	22
50-54	8	9	19	23	59	5	3	9	8	25
55-59	5	4	11	17	37	3	1	8	8	20
60-64	5	1	14	18	38	4	3	3	1	11
65-69	–	1	1	5	7	1	–	–	1	2
70+	2	4	6	3	15	1	1	1	2	5
Unknown	–	–	–	–	–	–	–	–	–	–
Total	91	59	343	415	908	49	37	252	267	605

Table S4.18. *Age by Sex, Birthplace and Slave-holding Size-group: St. Lucia, 1815*

Age group	Africans Males	Africans Females	Creoles Males	Creoles Females	Total	Africans Males	Africans Females	Creoles Males	Creoles Females	Total
			1-10 Slaves					*11-50 Slaves*		
0-4	–	–	200	207	407	–	–	344	385	729
5-9	–	–	133	169	303	1	1	330	310	642
10-14	7	1	161	162	332	1	1	297	299	598
15-19	18	18	67	141	246	17	12	221	199	449
20-24	37	46	102	149	336	57	40	195	238	530
25-29	36	50	83	140	311	91	44	210	220	567
30-34	36	46	60	97	241	72	57	133	145	407
35-39	33	50	33	64	182	72	63	75	142	352
40-44	16	51	22	74	164	53	80	42	104	281
45-49	10	23	17	43	93	49	49	39	96	233
50-54	12	30	8	32	82	29	55	22	68	174
55-59	7	16	9	15	47	21	27	21	38	107
60-64	9	11	9	20	50	25	35	13	30	104
65-69	5	5	2	13	25	9	27	5	20	61
70+	3	15	5	5	28	16	27	3	15	61
Unknown	2	–	4	1	7	2	1	6	3	14
Total	231	362	915	1,332	2,854*	515	519	1,956	2,312	5,309**

* Includes 14 slaves whose birthplace is unknown.
** Includes 7 slaves whose birthplace is unknown.

Table S4.18. *Age by Slave-holding Size-group: St. Lucia, 1815 (continued)*

Age group	Africans Males	Africans Females	Creoles Males	Creoles Females	Total	Africans Males	Africans Females	Creoles Males	Creoles Females	Total
	51-100 Slaves					*101-200 Slaves*				
0-4	–	–	189	250	439	–	–	148	183	331
5-9	–	1	193	199	394	–	–	139	148	287
10-14	1	–	230	196	427	2	–	137	141	280
15-19	9	2	140	152	303	9	4	123	101	237
20-24	21	19	155	153	348	32	21	99	109	261
25-29	39	25	155	139	358	52	39	99	123	313
30-34	48	44	111	139	342	51	25	89	84	250
35-39	54	33	69	89	246	38	42	52	86	218
40-44	38	51	45	90	225	44	46	28	53	171
45-49	35	56	27	66	185	36	40	31	44	151
50-54	37	44	34	45	160	22	23	18	36	99
55-59	24	28	10	41	105	12	28	9	26	75
60-64	22	35	12	45	114	16	32	12	26	86
65-69	7	15	7	14	44	11	14	4	10	39
70+	15	29	13	16	74	20	28	6	16	70
Unknown	–	–	3	4	12	1	–	1	–	2
Total	350	382	1,393	1,638	3,776*	346	342	995	1,186	2,870**
	201-300 Slaves					*301-400 Slaves*				
0-4	–	–	53	53	106	–	–	16	22	38
5-9	–	–	36	55	91	–	–	12	19	31
10-14	–	–	68	55	123	7	2	14	10	33
15-19	4	–	45	68	117	14	6	12	6	38
20-24	12	10	46	49	117	4	1	7	5	17
25-29	16	5	33	40	95	16	2	8	17	43
30-34	17	14	35	29	96	17	2	7	4	30
35-39	28	29	9	24	90	11	3	3	5	23
40-44	16	24	12	24	77	11	3	1	4	20
45-49	12	26	10	9	58	4	7	2	2	15
50-54	9	16	11	19	55	5	3	2	6	16
55-59	6	7	1	12	26	4	6	1	1	12
60-64	4	9	7	5	25	1	4	–	1	6
65-69	7	11	4	3	25	2	1	–	3	6
70+	6	13	4	7	30	2	2	2	2	8
Unknown	–	–	1	–	4	–	–	2	–	2
Total	137	164	375	452	1,135†	98	42	89	107	338††

* Includes 13 slaves whose birthplace is unknown.
** Includes 1 slave whose birthplace is unknown.
† Includes 7 slaves whose birthplace is unknown.
†† Includes 2 slaves whose birthplace is unknown.

Table S4.19. *Age by Sex, Birthplace and Slave-holding Size-group: St. Vincent, 1817*

Age group	Africans		Creoles		Total	Africans		Creoles		Total
	Males	Females	Males	Females		Males	Females	Males	Females	
	1-10 Slaves					*11-50 Slaves*				
0-4	–	–	128	146	274	–	–	137	120	257
5-9	–	–	118	137	255	–	–	132	115	247
10-14	2	–	146	137	285	–	–	129	114	243
15-19	8	4	70	99	181	12	6	85	68	171
20-24	26	41	67	60	194	67	20	48	59	194
25-29	68	84	37	61	250	121	69	41	42	273
30-34	77	105	28	45	255	151	86	28	43	308
35-39	48	71	22	29	170	111	66	20	36	233
40-44	40	74	5	23	142	69	53	9	21	152
45-49	26	38	8	17	89	43	27	13	9	92
50-54	20	20	6	10	56	26	22	7	13	68
55-59	5	4	6	4	19	17	8	4	5	34
60-64	8	12	4	8	32	15	5	2	3	25
65-69	3	2	–	–	5	4	4	2	1	11
70+	1	5	1	5	12	3	–	1	1	5
Unknown	–	5	–	2	7	–	–	2	–	2
Total	332	465	646	783	2,226	639	366	660	650	2,315
	51-100 Slaves					*101-200 Slaves*				
0-4	–	–	81	76	157	–	–	351	422	773
5-9	–	–	118	88	206	–	–	395	402	797
10-14	–	–	91	101	192	1	1	382	353	737
15-19	5	1	75	77	158	4	–	249	269	522
20-24	18	21	52	59	150	45	22	229	230	526
25-29	67	29	45	43	184	175	134	191	181	681
30-34	77	64	29	29	199	242	199	157	176	774
35-39	87	70	25	27	209	258	214	136	173	781
40-44	51	71	20	23	165	248	211	84	103	646
45-49	39	36	9	10	94	186	134	62	73	455
50-54	36	33	9	8	86	147	146	44	38	375
55-59	18	9	11	4	42	61	42	22	28	153
60-64	14	15	3	9	41	77	82	11	27	197
65-69	8	9	–	3	20	29	33	4	7	73
70+	9	9	1	5	24	64	76	10	22	172
Unknown	–	3	–	–	3	3	3	1	1	8
Total	429	370	569	562	1,930	1,540	1,297	2,328	2,505	7,670

Table S4.19. *Age by Slave-holding Size-group: St. Vincent, 1817 (continued)*

Age group	Africans		Creoles		Total	Africans		Creoles		Total
	Males	Females	Males	Females		Males	Females	Males	Females	
	201-300 Slaves					*301-400 Slaves*				
0-4	–	–	285	297	582	–	–	178	215	393
5-9	–	–	254	286	540	–	–	194	186	380
10-14	1	–	278	244	523	1	–	191	169	361
15-19	4	4	209	212	429	10	5	173	169	357
20-24	43	14	145	129	331	24	26	94	148	292
25-29	121	78	103	106	408	70	50	89	90	299
30-34	190	156	74	89	509	197	145	63	75	480
35-39	214	216	79	99	608	198	161	45	54	458
40-44	167	143	72	61	443	148	120	25	20	313
45-49	121	103	49	32	305	110	69	22	12	213
50-54	75	67	21	25	188	79	65	15	23	182
55-59	46	47	9	20	122	41	40	4	7	92
60-64	49	47	4	11	111	25	35	3	3	66
65-69	17	27	7	7	58	14	8	4	–	26
70+	15	31	3	8	57	17	10	4	1	32
Unknown	–	–	–	–	–	–	–	1	–	1
Total	1,063	933	1,592	1,626	5,214	934	734	1,105	1,172	3,945
	401-500 Slaves					*501-600 Slaves*				
0-4	–	–	49	49	98	–	–	63	61	124
5-9	–	–	53	35	88	–	–	60	54	114
10-14	1	–	44	33	78	–	–	66	57	123
15-19	1	–	30	37	68	2	1	57	68	128
20-24	10	7	23	32	72	11	2	51	80	144
25-29	21	15	15	17	68	7	3	28	27	65
30-34	38	22	5	17	82	6	5	16	21	48
35-39	40	48	10	10	108	21	25	11	16	73
40-44	30	28	6	6	70	38	37	8	23	106
45-49	20	19	3	4	46	21	35	5	9	70
50-54	8	4	2	1	15	42	33	3	4	82
55-59	6	9	1	3	19	22	16	3	1	42
60-64	4	4	1	5	14	20	13	–	2	35
65-69	–	2	1	1	4	9	5	1	–	15
70+	2	2	–	–	4	3	2	–	1	6
Unknown	–	–	–	–	–	–	–	–	–	–
Total	181	160	243	250	834	202	177	372	424	1,175

Table S4.20. *Age by Sex, Birthplace and Slave-holding Size-group: Tobago, 1819*

Age group	Africans		Creoles		Total	Africans		Creoles		Total
	Males	Females	Males	Females		Males	Females	Males	Females	
	1-10 Slaves					*11-50 Slaves*				
0-4	–	–	43	52	95	–	–	43	43	86
5-9	–	–	44	54	98	–	–	51	40	91
10-14	1	–	38	35	74	–	–	47	35	82
15-19	1	1	34	33	69	4	2	19	34	59
20-24	9	14	17	26	66	5	21	17	18	61
25-29	33	45	18	15	111	41	47	7	21	116
30-34	44	54	9	18	125	62	44	10	15	131
35-39	25	41	6	5	77	55	29	6	7	97
40-44	33	26	6	4	69	33	30	2	6	71
45-49	13	18	4	4	39	22	10	2	4	38
50-54	8	17	2	2	29	6	6	1	5	18
55-59	4	5	–	–	9	6	5	–	1	12
60-64	5	–	–	–	5	6	5	–	–	11
65-69	1	3	–	1	5	1	1	–	–	2
70+	1	2	–	–	3	–	–	–	–	–
Unknown	–	1	1	–	2	1	–	–	–	1
Total	178	227	222	249	876	242	200	205	229	876
	51-100 Slaves					*101-200 Slaves*				
0-4	–	–	40	53	93	–	–	285	331	616
5-9	–	–	49	51	100	–	–	315	312	627
10-14	–	–	48	44	92	–	–	294	258	552
15-19	3	1	34	28	66	3	1	253	236	493
20-24	19	13	36	37	105	16	7	201	224	448
25-29	52	24	20	24	120	71	40	185	239	535
30-34	49	53	16	22	140	189	138	156	180	663
35-39	42	33	10	13	98	273	218	122	140	753
40-44	38	26	3	11	78	253	229	50	67	599
45-49	33	31	3	4	71	139	142	20	26	327
50-54	13	26	–	3	42	124	161	11	15	311
55-59	14	13	1	–	28	73	115	4	7	199
60-64	7	6	–	1	14	99	120	3	2	224
65-69	4	7	1	2	14	32	36	3	1	72
70+	2	2	–	–	4	30	42	1	3	76
Unknown	–	–	–	–	–	–	–	1	–	1
Total	276	235	261	293	1,065	1,302	1,249	1,904	2,041	6,496

Age group	Africans Males	Females	Creoles Males	Females	Total	Africans Males	Females	Creoles Males	Females	Total
	201-300 Slaves					*301-400 Slaves*				
0-4	–	–	157	140	297	–	–	128	152	280
5-9	–	–	154	155	309	–	–	154	153	307
10-14	–	–	149	188	337	–	–	129	128	257
15-19	–	–	95	102	197	1	–	120	128	249
20-24	5	1	57	50	113	6	7	100	109	222
25-29	25	29	82	79	215	39	41	69	82	231
30-34	57	51	62	74	244	68	38	52	61	219
35-39	104	92	62	76	334	69	54	42	54	219
40-44	116	91	48	52	307	62	77	17	27	183
45-49	85	74	13	21	193	75	85	13	10	183
50-54	71	52	5	12	140	54	53	4	5	116
55-59	49	48	6	4	107	35	47	1	2	85
60-64	47	50	5	6	108	38	43	2	4	87
65-69	20	34	1	4	59	16	12	–	1	29
70+	18	22	1	2	43	9	16	–	–	25
Unknown	–	–	–	–	–	–	–	–	–	–
Total	597	544	897	965	3,003	472	473	831	916	2,692
	401-500 Slaves									
0-4	–	–	18	22	40					
5-9	–	–	35	25	60					
10-14	–	–	38	27	65					
15-19	–	–	24	23	47					
20-24	–	–	10	8	18					
25-29	2	1	13	11	27					
30-34	2	6	7	7	22					
35-39	8	9	5	6	28					
40-44	15	9	1	7	32					
45-49	16	11	1	–	28					
50-54	15	10	–	–	25					
55-59	12	13	–	–	25					
60-64	4	6	–	–	10					
65-69	6	5	–	1	12					
70+	5	4	–	1	10					
Unknown	–	–	–	–	–					
Total	85	74	152	138	449					

Table S4.21. *Age by Sex, Birthplace and Slave-holding Size-group: Berbice, 1819*

Age group	Africans		Creoles		Total	Africans		Creoles		Total
	Males	Females	Males	Females		Males	Females	Males	Females	
	1-10 Slaves					*11-50 Slaves*				
0-4	–	–	92	97	189	–	–	86	110	196
5-9	–	–	61	80	141	–	–	68	87	155
10-14	–	1	47	65	113	–	1	68	49	118
15-19	5	11	36	40	92	13	4	44	39	100
20-24	57	42	19	27	145	64	31	26	23	144
25-29	124	102	17	28	272	231	86	17	12	346
30-34	104	85	10	10	210	190	87	17	11	306
35-39	61	48	5	9	123	183	62	11	8	264
40-44	38	21	4	9	72	78	32	5	5	120
45-49	14	13	5	2	34	59	17	9	4	89
50-54	12	10	2	3	28	15	10	–	3	28
55-59	9	2	1	1	14	7	1	–	1	9
60-64	4	6	1	2	13	4	4	2	1	11
65-69	2	1	–	–	3	1	–	–	–	1
70+	1	2	1	1	5	1	1	1	1	4
Unknown	2	–	2	2	6	1	1	–	–	2
Total	433	344	303	376	1,460*	847	337	354	354	1,893**
	51-100 Slaves					*101-200 Slaves*				
0-4	–	–	178	175	353	–	–	551	574	1,125
5-9	–	–	147	168	316	–	–	445	514	959
10-14	1	–	143	144	288	1	3	433	393	830
15-19	6	3	98	90	197	17	2	269	244	532
20-24	63	41	25	39	168	98	62	135	150	445
25-29	280	182	34	41	537	514	415	147	191	1,267
30-34	263	173	22	26	484	624	459	118	129	1,330
35-39	341	147	21	22	531	859	497	104	120	1,580
40-44	173	67	13	12	265	422	207	55	55	739
45-49	92	34	13	3	142	245	115	41	44	445
50-54	30	17	4	10	61	105	74	12	27	218
55-59	19	9	2	1	31	49	56	16	16	137
60-64	14	9	–	1	24	58	59	9	9	135
65-69	5	2	2	1	10	18	20	5	7	50
70+	5	3	2	4	14	11	11	6	8	36
Unknown	–	–	–	–	–	19	1	5	3	44
Total	1,292	687	704	737	3,421†	3,040	1,981	2,351	2,484	9,872††

* Total includes 4 slaves whose birthplace is unknown.
** Total includes one slave whose birthplace is unknown.
† Total includes one slave whose birthplace is unknown.
†† Total includes 16 slaves whose birthplace is unknown.

Table S4.21. *Age by Slave-holding Size-group: Berbice, 1819 (continued)*

Age group	Africans		Creoles		Total	Africans		Creoles		Total
	Males	Females	Males	Females		Males	Females	Males	Females	
	201-300 Slaves					*301-400 Slaves*				
0-4	–	–	204	221	425	–	–	163	157	320
5-9	–	–	187	189	376	–	–	158	159	317
10-14	–	1	150	148	299	–	–	134	131	265
15-19	8	7	108	91	214	6	1	79	94	180
20-24	69	46	41	81	237	51	48	35	30	164
25-29	177	127	35	30	369	140	100	25	38	303
30-34	286	160	35	24	505	140	100	24	23	288
35-39	336	197	29	12	574	209	175	23	31	438
40-44	201	139	23	21	384	160	71	17	25	273
45-49	144	78	12	16	250	93	23	22	11	149
50-54	42	27	8	8	85	48	13	9	7	77
55-59	21	14	5	11	51	27	12	6	9	54
60-64	13	17	6	4	40	15	8	9	5	37
65-69	6	5	1	3	15	3	8	3	4	18
70+	4	5	2	1	12	10	10	4	10	34
Unknown	3	–	1	24	50	12	–	1	1	14
Total	1,310	823	847	884	3,886*	914	569	712	735	2,931**
	401-500 Slaves									
0-4	–	–	16	16	32					
5-9	–	–	16	7	23					
10-14	–	–	15	16	31					
15-19	–	–	4	4	8					
20-24	7	13	1	2	23					
25-29	68	69	7	3	147					
30-34	49	32	2	–	83					
35-39	18	10	1	–	29					
40-44	3	2	1	1	7					
45-49	–	3	–	1	4					
50-54	5	2	–	–	7					
55-59	1	–	–	–	1					
60-64	1	–	–	–	1					
65-69	–	–	–	–	–					
70+	–	–	–	–	–					
Unknown	4	1	–	–	5					
Total	156	132	63	50	401					

* Total includes 22 slaves whose birthplace is unknown.
** Total includes one slave whose birthplace is unknown.

Table S4.22. *Age by Sex, Birthplace and Slave-holding Size-group: Anguilla, 1827*

Age group	Africans Males	Africans Females	Creoles Males	Creoles Females	Total	Africans Males	Africans Females	Creoles Males	Creoles Females	Total
	1-10 Slaves					*11-50 Slaves*				
0-4	–	–	61	43	104	–	–	85	85	170
5-9	–	–	44	43	87	–	–	53	58	111
10-14	–	–	51	42	93	–	–	49	45	94
15-19	–	–	34	50	84	–	–	48	40	88
20-24	–	–	16	43	59	–	–	46	60	106
25-29	–	–	20	31	51	1	–	25	49	75
30-34	1	1	9	36	47	1	–	24	32	57
35-39	–	–	6	19	25	–	3	17	19	39
40-44	1	–	8	20	29	2	–	18	37	57
45-49	–	–	8	8	16	–	1	13	16	30
50-54	–	–	8	11	19	1	2	7	20	30
55-59	–	3	4	9	16	1	–	6	14	21
60-64	–	1	5	5	11	2	–	8	5	15
65-69	1	–	1	1	3	1	–	3	4	8
70+	–	1	1	1	3	–	–	3	6	9
Unknown	–	–	–	–	–	–	–	–	–	–
Total	3	6	276	362	647	9	6	405	490	910
	51-100 Slaves					*101-200 Slaves*				
0-4	–	–	35	41	76	–	–	14	16	30
5-9	–	–	19	32	51	–	–	19	22	41
10-14	–	–	23	31	54	–	–	16	10	26
15-19	–	–	18	14	32	–	–	11	20	31
20-24	–	–	16	16	32	–	–	9	8	17
25-29	1	–	21	18	40	–	–	6	9	15
30-34	2	–	12	19	33	1	–	4	9	14
35-39	–	–	11	15	26	–	–	6	12	18
40-44	–	–	7	14	21	1	–	4	1	6
45-49	–	–	4	4	8	2	1	1	2	6
50-54	2	1	8	9	20	2	2	1	7	12
55-59	–	2	2	8	12	2	–	2	2	6
60-64	1	1	3	5	10	1	1	–	4	6
65-69	–	–	1	2	3	–	–	–	–	–
70+	2	1	–	3	6	2	–	2	2	6
Unknown	–	–	–	–	–	–	–	–	–	–
Total	8	5	180	231	424	11	4	95	124	234

Table S4.22. *Age by Slave-holding Size-group: Anguilla, 1827 (continued)*

Age group	Africans		Creoles		Total
	Males	Females	Males	Females	
201-300 Slaves					
0-4	–	–	11	21	32
5-9	–	–	20	8	28
10-14	–	–	21	10	31
15-19	–	–	11	20	31
20-24	–	–	15	14	29
25-29	–	–	10	11	21
30-34	1	–	18	11	30
35-39	1	1	8	4	14
40-44	–	1	18	9	28
45-49	–	–	7	7	14
50-54	–	–	4	5	9
55-59	–	–	–	2	2
60-64	2	3	2	3	10
65-69	–	2	–	–	2
70+	–	3	–	4	7
Unknown	–	–	–	–	–
Total	4	10	145	129	288

Table S4.23. *Age by Sex, Birthplace and Slave-holding Size-group: Trinidad, 1813*

Age group	Africans			Creoles			Total
	Males	Females	Total	Males	Females	Total	
1-10 Slaves							
0-4	–	–	–	379	388	767	767
5-9	1	2	3	254	267	521	524
10-14	19	20	39	198	224	422	461
15-19	184	220	404	176	163	339	743
20-24	390	413	803	156	185	341	1,144
25-29	389	449	838	103	176	279	1,117
30-34	267	256	523	90	115	205	728
35-39	142	142	284	48	80	128	412
40-44	123	119	242	34	66	100	342
45-49	64	73	137	30	32	62	199
50-54	33	38	71	17	28	45	116
55-59	20	16	36	9	9	18	54
60-64	12	17	29	8	12	20	49
65-69	3	3	6	3	2	5	11
70+	4	2	6	–	2	2	8
Unknown	–	–	–	–	–	–	–
Total	1,651	1,770	3,421	1,505	1,749	3,254	6,675

Table S4.23. *Age by Slave-holding Size-group: Trinidad, 1813 (continued)*

Age group	Africans			Creoles			Total
	Males	Females	Total	Males	Females	Total	
11-50 Slaves							
0-4	1	1	2	505	536	1,041	1,043
5-9	2	–	2	354	348	702	704
10-14	27	8	35	258	246	504	539
15-19	253	123	376	182	148	330	706
20-24	510	349	859	168	182	350	1,209
25-29	686	462	1,148	191	157	348	1,496
30-34	580	320	900	148	122	270	1,170
35-39	366	164	530	94	73	167	697
40-44	262	134	396	57	78	135	531
45-49	154	90	244	43	50	93	337
50-54	84	51	135	34	27	61	196
55-59	25	18	43	12	13	25	68
60-64	38	26	64	10	14	24	88
65-69	9	7	16	3	5	8	24
70+	19	9	28	11	8	19	47
Unknown	–	–	–	–	–	–	–
Total	3,016	1,762	4,778	2,070	2,007	4,077	8,855
51-100 Slaves							
0-4	2	1	3	318	345	663	666
5-9	2	3	5	247	269	516	521
10-14	5	6	11	180	172	352	363
15-19	165	47	212	105	116	221	433
20-24	367	220	587	126	104	230	817
25-29	524	338	862	90	99	189	1,051
30-34	443	266	709	102	67	169	878
35-39	305	152	457	69	53	122	579
40-44	199	100	299	46	29	75	374
45-49	109	61	170	31	20	51	221
50-54	77	42	119	27	26	53	172
55-59	32	19	51	11	6	17	68
60-64	27	20	47	14	4	18	65
65-69	7	6	13	6	2	8	21
70+	18	8	26	6	6	12	38
Unknown	–	–	–	–	–	–	–
Total	2,282	1,289	3,571	1,378	1,318	2,696	6,267

Table S4.23. *Age by Slave-holding Size-group:*
Trinidad, 1813 (continued)

Age group	Africans			Creoles			Total
	Males	Females	Total	Males	Females	Total	
101-200 Slaves							
0-4	–	–	–	154	175	329	329
5-9	–	–	–	95	138	233	233
10-14	17	2	19	94	70	164	183
15-19	92	24	116	78	63	141	257
20-24	133	107	240	62	52	114	354
25-29	187	133	320	48	35	83	403
30-34	215	125	340	35	29	64	404
35-39	131	88	219	18	14	32	251
40-44	95	52	147	21	11	32	179
45-49	58	30	88	12	13	25	113
50-54	37	34	71	12	12	24	95
55-59	25	11	36	2	–	2	38
60-64	22	10	32	1	3	4	36
65-69	8	2	10	1	2	3	13
70+	8	7	15	5	5	10	25
Unknown	–	–	–	–	–	–	–
Total	1,028	625	1,653	638	622	1,260	2,913
201-300 Slaves							
0-4	–	–	–	59	51	110	110
5-9	–	1	1	34	40	74	75
10-14	1	4	5	30	20	50	55
15-19	17	3	20	8	7	15	35
20-24	26	24	50	8	9	17	67
25-29	61	52	113	9	9	18	131
30-34	81	53	134	14	8	22	156
35-39	66	36	102	7	9	16	118
40-44	37	19	56	5	1	6	62
45-49	11	17	28	7	2	9	37
50-54	13	13	26	5	1	6	32
55-59	6	9	15	1	1	2	17
60-64	3	2	5	–	–	–	5
65-69	3	1	4	–	–	–	4
70+	1	1	2	–	1	1	3
Unknown	–	–	–	–	–	–	–
Total	326	235	561	187	159	346	907

Table S4.24. *Mean Age of Slaves by Sex, Birthplace and Slave-holding Size-group: St. Lucia, 1815 and Berbice, 1819*

Slaves per holding	St. Lucia, 1815				Berbice, 1819			
	Africans		Creoles		Africans		Creoles	
	Males	Females	Males	Females	Males	Females	Males	Female
1	35.5	34.1	26.5	26.6	32.2	30.8	20.9	22.3
2	29.7	36.9	19.5	24.5	32.9	29.9	16.4	16.9
3	28.7	34.1	19.0	20.5	30.9	31.5	12.3	11.2
4	36.3	37.5	16.2	21.2	35.0	34.1	10.7	13.3
5	32.7	39.8	15.1	21.3	31.3	31.1	11.9	8.2
6-10	36.2	39.1	16.8	20.6	31.8	31.7	12.0	13.5
11-20	37.5	41.8	16.9	21.8	33.4	32.1	14.8	11.1
21-30	37.6	44.8	17.8	20.9	30.9	32.0	13.7	13.1
31-40	39.7	45.8	19.4	22.6	34.2	33.6	13.6	13.2
41-50	38.1	41.3	18.7	21.6	35.5	35.1	13.9	11.4
51-75	41.4	45.6	20.4	23.8	34.6	33.7	14.0	14.5
76-100	42.4	47.5	20.2	22.9	35.8	34.2	12.7	12.5
101-150	39.1	45.8	20.2	23.1	36.5	36.0	14.2	14.3
151-200	42.7	44.1	20.5	22.5	36.4	36.7	15.8	16.6
201-250	40.5	46.3	21.1	23.0	36.7	36.3	15.1	15.4
251-300	–	–	–	–	36.3	36.8	13.1	11.4
301-350	33.3	42.4	20.3	21.6	37.1	35.8	16.1	16.9
351-400	–	–	–	–	41.5	38.6	8.4	9.5
401-450	–	–	–	–	31.0	29.5	11.5	11.1
Total	38.7	43.5	19.0	22.3	35.7	35.3	14.5	14.7

Table S4.25. *Age-specific Slave Sex Ratios by Colony, 1813-34*

Age group	Males per 100 Females						
	Barbados, 1817	St. Kitts, 1817	Nevis, 1817	Antigua, 1832	Montserrat 1831	Virgin Islands, 1818	Jamaica, 1817
0-4	96.4	93.4	87.0	101.0	99.4	92.5	94.3
5-9	96.6	99.9	109.7	102.6	85.7	97.1	96.6
10-14	96.4	105.2	116.9	99.4	89.6	100.0	105.0
15-19	95.2	98.2	109.3	85.2	105.6	100.0	102.6
20-24	92.1	101.9	95.5	93.0	99.6	96.6	97.7
25-29	83.8	99.4	96.4	88.6	95.5	78.1	103.8
30-34	78.9	92.3	99.8	116.3	107.2	81.3	102.8
35-39	82.9	99.0	111.7	88.9	94.1	101.8	106.4
40-44	71.0	87.5	98.3	97.9	77.5	83.8	111.0
45-49	68.7	94.1	88.5	87.2	78.0	71.2	105.9
50-54	60.8	83.9	72.2	71.4	70.9	78.7	97.5
55-59	51.9	70.6	54.4	68.7	68.4	66.0	90.1
60-64	48.2	67.5	68.2	65.6	44.0	73.3	87.9
65-69	47.3	54.7	68.3	37.8	25.8	50.0	80.9
70+	35.6	57.8	47.1	38.9	26.8	52.5	72.3
Total	83.9	92.4	95.3	90.0	89.1	88.1	100.3

Table S4.25. *Age-specific Sex Ratios by Colony (continued)*

Age group	Males per 100 Females					
	Dominica, 1829	St. Lucia, 1815	St. Vincent, 1817	Grenada, 1817	Tobago, 1819	Trinidad, 1813
0-4	96.3	86.4	91.8	94.4	90.0	94.7
5-9	97.4	93.6	101.6	96.4	101.5	92.6
10-14	101.3	106.7	110.3	106.5	104.1	107.4
15-19	90.6	95.8	97.5	94.0	100.3	138.0
20-24	92.9	91.3	99.6	93.6	93.1	118.4
25-29	102.5	99.3	116.4	103.6	94.1	119.7
30-34	99.8	98.5	108.1	96.6	102.9	145.1
35-39	80.8	75.7	100.5	101.8	106.7	153.6
40-44	76.4	54.3	100.5	95.9	102.3	144.2
45-49	97.4	59.0	118.3	92.1	99.8	133.8
50-54	86.6	55.4	105.3	85.4	85.6	124.6
55-59	84.7	51.0	111.7	95.4	78.8	140.2
60-64	79.2	51.4	87.0	100.0	88.9	125.0
65-69	68.7	46.3	94.5	65.6	78.7	143.3
70+	75.9	54.3	75.7	66.4	71.3	146.9
Total	91.5	83.7	102.1	96.1	97.4	122.1

Age group	Males per 100 Females					
	Berbice, 1819	British Honduras, 1834	Cayman Islands, 1834	Bahamas, 1834	Anguilla, 1827	Barbuda, 1832
0-4	95.6	107.4	80.0	101.7	100.0	110.8
5-9	89.9	103.7	93.7	85.4	95.1	62.7
10-14	104.2	110.0	68.7	90.6	115.9	70.2
15-19	110.0	115.1	185.2	100.6	84.7	108.3
20-24	108.8	116.8	76.1	87.4	72.3	63.3
25-29	127.5	102.6	108.0	97.0	71.2	89.5
30-34	142.8	168.1	117.9	83.3	67.6	50.0
35-39	164.6	176.6	103.4	91.2	67.1	62.5
40-44	178.9	232.1	86.7	104.1	72.0	83.3
45-49	206.0	337.5	112.5	124.4	89.7	33.3
50-54	138.4	426.1	161.1	110.8	57.9	50.0
55-59	122.6	393.3	58.8	107.1	42.5	133.3
60-64	108.8	488.9	190.9	121.2	85.7	550.0
65-69	90.2	433.3	80.0	98.1	77.8	0.0
70+	84.2	283.3	60.0	102.9	47.6	20.0
Total	127.0	162.5	99.0	96.1	83.1	75.1

SECTION 5

Color

Table S5.1.   *Source:* T.71/378-79.

                       Note: This table excludes 44 slaves whose birthplace is unknown.

Table S5.2.   *Source:* T.71/493-94.

Table S5.3.   *Source:* T.71/438-39.

                       Note: This table excludes 45 slaves whose birthplace is unknown.

Table S5.4.   *Source:* T.71/520-22.

                       Notes: The slaves included in this table comprise all those registered as "coloured." "Bridgetown" comprises all slave-holdings in St. Michael not containing field laborers.

Table S5.5.   *Source:* T.71/461-62.

Table S5.6.   *Source:* T.71/501-503.

                       Note: African slaves registered as colored (17) are excluded.

Table S5.7.   *Source:* T.71/261.

                       Note: Another 10 slaves were registered as "mustee," "mongrel" or "coloured."

Table S5.1. *Color of Slaves by Sex and Birthplace: St. Lucia, 1815*

Color	Africans			Creoles		
	Males	Females	Total	Males	Females	Total
Negre	1,507	1,625	3,132	4,365	5,384	9,749
Negrit	–	–	–	–	10	10
Negrillon	–	–	–	4	–	4
Noir, Black	124	137	261	301	373	674
Noir claire	–	1	1	–	1	1
Peau noire	–	–	–	–	4	4
Yellow	–	1	1	–	1	1
Jaumatre	–	–	...	1	–	1
Peau claire	–	–	–	1	1	2
Rouge	18	19	37	63	105	168
Rougeatre	21	19	40	37	38	75
Reddish	–	–	–	5	6	11
Red	–	–	–	1	–	1
Roux	–	–	–	–	1	1
Rouge peau	–	–	–	6	7	13
Sambo	–	–	–	6	2	8
Capre, Negre capre	5	1	6	380	529	909
Capre rouge	–	–	–	3	5	8
Cap	–	–	–	1	2	3
Cobb	–	–	–	–	1	1
Copper	1	1	2	4	4	8
Mulatre	1	5	6	480	475	955
Griffe	–	–	–	25	29	54
Griffe rouge	–	–	–	1	–	1
Mulatre rouge	–	–	–	1	–	1
Carteron	–	–	–	–	1	1
Metive	–	–	–	19	29	48
Mestive	–	–	–	–	2	2
Mestee	–	–	–	3	3	6
Mustee	–	–	–	3	4	7
Metisse	–	–	–	–	1	1
Metive blanche	–	–	–	1	–	1
Mongrel	–	–	–	8	1	9
Brown	–	–	–	–	1	1
Unknown	–	2	2	4	7	11
Total	1,677	1,811	3,488	5,723	7,027	12,750

Table S5.2. *Color of Slaves by Sex: St. Vincent, 1817*

Color	Plantation Slaves			Unattached Slaves		
	Males	Females	Total	Males	Females	Total
Black	10,362	10,031	20,393	1,897	1,914	3,811
Yellow	1	2	3	–	–	–
Tawny	–	1	1	–	–	–
Sambo	1	–	1	–	–	–
Cabre	3	2	5	1	2	3
Cobb	1	2	3	–	–	–
Copper colour	–	–	–	1	1	2
Mulatto	264	241	505	116	137	253
Mustee	33	21	54	13	8	21
Mestif	2	3	5	–	–	–
Mongrel	82	49	131	53	53	106
Of colour	–	2	2	4	3	7
Albino	1	1	2	–	–	–
Total	10,750	10,355	21,105	2,085	2,118	4,203

Table S5.3. *Color of Slaves by Sex and Birthplace: Berbice, 1819*

Color	Africans			Creoles		
	Males	Females	Total	Males	Females	Total
Black	7,314	4,225	11,539	4,607	4,704	9,311
Negro	32	35	67	53	48	101
Very black	1	—	1	—	—	—
Black tawny	—	—	—	2	1	3
Light black	8	13	21	12	11	23
Clear black	—	—	—	2	2	4
White Negro	—	—	—	1	1	2
Yellow	144	156	300	99	155	254
Yellow skin	105	120	225	94	128	222
Yellowish	279	232	511	152	225	377
Yellowish black	4	2	6	1	—	1
Dark yellow	1	7	8	3	8	11
Very yellow	2	3	5	2	—	2
Rather yellow	3	—	3	—	—	—
Sickly yellow	13	11	24	7	4	11
Little yellow	2	2	4	1	—	1
Red	30	28	58	23	28	51
Reddish	18	26	44	12	29	41
Red skin	1	—	1	1	2	3
Red skinned	1	1	2	1	—	1
Reddish skin	2	3	5	1	4	5
Red skinned black	1	—	1	—	—	—
Sambo	—	—	—	22	21	43
Samba	—	—	—	—	3	3
Dark sambo	—	—	—	—	2	2
Cob	1	—	1	6	7	13
Cobre	3	1	4	1	1	2
Copper coloured	2	—	2	—	—	—
Mulatto	—	—	—	183	169	352
Mulat, mulate	—	1	1	8	8	16
Molato	—	—	—	—	1	1
Mustee	—	—	—	10	18	28
Mustice	—	—	—	2	2	4
Mestee	—	—	—	1	5	6
Mestize	—	—	—	3	2	5
Caboeger	—	1	1	7	7	14
Cabouger	1	2	3	5	4	9
Carboeger	—	—	—	—	1	1
Kabooger	—	—	—	1	1	2
Brownish	—	—	—	—	1	1
Brownish black	1	2	3	1	1	2
Coloured	—	—	—	1	5	6
Indian	—	—	—	2	8	10
Half a buck	—	—	—	1	—	1
Unknown	25	1	26	6	3	9
Total	7,969	4,871	12,840	5,328	5,617	10,945

Table S5.4. *Age Structure of Slaves of Color by Sex: Barbados, 1817*

Age group	Bridgetown		Rural St. Michael		St. Andrew		St. John	
	Males	Females	Males	Females	Males	Females	Males	Females
0-4	208	250	119	126	30	31	70	74
5-9	174	205	85	76	26	28	64	57
10-14	152	185	107	86	25	24	48	51
15-19	117	157	60	66	19	22	45	52
20-24	94	127	54	62	19	15	26	41
25-29	72	106	41	66	21	20	39	40
30-34	51	66	33	36	7	15	26	39
35-39	36	67	33	26	18	9	30	31
40-44	18	51	22	39	9	9	17	24
45-49	14	32	15	26	6	6	13	14
50-54	4	44	19	35	1	7	11	14
55-59	5	17	4	11	2	3	2	7
60-64	3	30	5	10	1	1	4	8
65-69	2	5	1	4	1	2	1	5
70+	3	24	1	9	–	2	1	8
Unknown	–	–	–	–	–	–	–	–
Total	953	1,366	599	678	185	194	397	465

Table S5.5. *Age Structure of Mulatto and Mestee Slaves by Sex: Tobago, 1819*

Age group	Plantation Slaves			Personal Slaves			Total
	Males	Females	Total	Males	Females	Total	
0-4	60	44	104	5	7	12	116
5-9	52	35	87	5	4	9	96
10-14	53	41	94	–	2	2	96
15-19	24	21	45	1	3	4	49
20-24	11	15	26	1	3	4	30
25-29	9	8	17	1	3	4	21
30-34	12	8	20	2	3	5	25
35-39	6	2	8	–	–	–	8
40-44	5	1	6	–	1	1	7
45-49	2	1	3	2	–	2	5
50-54	–	4	4	–	1	1	5
55-59	1	1	2	–	–	–	2
60-64	1	1	2	–	–	–	2
65-69	–	–	–	–	–	–	–
70+	–	–	–	–	–	–	–
Unknown	–	–	–	–	–	–	–
Total	236	182	418	17	27	44	462

Table S5.6. *Age Structure of Creole Slaves of Color by Sex, Urban and Rural: Trinidad, 1813*

| Age group | Rural Slaves | | | Urban Slaves | | | Total |
	Males	Females	Total	Males	Females	Total	
0-4	98	102	200	76	63	139	339
5-9	64	76	140	51	46	97	237
10-14	33	55	88	30	38	68	156
15-19	40	40	80	36	27	63	143
20-24	48	51	99	31	46	77	176
25-29	52	28	80	35	38	73	153
30-34	39	29	68	11	33	44	112
35-39	28	20	48	5	18	23	71
40-44	20	11	31	3	20	23	54
45-49	12	11	23	6	3	9	32
50-54	7	8	15	3	7	10	25
55-59	3	1	4	–	3	3	7
60-64	3	1	4	–	3	3	7
65-69	1	–	1	–	–	–	1
70+	5	2	7	–	1	1	8
Unknown	–	–	–	–	–	–	–
Total	453	435	888	287	346	633	1,521

Table S5.7. *Age Structure of Slaves by Color and Sex: Anguilla, 1827*

| Age group | Black | | Yellow | | Sambo | | Mulatto | |
	Males	Females	Males	Females	Males	Females	Males	Females
0-4	167	168	13	12	15	14	9	12
5-9	119	136	14	17	13	6	6	4
10-14	126	113	7	11	20	9	6	5
15-19	107	118	4	9	11	12	–	4
20-24	85	113	5	13	9	11	3	4
25-29	67	92	6	13	8	7	2	6
30-34	64	97	5	4	–	6	4	1
35-39	42	54	2	10	1	6	3	3
40-44	48	74	8	5	1	1	2	1
45-49	32	34	3	4	–	–	–	1
50-54	29	51	4	6	–	–	–	–
55-59	16	37	–	5	–	–	1	2
60-64	21	25	1	2	–	1	2	–
65-69	7	9	–	–	–	–	–	–
70+	8	16	1	2	1	1	–	2
Unknown	–	–	–	–	–	–	–	–
Total	938	1,133	73	113	79	74	38	45

SECTION 6

Stature

General Note

The heights in these tables are converted to centimeters using the following factors: 1 inch = 2.54 cm (for Trinidad and Berbice), and 1 inch or 1 pouce = 2.59 cm (St. Lucia). The derivation of these factors is discussed in Chapter 2.

Table S6.1.   *Sources:* T.71/501-503 (Trinidad), 378-79 (St. Lucia), 438-39 (Berbice).

Table S6.2.   *Source:* T.71/501-503.

Table S6.3.   *Source:* T.71/378-79.

Table S6.4.   *Source:* T.71/438-39.

Table S6.5.   *Source:* T.71/378-79.

Table S6.6.   *Source:* T.71/438-39.

Table S6.7.   *Source:* T.71/378-79.

Table S6.8.   *Source:* T.71/438-39.

Table S6.9.   *Source:* T.71/378-79.

Table S6.10.   *Source:* T.71/378-79.

Table S6.11.   *Source:* T.71/378-79.

Note: Only "plantation" slaves are included in this table; "personal" slaves, most of whom lived in towns, are excluded.

Table S6.12.   *Source:* T.71/378-79.

Notes: Some slaves aged less than 3 years were listed as field laborers or domestics, but are excluded here, since they are unlikely to have been actively employed. Slaves over 15 years of age with no occupation were generally invalids, and are excluded.

Table S6.1. *Heights (cm) of Creole Slaves by Sex and Age: Trinidad, St. Lucia and Berbice, 1813-19*

Age	Males			Females		
	No.	Mean	S.D.	No.	Mean	S.D.
Trinidad, 1813						
0+	144	64.5	5.1	148	63.0	4.3
1+	262	69.9	8.9	253	69.1	6.6
2+	226	76.7	9.1	283	75.4	8.9
3+	308	86.1	9.7	290	84.8	9.9
4+	238	91.2	10.9	250	91.7	10.9
5+	213	98.6	10.7	246	98.0	10.7
6+	211	104.6	11.2	205	104.6	11.7
7+	190	109.7	9.4	191	109.7	10.7
8+	172	113.3	10.7	178	114.3	9.9
9+	110	118.4	8.9	157	119.1	9.9
10+	154	125.7	9.7	152	120.7	9.4
11+	95	127.0	8.1	95	129.0	11.4
12+	126	132.8	8.9	127	134.6	10.4
13+	87	134.9	10.4	87	138.7	9.7
14+	101	142.2	12.2	94	141.2	11.4
15+	83	147.6	10.2	70	148.8	11.2
16+	64	150.1	9.4	77	152.4	8.1
17+	46	154.4	11.4	46	154.7	7.1
18+	77	158.2	8.6	73	154.9	8.4
19+	23	157.7	13.2	37	153.7	10.9
20+	69	163.8	7.9	81	156.2	8.9
21+	24	165.4	4.3	21	154.9	6.6
22+	49	164.6	7.6	41	157.5	6.9
St. Lucia, 1815						
0+	107	57.8	10.0	104	57.3	8.9
1+	167	67.0	9.2	187	68.3	10.6
2+	171	78.1	9.1	183	76.5	10.0
3+	163	85.9	13.0	205	86.0	11.6
4+	132	94.1	10.2	168	94.2	11.4
5+	145	98.6	12.1	153	100.8	10.7
6+	136	103.7	11.4	144	107.0	13.6
7+	117	110.2	9.8	138	110.0	10.0
8+	152	115.0	11.8	164	115.6	12.2
9+	141	119.8	12.7	151	120.3	10.1
10+	181	124.6	11.9	178	125.3	12.6
11+	102	127.4	10.0	127	130.9	11.4
12+	157	132.8	10.0	139	135.2	11.6
13+	148	137.6	11.1	119	139.1	10.2
14+	133	143.0	9.7	137	144.7	11.6
15+	133	147.1	13.3	124	149.9	10.3
16+	105	150.9	11.3	114	150.0	11.1
17+	71	154.6	10.8	76	150.7	8.9
18+	90	159.1	9.6	103	152.4	9.2
19+	62	160.1	9.4	81	154.3	7.3
20+	109	160.0	10.6	118	153.9	9.3
21+	82	160.7	9.8	85	153.3	9.1
22+	91	161.3	9.1	129	153.8	9.3

Table S6.1. *Heights of Creoles: Trinidad, St. Lucia and Berbice (continued)*

Age	Males			Females		
	No.	Mean	S.D.	No.	Mean	S.D.
Berbice, 1819						
0+	1	45.7	0.0	2	35.6	0.0
1+	4	76.8	6.4	3	63.5	15.5
2+	7	90.0	15.3	8	89.2	31.9
3+	7	98.3	31.8	7	85.3	9.9
4+	6	94.0	7.0	3	100.8	8.9
5+	6	99.1	5.6	3	95.7	16.9
6+	7	106.0	7.1	3	100.8	1.5
7+	6	113.0	6.2	2	104.1	14.4
8+	2	128.3	5.4	4	106.7	20.4
9+	7	121.2	3.5	7	117.6	7.7
10+	4	116.2	6.7	3	126.2	8.2
11+	3	124.5	17.8	6	128.3	5.0
12+	7	144.1	13.1	6	141.4	8.8
13+	11	132.3	12.9	6	141.4	11.7
14+	11	138.1	33.4	10	149.6	9.3
15+	16	145.9	29.6	13	150.1	11.8
16+	22	152.9	12.4	29	153.9	7.6
17+	19	157.1	11.2	28	155.3	6.1
18+	13	164.3	7.1	37	154.3	6.6
19+	25	160.2	7.9	42	156.9	8.8
20+	18	160.9	7.9	24	154.9	7.9
21+	32	162.8	7.4	43	153.8	4.5
22+	14	166.6	6.2	26	152.7	7.5

Table S6.2. *Heights (cm) of Slaves Aged 25-40 Years by Sex and Birthplace: Trinidad, 1813*

Birthplace	Males			Females		
	No.	Mean	S.D.	No.	Mean	S.D.
Africans						
Senegambia	568	166.1	8.4	286	156.7	7.9
Sierra Leone	121	164.6	7.9	73	152.9	6.6
Windward Coast	302	162.6	7.9	191	152.7	7.6
Gold Coast	364	163.6	8.1	236	154.4	7.6
Bight of Benin	361	165.9	8.1	276	155.7	8.1
Bight of Biafra	1,818	162.8	8.1	1,472	153.4	8.4
Central Africa	985	161.8	7.9	585	152.7	8.4
Mozambique	4	161.3	2.8	2	152.4	0.0
Other	388	164.6	8.1	210	155.4	8.1
Total	4,911	163.3	8.1	3,331	153.9	8.1
Creoles						
Trinidad	128	165.6	7.6	149	154.9	8.4
British sugar colonies	539	166.1	7.6	521	157.0	7.6
British marginal colonies	44	166.6	6.9	61	159.3	7.9
French colonies	377	166.1	7.6	360	156.7	8.1
Spanish colonies	19	166.4	9.4	11	149.9	8.9
Other	61	163.8	7.6	73	159.0	7.9
Total	1,168	165.9	7.6	1,175	157.0	7.9

Table S6.3. *Heights (cm) of Slaves Aged 25-40 Years by Sex and Birthplace: St. Lucia, 1815*

Birthplace	Males			Females		
	No.	Mean	S.D.	No.	Mean	S.D.
Africans						
Senegambia	38	166.2	10.3	12	158.7	9.4
Sierra Leone	5	165.3	3.8	4	159.3	8.0
Windward Coast	49	162.2	7.9	44	152.7	10.0
Gold Coast	53	164.1	8.9	34	153.6	8.9
Bight of Benin	14	161.7	12.2	20	155.0	6.1
Bight of Biafra	215	163.1	7.9	280	153.6	9.0
Central Africa	194	161.1	8.7	139	152.3	9.5
Other	219	163.6	7.0	151	151.6	11.3
Total	787	162.7	8.7	684	153.5	9.0
Creoles						
St. Lucia	930	164.5	9.2	1,307	155.2	9.2
British sugar colonies	41	166.4	8.7	38	158.8	8.7
British marginal colonies	7	169.1	6.6	5	165.3	6.7
French colonies	74	164.4	9.8	59	156.1	7.4
Other	232	165.9	8.9	279	155.8	8.8
Total	1,284	164.8	9.1	1,688	155.4	9.1

Table S6.4. *Heights (cm) of Slaves Aged 25-40 Years by Sex and Birthplace: Berbice, 1819*

Birthplace	Males			Females		
	No.	Mean	S.D.	No.	Mean	S.D.
Africans						
Senegambia	41	168.6	6.6	16	160.7	8.0
Sierra Leone	41	170.0	7.5	22	154.7	10.2
Windward Coast	20	162.6	6.2	16	152.7	6.8
Gold Coast	51	165.3	6.9	33	157.3	6.3
Bight of Benin	107	166.0	6.6	57	157.7	6.8
Bight of Biafra	59	163.0	5.3	51	152.8	6.0
Central Africa	87	161.0	6.9	59	151.5	6.8
Other	1,717	163.3	7.4	1,063	153.9	7.7
Total	2,123	163.6	7.4	1,317	154.1	7.6
Creoles						
Berbice	166	162.6	8.0	167	154.4	7.7
British sugar colonies	36	166.2	7.5	25	158.9	5.3
British marginal colonies	2	168.9	16.2	–	–	–
French colonies	3	177.8	5.1	–	–	–
Other	23	160.2	9.2	17	145.2	6.5
Total	230	163.2	8.3	209	154.2	7.7

Table S6.5. *Heights (cm) of Slaves Aged 25-40 Years by Sex, Birthplace and Color: St. Lucia, 1815*

Color	Males			Females		
	No.	Mean	S.D.	No.	Mean	S.D.
Africans						
Black	768	162.7	8.8	672	153.5	9.1
Colored	19	161.7	8.3	12	152.8	7.7
Total	787	162.7	8.7	684	153.5	9.0
Creoles						
Black	1,066	164.4	9.3	1,415	155.3	9.0
Colored	218	166.6	8.4	273	156.0	9.5
Total	1,284	164.8	9.1	1,688	155.4	9.1

Table S6.6. *Heights (cm) of Slaves Aged 25-40 Years by Sex, Birthplace and Color: Berbice, 1819*

Color	Males			Females		
	No.	Mean	S.D.	No.	Mean	S.D.
Africans						
Black	1,936	163.5	7.3	1,117	153.9	7.7
Colored	23	160.6	10.8	22	154.4	5.9
Yellow	168	165.1	7.4	179	154.9	7.3
Total	2,127	163.6	7.4	1,318	154.1	7.6
Creoles						
Black	194	163.1	8.0	159	154.5	8.4
Colored	17	162.9	11.5	28	155.8	6.4
Yellow	18	164.5	8.5	19	150.1	4.7
Total	229	163.2	8.3	206	154.2	7.7

Table S6.7. *Heights (cm) of Slaves Aged 25-40 Years by Sex,*
Birthplace and Occupation: St. Lucia, 1815

Occupation	Males			Females		
	No.	Mean	S.D.	No.	Mean	S.D.
Africans						
Field laborers	513	162.5	9.0	501	153.1	8.9
Drivers	14	163.4	12.3	–	–	–
Skilled tradespeople	119	163.2	8.1	–	–	–
Domestics	39	162.0	8.7	111	154.1	8.4
Washerwomen	–	–	–	25	158.9	8.1
Stockkeepers	9	162.9	6.1	3	150.2	6.8
Transport workers	38	164.8	7.1	–	–	–
Watchmen	12	165.1	6.7	1	176.1	0.0
Fishermen	8	158.3	10.6	–	–	–
Sellers	–	–	–	10	156.4	7.0
Laborers	7	163.2	11.8	9	146.5	11.1
Nurses	–	–	–	4	148.3	11.1
Sick or disabled	14	164.8	6.1	4	160.6	4.2
None	3	157.1	6.5	5	150.7	14.9
Total	776	162.7	8.7	673	153.5	9.0
Creoles						
Field laborers	654	163.8	9.0	1,112	155.5	8.5
Drivers	72	165.7	8.3	–	–	–
Skilled tradespeople	298	167.0	8.3	22	159.0	7.4
Domestics	78	165.7	8.5	369	155.5	9.4
Washerwomen	–	–	–	51	154.7	8.1
Stockkeepers	21	165.6	10.3	2	158.0	11.0
Transport workers	51	165.2	8.7	1	170.9	0.0
Watchmen	6	162.3	11.2	5	153.8	9.3
Fishermen	19	165.4	9.1	–	–	–
Sellers	1	150.2	0.0	25	156.4	7.1
Laborers	31	159.6	9.6	20	151.4	12.7
Nurses	1	170.9	0.0	9	158.0	9.7
Sick or disabled	16	162.8	14.2	23	156.4	8.0
None	7	159.8	18.5	19	150.9	21.9
Total	1,255	164.8	9.1	1,658	155.4	9.1

Table S6.8. *Heights (cm) of Slaves Aged 25-40 Years by Sex,*
Birthplace and Occupation: Berbice, 1819

Occupation	Males			Females		
	No.	Mean	S.D.	No.	Mean	S.D.
Africans						
Field laborers	1,435	163.3	7.5	1,020	153.9	7.6
Drivers	62	167.7	8.1	1	154.9	0.0
Skilled tradespeople	310	164.5	6.5	1	147.3	0.0
Domestics	44	162.5	8.6	77	154.9	8.6
Washerwomen	–	–	–	32	156.1	7.3
Stockkeepers	49	162.6	8.3	1	160.0	0.0
Transport workers	41	162.2	5.7	–	–	–
Watchmen	34	167.3	6.3	–	–	–
Fishermen	3	160.0	5.1	–	–	–
Sellers	–	–	–	4	152.4	4.1
Laborers	75	162.8	7.6	50	155.3	6.8
Nurses	8	167.3	7.1	24	156.4	5.8
Sick or disabled	61	163.3	6.8	74	154.6	8.1
None	2	161.3	9.0	9	152.4	9.8
Total	2,124	163.6	7.4	1,293	154.1	7.6
Creoles						
Field laborers	89	162.6	7.9	135	154.1	8.0
Drivers	15	163.9	6.8	1	162.6	0.0
Skilled tradespeople	93	163.3	8.5	1	144.8	0.0
Domestics	11	162.8	6.5	49	155.6	6.8
Washerwomen	–	–	–	9	154.4	7.0
Stockkeepers	4	164.5	9.1	–	–	–
Transport workers	2	175.3	7.2	–	–	–
Watchmen	1	149.9	0.0	–	–	–
Fishermen	–	–	–	–	–	–
Sellers	–	–	–	–	–	–
Laborers	4	163.2	13.5	2	158.8	1.8
Nurses	2	165.1	3.6	2	149.9	3.6
Sick or disabled	9	164.5	13.1	9	149.6	11.4
None	–	–	–	–	–	–
Total	230	163.2	8.3	208	154.2	7.7

Table S6.9. *Heights (cm) of Creole Slaves by Sex, Age and Color: St. Lucia, 1815*

Age	Males			Females		
	No.	Mean	S.D.	No.	Mean	S.D.
Black						
0+	91	59.2	12.9	93	57.2	9.4
1+	144	67.0	10.9	177	67.4	10.3
2+	161	78.3	8.8	169	76.8	10.2
3+	154	85.6	12.7	172	86.3	10.2
4+	125	93.5	10.3	154	93.4	11.3
5+	126	99.1	11.5	140	101.4	10.5
6+	128	104.0	11.7	136	107.2	11.8
7+	119	110.1	10.1	123	111.2	8.9
8+	143	114.5	12.0	152	115.5	12.5
9+	116	121.4	11.2	143	120.4	10.4
10+	163	124.3	11.7	178	125.6	12.2
11+	103	127.1	10.4	116	130.1	9.5
12+	164	132.0	10.6	147	135.2	12.9
13+	152	137.6	11.2	110	139.5	10.2
14+	141	143.4	10.3	138	144.9	11.8
15+	129	148.1	13.3	132	149.9	10.3
16+	124	151.2	10.8	122	150.5	10.8
17+	87	154.5	10.2	89	151.4	8.4
18+	97	158.6	9.5	111	153.6	8.8
19+	68	159.7	9.5	94	153.4	7.2
20+	123	160.4	10.4	133	153.4	9.2
21+	82	160.9	9.6	87	153.8	9.0
22+	98	160.8	8.5	131	154.4	9.1
Colored						
0+	30	57.9	9.7	32	57.1	7.8
1+	39	66.3	9.6	40	67.3	12.7
2+	31	76.4	8.2	48	75.5	9.7
3+	42	86.9	12.5	60	85.4	14.2
4+	32	94.9	9.0	44	94.8	11.1
5+	47	99.0	12.5	35	99.2	12.0
6+	36	104.0	9.1	33	105.0	19.2
7+	29	110.7	8.7	40	109.2	12.2
8+	32	117.5	10.3	36	114.8	10.1
9+	45	116.0	14.1	44	119.1	9.0
10+	46	125.4	11.2	39	124.5	13.7
11+	24	130.8	8.7	36	133.5	14.7
12+	44	133.6	9.3	30	134.9	9.8
13+	33	136.9	11.5	30	140.2	10.7
14+	25	141.2	6.6	29	147.0	10.1
15+	32	145.5	10.6	28	149.7	10.1
16+	14	151.0	12.2	27	151.3	8.1
17+	15	151.8	13.2	15	152.8	10.3
18+	20	156.3	13.3	19	149.7	10.5
19+	12	162.5	6.7	20	154.4	9.8
20+	26	164.6	8.2	26	155.3	7.0
21+	21	160.3	9.7	18	154.1	8.0
22+	28	163.3	9.8	33	154.1	10.9

Table S6.10. *Heights (cm) of Creole Slaves by Sex and Age, Urban and Rural: St. Lucia, 1815*

Age	Males			Females		
	No.	Mean	S.D.	No.	Mean	S.D.
Urban						
0+	26	55.0	12.0	14	54.4	11.4
1+	22	65.2	10.4	21	67.5	5.5
2+	23	78.3	8.8	34	75.9	10.0
3+	27	88.1	10.8	27	83.8	9.9
4+	20	94.1	7.4	25	95.3	13.1
5+	26	99.9	11.0	23	103.0	9.9
6+	19	103.3	10.6	13	107.6	11.9
7+	17	111.8	9.2	23	108.9	14.1
8+	16	113.5	12.1	23	115.4	11.5
9+	19	111.1	16.6	23	121.2	10.6
10+	21	121.4	10.6	19	124.5	9.9
11+	11	128.6	12.9	22	130.1	11.5
12+	34	130.4	7.8	31	136.7	10.2
13+	23	136.3	13.5	15	135.9	11.8
14+	16	144.6	9.4	19	146.0	11.7
15+	17	140.3	20.0	22	149.4	11.2
16+	17	151.1	8.7	22	150.3	9.6
17+	13	157.4	9.1	11	151.9	7.9
18+	8	158.3	6.3	19	154.7	6.6
19+	6	159.3	7.8	15	156.6	6.8
20+	19	165.1	7.6	24	156.5	5.9
21+	13	160.6	9.7	15	154.7	11.1
22+	17	162.6	10.7	27	154.0	11.5
Rural						
0+	95	60.0	12.1	110	57.4	8.7
1+	161	67.1	10.7	195	67.3	11.2
2+	168	78.0	8.8	183	76.6	10.1
3+	169	85.6	12.9	205	86.3	11.5
4+	137	93.7	10.4	173	93.5	11.0
5+	147	99.0	11.9	152	100.6	11.0
6+	144	104.1	11.3	156	106.7	13.7
7+	132	110.1	9.9	140	111.0	8.9
8+	159	115.2	11.7	165	115.4	12.2
9+	141	121.3	11.0	164	120.0	10.1
10+	189	125.0	11.6	198	125.5	12.7
11+	116	127.7	9.9	130	131.1	10.9
12+	174	132.7	10.7	146	134.8	12.9
13+	162	137.6	10.9	125	140.1	10.0
14+	150	143.0	9.9	147	145.2	11.6
15+	143	148.5	11.4	138	149.9	10.1
16+	121	151.2	11.2	127	150.7	10.5
17+	89	153.6	10.8	94	151.6	8.8
18+	109	158.2	10.5	112	152.8	9.5
19+	74	160.2	9.4	99	153.1	7.7
20+	130	160.6	10.4	134	153.2	9.3
21+	90	160.8	9.6	91	153.7	8.4
22+	109	161.2	8.6	137	154.4	9.1

Age	Males			Females		
	No.	Mean	S.D.	No.	Mean	S.D.
Sugar						
0+	30	58.9	9.4	47	59.0	7.3
1+	63	67.1	8.9	89	69.2	11.2
2+	54	80.7	8.2	74	78.3	8.6
3+	71	87.1	13.4	87	86.9	12.9
4+	48	94.0	11.0	62	94.3	10.6
5+	62	99.8	12.6	66	101.2	11.6
6+	64	104.7	12.7	67	109.4	11.1
7+	53	111.3	10.3	66	112.4	7.8
8+	67	117.7	11.0	55	118.6	12.2
9+	51	122.1	9.8	75	121.8	9.9
10+	86	125.1	11.5	82	126.1	12.8
11+	44	128.9	10.7	54	130.7	12.9
12+	85	133.4	10.8	73	136.8	12.1
13+	66	137.6	11.4	50	142.3	8.8
14+	64	142.8	9.5	62	145.8	13.0
15+	79	149.4	11.0	61	151.7	9.1
16+	66	152.6	10.6	57	152.2	10.9
17+	45	153.9	12.2	54	150.7	9.2
18+	50	160.9	9.0	59	153.1	10.6
19+	42	160.1	10.0	49	154.7	7.0
20+	63	161.1	9.8	55	154.1	7.8
21+	45	162.7	8.3	42	154.0	8.5
22+	53	161.6	8.7	59	155.2	7.7
Other agriculture						
0+	28	61.4	15.5	20	57.0	9.6
1+	53	65.7	13.4	49	64.7	9.1
2+	56	77.1	9.2	47	73.6	10.4
3+	48	81.6	11.5	45	84.9	12.3
4+	37	92.8	12.4	58	91.5	11.1
5+	40	98.5	11.9	40	98.7	11.9
6+	38	105.0	9.5	39	101.7	13.5
7+	37	107.7	9.6	32	110.6	8.6
8+	42	112.1	10.2	54	112.5	11.9
9+	38	119.2	12.3	37	118.6	10.1
10+	45	124.3	12.6	60	123.2	13.7
11+	36	127.9	9.1	32	131.4	8.6
12+	42	130.6	10.2	33	129.9	15.5
13+	46	137.6	10.0	31	136.4	11.0
14+	33	142.5	11.3	41	144.8	10.5
15+	28	144.0	10.0	28	147.7	9.7
16+	29	150.8	12.4	32	149.7	11.2
17+	23	152.2	9.8	17	151.0	7.6
18+	26	154.8	11.8	16	149.4	7.8
19+	13	157.2	11.0	26	151.0	8.9
20+	23	161.4	9.5	30	152.6	9.4
21+	25	158.8	9.2	28	152.5	8.9
22+	28	157.7	8.5	31	153.8	9.1

Table S6.12. *Heights (cm) of Creole Slaves by Sex, Age and Occupation: St. Lucia, 1815*

Age	Males			Females		
	No.	Mean	S.D.	No.	Mean	S.D.
Field laborers						
3+	8	91.9	18.1	7	85.1	11.8
4+	6	101.9	13.0	6	93.7	22.2
5+	9	98.1	16.5	4	101.7	8.6
6+	8	104.6	14.7	18	109.1	15.5
7+	10	119.4	13.6	10	111.4	10.7
8+	22	117.3	12.5	30	119.1	12.0
9+	22	123.5	10.9	31	120.3	14.1
10+	48	125.0	13.7	52	126.5	13.3
11+	28	128.9	10.3	39	131.4	11.0
12+	70	131.1	11.1	55	135.9	11.5
13+	76	138.0	11.7	62	140.6	9.5
14+	77	141.7	10.5	95	146.0	11.5
15+	90	149.2	11.0	106	151.0	9.7
16+	84	151.4	11.6	97	150.1	11.2
17+	67	154.9	10.3	73	151.7	8.6
18+	70	158.1	9.9	75	152.6	9.4
19+	51	157.8	9.0	76	152.6	7.8
20+	101	160.3	10.5	88	153.1	9.3
21+	63	160.1	10.1	68	153.6	8.1
22+	73	160.4	8.6	95	153.6	8.9
Domestics						
3+	11	87.4	9.3	7	86.6	6.0
4+	12	93.7	8.8	11	93.2	12.8
5+	17	101.8	14.6	5	104.1	7.6
6+	17	104.2	14.3	19	111.4	22.1
7+	22	112.2	9.9	27	111.8	11.7
8+	22	119.5	11.6	44	115.4	12.9
9+	33	122.2	14.6	50	118.8	9.9
10+	45	124.3	11.2	65	126.9	11.7
11+	42	127.3	10.0	58	130.5	11.9
12+	61	133.4	9.6	72	136.9	13.4
13+	53	135.6	11.7	56	139.2	10.8
14+	51	144.8	10.2	56	144.7	10.0
15+	38	144.4	12.1	43	148.3	11.4
16+	29	150.9	10.0	42	151.3	8.3
17+	12	152.6	12.0	27	151.6	9.6
18+	28	155.8	12.4	41	153.8	8.6
19+	11	165.3	7.5	24	155.8	7.3
20+	21	163.3	8.1	49	154.7	8.4
21+	8	159.9	10.6	25	154.3	11.1
22+	12	159.1	6.4	52	155.0	11.0

Table S6.12. *Heights by Age and Occupation: St. Lucia, 1815 (cont.)*

Age	Males			Females		
	No.	Mean	S.D.	No.	Mean	S.D.
Skilled tradespeople						
7+	1	101.0	0.0	–	–	–
8+	2	110.1	12.8	–	–	–
9+	1	124.3	0.0	–	–	–
10+	3	121.7	11.9	–	–	–
11+	4	138.6	4.5	–	–	–
12+	6	129.9	5.0	–	–	–
13+	4	141.2	8.6	–	–	–
14+	5	146.1	6.0	–	–	–
15+	15	144.3	21.6	–	–	–
16+	10	153.8	11.3	–	–	–
17+	9	153.1	9.0	–	–	–
18+	12	161.7	5.6	–	–	–
19+	9	165.2	6.3	–	–	–
20+	16	164.8	7.6	–	–	–
21+	22	164.3	7.4	–	–	–
22+	25	166.2	8.2	–	–	–
No occupation						
0+	115	59.5	11.9	118	56.9	8.9
1+	171	67.0	10.7	209	67.5	10.8
2+	181	78.2	8.8	200	76.2	9.8
3+	174	85.4	12.4	215	86.1	11.5
4+	134	93.5	9.8	178	93.6	10.8
5+	144	99.0	11.2	163	100.8	10.9
6+	128	103.8	10.7	127	105.8	11.6
7+	97	109.3	9.1	118	110.0	9.4
8+	100	114.7	11.7	93	114.5	11.0
9+	76	118.5	12.5	80	120.7	8.9
10+	57	124.4	12.1	72	124.5	13.0
11+	24	128.0	11.2	32	129.3	10.7
12+	28	131.7	12.7	27	133.2	9.3
13+	13	137.3	13.7	8	136.9	12.2
14+	5	141.9	3.4	4	144.4	14.7
15+	–	–	–	2	151.5	16.5

SECTION 7

Occupation

Table S7.1.   *Sources:* T.71/851; Robert M. Martin, *Statistics of the Colonies of the British Empire* (London, 1839), pp.29 and 95.

           Note: No classification was made for the Cayman Islands. The total for Demerara, Essequibo and Berbice is 82,824, whereas that given for British Guiana is 83,544 (T.71/851). For most colonies, the data in T.71/851 is broken down by parish, division or numbered compensation district.

Table S7.2.   *Source:* T.71/520-22.

           Notes: (1) The descriptions of occupations are taken directly from the registration returns. Variant spellings have generally been ignored and the first example only included in the list. Descriptions which appear to relate to the same occupation are grouped, separated by semicolons. (2) "Bridgetown" comprises all slave-holdings in St. Michael not containing field laborers.

Table S7.3.   *Source:* T.71/378-79.

           Notes: The method of listing is as for Table S7.2. But French and English equivalents occurring in the returns are given, separated by slashes; and translations are provided of most French terms, in square brackets.

Table S7.4.   *Source:* T.71/501-503.

           Note: For the method of listing, see notes to Table S7.2.

Table S7.5.   *Source:* T.71/438-39.

                    Note: For the method of listing, see notes to Table S7.2.

Table S7.6.   *Source:* T.71/261.

                    Note: For the method of listing, see notes to Table S7.2.

Table S7.7.   *Source:* T.71/493.

                    Note: Some slaveowners described all slaves under 10 years of age as domestics or house servants. Such slaves have been removed from the "domestic" category in this table and placed with the other juveniles.

Table S7.8.   *Source:* T.71/243.

Table S7.9.   *Source:* T.71/378-79.

Table S7.10.   *Source:* T.71/501-503.

Table S7.11.   *Source:* T.71/520-22.

Table S7.12.   *Source:* T.71/378-79.

Table S7.13.   *Source:* T.71/438-39.

Table S7.14.   *Source:* T.71/378-79.

Table S7.15.   *Source:* T.71/520-22.

Table S7.16.   *Source:* T.71/438-39.

Table S7.17.   *Source:* T.71/520-22.

Table S7.18.   *Source:* T.71/501-503.

Table S7.19.   *Source:* T.71/378-79.

Table S7.20.   *Source:* T.71/438-39.

Table S7.1. *Occupational Distribution of Slaves, as Classified for Compensation, 1834*

Category	Barbados	St. Kitts	Nevis	Antigua	Montserrat
Predial attached					
Head people	1,963	648	276	588	239
Tradesmen	1,821	367	319	978	102
Inferior tradesmen	784	155	42	297	50
Field labourers	27,693	4,973	2,986	11,204	2,364
Inferior field labourers	15,615	4,539	1,510	6,400	1,205
Predial unattached					
Head people	32	33	7	7	16
Tradesmen	224	15	16	34	6
Inferior tradesmen	163	15	3	7	12
Field labourers	2,330	296	104	373	357
Inferior field labourers	1,568	293	46	173	177
Non-predial					
Head tradesmen	391	130	88	254	46
Inferior tradesmen	408	80	25	214	23
Head people on wharves, shipping, etc.	64	165	498	77	42
Inferior people on wharves, shipping	1,071	77	112	191	9
Head domestic servants	3,815	1,204	909	302	235
Inferior domestic servants	8,695	981	304	1,902	173
Other					
Children under 6 years of age	14,732	2,741	1,263	4,216	1,130
Aged, diseased, non-effective	1,780	811	329	1,421	215
Runaways	–	–	–	–	–
Total	83,149	17,523	8,837	28,638	6,401

Category	Virgin Islands	Jamaica	Dominica	St. Lucia	St. Vincent
Predial attached					
Head people	137	14,043	620	332	927
Tradesmen	84	11,244	246	237	268
Inferior tradesmen	68	2,635	76	30	375
Field labourers	1,410	107,053	5,930	5,547	7,622
Inferior field labourers	1,097	63,923	2,951	2,181	5,605
Predial unattached					
Head people	25	1,329	11	7	23
Tradesmen	9	1,133	20	3	22
Inferior tradesmen	5	322	11	1	21
Field labourers	326	11,670	402	269	268
Inferior field labourers	256	5,104	190	107	178
Non-predial					
Head tradesmen	14	1,759	33	37	111
Inferior tradesmen	23	780	32	36	101
Head people on wharves, shipping, etc.	92	1,428	12	2	246
Inferior people on wharves, shipping	35	901	45	80	136
Head domestic servants	321	12,883	230	1,059	949
Inferior domestic servants	416	19,083	847	389	1,250
Other					
Children under 6 years of age	747	39,013	2,112	1,953	2,959
Aged, diseased, non-effective	70	15,692	397	1,005	1,189
Runaways	–	1,075	–	–	–
Total	5,135	311,070	14,165	13,275	22,250

Table S7.1. *Occupational Distribution of Slaves, 1834 (continued)*

Category	Grenada	Tobago	Trinidad	Demerara	Esse-quibo
Predial attached					
Head people	1,164	209	1,100	1,508	993
Tradesmen	741	348	345	691	456
Inferior tradesmen	278	243	333	227 ·	224
Field labourers	8,651	3,722	8,018	18,271	11,893
Inferior field labourers	5,728	3,558	2,448	6,030	3,947
Predial unattached					
Head people	9	6	86	94	17
Tradesmen	25	5	51	30	14
Inferior tradesmen	10	5	34	17	3
Field labourers	214	74	1,001	2,236	469
Inferior field labourers	125	68	357	984	285
Non-predial					
Head tradesmen	95	40	92	691	79
Inferior tradesmen	124	18	220	209	22
Head people on wharves, shipping, etc.	28	66	59	37	11
Inferior people on wharves, shipping	498	53	133	172	53
Head domestic servants	349	315	1,678	2,282	161
Inferior domestic servants	974	314	1,584	1,370	105
Other					
Children under 6 years of age	3,320	1,478	2,246	5,114	2,488
Aged, diseased, non-effective	1,312	1,025	872	1,471	969
Runaways	–	–	–	–	–
Total	23,645	11,547	20,657	41,434	22,189

Category	Berbice	British Honduras	Bahamas	Anguilla	Barbuda	TOTAL
Predial attached						
Head people	812	–	68	12	7	25,646
Tradesmen	463	–	–	3	19	18,732
Inferior tradesmen	167	–	–	2	11	5,997
Field labourers	9,029	–	2,668	580	161	239,775
Inferior field labourers	3,096	–	1,280	386	126	131,625
Predial unattached						
Head people	42	24	3	–	–	1,771
Tradesmen	18	15	–	–	–	1,640
Inferior tradesmen	6	6	–	1	–	642
Field labourers	873	524	184	124	–	22,094
Inferior field labourers	387	240	73	59	–	10,670
Non-predial						
Head tradesmen	102	10	162	8	–	4,142
Inferior tradesmen	44	13	48	10	–	2,430
Head people on wharves, shipping, etc.	1	9	459	18	3	3,317
Inferior people on wharves, shipping	5	10	321	8	11	3,921
Head domestic servants	536	399	1,264	243	–	29,134
Inferior domestic servants	417	338	1,186	238	19	40,585
Other						
Children under 6 years of age	2,291	219	1,986	459	113	90,580
Aged, diseased, non-effective	912	90	293	109	22	29,984
Runaways	–	–	–	–	–	1,075
Total	19,201	1,897	9,995	2,260	492	663,760

Table S7.2. *Occupations of Slaves: Barbados, 1817*

Occupation	Bridge-town	Rural St. Michael	St. John	St. Andrew
		Number of Slaves		
Field laborers				
Field	–	2,643	1,786	1,340
Field and cooper; field and carpenter	–	1	–	1
Field and clarifier; field and feeds mill; field and boiler; field and boson; field and stoker	–	7	11	1
Field and carter	–	3	–	–
Field and ploughman	–	–	1	–
Field and watch	–	3	–	1
Field and house; field and washer	–	–	1	1
First gang field labourer; field, first class	–	313	292	232
Second gang field	–	114	167	82
Third gang field; third gang grass gatherer	–	131	108	51
Fourth gang field	–	17	–	–
Grass gang; meat gang; meat picker; grass picker	–	305	507	207
Invalid gang	–	–	16	10
Ploughman	–	2	1	–
Liner; planter	–	1	–	1
Corn beater; pecker	–	2	–	–
Woodcutter; cuts firewood	–	–	1	1
Water carrier; water carrier to first gang; water carrier to second gang	–	12	21	4
Field cook	–	–	1	–
Cook (first gang; second gang; third gang; negroes; little negroes)	–	23	22	5
Attendant (first gang; second gang)	–	2	–	–
Attends children; attending small people; child tender	2	10	4	10
Gardener	7	20	3	2
Total	9	3,609	2,942	1,949
Drivers				
Driver	–	45	32	26
First gang driver	–	9	10	2
Second gang driver; second driver	–	12	16	4
Third gang driver	–	7	9	3
Fourth gang driver	–	2	2	1
Meat gang driver; driver to grass gatherers; driver to meat pickers	–	1	8	2
Invalid gang driver	–	–	–	1
Superintendent	–	4	2	3
Superintendent of first class field	–	–	2	–
Superintendent of second gang	–	–	2	–
Superintendent of third gang	–	–	2	–

Table S7.2. *Occupations: Barbados, 1817 (continued)*

Occupation	Bridge-town	Rural St. Michael	St. John	St. Andrew
		Number of Slaves		
Superintendent of the gang; superintendent of the field	—	1	4	5
Overseer	—	2	—	—
Ranger	—	18	8	10
Ranger and driver	—	—	—	1
Boatswain; millswain		4	2	1
Total	—	105	99	59
Skilled tradespeople				
Cooper	98	51	41	26
Cooper and mason	—	3	—	—
Apprentice cooper; in cooper's shop	8	7	1	—
Mason	58	83	31	20
Mason and boiler	—	1	—	—
Apprentice mason; mason's boy	1	7	2	3
Carpenter	255	189	56	37
Carpenter and joiner	—	1	—	—
Carpenter and shoemaker	1	—	—	—
Carpenter and sugar boiler	—	—	—	1
Ship carpenter	3	—	—	—
House carpenter	2	—	—	—
Mill Carpenter	—	1	—	—
Apprentice carpenter; carpenter's boy	17	14	5	1
Joiner	20	3	—	—
Apprentice joiner	5	—	—	—
Sawyer	4	—	—	—
Cabinet maker	15	2	—	—
Painter	4	4	1	1
Plumber	—	—	—	2
Shipwright	14	4	—	—
Caulker	14	1	—	—
Sailmaker	17	—	—	—
Wheelwright	4	1	1	—
Apprentice wheelwright	—	2	—	—
Millwright; millman	—	—	4	—
Cartwright	—	3	—	—
Blacksmith	14	10	9	8
Smith	1	4	2	1
Farrier	—	1	—	—
Coppersmith	17	2	3	—
Apprentice coppersmith	1	—	—	—
Goldsmith	3	—	—	—
Silversmith	1	—	—	—

Table S7.2. *Occupations: Barbados, 1817 (continued)*

Occupation	Number of Slaves			
	Bridge-town	Rural St. Michael	St. John	St. Andrew
Watchmaker	1	1	–	–
Printer's pressman; printing press and waiter; pressman at the printing office	2	1	–	–
Saddler; harness maker	5	6	2	–
Shoemaker; cordwainer; cobbler	137	37	13	5
Apprentice shoemaker	3	–	–	–
Sempstress	152	62	10	1
Neddlewoman; needlework; learning the needle	16	4	6	1
Sempstress and washer	1	–	–	–
Taylor	120	31	7	1
Apprentice tailor	4	1	–	–
Setter of linen [weaver]	1	–	–	–
Dyer	1	–	–	–
Baker	17	3	–	–
Bread baker; pastry cook	2	–	–	–
Butcher	14	2	–	–
Barber	2	2	–	–
Boiler; sugar boiler	–	6	5	9
Boiler and watch	–	1	2	–
Distiller	–	3	5	3
Distiller and field	–	1	6	–
Assistant distiller	–	1	–	–
Basket maker	–	–	4	–
Potter; pottery	–	–	–	10
Mechanic	–	1	11	–
Tradesman	7	5	17	2
Apprenticed	27	8	–	–
Total	1,089	570	244	132
Domestics				
Domestic	1,088	352	247	62
House servant	2,291	738	160	150
House	236	219	41	24
House maid; maid servant	37	10	2	1
Servant	6	6	1	–
House boy	–	1	–	–
Chamber maid	5	1	–	1
Waiting maid; lady's maid	10	3	–	–
Nursery maid; attends a child	2	4	–	1
Waits on the manager; overseer's servant; overseer's steward	–	2	2	–

Table S7.2. *Occupations: Barbados, 1817 (continued)*

Occupation	Number of Slaves			
	Bridge-town	Rural St. Michael	St. John	St. Andrew
Waits on white servants	–	1	–	–
Waits on driver	–	1	1	–
Waits on housekeeper	–	1	–	–
Housekeeper	5	6	2	2
Butler	96	43	16	3
Steward	–	1	–	–
Key keeper	–	–	1	–
Footman; footboy	1	1	–	–
Cook	302	135	47	28
Cook (family, servants, manager)	–	4	–	–
Cook and house servant	2	–	–	–
Assistant cook	1	2	–	–
Assistant cook for small negroes	–	–	1	–
Scullion; Butry maid	1	1	–	–
Waiter	–	2	–	–
Waterman	1	–	–	–
Drudge	7	4	–	–
Washer; laundress	557	185	29	14
Laundress and milk maid	–	1	–	–
Washer and cook	5	–	–	–
Attending masons	1	–	–	–
Attending on a lunatick [slave]	1	–	–	–
Groom and house servant	–	–	–	1
Postillion; messenger; errand boy	1	2	–	–
Counting house; office boy	1	1	1	–
Housewife; house and retailer of goods	3	–	–	–
Total	4,660	1,728	551	287
Stockkeepers				
Stockkeeper	–	111	77	46
Stockminder; minding stock; stock feeder	–	16	3	–
Herdsman	–	8	25	2
Assistant herdsman	–	–	1	–
Cattle keeper; attending cattle; cattle minder; ox keeper	–	128	100	62
Chief cattle keeper; head cattle keeper	–	5	4	–
Cattle boy	–	21	8	–
Calf keeper; attends calves	–	12	10	4
Dairy woman; milk maid	1	6	1	–
Shepherd; shepherdess; sheep keeper	–	14	6	6
Goat keeper	–	2	–	–
Attends young stock	–	1	–	–
About the stock yard, etc.	–	2	–	–

Table S7.2. *Occupations: Barbados, 1817 (continued)*

Occupation	Bridge-town	Rural St. Michael	St. John	St. Andrew
		Number of Slaves		
Groom	24	41	21	12
Assistant groom	–	1	1	–
Groom and gardener	1	–	–	–
Ostler	1	3	–	–
Stable; in care of horses	1	–	1	–
Stable boy	–	3	–	–
Minds asses	–	–	–	1
Hog keeper	–	15	7	6
Pig driver	–	–	2	–
Hog cook; cook for plough cattle	–	–	2	–
Feathered stockkeeper; keeper of fowls; turkey keeper	–	6	4	2
Total	28	395	273	141
Transport workers				
Sailor	84	7	3	–
Mariner	6	–	–	–
Boatman	135	7	3	–
Seaman	37	1	–	–
Carter	4	21	7	12
Head carter	–	2	–	–
Second carter	–	1	–	–
Waggoner	–	–	1	–
Coachman	–	1	–	–
Porter	160	27	–	–
Porter and groom	1	–	–	–
Cabin boy	2	–	–	–
Total	429	67	14	12
Watchmen				
Watchman	1	60	45	39
Watch, invalid	–	1	–	–
Constant watch	–	–	3	–
Total	1	61	48	39
Fishermen				
Fisherman	68	18	–	–

Table S7.2. *Occupations: Barbados, 1817 (continued)*

Occupation	Number of Slaves			
	Bridge-town	Rural St. Michael	St. John	St. Andrew
Sellers				
Seller of goods; vendor of goods; retailer of goods	35	4	–	–
Market woman	7	11	–	1
Huxter	4	–	–	–
Shopkeeper	2	–	–	–
Shopman	1	–	–	–
Retailer of dry goods	2	1	–	–
Milk seller: milk carrier	–	8	–	–
Total	51	24	–	1
Laborers				
Labourer	188	22	35	2
Pioneer	8	–	–	1
Total	196	22	35	3
Hired				
Hired out	31	5	1	–
Hired out as a seller of goods; hired to hospital; hired at the garrison; hired as a pioneer	3	1	–	–
On hire to herself as washer, etc.	1	–	–	–
Total	35	6	1	–
Nurses				
Nurse	6	10	8	10
Sick nurse	2	26	17	11
Hospital nurse	–	–	2	1
Nurse's assistant; sick nurse's assistant	–	1	1	–
Attending sick	–	1	–	–
Midwife	1	3	4	3
Midwife and sick nurse	–	1	–	–
Naval hospital	3	–	–	–
Dry nurse	–	1	2	–
Field nurse	–	–	2	–
Nurse to infants; nurse to little negroes; attending infants; with weaned children	–	18	19	4
In charge of invalids	–	–	1	–
Attending her infants; careing her children	2	3	1	–
Total	14	64	57	29

Table S7.2. *Occupations: Barbados, 1817 (continued)*

Occupation	Number of Slaves			
	Bridge-town	Rural St. Michael	St. John	St. Andrew
Sick or disabled				
Invalid; infirm	45	76	68	27
Leper	5	8	2	–
Cripple	1	1	–	1
Blind, none	4	1	–	1
Insane	3	1	–	–
Total	58	87	70	29
Absent				
Absent	20	12	3	2
Off the island	4	–	–	–
Total	24	12	3	2
None				
None	2,561	2,185	1,123	701
Superannuated	5	23	3	8
At school	26	3	1	–
Total	2,592	2,211	1,127	709
Unspecified				
Various	7	1	–	–
Scavenger; performs light jobs	1	1	–	–
Not stated	35	1	2	1
Total	43	3	2	1
TOTAL	9,297	8,982	5,466	3,393

Table S7.3. *Occupations of Slaves, Urban and Rural: St. Lucia, 1815*

Occupation	Number of Slaves	
	Rural	Urban
Field laborers		
Au jardin; de jardin [field]	3,208	68
Jardin et rafineur [field and sugar boiler]; jardin et rumier [field and distiller]; jardin et mulier [field and mule driver]	3	–
Au jardin et accoucheuse [field and midwife]	1	–
Laboureur/labourer	1,284	43
Laboureur à loyers [hired]	1	–
Cultivateur/cultivator	1,037	38
A la houe/hoe	568	8
A la culture	379	–
Travaillant la terre; à la terre	46	3
Field	66	–
Agriculteuse	28	–
Petit atelier/small gang; little gang	134	–
Garçon d'herbe/grass gang	82	–
Coupeur d'herbes/cutter of grass	16	–
Porteuse d'herbes; charoyeuse d'herbes [grass carrier]	6	–
Cane top cutter	1	–
Charoyeuse d'eau; porteuse d'eau/water carrier	5	1
Jardinier/gardener	31	3
Au petit jardin [gardener]	5	–
Petit herbes [herb garden]	5	–
Total	6,906	164
Drivers		
Commandeur/driver	164	–
Premier commandeur [first driver]	1	–
Second driver	1	–
Chef du petit atelier	1	–
Driver little grass gang	2	–
Total	169	–
Skilled tradespeople		
Tonnelier/cooper	171	24
Tonnelier et rafineur	1	–
Chef tonnelier/head cooper	1	1
Apprentif tonnelier [apprentice cooper]	2	–
Maçon/mason	120	28
Premier maçon	1	–
Apprentice mason	6	2

Table S7.3. *Occupations: St. Lucia, 1815 (continued)*

Occupation	Number of slaves	
	Rural	Urban
Charpentier/carpenter	175	38
Chef charpentier	1	–
Aide charpentier [carpenter's assistant]	1	–
Apprentice carpenter	10	1
Menuisier/joiner	3	1
Chantier [boat builder]	1	–
Calfaiteur/caulker	–	4
Scieur de long [sawyer]	9	–
Doleur d'essentes [shingle cutter]	1	–
Forgeron/blacksmith	8	8
Mahotier [smith]	1	–
Maréchal [farrier]	–	1
Faiseur de cordes [rope maker]	1	–
Cordonnier/cordwainer [shoemaker]	9	5
Perruquier [wig maker]	3	–
Hatter	–	1
Tailleur/tailor	–	4
Tailleur de lisieres [tailor, selvedges]	2	–
Couturiere/seamstress	32	23
Couturiere et marchande [seamstress and seller]	2	4
Apprentif couturiere	4	–
Brodeuse [embroiderer]	1	–
Lingère [sewing maid]	1	–
Bonbonnière [sweetmaker]	–	1
Faiseuse de cigares [cigarmaker]	1	1
Boulanger/baker	4	13
Boucher/butcher	2	3
Pottier [potter]	3	–
Rafineur/boiler [sugar boiler]	58	–
Second boiler	1	–
Rhumier/distiller	30	–
Stillman	1	–
Journallier [journeyman]	12	19
Apprentif; au métier, apprentif [apprenticed to a trade]	3	–
Total	682	182
Domestics		
Servante	672	401
Domestique/domestic	603	313
Servante domestique	2	–
Servante de maison/house servant; house servant of all work	7	24
A la maison; à l'entour de la maison; ménagère/house	25	15
House boy	–	1

Table S7.3. *Occupations: St. Lucia, 1815 (continued)*

Occupation	Number of slaves	
	Rural	Urban
Aff^e de tout service [general servant]	1	–
Petit servant	–	1
Servante au bourg [servant in town]	1	–
Domestique à loyer journallier [hired, journeyman domestic]	1	–
Matronne [housekeeper]	1	–
Maitre d'hotel/butler	2	1
Valet	126	55
Valet et cuisinier	1	–
Cuisinier/cook	110	53
Marmiton [scullion]	3	2
Servante de chambre/chambermaid	–	4
Blanchisseuse; lessiviere/washer	73	87
Washer and sempstress	–	1
Washer and itinerant retailer of dry goods	–	1
Gardien d'enfants/attending on children	41	2
Gardienne d'enfant blanc	1	–
Gardienne d'barriére; à la troue [gate keeper]	4	–
Messagère; commissionaire; employé à faires des commissions; affaires des commissions [messenger]	7	–
Petit commissionaire [errand boy]	–	1
Jouer de violon/fiddler	2	1
Total	1,683	963
Stockkeepers		
Gardien de animaux	98	–
Gardeur/stockkeeper	67	1
Gardien de troupeaux/herdsman	8	–
Gardien de bestieaux/cattleherd; takes care of cattle	51	–
Driver of cattle; cattle boy	4	–
Gardien de boeuf/cow keeper	25	2
Berger/shepherd	3	–
Gardien de mouton/takes care of sheep	12	–
Gardeur de mulets/takes care of mules	11	–
Mule boy	9	–
Palefrenier; panseur; ayant soin des chevaux/groom	10	1
Cabrouetier [head groom]	4	1
Hostler	–	1
Stable boy	2	–
A la savanne/pasture boy	10	–
Gardien des poules; gardien de poulailler	9	2
Gardien de volaille/takes care of the poultry	4	–
Gardien de lapins [rabbit keeper]	1	–
Total	328	8

Occupation	Number of slaves	
	Rural	Urban
Transport workers		
Matelot/sailor	32	65
Marin/mariner	–	9
Canotier/boatman	5	8
Maneuver [sailor]	–	1
De pirogue [canoe man]	14	14
Dans les pirogues et au jardin; sailor and labourer	10	–
En journee dans la pirogue [canoe, daily worker]	1	–
Patron; capitaine [skipper]	1	1
Patron de pirogue; patron de canot	4	1
Captain of schooner; captain of sloop	–	2
Mousse [cabin boy]	1	–
Cartman	2	–
Muletier [mule driver]	51	2
Chef muletier/mules captain	2	–
Mutelier et valet	1	–
Porter	–	1
Total	124	104
Watchmen		
Gardien; guardien/watchman	156	5
Chef de gardiens [head watchman]	1	–
Gardien et infirme	1	–
Gardeuse de savane [pasture]	58	–
Gardien de cannes [sugar canes]	21	–
Gardien de banane [plantains]	18	–
Gardien de verger [orchard]	3	–
Gardien du pottage; gardienne de polager [kitchen garden]	5	–
Gardeur de jardins	4	–
Gardien des jardins à Négre [slave grounds]	2	–
Gardienne de vivres [provisions]	8	–
Watchman and mill boatswain	1	–
Gardeur de batimens [buildings]	1	–
Gardeuse de magasin [shop]	2	–
Gardeuse de maison au bourg [town house]	1	–
Total	282	5
Fishermen		
Pecheur/fisherman	41	24
Seineur	3	–
Pecheur à loyers [hired]	1	–
Total	45	24

Table S7.3. *Occupations: St. Lucia, 1815 (continued)*

Occupation	Number of slaves	
	Rural	Urban
Sellers		
Marchand/huxter	15	36
Marchande et servante	7	1
Vendreuse; pourvoyeuse/seller	2	3
Itinerant retailer of dry goods	–	3
Storekeeper	1	–
Total	25	43
Laborers		
Ouvrier [worker]	24	8
Travailleur [worker]	15	9
En journée; à la journée; payant journée [daily worker]	18	38
Jobber	5	3
A l'equipage	3	–
Pécheur de chaux [coral fisher]	1	–
Fabrication d'la chaux; à la chaux [lime maker]	19	–
Charbonnier [charcoal burner]	–	1
Bruillant le café [coffee dryer]	4	–
Makes castor oil	1	–
Chasseur/huntsman; extra huntsman	4	–
Chasseur de rats; preneur de rats [rat catcher]	2	–
Total	96	59
Hired		
A loyers; louee/hired out	19	4
A loyers sur l'habitation dite ...	6	–
A loyer en ville	1	–
A loyers journallier [journeyman]	15	5
Servante à loyer journallier	2	–
Total	43	9
Nurses		
Nurse	5	1
A soigner des malades/sick nurse; attending the sick	5	–
Hospitalière; infirmière/hospital nurse	55	–
Yaws house nurse	1	–
Doctor	1	–
Sage femme; accoucheuse [midwife]	12	–
Garde une aveugle [minding a blind person]; au service de une vieille negresse libre [helping an old free black woman	2	–
Bonne du enfants [nursemaid]	1	–
Nurse to the children	6	–
Gardeuse de negrillons [minding slave children]	12	–
Gardien de ses sœurs [minding sisters]	2	–
Total	102	1

Table S7.3. *Occupations: St. Lucia, 1815 (continued)*

Occupation	Number of slaves	
	Rural	Urban
Sick or disabled		
Infirm	248	10
Infirme lunatique; infirm et folle	2	2
Infirme muet	1	–
Aveugle/blind	8	2
Paralisée [paralysed] ; mal caduc [elipepsy]	2	–
Folle [mad]	1	1
Impotente [helpless]/incapable	3	–
Repos [resting]	1	1
En traitement	3	–
Total	269	16
Absent		
Marron [runaway]	79	4
Off the island	1	–
Total	80	4
None		
Non/none	2,545	174
Enfant/infant	692	198
A la mamele [at the breast	18	2
Jouant [playing]	–	1
Vieux; suragée [old]	2	–
Superannuated	15	–
Hors de service [useless]	15	–
Total	3,287	375
Unspecified		
A tout [all work]	3	–
Travaux du morne	1	–
De confiance [trusted]	1	–
Pour être affranchi	15	1
Travaillant pour son affranchisement	9	–
Affranchie/free	3	–
Libre sans être affranchi	1	–
Not stated	84	69
Total	117	70
TOTAL*	14,238	2,027

* Excludes 17 slaves whose location is unknown.

Table S7.4. *Occupations of Slaves, Urban and Rural: Trinidad, 1813*

Occupation	Number of slaves	
	Rural	Urban
Field laborers		
Labourer	10,634	1,115
Labourer and boiler; labourer and distiller; labourer and fireman; labourer and carpenter	7	–
Labourer and carter; labourer and mule boy	7	–
Labourer and washer	1	–
Grass gang	95	–
Small grass gang; little grass gang	108	–
Little gang; small gang	80	5
Weeding gang	15	–
Small weeding gang	23	–
Small garden gang	3	–
Weak gang	8	–
Attending grass gang; care of little gang	2	–
Top cutter; hedge cutter, trimmer	7	–
Ploughman	2	–
Wood cutter	3	9
Water carrier	4	–
Gardener	15	7
Total	11,014	1,136
Drivers		
Driver	280	9
Driver and boiler; driver and mason	2	–
Head driver	1	–
Head driver and boiler	1	–
Second driver	5	–
Driver of the boys	1	–
Mill driver	1	–
Boatswain; mill boatswain	15	–
Chief of the mill; captain of the mill; windmill boatswain	3	–
Ranger	1	
Overseer	1	–
Total	311	9
Skilled tradespeople		
Cooper	335	70
Cooper and labourer	3	–
First cooper; master cooper	3	–
Apprentice cooper	3	–
Mason	150	162
Apprentice mason	1	1
Carpenter	398	227

Table S7.4. *Occupations: Trinidad, 1813 (continued)*

Occupation	Number of slaves	
	Rural	Urban
Carpenter and boiler; carpenter and labourer	3	–
First carpenter	1	–
Second carpenter	1	–
Third carpenter	1	–
Ship carpenter	–	1
Mill carpenter	3	–
House carpenter	–	1
Jobbing carpenter	1	–
Apprentice carpenter	4	2
Joiner	–	17
Sawyer	19	12
Sawyer and labourer	2	–
Cabinet maker	–	1
Apprentice cabinet maker	–	1
Painter	–	3
Bricklayer	1	1
Plumber	–	2
Caulker	–	1
Sail maker	–	3
Rope maker	1	–
Saddler	1	8
Wheelwright	2	3
Apprentice wheelwright	–	1
Cartwright	–	1
Millwright	4	–
Blacksmith	14	18
Smith	5	–
Coppersmith	–	1
Goldsmith	–	9
Apprentice goldsmith	–	1
Armourer	–	1
Tanner	–	13
Shoemaker; cobbler	10	30
Apprentice shoemaker	–	1
Seamstress	68	79
Tailor	13	28
Apprentice tailor	–	1
Butcher	–	7
Baker	3	58
Confectioner	2	–
Sugar baker	2	–
Pastry cook	1	4
Segar maker; segar manufacturer	–	43
Umbrella maker	–	1

Table S7.4. *Occupations: Trinidad, 1813 (continued)*

Occupation	Number of slaves	
	Rural	Urban
Potter	13	–
Boiler; sugar boiler; boiler man	233	2
Head boiler	1	–
Second boiler	1	–
Boiler and distiller; boiler and labourer	8	–
Head boiler	1	–
Second boiler	1	–
Boiler and distiller; boiler and labourer	8	–
Distiller; rum distiller	108	–
Distiller and carpenter; distiller and labourer	2	–
Refiner	8	–
Engineer	3	–
Journeyman	–	1
Tradesman	1	–
Apprentice	5	2
Total	1,435	818
Domestics		
Servant	1,127	1,395
Servant and carpenter; servant and labourer	–	4
Domestic	398	370
House servant	105	161
House servant and seamstress	1	–
House maid	3	37
House boy; house girl	16	20
Chamber maid	2	3
Waiting maid; lady's maid	1	1
Nursery maid; children's maid	–	2
Around the house	2	–
Housekeeper	3	–
Butler	–	1
Footman	1	–
Barber; hairdresser; barber's boy	1	6
Cook	169	206
Cook and washer	–	3
Scullion	–	1
Waiter	–	1
Washer	212	519
Washer and ironer; washer and house servant; washer and servant; washer and sempstress; washer and labourer	8	3
Laundress	5	7
Butter churner	1	–
Gatekeeper	1	–
Total	2,056	2,740

Table S7.4. *Occupations: Trinidad, 1813 (continued)*

Occupation	Number of slaves	
	Rural	Urban
Stockkeepers		
Stockkeeper	63	2
Herdsman	1	–
Cattle keeper; cattleherd; cowherd; watching the cattle	20	–
Cattle boy; cow boy; stock boy	15	2
Dairy maid; dairy woman	–	2
Sheep driver	2	–
Swine keeper	2	–
Mule keeper	9	–
Mule boy	129	1
Crook boy; crook corp; crook mules	6	1
Groom	11	9
Ostler; hostler	4	–
Pastureman; in the pastures	3	–
Pasture boy	50	–
Grass boy	1	–
Total	316	17
Transport workers		
Sailor	31	64
Sailor and labourer	4	–
Boatman; seaman	4	22
Boatman and labourer	–	1
Captain of the boat	1	–
Carter	133	43
Carter and carpenter; carter and labourer	11	–
Cartman	1	5
Mule driver; muleteer; mule boy and carter	9	–
Carrier	5	–
Porter	–	11
Total	199	146
Watchmen		
Watchman	107	–
In the watch house; pasture watchman	2	–
Total	109	–
Fishermen	26	64

Table S7.4. *Occupations: Trinidad, 1813 (continued)*

Occupation	Number of slaves	
	Rural	Urban
Sellers		
Huckster	21	142
Seller	–	1
Storekeeper	1	–
Bread seller	–	4
Total	22	147
Laborers		
Jobber	17	2
Brickmaker	34	–
Limemaker; lime burner	–	28
Quarrier; miner	–	24
Bark dryer; wood squarer	1	1
Cotton ginner	2	12
Syrup maker	–	1
Mattress maker	–	1
Fireman	22	–
Mill boy	1	–
Huntsman	1	–
Total	78	69
Nurses		
Nurse	27	5
Head nurse	1	3
Sick nurse	42	1
Hospital nurse	13	–
Midwife	6	–
Midwife and nurse	2	–
Dry nurse	2	–
Attending hospital	1	–
Yaws house	2	–
Hospital cook	1	–
Children's nurse; taking care of children	18	–
Taking care of her sisters	1	–
Total	116	9
Sick or disabled		
Invalid	103	5
Infirm	33	11
Dumb	–	1
Deranged	1	–
Total	137	17

Table S7.4. *Occupations: Trinidad, 1813 (continued)*

Occupation	Number of slaves	
	Rural	Urban
Absent		
Deserter	144	44
Labourer, deserter	6	1
Cooper, deserter; carpenter, deserter	2	–
Absent	–	1
Total	152	46
None		
None	3,397	946
None, 6 children	1	–
Superannuated	17	1
Infant; child	9	1
At school; keeps the children's school	1	4
In gaol	1	–
Useless	4	–
Total	3,430	952
TOTAL*	19,401	6,170

* Excludes 125 slaves whose location is unknown.

Table S7.5. *Occupations of Slaves by Sex: Berbice, 1819*

Occupation	Males	Females	Total
Field laborers			
Field	5,585	4,509	10,094
Field labourer	37	53	90
Field light work	29	22	51
Creole gang	14	28	42
Grass cutter	19	–	19
Field and liner; field and baler; field and jobber; field and logie	12	2	14
Field and sugar boiler; field and distiller; field and mill feeder; field and fireman; field and mason	26	–	26
Field and sailor; field and punt captain; field and punting; field work, punting, cook etc; field and boat	30	1	31
Field and breeder	–	12	12
Field and watchman; field and plantin minder	2	–	2
Field and midwife; field and nurse; field and creole nurse	–	7	7
Field and domestic	–	4	4
Field and cook	–	8	8
Mill feeder	2	–	2
Logie; in the logie	520	553	1,073
Droghery; in the drogery	21	27	48
Wood cutter; stave cutter etc.	32	–	32
Cotton cleaner	–	1	1
In the coffee lodge	40	31	71
Water carrier	11	2	13
Gardener	56	–	56
Total	6,436	5,260	11,696
Drivers			
Driver	208	2	210
Driver and head sugar boiler	1	–	1
Driver or carpenter	2	–	2
Driver and field	1	–	1
First driver; head driver	29	–	29
Second driver	14	2	16
Third driver	5	–	5
Fourth driver	2	–	2
Field men driver; men driver	6	–	6
Field women driver; women driver; woman driver	8	2	10
Creole driver; children driver	2	1	3
Logie driver	21	–	21
Logie driver and jobber	1	–	1
Droghery driver	1	–	1
Under driver	1	–	1
Carpenter driver	1	–	1
Old driver	1	–	1
Bush driver	1	–	1
Overseer	7	–	7
Boatswain of mill; mill boatswain and field	4	–	4
Ranger	2	–	2
Total	318	7	325

Occupation	Males	Females	Total
Skilled tradespeople			
Cooper	167	–	167
Cooper and mason; cooper and painter	2	–	2
Cooper and field	2	–	2
Head cooper	2	–	2
Apprentice cooper; cooper's boy	3	–	3
Invalid cooper	1	–	1
Mason	67	1	68
Mason's boy	1	–	1
Carpenter	883	–	883
Carpenter and cooper; carpenter and mason; carpenter and ginner; carpenter and engineer; carpenter and painter; carpenter and sawyer; carpenter, cooper and sawyer	17	–	17
Carpenter and sick nurse	1	–	1
Carpenter and field; carpenter and woodcutter	43	1	44
Carpenter and watchman	1	–	1
Carpenter and invalid	1	–	1
Carpenter hired in Demy [Demerara]	3	–	3
Carpentry and different work	9	–	9
Head carpenter; first carpenter; chief carpenter	13	–	13
Apprentice carpenter; carpenter's boy; by the carpenter	17	–	17
Head carpenter and driver; head carpenter and cooper	2	–	2
Sawyer	33	–	33
Sawyer and field	6	–	6
Cabinet maker	1	–	1
Painter	1	–	1
Woodcutter and carpenter	44	–	44
Shingles maker	9	–	9
Shingles maker and punt captain; shingles maker and punt negro	4	–	4
Blacksmith	12	–	12
Smith	24	–	24
Coppersmith	1	–	1
Boatbuilder	26	–	26
Shipwright	1	–	1
In the printing office	1	–	1
Saddle maker	1	–	1
Rope maker	1	–	1
Basket maker	12	–	12
Basket and rope maker	5	–	5
Shoemaker	4	–	4
Taylor	17	–	17
Seamstress	–	52	52
Seamstress and field	–	1	1
Learning to sew	–	3	3
Baker	1	–	1

Table S7.5. *Occupations: Berbice, 1819 (continued)*

Occupation	Males	Females	Total
Pastry cook	–	1	1
Butcher	4	–	4
Chocolate manufacturer	2	2	4
Segar manufacturer	1	–	1
Weaver	–	21	21
Cotton spinner	–	4	4
Weaver and ginner	1	–	1
Ginner and field	91	–	91
Engineer	9	–	9
Engineer and field; engineer and sick nurse	3	–	3
Boiler; sugar boiler	39	–	39
Boiler and field	3	–	3
Distiller	10	–	10
Tradesman	8	–	8
Apprentice	4	–	4
Total	1,614	86	1,700
Domestics			
Domestic	430	745	1,175
Domestic and nurse; domestic and washer	–	2	2
Domestic, carpenter etc.	1	–	1
Domestic, field etc.	–	3	3
Domestic, now in Holland with owner	–	1	1
House servant; house servant, released from slavery	41	128	169
House; in the house	10	23	33
House maid; servant maid	–	37	37
Near the house	–	1	1
Servant	14	17	31
Body servant	1	–	1
Servant and different work	1	–	1
House boy; house girl	60	9	69
House and field	–	1	1
Waiting boy	1	–	1
Attending domestic	–	1	1
Dress negro	2	–	2
Housekeeper	–	4	4
Housekeeper and seamstress	–	1	1
Butler	1	–	1
Cook	53	92	145
Cook and house servant; cook and domestic; cook and nurse; cook and washerwoman	1	3	4
Cook and sawyer	1	–	1
Cook and field	1	2	3
Cook and different work	1	–	1
Assistant cook; assistant to the cook	–	3	3
Children's cook	–	2	2

Table S7.5. *Occupations: Berbice, 1819 (continued)*

Occupation	Males	Females	Total
Learn cooking	–	1	1
Kitchen; assisting in the kitchen	–	2	2
Scullion	1	–	1
Drudge		1	1
Washer; laundress	3	171	174
Wash maid; assisting washerwoman	–	2	2
Washer and field	–	4	4
Attends the infants	5	22	27
Messenger, etc.	1	–	1
In town with ...	1	1	2
Total	630	1,279	1,909
Stockkeepers			
Stockkeeper	217	17	234
Stockkeeper and jobber	1	–	1
Assistant stockkeeper	2	1	3
Stock minder	5	4	9
Minder of small stock	–	1	1
Herdsman	19	–	19
Cowherd; cattleherd; cattle keeper; minding cattle	27	–	27
Cattle keeper and field	2	–	2
Assistant cattle keeper	2	–	2
Cattle driver	2	–	2
Cattle boy; cow boy	3	–	3
Dairy woman	–	1	1
Shepherd; shepherdess; sheep boy	15	1	16
Mule minder; mule boy	4	–	4
Groom	14	–	14
Groom and field	1	–	1
Ostler	17	–	17
Stable boy	1	–	1
Feather stockkeeper; attending poultry	–	2	2
Jockey	1	–	1
Total	333	27	360
Transport workers			
Sailor; mariner	38	–	38
Sailor and carpenter	1	–	1
Seaman	6	–	6
Boatman	43	–	43
Boat captain	10	–	10
Boat puller	5	–	5
In boat	1	–	1
Pilot	1	–	1
Ferryman; at Canje ferry	13	–	13
Punt captain; punt negro	9	–	9
Mule driver; muleteer	10	–	10
Porter	14	–	14
Porter and sawyer	2	–	2
Total	153	–	153

Occupation	Males	Females	Total
Watchmen			
Watchman	182	–	182
Field watchman	20	–	20
Plantation watchman; watchman by the provisions	10	–	10
Old ranger	3	2	5
Invalid watchman	1	–	1
Watchman and ginner	1	–	1
Total	217	2	219
Fishermen			
Fisherman	27	–	27
Fishing boy	4	–	4
Total	31	–	31
Sellers			
Huckster	–	24	24
Laborers			
Labourer	327	112	439
Jobber	118	91	209
Any light work; slight work; light work	93	97	190
About buildings; jobbing about buildings	28	51	79
About the works	24	18	42
Sundry light work about the buildings, drying cotton, cane megass etc.	12	19	31
About the yard	1	3	4
Coffee cleaner; clean coffee	–	22	22
Coffee cleaner and field	–	1	1
Baler	1	1	2
Fireman	1	–	1
Brickmaker	1	–	1
Huntsman	2	–	2
Light work in town	1	–	1
Factotum	1	–	1
Colony works	12	3	15
Colony stocks	3	1	4
Cook for chain gang	1	–	1
Total	626	419	1,045
Hired			
Hired to self	–	1	1
Working out	1	–	1
Total	1	1	2

Table S7.5. *Occupations: Berbice, 1819 (continued)*

Occupation	Males	Females	Total
Nurses			
Nurse	2	80	82
Sick nurse	38	12	50
Hospital nurse; sick nurse in the hospital	6	9	15
Assistant sick nurse	1	–	1
Assisting nurse; nurse tender	–	6	6
Nurse and invalid	–	1	1
Hospital assistant; hospital attendant; attending hospital; attending the sick	15	–	15
Hospital mate	1	–	1
Hospital cook	–	1	1
Hospital	1	–	1
Doctor	7	–	7
Apothecary	1	–	1
Midwife	–	33	33
Midwife and sick nurse	–	1	1
Yaws nurse	–	5	5
Yaws house	–	1	1
Creole nurse; minding creoles	–	15	15
Children's nurse	–	38	38
Dress nurse	1	–	1
Takes care of child who is her owner	–	1	1
Total	73	203	276
Sick or disabled			
Invalid	418	466	884
Old invalid	1	–	1
Leper	10	3	13
Sickly	1	2	3
In the yaws	4	5	9
Insane	3	1	4
Total	437	477	914
Absent			
Runaway (pre 1810)	45	3	48
Runaway	18	3	21
Deserter	1	–	1
In England	2	–	2
Confined in gaol	1	–	1
Total	67	6	73
None			
None	2,202	2,420	4,622
None – buildings	2	–	2
Superannuated	17	38	55

Table S7.5. *Occupations: Berbice, 1819 (continued)*

Occupation	Males	Females	Total
Infant sucking; at the breast	4	–	4
In the nursery; under the care of nurses; with nurses	126	138	264
Child; boy	25	6	31
Playing	10	8	18
At school	1	4	5
Exempted from work	–	1	1
Not able to work; useless; unserviceable	16	15	31
Total	2,403	2,630	5,033
Unspecified			
Variously employed	1	–	1
Fruiter	1	–	1
Drif Negro	1	–	1
Not stated	25	93	118
Total	28	93	121
TOTAL	13,367	10,514	23,881

Table S7.6. *Occupations of Slaves by Sex: Anguilla, 1827*

Occupation	Males	Females	Total
Field laborers			
Field	412	503	915
Cultivator	45	61	106
Water drawer	–	2	2
Total	457	566	1,023
Drivers			
Driver	9	–	9
Ranger	1	–	1
Total	10	–	10
Skilled tradespeople			
Carpenter	22	–	22
Mason	20	–	20
Cooper	16	–	16
Blacksmith	1	–	1
Shoemaker	17	–	17
Apprentice shoemaker	2	–	2
Seamstress	–	27	27
Tailor	11	–	11
Sugar boiler	7	–	7
Distiller	2	–	2
Basket maker	1	–	1
Apprentice	2	–	2
Total	101	27	128
Domestics			
Domestic	35	182	217
House servant	7	43	50
House boy	2	–	2
Cook	5	21	26
Washer	–	72	72
Drudge	1	–	1
Total	50	318	368
Stockkeepers			
Stockkeeper; stock minder	15	6	21
Stock boy	6	–	6
Shepherd	8	3	11
Herdsman	1	–	1
Cattle keeper; cattle minder	10	1	11
Groom	5	–	5
Turkey minder	–	2	2
Total	45	12	57

Table S7.6. *Occupations: Anguilla, 1827 (continued)*

Occupation	Males	Females	Total
Transport workers			
Sailor	11	–	11
Boatman	3	–	3
Total	14	–	14
Watchmen			
Watchman	9	–	9
Ground minder	2	4	6
Total	11	4	15
Fishermen	25	–	25
Sellers			
Seller	–	2	2
Huxter	–	1	1
Total	–	3	3
Nurses			
Sick nurse	–	1	1
Dry nurse	–	1	1
Midwife	–	6	6
Child minder	–	1	1
Total	–	9	9
Sick or disabled			
Infirm	8	5	13
Invalid	2	3	5
Diseased	2	2	4
Distempered; afflicted	1	1	2
Blind; lost arm	–	3	3
Total	13	14	27
Absent (runaway)	1	–	1
None			
None	392	393	785
Infant	12	17	29
Superannuated	2	–	2
Exempt	3	4	7
Total	409	414	823
TOTAL	1,136	1,367	2,503

Table S7.7. *Occupations of Slaves by Sex and Slave-holding Size-group: Kingstown, St. Vincent, 1817*

Occupation	Males	Females	Total
1-10 SLAVES			
Skilled tradespeople			
Carpenter	54	–	54
Apprentice carpenter	1	–	1
Cooper	31	–	31
Mason	15	–	15
Apprentice mason	1	–	1
Blacksmith	1	–	1
Gold and silver smith	2	–	2
Printer	2	–	2
Saddler	2	–	2
Sail maker	1	–	1
Seamstress	–	14	14
Seamstress and washer	–	4	4
Tailor	4	–	4
Baker	1	–	1
Tradesman	2	–	2
Apprentice	4	–	4
Total	121	18	139
Domestics			
Domestic	96	269	365
House servant; servant	44	83	127
Cook	11	8	19
Cook and house servant	1	–	1
Butler	1	–	1
Valet	2	–	2
Chamber maid	–	2	2
Nursery maid	–	1	1
Waiting boy	1	–	1
Washer	–	86	86
Washer and jobber	–	1	1
Groom; ostler	3	–	3
Gardener	1	–	1
Drudge	–	5	5
Total	160	455	615
Transport workers			
Sailor	42	–	42
Boatman	4	–	4
Sailor and cooper	1	–	1
Total	47	–	47

Table S7.7. *Occupations: Kingstown, 1817 (continued)*

Occupation	Males	Females	Total
Fishermen	7	–	7
Sellers			
Huckster	–	5	5
Seller	–	9	9
Total	–	14	14
Laborers			
Labourer	65	53	118
Gathering wood; charing wood	2	–	2
Total	67	53	120
Nurses			
Sick nurse	–	1	1
Sick or disabled			
Invalid	3	4	7
Blind, infirm	5	2	7
Total	8	6	14
Absent			
At large	–	10	10
None			
Under 10 years of age	128	170	298
Over 60 years of age	–	5	5
No trade yet	1	–	1
Idler; spinster	–	2	2
Total	129	177	306
TOTAL	539	734	1,273
11-50 SLAVES			
Skilled tradespeople			
Carpenter	53	–	53
Apprentice carpenter	3	–	3
Cooper	29	–	29
Apprentice cooper	2	–	2
Mason	9	–	9
Blacksmith	10	–	10
Coppersmith	2	–	2
Ship carpenter	1	–	1

Table S7.7. *Occupations: Kingstown, 1817 (continued)*

Occupation	Males	Females	Total
Sail maker	2	–	2
Caulker	6	–	6
Seamstress	–	14	14
Tailor	4	–	4
Baker	1	–	1
Butcher	1	–	1
Apprentice	1	–	1
Total	124	14	138
Domestics			
Domestic	39	94	133
House servant	48	61	109
Cook	7	7	14
Scullion	–	1	1
Chamber maid	–	1	1
Washer	–	48	48
Ironer	–	1	1
Groom	2	–	2
Drudge	–	2	2
Total	96	215	311
Transport workers			
Sailor	55	–	55
Boatman	28	–	28
Boatman and labourer	16	–	16
Porter	1	–	1
Total	100	–	100
Fishermen	6	–	6
Sellers			
Seller	–	7	7
Huckster	–	4	4
Total	–	11	11
Laborers			
Labourer	96	38	134
Stockkeeper	3	–	3
Total	99	38	137
Nurses			
Nurse	–	4	4
Sick nurse	–	2	2
Total	–	6	6

Table S7.7. *Occupations: Kingstown, 1817 (continued)*

Occupation	Males	Females	Total
Sick or disabled			
Blind, invalid	5	2	7
None			
Under 10 years of age	88	115	203
Over 60 years of age	3	1	4
Superannuated	1	1	2
Total	92	117	209
TOTAL	522	403	925
51-100 SLAVES			
Skilled tradespeople			
Cooper	2	–	2
Ship carpenter and sailor	1	–	1
Seamstress and house servant	–	2	2
Total	3	2	5
Domestics			
House servant	2	1	3
Cook, butler etc.	1	–	1
Washer	–	1	1
Washer and house servant	–	3	3
Total	3	5	8
Transport workers			
Sailor	35	–	35
Sailor and sail maker	2	–	2
Sailor and fisherman	1	–	1
Porter	2	–	2
Porter and sailor	1	–	1
Total	41	–	41
None			
Under 10 years of age	1	2	3
TOTAL	48	9	57

Table S7.8. *Occupations of Slaves by Age and Sex:*
   Cayman Islands, 1834

Occupation	Number of Slaves Aged							
	0-9	10-19	20-29	30-39	40-49	50-59	60-	Total
Males								
Field laborers	17	65	75	42	49	35	28	311
Carpenters	–	2	–	4	–	1	–	7
Sawyers	–	–	3	4	4	–	–	11
Caulkers	–	–	–	–	1	1	–	2
Coopers	–	–	–	–	–	–	1	1
Mechanics	–	–	–	–	2	–	1	3
Domestics	49	22	1	1	2	1	1	77
Mariners	–	1	7	4	1	1	–	14
Fishermen	–	3	3	6	2	–	1	15
Cripple	–	1	–	–	–	–	–	1
Runaway	–	–	–	1	–	–	–	1
None	45	–	–	1	1	–	–	47
Females								
Field laborers	2	19	28	22	30	22	13	136
Domestics	74	72	68	35	32	13	11	305
Midwives	–	–	–	–	–	–	2	2
None	52	–	–	–	–	–	–	52

Table S7.9. *Occupations of Slaves by Sex and Crop-type: St. Lucia, 1815*

Occupation	Percentage of Slaves						
	Sugar	Coffee	Cocoa	Cotton	Pro-visions	Per-sonal	Total
Males							
Field laborers	45.5	47.1	38.2	47.0	45.7	14.2	44.0
Drivers	2.6	3.4	1.6	2.4	0.0	0.1	2.4
Skilled tradespeople	12.8	5.8	4.9	3.6	4.3	13.4	1.6
Domestics	5.0	9.0	7.6	9.6	15.7	31.1	11.9
Stockkeepers	3.8	2.8	4.9	2.4	2.9	1.1	3.4
Transport workers	1.6	0.7	1.1	3.6	0.0	9.3	3.4
Watchmen	4.7	2.0	1.1	0.0	0.0	0.3	3.2
Fishermen	0.4	0.4	0.0	3.6	0.0	2.8	1.0
Sellers	0.0	0.0	0.0	0.0	0.0	0.2	0.1
Laborers	0.6	1.0	0.5	4.8	1.4	2.6	1.2
Hired	0.0	0.0	0.5	0.0	0.0	1.3	0.3
Nurses	0.0	0.2	0.0	0.0	0.0	0.0	0.0
Sick or disabled	1.6	0.5	1.6	0.0	1.4	0.4	1.5
Absent	1.4	0.2	0.5	2.4	0.0	0.3	0.9
None	20.0	26.9	37.5	20.6	28.6	22.9	25.1
Females							
Field laborers	59.7	50.7	48.9	51.1	48.5	13.4	47.4
Drivers	0.1	0.0	0.0	0.0	0.0	0.0	0.1
Skilled tradespeople	0.6	0.8	0.0	0.7	0.0	2.9	1.0
Domestics	8.5	15.9	16.2	14.6	21.7	58.2	21.3
Stockkeepers	1.2	1.5	0.4	1.5	1.0	0.2	1.0
Transport workers	0.0	0.0	0.4	0.0	0.0	0.0	0.0
Watchmen	1.7	1.3	1.8	0.0	0.0	0.1	1.1
Fishermen	0.0	0.0	0.0	0.0	0.0	0.0	0.0
Sellers	0.0	0.4	0.4	0.7	0.0	2.8	0.7
Laborers	0.2	0.8	0.9	1.5	4.0	2.2	0.7
Hired	0.0	0.3	0.9	2.2	0.0	1.5	0.4
Nurses	1.9	1.3	0.0	0.7	0.0	0.1	1.1
Sick or disabled	2.3	2.6	0.9	1.5	4.0	1.0	2.1
Absent	0.3	0.1	0.0	0.7	0.0	0.2	0.3
None	23.5	24.3	29.2	24.8	20.8	17.4	22.8

Table S7.10. *Occupations of Slaves by Sex and Crop-type:*
Trinidad, 1813

Occupation	Percentage of Slaves						
	Sugar	Coffee	Cocoa	Cotton	Pro-visions	Per-sonal	Total
Males							
Field laborers	55.1	68.2	66.2	65.7	60.4	31.7	50.1
Drivers	3.3	2.3	2.9	0.9	1.8	0.4	2.3
Skilled tradespeople	14.4	3.2	2.8	2.7	9.0	19.3	14.1
Domestics	3.4	10.2	7.3	3.9	7.4	23.2	10.1
Stockkeepers	3.7	0.2	0.5	0.0	0.5	0.5	2.2
Transport workers	2.3	0.3	0.5	0.0	1.4	3.7	2.4
Watchmen	1.4	0.0	0.0	0.3	0.0	0.0	0.8
Fishermen	0.1	0.3	0.0	1.5	0.7	1.7	0.6
Sellers	0.0	0.0	0.0	0.0	0.0	0.3	0.1
Laborers	0.7	0.6	0.7	0.8	0.6	2.1	0.7
Hired	0.0	0.0	0.0	0.0	0.0	0.0	0.0
Nurses	0.0	0.0	0.0	0.0	0.0	0.1	0.0
Sick or disabled	0.6	0.0	0.2	0.3	0.2	0.2	0.5
Absent	0.9	0.2	0.8	0.0	1.4	0.7	0.8
None	14.1	14.5	18.1	23.9	16.6	16.1	15.3
Females							
Field laborers	63.9	56.3	46.4	49.3	54.3	17.5	44.6
Drivers	0.0	0.0	0.0	0.0	0.0	0.0	0.0
Skilled tradespeople	0.7	0.2	1.1	0.0	1.4	3.4	1.7
Domestics	10.6	20.8	29.0	19.3	22.2	56.4	29.8
Stockkeepers	0.3	0.0	0.0	0.0	0.0	0.1	0.2
Transport workers	0.0	0.0	0.0	0.0	0.0	0.0	0.0
Watchmen	0.0	0.0	0.0	0.0	0.0	0.0	0.0
Fishermen	0.0	0.0	0.0	0.0	0.0	0.0	0.0
Sellers	0.1	0.6	0.0	0.0	0.0	3.4	1.4
Laborers	0.2	0.2	0.5	0.2	0.3	0.6	0.4
Hired	0.0	0.0	0.0	0.0	0.0	0.0	0.0
Nurses	1.8	0.0	0.5	0.0	0.0	0.3	1.0
Sick or disabled	1.0	0.4	0.7	0.0	0.3	0.3	0.8
Absent	0.2	0.0	0.0	0.7	0.9	0.5	0.3
None	21.2	21.5	21.8	30.5	20.6	17.5	19.8

Table S7.11.*Occupations of Slaves by Sex and Slave-holding Size-group: St. Andrew, Barbados, 1817*

Occupation	Percentage of Slaves						
	1-10 Slaves	11-50 Slaves	51-100 Slaves	101-150 Slaves	151-200 Slaves	201-300 Slaves	Total
Males							
Field laborers	47.5	51.0	51.3	57.2	53.0	56.6	54.4
Drivers	0.0	1.5	2.3	1.6	1.2	2.2	1.7
Skilled tradespeople	7.4	4.0	6.8	7.1	8.4	10.9	7.5
Domestics	10.7	4.5	4.9	3.3	3.6	2.8	4.2
Stockkeepers	8.2	6.1	6.8	6.4	12.0	5.6	6.7
Transport workers	0.0	0.0	1.9	0.6	1.2	0.6	0.7
Watchmen	0.0	2.0	2.7	1.4	3.6	4.7	2.3
Fishermen	0.0	0.0	0.0	0.0	0.0	0.0	0.0
Sellers	0.0	0.0	0.0	0.0	0.0	0.0	0.0
Laborers	0.8	0.0	0.0	0.3	0.0	0.0	0.2
Hired	0.0	0.0	0.0	0.0	0.0	0.0	0.0
Nurses	0.8	0.0	0.0	0.0	0.0	0.0	0.1
Sick or disabled	0.0	0.5	0.4	0.0	0.0	0.0	0.2
Absent	0.0	0.0	0.0	0.2	0.0	0.0	0.1
None	24.6	30.4	22.9	21.9	17.0	16.6	21.9
Females							
Field laborers	34.9	36.3	57.5	64.5	76.2	70.2	60.2
Drivers	0.0	0.0	1.9	1.2	2.9	1.4	1.2
Skilled tradespeople	0.0	4.4	0.0	0.1	0.0	0.0	0.4
Domestics	42.3	25.6	10.9	8.0	5.7	6.1	12.4
Stockkeepers	4.7	5.6	2.6	1.4	1.0	2.6	2.4
Transport workers	0.0	0.0	0.0	0.0	0.0	0.0	0.0
Watchmen	0.0	0.0	0.4	0.0	0.0	0.0	0.1
Fishermen	0.0	0.0	0.0	0.0	0.0	0.0	0.0
Sellers	0.7	0.0	0.0	0.0	0.0	0.0	0.1
Laborers	0.0	0.0	0.0	0.0	0.0	0.0	0.0
Hired	0.0	0.0	0.0	0.0	0.0	0.0	0.0
Nurses	0.7	0.0	1.5	1.6	2.9	2.3	1.6
Sick or disabled	1.3	0.6	0.4	2.3	0.0	1.7	1.5
Absent	0.0	0.0	0.0	0.1	0.0	0.0	0.1
None	15.4	27.5	24.8	20.8	11.3	15.7	20.0

Table S7.12.*Occupations of Slaves by Sex and Slave-holding Size-group: St. Lucia, 1815*

Occupation	Percentage of Slaves						
	1-10 Slaves	11-50 Slaves	51-100 Slaves	101-200 Slaves	201-300 Slaves	301-400 Slaves	Total
Males							
Field laborers	24.3	39.8	42.0	42.5	54.2	56.9	39.9
Drivers	0.3	2.6	2.9	2.5	2.4	1.6	2.2
Skilled tradespeople	9.9	8.4	11.9	14.4	12.4	9.0	10.8
Domestics	27.7	12.6	5.4	4.6	2.9	3.2	10.8
Stockkeepers	1.1	2.3	4.0	4.9	2.8	2.7	3.0
Transport workers	5.6	3.8	2.9	0.4	1.0	4.8	3.0
Watchmen	0.3	1.8	4.4	4.6	4.5	2.1	2.9
Fishermen	2.1	1.1	0.4	0.6	0.6	0.0	0.9
Sellers	0.3	0.0	0.1	0.0	0.0	0.0	0.1
Laborers	2.5	1.4	0.5	0.4	0.6	0.0	1.1
Hired	0.4	0.5	0.0	0.0	0.0	0.0	0.2
Nurses	0.0	0.1	0.0	0.0	0.0	0.5	0.0
Sick or disabled	0.5	1.2	1.7	2.0	0.8	2.7	1.4
Absent	0.6	0.5	0.6	2.1	0.0	1.1	0.8
None	24.4	23.9	23.2	21.0	17.8	15.4	22.9
Females							
Field laborers	21.7	45.2	54.9	59.3	71.7	58.4	47.4
Drivers	0.0	0.0	0.0	0.2	0.3	0.0	0.1
Skilled tradespeople	2.0	1.0	0.7	0.6	0.0	2.0	1.1
Domestics	51.2	23.4	10.5	7.1	4.2	4.0	21.3
Stockkeepers	0.1	1.3	1.6	1.2	0.2	0.0	1.0
Transport workers	0.0	0.0	0.0	0.0	0.0	0.0	0.0
Watchmen	0.1	1.2	1.8	1.4	0.7	0.7	1.1
Fishermen	0.0	0.0	0.0	0.0	0.0	0.0	0.0
Sellers	2.1	0.7	0.1	0.0	0.0	0.0	0.7
Laborers	2.3	0.5	0.3	0.3	0.2	0.0	0.7
Hired	0.7	0.9	0.0	0.0	0.0	0.0	0.4
Nurses	0.1	0.4	1.7	2.2	2.5	2.0	1.1
Sick or disabled	1.4	1.7	2.8	3.0	0.8	4.7	2.1
Absent	0.3	0.3	0.2	0.3	0.0	0.7	0.3
None	18.0	23.4	25.4	24.4	19.4	27.5	22.7

Table S7.13. *Occupations of Slaves by Sex and Slave-holding Size-group: Berbice, 1819*

Occupation	Percentage of Slaves							
	1-10 Slaves	11-50 Slaves	51-100 Slaves	101-200 Slaves	201-300 Slaves	301-400 Slaves	401-500 Slaves	Total
Males								
Field laborers	25.0	38.8	54.5	52.7	49.7	41.1	35.6	48.0
Drivers	0.3	1.8	2.9	2.7	2.2	2.0	2.3	2.3
Skilled tradespeople	18.3	16.7	8.6	9.8	11.1	16.8	27.9	12.1
Domestics	23.1	10.6	4.2	3.0	2.0	2.4	0.9	4.7
Stockkeepers	3.8	3.6	3.2	2.1	2.4	2.3	2.7	2.6
Transport workers	3.8	3.4	0.8	0.6	0.8	1.6	0.0	1.2
Watchmen	0.5	0.7	1.6	1.7	1.8	2.2	2.7	1.6
Fishermen	0.7	0.0	0.2	0.1	0.3	0.4	0.5	0.2
Sellers	0.0	0.0	0.0	0.0	0.0	0.0	0.0	0.0
Laborers	3.4	8.9	4.9	4.3	3.9	5.6	9.6	5.0
Hired	0.0	0.1	0.0	0.0	0.0	0.0	0.0	0.0
Nurses	0.0	0.2	0.6	0.5	0.6	0.6	0.9	0.5
Sick or disabled	1.8	2.3	2.8	3.8	3.4	3.8	0.0	3.3
Absent	0.3	0.3	0.0	0.4	1.0	0.7	1.8	0.5
None	19.0	12.6	15.7	18.3	20.8	20.5	15.1	18.0
Females								
Field laborers	5.1	26.2	57.6	56.7	53.8	49.2	55.8	49.9
Drivers	0.0	0.0	0.1	0.1	0.1	0.1	0.6	0.1
Skilled tradespeople	3.8	2.3	0.3	0.7	0.1	0.5	1.1	0.8
Domestics	59.7	36.4	9.2	6.7	4.7	6.3	9.9	12.3
Stockkeepers	0.4	0.7	0.6	0.1	0.1	0.3	1.1	0.3
Transport workers	0.0	0.0	0.6	0.4	0.0	0.0	0.0	0.3
Watchmen	0.0	0.0	0.1	0.0	0.1	0.0	0.0	0.0
Fishermen	0.0	0.0	0.0	0.0	0.0	0.0	0.0	0.0
Sellers	2.1	1.2	0.1	0.0	0.0	0.0	0.0	0.2
Laborers	1.4	3.9	3.0	4.1	6.2	7.6	14.4	4.8
Hired	0.1	0.0	0.0	0.0	0.0	0.0	0.0	0.0
Nurses	0.7	0.1	2.0	1.9	2.5	1.9	2.2	1.8
Sick or disabled	2.5	1.6	4.0	4.9	5.5	6.0	0.0	4.6
Absent	0.0	0.0	0.0	0.0	0.2	0.1	0.0	0.1
None	24.2	27.6	22.4	24.4	26.7	28.0	14.9	24.8

Table S7.14. *Occupations of Slaves by Sex, Age and Color, Rural and Urban: St. Lucia, 1815*

Occupation	Percentage of Slaves Aged							
	0-9	10-19	20-29	30-39	40-49	50-59	60-	Total
Black Males: Rural								
Field laborers	7.0	56.1	69.8	67.4	59.8	49.1	24.0	48.3
Drivers	0.0	0.2	1.5	4.8	8.2	7.9	4.7	2.5
Skilled tradespeople	0.2	3.4	14.8	14.9	12.6	13.4	12.4	8.7
Domestics	5.6	15.0	4.3	2.3	3.0	1.7	1.9	6.2
Stockkeepers	3.1	7.6	1.5	1.4	1.4	2.7	4.7	3.4
Transport workers	0.3	3.4	1.9	2.5	2.2	0.3	1.6	1.9
Watchmen	1.8	4.6	0.8	1.2	3.8	9.6	17.8	3.4
Fishermen	0.1	0.3	0.7	0.4	1.6	1.4	2.7	0.6
Sellers	0.0	0.0	0.0	0.0	0.2	0.0	0.0	0.0
Laborers	0.2	0.3	0.9	0.9	1.6	2.4	0.8	0.7
Hired	0.0	0.0	0.6	0.4	0.2	0.0	0.0	0.2
Nurses	0.2	0.0	0.0	0.0	0.0	0.0	0.0	0.0
Sick or disabled	0.1	0.2	1.0	1.7	3.4	2.7	9.7	1.5
Absent	0.2	0.7	1.3	1.3	0.8	2.7	0.4	0.9
None	81.2	8.2	0.9	0.8	1.2	6.1	19.3	21.7
Colored Males: Rural								
Field laborers	2.1	18.2	34.9	33.0	23.9	14.3	11.8	18.4
Drivers	0.0	0.0	4.1	8.5	13.0	14.3	0.0	2.8
Skilled tradespeople	0.0	9.8	35.9	39.6	39.1	28.5	17.6	17.8
Domestics	10.6	43.6	15.4	5.9	13.0	14.3	0.0	19.3
Stockkeepers	2.4	7.1	0.0	0.9	6.6	0.0	17.6	3.4
Transport workers	0.0	2.7	1.5	2.8	0.0	0.0	0.0	1.3
Watchmen	1.4	4.9	0.0	0.9	0.0	0.0	0.0	1.8
Fishermen	0.0	0.9	1.0	0.0	0.0	14.3	17.6	1.0
Sellers	0.0	0.0	0.5	0.0	0.0	0.0	0.0	0.1
Laborers	0.0	0.0	2.6	4.7	2.2	0.0	0.0	1.2
Hired	0.0	0.0	0.0	0.0	0.0	0.0	0.0	0.0
Nurses	0.0	0.0	0.0	0.9	0.0	0.0	0.0	0.1
Sick or disabled	0.0	0.0	3.1	0.9	2.2	14.3	11.8	1.3
Absent	0.0	0.0	0.5	1.9	0.0	0.0	0.0	0.3
None	83.5	12.8	0.5	0.0	0.0	0.0	23.6	31.2

Table S7.14. *Occupation by Age: St. Lucia, 1815 (continued)*

Occupation	Percentage of Slaves							
	0-9	10-19	20-29	30-39	40-49	50-59	60-	Total
Black Females: Rural								
Field laborers	8.0	60.5	80.7	82.9	80.1	69.4	32.7	57.8
Drivers	0.0	0.0	0.0	0.0	0.0	0.4	0.6	0.1
Skilled tradespeople	0.1	0.6	0.8	0.4	0.6	0.2	0.4	0.5
Domestics	5.8	22.1	13.9	12.1	10.2	9.7	8.5	12.1
Stockkeepers	2.4	2.9	0.2	0.2	0.0	0.6	1.4	1.2
Transport workers	0.0	0.0	0.0	0.1	0.0	0.0	0.0	0.0
Watchmen	0.8	1.8	0.2	0.4	0.8	3.3	5.4	1.3
Fishermen	0.0	0.0	0.0	0.0	0.0	0.0	0.2	0.0
Sellers	0.0	0.1	0.4	0.2	0.3	0.0	0.6	0.2
Laborers	0.2	0.4	0.6	0.4	0.5	0.0	0.8	0.4
Hired	0.0	0.6	0.5	0.6	0.2	1.2	0.0	0.4
Nurses	0.0	0.3	0.2	0.5	1.5	4.8	7.5	1.3
Sick or disabled	0.0	0.4	1.5	0.9	2.4	7.2	14.3	2.4
Absent	0.1	0.4	0.5	0.2	0.5	0.2	0.2	0.3
None	82.6	9.9	0.5	1.1	2.9	3.0	27.4	22.0
Colored Females: Rural								
Field laborers	1.1	25.6	34.6	39.0	45.6	28.6	36.0	22.0
Drivers	0.0	0.0	0.0	0.0	0.0	0.0	0.0	0.0
Skilled tradespeople	0.6	3.8	5.0	3.2	1.5	0.0	0.0	2.4
Domestics	10.5	53.0	54.2	51.3	42.7	46.9	20.0	36.4
Stockkeepers	0.6	1.4	0.0	0.8	0.0	2.0	0.0	0.7
Transport workers	0.0	0.0	0.0	0.0	0.0	0.0	0.0	0.0
Watchmen	0.0	1.4	0.6	0.0	0.0	2.0	8.0	0.7
Fishermen	0.0	0.0	0.0	0.0	0.0	0.0	0.0	0.0
Sellers	0.0	0.0	0.6	0.8	0.0	0.0	0.0	0.2
Laborers	0.0	0.5	0.6	1.6	0.0	0.0	0.0	0.4
Hired	0.0	0.9	1.1	0.0	0.0	0.0	0.0	0.4
Nurses	0.6	0.9	0.6	1.6	2.9	6.1	8.0	1.4
Sick or disabled	0.0	0.0	1.1	0.8	4.4	6.1	20.0	1.4
Absent	0.0	0.0	0.6	0.0	0.0	0.0	0.0	0.1
None	86.6	12.5	1.0	0.9	2.9	8.3	8.0	33.9

Table S7.14. *Occupation by Age: St. Lucia, 1815 (continued)*

Occupation	Percentage of Slaves							
	0-9	10-19	20-29	30-39	40-49	50-59	60-	Total
Black Males: Urban								
Field laborers	1.3	11.8	8.5	16.2	21.6	12.0	16.7	10.0
Drivers	0.0	0.0	0.0	0.0	0.0	0.0	0.0	0.0
Skilled tradespeople	0.6	9.6	27.5	25.7	13.7	24.0	33.3	16.5
Domestics	20.8	64.7	30.0	17.1	15.7	24.0	16.7	31.0
Stockkeepers	1.3	0.7	0.0	1.0	3.9	0.0	8.3	1.0
Transport workers	0.0	5.9	19.0	25.7	33.3	20.0	8.3	14.1
Watchmen	0.0	0.0	1.5	0.0	0.0	0.0	8.3	0.6
Fishermen	0.0	1.5	5.0	6.7	3.9	4.0	8.3	3.4
Sellers	0.6	0.0	0.0	0.0	0.0	0.0	0.0	0.1
Laborers	0.0	1.5	6.5	4.8	5.9	4.0	0.0	3.5
Hired	0.0	0.7	1.0	1.0	0.0	0.0	0.0	0.6
Nurses	0.0	0.0	0.0	0.0	0.0	0.0	0.0	0.0
Sick or disabled	0.0	0.0	0.0	1.8	2.0	8.0	0.0	0.7
Absent	0.0	0.0	1.0	0.0	0.0	0.0	0.0	0.3
None	75.4	3.6	0.0	0.0	0.0	4.0	0.1	18.2
Colored Males: Urban								
Field laborers	1.2	0.0	7.1	5.0	0.0	100.0	0.0	2.9
Drivers	0.0	0.0	0.0	0.0	0.0	0.0	0.0	0.0
Skilled tradespeople	1.2	26.3	50.0	40.0	50.0	0.0	0.0	20.2
Domestics	19.8	60.5	28.7	35.0	25.0	0.0	100.0	32.4
Stockkeepers	0.0	0.0	0.0	0.0	0.0	0.0	0.0	0.0
Transport workers	0.0	2.6	7.1	10.0	25.0	0.0	0.0	3.5
Watchmen	0.0	0.0	0.0	0.0	0.0	0.0	0.0	0.0
Fishermen	0.0	0.0	0.0	5.0	0.0	0.0	0.0	0.6
Sellers	0.0	0.0	0.0	5.0	0.0	0.0	0.0	0.6
Laborers	0.0	0.0	7.1	0.0	0.0	0.0	0.0	1.2
Hired	0.0	0.0	0.0	0.0	0.0	0.0	0.0	0.0
Nurses	0.0	0.0	0.0	0.0	0.0	0.0	0.0	0.0
Sick or disabled	0.0	0.0	0.0	0.0	0.0	0.0	0.0	0.0
Absent	0.0	0.0	0.0	0.0	0.0	0.0	0.0	0.0
None	77.8	10.6	0.0	0.0	0.0	0.0	0.0	38.6

Table S7.14. *Occupation by Age: St. Lucia, 1815 (continued)*

Occupation	Percentage of Slaves							
	0-9	10-19	20-29	30-39	40-49	50-59	60-	Total
Black Females: Urban								
Field laborers	1.3	10.1	9.7	14.3	18.8	16.4	8.1	10.2
Drivers	0.0	0.0	0.0	0.0	0.0	0.0	0.0	0.0
Skilled tradespeople	2.5	4.3	1.8	3.8	2.1	2.3	0.0	2.6
Domestics	28.1	76.8	77.1	64.7	59.4	74.4	51.3	62.3
Stockkeepers	0.0	0.0	0.0	0.0	0.0	0.0	0.0	0.0
Transport workers	0.0	0.0	0.0	0.0	0.0	0.0	0.0	0.0
Watchmen	0.0	0.0	0.4	0.0	0.0	0.0	0.0	0.1
Fishermen	0.0	0.0	0.0	0.0	0.0	0.0	0.0	0.0
Sellers	0.6	0.7	6.2	6.8	7.3	2.3	0.0	4.0
Laborers	0.0	1.4	3.1	6.0	10.4	2.3	2.7	3.5
Hired	0.0	0.7	0.0	1.5	1.0	0.0	2.7	0.6
Nurses	0.0	0.0	0.0	0.0	0.0	0.0	2.7	0.1
Sick or disabled	0.0	0.0	0.0	2.3	0.0	2.3	13.5	1.1
Absent	0.0	0.0	0.9	0.0	0.0	0.0	0.0	0.2
None	67.5	6.0	0.8	0.6	1.0	0.0	19.0	15.3
Colored Females: Urban								
Field laborers	0.0	1.6	3.5	3.7	4.3	0.0	0.0	1.9
Drivers	0.0	0.0	0.0	0.0	0.0	0.0	0.0	0.0
Skilled tradespeople	2.5	9.7	3.5	3.7	0.0	12.5	0.0	4.6
Domestics	25.3	83.8	89.5	77.8	69.6	75.0	50.0	64.6
Stockkeepers	0.0	0.0	0.0	0.0	0.0	0.0	25.0	0.4
Transport workers	0.0	0.0	0.0	0.0	0.0	0.0	0.0	0.0
Watchmen	0.0	0.0	0.0	0.0	0.0	0.0	0.0	0.0
Fishermen	0.0	0.0	0.0	0.0	0.0	0.0	0.0	0.0
Sellers	0.0	0.0	3.5	7.4	17.4	0.0	0.0	3.1
Laborers	0.0	1.6	0.0	3.7	8.7	12.5	0.0	1.9
Hired	0.0	0.0	0.0	0.0	0.0	0.0	0.0	0.0
Nurses	0.0	0.0	0.0	0.0	0.0	0 0	0.0	0.0
Sick or disabled	1.3	0.0	0.0	3.7	0.0	0.0	0.0	0.8
Absent	0.0	0.0	0.0	0.0	0.0	0.0	0.0	0.0
None	70.9	3.3	0.0	0.0	0.0	0.0	25.0	22.7

Table S7.15. *Occupations of Slaves by Sex, Age and Color: Bridgetown, Barbados, 1817*

Occupation	Percentage of Slaves							
	0-9	10-19	20-29	30-39	40-49	50-59	60-	Total
Black Males								
Field laborers	0.0	0.0	0.0	0.4	0.0	2.4	5.7	0.2
Drivers	0.0	0.0	0.0	0.0	0.0	0.0	0.0	0.0
Skilled tradespeople	2.4	30.8	30.9	26.6	18.9	20.7	20.8	21.0
Domestics	11.8	45.7	33.8	27.5	29.4	28.0	22.6	28.6
Stockkeepers	0.2	1.7	1.6	1.3	1.0	2.4	0.0	1.2
Transport workers	0.1	4.0	21.0	30.7	26.4	29.3	13.2	13.4
Watchmen	0.0	0.0	0.0	0.0	0.0	1.2	0.0	0.0
Fishermen	0.0	0.9	3.7	3.3	5.5	4.9	0.0	2.1
Sellers	0.0	0.0	0.0	0.2	0.5	0.0	0.0	0.1
Laborers	0.0	4.6	5.8	8.3	13.4	6.1	5.7	4.9
Hired	0.0	0.5	0.4	0.2	0.0	0.0	0.0	0.2
Nurses	0.0	0.0	0.0	0.0	0.0	0.0	0.0	0.0
Sick or disabled	0.0	0.6	1.0	0.2	2.0	3.7	5.7	0.7
Absent	0.0	0.3	0.4	0.0	0.5	0.0	1.9	0.2
None	85.5	10.9	1.4	1.3	2.4	1.3	24.4	27.4
Colored Males								
Field laborers	0.0	0.0	0.0	0.0	0.0	0.0	0.0	0.0
Drivers	0.0	0.0	0.0	0.0	0.0	0.0	0.0	0.0
Skilled tradespeople	1.8	34.2	56.0	54.0	37.5	11.1	12.5	26.5
Domestics	9.9	40.1	33.7	28.7	40.6	55.6	62.5	26.2
Stockkeepers	0.0	1.9	1.2	2.3	0.0	0.0	12.5	1.0
Transport workers	0.0	2.6	6.6	11.5	12.5	11.1	0.0	3.5
Watchmen	0.0	0.0	0.0	0.0	0.0	0.0	0.0	0.0
Fishermen	0.0	0.7	1.2	2.3	3.1	0.0	0.0	0.7
Sellers	0.0	0.0	0.0	0.0	0.0	0.0	0.0	0.0
Laborers	0.0	3.7	0.0	0.0	6.3	11.1	0.0	0.7
Hired	0.0	0.0	0.0	0.0	0.0	0.0	0.0	0.0
Nurses	0.0	0.0	0.0	0.0	0.0	0.0	0.0	0:0
Sick or disabled	0.0	0.0	0.0	0.0	0.0	11.1	0.0	0.1
Absent	0.0	0.0	0.6	0.0	0.0	0.0	0.0	0.1
None	88.3	16.8	0.7	1.2	0.0	0.0	12.5	41.2

Table S7.15. *Occupation by Age: Bridgetown, 1817 (continued)*

Occupation	Percentage of Slaves							
	0-9	10-19	20-29	30-39	40-49	50-59	60-	Total
Black Females								
Field laborers	0.1	0.0	0.0	0.0	0.0	0.0	0.0	0.0
Drivers	0.0	0.0	0.0	0.0	0.0	0.0	0.0	0.0
Skilled tradespeople	0.3	6.0	3.1	1.5	1.0	1.2	0.0	2.2
Domestics	14.2	79.2	88.6	91.4	87.7	83.2	58.8	69.6
Stockkeepers	0.0	0.0	0.0	0.0	0.0	0.0	0.0	0.0
Transport workers	0.0	0.0	0.0	0.0	0.0	0.0	0.0	0.0
Watchmen	0.0	0.0	0.0	0.0	0.0	0.0	0.0	0.0
Fishermen	0.0	0.0	0.0	0.0	0.0	0.0	0.0	0.0
Sellers	0.0	0.7	1.6	1.4	2.0	1.2	0.8	1.0
Laborers	0.1	1.5	2.1	1.7	3.0	2.8	1.2	1.6
Hired	0.0	0.3	1.0	0.9	0.8	1.2	0.0	0.6
Nurses	0.0	0.3	0.6	0.0	0.3	0.4	0.8	0.3
Sick or disabled	0.0	0.0	0.5	0.3	1.0	2.0	5.8	0.7
Absent	0.0	0.7	0.3	0.3	0.0	0.8	0.4	0.3
None	85.3	11.3	2.2	2.5	4.2	7.2	32.2	23.7
Colored Females								
Field laborers	0.0	0.0	0.0	0.0	0.0	0.0	0.0	0.0
Drivers	0.0	0.0	0.0	0.0	0.0	0.0	0.0	0.0
Skilled tradespeople	0.4	11.1	12.0	8.3	3.6	1.6	1.7	6.2
Domestics	11.4	74.0	82.4	83.5	88.0	85.2	64.4	56.5
Stockkeepers	0.0	0.3	0.0	0.0	0.0	0.0	0.0	0.1
Transport workers	0.0	0.0	0.0	0.0	0.0	0.0	0.0	0.0
Watchmen	0.0	0.0	0.0	0.0	0.0	0.0	0.0	0.0
Fishermen	0.0	0.0	0.0	0.0	0.0	0.0	0.0	0.0
Sellers	0.0	0.0	0.9	0.8	0.0	6.6	1.7	0.6
Laborers	0.0	0.6	0.4	4.5	0.0	0.0	0.0	0.7
Hired	0.0	0.9	0.4	0.0	0.0	0.0	0.0	0.3
Nurses	0.0	0.0	0.0	0.0	1.2	0.0	0.0	0.1
Sick or disabled	0.0	0.6	0.9	0.0	0.0	0.0	3.4	0.4
Absent	0.0	0.0	0.4	0.8	1.2	0.0	0.0	0.2
None	88.2	12.5	2.6	2.1	6.0	6.6	28.8	34.9

Table S7.16. *Occupations of Slaves by Sex, Age and Color: Berbice, 1819*

Occupation	Percentage of Slaves							
	0-9	10-19	20-29	30-39	40-49	50-59	60-	Total
Black Males								
Field laborers	7.4	44.2	58.7	67.1	62.3	31.6	18.1	49.5
Drivers	0.0	0.0	1.3	3.2	5.8	8.1	3.7	2.4
Skilled tradespeople	0.1	10.2	21.7	14.4	9.6	11.4	7.0	11.9
Domestics	2.1	18.3	5.6	1.7	1.1	0.8	1.4	4.5
Stockkeepers	0.5	5.4	1.9	2.3	3.2	7.1	1.9	2.6
Transport workers	0.1	2.0	2.0	1.3	1.0	1.0	0.0	1.2
Watchmen	0.0	0.2	0.5	1.6	4.2	11.9	3.3	1.7
Fishermen	0.0	0.6	0.2	0.2	0.1	1.0	1.4	0.2
Sellers	0.0	0.0	0.0	0.0	0.0	0.0	0.0	0.0
Laborers	3.1	7.8	5.1	4.1	5.0	5.9	1.4	4.7
Hired	0.0	0.0	0.0	0.0	0.1	0.0	0.0	0.0
Nurses	0.0	0.5	0.7	0.5	0.6	0.0	0.5	0.4
Sick or disabled	0.0	1.1	1.6	2.6	5.3	14.7	34.0	3.1
Absent	0.0	0.1	0.2	0.1	0.1	0.0	0.5	0.1
None	86.7	9.6	0.5	0.9	1.6	6.5	26.8	17.7
Colored Males								
Field laborers	0.7	10.8	14.3	45.0	36.1	27.3	0.0	14.2
Drivers	0.0	0.0	2.4	5.0	5.6	0.0	0.0	1.4
Skilled tradespeople	1.4	24.3	66.7	32.5	13.8	18.2	25.0	20.0
Domestics	3.6	41.9	11.8	2.5	11.1	0.0	0.0	13.3
Stockkeepers	0.0	1.4	2.4	2.5	5.6	0.0	0.0	1.4
Transport workers	0.0	1.4	0.0	2.5	2.8	0.0	0.0	0.9
Watchmen	0.0	0.0	0.0	2.5	0.0	9.0	50.0	1.2
Fishermen	0.0	0.0	0.0	0.0	0.0	0.0	0.0	0.0
Sellers	0.0	0.0	0.0	0.0	0.0	0.0	0.0	0.0
Laborers	1.4	6.8	0.0	2.5	5.6	0.0	0.0	2.9
Hired	0.0	0.0	0.0	0.0	0.0	0.0	0.0	0.0
Nurses	0.0	0.0	2.4	2.5	5.6	0.0	0.0	1.2
Sick or disabled	0.0	0.0	0.0	2.5	13.8	45.5	25.0	3.5
Absent	0.0	0.0	0.0	0.0	0.0	0.0	0.0	0.0
None	92.9	13.4	0.0	0.0	0.0	0.0	0.0	40.0

Table S7.16. *Occupation by Age: Berbice, 1819 (continued)*

Occupation	Percentage of Slaves							
	0-9	10-19	20-29	30-39	40-49	50-59	60-	Total
Black Females								
Field laborers	7.1	54.2	76.2	75.8	62.0	29.7	5.9	51.5
Drivers	0.0	0.0	0.1	0.0	0.2	0.4	0.0	0.1
Skilled tradespeople	0.0	0.7	1.3	0.8	0.2	0.7	0.5	0.6
Domestics	3.1	20.3	16.0	12.1	12.6	14.5	4.9	11.8
Stockkeepers	0.0	0.3	0.1	0.2	1.1	1.1	0.5	0.3
Transport workers	0.0	1.6	0.1	0.1	0.0	0.0	0.0	0.3
Watchmen	0.0	0.1	0.0	0.0	0.0	0.0	0.0	0.0
Fisherman	0.0	0.0	0.0	0.0	0.0	0.0	0.0	0.0
Sellers	0.0	0.0	0.3	0.5	0.1	0.0	0.0	0.2
Laborers	5.1	11.0	2.4	2.8	4.1	3.9	1.5	4.6
Hired	0.0	0.0	0.0	0.0	0.1	0.0	0.0	0.0
Nurses	0.0	0.4	0.8	1.7	5.0	14.5	5.4	1.7
Sick or disabled	0.2	0.7	1.8	4.3	11.2	20.5	43.6	4.3
Absent	0.0	0.0	0.0	0.0	0.0	0.0	0.0	0.0
None	84.5	10.7	0.9	1.7	3.4	14.7	37.7	24.6
Colored Females								
Field laborers	0.8	21.7	38.7	53.2	45.2	22.2	0.0	23.2
Drivers	0.0	0.0	0.0	0.0	0.0	0.0	0.0	0.0
Skilled tradespeople	0.8	8.7	9.7	10.6	6.5	0.0	0.0	5.8
Domestics	5.6	50.0	43.5	23.4	35.5	11.1	20.0	27.6
Stockkeepers	0.0	0.0	0.0	0.0	0.0	0.0	0.0	0.0
Transport workers	0.0	0.0	0.0	0.0	0.0	0.0	0.0	0.0
Watchmen	0.8	0.0	0.0	0.0	0.0	0.0	0.0	0.0
Fishermen	0.0	0.0	0.0	0.0	0.0	0.0	0.0	0.0
Sellers	0.0	0.0	0.0	0.0	0.0	0.0	0.0	0.0
Laborers	0.8	0.0	1.6	0.0	0.0	5.6	0.0	0.8
Hired	0.0	0.0	0.0	0.0	0.0	0.0	0.0	0.0
Nurses	0.0	0.0	0.0	0.0	0.0	5.6	0.0	0.3
Sick or disabled	0.0	2.2	4.8	10.6	9.7	50.0	60.0	6.6
Absent	0.0	0.0	0.0	0.0	0.0	0.0	0.0	0.0
None	91.2	17.4	1.7	2.2	3.1	5.5	20.0	35.7

Table S7.17. *Occupations of Slaves by Sex, Age and Color:*
St. John, Barbados, 1817

Occupation	Percentage of Slaves							
	0-9	10-19	20-29	30-39	40-49	50-59	60-	Total
Black Males								
Field laborers	22.8	70.0	70.8	67.3	58.7	47.5	22.7	53.2
Drivers	0.0	0.2	0.6	4.9	4.7	5.1	6.7	1.8
Skilled tradespeople	0.0	3.7	13.4	13.1	11.7	9.1	16.0	7.0
Domestics	1.0	5.2	7.3	4.6	2.8	9.1	4.0	4.2
Stockkeepers	3.8	16.7	4.4	4.9	9.9	13.1	14.7	8.7
Transport workers	0.0	0.0	0.6	1.3	2.3	3.0	0.0	0.6
Watchmen	0.0	0.0	1.2	2.9	7.5	6.1	12.0	2.0
Fishermen	0.0	0.0	0.0	0.0	0.0	0.0	0.0	0.0
Sellers	0.0	0.0	0.0	0.0	0.0	0.0	0.0	0.0
Laborers	0.0	0.7	1.2	0.3	0.9	0.0	0.0	0.5
Hired	0.0	0.0	0.0	0.0	0.0	0.0	0.0	0.0
Nurses	0.0	0.0	0.0	0.0	0.0	0.0	0.0	0.0
Sick or disabled	0.0	0.9	0.0	0.7	0.9	6.1	12.0	1.1
Absent	0.0	0.0	0.0	0.0	0.0	0.0	0.0	0.0
None	72.4	2.6	0.5	0.0	0.6	0.9	11.9	20.9
Colored Males								
Field laborers	13.4	43.0	41.5	42.8	33.3	15.4	16.7	30.7
Drivers	0.0	0.0	0.0	5.4	10.0	0.0	0.0	1.5
Skilled tradespeople	0.0	22.6	29.2	32.1	23.3	30.8	50.0	18.1
Domestics	6.0	18.3	24.6	16.1	16.7	23.1	16.7	14.9
Stockkeepers	1.5	11.8	4.6	1.8	6.7	23.1	0.0	5.5
Transport workers	0.0	0.0	0.0	0.0	0.0	0.0	0.0	0.0
Watchmen	0.0	0.0	0.0	1.8	10.0	0.0	0.0	1.0
Fishermen	0.0	0.0	0.0	0.0	0.0	0.0	0.0	0.0
Sellers	0.0	0.0	0.0	0.0	0.0	0.0	0.0	0.0
Laborers	0.0	0.0	0.0	0.0	0.0	0.0	0.0	0.0
Hired	0.0	0.0	0.0	0.0	0.0	0.0	0.0	0.0
Nurses	0.0	0.0	0.0	0.0	0.0	0.0	0.0	0.0
Sick or disabled	0.0	0.0	0.0	0.0	0.0	7.6	0.0	0.3
Absent	0.0	0.0	0.0	0.0	0.0	0.0	16.6	0.3
None	79.1	4.3	0.1	0.0	0.0	0.0	0.0	27.7

Table S7.17. *Occupation by Age: St. John, 1817 (continued)*

Occupation	Percentage of Slaves							
	0-9	10-19	20-29	30-39	40-49	50-59	60-	Total
Black Females								
Field laborers	21.9	77.4	83.7	84.5	74.2	49.7	24.9	60.1
Drivers	0.0	0.0	0.6	1.3	6.5	6.2	7.1	1.9
Skilled tradespeople	0.3	0.8	0.0	0.3	0.0	0.0	0.6	0.3
Domestics	2.3	12.5	12.7	9.6	10.9	22.4	20.7	10.6
Stockkeepers	1.3	4.4	0.3	1.9	1.5	8.7	9.5	2.9
Transport workers	0.0	0.0	0.0	0.0	0.0	0.0	0.0	0.0
Watchmen	0.0	0.0	0.0	0.0	0.0	0.0	0.0	0.0
Fishermen	0.0	0.0	0.0	0.0	0.0	0.0	0.0	0.0
Sellers	0.0	0.0	0.0	0.0	0.0	0.0	0.0	0.0
Laborers	0.0	1.2	1.4	1.1	2.2	1.9	0.0	1.0
Hired	0.0	0.0	0.0	0.0	0.0	0.0	0.0	0.0
Nurses	0.0	0.4	0.3	0.3	2.5	6.8	14.8	1.9
Sick or disabled	0.0	0.8	0.6	0.5	1.8	2.5	14.8	1.7
Absent	0.0	0.0	0.0	0.5	0.0	0.0	0.0	0.1
None	74.2	2.5	0.4	0.0	0.4	1.8	7.6	19.5
Colored Females								
Field laborers	21.4	59.2	56.8	54.3	55.3	14.3	14.3	43.0
Drivers	0.0	0.0	0.0	0.0	0.0	0.0	0.0	0.0
Skilled tradespeople	0.0	3.9	2.5	1.4	2.6	0.0	0.0	1.7
Domestics	10.7	30.1	37.0	42.9	31.6	71.4	42.9	30.6
Stockkeepers	0.8	1.0	0.0	1.4	0.0	0.0	4.8	0.9
Transport workers	0.0	0.0	0.0	0.0	0.0	0.0	0.0	0.0
Watchmen	0.0	0.0	0.0	0.0	0.0	0.0	0.0	0.0
Fishermen	0.0	0.0	0.0	0.0	0.0	0.0	0.0	0.0
Sellers	0.0	0.0	0.0	0.0	0.0	0.0	0.0	0.0
Laborers	0.0	0.0	0.0	0.0	0.0	0.0	0.0	0.0
Hired	0.0	0.0	0.0	0.0	2.6	0.0	0.0	0.2
Nurses	0.0	0.0	0.0	0.0	5.3	9.5	28.6	2.2
Sick or disabled	0.0	0.0	1.2	0.0	0.0	4.8	4.8	0.6
Absent	0.0	0.0	0.0	0.0	0.0	0.0	0.0	0.0
None	67.1	5.8	2.5	0.0	2.6	0.0	4.6	20.8

Table S7.18. *Occupations of Slaves by Sex and Age, Urban and Rural: Trinidad, 1813*

Occupation	Percentage of Slaves							
	0-9	10-19	20-29	30-39	40-49	50-59	60-	Total
Rural Males								
Field laborers	7.7	55.9	71.3	70.0	67.0	59.8	33.8	56.5
Drivers	0.0	0.3	2.7	3.8	6.1	7.7	5.2	2.8
Skilled tradespeople	0.1	5.5	16.3	17.6	16.4	18.4	9.9	12.4
Domestics	7.6	17.6	3.4	2.0	1.7	2.6	0.8	5.4
Stockkeepers	2.2	12.6	1.3	0.5	0.7	1.4	1.6	2.7
Transport workers	0.0	1.1	2.7	2.3	2.3	1.2	0.4	1.8
Watchmen	0.0	0.2	0.4	1.0	1.9	5.3	7.5	1.0
Fishermen	0.0	0.1	0.4	0.3	0.2	0.7	0.8	0.2
Sellers	0.0	0.1	0.0	0.0	0.0	0.0	0.0	0.0
Laborers	0.0	0.1	0.5	0.6	0.6	0.4	0.3	0.4
Hired	0.0	0.0	0.0	0.0	0.0	0.0	0.0	0.0
Nurses	0.0	0.0	0.0	0.0	0.1	0.0	0.0	0.0
Sick or disabled	0.0	0.3	0.2	0.5	0.9	1.4	7.5	0.5
Absent	0.2	0.3	0.5	1.1	1.3	0.5	20.6	1.1
None	82.2	5.9	0.3	0.3	0.8	0.6	11.6	15.2
Rural Females								
Field laborers	6.6	52.0	78.5	82.2	73.4	64.6	29.6	57.2
Drivers	0.0	0.0	0.0	0.0	0.0	0.0	0.0	0.0
Skilled tradespeople	0.3	1.9	0.9	0.9	0.9	0.3	0.0	0.8
Domestics	8.7	37.7	18.7	13.4	14.9	12.8	17.4	17.3
Stockkeepers	0.3	0.3	0.1	0.0	0.1	1.4	0.6	0.2
Transport workers	0.0	0.0	0.0	0.0	0.0	0.0	0.0	0.0
Watchmen	0.0	0.0	0.0	0.0	0.1	0.0	0.0	0.0
Fishermen	0.0	0.0	0.0	0.0	0.0	0.0	0.0	0.0
Sellers	0.0	0.2	0.4	0.4	0.3	0.3	0.0	0.2
Laborers	0.0	0.2	0.3	0.3	0.3	0.2	0.1	0.2
Hired	0.0	0.0	0.0	0.0	0.0	0.0	0.0	0.0
Nurses	0.1	0.2	0.4	1.2	5.5	7.9	7.7	1.3
Sick or disabled	0.0	0.3	0.2	0.9	1.7	7.6	13.5	0.9
Absent	0.0	0.2	0.2	0.4	0.7	0.3	7.1	0.4
None	84.0	7.0	0.3	0.3	2.1	4.6	24.0	21.5

Table S7.18. *Occupation by Age: Trinidad, 1813 (continued)*

Occupation	Percentage of Slaves							
	0-9	10-19	20-29	30-39	40-49	50-59	60-	Total
Urban Males								
Field laborers	0.9	19.5	33.6	41.4	45.9	44.8	22.1	26.2
Drivers	0.0	0.0	0.2	0.5	1.6	0.0	2.6	0.3
Skilled tradespeople	0.4	19.3	30.5	23.1	20.7	18.9	10.5	20.4
Domestics	20.3	54.8	22.1	16.5	18.1	18.9	23.7	26.9
Stockkeepers	0.0	0.7	0.7	0.4	0.0	0.0	0.0	0.5
Transport workers	0.0	1.3	7.2	8.0	6.7	3.8	2.6	4.7
Watchmen	0.0	0.0	0.0	0.0	0.0	0.0	0.0	0.0
Fishermen	0.0	0.2	3.3	3.8	1.6	7.5	0.0	2.1
Sellers	0.0	0.3	0.1	1.1	0.0	1.9	0.0	0.3
Laborers	0.0	0.2	0.8	3.2	2.9	2.3	1.6	2.0
Hired	0.0	0.0	0.0	0.0	0.0	0.0	0.0	0.0
Nurses	0.0	0.0	0.0	0.0	0.0	0.0	7.9	0.1
Sick or disabled	0.0	0.0	0.2	0.4	0.5	1.9	2.6	0.2
Absent	0.4	0.2	0.9	0.9	1.0	0.0	23.7	0.9
None	78.0	3.5	0.4	0.7	1.0	0.0	2.7	15.4
Urban Females								
Field laborers	0.7	8.7	12.2	16.2	20.7	14.5	11.2	10.7
Drivers	0.0	0.0	0.0	0.0	0.0	0.0	0.0	0.0
Skilled tradespeople	1.5	7.1	4.5	4.3	2.8	1.2	0.0	4.0
Domestics	23.0	75.8	74.3	72.2	70.1	65.1	50.0	63.4
Stockkeepers	0.0	0.2	0.1	0.0	0.0	1.2	0.0	0.1
Transport workers	0.0	0.0	0.0	0.0	0.0	0.0	0.0	0.0
Watchmen	0.0	0.0	0.0	0.0	0.0	0.0	0.0	0.0
Fishermen	0.0	0.0	0.0	0.0	0.0	0.0	0.0	0.0
Sellers	0.0	3.1	7.1	5.8	3.5	8.1	0.0	4.4
Laborers	0.1	0.2	0.4	0.5	0.6	0.6	0.2	0.5
Hired	0.0	0.0	0.0	0.0	0.0	0.0	0.0	0.0
Nurses	0.0	0.2	0.2	0.0	0.0	2.3	2.3	0.2
Sick or disabled	0.0	0.0	0.2	0.2	0.8	2.3	6.8	0.3
Absent	0.0	0.4	0.8	0.4	0.8	1.2	4.5	0.5
None	74.7	4.3	0.2	0.4	0.7	3.5	25.0	15.9

Table S7.19. *Mean Age of Slaves by Occupation, Sex and Birthplace: St. Lucia, 1815*

Occupation	Africans				Creoles			
	Males		Females		Males		Females	
	Mean	S.D.	Mean	S.D.	Mean	S.D.	Mean	S.D.
Field laborers	36.2	11.6	41.3	12.3	24.2	11.7	28.5	13.4
Drivers	48.9	12.9	64.0	–	37.8	9.9	59.3	7.8
Skilled tradespeople	37.5	14.0	46.3	23.6	29.7	11.2	23.2	12.3
Domestics	28.3	10.8	35.8	15.1	16.2	10.8	24.5	14.2
Stockkeepers	46.2	16.5	53.5	15.6	16.1	12.0	13.4	13.4
Transport workers	34.1	12.6	–	–	24.5	11.4	–	–
Watchmen	56.1	14.5	59.5	17.2	21.5	18.9	30.4	22.8
Fishermen	40.5	14.8	62.0	–	36.8	17.4	–	–
Sellers	–	–	32.1	11.4	19.7	16.9	33.1	11.5
Laborers	40.3	12.8	39.1	13.1	29.9	11.7	31.0	14.8
Hired	32.3	8.8	41.1	11.1	27.0	7.7	27.4	13.7
Nurses	–	–	59.0	13.1	14.0	13.9	50.2	17.8
Sick or disabled	52.8	18.9	62.3	14.3	39.5	17.8	44.5	17.6
Absent	36.4	17.5	45.7	9.0	29.2	13.8	28.2	14.5
None	60.8	18.5	66.3	13.7	5.9	9.7	8.0	14.3
Total	38.7	15.0	43.5	15.4	19.0	15.3	22.3	17.2

Table S7.20. *Mean Age of Slaves by Occupation, Sex and Birthplace: Berbice, 1819*

Occupation	Africans				Creoles			
	Males		Females		Males		Females	
	Mean	S.D.	Mean	S.D.	Mean	S.D.	Mean	S.D.
Field laborers	35.1	7.5	33.4	7.0	19.5	10.5	21.5	10.8
Drivers	39.4	8.7	41.5	9.9	41.4	9.1	32.7	8.0
Skilled tradespeople	32.5	7.9	32.9	9.5	27.8	11.1	24.3	7.9
Domestics	30.1	7.3	33.0	8.8	15.0	7.3	20.9	11.6
Stockkeepers	37.9	9.8	42.4	8.8	17.0	10.1	22.3	19.0
Transport workers	31.5	6.7	33.0	2.8	23.1	12.3	13.3	3.3
Watchmen	43.0	9.2	–	–	43.5	8.0	–	–
Fishermen	36.6	12.5	–	–	27.3	19.6	–	–
Sellers	–	–	29.3	6.0	–	–	34.3	3.1
Laborers	35.6	8.7	36.0	8.0	12.9	7.7	11.9	6.5
Hired	–	–	46.0	–	–	–	40.0	–
Nurses	35.7	8.1	43.1	9.8	29.2	11.7	43.4	15.5
Sick or disabled	44.8	12.6	45.4	12.5	37.4	20.2	40.6	18.3
Absent	33.6	7.4	–	-	31.8	21.0	–	–
None	48.1	15.0	48.6	16.4	5.3	8.0	5.9	9.7
Total	35.7	8.9	35.3	9.6	14.5	13.3	14.7	13.7

SECTION 8

Births and Deaths

Table S8.1.   *Sources: P.P.*, 1833, Vol. XXVI (539), "Slave Registration," pp.473-77, (700), "Slave Population," p.2, and 1835, LI (235), p.289; Index 10492, for Barbados, 1832 (P.R.O.); supplemented by various calculations from T.71, for particular colonies.

Notes: For exact dates of registration, see Table 2.1. Errors in addition in the published data, for St. Vincent, have been corrected. Where calculations derived directly from the registration returns (T.71) differ from the published data the former have been preferred, except in the cases of St. Lucia and Berbice, where the direct calculations are significantly less than the published figures (cf. Table S8.3.).

Table S8.2.   *Sources:* Calculated from data in Table S8.1., using model life table ratios to adjust for under-registration of births and deaths. See Tables 2.7 and 2.8 for the ratios used.

Notes: Where births or deaths are not available by sex in Table S8.1., the estimates are based on the sex ratio in proximate years. For Anguilla, the sex ratio of births is simply a halving. See also notes to Table S8.1.

Table S8.3.   *Sources:* T.71/254-55 (St. Kitts), 365 (Nevis), 371 (Virgin Islands), 380-81 (St. Lucia), 463-68 (Tobago), 440-41 (Berbice), and 261-63 (Anguilla).

Table S8.4.   *Source:* T.71/524-27.

Table S8.5.   *Source:* T.71/363.

Table S8.6.   *Source:* T.71/495-96.

Table S8.7.   *Source:* T.71/266-72.

Table S8.8.   *Source:* T.71/313-18.

Table S8.9.   *Source:* T.71/254-55.

Table S8.10.   *Source:* T.71/524-27.

Table S8.11.   *Source:* T.71/266-327.

Table S8.12.   *Source:* T.71/463-68.

Notes: The descriptions of causes of death in each class are taken directly from the registration returns. Minor variations in spelling have generally been ignored and the first example only included in the list.

Table S8.13.   *Source:* T.71/440-41.

Note: The method of listing follows that for Table S8.12.

Table S8.1. *Registered Slave Births and Deaths, by Sex and Colony, 1815-34*

Colony	Registration Interval (Months)	Registered Births			Registered Deaths		
		Males	Females	Total	Males	Females	Total
Barbados							
1817-20	36	3,805	3,913	7,718	3,317	3,286	6,603
1820-23	36	4,178	4,058	8,236	3,487	3,228	6,715
1823-26	36	4,788	4,814	9,602	3,409	3,304	6,713
1826-29	36	4,748	4,502	9,250	3,494	3,320	6,814
1829-32	36	n.c.	n.c.	9,975	n.c.	n.c.	8,587
1832-34	22	n.c.	n.c.	6,084	1,988	1,933	3,921
St. Kitts							
1817-22	55	1,132	1,187	2,319	1,424	1,415	2,839
1822-25	36	901	765	1,666	892	799	1,691
1825-28	36	858	848	1,706	845	758	1,603
1828-31	36	827	801	1,628	786	729	1,515
1831-34	36	n.c.	n.c.	1,762	735	773	1,508
Nevis							
1817-22	54	547	517	1,064	648	613	1,261
1822-25	36	349	316	665	358	335	693
1825-28	36	323	315	638	328	301	629
1828-31	36	334	309	643	343	336	679
1831-34	36	331	353	684	263	264	527
Antigua							
1817-21	48	1,193	1,146	2,339	1,497	1,388	2,885
1821-24	36	1,262	1,230	2,492	1,318	1,216	2,534
1824-28	42	1,109	1,194	2,303	1,146	1,131	2,277
1828-32	45	n.c.	n.c.	2,455	1,310	1,367	2.677
Montserrat							
1817-21	48	329	281	610	318	279	597
1821-24	36	313	289	602	327	286	613
1824-28	48	314	328	642	265	264	529
1828-31	36	n.c.	n.c.	713	256	278	534
Virgin Islands							
1818-22	48	289	260	549	432	359	791
1822-25	36	237	231	468	168	137	305
1825-28	36	238	221	459	157	125	282
1828-31	36	n.c.	n.c.	414	180	221	401
1831-34	36	207	175	382	189	175	364

Table S8.1. *Registered Births and Deaths by Colony (continued)*

Colony	Registration Interval (Months)	Registered Births			Registered Deaths		
		Males	Females	Total	Males	Females	Total
Jamaica							
1817-20	36	12,201	12,145	24,346	13,423	11,681	25,104
1820-23	36	11,685	11,564	23,249	14,030	12,321	26,351
1823-26	36	11,604	11,422	23,026	13,520	11,650	25,170
1826-29	36	10,986	10,742	21,728	13,435	11,702	25,137
1829-32	36	n.c.	n.c.	22,138	14,630	12,100	26,730
Dominica							
1817-20	36	729	704	1,433	915	833	1,748
1820-23	36	691	673	1,364	818	709	1,527
1823-26	36	659	650	1,309	766	727	1,493
1826-29	36	664	684	1,348	672	623	1,295
1829-32	36	n.c.	n.c.	1,305	575	602	1,177
St. Lucia							
1815-19	38	385	344	729	1,087	906	1,993
1819-22	36	478	446	924	691	643	1,334
1822-25	36	591	616	1,207	556	483	1,039
1825-28	36	587	606	1,193	586	416	1,002
1828-31	36	581	549	1,130	573	475	1,048
1831-34	36	n.c.	n.c.	n.c.	n.c.	n.c.	n.c.
St. Vincent							
1817-22	57	1,320	1,382	2,702	2,345	1,885	4,230
1822-25	36	918	934	1,852	1,157	949	2,106
1825-28	36	939	890	1,829	1,117	903	2,020
1828-31	36	919	862	1,781	1,230	1,036	2,266
1831-34	36	n.a.	n.a.	n.a.	n.a.	n.a.	n.a.
Grenada							
1817	8	212	239	451	478	424	902
1818	12	305	352	657	538	532	1,070
1819	12	339	375	714	585	584	1,169
1820	12	311	330	641	485	410	895
1821	12	352	330	682	506	422	928
1822	12	371	350	721	364	316	680
1823	12	361	358	719	398	426	824
1824	12	353	324	677	392	332	724
1825	12	337	340	677	399	360	759
1826	12	320	340	660	397	397	794
1827	12	369	335	704	360	309	669
1828	12	355	332	687	376	337	713
1829	12	377	359	736	372	358	730
1830	12	385	349	734	503	476	979
1831	12	348	336	684	500	428	928
1832	12	n.c.	n.c.	637	379	332	711
1833	12	n.c.	n.c.	808	348	307	655

Table S8.1. *Registered Births and Deaths by Colony (continued)*

Colony	Registration Interval (Months)	Registered Births			Registered Deaths		
		Males	Females	Total	Males	Females	Total
Tobago							
1819	12	141	163	304	416	384	800
1820	12	178	155	333	370	306	676
1821	12	159	158	317	367	303	670
1822	12	151	167	318	232	211	443
1823	12	166	157	323	371	290	661
1824	12	154	157	311	213	191	404
1825	12	168	160	328	362	328	690
1826	12	171	163	334	213	185	398
1827	12	178	191	369	289	249	538
1828	12	178	196	374	283	248	531
1829	12	165	155	320	288	220	508
1820	12	170	171	341	274	241	515
1831	12	145	161	306	298	253	551
1832	12	135	125	260	245	256	501
1833	12	153	157	310	238	195	433
Trinidad							
1813-16	33	939	933	1,872	1,373	965	2,338
1816-19	36	739	669	1,408	1,417	1,352	2,769
1819-22	36	757	731	1,488	1,303	1,101	2,404
1822-25	36	812	824	1,636	1,063	692	1,755
1825-28	36	710	759	1,469	1,079	767	1,846
1828-31	36	686	731	1,417	1,021	772	1,793
1831-34	38	644	626	1,270	1,040	866	1,906
Demerara-Essequibo							
1817-20	36	n.a.	n.a.	4,868	n.a.	n.a.	7,140
1820-23	36	2,233	2,279	4,512	4,328	2,860	7,188
1823-26	36	2,251	2,243	4,494	4,530	3,104	7,634
1826-29	36	2,319	2,365	4,684	3,517	2,214	5,731
1829-32	36	1,976	2,114	4,090	4,275	2,741	7,016
Berbice							
1817-19	14	n.a.	n.a.	n.a.	n.a.	n.a.	n.a.
1819-22	36	833	831	1,664	1,249	987	2,236
1822-25	36	773	740	1,513	1,348	1,052	2,400
1825-28	36	919	869	1,788	1,029	707	1,736
1828-31	36	820	770	1,590	1,092	795	1,887
1831-34	36	n.c.	n.c.	n.c.	n.c.	n.c.	n.c.

Table S8.1. *Registered Births and Deaths by Colony (continued)*

Colony	Registration Interval (Months)	Registered Births			Registered Deaths		
		Males	Females	Total	Males	Females	Total
Bahamas							
1822-25	36	417	392	809	266	162	428
1825-28	36	437	426	863	244	171	415
1828-31	36	n.c.	n.c.	1,100	n.c.	n.c.	433
1831-34	42	n.c.	n.c.	1,329	260	209	469
Anguilla							
1827-31	60	n.c.	n.c.	538	74	92	166
1831-34	30	n.c.	n.c.	193	112	91	203
Barbuda							
1817	48	n.c.	n.c.	43	n.c.	n.c.	17
1821-24	36	n.c.	n.c.	55	n.c.	n.c.	12
1824-28	42	n.c.	n.c.	53	n.c.	n.c.	18
1828-32	45	n.c.	n.c.	60	n.c.	n.c.	20

Table S8.2. *Estimated Slave Births and Deaths, Adjusted for Under-registration, by Sex and Colony, 1815-34*

Colony	Registration Interval (Months)	Estimated Births			Estimated Deaths		
		Males	Females	Total	Males	Females	Total
Barbados							
1817-20	36	5,444	5,598	11,042	4,989	4,941	9,930
1820-23	36	5,977	5,806	11,783	5,244	4,854	10,098
1823-26	36	6,850	6,887	13,737	5,126	4,968	10,094
1826-29	36	6,793	6,440	13,233	5,254	4,992	10,246
1829-32	36	7,325	6,945	14,270	6,586	6,327	12,913
1832-34	22	4,468	4,236	8,704	2,989	2,907	5,896
St. Kitts							
1817-22	55	1,594	1,672	3,266	1,901	1,889	3,790
1822-25	36	1,269	1,077	2,346	1,191	1,067	2,258
1825-28	36	1,209	1,194	2,403	1,128	1,012	2,140
1828-31	36	1,165	1,128	2,293	1,049	973	2,022
1831-34	36	1,261	1,221	2,482	981	1,032	2,013
Nevis							
1817-22	54	826	781	1,607	935	885	1,820
1822-25	36	527	478	1,005	517	483	1,000
1825-28	36	488	476	964	473	434	907
1828-31	36	505	466	971	495	485	980
1831-34	36	500	533	1,033	380	381	761
Antigua							
1817-21	48	1,772	1,703	3,475	2,163	2,006	4,169
1821-24	36	1,875	1,828	3,703	1,905	1,757	3,662
1824-28	42	1,648	1,774	3,422	1,656	1,634	3,290
1828-32	45	1,757	1,891	3,648	1,893	1,975	3,868
Montserrat							
1817-21	48	389	333	722	399	350	749
1821-24	36	370	342	712	410	359	769
1824-28	48	372	388	760	332	331	663
1828-31	36	413	431	844	321	349	670
Virgin Islands							
1818-22	48	445	401	846	610	507	1,117
1822-25	36	365	356	721	237	194	431
1825-28	36	367	340	707	222	177	399
1828-31	36	331	307	638	254	312	566
1831-34	36	319	270	589	267	247	514

Table S8.2. *Estimated Births and Deaths by Colony (continued)*

Colony	Registration Interval (Months)	Estimated Births			Estimated Deaths		
		Males	Females	Total	Males	Females	Total
Jamaica							
1817-20	36	15,063	14,994	30,057	16,450	14,315	30,765
1820-23	36	14,426	14,276	28,702	17,194	15,099	32,293
1823-26	36	14,326	14,101	28,427	16,569	14,277	30,846
1826-29	36	13,563	13,262	26,825	16,464	14,341	30,805
1829-32	36	13,819	13,512	27,331	17,929	14,828	32,757
Dominica							
1817-20	36	865	835	1,700	1,088	990	2,078
1820-23	36	820	798	1,618	973	843	1,816
1823-26	36	782	771	1,553	911	864	1,775
1826-29	36	788	811	1,599	799	741	1,540
1829-32	36	763	785	1,548	684	716	1,400
St. Lucia							
1815-19	38	671	599	1,270	1,381	1,151	2,532
1819-22	36	833	777	1,610	878	817	1,695
1822-25	36	1,030	1,073	2,103	706	614	1,320
1825-28	36	1,023	1,055	2,078	745	529	1,274
1828-31	36	1,012	957	1,969	728	604	1,332
1831-34	36	n.c.	n.c.	n.c.	n.c.	n.c.	n.c.
St. Vincent							
1817-22	57	1,673	1,752	3,425	2,648	2,247	4,895
1822-25	36	1,164	1,183	2,347	1,347	1,105	2,452
1825-28	36	1,190	1,128	2,318	1,300	1,051	2,351
1828-31	36	1,165	1,092	2,257	1,432	1,206	2,638
1831-34	36	n.a.	n.a.	n.a.	n.a.	n.a.	n.a.
Grenada							
1817	8	227	256	483	500	444	944
1818	12	327	377	704	563	556	1,119
1819	12	363	402	765	612	611	1,223
1820	12	333	354	687	507	430	937
1821	12	377	354	731	529	441	970
1822	12	398	375	773	381	331	712
1823	12	387	384	771	416	446	862
1824	12	378	348	726	410	347	757
1825	12	362	364	726	417	377	794
1826	12	343	364	707	415	415	830
1827	12	396	359	755	377	323	700
1828	12	380	356	736	393	353	746
1829	12	404	385	789	389	374	763
1830	12	413	374	787	526	498	1,024
1831	12	373	360	733	523	448	971
1832	12	347	335	682	396	347	743
1833	12	441	425	866	364	321	685

Table S8.2. *Estimated Births and Deaths by Colony (continued)*

Colony	Registration Interval (Months)	Estimated Births			Estimated Deaths		
		Males	Females	Total	Males	Females	Total
Tobago							
1819	12	169	195	364	451	416	867
1820	12	213	186	399	401	332	733
1821	12	191	189	380	398	328	726
1822	12	181	200	381	251	229	480
1823	12	199	188	387	402	314	716
1824	12	184	188	372	231	207	438
1825	12	201	192	393	392	355	747
1826	12	205	195	400	231	200	431
1827	12	213	229	442	313	270	583
1828	12	213	235	448	307	269	576
1829	12	198	185	383	312	238	550
1830	12	204	204	408	297	261	558
1831	12	174	192	366	323	274	597
1832	12	162	150	312	265	278	543
1833	12	183	188	371	258	211	469
Trinidad							
1813-16	33	1,560	1,550	3,110	1,836	1,290	3,126
1816-19	36	1,228	1,111	2,339	1,894	1,807	3,701
1819-22	36	1,257	1,215	2,472	1,742	1,472	3,214
1822-25	36	1,349	1,369	2,718	1,421	925	2,346
1825-28	36	1,179	1,261	2,440	1,443	1,025	2,468
1828-31	36	1,139	1,214	2,353	1,365	1,032	2,397
1831-34	38	1,070	1,040	2,110	1,390	1,158	2,548
Demerara-Essequibo							
1817-20	36	3,683	3,760	7,443	5,821	3,880	9,701
1820-23	36	3,414	3,485	6,899	5,880	3,886	9,766
1823-26	36	3,442	3,430	6,872	6,155	4,217	10,372
1826-29	36	3,546	3,616	7,162	4,779	3,008	7,787
1829-32	36	3,022	3,232	6,254	5,808	3,724	9,532
Berbice							
1817-19	14	n.a.	n.a.	n.a.	n.a.	n.a.	n.a.
1819-22	36	1,039	1,036	2,075	1,480	1,169	2,649
1822-25	36	964	923	1,887	1,597	1,246	2,843
1825-28	36	1,146	1,083	2,229	1,219	838	2,057
1828-31	36	1,023	960	1,983	1,294	942	2,236
1831-34	36	n.c.	n.c.	n.c.	n.c.	n.c.	n.c.

Table S8.2. *Estimated Births and Deaths by Colony (continued)*

Colony	Registration Interval (Months)	Estimated Births			Estimated Deaths		
		Males	Females	Total	Males	Females	Total
Bahamas							
1822-25	36	754	709	1,463	702	427	1,129
1825-28	36	790	770	1,560	644	451	1,095
1828-31	36	n.c.	n.c.	1,989	n.c.	n.c.	1,142
1831-34	42	n.c.	n.c.	2,403	686	552	1,238
Anguilla							
1827-31	60	349	348	697	145	180	325
1831-34	30	125	125	250	219	178	397
Barbuda							
1817-21	48	n.c.	n.c.	60	n.c.	n.c.	38
1821-24	36	n.c.	n.c.	77	n.c.	n.c.	27
1824-28	42	n.c.	n.c.	74	n.c.	n.c.	41
1828-32	45	n.c.	n.c.	84	n.c.	n.c.	45

Table S8.3. *Registered Slave Deaths by Age, Sex and Birthplace:*
St. Kitts, Nevis, Virgin Islands, St. Lucia, Tobago, Berbice and
Anguilla, 1815-34

Age group	Africans		Creoles		Africans		Creoles	
	Males	Females	Males	Females	Males	Females	Males	Females
	St. Kitts, 1817-22				*Nevis, 1817-22*			
0-4	–	–	390	406	–	–	138	126
5-9	–	–	69	71	–	–	40	25
10-14	–	–	56	54	1	–	28	21
15-19	7	3	43	45	1	2	22	18
20-24	14	10	43	49	9	6	21	17
25-29	37	34	48	45	14	8	26	30
30-34	55	32	63	64	20	6	25	29
35-39	29	9	61	46	21	21	22	25
40-44	33	24	59	64	27	17	34	19
45-49	31	10	61	44	10	3	27	33
50-54	29	21	58	61	10	11	32	25
55-59	25	18	23	36	10	11	14	24
60-64	42	25	22	51	17	14	21	31
65-69	17	14	21	39	7	9	9	9
70+	46	53	35	75	16	22	19	47
Unknown	4	3	6	12	2	2	5	2
Total	369	256	1,058	1,162	165	132	483	481
	Virgin Islands, 1818-22				*St. Lucia, 1815-19*			
0-4	–	–	59	60	–	–	180	174
5-9	–	–	25	21	1	–	56	50
10-14	–	–	21	24	1	–	42	39
15-19	2	–	20	16	3	5	35	34
20-24	6	3	19	10	17	16	41	38
25-29	9	6	20	25	25	10	39	36
30-34	14	8	24	21	29	16	32	30
35-39	17	4	19	16	40	20	16	34
40-44	16	4	32	17	36	26	14	28
45-49	11	5	11	11	22	32	14	33
50-54	14	9	20	12	24	37	20	26
55-59	6	2	8	10	17	24	10	18
60-64	9	9	17	17	17	27	9	24
65-69	3	3	3	11	13	23	5	8
70+	10	19	14	15	17	36	12	20
Unknown	–	–	3	1	2	1	4	2
Total	117	72	315	287	264	273	529	594

Table S8.3. *Deaths by Age: Seven Colonies (continued)*

Age group	Africans		Creoles		Africans		Creoles	
	Males	Females	Males	Females	Males	Females	Males	Females
	Tobago, 1819-21				*Berbice, 1819-22*			
0-4	–	–	136	175	–	–	172	187
5-9	–	–	69	49	–	–	44	33
10-14	–	–	48	29	–	–	29	29
15-19	1	–	22	30	7	2	30	21
20-24	3	6	38	37	16	19	15	20
25-29	42	23	48	37	83	60	20	21
30-34	70	47	22	31	115	70	17	18
35-39	94	42	24	31	150	95	20	28
40-44	98	81	20	19	101	57	17	14
45-49	85	65	8	11	72	34	15	10
50-54	83	59	8	4	51	24	6	9
55-59	47	54	2	3	22	14	6	7
60-64	78	60	–	1	30	27	3	6
65-69	32	31	2	2	12	7	5	2
70+	31	22	1	1	14	15	5	7
Unknown	1	–	5	6	94	58	82	86
Total	665	490	453	466	767	482	486	498
	Anguilla, 1827-31				*Anguilla, 1831-34*			
0-4	–	–	23	27	–	–	23	20
5-9	–	–	10	7	–	–	28	16
10-14	–	–	2	3	–	–	3	3
15-19	–	–	3	–	–	–	5	3
20-24	–	–	3	4	–	–	2	1
25-29	–	–	1	6	–	–	5	3
30-34	1	–	1	3	–	–	5	5
35-39	–	–	1	1	3	–	2	1
40-44	–	–	4	1	–	–	1	1
45-49	–	–	–	2	3	1	1	1
50-54	–	–	5	2	–	–	4	2
55-59	–	–	1	4	1	2	–	3
60-64	–	–	2	2	1	1	6	3
65-69	1	2	4	3	1	–	–	6
70+	–	–	–	1	2	1	7	14
Unknown	–	–	12	24	–	–	9	4
Total	2	2	72	90	11	5	101	86

Table S8.4. *Registered Slave Deaths by Age, Sex and Birthplace: Barbados, 1817-20 (Select Parishes)*

Age group	Africans		Creoles		Africans		Creoles	
	Males	Females	Males	Females	Males	Females	Males	Females
	St. Michael: Bridgetown				*St. Michael: Rural*			
0-4	–	–	67	69	–	–	60	63
5-9	–	–	18	12	–	–	15	10
10-14	–	–	14	9	–	–	10	7
15-19	4	2	12	9	–	–	8	5
20-24	12	5	6	14	2	1	11	10
25-29	13	5	10	16	15	3	9	9
30-34	10	3	19	14	8	2	8	15
35-39	12	5	11	10	7	3	10	9
40-44	3	1	13	11	3	–	14	11
45-49	2	3	9	9	1	–	12	18
50-54	6	1	3	17	2	2	11	17
55-59	3	2	–	5	1	–	9	13
60-64	4	2	4	12	1	2	7	16
65-69	2	3	2	4	1	–	6	5
70+	1	7	4	16	5	8	8	20
Unknown	–	–	–	–	–	–	–	–
Total	72	39	192	227	46	21	198	228
	St. John				*St. Andrew*			
0-4	–	–	58	58	–	–	29	20
5-9	–	–	14	8	–	–	10	7
10-14	–	–	7	9	–	–	3	5
15-19	1	–	6	6	–	–	4	4
20-24	1	–	9	6	–	–	9	6
25-29	1	–	12	8	–	1	4	9
30-34	4	3	11	7	5	2	4	7
35-39	2	2	15	9	2	–	5	7
40-44	1	2	8	10	1	–	5	7
45-49	–	3	16	15	1	–	7	5
50-54	5	2	19	6	1	–	4	9
55-59	1	2	4	10	–	2	11	9
60-64	1	4	2	9	–	–	6	5
65-69	–	–	4	10	–	1	3	4
70+	2	3	9	21	1	1	6	13
Unknown	–	–	–	–	–	–	–	–
Total	19	21	194	192	11	7	110	117

Table S8.5. *Registered Slave Deaths by Age, Sex and Parish: Dominica, 1829-32*

Age group	Males	Females	Males	Females	Males	Females	Males	Females
	Roseau		*St. George*		*St. Paul*		*St. Joseph*	
0-4	6	4	34	24	14	18	17	14
5-9	1	3	4	16	5	3	4	1
10-14	–	–	3	8	1	2	3	2
15-19	3	2	7	7	1	5	1	2
20-24	3	5	6	10	6	5	2	1
25-29	8	3	3	3	6	1	3	1
30-34	5	2	10	5	1	1	3	3
35-39	2	2	8	3	3	7	7	9
40-44	3	5	20	9	10	9	5	10
45-49	2	4	9	5	9	11	3	3
50-54	2	–	9	11	3	7	4	3
55-59	2	4	4	9	6	5	1	2
60-64	1	2	5	–	1	3	3	4
65-69	1	–	5	5	1	3	1	3
70+	1	2	3	8	3	5	1	1
Unknown	5	4	2	1	–	–	2	1
Total	45	42	132	124	70	85	60	60
	St. Peter		*St. John*		*St. Andrew*		*St. David*	
0-4	8	12	7	6	14	26	8	14
5-9	1	4	2	3	3	1	–	1
10-14	3	1	2	–	1	1	–	–
15-19	1	–	–	2	–	1	1	1
20-24	1	–	1	3	4	1	2	1
25-29	–	1	–	4	2	2	2	–
30-34	3	1	2	1	1	4	1	2
35-39	1	4	2	1	1	2	–	4
40-44	2	1	3	3	4	7	2	5
45-49	2	1	6	7	6	6	4	1
50-54	1	1	9	3	6	9	2	2
55-59	–	–	2	1	3	2	1	–
60-64	1	–	2	1	2	4	1	–
65-69	1	1	2	–	2	3	–	3
70+	3	1	3	1	2	2	1	2
Unknown	2	1	1	–	–	–	1	1
Total	30	29	44	36	51	71	26	37

Table S8.5. *Deaths by Age: Dominica, 1829-32 (continued)*

Age group	Males	Females	Males	Females	Males	Females	Males	Females
	St. Patrick		*St. Mark*		*St. Luke*		*Total*	
0-4	25	21	14	6	6	8	153	153
5-9	2	5	3	—	2	2	27	39
10-14	2	2	—	1	—	1	15	18
15-19	2	1	—	—	1	—	17	21
20-24	1	3	3	3	4	2	33	34
25-29	—	7	1	—	3	2	28	24
30-34	1	2	—	—	—	1	27	21
35-39	5	4	—	1	3	—	32	37
40-44	2	3	2	1	1	1	54	54
45-49	9	3	2	2	1	1	53	44
50-54	—	4	2	1	1	2	39	43
55-59	2	4	1	—	—	3	22	30
60-64	—	3	2	2	1	2	19	21
65-69	2	1	—	1	—	1	15	21
70+	2	6	2	2	2	1	23	31
Unknown	5	—	—	—	1	2	18	11
Total	60	69	32	20	26	29	575	602

Table S8.6. *Registered Slave Deaths by Age, Sex and Parish: St. Vincent, 1817-22*

Age group	Males	Females	Males	Females	Males	Females	Males	Females
	St. George		*St. Andrew*		*St. Patrick*		*St. David*	
0-4	142	143	29	34	38	27	47	33
5-9	30	30	13	14	10	8	7	13
10-14	29	20	12	14	6	6	4	7
15-19	30	26	9	11	5	10	2	3
20-24	32	22	14	15	12	11	9	9
25-29	55	42	16	13	16	12	8	5
30-34	66	58	27	17	21	17	10	13
35-39	81	46	24	17	22	23	20	28
40-44	74	38	20	19	22	18	15	12
45-49	51	26	12	3	10	11	6	5
50-54	51	26	11	14	15	6	11	5
55-59	24	20	9	7	5	3	5	2
60-64	36	27	6	7	8	12	4	6
65-69	20	24	2	8	2	2	4	3
70+	17	24	11	18	8	6	5	6
Unknown	127	112	6	6	53	37	5	3
Total	865	684	221	217	253	209	162	153
	Charlotte		*Grenadines*				*Total*	
0-4	132	150	26	26			414	413
5-9	32	20	7	4			99	89
10-14	24	18	6	6			81	71
15-19	29	11	3	2			78	63
20-24	28	15	3	4			98	76
25-29	33	22	5	3			133	97
30-34	55	42	6	15			185	162
35-39	64	41	8	8			219	163
40-44	65	34	20	8			216	129
45-49	59	31	8	6			146	82
50-54	54	33	14	9			156	93
55-59	23	11	4	2			70	45
60-64	23	15	10	2			87	69
65-69	11	7	4	2			43	46
70+	12	11	9	6			62	71
Unknown	50	48	17	10			258	216
Total	694	509	150	113			2,345	1,885

Table S8.7. *Registered Slave Deaths by Age and Sex: Grenada, 1817-19 (Select Parishes)*

Age group	Town of St. George		St. John & St. Mark		St. Andrew		Grenadines	
	Males	Females	Males	Females	Males	Females	Males	Females
0-4	38	27	46	49	77	77	68	65
5-9	5	4	9	12	17	20	19	9
10-14	2	3	3	6	11	5	13	7
15-19	–	2	6	4	6	10	6	10
20-24	5	4	6	4	10	12	5	6
25-29	8	10	8	9	22	22	5	4
30-34	11	5	14	10	35	28	6	9
35-39	12	7	18	15	25	24	5	6
40-44	8	9	12	14	26	23	11	7
45-49	6	5	25	23	26	19	14	10
50-54	1	3	14	13	18	25	15	11
55-59	2	2	10	7	20	15	9	8
60-64	4	4	10	10	20	23	15	11
65-69	–	3	6	5	6	18	3	5
70+	–	3	18	25	22	29	15	13
Unknown	2	2	–	3	–	–	–	–
Total	104	93	205	209	341	350	209	181

Table S8.8. *Registered Slave Deaths by Age and Sex: Grenada, 1830-32 (Select Parishes)*

Age group	Town of St. George		St. John & St. Mark		St. Andrew		Grenadines	
	Males	Females	Males	Females	Males	Females	Males	Females
0-4	17	12	74	44	63	52	53	44
5-9	2	2	7	2	9	7	10	3
10-14	3	1	2	2	6	4	2	1
15-19	3	3	4	3	8	11	3	2
20-24	2	6	5	7	10	8	3	–
25-29	2	5	5	4	9	17	7	2
30-34	6	3	5	6	15	12	4	3
35-39	5	3	9	8	17	13	5	4
40-44	11	5	15	16	37	15	3	4
45-49	8	5	18	11	30	22	1	1
50-54	9	8	18	10	22	28	3	7
55-59	4	4	12	8	24	20	6	8
60-64	4	3	13	11	25	16	3	7
65-69	2	1	5	1	14	10	5	9
70+	–	1	17	19	22	30	15	16
Unknown	–	–	–	–	–	–	–	–
Total	78	62	209	152	311	265	123	111

Table S8.9. *Registered Slave Deaths by Age, Sex, Birthplace and Slave-holding Size-group: St. Kitts, 1817-22*

Age group	Africans		Creoles		Africans		Creoles	
	Males	Females	Males	Females	Males	Females	Males	Females
	1-10 Slaves				*11-50 Slaves*			
0-4	–	–	37	56	–	–	17	16
5-9	–	–	6	6	–	–	5	3
10-14	–	–	6	3	–	–	8	3
15-19	1	1	6	4	–	–	4	1
20-24	2	–	2	4	1	–	2	6
25-29	3	4	1	6	6	2	2	2
30-34	8	4	7	11	9	3	5	5
35-39	2	–	5	6	2	–	4	4
40-44	3	4	5	2	1	1	2	5
45-49	5	1	3	3	5	1	–	3
50-54	3	3	1	1	1	2	2	2
55-59	1	2	–	2	2	1	–	–
60-64	1	2	1	1	1	3	–	2
65-69	1	2	1	–	–	1	–	3
70+	1	4	–	4	1	1	–	1
Unknown	3	3	5	6	1	–	–	3
Total	34	30	86	115	30	15	51	59
	51-100 Slaves				*101-200 Slaves*			
0-4	–	–	38	32	–	–	202	209
5-9	–	–	6	6	–	–	33	39
10-14	–	–	2	7	–	–	32	20
15-19	–	1	–	6	3	1	19	24
20-24	1	1	3	5	6	7	27	22
25-29	2	2	5	4	24	22	29	19
30-34	4	1	7	8	22	16	30	29
35-39	5	–	10	5	15	5	27	22
40-44	8	1	8	5	16	15	30	28
45-49	6	2	8	3	7	3	36	19
50-54	2	2	4	7	18	9	35	37
55-59	3	–	5	7	15	14	18	17
60-64	8	–	1	6	23	14	14	30
65-69	2	1	6	2	9	8	9	25
70+	5	6	8	9	31	32	13	46
Unknown	–	–	–	1	–	–	1	2
Total	46	17	111	113	189	146	555	588

Table S8.9. *Deaths by Age: St. Kitts, 1817-22 (continued)*

Age group	Africans		Creoles		Africans		Creoles	
	Males	Females	Males	Females	Males	Females	Males	Females
	201-300 Slaves				*301+ Slaves*			
0-4	–	–	66	60	–	–	30	33
5-9	–	–	11	13	–	–	8	4
10-14	–	–	6	10	–	–	2	11
15-19	–	–	5	4	3	–	9	6
20-24	–	1	7	9	4	1	2	3
25-29	1	1	7	9	1	3	4	5
30-34	5	5	13	6	7	3	1	5
35-39	2	2	10	5	3	2	5	4
40-44	1	2	12	18	4	1	2	6
45-49	5	1	10	9	3	2	4	7
50-54	4	4	11	12	1	1	5	2
55-59	2	–	–	6	2	1	–	4
60-64	5	4	6	9	4	2	–	3
65-69	4	2	5	4	1	–	–	5
70+	4	4	9	12	4	6	5	3
Unknown	–	–	–	–	–	–	–	–
Total	33	26	178	186	37	22	77	101

Table S8.10. *Registered Births and Deaths by Parish: Barbados, 1817-20*

Parish	Births			Deaths			Birth-deaths*
	Males	Females	Total	Males	Females	Total	
St. Michael	915	980	1,895	708	758	1,466	74
St. James	202	212	414	168	172	340	18
St. Peter	322	298	620	282	273	555	37
St. Lucy	263	247	510	257	236	493	14
St. Andrew	139	145	284	176	177	353	24
St. Joseph	178	177	355	170	161	331	2
St. John	225	281	506	259	196	455	18
St. Philip	434	450	884	433	434	867	61
Christ Church	524	569	1,093	347	333	680	55
St. George	380	305	685	287	314	601	41
St. Thomas	236	236	472	230	232	462	7
Total	3,818	3,900	7,718	3,317	3,286	6,603	351

* Registered children born within the triennium who died before its end.

Table S8.11. *Registered Slave Births and Deaths by Sex and Parish:*
Grenada, 1817-33

Year	Town of St. George	St. George	St. John & St. Mark	St. Patrick	St. Andrew	St. David	Grena-dines
Births							
1817	37	76	64	51	76	31	101
1818	77	113	88	87	105	38	148
1819	88	107	103	112	113	58	135
1820	57	96	92	81	131	58	131
1821	73	103	86	115	115	61	129
1822	64	118	106	135	116	64	134
1823	62	104	106	140	122	72	113
1824	60	117	102	106	113	54	125
1825	60	85	119	104	118	69	122
1826	47	116	88	98	112	55	148
1827	62	124	108	123	106	67	114
1828	47	109	103	104	114	59	151
1829	51	132	106	139	107	63	138
1830	55	94	109	145	128	74	129
1831	56	115	115	100	95	58	145
1832	45	93	102	87	122	54	134
1833	55	141	108	158	129	60	157
Deaths: Males							
1817	32	84	61	100	94	38	69
1818	30	89	83	114	117	45	63
1819	39	102	63	113	131	66	78
1820	34	87	63	110	104	38	49
1821	34	114	72	90	106	57	40
1822	23	76	62	64	86	22	28
1823	27	67	57	81	93	37	36
1824	26	69	59	84	66	37	51
1825	13	82	50	83	94	34	43
1826	26	71	45	87	84	43	41
1827	22	67	60	67	87	25	32
1828	18	66	44	67	102	46	33
1829	23	73	57	72	78	27	42
1830	22	88	74	139	109	32	39
1831	32	83	74	106	110	45	50
1832	26	73	59	65	92	27	37
1833	18	65	54	66	65	37	43

Table S8.11. *Births and Deaths by Parish: Grenada, 1817-33 (continued)*

Year	Town of St. George	St. George	St. John & St. Mark	St. Patrick	St. Andrew	St. David	Grena-dines
Deaths: Females							
1817	25	86	65	99	93	31	41
1818	38	85	82	108	114	37	68
1819	34	96	61	134	143	53	74
1820	23	74	54	89	94	41	51
1821	31	81	67	80	86	36	38
1822	21	58	54	59	70	20	33
1823	20	71	51	86	96	35	66
1824	16	57	39	77	68	37	38
1825	24	60	54	71	79	31	41
1826	27	60	47	79	90	51	43
1827	17	57	45	63	70	22	35
1828	14	81	37	65	68	35	37
1829	23	62	46	73	95	24	35
1830	26	101	54	115	108	42	30
1831	26	82	44	92	88	55	41
1832	12	60	53	72	69	25	41
1833	16	51	43	62	69	29	37

Table S8.12. *Causes of Slave Deaths: Tobago, 1819-21*

Cause	Number of Deaths
Diarrhea	
Flux	150
Dysentery	94
Bloody flux	19
Bilious diarrhoea; diarrhoea and old age	2
Dysentery causing dropsy; sores and dysentery; mal d'estomach and dysentery; elephantiasis and dysentery; rupture and dysentery	5
Flux and mal d'estomach; flux and sores; flux and consumption; mal d'estomach and flux; dirt eating and flux; debility and flux	9
Total	279
Old Age	
Old age	139
Old age and debility	53
Old age and infirmity	12
Old age and flux; old age and dysentery	17
Old age and dropsy; old age and rheumatism; old and liver complaint; old age and consumption; old age and ulcers; old age and elephantiasis; old age-scrofulous; debility, old age and scrufula; old age, dropsy, flux; old age and worms; old age and sores; old age and fever	20
Old age and decay of nature; age and long disease; old age and weakness; debility from age; old age and rupture; old age − blind; old age and bowel complaint; age, sores, debility; mal d'estomach and old age; mortification − age	15
Total	256
Dropsy	
Dropsy	141
Mal d'estomach and dropsy	19
Dropsy leading to flux; dropsy and dysentery; dropsy and hooping cough; dropsy and worms; dropsy and venereal; bowel complaint causing dropsy − leprosy; elephantiasis and dropsical; dirt eating and dropsy; blind, anasarcous swelling and worms	9
Total	169
Whooping cough	
Whooping cough	160
Chin cough	1
Hooping cough and yaws; hooping cough and fits; hooping cough and malformation of chest	7
Total	168
Fever	
Fever	70
Inflammatory fever	44
Bilious fever	13

Cause	Number of Deaths
Bilious and inflammatory fever; mal d'estomach caused by inflammatory fever; inflammatory and bilious fever; inflammation and bilious complaint; bilious fever and hooping cough; fever and fits; fever and debility; fever and yaws; fever and worms; bilious fever and worms; fever and bowel complaint; cough and fever; cold and fever	15
Cold; severe cold; violent cold; suddenly, a cold; a cough	6
Total	148
Tuberculosis	
Consumption	90
Consumption or decline; pulmonary consumption; consumptive cough; consumption and eating ashes and clay; scrofulous and consumption; rupture and consumption	7
Scrofula	14
Scrofulous sores; scrofulous ulcer; scrofula disorder; scrofula and age	12
Total	123
Digestive system diseases	
Bowel complaint	38
Inflammation of bowels; protracted bowel complaint with fever; bowel disease; inflammation at navel	9
Bowel complaint and worms; mal d'estomach and bowel complaint; cold and bowel complaint; obstructed and bowel complaint; decline and bowel complaint	5
Liver complaint	10
Affection of liver; diseased liver; inflammation of liver; under salivation for the liver complaint; mal d'estomach and liver complaint; liver complaint and dysentery; sores and liver complaint	11
Violent cholic	1
Dry belly ache	2
Ascites; iliac passion; mal d'estomach and ulcers	3
Rupture; strangulated rupture; inflammation from rupture	10
Strangulated hernia	1
Total	90
Nervous system diseases	
Apoplexy	21
Fits	12
Convulsions	9
Apoplectic fits; epileptic fits; convulsive fits; convulstions, fits; violent convulsive fits, far gone in pregnancy; spasms	13
Elipepsy; epilepsy from excessive drinking; falling sickness	6
Water in brain; water in head; brain fever; disease in head; mortification in head	12
Palsy; palsy and old age	2
Insane; insane – sores	2
Total	77

[625]

Table S8.12. *Causes of Death: Tobago, 1819-21 (continued)*

Cause	Number of Deaths
Leprosy	
Leprosy	53
Joint evil	1
Leprosy and bad sores; leprosy and old age; flux and leprosy; burst artery, leprosy; mal d'estomach and leprosy; mortification − leprosy	8
Total	62
Worms	
Worms	53
Worm fever	1
Worms and yaws; worms and hooping cough; worms and bowel complaint; worms and dirt eating	8
Total	62
Accidents	
Drowned	12
Lost in sea; drowned − having been thrown from a horse while washing it in the sea; supposed to be drowned	3
A fall; supposed by a fall from its mother; fall from a bridge; spine hurt by fall; fall, on a stick into his throat	8
Scorpion's bite; sting of a scorpion; bitten by a serpent	7
Scalded with boiling liquor; burnt to death in a cane piece; scorched in trying to stop a fire in a cane piece	4
But of a ram; mutilated by his own hog	2
Log of wood fell on him; heavy piece of timber fell on him	2
Severe bruise	1
Wound in the knee from the point of his cutlass; dislocation of neck	2
Suffocation; overlaid by mother	2
Accident	1
Total	44
Yaws	
Yaws	33
Yaws and dysentery; yaws and leprosy; yaws and dropsy; yaws and sores; yaws and debility	5
Total	38
Tetanus	
Locked jaw	33
Tetanus	1
Total	34

Table S8.12. *Causes of Death: Tobago, 1819-21 (continued)*

Cause	Number of Deaths
Respiratory diseases	
Pleurisy	7
Inflammation of lungs; violent inflammation of pleura and lungs; affection of lungs; abcess of lungs	6
Asthma	4
Water in chest; mortification in chest; extreme salivation – suffocated	4
Total	21
Maternity	
Child bed; child birth	17
Child bed, of the first child; retention of inability to pass off the meconium; puerperal fever – after bringing a dead child; abortion	4
Total	21
Scarlet fever	
Putrid sore throat	5
Inflammatory sore throat	5
Sore throat	4
Ulcerated sore throat; ulcer in throat; inflammation of throat; suffocation and putrid sore throat; putrid fever	5
Total	19
Venereal disease	
Venereal	10
Sore throat, from venereal; venereal and fever – having concealed her disease until the day before she died	2
Total	12
Teething	
Cutting teeth	5
Teething and fits; teething and worms; fever and cutting teeth; oppression on the breast and teething	4
Total	9
Suicide	
Hanged self	4
Shot self; drowned himself in a state of insanity	2
Total	6
Rheumatism	
Rheumatism	4
Rheumatism in stomach	1
Total	5

Table S8.12. *Causes of Death: Tobago, 1819-21 (continued)*

Cause	Number of Deaths
Urinary system diseases	
Ulcer in testicles; inflammation of bladder; mortification of bladder	3
Neoplasms	
Cancer	1
Debility	
Debility	43
General debility	4
Debility and sores; debility and leprosy; debility and elephantiasis; debility and disease of the head; debility and mal d'estomach; debility and long sickness; ulcers and debility, rupture and general debility; debility − insane; debility − blind	21
General decay; decay; decay of nature; weakly; weakness; weak from birth; born very weakly	23
Exhaustion; decline	8
Infirmity	6
Scurvy; rickets	2
Total	107
Mal d'estomac	
Mal d'estomach	164
Mal d'estomach and sores; mal d'estomach and rupture; inflammation and mal d'estomach	6
Mal d'estomach from dirt eating	1
Eating dirt; eating ashes and clay; eating dirt and ashes	7
Total	181
Undefined	
Suddenly; very suddenly	10
Found dead	5
Invalid; long sickly; lingering illness; sickly; complication of disorders	17
Infant; sickly child; sickly from birth	3
Default of nature	1
Total	36
Not classified	
Inflammation; inflammatory; inflammatory complaint; inflammation in back; inflammation and abcess	47
Sores; bad sores; sore in groin; putrid sores; mortification from sores; sores and diseased system; cripple from sores; sore leg; sore eyes	24
Ulcers; ulcer in leg; abcess in loins	7
Burst blood vessel	8
Obstructions	8
Elephantiasis	3

Table S8.12. *Causes of Death: Tobago, 1819-21 (continued)*

Cause	Number of Deaths
Swelling in neck; swelling in limbs; swelling in jaw; general swelling of head and stomach	4
Pains; malacia; cramp	3
Diseased from birth; lived only a few hours; a seven months child; premature birth	4
Poisoned by bitter cassava	5
Intoxication; overdose of rum and intoxication	3
Overdose of medicine	1
Of repletion	1
Of a rising in herself	1
Under the idea of obia	1
Hypochondriac	2
Total	122
Not stated	53
TOTAL	2,146

Table S8.13. *Causes of Slave Deaths: Berbice, 1819-22*

Cause	Number of Deaths
Diarrhea	
Dysentery	187
Dysentery and old age	3
Dysentery and flux; dysentery and dropsy; dysentery and leprosy; dysentery and ulcerated throat; dysentery and debility	5
Diarrhoea	27
Chronic diarrhoea	3
Bilious diarrhoea; ulcers and diarrhoea	2
Hepatitis	9
Chronic hepatitis	4
Hepatic disease	1
Bloody flux; flux; flux and apoplexy	3
Total	244
Nervous system diseases	
Convulsions	54
Apoplexy	40
Epilepsy	16
Apoplectic stroke; apoplectic fit	2
Fits	7
Fits and fever	1
Fainting fits	2
Spasm; hysteritis	2
Nervous fever	9
Nervous fever and fits; nervous fever and dysentery	2
Palsy	7
Paralysis	4
Stk. of paralysis	1
Water in the brain; water in head	3
Effusion of brain	2
Brain fever; fungus haematades of the brain; coneussis cerebri	4
Diseased spine; spinal marrow affection	2
Lumber abscess; injury of spine	4
Insanity	10
Diseased mind; lunacy; mad; mania	5
Total	177
Dropsy	
Dropsy	133
Dropsy on breast	11
Pectoral affection	7
Hydropsy; hydropisia	3
Hydropsy in breast	2
Hydrothorax	4
Water on chest	2

Table S8.13. *Causes of Death: Berbice, 1819-22 (continued)*

Cause	Number of Deaths
Anasarca	2
Ascites	2
Dropsy and yaws; dropsy and worms	4
Debility from dropsy	1
Total	171
Respiratory diseases	
Pleurisy	39
Pleurisy purulenta; pleurisy and bowel complaint	2
Pneumonia	22
Peripneumony	3
Inflammation of lungs	14
Inflammation on breast	4
Inflammation of lungs and debility	1
Effusion on lungs	2
Suffocation of lungs; ulcer in lungs; haemorrhage from lungs; diseased lungs; abcess in lungs; burst abscess of lungs; ruptured blood vessel in lungs	9
Asthma	19
Suffocation from asthma	2
Asthma and yaws; asthma and old age	2
Catarrhal fever	13
Catarrh	12
Bronchitis; bronchoceli; bronchocate	3
Compressed thorax; mortification of chest	2
Haemoptyses	1
Total	150
Tuberculosis	
Consumption	101
Pulmonary consumption; pulmonary disease; pulmonary; pulmonarie	9
Consumption and slow fever; debility of consumption	2
Scrofulous	16
Phthisis; phitis pulmonalis; phthises vera ulcerosa	8
Tabes mesenterica	1
Total	137
Yaws	
Yaws	91
Mortification from yaws; debility from yaws; gangrene from yaws	8
Yaws and dysentery; yaws and diarrhoea	2
Total	101

Cause	Number of Deaths
Fever	
Fever	65
Bilious fever; defluxion fever; hectic fever; obstinate fever	8
Debility from fever; fits from fever	2
Fever and worms; fever and yaws; fever and convulsions; fever and debility; fever and flux	15
Ague; typus putd.; violent cold	3
Total	93
Old age	
Old age	83
Debility from old age	4
Old age and infirmity; old age and decay of nature; old age and weakness; old age and pleurisy; old age, asthma and rheumatism	5
Total	92
Leprosy	
Leprosy	85
Leprous ulcerations; leprosy and venereal; leprosy and dropsy	3
Total	88
Digestive system diseases	
Diseased liver; liver complaint	13
Ulcerated liver; abscess of liver	4
Diseased liver and spleen; liver disease and hepetic dysentery	2
Inflammation of the bowels; inflammation of oroflagus and bowels	11
Bowel complaint; ruptured abscess in bowel	7
Colic; colicks; colica omlle	4
Belly ache; dry belly ache; cramp on belly; pressing of stomach	5
Visceral disease; thoreca viscera	3
Convul. stomach and diarrhoea; black vomit	2
Tympanitis	1
Enteritis	4
Jaundice; jaundice and dropsy	3
Piles	1
Thrush	2
Rupture	7
Hernia; strangulated hernia	2
Total	70

Table S8.13. *Causes of Death: Berbice, 1819-22 (continued)*

Cause	Number of Deaths
Worms	
Worms	48
Worm fever; vermes	6
Worms and convulsions; convulsions from worms; a fit, supposed from worms	4
Total	58
Accidents	
Drowned	31
Drowned at sea	2
Scalded; burnt; severe burns; burnt legs	7
Hit by a tree he was felling	2
Wounded from a fall; concussion of brain by a fall; fell from a coconut tree	3
Wound from a bull; overthrow by a cow; locked jaw from a wound from a bull	3
Injury; bit by a snake; wound in privy parts; discharge of a fowling piece	4
Total	52
Tetanus	
Tetanus	25
Locked jaw	16
Total	41
Venereal disease	
Venereal disease	25
Syphilis; pseudo syphilis	6
Venerial and consumption; diseased testis; ulcers caused by venery	3
Total	34
Maternity	
Child bed	16
Haemorrhage in labour; effusion of lungs in labour; exhaustion after delivery	3
Abortion	1
Purpl. fever [puerperal fever]	1
Total	21
Suicide	
Suicide	10
Hanged self	6
Stabbed self; wound self inflicted	2
Total	18

Table S8.13. *Causes of Death: Berbice, 1819-22 (continued)*

Cause	Number of Deaths
Scarlet fever	
Putrid fever	3
Inflammation of throat	3
Ulcerated throat; affection of throat; sore throat; cramp in throat; suffocation from ulcerated throat	5
Quinsy; cynanche pura.	2
Total	13
Neoplasms	
Cancer	8
Cancer of throat	2
Total	10
Violence	
Hanged	2
Murdered; violence on body; flogged by Wm. of Buze's Lust	3
Total	5
Female diseases	
Uterine hemorrhage	2
Prolapsus uteri; rupture of uterus; inflammation of womb	3
Total	5
Rheumatism	
Rheumatism	3
Rheumatism and debility	1
Total	4
Cholera	
Cholera morbus	2
Heart	
Syncope; disease of heart	2
Teething	2
Diphtheria	
Croup	2
Whooping cough	
Hooping cough	1
Urinary system diseases	
Kidneys complaint	1

Table S8.13. *Causes of Death: Berbice, 1819-22 (continued)*

Cause	Number of Deaths
Debility	
Debility	119
General debility	8
Debility of old sores; debility and old age; sores and debility; ulcers and general debility; cacheta and debility; sores and general emaciation	14
Decay; natural decay; tabes; gradual decay of nature; weakness	12
Atrophia; exhaustion	6
Decline; long decline	3
Infirmity	11
Bodily infirmity; corporal infirmity; disability	3
Total	176
Undefined	
Suddenly	15
Visitation of God	3
Diseased; lingering illness; invalid; bed ridden; compln. of disorders	8
Total	26
Not classified	
Cachexia	21
Mortification	12
Ulcers	7
Old ulcers; ulcer in arm; gangreen ulcer; mortification from ulcers	8
Incurable sores; bad sores; sores; old sores	7
Haemorrhage; bursting of blood vessel; rupture of blood vessel	4
Inflammation; inflammation in genital parts; swelling on knee; swelling in thigh and fever	6
Mortification inside; mortification of leg; mortification in arm; mortification in feet	6
Suffocation	2
Elephantiasis; oliphantism	3
Amputated legs	2
Mal de stomac	2
Poison; drunkenness; exposed self to colds while intoxicated; exhaustion from exposure to cold; taking cold while under influence of mercury	5
Contusion; uleus gangrena; tabies infanta; pus in shoulder; palm affection; cutaneous eruptions; disd. glands; illusia caries ossis; rebleures; Indian pocks; stiffness in limbs; a strong blood vomit; phumitis	14
Total	99
Not stated	341
TOTAL	2,236

SECTION 9

Vital Rates

Table S9.1.   *Source:* T.71/520-27 and 553-64.

                    Note: The rates are based on the populations living in 1817 and 1834.

Table S9.2.   *Source:* T.71/260.

                    Note: The rates are based on the populations living in 1834.

Table S9.3.   *Source:* T.71/250.

                    Note: The rates are based on the populations living in 1832.

Table S9.4.   *Source:* T.71/451.

                    Note: The rates are based on the populations living in 1831.

Table S9.5.   *Source:* T.71/374.

                    Note: The rates are based on the populations living in 1831.

Table S9.6.   *Source:* T.71/361-63.

                    Note: The rates are based on the populations living in 1829 and 1832.

Table S9.7.   *Source:* T.71/376-81.

                Note: The rates are based on the populations living in 1815.

Table S9.8.   *Source:* T.71/493-96.

                Note: The rates are based on the populations living in 1817.

Table S9.9.   *Source:* T.71/264-72 and 313-38.

                Note: The rates are based on the populations living in 1817
                and 1829.

Table S9.10.   *Source:* T.71/461-67.

                Note: The rates are based on the populations living in 1819.

Table S9.11.   *Source: P.P.,* 1833, Vol. XXVI (700), "Slave Population,"
                pp.10-11.

                Note: The rates are based on the populations living in 1832.

Table S9.12.   *Source:* T.71/553-64 (Barbados), 260 (St. Kitts), 376-81
                (St. Lucia), 493-96 (St. Vincent), 461-67 (Tobago), 438-41
                (Berbice), 261-62 (Anguilla).

                Note: The rates are based on the populations living in 1834,
                1817, 1815, 1817, 1819, 1819, and 1827, respectively.

Table S9.13.   *Source:* T.71/461-67.

                Notes: The rates are based on the populations living in
                1819. Unknowns have been distributed.

Table S9.14.   *Source:* T.71/260 (St. Kitts), 364-65 (Nevis), 370-71 (Virgin Islands), 376-81 (St. Lucia), 461-67 (Tobago), 438-41 (Berbice).

Notes: The rates are based on the populations living in 1817, 1817, 1818, 1815, 1819, and 1819, respectively. Unknowns have been distributed.

Table S9.15.   *Source:* T.71/361-63.

Notes: The rates are based on the populations living in 1829. Unknowns have been distributed.

Table S9.16.   *Source:* D. Gail Saunders, *The Slave Population of the Bahamas, 1783-1834* (M. Phil. thesis, University of the West Indies, 1978), pp. 142-46. (Derived from the registration data.)

Table S9.17.   *Source:* T.71/520-27.

Notes: The rates are based on the populations living in 1817. Unknowns have been distributed.

Table S9.18.   *Source:* T.71/493-96.

Notes: The rates are based on the populations living in 1817. Unknowns have been distributed.

Table S9.19.   *Source:* T.71/264-72 and 313-38.

Notes: The rates are based on the populations living in 1817 and 1829. Unknowns have been distributed.

Table S9.20.   *Source:* T.71/520-27.

Notes: The rates are based on the populations living in 1817. Unknowns have been distributed.

Table S9.21.   *Source:* T.71/376-81.

Notes: The rates are based on the populations living in 1815. Unknowns have been distributed.

Table S9.22.   *Source:* T.71/461-67.

Notes: The rates are based on the populations living in 1819. Unknowns have been distributed.

Table S9.23.   *Source:* T.71/376-81.

Notes: The rates are based on the populations living in 1815. Unknowns have been distributed.

Table S9.24.   *Source:* T.71/461-67.

Notes: The rates are based on the populations living in 1819. Unknowns have been distributed.

Table S9.25.   *[Source:]* T.71/376-81.

Notes: The rates are based on the populations living in 1815. Unknowns have been distributed.

Table S9.26.   *Source:* T.71/376-81.

Notes: The mean ages are based on age in 1815. Only cases for which age is known are included.

Table S9.27.   *Source:* T.71/438-41.

Notes: The mean ages are based on age in 1819. Only cases for which age is known are included.

Table S9.28.   *Source:* T.71/376-81.

Notes: The rates are based on the populations living in 1815. Unknowns have been distributed.

Table S9.29.   *Source:* T.71/520-27.

                 Notes: The rates are based on the populations living in 1817. Unknowns have been distributed.

Table S9.30.   *Source:* T.71/376-81.

                 Notes: The rates are based on the populations living in 1815. Unknowns have been distributed.

Table S9.31.   *Source:* T.71/438-41.

                 Notes: The rates are based on the populations living in 1819. Unknowns have been distributed.

Table S9.32.   *Source:* T.71/461-67.

                 Note: Based on location in 1819.

Table S9.33.   *Source:* T.71/438-41.

                 Note: Based on occupations in 1819.

Table S9.34.   *Source:* T.71/461-67.

Table S9.35.   *Source:* T.71/438-41.

Table S9.36.   *Source:* T.71/461-67.

                 Note: Based on location in 1819.

Table S9.37.   *Source:* T.71/264-72 and 313-38.

Table S9.38.   *Source:* T.71/438-41 and 461-67.

                 Note: Based on holding-size in 1819.

Table S9.39.   *Source:* T.71/461-67.

Table S9.40.   *Source:* T.71/438-41.

                 Note: Based on occupations in 1819.

Table S9.41.   *Source:* T.71/461-67.

                 Note: The mean ages are based on age in 1819.

Table S9.42.   *Source:* T.71/438-41.

                 Note: The mean ages are based on age in 1819.

Table S9.43.   *Source:* T.71/438-41 and 461-67.

                 Notes: The rates are based on the populations living in 1819. Unknowns have been distributed.

Table S9.44.   *Source:* T.71/376-81 (St. Lucia), 461-67 (Tobago), and 438-41 (Berbice).

                 Notes: The rates are based on the populations living in 1815, 1819, and 1819, respectively. Unknowns have been distributed. See Table 9.10 for rates adjusted for under-registration of births.

Table S9.45.   *Source: ibid.*

                 Notes: The rates are based on the populations living in 1815, 1819, and 1819, respectively. Unknowns have been distributed.

Table S9.46.   *Source:* T.71/376-81 and 461-67.

                 Notes: The rates are based on the populations living in 1815 and 1819, respectively. Unknowns have been distributed.

Table S9.47.   *Source:* T.71/376-81 (St. Lucia), 461-67 (Tobago), and 438-41 (Berbice).

Notes: The rates are based on the populations living in 1815, 1819, and 1819, respectively. Unknowns have been distributed.

Table S9.48.   *Source:* T.71/376-81 and 438-41.

Notes: The rates are based on the populations living in 1815 and 1819, respectively. Unknowns have been distributed.

Table S9.49.   *Sources:* T.71/337-63 (Dominica), 461-67 (Tobago), and 438-41 (Berbice); *Dominica Almanac* (Roseau, 1828).

Notes: Crop-type is based on identifications of sample plantations for 1827, in Dominica. Locations and occupations are based on data for 1819, in Tobago and Berbice.

Table S9.1. *Slave Birth Rates, Death Rates, Rates of Natural Increase and Sex Ratios, by Parish: Barbados, 1817-20 and 1832-34*

Parish	Males per 100 Females	(Registered) Births per 1,000	(Registered) Deaths per 1,000			Natural Increase per 1,000
			Males	Females	Total	
1817-20						
St. Michael	77.6	34.6	29.6	24.5	26.7	+7.9
St. James	88.6	35.3	30.5	27.7	29.0	+6.3
St. Peter	88.1	33.7	32.7	27.9	30.2	+3.5
St. Lucy	88.9	31.1	33.3	27.2	30.1	+1.0
St. Andrew	92.6	27.9	36.0	33.5	34.7	- 6.8
St. Joseph	80.8	34.1	36.5	28.0	31.8	+2.3
St. John	87.8	30.9	33.8	22.5	27.7	+3.2
St. Philip	83.5	30.9	33.3	27.8	30.3	+0.6
Christ Church	86.9	36.8	25.1	20.9	22.9	+13.9
St. George	84.8	33.7	30.8	28.6	29.6	+4.1
St. Thomas	86.2	30.5	32.1	27.9	29.8	+0.7
Total	84.3	33.2	31.2	26.1	28.4	+4.8
1832-34						
St. Michael	80.0	38.3	31.6	25.2	28.0	+10.3
St. James	93.4	41.9	34.7	29.6	32.4	+9.5
St. Peter	87.4	39.2	35.5	24.3	29.5	+9.7
St. Lucy	84.9	45.1	25.7	20.8	23.1	+22.0
St. Andrew	85.6	42.1	31.2	23.7	27.2	+14.9
St. Joseph	87.4	46.9	22.2	25.5	23.9	+23.0
St. John	86.9	44.1	32.9	22.6	27.4	+16.7
St. Philip	86.1	47.7	31.4	29.4	30.4	+17.3
Christ Church	87.7	37.5	24.2	21.6	22.8	+14.7
St. George	91.8	45.7	29.3	26.9	28.1	+17.6
St. Thomas	89.4	36.5	24.4	22.0	21.4	+15.1
Total	86.2	40.3	28.2	23.8	26.0	+14.3

Table S9.2. *Slave Birth Rates, Death Rates, Rates of Natural Increase and Sex Ratios, by Parish: St. Kitts, 1831-34*

Parish	(1834) Males per 100 Females	(Registered) Births per 1,000	(Registered) Deaths per 1,000			Natural Increase per 1,000
			Males	Females	Total	
Basseterre	83.1	35.1	22.6	20.3	21.1	+14.0
St. George	94.3	32.7	38.1	35.5	36.8	- 4.1
St. Peter	92.5	33.8	26.3	27.2	26.8	+7.0
Trinity	95.1	32.9	29.8	21.3	25.6	+7.3
St. Thomas	102.8	26.1	29.0	25.2	27.0	- 0.9
St. Ann	98.2	33.8	27.8	28.7	28.2	+5.6
St. Paul	89.3	29.4	28.4	26.7	27.5	+1.9
St. John	95.0	31.1	23.8	28.0	25.9	+5.2
Christ Church	83.9	39.7	29.1	31.0	30.8	+8.9
St. Mary	93.0	33.9	26.1	24.0	25.2	+8.7
Total*	93.1	31.7	27.5	26.8	27.1	+4.6

* Includes 21 slaves whose parish is unknown.

Table S9.3. *Slave Birth Rates, Death Rates, Rates of Natural Increase and Sex Ratios, by Parish and Division: Antigua, 1828-32*

Parish/Division	(1832) Males per 100 Females	(Registered) Births per 1,000	(Registered) Deaths per 1,000			Natural Increase per 1,000
			Males	Females	Total	
St. John's						
St. John Division	89.7	21.1	28.5	25.4	26.9	- 5.8
Town of St. John's	84.7	22.1	25.5	21.4	23.3	- 1.2
Dickinson's Bay Division	87.9	24.6	23.3	23.3	23.3	- 1.3
Five Islands Division	95.3	22.2	16.7	17.7	17.2	+5.0
Total	88.2	22.2	25.8	23.4	24.5	- 2.3
St. George's						
New North Sound Division	91.4	22.7	23.2	25.4	24.4	- 1.7
St. Peter's						
Old North Sound Division	97.0	22.5	30.6	31.3	31.0	- 8.5
Town of Parham	70.3	21.2	–	14.4	8.5	+12.7
Total	96.6	22.4	30.2	31.1	30.6	- 8.2
St. Philip's						
Belfast Division	94.7	25.2	23.7	21.5	22.6	+2.6
Nonsuch Division	89.5	27.5	19.1	21.6	20.4	+7.1
Total	91.5	26.6	21.0	21.5	21.3	+5.3
St. Paul's						
Falmouth Division	87.5	20.0	28.7	23.2	25.8	- 5.8
Town of English Harbour	93.4	22.1	25.0	25.3	25.2	- 3.1
Town of Falmouth	95.4	27.3	30.1	20.5	25.2	+2.1
Willoughby Bay Division	79.2	29.2	21.0	21.5	21.3	+7.9
Rendezvous Bay Division	70.5	17.8	34.4	18.2	24.9	- 7.1
Total	84.2	24.4	25.3	22.4	23.7	+0.7
St. Mary's						
New Division	91.7	23.2	22.9	17.1	19.9	+3.3
Bermudian Valley Division	85.7	21.5	23.6	20.8	22.1	- 0.6
Old Road Division	92.9	21.6	26.9	19.8	23.2	- 1.6
Total	90.6	22.2	24.5	19.0	21.6	+0.6
Unknown	87.0	16.8	19.5	17.0	18.2	- 1.4
TOTAL	90.1	22.1	24.9	23.	24.1	- 2.0

Table S9.4. *Slave Birth Rates, Death Rates, Rates of Natural Increase and Sex Ratios, by Parish: Montserrat, 1828-31*

Parish	(1831) Males per 100 Females	(Registered) Births per 1,000	(Registered) Deaths per 1,000			Natural Increase per 1,000
			Males	Females	Total	
Plymouth	78.2	38.8	12.4	26.7	20.4	+18.4
St. George	88.5	38.9	34.6	30.6	32.5	+6.4
St. Anthony	89.4	37.1	33.8	29.7	31.6	+5.5
St. Peter	89.0	33.4	21.6	22.7	22.2	+11.2
St. Patrick	94.6	44.4	26.3	25.7	26.0	+18.4
Unknown	120.7	20.8	9.5	34.5	20.8	0.0
Total	89.2	37.6	28.6	27.7	28.1	+9.5

Table S9.5. *Slave Birth Rates, Death Rates, Rates of Natural Increase and Sex Ratios, by Island: Virgin Islands, 1828-31*

Island	(1831) Males per 100 Females	(Registered) Births per 1,000	(Registered) Deaths per 1,000			Natural Increase per 1,000
			Males	Females	Total	
Tortola	86.2	25.8	29.1	32.6	31.0	- 5.2
Spanish Town	95.2	33.6	5.6	10.6	8.2	+25.4
Peter's Island	93.6	33.0	30.3	0.0	14.7	+18.3
Thatch Island	109.7	46.2	4.9	5.4	5.1	+41.1
Anegada	58.8	32.9	11.1	0.0	4.1	+28.8
Jos Van Dykes	83.7	29.5	0.0	15.5	8.4	+21.1
Beef Island	83.3	18.9	33.3	13.9	22.7	- 3.8
Frenchman's Quay	87.0	15.5	0.0	0.0	0.0	+15.5
Guana Island	90.0	35.1	18.5	0.0	8.8	+26.3
Quaymanas	44.0	37.0	0.0	0.0	0.0	+37.0
Salt Island	87.5	66.7	47.6	0.0	22.2	+44.5
Unknown	98.2	22.2	22.5	20.2	21.3	+0.9
Total	87.3	27.0	25.2	27.0	26.2	+0.8

Table S9.6. *Slave Birth Rates, Death Rates, Rates of Natural Increase and Sex Ratios, by Parish: Dominica, 1826-29 and 1829-32*

Parish	Males per 100 Females	(Registered) Births per 1,000	(Registered) Deaths per 1,000			Natural Increase per 1,000
			Males	Females	Total	
1826-29						
Roseau	73.6	23.2	31.1	25.1	27.6	- 4.4
St. George	96.4	29.1	31.0	25.2	28.0	- 1.1
St. Paul	86.6	28.1	38.4	35.1	36.6	- 8.5
St. Joseph	91.6	33.2	34.4	24.5	29.3	+3.9
St. Peter	100.4	42.8	25.2	23.4	24.3	+18.5
St. John	94.7	33.2	33.5	25.7	29.5	+3.7
St. Andrew	89.0	27.3	33.8,	25.8	29.6	- 2.3
St. David	95.8	24.5	44.0	35.1	39.4	- 14.9
St. Patrick	91.0	32.6	32.0	30.6	31.3	+1.3
St. Mark	99.2	34.3	17.0	26.0	21.5	+12.8
St. Luke	88.1	26.6	28.8	17.9	23.0	+3.6
Total	91.3	30.4	31.8	26.9	29.2	+1.2
1829-32						
Roseau	71.1	34.6	47.1	30.7	37.5	- 2.9
St. George	94.2	33.1	34.9	31.7	33.3	- 0.2
St. Paul	89.4	23.7	29.4	31.8	30.7	- 7.0
St. Joseph	91.0	26.7	30.9	28.2	29.5	- 2.8
St. Peter	98.0	33.3	22.4	23.5	23.0	+10.3
St. John	102.6	26.0	25.6	21.2	23.4	+2.6
St. Andrew	90.4	33.5	20.7	26.4	23.7	+9.8
St. David	102.6	30.5	31.3	45.7	38.4	- 7.9
St. Patrick	95.4	32.2	25.3	27.2	26.3	+5.9
St. Mark	97.7	26.2	23.3	14.9	19.1	+7.1
St. Luke	90.3	33.6	21.7	21.8	21.7	+11.9
Total	92.7	30.2	27.7	26.9	27.3	+2.9

Table S9.7. *Slave Birth Rates, Death Rates, Rates of Natural Increase and Sex Ratios, by Quarter: St. Lucia, 1815-19*

Quarter	(1815) Males per 100 Females	(Registered) Births per 1,000	(Registered) Deaths per 1,000			Natural Increase per 1,000
			Males	Females	Total	
Castries	92.9	12.0	45.5	44.1	44.8	- 32.8
Gros Islet	79.0	12.4	50.4	32.0	40.1	- 27.7
Dauphin	93.4	20.1	52.5	29.3	40.5	- 20.4
Dennery	69.8	17.4	35.4	18.8	25.7	- 8.3
Praslin	88.2	17.5	36.8	45.4	41.4	- 23.9
Micoud	77.3	8.9	45.6	42.4	43.8	- 34.9
Vieux Fort	81.3	11.3	60.1	38.1	48.0	- 36.7
Laborie	79.3	14.9	55.0	28.8	40.4	- 25.5
Choiseul	81.4	15.2	36.0	34.5	35.2	- 20.0
Soufriere	89.7	15.4	41.0	33.2	36.9	-21.5
Anse la Raye	88.2	13.6	55.4	37.2	45.7	- 32.1
Town of Castries	85.5	13.6	47.5	18.3	31.8	- 18.2
Town of Gros Islet	76.6	11.4	26.3	10.8	17.5	- 6.1
Town of Micoud	38.5	70.2	88.4	0.0	24.6	+45.6
Town of Vieux Fort	53.8	0.0	0.0	0.0	0.0	0.0
Town of Laborie	54.2	17.1	49.8	13.8	21.3	- 4.2
Town of Choiseul	37.8	0.0	31.6	0.0	8.7	- 8.7
Town of Soufriere	70.4	15.7	18.3	19.6	19.1	- 3.4
Total	83.9	14.3	46.9	32.7	39.8	- 25.5

Table S9.8. *Slave Birth Rates, Death Rates, Rates of Natural Increase and Sex Ratios, by Parish: St. Vincent, 1817-22*

Parish	(1817) Males per 100 Females	(Registered) Births per 1,000	(Registered) Deaths per 1,000			Natural Increase per 1,000
			Males	Females	Total	
St. George	101.4	22.5	41.6	33.4	37.5	- 15.0
St. Andrew	89.4	13.4	48.6	42.7	45.4	- 32.0
St. Patrick	100.3	21.2	41.2	34.2	37.7	- 16.5
St. David	100.3	27.0	37.9	35.9	36.9	- 9.9
Charlotte	109.9	24.1	38.0	30.7	34.5	- 10.4
Grenadines	104.3	22.9	21.5	16.9	19.3	+3.6
Total	102.9	22.5	38.5	31.8	35.2	- 12.7

Table S9.9. *Slave Birth Rates, Death Rates, Rates of Natural Increase and Sex Ratios, by Parish: Grenada, 1817-19 and 1830-32*

Parish	Males per 100 Females	(Registered) Births per 1,000	(Registered) Deaths per 1,000			Natural Increase per 1,000
			Males	Females	Total	
1817-19						
Town of St. George	86.1	28.8	31.1	25.7	28.2	+0.6
St. George	99.2	20.5	38.3	36.9	37.6	- 17.1
St. John & St. Mark	98.3	26.3	43.1	42.6	42.8	- 16.5
St. Patrick	97.9	20.0	52.8	53.9	53.3	- 33.3
St. Andrew	100.1	23.2	54.1	55.4	54.7	- 31.5
St. David	100.0	20.7	48.7	39.5	44.1	- 23.4
Grenadines	89.4	31.1	36.1	28.1	31.9	- 0.8
Total	96.1	24.2	44.0	41.1	42.5	- 18.3
1830-32						
Town of St. George	80.5	30.3	34.9	22.5	28.0	+2.3
St. George	95.0	24.2	40.2	38.0	39.1	- 14.9
St. John & St. Mark	99.4	31.4	40.0	29.0	34.5	- 3.1
St. Patrick	92.3	25.1	48.8	40.5	44.5	- 19.4
St. Andrew	98.1	23.4	42.5	35.6	39.0	- 15.6
St. David	92.7	32.8	38.1	41.5	39.9	- 7.1
Grenadines	92.1	40.9	26.3	21.6	23.9	+17.0
Total	94.0	28.7	39.8	33.5	36.5	- 7.8

Table S9.10. *Slave Birth Rates, Death Rates, Rates of Natural Increase and Sex Ratios, by Parish: Tobago, 1819-21*

Parish	(1819) Males per 100 Females	(Registered) Births per 1,000	(Registered) Deaths per 1,000			Natural Increase per 1,000
			Males	Females	Total	
St. Andrew	92.0	19.1	68.2	51.4	59.7	- 40.6
St. Patrick	91.9	23.8	55.7	50.5	53.3	- 29.5
St. David	101.4	22.7	44.5	39.4	42.3	- 19.6
St. John	99.6	20.2	34.2	27.8	31.2	- 11.0
St. Paul	99.6	18.7	42.2	39.0	40.8	- 22.1
St. Mary	92.9	20.2	54.6	46.5	50.8	- 30.6
St. George	106.5	18.0	59.2	42.5	51.4	- 33.4
Town of Scarborough	89.7	20.3	34.9	24.2	29.7	- 9.4
Town of Plymouth	138.3	14.9	51.3	49.6	50.6	- 35.7
Total	97.4	20.8	50.9	42.7	46.8	- 26.0

Table S9.11. *Slave Birth Rates, Death Rates, Rates of Natural Increase and Sex Ratios, by Parish: Demerara-Essequibo, 1829-32*

Parish	(1832) Males per 100 Females	(Registered) Births per 1,000	(Registered) Deaths per 1,000			Natural Increase per 1,000
			Males	Females	Total	
St. Mary	116.8	24.4	34.9	26.5	31.0	- 6.6
St. Paul	105.8	24.2	33.7	25.4	29.7	- 5.5
St. George & St. Andrew	98.8	23.9	33.9	19.3	26.6	- 2.7
St. Matthew	109.9	19.0	43.4	32.8	38.4	- 19.4
St. Mark	124.6	16.1	38.1	34.1	36.3	- 20.2
St. Swithin	111.2	17.7	49.2	42.3	46.0	- 28.3
St. Luke	112.5	21.7	45.2	30.1	38.0	- 16.3
St. Peter	105.0	18.9	53.1	34.2	43.9	- 25.0
St. James	104.2	15.0	58.3	31.5	45.2	- 30.2
St. John	115.1	19.6	45.1	31.4	38.7	- 19.1
Trinity	117.1	20.9	38.0	28.5	33.6	- 12.7
Total	110.2	20.2	41.5	29.3	34.7	- 14.5

Table S9.20. *Slave Age-specific Death Rates by Sex and Color:*
St. Michael, Barbados, 1817-20 (Registered Deaths per 1,000)

Age group	Bridgetown				Rural St. Michael			
	Black		Colored		Black		Colored	
	Males	Females	Males	Females	Males	Females	Males	Females
0-4	35	33	32	29	27	29	45	24
5-9	12	8	6	5	11	7	8	4
10-14	11	4	4	7	6	4	6	8
15-19	15	8	9	6	8	4	–	5
20-24	16	13	7	5	11	9	6	5
25-29	22	14	5	6	24	10	24	5
30-34	27	14	59	10	17	15	20	19
35-39	32	15	28	10	20	13	40	13
40-44	40	16	37	7	28	15	30	9
45-49	32	22	71	10	27	26	22	39
50-54	52	31	–	15	37	29	–	19
55-59	42	30	–	–	55	38	–	–
60-64	92	37	–	22	44	48	–	–
65-69	103	60	–	–	97	40	–	–
70+	152	66	–	56	131	97	–	–
Total	24	18	17	12	20	18	18	12

Table S9.21. *Slave Age-specific Death Rates by Sex and Color:*
St. Lucia, 1815-19 (Registered Deaths per 1,000)

Age group	Black			Colored		
	Males	Females	Total	Males	Females	Total
0-4	83	58	70	76	45	57
5-9	33	22	26	20	11	16
10-14	23	16	19	12	15	12
15-19	27	21	24	9	12	11
20-24	32	24	28	35	15	24
25-29	34	20	27	29	13	21
30-34	37	24	30	49	22	33
35-39	55	30	40	11	37	26
40-44	69	33	46	35	12	19
45-49	57	52	53	52	10	27
50-54	89	60	70	144	45	58
55-59	92	60	73	96	58	70
60-64	78	65	69	216	128	163
65-69	69	80	90	173	70	120
70+	143	109	119	–	209	100
Total	48	36	42	36	25	30

Table S9.22. *Slave Age-specific Death Rates by Sex and Color: Tobago, 1819-21 (Registered Deaths per 1,000)*

Age group	Black			Colored		
	Males	Females	Total	Males	Females	Total
0-4	66	75	71	51	72	57
5-9	29	20	25	23	26	24
10-14	22	13	18	19	16	17
15-19	14	17	15	–	14	7
20-24	27	27	27	56	19	33
25-29	45	29	37	67	30	48
30-34	38	35	36	119	30	80
35-39	48	31	40	56	–	42
40-44	59	52	55	–	–	–
45-49	72	58	65	–	333	67
50-54	97	58	76	–	–	–
55-59	80	73	76	–	–	–
60-64	121	84	101	–	–	–
65-69	133	102	116	–	–	–
70+	159	82	114	–	–	–
Total	49	41	45	36	33	35

Table S9.23. *Slave Age-specific Death Rates by Sex and Birthplace, Rural and Urban: St. Lucia, 1815-19 (Registered Deaths per 1,000)*

Age group	Africans		Creoles		Total		
	Males	Females	Males	Females	Males	Females	Total
Rural							
0-4	–	–	80	57	80	57	67
5-9	–	–	30	19	30	19	24
10-14	30	–	22	17	22	17	19
15-19	29	37	26	18	27	20	23
20-24	40	49	31	19	32	23	28
25-29	49	25	28	19	34	20	27
30-34	54	30	33	20	40	23	31
35-39	78	34	24	28	51	30	39
40-44	91	35	39	31	67	32	45
45-49	67	56	48	46	58	50	53
50-54	87	73	90	44	88	58	68
55-59	96	70	90	49	93	58	71
60-64	94	74	80	58	88	66	74
65-69	149	99	104	41	133	72	92
70+	118	106	158	108	132	107	116
Total	71	53	40	30	47	35	40
Urban							
0-4	–	–	94	19	94	19	56
5-9	–	–	20	15	20	15	18
10-14	–	–	–	3	–	3	2
15-19	–	53	14	7	12	10	11
20-24	58	9	22	12	35	11	22
25-29	19	7	37	13	30	11	19
30-34	45	13	26	20	34	18	26
35-39	25	–	83	20	56	13	28
40-44	65	28	53	–	60	9	26
45-49	49	20	55	18	52	19	27
50-54	144	55	106	18	126	33	67
55-59	142	75	–	–	95	41	56
60-64	147	32	–	102	63	71	70
65-69	–	163	–	45	–	100	76
70+	147	63	–	–	147	63	95
Total	48	26	38	14	41	17	27

Table S9.24. *Slave Age-specific Death Rates by Sex and Birthplace, Rural and Urban: Tobago, 1819-21 (Registered Deaths per 1,000)*

Age group	Africans		Creoles		Total		
	Males	Females	Males	Females	Males	Females	Total
Rural							
0-4	–	–	65	75	65	75	70
5-9	–	–	30	21	30	21	26
10-14	–	–	22	14	22	14	18
15-19	42	–	14	17	14	17	15
20-24	20	31	27	28	26	28	27
25-29	50	34	42	27	13	29	37
30-34	49	39	23	28	38	33	36
35-39	56	31	31	33	48	32	40
40-44	58	58	54	34	57	51	54
45-49	71	61	50	57	69	60	64
50-54	97	60	133	26	99	57	76
55-59	82	74	56	77	80	74	77
60-64	130	86	–	26	123	83	101
65-69	133	100	133	74	133	97	113
70+	156	80	167	56	157	78	110
Total	71	56	34	32	49	41	45
Urban							
0-4	–	–	44	56	44	56	51
5-9	–	–	12	12	12	12	12
10-14	–	–	20	–	20	–	11
15-19	–	–	–	8	–	8	4
20-24	–	33	67	–	44	14	25
25-29	53	26	–	16	39	23	31
30-34	47	38	33	–	45	28	37
35-39	32	16	–	95	29	28	28
40-44	52	20	–	111	46	34	40
45-49	101	18	–	–	90	14	53
50-54	37	67	–	83	28	70	54
55-59	67	56	–	–	67	48	56
60-64	42	333	–	–	42	333	74
65-69	–	–	–	–	–	–	–
70+	333	–	–	–	333	–	333
Total	51	30	21	22	36	26	31

Table S9.25. *Slave Age-specific Death Rates by Sex and Crop-type:*
St. Lucia, 1815-19 (Registered Deaths per 1,000)

Age group	Males	Females	Total	Males	Females	Total
		Sugar			*Coffee*	
0-4	89	69	77	95	53	75
5-9	30	26	28	38	18	27
10-14	26	16	21	17	18	18
15-19	30	23	27	29	19	24
20-24	44	24	35	14	36	25
25-29	45	25	35	27	20	24
30-34	41	23	33	34	22	28
35-39	58	39	48	7	41	25
40-44	78	35	53	76	50	58
45-49	62	55	58	56	45	48
50-54	117	64	86	59	81	73
55-59	110	61	76	66	47	54
60-64	82	78	79	100	46	60
65-69	162	70	102	63	21	34
70+	142	121	129	85	221	159
Total	54	40	47	41	36	39
	Coffee, Cocoa, Cotton, Provisions				*Personal*	
0-4	79	48	64	88	29	57
5-9	41	18	29	27	11	19
10-14	15	21	18	7	5	6
15-19	21	21	21	11	8	10
20-24	21	28	26	29	18	23
25-29	26	15	21	26	11	17
30-34	39	17	28	33	17	24
35-39	16	34	26	39	16	24
40-44	71	37	47	59	11	26
45-49	60	44	48	59	18	32
50-54	64	61	62	108	37	56
55-59	76	53	61	57	17	43
60-64	102	53	66	81	68	72
65-69	63	47	51	—	86	68
70+	71	165	136	55	23	34
Total	41	34	37	38	18	26

Table S9.26. *Mean Age of Slaves at Death, by Sex, Birthplace and Occupation: St. Lucia, 1815-19*

| Occupation | Africans | | | | Creoles | | | |
| | Males | | Females | | Males | | Females | |
	Mean	S.D.	Mean	S.D.	Mean	S.D.	Mean	S.D.
Field laborers	37.7	11.4	45.0	14.0	26.2	14.4	32.8	15.4
Drivers	52.5	17.7	64.0	–	42.3	11.3	–	–
Skilled tradespeople	45.7	13.3	–	–	32.9	15.2	25.0	20.8
Domestics	31.4	9.4	44.4	18.2	14.9	11.6	31.5	17.6
Stockkeepers	59.1	10.8	–	–	30.0	15.6	9.5	1.9
Transport workers	37.1	14.0	–	–	25.9	12.1	–	–
Watchmen	55.4	13.5	58.1	14.8	33.2	22.6	30.4	25.2
Fishermen	39.0	–	62.0	–	53.8	6.1	–	–
Sellers	–	–	40.0	–	–	–	–	–
Laborers	42.5	12.9	43.3	5.8	49.7	19.4	43.0	16.1
Hired	–	–	–	–	–	–	52.0	2.8
Nurses	–	–	64.8	8.1	–	–	60.5	15.8
Sick or disabled	58.3	21.7	63.9	14.3	48.4	19.9	46.1	19.8
Absent	37.0	2.6	–	–	33.2	16.6	43.5	24.7
None	66.1	13.1	66.6	12.4	6.6	15.4	9.6	20.6
Total	43.7	15.6	50.5	16.4	18.8	19.5	32.4	23.8

Table S9.27. *Mean Age of Slaves at Death, by Sex, Birthplace and Occupation: Berbice, 1819-22*

| Occupation | Africans | | | | Creoles | | | |
| | Males | | Females | | Males | | Females | |
	Mean	S.D.	Mean	S.D.	Mean	S.D.	Mean	S.D.
Field laborers	37.0	8.5	34.7	7.4	23.7	11.2	27.5	12.0
Drivers	44.4	9.5	–	–	41.5	8.9	–	–
Skilled tradespeople	36.2	8.9	43.0	16.7	37.6	11.0	32.5	2.1
Domestics	29.5	5.9	37.8	9.1	15.9	10.5	24.1	14.0
Stockkeepers	41.6	9.4	33.7	3.1	18.4	7.9	–	–
Transport workers	31.2	6.5	–	–	34.3	18.0	–	–
Watchmen	48.9	8.3	–	–	42.8	7.6	–	–
Fishermen	44.3	11.5	–	–	58.5	10.6	–	–
Sellers	–	–	29.0	–	–	–	–	–
Laborers	39.3	10.6	36.6	7.8	14.3	12.4	11.8	4.0
Hired	–	–	–	–	–	–	–	–
Nurses	39.7	9.4	48.2	10.5	32.0	7.4	41.4	17.2
Sick or disabled	47.8	13.8	46.5	13.8	43.6	19.5	44.5	18.6
Absent	47.0	–	–	–	–	–	–	–
None	50.8	17.5	47.8	17.0	5.5	13.7	6.4	15.4
Total	39.9	11.3	39.8	12.2	16.2	18.6	16.3	18.8

Table S9.28. *Slave Age-specific Death Rates by Sex, Birthplace, Occupation and Crop-type: St. Lucia, 1815-19 (Registered Deaths per 1,000)*

Age group	Sugar		Coffee, Cocoa, Cotton, Provisions		Personal	
	Field Laborers	Domestics, Skilled Tradespeople and Drivers	Field Laborers	Domestics, Skilled Tradespeople and Drivers	Field Laborers	Domestics, Skilled Tradespeople and Drivers
African males						
0-9	–	–	–	–	–	–
10-19	27	–	–	–	–	–
20-29	75	34	29	43	–	23
30-39	72	13	35	54	17	32
40-49	81	70	98	216	43	100
50-59	93	135	144	–	54	144
60+	76	96	–	108	72	108
Total	74	56	52	64	27	39
Creole males						
0-9	28	20	67	26	–	20
10-19	34	24	19	12	–	13
20-29	41	33	48	10	9	39
30-39	39	18	25	11	20	20
40-49	57	28	–	36	–	22
50-59	138	41	27	–	–	86
60+	118	48	62	432	–	–
Total	42	27	22	17	7	31
African females						
0-9	–	–	–	–	–	–
10-19	22	–	70	–	–	25
20-29	42	–	50	–	–	12
30-39	44	58	36	–	28	13
40-49	51	50	42	–	29	9
50-59	77	70	34	349	27	77
60+	129	77	55	116	–	–
Total	58	46	42	58	23	17
Creole females						
0-9	26	–	–	45	27	10
10-19	25	8	19	19	8	5
20-29	21	23	62	7	32	34
30-39	25	33	30	61	12	17
40-49	44	32	53	17	–	–
50-59	44	40	41	70	32	20
60+	85	35	–	–	174	65
Total	29	21	28	25	21	11

Table S9.29. *Slave Age-specific Death Rates by Sex and Occupation: Barbados, 1817-20 (Select Parishes) (Registered Deaths per 1,000)*

Age group	Bridgetown					
	Domestics		Skilled Tradespeople	Transport Workers	Sick or Disabled, or No Occupation	
	Males	Females	Males	Males	Males	Females
0-4	46	29	–	–	34	30
5-9	6	9	12	–	12	6
10-14	11	5	–	42	17	8
15-19	8	8	14	53	–	26
20-24	13	11	4	35	133	39
25-29	5	13	10	39	83	–
30-34	39	15	42	13	–	–
35-39	26	14	70	49	–	–
40-44	16	13	86	51	–	30
45-49	33	20	43	–	133	28
50-54	63	26	22	53	–	70
55-59	28	29	111	56	–	–
60-64	42	31	167	–	10	42
65-69	167	24	111	–	–	120
70+	95	65	111	–	167	67
Total	17	14	18	36	26	25

Age group	Rural St. Michael							
	Field Laborers		Domestics		Skilled Tradespeople and Drivers	Stock-keepers	Sick or Disabled, or No Occupation	
	Males	Females	Males	Females	Males	Males	Males	Females
0-4	–	37	–	–	–	–	30	29
5-9	15	6	–	18	42	8	10	3
10-14	5	3	6	7	–	5	17	6
15-19	5	2	4	6	–	17	74	42
20-24	11	10	7	5	10	–	–	67
25-29	20	10	8	7	31	20	67	111
30-34	17	17	33	11	12	30	–	–
35-39	17	12	38	16	20	74	–	–
40-44	18	10	28	22	38	59	83	111
45-49	30	29	61	23	–	48	–	83
50-54	30	22	–	24	49	–	–	200
55-59	67	61	–	16	–	133	67	83
60-64	30	20	83	32	30	–	167	111
65-69	–	–	167	–	–	–	267	48
70+	133	67	167	22	133	133	128	133
Total	16	12	14	12	16	18	28	29

Table S9.29. *Age-specific Death Rates: Barbados, 1817-20 (continued)*

Age group	St. John and St. Andrew							
	Field Laborers		Domestics		Skilled Tradespeople and Drivers	Stock-keepers	Sick or Disabled, or No Occupation	
	Males	Females	Males	Females	Males	Males	Males	Females
0-4	–	30	83	–	–	–	48	44
5-9	11	7	17	8	–	11	20	12
10-14	5	8	–	4	12	3	32	36
15-19	8	5	10	15	–	12	48	67
20-24	18	14	14	–	18	28	–	–
25-29	20	18	11	6	6	–	–	–
30-34	31	18	–	12	12	–	167	–
35-39	27	17	18	23	10	89	333	83
40-44	29	26	111	18	–	–	222	83
45-49	48	33	42	11	14	45	167	–
50-54	59	22	5	35	56	194	167	95
55-59	53	75	42	64	133	167	–	56
60-64	43	40	–	37	–	100	–	83
65-69	–	51	–	83	83	–	333	133
70+	56	83	–	56	67	83	185	146
Total	20	17	17	42	18	29	44	43

Table S9.30. *Slave Age-specific Death Rates by Sex and Occupation: St. Lucia, 1815-19 (Registered Deaths per 1,000)*

Age group	Field Laborers		Domestics		Skilled Tradespeople and Drivers	Stock-keepers	Watchmen		Sick or Disabled, or No Occupation	
	Males	Females	Males	Females	Males	Males	Males	Females	Males	Females
0-4	86	17	102	44	–	–	–	–	81	58
5-9	37	33	25	7	108	–	16	32	34	20
10-14	28	18	12	9	18	10	31	48	10	17
15-19	29	26	20	7	14	22	48	–	–	35
20-24	32	26	34	13	21	–	–	349	124	65
25-29	39	21	46	11	25	–	173	–	29	70
30-34	47	26	25	17	21	72	–	–	67	27
35-39	50	30	48	30	17	10	72	–	144	87
40-44	58	34	58	13	54	54	144	174	173	66
45-49	64	58	–	13	47	108	173	70	–	67
50-54	79	52	62	55	94	–	108	218	144	70
55-59	76	54	–	36	31	212	72	139	264	126
60-64	54	66	–	45	115	130	102	116	103	95
65-69	62	105	–	–	48	259	144	149	166	81
70+	108	116	–	87	72	432	72	105	184	119
Total	43	33	26	16	33	31	68	97	67	50

Table S9.31. *Slave Age-specific Death Rates by Sex and Occupation: Berbice, 1819-22 (Registered Deaths per 1,000)*

Age group	Field Laborers		Domestics		Skilled Tradespeople & Drivers	Stock-keepers	Watchmen	Sick or Disabled, or No Occupation	
	Males	Females	Males	Females	Males	Males	Males	Males	Females
0-4	64	85	–	38	–	–	–	51	54
5-9	8	5	24	–	–	32	–	15	12
10-14	9	10	9	19	–	13	–	10	9
15-19	22	12	17	9	9	40	–	106	18
20-24	23	25	7	9	4	35	–	55	144
25-29	20	21	16	10	16	27	38	86	92
30-34	22	26	28	12	26	47	29	106	84
35-39	28	31	15	31	22	22	30	86	96
40-44	33	32	24	42	39	24	31	80	89
45-49	32	39	38	31	44	79	77	90	81
50-54	45	43	–	32	87	70	108	80	94
55-59	41	46	–	–	49	64	67	98	56
60-64	67	48	–	48	45	–	128	106	105
65-69	77	–	–	–	64	–	–	178	82
70+	105	–	–	–	–	–	–	180	162
Total	25	24	15	17	24	36	56	49	49

Table S9.32. *Seasonality of Slave Deaths by Sex, Rural and Urban: Tobago, 1819-21*

Month	Percentage of Daily Average				
	Males	Females	Rural	Urban	Total
January	87.0	83.5	86.3	65.7	83.7
February	75.5	97.0	85.4	86.2	83.1
March	93.3	68.4	83.1	53.4	79.4
April	102.8	105.5	103.9	110.8	101.6
May	70.9	92.4	80.2	92.3	81.6
June	88.7	80.0	83.5	110.8	88.7
July	106.1	110.9	107.1	131.3	107.4
August	125.1	119.8	120.3	172.4	122.4
September	128.1	121.0	126.8	82.1	127.7
October	129.4	112.1	123.4	78.0	121.9
November	112.7	113.2	112.7	123.1	113.7
December	79.5	95.9	86.9	92.7	88.1
Total Number of Deaths	1,118	951	1,974	95	2,069

Table S9.33. *Seasonality of Slave Deaths by Occupation: Berbice, 1819-22*

Month	Percentage of Daily Average				
	Field Laborers	Domestics	Skilled Tradespeople & Drivers	Sick and Disabled	Total
January	89.7	98.8	67.7	97.3	91.3
February	83.1	30.1	94.3	79.7	80.2
March	90.6	124.6	132.6	108.5	93.6
April	84.8	98.8	197.4	90.9	94.7
May	83.1	55.9	38.3	113.2	88.5
June	123.6	85.9	58.9	100.5	115.0
July	134.6	124.6	85.4	97.3	123.3
August	106.5	43.0	103.1	82.9	96.4
September	107.9	128.9	88.4	127.6	116.8
October	117.5	55.9	85.4	108.5	109.5
November	77.3	214.9	88.4	111.6	93.8
December	92.3	137.5	56.0	82.9	92.6
Total Number of Deaths	1,262	85	124	229	2,064

Table S9.34. *Seasonality of Major Causes of Slave Deaths: Tobago, 1819-21*

| | Percentage of Daily Average | | | | | |
Month	Diarrhea	Dropsy	Whooping Cough	Fever	Tuberculosis	Digestive System Diseases
January	68.8	113.1	177.2	99.6	56.9	54.6
February	42.3	69.6	295.3	117.5	125.7	29.4
March	51.6	84.8	253.7	81.7	38.9	42.0
April	79.4	50.0	240.6	120.0	80.8	113.4
May	34.4	56.5	113.7	114.9	125.7	54.6
June	52.9	80.4	87.5	84.3	80.8	84.0
July	170.7	76.1	28.4	132.8	68.9	79.8
August	128.4	126.1	21.9	140.5	143.7	188.9
September	141.6	189.1	0.0	51.1	188.6	138.5
October	187.9	97.8	0.0	74.1	125.7	146.9
November	162.8	123.9	0.0	109.8	89.8	113.4
December	76.8	132.6	0.0	74.1	77.8	146.9
Total Number of Deaths	276	168	167	143	122	87

Month	Nervous System Diseases	Leprosy	Yaws	Respiratory Diseases	Debility	Old Age	Total
January	79.0	35.9	56.2	226.1	103.8	56.1	83.7
February	88.8	41.9	131.1	121.8	50.1	76.2	83.1
March	93.8	77.8	93.7	52.2	93.1	69.0	79.4
April	49.4	119.8	121.8	173.9	60.9	71.9	101.6
May	64.2	59.9	93.7	104.4	68.0	60.4	81.6
June	133.3	59.9	93.7	52.2	118.2	86.3	88.7
July	64.2	155.7	149.8	52.2	114.6	83.4	107.4
August	157.9	137.7	121.8	173.9	114.6	135.2	122.4
September	64.2	197.6	93.7	121.8	132.5	119.4	127.7
October	143.1	137.7	121.8	0.0	114.6	120.8	121.9
November	133.3	119.8	93.7	121.8	82.4	182.6	113.7
December	29.6	59.9	28.1	0.0	139.7	139.5	88.1
Total Number of Deaths	74	61	38	21	102	254	2,146

Table S9.35. *Seasonality of Major Causes of Slave Deaths: Berbice, 1819-22*

Month	Percentage of Daily Average					
	Diarrhea	Nervous System Diseases	Dropsy	Respiratory Diseases	Tuberculosis	Yaws
January	102.2	66.4	68.8	77.9	50.7	126.6
February	48.1	95.5	98.8	51.1	93.3	126.6
March	67.6	60.2	90.2	95.0	146.6	83.2
April	90.2	118.3	101.0	97.4	88.0	119.3
May	102.2	66.4	118.2	85.2	104.0	68.7
June	124.8	109.9	122.5	153.4	61.3	119.3
July	111.2	147.3	180.5	211.8	112.0	94.0
August	111.2	87.2	96.7	116.9	77.3	104.9
September	124.8	124.5	92.4	121.8	160.0	133.8
October	111.2	134.9	83.8	56.0	93.3	104.9
November	79,7	83.0	79.5	41.4	72.0	61.5
December	121.8	107.9	68.8	85.2	138.6	57.9
Total Number of Deaths	244	176	170	150	137	101

Month	Fever	Leprosy	Digestive System Diseases	Accidents	Debility	Old Age	Total
January	99.3	78.9	123.5	98.9	73.1	166.7	91.3
February	27.8	29.1	75.2	106.5	110.6	111.2	80.2
March	63.5	132.8	123.5	175.0	93.9	154.8	93.6
April	107.2	124.5	0.0	152.2	110.6	107.2	94.7
May	63.5	66.4	155.8	22.8	121.1	103.2	88.5
June	158.8	95.5	53.7	53.3	104.4	91.3	115.0
July	103.2	107.9	69.8	76.1	93.9	75.4	123.3
August	154.8	78.9	123.5	98.9	108.5	51.6	96.4
September	107.2	124.5	145.0	53.3	89.7	131.0	116.8
October	103.2	145.3	139.7	197.8	127.3	51.6	109.5
November	158.8	166.0	123.5	22.8	62.6	79.4	93.8
December	51.6	41.5	69.8	144.6	100.2	75.4	92.6
Total Number of Deaths	92	88	68	48	175	92	2,064

Table S9.36. *Causes of Slave Deaths by Sex, Rural and Urban: Tobago, 1819-21*

| Cause | Percentage of Deaths | | | | | |
| | Rural | | | Urban | | |
	Males	Females	Total	Males	Females	Total
Diarrhea	14.1	13.2	13.7	9.6	5.4	7.9
Dropsy	8.2	7.0	7.6	19.2	13.5	16.9
Whooping cough	7.1	10.0	8.4	1.9	2.7	2.2
Fever	7.1	5.9	6.5	13.5	21.6	16.9
Tuberculosis	6.3	5.2	5.8	7.7	10.8	9.0
Digestive system diseases	4.5	3.9	4.2	3.8	2.7	3.4
Nervous system diseases	4.5	2.3	3.5	5.8	2.7	4.5
Leprosy	3.3	2.7	3.0	1.9	–	1.1
Worms	2.5	3.3	2.9	3.8	5.4	4.5
Accidents	2.4	1.0	1.7	11.5	–	6.7
Yaws	1.9	2.0	1.9	–	2.7	1.1
Tetanus	1.3	1.9	1.6	1.9	–	1.1
Respiratory diseases	0.9	1.2	1.1	–	–	–
Maternity	–	1.9	0.9	–	5.4	2.2
Scarlet fever	0.4	1.1	0.9	–	–	–
Venereal disease	0.5	0.8	0.6	–	–	–
Teething	0.1	0.2	0.2	1.9	–	1.1
Suicide	0.6	–	0.3	–	–	–
Rheumatism	0.3	0.2	0.3	–	–	–
Urinary system diseases	0.3	–	0.2	–	–	–
Neoplasms	–	0.1	0.1	–	–	–
Debility	3.9	6.0	4.8	7.7	8.1	7.9
Old age	11.0	14.7	12.7	1.9	8.1	4.5
Unclassifiable/undefined	18.5	15.3	17.0	7.7	10.8	9.0
Total Number of Deaths	1,061	902	1,963	52	37	89

Table S9.37. *Causes of Slave Deaths: Grenada, 1817-32*
   (Select Parishes)

Cause	Percentage of Deaths					
	1817-19			1830-32		
	Town of St. George	St. Andrew	Grena-dines	Town of St. George	St. Andrew	Grena-dines
Diarrhea	6.2	19.5	6.6	5.2	10.9	2.3
Dropsy	7.5	17.7	15.0	13.0	13.3	6.8
Respiratory diseases	2.1	9.8	2.9	2.6	14.2	4.5
Nervous system diseases	6.8	9.0	11.0	11.3	11.8	10.6
Digestive system diseases	4.8	6.6	5.9	7.8	10.6	11.4
Fever	27.4	6.6	19.4	10.4	10.6	9.1
Tuberculosis	13.0	5.0	7.0	18.3	5.3	2.3
Marasmus	—	4.2	0.7	1.7	4.1	—
Tetanus	0.7	3.4	9.9	0.9	2.4	19.7
Worms	8.2	2.8	5.5	7.0	2.4	4.5
Accidents	3.4	2.8	1.8	8.7	2.4	6.1
Whooping cough	—	2.6	2.6	6.1	5.6	10.6
Leprosy	2.7	2.2	6.6	1.7	2.1	9.1
Scarlet fever	2.7	1.8	—	0.9	0.3	—
Yaws	—	1.4	—	—	0.6	—
Female diseases	—	1.0	0.7	0.9	0.9	0.8
Heart disease	1.4	0.6	—	—	—	0.8
Venereal disease	2.1	0.6	0.7	2.6	1.2	—
Suicide	—	0.6	—	—	0.3	—
Maternity	4.1	0.4	1.5	—	0.3	—
Measles	2.1	0.2	1.5	—	—	—
Neoplasms	—	0.2	—	—	0.3	0.8
Cholera	—	0.2	0.7	—	—	—
Rheumatism	1.4	0.2	—	—	0.6	—
Teething	3.4	0.2	—	0.9	—	0.8
Violence	—	0.2	—	—	—	—
	100.0	100.0	100.0	100.0	100.0	100.0
Total Number of Deaths	198	692	393	144	576	238
Not included above:						
Unclassified, undefined	31	72	20	16	41	9
Mal d'estomac, cachexy	8	36	41	1	72	7
Old age	4	68	44	9	97	47
Debility	9	18	15	3	27	43
Percentage of Total	26.3	28.0	30.5	20.1	41.1	44.5

Table S9.38. *Major Causes of Slave Deaths by Slave-holding Size-group: Tobago, 1819-21 and Berbice, 1819-22*

Cause	1-10 Slaves	11-50 Slaves	51-100 Slaves	101-200 Slaves	201-300 Slaves	301-400 Slaves	401-500 Slaves	Total
				Percentage of Deaths				
Tobago, 1819-21								
Diarrhea	8.2	11.4	20.4	14.1	12.0	11.7	11.9	13.4
Dropsy	9.6	17.7	9.9	8.2	6.7	6.1	4.8	8.0
Whooping cough	9.6	3.8	4.3	7.0	8.4	13.5	4.8	8.1
Fever	15.1	16.5	8.0	6.1	7.2	5.6	2.4	7.0
Tuberculosis	9.6	8.9	4.3	5.5	7.4	4.7	4.8	5.9
Digestive system diseases	5.5	7.6	1.2	4.0	6.2	2.9	4.8	4.3
Nervous system diseases	4.1	2.5	4.9	3.4	4.3	2.9	4.8	3.6
Leprosy	1.4	2.5	1.9	3.2	2.6	2.9	7.1	3.0
Yaws	1.4	1.3	0.6	1.6	1.9	3.5	2.4	1.9
Respiratory diseases	—	2.5	0.6	1.4	0.5	0.6	2.4	1.0
Debility	5.5	3.8	3.1	5.7	4.3	5.6	—	4.9
Old age	5.5	1.3	6.8	13.4	13.2	14.9	16.7	12.4
Other/not classified	24.5	20.2	34.0	26.4	25.3	25.1	33.1	26.5
Total Number of Deaths	73	79	162	951	417	342	42	2,146
Berbice, 1819-22								
Diarrhea	13.5	15.3	12.2	11.6	13.7	12.1	31.1	12.9
Nervous system diseases	14.6	11.0	7.8	9.1	11.2	7.4	2.2	9.3
Dropsy	5.6	14.4	4.4	8.6	9.5	12.1	8.9	9.1
Respiratory diseases	12.4	5.1	9.4	8.6	7.0	5.8	8.9	8.0
Tuberculosis	11.2	10.2	6.1	7.7	5.9	6.2	4.4	7.3
Yaws	—	1.7	6.1	6.9	5.3	3.5	4.4	5.4
Fever	4.5	5.9	4.4	5.6	4.2	3.9	2.2	4.9
Leprosy	5.6	1.7	2.8	3.8	7.0	6.6	4.4	4.7
Digestive system diseases	3.4	3.4	8.9	2.9	5.0	0.8	2.2	3.6
Accidents	3.4	6.8	3.9	1.3	3.1	3.5	—	2.6
Debility	2.2	3.4	7.8	11.3	9.5	8.2	11.1	9.3
Old age	4.5	0.8	3.9	6.0	2.8	6.6	6.7	4.9
Other/not classified	19.1	20.3	22.3	16.6	15.8	23.3	13.5	18.0
Total Number of Deaths	89	118	180	839	358	257	45	2,064

Table S9.39. *Causes of Slave Deaths by Sex, Birthplace and Color:*
Tobago, 1819-21

Cause	Africans		Creoles		Black		Colored		Total
	Males	Females	Males	Females	Males	Females	Males	Females	
Diarrhea	16.6	16.9	10.2	8.3	14.8	13.0	6.6	11.1	13.4
Dropsy	9.7	9.1	7.1	5.0	8.6	7.6	8.5	3.0	8.2
Whooping cough	0.3	0.4	16.4	19.5	6.9	9.4	6.6	12.1	8.1
Fever	6.4	3.1	8.9	10.3	7.2	6.3	9.4	9.1	7.0
Tuberculosis	6.1	5.8	6.9	5.0	6.4	5.3	6.6	6.1	5.9
Digestive system diseases	5.6	4.3	2.9	3.1	4.4	3.9	5.7	2.0	4.2
Nervous system diseases	3.9	1.2	5.8	3.5	4.6	2.5	5.7	1.0	3.6
Leprosy	3.2	3.3	3.3	2.0	3.1	2.8	4.7	1.0	3.0
Worms	–	0.2	6.2	6.8	2.4	3.2	3.8	5.1	3.0
Accidents	2.3	0.4	3.3	1.5	2.6	0.7	3.8	3.0	1.9
Yaws	0.5	0.2	3.8	3.9	1.9	1.9	0.9	3.0	1.9
Tetanus	0.9	1.0	2.0	2.9	1.4	2.1	0.9	–	1.6
Respiratory diseases	0.9	1.2	0.9	1.1	0.9	0.9	0.9	3.0	1.0
Maternity	–	0.8	–	3.5	–	2.0	–	3.0	1.0
Scarlet fever	0.6	1.4	0.9	0.7	0.6	1.1	1.9	1.0	0.8
Venereal disease	0.6	0.8	0.2	0.7	0.5	0.7	–	1.0	0.6
Teething	–	–	0.7	0.4	0.2	0.2	0.9	–	0.2
Suicide	0.6	–	0.2	–	0.5	–	–	–	0.2
Rheumatism	0.5	0.2	–	0.2	0.3	0.1	–	1.0	0.2
Urinary system diseases	0.5	–	–	–	0.2	–	0.9	–	0.1
Neoplasms	–	0.2	–	–	–	0.1	–	–	–
Debility	4.8	7.6	2.9	4.4	4.1	6.3	3.8	4.0	5.0
Old Age	16.9	26.7	1.3	1.8	10.8	14.6	8.5	15.2	12.4
Unclassifiable/undefined	19.3	15.0	16.2	15.2	17.8	15.1	19.8	15.1	16.8
Total Number of Deaths	661	486	451	456	1,006	844	106	99	2,146

Table S9.40. *Causes of Adult Slave Deaths by Sex and Occupation: Berbice, 1819-22 (Slaves Aged 20-50 Years)*

Cause	Percentage of Deaths					
	Males			Females		
	Field Laborers	Skilled Tradespeople & Drivers	Sick and Disabled	Field Laborers	Domestics	Sick and Disabled
Diarrhea	16.6	13.3	8.2	19.2	8.8	6.3
Nervous system diseases	9.4	12.2	1.6	6.7	2.9	9.5
Dropsy	8.0	15.3	9.8	8.6	14.7	6.3
Respiratory diseases	12.6	5.1	3.3	10.9	17.6	3.2
Tuberculosis	9.1	11.2	9.8	11.8	23.5	6.3
Yaws	0.5	–	–	1.0	–	–
Fever	4.0	6.1	1.6	3.8	2.9	–
Leprosy	5.3	–	23.0	2.6	5.9	22.2
Digestive system diseases	4.5	5.1	1.6	3.2	–	1.6
Worms	0.8	–	–	1.3	–	–
Accidents	5.6	9.2	1.6	0.3	–	–
Tetanus	0.8	2.0	–	1.6	2.9	3.2
Venereal disease	1.6	1.0	4.9	2.2	–	9.5
Maternity	–	–	–	4.2	2.9	–
Suicide	1.6	1.0	1.6	0.6	–	–
Neoplasms	–	–	–	1.0	–	3.2
Violence	0.3	1.0	–	0.6	–	–
Female diseases	–	–	–	1.0	2.9	1.6
Rheumatism	0.5	1.0	–	–	–	–
Debility	8.3	5.1	14.8	9.6	5.9	14.3
Old age	0.5	1.0	6.6	1.3	–	3.2
Unclassifiable/undefined	10.0	10.4	11.6	8.5	9.1	9.6
Total Number of Deaths	374	98	61	313	34	63

Table S9.41. *Mean Age of Slaves at Death, by Sex, Birthplace and Cause of Death: Tobago, 1819-21*

Cause	Africans				Creoles			
	Males		Females		Males		Females	
	Mean	S.D.	Mean	S.D.	Mean	S.D.	Mean	S.D.
Diarrhea	46.5	11.7	45.1	9.7	18.4	15.7	17.0	15.0
Dropsy	42.1	10.4	41.0	8.9	18.2	13.8	19.7	12.5
Whooping cough	45.0	7.1	52.0	4.2	2.7	2.6	3.0	4.0
Fever	41.5	8.5	49.0	8.6	11.2	9.4	10.8	11.2
Tuberculosis	43.7	10.1	43.2	12.0	25.3	13.6	26.9	11.4
Digestive system diseases	41.1	9.7	46.0	8.6	27.5	14.9	19.8	17.3
Nervous system diseases	44.0	11.6	44.5	10.7	17.4	13.8	18.8	16.2
Leprosy	41.9	10.4	42.4	10.1	25.3	7.4	27.3	15.4
Worms	−	−	27.0	−	4.8	6.8	4.0	6.9
Accidents	39.0	9.0	29.0	1.4	16.0	11.5	18.4	13.9
Yaws	41.0	20.8	37.0	−	6.1	8.7	1.5	1.6
Tetanus	38.5	9.5	39.6	10.7	19.8	11.5	18.2	15.1
Respiratory diseases	45.5	9.5	38.8	10.8	13.8	9.4	18.0	10.9
Maternity	−	−	34.3	7.6	−	−	26.1	6.5
Scarlet fever	43.0	13.4	51.6	13.7	16.3	12.3	10.3	13.6
Venereal disease	42.3	14.9	47.0	17.4	30.0	−	22.3	3.1
Teething	−	−	−	−	0.5	0.7	0.5	0.5
Suicide	48.8	7.5	−	−	42.0	−	−	−
Rheumatism	56.3	7.8	54.0	−	−	−	19.0	−
Urinary system diseases	47.7	11.2	−	−	−	−	−	−
Neoplasms	−	−	55.0	−	−	−	−	−
Debility	48.0	12.5	51.2	13.8	25.8	18.3	25.2	13.6
Old age	61.3	9.7	58.3	10.7	58.2	11.1	54.0	13.2
Unclassifiable/undefined	41.8	10.8	42.3	11.0	22.2	11.9	25.6	13.3
Total	46.4	12.7	48.1	12.6	16.0	14.7	15.7	15.3

Table S9.42. *Mean Age of Slaves at Death, by Sex, Birthplace and Cause of Death: Berbice, 1819-22*

Cause	Africans				Creoles			
	Males		Females		Males		Females	
	Mean	S.D.	Mean	S.D.	Mean	S.D.	Mean	S.D.
Diarrhea	38.5	11.5	36.7	8.7	14.2	18.5	15.4	17.6
Nervous system diseases	37.1	9.7	35.0	7.3	14.8	15.8	11.3	13.8
Dropsy	39.1	8.9	40.7	11.4	14.7	14.7	13.5	14.4
Respiratory diseases	38.1	9.0	36.2	11.2	18.1	16.5	20.1	16.2
Tuberculosis	35.8	8.1	40.1	8.8	20.4	16.8	28.7	12.9
Yaws	38.5	3.5	29.4	17.4	2.1	3.6	2.0	3.1
Fever	34.4	9.1	39.1	13.9	14.1	14.2	7.8	12.0
Leprosy	39.1	7.8	37.2	6.9	33.8	21.1	29.0	21.2
Digestive system diseases	40.9	9.6	34.0	4.6	18.4	19.5	8.9	9.1
Worms	37.0	10.5	37.7	1.2	2.6	3.0	3.1	4.7
Accidents	37.3	7.7	57.3	15.2	26.3	15.8	6.4	5.8
Tetanus	39.5	17.7	32.5	5.8	8.5	9.0	13.3	11.9
Venereal disease	34.5	10.0	36.8	4.4	30.8	25.0	39.2	18.9
Maternity	–	–	27.1	3.8	–	–	21.3	9.6
Suicide	43.0	12.5	23.0	–	27.3	9.6	29.0	–
Scarlet fever	32.0	11.5	32.5	4.9	9.0	11.3	24.0	41.6
Neoplasms	39.0	–	39.2	3.6	14.0	4.2	29.7	13.7
Violence	46.5	2.1	37.0	–	3.0	–	–	–
Female diseases	–	–	30.0	8.9	–	–	26.0	–
Rheumatism	47.7	15.9	–	–	28.0	–	–	–
Cholera	–	–	–	–	23.0	–	–	–
Heart diseases	–	–	–	–	3.0	–	15.0	–
Teething	–	–	–	–	0.5	–	0.5	–
Diphtheria	–	–	–	–	–	–	2.0	–
Urinary system diseases	–	–	–	–	29.0	–	–	–
Debility	45.8	13.1	43.0	13.3	23.5	23.9	31.8	26.5
Old age	58.4	13.2	59.2	9.9	63.9	10.8	53.2	19.4
Unclassifiable/undefined	39.0	8.5	35.4	8.7	23.3	24.0	19.4	17.9
Total	39.8	11.3	39.8	12.2	16.0	18.7	16.3	18.9

Table S9.43. *Age-specific Slave Death Rates by Major Causes of Death: Tobago, 1819-21 and Berbice, 1819-22 (Registered Deaths per 1,000)*

Cause	Age group							
	0-9	10-19	20-29	30-39	40-49	50-59	60-	Total
Tobago, 1819-21								
Diarrhea	3.4	1.9	3.6	5.6	10.7	15.1	10.3	6.0
Dropsy	2.0	1.3	3.6	3.9	6.3	6.4	2.5	3.6
Whooping cough	17.1	0.4	0.1	–	0.3	0.6	–	3.6
Fever	5.0	2.5	2.1	2.5	3.3	2.9	2.1	3.2
Tuberculosis	0.8	0.9	3.5	3.2	4.5	4.1	3.7	2.7
Digestive system diseases	1.0	0.4	0.8	2.4	4.2	3.8	1.2	1.9
Nervous system diseases	1.5	1.3	1.4	1.5	2.0	2.3	2.1	1.6
Leprosy	0.2	0.4	1.8	1.8	2.9	1.5	0.8	1.3
Worms	5.7	0.3	0.1	0.2	–	–	–	1.3
Accidents	0.9	0.6	1.0	0.9	1.5	–	0.4	0.9
Yaws	3.4	0.1	0.3	0.3	–	–	0.4	0.8
Tetanus	0.8	0.6	0.8	0.7	0.8	0.9	–	0.7
Respiratory diseases	0.3	0.3	0.6	0.6	0.5	0.6	0.4	0.5
Venereal disease	–	0.1	0.4	0.4	0.2	0.3	0.8	0.3
Suicide	–	–	–	–	0.6	–	0.4	0.1
Debility	0.5	1.1	1.1	1.8	3.0	5.8	9.0	2.2
Old age	–	–	–	0.6	4.5	20.4	61.5	5.5
Berbice, 1819-22								
Diarrhea	3.5	0.6	2.7	3.9	5.0	6.7	7.2	3.4
Nervous system diseases	3.0	2.5	1.8	2.2	2.9	3.8	2.2	2.5
Dropsy	2.6	1.2	1.8	2.0	4.3	5.0	3.6	2.4
Respiratory diseases	1.3	1.2	1.9	2.6	3.3	2.9	3.6	2.1
Tuberculosis	0.5	0.7	1.9	3.0	2.8	2.9	2.9	1.9
Yaws	6.2	0.2	0.1	0.2	0.2	–	–	1.4
Fever	2.4	1.1	0.1	1.0	0.2	2.5	1.4	1.3
Leprosy	0.3	0.2	0.5	1.9	2.8	3.3	1.4	1.2
Digestive system diseases	1.2	0.4	0.7	0.9	1.5	1.7	1.4	1.0
Worms	3.3	0.3	0.2	0.2	0.1	–	–	0.8
Accidents	0.3	0.4	0.4	0.8	1.3	0.8	1.4	0.7
Tetanus	1.2	0.6	0.3	0.4	0.2	0.4	0.7	0.6
Venereal disease	0.1	0.1	0.4	0.6	0.8	1.3	1.4	0.5
Suicide	–	0.1	0.4	0.2	0.6	0.4	0.7	0.3
Debility	1.5	0.3	1.2	2.2	3.8	8.7	24.5	2.4
Old age	–	–	–	0.2	1.1	10.4	36.7	1.3

Table S9.44. *Age-specific Slave Birth Rates by Birthplace: St. Lucia, 1815-19, Tobago, 1819-21, and Berbice, 1819-22 (Registered Births per 1,000 Females)*

Age group	St. Lucia, 1815-19			Tobago, 1819-21			Berbice, 1819-22		
	Africans	Creoles	Total	Africans	Creoles	Total	Africans	Creoles	Total
10-14	–	10	10	–	7	7	–	13	13
15-19	29	50	48	–	86	85	98	125	124
20-24	41	66	62	83	129	123	107	142	127
25-29	49	66	63	75	91	88	101	137	109
30-34	24	60	50	76	80	78	82	92	84
35-39	39	41	40	45	83	59	63	83	66
40-44	8	25	18	27	41	30	27	30	28
45-49	10	20	16	11	11	11	15	14	15
50-54	5	6	5	8	18	9	3	–	2
General Fertility Rate	28	55	48	47	91	71	73	119	87
Total Number of Births	107	622	729	284	670	954	972	692	1,664

Table S9.45. *Age-specific Slave Birth Rates by Color and Birthplace: St. Lucia, 1815-19, Tobago, 1819-21, and Berbice, 1819-22 (Registered Births per 1,000 Females)*

Age group	St. Lucia, 1815-19			Tobago, 1819-21			Berbice, 1819-22		
	Africans	Black Creoles	Colored Creoles	Africans	Black Creoles	Colored Creoles	Africans	Black Creoles	Colored Creoles
10-14	–	10	11	–	7	9	–	14	–
15-19	29	51	40	–	82	171	98	127	117
20-24	41	65	70	83	123	269	107	153	49
25-29	49	67	53	75	90	136	101	140	114
30-34	24	62	42	76	79	100	82	93	98
35-39	39	41	44	45	81	367	63	87	–
40-44	8	24	36	27	41	–	27	30	40
45-49	10	19	34	11	11	–	15	16	–
50-54	5	7	–	8	18	–	3	–	–
General Fertility Rate	28	55	54	47	88	184	73	120	80
Total Number of Births	107	535	83	284	628	38	972	661	34

Table S9.46. *Age-specific Slave Birth Rates by Birthplace, Rural and Urban: St. Lucia, 1815-19, and Tobago, 1819-21 (Registered Births per 1,000 Females)*

Age group	Rural Slaves			Urban Slaves		
	Africans	Creoles	Total	Africans	Creoles	Total
St. Lucia, 1815-19						
10-14	–	11	11	–	4	4
15-19	23	52	50	68	40	41
20-24	32	67	62	70	59	61
25-29	47	73	68	55	30	38
30-34	22	62	51	33	47	44
35-39	40	45	43	32	17	22
40-44	7	24	17	17	34	29
45-49	11	23	18	–	–	–
50-54	5	6	6	–	–	–
General Fertility Rate	26	58	50	41	38	39
Total Number of Births	84	560	644	23	62	85
Tobago, 1819-21						
10-14	–	7	7	–	8	8
15-19	–	86	85	–	71	67
20-24	95	126	123	55	141	106
25-29	89	91	90	64	71	66
30-34	76	79	78	64	61	63
35-39	47	85	62	18	–	15
40-44	26	42	30	22	–	19
45-49	12	12	12	–	–	–
50-54	8	19	10	–	–	–
General Fertility Rate	47	91	72	43	78	56
Total Number of Births	254	632	886	28	30	58

Table S9.47. *Age-specific Slave Birth Rates by Slave-holding Size-group: St. Lucia, 1815-19, Tobago, 1819-21, and Berbice, 1819-22 (Registered Births per 1,000 Females)*

Age group	1-10 Slaves	11-50 Slaves	51-100 Slaves	101-200 Slaves	201-300 Slaves	301-400 Slaves	401-500 Slaves	Total
St. Lucia, 1815-19								
10-14	7	9	6	14	–	100	–	10
15-19	56	38	55	54	47	–	–	48
20-24	45	61	66	68	103	68	–	62
25-29	40	58	57	82	72	191	–	63
30-34	22	38	73	59	57	137	–	50
35-39	18	41	36	50	53	133	–	40
40-44	16	13	20	20	33	–	–	18
45-49	12	11	20	24	12	–	–	16
50-54	7	7	5	–	–	46	–	5
General Fertility Rate	36	44	51	59	56	113	–	48
Total Number of Births	112	206	170	153	63	25	–	729
Tobago, 1819-21								
10-14	11	11	–	6	10	3	14	7
15-19	76	62	52	100	98	58	97	85
20-24	112	96	97	135	160	106	138	123
25-29	87	60	54	91	114	88	92	88
30-34	67	76	50	70	113	71	144	78
35-39	33	31	33	51	86	83	24	59
40-44	37	20	10	33	23	32	94	30
45-49	–	–	11	4	24	16	–	11
50-54	–	–	–	11	17	6	–	9
General Fertility Rate	72	61	48	75	90	68	87	71
Total Number of Births	64	50	45	409	204	156	26	954
Berbice, 1819-22								
10-14	18	15	8	9	26	12	25	13
15-19	114	109	100	112	150	164	192	124
20-24	73	122	102	128	138	184	104	127
25-29	90	87	92	117	138	144	49	109
30-34	37	71	43	92	118	123	37	84
35-39	21	39	64	63	89	79	–	66
40-44	13	52	35	13	37	44	–	28
45-49	27	–	–	10	33	12	–	15
50-54	–	–	–	–	–	–	4	2
General Fertility Rate	66	77	71	85	105	114	56	87
Total Number of Births	89	97	186	681	324	264	23	1,664

Table S9.48. *Age-specific Slave Birth Rates by Occupation and Birthplace: St. Lucia, 1815-19, and Berbice, 1819-22 (Registered Births per 1,000 Females)*

Age group	Field Laborers			Domestics		
	Africans	Creoles	Total	Africans	Creoles	Total
St. Lucia, 1815-19						
10-14	–	17	17	–	10	10
15-19	16	49	47	51	57	56
20-24	32	72	66	59	57	57
25-29	54	75	72	46	53	51
30-34	26	71	58	21	45	39
35-39	41	53	49	28	25	25
40-44	8	21	15	14	25	22
45-49	10	29	19	17	7	10
50-54	7	8	7	–	8	7
General Fertility Rate	27	61	52	36	50	45
Total Number of Births	441	76	517	148	28	176
Berbice, 1819-22						
10-14	–	13	13	–	17	17
15-19	64	136	134	273	167	174
20-24	135	168	152	99	155	132
25-29	117	162	127	88	130	100
30-34	97	118	100	83	72	81
35-39	71	97	74	40	74	51
40-44	29	41	31	47	37	43
45-49	20	31	22	13	22	16
50-54	–	–	–	–	–	–
General Fertility Rate	86	138	101	74	132	100
Total Number of Births	847	523	1,370	120	168	288

Table S9.49. *Seasonality of Slave Births: Dominica, 1817-32, Tobago, 1819-2* *and Berbice, 1819-22 (Percentage of Daily Average)*

Month of Birth	Dominica, 1817-32			Tobago, 1819-21			Berbice, 1819-22		
	Sugar Plantations	Coffee Plantations	Total	Rural	Urban	Total	Field Laborers	Domestics	Total
January	100	68	93	87	122	88	84	110	88
February	128	140	131	94	156	97	75	64	77
March	82	150	98	77	142	81	84	116	86
April	118	61	105	70	105	74	95	72	97
May	107	93	104	87	81	85	95	128	108
June	121	143	126	99	84	99	113	72	106
July	87	93	87	107	0	99	116	116	110
August	113	125	117	119	81	117	99	81	96
September	139	118	134	138	42	134	118	150	116
October	48	47	48	120	.41	113	104	93	103
November	82	82	82	101	189	105	121	96	115
December	79	82	80	101	163	108	96	99	98
Total Number of Births	342	102	444	883	58	941	1,185	203	1,581

SECTION 10

Manumissions

Table S10.1.   *Sources: P.P.,* 1823, Vol. XVIII (89), "Slave Population," pp. 6, 36, 46, 49, 65-69, 75-79, 105-107, 110, 114, and 118; *ibid.,* (347), pp.8-129, 146, and 151; *P.P.,* 1833, Vol. XXVI (539), "Slave Registration," pp.2-5; *ibid.,* (700), "Slave Population," p.2; supplemented by various calculations from T.71 for particular colonies.

Notes: Data from the slave registration returns (T.71) have been used wherever available. All data for years preceding registration are for calendar years, and overlap with the initial registration year has been distinguished. The sources do not always agree: see Chapter 10.

Table S10.2.   *Source:* T.71/520-27.

Note: "Bridgetown" comprises all slave-holdings in St. Michael lacking field laborers.

Table S10.3.   *Sources:* T.71/260, linked to locations in T.71/740-42 (Valuers' Returns).

Table S10.4.   *Source:* T.71/363.

Table S10.5.   *Source:* T.71/520-27.

Note: Bridgetown defined as for Table S10.2.

Table S10.6.   *Source:* T.71/376-81.

Table S10.7.   *Source:* T.71/520-27.

                Note: Bridgetown defined as for Table S10.2.

Table S10.1. *Manumissions of Slaves by Sex and Colony, 1808-34*

Colony	Period (Months)	Number Manumitted			Slaves Manumitted per 1,000 per annum		
		Males	Females	Total	Males	Females	Total
Barbados							
1808-10	36	145	250	395	n.a.	n.a.	1.7
1811-13	36	102	176	278	n.a.	n.a.	1.2
1814-16	36	167	244	411	n.a.	n.a.	1.8
1817	12	67	98	165	1.9	2.3	2.1
1817-20	36	108	142	250	1.0	1.1	1.1
1820-23	36	131	166	297	1.2	1.3	1.3
1823-26	36	126	196	322	1.1	1.5	1.3
1826-29	36	212	458	670	1.9	3.5	2.7
1829-32	36	n.c.	n.c.	1,089	n.c.	n.c.	4.4
1832-34	22	292	450	742	4.2	5.6	4.9
St. Kitts							
1808-10	36	1	9	10	n.a.	n.a.	0.2
1811-13	36	4	5	9	n.a.	n.a.	0.1
1814-16	36	98	116	214	n.a.	n.a.	3.5
1817	12	27	65	92	2.8	6.2	4.6
1817-22	55	62	155	217	1.3	3.3	2.4
1822-25	36	98	167	265	3.5	5.4	4.5
1825-28	36	101	142	243	3.6	4.7	4.2
1828-31	36	83	160	243	3.0	5.3	4.2
1831-34	36	125	161	286	4.7	5.6	5.1
Nevis							
1808-10	36	3	1	4	n.a.	n.a.	0.1
1811-13	36	4	3	7	n.a.	n.a.	0.2
1814-16	36	16	21	37	n.a.	n.a.	1.3
1817	12	4	5	9	0.9	1.0	0.9
1817-22	54	15	27	42	0.7	1.3	1.0
1822-25	36	11	27	38	0.8	1.9	1.4
1825-28	36	28	33	61	2.0	2.3	2.2
1828-31	36	29	37	66	2.1	2.7	2.4
1831-34	36	25	31	56	n.a.	n.a.	2.1
Antigua							
1808-10	36	98	178	276	n.a.	n.a.	2.5
1811-13	36	105	207	312	n.a.	n.a.	3.0
1814-16	36	149	242	391	n.a.	n.a.	3.9
1817	12	74	137	211	5.0	8.1	6.6
1817-21	48	69	139	208	1.2	2.1	1.7
1821-24	36	104	114	218	2.4	2.4	2.4
1824-28	42	93	135	228	1.9	2.5	2.2
1828-32	45	107	207	314	2.1	3.6	2.9

Table S10.1. *Manumissions by Colony, 1808-34 (continued)*

Colony	Period (Months)	Number Manumitted			Slaves Manumitted per 1,000 per annum		
		Males	Females	Total	Males	Females	Total
Montserrat							
1808-10	36	30	55	85	n.a.	n.a.	4.2
1811-13	36	38	58	96	n.a.	n.a.	4.7
1814-16	36	35	47	82	n.a.	n.a.	4.1
1817	12	9	12	21	3.0	3.4	3.2
1817-21	48	16	24	40	1.3	1.7	1.5
1821-24	36	13	19	32	1.5	1.8	1.7
1824-28	48	12	32	44	1.0	2.4	1.8
1828-31	36	13	33	46	1.5	3.3	2.4
Virgin Islands							
1808-10	36	n.a.	n.a.	60	n.a.	n.a.	2.6
1811-13	36	n.a.	n.a.	22	n.a.	n.a.	1.0
1814-16	36	n.a.	n.a.	57	n.a.	n.a.	2.7
1817-18	24	n.a.	n.a.	94	n.a.	n.a.	6.8
1818-22	48	35	51	86	2.8	3.6	3.2
1822-25	36	34	49	83	4.1	5.1	4.7
1825-28	36	43	47	90	5.7	5.4	5.5
1828-31	36	36	35	71	4.9	4.2	4.5
1831-34	36	28	47	75	3.9	5.7	4.9
Jamaica							
1817-20	36	366	650	1,016	0.7	1.3	1.0
1820-23	36	371	550	921	0.7	1.1	0.9
1823-26	36	346	611	957	0.7	1.2	1.0
1826-29	36	362	755	1,117	0.8	1.5	1.1
1829-32	36	558	804	1,362	1.2	1.6	1.4
Dominica							
1808-10	36	33	73	106	n.a.	n.a.	1.8
1811-13	36	73	129	202	n.a.	n.a.	3.6
1814-16	36	74	142	216	n.a.	n.a.	3.9
1817	12	33	52	85	3.8	5.6	4.7
1817-20	36	47	66	113	1.9	2.4	2.2
1820-23	36	49	54	103	2.1	2.1	2.1
1823-26	36	74	132	206	3.3	5.4	4.4
1826-29	36	109	185	294	5.0	7.8	6.5
1829-32	36	107	160	267	5.1	7.0	6.1

Table S10.1. *Manumissions by Colony, 1808-34 (continued)*

Colony	Period (Months)	Number Manumitted			Slaves Manumitted per 1,000 per annum		
		Males	Females	Total	Males	Females	Total
St. Lucia							
1815-19	38	29	32	61	1.3	1.2	1.2
1819-22	36	22	47	69	1.1	2.0	1.6
1822-25	36	57	127	184	3.0	5.7	4.5
1825-28	36	77	142	219	4.1	6.4	5.3
1828-31	36	151	215	366	8.1	9.8	9.0
1831-34	36	n.c.	n.c.	n.c.	n.c.	n.c.	n.c.
St. Vincent							
1817-22	57	46	68	114	0.8	1.2	1.0
1822-25	36	36	71	107	1.0	1.9	1.5
1825-28	36	74	79	153	2.1	2.2	2.1
1828-31	36	51	50	101	1.5	1.4	1.4
1831-34	36	n.a.	n.a.	n.a.	n.a.	n.a.	n.a.
Grenada							
1817-19	32	79	112	191	2.2	3.0	2.6
1820-22	36	62	104	166	1.6	2.6	2.1
1823-25	36	112	211	323	3.1	5.4	4.3
1826-28	36	97	168	265	2.7	4.4	3.6
1829-31	36	105	176	281	3.0	4.7	3.9
1832-33	24	64	74	138	2.8	3.1	2.9
Tobago							
1808-10	36	37	72	109	n.a.	n.a.	2.0
1811-13	36	36	78	114	n.a.	n.a.	2.2
1814-16	36	12	26	38	n.a.	n.a.	0.8
1817-19	36	5	10	15	n.a.	n.a.	0.3
1820-22	36	16	30	46	0.8	1.3	1.1
1823-25	36	20	26	46	1.0	1.2	1.1
1826-28	36	9	20	29	0.5	1.0	0.7
1829-31	36	21	44	65	1.2	2.2	1.7
1832-33	24	18	45	63	1.7	3.6	2.7
Trinidad							
1808-10	36	42	81	123	n.a.	n.a.	1.6
1811-12	24	60	108	168	n.a.	n.a.	3.2
1813	12	44	59	103	3.1	5.1	4.0
1813-16	33	94	146	240	2.4	4.6	3.5
1816-19	36	151	235	386	3.7	7.2	5.2
1819-22	36	190	277	467	4.8	8.9	6.6
1822-25	36	182	259	441	4.6	8.1	6.1
1825-28	36	177	241	418	4.5	7.2	5.8
1828-31	36	86	174	260	n.c.	n.c.	3.8
1831-34	38	168	182	350	n.c.	n.c.	5.1

Table S10.1. *Manumissions by Colony, 1808-34 (continued)*

Colony	Period (Months)	Number Manumitted			Slaves Manumitted per 1,000 per annum		
		Males	Females	Total	Males	Females	Total
Demerara-Essequibo							
1808-10	36	5	22	27	n.a.	n.a.	0.1
1811-13	36	22	50	72	n.a.	n.a.	0.3
1814-16	36	64	135	199	n.a.	n.a.	0.8
1817	12	12	29	41	0.3	0.9	0.5
1817-20	36	n.a.	n.a.	36	n.a.	n.a.	0.2
1820-23	36	n.a.	n.a.	72	n.a.	n.a.	0.3
1823-26	36	n.a.	n.a.	132	n.a.	n.a.	0.6
1826-29	36	100	154	254	0.9	1.6	1.2
1829-32	36	187	272	459	1.7	2.9	2.3
Berbice							
1808-10	36	n.a.	n.a.	17	n.a.	n.a.	0.2
1811-13	36	n.a.	n.a.	20	n.a.	n.a.	0.3
1814-16	36	n.a.	n.a.	30	n.a.	n.a.	0.4
1817-19	36	n.a.	n.a.	72	n.a.	n.a.	1.0
1819-22	36	3	15	18	0.1	0.5	0.3
1822-25	36	12	20	32	0.3	0.7	0.5
1825-28	36	47	56	103	1.4	1.9	1.6
1828-31	36	49	69	118	1.5	2.4	1.9
1831-34	36	n.c.	n.c.	n.c.	n.c.	n.c.	n.c.
Bahamas							
1808-10	36	37	55	92	n.a.	n.a.	3.1
1811-13	36	40	39	79	n.a.	n.a.	2.6
1814-16	36	68	91	159	n.a.	n.a.	5.0
1817-19	36	64	109	173	n.a.	n.a.	5.3
1820-22	36	74	74	148	n.a.	n.a.	4.5
1822-25	36	35	49	84	2.3	3.3	2.8
1825-28	36	52	66	118	3.7	4.8	4.2
1828-31	36	n.c.	n.c.	190	n.c.	n.c.	6.7
1831-34	42	206	187	393	12.2	10.7	11.4
Anguilla							
1827-31	60	37	72	109	6.2	10.3	8.4
1831-34	30	12	20	32	4.1	5.8	5.1
Barbuda							
1817-21	48	–	–	–	–	–	–
1821-24	36	–	–	–	–	–	–
1824-28	42	n.c.	n.c.	1	n.c.	n.c.	0.6
1828-32	45	2	–	2	2.5	–	1.1

Table S11.7. *Agricultural Production by Parish: Grenada,*
1819 and 1831

Parish	Sugar (Lbs.)	Rum (Gallons)	Molasses (Gallons)	Cotton (Lbs.)	Coffee (Lbs.)	Cocoa (Lbs.)
1819						
St. George	3,347,137	162,281	19,528	53,948	26,256	6,700
St. John	1,898,592	90,694.	7,670	–	22,387	75,180
St. Mark	1,360,526	60,068	13,287	–	17,785	50,993
St. Patrick	7,756,516	369,560	3,476	48,152	960	–
St. Andrew	7,755,812	368,986	6,965	600	1,360	20,211
St. David	2,453,678	139,010	1,100	4,500	2,306	330
Total	24,572,261	1,190,599	52,026	107,200	71,054	153,414
1831						
St. George	3,179,916	122,422	56,382	7,149	9,839	20,022
St. John	913,247	29,450	7,880	–	7,852	148,223
St. Mark	958,276	34,533	11,784	–	5,287	125,454
St. Patrick	6,214,350	275,891	3,997	600	500	–
St. Andrew	6,756,021	303,592	24,955	–	1,500	39,670
St. David	1,853,443	114,550	6,368	–	1,144	4,534
Total	19,875,253	880,438	111,366	7,749	26,122	337,903

Table S11.8. *Land Use by Crop: Trinidad, 1808, 1824 and 1832*

Crop	Acres		
	1808	1824	1832
Cane	13,976	22,425	27,724
Cocoa		9,369	10,380
Coffee		1,903	1,200
Cotton	1,740	669	146
Provisions	7,897	5,997	16,004
Negro grounds		10,010	
Pasture	9,260	11,974	10,694
Total	32,873	62,347	66,148

Table S11.9. *Distribution of Slaves by Crop and Parish: Demerara-Essequibo, 1832*

| Parish | Percentage of Slaves | | | | | | | Number of Slaves |
	Sugar	Cotton	Coffee	Cattle	Plantains	Timber	Urban	
Demerara								
St. Mary	74.7	22.1	–	3.2	–	–	–	6,301
St. Paul	78.1	19.7	–	2.2	–	–	–	8,772
St. George & St. Andrew	12.1	–	3.7	–	–	–	84.2	8,033
St. Matthew	88.5	–	11.5	–	–	–	–	5,604
St. Mark	66.0	8.8	32.3	–	–	1.7	–	4,633
St. Swithin	90.3	–	–	–	0.9	–	–	3,910
St. Luke	94.4	–	4.7	0.6	–	0.3	–	5,535
	68.5	8.1	6.3	1.0	0.1	0.2	15.8	42,788
Essequibo								
St. Peter	99.5	–	–	–	–	0.5	–	5,887
St. James	99.8	–	–	–	–	0.2	–	4,166
St. John	96.9	–	2.4	–	–	0.7	–	4,617
Trinity	94.4	4.8	0.7	–	–	0.1	–	8,059
	97.2	1.7	0.7	–	–	0.4	–	22,729
Total	78.5	5.9	4.4	0.7	0.0	0.2	10.3	65.617

Table S11.10. *Land Use by District: Berbice, 1832*

| District | Number of Holdings | | | |
	Sugar	Coffee	Cotton	Cattle Farms, Plantains, etc.
Corentyne Coast	6	–	2	1
East Coast	–	–	1	–
East Coast Canal	2	–	–	–
Canje Creek	8	6	–	–
East Bank	6	17	–	–
West Bank	3	17	–	–
West Coast	6	–	5	1
Total	31	40	8	2

Table S11.11. *Agricultural Production by Island: Bahamas, 1832*

Island	Cotton (Tons)	Indian and Guinea Corn ('00 Bushels)	Potatoes and Yams ('00 Lbs.)	Cassava and Arrow-root ('00 Lbs.)	Ochras ('00 Lbs.)	Cattle	Sheep and Goats
New Providence	–	8	17	100	150	300	1,000
Turk's Island	–	10	–	5	–	240	100
Caicos	–	5	3	7	10	300	700
Eleuthera	4	100	700	300	80	200	500
Crooked Island	5	20	35	20	10	350	400
Rum Key	5	17	22	10	7	250	1,000
Watling's Island	–	15	17	5	6	150	1,000
Long Island	11	15	85	7	30	1,000	700
Exuma	12	25	45	3	17	200	500
Heneagua, Mayaguana, etc.	3	15	27	5	7	25	50
Grand Bahama & Berry Island	–	45	17	11	45	50	100
Andros Island	–	17	25	12	17	–	40
Ragged Island	–	1	4	3	7	100	200
St. Salvador	2	20	17	17	60	550	1,500
Abaco	–	22	200	10	85	–	50
Harbour Island	–	–	–	–	–	50	50
Total	42	335	1,214	515	531	3,765	7,890

Notes

CHAPTER 1

1. For comparative studies see Cedric A. Yeo, "The Development of the Roman Plantation and Marketing of Farm Products," *Finanzarchiv* 13 (1952):321–42; Frederick Cooper, *Plantation Slavery on the East Coast of Africa* (1977); James L. Watson, ed., *Asian and African Systems of Slavery* (1980); Paul Lovejoy, "Plantations in the Economy of the Sokoto Caliphate," *Journal of African History* 19 (1978):341–68; Suzanne Miers and Igor Kopytoff, eds., *Slavery in Africa* (1977); Sidney M. Greenfield, "Plantations, Sugar Cane and Slavery," *Historical Reflections-Réflexions Historiques* 6 (1979):85–119.

2. M. I. Finley, *Ancient Slavery and Modern Ideology* (1980), p. 66.

3. Theda Skocpol and Margaret Somers, "The Uses of Comparative History in Macrosocial Inquiry," *Comparative Studies in Society and History* 22 (1980):174–97.

4. See Joseph C. Miller, *Slavery: A Comparative Teaching Bibliography* (Waltham, Mass., 1977), and subsequent updates in the journal *Slavery and Abolition*.

5. See especially Frank Tannenbaum, *Slave and Citizen* (1946); Carl Degler, *Neither Black Nor White* (1971); Herbert Klein, *Slavery in the Americas* (1967); H. Hoetink, *Slavery and Race Relations in the Americas* (1973); Laura Foner and Eugene D. Genovese, eds., *Slavery in the New World* (Englewood Cliffs, N.J., 1969); David Brion Davis, *The Problem of Slavery in Western Culture* (1966), pp. 223–61.

6. Eugene D. Genovese, *In Red and Black* (1968), p. 159.

7. Franklin W. Knight, *Slave Society in Cuba during the Nineteenth Century* (1970), pp. 193–94.

8. Herbert G. Gutman, *Slavery and the Numbers Game: A Critique of* Time on the Cross (1975); Paul A. David et al., *Reckoning with Slavery* (1976); Eugene D. Genovese, *Roll, Jordan, Roll* (1974); Marvin Harris, *Patterns of Race in the Americas* (New York, 1974), pp. 71–74; Al-Tony Gilmore, ed., *Revisiting Blassingame's* The Slave Community: *The Scholars Respond* (Westport, Conn., 1978).

9. David Lowenthal, *West Indian Societies* (1972), p. 40

10. Michael Craton, "Hobbesian or Panglossian? The Two Extremes of Slave Conditions in the British Caribbean, 1783 to 1834," *William and Mary Quarterly* 35 (1978):324–56; Richard S. Dunn, "A Tale of Two Plantations: Slave Life at Mesopotamia in Jamaica and Mount Airy in Virginia, 1799 to 1828," ibid., 34 (1977):32–65.

11. Based on data in Philip D. Curtin, *The Atlantic Slave Trade* (1969), pp. 34, 78, 85; Herbert S. Klein, *The Middle Passage* (1978), p. 117; Robert William Fogel and Stanley L. Engerman, *Time on the Cross* (1974), 1:29.

12. T.71/678–1 (bundle 16), 684, 851; *P.P.*, 1835, vol. 51 (235), "Slavery Abolition Proceedings," p. 289. See Cyril Outerbridge Packwood, *Chained on the Rock: Slavery in Bermuda* (1975); James E. Smith, *Slavery in Bermuda* (1976); Burton Benedict, "Slavery and Indenture in Mauritius and Seychelles," in Watson, *Asian and African Systems of Slavery;* Moses D. Nwulia, *The History of Slavery in Mauritius and the Seychelles, 1810–1875* (1981); Richard Elphick and Hermann Giliomee, eds., *The Shaping of South African Society, 1652–1820* (Cape Town, 1979).

13. But see William Law Mathieson, *British Slavery and Its Abolition* (1926); Michael Craton, *Sinews of Empire* (1974); William A.

Green, *British Slave Emancipation* (1976);
Eric Williams, *From Columbus to Castro*
(1970), pp. 282–85; idem, *History of the
People of Trinidad and Tobago* (1964), pp.
83–85.

14. Orlando Patterson, *The Sociology of
Slavery* (1967), p. 10; Edward Brathwaite, *The
Development of Creole Society in Jamaica,
1770–1820* (1971), pp. vii, 307. See also
B. W. Higman, *Slave Population and
Economy in Jamaica, 1807–1834* (1976).

15. Edward Brathwaite, *Contradictory
Omens* (1974), pp. 11, 67 n. 13.

16. Elsa V. Goveia, *Slave Society in the
British Leeward Islands at the End of the
Eighteenth Century* (1965), pp. vii, 311–12.

17. O. Nigel Bolland, *The Formation of a
Colonial Society* (1977), pp. 53, 85.

18. Bernard Marshall, *Society and Economy
in the British Windward Islands, 1763–1823*
(PhD. diss., University of the West Indies,
1972); D. Gail Saunders, *The Slave
Population of the Bahamas, 1783–1834*
(Master's thesis, University of the West
Indies, 1978). Jerome Handler is currently
completing a study of slavery in Barbados,
Gerald Friedman is working on the Trinidad
registration data, and Alvin Thompson is
working on Guyana.

19. Stanley L. Engerman, "Some Economic
and Demographic Comparisons of United
States and British West Indian Slavery,"
Economic History Review 29 (1976):258–75.

CHAPTER 2

1. Lowell Joseph Ragatz, *A Guide for the
Study of British Caribbean History,
1763–1834* (1932); E. C. Baker, *A Guide to
Records in the Leeward Islands* (1965); idem,
A Guide to Records in the Windward Islands
(1968); M. J. Chandler, *A Guide to Records in
Barbados* (1965); Jerome S. Handler, *A
Guide to Source Materials for the Study of
Barbados History, 1627–1834* (1971).

2. Betty Fladeland, "Abolitionist Pressures
on the Concert of Europe, 1814–22," *Journal
of Modern History* 38 (1966):355–73; D. J.
Murray, *The West Indies and the Development
of Colonial Government, 1801–1834* (1965);
Parliamentary Debates, 1st ser., vol. 17, pp.
659–89: 15 June 1810; vol. 19, pp. 233–40: 5
Mar. 1811.

3. C.O. 295/28, f. 208: James Stephen to
Robert Peel, 17 Jan. 1812; C.O. 295/28, f.
250: Order in Council, 26 Mar. 1812.

4. T.71 (Public Record Office, London).
Complete sets of the original registers survive
in Jamaica, the Bahamas, and Belize, and
incomplete sets in Grenada, Tobago,
Dominica, and St. Kitts.

5. C.O. 295/28, f. 148: Monro to
Bathurst, 4 Sept. 1812; f. 154: Murray to
Bathurst, 11 Sept. 1812; f. 160: Murray to
Monro, 7 Sept. 1812; f. 365: Murray to
Bathurst, 25 Oct. 1812; C.O. 295/29, f.23:
Monro to Bathurst, 5 Mar. 1813.

6. C.O. 295/29, f. 26: Proclamation, 27
Feb. 1813; f. 41: Murray to Monro, 17 May
1813; C.O. 295/32, f.52: Woodford to
Bathurst, 4 Jan. 1814; f. 150: Woodford to
Bathurst, 9 May 1814.

7. C.O. 295/30, f. 157: Proclamation, 14
Oct. 1813; C.O. 295/32, f. 135: Murray to
Woodford, 28 Feb. 1814.

8. C.O. 295/34, f. 13: James Stephen to
Henry Goulburn, 4 Feb. 1814. Cf. C.O.
295/32, f. 150: Woodford to Bathurst, 9 May
1814.

9. C.O. 295/42, no. 21: Registrar of
Slaves, 25 Jan. 1817 (enclosed in Woodford to
Bathurst, 9 Feb. 1817).

10. *P.P.*, 1823 (16), "Papers, Presented
Pursuant to Address, Relating to the Island of
Trinidad," p. 76 (Woodford to Bathurst, 9
Feb. 1817).

11. C.O. 295/33, f. 420: Order of
Government, 6 Dec. 1814.

12. C.O. 295/33, f. 114: Woodford to
Bathurst, 11 Apr. 1821.

13. *Barbados Mercury* (Bridgetown), 11
Jan., 20 May, 24 June 1817; 28 Aug. 1824
(obituary); *The Barbadian* (Bridgetown), 31
Aug. 1824, 8 and 22 Aug. 1828.

14. *P.P.*, 1817, vol. 17 (338), p. 5;
Barbados Mercury, 1 Mar. 1817.

15. M.C.P.D.E., 1817, p. 278: 12 Mar.
1817.

16. M.C.P.D.E., 1824, p. 329; 10 Mar.
1824.

17. M.C.P.D.E., 1826, vol. 2, p. 324: Petition, 9 Aug. 1826; 1827, vol. 1, p. 95:
Petition, 30 June 1827; 1828, vol. 2, p. 153:
Petition, 28 July 1828; *P.P.*, 1833, vol. 26
(700), pp. 427–49.

18. G.W. Roberts, "A Life Table for a

West Indian Slave Population," *Population Studies* 5 (1952):238–43.

19. *St. George's Chronicle* (Grenada), 6 Dec. 1823 and 20 July 1833; *Grenada Free Press,* 2 Dec. 1829; *St. Vincent Gazette,* 27 Aug. 1825.

20. James Crooks, Registrar for Tobago, owned Belmont Estate and 85 slaves: T.71/462, p. 228; Official Returns of Registrar of Slaves, Tobago, 1823 (T.A.). See also St. Kitts Bluebook, 1832, p. 66 (S.K.G.A.).

21. M.B.C., 1828–31, p. 291: 21 Dec. 1830. But this memorial was subsequently withdrawn—M.B.C., p. 329: 3 May 1831.

22. Michael Craton, "Hobbesian or Panglossian? The Two Extremes of Slave Conditions in the British Caribbean, 1783 to 1834," *William and Mary Quarterly* 35 (1978):324–56.

23. *P.P.,* 1817, vol. 17 (338), p. 6; T.71/524, p. 519; T.71/525, p. 746.

24. M.C.P.D.E., 1817, pp. 276, 361; *P.P.,* 1817, vol. 17 (338), p. 35.

25. T.71/522, pp. 180–81; index 10487, f. 93 (P.R.O.).

26. *P.P.,* 1817, vol. 17 (338), pp. 4, 30, 35, 47; *P.P.,* 1818, vol. 17 (433), pp. 32, 44, 84, 94, 105; T.71/250, p. 8.

27. C.O. 295/28, f. 251, For a contemporary critique, see *A Review of the Slave Registration Acts, in a Report of a Committee of the Board of Directors of the African Institution* (1820).

28. T.71/379, pp. 185, 708; T.71/501, p. 421.

29. *P.P.,* 1817, vol. 17 (338), p. 3.

30. Cf. Michael Craton, *Searching for the Invisible Man: Slaves and Plantation Life in Jamaica* (1978), pp. 156–60; Herbert Gutman, *The Black Family in Slavery and Freedom, 1750–1925* (1976), pp. 230–56; Stephen Gudeman, "Herbert Gutman's *The Black Family in Slavery and Freedom, 1750–1925:* An Anthropologist's View," *Social Science History* 3 (1979):56–65.

31. C.O. 295/37, f.177: Woodford to Goulburn, 15 Oct. 1815.

32. *P.P.,* 1836 (560), p. 402 (Augustus Hardin Beaumont).

33. T.71/438, p. 463.

34. See United Nations, *Methods of Estimating Basic Demographic Measures from Incomplete Data* (1967), p. 47.

35. Mortimer Spiegelman, *Introduction to Demography* (1976), p. 71.

36. Ibid., p. 71.

37. *P.P.,* 1817, vol. 17 (338), p. 4.

38. *P.P.,* 1823, vol. 18 (68), p. 5.

39. *P.P.,* 1817, vol. 17 (338), p. 23; C.O. 295/28, f. 252.

40. T.71/438, p. 509.

41. T.71/250, p. 634.

42. T.71/438, p. 653.

43. C.O. 295/28, f. 252.

44. T.71/438, pp. 353, 379, 389.

45. C.O. 295/33, f. 420: Order of Government 6 Dec. 1814; C.O. 295/37, f. 177: Woodford to Goulburn, 15 Oct. 1815.

46. T.71/379, p. 412.

47. Mrs. [A.C.] Carmichael, *Domestic Manners and Social Condition of the White, Coloured, and Negro Population of the West Indies* (1833), 2: 173–75.

48. One St. Lucia return in English specified "5$^{F.}$ French": T.71/378, f. 28; another "5$^{F.}$ 3$^{L.}$ ¾$^{L.}$": T.71/378, f. 89; and another "5$^{F.}$ 2$^{L.}$": T.71/378, f. 580. See Ronald Edward Zupko, *French Weights and Measures before the Revolution* (1978), p. 134.

49. T.71/438, pp. 463, 599.

50. T.71/438, p. 467, for example.

51. C.O. 295/28, f. 252.

52. *P.P.,* 1817, vol. 17 (338), p. 24.

53. C.O. 295/28, f. 251.

54. C.O. 295/28, f. 252.

55. C.O. 295/28, f. 255.

56. G. W. Roberts, "Movements in Slave Population of the Caribbean during the Period of Slave Registration", *Annals, New York Academy of Sciences* 292 (1977):148, is incorrect in stating that such births and deaths were "completely lost to the record." See also Roberts, "Life Table," p. 240; B. W. Higman, *Slave Population and Economy in Jamaica, 1807–1834* (1976), pp. 47–49.

57. Jerome S. Handler and Frederick W. Lange, *Plantation Slavery in Barbados* (1978), p. 287.

58. E. A. Wrigley, "Births and Baptisms," *Population Studies* 31 (1977):283; Robert Woods, *Population Analysis in Geography* (London, 1979), p. 44.

59. John Hancock, "Observations on Tetanus Infantum, or Lock-jaw of Infants," *Edinburgh Medical and Surgical Journal* 35 (1831):343.

60. Robert Renny, *A History of Jamaica* (1807), p. 207.

61. Jean Bourgeois-Pichat, "La Mesure de la Mortalité Infantile," *Population* 6 (1951):233–48, 459–80. For examples of the use of the method, see Roger Schofield and E. A. Wrigley, "Infant and Child Mortality in England in the Late Tudor and Early Stuart Period," in Charles Webster, ed., *Health, Medicine, and Mortality in the Sixteenth Century* (1979), pp. 73–74; Louis Henry, *Population: Analysis and Models* (1976), p. 149; Remy Clairin, "The Assessment of Infant and Child Mortality from the Data Available in Africa," in John C. Caldwell and Chukuka Okonjo, eds., *The Population of Tropical Africa* (1968) p. 204. See also John Knodel and Hallie Kinter, "The Impact of Breast Feeding Patterns on the Biometric Analysis of Infant Mortality," *Demography* 14 (1977): 391–409.

62. T.71/495, ff. 3, 9, 46: Rabacca Estate, with 255 slaves in 1817; Langley Park Estate, 302 slaves; Orange Hill Estate, 321 slaves.

63. T.71/255, ff. 64, 129: Abednego Matthew's plantation, with 130 slaves in 1817; John Willett Willett's, with 244 slaves.

64. James Thomson, *A Treatise on the Diseases of Negroes, as they Occur in the Island of Jamaica* (1820), p. 120.

65. The percentages of registered birth-deaths to total births employed in the estimate are those contained in table 2.5 or are assumed to be 13 percent (Antigua, Montserrat, and Trinidad), 10 percent (Bahamas), and 0 percent (Demerara-Essequibo). On Demerara-Essequibo see Roberts, "Life Table," p. 240. Child mortality (deaths of children born within a registration period and dying before its end) are assumed to be 40 percent in St. Kitts, Nevis, St. Lucia, St. Vincent, Trinidad, Berbice, and Anguilla, and 33 percent in the remaining colonies. The latter distinction is based on differences in the length of the registration intervals and on similarities in administrative practices and demographic characteristics between colonies.

66. The most commonly used tables are those in Ansley J. Coale and Paul Demeny, *Regional Model Life Tables and Stable Populations* (1966). See also Michael R. Haines, "The Use of Model Life Tables to Estimate Mortality for the United States in the Late Nineteenth Century," *Demography* 16 (1979):289–312; Youssef Courbage and Philippe Fargues, "A Method for Deriving Mortality Estimates from Incomplete Vital Statistics," *Population Studies* 33 (1979):165–80.

67. Roberts, "Life Table."

68. Cf. Craton, *Searching for the Invisible Man*, pp. 90–92, 115–17.

69. T.71/495, pp. 265, 267, 324.

70. See David Eltis, "The Impact of Abolition on the Atlantic Slave Trade," in David Eltis and James Walvin, eds., *The Abolition of the Atlantic Slave Trade* (1981), and D. Eltis, "The Traffic in Slaves between the British West Indian Colonies, 1807–1833," *Economic History Review* 25 (1972):55–64.

71. In the writer's previous study of Jamaica, it was argued that "both births and deaths should be inflated by roughly one third." The model life table estimate, however, suggests that an inflation of only 23 percent is required for both births and deaths. See Higman, *Slave Population and Economy in Jamaica*, p. 49.

72. In St. Vincent, runaways were generally listed at the end of the 1817 returns, most of them said to have been absent more than five years. These slaves are excluded from all calculations used in this book, as was the practice in contemporary registration computations.

73. T.71/685–851, 852–914, 915–42. See also R. E. P. Wastell, *The History of Slave Compensation, 1833 to 1845* (Master's thesis, University of London, 1932). The valuers' returns were printed forms, filled in by hand, the data concerning the slaves being much more scant than in the registration returns and of little value for direct analysis.

74. Higman, *Slave Population and Economy in Jamaica*, pp. 50–54.

CHAPTER 3

1. This section is based on B. W. Higman, *The Caribbean Today* (1975).

2. M.C.P.B.G., 24 May 1833: Petition of William Hilhouse.

3. For general accounts see Franklin W. Knight, *The Caribbean: The Genesis of a Fragmented Nationalism* (1978) and Eric Williams, *From Columbus to Castro* (1970). For the early period, Richard S. Dunn, *Sugar and Slaves* (1972) and Richard B. Sheridan, *Sugar and Slavery* (1974).

4. Philip D. Curtin, *The Atlantic Slave Trade* (1969), p. 56.

5. Elsa V. Goveia, *Slave Society in the British Leeward Islands at the End of the Eighteenth Century* (1965), pp. 52–58.

6. Narda Dobson, *A History of Belize* (1973); R. A. Humphreys, *The Diplomatic History of British Honduras, 1638–1901* (1961); Neville Williams, *A History of the Cayman Islands* (1970); Michael Craton, *A History of the Bahamas* (London: 1963); *Royal Gazette* (Nassau), 3 October 1804.

7. Richard Pares, *Merchants and Planters* (1960), p. 40.

8. Linda A. Newson, *Aboriginal and Spanish Colonial Trinidad* (1976), p. 180.

9. D.J. Murray, *The West Indies and the Development of Colonial Government, 1801–1834* (1965), pp. 67–68; James Millette, *The Genesis of Crown Colony Government: Trinidad 1783–1810* (1970).

10. Murray, *Development of Colonial Government*, pp. 56, 161; Lowell Joseph Ragatz, *The Fall of the Planter Class in the British Caribbean, 1763–1833* (1963), pp. 218, 332, 351.

11. Ragatz, *Fall of the Planter Class*, p. 332; Alan H. Adamson, *Sugar without Slaves* (1972), p. 24.

12. R. E. P. Wastell, *The History of Slave Compensation, 1833 to 1845* (Master's thesis, University of London, 1932), pp. 29–47; T.71/685–851; Lt. Governor's Correspondence, Tobago, 1835: 6 April 1835, "Report of the committee appointed to inspect the books of the Compensation Commissioners" (T.A.).

13. Wastell, *History of Slave Compensation*, p. 80; Woodville K. Marshall, ed., *The Colthurst Journal* (1977), pp. 68–69.

14. Wastell, *History of Slave Compensation*, p. 77. In Barbados, "field labourers" were aged 16–60 years and "inferior field labourers" 6–16 or 60–69 years, whereas in the Bahamas these ages were 15–49 and 6–14 or 50–70.

15. T.71/851.

16. Wastell, *History of Slave Compensation*, p. 77.

17. Index 10493, following Y; the index to T.71/553–64 (P.R.O.).

18. The original of the 1 August 1834 return for Drax Hall classified the plantation's slaves as follows:

	♀	♂	Total
Domestics	3	4	7
Labourers in sugar	61	77	138
Labourers in cotton	—	—	—
Labourers in agriculture	9	3	12
None	17	13	30

See Drax Hall Estate Papers (D.A.B.).

19. Cf. R. Keith Aufhauser, "Profitability of Slavery in the British Caribbean," *Journal of Interdisciplinary History* 5 (1974):51; and Barbados, Agents' Letterbooks, 1829–33: J. P. Mayers to Viscount Goderich, 2 March 1833 (D.A.B.).

20. For lists of mills by parish, see Minute Book, Barbados Agricultural Society, p. 31 (1811), p. 167 (1812), p. 245 (1813) (University of Keele); *Barbados Almanack*, 1818; Barrallier's map of Barbados (1827).

21. *The Barbadian*, 16 March 1833; *Barbados Almanack*, 1835, p. 65.

22. Robert Haynes to Thomas Lane, 12 and 24 February, and 23 June 1814 (Newton Estate Papers, University of London), MS 523/715, 716, 730.

23. J. S. Handler, "The History of Arrowroot and the Origin of Peasantries in the British West Indies," *Journal of Caribbean History*, 2 (1971): 46–93.

24. Barbados Acts of 4 November 1806 and 18 January 1822 (cotton), 28 May 1811 and 23 March 1813 (aloes), and 30 June and 27 August 1824 (ginger). See also *The Barbadian* (Bridgetown), 18 January 1825.

25. St. Kitts Bluebook, 1832, p. 148 (S.K.G.A.).

26. St. Kitts, Record Book of the Court of Special Sessions, 1815–25: 22 September 1820 (S.K.G.A.); Goveia, *Slave Society in the British Leeward Islands*, pp. 136–37; Douglas Hall, *Five of the Leewards* (1971), p. 29.

27. Richard Pares, *A West-India Fortune* (1950), p. 354; Gordon C. Merrill, *The His-*

torical Geography of St. Kitts and Nevis (1958).

28. Hall, *Five of the Leewards*, p. 4.

29. *P.P.*, Lords, 1832 (127), vol. 1, p. 354; *The Weekly Register* (Antigua), 8 October 1814, 14 January 1815, 13 May 1819; *Antigua Gazette*, 18 March 1819.

30. Hall, *Five of the Leewards*, p. 29.

31. Frances Armytage, *The Free Port System in the British West Indies* (1953), pp. 104, 141.

32. John Stobo, "Statistical Table of the British Virgin Islands at two periods, 1815 and 1823," April 1823, C.O. 239/9. Stobo put the total area of the Virgin Islands at 58,649 acres, rather than the actual 38,000. He put Tortola at 13,300 acres (instead of 15,360), Anegada at 21,200 (8,320), Virgin Gorda at 9,500 (5,760), and Jos Van Dykes at 3,200 (2,560). But if his remnant categories, "forest and brush wood" and "barren," are ignored, it is probable that the acres said to be under crop were close to the reality.

33. *Plan of Tortola, from Actual Survey by George King* (1798).

34. Armytage, *Free Port System*, p. 154; Robert Montgomery Martin, *Statistics of the Colonies of the British Empire* (1839), p. 101.

35. B. W. Higman, *Slave Population and Economy in Jamaica, 1807–1834* (1976), chaps. 2–4.

36. Census of Dominica in 1763, printed in *Dominica Chronicle*, 16 March 1825; Thomas Atwood, *The History of the Island of Dominica* (1791), pp. 82–83.

37. Planters' Petition to Council and Assembly [Dominica], n.d. (Archive Room, Old Ministerial Building, Roseau).

38. Martin, *Statistics of the Colonies*, p. 78.

39. See *Royal St. Vincent Gazette*, 1 January 1825, and 7 April and 22 December 1827. The returns were published in *An Account of the Number of Slaves Employed, and Quantity of Produce Grown, on the Several Estates in the Island of Saint Vincent and Its Dependencies, 1801–24* (1825).

40. Handler, "The History of Arrowroot," p. 70; Martin, *Statistics of the Colonies*, p. 59.

41. Charles Shephard, *An Historical Account of the Island of St. Vincent* (1831), p. 215.

42. C.O. 106/22, p. 154. For examples, see Grenada, Deeds, vols. M/5, pp. 280, 282; L/5, p. 271 (Supreme Court Registry, St. Georges).

43. *Proceedings of the Grenada Agricultural Society, 1820 and 1821* (1821); [Robert Wilkinson], *A Topographical Description of the Island of Grenada* (1805) (microfilm of typescript at U.W.I. Library, Mona).

44. *Proceedings of the Grenada Agricultural Society*, pp. 29–41.

45. Custom House, Tobago, Letterbook, 1814–26, p. 66 (T.A.); Martin, *Statistics of the Colonies*, p. 40; J.-C. Nardin, *La Mise en Valeur de l'ile de Tabago, 1763–1783* (1969), pp. 227–37; J.-C. Nardin, "Tabago, Antille Francaise, 1781–1793," *Annales des Antilles*, 14 (1966); Tobago Bluebook, 1838, p. 162 (T.A.).

46. Martin, *Statistics of the Colonies*, pp. 72–73; Ragatz, *Fall of the Planter Class*, p. 351.

47. C.O. 300/46.

48. *Port of Spain Gazette*, 17 May 1833; C.O. 295/14, f. 49.

49. C.O. 295/53, f. 341; 295/75, f. 138; 295/78, f. 55; 295/89, f. 152.

50. C.O. 300/40 (Report); 300/47, p. 162.

51. C.O. 295/21, f. 107; 295/33, f. 437; 295/66, f. 299; 295/46, p. 158; C.O. 300/40; *Port of Spain Gazette*, 17 May 1833.

52. C.O. 295/44, f. 15, 3 August 1817: Woodford to Goulburn; Protocols of Wills, Trinidad, 1826, f. 96, and 1829, p. 107 (Registrar General's Department, Port of Spain); T.71/501–3.

53. C.O. 300/40, f. 18; 300/46, p. 163; 300/47, p. 163; C.O. 295/78, f. 105; 295/85, f. 14; C.O. 298/6, 2 May 1826: Memorial of C. A. Whyte; T.71/501–3.

54. Adamson, *Sugar Without Slaves*, p. 25; Martin, *Statistics of the Colonies*, p. 135; M.C.P.D.E., 1833, vol. 1, p. 502: 19 March 1833.

55. *Demerary and Essequibo. The Annual Miscellany, or Local Guide, for 1817* (1817), p. 96.

56. M.C.P.D.E., 1833, vol. 1, p. 502: 19 March 1833.

57. Ibid.

58. T.71/251.

59. British Honduras, Mr. Miller's Mission

to England, 1834–35: Journal, 6 March 1835 (N.A.B.); Legislative Meetings, 1830–36, p. 166: 2 July 1833, and pp. 188–93: 4 November 1833 (Supreme Court Registry, Belize); Capt. Henderson, *An Account of the British Settlement of Honduras* (1809), pp. 39–43.

60. Martin, *Statistics of the Colonies,* p. 141; Alan K. Craig, "Logwood as a Factor in the Settlement of British Honduras," *Caribbean Studies,* 9 (1969):53–62; Dobson, *History of Belize,* p. 129.

61. Dobson, *History of Belize,* p. 130; Mr. Miller's Mission to England: Memoranda, 24 November 1834; British Honduras, Miscellaneous, Inwards and Outwards, 1830–39: Magistrates to Arthur, 16 January 1820 (N.A.B.).

62. Williams, *History of the Cayman Islands,* pp. 32–45; George S. S. Hirst, *Notes on the History of the Cayman Islands* (1910), pp. 119–21.

63. T.71/851. Another 425 slaves lived in the parish of Bodden Town.

64. Minutes of Meetings of the Commissioners of Correspondence, 1796–1833: 2 May 1816 (House of Assembly, Nassau).

65. Ibid., 31 January 1829.

66. T.71/851.

67. Martin, *Statistics of the Colonies,* p. 110; *Royal Gazette and Bahama Advertiser,* 26 May 1832.

68. *Royal Gazette and Bahama Advertiser,* 18 February 1832.

69. C.O. 239/12, No. 157, Maxwell to Bathurst, 10 January 1825 (Report of Pickwood and Rawlins, 1 December 1824).

70. Henry Nelson Coleridge, *Six Months in the West Indies in 1825* (1832), p. 212.

71. Ragatz, *Fall of the Planter Class,* p. 357; C.O. 239/9, Maxwell to Bathurst, 11 March 1823 and 28 August 1823; C.O. 239/10, Maxwell to Bathurst, 8 August 1824; Customs 34/721 and 726, James Hay, Waiter and Searcher, Anguilla, to Commissioners of Customs 10 October 1822 and 20 October 1823 (H.M. Customs and Excise Archives, London).

72. C.O. 239/29, No. 39, Nicolay to Goderich, 2 May 1832; *Grenada Free Press,* 19 September, 10 and 31 October 1832; *The Barbadian,* 6 February 1833.

73. David Lowenthal and Colin G. Clarke,

"Slave-Breeding in Barbuda: The Past of a Negro Myth," *Annals of the New York Academy of Sciences,* 292 (1977) 510–35; Hall, *Five of the Leewards,* pp. 59–60; Coleridge, *Six Months in the West Indies,* pp. 256–59.

CHAPTER 4

1. Philip D. Curtin, *The Atlantic Slave Trade* (1969), p. 66.

2. Cf. B. W. Higman, *Slave Population and Economy in Jamaica, 1807–1834* (1976), p. 76; Roderick A. McDonald, "Measuring the British Slave Trade to Jamaica, 1789–1808: A Comment," *Economic History Review* 33 (1980):253–58.

3. *Barbados Mercury* (Bridgetown), 1 August and 26 December 1807, 12 April and 11 October 1808.

4. Curtin, *Atlantic Slave Trade,* p. 68.

5. See T.71/1537-49; Lowell Joseph Ragatz, *The Fall of the Planter Class in the British Caribbean, 1763–1833* (1963), p. 453.

6. See D. Eltis, "The Traffic in Slaves between the British West Indian Colonies, 1807–1833," *Economic History Review* 25 (1972):55–64; Eric Williams, "The British West Indian Slave Trade after Its Abolition in 1807," *Journal of Negro History* 27 (1942):175–91.

7. 58 Geo. 3. See also 46, 47, 51, and 56 Geo. 3; Customs 34/214 (16), 24 June 1819 (H.M. Customs and Excise Archives, London).

8. Cf. Williams, "The British West Indian Slave Trade," pp. 179–90.

9. Eltis, "The Traffic in Slaves," p. 58. The data derive largely from published reports in *P.P.*

10. C.O. 28/102, p. 145; Skeete to Murray, 2 December 1828. Cf. R. Keith Aufhauser, "Profitability of Slavery in the British Caribbean," *Journal of Interdisciplinary History* 5 (1974): 45–67.

11. *Royal Gazette* (Nassau), 17 March 1832; 58 Geo. 3.

12. Bahamas, Registers of Slaves, 1822 (Nassau Public Library).

13. Ibid., 1821. For data on Bahamas slaves imported to Jamaica, see Returns of Registrations of Slaves, liber 35, ff. 115–21 (Jamaica Archives, Spanish Town).

14. Bahamas, Registers of Slaves, 1821 and 1822.

15. C.O. 295/53, f. 341: Young to Bathurst, 13 December 1821; 295/59, f. 241: Woodford to Bathurst, 6 November 1823; 295/66, f. 53: minutes of evidence, Burton Williams, 18 January 1825.

16. C.O. 295/71, f. 26: Woodford to Bathurst, 13 April 1826.

17. C.O. 295/78, f. 233: Farquharson to Secretary of State, 12 October 1828.

18. See Customs 34/871 (62), Colonial Office to Commissioners of Customs, Dominica, 30 July 1818; 34/214 (61), 11 November 1822 (Nassau); 34/412 (74), Buller to Moss, 7 October 1815.

19. The lists of slaves brought from the Bahamas to Jamaica are ordered in a manner suggestive of "family" groupings. Returns of Registrations of Slaves, liber 35, ff. 115–21 (Jamaica Archives).

20. T.71/520–27.

21. C.O. 295/78, f. 87: statement of Henry Fuller, Attorney General, Trinidad, 1828.

22. Customs 34/370 (61), Laidlaw, President, Dominica to Collector of Customs, 23 February 1828, and Collector of Customs, Trinidad, to Commissioners of Customs, London, 8 March 1828.

23. Dominica, Governor's Letterbook, Outgoing, 1827–29: Robe to Blanc, 13 June 1829; 1829–32: Blanc to Robe, 20 January 1830; 1832: Birmingham to Burgoyne, 25 April 1832 (Archive Room, Old Ministerial Building, Roseau).

24. C.O. 295/78, f. 74: Farquharson to Murray, 26 August 1828; 295/81, f. 1: Grant to Murray, 10 July 1829.

25. Customs 34/893, Collector of Customs, Demerara, to Commissioners, 1 June 1831.

26. Ibid.

27. Bahamas, Minutes of Meetings of the Commissioners of Correspondence, 1796–1833: 31 January 1829 and 21 August 1832 (House of Assembly, Nassau).

28. Customs 34/872, Collector of Customs, Nassau, to Commissioners, 4 May 1832.

29. An Official Letter from the Commissioners of Correspondence of the Bahama Islands (1823), p. 41; Minutes of the Meetings of the Commissioners of Correspondence, 1796–1833: 2 May 1816.

30. In 1809 some 69,369 slaves were returned for poll tax in Barbados, but it was notorious that these returns omitted many slaves belonging to small owners, especially those living in towns. If the slave population in 1809 was in fact 75,000 (table S1.2), the population of St. Michael may be inflated from 12,262 to 17,900, assuming most slaves omitted from poll tax were in that parish. See Minute Book of the Barbados Agricultural Society, p. 31 (University of Keele Library).

31. T.71/364 and 851. For 1817 see table S4.4.

32. T.71/451 and 851.

33. Higman, Slave Population and Economy in Jamaica, chap. 5.

34. An Account of the Number of Slaves Employed, and Quantity of Produce Grown, on the Several Estates in the Island of St. Vincent (1825), pp. 143, 235; R. M. Martin, Statistics of the Colonies, p. 59.

35. An Account of the Number of Slaves, pp. 143, 235; T.71/265, 311, 851.

36. M.C.P.D.E., 1820, p. 203; 1826, vol. 2, p. 479.

37. T.71/851.

38. Ibid.

39. Higman, Slave Population and Economy in Jamaica, p. 58.

40. See Franklin W. Knight, Slave Society in Cuba during the Nineteenth Century (1970), p. 63; Claudia Dale Goldin, Urban Slavery in the American South, 1820–1860 (1976), p. 52.

41. Robert V. Wells, The Population of the British Colonies in America before 1776 (1975), pp. 196–98; Higman, Slave Population and Economy in Jamaica, pp. 255–56.

42. Richard S. Dunn, Sugar and Slaves (1972), pp. 180, 312; Handler, The Unappropriated People, p. 20.

43. T.71/361–63.

44. Cf. Goldin, Urban Slavery in the American South, p. 52.

45. M.C.P.D.E., 1817, p. 484; P.P. 1833, vol. 26 (700), p. 432; C.O. 295/21, f. 107; C.O. 300/46, p. 118.

46. Cf. Handler, The Unappropriated People, p. 16; John W. Blassingame, Black New Orleans (Chicago, 1973), p. 16; Richard C. Wade, Slavery in the Cities (1964); John P. Radford, "Race, Residence and Ideology: Charleston, South Carolina in the Mid-

Nineteenth Century," *Journal of Historical Geography* 2 (1976):329–46.

47. F. W. N. Bayley, *Fours Years' Residence in the West Indies* (1830), pp. 191–92.

48. *Royal St. Vincent Gazette*, 18 March 1820.

49. Ibid., 20 May 1820. Cf. *British Guiana Courier*, 23 January 1835 (copy in T.71/1547).

50. Higman, *Slave Population and Economy in Jamaica*, p. 61; *The Columbian Magazine* (Kingston), 3 (1797): 8, 77, 168.

51. T.71/553–54, linked to T.71/790–803 and T.71/895. See table S1.15.

52. C.O. 30/20, Act no. 431, 27 August 1822: "An Act to Fix and Settle the Limits of the Town of St. Michael commonly called Bridge-Town." The streets, many of which disappeared or changed their names after the fire of 1845, have been identified from historical maps, "Place Names of Bridgetown and Its Environs," *Journal of the Barbados Museum and Historical Society* 25 (1958):127–38, and Warren Alleyne, *Historic Bridgetown* (Barbados, 1978).

53. See St. Michael, Assessment Book, 1802–10: 10 March 1806 (D.A.B.).

54. For 1830 the data are available by district only for whites and freedmen. M.C.P.D.E., 1830 vol. 1, p. 250.

55. Ibid., 1828, vol. 1, p. 353.

56. Ibid., 1815, p. 503: Petition of George Lacy.

CHAPTER 5

1. Eric Williams, *From Columbus to Castro* (1970), pp. 282–85. Williams found an average slaveholding size of only 14, using data derived from the compensation returns. But his data understate the size of the slave population by excluding children under six years and the aged, and he found 38,218 "owners" (compensation claims) compared to the 32,471 registration returns of c. 1832.

2. T.71/493.

3. B. W. Higman, *Slave Population and Economy in Jamaica, 1807–1834* (1976), p. 69.

4. Carl Campbell, "The Rise of a Free Coloured Plantocracy in Trinidad 1783–1813," *Boletin de Estudios Latino-americanos y del Caribe* 29 (1980):47; T.71/501–2.

5. I am grateful to Barry Gaspar for data permitting the identification of a further 22 freedman slaveowners in St. Lucia.

6. John Jeremie, *Four Essays on Colonial Slavery* (1831), pp. 50–51.

7. Jerome S. Handler, *The Unappropriated People* (1974), pp. 18–25.

8. Ibid., p. 150.

9. William A. Green, *British Slave Emancipation* (1976), p. 15.

10. C.O. 295/23, f. 57: Hislop to Liverpool, 16 April 1810.

11. Ibid., p. 7; Handler, *Unappropriated People*, p. 187; Edward Brathwaite, *The Development of Creole Society in Jamaica, 1770–1820* (1971), p. 268.

12. E. G. West, "Literacy and the Industrial Revolution," *Economic History Review* 31 (1978):380; Lawrence Stone, "Literacy and Education in England, 1640–1900," *Past and Present* 42 (1969):120.

13. Handler, *Unappropriated People*, p. 150. But the Barbados registration returns showed a fall in the number of freedman slaveowners from 650 in 1817 to 535 in 1820. Index 10488 (P.R.O.).

14. Ibid., pp. 56, 152; Mavis Christine Campbell, *The Dynamics of Change in a Slave Society* (Rutherford, 1976), p. 56; Gad J. Heuman, *Between Black and White* (1981), p. 14; F. W. N. Bayley, *Four Years' Residence in the West Indies* (1830), pp. 417–18.

15. Karl Watson, *The Civilised Island* (1979), p. 40.

16. Higman, *Slave Population and Economy in Jamaica*, p. 10.

17. T.71/462.

18. Elsa V. Goveia, *Slave Society in the British Leeward Islands at the End of the Eighteenth Century* (1965), p. 204; S. G. Checkland, *The Gladstones* (1971), pp. 124–26.

19. Douglas Hall, "Absentee-Proprietorship in the British West Indies to about 1850," *Jamaican Historical Review* 4 (1964) 15–35; William A. Green, "The Planter Class and British West Indian Sugar Production, before and after Emancipation," *Economic History Review* 26 (1973) 448–63.

20. R. E. P. Wastell, *The History of Slave*

Compensation, 1833 to 1845 (Master's thesis, University of London, 1932), p. 61.

21. T.71/1549, document H: Assistant Commissioners, Barbados, to Commissioners of Compensation, London, 28 November 1834.

22. T.71/363, f. 210–13. In St. David, Dominica in 1832 there were only 10 slave-holdings, comprising 1, 1, 1, 2, 3, 3, 3, 174, 177, and 182 slaves.

23. Herbert S. Klein, *The Middle Passage* (1978), p. 150; Richard B. Sheridan, "Slave Demography in the British West Indies and the Abolition of the Slave Trade," in *The Abolition of the Atlantic Slave Trade,* ed. David Eltis and James Walvin (1981), p. 276.

24. Calculated from T.71/520.

25. Higman, *Slave Population and Economy in Jamaica,* p. 123.

26. Ibid., p. 123.

27. Michael Craton, "Death, Disease, and Medicine on Jamaican Slave Plantations; the Example of Worthy Park, 1767–1838," *Histoire Sociale—Social History* 9 (1976):243; Peter Hogg, *Slavery: The Afro-American Experience* (London, 1979), p. 52.

28. *The Columbian Magazine* (Kingston), 2 (1797):701; George Pinckard, *Notes on the West Indies* (1806), 2: 223.

29. T.71/523.

30. T.71/501–3. See also B. W. Higman, "Urban Slavery in the British Caribbean," in *Perspectives on Caribbean Regional Identity,* ed. Elizabeth Thomas-Hope (1983).

31. Philip D. Curtin, *The Atlantic Slave Trade* (1969), p. 150; Klein, *Middle Passage,* p. 149.

32. But shipping data for 1804–5 do not demonstrate this change. See *P.P.,* 1806, vol. 13 (265), pp. 24–26.

33. Curtin, *Atlantic Slave Trade,* p. 150.

34. Sidney W. Mintz and Richard Price, *An Anthropological Approach to the Afro-American Past: A Caribbean Perspective* (1976), pp. 24–26.

35. T.71/378–79, 438–39.

36. *Columbian Magazine,* 2 (1797):699.

37. J. S. Handler, R. S. Corruccini, and R. J. Mutaw, "Tooth Mutilation in the Caribbean," *Journal of Human Evolution* 11 (1982):308–11.

38. Klein, *Middle Passage,* p. 151.

39. Albert J. Raboteau, *Slave Religion* (New York, 1978), p. 39.

40. Hogg, *Slavery,* p. 52. Cf. "Characteristic Traits of the Creolian and African Negroes in this Island," *Columbian Magazine* (1797).

41. Higman, *Slave Population and Economy in Jamaica,* p. 94.

42. Klein, *Middle Passage,* p. 150. For the definition of "boys" and "girls," see T.71/364, pp. 104, 107, 174.

43. For the old sugar colonies, the age structure of Antigua in 1817 has been estimated using St. Kitts as a model, and that of Montserrat using Nevis. Dominica has been estimated on the model of St. Lucia, and Demerara-Essequibo on Berbice.

44. David Lowenthal and Colin G. Clarke, "Slave-Breeding in Barbuda: The Past of a Negro Myth," *Annals of the New York Academy of Science* 292 (1977):519.

45. Higman, *Slave Population and Economy in Jamaica,* pp. 81–93.

46. Higman, "Urban Slavery."

47. Higman, *Slave Population and Economy in Jamaica,* p. 139.

48. In Tobago in 1819 some 470 Africans and 754 creoles were described as yellow, while the mulatto, mestee, and cobre slaves numbered only 498, all of them creoles. In Berbice 1,086 Africans and 879 creoles were designated yellow but another 122 Africans were attributed to other color types. In Nevis in 1817 only 194 slaves were listed as yellow, compared to 1,350 mulatto, sambo, and mustee slaves.

49. Higman, *Slave Population and Economy in Jamaica,* p. 142.

50. Brathwaite, *Creole Society,* p. 168; Green, *British Slave Emancipation,* p. 14.

51. Higman, *Slave Population and Economy in Jamaica,* p. 145. See also Richard H. Steckel, "Miscegenation and the American Slave Schedules," *Journal of Interdisciplinary History* 11 (1980):251–63.

52. Cf. Lowenthal and Clarke, "Slave-Breeding in Barbuda."

53. Edwin Lascelles et. al., *Instructions for the Management of a Plantation in Barbadoes* (1786), p. 20.

54. *A Report of a Committee of the Council of Barbadoes, Appointed to Inquire into the*

Actual Condition of the Slaves in this Island (1824), pp. 104, 118; also p. 111.

55. Higman, *Slave Population and Economy in Jamaica*, pp. 128, 147.

56. Ibid., p. 123.

57. Cf. H. Hoetink, *Slavery and Race Relations in the Americas* (1973), p. 9.

58. Higman, *Slave Population and Economy in Jamaica*, p. 139.

59. T.71/501, p. 575. See also Pierre Crépeau, *Classifications Raciales Populaires et Métissage* (Martinique, 1973).

60. See Jerome S. Handler, "The Amerindian Slave Population of Barbados in the Seventeenth and Early Eighteenth Centuries," *Caribbean Studies* 8 (1969):38–64; M.C.P.D.E., 1808, p. 201: 28 April 1808; Mary Noel Menezes, *British Policy towards the Amerindians in British Guiana, 1803–1873* (1977), p. 181; T.71/364, p. 81; *P.P.*, 1823, vol. 18 (457), "Slaves at Honduras," p. 60; Private Records, vol. P/BB, 1825–28, p. 301: Appraisement of goods and chattels of Ann Pattenett (Supreme Court Registry, Belize).

61. *The Impartial Expositor* (Bridgetown), 19 June 1805 (bound with *Barbados Mercury*). Cf. Jerome S. Handler, *A Guide to Source Materials for the Study of Barbados History* (1971), p. 118.

CHAPTER 6

1. See Richard B. Sheridan, *Sugar and Slavery* (1974), pp. 107–18; B. W. Higman, *Slave Population and Economy in Jamaica, 1807–1834* (1976), pp. 18–30, 188–201; Lowell Joseph Ragatz, *The Fall of the Planter Class in the British Caribbean, 1763–1833* (1928), pp. 56–63; Michael Craton and James Walvin, *A Jamaican Plantation* (1970), chap. 5; Michael Craton, *Searching for the Invisible Man* (1978), chap. 5; Orlando Patterson, *The Sociology of Slavery* (1967), pp. 52–69; William A. Green, *British Slave Emancipation* (1976), pp. 46–64; Thomas Roughley, *The Jamaica Planter's Guide* (1823), chaps. 5–7; *P.P.*, 1832 (127), House of Lords, "Report from the Select Committee on the State of the West India Colonies," pp. 45–49.

2. Cf. J. Durnin and R. Passmore, *Energy, Work, and Leisure* (London, 1967);

O. Edholm, *The Biology of Work* (New York, 1967).

3. William A. Green, "The Planter Class and British West Indian Sugar Production, before and after Emancipation," *Economic History Review* 26 (1973):449–51.

4. *Port of Spain Gazette*, 22 December 1830; *St. George's Chronicle and Grenada Gazette*, 27 September 1823 and 30 October 1824; *Grenada Free Press and Public Gazette*, 2 December 1829, 12 February and 19 March 1834.

5. Ragatz, *Fall of the Planter Class*, p. 66; Noel Deerr, *The History of Sugar* (1950), 2:353; *Dominica Chronicle*, 7 February 1821 (Antigua Agricultural Report, 1820).

6. Alan H. Adamson, *Sugar without Slaves* (1972), p. 169.

7. Deerr, *History of Sugar*, 2:352; Sheridan, *Sugar and Slavery*, p. 111; *P.P.*, 1832, vol. 20 (721), "Report from Select Committee on the Extinction of Slavery," p. 14; *P.P.*, 1832 (127), Lords, "Report from the Select Committee on the State of the West India Colonies," vol. 1, p. 47.

8. Deerr, *History of Sugar*, 1:174; Sheridan, *Sugar and Slavery*, pp. 110–11; Craton, *Searching for the Invisible Man*, pp. 136–37, 144–45. These references provide contemporary illustrations of the methods used in Antigua and Trinidad, which are idealized versions rather than "authentic" pictures.

9. *P.P.*, 1832 (127), Lords, vol. 1, p. 45; Richard Pares, *A West-India Fortune* (1950), p. 112.

10. *Dominica Chronicle*, 7 February 1821.

11. Minute Book of the [Barbados] Agricultural Society, 1812–16: 23 May 1812, pp. 63–64 (University of Keele).

12. *P.P.*, vol. 20 (721), p. 12. See also Gilbert Mathison, *Notices Respecting Jamaica* (1811), p. 38.

13. Higman, *Slave Population and Economy in Jamaica*, p. 20.

14. Minute Book of the Barbados Agricultural Society, pp. 28–29. This document contains numerous additional examples. See also Newton Estate Papers, items 128–31 (University of London); J. Nicholson, "A Sketch of the Cultivation and Manufacture of Sugar in Barbados," *Proceedings of the Grenada Agricultural Society*, 1822–27, p. 26.

15. Edwin Lascelles et al., *Instructions for the Management of a Plantation in Barbados* (1786), p. 1.

16. Cf. Adamson, *Sugar without Slaves,* pp. 112, 169–70.

17. Lascelles, *Instructions,* p. 6.

18. *P.P.,* 1832 (721), p. 431.

19. Higman, *Slave Population and Economy in Jamaica,* pp. 40–41.

20. Ibid., p. 238; Colletons Estate, Journal and Ledger, 1818–44 (B.M.H.S.); Mount Gay Plantation and Refinery Journal, 1809–36: May 1812, September 1813 (microfilm at Barbados Public Library).

21. Minute Book of the Barbados Agricultural Society, p. 30.

22. *P.P.,* 1832 (721), p. 14; C.O. 295/85, f. 388: Smith to Murray, 9 October 1830.

23. *P.P.,* 1832 (721), p. 598; S. G. Checkland, *The Gladstones* (1971), p. 265.

24. M.C.P.D.E., 1832, vol. 1, p. 429.

25. C.O. 295/21, f. 107; C.O. 300/40; *Port of Spain Gazette,* 17 May 1833; Adamson, *Sugar without Slaves,* p. 27; Ragatz, *Fall of the Planter Class,* p. 63.

26. *Local Guide of British Guiana* (Demerara, 1843), p. xxiv; Adamson, *Sugar without Slaves,* p. 27; Checkland, *The Gladstones,* p. 266.

27. *P.P.,* 1828, vol. 25 (261), "Slaves, Berbice and Demerara," p. 457.

28. Elsa V. Goveia, *Slave Society in the British Leeward Islands at the End of the Eighteenth Century* (1965), p. 131.

29. Rowland Fearon to Lord Penrhyn, 26 January 1805, Penrhyn Castle MS. 1355 (University College of North Wales, Bangor). I am indebted to Jean Lindsay for this reference.

30. *P.P.,* 1832 (721), p. 12.

31. Jerome S. Handler and Frederick W. Lange, *Plantation Slavery in Barbados* (1978), p. 72.

32. *P.P.,* 1832 (721), p. 598.

33. *Barbados Mercury,* 4 July 1815. Cf. Lewis Cecil Gray, *History of Agriculture in the Southern United States to 1860* (Washington, 1933), 1:548–50.

34. Alexander Winter, "Coffee Cultivation in Berbice, 50 Years Ago," *Timehri,* 1 (1882):275; Higman, *Slave Population and Economy in Jamaica,* pp. 21–25. For detailed accounts of pimento cultivation see Journals of James H. Archer, 1828–41, Add. MS. 33,294

(British Library, London), and Accounts and Letters of James H. Archer, M.D., 1822–45, Add. MS. 27,970.

35. Linda A. Newson, *Aboriginal and Spanish Colonial Trinidad* (1976), pp. 203–5.

36. *P.P.,* 1832 (721), p. 440.

37. Warren Dean, *Rio Claro* (1976), p. 30. Cf. Stanley J. Stein, *Vassouras* (1957), pp. 32–38.

38. Higman, *Slave Population and Economy in Jamaica,* pp. 24, 204.

39. Charles Farquharson, *A Relic of Slavery* (1957), provides an account of a small holding in the Bahamas.

40. *P.P.,* 1832 (721), p. 335.

41. Ibid., p. 15.

42. Ibid., pp. 46, 335; Minute Book of the Barbados Agricultural Society, pp. 130–31; *P.P.,* 1832 (127), Lords, vol. 1, pp. 550, 567. Cf. William L. Van Deburg, *The Slave Drivers* (Westport, 1979).

43. Handler and Lange, *Plantation Slavery in Barbados,* pp. 75–76. See also table S7.5; Higman, *Slave Population and Economy in Jamaica,* p. 228; *P.P.,* 1832 (127), Lords, vol. 1, p. 35.

44. *P.P.,* 1836, vol. 25 (560), "Report from the Select Committee on Negro Apprenticeship in the Colonies," p. 388.

45. Miscellaneous, Inwards and Outwards, 1820–39; Arthur to Bathurst, 26 July 1822, and Meeting called by Superintendent, 13 June 1834 (N.A.B.); *P.P.,* 1832 (127), Lords, vol. 1, p. 307.

46. Letter Book of C. Reevers, p. 153: 25 April 1828 (N.A.G.).

47. O. Nigel Bolland, *The Formation of a Colonial Society* (1977), p. 109.

48. "As Relate to the Treatment of Negroes in Demerary," uncatalogued, Gladstone Papers (Flintshire Record Office, Hawarden, North Wales). I am grateful to Richard Sheridan for this reference.

49. *P.P.,* 1832 (721), p. 86.

50. Ibid., p. 431; *P.P.,* 1832 (127), Lords, vol. 1, p. 48.

51. *P.P.,* 1832 (721), p. 431.

52. *P.P.,* 1832 (127), Lords, vol. 1, p. 48; *P.P.,* 1828, p. 499 (evidence of Thomas Moody); Sheridan, *Sugar and Slavery,* p. 115.

53. Joseph Sturge and Thomas Harvey, *The West Indies in 1837* (1838), pp. 229–30.

54. See Jerome S. Handler, "A Historical

ᴇtch of Pottery Manufacture in Barbados,"
Journal of the Barbados Museum and Historical Society 30 (1963):129–53; Handler and Lange, *Plantation Slavery in Barbados*, p. 139.

55. Cf. Handler and Lange, *Plantation Slavery in Barbados*, pp. 76–77; Craton and Walvin, *A Jamaican Plantation*, p. 139.

56. Karl Watson, *The Civilised Island* (1979), p. 75; Craton and Walvin, *A Jamaican Plantation*, p. 139; Handler and Lange, *Plantation Slavery in Barbados*, p. 77.

57. B. W. Higman, "Domestic Service in Jamaica since 1750," in *Trade, Government, and Society in Caribbean History*, ed. B. W. Higman (1983).

58. Patterson, *Sociology of Slavery*, pp. 58–61; Edward Brathwaite, *The Development of Creole Society in Jamaica* (1971), pp. 155–56.

59. George Pinckard, *Notes on the West Indies* (1806), 1:290–91. See also Mrs. [A. C.] Carmichael, *Domestic Manners and Social Condition of the White, Coloured, and Negro Population of the West Indies* (1833), 1:118.

60. Higman, *Slave Population and Economy in Jamaica*, pp. 25–26.

61. M.B.C., 1828–31, p. 291: 21 December 1830.

62. M.C.P.D.E., 1819, pp. 437–41: 29 July 1819, See also ibid., 1829, vol. 2, p. 379: 16 September 1829.

63. *The Weekly Register* (Antigua), 20 May 1815.

64. *P.P.*, 1826–27 (479), p. 47.

65. *P.P.*, 1832 (721), p. 76.

66. *Barbados Mercury*, 22 July 1809; Barbados Act 12 February 1809; Mount Gay Plantation Journal, January 1810.

67. Sturge and Harvey, *The West Indies in 1837*, p. 94. See also Richard Price, "Caribbean Fishing and Fishermen: A Historical Sketch," *American Anthropologist* 68 (1966):1363–83.

68. *Royal St. Vincent Gazette*, 18 November 1820.

69. Ibid., 1 July, 14 October, 14 November, and 30 December 1820; *St. George's Chronicle*, 29 January and 6 December 1820; Higman, *Slave Population and Economy in Jamaica*, p. 36; Price, "Caribbean Fishing," p. 1375.

70. C.O. 300/43, p. 158; C.O. 300/47, p.

162; Protocols of Wills, Trinidad, 1826, ff. 95–96 (Registrar General's Department, Port of Spain).

71. M.C.P.D.E., 1807, p. 304: 25 March 1807; 1808, pp. 255–60, 281–82: 2 July 1808.

72. Petitions, 1813–14, p. 52 (N.A.G.).

73. Ibid., 1820–21, p. 224: Petition of Park Benjamin and James H. Albouy, 15 May 1821; ibid., p. 226: Petition of John D. Paterson, 2 June 1821.

74. Pinckard, *Notes on the West Indies*, 3:299.

75. Park Benjamin to Francis Yates, 17 June 1813, Correspondence, box 12, Park Benjamin Papers (Butler Library, Columbia University, New York).

76. Inventories in British Honduras, Private Records, vol. P/AA, pp. 41, 207, 359; vol. P/ BB, p. 436 (Supreme Court Registry, Belize).

77. *Honduras Almanack*, 1827, quoted in *Port of Spain Gazette*, 4 and 8 August 1827; [George] Henderson, *An Account of the British Settlement of Honduras* (London, 1809), pp. 47– 53; *Honduras Gazette and Commercial Advertiser* (Belize), 16 September and 21 October 1826, 9 February 1828; Bolland, *Formation of a Colonial Society*, pp. 54–7.

78. *Royal Gazette and Bahama Advertiser* (Nassau), 4 September 1804, 20 January and 3 February 1810.

79. C.O. 239/58, no. 3, Colebrooke to Russell, 25 January 1840.

80. Ibid., C.O. 239/29, no. 39, Nicolay to Goderich, 2 May 1832 (Petition); Minutes of Meetings of the Commissioners of Correspondence, 1796–1833: 31 January 1829 (House of Assembly, Nassau); Thomas Pringle, ed., *The History of Mary Prince, A West Indian Slave* (1831), p. 10.

81. F. W. N. Bayley, *Four Years' Residence in the West Indies* (1830), p. 95. Cf. *A Report of a Committee of the Council of Barbadoes, Appointed to Inquire into the Actual Condition of the Slaves in this Island* (London, 1824), p. 110.

82. *P.P.*, 1831–32, vol. 20 (381), "Report from Select Committee on the Commercial State of the West India Colonies," p. 725.

83. Philip D. Morgan, "Work and Culture: The Task System and the World of Lowcountry Blacks, 1700–1880," *William and Mary Quarterly* 39 (1982):568–69.

84. *An Official Letter from the Commissioners of Correspondence of the Bahama Islands* (Nassau, 1823), p. 41. But the task-work system is not obvious in *Farquharson's Journal for 1831–32*.

85. British Honduras, Legislative Meetings, 1830–36, p. 181: Memorial to Superintendent, 26 October 1833 (Supreme Court Registry, Belize); *Port of Spain Gazette*, 8 August 1827.

86. *St. George's Chronicle*, 24 August 1833.

87. See Ragatz, *Fall of the Planter Class*, p. 415.

88. *P.P.*, 1826–27 (479), p. 46; *P.P.*, 1828 (261), p. 457; *P.P.*, 1831–32 (381), pp. 725, 933; William Law Mathieson, *British Slavery and Its Abolition* (1926), p. 178.

89. *P.P.*, 1832 (721), p. 596.

90. Higman, *Slave Population and Economy in Jamaica*, pp. 24–25.

91. C.O. 295/85, f. 388: Smith to Murray, 9 October 1830; *P.P.*, 1831–32 (381), pp. 725, 933; *P.P.*, 1832 (721), p. 596.

92. *P.P.*, 1832 (721), p. 14; C.O. 295/85, f. 388. *P.P.*, 1831–32 (381), p. 933; *P.P.*, 1826 (401), p. 18; *Port of Spain Gazette*, 8 August 1827.

93. Ordinance of Thomas Picton, 30 June 1800, published in Gertrude Carmichael, *The History of the West Indian Islands of Trinidad and Tobago (1961)*, pp. 380–82.

94. Goveia, *Slave Society in the British Leeward Islands*, p. 171; Handler and Lange, *Plantation Slavery in Barbados*, p. 82.

95. *A Report of a Committee of the Council of Barbadoes*, p. 116; Pinckard, *Notes on the West Indies*, 2:117.

96. *Farquharson's Journal for 1831–32*, pp. 24, 53.

97. Handler and Lange, *Plantation Slavery in Barbados*, p. 82; *Farquharson's Journal for 1831–32*; Peruvian Vale Estate, St. Vincent, Journal, 1807–8 (Supreme Court Registry, Kingstown); Rose Hall Journal, 1817–32, vol. 2 (Jamaica Archives, Spanish Town).

98. Eric Williams, *History of the People of Trinidad and Tobago* (1964), p. 77.

99. Letter Book, Lieutenant Governor, Tobago, 1824–26: Robinson to Sitting Magistrates, 9 January 1824, 30 April 1824 and 15 February 1826 (T.A.); Journals of James

McTear, 1825, vol. 1, pp. 174–6 (Library Congress, Washington). See also *P.P.*, 1o. (721), p. 331.

100. *P.P.*, 1816, vol. 19 (226), "Colonial Laws Respecting Slaves," p. 117. *P.P.*, 1818, vol. 17 (433), "Further Papers Relating to the Treatment of Slaves," p. 53.

101. *P.P.*, 1832 (721), p. 238.

102. J. Harry Bennett, *Bondsmen and Bishops* (1958), p. 103; Handler and Lange, *Plantation Slavery in Barbados*, pp. 82, 89; Bayley, *Four Years' Residence in the West Indies*, p. 106.

103. *P.P.*, 1832 (721), p. 523; John Jeremie, *Four Essays on Colonial Slavery* (1831), p. 19. *Farquharson's Journal for 1831–32*, p. 30.

104. *P.P.*, 1832 (721), pp. 169, 333, 430, 525.

105. *A Report of a Committee of the Council of Barbadoes*, pp. 108, 115; Bennett, *Bondsmen and Bishops*, p. 22; Bayley, *Four Years' Residence in the West Indies*, p. 137.

106. *P.P.*, 1818 (433), p. 130.

107. C.O. 295/85, f. 388: Smith to Murray, 9 October 1830. See also *P.P.*, 1818 (433), p. 277.

108. *P.P.*, 1832 (721), pp. 597–98.

109. See Higman, *Slave Population and Economy in Jamaica*, p. 21; Pares, *A West-India Fortune*, p. 115; C.O. 295/85, f. 388; Peruvian Vale Estate Journal, 1807–8; Newton Estate Papers, items 117, 129, Boiling House Books, 1798, 1799; Journals of James McTear, vol. 1, p. 174.

110. M.C.P.D.E., 1830, vol. 1, p. 568: 11 March 1830; *P.P.*, 1818 (433), p. 277.

111. Higman, *Slave Population and Economy in Jamaica*, pp. 23–25; Accounts and Letters of James H. Archer, 1822–45, p. 273, Add. MS. 27,970; Ripon Papers, ff. 480–511: Mulgrave to Goderich, 1832, Add. MS. 40,879, pt. 2 (British Library, London); G. Carmichael, *History of Trinidad and Tobago*, p. 383.

112. Peruvian Vale Estate Journal, 1807–8 (Supreme Court Registry, Kingstown).

113. Cf. Stein, *Vassouras*, p. 168.

114. M.C.P.D.E., 1825, vol. 2, pp. 354–56: 6 September 1825. Cf. ibid., 1828, vol. 2, pp. 103–6: 13 May 1828.

115. *P.P.*, 1803–4, vol. 10 (119), "Papers